AA Lifestyle Guides in
association with Moat House

are giving away **30** weekends for two

in 6 free prize draws

5 winners will be drawn every 2 months; on the last day of:

- December 1997
- February 1998
- April 1998
- June 1998
- August 1998
- October 1998

Choose your "Views of Britain" weekend break from a selection of over 50 properties in the Moat House Hotels group, a number of which enjoy water-front locations.

Moat House Hotels offer the highest standards of service and hospitality to ensure that your stay is one to remember. Selected hotels offer Club Moativation health and fitness clubs, where facilities include swimming pool, jacuzzi, sauna, solarium and fully equipped gym. At a few you'll even find a golf course!

For more information on Moat House Hotels or for your free copy of their "Views of Britain" weekend breaks brochure, call **0541 556 556** quoting "AA Lifestyle Guides".

MOAT HOUSE HOTELS

HOW TO ENTER

Just complete (in capitals, please) and send off this card or, alternatively, send your name and address on a **stamped** postcard to the address overleaf (no purchase required). Entries limited to one per household and to residents of the UK and Republic of Ireland. This card will require a stamp if posted in the Republic of Ireland.

MR/MRS/MISS/MS/OTHER, PLEASE STATE:

NAME:

ADDRESS:

POSTCODE:

TEL.NOS:

Are you an AA Member ?   Yes/No
Have you bought this or any other AA Lifestyle Guide before?   Yes/No
If yes, please indicate the year of the last edition you bought:

The AA Hotel Guide	19____	AA Camping and Caravanning (Europe)	19____
AA Best Restaurants	19____	AA Hotels in France	19____
AA Bed and Breakfast Guide	19____	AA Bed & Breakfast in France	19____
AA Camping & Caravanning (Britain & Ireland)	19____	AA Best Pubs & Inns	19____

If you do not wish to receive further information or special offers from
AA Publishing ☐   Moat House Hotels ☐ please tick the box

HF98

Terms and Conditions

1. Five winners will be drawn for each of six prize draws to take place on 31 December 1997, 28 February, 30 April, 30 June, 31 August, 31 October 1998.

2. Closing date for receipt of entries is midday on the relevant draw date. Final close date for receipt of entries is 31 October 1998.

3. Entries received after any draw date except the final one will go forward into the next available draw. Entries will be placed in one draw only. Only one entry per household accepted.

4. Winners will be notified by post within 14 days of the relevant draw date. Prizes will be valid for 3 months from the relevant draw date. Prizes are not transferable and there will be no cash alternative.

5. Each prize consists of a two night Views of Britain weekend break at a Moat House Hotel. The prize includes two nights' accommodation and full breakfast for two people sharing a twin or double bedded room. The prize does not include dinner, lunch or additional expenses such as drinks or travelling expenses Any additional expenses will be charged as taken and payable on departure.

6. All hotel accommodation, services and facilities are provided by Moat House Hotels and AA Publishing is not party to your agreement with Moat House Hotels in this regard.

7. The prize draw is open to anyone resident in the UK or the Republic of Ireland over the age of 18 other than employees of the Automobile Association or Moat House Hotels, their subsidiary companies, their families or agents

8. For a list of winners, please send a stamped, self-addressed envelope to AA Lifestyle Guide winners, Publishing Admin, Fanum House, Basing View, Basingstoke, Hants RG21 4EA.

9. If this card is posted in the Republic of Ireland it must have a stamp.

BUSINESS REPLY SERVICE
Licence No BZ 343

PLEASE NOTE: Requires a stamp if posted in Republic of Ireland

AA Lifestyle Guide Prize Draw

AA PUBLISHING

FANUM HOUSE

BASING VIEW

BASINGSTOKE

HANTS RG21 4EA

Hotels
in France
1998

The directory is compiled by the AA's Hotel and Touring Services
Department and generated from the AA's establishment database

The contents of this publication are believed correct at the time of printing.
Nevertheless, the publishers cannot be held responsible for any errors or
omissions or for changes in the details given in this guide or for the
consequences of any reliance on the information provided by the same. We
have tried to ensure accuracy in this guide but things do change and we
should be grateful if readers would advise us of any inaccuracies they may
encounter

Picture credits:
Front cover photograph: Assiette Champenoise, Tinqueux, Marne,
Champagne-Ardenne, by R Meulle
All other photographs were taken from the AA's picture library
(©AA photo library)
All other photos of establishments were supplied by the proprietors and
managers of the establishments featured in this guide

Editorial contributions from:
Jim Barker, Christopher Blackford and Sarah Catliff

French regional maps are based on maps supplied by the French Tourist
Office and reproduced with their kind permission.

Typeset and reprographics by Avonset, 1 Palace Yard Mews, Bath

Printed and bound by Gráficas Estella, SA, Navarra, Spain

Advertisement Sales:
Head of Advertisement Sales: Christopher Heard, direct line 01256 491544
Advertisement Production: Karen Weeks, direct line 01256 491545

A CIP catalogue record for this book is available from the British Library

ISBN: 0 7495 17557

AA ref no: 10058

Published by AA Publishing, a trading name of Automobile Association
Developments Limited, whose registered office is Norfolk House, Priestley
Road, Basingstoke, Hampshire, RG24 9NY. Registered number 1878835

■■Contents■■

Directory of Establishments

"Regions & *Départements*"

In this book France has been divided into 21 regions as numbered and colour-coded on the map opposite. Individual maps of these regions appear at the beginning of each section. The map also shows the *départements* into which France is divided. Each *département* has a standard number, as shown on the map and in the key, which for postal purposes replaces its name. These numbers also form part of the registration number of French cars, thus indicating the *département* in which the car was registered. The *départements* are listed alphabetically within their regions.

BRITTANY
Côtes d'Armor	22
Finistère	29
Ille-et-Vilaine	35
Morbihan	56

NORMANDY
Calvados	14
Eure	27
Manche	50
Orne	61
Seine-Maritime	76

NORD/PAS-DE-CALAIS
Nord	59
Pas-de-Calais	62

PICARDY
Aisne	02
Oise	60
Somme	80

CHAMPAGNE-ARDENNE
Ardennes	08
Aube	10
Haute-Marne	51
Marne	52

LORRAINE VOSGES
Meurthe-et-Moselle	54
Meuse	55
Moselle	57
Vosges	88

ALSACE
Bas-Rhin	67
Haut-Rhin	68

WESTERN LOIRE
Loire-Atlantique	44
Maine-et-Loire	49
Mayenne	53
Sarthe	72
Vendeé	85

VAL DE LOIRE
Cher	18
Eure-et-Loir	28
Indre	36
Indre-et-Loir	37
Loir-et-Cher	41
Loiret	45

PARIS & ILE DE FRANCE
Essonne	91
Hauts-de-Seine	92
Paris	75
Seine-et-Marne	77
Seine-St-Denis	93
Val-de-Marne	94
Val-d'Oise	95
Yvelines	78

BURGUNDY
Côte-d'Or	21
Nièvre	58
Saône-et-Loire	71
Yonne	89

FRANCHE-COMTE
Doubs	25
Haute-Saône	70
Jura	39
Territoire-de-Belfort	90

POITOU-CHARENTES
Charente	16
Charente-Maritime	17
Deux Sèvres	79
Vienne	86

LIMOUSIN
Corrèze	23
Creuse	19
Haute-Vienne	87

AUVERGNE
Allier	03
Cantal	15
Haute-Loire	43
Puy-de-Dôme	63

RHONE ALPES
Ain	01
Ardèche	07
Drôme	26
Haute-Savoie	74
Isère	38
Loire	42
Rhône	69
Savoie	73

AQUITAINE
Dordogne	24
Gironde	33
Landes	40
Lot-et-Garonne	47
Pyrénées-Atlantiques	64

MIDI-PYRENEES		LANGUEDOC-ROUSSILLON		PROVENCE	
Ariège	09	Aude	11	Alpes-de-Haute-Provence	04
Aveyron	12	Gard	30	Bouches-du-Rhône	13
Gers	32	Hérault	34	Hautes-Alpes	05
Haute-Garonne	31	Lozère	48	Var	83
Hautes-Pyrénées	65	Pyrénées-Roussillon	66	Vaucluse	84
Lot	46				
Tarn	81				
Tarn-et-Garonne	82				

COTE D'AZUR

Alpes Maritimes   06

■■Introduction■■

Welcome to the AA's second edition of **Hotels in France**, a guide to the wealth of luxury hotels, châteaux, small family-run hotels and budget-priced accommodation available to both the holidaymaker and business traveller alike.

To make the selection of hotels in this guide we have worked in close collaboration with the French Tourist Office in London and its regional departments throughout France to bring you more than 1,500 recommended hotels stretching the length and breadth of the country.

In the directory, hotels are listed under the village, town or city closest to them, which in turn are listed alphabetically under the appropriate region. Paris is divided into arrondissements (postal districts) and to help you find your way around Paris we have included a map of the Périphérique and central Paris on pages 24/5.

France is divided into twenty one regions (see the map on pages 4/5 showing all regions with their corresponding départements), each with its own character, tradition and cuisine. Each region in the directory begins with an **Essential Facts** introduction, giving information and insight into the history, attractions, a diary of events and festivals, (dates given were correct when we went to press, but should be checked on arrival - see below) plus the gastronomic delights of the area. Although we have also given the addresses and phone numbers of the major tourist offices for each region, on arrival at your holiday destination you should always find the local one, which will give you detailed information on the dates and venues of any events and festivals taking place during your stay.

To help you book your stay at a hotel, we have drawn up a standard booking letter and helpful phrases you may wish to use if booking by phone. To help you further we have included a **'France At A Glance'** section - see page 10 - which gives the addresses and phone numbers of all the major ferry companies which sail to the French ports. Also **'Motoring in France'** - see page 13 - which gives advice on motoring abroad, should be read before you set off on your trip.

Once you reach France and find you are spoilt for choice by the vast and varied array of food on offer, we hope our **What's On The Menu?** section will help you. See page 30. Equally, we hope our **Useful French Phrases** section, page 26, will come to your aid at the hotel, in the supermarket, or if your car breaks down.

At the back of the guide you will find an index of location names, with page numbers of where the entry is listed in the guide. We have tried to provide as much information as possible about the hotels in our directory, but if you require further information, write or telephone the hotel itself. Do remember to enclose an international reply coupon, and please quote this publication in any enquiry. Although we try to publish accurate and up-to-date information, please remember that any details, and particularly prices, are subject to change without notice. If you have a complaint we strongly advise you to take the matter up with the management there and then, in order to give the hotelier a chance to put things right, but we should be grateful if you let us know of any dissatisfaction. Please note that all the establishments listed have been classified and inspected by the French Tourist Board and not by the AA Hotel & Restaurant Inspectorate.

"Using the Guide"

★ ★ ★ **Typical Hotel**
3 rue General de Gaulle *29270*
☎123456789. FAX 12345678
From the motorway, follow signs to the centre of town.
Converted from an ancient priory, the hotel is situated
between two abbeys in the centre of Menton.
All bedrooms are furnished in traditional rustic style and are
charming and comfortable, many containing the priory's
original features of wooden beams and stone floors. The
restaurant specialises in local seafood and rustic dishes.
In wooded area Near motorway
24 rms (8 bth/shr), (7 with balcony). CTV in all bedrooms.
Child discount available 10 yrs Last d 21:30. Free parking.
ROOMS s260-490FF d300-610FF
MEALS Breakfast 50FF dinner fixed price 100-350FF
dinner alc 200-300FF
CARDS 🏧 💳 💳 Travellers cheques

1) TOWN NAME FOLLOWED BY DEPARTEMENT NAME

2) HOTEL NAME

3) PHONE NUMBER

4) ACCOMMODATION DESCRIPTION AND LOCATION DETAILS

5) HOTEL FACILITIES

6) MEALS & ROOMS

7) PAYMENT DETAILS

1. TOWN NAME

Listed in the directory in alphabetical order by region: Brittany, Normandy, Nord/Pas de Calais, Picardy, Champagne-Ardenne, Lorraine Vosges, Alsace, Western Loire, Val de Loire, Paris and the Ile de France, Burgundy, Franche-Comté, Poitou-Charentes, Limousin, Auvergne, Rhône Alpes, Aquitaine, Midi-Pyrénées, Languedoc-Rousillon, Provence, Côte d'Azur.

After the town name comes the département name. At the back of the book is an index of locations with page numbers of where the entry is listed in the guide. We have provided simple maps at the beginning of each regional section, so that you can see where in the region a town is, but for driving and precise orientation you will need a large-scale road atlas.

2. HOTEL NAME

The star rating precedes the hotel name. Hotels in this guide have a star rating given to them by the French Tourist Office; this is very similar, but not identical, to the AA's UK hotel classification scheme. The French Tourist Office description of the star ratings is as follows:

★★★★★ Large luxury hotel offering the highest international standards of accommodation, facilites, services and cuisine
★★★★ Large hotel with spacious accommodation where guests may expect high standards of comfort and food
★★★ Very comfortable hotel with en suite facilities
★★ Good, average hotel with some en suite facilities
★ Plain, comfortable and inexpensive hotel, usually with shared bathroom facilities
Please note that some private châteaux do not subscribe to the star rating scheme.
The postal address and telephone number follow the hotel name.

3 ADDRESS & TELEPHONE NUMBER

Please see the notes on page 11 about using the telephone in France. The postal code which appears in italics should be used in front of the town name for address purposes eg *29270* ANYTOWN.

4. DESCRIPTION & LOCATION

Descriptions and a summary of the location (e.g. Forest area Near motorway), have been provided by the hotels themselves.

We believe the details to be accurate and we have published them in good faith. Where a hotel has stated that it is 'In town centre' and 'Near Motorway', remember that 'Near Motorway' may refer to the town/village itself, and not to the hotel directly. Similarly, 'In Forest area' may refer to the town or village, not to the grounds of the hotel.

4. ACCOMMODATION DETAILS

The first figure shows the number of letting bedrooms, followed by the numbers of rooms that have en suite bath or shower and WC.

5. HOTEL FACILITIES

fmly	family bedrooms
CTV/TV	colour/black & white television in lounge or in bedrooms. Check when booking
STV	satellite TV channels at no extra cost, but check details when booking.
Night porter	at some hotels, the night porte may be there only between certain hours or on certain nights.
Last d	indicates the latest time at which dinner may be ordered

6. ROOMS & MEALS

Prices are provided by hoteliers in good faith and are indications not firm quotations. Hoteliers have also informed us of reductions for stays of more than one night, or special break offers. However, you must check when booking. In some hotels children can sleep in the parents' room at no extra cost. Please check when booking.

Details of the style of food and price range are given. If there is a fixed-price menu(s), this is the price range quoted. If the words '**& alc**' follow, it means an à la carte menu is available and its prices may be much higher than those on the table d'hôte menus.

V meals a choice of vegetarian dishes is normally available, but check first.

7. CREDIT & CHARGE CARDS

Mastercard
American Express
Visa
Diners
Travellers cheques

Check the position on credit cards when booking. They may be subject to a surcharge. See the note on payment below.

Useful Information

BOOKING

Book as early as possible, particularly during the peak holiday periods from the beginning of June to the end of September, at public holiday weekends and, in some parts of France, during the skiing season. Some hotels ask for a deposit, or even full payment in advance, especially for one-night bookings from chance callers. Not all hotels, however, will take advance bookings for bed and breakfast for overnight or short stays. Some may not make reservations from mid week in high season.

CANCELLATION

Once the booking has been confirmed, notify the hotel immediately if you are in any doubt as to whether you can keep to your reservation. If the hotel cannot re-let your accommodation you may be liable to pay about two-thirds of the price you would have paid if you had stayed there. A deposit will count towards this payment. Illness is not usually accepted as a release from this contract. You are advised to effect insurance cover, for example, AA Travelsure, against possible cancellation.

LICENCE TO SELL ALCOHOL

Unless otherwise stated, all establishments listed are licensed and resident guests should have no problem in obtaining drinks either with a meal or from the bar, if there is one, during he hours when it is open. The bar may or may not be open to non-residents.

PAYMENT

Most establishments will only accept Eurocheques in payment of accounts if notice is given and identification (e.g., a cheque card) produced. Not all take Eurocheques or travellers cheques, even from leading banks and agencies. If credit cards are accepted, the information is shown at the end of the entry.

PRICES

Throughout all prices are given in French francs and so will fluctuate with the exchange rate.

Prices given usually refer to the cost of a room per night rather than per person per night. Most hotels do not include the cost of breakfast in their room rates. Where we have been able to obtain a price for breakfast, it is shown.

An asterisk (*) against prices indicates 1997 prices have been given by the proprietor.

▌▌France at a Glance▐▐

What is it about France that draws millions of francophiles back year after year for a taste of la vie française? Is it the chic boulevards of Paris, the sparkling ski slopes of the Alps, sunlit vineyards and sun-baked beaches, coffee and croissants in an undiscovered village or a relaxing picnic in Provence, where the air is fragrant with wild herbs and lavender? France is a land of great contrasts, catering for all tastes and offering an endless choice of enticing destinations, a rich diversity of landscape, cuisine, climate and people, and an exceptional cultural heritage.

Next time you hop across the Channel, consider your destination with care. Before you head off yet again for your annual fix of Mediterranean sunshine, or to the alluring Dordogne, consider the delights of other little-known regions such as Franche-Comté, Gascony or Berry, whose sleepy villages offer visitors a chance to sample the true douceur de vivre of provincial France.

Whichever destination you choose, you won't be disappointed. Each region offers its own character, charm and attractions, and you will soon discover why the French stay at home for their holidays.

AT-A-GLANCE FACTS AND FIGURES

Capital: Paris
IDD code: 33. To call the UK dial 00 44
Currency: Franc (Fr1 = 100 centimes).
At the time of going to press £1 =Frs9.7
Local time: GMT + 1 (summer GMT + 2)
Emergency numbers: Police 17; Fire 18;
Ambulance - dial number given in callbox, or,
if no number given, the police
Business hours: Banks: Mon-Fri 09.00-12.00 &
14.00-16.00
Shops: Mon-Sat 09.00-18.00 (times may vary for
food shops)
Average daily temperature:

| Paris | Jan 3° C | May 13°C | Sep 15°C |
| | Mar 6°C | Jul 18°C | Nov 6°C |

TOURIST INFO:

French Tourist Office
178 Piccadilly, London W1V 0AL Tel: 0891 244123
(premium rate information line; 08.30-21.30 weekdays,
09.00-1700 Saturdays)
Monaco Government Tourist and
Convention Office
3-18 Chelsea Garden Market Chelsea Harbour
London SW10 0XE
British Embassy
75383 Paris, Cedex 08, 35 rue de Faubourg St-Honoré
Tel: 0144513100
Consular section
75008 Paris, 16 rue d'Anjou Tel: 0142663810
There are British Consulates in Bordeaux, Lille, Lyon and
Marseille; there are British Consulates with Honorary
Consuls in Biarritz, Boulogne-sur-Mer, Calais, Cherbourg,
Dunkerque (Dunkirk), Le Havre, Nantes, Nice, St Malo-
Dinard and Toulouse

USING THE PHONE IN FRANCE

For all calls inside France dial 0 before the 9-digit
number eg Paris 01 .. .., Marseille 04 .. ..
To call abroad from France dial 00 and country code.
To call the UK dial 00 44 followed by the UK number
ignoring the first digit (0).
For information and directory assistance dial 12

To use your mobile phone abroad:
● contact your service provider before you leave to
arrange international access

● take your mobile phone handbook with you to ensure
you know how to manually roam onto a foreign
network
● to call the UK dial 00 44 (or use the + key on the
keypad - see your handbook) followed by the UK
number ignoring the first digit (0)

HOW TO GET THERE

Apart from the direct crossing by the Channel Tunnel
(Folkestone-Calais, 35 mins, see French ABC, page 00), the
following ferry services are available:

Short ferry crossings
From Dover to Calais takes 75-90 mins or 45 mins by Lynx
Catamaran

Longer ferry crossings
From Ramsgate to Dunkirk takes 2 hrs 30 mins
From Newhaven to Dieppe takes 4 hrs or 2 hrs 15 mins by
Lynx Catamaran
From Portsmouth to Le Havre takes 5 hrs 30 mins (day); 7
hrs 30 mins / 8 hrs (night)
Caen takes 6 hrs
Cherbourg takes 5 hrs (day); 7 hrs / 8 hrs 15 mins (night)
St Malo takes 8 hrs 45 mins (day); 11 hrs 30 mins (night)
From Poole to Cherbourg takes 4 hrs 15 mins
From Poole to St Malo takes 8 hrs (summer service only)
From Plymouth to Roscoff takes 6 hrs
From Southampton to Cherbourg takes 5 hrs

FERRY COMPANIES

Brittany Ferries
Millbay Docks, Plymouth PL1 3EW
Tel: 01752 221321
The Brittany Centre, Wharf Road, Portsmouth
Tel: 01705 827701
Caen Tel: 31 96 88 80   Cherbourg Tel: 33 43 43 68
Roscoff Tel: 98 29 28 28   St-Malo Tel: 99 40 64 41

Hoverspeed Ltd
International Hoverport, Western Docks, Dover,
Kent CT17 9TG Tel: 01304 240241
Boulogne Tel: 21 30 27 26   Calais Tel: 21 46 14 14

P&O European Ferries
Channel House, Channel View Road, Dover CT17 9TJ
Tel: 01304 203388   Calais Tel: 21 46 04 40
Le Havre Tel: 35 19 78 50   Cherbourg Tel: 33 88 65 70

Sally Ferries

Sally Line Ltd, Argyle Centre, York Street, Ramsgate, Kent
CT11 9DS Tel: 01843 595522 0181 858 1127
Dunkirk Tel: 28 21 43 44

Stena Sealink

Charter House, Ashford, Kent Tel: 01233 647047
Calais Tel: 21 46 80 00   Cherbourg Tel: 33 20 43 38
Dieppe Tel: 35 06 39 00

Fast Hoverspeed services

Hoverspeed/Hovercraft from Dover to Calais takes 35
mins. Hoverspeed/Seacat catamaran from Folkestone to
Boulogne takes 55 mins.

Car sleeper trains

A daily service operates from Calais to the south of the
country

For details of the AA European Routes Service see page 393.

For details of the AA European Routes Service see page 393.

ON THE ROAD

Please refer to Motoring in France on page 13. Remember
that during peak holiday times traffic will be very heavy
and delays are likely in some places. Remember too that
during the month of August most Parisians leave the city
for the coast, so all roads leading out of Paris will be
packed. In general, times to avoid travelling are at
weekends, at the beginning and end of school holidays,
before and after public holidays and religious feasts and
festival days at religious centres (see list below). Contact
local tourist boards for information on road congestion.

Public Holidays

New Year's Day	January 1
Easter Sunday	April 12
Easter Monday	April 13
Labour Day	May 1
V.E Day	May 8
Ascension Day	May 31 - June 1
Bastille Day	July 14
Assumption Day	August 15
All Saints' Day	November 1
Remembrance Day	November 11
Christmas Day	December 25

French School Holidays for 1998

(staggered throughout France)

Winter half-term	February 6th - March 9th
Easter/Spring holiday	April 2 - April 27
Summer	June 30 - September 2
Autumn half-term	October 23 - November 3
Christmas	December 19 - January 4

Garages and service stations

In France garages are generally open from 08.00 to 18.00
(sometimes with a break at midday, 12.00 to 15.00),
Monday to Saturday. On Sunday and public holidays fuel
and service are often unobtainable, and in some rural
areas of France it may be difficult to get repairs done in
August, when many firms close for the annual holidays.
Ask your local dealer for a list of franchised repairers in
Europe before you leave.

   Always ask for an estimate before you have your
repairs done; it can save disputes later. Always settle any
dispute with a garage before you leave; subsequent
negotiations by post are usually lengthy and
unsatisfactory.

Road signs

Although most road signs are the same and therefore
easily identifiable throughout the Continent, below are
explanations of specifically French ones:

Allumez vos phares - Switch on your headlights
Attention travaux - Road works ahead
Chaussée déformée - Uneven road surface
Fin d'interdiction de stationner - End of restricted
parking
Gravillons - Loose chippings
Haute tension - Electrified lines
Interdit aux piétons - No pedestrians
Nids de poules - Potholes
Priorité à droite - Give way to traffic on the right
(see Priority including roundabouts on page 00)
Passage protégé - Your right of way
Rappel 50 - Remember 50 kph or whatever speed
is relevant)
Route barrée - Road closed

   And finally, remember always when driving through
France, **drive on the right** and **overtake carefully
on the left**.

Safe motoring - and enjoy your holiday!

"Motoring in France"
General Information

Motoring in France should cause little difficulty to British motorists, but remember to drive on the right-hand side of the road, and take particular care when approaching junctions, traffic lights, roundabouts, etc. Also ensure that you comply with signs showing speed limits.

Ensure that your vehicle is in good order mechanically. We recommend a full service by a franchised dealer. AA members can arrange a thorough check of their car by an experienced AA engineer. Any AA shop can organise this, given a few days' notice. There is a fee for this service, and for more information or, if you wish to book an inspection, please telephone 0345 500610.

"A"

ACCIDENTS AND EMERGENCIES

In the event of an accident, you must stop. In the event of injury or damage, you should inform the police, and notify your insurers by letter if possible within 24 hours. If a third party is injured your insurers will advise you, or, if you have a Green Card (see Motor Insurance below), contact the company or bureau given on the back of the card for advice over claims for compensation

"B"

BANKING HOURS

Banks close at midday on the day prior to a national holiday, and all day on Monday if the holiday falls on a Tuesday. Otherwise hours are similar to those in Britain. Most French banks will no longer cash Eurocheques, but if you have a Eurocheque or credit card with a PIN you can withdraw cash from a network of around 15,000 cash dispensers. Eurocheques are quite widely accepted in shops in large towns. See also Fuel/Petrol and Money.

BBC WORLD SERVICE

The BBC World Service broadcasts globally in 45 languages, including a 24 hour-a-day English service. If your are travelling in north-west Europe, you can listen on medium wave and long wave at these times:

kHz	Metres	Summer broadcasting times GMT
198	151	52345-0500
648	463	0000-0800;
		0830-1200; 1215-1530;
		1600-1730; 1800-2400

BBC World Service also transmits on short wave, and comprehensive details of all frequencies are available in a free programme guide from BBC World Service, PO Box 76, Bush House, London WC2B 4PH. A digitally tuned radio makes it easier to find frequencies than the traditional 'dial and pointer' set. A monthly magazine, BBC On Air, provides details of all World Service programmes. It costs £2 per issue, or £18.00 (30 US$) for an annual subscription. For information, telephone 0171 557 2211.

BRITISH EMBASSY/CONSULATE

The British Embassy is at 75383 Paris Cedex 08, 35 rue du Faubourg St Honoré, telephone 144513100; consular section 16 rue d'Anjou, telephone 142663810. There are British Consulates in Bordeaux, Lille, Lyon and Marseille; there are British Consulates with Honorary Consuls in Biarritz, Boulogne-sur-Mer, Calais, Cherbourg, Dunkerque (Dunkirk), Le Havre, Nantes, Nice, St Malo-Dinard and Toulouse.

"C"

CHILDREN IN CARS

A child under 10 years old may not travel as a front-seat passenger. A baby of up to 9 months and weighing less than 9kg may travel in the front of the car in a rear-facing seat. Children under 10 years old in rear seats must use a restraint system appropriate to their age and weight.

Note; in no circumstances should a rear-facing restraint be used in a front seat with an airbag.

CUSTOMS AND EXCISE

When you enter the UK from another EC country without having travelled to or through a non-EC country you do not need to go through the red or green channels. Look for the blue channel or blue exit reserved for EC travellers. But please remember that, although the limits on duty and tax paid goods bought within the EC ended on 31 December 1992, EC law sets out limits on purchases from duty-free and tax-free shops. It also establishes guidence levels for tobacco goods and wines and spirits bought elsewhere within the EC. Additionally the importation of certain goods into the UK is prohibited or restricted.

The quantities shown below may be bought from duty-free and tax-free shops for personal use. This is your entitlement each time you travel to and from another EC country.

Tobacco goods: 200 cigarettes; or 100 cigarillos; or 50 cigars; or 250gms of tobacco

Wines & Spirits: 2 litres of still table wine and 1 litre of spirits or strong liqueurs over 22% volume; or 2 litres of fortified wine, sparkling wine or other liqueurs

Perfume: 60cc/ml of perfume and 250cc/ml of toilet water

Other Goods: £75 worth of all other goods, including gifts and souvenirs

Note: Under 17s cannot have tobacco or alcohol allowance

The guidence levels, which include any duty-free purchases, are the amounts you may bring in for your personal use. If you bring in more, and cannot prove that the goods are for your personal use, they may be seized. The levels for tobacco goods are 800 cigarettes, 400 cigarillos, 200 cigars and 1kg smoking tobacco; for wines and spirits 10 litres of spirits, 20 litres of fortified wine (such as port and sherry), 90 litres of wine (of which not more than 60 litres are sparkling) and 110 litres of beer. Prohibited or restricted goods include drugs, firearms, ammunition, offensive weapons (such as flick knives), explosives, obscene material, indecent and obscene material featuring children, unlicensed animals that could be carrying rabies (such as cats, dogs and mice).

When you enter the UK from a non-EC country or an EC country having travelled to or through a non-EC country, you must go through Customs. If you have more than the customs allowances or any prohibited, restricted or commercial goods, go through the red channel. Only go through the green channel if you are sure that you have "nothing to declare".

For customs allowances see babove, but for "other goods" read £145 not £75.

Prohibited goods include unlicensed drugs; offensive weapons; obscene material; counterfeit and copied goods.

Restricted goods include firearms, explosives and ammunition; dogs, cats and other animals; live birds; endangered species; meat and poultry; certain plants; radio transmitters.

Don't be tempted to hide anything or to mislead the Customs. Penalties are severe and articles not properly declaredmay be forfeit. If articles are hidden in a vehicle that too becomes liable to forfeiture. Customs officers are legally entitiled to examine your luggage. You are responsible for opening, unpacking and repacking it. If you require more information, obtain a copy of Customs

Notice 1, available at UK points of entry and exit, or telephone an Excise and Inland Customs Advice Centre (see Customs and Excise in the telephone directory).

"D"

DIESEL

See Fuel/Petrol

DOCUMENTS

A tourist driving abroad should always carry a current passport, and a full, valid national driving licence, even if an International Driving Permit (IDP) is also held, the vehicle registration document and certificate of motor insurance. (See Motor Insurance below). Any AA shop will advise you of the procedure for personal or postal applications for an IDP, for which a statutory charge is made. If you have no registration document, apply to a Vehicle Registration Office (in Northern Ireland a Local Vehicle Licensing Office) for a temporary certificate of registration (V379) to cover the period abroad. Consult the local telephone directory for addresses, or leaflet V100, available from post offices. Apply well in advance of your journey.

The proper International Distinguishing Sign should be displayed on the rear of the vehicle and any trailer.

Remember that foreign vehicles are often subject to spot checks, so to avoid delay or a possible police fine, ensure that your papers are in order and that your International Distinguishing Sign is of the approved standard design (oval with black letters - GB for UK residents - on a white background at least 6.9 in by 4.5 in and affixed to the rear of the vehicle). If you are carrying skis, ensure that their tips point to the rear. If you have cycle rack, ensure that it does not obscure the number plate or IDS.

"E"

EMERGENCY MESSAGES

In emergencies the AA will help in the passing on of messages to tourists wherever possible. Members wishing to use this service should telephone the AA Information Centre on 0990 500600. The AA can arrange for messages to be published in the overseas editions of the Daily Mail, and in the case of extreme emergency (death or serious illness) undertake to pass on messages to the appropriate authorities so they can be broadcast. The AA cannot guarantee that messages will be broadcast, nor can the AA or Daily Mail accept any responsibility for the authenticity of messages.

EUROCHEQUES

Most French banks will no longer cash Eurocheques, but they are widely accepted in shops. See also Banking Hours and Money.

EUROTUNNEL

Eurotunnel's Le Shuttle car passenger service provides up to four departures per hour at peak times from Folkestone to Calais. Services operate 24 hours a day with up to four departures an hour at peak times. The journey takes only 35 minutes from platform to platform (45 minutes at night), and just over an hour from the M20 in Kent to the A16 at Calais.

Motorists leave the M20 at Exit 11a (clearly signposted to the Channel Tunnel) and buy a ticket on arrival at the tollbooths by cash, check or payment card (charge/credit/debit) or in advance from the Le Shuttle Customer Service Centre, travel agents or any AA shop. For more information telephone Le Shuttle Customer Service Centre on 0990 353535 or write to PO Box 300, Folkestone, Kent CT19 4QW. Remember, vehicles with LPG or duel fuel systems or petrol cans cannot be carried aboard LeShuttle.

The Eurostar passenger service to Paris leaves from Waterloo Station in London and may also be boarded at Ashford in Kent.

F

FUEL/PETROL

Motorists will find comparable grades of petrol and familiar brand names along main routes. You will normally have to buy a minimum of 5 litres (just over a gallon), but it is wise to keep the tank topped up, especially in rural areas, and on Sundays and National Holidays when many local service stations may close. Fuel is generally available with 24-hr service on motorways, but on other roads, some service stations may close between 12 noon and 15.00 hours. Do not assume that service stations will accept credit cards. See also Money. Leaded, unleaded, diesel fuel are all available. Unleaded (sans plomb) and leaded are both available as 'normal' and 'super'. You may also find unleaded 98 octane instead of or as well as 95 octane. It may also be described as 'super plus' or 'premium'. Take care to use the recommended fuel, especially if your car is fitted with a catalytic converter. The octane grade should be the same or higher. If you accidentally fill the tank of a catalyst-equipped car with leaded fuel the best course is to have the tank drained and refilled with unleaded.

Diesel fuel is generally known as diesel or gas oil. It is normally available, but do ensure that you keep the tank topped up. If you accidentally put more than about a gallon of petrol into a diesel car (or vice versa), you must drain the tank and refill with the correct fuel before starting the engine.

Note: ferry operators and motorail forbid the carriage of fuel in spare cans, though empty cans may be carried.

L

LIGHTS

Headlights should be altered so that the dipped beam does not dazzle other drivers. Easily fitted headlamp beam converter kits are on sale at AA shops, but remember to remove them as soon as you return to the UK.

Dipped headlights should be used in tunnels, irrespective of length and lighting. Police may wait at the end of a tunnel to check vehicles. In the dark or in poor visibility, you must use headlights, as driving on side lights only is not permitted. Yellow-tinted headlights, however, are no longer necessary. In fog or mist, two dipped headlights or two fog lights must be switched on. Headlight flashing is used only to signal approach or when overtaking at night. If used at other times, it could be taken as a sign of irritation and lead to misunderstandings. See also Spares.

M

MEDICAL TREATMENT

Travellers who normally take certain medicines should ensure they have a sufficient supply as they may be difficult to obtain abroad. Those with certain medical conditions (diabetes, coronary artery diseases) should get a letter from their doctor giving treatment details and obtain a translation. The AA cannot make translations.

Travellers who, for legitimate health reasons, carry drugs (see also Customs regulations for the United Kingdom) or appliances (e.g., a hypodermic syringe), may have difficulty with Customs or other authorities. They should carry translations which describe their special condition and appropriate treatment in the language of the country they intend to visit to present to

Customs. Similarly, people with special dietary requirements may find translations helpful in hotels and restaurants.

The National Health Service is available in the UK only, and medical expenses incurred overseas cannot generally be reimbursed by the UK Government. There is a reciprocal health agreement with France, but you should not rely exclusively on this arrangement, as the cover provided may not be comprehensive. (For instance, the cost of bringing a person back to the UK in the event of illness or death is not covered). You are strongly advised to take out adequate insurance before leaving the UK, such as the AA's Personal Travel Insurance.

Urgent medical treatment in the event of an accident or unforeseen illness is available for most visitors at reduced costs, from the health care schemes of those countries with whom the UK has health-care arrangements. Details are in the Department of Health booklet T5 which also gives advice about health precautions and vaccinations. Free copies are available from main post offices or by ringing the Health Literature Line on 0800 555 777 any time, free of charge. In some of these countries, visitors can obtain urgently needed treatment by showing their UK passport, but in some an NHS medical card must be produced, and in most European Economic Area countries a certificate of entitlement (E111) is necessary. The E111 can be obtained over the counter of the post office on completion of the forms incorporated in booklet T5. However, the E111 must be stamped and signed by the post office clerk to be valid. Residents of the Republic of Ireland must apply to their Regional Health Board for an E111.

MONEY

You should carry enough local currency notes for immediate needs and also local currency travellers cheques which can often be used like cash. Sterling travellers cheques can be cashed at banks, and you will need your

passport with you. Credit cards are widely accepted, and there are about 15,000 automatic cash dispense machines which you can use to obtain cash. See also Eurocheques.

MOTORING CLUB

The AA is affiliated to the Automobile Club National (ACN) whose office is at 75009 Paris, 5 rue Auber. Telephone 144515399.

MOTOR INSURANCE

When driving abroad you must carry your certificate of motor insurance with you at all times. Third-party is the minimum legal requirement in most countries. Before taking your vehicle abroad, contact your insurer or broker to ask for advice. Some insurers will extend your UK or Republic of Ireland motor policy to apply in the countries you intend visiting free of charge; others may charge an additional premium. It is most important to know the level of cover you will actually have, and what documents you will need to prove it.

A Green Card is not essential in France. This document issued by your motor insurer provides internationally recognised proof of insurance. It must be signed on receipt as it will not be accepted without the signature of the insured person. Motorists can obtain expert advice through AA Insurance Services for all types of insurance. Ask at your local AA shop or contact AA Insurance Services Ltd, PO Box 2AA Newcastle upon Tyne NE99 2AA. Do also check that you are insured for damage in transit other than when the vehicle is being driven (e.g. on the ferry).

❚❚P❚❚

PARKING

As a general rule, park on the right hand side of the road so as not to obstruct traffic or a cycle lane, etc., but better still, park in an authorised place as regulations are stringent, especially in large towns and cities and fines are heavy. In Paris it is absolutely forbidden to stop or park on a red route. The east-west route includes the left bank of the Seine and the Quai de la Megisserie; the north-south route includes the Avenue du Général Leclerc, part of the Boulevard St Michel, the Rue de Rivoli, the Boulevards Sébastopol, Strasbourg, Barbès and Ornano, the Rue Lafayette and the Avenue Jean Jaurès. Parking is also absolutely forbidden in some parts of the green zone.

PASSPORTS

Each person must hold, or be named on, a valid passport and should carry it with them at all times. For security, keep a separate note of the number, date and place of issue. If it is lost, report the matter to the police. There is now only one type of passport, the standard 10 year passport. Full information and application forms are available from main Post Offices, branches of Lloyds Bank, Artac World Choice travel agents or from one of the passport offices in Belfast, Douglas (Isle of Man), Glasgow, Liverpool, London, Newport (Gwent), Peterborough, St Helier (Jersey), St Peter Port (Guernsey). Allow at least 15 working days at peak periods.

PETROL

See Fuel/Petrol

POLICE FINES

In France, the police may impose an immediate deposit for a traffic infringement and subsequently may levy a fine which must normally be paid in cash in French francs either to the police or at a post office against a ticket issued by the police. The amount can, for serious offences, exceed the equivalent of £1000. A receipt should be obtained, but motorists should be aware that disputing a fine usually leads to a court appearance with all the extra costs and delays that may entail.

PRIORITÉ À DROITE

Probably the most unfamiliar aspect of driving in France to British motorists is the rule giving priority to traffic coming from the right - priorité à droite - and unless this priority is varied by signs, it must be strictly observed. In built-up areas (including small villages) you must give way to traffic coming from the right. Also remember that farm vehicles and buses may expect to be given priority. At roundabouts, priority is generally given to vehicles entering the roundabout (the opposite of the rule in Britain). However, at roundabouts bearing the words 'Vous n'avez pas la priorité' or 'Cédez le passage', traffic on the roundabout has the priority.

Outside built up areas, all main roads of any importance have right of way. This is indicated by one of three signs: a red-bordered triangle showing a black cross on a white background with the words 'Passage Protégé' underneath; a red-bordered triangle showing a pointed black upright with horizontal bar on a white background; or a yellow square within a white square with points vertical.

"R"

ROADS

Roads in France are generally very good, but the camber is often severe and edges can be rough. In July and August, especially at weekends, traffic is likely to be very heavy. Special signs are erected to indicate alternative routes and it is usually advantageous to follow them, though they are not guaranteed to save time. A free road map showing marked alternative routes is available from service stations display the 'Bison Futé' poster (a Red Indian chief in full war bonnet). These maps are also available from Syndicats d'Initiative and Information Offices.

S

SPARES

Motorists are recommended to carry a set of replacement bulbs. If you are able to replace a faulty bulb when asked to do so by the police, you may still have to pay a fine but you may avoid the cost and inconvenience of a garage call out. Other useful items are windscreen wiper blades, a length of electrical cable and a torch.

Remember when ordering spare parts for dispatch abroad you must be able to identify them clearly - by the manufacturer's part numbers if known. Always quote your engine and vehicle identification number (VIN).

SPEED LIMITS

On normal roads - Built up areas: 50kph (31mph)
Outside built up areas: 90kph (55mph). **Dual Carriage-ways with central reservation:**110kph (69mph)
On motorways- 130kph (80mph)

Note: minimum speed in the fast lane on a level stretch of motorway in good daytime visibility is 80kph (49mph).

Maximum speed on the Paris Périphérique is 80kph (49mph); on other urban stretches of motorway, 1109kph (69kph).

In fog, when visibility is reduced to 50 metres, the speed limit on all roads is 50kph (31mph) and in wet weather speed limits outside built-up areas are reduced to 80kph (49mph), 100kph (62mph) on dual carriageways and 110kph (69mph) on other motoways.

Drivers who have held a licence for less than two years must at all times observe these reduced speed limits.

T

TAX DISC

See Vehicle Excise Licence

TOLL ROADS (PÉAGE)

Tolls are payable on most motorways in France, and over long distances charges can be considerable. Motorists collect a ticket on entering the motorway and pay at the exit. You must have local currency or a credit card. Travellers' cheques and Eurocheques are not accepted. Please note that (for a UK driver) booths are virtually always on the passenger side of the car).

TRAFFIC LIGHTS

Traffic lights are similar to those in the UK, except that they turn directly from red to green, but from green through amber to red. The intensity of the light is poor, and they could be easily missed, especially those overhead. There is usually only one set by the right-hand side of the road, at some distance before the junction and if you stop too close to the corner, you may not be able to see them change. Watch for 'filter' lights enabling you to turn right and enter the appropriate lane.

TRAMS

Trams have priority over other vehicles. Never obstruct the passage of a tram. Always give way to passengers boarding and alighting. Trams must be overtaken on the right except in one-way streets.

V

VEHICLE EXCISE LICENCE

Remember that your tax disc needs to be valid on your return from abroad, so if it is due to expire while you are away, you can apply by post to a Head Post Office up to 42 days in advance of the expiry date. You should explain why you need it and ask for it to be posted either to your home address or your address abroad. The application form must be completed with your UK address, however.

Residents of the Republic of Ireland should contact their local Vehicle Registration Office.

Residents of Northern Ireland should apply to the Driver and Vehicle Licensing Northern Ireland, Vehicle licensing Division, County Hall, Coleraine BT51 3HS.

‖ W ‖

WARNING TRIANGLE

If you should break down or be involved in an accident, the use of a warning triangle or hazard warning lights is compulsory. As hazard warning lights may be damaged, we recommend that you carry a warning triangle, which should be placed 30 metres behind the vehicle (100 metres on motorways), about 60 cm from the edge of the road, but not in such a position as to present a danger to oncoming traffic, and be clearly visible from 100 metres, by day and night.

WEATHER INFORMATION

UK Regional weather reports are provided direct from the Met. Office by the AA Weatherwatch recorded information service.

National Forecast*	**0336 401 130**
London & SE England	**0336 401 131**
West Country	**0336 401 132**
Wales	**0336 401 133**
Midlands	**0336 401 134**
East Anglia	**0336 401 135**
NW England	**0336 401 136**
NE England	**0336 401 137**
Scotland	**0336 401 138**
Northern Ireland	**0336 401 139**

For weather reports for crossing the Channel and northern France, call 0336 401 361, whilst Continental Roadwatch on 0336 401 904 provides information on traffic conditions to and from ferry ports, ferry news and details of major European events. A world-wide, city-by-city six-day weather forecast is also available on 0336 411 212.

For other weather information for the UK and the Continent (but not road conditions) please contact:

The Met Office
Enquiries Officer, London Road
Bracknell, Berkshire RG12 2SZ

or telephone 01344 854455 during normal office hours.

* Calls are charged at 50p per minute at all times.

★★★
ℙRIMOTEL GROUP

When in Paris, the ideal location for business and pleasure

The Primotel ★★★ Empire is a few steps away from the Place de l'Etoile and the famous Champs Elysées. 49 rooms – Meeting room.

Primotel ★★★ Empire:
3 Rue Montenotte 75017 PARIS
Tel: (33) (0)1 43 80 14 55 –
Fax: (33) (0)1 47 66 04 33

3-Star comfort in Marseille's Airport area

The Primotel ★★★ offers you an ideal location for business lunches and meetings. 120 rooms – 5 meeting-rooms, restaurant, swimming-pool, tennis.

Primotel ★★★ Aeroport Marseille Provence: Face à lAéroport 13127 VITROLLES
Tel: (33) (0)4 42 79 79 19 – Fax: (33) (0)4 42 89 69 18

The charm of Provence Region

A few minutes away from the Historic City of Arles, you will find the Primotel ★★★ Camargue 144 rooms, a traditional restaurant, 4 meeting-rooms, a swimming-pool, 2 tennis courts and a large private car park.

Primotel ★ ★ ★ Camargue:
Face au Palais des Congrès 13200 ARLES
Tel: (33) (0)4 90 93 80 – Fax: (33) (0)4 90 49 92 76

In the heart of the old town of Avignon

The 70 room Primotel ★ ★ ★ Horloge is situated a few steps away from the Palais des Papes, in the pedestrian area of the Place de l'Horloge, with its typical cafes and restaurants.

Primotel ★★★ Horloge:
Place de l'Horloge 84000 AVIGNON
Tel: (33) (0)4 90 86 88 61 – Fax: (33) (0)4 90 82 17 32

In the city of Stars!

The Primotel ★★★ Canberra opens its doors onto the famous Rue d'Antibes, the shopping area of Cannes and just 100 metres away, the Croisette and the Festival Hall. 44 rooms. Private car-park.

Primotel ★★★ Canberra: 120 Rue d'Antibes 06400 CANNES
Tel: (33) (0)4 93 38 20 70 – Fax: (33) (0)4 92 98 03 47

A scenic view of the Baie des Anges

Right on the Promenade des Anglais, the Primotel ★★★ Suisse benefits a wonderful view over the Baie des Anges. The old town, its flower markets, its typical restaurants are in a walking distance of the hotel. 42 rooms. Meeting room.

Primotel ★★★ Suisse:
15 Quai Raubà Capéù 06300 NICE
Tel: (33) (0)4 92 17 39 00 – Fax: (33) (0)4 93 85 30 70

■■Booking Accommodation■■

Below is a standard letter which can be sent out to the place you're planning to stay. Do remember to enclose an international reply coupon with your letter. These are available from all post offices and at the time of going to press cost 60p. In Britain, a room with bath/shower automatically includes a WC. In France you need to ask. **Please do not send an SAE with your letter, as English stamps are invalid in France**.

ENGLISH

Your address
in full
with post-code
and country

Hotel's
address
in full
with
country

00.00.98

Dear Sir/Madam

I should be very grateful if you would send me by return of post your prices for, and the availabilty of, accommodation with full board/half board/bed and breakfast from 00.00.98 until 00.00.98.

I should like to reserve ... single room(s) with/without bath/shower & WC   ... double room(s) with/without bath/ shower & WC   ... twin room(s) with/without bath/ shower & WC   ... cot(s) in the parents' room

We are a party of ..., comprising ... adult(s), and ... child(ren) aged .../both under ... years.

Please find enclosed an International Reply Coupon.

I would like to take this opportunity to thank you in advance, and look forward to hearing from you soon.

Yours faithfully

FRENCH

Your address
in full
with post-code
and country

Hotel's
address
in full with
country

00.00.98

Monsieur le Directeur/Madame la Directrice

Je vous serais reconnaissant de bien vouloir me communiquer, par retour du courrier, vos tarifs et la disponibilité d'un séjour en pension complet/demi-pension/chambre et petit déjeuner du 00.00.98 jusq'au 00.00.98.

Je voudrais retenir... chambre(s) pour une personne avec/sans bain/douche et toilette
... chambre(s) avec un grand lit avec/sans bain/douche et toilette
... chambre(s) à deux lits avec/sans bain/douche et toilette
... lit(s) d'enfants avec petit lit dans la chambre des parents.

Nous sommes ..., ... adulte(s), et ... enfant(s) de ... ans/touts moins ... ans. Ci-inclus un coupon-réponse international.

J'attends vos renseignements et vous remercie par avance. Je vous prie, monsieur le directeur/madame la directrice, d'agréer l'expression de mes sentiments distingués.

▮▮Booking by Telephone▮▮

Remember, even if you make a reservation by telephone, it is always advisable to then write to the establishment confirming your booking arrangements. The French for numbers, days of the week, months and telling the time can be found on pages 26.

ENGLISH	FRENCH
Hello, I'd like to make a reservation please_____	Bonjour, je voudrais faire une réservation
We shall need xx rooms with bath/shower and WC for__	Il nous faut xx chambre(s) avec bain/douche et toilette pour
xx nights from (10 July to 13 July):_____	xx nuits, du (dix juillet jusqu'au treize juillet):
xx single rooms_____	xx chambres pour une personne
xx twin-bedded rooms_____	xx chambres à deux lits
xx double rooms _____	xx chambres à grand lit
There are (four) people with a baby and a child of_____	Nous sommes (quatre) personne(s) accompagnés d'un bébé et
(10) years	d'un enfant âgé de (dix) ans
Reply a) - I'm sorry, we are fully booked _____	Reply a) - Je suis désolé, mais l'hôtel est complet
Reply b) - Of course; we have rooms available _____	Reply b) - Bien sûr; nous avons des chambres
I'll arrive about midday/4 pm on 10 July_____	J'arriverai vers midi/quatres heures de l'après midi le
	dix juillet
How long will you be staying? _____	Pour combien de temps voulez-vous rester?
For ... nights, please _____	Pour ... nuits
Would you like full board, half-board, or bed and_____	Voulez-vous rester avec pension complet, demi pension, ou
breakfast?	chambre avec petit déjeuner?
How much does full board/half-board/bed and_____	C'est combien pour rester avec pension complet /demi-
breakfast cost?	pension/ chambre avec petit déjeuner?
It costs ... francs_____	ça coute ... franc
I'd like full board,/half-board,/bed and breakfast _____	Je voudrais rester avec pension complet/demi pension/chambre
please	avec petit déjeuner, s'il vous plaît
a) - Certainly sir/madam; your name, address and_____	a) - Bien sûr, monsieur/ madame; votre nom, adresse et
telephone number?	nombre de téléphone?
b) - How many are there in your party? _____	b) - Vous êtes combien?
There are ... of us; ... adult(s) and ... child(ren)_____	Nous sommes ..., ... adulte(s) et ... enfant(s)
How old is/are your child(ren)_____	Quel age a/ont l'(les) enfant(s)?
a) - ...and ... years old_____	a) - Ils ont ... ans et ... ans
b) - The girl/boy is ... years old _____	b) - La fille/le garçon a xx ans
I'd like a double room and a twin-bedded room _____	J'aimerais une chambre à grand lit, et une chambre
	à deux lits
I'm sorry but we only have two double rooms - _____	Je suis désolé, mais nous n'avons que deux chambres à grand
will that be alright?	lit – ça va bien?
With shower or bath?_____	Avec bain ou douche?
Could you put a cot in the parents' room? _____	Pouvez-vous mettre un petit lit dans la chambre des parents?
Certainly sir/madam, thank you_____	Bien sûr monsieur/madame, merci.

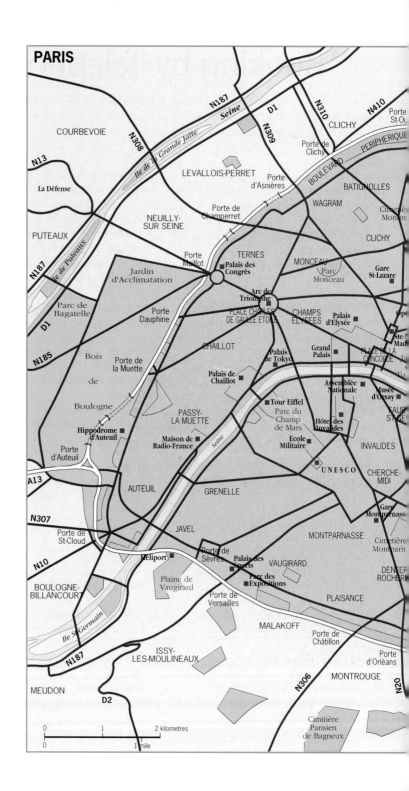

PARIS

COURBEVOIE

CLICHY

Porte St-Ou

Seine

Ile de la Grande Jatte

Porte de Clichy

PERIPHERIQUE

La Défense

LEVALLOIS-PERRET

Porte d'Asnières

BATIGNOLLES

BOULEVARD

WAGRAM

Porte de Champerret

Cimetière Montm

NEUILLY-SUR SEINE

PUTEAUX

CLICHY

Ile de Puteaux

Jardin d'Acclimatation

Porte Maillot

Palais des Congrès

TERNES

MONCEAU

Parc Monceau

Gare St-Lazare

Arc de Triomphe

Parc de Bagatelle

Porte Dauphine

PLACE CHARLES DE GAULLE ETOILE

CHAMPS ELYSEES

Palais d'Elysée

Op

Bois

Porte de la Muette

CHAILLOT

Palais de Tokyo

Grand Palais

PLACE DE LA CONCORDE

Ste-Mad

de

Palais de Chaillot

Assemblée Nationale

Musée d'Orsay

Boulogne

Tour Eiffel

PASSY-LA MUETTE

Parc du Champ de Mars

Hôtel des Invalides

Hippodrome d'Auteuil

Maison de Radio-France

Seine

Ecole Militaire

INVALIDES

Porte d'Auteuil

AUTEUIL

GRENELLE

UNESCO

CHERCHE-MIDI

Gare Montparnass

Porte de St-Cloud

JAVEL

MONTPARNASSE

Cimetière Montparn

Héliport

Porte de Sèvres

Palais des Sports

VAUGIRARD

DENFER ROCHER

BOULOGNE-BILLANCOURT

Plaine de Vaugirard

Parc des Expositions

PLAISANCE

Porte de Versailles

Ile St-Germain

MALAKOFF

Porte de Châtillon

Porte d'Orléans

N187

ISSY-LES-MOULINEAUX

MONTROUGE

MEUDON

D2

Cimitière Parisien de Bagneux

0   1   2 kilometres

0   1 mile

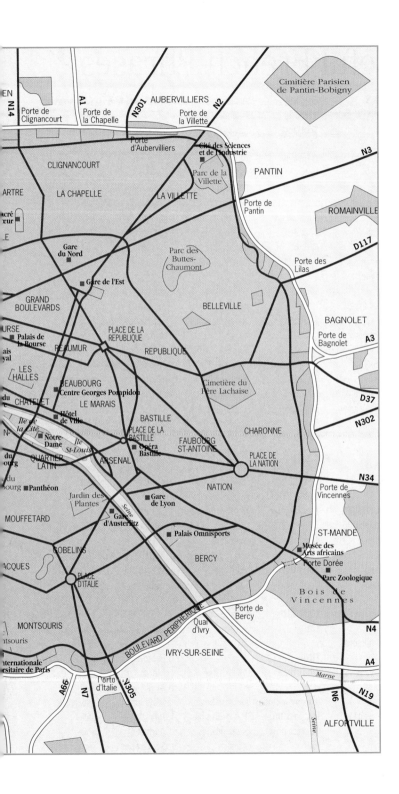

"Useful French Phrases"

GENERAL EXPRESSIONS

Hello _____	Bonjour
Goodbye _____	Au revoir
Good morning _	Bonjour
Good evening _	Bonsoir
Good night ____	Bonne nuit
See you later __	A bientôt
Please/ _____	S'il vous plaît/
thankyou	merci
You're _____	Je vous en prie
welcome	
Yes/no _____	Oui/non
Excuse me ____	Excusez-moi
I'm sorry _____	Pardon
How are you? _	Comment allez-vous?
I'm fine, thanks	Très bien merci
My name is ____	Je m'appelle
Mr/Mrs/Miss	Monsieur/ Madame/ Mademoiselle
I like/don't ____	J'aime/je n'aime
like ...	pas ...
That's fine/OK _	Ça va
What time ____	A quelle heure
do you open/	vous ouvrez/
close?	fermez?

LANGUAGES AND COUNTRIES

I am English ___	Je suis Anglais(e)
Scottish	Ecossais(e)
Welsh / Irish ...	Gallois(e) / Irlandais(e) ...
Do you speak _	Parlez-vous
English?	anglais?
I don't speak __	Je ne parle pas
French	français
I don't _____	Je ne comprends
understand	pas
Could you_____	Pourriez-vous
speak more	parler plus
slowly please?	lentement, s'il vous plaît?

England _____	Angleterre
Ireland _____	Irelande
Scotland _____	Écosse
Wales_____	Pays de Galles
Germany _____	Allemagne
Italy _____	Italie
Spain _____	Espagne

NUMBERS

1, 2, 3 _____	un, deux, trois
4, 5, 6 _____	quatre, cinq, six
7, 8, 9, 10 _____	sept, huit, neuf, dix
11, 12, 13 _____	onze, douze, treize
14, 15, 16 _____	quatorze, quinze, seize
17, 18, 19 _____	dix-sept, dix-huit, dix-neuf
20, 21, 22 _____	vingt, vingt-et -un, vingt-deux
30, 40, 50 _____	trente, quarante, cinquante
60, 70, 80 _____	soixante, soixante-dix, quatre-vingts
90, 100, 101 ___	quatre-vingts-dix, cent, cent-et-un
1000, 2000 ____	mille, deux milles
1st, 2nd, 3rd___	premier, deuxième, troisième
4th, 5th, 6th ___	quatrième, cinquième, sixième
7th, 8th, 9th ___	septième, huitième, neuvième
10th, 11th,_____	dixième, onzième, douzième
12th	

TIME

What time ____	Quelle heure
is it?	est-il?
It's one o'clock	Il est une heure
Ten past three _	Trois heures dix
Quarter past___	Quatre heures
four	et quart

Half past five__	Cinq heure set demi
Twenty to six __	Six heures moins vingt
Quarter to ____	Sept heures moins
seven	le quart
This morning/ _	Ce matin/soir
evening	
Now _____	Maintenant
At once _____	Tout de suite
It's late/early __	Il est tard/tôt
Sorry I'm late _	Je suis désolé d'être en retard
second,_____	seconde,
minute, hour	minute, heure
yesterday,_____	hier,
today,	aujourd'hui,
tomorrow	demain
midday _____	midi
midnight _____	minuit
day, night_____	le jour, la nuit

DAYS OF THE WEEK

Monday _____	lundi
Tuesday _____	mardi
Wednesday ____	mercredi
Thursday _____	jeudi
Friday _____	vendredi
Saturday _____	samedi
Sunday _____	dimanche

MONTHS AND DATES

What's the ____	Quelle est la
date?	date?
It's the first____	Nous sommes le
of July /	premier juillet / le
2nd August	deux août
January_____	janvier
February _____	février
March _____	mars
April_____	avril
May, June _____	mai, juin
July _____	juillet
August _____	août
September____	septembre

October _____ octobre
November _____ novembre
December_____ décembre

SHOPPING
How much?____ Combien?
I'm just_____ Je regarde
looking   seulement
That's enough, _ Ça suffit, merci
thank you
May I have a ___ Puis-je avoir un
bag please?   sac, s'il vous plaît?
Have you got...? Est-ce que vous
                 avez ... ?
I'd like ..._____ Je voudrai ...
Could you_____ Pouvez-vous me
show me ... ?   montrer
supermarket___ supermarché
newsagent_____ marchand de
                 journaux
newspaper_____ journal
bookshop_____ librairie
writing paper _ papier à lettres
envelopes_____ envelopes
a map _____ une carte
(of the area)   (de la région)
town plan_____ plan de la ville
a colour/black _ une pellicule
and white film   couleur/noir et
                 blanc
tights_____ un collant
a guide book __ un guide
an umbrella ___ un parapluie
coins_____ des pièces
change _____ la monnaie

CHEMIST _____ LA PHARMACIE
I've got a _____ J'ai mal à
headache   la tête
stomach ache _ mal au ventre
I've got a cold _ Je suis enrhumé
aspirin_____ de l'aspirine
antiseptic_____ antiseptique
cotton wool ___ du coton
disposable ____ couches en
nappies   cellulose
paper tissues __ Kleenex

sanitary towels couches
                périodiques
tampons _____ tampons
                périodiques
suntan oil_____ huile solaire
toilet paper___ papier hygiénique
razor blades ___ lames de rasoir
plasters _____ pansements
                adhésifs
soap _____ savon
toothpaste____ dentifrice

POST OFFICE __ LA POSTE
How much is __ Combien coûte un
a stamp for   timbre pour
England?   l'Angleterre?
Where can I____ Où puis-je
telephone?   téléphoner?
letter _____ lettre
postcard _____ carte postale
parcel _____ paquet
post box _____ boîte aux lettres
phone box ____ cabinet
                téléphonique
tobacconist ___ bureau de tabac
A packet of ...__ Un paquet de ...
please   s'il vous plaît
cigarettes_____ cigarettes
cigars_____ cigares
tobacco _____ tabac
matches_____ allumettes
lighter _____ briquet

FOOD SHOPPING
BAKER/CAKE___ BOULANGERIE/
SHOP   PÂTISSERIE
pastries _____ pâtisseries
bread_____ pain
French stick ___ baguette
cake _____ gâteau
rolls_____ petits pains
butcher/_____ boucherie/
delicatessen   charcuterie
one/two_____ une/deux
slice(s) of ...   tranche(s) de ...
half a kilo of ... un demi-kilo de ...
a pound_____ une livre
(weight)

250 grams of ... deux cent
                 cinquante
                 grammes de
fresh, raw, ____ frais, cru, cuit,
cooked,   fumé
smoked
cheese_____ fromage
ham _____ jambon
kidneys_____ rognons
liver _____ foie
mince_____ viande hachée
pâté _____ pâté
sausage _____ saucisse

FISHMONGER__ POISSONNERIE
anchovies_____ anchois
mussels _____ moules
oysters _____ huîtres
prawns _____ crevettes roses
sardines_____ sardines
crab _____ crabe
lobster _____ homard
squid _____ calmar
octopus _____ poulpe
GREENGROCER_ MARCHAND DE
                 FRUITS ET
                 LÉGUMES
apples_____ pommes
bananas_____ bananes
grapefruit_____ pamplemousse
grapes_____ raisins
melon _____ melon
oranges _____ oranges
peaches _____ pêches
raspberries ___ framboises
strawberries ___ fraises
carrots _____ carottes
cucumber _____ concombre
garlic _____ ail
green beans ___ haricots verts
lettuce _____ laitue
mushrooms ___ champignons
onions_____ oignons
peas _____ petit pois
potatoes _____ pommes de terre
tomatoes _____ tomates

DIRECTIONS

Where is/are ...	Où se trouve/ trouvent ...
Turn left / right	Tournez à gauche /à droite
Go straight on	Continuez tout droit
Take the first left/right	Prenez la première à gauche / droite

AT THE HOTEL

I have a booking, my name is ...	J'ai une réservation, je m'appelle
What floor is the room on?	À quel étage se trouve la chambre?
Is there a lift?	Y a-t-il un ascenseur?
Could I see the room?	Pourrais-je voir la chambre?
Does the price include ...?	Est-ce que le prix comprend?
The key for room ... please	La clef pour chambre s'il vous plaît
Please call me at ...	S'il vous plaît, réveillez-moi à ...
Where can I park?	Où puis-je garer la voiture?
Are there any letters for me?	Y a-t-il des lettres pour moi?
The bill please?	La note, s'il vous plaît?
guesthouse	pension
inn	auberge
single room	chambre à un lit
twin bedded room	chambre à deux lits
double room	chambre à grand lit
blanket	couverture
coat hanger	cintre

chambermaid	femme de chambre
manager	directeur
porter	concierge
pillow	oreiller
room service	service d'étage
sheets	draps
towel	serviette de toilette

TRAVEL
(See also Directions)

ON THE ROAD	SUR LA ROUTE
Fill it up, please	Faites le plein, s'il vous plaît
(10) litres of 4 star, please	(10) litres de super, s'il vous plaît
unleaded	sans plomb
diesel	diesel / gas oil
LPG	gaz de pétrole liquéfié (GPL)
Please check water level	Veuillez vérifier niveau d'eau
antifreeze	l'antigel
battery	la batterie
brake fluid	le liquide des freins
oil	huile
oil filter	le filtre à huile
My car.... won't start	Ma voiture ...ne démarre pas
has broken down	est en panne
I've lost my car key	J'ai perdu ma clef de contact
It won't go	Il ne marche pas
I have no petrol	Je n'ai plus d'essence
to hire a car	louer une voiture
the bill?	la facture?
broken	cassé
engine	le moteur

exhaust	l'échappement
handbrake	frein à main
horn	klaxon
ignition	l'allumage
puncture	crevaison
tow	remorquer
windscreen	pare-brise

AT THE STATION À LA GARE
[Note: at railway stations, when you have purchased your ticket, you must validate it (i.e. get it date-stamped) in one of the machines you will find on your way to the platform. If you forget to do this, you may incur a fine.]

by rail/bus	par train /autobus
railway/bus station	gare / gare routière
a single to	un billet simple pour
a return	un aller-et-retour pour
When is the next bus/train to ...?	A quelle heure part le prochain autobus/train pour?
Is this the train/bus for...?	Est-ce bien le train / le bus pour?...
Do I have to change?	Faut-il changer?
platform	quai
bus stop	arrêt d'autobus
entry/exit	entrée/sortie
seat	la place
Is this seat taken?	Est-ce que cette place est occupée?
ticket collector	le contrôleur
ticket office	le guichet
timetable	horaire

BONSAÏ HOTELS®

20 hotels across France classified in 3 labels

HOTEL
BONSAÏ ESCALE

149FF

per room
for 1, 2 or 3 persons

298FF

family suite
for up to 6 persons

HOTEL
BONSAÏ ETAPE

169FF

per room
for 1, 2 or 3 persons

338FF

family suite
for up to 5 persons

HOTEL   RESTAURANT
BONSAÏ RELAIS

from

195FF

per double or twin room
gourmet restaurant
conference rooms

For information and bookings, please call ☎ 0 0 3 3 5 5 7 2 5 2 5 0 7

"What's on the Menu"

A holiday in France can be the gastronome's idea of heaven. Each region has a different specialty or drink associated with it, but wherever you are, always look out for the set menu (menu à prix fixé), which will give you the best value for money.

Below is a list of phrases which should be useful when ordering a meal in a restaurant, and the list also includes words for the types of foods and dishes you will come across on the menu. Each section lists some traditional dishes, as well as ordinary menu terms.

recommend?	recommandez?
I'd like ... please	Je voudrais ... s'il vous plaît
Do you have ...?	Avez-vous ...?
tourist menu	menu touristique
knife, fork	couteau, fourchette
spoon	cuillière
cup, saucer	tasse, soucoupe
plate, dish	assiette, plat
napkin	serviette
pepper/salt	poivre/sel

PROBLEMS

Where are our drinks?	Où sont nos boissons?
The food is cold	Le plat est froid
It is not properly cooked	Ce n'est pas bien cuit

PAYING

May I have the bill?	L'addition s'il vous plaît?
Is service included?	Le service, est-il compris?
Do you take credit cards/traveller's cheques?	Acceptez-vous les cartes de crédit/ les chèques de voyage?
Thank you, the meal was wonderful	Merci, c'était très bon

BOOKING AND ARRIVING

I'd like to book a table for two at eight o'clock	Je voudrais réserver une table pour deux à huit heures
I've booked a table	J'ai reservé une table
A table for ... please	Une table pour ... s'il vous plaît
Is this table taken?	Cette table est-elle libre?
May we have an ashtray please?	Pouvons-nous avoir un cendrier, s'il vous plaît?
Where is the cloakroom?	Où se trouvent les toilettes?
self service café	libre-service
bar	bar
take-away	mets à emporter

ORDERING

Is there a set menu?	Y a-t-il un menu à prix fixe?
Do you serve children's portions?	Servez-vous des portions d'enfant?
What is the regional speciality?	Quelle est la spécialité du pays?
What is the dish of the day?	Quel est le plat du jour?
What do you	Qu'est-ce que vous

THE MENU

starter	hors d'oeuvres
main course	entrée
dessert	dessert
meat	viande
chop, cutlet	côtelette
escalope	escalope
grilled, fried	grillé(e), frit(e)
rare, medium,	saignant, à point,
well done	bien cuit
roast, boiled	rôti(e), bouilli(e)
stewed, baked	à l'étouffée, au four

beef _____ boeuf
chicken _____ poulet
ham _____ jambon
lamb _____ agneau
pork _____ porc
steak _____ bifteck
veal _____ veau

andouille _____ smoky flavoured sausage
boeuf bourguignon __ rich beef stew made with red
wine, mushrooms and onions
boudin blanc _____ white sausage made with a
variety of meats
carbonnade de boeuf_ a beef and beer stew
carré d'agneau _____ loin of lamb, cooked with herbs
Châteaubriand _____ a thick fillet steak
cochon de lait _____ sucking pig
crépinettes _____ small sausages enriched with
herbs and brandy
jambon persillé _____ a Burgundy speciality of jellied
ham and parsley
potée auvergnate _____ a salt pork and vegetable stew
from the Auvergne and
Languedoc
tripes à la mode _____ traditional Norman dish of tripe,
de Caen with onions and carrots

FISH/SHELLFISH _____ POISSON/FRUITS DE MER
fish _____ poisson
carp _____ carpe
clams _____ palourdes
cod _____ morue
crab _____ crabe
Dublin Bay prawns/ __ langoustines
scampi
freshwater crayfish __ écrevisses
lobster _____ homard
mackerel _____ maquereau
monkfish _____ lotte
mussels _____ moules
octopus _____ poulpe
oysters _____ huîtres
rock lobster _____ langouste
salmon _____ saumon
sardines _____ sardines
sea bass _____ loup de mer

sea urchin _____ oursin
shellfish _____ fruits de mer
shrimps/prawns _____ crevettes
skate _____ raie
sole _____ sole
squid _____ calmar
trout _____ truite
tuna _____ thon
turbot _____ turbot
whiting _____ merlan

assiettes de fruit _____ a mixed platter of cooked
de mer seafood and assorted shellfish
bisque de homard _____ lobster soup
bouillabaisse _____ a Mediterranean fish stew
moules marinières _____ mussels in a white wine sauce
quenelles de brochet _ a classic dish of pike rissoles
salade Niçoise _____ tuna salad, from Provence
sole Véronique _____ sole garnished with grapes

POULTRY/GAME _____ VOLAILLE/GIBIER
wing _____ aile
breast _____ blanc/suprême
chicken _____ poulet
duck _____ canard
goose _____ oie
partridge _____ perdreau
quail _____ caille
rabbit _____ lapin
spring chicken _____ poussin
turkey _____ dinde
venison _____ chevreuil
wild boar _____ sanglier

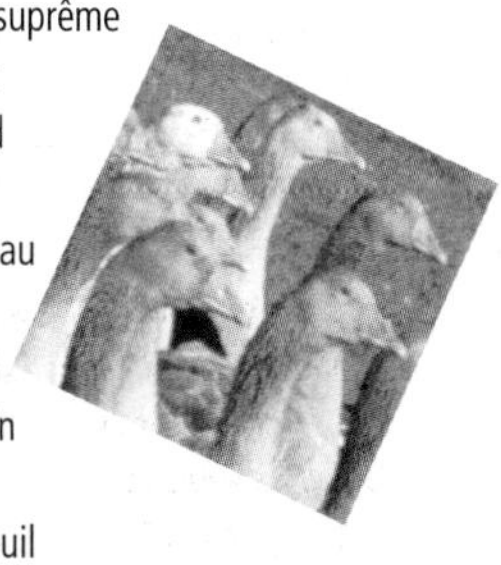

canard à l'orange _____ duck in orange sauce
caneton à la _____ pink-fleshed duck
Rouennais
civet de lièvre _____ jugged hare
confit de canard/ _____ wings or legs of duck or goose,
d'oie preserved in their own fat, found
especially in the Perigord and
Quercy areas
coq au vin _____ chicken in red wine, onions,
bacon and mushrooms
foie gras _____ goose liver, often made into a
very rich pâté

EGGS	ŒUFS
boiled, fried,	à la coq, sur le plat, brouillés,
scrambled, poached	pochés
savoury omelette	omlette aux fines herbes
soufflé	soufflé

œufs à la mayonnaise	egg mayonnaise
pipérade	scrambled eggs prepared with peppers and tomatoes
Quiche Lorraine	an open savoury tart filled with a rich egg custard filling with bacon and onion

VEGETABLES/	LÉGUMES/
SIDE DISHES	GARNITURES
artichoke hearts	fonds d'artichauts
chips	frites
French dressing	vinaigrette
green salad	salade verte
mixed salad	salade panachée
oil	huile
pasta	pâtes
pepper	poivre
rice	riz
vinegar	vinaigre

aioli	garlic mayonnaise
choucroute	sauerkraut
cousinat	chestnut, cream and fruit stew
galettes	buckwheat pancakes
mojettes	kidney beans in butter made from pasteurised cream, west coast speciality
truffes	truffles
pissaladière	onion tart
potage julienne	vegetable soup
ratatouille	tomato, aubergine, onion and pepper stew
vichyssoise	creamy leek and potato soup

FRUIT AND NUTS	FRUITS ET NOIX
(See also Food Shopping)	
cherry	cerise
chestnut	marron
fig	figue
hazelnut	noisette
lemon	citron
pineapple	ananas
plum	prune
raisin	raisin sec
raspberry	framboise
walnut	noix
water melon	pastèque
wild strawberries	fraises des bois

DESSERT	DESSERT
cake	gâteau
cheese	fromage
fritters	beignets
fruit salad	salade de fruits
ice cream	glace
pancakes	crêpes
(strawberry) tart	tarte (aux fraises)

DRINKS	BOISSONS
black/white coffee	café noir/au lait
fruit juice	jus de fruit
beer	bière
lemonade	limonade
mineral water	eau minérale
fizzy	gazeuse
orangeade	orangeade

tea with milk/lemon __	thé au lait/avec citron
red/white/rosé wine __	vin rouge/blanc/rosé
dry/sweet _____	sec/doux
sparkling _____	pétillant/mousseux
glass _____	verre
half bottle/bottle _____	demi bouteille/bouteille

SOME TRADITIONAL DRINKS

Bénédictine _____	liqueur made from aromatic herbs by the monks of Fécamp
Calvados _____	apple brandy from Normandy and Brittany
cassis _____	either a sweet blackcurrant liqueur or a provençal wine traditionally drunk with bouillabaisse
Champagne _____	champagne
cidre _____	cider
cognac _____	brandy fom Bordeaux
pastis _____	an aniseed aperitif
vin de Xérès _____	sherry

CHEESE

France is justly famous for its many different cheeses. Here are just a few to look out for

Boursin _____	Garlic and herb cheese
Brie _____	Originally from the Ile de France region but widely available, combining a creamy texture with a full taste
Camembert _____	A creamy cheese from Normandy
Cantal _____	hard and yellow, with a 2000 year-old tradition, from Auvergne
Epoisses _____	a ripe Burgundian speciality
Gruyère _____	a hard, full-fat cheese with a nutty taste
Livarot _____	a Normandy speciality, with a strong taste
Munster _____	highly aromatic, with a sharp taste, developed in the Alsace region by monks during the 7th century
Reblochon _____	a soft, fruity Alpine cheese

"World Cup"
Tourist Offices and Fixtures

WORLD CUP CONTACTS
French tourist office contacts for the towns and cities that are hosting the various rounds for the World Cup:

BORDEUX
Jean-Daniel Terrassin, Office de Tourisme, 19 Cours du 30 Juillet, 333080 Bordeaux.
Tel 0033 556442841 Fax 0033 556818921

LENS
Yves Silvain, Office de Tourisme, 26 rue de la Paix, 63200 Lens.
Tel 0033 321676666 Fax 0033 321676566

LYONS
Eriv Ballarin, Office de Tourisme, Place Bellecour, BP 2254, 69214 Lyon.
Tel 0033 472777230 Fax 0033 178370206

MARSEILLES
Maxime Tissot, Office de Tourisme 4 La Canabiere, 13000 Marseille
Tel 0033 491138900 Fax 0033491138920

MONTPELLIER
Helene Schneider, Office de Tourisme 78 Avenue du Piree, 34000 Montpellier
Tel 0033 467606060 Fax 0033 467606061

NANTES
Michele Guillossiou, Office de Tourisme 7 rue Valmy, 44041 Nantes Cedex 01
Tel 0033 251882020 Fax 0033 240891199

PARIS
Stephanie Bertrand, Office de Tourisme 127 avenue des Champs Elysees. 75008 Paris
Tel 0033 149525381 Fax 0033 149525310

SAINT-DENIS
Theodoulitsa Kouloumbri, Office de Tourisme, 1 rue de la Republique, 93200 Saint-Denis
Tel 0033 155870870 Fax 0033 148202411

SAINT ETIENNE
Dominique Vettier, 3 place Roannelle, 42029 Saint Etienne, Cedex 1
Tel 0033 477251214 Fax 0033 477322728

TOULOUSE
Marc Julia, Office de Tourisme, Donjon du Capitol 31080 Toulouse
Tel 0033 561110222 Fax 0033 561220303

FIXTURES CALENDAR
A useful tool for those that wish to attend World Cup events and those who would prefer to avoid them.

FIRST ROUND

MONTPELLIER
Stade de la Mosson
Wed 10/6 Fri 12/6 Wed 17/6
Mon 22/6 Thur 25/6 Mon 29/6

SAINT-DENIS
Stade de France
Wed 10/6 Sat 13/6 Thur 18/6
Tue 23/6 Fri 26/6 28/6

BORDEAUX
Stade Lescure
Thur 11/6 Tue 16/6 Sat 20/6 Wed 24/6
Fri 26/6 Tues 30/6

TOULOUSE
Stadium Municipal
Thur 11/6 Sun 14/6 Thur 18/6
Mon 22/6 Wed 24/6 Mon 29/6

LENS
Stade Felix-Bollaert
Fri 12/6 Sun 14/6 Sun 21/6 Wed 24/6
Fri 26/6 Sun 28/6

LYONS
Stade de Gerland
Sat 13/6 Mon 15/6 Sun 21/6
Wed 24/6 Fri 26/6

MARSEILLES
Stade Municipal
Sat 13/6 Mon 15/6 Sat 20/6 Tues 23/6
Sat 27/6

NANTES
Stade de la Beaujoire
Sat 13/6 Tues 16/6 Sat 20/6 Tues 23/6
Thur 25/6

SAINT-ETIENNE
Stade Geoffroy-Guihard
Sun 14/6 Wed 17/6 Fri 19/6 Tue 23/6
Fri 26/6 Tues 30/6

PARIS
Parc des Princes
Mon 15/6 Fri19/6 Sun 21/6
Thur 25/6 Sat 27/6

QUARTER FINALS

NANTES
Stade de la Beaujoire
Fri 3/7

SAINT-DENIS
Stade de France
Fri 3/7

LYONS
Stade de Gerland
Sat 4/7

MARSEILLES
Stade Municipal
Sat 4/7

SEMI FINALS

MARSEILLES
Stade Municipal
Tues 7/7

SAINT-DENIS
Stade de France
Wed 8/7

FINALS

PARIS
Parc des Princes
Sat 11/7

SAINT-DENIS
Stade de France
Sun 12/7

Brittany

Of all France, Brittany most preserves an individuality and character of its own. Partly attributable to the religious heritage of its inhabitants, but also to its geographical location as the most westerly region; once it was almost inaccessible to the rest of the country. Early Christians of the 5th and 6th centuries arrived and built monasteries here. Breton, its native language, similar to old Cornish and Welsh, is still spoken; traditional costumes still worn; old Celtic customs and pilgrimage-processions adhered to. Away from the mystical aura, one finds countless little coves and miles of glorious, sandy beaches around its rocky coastline.

(Top): Trecesson is one of the many châteaux in a region which often needed to protect itself from its worst enemy of the middle ages, - France!

(Bottom): Seafood platter is on the menu at this Cancale restaurant. The town is best known for its oysters.

ESSENTIAL FACTS

Départements:	Côtes d'Armor, Finistère, Ille-et-Vilaine, Morbihan
PRINCIPAL TOWNS	Rennes, Fougères, St Brieuc, Brest, Quimper, Lorient,Vannes, St Malo
PLACES TO VISIT:	The standing stones at Carnac; the castles and fortresses of inland Brittany: Josselin, Vitré, Fourgères and Combourg; the medieval town of Dinan; the pilgrimage procession at Carantec on the first Sunday after 15 August
REGIONAL TOURIST OFFICE	74B r de Paris, 35069 Rennes Tel: 99 28 44 40
LOCAL GASTRONOMIC DELIGHTS	Assiette de fruits de mer, a seafood platter which may include lobster, langoustines, crab, mussels, sea perch, oyster and other seafood; cotriade, a seafood stew; coquilles-St-Jacques; the classic homard à l'armoricaine; far, a local pudding; galettes, savoury pancakes made with buckwheat flour; crêpes, sweet pancakes
DRINKS	Heady Breton cider, strong local beer, poiré, pear cider and lambig, fiery cider brandy
LOCAL CRAFTS WHAT TO BUY	Pottery and textiles from Quimper, numerous traditional craftsmen including woodcarvers, glass-blowers, weavers, engravers and turners are resident in Dinan

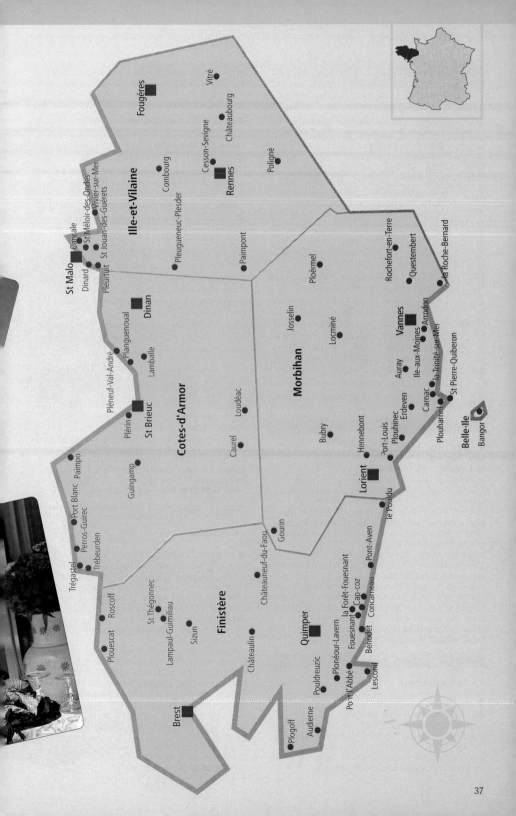

EVENTS & FESTIVALS

Mar	Rennes International Fair
Apr	St-Quay-Portrieux Festival of The Scallop
May	St-Malo Festival of Travel Writers, Tréguier
	St-Yves'Pardon (patron saint of lawyers)
Jun	Rumengol, le Faou Pardon of Our Lady of
	Rumengol; La Faouet, Pardon of Sainte
	Barbe;
Jul	La Pauline Festival (old sailing ships) at
	Pléneuf-Val-André; Pont-l'Abbé Embroider
	Festival; Josselin Medieval Festival; Gourin
	Pancake Fête; Quiberon Festival of Sea-
	Shanties; Fouesnant Apple-Tree Festival;
	Quimper Festival of Celtic Music; Vannes Jazz
	Festival; Concarneau Maritime Book Festival;
	Paimpol Festival of Newfoundland & Iceland
	Fishermen; Pontivy Musical Summer;
	Guingamp Folk Dancing Festival for Children;
	Camaret Musical Mondays; Auray Music &
	Folklore Festival; Plozevet Folklore Festival;
	Auray Pardon of Sainte-Anne Procession;
Aug	Lorient Interceltic Festival; Concarneau Fête
	Les Filets Bleus; Guingamp Dance Festival &
	Fête de St Loup; Étel Tuna Fair; Plomodiern
	Folklore Menez-Hom Festival; Arvor Folklore
	Festival; Vannes Arvor Folklore Festival;
	Perrros-Guirec Pardon of Notre Dame de la
	Clarté; Lamballe Fête des battages St-Aaron

Sep	Free concerts (classical, jazz, rock) on Brest
	waterfront; Plouha Pardon of Kermaria-en
	Isquit
Oct	St-Brieuc Art Rock Festival
Dec	Les Transmusicales (rock) at Rennes

Saints and Remedies

Saints are an integral part of Britanny's rich traditional culture. No other part of France venerates as many, as you'll discover from their statues in the numerous, fascinating chapels which are well worth visiting. Quimper diocese claims around 7,500 alone, yet only three of them get the Vatican's seal of approval. Bretons seem to have a saint to call on for every ailment and problem. Saint Livertin, whose statue is outside the chapel of Notre-Dame-du-Haut in Trédaniel, is the headache specialist; Saint Mammert takes care of stomach aches. Saints Nicodemus and Tugen are invoked at times of epidemics and rabies respectively; you can visit the former's holy well at Saint-Nicolas-des-Eaux. Women saints like Nonna, Ivy and Derrien are said to help with childhood illnesses. There's even a saint (Agatha) who helps mothers' problems with babies.

ARRADON Morbihan

★ ★ ★ **Le Logis de Parc er Gréo**
9 rue Mane Guen le Gréo *56610*
☎ 297447303 FAX 297448048
(leave N165 at 'Vannes Ouest' and follow signs towards Arradon until you pick up D101 to Moustoir then follow signs to Le Gréo)
Beside the Golf of Morbihan, at the end of a tree lined drive you will discover this charming, elegant hotel. The antique furniture, watercolours and model boats create an atmosphere of warmth and refinement.
Near sea Near beach Forest area
12 en suite (bth/shr) (3 fmly) No smoking in 2 bedrooms TV in all bedrooms Direct dial from all bedrooms Licensed Full central heating Open parking available Child discount available 9yrs Outdoor swimming pool (heated) Bicycle rental Covered terrace Last d 21.00hrs Languages spoken: English
ROOMS: (room only) s 304-438FF; d 416-498FF
MEALS: Full breakfast 46FF Dinner 120FF
CARDS: ⊕ ■ ⊞ ␌ Travellers cheques

AUDIERNE Finistère

★ ★ **Au Roi Gradlon**
29770
☎ 298700451 FAX 298701473
With its sea-front location, the hotel affords a magnificent view over the Atlantic Ocean and has direct access to the fine sandy beach. The south-facing bedrooms are all well equipped and have sea views. It is the ideal location for a relaxing holiday with a variety of sporting activities nearby. The restaurant has a good choice of seafood delicacies on the menu.

Near river Near sea Forest area
15 en suite (bth) (9 fmly) (7 with balcony) TV in all bedrooms STV Direct dial from all bedrooms Licensed Full central heating Open parking available Supervised Child discount available 10yrs Bicycle rental Open terrace Sports Centre close by Last d 21.00hrs Languages spoken: English
CARDS: ⊕ ■ ⊞ ␌ Travellers cheques

AURAY Morbihan

★ ★ ★ **Fairway**
56400
☎ 297568888 FAX 297568828
This hotel is the ideal venue for combining an active holiday with an appreciation of excellent cuisine. The bedrooms are bright and airy and offer modern day facilities, whilst the public areas are decorated with tasteful contemporary fabrics and furniture. The restaurant serves an array of classic dishes, whilst the wine list features several outstanding examples.
Near river Near sea Near beach Forest area
Closed 26 Dec-4 Jan
42 en suite (bth/shr) (8 fmly) (42 with balcony) No smoking in 21 bedrooms TV in all bedrooms STV Radio in rooms Direct dial from all bedrooms Licensed Night porter Full central heating Open parking available Supervised Child discount available 12yrs Outdoor swimming pool (heated) Golf 9 Tennis Sauna Solarium Gym Pool table Boule Jacuzzi/spa Bicycle rental Open terrace Covered terrace Sailing boats Last d 22.00hrs Languages spoken: English, German and Spanish
MEALS: Full breakfast 48FF Continental breakfast 48FF Lunch 80-130FF&alc Dinner 80-130FF&alc✱
CARDS: ⊕ ■ ⊞ ␌ Travellers cheques

★ ★ ★ Hotel-Village la Désirade
Le Petit Cosquet *56360*
☎ 297317070 FAX 297318963
The hotel La Désirade is almost unique. It has combined many styles from different countries in guests' accommodation: one room reflects the decor of a Tuscan villa whilst the other is furnished in oriental style. Surrounded by flowerbeds it provides a charming setting in which to unwind and recharge one's batteries.
Near sea
Closed early Jan-mid Feb
24 en suite (bth/shr) TV in all bedrooms STV Direct dial from all bedrooms Licensed Full central heating Open parking available Child discount available Outdoor swimming pool (heated) Bicycle rental Open terrace V meals Last d 21.30hrs Languages spoken: English,Spanish
MEALS: Full breakfast 60FF Dinner fr 200FF✱
CARDS: 🌑 ■ ☰ ⑨ Travellers cheques

★ ★ ★ Armoric Hotel
3 rue de Penfoul *29950*
☎ 298570403 FAX 298572128
(From the direction of Quimper towards Bénodet, hotel is first on right coming from the beach)
Benodet is a well-known sea-side resort on the South Brittany coast. Surrounded by peaceful flower-filled gardens, and close to the yachting harbour and beach, the Armoric hotel features smartly furnished bedrooms - with en-suite facilities overlooking a park - whilst a congenial bar and terrace invite visitors to relax or soak up the sun.
Near river Near sea Forest area In town centre Near motorway
30 en suite (bth/shr) 10 rooms in annexe (5 fmly) (4 with balcony) TV in all bedrooms Radio in rooms Mini-bar in 7 bedrooms Licensed Lift Night porter Full central heating Open parking available Covered parking available (charged) Supervised Child discount available 12yrs Outdoor swimming pool (heated) Tennis Boule Bicycle rental Open terrace V meals Languages spoken: English,Danish & German
ROOMS: (room only) s 395-495FF; d 395-875FF
Reductions over 1 night Special breaks
MEALS: Continental breakfast 45FF Lunch 130-240FF
CARDS: 🌑 ■ ☰ ⑨ Travellers cheques

★ ★ ★ Hotel Residence Eurogreen
Golf de l'Odet *29950*
☎ 298517300 FAX 298517349
(from Quimper take direction of Bénodet D34, in 10km at Le Drennel take direction of Clohars-Fouesnant D134, then follow signs Golf de l'Odet or Eurogreen)
The hotel overlooks the 10th fairway of the Golf de l'Odet, a quality 18 hole, 6235m, par 72 golf course, where hotel guests have priority at peak times. The hotel complex is spread out and comprises a main building and row of maisonettes; rooms and apartments are well equipped, and there is also self catering accommodation.
Closed 4-24 Apr
43 en suite (bth/shr) (37 fmly) (14 with balcony) TV in all bedrooms STV Direct dial from all bedrooms Licensed Full central heating Open parking available Supervised Outdoor swimming pool (heated) Golf 18 Tennis Sauna Solarium

Gym Bicycle rental Languages spoken: English
ROOMS: (room only) s 300-380FF; d 300-380FF
CARDS: 🌑 ☰

★ ★ Ker Vennaik
45 av de la Plage *29950*
☎ 298571540 FAX 298572748
(15km S of Quimper towards the sea via D34)
The hotel is located in the heart of Benodet, well known for its superb marina and lush vegetation. The pleasant bedrooms offer peaceful accommodation and have views of the flower-filled garden. In addition there is a bar and brasserie, and the restaurant can be found at the neighbouring hotel de la Poste.
Near river Near sea Near beach In town centre
Closed Nov-Mar
16 en suite (bth/shr) (2 fmly) (5 with balcony) TV in all bedrooms STV Radio in rooms Direct dial from all bedrooms Mini-bar in all bedrooms Room-safe Full central heating Open parking available Covered parking available Supervised Child discount available Pool table Open terrace Languages spoken: English
ROOMS: (room only) s 200-300FF; d 200-400FF ✱
CARDS: 🌑 ■ ☰ Travellers cheques

★ ★ Le Minaret
Corniche de l'Estuaire *29950*
☎ 298570313 FAX 298662372
This Moorish style house was built in 1925. Situated on an estuary, it offers panoramic views of the Atlantic ocean. The airy bedrooms are spacious and well equipped with modern amenities. The landscaped gardens are made to resemble the grounds of the Alhambra palace in Granada. The quality cuisine features a good choice of classic dishes and fish specialities.
Near river Near beach In town centre
Closed 4Nov-3 Apr
20 en suite (bth/shr) (6 with balcony) TV in all bedrooms STV Direct dial from 22 bedrooms Licensed Lift Full central heating Open parking available Open terrace Last d 21.45hrs Languages spoken: English
ROOMS: (room only) d 275-400FF ✱
MEALS: Full breakfast 45FF Continental breakfast 45FF Lunch 90-220FF Dinner 90-220FF✱
CARDS: 🌑 ☰ Travellers cheques

★ ★ ★ Château Hotel de Brélidy
22140
☎ 296056938 FAX 296951803
(from N12 Paris-Brest exit in direction Lannion/Begard on D767 then direction off Treouier, then D15 to Brelidy)
In a restful setting of woods and river, you will savour the peace and tranquility of this 16th century residence, with its refined but welcoming atmosphere.
Near river Near lake Forest area
Closed 3 Nov-11 Apr
10 en suite (bth/shr) Some rooms in annexe (2 fmly) TV in all bedrooms Direct dial from all bedrooms Licensed Full central heating Open parking available Covered parking available Child discount available 12yrs Fishing Jacuzzi/spa Bicycle rental Covered terrace Last d 21.00hrs Languages spoken: English
ROOMS: (room only) s 380-450FF; d 420-790FF
MEALS: Full breakfast 50FF Dinner 145-185FF
CARDS: 🌑 ■ ☰ Travellers cheques

BREST Finistère

★ ★ ★ Hotel Mercure
24 rue de Lyon *29200*
☎ 298805040 FAX 298431747
(Approach via N12 from Rennes or N165 from Nantes)
Situated in the centre of the town, this hotel offers the visitor comfortable, well furnished accommodation with soundproofed rooms ensuring a quiet stay.
In town centre
75 en suite (bth/shr) (17 fmly) (16 with balcony) No smoking in 14 bedrooms TV in all bedrooms STV Radio in rooms Direct dial from all bedrooms Mini-bar in 21 bedrooms Licensed Lift Night porter Full central heating Child discount available 16yrs Pool table Languages spoken: English,German,Spanish,Italian
ROOMS: (room only) s 460-590FF; d 500-630FF ✱
CARDS: ●● ■■ ☎ ◗ Travellers cheques

BUBRY Morbihan

★ ★ Auberge de Coet Diquel
56310
☎ 297517070 FAX 297517308
(In town take the road opposite the entrance to the church for 500mtrs)

This traditional hotel is situated amidst green surroundings on the banks of a river. The individually appointed bedrooms have modern facilities, and the chef-owner Mr Romieux is responsible for the light, creative cuisine served in the restaurant. The hotel is well placed to explore the splendid Brittany countryside and excellent coastline and beaches, whilst it is equally suitable for an overnight stop en route to further holiday destinations.
Near river Forest area
Closed Jan
20 en suite (bth/shr) TV in all bedrooms Radio in rooms Direct dial from all bedrooms Licensed Full central heating Open parking available Child discount available 12yrs Indoor swimming pool (heated) Tennis Pool table Boule Open terrace Last d 22.00hrs Languages spoken: English
ROOMS: (room only) d 260-306FF
MEALS: Continental breakfast 40FF Lunch 83-200FF Dinner 83-200FF
CARDS: ●● ■■ Travellers cheques

CANCALE Ille-et-Vilaine

★ ★ Emeraude
7 Quai Albert Thomas *35260*
☎ 299896176 FAX 299898821
The small characterful hotel Emeraude enjoys a splendid

location in this little Breton harbour town, and offers fine views of the oyster farms and the open sea. Decorated throughout with bric-à-brac and paintings, and with an open fire lit in winter, it provides the cosy setting for a comfortable stay. Fresh fish specialities feature strongly on the menu and are complemented with a range of imaginative seasonal dishes. The spacious bedrooms are traditionally furnished and comfortable.
Near sea In town centre Near motorway
16 en suite (bth/shr) 5 rooms in annexe (2 fmly) (4 with balcony) TV in all bedrooms Licensed Full central heating Child discount available Open terrace Last d 22.00hrs Languages spoken: English
MEALS: Continental breakfast 42FF Lunch 100-300FF&alc Dinner 100-300FF✱
CARDS: ●● ■■ ■■ Travellers cheques

CAP-COZ Finistère

★ ★ Belle Vue
30 descente de Belle Vue *29170*
☎ 298560033 FAX 298516085
Near sea Forest area
Closed Nov-Feb
20 rms (3 fmly) Direct dial from all bedrooms Licensed Full central heating Open parking available Child discount available 12yrs Open terrace Last d 21.00hrs Languages spoken: English,German,Italian
CARDS: ●● ■■ Travellers cheques

CARNAC Morbihan

★ ★ ★ ★ Le Diana
21 bd de la Plage *56340*
☎ 297520538 FAX 297528791
The hotel is located just opposite the beach in Carnac, a place well known for its historic monuments and pleasant climate. It features individually styled bedrooms offering a high standard of comfort and cosy public areas including an attractive restaurant with panoramic views of the ocean. The menu lists a wide choice of fresh seafood specialities, whilst a bar and terrace complement this attractive setting.
Near sea
Closed Oct-Etr
32 en suite (bth/shr) (6 fmly) (30 with balcony) TV in all bedrooms STV Mini-bar in all bedrooms Licensed Lift Night porter Full central heating Open parking available Child discount available 5yrs Last d 22.00hrs Languages spoken: English
CARDS: ●● ■■ ◗ Travellers cheques

★ ★ Ibis Hotel
Av de l'Atlantique *56343*
☎ 297525354
(head towards Carnac/Quiberon then Carnac Beach, hotel near yacht club)
The Ibis hotel welcomes you in a cosy and comfortable ambiance. There is a welcoming bar and a restaurant with panoramic views over the salt lakes. A variety of activities is offered including thalassotherapy, tennis, golf and sailing.
Near lake Near sea Near beach
119 en suite (shr) (23 fmly) (115 with balcony) No smoking in 33 bedrooms TV in all bedrooms STV Direct dial from all bedrooms Licensed Lift Night porter Full central heating Open parking available Child discount available 12yrs Indoor swimming pool (heated) Tennis Riding Sauna Solarium Gym Boule Jacuzzi/spa Bicycle rental Covered terrace

Last d 22.00hrs Languages spoken: English
ROOMS: (room only) s 350-560FF; d 390-600FF
MEALS: Full breakfast 43FF Lunch 125FF&alc Dinner
125FF&alc
CARDS: ● ▤ ▦ ⑩ Travellers cheques

★ ★ **Tumulus**
31 rue du Tumulus *56340*
☎ 297520821 FAX 297528188
This hotel is peacefully situated at the foot of the St Michel
Tumulus (a protected site of historic significance) and offers
visitors comfortable bedrooms - some housed in small
bungalows with private gardens overlooking the park - and a
Breton-style restaurant with an unrivalled view of the bay.
There is an outdoor heated swimming pool and the
opportunity to play volley-ball and ping-pong.
Near sea Forest area
Closed Oct-Dec
27 rms (16 bth 10 shr) 6 rooms in annexe (5 fmly) (7 with
balcony) TV in 12 bedrooms Direct dial from all bedrooms
Licensed Full central heating Open parking available Child
discount available Outdoor swimming pool (heated) Boule
Jacuzzi/spa Bicycle rental Open terrace Volley-Ball V meals
Last d 21.30hrs Languages spoken: English, Italian & Spanish
ROOMS: (room only) d 260-395FF **Reductions over 1
night**
CARDS: ● ▤ ▦ ⑩ Travellers cheques

CARNAC-PLAGE Morbihan

★ ★ ★ **Hotel Celtique** (Best Western)
17 av de Kermario *56340*
☎ 297521149 FAX 297527110
A recently renovated hotel, quietly situated amongst pine
trees.
Near beach In town centre
53 en suite (bth/shr) 3 rooms in annexe (7 fmly) (15 with
balcony) No smoking in 9 bedrooms TV in all bedrooms STV
Direct dial from all bedrooms Licensed Lift Full central
heating Open parking available Child discount available 12yrs
Outdoor swimming pool (heated) Sauna Jacuzzi/spa Bicycle
rental Open terrace Languages spoken: English, German &
Spanish
ROOMS: (room only) s 300-405FF; d 295-695FF
CARDS: ● ▤ ▦ ⑩ Travellers cheques

CAUREL Côtes-D'Armor

★ ★ **Le Beau Rivage**
22530
☎ 296285215 FAX 296260116
(S of town on the Lac de Guerlédan)

On the shores of the Guerdélan lake, the hotel Beau Rivage
offers attractive accommodation in pleasant surroundings. The
restaurant serves skilfully prepared dishes.
Near lake Near sea Forest area
8 en suite (bth) TV in all bedrooms STV Licensed Full central
heating Open parking available Open terrace Covered
terrace Last d 21.00hrs Languages spoken: English
ROOMS: (room only) s 250-300FF; d 270-320FF ✱
MEALS: Full breakfast 35FF Continental breakfast 35FF Lunch
85-300FF Dinner 85-300FF✱
CARDS: ● ▤ ▦ Travellers cheques

CESSON-SEVIGNE Ille-et-Vilaine

★ ★ ★ **Germinal**
9 cours se la Vilaine *35510*
☎ 299831101 FAX 299834516
The hotel Germinal is an old mill which dates back to 1883.
Built on the tiny island of Vilaine, it features well-appointed
bedrooms decorated with high quality furniture made of
cherry-wood, and the atmosphere is relaxed. The dining room
with its large windows offers splendid views over the
surroundings and serves a choice of dishes.
Near river Near lake Forest area In town centre Near
motorway
(2 fmly) (2 with balcony) TV in 20 bedrooms Direct dial from
20 bedrooms Licensed Lift Full central heating Open parking
available Fishing Open terrace Covered terrace Last d
21.30hrs Languages spoken: English
MEALS: Full breakfast 40FF Continental breakfast 45FF Lunch
92-230FF&alc Dinner 92-230FF&alc✱

CHÂTEAUBOURG Ille-et-Vilaine

★ ★ ★ **Ar-Milin**
30 rue de Paris *35220*
☎ 299003091 FAX 299003756
A handsome granite and timber converted mill with attractive
features such as fine stone fireplaces, sluices and mill-pools. It
is surrounded by five hectares of superb woodland which
houses brightly-coloured butterflies and over 50 different
species of birds. The river Vilaine counts carp, pike-perch and
pike among its many inhabitants. The hotel offers attractive,
individually appointed bedrooms, a cosy bar, and a gourmet
restaurant serving a wide choice of regional cuisine.
Near river In town centre Near motorway
Closed end Dec-early Jan
31 en suite (bth/shr) 20 rooms in annexe (13 with balcony) TV
in all bedrooms Licensed Lift Full central heating Open
parking available Child discount available Tennis Fishing
Boule Bicycle rental Open terrace Last d 21.30hrs Languages
spoken: English,German,Spanish
MEALS: Full breakfast 50FF Continental breakfast 50FF Lunch
100-198FF&alc Dinner 100-198FF&alc✱
CARDS: ● ▤ ▦ ⑩ Travellers cheques

CHÂTEAULIN Finistère

★ ★ **Au Bon Accueil**
A Port Launay *29150*
☎ 298861577 FAX 298063625
Located in the heart of Finistère, the hotel stands just opposite
the river Aulne. It has comfortable rooms - some are adapted
to individual needs - which are fully equipped with private
facilities. Guests can relax in the TV lounge and bar, whilst
there is no shortage of things to do and explore in the
immediate vicinity. The restaurant has a choice of regional and
seafood dishes on the menu, which are prepared with the
contd.

finest local produce.
Near river Forest area
Closed 31Dec-1Feb
59 rms TV in all bedrooms Radio in rooms Licensed Lift Full
central heating Open parking available Child discount
available 12yrs Outdoor swimming pool (heated) Fishing
Sauna Mini-golf Open terrace Last d 21.15hrs Languages
spoken: English
MEALS: Full breakfast 37FF Continental breakfast 37FF Lunch
75-280FF&alc Dinner 75-280FF&alc✱
CARDS: ✱ ⬜ Travellers cheques

CHÂTEAUNEUF-DU-FAOU Finistère

★ ★ Relais de Cornouaille
9 rue Paul Serusier 29520
☎ 298817536 FAX 298818132
Located just 40 minutes from Finistère, this hotel features
bedrooms offering an adequate level of comfort and a cosy
dining room which serves a good regional cuisine including
seafood and fish specialities.
Near river Forest area In town centre Near motorway
28 en suite (bth/shr) (4 fmly) TV in all bedrooms Direct dial
from all bedrooms Licensed Lift Full central heating Open
parking available Covered parking available (charged) Child
discount available V meals Last d 21.00hrs Languages
spoken: English
MEALS: Full breakfast 35FF Lunch 66-155FF&alc Dinner 66-
155FF&alc✱
CARDS: ✱ ⬜ Travellers cheques

COMBOURG Ille-et-Vilaine

★ ★ Château et des Voyageurs
1 pl Châteaubriant 35270
☎ 299730038 FAX 299732579
Situated between the medieval castle Château de Combourg
and the lake, this hotel offers its visitors attractive comfortable
accommodation. It has well equipped bedrooms - divided
between two buildings - public lounge with open fireplace, a
pleasant garden and a gourmand restaurant with splendid
views over the lake. The surrounding area has many points of
interest, such as historic monuments and castles, museums,
forests, a challenging golf course and horse-riding.
Near river Near lake In town centre Near motorway
Closed mid Dec-mid Jan
35 en suite (bth/shr) (3 fmly) TV in all bedrooms STV Direct
dial from all bedrooms Mini-bar in all bedrooms Licensed
Night porter Full central heating Open parking available
Covered parking available Child discount available Boule
Open terrace V meals Last d 22.00hrs Languages spoken:
English,German
ROOMS: (room only) s 260-650FF; d 260-650FF ✱
Reductions over 1 night Special breaks
MEALS: Full breakfast 47FF Lunch 92-280FF&alc Dinner 92-
280FF&alc✱
CARDS: ✱ ⬜⬜ ⬜ ⬤ Travellers cheques

★ ★ Du Lac
2 pl Châteaubriant 35270
☎ 299730565 FAX 299732334
(From St Malo on N137 exit at Hede)
Visitors are met upon arrival by the friendly proprietors Mr
and Mrs Hamon who provide warm hospitality and attentive
service throughout your stay. Situated at the foot of a castle,
the hotel occupies a pleasant location on the shores of a lake.
It features a pleasant day room with open fireplace and

bedrooms offering a good standard of accommodation. A
range of wholesome dishes, carefully prepared by the host, are
on offer in the restaurant.
Near river Near lake Forest area Near motorway
Closed Nov
28 en suite (bth/shr) 6 rooms in annexe (2 fmly) TV in all
bedrooms Direct dial from all bedrooms Licensed Night
porter Full central heating Open parking available Covered
parking available Child discount available 10yrs Open
terrace V meals Last d 21.30hrs Languages spoken: English,
German
CARDS: ✱ ⬜⬜ ⬜ ⬤ Travellers cheques

CONCARNEAU Finistère

★ ★ Des Sables Blancs
Plage des Sables Blancs 29110
☎ 298970139 FAX 298506588
Situated just one kilometre from the town and large fishing
port, the hotel is located directly on the seaside, and guests
only have to go down a few steps from the hotel to set foot on
the fine sandy beach. It features bedrooms - some with
excellent views of the beach and the sea - and a fine restaurant
where seafood takes pride of place on the menu. With a choice
of fitness and leisure facilities in the vicinity it is a good venue
for a relaxing holiday on the coast.
Near sea Forest area Near motorway
Closed 10 Oct-4 Apr
48 rms (9 fmly) (25 with balcony) TV in all bedrooms
Licensed Full central heating Child discount available 5yrs
Open terrace V meals Last d 21.00hrs Languages spoken:
English,German,Spanish
MEALS: Full breakfast 34FF Continental breakfast 34FF Lunch
85-195FF&alc Dinner 85-195FF&alc✱
CARDS: ✱ ⬜⬜ ⬜ ⬤ Travellers cheques

DINARD Ille-et-Vilaine

★ ★ Altair
18 bld Féart 35800
☎ 299461358 FAX 299882049
(Follow signs for 'Plage')
The hotel is a charming, peaceful establishment with a small
garden and terrace, situated in the centre of town and just 100
metres from the main beach. The bedrooms have modern
facilities and provide an adequate level of comfort, whilst the
cuisine has a good reputation in the area and consists of
regional dishes with a modern accent.
Near sea Near beach In town centre
RS Mon in winter
21 en suite (bth/shr) (7 fmly) (2 with balcony) TV in all
bedrooms Direct dial from all bedrooms Licensed Full central
heating Child discount available Last d 21.30hrs Languages
spoken: English
ROOMS: (room only) s 250-390FF; d 310-390FF ✱
MEALS: Full breakfast 35FF Continental breakfast 35FF Lunch
88-200FF&alc Dinner 88-200FF&alc✱
CARDS: ✱ ⬜⬜ ⬜ ⬤ Travellers cheques

★ ★ Hotel Amethyste
pl du Calvaire 35800
☎ 299466181 FAX 299469691
Set in the centre of town at only 100 metres from the beach and
close to the town centre, the hotel welcomes its visitors in a warm,
family atmosphere. All the bedrooms have modern facilities and
provide a good level of comfort. There is a bar and an ice-cream
parlour with tables and chairs set out in the sunshine.

Near sea Near beach In town centre
20 en suite (shr) (3 fmly) (2 with balcony) TV in all bedrooms
Direct dial from all bedrooms Licensed Full central heating
Open parking available Supervised Bicycle rental Open
terrace Languages spoken: English & Italian
Rooms: (room only) d 280-350FF
Cards: ●● ■■ ᴣ Travellers cheques

★ ★ Inter Hotel Balmoral
26 rue du Ml-Leclerc *35800*
☎ 299461697 FAX 299882048
Set in the centre of Dinard, the hotel is only 200 metres from
the beach, casino and seaside promenade. It has an informal
interior where a relaxed atmosphere prevails throughout, and
offers guest rooms decorated with traditional furnishings and
well equipped private facilities. It has a congenial bar where
guests can enjoy an aperitif, before seeking out one of the
restaurants in the vicinity.
Near sea Near beach In town centre
Closed Jan
31 en suite (bth/shr) (2 fmly) TV in all bedrooms Direct dial
from all bedrooms Licensed Lift Night porter Full central
heating Languages spoken: English,German
Cards: ●● ■■ ᴣ ❿ Travellers cheques

★ ★ ★ Roche Corneilée
4 rue Georges Clemenceau *35800*
☎ 299461447 FAX 299464080
This elegant hotel offers its visitors a restful stay in discreet,
charming surroundings. The bedrooms are airy and well
equipped with matching furnishings, and offer maximum
comfort. The dining room with its attractive fireplace serves
enjoyable meals in informal surroundings.
Near sea In town centre Near motorway
Closed mid Nov-mid Mar
28 en suite (bth/shr) (3 fmly) (5 with balcony) TV in all
bedrooms Direct dial from all bedrooms Licensed Lift Full
central heating Child discount available 12yrs Last d 21.30hrs
Languages spoken: English
Cards: ●● ■■ ᴣ Travellers cheques

★ ★ La Vallée
6 av George V *35800*
☎ 299469400 FAX 299882247
(On the western extremity of the town overlooking the sea)

The hotel enjoys a peaceful location by the sea, yet is situated
just seconds away from the centre, providing a suitable base
from which to explore the town as well as to relax near the
seaside. It offers rooms with all modern conveniences and a
gourmet restaurant where lobster and other seafood
specialities feature strongly on the menu.

Near sea
RS Tue in low season
23 en suite (bth/shr) (6 fmly) (6 with balcony) TV in all
bedrooms Direct dial from all bedrooms Licensed Lift Full
central heating Open parking available (charged) Child
discount available 8yrs Bicycle rental Open terrace Covered
terrace V meals Last d 21.00hrs Languages spoken: English,
German & Italian
Rooms: (room only) d 350-450FF
Meals: Continental breakfast 40FF Lunch 110-300FF&alc
Dinner 110-300FF&alc
Cards: ●● ᴣ Travellers cheques

ERDEVEN Morbihan

★ ★ Auberge du Sous Bois
rte de Pont Lorois *56410*
☎ 297556610 FAX 297556882
This is a typical Breton hotel situated in a park with pine trees,
where the proprietor and his family offer their visitors a warm
welcome. The rooms are equipped with modern amenities and

provide a high standard of comfort. The menu comprises
traditional dishes combined with fresh seafood specialities.
Near sea Near beach Forest area
Closed Oct-Mar
21 en suite (bth/shr) TV in all bedrooms STV Direct dial from
all bedrooms Licensed Full central heating Open parking
available Child discount available Open terrace Last d
21.00hrs Languages spoken: English
Rooms: (room only) s 180-380FF; d 180-380FF
Reductions over 1 night
Meals: Full breakfast 45FF Lunch 66-185FF Dinner 82-185FF
Cards: ●● ■■ ᴣ ❿ Travellers cheques

★ ★ Des Voyageurs
14 rue de l'Océan *56410*
☎ 297556447 FAX 297556424
The hotel des Voyageurs is a traditional, family hotel located in
a quiet street, not far from the shops and about two kilometres
from the beach. Rooms are well equipped and provide an
adequate level of comfort, whilst the cooking is accomplished
and includes numerous seafood specialities prepared with
fresh local produce.
Near sea Near beach Forest area In town centre Near
motorway
Closed Oct-Mar
20 rms (1 fmly) (4 with balcony) TV in all bedrooms Licensed
Open parking available Child discount available V meals Last
d 21.00hrs Languages spoken: English
Cards: ●● ᴣ Travellers cheques

FORÊT-FOUESNANT, LA Finistère

★ ★ Aux Cerisiers
3 rue des Cersiers *29940*
☎ 298569724
Situated between a cove and lakes, the fishing village of La Fôret-Fouesnant enjoys a sheltered location in the bay. Standing near the 16th-century church, this cheerful hotel offers warm hospitality and a comfortable stay. The bedrooms have good amenities and the fine cuisine includes a choice of regional dishes as well as fresh seafood produce.
16 en suite (shr) TV available STV Licensed Full central heating Open parking available Supervised Child discount available Golf Open terrace Last d 21.30hrs Languages spoken: English
MEALS: Full breakfast 35FF Lunch 85-240FF Dinner 85-240FF✱
CARDS: ●● ▆

★ ★ Hotel de l'Espérance
6 rue Charles-de-Gaulle *29940*
☎ 298569658 FAX 298514225
(From Quimper take D783 towards Coccarneau)
Situated in the heart of a small fishing village, the hotel features spacious bedrooms with modern amenities, a lounge for relaxation, and a friendly restaurant where fresh shellfish features strongly on the menu.
Near sea Forest area In town centre Near motorway Closed Oct-Etr
27 rms (24 bth/shr) 18 rooms in annexe (9 fmly) (2 with balcony) TV in all bedrooms Direct dial from all bedrooms Licensed Full central heating Open parking available Child discount available 12yrs Open terrace Last d 21.00hrs Languages spoken: English,German
ROOMS: (room only) s 168-272FF; d 210-340FF
Reductions over 1 night
MEALS: Continental breakfast 35FF Lunch 90-220FF&alc Dinner 90-220FF&alc
CARDS: ●● ▆ Travellers cheques

★ ★ ★ Manoir du Stang
29940
☎ 298569737 FAX 298569737
(From N165 take Concarneau/Fouesnant exit and follow D783 to hotel on private drive)
Near sea Forest area
24 en suite (bth/shr) Direct dial from all bedrooms Licensed Lift Full central heating Open parking available Child discount available 10yrs Golf 18 Covered terrace Last d 20.30hrs
ROOMS: (room only) s 360-570FF; d 580-950FF
Reductions over 1 night
MEALS: Continental breakfast 45FF Dinner 170-180FF
CARDS: Travellers cheques

FOUESNANT Finistère

★ ★ De la Pointe de Mousterlin
Mousterlin Plages *29170*
☎ 298560412 FAX 298566102
(From Quimper enter Fouesnant and turn right after the cinema)
This comfortable family hotel is tucked away amidst rocks with a beautiful beach either side and has fine views of the small fishing harbour. All the bedrooms have en suite facilities, whilst a number of larger rooms also have balconies. The restaurant serves local fresh fish produce as well as shellfish.

The comfortable lounge invites guests for a game of bridge or chess, whilst a large choice of leisure facilities is available for the more energetic.
Near sea Near beach
Closed 30 Sep-12 Apr
50 en suite (bth/shr) 20 rooms in annexe (40 fmly) (30 with balcony) TV in all bedrooms Direct dial from all bedrooms Licensed Lift Full central heating Open parking available Covered parking available Supervised Child discount available Tennis Sauna Gym Boule Mini-golf Jacuzzi/spa Bicycle rental Open terrace V meals Last d 22.00hrs Languages spoken: Englis & German
ROOMS: (room only) d 265-455FF
MEALS: Full breakfast 42FF Lunch 90-200FF Dinner 90-200FF

HENNEBONT Morbihan

★ ★ ★ ★ Château de Locguénolé
rte de Port-Louis *56700*
☎ 297762904 FAX 297768235
A most charming historic residence, situated in the centre of a 120 hectare wooded parkland. Beauty, comfort and charm are the key words of this hotel. Guest rooms and public rooms are luxurious, enhanced by the warmth of the woodwork and the authentic furnishings. The gourmet cuisine includes ingredients from the Breton vegetable garden and fish caught on the line.
Near river Near sea Near beach Forest area
Closed 4 Jan-5 Feb
22 en suite (bth) 10 rooms in annexe (5 fmly) TV in all bedrooms STV Direct dial from all bedrooms Mini-bar in all bedrooms Room-safe Licensed Full central heating Open parking available Child discount available 12yrs Outdoor swimming pool (heated) Tennis Fishing Sauna Solarium Bicycle rental Open terrace V meals Last d 21.30hrs Languages spoken: English, German & Italian
ROOMS: (room only) s 660-1480FF; d 660-1480FF
Reductions over 1 night
MEALS: Full breakfast 132FF Continental breakfast 82FF Lunch 180-490FF&alc Dinner 180-490FF&alc
CARDS: ●● ▆▆ ▆ ◑ Travellers cheques

ILE-AUX-MOINES Morbihan

Le San Francisco
Le Port *56780*
☎ 297263152 FAX 297263559
The hotel San Francisco apparently got its name from an order of nuns called the Sisters of St Francis. It has fine stone walls and was completely renovated in 1991. It now offers attractive bedrooms with good amenities and a restaurant which serves a range of enjoyable meals. In addition, guests can relax on the terrace which provides fine views of the surrounding area.
Near lake Near sea Near beach Forest area
Etr-2 Nov
8 en suite (bth/shr) (1 fmly) (1 with balcony) TV in all bedrooms Direct dial from all bedrooms Licensed Child discount available Open terrace Last d 20.30hrs Languages spoken: English, German
ROOMS: (room only) s 370-535FF; d 370-535FF
MEALS: Full breakfast 45FF Lunch 110-230FF&alc Dinner 110-230FF&alc
CARDS: ●● ▆▆ ▆ ◑ Travellers cheques

LAMBALLE Côtes-D'Armor

★★ Alizes
La Ville es Lan *22400*
☎ 296311637 FAX 296312389
In the heart of a delightful area not far from the Rennes-Brest motorway, the hotel features a contemporary yet intimate interior, and is the ideal venue to explore the countryside between Ile de Bríhat and St-Malo. Charming bedrooms are equipped with modern amenities, whilst the restaurant serves imaginative cuisine incorporating well-balanced dishes with a personal touch.
Near lake Near motorway
Closed 24 Dec-8 Jan
72 rms (3 fmly) (16 with balcony) TV in all bedrooms Direct dial from all bedrooms Mini-bar in all bedrooms Licensed Night porter Full central heating Open parking available Tennis Pool table Open terrace V meals Last d 21.45hrs Languages spoken: English,Portuguese,Spanish
MEALS: Full breakfast 35FF Continental breakfast 35FF Lunch 78-159FF&alc Dinner 87-159FF&alc✱
CARDS: ●● ▨ ☲ Travellers cheques

★★★ D'Angleterre
29 bd Jobert M Toublanc *22400*
☎ 296310016 FAX 296319154
Set in the heart of a town with an historic past going back some 1000 years, and centrally situated for the most beautiful beaches on the Côte d'Emeraude, the hotel has renovated bedrooms with modern appointments which provide a high standard of comfort. Guests can sample high quality cuisine in the restaurant which has a good reputation locally, and which serves excellent dishes of good flavour.
In town centre
20 rms (19 bth/shr) TV in all bedrooms Radio in rooms Direct dial from all bedrooms Mini-bar in all bedrooms Licensed Lift Night porter Full central heating Covered parking available (charged) Supervised Child discount available 8yrs Bicycle rental Open terrace V meals Last d 21.30hrs Languages spoken: English
MEALS: Full breakfast 50FF Continental breakfast 38FF Lunch 92-300FF&alc Dinner 92-300FF&alc✱

LAMPAUL-GUIMILIAU Finistère

★★ Hotel de L'Enclos
rte de St-Jacques *29400*
☎ 298687708 FAX 298686106
(leave N12 at Landivisau exit, turn right at 1st roundabout & left at 2nd roundabout)
Near river Forest area Near motorway
36 en suite (bth) TV in all bedrooms Direct dial from all bedrooms Licensed Open parking available Child discount available 12yrs Open terrace V meals Last d 21.30hrs Languages spoken: English
ROOMS: (room only) s 232FF; d 270FF ✱
MEALS: Full breakfast 32FF Continental breakfast 32FF Lunch 69-200FF Dinner 69-200FF
CARDS: ●● ▨ ☲ ◑ Travellers cheques

LESCONIL Finistère

★★ Atlantic
11 rue Jean Jaurès *29740*
☎ 298878106 FAX 298878804
(Approach via Quimper. Hotel close to Port de Pêche)
Situated in green surroundings and set in a flower-filled garden, the Hotel Atlantic offers its visitors the tranquillity and delicious cuisine of the Bigouden region. The sound-proofed guest rooms offer a good level of comfort, whilst in the restaurant the chef Laurent Toulemont has created a menu where fresh fish, shellfish and seafood feature strongly.
Near sea Forest area In town centre
Closed 30 Sep-1 Apr
24 en suite (bth/shr) (2 fmly) TV in all bedrooms Direct dial from all bedrooms Licensed Full central heating Air conditioning in bedrooms Open parking available Supervised Child discount available 10yrs Riding Boule Bicycle rental Open terrace Covered terrace ping pong Last d 21.00hrs Languages spoken: English
ROOMS: (room only) s 220-240FF; d 240-280FF ✱
MEALS: Continental breakfast 35FF Lunch 85-220FF&alc Dinner 85-220FF&alc✱
CARDS: ●● ▨ ☲ Travellers cheques

LOCMINÉ Morbihan

★★ L'Argoat
pl Anne de Bretagne *56500*
☎ 297600102 FAX 297442055
The town of Locminé is situated in the heart of Morbihan in Brittany, and surrounded by meadows, moors and woodland whilst a light breeze comes from the Atlantic Ocean. This friendly establishment offers its visitors excellent Breton cooking and a peaceful night's sleep. The walls in the attractive restaurant are adorned with numerous paintings which create a cosy atmosphere where guests can sample a choice of tasty dishes, whilst the bar is also a meeting place for the locals who are always willing to give advice about the best fishing grounds.
Forest area In town centre
Closed 15 Dec-15 Jan
TV available Licensed Full central heating Open parking available Covered parking available Supervised Child discount available V meals Last d 21.00hrs Languages spoken: English,Spanish
MEALS: Full breakfast 30FF Continental breakfast 30FF Lunch 70-150FF&alc Dinner 70-150FF&alc✱
CARDS: ☲ Travellers cheques

LOUDÉAC Côtes-D'Armor

★★ Des Voyageurs
10 rue de Cadélac *22600*
☎ 296280047 FAX 296282230
(SW of town centre)
Entirely renovated in 1996, the hotel now features individually styled bedrooms with modern amenities offering restful accommodation. The restaurant, where seafood specialities feature strongly on the menu, offers a high standard of cooking served by an attentive and friendly staff
Near lake Forest area In town centre
28 en suite (bth/shr) (2 fmly) (12 with balcony) TV in all bedrooms STV Direct dial from all bedrooms Mini-bar in 4 bedrooms Licensed Lift Full central heating Covered parking available Supervised Child discount available 12yrs Bicycle rental V meals Last d 21.30hrs Languages spoken: English, German
ROOMS: (room only) s 160-250FF; d 220-300FF
Reductions over 1 night
MEALS: Full breakfast 45FF Continental breakfast 45FF Lunch 70-250FF&alc Dinner 70-250FF&alc
CARDS: ●● ▨ ☲ ◑ Travellers cheques

PAIMPOL Côtes-D'Armor

★ ★ ★ Le Barbu
Pointe de l'Arcouest *22620*
☎ 296558698 FAX 296557387
Surrounded by sea and countryside, the hotel has a panoramic restaurant which serves a range of seafood specialities, and comfortable guest rooms with views of the flower-filled Isle of Bréhat. In addition guests can relax by the side of the swimming pool, the bar, or television lounge.
Near sea Near beach
20 en suite (bth/shr) (6 fmly) No smoking in 2 bedrooms TV in all bedrooms Direct dial from all bedrooms Licensed Full central heating Open parking available Covered parking available Supervised Child discount available 8yrs Outdoor swimming pool (heated) Sauna Solarium Gym Bicycle rental Open terrace Covered terrace Last d 21.00hrs Languages spoken: English
MEALS: Lunch 150-200FF&alc Dinner 150-200FF&alc✱
CARDS: ●● ■■ ⊞ Travellers cheques

★ ★ ★ Répaire de Kerroch
29 quai Morand *22500*
☎ 296205013 FAX 296220746
This building dates back to the 18th century and was built by the pirates of St Malo in the distinct architectural style of the town. Overlooking the port of Paimpol, it is now classified as a historic building and features comfortable guest rooms and a fine restaurant which has acquired accolades over the years.
In town centre Near motorway
13 en suite (bth/shr) (1 fmly) (2 with balcony) TV in all bedrooms Licensed Lift Full central heating Open terrace Last d 21.30hrs Languages spoken: English,Spanish
CARDS: ●● ⊞ Travellers cheques

PAIMPONT Ille-et-Vilaine

★ ★ Relais de Broceliande
5 rue des Forges *35380*
☎ 299078107 FAX 299078108
The hotel is located in the heart of the Brocéliande Forest, which according to local tales was once the home of the nymph Viviane and Merlin the magician. It offers a peaceful location for a relaxing stay; attractive bedrooms with good amenities, and a large restaurant with an informal country-style decor serving a high standard of cooking by the chef-proprietor.
Near river Near lake Forest area
23 rms 15 rooms in annexe (6 fmly) TV in all bedrooms Licensed Full central heating Open parking available Supervised Child discount available 10yrs Tennis Fishing Boule Open terrace Covered terrace Casino V meals Last d 21.00hrs Languages spoken: English,German
CARDS: ●● ■■ ⊙ Travellers cheques

PERROS-GUIREC Côtes-D'Armor

★ ★ Hermitage Hotel
20 rue le Montréer *22700*
☎ 296232122 FAX 296911656
The hotel is located in the centre of the town and is surrounded by a large garden. It offers a relaxing stay in a warm and friendly atmosphere, where the guest rooms are equipped with every modern convenience and provide a good level of comfort. The restaurant - only open in the evening - serves a range of dishes to suit most tastes.
Near sea Forest area In town centre

Closed Oct-Apr
25 en suite (bth/shr) (2 fmly) TV in all bedrooms STV Licensed Full central heating Open parking available Child discount available 10yrs Open terrace Last d 20.30hrs Languages spoken: English
CARDS: ●● ■■ ⊞ Travellers cheques

PLANGUENOUAL Côtes-D'Armor

★ ★ ★ Domaine du Val
22400
☎ 296327540 FAX 296327150
The chateau-hotel Domaine du Val consists of guest rooms and apartments situated in large grounds and equipped with every modern convenience. The guest rooms are decorated with period furniture whilst the spacious apartments provide the ideal family accommodation for a weekend or a longer break. With comprehensive indoor leisure facilities available and close to all the main tourist sights in Brittany it is the ideal setting for an enjoyable stay.
Near river Near sea Forest area
53 en suite (bth) 19 rooms in annexe (6 fmly) (1 with balcony) TV in all bedrooms Direct dial from all bedrooms Licensed Night porter Full central heating Open parking available Child discount available 12yrs Indoor swimming pool (heated) Tennis Fishing Squash Sauna Solarium Gym Boule Jacuzzi/spa Open terrace Covered terrace V meals Last d 22.00hrs Languages spoken: English
ROOMS: (room only) s 460-1200FF; d 460-1200FF ✱
MEALS: Full breakfast 50FF Lunch 140-345FF&alc Dinner 140-345FF&alc
CARDS: ●● ⊞ Travellers cheques

PLÉRIN Côtes-D'Armor

★ ★ Chêne Vert
rte de St-Laurent-de-la-Mer *22190*
☎ 296798020 FAX 296798021
The hotel is surrounded by green scenery as far as the eye can see. The interior has been designed with the comfort of guests in mind and features two lounges, a congenial bar and pleasant guest accommodation. The informal restaurant serves seafood specialities all year round, which are complemented by fine wines from the well-stocked house cellar.
Near sea Near beach Forest area Near motorway
70 en suite (bth/shr) 16 rooms in annexe (10 fmly) No smoking in 10 bedrooms TV in all bedrooms STV Radio in rooms Direct dial from all bedrooms Mini-bar in 13 bedrooms Licensed Full central heating Open parking available Child discount available 12yrs Squash Boule Open terrace Sqaush courts Last d 22.00hrs Languages spoken: English,German,Spanish
ROOMS: (room only) s 78-278FF; d 298-298FF
MEALS: Full breakfast 48FF Continental breakfast 38FF Lunch 75-160FF&alc Dinner 75-160FF&alc
CARDS: ●● ■■ ⊞ ⊙ Travellers cheques

PLEUGUENEUC-PLESDER Ille-et-Vilaine

★ ★ ★ Château de la Motte-Beaumanoir
La Motte-Beaumanoir *35720*
☎ 299694601 FAX 299694249
The residence is situated in a park of 60 acres dating back to the 15th century. Completely renovated, it offers elegant accommodation with excellent facilities which will satisfy any discerning visitor. The guest rooms are decorated with high quality furniture and fabrics and offer fine views of

the park. The cuisine combines classic dishes with imaginative and innovative combinations of ingredients which are served in the sophisticated restaurant.
Near lake Forest area Near motorway
6 en suite (bth) (2 fmly) Licensed Full central heating Open parking available Supervised Child discount available 3yrs Outdoor swimming pool (heated) Tennis Fishing Solarium Bicycle rental Open terrace Languages spoken: English
CARDS: ●● ■■ ☲ Travellers cheques

PLEURTUIT Ille-et-Vilaine

★ ★ ★ **Manoir de la Rance**
Château de Jourvente *35730*
☎ 299885376 FAX 299886303
The Manoir de la Rance is a 19th-century residence surrounded by extensive woodland on the banks of the river Rance. All the guest rooms are individually styled, equipped with modern facilities and offer fine views over the sea. Guests can relax on the terraces or take a stroll in the flower-filled gardens.
Near river Near lake Near sea Forest area
Closed early Jan-mid Mar
10 en suite (bth/shr) 3 rooms in annexe (2 fmly) (1 with balcony) TV in all bedrooms Licensed Full central heating Open parking available Fishing Open terrace Languages spoken: English,German
CARDS: ●● ☲ Travellers cheques

PLÉVEN Côtes-D'Armor

★ ★ ★ ★ **Manoir du Vaumadeuc**
22130
☎ 296844617 FAX 296844016

A magnificent location in the heart of Penthièvre, a 15th century building that will delight guests with its authenticity and the warm welcome of the owners. The manor, which has been in the same family for 200 years, has award-winning formal French gardens.
Near river Near lake Forest area
Closed early Nov-Etr
13 en suite (bth/shr) 2 rooms in annexe (4 fmly) Direct dial from all bedrooms Licensed Full central heating Open parking available Child discount available 5yrs Fishing Open terrace Last d 21.00hrs Languages spoken: English & Spanish
ROOMS: (room only) s 590-1050FF; d 590-1050FF
Reductions over 1 night Special breaks
MEALS: Full breakfast 50FF Continental breakfast 50FF Dinner fr 195FF&alc
CARDS: ●● ■■ ☲ ⍉ Travellers cheques

PLOËRMEL Morbihan

★ ★ ★ **Golf Hotel du Roi Arthur**
Le Lac au Duc *56800*
☎ 297736464 FAX 297736450
(follow direction of Le Lac au Duc from Rennes or Vannes roads)

The hotel with 46 comfortable bedrooms and 12 apartments is situated beside the legendary forest of Broceliand. Set in 62 acres of grounds, which include a 9 hole golf course, a swimming pool and gym, the hotel also overlooks the Lac au Duc, the largest natural lake in Brittany.
Near lake Near beach Forest area
46 en suite (bth/shr) (41 fmly) TV in all bedrooms STV Direct dial from all bedrooms Licensed Lift Night porter Full central heating Open parking available Supervised Indoor swimming pool (heated) Golf 9 Fishing Riding Sauna Solarium Gym Boule Jacuzzi/spa Bicycle rental Open terrace Last d 21.30hrs Languages spoken: English, German & Spanish
ROOMS: (room only) s 330-400FF; d 380-480FF
MEALS: Continental breakfast 58FF Lunch 100-220FF&alc Dinner 138-220FF&alc
CARDS: ●● ■■ ☲ ⍉ Travellers cheques

PLOGOFF Finistère

★ ★ **Ker Moor**
Plague de Loch-Pointe du Raz *29770*
☎ 298706206 FAX 298703269
The hotel occupies an enviable position with unrivalled views over the Atlantic ocean. The fully equipped bedrooms provide comfortable guest accommodation. The cuisine is based on fresh sea fish produce and is skilfully executed by the chef-proprietor Mr Cassegrain. Open all year round it provides the ideal venue for banquets, conferences and family events.
Near sea
16 rms (8 bth 4 shr) (2 fmly) No smoking in 1 bedroom TV in all bedrooms Licensed Full central heating Open parking available Boule Bicycle rental Open terrace Last d 21.30hrs Languages spoken: English,Spanish
CARDS: ●● ☲ Travellers cheques

PLONÉOUR-LAVERN Finistère

★ ★ **De La Mairie**
3 rue Jules Ferry *29720*
☎ 298876134 FAX 298877704
The Hotel de la Mairie is set in the heart of Cornouaille, just five minutes from the beach and picturesque fishing ports. Its cosy interior is decorated with country-style furnishings and complemented by paintings and assorted antiques.
The hostess provides a friendly welcome upon arrival, *contd.*

and the host is responsible for the imaginative dishes served in the restaurant.
18 rms (1 fmly) TV in all bedrooms Licensed Full central heating Open parking available Child discount available Boule Bicycle rental Open terrace V meals Last d 21.00hrs
CARDS: ●● ▆ Travellers cheques

★ ★ ★ Manoir de Kerhuel
Kaerhuel *29720*
☎ 298826057 FAX 298826179
Located in the heart of the 'Bigouden country', a region with a wealth of art, culture and history, the hotel is surrounded by mature trees just a few minutes from Quimper. It has comfortable guest rooms with good modern facilities and an informal restaurant where a range of regional delicacies is served by an attentive and friendly staff.
Near river Near lake Near sea Forest area
26 en suite (bth/shr) 3 rooms in annexe (6 fmly) (1 with balcony) TV in all bedrooms Licensed Full central heating Open parking available Supervised Child discount available 12yrs Outdoor swimming pool (heated) Sauna Gym Pool table Jacuzzi/spa Open terrace V meals Last d 21.30hrs Languages spoken: English,German
CARDS: ▆ Travellers cheques

PLOUËR-SUR-RANCE Côtes-D'Armor

★ ★ Manoir de Rigourdaine
rte de Langrolay *22490*
☎ 296868996 FAX 296869246

(from St Malo, take dual-carriageway towards Rennes (N137), after 15km follow the road signposted Dinan/St Brieuc (N176). Leave the dual-carriageway, after the bridge on the Rance, take Plouër exit. Take the road to Langrolay, then follow sign)
A charming stone-built, historic house with beams and open fireplace. Set in extensive grounds with views of the Breton estuary.
Near river Near sea Near beach Forest area
Closed mid Nov-Mar
19 en suite (bth/shr) (6 fmly) TV in all bedrooms Direct dial from all bedrooms Licensed Open parking available Supervised Fishing Boule Open terrace Languages spoken: English & German
ROOMS: (room only) s 290-300FF; d 300-420FF
CARDS: ●● ▆▆ ▆ Travellers cheques

PLOUESCAT Finistère

★ ★ La Caravelle
20 rue du Calvaire *29430*
☎ 298696175 FAX 298619261

(from ferry terminal follow D769 then D10 to Plouescat)
Hotel la Caravelle is located in the small seaside village of Plouescat which has only 4000 inhabitants, and at only 15 minutes from the ferry terminal in Roscoff, it's a good venue for an overnight stop. Bedrooms are furnished in a simple fashion and provide good levels of comfort, while the restaurant offers a high standard of home-cooked dishes including seafood specialities.
Near sea Near beach Near motorway
17 en suite (bth/shr) (1 fmly) TV in all bedrooms Radio in rooms Direct dial from all bedrooms Licensed Full central heating Child discount available 13yrs Boule Bicycle rental V meals Last d 21.00hrs Languages spoken: English & German
ROOMS: (room only) d 270-290FF
MEALS: Continental breakfast 32FF Lunch 68-190FF Dinner 68-190FF✱
CARDS: ●● ▆▆ ▆ ⓓ Travellers cheques

PLOUHARNEL Morbihan

★ ★ Hostellerie les Ajoncs D'Or
Kerbachique *56340*
☎ 297523202 FAX 297524036
(from Auray take D768 to Plouharnel, then road to Carnac) This friendly inn is set amidst leafy parkland in the heart of Brittany. Situated only a few minutes away from fine, sandy beaches, it is a good base for excursions to Quiberon, the Gulf of Morbihan, and other points of interest. The cuisine consists of regional dishes, prepared with fresh farm and sea produce.
Near sea Near beach Forest area
Closed 3 Nov-15 Mar
17 rms (2 bth 14 shr) (4 fmly) TV in all bedrooms STV Direct dial from 16 bedrooms Licensed Full central heating Open parking available Supervised Child discount available 2yrs · Boule Open terrace V meals Last d 21.00hrs Languages spoken: English
ROOMS: (room only) s fr 270FF; d 310-420FF ✱
CARDS: ●● ▆ Travellers cheques

PLOUHINEC Morbihan

★ ★ Hotel de Kerlon
56680
☎ 297367703 FAX 297858114
(leave N165 at Hennebont & take D194 in direction of Carnac/Quiberon, then onto D9)
A warm welcome awaits you from the friendly proprietors of this charming hotel. Situated in a beautiful area of peaceful countryside, only 5kms from the beach, the hotel is surrounded by extensive gardens with a play area. Breakfast is continental style, whilst good value local dishes are prepared in the rustic dinning room. Half-board only available in July and August.
16 rms (15 bth/shr) (1 fmly) TV in 15 bedrooms Direct dial from all bedrooms Licensed Full central heating Open parking available Supervised Child discount available 12yrs Bicycle rental Open terrace Last d 21.00hrs Languages spoken: English
ROOMS: (room only) s 260-290FF; d 290-320FF
MEALS: Continental breakfast 40FF Dinner 82-160FF✱
CARDS: ●● ▆▆ ▆ ⓓ Travellers cheques

POLIGNÉ Ille-et-Vilaine

Château du Bois Glaume
35320
☎ 299438305 FAX 299437940
The residence dates back to the beginning of the 18th century, and is together with its chapel, classified as an historic

monument. Situated in an extensive park with hundred-year old oak trees and a lake, it features an elegant interior with cosy public areas and excellent bedrooms with modern facilities. It has an extraordinary roof where the tiles are laid like fish scales and which is the only one of its kind in France.
Near river Near lake Forest area Near motorway
4 en suite (bth/shr) (2 fmly) (1 with balcony) TV in all bedrooms Radio in rooms Mini-bar in all bedrooms Full central heating Open parking available Supervised Child discount available 12yrs Fishing Languages spoken: Spanish
MEALS: Full breakfast 50FF Continental breakfast 35FF Lunch fr 150FF Dinner fr 150FF✱
CARDS: Eurocheques

PONT-AVEN Finistère

★ ★ ★ Roz-Aven
11 quai Théodore Botrel 29930
☎ 298061306 FAX 298060389
The city of Pont-Aven is situated opposite the mouth of a river, and is known as the town of painters and mills, made famous by Gauguin and his disciples. A combination of an 18th-century thatched cottage, a modern extension and a house from the last century, and located in wooded parklands, it offers bedrooms with private facilities, most of which have views over the tidal harbour. Although bustling with activity during the day in holiday season, this small corner of the port becomes very peaceful as soon as night falls.
Near river Near sea Near beach Forest area Near motorway
Closed 16 Dec-14 Feb
25 en suite (bth/shr) 8 rooms in annexe (3 fmly) TV in all bedrooms Mini-bar in 3 bedrooms Licensed Full central heating Open parking available Child discount available 12yrs Pool table Open terrace Languages spoken: English,German
CARDS: ●● ⅈ Travellers cheques

PONT-L'ABBÉ Finistère

★ ★ Château Hotel de Kernuz
rte de Penmarc'h 29120
☎ 298870159 FAX 298660236
This 16th-century residence has been in the hands of the Chatellier family for two centuries. Set in secluded grounds with ancient oak trees, it features a dovecote, a chapel, fortifications, lawns and terraces. The interior is exquisitely decorated with polished wood and period furniture, while the bedrooms and apartments provide a good standard of comfort. The restaurant serves a combination of classic cuisine and fresh fish produce.
Near sea Forest area
Closed Oct-Mar
24 rms 7 rooms in annexe (8 fmly) (1 with balcony) Licensed Full central heating Open parking available Child discount available 10yrs Outdoor swimming pool Tennis Pool table Bicycle rental Open terrace Last d 21.30hrs Languages spoken: English,Spanish
CARDS: ●● ⅈ Travellers cheques

★ ★ D'Auvergne
22 pl Gambetta 29120
☎ 298870047 FAX 298823378
This family hotel is situated at Pont-l'Abbé. With the beaches and the ports just five minutes away, it provides a good venue for an overnight-stop or break at the seaside. The guest accommodation is functional, has good facilities and provides straightforward comfort.
Near river In town centre Near motorway

27 en suite (bth/shr) TV in all bedrooms STV Licensed Full central heating Child discount available 12yrs Bicycle rental Languages spoken: English
CARDS: ■■ ⅈ Travellers cheques

PORT BLANC Côtes-D'Armor

★ ★ Grand Hotel
bd de la Mer 22710
☎ 296926652 FAX 296928157
The hotel occupies a fine location on the Brittany coast and offers beautiful views across the sea. The cheerful interior and informal atmosphere create a feeling of well being in this attractive hotel. The restaurant offers a range of well-prepared dishes, while the gardens and play area provide a carefree place for children to enjoy themselves.
Near sea
Closed Nov-mid Mar RS Half board obligatory Jul-Aug
29 rms (12 bth 9 shr) (4 fmly) Licensed Full central heating Open parking available Child discount available 10yrs Tennis Pool table Open terrace Table Tennis V meals Last d 22.00hrs Languages spoken: English
ROOMS: (room only) s 250-290FF; d 280-320FF **Special breaks**
MEALS: Continental breakfast 30FF Lunch fr 90FF Dinner fr 90FF
CARDS: ●● ⅈ Travellers cheques

PORT-LOUIS Morbihan

★ ★ Du Commerce
1 pl du Marché 56290
☎ 297824605 FAX 297821102
Sheltered by the ramparts of the historic town Port Louis, the hotel is situated just 250 metres from the beach. It offers its visitors pleasant guest rooms with good modern facilities, a delightful garden and a restaurant where Mr Boutbien, the chef-proprietor, introduces his guests to a gastronomic delights of the area.
Near sea Near beach In town centre Near motorway
36 rms (14 bth 17 shr) 11 rooms in annexe (2 fmly) TV in all bedrooms Direct dial from all bedrooms Licensed Full central heating Child discount available 8yrs Open terrace V meals Last d 21.30hrs Languages spoken: English
MEALS: Continental breakfast 40FF Lunch 65-245FF&alc Dinner 110-245FF&alc✱
CARDS: ●● ⅈ Travellers cheques

POULDREUZIC Finistère

★ ★ ★ Ker Ansquer
Lababan 29710
☎ 298544183 FAX 495543224
This handsome building is set in peaceful surroundings only three kilometres from the sea. It features a delightful garden with shaded terrace, and a number of guest rooms and apartments which offer a high standard of comfort. The cuisine is based on regional recipes where typical Breton dishes take pride of place.
Near sea Near beach
Closed Nov-Apr
16 en suite (bth/shr) 10 rooms in annexe (2 fmly) TV in all bedrooms Direct dial from all bedrooms Mini-bar in all bedrooms Licensed Full central heating Open parking available Supervised Child discount available Pool table Boule Open terrace Last d 21.00hrs Languages spoken: English

contd.

49

MEALS: Full breakfast 38FF Lunch 100-300FFalc Dinner fr 100FFalc✷
CARDS: ●● ▨

POULDU, LE Finistère

★ ★ ★ Armen
rte du Port, Le Pouldu 29360
☎ 298399044 FAX 298399869
(From N165 exit Quimperle, take D49 to Le Pouldu)
This traditional family hotel offers its clientele an informal atmosphere and warm hospitality. The bedrooms have good amenities and provide comfortable accommodation, there is a cosy bar, and the restaurant serves a regional cuisine including fresh fish and seafood. The surrounding area has a multitude of leisure opportunities on offer, such as fine sandy beaches, forests with numerous footpaths, and walks along the splendid coastline.
Near river Near sea Near beach Forest area
Closed end Sep-end Apr
75 en suite (bth/shr) (3 fmly) (9 with balcony) TV in all bedrooms Direct dial from all bedrooms Licensed Lift Full central heating Open parking available Covered parking available Child discount available 12yrs Bicycle rental Open terrace Last d 21.00hrs Languages spoken: English,German
ROOMS: (room only) s 270-380FF; d 290-480FF ✷
MEALS: Full breakfast 55FF Lunch 95-230FF&alc Dinner 95-230FF&alc
CARDS: ●● ▨ ▨ Travellers cheques

QUESTEMBERT Morbihan

★ ★ ★ Bretagne
13 rue St-Michel 56230
☎ 297261112 FAX 297261237
(leave N24 at Ploermel in direction of Vannes, then N166 to Questembert)
Situated in the quiet village of Questembert, with its covered market, fountain and 18th-century houses, the Hotel Bretagne is a home from home. The hotel has all the charm of a private residence and features pretty, intimate bedrooms which open on to the garden and are equipped with every modern convenience. The elegant wood-panelled restaurant serves a delightful cuisine where artichokes and foie gras, truffles, lobster and wild mushrooms take pride of place on the menu.
Near river Near lake Forest area In town centre Near motorway
Closed 5-30 Jan
9 en suite (bth/shr) 9 rooms in annexe (1 fmly) (3 with balcony) No smoking in 4 bedrooms TV in all bedrooms Direct dial from all bedrooms Mini-bar in all bedrooms Licensed Full central heating Air conditioning in bedrooms Open parking available Supervised Child discount available 12yrs Indoor swimming pool (heated) Golf Tennis Fishing Riding Solarium Gym Bicycle rental Open terrace Covered terrace V meals Last d 22.00hrs Languages spoken: English & Spanish
ROOMS: (room only) s 780-980FF; d 980-1200FF ✷
MEALS: Full breakfast 90FF Lunch 210-490FF&alc Dinner 295-490FF&alc
CARDS: ●● ▨ ▨

QUIMPER Finistère

★ ★ Hotel Mascotte
6 rue Théodore le Hars 29000
☎ 298533737 FAX 298903151

The hotel can be found the in the centre of the town close to the cathedral and is surrounded by lively streets. It features modern bedrooms with good amenities, comfortable lounge, bar and a restaurant.
Near river Near motorway
63 en suite (bth/shr) (2 fmly) No smoking in 6 bedrooms TV in all bedrooms STV Radio in rooms Direct dial from all bedrooms Licensed Lift Night porter Full central heating Child discount available 12yrs V meals Last d 22.00hrs Languages spoken: English,German
MEALS: Full breakfast 70FF Continental breakfast 42FF Lunch 78-145FF Dinner 70-145FF✷
CARDS: ●● ▨ ▨ ●) Travellers cheques

RENNES Ille-et-Vilaine

★ ★ ★ ★ Hotel Lecoq-Gadby
156 rue d'Antrain 35000
☎ 299380555 FAX 299385340
(from the centre of town, head in the direction of Mont St Michel to find Antrain St, hotel by Thabor Park)
Le Coq-Gadby is quite an institution. Many personalities have stayed at this hotel which is elegantly furnished with antiques and provides a comfortably, relaxing atmosphere. The restaurant offers both fixed price menu and à la carte
In town centre Near motorway
11 en suite (bth/shr) (4 fmly) (3 with balcony) TV in all bedrooms Direct dial from all bedrooms Mini-bar in all bedrooms Licensed Lift Night porter Full central heating Open parking available Child discount available 14yrs Solarium Open terrace Covered terrace Last d 21.30hrs Languages spoken: English & Spanish
ROOMS: (room only) s fr 550FF; d 650-750FF **Reductions over 1 night Special breaks**
MEALS: Continental breakfast 60FF Lunch 90-180FF&alc Dinner 140-225FF&alc
CARDS: ●● ▨ ▨ ●) Travellers cheques

ROCHE-BERNARD, LA Morbihan

★ ★ Auberge des Deux Magots
pl du Bouffay 56130
☎ 299906075 FAX 299908787
Near river Near sea Near beach In town centre Near motorway
Closed 20Dec-20Jan
36 rms (14 bth/shr) (4 fmly) TV in 15 bedrooms STV Licensed Full central heating Languages spoken: English
MEALS: Lunch 80-320FFalc✷
CARDS: ●● ▨ Travellers cheques

★ ★ ★ Domaine de Bodeuc
Nivillac 56130
☎ 299908963 FAX 299909032
Situated in the peaceful surroundings of a park, the establishment features individually styled guest rooms with modern facilities and elegant public areas. After dinner, guests can retire to the lounge or play a game of billiards.
Near river Near sea Forest area
Closed Mar
8 en suite (bth/shr) TV in all bedrooms Licensed Lift Full central heating Open parking available Child discount available Outdoor swimming pool (heated) Pool table Boule Last d 21.00hrs Languages spoken: English
MEALS: Continental breakfast 45FF Dinner fr 70FF✷
CARDS: ●● ▨ ▨ ●) Travellers cheques

★ ★ ★ L'Auberge Bretonne
2 pl Duguesclin *56130*
☎ 299906028 FAX 299908500
Near river Near sea In town centre Near motorway
Closed mid Nov-early Dec & early Jan-end Jan
10 en suite (bth/shr) (3 fmly) TV in all bedrooms Licensed Lift
Full central heating Open parking available (charged)
Covered parking available (charged) Supervised Open terrace
V meals Last d 21.00hrs Languages spoken: English
ROOMS: (room only) d 500-1400FF ✷
MEALS: Continental breakfast 85FF Lunch 150-600FF&alc
Dinner 150-600FF&alc✷
CARDS: 😇 💳 ⚏

ROCHEFORT-EN-TERRE Morbihan

Château de Talhouet
56220
☎ 297433472 FAX 297433504
Near river Forest area
8 en suite (bth/shr) Full central heating Open parking
available Pool table Open terrace V meals Last d 21.30hrs
Languages spoken: English
CARDS: 💳 ⚏

ROSCOFF Finistère

★ ★ ★ Hotel Brittany
blvd St Barbe, BP47 *29681*
☎ 298697078 FAX 298611329
Elegant, stylish, friendly and refined, the manor house offers an
ideal setting for all occasions. The renowned gourmet restaurant,
overlooking the sea, offers the flavour of local specialities.
Near sea Near beach
Closed Nov-mid Mar
25 en suite (bth/shr) (3 fmly) (6 with balcony) TV in all bedrooms
STV Direct dial from all bedrooms Licensed Lift Night porter
Full central heating Open parking available Supervised Child
discount available 10yrs Indoor swimming pool (heated) Sauna
Solarium Jacuzzi/spa Open terrace V meals Last d 21.15hrs
Languages spoken: English German & Italian
ROOMS: (room only) s 400-590FF; d 490-990FF
Reductions over 1 night
MEALS: Full breakfast 58FF Lunch 220-300FFalc Dinner 220-
300FFalc
CARDS: 😇 💳 ⚏ Travellers cheques

ST-CAST-LE-GUILDO Côtes-D'Armor

★ ★ ★ Les Arcades
22380
☎ 296418050 FAX 296417734
Near sea Near beach In town centre
Closed 16 Sep-Mar
32 en suite (bth/shr) (18 with balcony) TV in all bedrooms
STV Direct dial from all bedrooms Licensed Lift Child
discount available Open terrace Covered terrace Last d
23.00hrs Languages spoken: English & Spanish
ROOMS: (room only) d 295-480FF
MEALS: Full breakfast 40FF Lunch 78-158FF Dinner 78-
158FF✷
CARDS: 😇 💳 ⚏ 💿 Travellers cheques

★ ★ Des Dunes
22380
☎ 296418031 FAX 296418534
Behind the handsome façade of this establishment is a cosy

interior where individually appointed bedrooms - some with
balconies - have modern facilities and provide a good level of
comfort. A family hotel since 1938, it is only 50 metres from
the beach and has a sheltered garden and tennis court at the
back, whilst the restaurant serves fine local seafood and fresh
fish specialities prepared by Monsieur Feret the chef-
proprietor.
Near sea Near beach In town centre
Closed early Nov-mid Mar
29 rms (20 bth 7 shr) (2 fmly) (8 with balcony) TV in all
bedrooms Full central heating Open parking available Child
discount available 7yrs Tennis Last d 21.30hrs Languages
spoken: English
MEALS: Continental breakfast 40FF Lunch 110-380FF&alc
Dinner 110-380FF&alc✷
CARDS: 😇 ⚏ Travellers cheques

★ ★ Les Mielles
22380
☎ 296418095 FAX 296417734
In pleasant and cosy surroundings the hotel Les Mielles offers
its visitors comfortable bedrooms with straightforward
amenities, a lounge for reading or relaxation, a pleasure
garden and a restaurant which serves fresh salads, patés,
seafood and grilled meat and fish.
Near sea In town centre
Closed 16 Sep-Mar
19 en suite (bth/shr) 5 rooms in annexe (5 fmly) (2 with
balcony) TV in all bedrooms STV Direct dial from all
bedrooms Licensed Child discount available Open terrace
Covered terrace Last d 22.30hrs Languages spoken: English &
Spanish
ROOMS: (room only) s 250-330FF; d 250-330FF ✷
MEALS: Full breakfast 40FF Lunch 75-115FF Dinner 75-
115FF✷
CARDS: 😇 💳 ⚏ 💿 Travellers cheques

ST-JOUAN-DES-GUÉRETS Ille-et-Vilaine

★ ★ ★ Malouinière des Longchamps
Les Longchamps *35430*
☎ 299827400 FAX 299827414
Standing on the edge of the 'pirate quarter', this charming
house welcomes its visitors in an informal family atmosphere.
Because of its good location, guests can make day-trips to
Mont-Saint-Michel or the medieval town of Dinan. There are
pretty bedrooms with modern appointments and a popular,
cosy restaurant which serves a range of tasty dishes, prepared
with fresh farm and regional produce.
Near river Near sea Near motorway
Closed Nov-1 Apr
9 en suite (bth/shr) No smoking in 4 bedrooms TV in all
bedrooms STV Direct dial from all bedrooms Licensed Full
central heating Open parking available Covered parking
available Child discount available 10yrs Outdoor swimming
pool (heated) Tennis Pool table Boule Mini-golf Bicycle
rental Open terrace Languages spoken: English,German
CARDS: 😇 💳 ⚏ Travellers cheques

ST-MALO Ille et Vilaine

★ ★ ★ Hotel Antinea
55 Chaussée de Sillon *35400*
☎ 299561075 FAX 299562211
The Atinea is a charming waterfront hotel situated only 200
metres from the spa. It features pleasant bedrooms with fully
equipped bathroom facilities, modern public areas and *contd.*

a terrace. The hotel has no restaurant but there are a number of attractive eating options nearby.
Near sea Near beach
25 en suite (bth/shr) (2 fmly) (6 with balcony) TV in all bedrooms STV Direct dial from all bedrooms Mini-bar in all bedrooms Licensed Lift Full central heating Open parking available (charged) Child discount available 12yrs Open terrace Languages spoken: English
CARDS: ●● ■■ ■■ ●) Travellers cheques

★ ★ ★ L'Ascott
35 rue du Chapitre *35400*
☎ 299818993 FAX 299817740
On the estuary of the River Rance between St Malo and Dinard, the Ascott Hotel provides an ideal stop-over to discover the charms of the Emerald coast. An elegantly renovated 19th-century manor house in picturesque gardens.
Near sea Near beach Forest area In town centre Near motorway
10 en suite (bth/shr) (2 fmly) (1 with balcony) TV in all bedrooms Direct dial from all bedrooms Licensed Night porter Full central heating Open parking available Solarium Covered terrace Languages spoken: English
ROOMS: s 400-500FF; d 600-700FF ✱
CARDS: ●● ■■ Travellers cheques

★ ★ ★ Elizabeth Hotel
2 rue des Cordiers *35400*
☎ 299562498 FAX 299563924
Situated near Mont-St-Michel and located inside the ramparts of the old pirate city. The 16th-century façade of the building conceals individually styled guest rooms and apartments - decorated in Louis XIII-style or a colonial theme - which are equipped with modern amenities, as well as a lounge bar in the original cellars. Located just half an hour from all the area's famous sights it is a suitable venue for a short stop or for visits in the region.
Near river Near sea Near beach In town centre
17 en suite (bth/shr) 7 rooms in annexe (5 fmly) TV in all bedrooms STV Radio in rooms Direct dial from all bedrooms Licensed Lift Night porter Full central heating Covered parking available (charged) Supervised Child discount available 12yrs Languages spoken: English,Spanish,German,Japanese
CARDS: ●● ■■ ■■ ●) Travellers cheques

★ ★ Hotel France & Châteaubriand
B P 77 *35412*
☎ 299566652 FAX 299401004
Built in the distinct Napoleon III style architecture, the hotel is situated in the historic heart of the 'pirate city' and just a few steps from the beach. It has comfortable bedrooms with views over the sea or the yachting harbour, and a restaurant which serves a choice of fresh fish and seafood.
78 en suite (bth/shr) 41 rooms in annexe (10 fmly) TV in all bedrooms STV Direct dial from all bedrooms Licensed Lift Night porter Full central heating Open parking available (charged) Covered parking available (charged) Supervised Pool table Bicycle rental Open terrace V meals Languages spoken: English, German, Italian & Spanish
ROOMS: (room only) s 346-403FF; d 411-532FF
CARDS: ●● ■■ ■■ ●) Travellers cheques

★ ★ ★ Grand Hotel des Thermes
100 blvd Hebert *35400*
☎ 299407575 FAX 290407600
Alongside a beautiful sandy beach, close to the historical

walled city. This hotel has comfortable bedrooms, two restaurants, several public rooms, a health club and beauty salon. It is also renowned for its Thalassotherapy Centre offering sea water treatments under medical control.
Near sea Near beach In town centre
Closed 4-14 Jan
185 en suite (bth/shr) 27 rooms in annexe (24 fmly) (20 with balcony) TV in all bedrooms STV Direct dial from all bedrooms Mini-bar in 150 bedrooms Licensed Lift Night porter Full central heating Open parking available Covered parking available (charged) Child discount available 12yrs Indoor swimming pool (heated) Sauna Solarium Gym Jacuzzi/spa Bicycle rental Open terrace Covered terrace Last d 21.30hrs Languages spoken: English, German & Italian
ROOMS: (room only) s 260-1350FF; d 430-1450FF
Reductions over 1 night
MEALS: Full breakfast 100FF Continental breakfast 70FF Lunch 130-295FF&alc Dinner 130-295FF&alc
CARDS: ●● ■■ ■■ ●) Travellers cheques

★ ★ Hotel Albatros
8 pl Duguesclin *35400*
☎ 299404711 FAX 299561049
This hotel is located near the harbour in the heart of the old pirate quarter just 50 metres from the beach. There is a large comfortable day room with cosy armchairs for relaxation and newly refurbished bedrooms which offer peaceful accommodation.
Near sea Near beach In town centre
22 en suite (bth/shr) (3 fmly) (3 with balcony) No smoking in 6 bedrooms TV in all bedrooms STV Direct dial from all bedrooms Licensed Lift Full central heating Open parking available Supervised Child discount available 10yrs Sauna Solarium Gym Jacuzzi/spa Bicycle rental Languages spoken: English,German
CARDS: ●● ■■ ■■ Travellers cheques

★ ★ ★ Hotel Central (Best Western)
6 Grande Rue *35400*
☎ 299408770 FAX 299404757
Town centre
Located in the heart of the old walled city of Saint-Malo, the hotel is ideally situated for both a business or leisure stay. Entirely refurbished, it features attractive guest rooms with modern amenities, a cosy bar serving a large selection of cocktails and a restaurant which offers an inventive cuisine based mainly on fresh fish and seafood produce. Staff are extremely helpful, providing an attentive service and putting a lot of effort into caring for their guests.
Near sea Near beach In town centre
46 en suite (bth/shr) (2 fmly) (10 with balcony) TV in all bedrooms STV Direct dial from all bedrooms Licensed Lift Night porter Full central heating Open parking available (charged) Covered parking available (charged) Supervised Child discount available 12yrs V meals Languages spoken: English,German,Italian
CARDS: ●● ■■ ■■ ●) JCB Travellers cheques

★ ★ Ibis
58 Chaussée du Sillon *35400*
☎ 299405777 FAX 299405778
The hotel occupies a superb location overlooking the sea, just ten minutes from the ramparts of the old town. The bedrooms are divided over three floors and offer fully equipped en suite facilities, and guests can start off the day with a generous buffet breakfast. There is a south-facing terrace garden and a splendid beach nearby.

Near sea Near beach In town centre Near motorway
60 en suite (bth/shr) (2 fmly) No smoking in 6 bedrooms TV in
all bedrooms STV Direct dial from all bedrooms Licensed
Lift Night porter Full central heating Open parking available
(charged) Covered parking available (charged) Supervised
Child discount available 12yrs Languages spoken:
English,German,Italian,Spanish
CARDS: ⊕ ▦ ▆ ➒ Travellers cheques

★ ★ Inter Hotel Ligne Bleue
138 bd des Talards *35400*
☎ 299820510 FAX 299817910
All the hotels in the Inter Hotel group offer guest
accommodation which is designed with the individual needs of
its clientele in mind. Whether situated in the capital or in a
seaside resort, they offer old-fashioned hospitality and up-to-
date modern amenities. Staff are friendly and helpful
throughout, and provide a degree of personal service which is
difficult to match, making a stay, whether for business or
pleasure an enjoyable experience to look back upon.
Near sea In town centre
Closed Nov-mid Mar
60 en suite (bth/shr) (3 fmly) TV available Direct dial from all
bedrooms Licensed Lift Full central heating Open parking
available Covered parking available (charged) Child discount
available 12yrs Last d 21.30hrs Languages spoken:
English,German
MEALS: Full breakfast 39FF Continental breakfast 39FF
Dinner 87-175FF✱
CARDS: ⊕ ▦ ▆ ➒ Travellers cheques

★ ★ Hotel Mascotte
76 Chaussée du Sillon *35400*
☎ 299403636 FAX 299401878
This modern hotel offers up-to-date guest rooms with fully
equipped en suite facilities, conference rooms, a cosy bar and a
restaurant which caters for all tastes.
Near sea Near beach
88 rms (14 fmly) (3 with balcony) No smoking in 8 bedrooms
TV in all bedrooms Radio in rooms Direct dial from all
bedrooms Licensed Lift Night porter Full central heating
Covered parking available (charged) Pool table Open terrace

★ ★ ★ Valmarin
7 rue Jean XX111 *35400*
☎ 299819476 FAX 299811003
(go to old city (intra muros) and follow walls from outside, pass
bridges of ferry terminal and turn right at second roundabout)
This 18th century manor, originally owned by a famous ship
owning family, offers comfortable and spacious
accommodation set in attractive grounds.
Near sea Near beach In town centre
Closed 16 Nov-24 Dec/7 Jan-part Feb
12 en suite (bth/shr) (3 fmly) TV in all bedrooms Radio in
rooms Direct dial from all bedrooms Mini-bar in all bedrooms
Licensed Full central heating Open parking available
Supervised Open terrace Languages spoken:
English,German,Italian
ROOMS: (room only) s 500-650FF; d 500-650FF
CARDS: ⊕ ▦ ▆ Travellers cheques

★ ★ ★ Villefromoy
7 bd Hebert *35400*
☎ 299409220 FAX 299567949
Located in a residential area on the edge of a fine sandy beach,
the hotel dates back to the Second Empire. Victorian-style
furnishings, model sailing ships and Neapolitan water-colours

acquired by pirates adorn the interior and blend harmoniously
with modern comfort. Most bedrooms have views of the sea
and are equipped with every convenience. With a promenade
running along the seafront, a health-centre and numerous
restaurant within easy walking distance, it provides the venue
for an enjoyable stay.
Near sea Near beach
Closed 16 Nov-14 Mar
22 en suite (bth) (3 fmly) (6 with balcony) No smoking in 1
bedroom TV in all bedrooms STV Radio in rooms Direct dial
from all bedrooms Licensed Lift Night porter Full central
heating Open parking available Supervised Open terrace
Languages spoken: English,German,Spanish
CARDS: ⊕ ▦ ▆ ➒ Travellers cheques

ST-MÉLOIR-DES-ONDES Ille-et-Vilaine

★ ★ ★ Tirel & Guerin
Gare de la Gouesnière *35350*
☎ 299891046
(from St Malo head for Rennes, then off the double
carriageway towards La Govesniere. First rdbt turn left
towards Cancale D76, 600m down road on the left.)
This traditionally furnished hotel has guest rooms and
apartments which are all equipped with modern amenities
offering a high level of comfort. There is a cosy bar and a
restaurant with a comprehensive menu featuring fresh fish
and seafood delicacies, as well as a choice of meat specialities,
augmented by an extensive selection of fine wines.
Near sea Near beach
15 Jan - 20 Dec
63 en suite (bth/shr) (5 fmly) (23 with balcony) TV in all
bedrooms STV Direct dial from all bedrooms Mini-bar in 12
bedrooms Licensed Night porter Full central heating Open
parking available Covered parking available (charged)
Supervised Child discount available 10yrs Indoor swimming
pool (heated) Tennis Sauna Solarium Gym Jacuzzi/spa Open
terrace Last d 21.30hrs Languages spoken: English & German
MEALS: Full breakfast 50FF Continental breakfast 50FF Lunch
125-400FF&alc Dinner 125-400FF&alc
CARDS: ⊕ ▦ ▆ ➒ Travellers cheques

ST-PIERRE-QUIBERON Morbihan

★ ★ ★ De La Plage
BP 6 *56510*
☎ 297309210 FAX 297309961
This hotel enjoys a splendid seaside location on the Quiberon
peninsula. The comfortable bedrooms have fine views over the
open sea, whilst the restaurant with panoramic terrace serves a
wide range of dishes. Because of its location, the hotel provides
a suitable base to explore the attractive Breton countryside.
Near sea In town centre
Closed Oct-Apr
49 en suite (bth/shr) (4 fmly) (28 with balcony) TV in all
bedrooms STV Direct dial from all bedrooms Licensed Lift
Full central heating Open parking available Supervised Child
discount available 6yrs Solarium Open terrace Last d
20.45hrs Languages spoken: English,German
CARDS: ⊕ ▦ ▆ ➒ Travellers cheques

★ ★ Hotel St Pierre
34 rte de Quiberon *56510*
☎ 297502690 FAX 297503798
Located in a sunny position at the very heart of the Quiberon
peninsula the hotel is just 100 metres from the beach. The
bedrooms have modern facilities and are quietly
contd.

situated, providing relaxing accommodation. A traditional cuisine, as well as seafood specialities are served in the homely restaurant, whilst the nearby Côte Sauvage is one of the most popular areas in Brittany.
Near lake Near sea Forest area Near motorway
Closed Nov-Mar
30 en suite (bth/shr) (5 fmly) No smoking in 5 bedrooms TV available STV Licensed Full central heating Open parking available Supervised Child discount available Tennis Boule Bicycle rental Open terrace V meals Last d 22.00hrs
Languages spoken: English,German
CARDS: ● ● ● ● Travellers cheques

ST-THÉGONNEC Finistère

★ ★ ★ Auberge St-Thégonnec
6 pl de la Mairie 29222
☎ 298796118 FAX 298627110
Situated in the heart of the parish enclosure of St-Thégonnec, this peaceful hotel offers comfortable guest accommodation, with bedrooms tastefully decorated in pastel shades, and fresh, imaginative cuisine, consisting of an array of commendable dishes.
Forest area In town centre Near motorway
19 en suite (bth/shr) (2 fmly) (3 with balcony) TV in all bedrooms Licensed Night porter Full central heating Open parking available Supervised Child discount available 10yrs Open terrace V meals Last d 21.00hrs Languages spoken: English,German
CARDS: ● ● ● ● Travellers cheques

SIZUN Finistère

★ ★ Le Clos des 4 Saisons
2 rue de la Paix 29450
☎ 298688019 FAX 298241193
This hotel opened its doors in 1990, and is housed in a building full of character, set in a flower-filled park. The bedrooms are well positioned to ensure peaceful accommodation, whilst the restaurant, which is located in the oldest part of the building, serves an inventive cuisine based on local produce and fish specialities.
Near river
19 rms (15 bth/shr) TV in all bedrooms Licensed Full central heating Open parking available Child discount available Last d 21.00hrs
ROOMS: (room only) s 200FF; d 230FF **Reductions over 1 night**
MEALS: Continental breakfast 37FF Lunch 59-119FF Dinner 59-119FF
CARDS: ● ● ● ● Travellers cheques

TRÉBEURDEN Côtes-D'Armor

★ ★ ★ Ti Al Lannec
allée de Mézo Guen 22560
☎ 296235726 FAX 296236214
The hotel is situated on one of the most spectacular stretches of coast in Brittany, and dates back to the turn of the century. Lovingly restored and renovated by the present owners, it offers a charming interior, where attractive furniture and well chosen fabrics and shades create a warm and comfortable atmosphere. Guests can enjoy breakfast in the flowered garden or soak up the sun on the terraces which go all the way down to the sea. There is a choice of in-house facilities available as well as many water sports in the vicinity.
Near sea Forest area Near motorway
Closed mid Nov-mid Mar

29 en suite (bth/shr) (7 fmly) (14 with balcony) TV in all bedrooms STV Direct dial from all bedrooms Licensed Lift Full central heating Open parking available Child discount available 14yrs Sauna Solarium Gym Pool table Jacuzzi/spa Open terrace Covered terrace V meals Last d 21.30hrs
Languages spoken: English,German
MEALS: Full breakfast 90FF Continental breakfast 65FF Lunch 108-390FF Dinner 185-390FF✱
CARDS: ● ● ● ● Travellers cheques

TRÉGASTEL Côtes-D'Armor

★ ★ Beau Séjour
22730
☎ 296238802 FAX 296234973
Situated in the heart of the 'Côte de Granite Rose' the hotel enjoys a seaside location. The bar and terrace skirt the beach, whilst the restaurant serves an array of seafood dishes and gastronomic specialties carefully prepared by the chef Mr Lavéant. The comfortable sound-proofed bedrooms are fitted with modern facilities.
Near sea Near beach
Closed 15 Nov-15 Feb
16 en suite (bth/shr) (6 fmly) (2 with balcony) TV in all bedrooms STV Direct dial from all bedrooms Licensed Full central heating Open parking available Child discount available Open terrace V meals Last d 22.30hrs Languages spoken: English,German
ROOMS: (room only) d 280-360FF
MEALS: Continental breakfast 40FF Lunch 75-190FFalc Dinner 75-190FFalc✱
CARDS: ● ● ● ● Travellers cheques

★ ★ ★ Belle-Vue
rue des Calculots 22730
☎ 296238818 FAX 296238991
Situated only 300 yards away from the magnificent 'Côte de Granite Rose', the hotel offers everything which makes Brittany such a charming place: a warm welcome, absolute tranquility and excellent food. The well equipped bedrooms have fine views over the Sept-Iles and offer a high degree of comfort. There is a homely day room and a cosy bar for a relaxing drink, whilst the restaurant serves a refined cuisine including seafood specialties.
Near sea
Closed Oct-Easter
31 en suite (bth/shr) (1 fmly) (4 with balcony) TV in all bedrooms Direct dial from all bedrooms Licensed Night porter Full central heating Open parking available Supervised No children Child discount available 6yrs Boule V meals Last d 21.15hrs Languages spoken: English,Italian
CARDS: ● ● ● ● Travellers cheques

TRINITÉ-SUR-MER, LA Morbihan

★ ★ Aux Algues Brunes
Le Bourg-St-Philbert 56470
☎ 297550878 FAX 297551859
Near river Near sea
20 rms (2 fmly) (14 with balcony) TV available Licensed Open parking available Supervised Child discount available 12yrs Open terrace Languages spoken: English,Italian

★ ★ Le Rouzic
17 cours des Quais 56470
☎ 297557206 FAX 297558225
(From N165 take D28,then D781, then D186 to La Trinite-sur-Mer)

Standing opposite the marina, the hotel offers traditional hospitality spiced with Breton charm. The wood-panelled interior features local hand-crafted furniture which creates a rustic atmosphere, whilst the restaurant with its granite fireplace serves traditional cuisine and fish specialities. The bedrooms are fitted with modern amenities and offer a good standard of comfort.
Near sea Near beach In town centre Near motorway
Closed 3-14 Jan and 16 Nov-14 Dec
32 en suite (bth/shr) (4 with balcony) TV in all bedrooms
Direct dial from all bedrooms Licensed Lift Full central heating Last d 21.00hrs
MEALS: Full breakfast 37FF Lunch 95-150FF&alc Dinner 95-150FF&alc✷
CARDS: ● ▅ ▆ ☼ Travellers cheques

VANNES Morbihan

★ ★ Hotel Mascotte
av Jean Monnet 56000
☎ 297475960 FAX 297470754
(follow directions for town centre, in front of Palais des Arts et des Congres)
The hotel is situated close to the historic centre of Vannes and the splendid bay of Morbihan, and provides the ideal setting to explore the fascinating past of this town at your own pace. The hotel features sound-proofed bedrooms equipped with the latest modern facilities, and a restaurant which serves a simple, light cuisine.
In town centre
65 en suite (bth/shr) (2 fmly) No smoking in 6 bedrooms TV in all bedrooms STV Radio in rooms Direct dial from all bedrooms Licensed Lift Night porter Full central heating Open parking available Covered parking available (charged) Child discount available 12yrs Pool table Last d 22.00hrs
Languages spoken: English,German,Italian,Spanish
MEALS: Full breakfast 45FF Lunch 69-89FF&alc Dinner 69-89FF&alc
CARDS: ● ▅ ▆ ☼

★ ★ ★ Manche Océan
31 rue du Lieut Col Maury 56000
☎ 297472646 FAX 297473086
(In the centre of Vannes. From Le Port, follow the walls (ramparts) and then head towards Pontiny, Lorient.)
This family hotel is situated on the edge of the historic quarter of the town, close to the shops, restaurants and tourist attractions. It features peacefully situated, comfortable bedrooms, fitted with modern amenities. Guests receive a friendly welcome from the owners Kareen and François Taillandier and their staff who provide a helpful and attentive service.
Near sea Near beach In town centre Near motorway
41 en suite (bth/shr) (5 fmly) (6 with balcony) TV in all bedrooms Direct dial from all bedrooms Mini-bar in all bedrooms Lift Night porter Full central heating Open parking available (charged) Covered parking available (charged) Supervised Child discount available 12yrs
Languages spoken: English
ROOMS: (room only) s 270-335FF; d 315-370FF
CARDS: ● ▅ ▆ ☼ Travellers cheques

VITRE Ille-et-Vilaine

★ ★ Hotel Perceval
Aire d'Erbrée 35500
☎ 299494999 FAX 299493022
(From motorway toll booth continue towards Rennes and take exit 'Aire d'Erbrée')
Constructed in 1988, the hotel is situated near an orchard and woods, and features a welcoming interior, where competent staff provide a 'round the clock' attentive service. An attractively decorated restaurant has a menu where regional specialities based on local ingredients from the Brocéliande forest take pride of place. Guests can relax in the comfortable TV lounge or on the flower-decked terrace and patio. The bedrooms are equipped with modern appointments - some with their own video-player - and offer a good level of comfort.
Forest area Near motorway
46 en suite (bth/shr) (2 fmly) TV in all bedrooms STV Direct dial from all bedrooms Night porter Full central heating Open parking available Pool table Open terrace V meals Last d 21.30hrs Languages spoken: English,Spanish
ROOMS: (room only) s 160-260FF; d 260FF
CARDS: ● ▅ ▆ ☼ Travellers cheques

VIVIER-SUR-MER, LE Ille-et-Vilaine

★ ★ Hotel Le Bretagne
6 Rond Point du Centre 35960
☎ 299489174 FAX 299488110
The informal hotel Le Bretagne has been skilfully managed by the same family for three generations. It stands on the shores of the Baie du Mont Saint-Michel and offers unrivalled views over the open sea. The attractively furnished bedrooms are well equipped and provide comfortable accommodation. The restaurant serves a traditional cuisine which includes many seafood delicacies and excellent desserts, which are freshly prepared on the premises.
Near sea Near beach Forest area In town centre Near motorway
Closed 30 Nov-15 Feb
16 en suite (bth/shr) 10 rooms in annexe (3 fmly) TV in all bedrooms Direct dial from all bedrooms Licensed Full central heating Open parking available Child discount available 12yrs Sauna Solarium Bicycle rental V meals Last d 20.45hrs
Languages spoken: English
MEALS: Full breakfast 40FF Continental breakfast 40FF Lunch 100-350FF&alc Dinner 100-350FF&alc✷
CARDS: ● ▅ ▆ ☼

Taking your mobile phone to France?
See page 11

Normandy

Normandy is without doubt a most beautiful area and much seems to be untouched by the twentieth century. Just a hop across the Channel, Normandy is close enough for a weekend break and full of interest for a longer visit. A vast region, full of variety which stretches from the majestic Mont-Saint-Michel in the west to almost the outer reaches of Paris, but far removed from Parisienne chic. Much of the region's economy is derived from the rich harvests from both the sea and the land and there are many gastronomic delights to sample and savour.

ESSENTIAL FACTS

DÉPARTEMENTS:	Calvados, Eure, Manche, Orne, Seine-Maritime
PRINCIPAL TOWNS	Bayeux, Caen, Alençon, Rouen, Le Havre, Cherbourg, Lisieux, Dieppe, Evreux.
PLACES TO VISIT:	The famous Bayeux Tapestry at Bayeux; the D-Day beaches; Chateau Gaillard; Monet's garden at Giverny; Mont-St-Michel
REGIONAL TOURIST OFFICE	30 Le Doyenné, 14 rue Charles-Corbeau, 27000 Evreux Tel 32 33 79 00
LOCAL GASTRONOMIC DELIGHTS	Chicken or pork with apples, cream and cider; creamy cheese such as Pont l'Evêque, Livarot and Camembert; duckling à la Rouenais (a pink fleshed duck); tripes à la mode de Caen (traditional dish featuring tripe); sole Dieppoise, a seafood speciality from Dieppe.
DRINKS	Calvados (apple-flavoured brandy); doux (sweet), sec (dry) and bouché (sparkling) cider; Pommeau, a local apple liqueur; Benedictine, a liqueur made by the monks of Fécamp from the aromatic herbs of the Pays de Ceux; poire pear cider
LOCAL CRAFTS WHAT TO BUY	Lace from Alençon and Bayeux; copper-ware and pewter from Villedieu-les-Poeles; stone-carving from the areas of Avrancles and Mortain; cloth and textiles from Louviers; linen from Orbec

(Top): The Allied invasion of occupied France in 1941 is commemorated by this beautiful stained glass window at Sainte-Mère-Église

(Bottom): The high chalk cliffs at Étretat have been worn into strange shapes by the constant action of the sea.

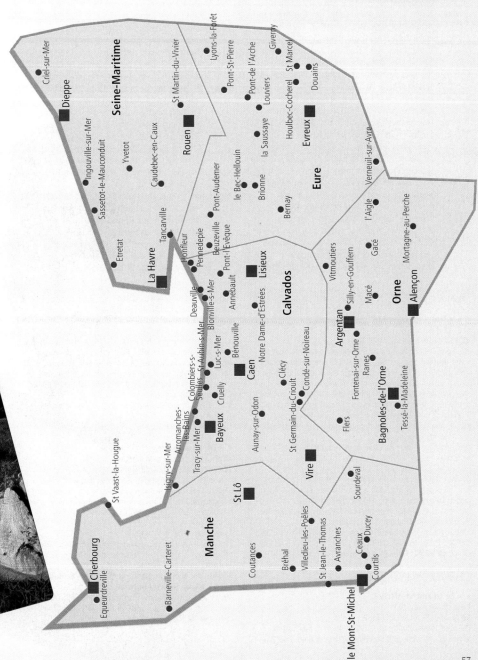

Criel-sur-Mer

Dieppe

Seine-Maritime

Lyons-la-Forêt

St Martin-du-Vivier

Pont-St-Pierre

Pont-de l'Arche

Giverny

St Marcel

Houlbec-Cocherel

Douains

Evreux

Ingouville-sur-Mer

Yvetot

Caudebec-en-Caux

Rouen

Verneuil-sur-Avre

Sassetot-le-Mauconduit

Pont-Audemer

le Bec-Hellouin

la Saussaye

Louviers

Eure

l'Aigle

Mortagne-au-Perche

Etretat

Tancarville

Honfleur

Pennedepie

Beuzeville

Brionne

Bernay

Gacé

Pont-l'Evêque

Vitmoutiers

La Havre

Deauville

Blonville-s-Mer

Annebault

Lisieux

Macé

Orne

Alençon

Colombiers-s-

St Aubin-s-Mer

Notre Dame-d'Estrées

Calvados

Silly-en-Gouffern

Seulles

Luc-s-Mer

Bénouville

Conté-sur-Noireau

Argentan

St Vaast-la-Hougue

Arromanches-

les-Bains

Tracy-sur-Mer

Bayeux

Cruelly

Caen

Clécy

Ranes

Fontenai-sur-Orne

Bagnoles-de-l'Orne

Isigny-sur-Mer

Aunay-sur-Odon

St Germain-du-Crioult

Flers

Tesse-la-Madeleine

Vire

St Lô

Sourdeval

Manche

Villedieu-les-Poêles

Ceaux

Ducey

Barneville-Carteret

Coutances

Bréhal

St Jean-le-Thomas

Avranches

Courtils

Cherbourg

Equeurdreville

le Mont-St-Michel

EVENTS & FESTIVALS

Mar Lisieux Tree Fair; Mortagne Pudding Fair; Rouen Scandinavian Film Festival; Caen Contemporary Music; Rouen International Fair

Apr Deauville 'Scales of Deauville'; Rouen Water Motor Sports

May Mortrée Vintage and Collectors Car Meeting; Mont-St-Michel Spring Festival; Coutances 'Jazz Under the Apple Trees' Festival; Cambremer AOC Festival; Argentan Antiques Show; Eure Département King Richard Calvalcade; Honfleur Seafarers' Pilgrimage; Rouen Joan of Arc Festival;

Jun Lisieux Son et Lumière 'From the Vikings to Thérèse'; Trouville Folklore Festival; Luneray Jazz Festival; Le Havre Blessing of the Sea Festival; Cabourg Romantic Film Festival; Flers Vibrations Festival; Blainville-Crévon Archeojazz; Le Pin-au-Haras 'Thursdays at The Stud du Pin' stallion musical show

Jul Bayeux Medieval Festival, La Haye de Routot Feast of St Clair; Forges les Eaux Horse Festival; Dives sur Mer Puppet Festival; Trouville 'Terrasses Musicales' Festival (*concerts on the pavements & beaches*); Sées Cathedral Son et Lumière; Deauville Bridge Festival; Le Pin-au-Haras 'Thursdays at The Stud du Pin' stallion musical show 3pm Thurs;

Trouville Festival of The Sea & The Mackerel; La Hay de Routot, Feast of St Clair; Mont-St Michel Pilgrimage across the beaches;

Aug Dieppe Ancient Music Festival; Bagnoles-de l'Orne Fireworks and Musical Show on the Lake; Livarot Cheese Fair; Ile de Tatihou 'Les Traversées' (*traditional dancing*); Le Pin-au Haras 'Thursdays at The Stud du Pin' stallion musical show 3pm Thurs; Deauville Thoroughbred Yearling Auction; Domfront Medieval Market; Lisieux Turkey Market; Saint-Lô 'Thursdays at the National Stud';

Sep Belleme International Mushroom Fair; Caen International Fair; Deauville American Film Festival; Lessay Ancient St Croix Fair; Le Neubourg Horse Show at Champ de Bataille Castle; Le Pin-au-Haras 'Thursdays at The Stud du Pin' stallion musical show 3pm Thurs; Le Havre Celebration of the sea; Lisieux Grand Feast of Ste Theresa; Le Pin-au-Haras horse racing & parade;

Oct Beuvron-en-Auge Grand Cider Market & Festival; Lisieux International Flower Festival; Honfleur Shrimp Festival; Rouen National Antique Fair; October in Normandy at Rouen, Dieppe, Le Havre; Lisieux Blues Festival; Calvados Equi'days (*horse riding competition & sale*); Vimoutiers Apple Festival;

AIGLE, L' Orne

★ ★ ★ Hotel du Dauphin (Best Western)
pl de la Halle *63100*
☎ 233841800 FAX 233340928
The hotel Dauphin dates back to 1618 and offers its clientele lavish hospitality and excellent food. The interior is tastefully furnished in a style befitting its origin and features an elegant lounge with superb open fire place as well as a cosy bar. The attractive bedrooms offer a high standard of comfort and are individually styled with high quality fabrics and furnishings. The cuisine combines a choice of classic and imaginative dishes incorporating the finest local produce. In addition there is a 1920s style brasserie.
Near river Near lake Forest area In town centre Near motorway
Closed 17 Feb-9 Mar & 4-17 Apr
30 rms (28 bth) (6 fmly) TV in all bedrooms STV Direct dial from all bedrooms Mini-bar in all bedrooms Licensed Night porter Full central heating Open parking available Supervised Child discount available 12yrs Open terrace Last d 23.00hrs Languages spoken: English
MEALS: Full breakfast 60FF Continental breakfast 45FF Lunch 150-358FF Dinner 150-358FF✱
CARDS: ●● ■■ ⯊ ·⯑ Travellers cheques

ALENÇON Orne

★ ★ Le Grand St-Michel
7 rue du Temple *61000*
☎ 233260477 FAX 233267182
The hotel is peacefully situated in the heart of this historic town and offers cheerful bedrooms. The proprietor-chef has

earned a well-deserved reputation throughout the region for his imaginative and classic French cuisine.
Forest area In town centre Near motorway
Closed Jul
13 en suite (bth/shr) (3 fmly) TV in all bedrooms Direct dial from all bedrooms Licensed Full central heating Air conditioning in bedrooms Open parking available Covered parking available (charged) Supervised Child discount available 10yrs V meals Last d 22.00hrs Languages spoken: German,Italian,Spanish
MEALS: Full breakfast 28FF Lunch 95-175FF Dinner 95-175FF✱
CARDS: ●● ■■ ⯊ ·⯑ Travellers cheques

★ ★ De L'Industrie
22 pl Général-de-Gaulle *61000*
☎ 233271930 FAX 233284956
This small hotel is pleasantly decorated throughout in fine pastel shades and has bedrooms offering a good standard of accommodation. The brasserie-style restaurant serves a selection of dishes including foie gras and fresh fish specialities.
In town centre Near motorway
7 en suite (shr) TV in all bedrooms Direct dial from all bedrooms Licensed Full central heating Child discount available 12yrs Last d 21.30hrs Languages spoken: English
ROOMS: (room only) s 180FF; d 230-260FF **Reductions over 1 night Special breaks**
MEALS: Full breakfast 35FF Lunch 75-170FF&alc Dinner 75-170FF&alc
CARDS: ●● ⯊ Travellers cheques

ANNEBAULT Calvados

★ ★ Le Cardinal
14430
☎ 231648196 FAX 231646465
An ideal establishment for nature lover and gourmet alike, the auberge 'Le Cardinal' offers visitors old-fashioned hospitality and excellent cuisine. The peaceful accommodation is equipped with en-suite facilities and provides maximum comfort. The charming restaurant with open fireplace serves an array of specialities such as duck foie gras, freshly smoked salmon and seasonal seafood delicacies.
Near lake Near sea Near beach In town centre Near motorway
Closed mid Jan-Feb
7 rms (6 shr) TV in all bedrooms STV Direct dial from all bedrooms Licensed Full central heating Air conditioning in bedrooms Open parking available Child discount available 12yrs Boule Open terrace Last d 21.00hrs Languages spoken: English
ROOMS: (room only) s 250-290FF; d 290-350FF
CARDS: ●● ▆▆

ARROMANCHES-LES-BAINS Calvados

★ ★ D'Arromanches
2 rue du Colonel René Michel *14117*
☎ 231223626 FAX 231222329
(access from Caen via N13)
This small hotel has undergone extensive renovation over the years, with the emphasis being on the bathrooms and the decoration of the bedrooms, and it now offers comfortable accommodation. The owner takes pride in his cooking and the lady of the house is a charming host.
Near sea Near beach In town centre
Closed Jan
9 en suite (bth/shr) (2 fmly) TV in all bedrooms STV Licensed Full central heating Open parking available Supervised Open terrace Last d 21.00hrs Languages spoken: English
ROOMS: (room only) d 290-320FF
MEALS: Full breakfast 3700FF Continental breakfast 37FF Lunch 78-160FF&alc Dinner 78-160FF&alc
CARDS: ●● ▆▆ Travellers cheques

★ ★ De La Marine
2 quai La Marine *14117*
☎ 231223419 FAX 231229880
Situated beside the sea, the hotel offers magnificent views from both the restaurant, and the guest-rooms which are equipped with good, modern amenities. The restaurant serves an array of delightful fresh seafood (arriving daily) and other fish specialities. Due to the geographical location, it is a good base for either a beach holiday or day trips in Normandy.
Near sea Near beach
Closed 15 Nov-15 Feb
30 rms (26 bth/shr) (2 fmly) TV in all bedrooms Radio in rooms Direct dial from all bedrooms Mini-bar in all bedrooms Licensed Full central heating Open parking available Supervised Child discount available 8yrs Fishing Bicycle rental Open terrace V meals Last d 21.30hrs Languages spoken: English
MEALS: Full breakfast 40FF Lunch 85-180FF&alc Dinner 85-180FF&alc✱
CARDS: ▆▆ ▆▆ Travellers cheques

AUNAY-SUR-ODON Calvados

★ ★ De la Place
rue du 12 Juin *14260*
☎ 231776073 FAX 231779007
The hotel is ideally located for visits to the surrounding sights. It offers functional bedrooms and a restaurant - furnished in typically French style - which provides a good choice of enjoyable meals.
Near river Near lake Forest area In town centre Near motorway
19 rms (13 shr) (1 fmly) (1 with balcony) TV available Licensed Full central heating Open parking available Covered parking available Supervised Child discount available 10yrs Boule Open terrace Covered terrace V meals Last d 21.00hrs Languages spoken: English
MEALS: Full breakfast 38FF Continental breakfast 30FF Lunch 70-175FF&alc Dinner 70-175FF&alc✱
CARDS: ●● ▆▆ ▆▆ Travellers cheques

AVRANCHES Manche

★ ★ Abrincates
37 bd du Luxembourg *50300*
☎ 233586664 FAX 233584011
(S of Avranches on N175)
This modern hotel is situated in Avranches which offers superb views across the bay of Mont-Saint-Michel. The attractive bedrooms are comfortable and fully equipped. There is a friendly bar and a mini-boutique selling Calvados, postcards and brochures. The cuisine is excellent and ranges from traditional regional dishes to fish specialities. A function room with a panoramic view of the surroundings can accommodate up to 25 people.
In town centre Near motorway
Closed 21 Dec-6 Jan RS Sun evening Oct-May
29 en suite (bth/shr) (1 fmly) (27 with balcony) TV in all bedrooms STV Direct dial from all bedrooms Licensed Lift Full central heating Open parking available Supervised Child discount available 12yrs Boule Bicycle rental Open terrace Last d 22.30hrs Languages spoken: English
ROOMS: (room only) s 250-290FF; d 270-360FF
Reductions over 1 night
MEALS: Continental breakfast 35FF Lunch 66-140FF&alc Dinner 66-140FF&alc
CARDS: ●● ▆▆ JCB Travellers cheques

★ ★ Du Jardin des Plantes
10 pl Carnot *50300*
☎ 233580368 FAX 233600172
This is a charming hotel situated near the Jardin des Plantes, offering bedrooms equipped with modern day amenities and an attractive dining room serving a good choice of enjoyable meals in informal surroundings.
Near sea In town centre Near motorway
26 rms (22 bth/shr) (9 fmly) (3 with balcony) TV in all bedrooms Licensed Night porter Full central heating Open parking available Supervised Open terrace V meals Last d 21.30hrs Languages spoken: English
CARDS: ●● ▆▆ JCB Travellers cheques

BAGNOLES-DE-L'ORNE Orne

★ ★ Beaumont
26 bd Lémeunier de la Raillère *61140*
☎ 233379177 FAX 233389061
This charming turn-of-the century building is
contd.

peacefully situated in a flower-filled park just five minutes from the town centre. It has cosy lounges, an attractive conservatory, congenial bar, and delightful garden. The bedrooms are well-equipped, and meals are served in the romantic atmosphere of the candlelit restaurant.
Near river Near lake Forest area
Closed end Nov-early Mar
40 rms 17 rooms in annexe (1 fmly) (2 with balcony) TV in all bedrooms Direct dial from all bedrooms Mini-bar in all bedrooms Licensed Night porter Full central heating Open parking available Supervised Child discount available Open

terrace Last d 21.30hrs Languages spoken: English
CARDS: ●● ▆▆ ▆▆ ◑ Euro charge & Euro cheque Travellers cheques

★ ★ ★ **Bois Joli** (Minotel)
av Philippe-du-Rozier *61140*
☎ 233379277 FAX 233370756
This Anglo-Norman timbered villa dates back to 1870 and is set in a 3000 square metre park near a lake. The restaurant and wine-cellar have earned a reputation in the area for both their first-class cuisine and comprehensive wine list. The bedrooms - some with balconies - offer a good standard of comfort, and in-house leisure facilities comprise a fitness room, sauna, Turkish bath and solarium.
Near river Near lake Forest area In town centre Near motorway
20 rms (14 bth 5 shr) (2 with balcony) TV in all bedrooms Direct dial from all bedrooms Licensed Lift Full central heating Open parking available Supervised Child discount available 12yrs Sauna Solarium Gym Bicycle rental Open terrace Last d 22.00hrs
CARDS: ●● ▆▆ ▆▆ ◑ Travellers cheques

★ ★ ★ **Lutétia**
bd Paul Chalvet *61140*
☎ 233379477 FAX 233300987
Set in the heart of Bagnoles-de-L'Orne, a well-known tourist resort and thermal spa in the west of France, Hôtel Lutétia and its restaurant Reine-Astrid welcome their guests in peaceful and relaxing surroundings. Situated in the centre of the 'Belle Époque' district, the Lutétia offers modern amenities whilst individually appointed bedrooms whilst still retaining traditional charm. An attractive residence for an overnight stop or holiday in Normandy.
Near lake Forest area In town centre Near motorway
Closed mid Oct-early April
34 rms (20 bth 10 shr) 14 rooms in annexe TV in all bedrooms STV Licensed Lift Full central heating Open parking available Supervised Child discount available Boule Covered terrace Last d 21.00hrs Languages spoken: English,German & Italian
CARDS: ●● ▆▆ ▆▆ ◑ Travellers cheques

★ ★ ★ **Manoir du Lys**
La Croix Gauthier, rte de Juvigny *61140*
☎ 233378069 FAX 233300580
(In direction of Juvigny-sous-Andaines pass golf course on right)
A charming Norman manor house in the heart of Normandy, at the edge of a forest. Guest rooms and public areas are tastefully furnished and a pleasant quiet stay in a family-like atmosphere is the aim of the staff.
Near lake Forest area
Closed 4 Jan-14 Feb RS Nov-3 Jan & 15 Feb-Etr
24 en suite (bth/shr) (3 fmly) (7 with balcony) Licensed Lift Full central heating Open parking available Child discount available Indoor swimming pool (heated) Outdoor swimming pool (heated) Tennis Fishing Boule Bicycle rental Open terrace Last d 21.00hrs
ROOMS: (room only) d 300-800FF ✱
MEALS: Continental breakfast 60FF Lunch 130-265FF&alc Dinner 130-265FF
CARDS: ●● ▆▆ ▆▆ ◑

★ ★ **De Normandie**
2 av du Dr Paul Lémuet *61140*
☎ 233308016 FAX 233370619
Located three hours from Paris, Bagnoles-de l'Orne is the most famous spa town in the western part of France. Situated opposite an extensive forest, the hotel provides the ideal venue for an overnight stop and features attractively decorated bedrooms, a delightful well maintained garden and terrace, whilst the restaurant serves a wide choice of delicious seafood specialities.
Near lake Forest area In town centre
Closed 6 Nov-Mar
22 rms (5 bth 13 shr) (3 fmly) (2 with balcony) TV in all bedrooms Direct dial from all bedrooms Licensed Full central heating Open parking available Covered parking available Supervised Child discount available 5yrs Bicycle rental Open terrace V meals Last d 21.00hrs Languages spoken: English
ROOMS: (room only) s 200FF; d 220FF ✱ **Special breaks: weekend breaks**
MEALS: Full breakfast 35FF Continental breakfast 35FF Lunch 78-185FF&alc Dinner 78-185FF&alc✱
CARDS: ●● ▆▆ ▆▆ ◑ Travellers cheques

★ ★ **Nouvel Hotel**
8 av Albert Christophle, Tessé-la-Madeleine *61140*
☎ 233378122 FAX 233380468
(Near the church and the castle, 400mtrs from the thermal baths)
In the centre of Tessé-la-Madeleine, the hotel is located close to the church and only 400 metres from the thermal baths. Entirely renovated, it now offers cosy bedrooms with modern appointments, and a restaurant which serves a sound, honest cuisine based on fresh local produce, which can be adapted to meet individual needs. In addition, guests can relax in the flower-filled garden or retire to one of the comfortable lounges, which are stocked with plenty of reading material and board-games for entertainment.
Near river Near lake Forest area In town centre Near motorway
Closed Nov-Mar
30 en suite (bth/shr) (1 fmly) (2 with balcony) TV in all bedrooms Direct dial from all bedrooms Room-safe Licensed Lift Night porter Full central heating Open parking available Supervised Child discount available 10yrs Boule Open terrace Wkly live entertainment V meals Last d 21.00hrs Languages spoken: English

ROOMS: (room only) s 230-260FF; d 240-345FF
MEALS: Continental breakfast 32FF Lunch 88-155FF Dinner 88-155FF✱
CARDS: ✪ ☲

BARNEVILLE-CARTERET Manche

★ ★ Les Isles
50270
☎ 233049076 FAX 233945383
(Approach from Cherbourg via D904)
The hotel Les Isles provides informal surroundings for a relaxing seaside holiday. The bedrooms have modern amenities and offer comfortable accommodation. The restaurant with its fine views of the garden and the sea beyond, serves an extensive array of specialities including fresh sea and shellfish.
Near sea Near beach
Closed 16 Nov-Jan
32 rms (30 bth) (3 fmly) (7 with balcony) TV in all bedrooms Direct dial from all bedrooms Licensed Full central heating Open parking available Child discount available Solarium Bicycle rental Open terrace Water skiing, Cycling Last d 21.30hrs Languages spoken: English
ROOMS: (room only) s fr 205FF; d 205-325FF **Reductions over 1 night**
MEALS: Full breakfast 35FF Continental breakfast 35FF Lunch 68-180FF&alc Dinner 68-180FF✱
CARDS: ✪ ▦ ☲ Travellers cheques

BAYEUX Calvados

★ ★ De Brunville
9 rue Génas Duhomme *14400*
☎ 231211800 FAX 231517089
In the heart of a historic village this establishment offers comfortable accommodation with good facilities, including well equipped bedrooms and a warm, friendly atmosphere. The restaurant 'La Marmite' serves a large choice of generously sized regional dishes. Guests can also enjoy their meals on the covered, heated terrace.
In town centre
38 en suite (bth/shr) 5 rooms in annexe (2 fmly) (1 with balcony) TV in all bedrooms STV Licensed Lift Full central heating Open parking available Open terrace Covered terrace Last d 22.00hrs Languages spoken: English
ROOMS: (room only) s 230-300FF; d 230-350FF ✱
MEALS: Full breakfast 40FF Continental breakfast 40FF Lunch 69-149FF Dinner 69-149FF
CARDS: ✪ ▦ ☲ Travellers cheques

★ ★ ★ Château de Bellefontaine
49 rue de Bellefontaine *14400*
☎ 231220010 FAX 231221909
This 18th-century building is set in private grounds surrounded by a stretch of a river and is not far from the centre of Bayeux. The elegant interior, complemented by attractive bedrooms with modern facilities, provides a pleasant setting for a relaxing stay.
Near river Forest area Near motorway
15 en suite (bth/shr) (3 fmly) No smoking in 1 bedroom TV in all bedrooms Direct dial from all bedrooms Licensed Lift Night porter Full central heating Open parking available Supervised Child discount available Tennis Bicycle rental Open terrace Languages spoken: English
ROOMS: (room only) s 400-450FF; d 450-650FF
CARDS: ✪ ▦ ☲ ➋

★ ★ ★ Hotel Churchill
14-16 rue St-Jean *14404*
☎ 231213180 FAX 231214166
Situated in the old quarter of the town, Monsieur and Madame Selmi welcome their visitors into a warm, informal atmosphere. The guest rooms are individually styled and offer a high standard of comfort; and the cuisine incorporates quality home cooking and regional specialities.
Forest area In town centre Near motorway
Closed mid Nov-mid Mar
32 en suite (bth/shr) (6 fmly) TV in all bedrooms STV Direct dial from all bedrooms Mini-bar in 5 bedrooms Full central heating V meals Languages spoken: English
ROOMS: (room only) s fr 360FF; d 360-520FF **Reductions over 1 night**
MEALS: Full breakfast 57FF Continental breakfast 42FF Lunch 75-135FF&alc Dinner 75-135FF&alc✱
CARDS: ✪ ▦ ☲ ➋ Travellers cheques

★ ★ ★ Grand Hotel du Luxembourg (Best Western)
25 rue des Bouches *14400*
☎ 231920004 FAX 231925426
The hotel is set in the heart of the town of Bayeux, famous for its history and tapestry. The building dates back to the 17th century and has comfortable and spacious guest rooms, whilst the restaurant serves an extensive choice of dishes incorporating good quality ingredients from the region.
Near sea Forest area In town centre Near motorway
22 en suite (bth/shr) 5 rooms in annexe (1 with balcony) TV in all bedrooms STV Radio in rooms Lift Full central heating Open parking available Covered parking available Child discount available 12yrs Last d 21.30hrs Languages spoken: English
MEALS: Full breakfast 50FF Lunch 103-290FF Dinner 103-290FF✱
CARDS: ✪ ▦ ☲ Travellers cheques

★ ★ ★ Lion d'Or
71 rue St-Jean *14400*
☎ 231920690 FAX 231221564
(From A13 follow directions to SNCF station. Then at station take 1st right, then straight ahead following arrows)
The characterful hotel Lion d'Or is a former coaching inn dating back to the 17th century. It has tastefully furnished guest-rooms offering a high standard of accommodation, cosy bar-lounge with open fireplace and a peaceful flower-filled courtyard. The menu features traditional, skilfully prepared dishes, served by a friendly, attentive staff.
Near river In town centre
Closed 20 Dec-20 Jan
25 en suite (bth/shr) (8 fmly) TV in all bedrooms STV Direct dial from all bedrooms Mini-bar in all bedrooms Licensed Night porter Full central heating Open parking available Covered parking available Supervised Child discount available 12yrs Open terrace V meals Last d 21.30hrs Languages spoken: English
ROOMS: (room only) s 430-460FF; d 430-480FF **Reductions over 1 night**
MEALS: Full breakfast 50FF Continental breakfast 60FF Lunch 100-230FF&alc Dinner 150-230FF&alc
CARDS: ✪ ▦ ☲ ➋ Travellers cheques

★ ★ ★ Novotel Bayeux
rue St-Patrice *14400*
☎ 231921611 FAX 231218876
Novotel offer their clients good quality accommodation in modern, well equipped bedrooms and boast refined

contd.

restaurants serving good quality cuisine They have excellent business meeting and conference facilities and some have food and beverages available 24 hours a day. All their hotels have at least one bedroom for disabled guests.
Near motorway
77 en suite (bth/shr) (25 fmly) No smoking in 30 bedrooms TV in all bedrooms Radio in rooms Direct dial from all bedrooms Mini-bar in all bedrooms Licensed Lift Night porter Full central heating Air conditioning in bedrooms Open parking available Child discount available 15yrs Outdoor swimming pool Pool table Open terrace Covered terrace V meals Last d 22.30hrs Languages spoken: English
ROOMS: (room only) s 395-405FF; d 435-405FF
MEALS: Full breakfast 55FF Continental breakfast 55FF Lunch 75-150FF Dinner 75-150FF✱
CARDS: ● ■ ⚏ ⁕ Travellers cheques

BEC-HELLOUIN, LE Eure

★ ★ ★ **Auberge de l'Abbaye**
27800
☎ 232448602 FAX 232463223
A very pretty, rustically furnished 18th century auberge in a little village in the heart of the Normandy countryside. Bedrooms are sympathetically furnished and are in keeping with the style of the exterior. The restaurant has a good reputation in the area - people come from miles around for the apple pie alone! Lots to see and do nearby.
Near river Forest area In town centre Near motorway
10 en suite (bth/shr) (1 fmly) No smoking in 1 bedroom Direct dial from all bedrooms Mini-bar in all bedrooms Licensed Full central heating Open parking available Covered parking available Supervised Child discount available Boule Bicycle rental Open terrace V meals Last d 22.00hrs Languages spoken: English
ROOMS: (room only) d 400-450FF ✱ **Reductions over 1 night**
MEALS: Full breakfast 45FF Lunch fr 140FF&alc Dinner fr 200FF&alc✱
CARDS: ● ■ ⚏ Travellers cheques

BÉNOUVILLE Calvados

★ ★ ★ **Glycine**
11 pl du Commando *14970*
☎ 231446194 FAX 231436730
This charming hotel is housed in a building with original exposed brickwork. The bedrooms are decorated in pastel shades and offer good comfort - some have private entries and are situated around a pretty patio with a small garden.
Near river Near sea Near motorway
25 en suite (bth/shr) (8 fmly) TV in all bedrooms STV Direct dial from all bedrooms Mini-bar in all bedrooms Licensed Full central heating Open parking available Supervised Open terrace Last d 21.45hrs Languages spoken: English
MEALS: Continental breakfast 33FF Lunch 95-230FF Dinner 95-230FF✱
CARDS: ● ⚏

BERNAY Eure

★ ★ **Le Lion d'Or**
48 rue du Général-de-Gaulle *27300*
☎ 232431206 FAX 232466058
(In the town centre near the Tourist Office)
This 150-year old former coaching inn is set in the heart of the town of Bernay and offers its visitors quality Normandy

cuisine and traditional hospitality. Built in the distinct architecture of the region and featuring an interior courtyard, it offers comfortable bedrooms with private facilities and an informal restaurant which serves a large choice of local produce.
Near river Forest area In town centre Near motorway
26 en suite (bth/shr) (8 fmly) (1 with balcony) No smoking in 6 bedrooms TV in all bedrooms STV Direct dial from all bedrooms Licensed Lift Full central heating Open parking available Supervised Child discount available 12yrs Open terrace V meals Last d 21.30hrs Languages spoken: English
ROOMS: (room only) s 185-200FF; d 220-275FF
Reductions over 1 night
MEALS: Continental breakfast 35FF Lunch 100-245FF&alc Dinner 100-245FF✱
CARDS: ● ■ ⚏ Travellers cheques

BEUZEVILLE Eure

★ ★ **Cochon d'Or et Petit Castel**
pl du Général-de-Gaulle *27210*
☎ 232577046 FAX 232422570
Whether situated on the garden or village side, the bedrooms in this establishment ensure peaceful accommodation. Tastefully decorated, they offer modern amenities and are suitable for both business and leisure travellers. Imaginative and plentiful are the hallmarks of the cuisine served in the elegant restaurant.
In town centre
Closed 16 Dec-16 Jan
20 rms 16 rooms in annexe (3 fmly) TV in all bedrooms Direct dial from all bedrooms Licensed Full central heating Open parking available V meals Last d 21.00hrs Languages spoken: English
MEALS: Continental breakfast 35FF Lunch 160-300FF&alc Dinner 81-240FF&alc✱
CARDS: ● ⚏ Travellers cheques

★ ★ **De la Poste**
60 rue Constant Fouché *27210*
☎ 232577104 FAX 232421101
(On N175 between Caen and Rouen)

This old coaching inn was built in 1844, and features cheerfully decorated bedrooms with good modern amenities and a classic French-style restaurant, offering a well balanced choice of dishes served by attentive staff. A golf course and mini-golf can be found within driving distance of the hotel.
Forest area In town centre Near motorway
Closed mid Nov-mid Mar
16 rms (4 bth 10 shr) (2 fmly) (3 with balcony) TV in 12 bedrooms Direct dial from 14 bedrooms Licensed Full central

heating Open parking available Child discount available 12yrs
Open terrace V meals Last d 21.00hrs Languages spoken:
English
ROOMS: (room only) d 290-310FF
MEALS: Full breakfast 40FF Continental breakfast 35FF Lunch
99-189FF Dinner 99-189FF✱
CARDS: ✹ ■ ☲

BLONVILLE-SUR-MER Calvados

★ ★ L'Epi d'Or
23 av Michel d'Ornano *14910*
☎ 231879048 FAX 231870898
(Access via Deauville heading towards Blonville & Villers)
Built in typical Normandy style and situated near a fine sandy
beach, the hotel provides a suitable setting for a seaside family
holiday. The bedrooms have fine views over the open sea and
are equipped with modern amenities, while the restaurant
serves a range of dishes to suit all tastes.
Near sea Near beach In town centre
12 en suite (bth/shr) (2 fmly) (4 with balcony) TV in all
bedrooms Direct dial from all bedrooms Mini-bar in all
bedrooms Licensed Lift Full central heating Open parking
available Child discount available 10yrs Open terrace
Covered terrace V meals Last d 22.00hrs Languages spoken:
English,Spanish
ROOMS: (room only) s 360-380FF; d 380-420FF
Reductions over 1 night
MEALS: Full breakfast 35FF Continental breakfast 35FF Lunch
90-360FF&alc Dinner 90-360FF&alc
CARDS: ✹ ■ ☲ Travellers cheques

BRÉHAL Manche

★ ★ De La Gare
1 pl Commandant Codart *50290*
☎ 23361611 FAX 233611802
(Approach via D971 (Granville-Coutances) exit Bréhal)
This superb small hotel has been entirely renovated and is
impeccably managed by its proprietors. The host presides over
the kitchen, whilst his wife provides an attentive, cheerful
service in the foyer and restaurant. The hotel is close to the
sea, the beaches and various leisure pursuits and offers a
pleasant setting for an enjoyable stay.
Near sea In town centre
9 rms (8 bth/shr) (2 fmly) TV in all bedrooms Direct dial from
all bedrooms Licensed Night porter Full central heating
Open parking available Covered parking available Child
discount available 10yrs Open terrace V meals Last d
21.30hrs Languages spoken: English
ROOMS: (room only) s 160FF; d 280FF **Reductions over 1
night**
MEALS: Full breakfast 38FF Continental breakfast 38FF Lunch
72-190FF&alc Dinner 72-190FF&alc
CARDS: ✹ ■ ☲ Travellers cheques

BRIONNE Eure

★ ★ ★ Le Logis de Brionne
1 pl St Denis *27800*
☎ 232448173 FAX 232451092
Near lake Forest area
12 en suite (bth/shr) (3 fmly) TV in all bedrooms Licensed
Full central heating Open parking available Covered parking
available Open terrace V meals Last d 21.15hrs Languages
spoken: English,Spanish

CAEN Calvados

★ Hotel Bernières
50 rue de Bernières *14000*
☎ 231860126 FAX 231865176
(In town centre follow signs 'Château', then the one-way
system around the castle to take 4th street on left shortly after
St-Pierre church)
Situated in the heart of Caen, the hotel offers well furnished
bedrooms of which most have private facilities. An entirely
renovated interior provides a cosy atmosphere where guests
are made to feel at home and where the proprietors offer a
friendly and attentive service.
In town centre
17 rms (1 bth 9 shr) (2 fmly) (3 with balcony) TV in all
bedrooms Direct dial from all bedrooms Licensed Night
porter Full central heating Languages spoken: English
ROOMS: (room only) s 155-210FF; d 175-230FF
✱ **Reductions over 1 night**
CARDS: ✹ ■ ☲ Travellers cheques

★ ★ Climat de France
av Montgomery, Quartier du Memorial *14000*
☎ 231443636 Cen Res 64460123 FAX 231956262
(off N22)
Situated in Caen, the hotel features bedrooms equipped with
every modern convenience. The restaurant serves a generous
and traditional cuisine in a friendly atmosphere, and guests
can help themselves to as many starters and sweets as they like
from the tempting buffet, whilst also barbecue and fondue
evenings are organised on a regular basis.
72 en suite (bth) (3 fmly) TV in all bedrooms Radio in rooms
Direct dial from all bedrooms Licensed Full central heating
Open parking available Supervised Pool table Open terrace
Covered terrace Last d 10pm Languages spoken: English,
German & Spanish
CARDS: ✹ ■ ☲ ◗ Travellers cheques

★ ★ ★ Dauphin
29 rue Gémare *14000*
☎ 231862226 FAX 231863514
Visitors receive a friendly welcome in this ancient former
priory, which stands between the two abbeys. Normandy
cuisine features prominently on the menu, and the restaurant
also serves a range of innovative dishes with the emphasis on
fresh fish specialities. The attractive bedrooms have modern
facilities, and some feature Normandy-style half-timbered
walls.
Forest area
22 en suite (bth/shr) 7 rooms in annexe TV in all bedrooms
Direct dial from all bedrooms Mini-bar in 11 bedrooms
Licensed Full central heating Open parking available Child
discount available Last d 21.30hrs Languages spoken: English
MEALS: Full breakfast 50FF Continental breakfast 45FF Lunch
100-310FF&alc Dinner 100-310FF&alc✱
CARDS: ✹ ■ ☲ ◗ Travellers cheques

CAUDEBEC-EN-CAUX Seine-Maritime

Normotel
18 quai Gauilbaud *76490*
☎ 235962011 FAX 235565440
Standing on the banks of the river Seine, this hotel features
comfortable bedrooms with views over the river, a cosy bar to
relax with a drink, and a restaurant where guests can enjoy
traditional cuisine, complemented by regional dishes, whilst
taking in the view of the passing boats on the river. *contd.*

Near river Forest area In town centre Near motorway
31 rms (6 fmly) (24 with balcony) TV in all bedrooms STV
Direct dial from all bedrooms Licensed Lift Full central
heating Open parking available (charged) Covered parking
available (charged) Supervised Child discount available 12yrs
Open terrace Last d 21.00hrs Languages spoken: English
CARDS: ▇▇ ▇▇ Travellers cheques

CEAUX Manche

★ ★ Le Relais du Mont
50220
☎ 233709255 FAX 233709457
Situated in the bay of Mont Saint-Michel, the establishment
has the informal atmosphere of a country hotel and offers its
visitors an attractive co-ordinated interior and modern
comfort. Guests are met upon arrival by the proprietor and are
well looked after in the restaurant by the chef who presides
over the kitchen. Situated between the D-Day landing beaches
and St Malo, it is an ideal venue for day-trips into the
surrounding region.
Near sea Forest area Near motorway
30 en suite (bth/shr) (14 fmly) TV in all bedrooms Licensed
Full central heating Open parking available Supervised Child
discount available 12yrs Boule Jacuzzi/spa Open terrace V
meals Last d 21.30hrs Languages spoken:
English,German,Italian
CARDS: ●● ▇▇ ▇▇ Travellers cheques

CHERBOURG Manche

★ ★ La Régence
42 Quai de Caligny *50100*
☎ 233430516 FAX 233439837
Situated in the old quarter of Cherbourg, the hotel offers
excellent views of the harbour and is just a few minutes away
from the ferry terminal and the town centre. The bright,
attractively decorated bedrooms have modern facilities and the
restaurant serves regional Normandy cuisine as well as a
range of seafood specialities.
Near sea In town centre
21 rms (18 bth/shr) (2 fmly) TV in all bedrooms Direct dial
from all bedrooms Full central heating Open parking
available (charged) Supervised Child discount available Last
d 22.00hrs Languages spoken: English
MEALS: Continental breakfast 35FF Dinner fr 89FFalc✱
CARDS: ●● ▇▇ ▇▇ Travellers cheques

CLÉCY Calvados

★ ★ ★ Hostellerie du Moulin du Vey
Le Vey *14570*
☎ 231697108 FAX 231691414
In the heart of the picturesque valley of the river L'Orne, this
former mill occupies a delightful river-side location and offers
guests a peaceful stay in unspoilt rural surroundings. It has
been renovated with precise attention to detail and has
retained all of its original character. The well equipped
bedrooms vary in style. Weather permitting, meals are served
on the terrace with views of a charming, well-tended flower
garden. Guests can seek out various places such as the
Normandy beaches, Mont Saint-Michel and the museums of
Clécy.
Near river Forest area
25 en suite (bth/shr) 2 rooms in annexe (2 fmly) (3 with
balcony) TV in all bedrooms Direct dial from all bedrooms
Licensed Full central heating Open parking available

Supervised Child discount available 10yrs Fishing Boule
Open terrace Last d 21.00hrs Languages spoken:
English,Spanish
CARDS: ●● ▇▇ ▇▇ ❿ Travellers cheques

★ ★ Au Site Normand
1 rue des Châtelets *14570*
☎ 231697105 FAX 231694851
(centre of village)
Clecy is the capital of the region in Normandy which is known
as 'Swiss Normandy', a rural, unspoilt area with woodlands
and pastures. The hotel features bedrooms with modern
amenities offering a good level of comfort and a traditionally
furnished restaurant which serves imaginative meals. In
addition there is a quiet lounge and a cosy bar for relaxation.
Near river Forest area
RS 24-31 Dec (restaurant closed evenings)
18 en suite (bth/shr) (1 fmly) (4 with balcony) TV in all
bedrooms Direct dial from all bedrooms Licensed Full central
heating Open parking available Child discount available 10yrs
Solarium Gym Open terrace V meals Languages spoken:
English
ROOMS: (room only) s 240FF; d 240-330FF **Reductions
over 1 night**
MEALS: Full breakfast 40FF Lunch 99-280FF&alc
CARDS: ●● ▇▇ Travellers cheques

COLOMBIERS-SUR-SEULLES Calvados

★ ★ Château du Baffy
Le Bourg *14480*
☎ 231080457 FAX 231080829
Near river Forest area
Closed Jan-Feb
35 en suite (bth/shr) Some rooms in annexe (2 fmly) TV in 5
bedrooms Licensed Full central heating Open parking
available Child discount available Tennis Fishing Riding
Gym Boule Bicycle rental Open terrace Last d 21.30hrs
Languages spoken: English
MEALS: Full breakfast 40FF Lunch 125-225FF&alc Dinner fr
125FF&alc✱
CARDS: ●● ▇▇ ▇▇ ❿ Travellers cheques

CONDÉ-SUR-NOIREAU Calvados

★ ★ Du Cerf
18 rue du Chêne *14110*
☎ 231694055 FAX 231697829
(from ferry at Ouistreham/Caen in direction Flers/Laval)
Peacefully situated in the serene surroundings of Swiss
Normandy, this hotel provides the setting for a relaxing stay.
The friendly proprietors are always present to offer service or
to provide information about the points of interest in the
region. The guest rooms are comfortable and the cuisine
consists of regional dishes prepared with fine local produce.
Near river In town centre
Closed 31 Oct-15 Nov RS Sun evening
9 en suite (bth/shr) (2 fmly) TV in all bedrooms Direct dial
from all bedrooms Licensed Full central heating Open
parking available Child discount available 12yrs Open terrace
V meals Last d 21.15hrs Languages spoken: English
ROOMS: (room only) s 204-224FF; d 204-224FF ✱
MEALS: Full breakfast 28FF Continental breakfast 28FF Lunch
67-180FF&alc Dinner 67-180FF&alc
CARDS: ●● ▇▇ ▇▇ ❿ Travellers cheques

COURTILS Manche

★ ★ ★ Manoir de la Roche Torin
La Roche Torin *50220*
☎ 233709655 FAX 233483520
This ivy-clad residence stands on the sandy shores of Mont-St-Michel and welcomes its visitors with a friendly, informal atmosphere in rural surroundings. It has individually appointed bedrooms with modern facilities including direct-dial phone and colour TV. The panoramic restaurant offers splendid views towards Mont-St-Michel and serves an array of tantalising dishes with salt-meadow lamb and fresh seafood specialities featuring on the menu
Near river
Closed 16 Nov-14 Feb ex Xmas & New Year
13 en suite (bth/shr) Some rooms in annexe (1 fmly) TV in all bedrooms Direct dial from all bedrooms Mini-bar in 3 bedrooms Licensed Full central heating Open parking available Child discount available 12yrs Boule Bicycle rental Open terrace Covered terrace Last d 21.00hrs Languages spoken: English,German
MEALS: Full breakfast 55FF Lunch 110-250FF Dinner 150-250FF✱
CARDS: ●● ▦ ▆▆ ❍ Travellers cheques

COUTANCES Manche

★ ★ Cositel Coutances
rte de Coutainville, BP 231 *50200*
☎ 233075164 FAX 233070623
This charming hotel, peacefully situated at the heart of the Cherbourg peninsula, features two restaurants, modern, comfortable bedrooms and function rooms for meetings and social events. With a wide choice of tourist attractions such as the fine sandy beaches, D-Day landing-places, Bayeux Tapestry and Mont-St-Michel nearby, it is the ideal venue for spending a leisurely holiday. The restaurant 'Le Pommeau' offers panoramic views over the surrounding countryside and serves well-presented delicious food.
Forest area
55 en suite (bth/shr) (7 fmly) No smoking in 4 bedrooms TV in all bedrooms STV Direct dial from all bedrooms Mini-bar in all bedrooms Licensed Night porter Full central heating Open parking available Covered parking available (charged) Supervised Child discount available 14yrs Mini-golf Open terrace Covered terrace V meals Last d 23.00hrs Languages spoken: English,German
ROOMS: (room only) s 280-295FF; d 295-350FF
MEALS: Full breakfast 42FF Continental breakfast 42FF Lunch 118-190FF&alc Dinner 118-190FF&alc✱
CARDS: ●● ▦ ▆▆ ❍ Travellers cheques

CREULLY Calvados

★ ★ Ferme de la Ranconnière
rte d'Arromanches *14480*
☎ 231222173 FAX 231229839
This ancient farmhouse dates back to the 18th-century and is classified as an historic monument. The bedrooms are furnished with period pieces and offer en-suite facilities. The cuisine incorporates high quality ingredients with seasonal produce.
Near sea
34 en suite (bth/shr) 7 rooms in annexe (5 fmly) TV in all bedrooms Licensed Full central heating Open parking available Child discount available Fishing Last d 21.30hrs

Languages spoken: English
MEALS: Full breakfast 45FF Lunch 88-225FF&alc Dinner 88-225FF&alc✱
CARDS: ●● ▦ ▆▆ ❍ Travellers cheques

CRIEL-SUR-MER Seine-Maritime

★ ★ Hostellerie de la Veille Ferme
23 rue de la Mer-Mesnil Val *76910*
☎ 235867218 FAX 235861264
Only 300 metres from the beach, this old Normandy farmhouse stands in attractive leafy surroundings and offers guests a friendly, relaxed atmosphere. There is a sunny terrace and an old cider press, a reminder of its working days as a farm. The cuisine features a wide range of fresh seafood and specialities, and makes extensive use of local produce.
Near sea
Closed Jan
22 rooms in annexe (3 fmly) TV in 33 bedrooms Direct dial from 33 bedrooms Licensed Full central heating Open parking available Child discount available 9yrs Open terrace Last d 20.30hrs Languages spoken: English
CARDS: ●● ▦ ▆▆ ❍

DEAUVILLE Calvados

★ ★ ★ Hotel du Golf
Mont Canisy, St-Arnoult *14800*
☎ 231142400 FAX 231142401
Situated in the centre of a large golf course, the hotel occupies a peaceful setting in the countryside. Individually appointed guest-rooms offer maximum comfort, and the dining rooms serve an extensive choice of well prepared dishes.
Near river Near sea Forest area Near motorway
Closed 3 Nov-28 Dec & 9 Feb-20 Mar
178 en suite (bth/shr) (66 fmly) (3 with balcony) No smoking in 12 bedrooms TV in all bedrooms Direct-dial available Mini-bar in all bedrooms Licensed Lift Night porter Full central heating Open parking available Child discount available 12yrs Outdoor swimming pool (heated) Golf Tennis Sauna Solarium Gym Boule Bicycle rental Open terrace Covered terrace V meals Last d 22.30hrs Languages spoken: English,German,Italian,Spanish
CARDS: ●● ▦ ▆▆ ❍

★ ★ ★ Hotel Royal
bd Cornuche *14800*
☎ 231986633 FAX 231986634
(From A13 exit 'Deauville/Trouville' follow signs for 'Deauville' and 'Plage')
The Royal hotel offers its guests a friendly reception in sumptuous surroundings. The staff are dedicated and efficient, making sure that visitors want for nothing. There is a cosy bar with a choice of meals, and an elegant restaurant serving a high quality cuisine. The rooms are spacious with smart furnishings and are equipped with many extras.
Near sea Near beach In town centre Near motorway
Closed early Nov-Mar
245 en suite (bth/shr) (8 fmly) (50 with balcony) TV in all bedrooms STV Radio in rooms Direct dial from all bedrooms Mini-bar in all bedrooms Room-safe Licensed Lift Night porter Full central heating Open parking available Outdoor swimming pool (heated) Golf 27 Tennis Sauna Solarium Gym Mini-golf Bicycle rental Open terrace Wkly live entertainment Casino Last d 22.00hrs Languages spoken: English, German & Spanish

contd.

ROOMS: (room only) d 1150-2300FF
MEALS: Full breakfast 120FF Lunch 225-300FF&alc Dinner 225-300FF&alc*
CARDS: ✱✱ ▦ ☲ ☜ JCB

★ ★ ★ ★ Hotel Normandy
38 rue Jean Mermoz *14800*
☎ 231986622 FAX 231986623
(From A13 exit 'Deauville/Trouville' follow signs for 'Deauville' and 'Plage')
This large, splendid Anglo-Norman manor house occupies a unique location on the sea-front. The bedrooms are elegantly furnished and offer an extensive range of facilities. The hotel has a wide choice of dishes on offer to suit all tastes.
Near sea Near beach In town centre
308 en suite (bth) TV in all bedrooms STV Radio in rooms Direct dial from all bedrooms Mini-bar in all bedrooms Licensed Lift Night porter Full central heating open parking spaces (charged) Covered parking available (charged) Indoor swimming pool (heated) Golf 27 Tennis Sauna Solarium Gym Pool table Mini-golf Bicycle rental Open terrace Wkly live entertainment Casino Last d 22.00hrs Languages spoken: English, German, Spanish
ROOMS: (room only) d 1100-2200FF **Reductions over 1 night**
MEALS: Full breakfast 120FF Lunch 225-300FF&alc Dinner 225-300FF&alc*
CARDS: ✱✱ ▦ ☲ ☜ JCB

★ ★ ★ Park Hotel
81 av de la République *14800*
☎ 231880971 FAX 231879949
A family atmosphere prevails throughout the hotel, where spacious guest-rooms provide a good standard of accommodation. Originally a private villa, it has undergone extensive renovation over the years and now features an attractive interior with a relaxing lounge and pleasant dining room.
Near sea In town centre Near motorway
15 en suite (bth/shr) (3 fmly) (5 with balcony) TV in all bedrooms Direct-dial available Licensed Full central heating Open parking available Child discount available 13yrs Bicycle rental Open terrace Languages spoken: English
CARDS: ✱✱ ▦ ☲ ☜

DOUAINS Eure

★ ★ ★ ★ Château de Brécourt
27120
☎ 232524050 FAX 232526965
Standing on the borders with Normandy, this elegant castle is surrounded by a moat and extensive wooded parklands. It offers individually styled bedrooms with modern amenities, which vary in size and are decorated with smart furnishings. In addition, there are spacious lounges and a restaurant with a tall open fireplace which serves an array of specialities including fresh seafood delicacies.
Forest area Near motorway
31 en suite (bth) (5 fmly) Licensed Full central heating Open parking available Child discount available 12yrs Indoor swimming pool (heated) Tennis Boule Jacuzzi/spa Bicycle rental Open terrace Covered terrace V meals Last d 21.30hrs Languages spoken: German,Spanish
MEALS: Full breakfast 73FF Continental breakfast 73FF Lunch 190-350FF&alc Dinner 235-350FF&alc*
CARDS: ✱✱ ▦ ☲ ☜ Travellers cheques

DUCEY Manche

★ ★ Auberge de la Sélune
2 rue St-Germain *50220*
☎ 233485362 FAX 233489030
Situated amidst delightful scenery, the hotel provides a suitable setting for an overnight stop. It features individually styled rooms with modern facilities, a peaceful day room and attractive garden with terrace.
Near river Forest area Near motorway
3 rooms in annexe (1 fmly) Licensed Full central heating Open parking available Child discount available Fishing Open terrace Last d 20.30hrs Languages spoken: English,Spanish
MEALS: Continental breakfast 40FF Lunch 80-200FF&alc Dinner 80-200FF&alc*
CARDS: ✱✱ ▦ ☲ ☜

EQUEURDREVILLE Manche

★ ★ Climat de France
200 rue de la Paix *50120*
☎ 233934294 Cen Res 64460123 FAX 233934554
Near sea
42 en suite (bth) TV in all bedrooms Radio in rooms Direct dial from all bedrooms Licensed Full central heating Open parking available V meals Languages spoken: English
CARDS: ✱✱ ☲

ÉTRETAT Seine-Maritime

★ ★ ★ Donjon
Chemin de St-Clair *76790*
☎ 235270823 FAX 235299224
The hotel Donjon is a small, charming residence peacefully set in extensive parklands overlooking the village and sea. The menu features traditional cuisine and meals are served in the elegant restaurant by friendly, attentive staff. From the day rooms guests can enjoy stunning views over the surrounding Falaises d'Entretat.
Near sea
10 en suite (bth/shr) (4 fmly) (1 with balcony) TV in all bedrooms Mini-bar in all bedrooms Full central heating Open parking available Child discount available 10yrs Outdoor swimming pool Jacuzzi/spa Open terrace Last d 22.30hrs Languages spoken: English
CARDS: ✱✱ ▦ ☲ ☜ Travellers cheques

ÉVREUX Eure

★ ★ France
29 rue St-Thomas *27000*
☎ 232390925 & 0117 986 0386 (UK booking) FAX 232383856
This traditional hotel occupies a tranquil location in the centre of Evreux, and offers its clientele pleasant bedrooms with private amenities and outstanding cuisine, incorporating classic dishes with a contemporary touch, augmented by an interesting wine-list.
Near river In town centre
RS restaurant closed Sun evening/Mon
16 en suite (bth/shr) (2 fmly) TV in all bedrooms Direct dial from all bedrooms Licensed Full central heating Open parking available Covered parking available Child discount available 12yrs Bicycle rental V meals Last d 22.00hrs Languages spoken: English,Spanish,German

ROOMS: (room only) s 245-270FF; d 300-335FF
Special breaks: Golf and gastronomic fixed price breaks
MEALS: Full breakfast 35FF Lunch 155-200FF Dinner 155-200FF
CARDS: 💳 🟦 🟰 💠 Travellers cheques

FONTENAI-SUR-ORNE Orne

★ ★ Le Faisan Doré
61200
☎ 233671811 FAX 233358215
(On road to Flers, 3km from Argentan)
This half-timbered inn is built in a style typical of the Normandy region. Standing amidst landscaped gardens, it provides the ideal setting for an enjoyable stay. The cosy bedrooms are well equipped and offer a high degree of comfort. The intimate dining-rooms offer a wide choice of delicious specialities with the emphasis on presentation and flavour. There is a bar for relaxation, and in the summer meals are served in the garden.
Forest area
Closed early Feb-early Mar
15 en suite (bth/shr) (2 fmly) (1 with balcony) No smoking in 2 bedrooms TV in all bedrooms Direct dial from all bedrooms Licensed Full central heating Open parking available Supervised Child discount available 10yrs Pool table Open terrace V meals Last d 22.00hrs Languages spoken: English & German
ROOMS: (room only) s 265-300FF; d 315-350FF
MEALS: Full breakfast 40FF Continental breakfast 40FF Lunch 95-295FF&alc Dinner 95-295FF&alc
CARDS: 💳 🟦 🟰 Travellers cheques

GACÉ Orne

★ ★ Hostellerie les Champs
rte d'Alençon-Rouen, RN 138 *61230*
☎ 233390905 FAX 233368126
Surrounded by the lush scenery of the Normandy countryside this manor house dates back to the mid 1800s. It offers its visitors a peaceful stay in the elegant interior of an ancient mansion. Bedrooms are tastefully furnished and feature modern facilities, whilst the restaurant serves a wide range of superb dishes.
Near river Forest area Near motorway
14 en suite (bth/shr) (3 fmly) Direct dial from all bedrooms Licensed Full central heating Open parking available Covered parking available (charged) Supervised Outdoor swimming pool Tennis Open terrace Last d 21.30hrs
CARDS: 💳 🟰 Travellers cheques

★ ★ ★ Hotel Antares
La Rivière St-Sauveur *14600*
☎ 231891010 FAX 231895857
(from A13 take the exit 'Honfleur', 15kms before Honfleur take direction 'Caen-Pont L'Eveque', hotel 100ms on left. From Le Havre, take Normandy Bridge, then follow signs Caen Pont L'Eveque)
At the entrance of Honfleur, with panoramic views of the Normandy Bridge. Hotel Antares has pleasant décor, comfortable bedrooms and a selection of leisure facilities.
Near sea Near beach Forest area Near motorway
Closed 2-26 Jan
48 en suite (bth/shr) (16 fmly) TV in all bedrooms STV Direct dial from all bedrooms Licensed Lift Night porter Full central heating Open parking available Child discount available 11yrs Indoor swimming pool (heated) Sauna Solarium Gym Open terrace Last d 21.00hrs Languages spoken: English & Spanish
ROOMS: (room only) s 295-540FF; d 320-740FF ★
Reductions over 1 night
MEALS: Continental breakfast 50FF Dinner 98FF
CARDS: 💳 🟦 🟰 💠 Travellers cheques

★ ★ ★ ★ La Chaumière
rte du Littoral *14600*
☎ 231816320 FAX 231895923
This ancient Norman farmhouse is situated amidst green meadows on the banks of an estuary of the river Seine and provides the ideal venue to recharge your batteries in peaceful surroundings. It features cosy bedrooms with good amenities and the restaurant offers a comprehensive menu with a large choice of classic and regional cuisine, augmented by a wine list featuring some outstanding wines.
Near sea Near beach Forest area
9 en suite (bth/shr) (1 fmly) TV in all bedrooms STV Licensed Full central heating Open parking available Supervised Child discount available Bicycle rental Open terrace V meals Last d 21.30hrs
MEALS: Continental breakfast 85FF Lunch 190-380FF&alc Dinner 190-380FF&alc✱
CARDS: 💳 🟦 🟰 Travellers cheques

★ ★ ★ Écrin
19 rue Eugène Boudin *14600*
☎ 231144345 FAX 231892441
In town centre
22 en suite (bth/shr) (6 fmly) (1 with balcony) TV in all bedrooms Mini-bar in all bedrooms Licensed Night porter Full central heating Open parking available Supervised Sauna Pool table Open terrace Covered terrace Languages spoken: English,German
CARDS: 💳 🟦 🟰 💠 Travellers cheques

★ ★ ★ ★ Le Ferme Saint-Simeon
Adolphe Marais *14600*
☎ 231892361 FAX 231894848
The house dates back to the 17th century and offers a combination of modern-day comfort blended with the lavish hospitality of a byegone age. Many of the original features have been preserved, and furnishings are completely in style with the architecture of the building. The guest accommodation is luxurious and furnished with great attention to detail. The cuisine offers some outstanding dishes incorporating regional produce, and the establishment provides the ideal venue for a weekend-break or a longer holiday. *contd.*

Near river Near sea Near beach
34 en suite (bth/shr) (8 fmly) (8 with balcony) TV in all
bedrooms STV Mini-bar in all bedrooms Licensed Lift Night
porter Full central heating Open parking available
Supervised Indoor swimming pool (heated) Sauna Solarium
Jacuzzi/spa Bicycle rental Open terrace V meals Last d
21.30hrs
CARDS: ●● ▦ � JCB Travellers cheques

HOULBEC-COCHEREL Eure

★ ★ ★ Ferme de Cocherel
rte de la Vallée d'Eure *27120*
☎ 232366827 FAX 232262818
(From A13 take exit 16)
The hotel is located in a small village surrounded by unspoilt
countryside. Maisonette-style rooms are situated in the
garden, and are equipped with modern facilities which offer a
good standard of comfort. There is a restaurant, and with Paris
and the coast just one hour's drive away, it provides a good
base for touring the surrounding region.
Near river Near lake Forest area Near motorway
Closed 3 wks Jan and 1 week Sep
3 en suite (bth/shr) Licensed Full central heating Open
parking available Supervised Open terrace Last d 21.15hrs
CARDS: ●● ▦ ▬ ◑ Travellers cheques

INGOUVILLE-SUR-MER Seine-Maritime

Les Hêtres
rue des Fleurs-le Bourg *76460*
☎ 235570930 FAX 235570931
This authentic Norman house dates back to 1627 and is
surrounded by a vast park. The bedroom capacity has been
purposely kept small to ensure a restful stay in traditional
surroundings. The charming bedrooms offer modern comfort
and are furnished with good quality pieces. There is a cosy
lounge and the restaurant, with its ancient fireplace, serves
delicious food in an informal atmosphere.
4 en suite (bth/shr) TV in all bedrooms Radio in rooms Direct
dial from all bedrooms Mini-bar in all bedrooms Licensed
Night porter Full central heating Open parking available
Covered parking available Boule Jacuzzi/spa Bicycle rental
Open terrace Last d 22.00hrs Languages spoken: English
MEALS: Continental breakfast 65FF Lunch 160-350FF&alc
Dinner 160-350FF&alc*
CARDS: ●● ▬ Travellers cheques

ISIGNY-SUR-MER Calvados

★ ★ De France
13-15 rue Emile Demagny *14230*
☎ 231220033 FAX 231227919
The hotel has been in the hands of the same family for the last
40 years, and a warm welcome and friendly service awaits
guests on arrival. The bedrooms are well equipped and of a
good size, whilst the cuisine incorporates a choice of
specialities from the region served in the recently refurbished
restaurant.
Near river Near lake Forest area In town centre Near
motorway
Closed 15 Nov-15 Feb
19 rms (16 bth/shr) 3 rooms in annexe (5 fmly) TV in all
bedrooms Direct dial from all bedrooms Licensed Night
porter Full central heating Open parking available
Supervised Child discount available 12yrs Outdoor swimming
pool (heated) Fishing Boule Bicycle rental V meals

Last d 21.30hrs Languages spoken: English, German
ROOMS: (room only) s 140-220FF; d 160-280FF ★
Reductions over 1 night
MEALS: Full breakfast 32FF Continental breakfast 32FF Lunch
69-185FF&alc Dinner 69-185FF&alc
CARDS: ●● ▦ ▬ Access/ Eurocard Travellers cheques

LOUVIERS Eure

★ ★ ★ Haye Le Comté
4 rte de la Haye-le-Comté *27400*
☎ 232400040 FAX 232250385
(A13 exit 18 to Louviers, then take D133 towards le Neubourg.
Take left turn following signs for La Haye le Comte)
Once two separate buildings, this 17th-century manor house
and ancient farm now offer a spacious interior where
contemporary features and traditional furnishings go hand in
hand. Surrounded by an extensive park and various leisure
pursuits it provides the ideal base for walking and exploring
the surroundings. The menu lists a choice of seasonal dishes
and specialities from the Normandy region.
Forest area
Closed Dec-Mar
16 en suite (bth/shr) (1 fmly) No smoking in 11 bedrooms TV
in all bedrooms STV Direct dial from all bedrooms Licensed
Full central heating Open parking available Child discount
available Tennis Boule Bicycle rental Open terrace Table
tennis V meals Last d 21.00hrs Languages spoken: English
ROOMS: (room only) s 360-510FF; d 360-510FF **Reductions
over 1 night Special breaks: 3 day breaks**
CARDS: ●● ▦ ▬ ◑ Travellers cheques

LUC-SUR-MER Calvados

★ ★ ★ Hotel des Thermes et du Casino
av Guynémer *14530*
☎ 231973237 FAX 231967257
The hotel enjoys an exceptional seaside location, with an
extensive park where apple trees shelter the open-air
swimming pool. The bedrooms are well equipped and offer
comfortable accommodation, while the restaurant with its
panoramic views over the open sea, serves a large choice of
fish and seafood specialities. In addition there is a sunny
terrace and a conservatory for reading or relaxing.
Near sea Near beach In town centre
Closed 16 Nov-Mar
48 en suite (bth/shr) (18 with balcony) TV in all bedrooms
STV Direct dial from all bedrooms Licensed Lift Full central
heating Open parking available Covered parking available
(charged) Supervised Child discount available Indoor
swimming pool (heated) Outdoor swimming pool (heated)
Sauna Gym Jacuzzi/spa Open terrace Last d 22.00hrs
Languages spoken: English, Spanish
MEALS: Full breakfast 45FF Lunch 125-260FF&alc Dinner 125-
260FF&alc*
CARDS: ●● ▦ ▬ ◑ Travellers cheques

LYONS-LA-FORÊT Eure

★ ★ Domaine St-Paul
27480
☎ 232496057 FAX 232595605
The hotel is situated on the edge of the typical Normandy
village of Lyons-La-Forêt and surrounded by the most
extensive beech-tree forest in France. Owned and run by the
Lorrain family it extends a warm welcome to its visitors.
Set in its own grounds, it offers charming guest-rooms with

modern amenities as well as classical French cuisine.
Near river Forest area
Closed 2 Nov-2 Apr
17 en suite (bth/shr) (1 fmly) Direct dial from all bedrooms
Licensed Full central heating Open parking available
Supervised Child discount available 10yrs Outdoor swimming
pool Solarium Pool table Boule Bicycle rental Open terrace
Covered terrace Table tennis Last d 21.00hrs Languages
spoken: English,German
ROOMS: (incl. dinner) s 435-615FF; d 620-800FF

MEALS: Continental breakfast 45FF Lunch 120-200FF Dinner
145-200FF
CARDS: ● ▆ Travellers cheques

★★★ **Licorne**
27 pl Bensérade *27480*
☎ 232496202 FAX 232498009
The hotel Licorne is located in a charming village in the heart
of the Forêt de Lyons. Individually styled bedrooms and
apartments provide the setting for a relaxing, peaceful stay
and are equipped with up-to-date facilities. The splendid
cuisine includes traditional dishes comprising fresh local and
seasonal produce. The Normandy region provides a wealth of
historic and cultural sights.
Near river Forest area In town centre
Closed 20 Dec-20 Jan RS Sun evening & Mon
19 en suite (bth/shr) 2 rooms in annexe (1 fmly) TV in all
bedrooms STV Licensed Full central heating Open parking
available Supervised Child discount available Mini-golf
Bicycle rental Open terrace Last d 21.30hrs Languages
spoken: English
ROOMS: (room only) s 385FF; d 480-750FF ✴
MEALS: Full breakfast 55FF Lunch 185FF&alc Dinner
185FF&alc✴
CARDS: ● ▆ ▆ ⬥ Travellers cheques

MACÉ Orne

★★ **Ile de Sées**
61500
☎ 233279865 FAX 233284122
This charming establishment is full of character and stands
amidst lush vegetation, sheltering it from the roads and traffic
noise. The bedrooms offer adequate comfort and have good
amenities, while the informal restaurant serves meals to suit all
tastes.
Near river Forest area
Closed 15 Jan-15 Mar
16 en suite (bth/shr) (4 fmly) TV in all bedrooms Direct dial
from all bedrooms Licensed Full central heating Open
parking available Child discount available 2yrs Tennis

Open terrace Last d 21.00hrs Languages spoken: English
MEALS: Full breakfast 38FF Lunch 78-175FF Dinner 98-
175FF✴
CARDS: ● ▆

MONT-ST-MICHEL, LE Manche

★★★ **De La Digue**
50116
☎ 233601402 FAX 233603759
Situated at two kilometres from Mont St-Michel, the hotel offers
fine views towards this famous landmark, which is surrounded
by radiant blue sky during the day, and offers a fabulous flood-
lit spectacle by night. There are charming guest rooms with
modern facilities and a panoramic restaurant which serves an
array of seafood specialities. It offers a choice of leisure facilities
nearby, whilst guests also may want to visit the towns of Saint-
Malo and Dinan or explore the attractive countryside of Brittany.
Near river
Closed 15 Nov-25 Mar
36 en suite (bth/shr) (5 fmly) (9 with balcony) TV in all
bedrooms STV Direct dial from all bedrooms Licensed Full
central heating Open parking available Child discount
available 10yrs Bicycle rental Open terrace Covered terrace
V meals Last d 21.30hrs Languages spoken: English, German
MEALS: Full breakfast 50FF Lunch 88-210FF&alc Dinner 88-
210FF&alc✴
CARDS: ● ▆ ▆ ⬥ Travellers cheques

★★★ **Relais du Roy**
50116
☎ 233601425 FAX 233603769
(Approach via Avranches)

The hotel building with its 14th and 15th century fireplaces has
been a family hotel for many generations. It was entirely
refurbished in recent years, and now offers pleasant bedrooms
with modern facilities, which have splendid views of Mont-St-
Michel and across the sea. The head-chef Yann Galton is a very
accomplished 'cuisinier' and has acquired many accolades in
his field.
Near river Forest area
Closed Dec-mid Mar
27 en suite (bth/shr) (20 with balcony) TV in all bedrooms
STV Direct dial from all bedrooms Licensed Night porter
Full central heating Open parking available Open terrace V
meals Last d 21.00hrs Languages spoken:
English,German,Italian & Spanish
ROOMS: (room only) s 350FF; d 440FF
MEALS: Full breakfast 50FF Lunch 90-200FF&alc Dinner 90-
200FF&alc✴
CARDS: ● ▆ ▆ Travellers cheques

★ ★ ★ Terrasses Poulard
Grande Rue *50116*
☎ 233601409 FAX 233603731
(Approach via Avranches)
The hotel is set in the heart of Mont Saint-Michel with views over the bay and has pleasant guest accommodation with good modern amenities. The panoramic dining rooms offer exceptional views over the bay and serve tasty regional dishes prepared with local produce throughout the day.
Near river Near motorway
29 en suite (bth/shr) 12 rooms in annexe (5 fmly) (4 with balcony) TV in all bedrooms STV Direct dial from all bedrooms Mini-bar in all bedrooms Licensed Night porter Full central heating Supervised Child discount available 12yrs V meals Last d 22.00hrs Languages spoken: English & German
ROOMS: (room only) d 200-900FF
MEALS: Continental breakfast 40FF Lunch 75-130FFalc Dinner 75-130FFalc
CARDS: ● ■ ■ ● Travellers cheques

MORTAGNE-AU-PERCHE Orne

★ ★ Du Tribunal
4 pl du Palais *61400*
☎ 233250477 FAX 233836083
The building dates back to the 16th century and is situated in the old centre of Montagne in the heart of the Normandy forests. When visitors step over the threshold, they are transported to the past; silk fabrics and fine polished woods, a flower-filled enclosed garden with terrace, and exposed beams in the bar and lounges create the charming atmosphere of yesteryear. The bedrooms offer comfortable accommodation whilst the restaurant serves a splendid cuisine to suit most palates.
Forest area In town centre
11 en suite (bth/shr) (3 fmly) TV in all bedrooms STV Direct dial from all bedrooms Licensed Full central heating Child discount available 3yrs Open terrace V meals Last d 21.00hrs Languages spoken: English
ROOMS: (room only) d 220-320FF
MEALS: Continental breakfast 40FF Lunch 90-200FF&alc Dinner 90-200FF&alc
CARDS: ● ■ Travellers cheques

NOTRE-DAME-D'ESTRÉES Calvados

★ ★ Au Repos des Chineurs
Chemin de l'Église *14340*
☎ 231637251 FAX 231636238
This charming hotel is set in the lush Auge countryside and provides a delightful setting for a relaxing stay. The house dates back to the 17th century and has been furnished throughout with period furniture and antiques, creating an atmosphere in which guests can unwind and relax. The attractive bedrooms are equipped with modern amenities and offer a good level of comfort.
Forest area
10 en suite (bth/shr) (2 fmly) (1 with balcony) Licensed Night porter Full central heating Open parking available Supervised Child discount available Languages spoken: English
CARDS: ● ■ Travellers cheques

PENNEDEPIE Calvados

★ ★ Romantica
Chemin du Petit Paris *14600*
☎ 231811400 FAX 231815478
Situated midway between Honfleur and Deauville, the hotel provides a setting for a relaxing stay. With views over both the sea and River Seine, and a fine sandy beach nearby, it offers pleasant bedrooms and an informal restaurant with terrace, where meals are served when the weather is fine.
Near sea Forest area
18 en suite (bth/shr) (1 fmly) (9 with balcony) TV in all bedrooms Direct dial from all bedrooms Mini-bar in all bedrooms Full central heating Open parking available Covered parking available Supervised Child discount available Outdoor swimming pool (heated) Open terrace Last d 22.00hrs Languages spoken: English,German,Italian
CARDS: ● ■ ■ ●

PONT-AUDEMER Eure

★ ★ Auberge Du Vieux Puits
6 rue Notre-Dame-du-Pré *27500*
☎ 232410148 FAX 232423728
This 'Old Well Inn' is housed in a group of 17th-century timbered buildings which are grouped around an interior courtyard, 400 metres from Pont-Audemer. The bedrooms vary in style and size; some are compact with traditional furnishings offering basic comfort, whereas those in the recently opened wing are spacious with up-to-date modern facilities. The cuisine is based on a choice of house specialities which use fresh seasonal produce.
In town centre
Closed 21 Dec-Jan, and every Mon-Tue ex summer
12 rms (11 bth/shr) (2 fmly) TV available Licensed Full central heating Open parking available Supervised Child discount available Open terrace V meals Last d 21.00hrs Languages spoken: English, Italian
MEALS: Continental breakfast 46FF Lunch 160-310FF&alc Dinner 160-310FF&alc✱
CARDS: ● ■ Travellers cheques

★ ★ ★ ★ Belle Isle Sur Risle
112 rte de Rouen *27500*
☎ 232569622 FAX 232428896
This handsome residence dates back to 1856 and occupies a superb location on an island in the River Risle. Surrounded by a park with mature trees, it offers cosy lounges, a bar, a winter garden and a range of leisure facilities. The bedrooms are elegantly furnished and provide the comfort and amenities expected of an hotel of this calibre. The smart restaurant serves an outstanding cuisine.
Near river Near sea Forest area Near motorway
19 en suite (bth) (4 fmly) (4 with balcony) No smoking in 4 bedrooms TV in all bedrooms STV Mini-bar in all bedrooms Licensed Night porter Full central heating Open parking available Supervised Child discount available 10yrs Indoor swimming pool (heated) Outdoor swimming pool (heated) Golf 3 Fishing Riding Sauna Solarium Gym Mini-golf Jacuzzi/spa Bicycle rental Open terrace ping pong,canoeing Wkly live entertainment Last d 21.30hrs Languages spoken: English,Arabic
CARDS: ● ■ ■ ● Travellers cheques

★★★★ Petit Coq Aux Champs
Campigny *27500*
☎ 232410419 FAX 232560625
This thatched cottage is situated in lush green surroundings and provides the perfect hideaway for those who prefer a relaxing, peaceful holiday. Tastefully decorated bedrooms offer comfortable guest accommodation, whilst the elegant beamed restaurant serves an imaginative choice of dishes, where classic recipes blend with innovative ingredients.
Forest area
Closed 6-26Jan
25 rms (1 fmly) (12 with balcony) TV in all bedrooms STV Direct dial from all bedrooms Licensed Night porter Full central heating Open parking available Supervised Child discount available 12yrs Outdoor swimming pool (heated) Boule Bicycle rental Open terrace Wkly live entertainment V meals Last d 21.30hrs Languages spoken: English
MEALS: Full breakfast 57FF Lunch 185-310FF&alc Dinner 185-310FF&alc✱
CARDS: ●● 📇 ⅀ ⑨ Travellers cheques

PONT-DE-L'ARCHE Eure

★★ Hotel de la Tour
41 quai Foch *27340*
☎ 235230099 FAX 235234622
(leave A13 exit 20 & continue for 3km)
The Hotel de la Tour is an 18th-century building situated just a few steps away from the medieval alleyways and streets in the town of Pont-de-l'Arche. Its delightful terraced-garden backs against the ramparts of the town and offers fine views over the River Seine. The bedrooms have modern facilities and offer a good level of comfort.
Near river Near lake Near sea Forest area
16 en suite (bth/shr) (4 fmly) TV in all bedrooms STV Direct dial from all bedrooms Full central heating Open parking available Supervised Open terrace Languages spoken: English & German
ROOMS: (room only) s 280-320FF; d 280-320FF ★
Reductions over 1 night
CARDS: ●● 📇 ⅀ ⑨ Travellers cheques

PONT-L'ÉVÊQUE Calvados

★★ Climat de France
14130
Centre de Loisirs du Lac-CD 48
☎ 231646400 Cen Res 64460123 FAX 231641228
(off A13 signed 'Pont l'Eveque')
Located on the banks of the lake, the hotel provides a peaceful setting for a relaxing holiday. With Deauville, its casino and varied entertainment, as well the old fishing port of Honfleur nearby, it is a good base for touring the surrounding region. Pleasant bedrooms provide comfortable accommodation, whilst the restaurant with open fireplace serves a traditional cuisine of good flavour.
Near lake Forest area Near motorway
Closed Jan
57 en suite (bth/shr) (3 fmly) TV in all bedrooms Direct dial from all bedrooms Licensed Full central heating Open parking available Fishing Pool table Open terrace Covered terrace Pedalos Canoe hire V meals Languages spoken: English, Dutch, German, Greek & Italian
CARDS: ●● ⅀

★★★ Clos Saint Gatien
St-Gatien des Bois *14130*
☎ 231651608 FAX 231651027
The hotel occupies a peaceful location between the towns of Deauville, Trouville and Honfleur. Situated next to a forest, it has a comfortable and informal interior, where the bedrooms are cheerfully decorated and have private facilities. In addition there is an attractive restaurant and a choice of leisure pursuits.
Near sea Forest area Near motorway
60 en suite (bth/shr) (5 fmly) (5 with balcony) TV in all bedrooms Licensed Lift Night porter Full central heating Open parking available Child discount available 10yrs Indoor swimming pool (heated) Outdoor swimming pool (heated) Tennis Riding Sauna Gym Pool table Boule Jacuzzi/spa Bicycle rental Open terrace V meals Last d 21.30hrs Languages spoken: English
MEALS: Lunch 130-345FF&alc Dinner 130-345FF&alc✱
CARDS: ●● 📇 ⅀ ⑨ Travellers cheques

PONT-ST-PIERRE Eure

★★★ Hostellerie La Bonne Marmite
10 rue Réné Raban *27360*
☎ 232497024 FAX 232481241
Standing in the pretty village of Pont-Saint-Pierre, this delightful former posting inn has an interior courtyard. The candlelit restaurant and the flower arrangements which feature throughout the house provide a charming setting for a romantic stay. The stylish guest rooms are comfortable with modern facilities and the restaurant with its coffered ceiling and Louis XVI-style decor serves a choice of splendid dishes, prepared by the chef-proprietor who has won many gastronomic competitions with his cuisine.
Near river Forest area In town centre Near motorway
9 en suite (bth/shr) (2 with balcony) TV in all bedrooms STV Direct dial from all bedrooms Mini bar in all bedrooms Licensed Full central heating Open parking available Supervised Child discount available 11yrs Last d 21.15hrs Languages spoken: English
CARDS: ●● 📇 ⅀ ⑨ Travellers cheques

RANES Orne

★★ St-Pierre
61150
☎ 233397514 FAX 233354923
(On D909)
Forest area In town centre
12 en suite (bth/shr) TV in all bedrooms STV Direct dial from all bedrooms Licensed Full central heating Open parking available Child discount available 12yrs Tennis Fishing Boule Mini-golf Open terrace V meals Last d 21.00hrs
ROOMS: (room only) d 245-345FF
MEALS: Continental breakfast 38FF Lunch 75-200FF Dinner 105-200FF&alc
CARDS: ●● 📇 ⅀ ⑨ Travellers cheques

ROUEN Seine-Maritime

★★ Climat de France
55 av de la Libération *76000*
☎ 235234242 FAX 235720600
Located at five minutes from the historic centre of Rouen, this attractive establishment features an informal interior, where pleasant bedrooms are fitted with private facilities. The restaurant 'La Soupière' serves a generous, traditional

contd.

cuisine with a choice of regional specialities and has a menu which changes according to the seasons.
Forest area Near motorway
49 en suite (shr) TV in all bedrooms Radio in rooms Direct dial from all bedrooms Full central heating Open parking available Child discount available 13yrs Open terrace V meals Last d 22.00hrs Languages spoken: English German & Spanish
ROOMS: (room only) s fr 270FF; d fr 270FF **Reductions over 1 night Special breaks**
MEALS: Continental breakfast 35FF Lunch 59-150FFalc Dinner 59-150FFalc
CARDS: ●● ▆▆ ▆▆

★ ★ ★ Hotel de Dieppe (Best Western)
pl Bernard Tissot *76000*
☎ 235719600 FAX 235896521
(in front of railway station)
Ideally situated in the heart of this historic city. Founded in 1880, the interior has been gradually transformed and now provides attractive modern surroundings. The bedrooms are all tastefully decorated and well-equipped and there is an inviting cocktail bar and grill where breakfast is also taken.
In town centre Near motorway
41 en suite (bth/shr) (4 fmly) TV in all bedrooms STV Direct dial from all bedrooms Licensed Lift Night porter Full central heating Child discount available 12yrs Last d 22.30hrs Languages spoken: English,German
ROOMS: (room only) s 398-498FF; d 510-610FF
MEALS: Full breakfast 45FF Lunch 138-218FF&alc Dinner 138-218FF&alc
CARDS: ●● ▆▆ ▆▆ ◑ JCB Travellers cheques

★ ★ ★ Hotel Frantour
15 rue de la Pie *76000*
☎ 235710088 FAX 235707594
In the very centre of this historic town, the Frantour, refurbished in 1995, offers comfortable well-appointed accommodation. There is a private bar, a breakfast room and an underground garage for secure parking.
In town centre
48 en suite (bth/shr) (3 fmly) (4 with balcony) TV in all bedrooms STV Direct dial from all bedrooms Mini-bar in all bedrooms Licensed Lift Night porter Full central heating Open parking available Covered parking available Supervised Child discount available 12yrs Languages spoken: English German & Italian
ROOMS: (room only) s fr 435FF; d fr 495FF
CARDS: ●● ▆▆ ▆▆ ◑ Travellers cheques

★ ★ Vidéotel
20 pl de Liéglise, St-Sever *76000*
☎ 235628182 FAX 235639362

The hotels in the Videotel group all have bedrooms with pleasant furnishings and are equipped with the comfort of their clientele in mind. The restaurants serve a good quality gourmet cuisine with a range of prix-fixe menus, regional specialities and 'eat your fill buffet'. The management couples and their dedicated teams offer a 'round the clock' efficient service, where the well-being and satisfaction of guests is the prime consideration.
In town centre
139 en suite (shr) (27 fmly) No smoking in 16 bedrooms TV in all bedrooms Direct dial from all bedrooms Licensed Lift Night porter Full central heating Open parking available Covered parking available Child discount available 12yrs Pool table V meals Last d 22.00hrs Languages spoken: English
ROOMS: (room only) s 290FF; d 290FF ✱
MEALS: Full breakfast 34FF Lunch fr 52FF Dinner fr 52FF✱
CARDS: ●● ▆▆ ▆▆ Travellers cheques

ST-AUBIN-SUR-MER Calvados

★ ★ Clos-Normand
Les Pieds dans L'Eua, Digue Guynemer *14750*
☎ 231973047 FAX 231964623
(from A13 exit 4 in direction of Douvres, then Langrune & St Aubin-sur-Mer)

The hotel is directly situated on the seaside and enjoys a quiet position. It has an enclosed terrace overlooking the beach and the sea, a congenial bar and a secluded garden. The informal restaurant with attractive open fireplace serves a choice of specialities from the region and seafood delicacies. The guest rooms and suites are equipped with modern facilities and provide a good level of comfort.
Near sea Near beach
Closed 16 Nov-1 Mar
31 en suite (bth/shr) (3 fmly) (2 with balcony) No smoking in 1 bedroom TV in all bedrooms Direct dial from all bedrooms Licensed Full central heating Open parking available Child discount available 12yrs Open terrace V meals Last d 21.30hrs Languages spoken: English & German
ROOMS: (room only) d 320-380FF
MEALS: Continental breakfast 36FF Lunch 70-280FF&alc Dinner 100-280FF&alc
CARDS: ●● ▆▆ ▆▆ Travellers cheques

ST-GERMAIN-DU-CRIOULT Calvados

★ ★ Auberge Saint-Germain
14110
☎ 231690810 FAX 231691467
This country inn enjoys a peaceful countryside setting beside the village church. It has a number of pleasant bedrooms

located in the annexe which are appointed with modern facilities. The surrounding region, 'La Suisse Normande' is so called for its resemblance with the Swiss scenery and is a popular area with tourists. A good range of regional dishes, available according to the seasons is available at the auberge.
Near motorway
Closed 20 Dec-10 Jan
9 en suite (bth/shr) 9 rooms in annexe (1 fmly) TV in 6 bedrooms Direct dial from all bedrooms Licensed Full central heating Open parking available Covered parking available Child discount available 8yrs Last d 21.00hrs
ROOMS: (room only) s 190-210FF; d 200-225FF
MEALS: Continental breakfast 23FF Lunch 72-155FF&alc Dinner 140-215FFalc
CARDS: ●● ▦ ▦ Travellers cheques

ST-JEAN-LE-THOMAS Manche

★ ★ Des Bains
8 allée Clemenceau *50530*
☎ 233488420 FAX 233486642
((On D911 towards Jullouville)

Located in a thousand-year old village on the coastal road between Granville and Avranches, the hotel has been in the hands of the same family for four generations. Its attractive interior is enhanced by pretty flower arrangements which create a warm and friendly atmosphere. Most of the guest rooms have modern amenities and provide a good level of comfort. The restaurant serves an honest cuisine, consisting of a choice of well-prepared, tasty dishes.
Near sea Near beach Forest area In town centre
Closed 2 Nov-31 Mar
30 rms (16 bth 11 shr) 6 rooms in annexe (15 fmly) (10 with balcony) TV in all bedrooms Direct dial from all bedrooms Licensed Full central heating Open parking available Supervised Child discount available Outdoor swimming pool (heated) Pool table Boule Open terrace Last d 21.00hrs
Languages spoken: English
ROOMS: (room only) s 165-350FF; d 165-350FF
Reductions over 1 night
MEALS: Full breakfast 33FF Continental breakfast 33FF Lunch 78-185FF Dinner 78-185FF
CARDS: ●● ▦ ▦ ● Travellers cheques

ST-MARCEL Eure

★ ★ Climat de France
17 rue de la Poste *27950*
☎ 233212500 Cen Res 164460123 FAX 233212325
(off A13 at Véron exit onto D181)
This recently built hotel offers pleasant guest rooms which are

equipped with private facilities and provide a good quality level of comfort. The restaurant welcomes guests for breakfast, lunches and dinners, and serves besides a generous buffet for appetisers and desserts, classic French cuisine in a warm atmosphere.
Near river Forest area Near motorway
44 en suite (bth/shr) TV in all bedrooms Direct dial from all bedrooms Licensed Night porter Full central heating Open parking available Pool table Open terrace Wkly live entertainment Casino Languages spoken: English, German & Italian
CARDS: ●● ▦

ST-MARTIN-DU-VIVIER Seine-Maritime

★ ★ ★ La Bertelière
76160
☎ 235604400 FAX 235615663

Built in 1987, this modern hotel is located in the countryside just ten minutes from the centre of Rouen, and features spacious public areas and contemporary bedrooms providing a good level of comfort. The gastronomic restaurant serves a high standard of cooking incorporating various dishes which will please most palates. In addition there is a piano-bar and a terrace for a chat or relaxation.
Forest area Near motorway
44 en suite (bth/shr) (4 fmly) TV in all bedrooms STV Direct dial from all bedrooms Mini-bar in all bedrooms Licensed Night porter Full central heating Open parking available Supervised Child discount available 15yrs Pool table Bicycle rental Open terrace Table tennis V meals Last d 22.00hrs
Languages spoken: English
CARDS: ●● ▦ ▦ ● Travellers cheques

ST-VAAST-LA-HOUGUE Manche

★ ★ France Fuchsias
20 rue Ml-Foch *50550*
☎ 233544226 FAX 233434679
(From Quettehou on D1 enter town and continue straight ahead into Rue Maréchal Foch)
A pleasant hotel close to the port and the marina, surrounded by a luxuriant private garden and noted for its fine cuisine.
Near sea In town centre
Closed early Jan-late Feb
33 rms (15 bth 14 shr) 13 rooms in annexe (3 fmly) TV in all bedrooms STV Direct dial from all bedrooms Licensed Full central heating Child discount available 8yrs Bicycle rental Open terrace V meals Last d 21.15hrs Languages spoken: English
ROOMS: (room only) s 155-310FF; d 200-435FF
contd.

Reductions over 1 night
MEALS: Full breakfast 43FF Continental breakfast 43FF Lunch 83-280FF Dinner 83-280FF&alc✱
CARDS: ● ▦ ▆ ● Travellers cheques

★ ★ ★ **Granitière**
74 r du Ml-Foch *50550*
☎ 233545899 FAX 233203491
(From Quettehou on D1 enter town and continue straight ahead into Rue Maréchal Foch)
An impressive granite building with marble floors, stained glass windows and rich wall coverings and stylishly decorated bedrooms.
Near sea In town centre
Closed mid Feb-mid Mar
10 rms (8 bth/shr) (2 fmly) (2 with balcony) TV in all bedrooms Licensed Full central heating Open parking available Supervised Child discount available 12yrs Bicycle rental Open terrace V meals Last d 21.00hrs Languages spoken: English
MEALS: Continental breakfast 42FF Dinner 85-190FF&alc
CARDS: ● ▦ ▆ ● Travellers cheques

SASSETOT-LE-MAUCONDUIT Seine-Maritime

★ ★ **Château de Sassetot**
Le Mauconduit *76540*
☎ 235280011 FAX 235285000
Near river Near lake Near sea Forest area In town centre
Near motorway
Closed end Dec-Feb
TV available STV Direct-dial available Licensed Night porter Full central heating Open parking available Supervised Child discount available Riding Sauna Pool table Boule Bicycle rental Open terrace V meals
CARDS: ● ▦ ▆ ● Travellers cheques

SAUSSAYE, LA Eure

Le Manoir des Saules
2 pl St-Martin *27370*
☎ 235872565 FAX 235874939
This charming Norman manor house with its original, beamed façade offers its visitors a memorable experience. It provides charming bedrooms featuring many personal touches. It also has a terrace and a delightful garden which is especially popular in summer.
Near river Near lake Forest area Near motorway
Closed Nov-Feb
9 en suite (bth/shr) (3 fmly) (1 with balcony) TV in all bedrooms Radio in rooms Direct dial from all bedrooms Licensed Full central heating Open parking available Covered parking available Supervised Bicycle rental Open terrace V meals Last d 21.00hrs Languages spoken: English
CARDS: ● ▦ ▆ ● Travellers cheques

SILLY-EN-GOUFFERN Orne

★ ★ ★ **Pavillon De Gouffern**
Le Pavillon *61310*
☎ 233366426 FAX 233365381
Set in its own extensive grounds, this former hunting lodge promises an unforgettable stay in charming and relaxing surroundings. Cosy lounges with comfortable armchairs, splendid fireplaces and elegant bedrooms create a warm, informal atmosphere. A creative selection of dishes is served in

the attractive restaurant which has fine views of the green surroundings.
Near river Near lake Forest area
20 en suite (bth) 7 rooms in annexe TV in all bedrooms Direct dial from all bedrooms Licensed Full central heating Open parking available Tennis Fishing Pool table Boule Bicycle rental Open terrace

SOURDEVAL Manche

★ ★ **Le Temps de Vivre**
12 rue St-Martin *50150*
☎ 233596041 FAX 233598834
This comfortable hotel is situated in a small, flower-filled village in a valley in the Normandy region. The beautiful surrounding area has plenty of green countryside, valleys and rivers, and provides the relaxing setting for an enjoyable holiday. There is a restaurant with a terrace, whilst most of the bedrooms in this hotel have modern amenities and offer a straight-forward level of comfort.
Near river Forest area In town centre
7 rms (6 shr) (1 fmly) (1 with balcony) TV in all bedrooms Radio in rooms Licensed Full central heating Open parking available Child discount available 9yrs Open terrace V meals Last d 21.00hrs
MEALS: Continental breakfast 25FF Lunch 56-165FF Dinner 56-165FF✱
CARDS: ● ▆ Travellers cheques

TANCARVILLE Seine-Maritime

★ ★ ★ **De La Marine**
Au Pied du Pont *76430*
☎ 235397715 FAX 235380330
(On D982 near the river bridge)
Set at the foot of the Tancarville bridge across the River Seine, the hotel has individually-appointed bedrooms with modern amenities which have views of the riverside gardens and the bridge. Seafood delicacies take pride of place on the menu and are skilfully prepared by Jean-Pierre Sedon who presides over the kitchen.
Near river
RS Sun & Mon evening
9 en suite (bth/shr) (1 fmly) TV in all bedrooms Direct dial from all bedrooms Mini-bar in all bedrooms Licensed Full central heating Open parking available Supervised Child discount available Bicycle rental Open terrace Last d 21.00hrs Languages spoken: English
ROOMS: (room only) s 250FF; d 250-340FF
MEALS: Full breakfast 45FF Lunch 140-230FF&alc Dinner 140-230FF&alc✱
CARDS: ● ▦ ▆ CB

TESSÉ-LA-MADELEINE Orne

★ ★ **Residence du Pont Bridge Hotel**
7 pl du Pont, 1 av des Thermes *61140*
☎ 466476003 FAX 466476278
(From Mende take N88 towards Langogne,then take D901 to Bagnols-les-Bains)
Standing in a privileged location in the Lot valley, the hotel extends a warm welcome to its visitors. Having a long-standing reputation in the hospitality trade, it offers peacefully situated guest rooms with modern facilities, congenial public areas and an attractive restaurant. With an array of leisure pursuits on offer, it is the ideal venue for both relaxing and active holidays.

Near river Forest area Near motorway
Closed 15 Oct-30 Mar
26 en suite (bth/shr) (4 fmly) (9 with balcony) TV in all
bedrooms Direct dial from all bedrooms Licensed Lift Full
central heating Open parking available Covered parking
available (charged) Supervised Child discount available 7yrs
Outdoor swimming pool Solarium Open terrace Covered
terrace Last d 21.00hrs Languages spoken: English, Spanish
MEALS: Full breakfast 50FF Continental breakfast 38FF Lunch
70-150FF&alc Dinner 70-150FF&alc✱
CARDS: ❀ ☲ Travellers cheques

★ ★ Hotel de Tessé
1 av de la Baillée *61140*
☎ 233308007 FAX 233385192
The hotel is situated in Bagnoles de l'Orne, a spa resort at the
very heart of the Andaine forest and provides a good starting
point for visits to the region. It has a country-style interior,
where bedrooms have modern amenities and provide a good
level of comfort. The restaurant caters for most tastes, whilst
also the surrounding region offers a range of leisure pursuits.
Near river Near lake Forest area
Closed end Oct-beg Apr
43 en suite (bth/shr) (2 fmly) (16 with balcony) TV in all
bedrooms Licensed Lift Night porter Full central heating
Open parking available Covered parking available (charged)
Supervised Child discount available 12yrs Last d 21.00hrs
Languages spoken: English, Spanish
MEALS: Full breakfast 30FF Lunch 85-110FF Dinner 85-
110FF✱
CARDS: ❀ ☲ ❂ Travellers cheques

★ ★ Victoria
24 chemin de l'Église, BP5 *14117*
☎ 231223537 FAX 231214166
The Victoria Hotel is a 19th-century manor house of traditional
appearance set in peaceful green surroundings 7 km from
Bayeux with its famous tapestry, imposing 11th-century
cathedral and museums. The D-Day landing beaches are also
within easy reach. It offers spacious, elegantly-furnished
bedrooms with fine views of the park or the flower-filled
courtyard.
Near sea Forest area
Closed early Oct-Mar
14 en suite (bth/shr) (4 fmly) TV in all bedrooms Direct dial
from all bedrooms Full central heating Open parking
available Supervised Open terrace
ROOMS: (room only) s fr 300FF; d 300-560FF **Reductions
over 1 night**
CARDS: ❀ ☲

★ ★ ★ Hostellerie du Clos
98 rue de la Ferté Vidame *27130*
☎ 232322181 FAX 232322136
Hidden away in delightful mature woodland, this handsome
manor house features a peaceful interior where cosy
bedrooms and intimate suites offer a high standard of guest
accommodation. The tastefully decorated lounges provide
comfortable surroundings for relaxing or reading, whilst the
restaurant, with magnificent flower arrangements, fine old
silver and porcelain, offers the setting for a refined cuisine.
Near river Forest area Near motorway
Closed 16 Dec-15 Jan

10 en suite (bth/shr) 3 rooms in annexe (3 fmly) TV in all
bedrooms STV Licensed Full central heating Open parking
available Supervised Child discount available 8yrs Tennis
Sauna Jacuzzi/spa Bicycle rental Open terrace Covered
terrace V meals Last d 21.00hrs Languages spoken:
English, Spanish, German, Portuguese
MEALS: Full breakfast 80FF Lunch 180-330FF&alc Dinner 180-
330FF&alc✱
CARDS: ❀ ☲☲ ❂ Travellers cheques

★ ★ Moulin de Balisne
RN12, Balisne *27130*
☎ 232320348 FAX 232601122
This 18th-century mill is located in extensive landscaped
gardens with rivers and lakes. The interior is adorned with
assorted knick-knacks which create a homely, personal
atmosphere. Inventive cuisine is served in the restaurant,
prepared with only the finest fresh produce and including a
whole range of home-made house specialities. The bedrooms
are full of character, and are equipped with good modern
amenities.
Near river Near lake Forest area Near motorway
12 en suite (bth/shr) (2 fmly) TV in all bedrooms Direct dial
from all bedrooms Mini-bar in all bedrooms Licensed Full
central heating Open parking available Child discount
available 10yrs Boule Bicycle rental Open terrace canoeing
V meals Last d 21.30hrs Languages spoken: English
CARDS: ❀ ☲☲ ❂ Travellers cheques

★ ★ Le Fruitier
pl des Costils *50800*
☎ 233905100 FAX 233905101
The hotel is situated in the centre of the charming village of
Villedieu-les-Poêles, famous for its copper industry and
located between Mont St-Michel and the D Day Beaches. A
friendly welcome awaits guests upon arrival in this
establishment, where the bedrooms are comfortable and
elegantly furnished, whilst the restaurant specialises in
seafood dishes and regional specialties. In addition, there is a
spacious lounge with congenial bar as well as a billiard room
for entertainment.
Near river Forest area In town centre Near motorway
Closed 23 Dec-5 Jan
48 en suite (bth/shr) (10 fmly) TV in all bedrooms STV Direct
dial from all bedrooms Licensed Lift Full central heating
Open parking available Covered parking available (charged)
Supervised Pool table V meals Last d 21.30hrs Languages
spoken: Englsih
CARDS: ❀ ☲ Travellers cheques

★ ★ L'Escale du Vitou
rte d'Argentan *61120*
☎ 233391204 FAX 233361334
Near river Near beach Forest area
17 en suite (bth/shr) 18 rooms in annexe TV in all bedrooms
Radio in rooms Direct dial from all bedrooms Licensed Full
central heating Air conditioning in bedrooms Open parking
available Outdoor swimming pool (heated) Tennis Fishing
Riding Boule Last d 22.45hrs Languages spoken: English
CARDS: ❀ ☲

VIRE Calvados

★ ★ Hotel de France
4 rue d'Aignaux *14500*
☎ 231680035 FAX 231682265
A hotel with modern comforts and specially adapted rooms for disabled guests.
In town centre Near motorway
50 en suite (bth/shr) TV in all bedrooms Direct dial from all bedrooms Licensed Lift Night porter Full central heating Open parking available Covered parking available (charged) Child discount available 8yrs V meals Last d 22.00hrs
Languages spoken: English
ROOMS: (room only) d 190-350FF **Reductions over 1 night**
MEALS: Full breakfast 35FF Continental breakfast 35FF Lunch 70-220FF&alc Dinner 70-220FF&alc
CARDS: ● ▆ ▆ Travellers cheques

YVETOT Seine-Maritime

Auberge du Val au Cesne
76190
☎ 235566306 FAX 235569278
(3km SW of Yvetot via D5)
A warm welcome awaits you at the auberge, situated in the heart of the Caux region. A high degree of comfort is offered here, including individually decorated bedrooms and traditional dining room with open fireplace. In summer, meals are served on the terrace.
Forest area Near motorway
5 en suite (bth/shr) (3 fmly) (5 with balcony) TV in all bedrooms Direct dial from all bedrooms Licensed Night porter Full central heating Open parking available Supervised Bicycle rental Open terrace Last d 21.00hrs
Languages spoken: English
ROOMS: (room only) d 400FF
MEALS: Continental breakfast 50FF Lunch fr 150FF Dinner fr 150FF
CARDS: ● ▆ ▆

TWO NORMANDY TOWNS

Bayeux

Situated in the romantic and wild Bessin area, Bayeux is an ancient Roman town whose centuries of rich heritage has been well preserved. The beauty of the old streets, with their fine historic buildings, the narrow bridges and the gleaming stonework of the mills on the River Aure invite the visitor for a peaceful stroll around this town.

The impressive Notre Dame Cathedral, the Musée Baron Gerard and the Bayeux School of Lace are all important features of Bayeux, but slide into insignificance against the priceless Bayeux Tapestry. This 11th-century

One of the beautiful stained glass windows of Notre Dame Cathedral.

masterpiece, housed in the Centre Guillaume le Conquerant (William the Conqueror), depicts the conquest of England in 1066 in colourful and lively scenes. An added treat may be in store if you are visiting this town in early July when the Medieval market takes place.

Villedieu-les-Poêles

A short drive south-west lies the charming and typically Norman town of Villedieu-les-Poêles, formerly a fort for the Knights of the Order of Malta. A visit to this small, delightful town is highly recommended. The town owes its name to its 800-year-old tradition of copper pot and pan making, hence the literal translation: city of god of the frying pans.

For many centuries this town has been a famous centre for craftsmen and metalworkers continuing this great tradition, displays of hand-beaten copper and examples of pewter-ware and lace-making are available together with the bell foundry and a museum of Norman furniture. Villedieu-les-Poêles makes an excellent stop for gift buying and if you fancy an experience in complete contrast try the underground adventure brought to life by the laser technology of Souterroscope at Caumont l'Evente.

Nord/Pas de Calais

An underestimated tourist area as French regions go, the Nord/Pas de Calais has much to reward the inquisitive visitor. Distinctive bell towers, prominent in each town, were formerly watch towers erected by the towns' burgomasters as a symbol of State power to rival the Church's spires, which are dominant features of the flat countryside. Locals call their sandy, grassy coastline — the northernmost in France — the Opal Coast because of its mysterious, bluish-purple light. Inland, rivers and canals are dotted with windmills, and picturesque villages spring to life in uproarious festivals celebrating the myths and legends of the past.

(Top): Cheese and wine from the village of Maroilles. The cheese is rinsed in beer to make a richly flavoured cheese tart.

(Bottom): Rodin's famous statue is a tribute to the 'Burghers of Calais', who risked their lives to save the town from destruction in 1347.

ESSENTIAL FACTS

DÉPARTEMENTS:	Nord, Pas-de-Calais
PRINCIPAL TOWNS	Calais, Lille, Arras, Boulogne-sur-Mer, Cambrai, Dunkerque, Valenciennes
PLACES TO VISIT:	The medieval Château Comtal at Boulogne-sur-Mer; the important Musée des Beaux-Arts at Lille; Vaucelles Abbey, founded by the Cisterian order in 1132 at Les Rues des Vignes; family amusement park in the Parc de Bagatelle at Merlimont
REGIONAL TOURIST OFFICE	6 place Mendès France, 59800 Lille. Tel: 20 14 57 57
LOCAL GASTRONOMIC DELIGHTS	Favourite regional dishes include flambee coffee and chicory Charlotte with caramel gin sauce and brown sugar; licques chicken and waterzoi; crab Charlotte from the Opal Coast; fish (cod and turbot) carbonade with beer
DRINKS	Many breweries produce lager as well as top-fermented ale like beers in the Belgian style. Houlle and Wambrechies are well known for their gin, while mead is brewed in Bavay and Bouin-Plumoison.
LOCAL CRAFTS WHAT TO BUY	Glass engraving from Bellignies, puppets from Camphin-en-Carembault, wood sculpture from Cassel, pottery and ceramics from Desvres, miniature paintings from Masny, silk painting from St-Laurent-Blangy

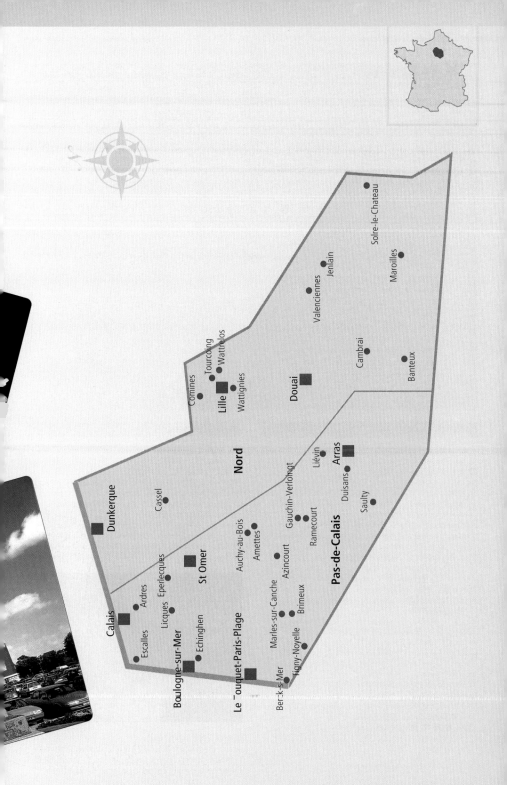

Solre-le-Chateau

Jenlain

Maroilles

Valenciennes

Tourcoing

Wattrelos

Cambrai

Banteux

Comines

Lille

Wattignies

Douai

Nord

Liévin

Arras

Dunkerque

Cassel

Duisans

Saulty

Gauchin-Verlohgt

Ramecourt

Auchy-au-Bois

Amettes

Azincourt

Pas-de-Calais

St Omer

Eperlecques

Ardres

Licques

Boulogne-sur-Mer

Echinghen

Marles-sur-Canche

Brimeux

Escalles

Le Touquet-Paris-Plage

Tigny-Noyelle

Berck-s-Mer

Calais

EVENTS & FESTIVALS

Feb Lille Mozart Festival; Carnivals at Dunkirk & Equihen-plage

Mar Carnivals at Cassel and Dunkerque; Berck Kite Festival; Valenciennes Cultural Spring Festival; Cassel Carnival & Parade of giant effigies; Aire-sur-la-Lys Carnival Parade

Apr Avesnes-sur-Helpe Fly Fair (*traditional celebration*); Roost Warendin Fête du Pureux - traditional feast & parade with giant effigy; Walled City Day: 14 walled cities have historical pageants, concerts, bell-ringing, theatre etc

May Tourcoing Medieval Festival

Jun Maroilles Flea market; Samer Strawberry Festival; Lille Festival

Jul Douai Gayant Procession & Festival; Boulogne-sur-Mer Napoleon Festival; Opal Coast Contemporary Music Festival; Neuville en-Ferrin Carnival & Festival; Wimereux Mussel Festival

Aug Hardelot Music Festival; Les Quesnoy Carnival with giant Pierre Bimberlot; Maroilles Fête de la Flamiche (a local delicacy); Cambrai Historical Parade with giant figures; Arras Carnival & Festival with giant figures; Le Touquet Music Festival

Sep Lille Giant Street market; Wattrelos Berlouffes Festival (commemorating the Beggars' Revolt); Arleux Garlic Fair; Aire-sur-la-Lys Andouille Festival; Armentieres Nieulles Festival (small cakes thrown down from town hall)

Oct Lille Festival; Comines Carnival Parade with giant figures; Bailleul Monts des Cats St Hubert Festival

Nov Tourcoing Jazz Festival

Dec Licques Turkey Festival; Boulogne-sur-Mer Guénels (hollowed-out beetroot) Festival

---

★ ★ ★ ★ Hostellerie des 3 Mousquetaires
Château du Fort de la Rédoute *62120*
☎ 321390111 FAX 321395010
(from Calais A26 exit4, direction of Aire-sur-la-Lys, on N43)
This 19th-century château is splendidly located in seven and a half acres of gardens, parkland and lakes. A warm welcome awaits guests at this establishment which is furnished in a style befitting its origins. Through the use of different fabrics each bedroom has its own character - some even have canopy beds. Visitors can try the challenging 18-hole golf course, enjoy a cocktail in one of the lounges in front of an open fire, or take a stroll in the garden, before pampering their palates with gastronomic specialities served in the restaurant which offers fine views over the Lys Valley.
Near river Near lake Forest area Near motorway
Closed 20 Jan-20 Jan
33 en suite (bth/shr) 3 rooms in annexe (2 fmly) (2 with balcony) TV in all bedrooms STV Direct dial from all bedrooms Licensed Full central heating Open parking available Supervised Child discount available 12yrs Boule Mini-golf Open terrace V meals Last d 21.45hrs Languages spoken: English
ROOMS: (room only) s 250-480FF; d 480-595FF **Special breaks**
MEALS: Full breakfast 55FF Continental breakfast 75FF Lunch 170-250FF&alc Dinner fr 250FF&alc
CARDS: 💳 ▥ ▩ 🐾 Travellers cheques

★ ★ Trois Luppars
49 Grand Place *62000*
☎ 321074141 FAX 321242480
The hotel is housed in the oldest building in the town of Arras and dates back as far as 1430. Situated on one of the historic squares in the centre of town, it is just a few steps away from the cafes, restaurants and varied entertainment. The guest rooms are protected by the Ancient Monuments Society and feature exposed beams and 15th-century wooden shutters on the inside, which are complemented by an inner courtyard full of flowers.

In town centre Near motorway
42 en suite (bth/shr) (8 fmly) TV in all bedrooms Direct dial from all bedrooms Mini-bar in 2 bedrooms Licensed Lift Full central heating Covered parking available (charged) *contd.*

Welcome to the GREAT NAUSICAÄ from 30th May 1998

NAUSICAÄ will be twice as big and invite you to live the Sea

Dive in an unbelievable Sub-Marine observatory and come nose to nose with the Sea-Lions

Come and discover the blue lagoon village and its superb coral reef

Open every day, minimum from 9.30 am to 6.30 pm
Rates from 30th May 1998 : Adults : 65 FF - Children (3 to 12 years) : 45 FF
NAUSICAA, Boulevard Sainte-Beuve 62200 BOULOGNE sur MER France
Tél. 00 33 3 21 30 98 98
http ://www. NAUSICAÄ-SEA-CENTRES.COM

NAUSICAÄ
Centre National de la Mer

Boulogne/Mer FRANCE

Child discount available 6yrs Sauna Bicycle rental Languages spoken: English
ROOMS: (room only) s fr 240FF; d fr 260FF **Reductions over 1 night**
CARDS: ✺ ▦ ☎ ➍ Travellers cheques

BAILLEUL Nord

★ ★ ★ Belle Hotel
19 rue de Lille *59270*
☎ 328491900 FAX 328492211
(from A25 take exit 10 in the direction of town centre)
This renovated, country-style establishment has retained all the charm of a typical Flemish house and is located deep in the heart of the 'Monts des Flandres' region. It has tastefully decorated and individually appointed bedrooms with modern amenities which offer a high level of comfort. The hotel has no restaurant facilities, but guests can enjoy a full three-course meal in their bedroom upon request, or seek out the eating establishments in the town.
In town centre Near motorway
31 en suite (bth/shr) (10 fmly) No smoking in 12 bedrooms TV in all bedrooms Licensed Full central heating Open parking available Supervised Child discount available 11yrs Languages spoken: English, Portuguese
ROOMS: (room only) s fr 350FF; d 390-500FF
CARDS: ✺ ▦ ☎ ➍

BERCK-SUR-MER Pas-de-Calais

★ ★ Les Flots Bleus
17 rue du Calvaire *62600*
☎ 321090342 FAX 321847524
(on arriving in Berck take Impératrice rue in direction of the beach and turn right after the tourist office)
The hotel located only 40metres from the beach and town, offers nine comfortable rooms. Wood fire grill and fish specialities are available in the restaurant.
Near sea Near beach Forest area In town centre Near motorway
Closed Dec & Jan
8 en suite (bth/shr) (1 fmly) No smoking in 3 bedrooms TV in all bedrooms STV Direct dial from all bedrooms Mini-bar in all bedrooms Licensed Full central heating Child discount available 12yrs Last d 21.30hrs Languages spoken: English
ROOMS: (room only) s 240-290FF; d 240-290FF; wkly hb 285-300FF
MEALS: Continental breakfast 35FF Lunch fr 85FF&alc Dinner fr 85FF&alc
CARDS: ✺ ▦ ☎ ➍ Travellers cheques

BOLLEZEELE Nord

★ ★ ★ Hostellerie Saint-Louis
47 rue de l'Eglise *59470*
☎ 328688183 FAX 328680117
(A25 Lille-Dunkerque exit 16 Bergues in direction St Omer for 10km to Bollezeele)
The Hostellerie St Louis is a country house in the tiny village of Bollezeele, which is between Dunkerque and St Omer. The spacious bedrooms are elegantly furnished and have views of the countryside or gardens. Philippe Dubreucq, the owner, prepares a three course menu which includes some of his specialities like warm foie gras, local poultry or fish, and patisseries.
Near sea Near beach Forest area In town centre Near motorway

Closed 2-16 Jan & 18-25 Feb
38 rms (19 bth 9 shr) (3 fmly) TV in 28 bedrooms STV Direct dial from 28 bedrooms Licensed Lift Full central heating Open parking available Open terrace Table tennis V meals Last d 21.00hrs Languages spoken: English & Dutch
ROOMS: (room only) s 250-300FF; d 320-450FF
MEALS: Full breakfast 35FF Dinner 140-290FF&alc✱
CARDS: ✺ ▦ ☎ Travellers cheques

BOULOGNE-SUR-MER Pas-de-Calais

★ ★ ★ Metropole
51 rue Thiers *62200*
☎ 321315430 FAX 321304572
In town centre
Closed 21 Dec-5 Jan
25 en suite (bth/shr) (2 fmly) (7 with balcony) TV in all bedrooms Direct dial from all bedrooms Mini-bar in all bedrooms Licensed Lift Night porter Full central heating Open parking available (charged) Covered parking available (charged) Languages spoken: English
ROOMS: (room only) s 340-370FF; d 400-440FF
MEALS: Continental breakfast 45FF
CARDS: ✺ ▦ ☎ ➍ Travellers cheques

BROUCKERQUE Nord

Le Middel-Houck
6 pl du Village *59630*
☎ 328271346 FAX 328271510
(approach via A16 exit 24b or 25)
This family hotel is housed in an 18th-century building in the heart of the village Brouckerque. Entirely renovated throughout, it offers well-equipped guest rooms and a skilfully executed cuisine which incorporates many regional specialities prepared with only high quality local produce, complemented by home-baked bread and patisseries.
Near lake In town centre Near motorway
4 en suite (shr) TV in all bedrooms Full central heating Last d 21.30hrs Languages spoken: English,German
ROOMS: (room only) d 215FF ✱
MEALS: Continental breakfast 28FF Lunch 90-178FF&alc Dinner 90-178FF&alc✱
CARDS: ✺ ▦ ☎ ➍ Travellers cheques

CALAIS Pas-de-Calais

★ ★ ★ George-V
36 rue Royale *62100*
☎ 321976800 FAX 321973473
(In the NW area of the town between the station and the ferry terminal)
Although situated in the centre of the town and just minutes away from both ferry terminals and Channel Tunnel, this charming hotel offers its guests a peaceful stay. Courteous staff provide attentive service in an amiable atmosphere. The modern bedrooms are well equipped and furnished in attractive pastel colours. There is a lounge-bar open to hotel residents only, whilst visitors are spoilt for choice by the two restaurants with delicious starters, grills, fresh fish specialities and patisseries Maison.
In town centre
42 en suite (bth/shr) (3 fmly) (12 with balcony) TV in all bedrooms STV Direct dial from all bedrooms Mini-bar in 16 bedrooms Licensed Lift Night porter Full central heating Open parking available Supervised Child discount available 12yrs V meals Last d 22.00hrs Languages spoken: English

ROOMS: (room only) d 310-470FF **Reductions over 1 night**
MEALS: Full breakfast 42FF Lunch 95-160FF Dinner 95-160FF✱
CARDS: ❤ ▦ ▭ ⏸ Travellers cheques

★ ★ ★ Holiday Inn Garden Court
6 bd des Allies
☎ 321346969 FAX 321970915
(Follow signs for 'Calais Nord' or 'Calais Port')
Because of its ideal geographical location, the town of Calais has been the traditional landfall on the European mainland for generations of British travellers. The hotel is situated in the centre of the town and offers a magnificent view over the yachting harbour and the sea, and is well positioned near the ferry terminal and Eurotunnel. The bedrooms have high quality bedding and are equipped with every modern convenience, whilst the restaurant caters for most tastes and offers a choice of enjoyable dishes.
Near sea In town centre Near motorway
65 en suite (bth/shr) (17 fmly) (6 with balcony) No smoking in 30 bedrooms TV in all bedrooms STV Direct dial from all bedrooms Mini-bar in all bedrooms Licensed Lift Night porter Full central heating Open parking available Covered parking available Supervised Sauna Fitness room V meals Last d 22.30hrs Languages spoken: English German & Dutch
ROOMS: (room only) d 570-590FF
CARDS: ❤ ▦ ▭ ⏸ JCB Travellers cheques

★ ★ ★ Metropol Hotel
45 quai de Rhin 62100
☎ 321975400 FAX 321966970
(From motorway exit 14 head towards town centre. Straight on at first rdbt, then right at traffic lights and next right)
The Metropol hotel was completely renovated in 1988 and decorated throughout in English style. It is ideally situated in the centre of the town and is just a few minutes away from the shuttle and ferries. It has functional bedrooms with en suite facilities, a stylish foyer and bar, and a spacious lounge with high quality furniture to relax in. The attractive restaurant features a good selection of dishes.
Near sea Near beach In town centre
Closed 19 Dec-3 Jan
40 en suite (bth/shr) (5 fmly) No smoking in 2 bedrooms TV in all bedrooms Radio in rooms Direct dial from all bedrooms Mini-bar in 10 bedrooms Licensed Lift Night porter Full central heating Open parking available Covered parking available (charged) Supervised Child discount available 12yrs Languages spoken: English
ROOMS: (room only) s 200-280FF; d 300-380FF
Reductions over 1 night
CARDS: ❤ ▦ ▭ ⏸

★ ★ ★ Meurice
5 rue E-Roche 62100
☎ 321345703 FAX 321341471
The Hotel Meurice is situated in the heart of Calais and dates back to 1771. After being destroyed during the second World War, it was completely rebuilt in 1954. It offers its visitors an enjoyable stay in a relaxed and friendly atmosphere. All the smartly furnished bedrooms have en-suite bathrooms, TV, and direct-dial telephones. Guests can relax in the cosy intimacy of the bar or in the conservatory which overlooks the interior garden. The exceptional cuisine features fresh market produce and seasonal ingredients.
Near sea Forest area In town centre
39 en suite (bth/shr) (1 fmly) No smoking in 2 bedrooms TV in

all bedrooms Direct dial from all bedrooms Licensed Lift Night porter Full central heating Open parking available Covered parking available (charged) Child discount available 12yrs V meals Last d 23.00hrs Languages spoken: English
MEALS: Full breakfast 56FF Continental breakfast 41FF Lunch 100-190FF&alc Dinner 100-190FF&alc✱
CARDS: ❤ ▦ ▭ ⏸ Travellers cheques

CAMBRAI Nord

★ ★ ★ Beatus
718 av de Paris 59400
☎ 327814570 FAX 327780083

With its secluded location in shaded parkland, the hotel Beatus is a haven of peace and tranquillity. Visitors are offered a warm and friendly welcome by dedicated staff for whom the well-being and satisfaction of the guests is the prime consideration. All the bedrooms offer a high standard of comfort, and are furnished and decorated in various styles ranging from Louis XV to contemporary. Breakfast is served in a charming room with a view of the garden.
In town centre
32 en suite (bth/shr) (1 fmly) TV in all bedrooms STV Direct dial from all bedrooms Licensed Night porter Full central heating Open parking available Covered parking available (charged) Supervised Bicycle rental Open terrace Last d 21.00hrs Languages spoken: English German & Polish
ROOMS: (room only) s 330-550FF; d 360-620FF ✱
MEALS: Full breakfast 50FF Continental breakfast 50FF Dinner 130FF✱
CARDS: ❤ ▦ ▭ ⏸ Travellers cheques

★ ★ ★ Château de la Motte Fenélon
sq du Château 59400
☎ 327836138 FAX 327837161
(N of town centre towards Valenciennes)
Standing in 20 acres of extensive parklands this 18th-century residence offers elegantly furnished bedrooms which are divided between the main building and its adjoining wings. The fabulous Louis-style lounges - decorated with gold trim and frescoes - and vaulted restaurant, create the stylish setting for an enjoyable overnight stop or weekend-end break. The excellent cuisine features a range of sophisticated dishes with well-balanced ingredients and flavours.
Forest area
40 en suite (bth/shr) TV in all bedrooms Direct dial from all bedrooms Mini-bar in all bedrooms Licensed Lift Night porter Full central heating Open parking available Supervised Child discount available 12yrs Tennis Pool table Open terrace Covered terrace Last d 22.00hrs Languages spoken: English & German
contd.

ROOMS: (room only) d 310-1000FF
MEALS: Full breakfast 55FF Continental breakfast 55FF Lunch 140-230FF&alc Dinner 140-230FF&alc
CARDS: ☎ ▦ ▦ ☞ Travellers cheques

★ ★ ★ Au Mouton Blanc
33 rue d'Alsace Lorraine *59400*
☎ 327813016 FAX 327818354
The hotel Mouton Blanc was built in the last century and has faithfully maintained its old world charm whilst offering modern day comfort. A warm atmosphere prevails throughout and it provides its visitors with cosy bedroom accommodation and excellent food. Because of its central location it is a good base from which to explore the sights.
In town centre
32 en suite (bth/shr) Some rooms in annexe (5 fmly) (4 with balcony) TV in all bedrooms Direct-dial available Lift Night porter Full central heating Open parking available Covered parking available V meals Last d 21.30hrs Languages spoken: English
MEALS: Lunch 98-215FF Dinner 98-218FF✱

CAMIERS Pas-de-Calais

★ ★ Les Cèdres
64 rue du Vieux Moulin *62176*
☎ 321849454 FAX 321092329
(6km S of Hardelot)
Situated close to the sea and the fine sandy beaches, the hotel is in peaceful leafy surroundings and provides the ideal venue for an overnight stop or weekend-break. It features a cosy lounge-reading room and well equipped bedrooms. The restaurant serves a range of well-prepared meat and fish specialities in an attractive interior.
Near sea Forest area Near motorway
Closed 16 Dec-4 Jan RS Sun
29 rms (17 bth 6 shr) (3 fmly) TV in all bedrooms Direct dial from all bedrooms Mini-bar in 25 bedrooms Licensed Full central heating Open parking available Supervised Child discount available Bicycle rental Open terrace V meals Last d 21.00hrs Languages spoken: English German Italian & Spanish
ROOMS: (room only) s 160-295FF; d 235-315FF ✱
MEALS: Full breakfast 35FF Lunch 80-250FF&alc Dinner 80-250FF&alc✱
CARDS: ☎ ▦ ▦ ☞ Travellers cheques

COQUELLES Pas-de-Calais

★ ★ ★ Hotel Copthorne
av Charles de Gaulle *62231*
☎ 321466060 FAX 321857676
(Close to the Channel Tunnel, ferry terminal, the A26 & A16 motorways)
A stylish new hotel surrounded by woodland and close to Calais, the shopping centre 'Cite Europe', Channel tunnel terminal and Eurostar station. Leisure club facilities available.
Near river Near lake
118 en suite (bth/shr) No smoking in 13 bedrooms TV in all bedrooms STV Direct dial from all bedrooms Mini-bar in 20 bedrooms Licensed Lift Night porter Full central heating Open parking available Covered parking available Child discount available 12yrs Indoor swimming pool (heated) Squash Sauna Solarium Gym Pool table Covered terrace V meals Last d 22.30hrs Languages spoken: English, Dutch & German

ROOMS: (room only) s 580-680FF; d 580-680FF
MEALS: Full breakfast 60FF Continental breakfast 30FF Lunch fr 130FF&alc Dinner fr 130FF&alc
CARDS: ☎ ▦ ▦ ☞ Travellers cheques

★ ★ Vidéotel
RN 1 *62231*
☎ 321368181 FAX 321368787

The hotels in the Vidéotel group all have bedrooms with pleasant furnishings and are equipped with the comfort of their clientele in mind. The restaurants serve a good quality gourmet cuisine with a range of prix-fixe menus, regional specialities and 'eat your fill buffet'. The management couples and their dedicated teams offer a 'round the clock' efficient service, where the well-being and satisfaction of guests is the prime consideration.
Near sea Near motorway
43 en suite (bth/shr) (3 fmly) No smoking in 8 bedrooms TV in all bedrooms STV Direct dial from all bedrooms Licensed Full central heating Open parking available Supervised Child discount available 12yrs Open terrace Last d 22.00hrs Languages spoken: English
ROOMS: (room only) s 280-299FF; d 280-299FF ✱
MEALS: Full breakfast 34FF Lunch 52-88FF Dinner 52-88FF✱
CARDS: ☎ ▦ ▦ ☞

DOUAI Nord

★ ★ ★ La Terrasse
36 Terrasse St-Pierre *59500*
☎ 327887004 FAX 327883605
(A1 exit Fresues les Bautaubau in direction Douai)
The Hotel La Terrasse combines elegant surroundings and luxurious bedrooms with a restaurant where an extensive menu features a choice of exquisite dishes, prepared with ingredients of the highest quality. The wine cellar is among the best in France and is stocked with more than 750 different wines and liqueurs, some dating back to 1920. Situated in the town of Douai, with its numerous historical sights and charming atmosphere, this attractive establishment is recommended to visitors to the north of France.
In town centre Near motorway
26 en suite (bth/shr) TV in all bedrooms STV Direct dial from all bedrooms Mini-bar in all bedrooms Licensed Night porter Full central heating Open parking available V meals Last d 22.00hrs
ROOMS: (room only) s 295-350FF; d 350-600FF
MEALS: Full breakfast 45FF Lunch fr 135FF&alc Dinner fr 135FF&alc
CARDS: ☎ ▦ ▦ ☞ Travellers cheques

DUNKERQUE Nord

★ ★ ★ Hotel Borel
6 rue l'Hermitte *59140*
☎ 328665180 FAX 328593382
The hotel Borel stands in the heart of the town, just a few steps away from the yachting harbour. It features a spacious, cosy lounge and well equipped bedrooms, some of which have views over the harbour.
Near sea In town centre
48 en suite (bth/shr) (6 fmly) No smoking in 10 bedrooms TV available Mini-bar in all bedrooms Licensed Lift Night porter Full central heating Languages spoken: English,German
CARDS: ●● ▥ ▨ ●)

★ ★ ★ Welcome
37 r Poincare *59140*
☎ 328592074 FAX 328210349
(from motorway A16 or A25 take exit "centre ville", at 3rd set of traffic lights turn left. At the 4th traffic lights turn right and first left)
Located in the heart of Dunkerque, within walking distance of Malo Beach and numerous museums.
Near sea Near beach In town centre Near motorway
39 en suite (bth/shr) (1 fmly) TV in all bedrooms STV Direct dial from all bedrooms Licensed Lift Night porter Full central heating Covered parking available (charged) Child discount available 12yrs V meals Last d 22.45hrs Languages spoken: English & German
ROOMS: (room only) s 357FF; d 402FF
MEALS: Continental breakfast 48FF Lunch 65-250FF&alc Dinner 102-250FF&alc✱
CARDS: ●● ▥ ▨

EMMERIN Nord

★ ★ ★ ★ La Howarderie
1 rue des Fusilles *59320*
☎ 320103100 FAX 320103109
(From Calais/Dunkerque A25 exit 7, follow in direction of Lens then Houbourdin & Emmerin.)
An old Flemish farmhouse, built around a paved courtyard, with a 17th century barn. The accommodation blends tastefully in this historic setting, combining traditional architecture with up to the minute comfort and luxury.
Near river Near lake Near sea Forest area Near motorway
Closed New Year-Etr,Xmas & 15 days Aug
8 en suite (bth/shr) TV in all bedrooms STV Direct dial from all bedrooms Full central heating Open parking available Child discount available 12yrs Languages spoken: English & German
ROOMS: (room only) s 450-650FF; d 800-1500FF
Reductions over 1 night
MEALS: Continental breakfast 70FF
CARDS: ●● ▥ ▨ ●)

ENGLOS Nord

★ ★ ★ Novotel Lille Englos
Autoroute Lille Dunkerque - *59320*
☎ 320070999 FAX 320447458
Novotel offer their clients good quality accommodation in modern, well equipped bedrooms and have refined restaurants serving good quality cuisine They have excellent business meeting and conference facilities and some have food and beverages available 24 hours a day. All their hotels have at least one bedroom for disabled guests.

Near motorway
124 en suite (bth/shr) (13 fmly) No smoking in 20 bedrooms TV in all bedrooms STV Radio in rooms Direct dial from all bedrooms Mini-bar in all bedrooms Licensed Night porter Full central heating Open parking available Supervised Child discount available 15yrs Outdoor swimming pool Boule Bicycle rental Open terrace Covered terrace Last d 24.00hrs Languages spoken: English & German
ROOMS: (room only) s 430-450FF; d 470-490FF
Reductions over 1 night
MEALS: Full breakfast 55FF Lunch 80-100FF&alc Dinner 95-150FFalc
CARDS: ●● ▥ ▨ ●) Travellers cheques

GAVRELLE Pas-de-Calais

★ ★ Manoir
35 rue Nationale *62580*
☎ 321586858 FAX 321553787
Situated amidst leafy surroundings, 'Le Manoir' has entirely renovated rooms with attractive furnishings and modern appointments. It has a pleasant restaurant with open fireplace, where the accent is on informality, and which serves a selection of tasty meals to suit most palates.
Near lake Forest area Near motorway
Closed 1-18 Aug
20 en suite (bth) (1 fmly) TV in all bedrooms Radio in rooms Direct dial from all bedrooms Licensed Full central heating Open parking available Covered parking available (charged) Supervised Child discount available 10yrs Pool table Boule Open terrace Last d 21.00hrs Languages spoken: English,German
CARDS: ●● ▥ ▨ Travellers cheques

GOSNAY Pas-de-Calais

★ ★ ★ ★ La Chartreuse du Val Saint-Esprit
1 rue Fouquières *62199*
☎ 321628088 FAX 321624250
(A26 exit 6)
The legend that gave its name to the valley and the decoration of La Chartreuse contribute to the charming atmosphere of the 18th century château. Beautifully restored by its owners, the hotel is an ideal place for gastronomy and holiday.
Forest area Near motorway
56 en suite (bth/shr) 11 rooms in annexe (3 fmly) TV in all bedrooms STV Direct dial from all bedrooms Mini-bar in all bedrooms Licensed Lift Night porter Full central heating Open parking available Child discount available 12yrs Tennis Open terrace V meals Last d 21.30hrs Languages spoken: English
ROOMS: (room only) s 410-600FF; d 480-860FF
MEALS: Continental breakfast 60FF Lunch 285-365FF&alc Dinner 285-365FF&alc
CARDS: ●● ▥ ▨ ●) Travellers cheques

GUÎNES Pas-de-Calais

Auberge du Colombier
la Bien Assise *62340*
☎ 321369300 FAX 321367920
Delightful hotel and restaurant in large secluded gardens.
7 en suite (bth/shr) (2 fmly) No smoking in 2 bedrooms TV in all bedrooms Direct dial from all bedrooms Licensed Open parking available Covered parking available Supervised Child discount available

contd.

Outdoor swimming pool (heated) Pool table Boule Mini-golf
Bicycle rental V meals Languages spoken: English
ROOMS: (room only) d 280FF **Reductions over 1 night**
CARDS: ✪ ▆

HARDELOT-PLAGE Pas-de-Calais

★ ★ ★ Hotel du Parc
av François-1er *62152*
☎ 321332211 FAX 321832971
(From Calais take A16 to Boulogne then D940 signed Le
Touquet. From Paris A1, then A26 exit Boulogne/Mer)
This is an attractive establishment, which through its
geographical location is suitable for either an active holiday or
a weekend break. Set in the heart of a pine forest, it offers
visitors informal lounges with cosy seating arrangements for
relaxation, and well equipped bedrooms with modern
conveniences, whilst the restaurant serves a wide range of
outstanding dishes from an inspired menu.
Near lake Near sea Near beach Forest area Near motorway
Closed 16-31 Dec
81 en suite (bth/shr) (81 fmly) (51 with balcony) No smoking
in 27 bedrooms TV in all bedrooms STV Radio in rooms
Direct dial from all bedrooms Mini-bar in all bedrooms
Licensed Lift Night porter Full central heating Open parking
available Supervised Child discount available 12yrs Outdoor
swimming pool (heated) Golf 18 Tennis Riding Sauna Gym
Pool table Boule Bicycle rental Open terrace Covered terrace
Childrens play area V meals Last d 22.30hrs Languages
spoken: English,German,Spanish
MEALS: Full breakfast 52FF Continental breakfast 52FF Lunch
135-180FF&alc Dinner 135-180FF&alc✱
CARDS: ✪ ▆ ▆ ᗞ Travellers cheques

HAZEBROUCK Nord

★ ★ Auberge de la Forêt
La Motte au Bois *59190*
☎ 328480878 FAX 328407776

This rustic inn is situated in the heart of the forest of Nieppe. A
warm and friendly atmosphere prevails, the bedrooms are
cosy with good amenities, while the restaurant with open
fireplace serves a good range of specialities and innovative
dishes, complemented by some great wines from the house
cellar.
Forest area
12 en suite (bth/shr) TV in all bedrooms Direct dial from all
bedrooms Licensed Full central heating Open parking
available Open terrace V meals Last d 21.00hrs Languages
spoken: English

ROOMS: (room only) s fr 240FF; d 300-320FF
MEALS: Continental breakfast 35FF Lunch 135-275FF&alc
Dinner 135-275FF&alc
CARDS: ✪ ▆ Travellers cheques

HESDIN Pas-de-Calais

★ La Chope
48 rue d'Arras *62140*
☎ 321868273
This small family hotel features bedrooms with good amenities
and offers a friendly attentive service to its visitors. The cuisine
is well respected throughout the region for its Flemish
specialities skilfully prepared by the proprietor.
Near river Forest area In town centre Near motorway
Closed Nov
7 rms (3 shr) (2 fmly) No smoking on premises Licensed Full
central heating Air conditioning in bedrooms Open parking
available Child discount available V meals Last d 20.45hrs
Languages spoken: English, Dutch, Flemish
CARDS: ✪ ▆ ▆ ᗞ Travellers cheques

★ ★ Les Flandries
22 rue d'Arras *62140*
☎ 321868021 FAX 321862801
Located amidst picturesque, leafy surroundings, this friendly
family hotel welcomes its visitors in an informal interior.
Entirely renovated throughout, it features comfortable
bedrooms which guarantee a restful night's sleep, and a
restaurant where a high standard of cooking has acquired a
faithful following amongst British visitors.
Near river Forest area In town centre Near motorway
Closed 20 Dec-10 Jan & 28 Jun-13 Jul
14 en suite (bth/shr) (2 fmly) TV in all bedrooms Direct dial
from all bedrooms Licensed Full central heating Open
parking available Covered parking available Supervised
Child discount available 8yrs V meals Last d 21.00hrs
Languages spoken: English
MEALS: Full breakfast 43FF Continental breakfast 38FF Lunch
90-188FF&alc Dinner 90-188FF&alc✱
CARDS: ✪ ▆

INXENT Pas-de-Calais

★ ★ Auberge d'Inxent
318 rue de la Vallée *62170*
☎ 321907119 FAX 321863167

(from Boulogne take N1 towards Montreuil.Take D149 to
Recques-sur-Course then D127 to Inxent)
This typical 18th-century inn stands on the banks of a river and
features completely renovated bedrooms offering comfortable

accommodation. The informal restaurant with ancient fireplace, serves a range of regional dishes prepared with fresh market produce.
Near river Near sea Near beach Forest area Near motorway Closed Jan RS Tue evening & Wed in high season
6 en suite (bth/shr) (2 fmly) STV Licensed Full central heating Open parking available Covered parking available Child discount available 12yrs Fishing Riding Boule Bicycle rental Open terrace V meals Last d 21.00hrs Languages spoken: English
ROOMS: (room only) s 255-310FF; d 295-350FF **Special breaks**
MEALS: Continental breakfast 35FF Lunch 79-195FF&alc Dinner 79-195FF&alc
CARDS: ✹ ⚏ Travellers cheques

LILLE Nord

★ ★ ★ ★ Hotel Alliance Lille
17 Quai du Wault, Lille Couvent des Minimes *59000*
☎ 320306262 FAX 320429425
(In town centre)
This building dates back to the 17th century, when it used to be a convent. Its imposing façade conceals the tranquil cloisters which house the hotel, where comfort and space blend harmoniously with the splendid Flemish architecture of the period. Bedrooms are tastefully furnished and offer a high standard of comfort, plus there is an informal piano-bar, delightful garden and a restaurant serving traditional cuisine.
Near river Near lake Forest area In town centre Near motorway
83 en suite (bth/shr) (8 fmly) No smoking in 4 bedrooms TV in all bedrooms STV Direct dial from all bedrooms Mini-bar in all bedrooms Room-safe Licensed Lift Night porter Full central heating Open parking available Child discount available 12yrs Wkly live entertainment Last d 22.30hrs Languages spoken: English
ROOMS: (room only) s 655-1500FF; d 770-15FF
Reductions over 1 night Special breaks: Weekend/Bed-Breakfast & Dinner
MEALS: Full breakfast 70FF Lunch 110-160FF&alc Dinner 110-160FF&alc
CARDS: ✹ ▤ ⚏ ⚏ Travellers cheques

★ ★ ★ ★ Carlton
3 rue de Paris *59000*
☎ 320133313 FAX 320514817
(From Eastern Ring Road follow signs 'Centre Ville', then right at 4th set of traffic lights and continue)
Because of its unique setting close to the Grand Palais and Opera, the Carlton hotel is the best in the city. The bedrooms are furnished in Louis XIV style and have luxury marbled bathrooms, while courteous staff render an attentive and friendly service. It offers a number of eating options alternating between classic French cuisine and regional dishes served in the Bistrot Opera and Brasserie Jean
In town centre
60 en suite (bth/shr) (40 with balcony) No smoking in 13 bedrooms TV in all bedrooms STV Direct dial from all bedrooms Mini-bar in all bedrooms Room-safe Licensed Lift Night porter Full central heating Air conditioning in bedrooms Open parking available (charged) Covered parking available (charged) Supervised Child discount available 12yrs Open terrace V meals Last d 00.30hrs Languages spoken: English German & Italian
ROOMS: (room only) s 820-1025FF; d 860-1075FF
CARDS: ✹ ▤ ⚏ ⚏ JCB Travellers cheques

★ ★ Climat de France
1 rue Christophe-Colomb *59000*
☎ 320552155 Cen Res 164460123 FAX 320558749
(Follow signs Lille Centre and take exit marked Nr 4 off La Madeleine)
Located in pleasant surroundings, the hotel has fine views over an extensive park, and features a warm and friendly interior where attractive bedrooms are equipped with up-to-date modern amenities. An informal restaurant offers a selection of carefully-prepared traditional dishes, as well as a generous 'as much as you can eat' buffet. The congenial cocktail bar is the right place for a drink and chat, whilst the comfortable lounge with board games and the billiard room provide entertainment for the guests.
Forest area In town centre Near motorway
60 en suite (shr) (4 fmly) No smoking in 15 bedrooms TV in all bedrooms Direct-dial available Licensed Lift Night porter Full central heating Open parking available Covered parking available (charged) Supervised Languages spoken: English
CARDS: ✹ ⚏

★ ★ ★ Grand Hotel Bellevue (Best Western)
5 rue Jean Roisin *59000*
☎ 320574564 FAX 320400793
Town centre
The Grand Hotel Bellevue offers fine views of Le Grand Place and the city. Elegantly decorated throughout, it features individually styled bedrooms with modern amenities, a cosy piano-bar and an attractive dining room, where breakfast and lunch are served. In addition, it is ideally situated close to all the main transport services.
In town centre Near motorway
61 rms (4 fmly) (4 with balcony) No smoking in 16 bedrooms TV in all bedrooms Direct dial from all bedrooms Mini-bar in all bedrooms Licensed Lift Full central heating Languages spoken: German, Spanish
CARDS: ✹ ▤ ⚏ ⚏ Travellers cheques

★ ★ Ibis Opéra
21 rue Lépelletier *59000*
☎ 320062195 FAX 320749130
This charming hotel is located in the heart of the old quarter of Lille, with all the shops, restaurants and main services just a short distance away. Because of the ideal location it is suitable for both commercial and leisure travellers. It offers guest rooms equipped with modern facilities and a restaurant which caters for all tastes.
In town centre
60 en suite (bth/shr) (4 fmly) (2 with balcony) No smoking in 7 bedrooms TV in 55 bedrooms Radio in rooms Lift Night porter Full central heating Child discount available 12yrs Languages spoken: English,German,Portuguese
CARDS: ✹ ▤ ⚏ ⚏

LOMME Nord

★ ★ Climat de France
rue du Grand But *59160*
☎ 320082054 Cen Res 164460123 FAX 320082057
(off A25)
This pleasant establishment has a warm and friendly interior where attractive bedrooms are equipped with up-to-date modern amenities. An informal restaurant offers a selection of carefully prepared traditional dishes, as well as a generous 'as much as you can eat' buffet.
Forest area Near motorway
56 en suite (bth/shr) TV in all bedrooms Radio in rooms
contd.

Direct dial from all bedrooms Licensed Lift Full central heating Open parking available Pool table Open terrace V meals Languages spoken: English, German & Spanish
CARDS: 💳 ▨

MAUBEUGE Nord

★ ★ Le Grand Hotel
1 Porte de Paris *59600*
☎ 327646316 FAX 327650576
This traditional hotel welcomes its visitors in a friendly informal atmosphere and offers pleasant bedrooms and a restaurant which serves dishes to suit most pockets and palates. Situated in the town of Maubeuge it provides a central base for touring the region with its many tourist attractions.
In town centre Near motorway
31 rms (28 bth/shr) (7 fmly) TV in all bedrooms STV Direct dial from all bedrooms Licensed Lift Night porter Full central heating Open parking available Covered parking available (charged) Supervised Child discount available 11yrs Open terrace Wkly live entertainment V meals Last d 22.00hrs Languages spoken: English
ROOMS: (room only) s 230-340FF; d 250-360FF ✱
Reductions over 1 night Special breaks
MEALS: Full breakfast 60FF Continental breakfast 35FF Lunch 78-340FF&alc Dinner 78-340FF&alc✱
CARDS: 💳 ▨ ▨ ◑ Travellers cheques

MONTREUIL-SUR-MER Pas-de-Calais

★ ★ ★ Les Hautes de Montreuil
21-23 rue Pierre Lédent *62170*
☎ 321819592 FAX 321862883
This authentic building dates back to 1537 and has 16th-century vaulted cellars which house delicious cheeses and well as wines and spirits. There is a shop where visitors can sample the regional produce. In summer guests can relax on the terrace in the garden beside a fountain. The restaurant serves a choice of dishes which are changed every season and are carefully prepared to a high standard, whilst the guest rooms are comfortably furnished with private facilities. There is free parking, and from the hotel it is only a short walk to the medieval ramparts of the town which offer splendid panoramic views over the surrounding area.
Near river In town centre
Closed 4 Jan-6 Feb

27 en suite (bth/shr) (4 fmly) (4 with balcony) TV in all bedrooms STV Direct dial from all bedrooms Mini-bar in 21 bedrooms Room-safe Licensed Full central heating Open parking available covered parking spaces Supervised Child discount available 2yrs Pool table V meals Last d 22.00hrs

Languages spoken: English & German
ROOMS: (room only) s 430-500FF; d 430-500FF
Reductions over 1 night
MEALS: Continental breakfast 60FF Lunch 100-245FF&alc Dinner 100-245FF&alc
CARDS: 💳 ▨ ▨ ◑ Travellers cheques

★ ★ ★ ★ Relais et Château de Montreuil
4 Chaussée des Capucins *62170*
☎ 321815304 FAX 321813643
(Opposite the Roman Citadel)
Château de Montreuil is a family run and privately owned hotel set in beautiful English-style gardens within the walled historic town of Montreuil-sur-Mer, just opposite the Roman Citadel. Only one hour's drive from Calais, it is ideally positioned for a first or last overnight stop or for a weekend break. The restaurant offers an excellent selection of dishes based on a traditional cuisine with a modern touch, whilst in summer lunches are also served in the garden. The individually appointed bedrooms provide elegant accommodation and are equipped with modern day amenities.
In town centre
Closed mid Dec-beg Feb
14 en suite (bth/shr) 3 rooms in annexe (2 fmly) (1 with balcony) TV in all bedrooms STV Direct dial from all bedrooms Licensed Night porter Full central heating Open parking available (charged) Covered parking available (charged) Supervised Child discount available 12yrs Bicycle rental Open terrace Covered terrace Last d 21.30hrs Languages spoken: English
ROOMS: (room only) s 760-910FF; d 810-1010FF
MEALS: Continental breakfast 70FF Lunch fr 200FF&alc Dinner 300-400FF&alc
CARDS: 💳 ▨ ▨ ◑ Travellers cheques

NEUVILLE-EN-FERRAIN Nord

★ ★ ★ Acacias
39 rue du Dronckaert *59960*
☎ 320378927 FAX 320463859
This peaceful establishment is only 30 minutes from the Belgian town of Bruges and ten minutes from Lille. It has comfortable bedrooms with private facilities, which have views of the park, whilst the restaurant enjoys a good reputation locally and serves traditional cuisine with the emphasis on regional specialities.
Forest area Near motorway
42 en suite (bth/shr) (2 fmly) No smoking in 5 bedrooms TV in all bedrooms STV Direct dial from all bedrooms Mini-bar in all bedrooms Licensed Lift Night porter Full central heating Open parking available Covered parking available (charged) Supervised Child discount available 12yrs Solarium Boule Open terrace V meals Last d 22.00hrs Languages spoken: English, German, Dutch
MEALS: Full breakfast 42FF Lunch 73-210FF&alc Dinner 73-210FF&alc✱
CARDS: 💳 ▨ ▨ ◑ Travellers cheques

ORCHIES Nord

★ ★ ★ Manoir
rte de Séclin *59310*
☎ 320646868 FAX 320646869
(Near A23 motorway, 500m from intersection of Orchies, exit 2 towards Seclin)
Pleasantly situated in leafy surroundings the Hotel Le Manoir offers modern facilities and services. The bedroom

accommodation is comfortable and features many little extras such as bathrobes and bathroom essentials. There are two public lounges and a restaurant which offers enjoyable meals served by friendly efficient staff.
Forest area Near motorway
34 en suite (bth/shr) (2 fmly) TV in all bedrooms STV Radio in rooms Direct dial from all bedrooms Mini-bar in all bedrooms Licensed Lift Night porter Full central heating Open parking available Supervised Child discount available Boule Open terrace Last d 22.00hrs Languages spoken: English
Rooms: (room only) s 300-330FF; d 380-380FF
Reductions over 1 night
Meals: Full breakfast 39FF Lunch 75-300FF Dinner 75-300FF
Cards: 💳 🏧 💳 🔟 Travellers cheques

PONT-DE-BRIQUES Pas-de-Calais

★ ★ Hostellerie de La Rivière
17 rue de la gare 62360
☎ 321322281 FAX 321874548
(from Boulogne, take direction of Montreuil/Le Touquet, hotel close to railway station)
A very charming hotel not far from Boulogne. The comfortable bedrooms are decorated in warm pastel colours. In the comfortable restaurant you can savour the cuisine of Mr Martin and his son Dominique and select a wine from the attractive list offered by Mrs Odette Martin.
In town centre Near motorway
Closed 17 Aug-7 Sep
8 en suite (bth/shr) TV in 5 bedrooms Direct dial from all bedrooms Licensed Full central heating Open parking available Child discount available 12yrs Open terrace V meals Last d 21.15hrs Languages spoken: English
Rooms: (room only) s 270-305FF; d 290-320FF
Reductions over 1 night
Meals: Continental breakfast 45FF Lunch fr 160FF&alc Dinner fr 160FF
Cards: 💳 🏧 💳 Travellers cheques

ST-OMER Pas-de-Calais

★ ★ Au Vivier
22 rue Louis Martel 62500
☎ 321957600 FAX 321954220
Despite being located in the busy centre of Saint Omer, the hotel features peaceful guest rooms with modern appointments. Entirely renovated throughout, decorated with good quality furnishings and conveniently situated close to the ferry ports, it provides a pleasant setting for an overnight stop. The restaurant has a varied menu where fresh fish, oysters and seafood take pride of place.
Forest area In town centre Near motorway
7 en suite (bth/shr) (3 fmly) TV in all bedrooms Direct dial from all bedrooms Mini-bar in all bedrooms Licensed Full central heating Open terrace V meals Last d 21.30hrs
Rooms: (room only) s 230FF; d fr 275FF
Meals: Continental breakfast 40FF Lunch 85-240FF Dinner 85-240FF
Cards: 💳 🏧 💳 🔟 Travellers cheques

★ ★ ★ Bretagne
2 pl du Vainquai 62500
☎ 321382578 FAX 321935122
The hotel Le Bretagne opened its doors in 1972 but was then entirely renovated and extended in 1990. Being one of the most popular hotels in the region, it now features modern guest rooms with up-to-date facilities and two restaurants; 'Le

Gastronomique' which serves a refined, classic cuisine, and 'Le Maeva Grill' which offers a choice of tasty meals to suit all palates.
Near river Forest area In town centre
75 en suite (bth/shr) 12 rooms in annexe TV in all bedrooms Direct dial from all bedrooms Licensed Lift Night porter Full central heating Open parking available Supervised Child discount available 12yrs V meals Last d 21.30hrs Languages spoken: English & German
Rooms: (room only) s fr 230FF; d fr 400FF **Reductions over 1 night Special breaks**
Meals: Full breakfast 45FF Lunch fr 160FF&alc Dinner fr 160FF&alc
Cards: 💳 🏧 💳 🔟 Travellers cheques

★ ★ Les Frangins
3 rue Carnot 62500
☎ 321381247 FAX 321987278
Forest area In town centre Near motorway
20 en suite (bth/shr) (1 fmly) No smoking in 2 bedrooms TV in all bedrooms Direct dial from all bedrooms Licensed Lift Full central heating Covered parking available (charged) Child discount available 4yrs Open terrace V meals Last d 22.00hrs Languages spoken: English
Rooms: (room only) s 285FF; d 330FF **Reductions over 1 night**
Meals: Full breakfast 37FF Continental breakfast 37FF Lunch 76-180FF&alc Dinner 76-180FF&alc
Cards: 💳 🏧 💳 🔟 Travellers cheques

SECLIN Nord

★ ★ ★ Auberge Du Forgeron
17 rue Bourvy 59113
☎ 320900952 FAX 320327087
An attractive establishment with cosy, fully equipped bedrooms offering a good level of comfort. Under the impeccable management of Mr and Mrs Belot and their dedicated team, guests are well looked after during the course of their stay. The restaurant is well known for its cuisine which consists of a creative selection of dishes skilfully prepared by the 'patron'.
19 rms (16 shr) TV in all bedrooms Direct dial from all bedrooms Licensed Full central heating Air conditioning in bedrooms Open parking available (charged) Supervised Child discount available Open terrace V meals Last d 21.30hrs Languages spoken: English,German,Spanish
Cards: 💳 🏧 💳 Travellers cheques

TOUQUET-PARIS-PLAGE, LE Pas-de-Calais

Red Fox
Angle rue St-Jean/rue de Metz 62520
☎ 321052758 FAX 321052756
(In town follow signs to 'Centre Ville'. From Boulevard Da Loz turn left into Rue St-Jean)
The hotel and its dedicated staff offer a 'round the clock' welcome to their visitors, and features fully equipped bedrooms, which are attractively decorated and provide a good level of comfort.
Near sea Forest area In town centre Near motorway
48 en suite (bth/shr) (3 fmly) No smoking in 10 bedrooms TV in all bedrooms STV Direct dial from all bedrooms Licensed Lift Night porter Open parking available (charged) Covered parking available (charged) Golf Languages spoken: English
Cards: 💳 🏧 💳 🔟 Travellers cheques

★ ★ Résidence Hippotel
av de l'Hippodrome *62520*
☎ 321050711 FAX 321054488

(from Channel ports take A16 to Etaples (last section due to open Spring 1998) then follow signs for Le Touquet, hotel is signed from the main road leading to Le Touquet)
In peaceful woodlands, a short walk from the town centre and beach. Spacious rooms ideal for couples and families supervised by an English manageress. The restaurant overlooks the park and racecourse.
Near sea Near beach Forest area Near motorway
72 en suite (bth/shr) (72 fmly) (72 with balcony) TV in 50 bedrooms Licensed Night porter Full central heating Open parking available Child discount available 12yrs Bicycle rental Open terrace Languages spoken: English
ROOMS: (room only) s 300-380FF; d 320-400FF
MEALS: Continental breakfast 32FF Lunch 60-80FF Dinner 60-80FF
CARDS: ●● ▆▆ ▆▆ Travellers cheques

★ ★ ★ Westminster Hotel
av du Verger *62520*
☎ 321054848 FAX 321054545
Situated on 'La Côte d'Opale' in the town of Le Touquet, the Hotel Westminster has been a fashionable 'rendez-vous' for high society since the 1930s, and is also nowadays the obvious choice for conventions and social gatherings at any time of the year. It has elegant lounges and delightfully furnished bedrooms with excellent modern amenities. The restaurant serves an outstanding cuisine where equal emphasis is placed on presentation and flavour, and is complemented by a large wine list with a choice of vintage wines.
Near sea Forest area In town centre
Closed 6 Jan-22 Feb
115 en suite (bth/shr) TV in all bedrooms STV Radio in rooms Direct dial from all bedrooms Mini-bar in all bedrooms Licensed Lift Night porter Full central heating Open parking available Child discount available Indoor swimming pool (heated) Tennis Riding Sauna Pool table Mini-golf Jacuzzi/spa Bicycle rental Open terrace
Languages spoken: English
ROOMS: (room only) s 580-1050FF; d 680-1150FF
✻ Reductions over 1 night
CARDS: ●● ▆▆ ▆▆ ●● Travellers cheques

Taking your mobile phone to France?
See page 11

90

TOURNEHEM-SUR-LA-HEM Pas-de-Calais

★ ★ Bal Parc Hotel
500 rue de Vieux Chateau *62890*
☎ 321356590 FAX 321351857
(A26 exit 2 or N43 then D218 or D217)
Situated just 7 minutes from Calais, the hotel offers a peaceful stay, and is (because of its convenient location) an ideal venue for those who require an overnight stop on the way to further destinations. The sound-proofed rooms are equipped with every modern amenity whilst tennis and miniature golf can be found nearby.
Near river Near lake Near sea Near beach Forest area Near motorway
26 en suite (bth/shr) TV in all bedrooms Direct dial from all bedrooms Licensed Night porter Full central heating Air conditioning in bedrooms Open parking available Tennis Mini-golf Languages spoken: English
ROOMS: (room only) s fr 205FF; d 205-225FF
MEALS: Full breakfast 25FF Continental breakfast 25FF Lunch fr 75FF&alc Dinner fr 75FF&alc
CARDS: ●● ▆▆ ▆▆ ●● Travellers cheques

VALENCIENNES Nord

★ ★ ★ Auberge Du Bon Fermier
64-66 r de Famars *59300*
☎ 37466825 FAX 327466825
Feel the history and enjoy the secrets of regional cuisine in an authentic 17th century setting. Dating back to to 1560 the building became an inn in 1840 and is classified as an historic monument. Painstakingly restored by its owners, Auberge du Bon Fermier is full of atmosphere, with oak floors and beams, and sparkling copper and pewterware. Bedrooms are stylish with modern comforts tastefully incorporated. In the restaurant, there is old-fashioned cooking over a wood fire, meat and game cooked on a spit, lobster from the tank and fresh fish.
In town centre
16 en suite (bth/shr) TV in all bedrooms STV Direct dial from all bedrooms Mini-bar in all bedrooms Licensed Night porter Full central heating Open parking available Covered parking available (charged) Supervised V meals Last d 22.30hrs Languages spoken: English & German
ROOMS: (room only) s 480-600FF; d 530-700FF
MEALS: Full breakfast 45FF Lunch 120-350FF&alc Dinner 120-350FF&alc
CARDS: ●● ▆▆ ▆▆ ●●

WIERRE-EFFROY Pas-de-Calais

★ ★ ★ Ferme du Vert
rte du Paon *62720*
☎ 321876700 FAX 321832262
(between Calais & Boulogne, leave A16 at Marquise to town centre and follow signs for "Ferme du Vert")
Forest area Near motorway
Closed mid Dec-mid Jan
15 en suite (bth/shr) (3 fmly) TV in all bedrooms Direct dial from all bedrooms Mini-bar in 4 bedrooms Licensed Full central heating Open parking available Child discount available 12yrs Bicycle rental Last d 21.00hrs
ROOMS: (room only) s 300-450FF; d 340-580FF
Reductions over 1 night
MEALS: Full breakfast 50FF Dinner 135-210FF
CARDS: ●● ▆▆ ▆▆ Travellers cheques

WIMEREUX Pas-de-Calais

★ ★ **Centre**
78 rue Carnot *62930*
☎ 321324108 FAX 321338248
(From Calais via A16 exit 'Wimereux Nord' follow signs for
'Centre Ville')
Family-run hotel situated in the centre of town yet very close
to the seafront. Rooms are functional and comfortable while
the restaurant serves a variety of dishes but specialises in
seafood. An ideal place to stay for a seaside-based holiday.
Near sea In town centre Near motorway
25 en suite (bth/shr) (5 fmly) TV in all bedrooms Direct dial
from all bedrooms Licensed Full central heating Open
parking available (charged) Covered parking available
(charged) Supervised Child discount available 3yrs Open
terrace Last d 21.30hrs Languages spoken: English
ROOMS: (room only) s 235-280FF; d 260-320FF ✱
MEALS: Continental breakfast 35FF Lunch 98-170FF&alc
Dinner 98-170FF&alc
CARDS: ●● ⚏ Travellers cheques

Picardy

France was said to have been born in Picardy. The region has been a crossroads of history and there is much to discover here, from ancient times through to the present day. The easily accessible capital, Amiens, is an action-packed city which has successfully married a rich heritage and impressive buildings with 20th-century innovations: elegant modern architecture and a lively contemporary arts scene have been sensitively integrated with the past. Take time to leave the motorways, you will be surprised and rewarded, not to mention seduced by the Picardy cuisine.

(Bottom): The waterfront at Amiens, the capital of Picardy, built on the banks of the Somme.

(Top): This quaint doorway is in the village of Gerberoy which was restored by a community of artists in the 19th century.

ESSENTIAL FACTS

DÉPARTEMENTS:	Aisne, Oise, Somme
PRINCIPAL TOWNS	Amiens, Beauvais, Abbeville, Noyon, Compiègne, St-Quentin, Soissons, Château-Thierry.
PLACES TO VISIT:	The cathedrals of Amiens and Beauvais; the battlefields and millitary cemeteries of the Somme; the sandy beaches and conservation areas in the Somme estuary.
REGIONAL TOURIST OFFICE	12, rue Chapeau de Violettes, Amiens Tel: 22 91 79 28 1; place de l'Admiral Courbet, 80100 AbbevilleTel: 22 24 27 92
LOCAL GASTRONOMIC DELIGHTS	Eels in a variety of guises: beer, smoked and as a pâté; duck pâté; delicious melting macaroons from Amiens; sauterelles, grey shrimps caught off the Picardy coast; savoury stuffed pancakes; gateau battu; mussels reared on farms in Marquenterre; lamb with a distinctive flavour due to salt marsh grazing methods
DRINKS	Locally produced cider; red berry spirits; top-fermented ales and of course, champagne.
LOCAL CRAFTS WHAT TO BUY	Pottery from the Pays de Bray; lace and tapestries are on sale throughout the region, huge selection of pastel paintings locally produced.

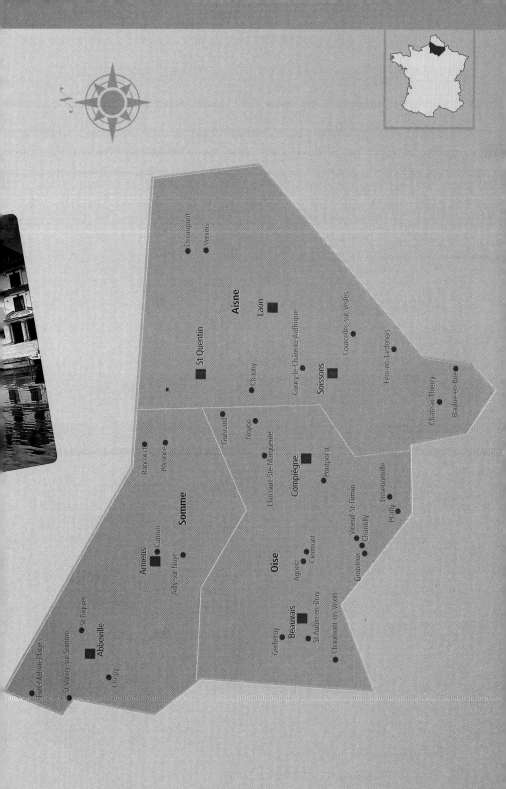

Étréaupont
Vervins

Aisne
Laon

St Quentin

Chauny

Courcy-le-Château-Auffique
Courcelles-sur-Vesles

Soissons

Fère-en-Tardenois

Château-Thierry
Baulne-en-Brie

Guiscard

Noyon

Rancourt
Péronne

Élincourt-Ste-Marguerite

Compiègne
Pontpoint

Somme

Ermenonville

Vineuil-St-Firmin
Chantilly

Clairoix
Gouvieux
Pailly

Oise

Camon

Ailly-sur-Noye

Amiens

Agnetz
Clermont

St Riquier

Abbeville

St Valéry-sur-Somme
Chepy

Fort-Mahon-Plage

Gerberoy

Beauvais
St Aubin-en-Bray
Chaumont-en-Vexin

93

EVENTS & FESTIVALS:

Mar St-Quentin Comic Book Festival; Beauvais Festival of Wildlife Films; Laon International Children's Film Festival

Apr Abbeville Bird Film Festival; St Aubin en Bray Dance Festival; Compiègne Lily of the Valley Festival

May Compiègne Joan of Arc Festival; Amiens Jazz Festival; Amiens Carnival; Chaumont-en Vexin Music Festival; Camon Festival of the Moors; Compiègne International Horse Show; St-Quentin Jesters' Festival

Jun Verneuil-en-Halatte Rock Festival; Doullens Gardening Days in the Citadelle; Amiens Town Festival; Château-Thierry 'Jean de la Fontaine' Festival (entertainment based on the fables, procession, fireworks); Coucy-le-Château Medieval Festival; Chantilly Horse Racing; St-Valéry sur Somme William the Conqueror Festival; Gerberoy Rose Festival; Beauvais 'Jeanne Hachette' Festival (commemorating the town's resistance in 1472)

Jul Guiscard, Noyonnais Son et Lumière Festival; Pierrefonds Festival; St-Michel-en-Tiérache, Holy, Ancient & Baroque Music Festival; Noyon Red Fruits Festival; Laon 'Promenades au crepuscule' (visits & entertainment); St Riquier Classical Music Festival

Aug Laon Music and Monuments; Ailly sur Noye Son et Lumière

Sep Amiens Water Festival; La Capelle International Cheese Festival; Ailly sur Noye Son et Lumière; Guise Festival at the Castle; throughout Picardy 'Festival of the Cathedrals' (classical & choral music); Pontpoint Jazz in Moncel Abbey; Laon French Music Festival

Oct Oise Classical Music Festival; Versigny Plant Fair

Nov Amiens International Film Festival

Dec Chantilly, 'Christmas, the horse and the child' (riding show in costume at the Living Museum of the Horse)

Home of the Impressionist Movement

The visual intensity of Picardy's scenery has inspired many artists; particularly those of the Impressionist movement, which has its roots here. The light Claude Monet discovered in Giverny so impressed him that he lived there for most of his life. You can enjoy the collection of Japanese prints exhibited in his house, then stroll in the sun-filled gardens which inspired so many of his pictures. Walk across the Japanese-style wooden bridge and you can almost imagine yourself in one of his famous water lily paintings.

AGNETZ Oise

★ ★ Le Clermotel
N31, Zone Hotelière 60600
☎ 344500990 FAX 344501300
(take Agnetz exit from A1 in the direction of Creil Puis Amiens Hotel on N31 on L'Axe Reims to Rouen in the Zone Hotelliere)
The Hotel Clermotel has been built in contemporary motel-style and is a peaceful haven situated in the countryside on the edge of the magnificent Fôret de Hez. The bedrooms, restaurant, bar and four fully-equipped conference rooms are all on ground-floor level. The restaurant serves a combination of innovative and regional dishes. There is a variety of leisure facilities available to suit everyone.
Near river Forest area Near motorway
37 en suite (bth/shr) (4 fmly) No smoking in 2 bedrooms TV in all bedrooms Direct dial from all bedrooms Licensed Full central heating Open parking available Child discount available 10yrs Tennis Boule Bicycle rental Open terrace Ping pong,Volley ball V meals Last d 22.00hrs Languages spoken: English & German
ROOMS: (room only) s 262-267FF; d 297-302FF
Reductions over 1 night Special breaks
ROOMS: (room only) s 270-305FF; d 290-320FF
MEALS: Full breakfast 37FF Lunch 94-151 FF&alc
Dinner 94-151FF
CARDS: ♥ ▦ ▱ Travellers cheques

AMIENS Somme

★ ★ ★ Grand Hotel de l'Univers (Best Western)
2 rue de Noyon 80000
☎ 322915251 FAX 322928166
(in the village centre 150m from La Gare)
In the heart of Amiens between the station and its great Cathedral stands the Grand Hotel De L'Univers, a homely establishment offering basic yet attractive rooms. Visitors will experience traditional French hospitality from the attentive and friendly staff. Light meals are available, and there are well-equipped function rooms.
In town centre Near motorway
41 rms (25 bth 15 shr) TV in all bedrooms STV Direct dial from all bedrooms Mini-bar in all bedrooms Licensed Lift Night porter Full central heating Child discount available 12yrs Languages spoken: English Italian & Spanish
CARDS: ♥ ▦ ▱ ♪ Travellers cheques

★ ★ Vidéotel
rue le Greco, Zac Vallée St-Iadre 80085
☎ 322520404 FAX 322449495
(From A16 exit 'Amiens Nord', take Amiens-Arras road and follow signs for 'Amiens Centre' and 'Centre Commercial Continent')
The hotels in the Videotel group all have bedrooms with pleasant furnishings and are equipped with the comfort of their clientele in mind. The restaurants serve a good quality gourmet cuisine with a range of prix-fixe menus, regional specialities and 'eat your fill buffet'. The management couples and their dedicated teams offer a 'round the clock' efficient service, where the well-being and satisfaction of guests is the prime consideration.
Near motorway

Taking your mobile phone to France?
See page 11

44 en suite (bth/shr) (26 fmly) No smoking in 8 bedrooms TV in all bedrooms Direct dial from all bedrooms Licensed Full central heating Open parking available Supervised Child discount available 12yrs Open terrace V meals Last d 22.00hrs Languages spoken: English & German

ROOMS: (room only) d 280FF ✱
MEALS: Full breakfast 34FF Lunch 52-88FF&alc Dinner 52-88FF&alc✱
CARDS: ●● ■■ ══ ⑩ Travellers cheques

ARGOULES Somme

★ ★ **Auberge le Gros Tilleul**
pl du Chateau *80120*
☎ 322299100 FAX 322239164
(from Calais or Boulogne take N1 or A16 in the direction

Montreuil/Mer-Abbeville to Nampout-St-Martin turn left in direction Argoules)
The Beugé family welcomes you warmly to their auberge, nestling in the village of Argoules amid the quiet beauty of the Authie valley. It is full of country charm, with small but pretty beamed bedrooms and a rustic dining room in which to enjoy the traditional country cooking.
Near river Forest area Near motorway
RS Monday
15 en suite (bth/shr) (3 fmly) TV in all bedrooms STV Direct dial from all bedrooms Mini-bar in 5 bedrooms Licensed Night porter Full central heating Open parking available (charged) Child discount available 10yrs Outdoor swimming pool (heated) Solarium Boule Bicycle rental Covered terrace Last d 21.00hrs Languages spoken: English & Spanish
ROOMS: (room only) s 350-450FF; d 540-580FF **Special breaks**
MEALS: Full breakfast 45FF Continental breakfast 38FF Lunch 75-195FF&alc Dinner 50-180FFalc✱
CARDS: ●● ■■ ══ ⑩ Travellers cheques

BAULNE-EN-BRIE Aisne

★ ★ **Auberge de l'Omois**
Grande rue *02330*
☎ 323820813 FAX 323826988
This small country inn is situated amidst the extensive vineyards of the Champagne region. It offers comfortable accommodation with modern amenities and provides a good base from which to explore the surroundings.
Near river Forest area Near motorway
7 en suite (bth/shr) Licensed Night porter Full central heating Open parking available Supervised Child discount available Tennis Fishing Riding Boule Bicycle rental Open terrace Wkly live entertainment V meals Last d 22.00hrs Languages spoken: English
MEALS: Full breakfast 35FF Lunch 100-158FF&alc Dinner 58-95FFalc✱
CARDS: ●● ■■ ══ ⑩ Travellers cheques

BEAUVAIS Oise

★ ★ ★ **Chenal Hotel**
63 blvd du Général de Gaulle *60000*
☎ 344060460 FAX 344485517
Located in the heart of the commercial, industrial & business centre of Beauvais, the hotel offers comfortable accommodation and attentive service.
Forest area In town centre Near motorway
29 en suite (bth/shr) 8 rooms in annexe (3 fmly) (3 with balcony) No smoking in 7 bedrooms TV in all bedrooms STV Direct dial from all bedrooms Licensed Lift Night porter Full central heating Open parking available Supervised Languages spoken: English & Spanish
ROOMS: (room only) s 260-310FF; d 320-400FF
CARDS: ●● ■■ ══

★ ★ ★ **Hostellerie St-Vincent**
rue de Clermont *60000*
☎ 344054999 FAX 344055294
In the heart of a lush green valley, the hotel offers spacious, well-equipped bedrooms, some with jacuzzis and some suitable for the disabled. Traditional and creative cuisine is offered with personal service.
48 en suite (bth/shr) (2 fmly) No smoking in 10 bedrooms TV in all bedrooms Direct dial from all bedrooms Licensed Night porter Full central heating Open parking available Child discount available 10yrs Open terrace V meals Last d 22.00hrs Languages spoken: English
ROOMS: (room only) s 298FF; d 298FF **Reductions over 1 night**
MEALS: Full breakfast 37FF Lunch 75-180FF&alc Dinner 75-180FF&alc

CHANTILLY Oise

★ ★ ★ **Hotel du Parc** (Best Western)
36 av Maréchal Joffe *60500*
☎ 344582000 FAX 344573110
(From A1(Paris to Lille)exit 8 (Senlis), follow signs for Chantilly, approx 10kms)
Situated in wooded grounds in the town centre of Chantilly and equipped with a range of facilities, the hotel offers excellent accommodation for both commercial and leisure guests. It features a well-stocked bar, individually appointed, spacious bedrooms offering a high level of comfort, and a large lounge where a comprehensive American-style breakfast is served.
Located just a few steps away from the race course   *contd.*

with its magnificent 18th-century stables, it provides a suitable setting for a visit to this charming town.
Forest area In town centre Near motorway 58 en suite (bth/shr) (4 fmly) (12 with balcony) No smoking in 25 bedrooms TV in 52 bedrooms STV Direct dial from 52 bedrooms Licensed Lift Night porter Full central heating Open parking available (charged) Covered parking available (charged) Supervised Child discount available 12yrs Bicycle rental Open terrace Wkly live entertainment Languages spoken: English, German, Portuguese
CARDS: ●● ██ ▓▓ ⑨ Travellers cheques

CHAUMONT-EN-VEXIN Oise

★ ★ **La Grange de St-Nicolas**
17 rue de la République *60240*
☎ 344491100 FAX 344499997
This motel-style hotel used to be a coaching inn but now offers restful accommodation away from the main road. The bedrooms are well equipped and have good quality beds with country-style furniture. There is a restaurant and an interesting 'gourmet' shop selling fine wines, patés and gift baskets.
Near river Forest area In town centre Near motorway RS 20 Dec-5 Jan
11 en suite (bth/shr) (8 fmly) TV in all bedrooms STV Direct dial from all bedrooms Mini-bar in 6 bedrooms Full c/heating Open parking available Supervised Child discount available 16yrs V meals Last d 21.30hrs Languages spoken: English
ROOMS: (room only) s 250FF; d 280FF **Special breaks: Golf Club/weekends Oct-Mar**
MEALS: Continental breakfast 30FF Lunch 62-98FF&alc Dinner 62-98FF&alc
CARDS: ●● ██ ▓▓ ⑨ Travellers cheques

CHAUNY Aisne

★ ★ ★ **La Toque Blanche**
24 av Victor Hugo *02300*
☎ 323399898 FAX 323523279
Véronique and Vincent Lequeux are the charming hosts in this attractive establishment. This 'home from home' is set in a large park and offers individually and tastefully furnished bedrooms with private facilities, three cosy lounges and a restaurant where guests are served subtly flavoured dishes which are both inventive and generous.
In town centre
Closed 1-12 Jan, 15-23 Feb & 2-24 Aug
6 en suite (bth/shr) No smoking in 2 bedrooms TV in all bedrooms Direct dial from all bedrooms Mini-bar in all bedrooms Licensed Full central heating Open parking available Tennis Last d 21.00hrs Languages spoken: English
ROOMS: (room only) d 310-480FF
MEALS: Full breakfast 60FF Continental breakfast 60FF Lunch 170-390FF&alc Dinner 170-390FF&alc
CARDS: ●● ▓▓ Travellers cheques

CHEPY Somme

★ ★ **Auberge Picarde**
pl de la Gare *80210*
☎ 322262078 FAX 322263334
The contemporary Auberge Picarde is located in the open countryside, just a stone's throw away from the shores of the Channel. The hotel is a popular venue with business travellers and holiday makers alike, and has personalised bedrooms with up-to-date modern facilities. The bright, comfortable lounge and terrace offer good relaxation, whilst the billiard room

provides pleasant entertainment. The light, refined cuisine is skilfully prepared by the chef Alain Henocque and incorporates fresh market produce.
Near motorway
Closed 16-25 Aug & 26 Dec-4 Jan
25 en suite (bth/shr) (3 fmly) TV in all bedrooms Direct dial from all bedrooms Licensed Full central heating Open parking available Sauna Pool table Open terrace V meals Last d 21.00hrs
ROOMS: (room only) s 230-360FF; d 255-385FF ✱
MEALS: Full breakfast 30FF Lunch 85-185FF&alc Dinner 85-185FF&alc✱
CARDS: ●● ██ ▓▓ Travellers cheques

COURCELLES-SUR-VESLES Aisne

★ ★ ★ ★ **Château de Courcelles**
02220
☎ 323741353 FAX 323740641
Surrounded by a splendid park containing a formal French garden, this handsome building dates back to 1690 and has been patronised by some eminent visitors over the years. The guest accommodation offers spacious bedrooms with high quality furniture which are decorated with well co-ordinating fabrics and shades. The restaurant serves a fine cuisine with a choice of dishes incorporating delicious ingredients from the region.
Forest area
14 en suite (bth/shr) (1 with balcony) TV in all bedrooms Licensed Full central heating Open parking available Supervised Outdoor swimming pool (heated) Tennis Fishing Sauna Bicycle rental Open terrace Covered terrace 3 jogging circuits Last d 21.30hrs Languages spoken: English
MEALS: Full breakfast 85FF Lunch 230-360FF&alc Dinner 230-360FF&alc✱
CARDS: ●● ██ ▓▓ Travellers cheques

ÉLINCOURT-STE-MARGUERITE Oise

★ ★ ★ ★ **Château de Bellinglise**
rte de Lassigny *60157*
☎ 344960033 FAX 344960300
(A1 exit 11, D82 to Ressons sur Matz, then D15)
Each of the guest rooms in this enchanting establishment is individually styled and offers a very high standard of accommodation. The exquisite fabrics and furnishing, and luxurious bathrooms are second to none, whilst the interior of the building is a maze of secret rooms and winding staircases. Wood panelling, chandeliers, and an open fireplace create a warm atmosphere in the restaurant, where traditional cuisine offers an innovative combination of delicate flavours and first-class ingredients.
Near river Near lake Forest area
45 en suite (bth) 10 rooms in annexe (1 fmly) (4 with balcony) TV in all bedrooms Direct dial from all bedrooms Mini-bar in all bedrooms Licensed Lift Night porter Full central heating Open parking available Child discount available 12yrs Tennis Fishing Pool table Boule Bicycle rental Open terrace Table tennis, Volley ball Last d 21.00hrs Languages spoken: English German & Spanish
CARDS: ●● ██ ▓▓ ⑨ Travellers cheques

ERMENONVILLE Oise

★ ★ **Hotel de la Croix d'Or**
2 rue Prince *60950*
☎ 344540004 FAX 344540544
Situated near Parc Astérix and EuroDisney, this hotel provides the ideal venue for a restful stay. It features rustic decor

throughout, and offers pleasant bedrooms with modern amenities, an attractive garden and a wonderful restaurant.
Near river Near lake Forest area In town centre Near motorway
Closed late Dec-late Jan
8 en suite (bth/shr) (1 fmly) TV in all bedrooms Licensed Full central heating Open parking available No children Last d 21.00hrs Languages spoken: English
MEALS: Continental breakfast 30FF Lunch 95-175FF&alc Dinner 95-175FF&alc✱
CARDS: 😑 💳 Travellers cheques

ÉTRÉAUPONT Aisne

★ ★ Le Clos du Montvinage
8 rue Albert Ledent *02580*
☎ 323974018 FAX 323974892
(5m N of Vervius via N2)
This delightful hotel, created from a late 19th century mansion, is in the heart of the Thierache region close to the Belgian border.
Near river Near motorway
Closed seasonal holidays
20 en suite (bth/shr) TV in all bedrooms STV Direct dial from all bedrooms Licensed Night porter Full central heating Open parking available Child discount available 12yrs Tennis V meals Last d 21.15hrs Languages spoken: English
ROOMS: (room only) s 290-445FF; d 340-500FF
Reductions over 1 night Special breaks
MEALS: Continental breakfast 40FF Lunch 92-225FF&alc Dinner 92-225FF&alc
CARDS: 😑 💳 💳 🌐

FÈRE-EN-TARDENOIS Aisne

★ ★ ★ ★ Château de Fére
rte de Fismes *02130*
☎ 323822113 FAX 323823781
This imposing mansion stands in 66 hectares of woodlands and features an elegant interior incorporating several dining rooms and sophisticated public areas. Every bedrooms has its own individual style, and carefully blends with the architecture of the building. The imaginative cuisine offers a selection of creative dishes carefully prepared by Christophe Turquier.
Near lake Forest area
Closed mid Jan-mid Feb
25 rms (24 bth) (6 fmly) TV in all bedrooms Mini-bar in all bedrooms Licensed Night porter Full central heating Open parking available Supervised Outdoor swimming pool (heated) Tennis Boule Bicycle rental Open terrace Last d 21.30hrs Languages spoken: English
CARDS: 😑 💳 💳 🌐 Travellers cheques

FORT-MAHON-PLAGE Somme

★ ★ ★ Hotel de la Terrasse
1461 av de la Plage *80790*
☎ 322233777 FAX 322233674
Overlooking the sea, the hotel offers refined comfort in pleasant bedrooms. The restaurant is an invitation to enjoy specialities
Near sea Near beach
56 en suite (bth/shr) (2 fmly) (24 with balcony) TV in all bedrooms Direct dial from all bedrooms Licensed Lift Full central heating Open parking available (charged) Covered parking available (charged) Supervised V meals Last d 21.30hrs
ROOMS: (room only) s 200-450FF; d 200-450FF
MEALS: Continental breakfast 45FF Lunch 120-250FF Dinner 75-295FF&alc
CARDS: 😑 💳 💳 🌐 Travellers cheques

GOUVIEUX Oise

★ ★ ★ Château de la Tour
ch de la Chaussée *60270*
☎ 344570739 FAX 344573197
This magnificent turn-of-the century mansion is set in an elevated position overlooking the forest. A warm welcome awaits visitors to this splendid mansion, which features guest rooms with excellent amenities and a splendid restaurant serving a good choice of outstanding dishes. Guests may want to retire after dinner to one the elegant lounges which are furnished with period pieces and rich fabrics.
Forest area
41 en suite (bth/shr) (2 fmly) TV in all bedrooms STV Licensed Night porter Open parking available Child discount available 12yrs Outdoor swimming pool (heated) Tennis Pool table Open terrace Last d 21.30hrs Languages spoken: English,German
MEALS: Full breakfast 65FF Lunch 195-290FF&alc Dinner 195-290FF&alc✱
CARDS: 😑 💳 💳 🌐 Travellers cheques

LAON Aisne

★ ★ ★ Hotel de la Banniere de France
11 rue Franklin Roosevelt *02000*
☎ 323232144 FAX 323233156
(A26 exit 13 follow signs to Ville Haute, hotel clearly signed)
Original posting inn dating from 1685, a traditional hotel in the best sense. Comfortable bedrooms and an attractive restaurant serving classic cuisine. On the direct motorway route two hours from Calais, the hotel has the advantage of garage parking. Within easy reach of Reims and Epernay.
In town centre
Closed 20 Dec-20 Jan & 1 May
18 rms (16 bth/shr) (6 fmly) TV in all bedrooms STV Direct dial from all bedrooms Licensed Full central heating Open parking available (charged) Covered parking available (charged) Supervised Child discount available V meals Last d 21.30hrs Languages spoken: English & Spanish
ROOMS: (room only) s 230-255FF; d 310-385FF
Reductions over 1 night
MEALS: Continental breakfast 42FF Lunch 120-320FF&alc Dinner 120-320FF&alc
CARDS: 😑 💳 💳 🌐 Travellers cheques

NOYON Oise

★ ★ Le Cèdre
8 rue de l'Evêché *60400*
☎ 344442324 FAX 344095379
(A1 exit 12)

contd.

In the shadow of Noyon's imposing cathedral, Le Cèdre is an ideal setting from which to discover the treasures of this city and the delights of Picardy.
Forest area In town centre Near motorway
34 en suite (bth/shr) TV in all bedrooms STV Direct dial from all bedrooms Licensed Night porter Full central heating Open parking available Supervised Child discount available 5yrs Bicycle rental Open terrace Billiards V meals Last d 21.30hrs Languages spoken: English
ROOMS: (room only) s 290FF; d 350FF **Reductions over 1 night Special breaks**
MEALS: Full breakfast 38FF Lunch 80-130FF&alc Dinner 80-130FF&alc
CARDS: 💳 🏧 💳 Travellers cheques

PÉRONNE Somme

★ ★ **Hostellerie des Remparts**
21 rue Beaubois *80200*
☎ 322840122 FAX 322843196

(A1/A2 exit Maurepas & take direction of Peronne, approx 5km)
Tucked away in the ramparts of the old town, the hotel provides comfortably en suite bedrooms. An excellent restaurant offers both fixed price and à la carte menu.
Near lake In town centre Near motorway
16 en suite (bth/shr) (4 fmly) TV in all bedrooms STV Direct dial from all bedrooms Licensed Night porter Full central heating Open parking available Covered parking available (charged) Supervised Child discount available 12yrs Fishing Riding Bicycle rental Open terrace V meals Last d 21.30hrs Languages spoken: English
ROOMS: (room only) s 220FF; d 280FF **Reductions over 1 night Special breaks**
MEALS: Continental breakfast 35FF Lunch 90-280FF&alc Dinner 95-280FF&alc
CARDS: 💳 🏧 💳 💳 Travellers cheques

PLAILLY Oise

★ ★ **Auberge du Petit Cheval d'Or**
rue de Paris *60128*
☎ 344543633 FAX 344543802
(leave A1 exit 7/Survilliers in direction of Ermenonville)
The hotel is in peaceful surroundings. Of the 27 rooms seven are spacious and the rest whilst small contain every comfort. In summer you may dine in the garden in the shadow of magnolias and weeping willows, whilst in winter the dining room with its rustic charm and comfortable decoration is welcoming. The chef offers different menus of traditional, carefully prepared dishes, and a generous list of wines is

available to complement the meal.
Forest area Near motorway
27 rms (25 bth/shr) (6 fmly) (1 with balcony) TV in all bedrooms Direct dial from all bedrooms Mini-bar in 12 bedrooms Licensed Lift Full central heating Open parking available Child discount available 12yrs Boule Bicycle rental Open terrace Last d 22.00hrs Languages spoken: English
ROOMS: (room only) s 180-600FF; d 210-600FF ✱
MEALS: Full breakfast 58FF Continental breakfast 36FF Lunch 110-150FF Dinner 110-150FF&alc✱
CARDS: 💳 🏧 💳 💳 Travellers cheques

RANCOURT Somme

★ ★ **Prieure**
RN 17 *80360*
☎ 322850443 FAX 322850669
Near motorway
27 en suite (bth/shr) (6 fmly) No smoking in 2 bedrooms TV in all bedrooms STV Licensed Night porter Full central heating Open parking available Supervised Child discount available 12yrs Tennis V meals Languages spoken: English,German,Italian
MEALS: Full breakfast 35FF Lunch 99-240FF&alc✱

ST-QUENTIN Aisne

★ ★ ★ **Hotel des Canonniers**
15 rue des Canonniers *02100*
☎ 323628787 FAX 323628786
(From A25 or A1 follow signs 'Centre Ville')
Situated in a quiet street, and just a few steps away from the town centre, this former private residence dates back to the 18th century. Bought in 1990 and renovated throughout by the present owners, it has the atmosphere of a private house with the added convenience of attentive service. Elegant lounges are decorated with fine period furniture and rich fabrics, there are splendid suites, and bedrooms with ancient exposed beams which are mostly situated in the old attic. In addition there is a small shaded park for relaxation.
In town centre Near motorway
Closed 2nd & 3rd weeks Aug
9 en suite (bth/shr) (4 fmly) (1 with balcony) TV in all bedrooms STV Direct dial from all bedrooms Mini-bar in all bedrooms Licensed Night porter Full central heating Open parking available Supervised Pool table Open terrace V meals Languages spoken: English & German
ROOMS: (room only) s 260-420FF; d 280-650FF
Reductions over 1 night
CARDS: 💳 🏧 💳 💳

★ ★ ★ **Le Grand Hotel**
6 rue Dachery *02100*
☎ 323626977 FAX 323625352
The hotel is set in the heart of St Quentin in Upper Picardy, also known as the land of the roses. It features a stylish interior, and has attentive staff who provide a discreet, but dedicated service. The pleasant bedrooms have superb facilities and are decorated with well-matching fabrics and shades. Guests can take their breakfast in the intimacy of their room or in the lounge with views of the flower-filled patio. With its fully equipped conference room, it is also a suitable venue for business. In addition, the restaurant offers excellent cuisine, accompanied by a fine wine list.
In town centre
24 en suite (bth/shr) (2 fmly) TV in all bedrooms STV Radio in rooms Direct dial from all bedrooms Mini-bar in all bedrooms

Licensed Lift Night porter Full central heating Open parking available Supervised Child discount available 10yrs V meals Last d 22.00hrs Languages spoken: English German Italian & Spanish
MEALS: Full breakfast 60FF Lunch fr 180FF&alc Dinner fr 180FF&alc✱
CARDS: ✹ ▦ ☎ ☺ Travellers cheques

★ ★ **Hotel de la Paix et Albert 1er**
3 pl du 8-Octobre *02100*
☎ 323627762 FAX 323625352
In the centre of St Quentin, this hotel offers charming regional accommodation and a restaurant with fixed price and à la carte menu.
Near river Near lake Forest area In town centre Near motorway
52 en suite (bth/shr) (4 fmly) TV in all bedrooms STV Direct dial from all bedrooms Mini-bar in all bedrooms Licensed Lift Night porter Full central heating Open parking available Covered parking available Supervised Child discount available 12yrs V meals Last d 0.45hrs Languages spoken: English & Spanish
ROOMS: (incl. full-board) s 200-280FF; d 280-310FF
MEALS: Full breakfast 38FF Continental breakfast 38FF Lunch 98-160FF&alc Dinner 98-160FF&alc
CARDS: ✹ ▦ ☎ ☺ Travellers cheques

ST-RIQUIER Somme

★ ★ ★ **Jean de Bruges**
18 pl de l'Église *80135*
☎ 322283030 FAX 322280069
(from Calais/Paris motorway exit Abbeville and take D925 in the direction Saint-Riquier)

This splendid 17th-century mansion is situated in a traffic-free area near the abbey in Saint-Riquier. Completely renovated and brought back to its former splendour, the hotel welcomes its visitors in a cosy, almost serene atmosphere. It features tastefully furnished bedrooms with modern facilities as well as an intimate lounge and bar.
Near river Near sea Forest area In town centre Near motorway
Closed Jan
8 en suite (bth/shr) (2 fmly) No smoking in 1 bedroom TV in all bedrooms Direct dial from all bedrooms Mini-bar in all bedrooms Licensed Lift Night porter Full central heating Open parking available Covered parking available (charged) Tennis Covered terrace V meals Last d 21.00hrs Languages spoken: English, Dutch & German

ROOMS: (room only) s 400-500FF; d 500-600FF
MEALS: Full breakfast 60FF Continental breakfast 60FF Lunch 40-80FFalc Dinner 40-80FFalc
CARDS: ✹ ▦ ☎ Travellers cheques

VERVINS Aisne

★ ★ ★ **Tour Du Roy**
45 rue Général Leclerc *02140*
☎ 323980011 FAX 323980072
This handsome manor house was the historic setting for the announcement of Henry IV 's ascencion to the throne, and welcomed also in later years many eminent heads of state. Stained-glass windows and hand-painted bathrooms are just a few of the features which make this a lovely venue to spend an overnight stop or extended break. Fully renovated, the bedrooms have fine views of the terraces, park and landscaped square, and are equipped with modern facilities. The cuisine consists of a choice of skilfully executed dishes by chef Annie Desvignes, which are served in the elegant restaurant.
Near lake Forest area In town centre Near motorway
18 en suite (bth/shr) 3 rooms in annexe (4 fmly) (2 with balcony) No smoking in 2 bedrooms TV in all bedrooms STV Mini-bar in 17 bedrooms Licensed Full central heating Open parking available Supervised Child discount available 12yrs Open terrace V meals Last d 21.30hrs Languages spoken: English
CARDS: ✹ ▦ ☎ ☺ Travellers cheques

VINEUIL-ST-FIRMIN Oise

★ ★ ★ **Golf Hotel Blue-Green**
rte d'Apremont *60500*
☎ 344584777 FAX 344585011

(A1 exit Chantilly, follow signs until you arrive at Château de Chantilly)
In the heart of the beautiful forest of Chantilly, just 40km north of Paris, this elegant hotel with its own golf course offers a complete change of enviroment in a magnificent setting. Every effort is made to ensure your stay is enjoyable.
Forest area Near motorway
111 en suite (bth/shr) TV in all bedrooms STV Direct dial from all bedrooms Mini-bar in all bedrooms Licensed Lift Night porter Full central heating Open parking available Child discount available 12yrs Golf 18 Tennis Bicycle rental Covered terrace Archery Table tennis Volleyball Last d 22.00hrs Languages spoken: English
ROOMS: (room only) s 710-1100FF; d 710-1100FF **Special breaks: Golf**
MEALS: Full breakfast 80FF Lunch 130FF Dinner 200FF
CARDS: ✹ ▦ ☎ ☺

Champagne-Ardenne

The region of Champagne-Ardenne is world famous for its wine and it is worth taking the opportunity to visit one of the many vineyards to gain an insight into how the emperor of celebratory wines is made. Champagne-Ardenne offers a huge variety of sights and attractions that a short break or longer holiday can be enjoyed at any time of year. Stretching from the Belgian border, and not an onerous drive from Calais, this region has all the assets for an ideal family destination: active holidays amidst protected countryside with wonderful food and traditions rooted in a landscape steeped in history. Champagne-Ardenne is a region of variety and many pleasures, but beware, the sampling the rich history of gastronomy could put pressure on your waistline after a visit here.

(Top): The impressive interior of a church at St-Amand-sur-Fion.

(Bottom): An atmospheric scene from the Mercier Champagne catacombs in Épernay.

ESSENTIAL FACTS

DÉPARTEMENTS:	Ardennes, Aube, Haute-Marne, Marne
PRINCIPAL TOWNS	Troyes, Charleville-Mézière, Reims, Chaumont, Chalons-Sur-Marne, Langres
PLACES TO VISIT:	Reims cathedral; Montmort-Lucy castle; the Saturday market at Charleville-Mézière and see their animated clock come alive on the hour; the viaduct at Chaumont and the lapidary exhibits in the Museum of Archeology
REGIONAL TOURIST OFFICE	16 boulevard Carnot, 10000 Troyes. Tel: 25 82 62 70 3 quai des Arts, 51000 Chalons-Sur-Marne. Tel: 26 65 17 89
LOCAL GASTRONOMIC DELIGHTS	Wild boar; boudin blanc - a white pudding from Rethel; smoked Ardennes ham; folies Troyennes - praline pastry puffs; local cheeses such as brie de Meaux and chaource
DRINKS	Casibel - cider with cassis and lemon; ratafia - a champagne liqueur; and that most famous of drinks: champagne
LOCAL CRAFTS WHAT TO BUY	Crystal glass from Bayel; cutlery from Nogent; basket work and willow weaving from Fayl-Billot; puppets from Charleville-Mézières

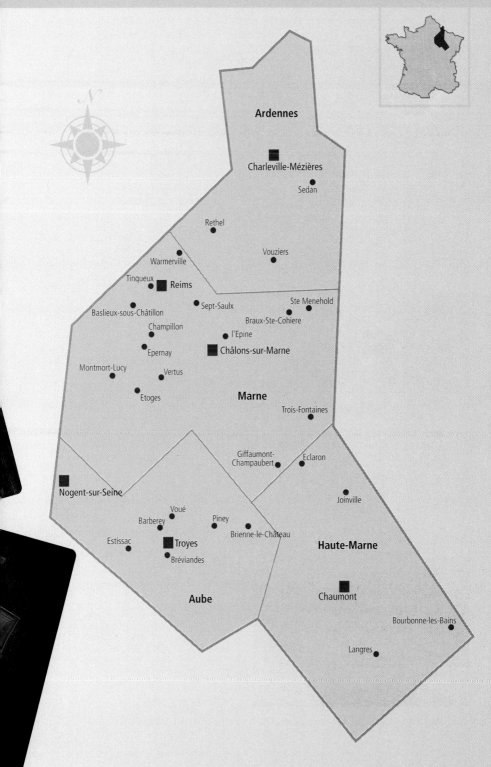

Ardennes

Charleville-Mézières

Sedan

Rethel

Vouziers

Warmerville

Tinqueux

Reims

Sept-Saulx

Ste Menehold

Baslieux-sous-Châtillon

Braux-Ste-Cohiere

Champillon

l'Epine

Epernay

Châlons-sur-Marne

Montmort-Lucy

Vertus

Marne

Etoges

Trois-Fontaines

Giffaumont-
Champaubert

Eclaron

Nogent-sur-Seine

Joinville

Voué

Barberey

Piney

Estissac

Brienne-le-Château

Haute-Marne

Troyes

Bréviandes

Chaumont

Aube

Bourbonne-les-Bains

Langres

EVENTS & FESTIVALS:

Jan Joinville Winter Festival

Mar Poucy La Nuit de la Chouette; Tintamars (March Madness) - music & comedy in numerous villages in southern Haute-Marne;

Apr Sedan Arts Festival & Craft Market;

May Sedan European Rally Jamboree; Revin Bread Festival; Troyes Champagne Fair;

Jun Sedan Medieval Fair; Reims Folklore Festival Celebration of St Joan; Trois-Fontaines Horse & Carriage Festival; Chaumont International Graphic Art Fair; Châlons-Sur-Marne Furies Festival (street theatre & circus artists); Launois-sur- Vence Art & Creative Crafts Festival; Braux Ste-Cohière Festival at the Castle (chamber music & exhibitions) (till early Sept); Reims Summer Music Festival (150 free concerts until mid-Aug)

Jul Aube Wine Festival; Bastieux-sur-Châtillon Champagne Festival Tourist Route; Langres July Festival (Sats & Suns); Vendresse Light & Sound Show at Cassina Castle; Joinville "Grand Jardin" concert in the castle & all over the department (till Aug); Chaumont L'Eté en Fête (till mid-Aug);

Aug Estissac Local Food Fair; Aube Wine Festival; Langres Halbardiers' Round - spectators mix with the cast & become actors for an evening (Fris & Sats); Aube (Othe & Amance) Festival - theatre, jazz, rock;

Sep Brienne-le-Château Choucroute Festival; Montier-en-Der Thursdays at The Stud (Haras) - horses & carriages in ceremonial dress at 3pm; Brienne-le-Château Sauerkraut Fair; Charleville-Mézières World Puppet heatre Festival

Oct Sedan Model Collectors Fair; Reims Marathon; Montier-en-Der Thursdays at The Stud (Haras) - horses & carriages in ceremonial dress at 3pm; Reims Marathon; Reims Octob'rock festival; Troyes Nights of Champagne (voice festival)

Nov Montier-en-Der Thursdays at The Stud Farm - horses & carriages in ceremonial dress at 3pm

Dec Braux-Ste-Cohière Shepherds' Christmas - traditional gathering of shepherds in the Castle on Christmas Eve, with music followed by midnight mass.

BARBERY Aube

★ ★ ★ Novotel RN19
RN 19 *10600*
☎ 325745995 FAX 325780573
(From A5 exit 20 follow 'Aéroport' signs, or from A26 exit 31 towards Troyes and Provins then follow signs for airport) Novotel offer their clients good quality accommodation in modern, well equipped bedrooms and have refined restaurants serving good quality cuisine They have excellent business meeting and conference facilities and some have food and beverages available 24 hours a day. All their hotels have at least one bedroom for disabled guests.

83 en suite (bth/shr) (40 fmly) No smoking in 18 bedrooms TV in all bedrooms STV Direct dial from all bedrooms Mini-bar in all bedrooms Licensed Night porter Full central heating Open parking available Supervised Child discount

available 16yrs Outdoor swimming pool Boule Open terrace Covered terrace ping pong,badminton,video games,karting, V meals Languages spoken: English,German,Spanish
Rooms: (room only) s 420-440FF; d 460-490FF
Meals: Full breakfast 55FF Continental breakfast 55FF✱
Cards: ●● ■■ ■■ ●〉 Travellers cheques

BOURBONNE-LES-BAINS Haute-Marne

★ ★ ★ Jeanne d'Arc
12 rue Amiral *52400*
☎ 325904600 FAX 325887871
Situated just five minutes away from the town and thermal baths, the hotel features cosy, comfortable bedrooms, a flower-filled garden with trees and a restaurant which serves delicious food in pretty surroundings.
Forest area In town centre
Closed 30 Nov-2 Mar
32 en suite (bth/shr) (2 fmly) TV in all bedrooms STV Direct dial from all bedrooms Mini-bar in all bedrooms Licensed Lift Full central heating Open parking available (charged) Covered parking available (charged) Supervised Child discount available Outdoor swimming pool Solarium Open terrace Languages spoken: English
Cards: ●● ■■ ■■ Travellers cheques

★ ★ Moulin de L'Achat
Enfonvelle *52400*
☎ 325900954 FAX 325902182
This 19th-century former mill is situated in tranquil countryside, and combines the rustic charm of the past with the modern comfort of the present. Pleasant bedrooms with

modern amenities, and an informal restaurant serving good food are complemented by a multitude of leisure facilities.
Near river Forest area
Closed 2 Nov-Etr
13 en suite (bth/shr) (2 fmly) (2 with balcony) No smoking in 1 bedroom Direct dial from all bedrooms Mini-bar in all bedrooms Licensed Full central heating Open parking available Supervised Child discount available Outdoor swimming pool Tennis Fishing Riding Sauna Gym Boule Bicycle rental Open terrace Covered terrace V meals Last d 22.30hrs Languages spoken: English
MEALS: Full breakfast 45FF Continental breakfast 35FF Lunch 97-170FF&alc Dinner 97-170FF&alc✱
CARDS: ✱✱ ■■ ☰ Travellers cheques

BRÉVIANDES Aube

★ ★ Du Pan De Bois
35 av Général Leclerc, rte de Dijon *10450*
☎ 325750231 FAX 325496784
The Hotel le Pan de Bois is set in a peaceful garden outside the town of Breviandes. It features bedrooms with modern amenities and a restaurant which has a faithful clientele who return time and time again to savour the delicious food and great vintage wines. With the town of Troyes and the Orient forest with lakes nearby, the hotel is an ideal venue for both culture and nature lovers.
Forest area Near motorway
31 en suite (bth/shr) TV in all bedrooms STV Radio in rooms Direct dial from all bedrooms Full central heating Open parking available Covered parking available (charged) Open terrace Last d 22.00hrs Languages spoken: English
CARDS: ✱✱ ☰ Travellers cheques

CHÂLONS-SUR-MARNE Marne

★ ★ ★ Angleterre
19 pl Monseigneur Tissier *51000*
☎ 326682151 FAX 326705167
(In the town centre between the church of Notre-Dame-en-Vaux and the Hôtel de la Préfecture)
Due to the impeccable management of the hosts Elisabeth and Jacky Michel, visitors to the hotel Angleterre will look back on their stay as a delightful experience. The hotel features pretty bedrooms with well co-ordinated decor and soft furnishings, and a private lounge for functions and social events. The restaurant has earned a first-class reputation in the Champagne-Ardenne region.
In town centre
Closed Xmas & 14 Jul-5 Aug
18 en suite (bth/shr) (2 fmly) TV in all bedrooms STV Direct dial from all bedrooms Mini-bar in all bedrooms Licensed Full central heating Air conditioning in bedrooms Open parking available Covered parking available (charged) Open terrace V meals Last d 21.30hrs Languages spoken: English & German
ROOMS: (room only) s 390-450FF; d 400-520FF
MEALS: Full breakfast 65FF Lunch 160-450FFalc Dinner 160-450FFalc
CARDS: ✱✱ ■■ ☰ ⏺ Travellers cheques

★ ★ ★ Le Rénard
24 pl de la République *51000*
☎ 326680378 FAX 326645007
The hotel Le Renard is a modern hotel with a homely atmosphere situated in Châlons-sur-Marne, with green parks and recreational areas nearby. It features spacious bedrooms

with private en suite facilities and two comfortable day rooms. The restaurant offers a good choice of set menus and à la carte dishes.
Near river Near lake In town centre Near motorway
35 en suite (bth/shr) (4 fmly) No smoking in 12 bedrooms TV in all bedrooms STV Mini-bar in all bedrooms Licensed Full central heating Open parking available Supervised Child discount available 10yrs V meals Languages spoken: English,Spanish
MEALS: Full breakfast 45FF Continental breakfast 45FF Lunch fr 100FF✱
CARDS: ✱✱ ■■ ☰ Travellers cheques

CHAMPILLON Marne

★ ★ ★ ★ Royal Champagne
Bellevue *51160*
☎ 326528711 FAX 326528969
Set in an elevated position overlooking the vineyards, this charming coaching inn dates back to the 18th century and offers its visitors a peaceful stay complemented by outstanding cuisine. Luxurious guest rooms with terraces provide the maximum of comfort, whilst the surrounding area offers many leisure options including tennis and a putting green; a large forest and stunning natural scenery provide ample possibilities for walking.
Forest area Near motorway
TV in 30 bedrooms STV Radio in rooms Direct dial from 30 bedrooms Mini-bar in 30 bedrooms Licensed Night porter Full central heating Open parking available Covered parking available Child discount available Tennis Solarium Bicycle rental Last d 21.30hrs Languages spoken: English & German
CARDS: ✱✱ ■■ ☰ ⏺ Travellers cheques

ECLARON Haute-Marne

★ ★ Hotellerie du Moulin
Rue du Moulin *52290*
☎ 325041776 FAX 325556701
This old wooden mill is situated on the banks of a river in lush green surroundings. The establishment offers its visitors a warm and friendly atmosphere and good traditional cuisine. Visitors can be assured of a good night's sleep in the spacious guest accommodation, where the only sound to be heard is the murmur of the river. In addition the hotel is close the Lac du Der-Chantecoq, the largest artificial lake in Europe.
Near river Near lake Near beach Forest area
Closed Jan
5 en suite (bth/shr) (2 fmly) TV in all bedrooms Direct dial from all bedrooms Licensed Full central heating Open parking available Open terrace V meals Last d 21.00hrs Languages spoken: English German & Spanish
ROOMS: (room only) s fr 240FF; d fr 240FF **Reductions over 1 night**
MEALS: Full breakfast 35FF Continental breakfast 35FF Lunch 80-165FF&alc Dinner 80-165FF&alc
CARDS: ✱✱ ☰ Travellers cheques

ÉPERNAY Marne

★ ★ Climat de France
Rue de Lorraine *51200*
☎ 326541739 Cen Res 64460123 FAX 326518878
(near village centre)
Situated in the town of Epernay, the hotel features pleasantly decorated, comfortable bedrooms with good modern facilities.

contd.

The restaurant serves a variety of menus, including a 'no-limits' hors d'oeuvre buffet, as well as the children's 'Soupière Junior'.
Near river Forest area In town centre Near motorway 33 en suite (bth/shr) TV in all bedrooms Radio in rooms Direct dial from all bedrooms Licensed Full central heating Open parking available Open terrace Covered terrace Languages spoken: English
CARDS: ●● ▆▆

ÉPINE, L' Marne

★ ★ ★ ★ Aux Armes de Champagne
pl de la Basilique *51460*
☎ 326693030 FAX 326669231
(on N3, Metz-Verdun)
This charming establishment offers its visitors a warm welcome in an informal atmosphere. The elegant lounges, with their tasteful furnishings and assorted antiques are evocative of a bygone age. The spotless bedrooms have modern facilities and are decorated with flair. There is a cosy bar and the cuisine offers a wide selection of delicately-flavoured dishes from the region.
Closed early Jan-mid Feb RS Nov-May (closed Sun evening/Monday)
37 en suite (bth/shr) 16 rooms in annexe (3 fmly) TV in all bedrooms Direct dial from all bedrooms Mini-bar in all bedrooms Licensed Full central heating Open parking available Child discount available 12yrs Tennis Mini-golf V meals Last d 21.00hrs Languages spoken: English
ROOMS: (room only) s 320-725FF; d 400-725FF ✱
MEALS: Full breakfast 65FF Lunch 220-490FF&alc Dinner 220-490FF&alc
CARDS: ●● ▆▆ ▆▆ ⑨ Travellers cheques

ÉTOGES Marne

★ ★ ★ Château d'Etoges
par Montmort-Lucy *51270*
☎ 326593008 FAX 326593557
Built at the beginning of the 17th century, the Château d'Etoges soon became famous for the hospitality it offered to passing visitors. It occupies a splendid setting amidst delightful grounds, and offers intimate bedrooms, decorated with rich period furnishings and fabrics. The menu features regional specialities complemented by a fine selection of wines.
Near river Near lake Forest area Near motorway 21 rms (20 bth/shr) (3 fmly) TV available Direct dial from all bedrooms Licensed Full central heating Open parking available Covered parking available Supervised Child discount available 10yrs Fishing Pool table Bicycle rental Open terrace Boating Croquet Last d 21.30hrs Languages spoken: English & German
ROOMS: (room only) s 400-700FF; d 600-1200FF
Reductions over 1 night Special breaks
MEALS: Continental breakfast 70FF Lunch 180-310FF Dinner 180-310FF
CARDS: ●● ▆▆ ▆▆ ⑨ Travellers cheques

GIFFAUMONT-CHAMPAUBERT Marne

★ ★ Le Cheval Blanc
rue du Lac *51290*
☎ 326726265 FAX 326739697
The hotel enjoys a peaceful setting in the heart of the Champagne countryside. With its warm, rustic interior it offers well equipped bedrooms, dining rooms and a large covered

terrace. The cuisine comprises a good choice of fresh fish specialities augmented by a good wine list.
Near river Near lake Forest area Near motorway 16 rms (8 bth 6 shr) TV in all bedrooms Direct dial from all bedrooms Licensed Full central heating Open parking available Supervised Child discount available 12yrs Open terrace Last d 21.30hrs Languages spoken: English German & Spanish
CARDS: ●● ▆▆ ▆▆ Travellers cheques

JOINVILLE Haute-Marne

★ ★ Poste
pl de la Grêve *52300*
☎ 325941263 FAX 325943623
This traditional hotel offers individually appointed bedrooms with country-style furnishings. Guests can enjoy an aperitif on the terrace before sampling one of the classic or regional dishes which are on offer in the restaurant.
Near river In town centre Near motorway
Closed 10-end Jan
10 en suite (bth/shr) (3 fmly) TV in all bedrooms Direct dial from all bedrooms Licensed Full central heating Open parking available Covered parking available (charged) Supervised Child discount available 11yrs Boule Open terrace Last d 21.30hrs Languages spoken: English & German
ROOMS: (room only) s 200-250FF; d 200-250FF
MEALS: Full breakfast 25FF Continental breakfast 25FF Lunch 80-210FF&alc Dinner 80-210FF
CARDS: ●● ▆▆ ▆▆ ⑨ Travellers cheques

LANGRES Haute-Marne

★ ★ Auberge des Voiliers
1 rue des Voiliers, Lac de La Liez *52200*

☎ 325870574 FAX 325872422
(Follow signs to Lac de Liez. Hotel is on lake shore)
The Auberge des Voiliers stands on the shores of Lac de la Liez, the largest lake in the region, and offers a stunning view of the lake and the fortified city. For those guests who want to relax and take in the sun, the beach is just a few steps away from the hotel, whilst a large choice of leisure pursuits is available for the more energetic. The bedrooms are comfortable with good amenities, and the restaurant serves a wide range of fresh fish delicacies and regional dishes.
Near lake Near beach Forest area
Closed 31 Jan-14 Mar
8 en suite (bth/shr) 3 rooms in annexe (1 fmly) (4 with balcony) TV in all bedrooms STV Direct dial from all bedrooms Licensed Full central heating Open parking available Child discount available 10yrs Open terrace

Childrens play area Last d 22.00hrs Languages spoken: English, German
Rooms: (room only) s 220FF; d 220-350FF **Special breaks: Fishing breaks, 5 day cooking courses in Nov**
Meals: Full breakfast 35FF Continental breakfast 22FF Lunch fr 80FF&alc Dinner fr 100FF&alc
Cards: ●● ▆▆ Travellers cheques

NOGENT-SUR-SEINE Aube

★ ★ **Le Beau Rivage**
20 rue Villiers aux Choux *10400*
☎ 325398422 FAX 325391832
(On N19 between Provins and Troyes)
Near river
Closed 3 wks Feb
7 en suite (bth/shr) TV in all bedrooms STV Direct dial from all bedrooms Licensed Full central heating Open terrace Last d 21.00hrs Languages spoken: English
Rooms: (room only) s 250-260FF; d 280-290FF
Meals: Full breakfast 35FF Lunch 78-190FF&alc Dinner 78-190FF&alc
Cards: ●● ▆▆ Travellers cheques

PINEY Aube

★ ★ **Le Tadorne**
3 pl de la Halle *10220*
☎ 325463035 FAX 325463649
The hotel is housed in an 18th century building which is built in the distinct half-timbered style of the region. All the bedrooms are individually appointed - some have exposed beams and timbered walls - equipped with modern amenities, and decorated with high quality beds and furniture. The restaurant serves a regional cuisine and house specialities include home-made foie gras and mille feuille de St Jacques à la ciboulette.
Near river Near lake Forest area In town centre Near motorway
20 rms (17 bth/shr) 5 rooms in annexe TV in all bedrooms STV Licensed Night porter Full central heating Open parking available Supervised Child discount available 3yrs Outdoor swimming pool (heated) Pool table Boule Mini-golf Bicycle rental Open terrace V meals Last d 22.00hrs Languages spoken: English & German
Cards: ●● ▆▆ Travellers cheques

REIMS Marne

★ ★ ★ ★ **Boyer Les Crayeres**
64 bd Henri Vasnier *51100*
☎ 326828080 FAX 326826552
(From A4 take exit Reims St-Remi, then head towards Luxembourg & Charleville. Turn right at rdbt towards Reims Prunay)
Forest area Near motorway
Closed 23 Dec-13 Jan
19 en suite (bth/shr) 3 rooms in annexe TV in all bedrooms STV Radio in rooms Direct dial from all bedrooms Mini-bar in all bedrooms Licensed Lift Night porter Full central heating Air conditioning in bedrooms Open parking available Covered parking available (charged) Supervised Tennis Open terrace V meals Last d 22.30hrs Languages spoken: English,German,Italian
Rooms: (room only) d 1270-1900FF
Meals: Continental breakfast 110FF Lunch 880-950FF&alc Dinner 880-950FF&alc
Cards: ●● ▆▆ ▆▆ ◑ Travellers cheques

★ ★ **Climat de France**
Rue Bertrand Russel *51100*
☎ 326096273 Cen Res 164460123 FAX 326874608
(off A4 or A26)
This recently-constructed establishment has a cosy atmosphere and features well-equipped bedrooms, which are attractively furnished and offer a good standard of comfort. Each floor has a tea maker, so guests may help themselves to free hot drinks. The country-style restaurant serves an array of appetising meals to suit most tastes, whilst the flexible conference facilities make it a good business venue.
Near motorway
38 en suite (bth) TV in all bedrooms Radio in rooms Direct dial from all bedrooms Licensed Full central heating Open parking available (charged) Covered parking available (charged) Supervised Languages spoken: English
Cards: ●● ▆▆

★ ★ ★ **Hotel Holiday Inn Garden Court**
46 rue Buirette *51100*
☎ 326475600 FAX 326474575
In town centre Near motorway
82 en suite (bth/shr) (5 fmly) (16 with balcony) No smoking in 40 bedrooms TV in all bedrooms STV Radio in rooms Direct dial from all bedrooms Mini-bar in all bedrooms Licensed Lift Night porter Full central heating Air conditioning in bedrooms Covered parking available (charged) Child discount available Open terrace Last d 22.00hrs Languages spoken: English,German
Cards: ●● ▆▆ ▆▆ ◑ Travellers cheques

★ ★ ★ **Hotel de la Paix** (Best Western)
9 rue Buirette *51100*
☎ 326400408 FAX 326477504
In town centre
106 rms (102 bth) (15 fmly) No smoking in 4 bedrooms TV in all bedrooms STV Direct dial from all bedrooms Mini-bar in all bedrooms Licensed Lift Night porter Full central heating Air conditioning in bedrooms Open parking available (charged) Covered parking available (charged) Child discount available 12yrs Outdoor swimming pool Open terrace V meals Languages spoken: English German Italian & Spanish
Rooms: (room only) s 390-500FF; d 420-660FF
Cards: ●● ▆▆ ▆▆ ◑ JCB Travellers cheques

★ ★ ★ **New Hotel Europe**
29 rue Buirette *51100*
☎ 326473939 FAX 326401437
(From A4 exit 'Reims Centre' follow signs for 'Hôtels Buirette')
In town centre Near motorway
54 en suite (bth/shr) (3 fmly) (3 with balcony) No smoking in 10 bedrooms TV in all bedrooms STV Radio in rooms Direct dial from all bedrooms Mini-bar in all bedrooms Room-safe Licensed Lift Night porter Full central heating Air conditioning in bedrooms Open parking available (charged) Supervised Child discount available 12yrs Open terrace Languages spoken: English,German
Rooms: (room only) s 380FF; d 420FF
Meals: Full breakfast 52FF Continental breakfast 45FF★
Cards: ●● ▆▆ ▆▆ ◑ JCB Travellers cheques

★ ★ ★ **Quality Hotel**
37 bd Paul Doumer *51100*
☎ 326400108 FAX 326403413
Near lake In town centre Near motorway
79 en suite (bth/shr) (4 fmly) (1 with balcony) No smoking in 12 bedrooms TV in all bedrooms STV
contd.

105

Direct dial from all bedrooms Mini-bar in all bedrooms Licensed Lift Night porter Full central heating Air conditioning in bedrooms Open parking available (charged) Covered parking available (charged) Child discount available 12yrs Open terrace Last d 22.00hrs Languages spoken: English
CARDS: ●● ■■ ☲ ☺ Travellers cheques

★ ★ ★ Reflets Bleus
12 rue Gabriel Voisin *51100*
☎ 326825979 FAX 326825392
Near motorway
41 rms (4 fmly) No smoking in 2 bedrooms TV in all bedrooms Radio in rooms Direct-dial available Mini-bar in all bedrooms Licensed Night porter Full central heating Open parking available Supervised Child discount available 12yrs Open terrace V meals Languages spoken: English & German
CARDS: ●● ■■ ☲ ☺ Travellers cheques

STE-MENEHOULD Marne

★ ★ Du Cheval Rouge
1 rue Chanzy *51800*
☎ 326608104 FAX 326609611
The hotel is housed in an 18th-century building and features completely renovated guest rooms, which are fully equipped and provide a good level of comfort. The restaurant, with its magnificent open fire place, offers an informal setting for enjoyable meals served by young, attentive staff.
Near river Forest area In town centre Near motorway
Closed 18 Nov-10 Dec
20 en suite (bth/shr) (1 fmly) TV in all bedrooms STV Radio in rooms Direct dial from all bedrooms Licensed Full central heating V meals Last d 22.00hrs Languages spoken: English & Spanish
ROOMS: (room only) s 240-270FF; d 240-270FF
MEALS: Full breakfast 45FF Continental breakfast 45FF Lunch 90-210FF Dinner 90-210FF
CARDS: ●● ■■ ☲ ☺ Travellers cheques

SEPT-SAULX Marne

★ ★ ★ Cheval Blanc
rue du Moulin *51400*
☎ 326039027 FAX 326039709
(from Reims-A4-exit 'Cormontreuil' towards Chalons-sur-Marne-N44-exit Les Petites Loges/Sept Saulx. from Troyes-A26-exit Laveuve/Metz towards Reims-N44-exit les Petites Loges/Sept Saulx.)
In the heart of Champagne and its famous vineyards, the fifth generation of the Robert family offers their visitors a warm welcome in this former coaching inn. The hotel is surrounded by a large park with a river, and features pretty bedrooms and country-style apartments overlooking the flower-filled courtyard. The restaurant serves a light, regional cuisine which combines imaginative dishes and tasty specialities, prepared by the young chef who presides over the kitchen.
Near river Forest area Near motorway
Closed 22 Jan-22 Feb

25 en suite (bth/shr) 4 rooms in annexe (1 fmly) (11 with balcony) TV in all bedrooms Direct dial from all bedrooms Mini-bar in all bedrooms Licensed Full central heating Open parking available Covered parking available Supervised Child discount available 10yrs Tennis Fishing Mini-golf Bicycle rental Open terrace V meals Last d 21.30hrs Languages spoken: English German & Spanish
ROOMS: (room only) s 350-800FF; d 390-980FF **Reductions over 1 night Special breaks: (1,2 or 3 day breaks)**
MEALS: Full breakfast 50FF Lunch 150-360FF&alc Dinner 180-360FF&alc
CARDS: ●● ■■ ☲ ☺

TINQUEUX Marne

★ ★ ★ ★ Assiette Champenoise
40 av P V Couturier *51430*
☎ 326846464 FAX 326041569
(Access via A4)
Two kilometres from Reims and just a few minutes away from the vineyards, this charming establishment is set in its own beautiful grounds. The interior is decorated with flair and good taste by the proprietor Colette Lallement, and offers spacious bedrooms with every day modern amenities, a congenial bar for a relaxing drink or chat with fellow guests, and splendid cuisine skilfully executed by Jean-Pierre Lallement.
In town centre Near motorway
62 en suite (bth/shr) TV in all bedrooms STV Direct dial from all bedrooms Mini-bar in all bedrooms Room-safe Licensed Lift Night porter Full central heating Open parking available Supervised Child discount available 12yrs Indoor swimming pool (heated) Sauna Open terrace V meals Last d 22.00hrs Languages spoken: English, German & Italian
ROOMS: (room only) s 505-1100FF; d 545-1100FF ✱
MEALS: Full breakfast 70FF Continental breakfast 70FF Lunch 295-495FF&alc Dinner 295-495FF&alc✱
CARDS: ●● ■■ ☲ ☺ Travellers cheques

★ ★ ★ Novotel Reims Tinqueux
rte de Soissons BP 12 *51430*
☎ 326081161 FAX 326087205
(From A4/A26 take exit Reims-Tinqueux)
Novotel offer their clients good quality accommodation in modern, well equipped bedrooms and have refined restaurants serving good quality cuisine They have excellent business meeting and conference facilities and some have food and beverages available 24 hours a day. All their hotels have at least one bedroom for handicapped guests.
Forest area Near motorway
127 en suite (bth/shr) (50 fmly) No smoking in 38 bedrooms TV in all bedrooms STV Radio in rooms Direct dial from all bedrooms Mini-bar in all bedrooms Licensed Night porter Full central heating Air conditioning in bedrooms Open parking available Supervised Child discount available 16yrs Outdoor swimming pool (heated) Solarium Bicycle rental Open terrace V meals Last d 24.00hrs Languages spoken: English,German,Italian,Spanish
ROOMS: (room only) s 450-460FF; d 480-490FF
MEALS: Full breakfast 60FF Continental breakfast 60FF Lunch 90-120FF&alc Dinner 90-120FF&alc
CARDS: ●● ■■ ☲ ☺

Taking your mobile phone to France?
See page 11

TROYES Aube

★ ★ ★ Royal Hotel
22 bld Carnot *10000*
☎ 325731999 FAX 325734785
(leave A26 in direction of Troyes centre, then follow signs "gare SNCF" or "Office of Tourisme", hotel close to the boulevard overlooking public gardens)
The Royal hotel is one of the many handsome buildings which can be found in the town centre of Troyes. Completely renovated and refurbished, it features comfortable bedrooms with functional, modern facilities. The elegant restaurant overlooks the shaded square and serves an inventive, regional cuisine complemented by the attentive service of the proprietors Philippe and Catherine Vos and their competent team.
In town centre
Closed 20 Dec-12 Jan
37 en suite (bth/shr) (3 fmly) (7 with balcony) TV in all bedrooms STV Radio in rooms Direct dial from all bedrooms Licensed Lift Night porter Full central heating Child discount available 12yrs Pool table V meals Last d 21.30hrs Languages spoken: English,Dutch,German
ROOMS: (room only) s 295-355FF; d 340-435FF
MEALS: Full breakfast 45FF Lunch 115-165FF&alc Dinner 115-165FF&alc✱
CARDS: ●● ▦ ▆ ◑

VERTUS Marne

★ ★ Le Thibault IV
2 pl de la République *51130*
☎ 326520124 FAX 326521659
(off A26)
Located along the tourist route to Champagne, this hotel is popular with business travellers and tourists alike. It has modern bedrooms fitted with every modern convenience, and a restaurant which serves a choice of specialities from the Champagne region.
Forest area
Closed 18 Feb-4 Mar
17 en suite (bth/shr) (4 fmly) TV in all bedrooms Direct dial from all bedrooms Licensed Full central heating Child discount available V meals Last d 21.30hrs Languages spoken: English,German

ROOMS: (room only) s 250FF; d 290FF **Special breaks**
MEALS: Full breakfast 40FF Continental breakfast 40FF Lunch 100-195FF&alc Dinner 100-195FF&alc
CARDS: ●● ▆ Travellers cheques

VOUÉ Aube

★ ★ ★ Le Marais
39 rte Imperiale *10150*
☎ 325375533 FAX 325375329
(Approach via A26 exit 30/31)
This contemporary family establishment features sound-proofed bedrooms with modern appointments, a comfortable lounge and terrace, complemented by a pleasant restaurant which serves good quality home-cooking by the chef-proprietor.
Near river Near lake Near motorway
20 en suite (bth/shr) (2 fmly) TV in all bedrooms Direct dial from all bedrooms Night porter Full central heating Open parking available Child discount available 3yrs Outdoor swimming pool Pool table Open terrace Last d 21.00hrs Languages spoken: English,German
ROOMS: (room only) s 250-280FF; d 295-390FF ✱
Reductions over 1 night Special breaks: 3 night breaks
MEALS: Full breakfast 40FF Lunch 90-240FF Dinner 90-240FF✱
CARDS: ●● ▆ Travellers cheques

WARMERIVILLE Marne

★ ★ Auberge du Val des Bois
3 rue du 8 Mai 1945 *51110*
☎ 326033209 FAX 326033784
Located close to the centre of Reims, this country-style hotel guarantees a peaceful, relaxing stay. Comfortable, prettily-decorated bedrooms offer all modern amenities while a range of reasonably-priced dishes are available from the restaurant. While staying here you must try the local champagne!
Near river Forest area
Closed 15 Dec-15 Jan
19 rms TV in all bedrooms Direct dial from all bedrooms Licensed Full central heating No children Open terrace V meals Last d 21.00hrs
CARDS: ●● ▆

Lorraine Vosges

This northern region is best known for its spa towns, lakes, winter sports resorts and eclectic architectural heritage, which includes Gothic cathedrals in Metz and Toul, Gallo-Roman remains in Bliesbruck, and ravishing Art Nouveau in Nancy. It also possesses the largest area of woodland in France, notably the Haye Forest, Charlemagne's former hunting ground. Even a high-tech industrial city like Nancy is not without a natural charm, being completely surrounded by a network of delightful waterways. Lorraine's social calendar is impressively wide-ranging. Events range from medieval fairs and avant-garde music, to the curious Trout and Ice Cream Festival.

(Top): These elegant gates in Nancy are a fine example of the largely intact 18th-century planning which makes the heart of the town so attractive.

(Bottom): Unusual monument to the children of Hattonchâtel killed in WWI.

ESSENTIAL FACTS

DÉPARTEMENTS:	Moselle, Meuse, Meurthe-en-Moselle, Vosges
PRINCIPAL TOWNS	Bar-Le-Duc, Briey, Metz, Nancy, Epinal, Verdun
PLACES TO VISIT:	The many vineyards of the Vosges; the splendid red sandstone church of Marmoutier; Notre-Dame Cathedral at Verdun; the 16th Century Château de la Varenne at Haironville; Nancy School Museum at Nancy
REGIONAL TOURIST OFFICE	1 place Gabriel Hocquard, BP 81004, 57036 Metz. Tel: 87 37 02 16
LOCAL GASTRONOMIC DELIGHTS	Rabbit in Mirabelle Jelly; Quiche Lorraine; Carp with Glasswort; vol-au-vents; frogs legs pie; choux puff buns filled with Mirabelle plums; walnut and Vosges honey cake
DRINKS	White wines such as Riesling, Muscat, Sylvaner, Tokay, Pinot Blanc and Pinot Noir. Beer is brewed at the famous Tourtel Brewery in Tantonville. Mineral water from Vittel and Contrexéville
LOCAL CRAFTS WHAT TO BUY	Glassware from Baccarat, Daum, Hartzviller, Portieux, Meisenthal, St-Louis and Vannes-le-Châtel; pottery, enamelware and "Chinese ware" from Lunéville, St-Clement and Longwy

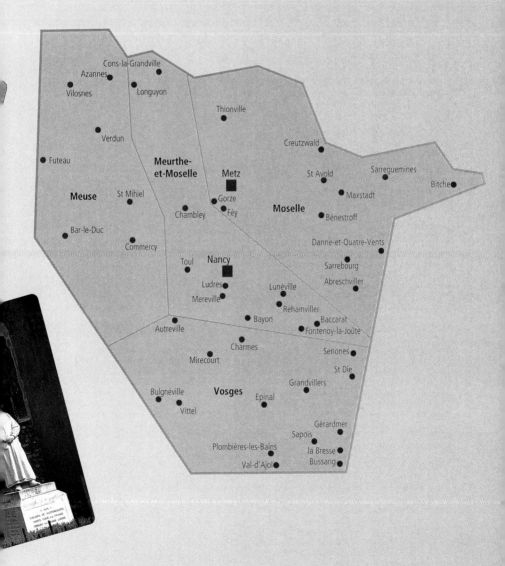

Cons-la-Grandville

Azannes

Vilosnes

Longuyon

Thionville

Verdun

Creutzwald

Futeau

Meurthe-et-Moselle

Metz

St Avold

Sarreguemines

Meuse

St Mihiel

Gorze

Maxstadt

Bitche

Chambley

Féy

Moselle

Bénestroff

Bar-le-Duc

Commercy

Danne-et-Quatre-Vents

Toul

Nancy

Sarrebourg

Ludres

Lunéville

Abreschviller

Mereville

Rehainviller

Autreville

Bayon

Baccarat

Fontenoy-la-Joûte

Charmes

Senones

Mirecourt

St Dié

Bulgnéville

Vosges

Grandvillers

Epinal

Vittel

Gérardmer

Sapois

Plombières-les-Bains

la Bresse

Val-d'Ajol

Bussang

EVENTS & FESTIVALS

Jan Gérardmer Adventure Film Festival; Nancy Photographic Exhibition

Feb Epinal Paper Boat Festival; Nancy Strip Cartoon Festival; Sarreguemines Carnival

Mar Commercy Jazz Festival; Creutzwald Carnival & Pageants; Epinal Classical Music Festival

Apr Toul French Wine Fair; Sarrebourg Ancient Music Festival

May Azannes Romagnes Crafts Festival each Sunday; La Bresse Woodcarving Festival; Domrémy Joan of Arc Festival; Vandoeuvre lès-Nancy Avant-garde Music Festival; Epinal Caricature Festival; Gorze Medieval Fair; Nancy Choral Song Festival; Montmedy City Walls Festival

Jun Lunéville Tableware Festival; Metz Summer Book Festival; Meuse Festival of Organ Music; Nancy Masquerade Puppet Event; Epinal Street Entertainment Festival

Jul La Bresse Forest Festival; Threshing Festival at Maxstadt; Plombières-les-Bains Trout and Ice Festival; St-Dié des Vosges Freedom Week - traditional entertainment & games; Contrexéville Old Crafts & Scenes from 19th century life

Aug Bénéstroff Harvest Festival; Cons-la Grandville Medieval Festival; Contrexéville Fireworks Display; Metz Mirabelle Plum estival; Sapois Loggers Sledging Festival; Madine Lake Festival - concert & fireworks; Jaulny Medieval entertainment plus fireworks; Gérardmer Lights on the Lake - show & fireworks

Sep Baccarat Lorraine Pâté Festival; Lunéville Pumpkin Festival; Vittel International Horse Show

Oct Epinal Theatrical Farce Festival; Nancy International Jazz Festival; Vandoeuvre-lès Nancy Mushers' Race (sledge dog racing); Metz International Fair

Nov Lachaussée Fish Festival; Lindre Basse Grand Fishing Festival; Metz Sacred Songs Festival

Dec St Nicholas Festivals at St-Nicholas-de-Port, Epinal, Metz & Nancy; Christmas markets at Metz & Nancy

---

ABRESCHVILLER Moselle

★★ Cigognes
74 rue Jordy 57560
☎ 387037009 FAX 387097906
(A4 then Phalsbourg N4 and D44 to Abreschviller)
This family hotel, part of the Minotel group, is situated near the Donon fir forest. Guest rooms with a terrace overlook the garden, where on fine days breakfast and dinner may be taken. Several set price menus are offered, and à la carte with specialities from Alsace and Lorraine.
Near river Forest area
29 rms (14 bth 13 shr) (1 fmly) (10 with balcony) TV in all bedrooms STV Direct dial from all bedrooms Licensed Full central heating Open parking available Child discount available 10yra Indoor swimming pool (heated) Sauna Open terrace Last d 19.00hrs Languages spoken: English & German
ROOMS: (room only) s 150FF; d 210-340FF
MEALS: Full breakfast 37FF Lunch 72-185FF&alc Dinner 72-185FF&alc
CARDS: ● ● ■ ■ ● Travellers cheques

AUTREVILLE Vosges

★★ Le Relais Rose
88300
☎ 383520498 383528237 FAX 383520603
This charming establishment features an informal homely interior where the bedrooms are decorated in individual styles, have high quality en-suite facilities, and offer an above average level of comfort. The menu has a choice of skilfully prepared dishes augmented by more than 200 selected wines from the family cellar.

Forest area Near motorway
17 rms (13 bth/shr) (5 fmly) (6 with balcony) No smoking in 2 bedrooms STV Direct dial from all bedrooms Licensed Full central heating Open parking available Covered parking available (charged) Supervised Child discount available 10yrs Open terrace V meals Languages spoken: English, German
MEALS: Full breakfast 40FF Lunch 110-145FF★
CARDS: ● ● ■ ■ Travellers cheques

BAYON Meurthe-et-Moselle

De l'Est
6 pl du Château 54290
☎ 383725368 FAX 383725906
This inn is situated in the town of Bayone, where the unspoilt surroundings offer a wide choice of leisure opportunities and historic sights. The bedrooms offer a straightforward level of comfort and are equipped with good amenities, whilst the restaurant serves a choice of dishes to suit most tastes.
Near river Forest area In town centre Near motorway
Closed 16-31 Oct
16 rms (5 bth 2 shr) (2 fmly) (2 with balcony) TV in all bedrooms Radio in rooms Licensed Full central heating Child discount available Fishing Bicycle rental V meals Last d 21.00hrs Languages spoken: English
MEALS: Full breakfast 26FF Continental breakfast 50FF Lunch 56-150FF Dinner 56-150FF★
CARDS: ● ● ■ Travellers cheques

Taking your mobile phone to France?
See page 11

110

BITCHE Moselle

★ ★ Relais des Châteaux Forts
6 quai Branly *57230*
☎ 387961414 FAX 387960736
A warm welcome awaits visitors as soon as they step over the threshold in this charming establishment. Set in leafy surroundings, it offers bedrooms with every modern convenience. The restaurant has views of the famous citadel and serves a range of fine, good value dishes.
Near lake Forest area Near motorway
30 en suite (bth/shr) (5 fmly) (15 with balcony) No smoking in 2 bedrooms TV in all bedrooms Direct dial from all bedrooms Licensed Full central heating Open parking available Supervised Child discount available 3yrs Sauna Jacuzzi/spa Bicycle rental Open terrace V meals Last d 21.00hrs
Languages spoken: English,German
MEALS: Full breakfast 42FF Lunch 110-170FF&alc Dinner 110-170FF&alc✱
CARDS: Eurocard

BRESSE, LA Vosges

★ ★ ★ Hotel Les Vallées
31 rue Paul Claudel *88250*
☎ 329254139 FAX 329256438
(Approach from remiremont via D417 and D34)
Whether it is for a family holiday, weekend break, meetings or seminars, Remy Loisirs, set in the heart of Ballons des Vosges Nature Park, offers accommodation and leisure facilities to suit everybody. In addition to the guest bedrooms, there are 60 apartments and two restaurants. It has a fabulous ski area with snow guaranteed (220 snow guns) equipment for hire, slopes for summer sledging, swimming-pool, tennis, squash and mountain-biking and is the ideal venue for those who want an active holiday.
Near river Near lake Forest area In town centre
53 en suite (bth) 60 rooms in annexe (27 fmly) (23 with balcony) TV in all bedrooms STV Radio in rooms Direct dial from all bedrooms Licensed Lift Night porter Full central heating Open parking available Covered parking available (charged) Supervised Child discount available 12yrs Indoor swimming pool (heated) Tennis Squash Sauna Solarium Gym Boule Bicycle rental Open terrace Last d 21.30hrs
Languages spoken: English,German,Dutch
ROOMS: (room only) s 280-335FF
MEALS: Full breakfast 40FF Lunch 90-275FF&alc Dinner 90-275FF&alc
CARDS: ✹ ▦ ▆ ⬤ Travellers cheques

BULGNÉVILLE Vosges

★ ★ Le Colibri
rte de Neufchâteau *88140*
☎ 329091570 FAX 329092140
Standing at the water's edge, Le Colibri occupies a restful position just five minutes from the spa towns of Vittel and Contrex. The hotel features a cosy interior with comfortable accommodation providing a good level of comfort. The restaurant offers a traditional cuisine prepared with fresh local produce.
Near river Near lake Forest area Near motorway
20 rms Some rooms in annexe TV in all bedrooms STV Direct dial from all bedrooms Licensed Full central heating Open parking available Supervised Child discount available 10yrs Fishing Solarium Boule Open terrace V meals

Last d 22.00hrs Languages spoken: English, German
MEALS: Full breakfast 22FF Continental breakfast 34FF Lunch 68-200FF&alc Dinner 68-2000FF&alc✱
CARDS: ✹ ▦ ▆

BUSSANG Vosges

★ ★ Des Sources
12 rte des Sources *88540*
☎ 329615194 FAX 329616061
The hotel des Sources is a handsome building which stands in the centre of the small town of Contrexeville. It features pleasant bedrooms decorated with co-ordinated fabrics and shades, which are equipped with modern appointments. There is a pretty restaurant with views of the fountains, which serves traditional cuisine including a range of popular dishes as well as meals to suit individual needs.
Near lake Forest area In town centre Near motorway
Closed 10 Oct-5 Apr
40 rms 10 rooms in annexe (6 fmly) (11 with balcony) Direct dial from all bedrooms Licensed Full central heating Child discount available Solarium Open terrace Last d 21.00hrs
Languages spoken: English,Portuguese,Spanish
CARDS: ▆ ⬤ Travellers cheques

★ ★ Du Tremplin
rue du 3 ème R.T.A. *88540*
☎ 329615030 FAX 329615089
(Between Epinal and Mulhouse on N66)
This comfortable family-run hotel provides a pleasant setting for an overnight stop or a longer break. Set in a picturesque valley in the upper part of the Vosges region, it features well equipped bedrooms, a bar and cosy lounge. The dining room with its impressive fireplace serves a wide choice of dishes from Alsace-Lorraine as well as some imaginative creations by the chef.
In town centre Near motorway
RS Sun
18 rms (13 shr) (6 fmly) No smoking in 2 bedrooms TV in all bedrooms STV Direct dial from all bedrooms Licensed Full central heating Open parking available Covered parking available (charged) Child discount available 8yrs V meals Last d 21.00hrs Languages spoken: English & German
ROOMS: (room only) s 160-250FF; d 200-340FF
Reductions over 1 night
MEALS: Full breakfast 35FF Lunch 75-300FF&alc Dinner 75-300FF&alc
CARDS: ✹ ▦ ▆ ⬤ Travellers cheques

CHARMES Vosges

★ ★ Dancourt
6 pl de Hôtel-de-Ville *88130*
☎ 329388080 FAX 329380915
(From Voie Rapide 57 take exit 'Charmes/Mirecourt' and follow signs for town centre)
This small establishment offers comfortable bedrooms with modern amenities and has a contemporary style dining room which serves a high standard of home cooking by the chef proprietor. The menu features a choice of classic dishes incorporating fresh ingredients from the region, plus a selection of house specials.
Near river Forest area In town centre Near motorway
Closed 15 Dec-15 Jan
15 en suite (bth/shr) (4 fmly) TV in all bedrooms Radio in rooms Direct dial from all bedrooms Licensed Full central heating Open parking available

contd.

Covered parking available (charged) Supervised Child discount available 2yrs Boule Bicycle rental Open terrace V meals Last d 21.30hrs Languages spoken: English & German
ROOMS: (room only) s 190-240FF; d 220-290FF
Reductions over 1 night
MEALS: Continental breakfast 38FF Lunch 110-300FF&alc Dinner 110-300FF&alc✱
CARDS: ✏ ▦ ▆ Travellers cheques

DANNE-ET-QUATRE-VENTS Moselle

★ ★ **Notre-Dame-de-Bonne-Fontaine**
57370
☎ 387243433 FAX 387242464
Surrounded by a large forest and with plenty of fresh air, the hotel provides the right setting for a restful stay. With attractive rustic furnishings in a modern decor, it blends the typical style of the region with the demands of modern comfort. Each bedroom has modern facilities, while the restaurant serves a large choice of regional dishes. In addition there is a cosy bar and piano-lounge complemented by a range of leisure facilities.
Forest area Near motorway
RS 30 Jan-20 Feb
34 en suite (bth/shr) 1 rooms in annexe (3 fmly) (19 with balcony) TV in all bedrooms Direct dial from all bedrooms Licensed Lift Full central heating Open parking available Child discount available 12yrs Indoor swimming pool (heated) Sauna Open terrace Covered terrace Last d 20.50hrs Languages spoken: English & German
ROOMS: (room only) s 250-320FF; d 320-420FF ✱
MEALS: Lunch 85-250FF&alc Dinner 85-250FF&alc
CARDS: ✏ ▦ ▆ ➄ Travellers cheques

ÉPINAL Vosges

Hotel La Fayette (Best Western)
Parc Economique, "Le Saut-le-Cerf" *88000*
☎ 329811515 FAX 329310708
Close to town, facing a golf course, this modern hotel with air-conditioning offers traditional cuisine and extensive fitness facilities. Excellent for business or leisure.
Near motorway
48 en suite (bth/shr) (3 with balcony) No smoking in 9 bedrooms TV in all bedrooms STV Radio in rooms Direct dial from all bedrooms Mini-bar in all bedrooms Licensed Night porter Full central heating Air conditioning in bedrooms Open parking available Covered parking available (charged) Supervised Child discount available 12yrs Indoor swimming pool (heated) Tennis Sauna Jacuzzi/spa Open terrace Last d 21.30hrs Languages spoken: English & German
ROOMS: (room only) s fr 440FF **Special breaks**
MEALS: Full breakfast 50FF Continental breakfast 50FF Lunch 110-280FF&alc Dinner 110-280FF&alc✱
CARDS: ✏ ▦ ▆ ➄ Travellers cheques

FÉY Moselle

★ ★ **Les Tuilleries**
rte de Curry *57420*
☎ 387520303 FAX 387528424
This is a cheerful contemporary style hotel offering good guest accommodation with modern facilities. Set in green surroundings, it has its own private park and garden, and it features a spacious informal restaurant serving a good choice of dishes.
Forest area Near motorway

41 en suite (bth/shr) (2 fmly) No smoking in 2 bedrooms TV in all bedrooms Direct dial from all bedrooms Licensed Night porter Open parking available Child discount available 12yrs Sauna Boule Bicycle rental Open terrace Last d 22.00hrs Languages spoken: English,German,Italian
CARDS: ✏ ▦ ▆ ➄ Travellers cheques

FUTEAU Meuse

★ ★ **Orée du Boise**
55120
☎ 329882841 FAX 329882452
In a setting beside a forest, the hotel commands fine views of the woodlands and surrounding countryside. This peaceful establishment offers visitors a relaxing stay and features fine oak furnishings in the restaurant and public areas. The bedrooms are equipped with modern facilities and offer a high degree of comfort. The menu comprises a host of sea and shellfish specialities served in the informal surroundings of the restaurant.
Forest area Near motorway
Closed Jan
7 en suite (bth/shr) TV in all bedrooms Licensed Full central heating Open parking available Child discount available Open terrace Last d 21.30hrs Languages spoken: English
MEALS: Continental breakfast 50FF Lunch 115-350FF&alc Dinner 115-350FF&alc✱

GÉRARDMER Vosges

★ ★ **Auberge de Martimprey**
26 Col de Martimpré *88400*
☎ 329630684 FAX 329630685
This small, pleasant hotel is located at the very heart of the Vosges mountains and is a suitable place for those who like to explore the surrounding countryside. It offers warm hospitality, well equipped bedrooms, and a menu which features regional cuisine.
Near lake Near beach Forest area
11 rms (10 bth/shr) (3 fmly) (2 with balcony) TV in 6 bedrooms Licensed Full central heating Open parking available Child discount available 15yrs Pool table Open terrace Last d 21.30hrs Languages spoken: English & German
ROOMS: (room only) s 200-265FF; d 200-265FF
MEALS: Full breakfast 30FF Continental breakfast 30FF Lunch 70-175FF&alc Dinner 98-175FF
CARDS: ▆ ➄ Travellers cheques

★ ★ ★ **Hostellerie des Bas-Rupts et son Chalet**
rte de la Bresse Fleuri *88400*
☎ 329630925 FAX 329630040
The hotel offers the irresistible combination of excellent food, comfortable accommodation and attentive service in pleasant surroundings. The elegant guest-rooms have individually styled interiors, whilst the restaurant serves classic dishes augmented by imaginative combinations of ingredients.
Near lake Forest area
?1 en suite (bth/shr) Some rooms in annexe (1 fmly) (25 with balcony) TV in all bedrooms Mini-bar in 25 bedrooms Licensed Full central heating Open parking available Covered parking available (charged) Supervised Child discount available Outdoor swimming pool (heated) Tennis Bicycle rental Open terrace V meals Last d 21.30hrs Languages spoken: English,German
MEALS: Full breakfast 80FF Lunch 160-400FF&alc Dinner 160-400FF&alc✱
CARDS: ✏ ▦ ▆ Travellers cheques

★ ★ ★ Grand Hotel Bragard
17-19 Charles-de-Gaulle, pl du Tilleul *88400*
☎ 329630631 FAX 329634681
The hotel is situated in Gerardmer, a popular holiday and ski resort set in unspoilt countryside and famous for the production of high quality textiles. Visitors receive a warm welcome from the proprietors Fabienne and Claude Remy and their team. Set between the lake and an extensive pine forest, the hotel provides excellent facilities for a relaxing winter holiday - a Louis XIII style bar with open fireplace, fitness room and sauna - and is equally well equipped for a summer stay with a swimming-pool and a park filled with flowers. The spacious guest rooms and suites are comfortable and some have a terrace. The gastronomic restaurant 'Le Grand Cerf' invites guests to savour a choice of refined dishes in elegant surroundings.
Near lake In town centre
62 en suite (bth/shr) (18 fmly) (9 with balcony) No smoking in 12 bedrooms TV in all bedrooms STV Direct dial from all bedrooms Licensed Lift Night porter Full central heating Open parking available Covered parking available (charged) Supervised Child discount available 12yrs Outdoor swimming pool (heated) Sauna Pool table Boule Open terrace Last d 21.30hrs Languages spoken: English & German
ROOMS: s 380-550FF; d 540-850FF **Special breaks**
MEALS: Continental breakfast 60FF Lunch 125-360FF&alc Dinner 125-360FF&alc✱
CARDS: 💳 📧 🖃 ⑩ Travellers cheques

★ ★ Du Parc
12-14 av de la Ville de Vichy *88400*
☎ 329633243 FAX 329631703
(From Remiremont keep to the side of the lake. Hotel in first turning on right near the Casino)

The hotel occupies an attractive location and offers views over the park and lake. The interior is decorated with fine pastel shades and good quality furniture, whilst the bedrooms with their pine-clad walls provide comfortable accommodation.
Near lake Forest area In town centre Near motorway
Closed mid Oct-mid Dec & mid Mar-mid Apr
30 en suite (bth/shr) 14 rooms in annexe (2 fmly) (4 with balcony) TV in all bedrooms Radio in rooms Direct dial from all bedrooms Full central heating Open parking available Covered parking available (charged) Child discount available 10yrs Outdoor swimming pool (heated) Open terrace Last d 21.00hrs Languages spoken: English & German
ROOMS: (room only) d 275-360FF
MEALS: Full breakfast 44FF Lunch 105-280FF&alc Dinner 105-280FF&alc
CARDS: 💳 📧 🖃 Travellers cheques

GRANDVILLERS Vosges

★ ★ ★ Hotel du Commerce et de l'Europe
88600
☎ 329657117 FAX 329658523
This family hotel offers peaceful accommodation, modern comfort and good food as well as an attentive service by the friendly owners Mr and Mrs Bastien. Because of its good geographical situation it is a good venue for an overnight stop or touring the region. The guest rooms are decorated with flair and furnished with good quality fabrics. There is an elegant restaurant where guests can sample an array of tasty dishes of a high standard.
Near river Near lake Forest area
20 en suite (bth/shr) 5 rooms in annexe (3 fmly) (11 with balcony) TV in all bedrooms Direct dial from all bedrooms Licensed Full central heating Open parking available Covered parking available (charged) Child discount available 12yrs Tennis Fishing Riding Gym Pool table Boule Bicycle rental Open terrace V meals Last d 21.15hrs Languages spoken: English,German,Spanish
MEALS: Full breakfast 30FF Lunch 70-200FF&alc Dinner 70-200FF&alc✱
CARDS: 💳 🖃 Travellers cheques

LONGUYON Meurthe-et-Moselle

★ ★ Lorraine
pl de la Gare *54260*
☎ 382265007 FAX 382392609
Standing at the cross-roads of Belgium, Luxembourg and France, this ancient, informal establishment warmly welcomes its visitors. Entirely renovated bedrooms are comfortable and the restaurant serves an imaginative cuisine incorporating fresh seasonal and market produce, complemented by some excellent wines from the house cellar.
Near river Forest area In town centre Near motorway
Closed 3 wks in Jan
14 en suite (bth/shr) (3 fmly) TV in all bedrooms STV Licensed Full central heating Covered parking available (charged) Supervised Open terrace Covered terrace Last d 21.30hrs Languages spoken: English & German
ROOMS: (room only) s 235FF; d 310FF **Special breaks: (gastronomic weekends)**
MEALS: Continental breakfast 35FF Lunch 120-360FF Dinner 120-360FF
CARDS: 💳 📧 🖃 ⑩ JB Travellers cheques

LUDRES Meurthe-et-Moselle

★ ★ Climat de France
338 Impane Bertholes *54710*
☎ Cen Res 164460123
This pleasant hotel is located between town and countryside and ensures a peaceful stay as well as good food. The bedrooms are attractively furnished with well-matched fabrics and shades and fitted with modern facilities. The restaurant serves a traditional cuisine, complemented by a generous 'no-limits' buffet and a special menu for the younger guests.
Forest area Near motorway
37 en suite (bth) TV available Direct-dial available Licensed Full central heating Open parking available Open terrace Languages spoken: English
CARDS: 💳 🖃

LUNÉVILLE Meurthe-et-Moselle

★ ★ ★ Hotel Oasis
3 av Voltaire *54300*
☎ 383735285 FAX 383730228
Near river Near lake Forest area Near motorway
Closed 20Dec-5Jan
32 en suite (bth/shr) (3 fmly) (3 with balcony) No smoking in 3
bedrooms TV in all bedrooms Radio in rooms Direct dial
from all bedrooms Lift Full central heating Open parking
available Supervised Indoor swimming pool (heated)
Outdoor swimming pool (heated) Pool table Boule Bicycle
rental Open terrace Languages spoken: English, Spanish
MEALS: Full breakfast 35FF Continental breakfast 35FF✱
CARDS: ✺ ▦ ▨ ◗ Travellers cheques

★ ★ ★ Hotel des Pages
5 quai des Petits Bosquets *54300*
☎ 383741142 FAX 383734663
Near river Forest area In town centre
30 en suite (bth/shr) TV in all bedrooms Direct dial from all
bedrooms Licensed Lift Night porter Full central heating Air
conditioning in bedrooms Open parking available Child
discount available 12yrs Bicycle rental Covered terrace Last d
22.30hrs Languages spoken: English
ROOMS: (room only) s 230-260FF; d 260-300FF
Reductions over 1 night
MEALS: Full breakfast 35FF Continental breakfast 35FF Lunch
98-120FF&alc Dinner 98-120FF&alc
CARDS: ✺ ▦ ▨ Travellers cheques

MEREVILLE Meurthe-et-Moselle

★ ★ ★ Maison Carrée
12 rue du Bac *54850*
☎ 383470923 FAX 383475075
(A330 exit6, D331 to Mereville)
Amidst peaceful countryside, and situated on the banks of the
River Moselle, the hotel offers a relaxing stay complemented
by excellent food. Situated ten kilometres from Nancy with its
rich historic and cultural heritage, it features pleasant guest
accommodation and sumptuous cuisine which includes home-
made foie gras, freshly smoked salmon and game depending
on the season, complemented by fine wines from the region.
Near river Near lake Forest area Near motorway
23 en suite (bth/shr) (4 fmly) (10 with balcony) TV in all
bedrooms STV Radio in rooms Direct dial from all bedrooms
Mini-bar in all bedrooms Licensed Full central heating Open
parking available Covered parking available (charged)
Supervised Child discount available 12yrs Outdoor swimming
pool (heated) Tennis Boule Bicycle rental Open terrace
Covered terrace Table tennis Last d 21.30hrs Languages
spoken: English, German
ROOMS: (room only) s 280-330FF; d 330-410FF **Special
breaks**
MEALS: Continental breakfast 40FF Lunch 128-248FFalc
Dinner 128-248FFalc✱
CARDS: ✺ ▨ Travellers cheques

METZ Moselle

★ ★ Grand Hotel de Metz
3 rue des Clercs *57000*
☎ 387361633 FAX 387741704
This hotel is located in a quiet pedestrian street just a few steps
away from the cathedral, and with many points of interest
nearby it provides the ideal venue from where to explore the

city. It offers peaceful rooms equipped with all modern
conveniences and pleasant public rooms to relax in. In addition
there is a dining room where a large breakfast is served in the
morning.
In town centre Near motorway
62 en suite (bth) (10 fmly) No smoking in 2 bedrooms TV in all
bedrooms STV Lift Night porter Full central heating Open
parking available (charged) Covered parking available
(charged) Child discount available Languages spoken:
English, German, Italian
CARDS: ✺ ▦ ▨ ◗ Travellers cheques

★ ★ ★ Novotel Metz Centre
Ctre St-Jacques, pl des Paraiges *57000*
☎ 387373839 FAX 387361000
Novotel offer their clients good quality accommodation in
modern, well-equipped bedrooms and have refined
restaurants serving good quality cuisine They have excellent
business meeting and conference facilities and some have food
and beverages available 24 hours a day. All their hotels have at
least one bedroom for disabled guests.
Near river Forest area In town centre Near motorway
120 en suite (bth) (15 fmly) No smoking in 26 bedrooms TV in
all bedrooms STV Radio in rooms Direct dial from all
bedrooms Mini-bar in all bedrooms Licensed Lift Night
porter Full central heating Air conditioning in bedrooms
Open parking available (charged) Covered parking available
(charged) Supervised Child discount available 16yrs Outdoor
swimming pool Pool table Bicycle rental Open terrace
Languages spoken: English & German
CARDS: ✺ ▦ ▨ ◗ Travellers cheques

★ ★ ★ Hotel Royal Concorde Bleu Marine
23 av Foch *57000*
☎ 387668111 FAX 387561316
This hotel is architecturally stunning and dates back to the
beginning of the century. Carefully renovated with great
attention to detail, it features comfortable bedrooms equipped
with modern amenities and an attractive restaurant where
traditional cuisine is served. Located close to the centre with
its historic sights and assorted entertainment, it provides the
ideal venue for an overnight stop or longer holiday break.
Near lake In town centre Near motorway
62 en suite (bth/shr) No smoking in 18 bedrooms TV in all
bedrooms STV Radio in rooms Direct dial from all bedrooms
Mini-bar in all bedrooms Licensed Lift Night porter Full
central heating No children Child discount available 16yrs
Sauna V meals Last d 23.00hrs Languages spoken: English
German & Spanish
CARDS: ✺ ▦ ▨ ◗ Travellers cheques

★ ★ ★ Hotel du Théâtre
Port St-Marcel, 3 rue du Pont St-Marcel *57000*
☎ 387311010 FAX 387300466
The hotel stands on the banks of the River Moselle in the
historic heart of Metz and provides the ideal base from which
to discover this 3000-year old city. The bedrooms are spacious
and well equipped with luxury en suite facilities offering a high
level of comfort. The restaurant is housed in a 17th-century
building and offers a wide choice of dishes from the region,
served by attentive staff in traditional Lorraine costume.
Near river Near lake In town centre Near motorway
36 en suite (bth/shr) (5 fmly) No smoking in 3 bedrooms TV in
all bedrooms STV Direct dial from all bedrooms Mini-bar in
all bedrooms Licensed Lift Night porter Full central heating
Open parking available Covered parking available Child
discount available 10yrs Outdoor swimming pool

Fishing Sauna Solarium Gym Pool table Jacuzzi/spa Bicycle rental Open terrace V meals Last d 23.00hrs Languages spoken: English German Italian & Spanish

ROOMS: (room only) s 395-550FF; d 490-990FF
Reductions over 1 night Special breaks
MEALS: Full breakfast 55FF Continental breakfast 55FF Lunch 98-168FF&alc Dinner 98-168FF&alc
CARDS: ●● ▆▆ ▆▆ ◉ Travellers cheques

MIRECOURT Vosges

★ ★ Le Luth
av de Chamiec 88500
☎ 329271212 FAX 329372344
The town of Mirecourt is the capital of the violin makers in France and also the setting for the contemporary hotel 'Le Luth'. The interior is decorated in pink and grey pastel shades and features charming bedrooms which provide a peaceful night's sleep. The restaurant serves light, delicious cuisine which consists of well-flavoured dishes of good quality and will please the most discerning gourmet. A choice of sporting and sight-seeing opportunities is available to those visitors who like an action-packed stay.
Forest area Near motorway
29 en suite (bth/shr) 17 rooms in annexe (8 fmly) (7 with balcony) TV in all bedrooms Licensed Full central heating Open parking available Child discount available Bicycle rental Open terrace V meals Last d 21.15hrs
MEALS: Full breakfast 45FF Continental breakfast 38FF Lunch 80-165FF&alc Dinner 80-165FF&alcCARDS: ●● ▆▆ ▆▆ Travellers cheques

NANCY Meurthe-et-Moselle

★ ★ Albert 1er - Astoria
3 rue de l'Armée Patton 54000
☎ 383403124 FAX 383284778
The historic town of Nancy is the capital of Lorraine and famous for its Place Stanislas, where this hotel is located. It features fully equipped bedrooms overlooking an interior garden and an English-style bar. With its excllent conference and leisure facilities it is also a good venue for business meetings and seminars.
In town centre Near motorway
125 en suite (bth/shr) TV in all bedrooms Direct dial from all bedrooms Licensed Lift Night porter Full central heating Open parking available Covered parking available (charged) Child discount available 4yrs Pool table Open terrace Languages spoken: English & German
CARDS: ●● ▆▆ ▆▆ ◉ JCB Travellers cheques

★ ★ ★ La Résidence
30 blvd Jean Jaurés 54000
☎ 383403356 FAX 383901628
Pleasant and modern hotel in the downtown area of Nancy. All bedrooms are soundproofed.
In town centre
22 en suite (bth/shr) (5 with balcony) No smoking in 4 bedrooms TV in all bedrooms Direct dial from all bedrooms Licensed Lift Full central heating Child discount available 10yrs Languages spoken: English & German
ROOMS: (room only) s 270-350FF; d 270-350FF
CARDS: ●● ▆▆ ▆▆ ◉

REHAINVILLER Meurthe-et-Moselle

★ ★ ★ Château d'Adomenil
54300
☎ 383740481 FAX 383742178
Near river Forest area
12 en suite (bth/shr) 9 rooms in annexe (1 fmly) (1 with balcony) TV in all bedrooms STV Mini-bar in all bedrooms Licensed Full central heating Air conditioning in bedrooms Open parking available Supervised Child discount available Outdoor swimming pool (heated) Fishing Bicycle rental Open terrace Last d 21.30hrs Languages spoken: English
CARDS: ●● ▆▆ ▆▆ ◉ Travellers cheques

ST-AVOLD Moselle

★ ★ ★ De L'Europe
7 rue Altmayer 57500
☎ 387920033 FAX 387920123
As soon as guests step over the threshold in this hotel, they are met with a friendly smile and warm hospitality. Stylishly decorated throughout, it offers pleasant guest rooms with modern amenities and a renowned restaurant which has earned many recommendations in gastronomic guides. The outstanding cuisine serves classic dishes and a choice of fresh fish and seafood specialities, complemented by a splendid selection of great French vintages and equally rated Alsace wines.
Forest area Near motorway
34 en suite (bth/shr) (3 fmly) TV available STV Direct dial from all bedrooms Licensed Lift Full central heating Open parking available Covered parking available (charged) Supervised Child discount available 12yrs Open terrace V meals Last d 22.00hrs Languages spoken: English German & Italian
CARDS: ●● ▆▆ ▆▆

★ ★ ★ Novotel Saint-Avold
RN 33- Autoroute A4 57500
☎ 387922593 FAX 387920247
(from St Avold town take direction of American Cemetery/motorway, from motorway exit St Avold in direction of town)
Forest area Near motorway
61 en suite (bth/shr) (10 fmly) No smoking in 11 bedrooms TV in all bedrooms STV Radio in rooms Direct dial from all bedrooms Mini-bar in all bedrooms Licensed Night porter Open parking available Child discount available 16yrs Outdoor swimming pool Boule Bicycle rental Open terrace Last d 24.00hrs Languages spoken: German
ROOMS: (room only) s fr 440FF; d fr 470FF **Special breaks**
MEALS: Full breakfast 55FF Continental breakfast 55FF Lunch 70-250FFalc Dinner 70-250FFalc
CARDS: ●● ▆▆ ▆▆ ◉ Travellers cheques

ST-MIHIEL Meuse

★★ Le Rive Gauge
pl de l'Ancienne Gare *55300*
☎ 329891583 FAX 329891535
The hotel is situated nine miles from the Lac de Madine and welcomes its visitors into a warm family atmosphere. The comfortable bedrooms have modern facilities and offer peaceful accommodation. There is a country-style restaurant which serves a range of tasty regional dishes and local specialities, plus a congenial bar, and guests are well looked afters by an attentive and courteous staff.
Near river
10 en suite (bth/shr) TV in all bedrooms STV Direct dial from all bedrooms Licensed Full central heating Air conditioning in bedrooms Open parking available Child discount available Outdoor swimming pool Pool table Open terrace V meals Languages spoken: English
ROOMS: (room only) s 200-240FF; d 220-240FF
Reductions over 1 night Special breaks
MEALS: Full breakfast 30FF Continental breakfast 40FF Lunch 60-148FF&alc
CARDS: ●● ☲ ⑨ Travellers cheques

SARREBOURG Moselle

★★ Hotel les Cèdres
Zone Loisirs, chemin d'Imling *57400*
☎ 387035555 FAX 387036633
Near lake Near motorway
44 en suite (bth/shr) (5 fmly) No smoking in 3 bedrooms TV in all bedrooms STV Direct dial from all bedrooms Licensed Lift Night porter Full central heating Open parking available Supervised Child discount available Pool table Bicycle rental Open terrace Covered terrace Games for children V meals Last d 22.00hrs Languages spoken: English German Italian & Dutch
ROOMS: (room only) s 328-535FF; d 358-535FF ✶ **Special breaks**
CARDS: ●● ▦ ☲ Travellers cheques

SARREGUEMINES Moselle

★★★ Hotel a'Alsace
10 rue Poincaré *57200*
☎ 387984432 FAX 387983985
Near river Forest area In town centre Near motorway
Closed 24 Dec & Good Fri
28 en suite (bth/shr) No smoking in 7 bedrooms TV in all bedrooms Direct dial from all bedrooms Licensed Lift Night porter Full central heating Open parking available Supervised Open terrace V meals Last d 22.00hrs Languages spoken: English,German,Italian
CARDS: ●● ▦ ☲ ⑨ Travellers cheques

SENONES Vosges

★★ Au Bon Gite
3 pl Vautrin *88210*
☎ 329579246 FAX 329579392
Situated in the heart of the Alsace, Senones is one of the most fascinating towns of the Vosges region and also the location for this charming establishment. The hotel features an attractive interior where the bedrooms are tastefully furnished with well co-ordinated shades and fabrics. The restaurant, with large bay window, serves tasty regional dishes, complemented by a choice of fine wines.

Near river In town centre
7 en suite (bth/shr) TV in all bedrooms Licensed Full central heating Open parking available (charged) Covered parking available (charged) Child discount available Jacuzzi/spa Open terrace V meals Last d 21.30hrs Languages spoken: English
CARDS: ●● ▦ ☲ Travellers cheques

VAL-D'AJOL Vosges

★★★ La Résidence
5 rue des Mousses *88340*
☎ 329306852/329306460 FAX 329665300
This 19th-century building used to be a private residence and is situated in five acres of peaceful parkland. The rooms have either contemporary or period furnishings, and are equipped with modern facilities. The spacious dining-room with large open fire place opens on to the park with ancient trees, and serves a range of dishes from a generous cuisine. There is no shortage of places to be seen and plenty of out door activities in the vicinity.
Forest area
Closed 15 Nov-15 Dec
55 rms (29 bth 24 shr) 30 rooms in annexe (23 fmly) (3 with balcony) TV in all bedrooms Licensed Full central heating Open parking available Child discount available 12yrs Outdoor swimming pool (heated) Tennis Fishing Riding Bicycle rental Open terrace Covered terrace Games for children Last d 21.30hrs Languages spoken: English,German,Spanish
ROOMS: (room only) s 230-320FF; d 300-400FF
MEALS: Full breakfast 45FF Lunch 135-255FF Dinner 135-255FF
CARDS: ●● ▦ ☲ ⑨ Travellers cheques

VERDUN Meuse

★★ Orchidées
Z I de d'Etain *55100*
☎ 329864646 FAX 329861020
The hotel can be found on the ring-road around Verdun and is located amidst green surroundings. It features peaceful bedrooms with modern facilities, inviting foyer and an attractive restaurant. Situated onhe main access road, it is a good venue for those who want to break their journey en route to further holiday destinations.
Forest area Near motorway
Closed 19 Dec-6 Jan
42 en suite (shr) (2 fmly) No smoking in 3 bedrooms TV in all bedrooms STV Direct dial from all bedrooms Licensed Full central heating Open parking available Outdoor swimming pool Tennis Open terrace Last d 21.30hrs Languages spoken: English
ROOMS: (room only) s 240FF; d 260FF
MEALS: Full breakfast 35FF Continental breakfast 35FF Lunch 60-140FF&alc Dinner 60-140FF&alc
CARDS: ●● ▦ ☲ Travellers cheques

VILOSNES Meuse

★★ Le Vieux Moulin
3 rue des Petits Ponts *55110*
☎ 329858152 FAX 329858819
Located in a charming small village in the northern Meuse region, the hotel welcomes its visitors in an attractive setting with a terrace overlooking the river. The building goes back as far as the year 1800, and offers refurbished bedrooms with every modern convenience, whilst the restaurant serves

innovative dishes of high quality. The surrounding area offers various leisure options, and because of its good geographical position, guests may want to visit the nearby Verdun battlefields or Belgium and Luxembourg to the north.
Near river Forest area Near motorway
Closed Feb/Xmas & New Year
18 rms (2 fmly) TV in all bedrooms Direct dial from all bedrooms Full central heating Open parking available
Covered parking available Supervised Child discount available Bicycle rental Open terrace V meals Languages spoken: English
CARDS: ♥ ▰ ▰ ◑ Travellers cheques

VITTEL Vosges

★ ★ ★ Angleterre
rue de Charmey *88800*
☎ 329080842 FAX 329080748
(From A31 exit Bulgneville continue through Contrexeville to Vittel)
The Hotel d'Angleterre is located in the town of Vittel, which is tucked away in a pretty valley amidst wooded hills. It features attractive guest rooms with every modern day convenience, as well as comfortable lounges, and a restaurant featuring set and à la carte menus with a large choice of appetising dishes to suit all palates.
Forest area In town centre Near motorway
61 en suite (bth/shr) TV in all bedrooms STV Direct dial from all bedrooms Licensed Lift Night porter Full central heating

Open parking available Child discount available 10yrs Bicycle rental Open terrace V meals Last d 21.00hrs Languages spoken: English,German,Italian
ROOMS: (room only) s 330-380FF; d 380-480FF
CARDS: ♥ ▰ ▰ ◑ Travellers cheques

★ ★ ★ Bellevue
503 av de Chatillon *88800*
☎ 329080798 FAX 329084189
In the heart of the Vosges mountains this family hotel is situated opposite a pine forest, in the famous spa resort of Vittel. It features comfortable bedrooms with good amenities and a restaurant which offers a fine cuisine which can be adapted to individual needs. All this is complemented by a pleasant day room, and a park with summer terrace where children can play freely.
Forest area Near motorway
Closed 16 Oct-15 Apr
36 en suite (bth/shr) (2 fmly) (4 with balcony) No smoking in 2 bedrooms TV in all bedrooms STV Direct dial from all bedrooms Licensed Full central heating Open parking available Covered parking available Child discount available 14yrs Boule Bicycle rental Open terrace V meals Last d 21.00hrs Languages spoken: English
ROOMS: (room only) s 240-300FF; d 300-380FF ✱
Reductions over 1 night
MEALS: Continental breakfast 45FF Lunch 95-160FF&alc Dinner 95-160FF&alc
CARDS: ♥ ▰ ▰ ◑ Travellers cheques

Alsace

Alsace prides itself on being the smallest region in France and with its unique blend of German and French influences, distilled over a thousand years, makes this tiny province a popular tourist destination. Enjoying its own special identity, which is not quite German nor wholly French, the local customs, folklore, dances and dialects are fervently preserved.

(Top): The black grapes of the Rhein Valley.

(Bottom): The château and church at Eguisheim, home of the 11th-century Pope Léon IX. Much of the town is built on a plan of concentric circles which was used for 1200 years.

ESSENTIAL FACTS

DÉPARTEMENTS:	Bas-Rhin, Haut-Rhin
PRINCIPAL TOWNS	Strasbourg, Colmar, Mulhouse, Haguenau
PLACES TO VISIT:	Petite France area of Strasbourg; the Krutenau district of Colmar, Castle of Haut-Koenigsbourg; old St Bartélemy mine at Ste-Marie-aux-Mines; Mont Ste-Odile pilgrimage centre plus the opportunity to walk some of the old pilgrim paths in the area; the Éco-musée de Haut Alsace near Guebwiller, reconstruction of traditional homes, farms and workshops showing the domestic life of past generations
REGIONAL TOURIST OFFICE	26 avenue de la Paix, 67080 Strasbourg Tel 88 25 01 66
LOCAL GASTRONOMIC DELIGHTS	Munster cheese, choucroute/sauerkraut (cabbage) cooked in Riesling or Kirsch, perhaps with Strasbourg sausage or pork chops; turkey cooked with chestnuts; fricassée of chicken with cream; pâté de foie gras with trufffles; kougelhopf, Alsatian cake; baeckoffe, stew; trout; venison; snails; blueberries; cherries; gingerbread
DRINKS	Famed white wines such as Riesling, Sylvaner, Gerwürztraminer, Tokay; Crémant is a sparkling Alsace wine made using the Champagne method; German-sounding beers brewed in the region; eaux de vies of Kirsch (cherry), Mirabelle (plum) or Framboise (raspberry).

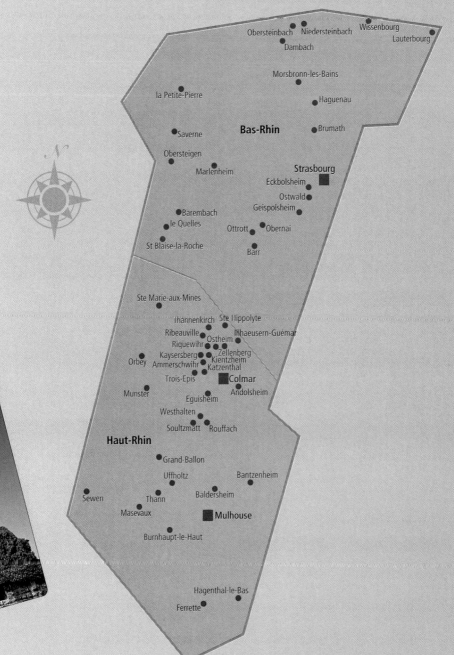

Obersteinbach
Niedersteinbach
Wissenbourg
Lauterbourg
Dambach

Morsbronn-les-Bains

la Petite-Pierre

Haguenau

Bas-Rhin

Saverne

Brumath

Obersteigen

Marlenheim

Strasbourg

Eckbolsheim

Ostwald
Geispolsheim

Barembach
le Quelles

Ottrott
Obernai

St Blaise-la-Roche

Barr

Ste Marie-aux-Mines

Thannenkirch
Ste Hippolyte

Ribeauvillé
Ilhaeusern-Guémar

Riquewihr
Ostheim

Kaysersberg
Zellenberg

Orbey
Ammerschwihr
Kientzheim

Trois-Epis
Katzenthal

Colmar

Munster
Andolsheim

Eguisheim

Westhalten

Soultzmatt
Rouffach

Haut-Rhin

Grand-Ballon

Uffholtz
Bantzenheim

Sewen
Baldersheim

Thann

Masevaux
Mulhouse

Burnhaupt-le-Haut

Hagenthal-le-Bas

Ferrette

119

EVENTS & FESTIVALS

Mar Masevaux Passion Play; Strasbourg Carnival and International Calvacade;

Apr Kayserberg Painted Easter Egg Market; Osenbach Snail Festival; Strasbourg Light & Sound Show at the Cathedral;

May Haguenau Humorous Notes Festival; Mulhouse Bach Festival; Strasbourg Light & Sound Show at the Cathedral; Guebwiller Wines Fair; Mulhouse International Exhibition and Fair

Jun Riebauville Kougelhopf Festival; Mulhouse Bach Festival; Strasbourg Music Festival; Turckheim Round of the Night Watch; Colmar Folk Art Performances; Saverne Rose Fair; Ste-Marie-aux-Mines International Mineral Market;

Jul Colmar Classical Music Festival; Strasbourg Music Festival; St-Pierre-Bois Light & Sound Show; Strasbourg Light & Sound Show at the Cathedral; Colmar Folk Art Performances; Zellenberg 'S'Wielada" (*Alsatian wine-making traditions*); Orschwihr Grand Crémant Night; Illhaeusern Boatmen's Fair; Thannenkirch Cherry Festival; Mutzig Parade of the 'Sans-Culottes'; Rouffach Witch Festival; Husseren-les-Châteaux Open-Air Café Festival; Dambach Blueberry Festival; Hunawihr Ami

Fritz Folklore Festival; Stotzheim Harvest Festival

Aug Lauterbourg Rock Festival; Thann Classical Music Festival; Mulhouse Jazz Festival; Strasbourg Romanesque Festival (*medieval music in the churches along the Romanesque route*); Strasbourg Light & Sound Show at the Cathedral; Turckheim Round of the Night Watch; Zellenberg 'S'Wielada" (*Alsatian wine-making traditions*); Guebwiller Open Air Folk Festival; Colmar Wines Fair; Rosheim Munster Cheese & Folk Festival; Gertwiller Gingerbread & Wine Festival

Sep Sélestat Gregorian Music Festival in Ste-Foix Church; Ribeauvillé Ancient Music Festival; Strasbourg Musica (contemporary music); Strasbourg European Fair; Riquewihr Wine Festival; Meistratzheim Sauerkraut Festival; Wuenheim New Wine Festival & Procession

Oct Strasbourg Light & Sound Show at the Cathedral; Turckheim Round of the Night Watch; Grape Harvest Festivals at Barr & Obernai;

Nov Mulhouse Antiques Fair; Christmas Markets at Strasbourg and Kaysersberg

Dec Christmas Markets at Strasbourg and Kaysersberg; Huningue Feast of St Nicholas; Riquewihr Christmas Market

---

AMMERSCHWIHR Haut-Rhin

★★À l'Arbre Vert
7 rue des Cigognes *68770*
☎ 389471223 FAX 389782721
Situated amongst extensive vineyards, this picturesque hotel offers an informal restaurant with wood-panelled walls featuring interesting carvings, and a menu containing well-flavoured regional dishes. A warm welcome and comfortable accommodation are assured by the friendly hosts, the Gebel-Fournier family.
Forest area In town centre
Closed 17 Nov-29 Nov & 9 Feb-21 Mar RS high season (half board only)
17 en suite (bth/shr) 4 rooms in annexe (4 fmly) TV in all bedrooms Direct dial from all bedrooms Mini-bar in all bedrooms Licensed Full central heating V meals Last d 21.15hrs Languages spoken: English,German,Italian,,Japanese
ROOMS: (room only) s 140-220FF; d 290-350FF
MEALS: Full breakfast 35FF Continental breakfast 35FF Lunch 85-230FF&alc Dinner 85-230FF&alc*
CARDS: ●● ▆▆ ▆ ·》 Travellers cheques

ANDOLSHEIM Haut-Rhin

★★Du Soleil
1 rue de Colmar *68280*
☎ 389714053 FAX 389714036
Visitors can expect a warm welcome and efficient, friendly service in this establishment situated in a quiet village. Pleasant, informal public areas and cosy bedrooms are comfortably furnished and offer a high level of comfort. The restaurant serves a selection of skilfully executed regional

dishes which are augmented by an excellent wine list.
Forest area Near motorway
Closed 26 Jan-5 Mar
18 rms (8 bth 5 shr) (3 fmly) (1 with balcony) TV in all bedrooms Licensed Full central heating Open parking available Covered parking available (charged) Supervised V meals Last d 21.00hrs Languages spoken: English,German
ROOMS: (room only) s 130-280FF; d 130-280FF
MEALS: Full breakfast 33FF Continental breakfast 33FF Lunch 120-220FF Dinner 120-220FF
CARDS: ●● ▆▆ ▆ ·》 Travellers cheques

BALDERSHEIM Haut-Rhin

★★Au Cheval Blanc
27 rue Principale *68390*
☎ 389454544 FAX 389562893
This attractive building is situated in the heart of the village of Baldersheim. It has been in the hands of the same family for more than 100 years, during which time the art of hospitality has been passed down from father to son. The bedrooms are comfortable and equipped with modern amenities. The menu features first-class cuisine and is particularly noted for its specialities from the Alsace; it is complemented by a good selection of French and regional wines.
Forest area Near motorway
83 en suite (bth/shr) 30 rooms in annexe (4 fmly) (6 with balcony) No smoking in 6 bedrooms TV in all bedrooms Mini-bar in all bedrooms Licensed Lift Full central heating Open parking available Indoor swimming pool (heated) Sauna Solarium Jacuzzi/spa Last d 22.40hrs Languages spoken: English & German
CARDS: ●● ▆ Travellers cheques

BANTZENHEIM Haut-Rhin

★★ De La Poste
1 rue de Bale *68490*
☎ 389260426
The hotel offers its visitors comfortable accommodation in pleasant, informal surroundings. The bedrooms provide modern amenities and adequate comfort. The restaurant serves a good range of regional specialities prepared with local market-produce. The hotel is a good base for visits to nearby Germany (3km) and Switzerland (32km).
Forest area
19 rms (15 bth/shr) (4 fmly) TV in all bedrooms Licensed Full central heating Open parking available Child discount available 10yrs Boule Last d 20.30hrs Languages spoken: English,German
MEALS: Continental breakfast 25FF Lunch 50-100FF&alc Dinner 50-100FF&alc✱
CARDS: ➡ ☎ Travellers cheques

BAREMBACH Bas-Rhin

★★★ Château de Barembach
5 rue Maréchal-de-Lattre *67130*
☎ 388979750 FAX 388471719
A small 'Renaissance ' castle situated in a peaceful little mountain village. The building dates back to 1892, and was used as a private residence until 1983. After careful renovation it was transformed into a charming hotel where the restaurant serves an excellent cuisine. The lush green surroundings offer splendid skiing facilities in winter, and is a paradise for walkers in the summer. In addition, the attractive bedrooms have modern facilities and provide relaxing accommodation.
Near river Near lake Forest area Near motorway
15 en suite (bth/shr) (1 with balcony) TV in all bedrooms Radio in rooms Direct dial from all bedrooms Mini-bar in all bedrooms Licensed Full central heating Open parking available Child discount available 12yrs Open terrace V meals Last d 21.30hrs Languages spoken: English,German,Danish,Italian
ROOMS: (room only) s 385-720FF; d 475-895FF **Special breaks**
MEALS: Full breakfast 55FF Lunch 120-398FF&alc Dinner 195-398FF&alc✱
CARDS: ➡ ☎ ☎ ◑ Travellers cheques

BARR Bas-Rhin

★★ Le Brochet
9 pl de l'Hôtel-de-Ville *67140*
☎ 388089242 FAX 388084815
(Approach via A35)
Set in the lively village of Barr, in the heart of the Alsace. The cosy bedrooms are furnished to create the atmosphere of a real Alsation home and are equipped with every modern convenience. The menu features a wide range of regional specialities prepared with high quality ingredients.
Forest area In town centre
Closed Jan-8 Feb
23 en suite (bth/shr) TV in all bedrooms Direct dial from all bedrooms Licensed Full central heating Open parking available Covered parking available Supervised Child discount available 12yrs Open terrace V meals Last d 22.00hrs Languages spoken: English, German
ROOMS: (room only) d 280-320FF
MEALS: Full breakfast 40FF Lunch 125-185FF&alc Dinner 125-185FF&alc
CARDS: ➡ ☎ ☎

★★ Du Château d'Andlau
113 Vallée St-Ulrich *67140*
☎ 388089678 388089403 FAX 388080093
The hotel occupies a tranquil location just outside the town of Barr, and features a homely interior enhanced by fresh bouquets of flowers and rustic furniture. The cosy bar, shaded garden and friendly restaurant provide the informal setting for a relaxing stay. The bedrooms are attractively appointed and equipped with modern facilities.
Near river Forest area
23 rms (7 bth 15 shr) TV in all bedrooms Licensed Full central heating Open parking available Supervised Open terrace Languages spoken: English, German
CARDS: ➡ ☎ Travellers cheques

BRUMATH Bas-Rhin

★★ L'Écrevisse
4 av de Strasbourg *67170*
☎ 385511108 FAX 388518902
Since 1844 the hotel has been in the hands of the Orth family. Seven generations have presided over the kitchen and have been responsible for the outstanding combinations of traditional cuisine from the Alsace and contemporary dishes, complemented by a prestigious wine list. The guest-rooms are attractively furnished and offer modern day comfort combined with traditional hospitality.
Forest area In town centre Near motorway
36 rms (1 with balcony) TV in all bedrooms Licensed Lift Full central heating Open parking available Covered parking available Sauna Gym Jacuzzi/spa Open terrace V meals Languages spoken: English,German
CARDS: ➡ ☎ ☎ ◑ Travellers cheques

BURNHAUPT-LE-HAUT Haut-Rhin

★★★ Hotel de l'Aigle d'Or
24 rue du Pont d'Aspach *68520*
☎ 389831010 FAX 389831033
(From Lyon on A6 take exit 15 towards Belfort)
This contemporary hotel was built in 1993 and offers up-to-date accommodation in cheerful, attractive surroundings. It features a day room with fire place which provides cosy seating, a bar, terrace and a garden where guests may want to go for a stroll and where children can play. The bedrooms are equipped with modern amenities and the elegant restaurant serves a cuisine to suit all tastes.
Forest area Near motorway
26 en suite (bth/shr) (2 fmly) TV in all bedrooms STV Radio in rooms Direct dial from all bedrooms Licensed Night porter Full central heating Open parking available Covered parking available Supervised Boule Bicycle rental Open terrace Languages spoken: English,German,Italian
ROOMS: (room only) d 275-350FF
MEALS: Full breakfast 42FF Lunch 79-285FFalc
CARDS: ➡ ☎ ☎ ◑ Travellers cheques

COLMAR Haut-Rhin

★★★ Bristol (Best Western)
7 pl de la Gare *68000*
☎ 389235959 FAX 389239226
Situated in the town of Colmar, the Hotel Bristol extends a warm welcome to its visitors. It is set in the gardens and walkways of Château d'Eau and the Champ de Mars. The interior features a well-balanced choice of selected furnishings, whilst the bedrooms are individually

contd.

appointed with every modern amenity. The restaurant 'Rendez-vous de Chasse' is a true reflection of its name, and guests can sample specialities from the Alsace prepared with fresh regional ingredients, complemented by a wine-list offering a selection of fine, fruity Alsace wines.
In town centre
70 en suite (bth/shr) (15 fmly) (19 with balcony) No smoking in 20 bedrooms TV in all bedrooms STV Radio in rooms Direct dial from all bedrooms Mini-bar in all bedrooms Licensed Lift Night porter Full central heating Open parking available Child discount available 12yrs Open terrace Covered terrace V meals Last d 22.00hrs Languages spoken: English,German
ROOMS: (room only) s 350-550FF; d 400-750FF
Reductions over 1 night Special breaks
MEALS: Full breakfast 56FF Lunch 160-390FF&alc Dinner 160-390FF&alc
CARDS: 💳 ▦ 🎫 🌐 Travellers cheques

★ ★ Climat de France
1 rue de la Gare *68000*
☎ 389413480 Cen Res 64460123 FAX 389412784
(in village centre)
This recently renovated hotel is situated in the very heart of Colmar and offers pleasant bedrooms with private facilities. The restaurant serves a choice of regional dishes of good flavour and quality.
In town centre
41 en suite (bth/shr) (4 with balcony) TV in all bedrooms Radio in rooms Direct-dial available Licensed Lift Night porter Full central heating No children Languages spoken: English & German
CARDS: 💳 🎫

★ ★ ★ Fecht
1 rue de la Fecht *68000*
☎ 389413408 FAX 389238028
The Hotel de la Fecht is situated close to the picturesque quarter of the old town and features an entirely renovated, comfortable interior. Bedrooms are tastefully decorated, with modern appointments, and there is a bright, airy lounge for relaxation, whilst an assortment of dishes is served in the 'Decapole' restaurant and charming 'Moris Stub' which is housed in the cellar. In addition guests can take a stroll in the magnificent garden.
In town centre
39 en suite (bth/shr) Some rooms in annexe (1 with balcony) No smoking in 4 bedrooms TV in all bedrooms Mini-bar in all bedrooms Licensed Night porter Full central heating Open parking available (charged) Covered parking available (charged) Supervised Child discount available 12yrs Sauna Bicycle rental Open terrace Last d 22.00hrs Languages spoken: English,German
CARDS: 💳 ▦ 🎫 🌐 Travellers cheques

★ ★ ★ ★ Hostellerie Le Maréchal
4 pl des Six Montagnes Noires *68000*
☎ 389416032 FAX 389245940
(From A35 exit at Colmar Sud,follow directions for town centre,then signs for 'Le Maréchal')
The hotel dates back to 1534 and is situated in the most beautiful part of the old town, called 'Little Venice'
Surrounded by half-timbered houses with waterside terraces and gardens, the hotel provides a romantic setting for a memorable stay. Exquisitely furnished guest rooms with spacious en-suite facilities offer the highest level of comfort, whilst the cuisine incorporates outstanding dishes, unique in

flavour and presentation, executed by some of the most skilled chefs in the whole of France.
Near river In town centre
30 en suite (bth/shr) (1 fmly) No smoking in 4 bedrooms TV in all bedrooms STV Direct dial from all bedrooms Licensed Lift Night porter Full central heating Air conditioning in bedrooms Open parking available (charged) Sauna Jacuzzi/spa Open terrace Covered terrace V meals Last d 23.00hrs Languages spoken: English, German
MEALS: Full breakfast 75FF Continental breakfast 50FF Lunch 140-365FF&alc Dinner 195-365FF&alc✱
CARDS: 💳 🎫 Travellers cheques

★ ★ ★ Novotel Colmar
49 rte de Strasbourg *68000*
☎ 389414914 FAX 389412256
Novotel offer their clients good quality accommodation in modern, well equipped bedrooms and have refined restaurants serving good quality cuisine They have excellent business meeting and conference facilities and some have food and beverages available 24 hours a day. All their hotels have at least one bedroom for disabled guests.
Near motorway
66 rms 36 rooms in annexe (30 fmly) No smoking in 12 bedrooms TV in 170 bedrooms STV Radio in rooms Direct dial from 170 bedrooms Mini-bar in 170 bedrooms Licensed Night porter Full central heating Air conditioning in bedrooms Open parking available Supervised Child discount available 16yrs Outdoor swimming pool Open terrace V meals Last d 24.00hrs Languages spoken: English,German
CARDS: ▦ 🎫 🌐 Travellers cheques

★ ★ ★ Hotel St-Martin
38 Grand Rue *68000*
☎ 389241151 FAX 389234778

Town centre
Ideally located in the heart of the old quarter of Colmar, the Hotel Saint Martin was originally a coaching inn and dates back to 1361. All of its magnificent period architecture has been preserved, especially its façade and Renaissance turret at the rear of the building, flanked by a handsome 17th-century spiral staircase. The cosy bedrooms have modern facilities and the hotel is perfectly placed for sightseeing and all the shops and restaurants.
In town centre
Closed Jan-Feb
24 en suite (bth/shr) (4 fmly) (2 with balcony) TV in all bedrooms Direct dial from all bedrooms Mini-bar in 13 bedrooms Room-safe Lift Night porter Full central heating Air conditioning in bedrooms Child discount available 12yrs

Open terrace Languages spoken: English, German
ROOMS: (room only) s 290-450FF; d 350-650FF
Reductions over 1 night Special breaks: Christmas breaks
CARDS: ●● ▆▆ ▆▆ ●) Travellers cheques

EGUISHEIM Haut-Rhin

★★ Auberge des Comtes
1 pl Charles-de-Gaulle *68420*
☎ 389411699 FAX 389249710
Standing at the foot of the 13th-century ramparts in the town of Eguisheim, the modern-built Auberge des Comtes offers its visitors a warm welcome in tastefully decorated surroundings. It features sound-proofed bedrooms - most equipped with modern amenities - pleasant foyer and a summer terrace. The restaurant offers a good choice of dishes incorporating delicacies from the Alsace which are skilfully prepared by the chef-proprietor.
Forest area In town centre Near motorway
18 rms (14 bth) (3 with balcony) Licensed Lift Full central heating Open parking available Supervised Child discount available 12yrs Open terrace Languages spoken: German
CARDS: ●● ▆▆

★★★ Hostellerie du Pape
10 Grande'Rue *68420*
☎ 389414121 FAX 389414131
The hotel provides a charming setting for an enjoyable stay in this typical Alsace village. Surrounded by extensive, vineyards it features restful accommodation offering a good level of comfort, a shaded terrace in the flower-filled courtyard and a high quality country cuisine. In addition, culinary enthusiasts can brush up their skills by enrolling in a cooking course conducted by Annie Huber.
Forest area In town centre Near motorway
Closed early Jan-mid Feb
33 en suite (bth) (3 fmly) TV in all bedrooms Licensed Lift Full central heating Open parking available Child discount available 12yrs Open terrace V meals Last d 21.00hrs
Languages spoken: English,German
MEALS: Full breakfast 50FF Continental breakfast 50FF Lunch 90-250FF&alc Dinner 90-250FF&alc✱
CARDS: ●● ▆▆ ▆▆ ●) Travellers cheques

FERRETTE Haut-Rhin

★★ Collin
68480
☎ 389404072 FAX 389403826
In the very south of the Alsace region the medieval village of Ferrette is set against the side of an enormous rock which bears the ruins of two castles. At an altitude of 600 metres and close to the Swiss border, it is the charming setting for the hotel Collin. The chef-proprietor presides over the kitchen, and is responsible for the tempting dishes which are prepared with great care and skill. The guest rooms are traditionally furnished and have modern facilities.
Forest area
Closed 13 Jan-1 Feb/8 Sep-2 Oct
9 en suite (bth/shr) TV in 20 bedrooms STV Direct dial from 20 bedrooms Licensed Full central heating Child discount available 12yrs Open terrace V meals Last d 21.00hrs
Languages spoken: English,German
CARDS: ●● ▆▆ Travellers cheques

GEISPOLSHEIM Bas-Rhin

★★★ Novotel Strasbourg Sud
rte de Colmar *67400*
☎ 388662156 FAX 388672163
Novotel offer their clients good quality accommodation in modern, well-equipped bedrooms and have refined restaurants serving good quality cuisine They have excellent business meeting and conference facilities and some have food and beverages available 24 hours a day. All their hotels have at least one bedroom for disabled guests.
Near motorway
76 en suite (bth) (76 fmly) No smoking in 20 bedrooms TV in all bedrooms Radio in rooms Direct dial from all bedrooms Mini-bar in all bedrooms Licensed Night porter Full central heating Air conditioning in bedrooms Open parking available Child discount available Outdoor swimming pool Golf 18 Mini-golf Bicycle rental Open terrace Covered terrace ping pong,volley ball Last d 24.00hrs Languages spoken: English,German,Italian,Spanish
CARDS: ●● ▆▆ ▆▆ ●) Travellers cheques

GRAND-BALLON Haut-Rhin

★★ Du Grand Ballon
68760
☎ 389768335 FAX 389831063
This rustic establishment is situated at the highest point in the Vosges mountains, and has an interior where wood-panelled dining-rooms and guest accommodation create a warm, informal atmosphere. As well as being a good starting point for numerous walks, it is also the ideal venue for a skiing holiday. It has a renowned cuisine which offers regional specialities, and comfortable bedrooms with private facilities.
Near lake Forest area Near motorway
18 rms (5 fmly) Licensed Full central heating Open parking available Supervised Child discount available 8yrs Open terrace V meals Last d 20.30hrs Languages spoken: English,German
MEALS: Continental breakfast 30FF Lunch 90-205FF&alc Dinner 90-205FF&alc✱
CARDS: ●● ▆▆ Travellers cheques

HAGENTHAL-LE-BAS Haut-Rhin

★★★ Jenny
84 rue de Hagenheim *68220*
☎ 389685009 FAX 389685864
The hotel is the ideal venue for an overnight stop or a short break. The elegant bedrooms are equipped with modern facilities and offer peaceful accommodation. The menu features imaginatively cooked dishes and an excellent choice of fine wines.
Near river Forest area Near motorway
Closed 20 Dec-30 Dec
26 en suite (bth/shr) (3 fmly) (21 with balcony) TV in all bedrooms Radio in rooms Licensed Lift Full central heating Open parking available Supervised Indoor swimming pool (heated) Fishing Sauna Solarium Bicycle rental Open terrace Covered terrace V meals Last d 21.30hrs Languages spoken: English,German
CARDS: ●● ▆▆ ▆▆ ●) Travellers cheques

Taking your mobile phone to France?
See page 11

123

HAGUENAU Bas-Rhin⁻

★ ★ **Climat de France**
rte de Bitche, chemin de Sandlach *67500*
☎ 388730666 Cen Res 64460123 FAX 388734961
(from A4 take the A440 then N63 to the N62)
Forest area Near motorway
47 en suite (bth/shr) (1 fmly) TV in all bedrooms Direct-dial available Licensed Full central heating Open parking available Open terrace Languages spoken: English, German, Italian & Spanish
CARDS: ●● ⬛

ILLHAEUSERN-GUÉMAR Haut-Rhin

★ ★ ★ **Clairère**
rte de Guemar *68970*
☎ 389718080 FAX 389718622
The hotel is situated in the heart of the Alsace region and provides a good base for exploring the region or for trying out some of the excellent restaurant in the locality. Equipped with modern day facilities, the bedrooms are decorated with flair and feature some nice personal touches.
Forest area Near motorway
Closed Jan-Feb
25 en suite (bth) (8 with balcony) TV in all bedrooms Direct-dial available Mini-bar in all bedrooms Licensed Lift Open parking available (charged) Outdoor swimming pool (heated) Tennis Boule Bicycle rental Languages spoken: English,German
CARDS: ●● ⬛ Travellers cheques

KATZENTHAL Haut-Rhin

★ ★ **A l'Agneau**
16 Grande Rue *68230*
☎ 389809025 FAX 389275958
(From Ingersheim and Ammerschwihr on the Wine Road)
This informal establishment is located in the heart of a peaceful village surrounded by the vineyards of the Alsace. The peaceful bedrooms are attractively appointed and offer a good standard of comfort. The restaurant serves a large choice of Alsatian specialities complemented by the splendid wines. Wine tasting can be arranged for guests.
Forest area Near motorway
Closed 21 Dec-Feb
11 en suite (bth/shr) 2 rooms in annexe (1 fmly) (1 with balcony) TV in 3 bedrooms STV Direct dial from all bedrooms Licensed Full central heating Open parking available Supervised Child discount available 12yrs Open terrace Last d 22.00hrs Languages spoken: English,German·
ROOMS: (room only) d 260-320FF
MEALS: Continental breakfast 35FF Lunch 70-280FF&alc Dinner 95-280FF&alc
CARDS: ●● ⬛ Travellers cheques

KAYSERSBERG Haut-Rhin

★ ★ ★ **Les Remparts**
4 rue Flieh *68240*
☎ 389471212 FAX 389473724
The hotel is located in the medieval village of Kaysersberg. With its newly acquired annexe offering spacious bedrooms, it is an ideal venue for a family holiday. Guest are ensured of a comfortable stay under the impeccable management of the untiring proprietor Christiane Keller. In addition, the

surrounding area offers a multitude of leisure facilities and places of interest to visit.
Near river Forest area Near motorway
43 en suite (bth/shr) 15 rooms in annexe (8 fmly) (18 with balcony) No smoking in 2 bedrooms TV in all bedrooms STV Mini-bar in all bedrooms Licensed Lift Full central heating Open parking available Covered parking available (charged) Sauna Pool table Open terrace Languages spoken: English,German
CARDS: ●● ⬛ ⬛ Travellers cheques

KIENTZHEIM Haut-Rhin

★ ★ **Hostellerie Schwendi**
2 pl Schwendi *68240*
☎ 389473050 FAX 389490449
(E of Kaysersberg)
The Hostelry Schwendi is located in Kientzheim, a small medieval market town adorned with the typical frame-work houses of the region. It features individually styled guest accommodation with modern amenities and offers a first-class cuisine, skilfully prepared by the proprietor's son Fabien.
Forest area
Closed 24 Dec-16 Mar
17 en suite (bth) TV in all bedrooms Direct dial from all bedrooms Licensed Full central heating Open parking available Open terrace V meals Last d 21.00hrs Languages spoken: English
ROOMS: (room only) d 320-370FF
MEALS: Full breakfast 36FF Continental breakfast 36FF Lunch 95-300FF&alc Dinner 95-300FF&alc✱
CARDS: ●● ⬛ ⬛ ●》

MARLENHEIM Bas-Rhin

★ ★ ★ **Cerf**
30 rue du Général-de-Gaulle *67520*
☎ 388877373 FAX 388876808
In 1938, this former coaching inn was transformed into the charming establishment it is today. Its bedrooms are equipped with modern facilities offering a good standard of comfort. The cuisine is based on traditional recipes from the Alsace, which are enhanced by innovative combinations of ingredients.
Forest area In town centre Near motorway
15 rms (7 bth 6 shr) (2 fmly) TV in all bedrooms Direct dial from all bedrooms Mini-bar in 3 bedrooms Licensed Full central heating Open parking available (charged) Child discount available Open terrace Last d 21.30hrs Languages spoken: English,German
ROOMS: (room only) s 285-550FF; d 410-850FF
MEALS: Full breakfast 60FF Lunch 250-550FF&alc Dinner 295-550FF&alc
CARDS: ●● ⬛ ⬛ ●》 Travellers cheques

MORSBRONN-LES-BAINS Bas-Rhin

★ ★ **Ritter Hoft**
23 rue Principale *67360*
☎ 388540737 FAX 388093339
This modern establishment is situated in a village with thermal baths and remedial services. Pretty bedrooms provide pleasant accommodation and are appointed with private facilities. There is a cosy TV lounge/reading room, and the restaurant offers a refined cuisine incorporating a choice of gourmet dishes augmented by excellent wines.
Forest area

17 en suite (bth/shr) Some rooms in annexe (4 with balcony)
TV in all bedrooms Direct dial from all bedrooms Licensed
Lift Full central heating Air conditioning in bedrooms Open
parking available Supervised Child discount available 12yrs
Indoor swimming pool (heated) Sauna Boule Jacuzzi/spa
Bicycle rental Open terrace V meals Last d 1.30hrs
Languages spoken: English & German
MEALS: Full breakfast 50FF Continental breakfast 35FF Lunch
70-240FF&alc Dinner 70-240FF&alc✱
CARDS: ●● 💳 Travellers cheques

MUNSTER Haut-Rhin

★ ★ Aux Deux Sapins
49 rue du 9ème Zouaves *68140*
☎ 389773396 FAX 389770390
This friendly establishment provides the pleasant combination
of good food, modern comfort and a cheerful welcome by the
owners. The discreetly furnished guest rooms have modern
amenities, whilst the proprietor Mr Rousselet is responsible for
the delicious, light cuisine served in the restaurant.
Near river Forest area Near motorway
Closed 20 Nov-19 Dec
25 en suite (bth/shr) 6 rooms in annexe (7 fmly) (3 with
balcony) TV in all bedrooms STV Direct dial from all
bedrooms Mini-bar in all bedrooms Licensed Lift Full central
heating Open parking available Supervised Child discount
available 8yrs Boule Bicycle rental Open terrace Last d
21.00hrs Languages spoken: English,German
ROOMS: (room only) s 240-300FF; d 240-320FF
MEALS: Continental breakfast 32FF Lunch 70-200FF Dinner
70-200FF
CARDS: ●● 💳 🔷 Travellers cheques

NIEDERSTEINBACH Bas-Rhin

★ ★ Cheval Blanc
67510
☎ 388095531 FAX 388095024
Located at 65 kilometres from Strasbourg and close to the
German border, this large residence with an architecture
typical of the Alsace region, is situated in a tiny picturesque
village with only 170 inhabitants. It offers its visitors a warm
welcome upon arrival and has comfortable bedrooms and a
gourmet cuisine, as well as a multitude of attractions available.
Because of its geographical position it is a good base to
explore the forests and nearby lakes as well the as surrounding
châteaux.
Near river Near lake Forest area Near motorway
Closed 15 days Jun & 10 days Dec
26 rms (8 bth 16 shr) 4 rooms in annexe (5 fmly) (3 with
balcony) TV in all bedrooms Direct dial from all bedrooms
Licensed Lift Open parking available Child discount available
13yrs Outdoor swimming pool (heated) Tennis Fishing Boule
Bicycle rental Open terrace Childrens play area,table tennis V
meals Languages spoken: English,German
CARDS: ●● 💳 Travellers cheques

OBERNAI Bas-Rhin

★ ★ Hostellerie la Diligence
23 pl de la Mairie *67210*
☎ 388955569 FAX 388954246
(A35 exit Obernai onto N422)
The hotel is situated on the Place de la Mairie in the historic
centre of the picturesque town of Obernai. The comfortable
bedrooms have good modern amenities and guests can enjoy a

true gourmet breakfast in the morning before exploring the
beautiful Alsace countryside.
Forest area In town centre Near motorway
41 rms (27 bth 12 shr) 15 rooms in annexe (9 fmly) TV in all
bedrooms STV Direct dial from all bedrooms Mini-bar in 15
bedrooms Licensed Lift Full central heating Open parking
available (charged) Supervised Open terrace Languages
spoken: English, German
ROOMS: (room only) s 168-465FF; d 168-465FF ✱
CARDS: ●● 💳 💳 Travellers cheques

★ ★ ★ Hotel le Parc
169 rte d'Ottrott *67210*
☎ 388955008 FAX 388953729
The Hotel Le Parc is the result of a success story, where the
talent and determination of a family transformed a simple
house into a grand hotel. It features spacious guest rooms and
apartments - some are situated under the eaves - with good
quality beds providing an excellent night's sleep. The
restaurant serves an outstanding cuisine accompanied by the
fine wines and beers from the region. There are numerous
leisure facilities on offer inside, whilst the surrounding region
is rich in places of interest and extensive natural scenery.
Forest area
Closed Dec
50 en suite (bth) TV in all bedrooms STV Direct dial from all
bedrooms Licensed Lift Night porter Full central heating Air
conditioning in bedrooms Open parking available Supervised
Child discount available 8yrs Indoor swimming pool (heated)
Outdoor swimming pool (heated) Riding Sauna Solarium
Pool table Boule Jacuzzi/spa Bicycle rental Open terrace V
meals Last d 21.00hrs Languages spoken: English & German
ROOMS: (room only) s fr 530FF; d 650-990FF ✱ **Special**
breaks: Jan-Mar breaks
MEALS: Full breakfast 75FF Lunch fr 190FF&alc Dinner fr
190FF&alc
CARDS: ●● 💳 💳 Travellers cheques

OBERSTEIGEN Bas-Rhin

★ ★ ★ Hostellerie Belle-Vue
16 rte de Dabo *67710*
☎ 388873239 FAX 388873777
(From A4(Paris to Strasbourg) exit at Saverne, follow directions
for Wangenbourg/Dabo)
This family run hotel is situated in the largest forested area of
the Vosges region and offers the ideal venue for resting,
relaxing and getting fit. The hotel hides behind a large wall of
dense forests and sandstone massifs. It features individually
styled bedrooms appointed with modern amenities, a
congenial bar and an informal restaurant where friendly,
cheerful staff serve a selection of rustic home-cooked dishes.
Forest area
Closed 6 Jan-10 Apr
38 en suite (bth/shr) 3 rooms in annexe (1 fmly) (8 with
balcony) TV in all bedrooms Direct dial from all bedrooms
Mini-bar in 7 bedrooms Licensed Lift Full central heating
Open parking available Covered parking available (charged)
Supervised Child discount available 12yrs Outdoor swimming
pool (heated) Sauna Solarium Gym Pool table Boule
Jacuzzi/spa Bicycle rental Open terrace Covered terrace Last
d 21.00hrs Languages spoken: English & German
ROOMS: s 350-430FF; d fr 480FF
MEALS: Full breakfast 50FF Lunch 85-200FF&alc Dinner 85-
200FF&alc
CARDS: ●● 💳 💳 Travellers cheques

OBERSTEINBACH Bas-Rhin

★ ★ Alsace Villages
49 rue Principale *67510*
☎ 388095059 FAX 388095356
The hotel features apartment-style guest accommodation and
is situated in Obersteinbach in the Sauer valley. The guest
rooms are comfortable, equipped with good quality beds and
modern facilities. The restaurant offers a varied menu
including many regional dishes prepared with local produce.
Near river Near beach Forest area
Closed 12 Nov-10 Dec
12 en suite (shr) (4 fmly) (5 with balcony) No smoking in 2
bedrooms TV in all bedrooms Licensed Full central heating
Open parking available Supervised Child discount available
11yrs Riding Boule Bicycle rental Open terrace V meals
Last d 21.00hrs Languages spoken: English, German
MEALS: Full breakfast 59FF Continental breakfast 39FF Lunch
95-125FF&alc Dinner 95-125FF&alc✱
CARDS: ●● ▥ Carte Blanche Travellers cheques

ORBEY Haut-Rhin

★ ★ ★ Hostellerie Motel Au Bois Le Sire
20 rue Général de Gaulle *68370*
☎ 389712525 FAX 389713075
(from A35 take N415, then D48)
The establishment is located in the Orbey valley at the foot of
the Vosges mountain range, and is surrounded by woodlands,
pine forests and hundreds of little streams. Because of its ideal
location it provides a good base for touring the countryside or
visiting the numerous places of interest. The bedrooms which
are divided over the main building and the adjacent motel,
provide comfortable accommodation and adequate comfort.
The menu features a range of well-prepared dishes.
Near river Forest area In town centre
Closed 6 Jan-4 Feb
36 rms (12 bth/shr) 24 rooms in annexe (3 fmly) (6 with
balcony) TV in 25 bedrooms STV Direct dial from all
bedrooms Mini-bar in 23 bedrooms Licensed Full central
heating Open parking available Child discount available 10yrs
Indoor swimming pool (heated) Sauna Jacuzzi/spa Open
terrace V meals Last d 21.00hrs Languages spoken: English &
German
ROOMS: (room only) s 230-360FF; d 240-380FF
Reductions over 1 night
MEALS: Full breakfast 50FF Lunch 53-320FF&alc Dinner 90-
320FF&alc
CARDS: ●● ▥▥ ▥ Travellers cheques

★ ★ Les Bruyères
35 rue Général de Gaulle *68370*
☎ 389712036 FAX 389713530
(exit Colmar from A35 onto N83, then onto N415. At
Kaysenberg take D to Orbey)
This completely renovated hotel stands opposite a splendid
park and is within walking distance of all the shops and
restaurants. Located in a popular tourist area in the Alsace, it
provides a good base to visit the beautiful castles and medieval
villages which are situated along the wine route. Well
equipped bedroom accommodation and a selection of
imaginative dishes on offer in the restaurant provide the
important ingredients for a pleasant stay.
Near river Forest area In town centre Near motorway
Closed 15 Nov-20 Dec/2 Jan-15 Feb
29 en suite (bth/shr) 4 rooms in annexe (11 fmly) (14 with
balcony) TV in all bedrooms STV Direct dial from all

bedrooms Licensed Lift Full central heating Open parking
available Child discount available 12yrs Sauna Boule Open
terrace Covered terrace V meals Last d 21.15hrs Languages
spoken: English German & Italian
ROOMS: (room only) s 230-300FF; d 230-350FF
MEALS: Full breakfast 38FF Lunch 75-165FF&alc Dinner 75-
165FF&alc
CARDS: ●● ▥▥ ▥ ◑ Travellers cheques

OSTHEIM Haut-Rhin

★ ★ ★ Au Nid de Gogognes
2 rte de Colmar *68150*
☎ 389479144 FAX 389479988
This beautiful Alsace-style inn is situated close to the towns of
Colmar and Kaysersberg and provides a good base from
which to visit places of interest in the region. It has peaceful
guest accommodation with good modern facilities, cosy
lounges, exhibition rooms and conference rooms, and a
restaurant where good quality home-cooking is complemented
by the best wines of the Alsace.
Near river Forest area In town centre Near motorway
Closed Feb-22 Mar
49 rms (21 bth 16 shr) 12 rooms in annexe (2 fmly) (9 with
balcony) TV in all bedrooms Radio in rooms Direct dial from
all bedrooms Licensed Lift Full central heating Open parking
available Covered parking available Child discount available
Boule Bicycle rental Open terrace Wkly live entertainment
Last d 21.30hrs Languages spoken: English,German
MEALS: Full breakfast 35FF Lunch 68-195FF&alc Dinner 68-
195FF&alc✱
CARDS: ●● ▥ Travellers cheques

OSTWALD Bas-Rhin

★ ★ ★ ★ Château de l'Ile
4 Quai Heydt *67540*
☎ 388668500 FAX 388668549
(from A35 exit 7 towards Ostwald and follow signs for Chateau
de l'Ile)
Standing midway between Strasbourg and the international
airport, the Château de l'Ile is surrounded by an extensive park.
The hotel consists of various half-timbered buildings built in
the distinct style of the Alsace, and offers elegant bedrooms
which are decorated with traditional period furnishings. Guests
can choose from a gourmet restaurant which serves regional
dishes, or enjoy a meal on the riverside terrace. There is an
unrivalled choice of leisure facilities indoors, and the
surrounding region has numerous places of interest to visit.
Near river Forest area Near motorway
62 en suite (bth/shr) (1 fmly) (14 with balcony) TV in all
bedrooms STV Radio in rooms Direct dial from all bedrooms
Mini-bar in all bedrooms Licensed Lift Night porter Full
central heating Air conditioning in bedrooms Open parking
available Supervised Child discount available 12yrs Indoor
swimming pool (heated) Fishing Sauna Solarium Gym
Jacuzzi/spa Bicycle rental Open terrace V meals Last d
22.00hrs Languages spoken: English, German, Italian, Spanish
CARDS: ●● ▥▥ ▥ ◑ JCB Travellers cheques

OTTROTT Bas-Rhin

★ ★ ★ Hostellerie des Châteaux
11 rue des Châteaux *67530*
☎ 388481414 FAX 388959520
The building stands on the edge of a forest and reflects in its
interior the traditional charm of the Alsace. Stained glass

windows and wood-panelled ceilings and walls create a warm informal atmosphere where guests can relax and unwind. Luxurious bedrooms offer comfortable accommodation and the cosy restaurant which serves imaginative combinations of ingredients such as crayfish, sole, spinach and foie gras, are complemented by excellent Alsace wines.
Near river Forest area
Closed Feb
67 en suite (bth/shr) 18 rooms in annexe (5 fmly) (32 with balcony) TV in all bedrooms Direct dial from all bedrooms Licensed Lift Full central heating Open parking available Supervised Child discount available 5yrs Indoor swimming pool (heated) Riding Sauna Solarium Gym Pool table Jacuzzi/spa Bicycle rental Open terrace Last d 21.00hrs Languages spoken: English,German
MEALS: Full breakfast 65FF Lunch 180-430FF&alc Dinner 180-430FF&alc✱
CARDS: ● ■ ■ ● Travellers cheques

PETITE-PIERRE, LA Bas-Rhin

★ ★ Au Lion d'Or
15 rue Principale 67290
☎ 388704506 FAX 388704556
Surrounded by extensive forest scenery, the fortified village of La Petite-Pierre combines the charm of the past with the beauty of the splendid countryside, and provides the setting for this friendly establishment. The bedrooms have private facilities while delicious meals are served in the panoramic restaurant.
Forest area Near motorway
Closed 5 Jan-5 Feb & 29 Jun-4 Jul
40 en suite (bth/shr) (2 fmly) (13 with balcony) TV in all bedrooms STV Direct dial from all bedrooms Licensed Lift Full central heating Open parking available Supervised Child discount available 12yrs Indoor swimming pool (heated) Tennis Sauna Jacuzzi/spa Bicycle rental Open terrace V meals Last d 21.00hrs Languages spoken: English, German
ROOMS: (room only) s 250-290FF; d 370-450FF
MEALS: Full breakfast 55FF Continental breakfast 35FF Lunch 98-260FF&alc Dinner 98-260FF&alc
CARDS: ● ■ ■ ● Travellers cheques

★ ★ ★ Clairière
63 rte d'Ingwiller 67290
☎ 388717500 FAX 388704105
This family establishment occupies an exceptional location in the heart of a forest and provides a good base for walks in the surrounding region. The restaurant serves a traditional cuisine incorporating game specialities from the forest and regional dishes. There is an English-style bar and a range of leisure facilities, and the bedrooms are attractively furnished and appointed with en suite amenities.
Forest area
50 en suite (bth/shr) (20 fmly) (36 with balcony) TV in all bedrooms STV Direct dial from all bedrooms Mini-bar in all bedrooms Licensed Lift Full central heating Open parking available Indoor swimming pool (heated) Sauna Solarium Pool table Boule Jacuzzi/spa Open terrace V meals Last d 21.30hrs Languages spoken: English,Dutch,German
MEALS: Full breakfast 40FF Lunch 132-335FF&alc Dinner 132-335FF&alc✱
CARDS: ● ■ ■ ● Travellers cheques

★ ★ Auberge d'Imsthal
rte Forestière sur CD 178 67290
☎ 388014900 FAX 388704026
The inn is located in the heart of the Vosges forest, and provides the ideal venue for nature lovers and ramblers with its numerous footpaths, and forest and lake nearby. The bedrooms have views of the surrounding area and offer comfortable accommodation, while the restaurant serves a traditional cuisine based on regional ingredients.
Near river Forest area
23 rms (20 bth/shr) (3 fmly) (4 with balcony) TV in all bedrooms STV Direct dial from all bedrooms Licensed Lift Full central heating Open parking available Child discount available Fishing Sauna Solarium Pool table Mini-golf Jacuzzi/spa Open terrace V meals Last d 21.00hrs Languages spoken: English,German
CARDS: ● ■ ■ ● Travellers cheques

QUELLES, LES Bas-Rhin

★ ★ Neuhauser
67130
☎ 388970681 FAX 388971429
This peaceful establishment is located in an open space amidst pine woods, and is completely sheltered from the noise of the passing traffic. It has been in the same family for four generations and features well-equipped guest accommodation which offers a good degree of comfort, and a restaurant with a range of dishes to suit most tastes.
Forest area
17 rms (5 shr) 6 rooms in annexe (3 fmly) TV in all bedrooms STV Licensed Full central heating Open parking available Child discount available 10yrs Outdoor swimming pool (heated) Tennis Jacuzzi/spa Bicycle rental Open terrace Last d 20.45hrs Languages spoken: English
MEALS: Full breakfast 45FF Lunch 130-300FF&alc Dinner 130-300FF&alc✱
CARDS: ● ■ Travellers cheques

RIBEAUVILLÉ Haut-Rhin

★ ★ Au Cheval Blanc
122 Grande Rue 68150
☎ 389736138 FAX 389733703
Like most houses in the Alsace region, the façade of this hotel is adorned with flowers as a sign of welcome. Upon arrival visitors are met by the friendly owners Mr and Mrs Leber who show old fashioned hospitality. The rustic bedrooms offer a good level of comfort, and the restaurant serves generous portions of regional cooking accompanied by the best wines of the Alsace. In winter guests can rest in the lounge with large open fireplace, whilst in summer the flower-decked terrace provides an attractive setting for relaxation.
Forest area In town centre Near motorway
25 rms (20 shr) (6 fmly) Licensed Full central heating

★ ★ De La Tour
1 rue de la Mairie 68150
☎ 389737273 FAX 389733874
(off N83)
In town centre
Closed Jan-mid Mar
35 en suite (bth/shr) (8 fmly) TV in 18 bedrooms STV Licensed Lift Full central heating Open parking available (charged) Covered parking available (charged) Tennis Sauna Solarium Jacuzzi/spa Bicycle rental Open terrace Languages spoken: English & German
CARDS: ● ■ ●

ALSACE

RIQUEWIHR Haut-Rhin

★★ Du Cerf
5 rue Général-de-Gaulle *68340*
☎ 389479218 FAX 389490458
Located in the town of Riquewihr, which is known widely as the pearl of Alsace, the hotel is a favourite meeting place for all the local wine growers. The guest rooms are individually furnished and fully equipped with good quality beds and private facilities, whilst the informal restaurant serves a choice of culinary delights, complemented by a personal selection of fine wines.
In town centre
15 en suite (bth/shr) 2 rooms in annexe (1 fmly) (2 with balcony) TV in all bedrooms Licensed Full central heating Open terrace Last d 21.15hrs Languages spoken: English,German
CARDS: 🗢 💳 Travellers cheques

ROTHAU Bas-Rhin

La Rubanerie
67570
☎ 388970195 FAX 388471734
Near river Forest area
16 en suite (bth/shr) (6 fmly) TV in 8 bedrooms STV Direct dial from all bedrooms Full central heating Open parking available Outdoor swimming pool (heated) Sauna Boule Bicycle rental Open terrace V meals Last d 20.30hrs
ROOMS: (room only) s 290-340FF; d 315-440FF
Reductions over 1 night
MEALS: Full breakfast 55FF Continental breakfast 42FF Dinner 140-250FF&alc✱
CARDS: 🗢 💳💳 🕦 Travellers cheques

ROUFFACH Haut-Rhin

★★★★ Château d'Isenbourg (Relais et Châteaux)
68250
☎ 389496353 FAX 389785370
(from Colmar take N83 towards Belfort, exit at Rouffach Nord. At first traffic lights turn right, then second right. Château on right after crossroads)
Dating from medieval times, the Château d'Isenbourg stands on a hillside overlooking the town of Rouffach and the Rhine Valley. The Château with its 40 rooms and imposing vaulted cellars is run with care to create a friendly atmosphere in top quality surroundings.
Forest area Near motorway
Closed mid Jan-mid Mar
40 en suite (bth/shr) 8 rooms in annexe (1 fmly) (2 with balcony) TV in all bedrooms Direct dial from all bedrooms Mini-bar in all bedrooms Licensed Lift Night porter Full central heating Open parking available Supervised Child discount available 12yrs Indoor swimming pool (heated) Outdoor swimming pool (heated) Tennis Sauna Gym Boule Jacuzzi/spa Bicycle rental Open terrace Covered terrace Table tennis, Massage V meals Last d 21.30hrs Languages spoken: English, German
ROOMS: (room only) s 865-1480FF; d 865-1990FF **Special breaks**
MEALS: Full breakfast 130FF Continental breakfast 85FF Lunch 270-370FF&alc Dinner 270-370FF&alc
CARDS: 🗢 💳💳 🕦 JCB Travellers cheques

ST-BLAISE-LA-ROCHE Bas-Rhin

★★ Auberge de la Bruche
rue Principale *67420*
☎ 388976868 FAX 388472222
Ideally situated near all the main access roads in the region, the hotel is a good starting point for exploring the surrounding sights or walks in the nearby forests. It features fully equipped bedrooms which provide relaxing accommodation, and a restaurant which offers a regional cuisine, augmented by selected Alsace wines.
Forest area Near motorway
Closed 23 Dec-23 Jan
13 en suite (bth/shr) 2 rooms in annexe TV in all bedrooms Direct dial from all bedrooms Licensed Full central heating Open parking available Covered parking available (charged) Supervised Child discount available 8yrs Indoor swimming pool (heated) Outdoor swimming pool (heated) Sauna Solarium Boule Jacuzzi/spa Open terrace Last d 20.45hrs Languages spoken: English
ROOMS: (room only) s 255-300FF; d 255-300FF
MEALS: Continental breakfast 40FF Lunch 120-165FF&alc Dinner 120-165FF&alc
CARDS: 🗢 💳 Travellers cheques

ST-HIPPOLYTE Haut-Rhin

★★★ Hostellerie Munsch Aux Ducs de Lorraine
68590
☎ 389730009 FAX 389730546
(From A35 (Mulhouse-Strasbourg) take exit 12 to St-Hippolyte)

This traditional inn is located at the foot of the Haut Koenigsbourg castle and has a friendly, country-style interior where the bedrooms are tastefully decorated with co-ordinated fabrics and furnishings, offering a high standard of comfort. The restaurant affords splendid views of the rolling countryside and serves a traditional cuisine, prepared with the freshest produce available in the region. Staff are courteous and provide a friendly service at all times.
15 Feb-24 Nov, and 10 Dec-10 Jan
42 en suite (bth/shr) (9 fmly) (32 with balcony) TV in all bedrooms Radio in rooms Direct dial from all bedrooms Mini-bar in 1 bedroom Licensed Lift Full central heating Open parking available Covered parking available (charged) Child discount available 12yrs Tennis Bicycle rental Open terrace Last d 21.30hrs Languages spoken: English,German
ROOMS: (room only) s 300-400FF; d 400-700FF
MEALS: Continental breakfast 60FF Lunch 95-315FF&alc Dinner 115-310FF&alc
CARDS: 🗢 💳 Travellers cheques

SAVERNE Bas-Rhin

★ ★ Chez Jean Winstub S'Rosestube
3 rue de la Gare *67700*
☎ 388911019 FAX 388912745
This hotel has been completely renovated and the bedrooms
offer a high level of comfort combined with decor of the
region. It incorporates two restaurants, one specialising in
food of Alsace.
Near river Forest area In town centre
25 en suite (bth/shr) (6 fmly) (4 with balcony) TV in all
bedrooms STV Radio in rooms Direct dial from all bedrooms
Room-safe Licensed Lift Full central heating Covered
parking available (charged) Supervised Child discount
available Sauna Solarium Bicycle rental Open terrace
Covered terrace V meals Last d 21.15hrs Languages spoken:
English,German
ROOMS: (room only) s 328-368FF; d 428-468FF
MEALS: Full breakfast 50FF Lunch 90-165FF&alc Dinner 90-
165FF&alc
CARDS: 💳 🏧 💳 💳

SEWEN Haut-Rhin

★ ★ Des Vosges
38 Grande rue *68290*
☎ 389820043 FAX 389820833
The hotel is located in Sewen, a charming village at the foot
of the Ballon d'Alsace, surrounded by the forests of the
Vosges mountains. This family-run establishment is the ideal
venue for those who prefer a peaceful place to relax, and has
bedrooms - some with balcony - fitted with modern
amenities. There is an extensive garden with trees on the
banks of the river Doller, and a tastefully decorated
restaurant where Jean Michel Kieffer - a former pupil of the
famous chef Paul Bocuse - is responsible for the delicacies on
offer.
Near river Near lake Forest area
Closed 1-27Dec approx
17 rms (8 bth 7 shr) (3 fmly) (6 with balcony) TV in all
bedrooms Direct dial from all bedrooms Licensed Full central
heating Open parking available Covered parking available
(charged) Child discount available 15yrs Bicycle rental Open
terrace Covered terrace V meals Last d 20.30hrs Languages
spoken: German
MEALS: Full breakfast 35FF Continental breakfast 35FF Lunch
60-250FF&alc Dinner 90-250FF&alc*
CARDS: 💳 💳 Travellers cheques

SOULTZMATT Haut-Rhin

★ ★ Klein
44 rue de la Vallée *68570*
☎ 389470010 FAX 389476503
(Off N83 between Rouffach & Guebwiller)
This charming, cosy inn can be found in the village of
Soultzmatt, which is surrounded by vineyards and produces
renowned wines and mineral water. It has personally-styled
bedrooms, which are decorated in a discreet fashion and
provide relaxing accommodation, whilst the main dining-room
with attractive mezzanine serves a range of sophisticated
classic dishes and tasty, local specialities.
11 rms (1 bth 5 shr) TV in 4 bedrooms Direct dial from 4
bedrooms Licensed Full central heating Open parking
available Supervised Open terrace V meals Last d 21.00hrs
Languages spoken: English,German,Spanish

ROOMS: (room only) s 200-300FF; d 250-350FF *
MEALS: Continental breakfast 40FF Lunch 95-250FF&alc
Dinner 95-250FF&alc*
CARDS: 💳 🏧 💳 💳 Travellers cheques

STRASBOURG Bas-Rhin

★ ★ ★ Baumann
16 pl Cathédrale *67000*
☎ 388324214 FAX 388230392
Built in 1427, this is one of the most beautiful buildings in
Strasbourg, 'Maison Kammerzell', which houses a famous
restaurant and hotel in one. The house stands at the foot of the
famous cathedral and is a masterpiece of architecture from the
Middle Ages. It conceals a fabulous interior where ancient
woodwork and murals can be seen in abundance. The guest
accommodation is decorated in a completely different style
from the rest of the house and offers excellent private facilities.
There are four restaurants with vaulted ceilings and frescoes,
which serve an excellent cuisine incorporating classic and fine
regional dishes executed to perfection.
In town centre
9 en suite (bth/shr) (3 fmly) TV in all bedrooms STV Radio in
rooms Direct dial from all bedrooms Mini-bar in all bedrooms
Licensed Lift Night porter Full central heating Air
conditioning in bedrooms Child discount available 10yrs Golf
Tennis Squash Riding Gym Pool table Bicycle rental Open
terrace V meals Last d 23.30hrs Languages spoken:
English,German,Italian
CARDS: 💳 🏧 💳 💳 Travellers cheques

★ ★ Climat de France
14 rue des Corroyeurs *67200*
☎ 388290606 Cen Res 164460123 FAX 388293666
(off A4 at Montagne junction)
This attractive establishment is built in the distinct style of the
region and features comfortable bedrooms with every modern
convenience, as well as a restaurant which serves a
comprehensive buffet and a choice of traditional dishes with a
regional touch.
Near river In town centre Near motorway
66 en suite (bth/shr) TV in all bedrooms Radio in rooms
Direct dial from all bedrooms Licensed Lift Full central
heating Open parking available Open terrace Languages
spoken: English & Spanish
CARDS: 💳 🏧

★ ★ ★ Comfort Hotel Plaza
10 pl de la Gare *67000*
☎ 388151717 FAX 388151715
(Opposite the railway station)
Situated in the lively Place de la Gare, the hotel is just a stone's
throw from all the main sights in the city. It features charming,
traditionally furnished bedrooms with excellent modern
facilities, and a congenial restaurant-brasserie with a splendid
terrace. The banqueting hall is an exact replica of a castle
chamber, and is fitted with an authentic open fire place.
In town centre
78 en suite (bth/shr) (12 fmly) No smoking in 14 bedrooms TV
in all bedrooms STV Direct dial from all bedrooms Mini-bar
in all bedrooms Licensed Lift Night porter Full central
heating Child discount available 12yrs Open terrace V meals
Last d 23.00hrs Languages spoken: English,German
ROOMS: (room only) s 480FF; d 560FF *
MEALS: Full breakfast 58FF Lunch 51FF&alc Dinner 95FF&alc
CARDS: 💳 🏧 💳 💳 Travellers cheques

★ ★ ★ Grand Hotel Concorde
12 pl de la Gare *67000*
☎ 388528484 FAX 388528400
(Opposite the railway station)
A town centre hotel with well equipped, comfortable
bedrooms close to the main historical sites.
Near river Forest area In town centre Near motorway
83 en suite (bth/shr) (10 fmly) (39 with balcony) TV in all
bedrooms STV Direct dial from all bedrooms Mini-bar in all
bedrooms Licensed Lift Night porter Full central heating
Child discount available 12yrs Open terrace Languages
spoken: English,Italian,German
ROOMS: (room only) s 395-550FF; d 395-610FF
Reductions over 1 night Special breaks
CARDS: ●● � ══ ●》 Travellers cheques

★ ★ ★ Hotel Cathedrale
12 pl de la Cathédrale *67061*
☎ 388221212 FAX 388232800
(From A4 or A35 take exit 4 'Place de l'Étoile' and follow signs
for town centre and cathedral)
This entirely renovated luxurious hotel stands opposite the
Gothic cathedral in Strasbourg. The personally styled rooms
and suites feature refined, pastel-shaded furnishings and are
equipped with modern facilities. With its wood-panelling and
exposed brickwork the hotel offers the cosy setting for an
enjoyable stay, complemented by cheerful staff who provide an
attentive and discreet service. In addition there is an elegant
bar with panoramic views of the cathedral and the famous
'Maison Kammerzell'.
In town centre Near motorway
35 en suite (bth/shr) 5 rooms in annexe No smoking in 2
bedrooms TV in all bedrooms STV Radio in rooms Direct
dial from all bedrooms Mini-bar in all bedrooms Licensed
Lift Night porter Full central heating Child discount available
15yrs Languages spoken: English,German
ROOMS: d 340-790FF
CARDS: ●● � ══ ●》 Travellers cheques

★ ★ ★ Maison Rouge
4 r des Frances-Bourgeois *67000*
☎ 388320860 FAX 388224373
Concealed behind its scarlet façade, the hotel features an
elegant, peaceful interior where efficient staff offer a degree of
personal service which is difficult to match. Fine period
furniture and splendid fabrics create an atmosphere of well-
being throughout, whilst the charming guest rooms with
luxurious facilities offer a high degree of comfort. Because of
its location between the cathedral and Petit France district, the
hotel is close to all the main activities and surrounded by the
best restaurants.
In town centre
142 en suite (bth/shr) (8 fmly) (90 with balcony) TV in all
bedrooms STV Radio in rooms Direct dial from all bedrooms
Mini-bar in all bedrooms Licensed Lift Night porter Full
central heating Open parking available (charged) Supervised
Languages spoken: English,German,Italian
ROOMS: (room only) s 430-540FF; d 460-590FF
CARDS: ●● ▪▪ ══ ●》 Travellers cheques

★ ★ ★ Rohan
17 rue du Maroquin *67000*
☎ 388328511 FAX 388756537
This small, peaceful hotel is situated next to the cathedral in the
historic town centre. The bedrooms are furnished in varied
styles, alternating between rustic and Louis XV, and are
equipped with every modern convenience. Porters are on hand

upon arrival to carry guests' luggage from the surrounding
parking places to the hotel, which is located in a pedestrianised
area.
In town centre
36 en suite (bth/shr) (4 fmly) No smoking on premises TV in
all bedrooms STV Radio in rooms Direct dial from all
bedrooms Mini-bar in all bedrooms Room-safe Licensed Lift
Night porter Full central heating Air conditioning in
bedrooms Child discount available Languages spoken:
English German
ROOMS: (room only) s 360-700FF; d 495-795FF
CARDS: ●● ▪▪ ══ ●》 Travellers cheques

★ ★ ★ ★ Sofitel
4 pl St-Pierre-le-Jeune *67000*
☎ 388362626 FAX 388371370
The Sofitel chain comprises of a group of very fine modern,
comfortable hotels at the four star level. Bedrooms have been
carefully designed to cater to guests' relaxation and well being
and the restaurant facilities offer fine cuisine in pleasant
surroundings. Ideal for business clientele with excellent
conference and meeting facilities.
Near river In town centre Near motorway
158 en suite (bth/shr) (15 with balcony) TV in all bedrooms
STV Radio in rooms Direct dial from all bedrooms Mini-bar
in all bedrooms Licensed Lift Night porter Full central
heating Air conditioning in bedrooms Open parking available
(charged) Covered parking available (charged) Open terrace
V meals Languages spoken: English,German,Italian
CARDS: ●● ▪▪ ══ ●》 Travellers cheques

★ ★ Tour Service Hotel
18 rue de la Tour-Koenigshoffe *67000*
☎ 388294141 FAX 388295770
Entirely renovated in 1995, the hotel is situated in a pleasant,
quiet area, three minutes' drive from the town centre and transport services. The modern guest accommodation has private
facilities and provides a good level of comfort, whilst the restaurant is housed in an attractively decorated cellar with flower-
decked terrace, and serves classic as well as a regional cuisine.
In town centre
38 en suite (bth/shr) 10 rooms in annexe (7 fmly) TV in all
bedrooms STV Licensed Full central heating Open parking
available Child discount available 12yrs Open terrace V meals
Last d 22.00hrs Languages spoken: English,German,Italian
MEALS: Full breakfast 42FF Lunch fr 70FF&alc Dinner fr
130FF&alc✱
CARDS: ●● ══ Travellers cheques

★ ★ YG Hotel
14 rue Jean Monnet *67201*
☎ 388778560 FAX 388778533
The hotel is located only four minutes from the centre of town
and has attractively decorated bedrooms which are fitted with
every modern convenience. The restaurant offers a choice of
eating options including 'have as much as you can eat' from
the buffet and a range of regional specialities from the menu.
In addition there is a cosy bar to relax in and good leisure
facilities on offer.
Near motorway
67 en suite (bth/shr) (4 fmly) (3 with balcony) TV in all
bedrooms STV Direct dial from all bedrooms Licensed Night
porter Full central heating Open parking available
Supervised Child discount available 12yrs Indoor swimming
pool Outdoor swimming pool Tennis Pool table Boule Open
terrace V meals Languages spoken: English,German,Italian
CARDS: ●● ▪▪ ══ Travellers cheques

THANNENKIRCH Haut-Rhin

★ ★ Auberge la Meuniére
30 rue Ste Anne *68590*
☎ 389731047 FAX 389731231
(on the Colmar to Strasbourg road N83 take 2nd exit for
Bergheim then signed to Thannenkirch)
A cosy hotel with beautiful views to Haut Koenigsbourg Castle
and mountains.
Forest area
Closed 22 Dec-24 Mar
23 en suite (bth/shr) 4 rooms in annexe (9 fmly) (12 with
balcony) TV in all bedrooms Direct dial from all bedrooms
Licensed Lift Full central heating Open parking available
Covered parking available (charged) Child discount available
12yrs Sauna Gym Jacuzzi/spa Bicycle rental Open terrace
Covered terrace V meals Last d 21.00hrs Languages spoken:
English, German, Italian & Spanish
ROOMS: (room only) s 290FF; d 300-380FF
MEALS: Full breakfast 55FF Continental breakfast 35FF Lunch
95-235FF&alc Dinner 100-235FF&alc
CARDS: 🔴 💳 💳 Travellers cheques

THANN Haut-Rhin

★ ★ Du Parc
23 rue Kléber *68800*
☎ 389373747 FAX 389375623
Forest area Near motorway
20 en suite (bth/shr) (3 fmly) (1 with balcony) No smoking in 5
bedrooms TV in all bedrooms STV Direct dial from all
bedrooms Licensed Full central heating Open parking
available Child discount available 13yrs Outdoor swimming
pool (heated) Tennis Riding Bicycle rental Open terrace
Wkly live entertainment V meals Last d 21.30hrs Languages
spoken: English, Italian, Portuguese,German
MEALS: Full breakfast 50FF Continental breakfast 40FF Lunch
98-225FF&alc Dinner 145-225FF&alc✱
CARDS: 🔴 💳 💳 ⑨ Travellers cheques

TROIS-ÉPIS Haut-Rhin

★ ★ Villa Rosa
68410
☎ 389498119 FAX 389789045
This former private house was transformed into an hotel which
offers a warm and friendly atmosphere, cosy bedrooms and an
excellent cuisine . The pleasant interior comprises a
comfortable lounge with light woods and attractive furniture,
whilst the restaurant with pretty flower displays, serves a
cuisine which covers a wide seasonal repertoire of ingredients,
lovingly prepared by Alain Denis the chef-proprietor.
Forest area
Closed 12Feb-1Apr
10 en suite (bth/shr) (4 fmly) (4 with balcony) No smoking in all
bedrooms Direct dial from all bedrooms Licensed Full central
heating Child discount available 15yrs Outdoor swimming pool
(heated) Sauna Jacuzzi/spa Bicycle rental Open terrace Last d
20.30hrs Languages spoken: English,German
MEALS: Full breakfast 48FF Continental breakfast 25FF
Dinner 100-150FF&alc✱
CARDS: 🔴 💳 Travellers cheques

Taking your mobile phone to France?
See page 11

UFFHOLTZ Haut-Rhin

★ ★ Frantz
41 rue de Soultz *68700*
☎ 389755452 FAX 389757051
The hotel is located in the town of Uffholtz, situated at an
altitude of 310 metres at the foot of the Vosges mountain range.
The bedrooms are divided over the main building and very
peaceful annexe, and are mostly equipped with modern
facilities. The restaurant which enjoys a good reputation
locally, has a comprehensive menu complemented by fine
wines from the house cellar.
Forest area In town centre Near motorway
50 rms 8 rooms in annexe (1 with balcony) TV in all bedrooms
Direct dial from all bedrooms Licensed Full central heating
Open parking available Child discount available Boule
Bicycle rental Open terrace V meals Last d 21.30hrs
Languages spoken: English,German
MEALS: Full breakfast 35FF Continental breakfast 35FF Lunch
87-330FF&alc Dinner 87-330FF&alc✱
CARDS: 🔴 💳 💳 ⑨ Travellers cheques

WESTHALTEN Haut-Rhin

★ ★ ★ Auberge du Cheval Blanc
20 rue de Rouffach *68250*
☎ 389470116 FAX 389476440
(Access via Rouffach on N83)
Located in a pretty village surrounded by vineyards and
orchards. The auberge is decorated in typical Alsatian style and
you can expect a warm welcome on arrival from the proprietors.
Bedrooms are prettily decorated and have all modern facilities,
including facilities for disabled guests. The family-run restaurant
prepares regional dishes accompanied by home-produced wines.
Forest area
Closed 2-26 Feb & 29 Jun-9 Jul
12 en suite (bth/shr) (2 fmly) (4 with balcony) TV in all
bedrooms Direct dial from all bedrooms Mini-bar in all
bedrooms Licensed Lift Full central heating Air conditioning
in bedrooms Open parking available Child discount available
12yrs Open terrace Last d 21.00hrs Languages spoken:
English,German
ROOMS: (room only) s 350-450FF; d 400-480FF ✱
MEALS: Full breakfast 55FF Lunch 185-410FF&alc Dinner 155-
410FF&alc✱
CARDS: 🔴 💳

ZELLENBERG Haut-Rhin

★ ★ Au Riesling
5 rte du Vin *68340*
☎ 389478585 FAX 389479208
This friendly family hotel is situated amidst extensive
vineyards along the famous wine route, and offers stunning
views over the surrounding countryside. Inside, it features a
cosy interior, where attractive wood-panelling on walls and
ceilings create a homely atmosphere. A choice of delicious
specialities from the region is served in the attractive, spacious
dining-rooms with views over the countryside and the
picture-postcard village of Zellenberg.
Forest area
Closed Jan-10 Feb
36 en suite (bth/shr) (6 with balcony) Direct dial from all
bedrooms Licensed Lift Open parking available Covered
parking available Child discount available 10yrs Open terrace
V meals Last d 21.00hrs Languages spoken: German
MEALS: Full breakfast 42FF Lunch 98-190FF Dinner 98-250FF★

Western Loire

The Atlantic coast is a serious rival to the Riviera. There are 140 km of fine, white sandy beaches which stretch out to the horizon; rocky creeks wait to surprise and delight and with 210 days of sunshine each year, this must be a perfect holiday destination. The coastline is splashed with charming fishing villages and sophisticated resorts offering extensive sports and leisure facilities. The invigorating sea air and famously clear waters should give you an appetite for sampling some of the delicious seafood and regional wines.

(Top): Wherever you go in France it's certain that a wide selection of fresh vegetables will await you at market.

(Bottom): A bizarre inhabitant of the Magic Museum at Saumur.

ESSENTIAL FACTS

DÉPARTEMENTS:	Loire-Atlantique, Maine-et-Loire, Mayenne, Sarthe, Vendée
PRINCIPAL TOWNS	La Roche-sur-Yon, Nantes, Angers, Fontenay-le-Compte, Chateaubriant, les Sables-d'Olonne, Saumur, Le Mans, Laval, Cholet
PLACES TO VISIT:	Visit the Troglodyte caves near Saumur; the Cadre Noir (High School Riding) at Saumur; the historic theme park of the Puy du Fou, the brilliant crescent-shaped beach of les Sables-de-Olonne; the notable châteaux of Brissac, le Plessis-Bourre, le Lude, and Montreuil-Bellay
REGIONAL TOURIST OFFICE	2 rue de la Loire, 44204 Nantes Tel: 40 48 24 20
LOCAL GASTRONOMIC DELIGHTS	Beurre-blanc, a butter sauce usually served with shad or pike; matelote d'anguille, eels stewed in wine; noisette de porc aux pruneaux, fillet of pork in a cream and prune sauce; citrouillat, pumpkin pie; cotignac, delicate apple and almond paste; Petit Lu, these crisp butter biscuits from Nantes have been part of the tradition since the Middle Ages when they were the staple diet of sailors; charcuterie of rillettes, terrines and pâtés of game and foie gras.
DRINKS	Cider and Saumar-Champigny, a light and fruity red wine.
LOCAL CRAFTS WHAT TO BUY	Cloth from Clisson and Cholet famous for their textile industry; traditional wooden crafts from Jupilles; pottery from le Fuilet; fine china from the workshops in Malicorne; silk from the farms in Montreuil-Bellay

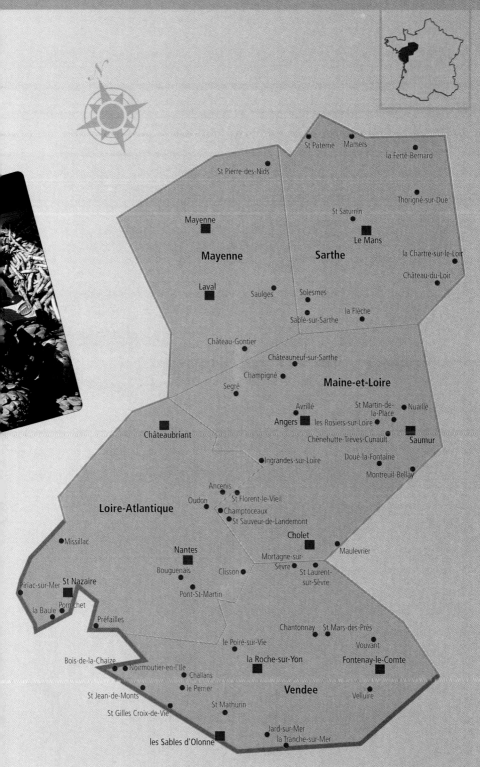

St Paterne Mamers

la Ferté-Bernard

St Pierre-des-Nids

Thorigné-sur-Due

St Saturnin

Mayenne

Le Mans

Mayenne   **Sarthe**

la Chartre-sur-le-Loir

Château-du-Loir

Laval

Saulges   Solesmes

Château-Gontier

la Flèche

Sablé-sur-Sarthe

Châteauneuf-sur-Sarthe

Champigné

Maine-et-Loire

Segré

Avrillé   St Martin-de-   Nuaillé
            la-Place

Angers   les Rosiers-sur-Loire

Châteaubriant

Chênehutte-Trèves-Cunault   **Saumur**

Doué-la-Fontaine

Ingrandes-sur-Loire

Montreuil-Bellay

Ancenis

Oudon   St Florent-le-Vieil

Loire-Atlantique   Champtoceaux

St Sauveur-de-Landemont

Cholet

Missillac

Mortagne-sur-   Maulevrier
Nantes   Sèvre

Bouguenais   Clisson   St Laurent-
                        sur-Sèvre

Piriac-sur-Mer   **St Nazaire**

Pont-St-Martin

la Baule Pornichet

Préfailles

Chantonnay   St Mars-des-Prés

le Poiré-sur-Vie

Vouvant

Bois-de-la-Chaize

Noirmoutier-en-l'Île   **la Roche-sur-Yon**   **Fontenay-le-Comte**

Challans

St Jean-de-Monts   le Perrier

Vendee

Velluire

St Mathurin

St Gilles Croix-de-Vie

Jard-sur-Mer

les Sables d'Olonne   la Tranché-sur-Mer

133

EVENTS & FESTIVALS

Mar Nantes Children's Carnival & Parade; Fontevraud, Holy Week in the Royal Abbey Church (*holy music & medieval games*); Sablé sur-Sarthe Carnival; Champagné 'Lances' Festival (*historical pageant*); St-Etienne de Montluc Daffodil Carnival;

Apr Cholet Harlequin Festival, & Carnival; International Fairs at Nantes & Angers; Le Mans 24-hours of Motorcycling; Nantes Grand Night Parade; Saumur International Horse Show; St Nazaire 'Theatre at Play' Festival; Saumur, Cadre Noir Riding School Displays

May Saumur, Loire Festival & Wine Fair; Nantes Spring Arts Festival; St Gilles-Croix-de-Vie Jazz Festival; Le Mans Festival of Epau Abbey; Saumur International Horse Show;

Jun Anjou Festival, throughout Maine-et-Loire; St Florent-le-Vieil, Asia-West Festival (*music & dance*); Gala evenings at the Cadre Noir Riding School, Saumur;

Jul Doué-la-Fontaine Rose Days (*rose & flower shows*); Challans Historic Fair; Clisson Music Festival; Nantes Summer Festival; Mayenne Nights: concerts in castles & churches throughout Mayenne; La Flèche, Street Theatre Festival; Saumur, Gala evenings at the

Cadre Noir Riding School; Le Mans 'Les Cénomanies' (*historical celebrations*); La Ménitré Headwear Festival; Sablé-sur-Sarthe Rockissimo (*children's rock festival*); Clisson Medieval & Classical Music Festival; La Baule International Dance Encounters; Saumur Military Tattoo

Aug Sablé-sur-Sarthe Ancient Dance & Music Festival, & Baroque Festival; St Nazaire Chamber Music 'Consonances' Festival; Angrie Harvest & Old Crafts Festival; Challans Historic Fair; Noirmoutier Vintage Sailing Ship Regatta; Le Perrier Village Fête (*unusual & traditional event*); La Baule Elegance Automobile; Noirmoutier Island Festival (*theatre in castle courtyard*)

Sep Nantes Les Rendez-vous de l'Edre, Saumur International Horse Show; Cadre Noir Riding School Displays, Saumur

Oct Le Mans 24-hours Book Fair; Durtal Curiosity and Bric-à-Brac Fair; Le Mans 24-hours Truck Race; Angers International Horse Show; Angers Antiques Show; Saumur, Cadre Noir Riding School Displays

Nov Nantes Antiques Show; Nantes Three Continents Festival

Dec Brissac Carols & Christmas Market at Castel Festival

ANCENIS Loire-Atlantique

★★ Le Val de Loire
rte d'Angers *44150*
☎ 240960003 FAX 240831730
(on N23, from Ancenis in direction of Angers)
Ideally situated for exploring the surrounding countryside, the hotel is peacefully situated and offers comfortable guest accommodation with good amenities. The restaurant is noted in the region for the high standard of cuisine and interesting wine list.
Near river Near sea Forest area Near motorway
41 en suite (bth/shr) (11 with balcony) TV in 16 bedrooms Direct dial from all bedrooms Licensed Full central heating Open parking available Child discount available Golf Tennis Gym Boule Mini-golf Open terrace Covered terrace Last d 21.15hrs Languages spoken: English,German,Spanish
ROOMS: (room only) s 215-243FF; d 250-300FF
MEALS: Full breakfast 26FF Continental breakfast 26FF Lunch 64-189FF&alc Dinner 64-189FF&alc✱
CARDS: ●● ▥ Travellers cheques

ANGERS Maine-et-Loire

★★★ D'Anjou (BW)
1 bd Maréchal-Foch *49100*
☎ 241882482 FAX 241872221
This elegantly furnished hotel, set in the centre of Angers, offers its guests comfortable bedrooms equipped with all modern amenities. The restaurant La Salamandre with its splendid neo-Gothic décor is one of the best in town and features an imaginative gourmand menu with an extensive choice of specialities. Function rooms are available for meetings and conferences.

In town centre Near motorway
53 en suite (bth/shr) (4 fmly) TV in all bedrooms Mini-bar in all bedrooms Licensed Lift Night porter Full central heating Open parking available (charged) Covered parking available (charged) V meals Languages spoken: English German Italian & Spanish
CARDS: ●● ▤ ▥ ➋ Travellers cheques

★★ Hotel du Mail
8 rue des Ursules *49100*
☎ 241250525 FAX 241869120
(behind Hotel de Ville in town centre)
A peacefully situated mansion in the heart of Angers, a city famous for its history, arts and festivals - and popular with visitors for its proximity to the Loire. All bedrooms offer every modern amenity and provide maximum comfort. The hotel caters for commercial and leisure guests alike, and the friendly, efficient staff ensure an enjoyable stay.
Near river Near lake Near sea Near beach Forest area In town centre Near motorway
27 en suite (bth/shr) (6 fmly) TV in all bedrooms Direct dial from all bedrooms Mini-bar in all bedrooms Full central heating Open parking available (charged) Supervised Open terrace Languages spoken: English
ROOMS: (room only) s 235-355FF; d 245-375FF
CARDS: ●● ▤ ▥ ➋ Travellers cheques

★★★ Quality Hotel
8 pl de la Gare *49100*
☎ 241884942 FAX 241867670
(leave the Paris/Nantes motorway at Angers, take the direction Cholet-Potiers and follow signs for Chateau and railway station)

134

The Hotel de France is an old building dating from 1893. Situated in a lively quarter of the city centre, the fourth generation of the Bouyer family continue the tradition of French hospitality.
Near river Near lake Forest area In town centre Near motorway
57 rms (54 bth 2 shr) No smoking in 3 bedrooms TV in all bedrooms Direct dial from all bedrooms Mini-bar in 55 bedrooms Licensed Lift Night porter Full central heating Covered parking available (charged) Supervised Child discount available Last d 23.00hrs Languages spoken: English & German
ROOMS: (room only) s 330-380FF; d 380-480FF ✱
Reductions over 1 night
MEALS: Full breakfast 50FF Continental breakfast 50FF Lunch 70-153FF Dinner 70-153FF
CARDS: 💳 💳 💳 💳

★ ★ Hotel de l'Univers
2 pl de la Gare *49100*
☎ 241884358 FAX 241869728
(from A11 exit at the sign 'Château, Maison du Tourisme' then after traffic lights follow signs 'La Gare' or 'Hotel l'Univers')

A comfortably furnished town centre hotel, facing the station and within walking distance of the castle and cathedral.
Near river Near lake In town centre Near motorway
45 rms (35 bth/shr) (6 fmly) (10 with balcony) TV in all bedrooms Direct dial from all bedrooms Licensed Lift Night porter Full central heating
ROOMS: (room only) s 150-280FF **Reductions over 1 night**
CARDS: 💳 💳 💳 💳 Travellers cheques

★ ★ Cavier
rte de Laval *49240*
☎ 241423045 FAX 241424032
This charming hotel is housed in an old mill, which is classified as a tourist attraction, and with its restful setting of old buildings provides the place for a relaxing stay. There are two restaurants; one with a varied family cuisine, whilst the other, situated in a windmill, serves a more traditional choice of dishes. The functional bedrooms are equipped with modern appointments and provide an adequate level of comfort. In addition, there are a number of chateaux well worth a visit, and leisure facilities available in the surrounding region.
Near river Near motorway
43 en suite (bth/shr) (7 fmly) TV in all bedrooms STV Radio in rooms Licensed Night porter Full central heating Open parking available Child discount available 10yrs Outdoor swimming pool (heated) Boule Open terrace Last d 21.30hrs Languages spoken: English
MEALS: Full breakfast 35FF Continental breakfast 45FF Lunch 102-166FF&alc Dinner 102-166FF&alc✱
CARDS: 💳 💳 💳 💳 Travellers cheques

★ ★ Le Lutetia
13 av des Evens *44500*
☎ 240602581 FAX 240427352
The hotel stands just a short distance away from what is reputedly Europe's finest beach. Concealed behind its original façade is an entirely renovated interior offering fully equipped bedrooms providing pleasant, relaxing accommodation. In addition, the elegant restaurant serves a regional cuisine incorporating high quality local produce.
Near sea Near beach In town centre
14 rms (1 fmly) (6 with balcony) TV in all bedrooms Riding Open terrace Languages spoken: English
CARDS: 💳 💳 💳 Travellers cheques

★ ★ La Palmeraie
7 allée des Cormorans *44500*
☎ 240602441 FAX 240427371
Situated amongst the pine trees, this entirely renovated hotel offers the ideal setting for a relaxing holiday near the seaside. The restaurant serves an array of well-prepared dishes, whilst the bedrooms provide comfortable accommodation. Guests can relax in the bar, cosy lounge or shaded terrace, or may stroll in the delightful garden under the palm trees.
Near sea Near beach In town centre Near motorway
Closed Oct-beg Apr
23 en suite (shr) (8 with balcony) TV in all bedrooms STV Direct dial from all bedrooms Full central heating Child discount available 6yrs Jacuzzi/spa Open terrace Covered terrace Last d 21.00hrs Languages spoken: English
ROOMS: (room only) d 340-450FF ✱
MEALS: Full breakfast 43FF Continental breakfast 43FF Lunch 130-160FF Dinner 130-160FF✱
CARDS: 💳 💳 💳 💳 Travellers cheques

★ ★ St-Christophe
pl Notre Dame *44500*
☎ 240603535 FAX 240601174
(From the first main junction in La Baule follow avenue de Gaulle, passing the Office de Tourisme. Turn right at the end into boulevard de Mer, then right again into avenue des Impairs. Hotel 100mtrs)
800 metres from the beach the hotel is a fine example of turn-of-the-century seaside architecture. Guests can expect a warm reception from the friendly, diligent staff, whilst the comfortable accommodation, which is divided over three villas, is elegantly furnished and offers good amenities. On fine days, meals are served on the terrace with views of the delightful garden.
Near sea Near beach In town centre
33 rms (20 bth 11 shr) (5 fmly) (11 with balcony) TV in all bedrooms STV Direct dial from all bedrooms Licensed Full central heating Open parking available Child discount available 12yrs Open terrace Last d 22.00hrs Languages spoken: English
ROOMS: (incl. full-board) d 450-690FF ✱
MEALS: Full breakfast 45FF Continental breakfast 45FF Lunch 90-190FF&alc Dinner 90-190FF&alc✱
CARDS: 💳 💳 💳 Travellers cheques

BOIS-DE-LA-CHAIZE Vendée

★ ★ ★ Hotel St-Paul
Bois de la Chaize
☎ 51390563 FAX 51397398
Near sea Forest area
Closed early Nov-mid March
(10 fmly) (20 with balcony) TV in 37 bedrooms Mini-bar in 37
bedrooms Licensed Full central heating Open parking
available Child discount available Indoor swimming pool
(heated) Outdoor swimming pool (heated) Tennis Last d
22.00hrs Languages spoken: English
CARDS: ●● ▦ ▆ Travellers cheques

BOUGUENAIS Loire-Atlantique

★ ★ ★ Hotel Océania
Aéroport de Nautes Atlantique *44340*
☎ 240050566 FAX 240051203
Near motorway
87 en suite (bth/shr) (70 fmly) No smoking in 30 bedrooms TV
in all bedrooms STV Radio in rooms Direct dial from all
bedrooms Mini-bar in all bedrooms Licensed Lift Night
porter Full central heating Air conditioning in bedrooms
Open parking available Child discount available 12yrs
Outdoor swimming pool (heated) Tennis Sauna Gym Pool
table Covered terrace Last d 23.30hrs Languages spoken:
English,German,Spanish
CARDS: ●● ▦ ▆ ● Travellers cheques

CHAMPIGNÉ Maine-et-Loire

Château des Briottières
49330
☎ 241420002 FAX 241420155
(4km from the village. Signposted)

This magnificent 18th-century residence has been in the hands
of the same family for six generations. Surrounded by 40
hectares of parkland, guests receive a warm welcome in the
grand surroundings of a typical French château. Impeccable
service and good old-fashioned hospitality here go hand in
hand. Places of interest in the vicinity are the many chateaux of
the Anjou region, Angers with its famous tapestries, and the
Cointreau distillery.
Near lake
10 rms (9 bth/shr) (2 fmly) (1 with balcony) No smoking in 1
bedroom TV in 1 bedroom Direct dial from all bedrooms
Licensed Open parking available Covered parking available
Child discount available 7yrs Outdoor swimming pool (heated)
Fishing Pool table Boule Bicycle rental Open terrace

V meals Last d 21.30hrs Languages spoken: English,Spanish
ROOMS: (room only) d 650-1200FF
MEALS: Continental breakfast 50FF Dinner 300FF
CARDS: ●● ▦ ▆ ● Travellers cheques

CHAMPTOCEAUX Maine-et-Loire

★ ★ Champalud
Promenade du Champalud *49270*
☎ 240835009 FAX 240835381
(From A6 exit 'Ancenis' take Nantes road for 8km then to
Dudon)
The hotel is situated on a elevated position in a charming little
village and offers views over the Loire valley. Most of the
bedrooms are equipped with modern facilities and all offer
adequate comfort. The restaurant serves regional dishes
complemented by some good wines while the bar has a large
choice of international lagers and beers on offer.
Near river In town centre Near motorway
16 rms (11 bth/shr) (3 fmly) TV in 10 bedrooms Radio in
rooms Direct dial from all bedrooms Licensed Full central
heating Child discount available 10yrs Pool table Bicycle
rental Open terrace Last d 21.30hrs Languages spoken:
English
ROOMS: (room only) s 180-220FF; d 200-280FF ✱
Reductions over 1 night Special breaks
MEALS: Full breakfast 34FF Lunch 61-250FF&alc Dinner 61-
250FF&alc
CARDS: ●● ▆ Travellers cheques

CHANTONNAY Vendée

★ ★ Moulin Neuf
85110
☎ 251943027 FAX 251945776
The Hotel Moulin Neuf occupies a splendid lakeside position
and is the ideal venue for both commercial and leisure
traveller. It offers airy, well-equipped bedrooms, a lounge and
a congenial bar, or guests can relax on the terrace with fine
views over the lake. The menu features a good choice of fresh
seafood and fish specialities from the lake, complemented by
regional dishes. Sporting facilities include mini-golf, archery,
two tennis courts, sauna and outdoor heated swimming pool.
Near river Near lake Forest area Near motorway
60 en suite (bth/shr) 22 rooms in annexe (29 with balcony) TV
in all bedrooms STV Direct dial from all bedrooms Mini-bar
in 3 bedrooms Licensed Full central heating Open parking
available Child discount available 10yrs Outdoor swimming
pool (heated) Tennis Sauna Solarium Pool table Boule Mini-
golf Bicycle rental Open terrace Covered terrace V meals
Last d 21.00hrs Languages spoken: English
MEALS: Continental breakfast 40FF Lunch 65-180FF Dinner
65-180FF✱
CARDS: ●● ▦ ▆ ● Travellers cheques

CHARTRE-SUR-LE-LOIR Sarthe

★ ★ Hotel de France
20 pl de la République *72340*
☎ 243444016 FAX 243796220
The hotel is located in the centre of the village and has an
abundance of flowers adorning its façade and terrace. Its rustic
interior features a spacious foyer with cosy armchairs and
large windows, a congenial bar and a handsome wooden
staircase leading to the bedrooms. All guest rooms have
modern facilities.

Near river Forest area In town centre Near motorway
Closed Feb-7 Nov RS Jul-Aug
28 en suite (bth/shr) 12 rooms in annexe (3 fmly) TV in all
bedrooms Direct dial from all bedrooms Licensed Full central
heating Open parking available Supervised Child discount
available 10yrs Fishing Bicycle rental Open terrace
Last d 21.30hrs Languages spoken: English
Rooms: (room only) s 220FF; d 260-320FF **Special
breaks: weekend breaks**

MEALS: Full breakfast 35FF Continental breakfast 35FF Lunch
74-200FF&alc Dinner 74-200FF
CARDS: ● ● Travellers cheques

CHÂTEAUBRIANT Loire-Atlantique

★ ★ ★ Hostellerie de la Ferrièrre
rte de Nantes *44110*
☎ 440280028 FAX 440282921
(On D963)
Situated in a peaceful, flower-filled park. The guest rooms vary
in style and size and offer comfortable accommodation. The
menu features an excellent selection of house specialities. The
surrounding area offers lakes and forests to explore, whilst
sporting facilities nearby include tennis, a swimming pool,
horse-riding and golf.
Forest area Near motorway
25 en suite (bth) 14 rooms in annexe (4 fmly) TV in all
bedrooms Mini-bar in all bedrooms Licensed Full central
heating Open parking available Child discount available 12yrs
Fishing Riding Boule Bicycle rental Open terrace Last d
22.00hrs Languages spoken: Engish
Rooms: (room only) s 270-340FF; d 340-400FF ✱
Reductions over 1 night
MEALS: Full breakfast 60FF Continental breakfast 40FF Lunch
80-210FF&alc Dinner 80-210FF&alc✱
CARDS: ● ● ● ● Travellers cheques

CHÂTEAU-GONTIER Mayenne

★ ★ Hostellerie de Mirwault
rue du Val de la Mayenne *53200*
☎ 243071317 FAX 243071413
(From S enter town on N162, cross bridge and follow the river
to the right towards Ecluse-de-Mirwault)
This family-run hotel stands on a peaceful stretch of the River
Mayenne just outside the historic town of Château-Gontier,
making it the ideal spot for relaxing or touring the Loire valley.
It features bedrooms with good amenities offering a
straightforward level of comfort, and an attractive restaurant.
Near river Near motorway
Closed 23 Dec-14 Jan & 26 Jul-3 Aug

11 en suite (bth/shr) (2 fmly) (3 with balcony) TV in all
bedrooms STV Direct dial from all bedrooms Mini-bar in all
bedrooms Licensed Full central heating Air conditioning in
bedrooms Open parking available Child discount available
12yrs Fishing Open terrace Boating V meals Last d 21.00hrs
Languages spoken: English, Spanish, German
MEALS: Full breakfast 35FF Lunch 80-170FF&alc Dinner 80-
170FF&alc
CARDS: ● ● ● ● Travellers cheques

CHÂTEAUNEUF-SUR-SARTHE Maine-et-Loire

★ ★ Les Ondines
Quai de la Sarthe *49330*
☎ 241698438 FAX 241698359
(From A11 exit at Durtal,take D859 to Châteauneuf)
Standing on the banks of the River Sarthe, the hotel provides a
good base for exploring the surrounding region, and with
many leisure facilities on offer nearby, it is suitable for both
sporty guests and nature lovers. The bedrooms have modern
amenities and there is a riverside terrace and grill.
Near river
24 en suite (bth/shr) (4 fmly) (7 with balcony) TV in 20
bedrooms Direct dial from all bedrooms Licensed Lift Full
central heating Open parking available Supervised Fishing
Open terrace Covered terrace Last d 21.30hrs Languages
spoken: English
Rooms: (room only) s 229-298FF; d 261-356FF
Reductions over 1 night
MEALS: Full breakfast 35FF Lunch 65-198FF Dinner 88-198FF
CARDS: ● ● ● ● Travellers cheques

★ De La Sarthe
1 rue du Port *49330*
☎ 241698529
(From A11 exit at Durtal, take D859 to Châteauneuf)
This small family inn stands on the banks of the River Sarthe
and features an outside terrace, country-style restaurant and
individually appointed bedrooms with fine views over the
river. The classic cuisine incorporates the finest fresh market
produce and is skilfully prepared by the chef-proprietor Jean-
Pierre Houdebine.
Near river In town centre Near motorway
Closed 6-31 Oct
7 rms (2 bth 4 shr) (1 fmly) (1 with balcony) Licensed Full
central heating Open parking available Supervised Child
discount available 10yrs Open terrace V meals Last d
21.15hrs Languages spoken: English
Rooms: (room only) s 200-280FF; d 230-280FF
MEALS: Full breakfast 30FF Continental breakfast 30FF Lunch
90-210FF&alc Dinner 90-210FF&alc
CARDS: ● ● ● Travellers cheques

CHÊNEHUTTE-TRÈVES-CUNAULT Maine-et-Loire

★ ★ ★ Hostellerie du Prieuré
49350
☎ 241679014 FAX 241679224
This gracious Renaissance manor house dates back to the 12th
century and occupies a magnificent location surrounded by 65
acres of parkland, with splendid views over the River Loire
and the glorious scenery of its valley. The elegant bedrooms
are furnished to a very high standard and offer every
conceivable amenity. Leisure facilities include a tennis court,
open-air heated swimming pool, mini-golf and pétanque.
Guests can pay a visit to the famous vineyards, the town of
Saumur or L'Abbaye de Fontevraud. The panoramic

contd.

restaurant serves a wide choice of regional specialities and is complemented by a wine-list featuring the delightful wines of the Loire region.
Near river Forest area
35 en suite (bth/shr) 15 rooms in annexe (5 with balcony) TV in all bedrooms Direct dial from all bedrooms Mini-bar in all bedrooms Licensed Night porter Full central heating Open parking available Child discount available 12yrs Tennis Boule Mini-golf Bicycle rental V meals Last d 22.00hrs Languages spoken: English,Italian,Spanish
MEALS: Full breakfast 130FF Continental breakfast 85FF Lunch fr 160FF&alc Dinner fr 230FF&alc✱
CARDS: ▨ ◑

CHOLET Maine-et-Loire

★★ Grand Hotel de la Poste
26 bd Gustave Richard 49300
☎ 241620720 FAX 241585410
(follow station and town centre signs, hotel is in front of Jardin de Verre theatre)
In the middle of the town the Grand Hotel de la Poste offers elegant interiors and high standards of comfort. Christian Monange, a young and inventive chef creates delicious menus in the Rotonde restaurant.
In town centre
Closed Xmas & New Year
53 en suite (bth/shr) (9 fmly) TV in all bedrooms STV Direct dial from all bedrooms Licensed Lift Night porter Full central heating Open parking available (charged) Covered parking available (charged) Covered terrace Last d 21.30hrs Languages spoken: English & German
ROOMS: (room only) s 270-400FF; d 298-480FF
MEALS: Full breakfast 42FF Lunch 80-295FF&alc Dinner 98-295FF&alc
CARDS: ◐▨ ▨ ◑

FERTÉ-BERNARD, LA Sarthe

★★ Climat de France
43 bd Général-de-Gaulle 72400
☎ 243938470 Cen Res 64460123 FAX 243712814
(off A11 in Le Mans direction)
Located close to the bay and the centre of town, this charming establishment provides the peaceful setting for an enjoyable break or a relaxing holiday. Guests can take boat rides on the lake or use one of the nearby leisure facilities, whilst the half-timbered houses of the town create a picturesque atmosphere. It has a warm and friendly interior where attractive bedrooms are equipped with up-to-date modern amenities and an informal restaurant where a selection of carefully prepared traditional dishes are complemented by fine quality local specialities.
Near river Near lake Near motorway
50 en suite (bth) (11 fmly) TV in all bedrooms Licensed Full central heating Open parking available Supervised Open terrace V meals Languages spoken: English, German & Portuguese
CARDS: ◐▨ ▨

FLÈCHE, LA Sarthe

★★ Le Vert Galant
70 Grande Rue 72200
☎ 243940051 FAX 243451124
This attractive residence dates back to the 18th century. There is a spacious lounge and the bedrooms, all equipped with

modern amenities, provide comfortable accommodation. The menu features first-class dishes prepared with fine local produce.
Near river Near lake Forest area In town centre Near motorway
9 en suite (bth/shr) (4 fmly) TV in all bedrooms Licensed Full central heating Open parking available Fishing Open terrace V meals Last d 21.00hrs Languages spoken: English
CARDS: ◐▨ ▨ Travellers cheques

FONTENAY-LE-COMTE Vendée

★★ Le Rabelais
rte de Parthenay 85200
☎ 251698620 FAX 251698045
(Approach via A83 exit 8)
This contemporary hotel is located in the peaceful surroundings of a park within driving distance of the sea. The bedrooms are equipped with modern day conveniences and are of a good size. The cuisine features a range of dishes prepared with first-class ingredients.
Near river Forest area In town centre Near motorway
54 en suite (bth/shr) (3 fmly) (15 with balcony) TV in all bedrooms Radio in rooms Direct dial from all bedrooms Licensed Lift Night porter Full central heating Open parking available Covered parking available (charged) Child discount available 12yrs Outdoor swimming pool Boule Bicycle rental Open terrace Table tennis Last d 21.30hrs Languages spoken: English,Spanish
ROOMS: (room only) s 260-290FF; d 280-330FF
Reductions over 1 night
MEALS: Full breakfast 40FF Lunch 65-140FFalc Dinner 65-140FFalc
CARDS: ◐▨ ▨ ▨ ◑ Travellers cheques

FONTEVRAUD-L'ABBAYE Maine-et-Loire

★★ Croix Blanche
7 pl des Plantagenets 49590
☎ 241517111 FAX 241381538
(16kms from Saumur A85, D947)

Dating back to the 17th century, the auberge has preserved its past traditions whilst transforming into a comfortable contemporary hotel.
Forest area In town centre Near motorway
Closed 1-13 Nov
21 en suite (bth/shr) (2 fmly) TV in 20 bedrooms Direct dial from all bedrooms Mini-bar in 20 bedrooms Licensed Full central heating Open parking available Child discount available Bicycle rental Open terrace V meals Last d 21.00hrs Languages spoken: English

ROOMS: (room only) s 290-400FF; d 305-450FF
MEALS: Continental breakfast 37FF Lunch 99-215FF&alc
Dinner 99-215FF&alc
CARDS: ✹ ▦ ☲ Travellers cheques

INGRANDES-SUR-LOIRE Maine-et-Loire

★ ★ Lion d'Or
26 rue du Pont *49123*
☎ 241392008 FAX 241392103
(Between Angers and Nantes by the nationale 23, heading
towards Ingrandes)
The Hotel Lion d'Or dates back to 1660 and was reputedly the
first hotel in the town. Guests can enjoy a peaceful stay and
relax in entirely renovated surroundings. Bedrooms are
comfortable and equipped with modern conveniences, whilst
the hotel provides a suitable base for exploring the Loire region.
16 rms (4 bth 6 shr) (2 fmly) (2 with balcony) TV in all
bedrooms STV Licensed Full central heating Open parking
available Covered parking available Child discount available
2yrs Last d 21.00hrs Languages spoken: English
ROOMS: (room only) s 160-230FF; d 160-230FF
MEALS: Continental breakfast 25FF Lunch 65-180FF&alc
Dinner 65-180FF
CARDS: ✹ ▦ ☲ Travellers cheques

JARD-SUR-MER Vendée

★ ★ ★ Hotel du Parc de la Grange (Best Western)
rte de l'Abbaye *85520*
☎ 251334488 FAX 251334058
This contemporary establishment is set in the heart of a pine
forest just 300 metres from the sea. It has undergone extensive
renovation and now offers brightly decorated bedrooms with
modern facilities, attractive public areas and a restaurant
which serves a varied choice of dishes. The hotel is ideally
suited for those who like an active holiday.
Near sea Near beach Forest area
RS Half board obligatory at high season
48 en suite (bth/shr) (16 fmly) (40 with balcony) TV in all
bedrooms STV Radio in rooms Direct dial from all bedrooms
Licensed Night porter Full central heating Open parking
available Outdoor swimming pool (heated) Tennis Solarium
Gym Pool table Boule Bicycle rental Open terrace Covered
terrace Last d 21.00hrs Languages spoken: English, German,
Spanish
ROOMS: s 385-440FF; d 560-665FF
MEALS: Lunch 120-180FF&alc Dinner 120-180FF&alc
CARDS: ✹ ▦ ☲ ➲ Travellers cheques

LAVAL Mayenne

★ ★ Climat de France
bd des Trappistines *53000*
☎ 243028888 Cen Res 64460123 FAX 243028700
(off N157/N171)
This pleasant establishment has a warm and friendly interior
where attractive bedrooms are equipped with up-to-date
modern amenities. An informal restaurant offers a selection of
carefully prepared traditional dishes, as well as a generous as
much as you can eat' buffet.
Near river Forest area Near motorway
44 en suite (bth/shr) Some rooms in annexe (8 fmly) TV in all
bedrooms Radio in rooms Direct dial from all bedrooms
Licensed Open parking available V meals Languages spoken:
English & Italian
CARDS: ✹ ☲

MANS, LE Sarthe

★ ★ Vidéotel
av Paul Courboulay
☎ 243244724 FAX 243245841
The hotels in the Vidéotel group all have bedrooms with
pleasant furnishings and are equipped with the comfort of
their clientele in mind. The restaurants serve a good quality
gourmet cuisine with a range of prix-fixe menus, regional
specialities and 'eat your fill buffet'. The management couples
and their dedicated teams offer a 'round the clock' efficient
service, where the well-being and satisfaction of guests is the
prime consideration.
Near river In town centre
91 en suite (shr) (17 fmly) No smoking in 12 bedrooms TV in
all bedrooms Direct dial from all bedrooms Mini-bar in all
bedrooms Licensed Lift Night porter Full central heating
Open parking available Covered parking available (charged)
Supervised Child discount available 12yrs Pool table V meals
Last d 22.00hrs Languages spoken: English
ROOMS: (room only) s 280FF; d 280FF
MEALS: Full breakfast 34FF Lunch 52-88FF&alc Dinner 52-
88FF&alc
CARDS: ✹ ▦ ☲ ➲ JCB Travellers cheques

MAULEVRIER Maine-et-Loire

★ ★ Château Colbert
49360
☎ 241555133 FAX 241550902
This handsome building dates back to the 18th century and is
situated right in the heart of all the main tourist attractions. It has
a splendid park with a delightful Japanese garden - which is
classified as the largest Oriental park in Europe - as well as an
international greyhound racing-track. Guests are well looked
after by a dedicated and friendly staff. Bedrooms are attractive
and offer a good level of comfort, while the elegant lounges and
restaurant provide a setting for relaxation and an enjoyable meal.
Near river Near lake Forest area In town centre Near
motorway
26 en suite (bth/shr) (5 fmly) TV in all bedrooms Direct dial
from all bedrooms Mini-bar in all bedrooms Licensed Lift
Full central heating Air conditioning in bedrooms Supervised
Child discount available 12yrs Fishing Boule Open terrace
Last d 21.00hrs Languages spoken: English
ROOMS: s 320-650FF; d 350-700FF Reductions over 1
night Special breaks
MEALS: Full breakfast 45FF Continental breakfast 45FF Lunch
95-185FF Dinner 95-185FF
CARDS: ✹ ▦ ☲ ➲ Travellers cheques

MAYENNE Mayenne

★ ★ ★ Grand Hotel
2 rue Ambroise-de-Loré *53100*
☎ 243009600 FAX 243320849
Near river In town centre Near motorway
28 en suite (bth/shr) (4 fmly) TV in all bedrooms STV Direct
dial from all bedrooms Licensed Full central heating Open
parking available Covered parking available Supervised
Child discount available 10yrs Bicycle rental Open terrace V
meals Last d 21.30hrs Languages spoken: English
ROOMS: (room only) s 175-299FF; d 215-389FF ✶
Reductions over 1 night
MEALS: Full breakfast 40FF Lunch 70-199FF&alc Dinner 70-
199FF&alc
CARDS: ✹ ▦ ☲ Travellers cheques

MISSILLAC Loire-Atlantique

★ ★ ★ Hotel de la Bretèsche
44780
☎ 251768696 FAX 240669947

The hotel stands on the shores of the lake and offers views over the water and the castle. Surrounded by a magnificent forest which used to be royal hunting grounds, it is an ideal place for business travellers and holiday makers alike. The bedrooms are furnished with well-matched fabrics and offer restful accommodation; there is a cosy lounge and a congenial bar in which to relax or have a drink before sampling regional dishes in the restaurant.
Near river Near lake Forest area Near motorway
Closed Feb
48 en suite (bth/shr) (24 fmly) TV in all bedrooms STV Radio in rooms Licensed Lift Full central heating Open parking available Supervised Child discount available Outdoor swimming pool (heated) Golf Tennis Open terrace V meals Last d 21.30hrs Languages spoken: English,German,Italian,Portuguese,Spanish
CARDS: ●● ■■ ■■ ●〉 Travellers cheques

MONTREUIL-BELLAY Maine-et-Loire

★ ★ Splendid Hotel
139 rue du Dr Gaudrez *49260*
☎ 241531000 FAX 241524517
This 15th-century establishment is situated on the banks of the river against a backdrop of vineyards and just a stone's throw from a 17th century castle. Set in pleasant grounds, it offers charming bedrooms which vary in style and size and offer modern facilities. With its lounges, billiard room and restaurant serving regional cuisine, it provides an attractive base from which to explore the Anjou region.
Near river Forest area In town centre
Some rooms in annexe (8 fmly) TV available Radio in rooms Licensed Lift Full central heating Open parking available Supervised Child discount available 10yrs Indoor swimming pool (heated) Outdoor swimming pool (heated) Fishing Sauna Pool table Jacuzzi/spa Bicycle rental Open terrace V meals Last d 22.00hrs Languages spoken: English
MEALS: Full breakfast 35FF Continental breakfast 35FF Lunch 75-220FF&alc Dinner 75-220FF&alc✱
CARDS: ●● ■■ Travellers cheques

MOREILLES Vendée

Le Château
85450
☎ 251561756 FAX 251563030
(A83 Nantes-Bordeaux take exit 7 Ste Hermine then N137 towards Rochelle and in 12km the Château is at end of village)

All the delights of the countryside only thirty minutes from La Rochelle. The owners aim to achieve a home-from-home atmosphere, refined and tastefully balanced.
Near motorway
8 en suite (bth/shr) 2 rooms in annexe (3 fmly) Direct dial from all bedrooms Licensed Full central heating Open parking available Covered parking available Supervised Child discount available 12yrs Outdoor swimming pool Boule Bicycle rental Covered terrace V meals Last d 21.00hrs
ROOMS: (room only) s 300-400FF; d 400-600FF
MEALS: Full breakfast 55FF Continental breakfast 55FF Dinner fr 195FF
CARDS: Travellers cheques

MORTAGNE-SUR-SÈVRE Vendée

★ ★ Hotel de France & Restaurant La Taverne
(Minotel)
4 pl du Dr Pichat *85290*
☎ 251650337 FAX 251672783
(at intersection N160/N149)

This elegant ivy-clad hotel dates back as far as 1604 and is reputedly one of the oldest coaching inns in the Vendée region. It has recently been completely renovated and offers guest rooms, a choice of restaurants, and leisure facilities. With a large choice of places of interest nearby it makes it a comfortable base for visits in the region.
Near river Near lake Near motorway
Closed 28 Jul-9 Aug
25 rms (23 bth/shr) Some rooms in annexe (3 fmly) (10 with balcony) TV in all bedrooms STV Direct dial from all bedrooms Mini-bar in all bedrooms Licensed Lift Full central heating Open parking available Covered parking available (charged) Supervised Child discount available 10yrs Indoor swimming pool (heated) Fishing Riding Boule Bicycle rental Open terrace Last d 21.30hrs Languages spoken: English, German
ROOMS: (room only) s 160-250FF; d 190-370FF
MEALS: Full breakfast 45FF Continental breakfast 45FF Lunch 80-245FF&alc Dinner 99-310FF&alc✱
CARDS: ●● ■■ ■■ ●〉 Travellers cheques

NANTES Loire-Atlantique

★ ★ ★ Hotel Le Jules Verne (Best Western)
3 rue du Couédic *44000*
☎ 240357450 FAX 240200935
Situated in the heart of Nantes, the hotel is situated on a leafy square, just a stone's throw from the main places of interest. The attractively furnished bedrooms combine functionality with good taste and have a cosy atmosphere. Breakfast is served in the lounge and consists of fruit, home-made jam and the best croissants in town.
In town centre
65 en suite (bth) TV in all bedrooms Direct dial from all bedrooms Lift Full central heating Air conditioning in bedrooms Child discount available 12yrs Languages spoken: English, German, Spanish, Russian
MEALS: Full breakfast 45FF Continental breakfast 45FF✱
CARDS: ●● ▭▭ ▭▭ ◑ Travellers cheques

★ ★ ★ Novotel Nantes
Cité des Congrés, 3 rue de Valmy *44000*
☎ 251820000 FAX 251820740
Novotel offer their clients good quality accommodation in modern, well-equipped bedrooms and have refined restaurants serving good quality cuisine They have excellent business meeting and conference facilities and some have food and beverages available 24 hours a day. All their hotels have at least one bedroom for disabled guests.
In town centre
105 rms (28 fmly) No smoking in 28 bedrooms TV in all bedrooms STV Radio in rooms Direct dial from all bedrooms Mini-bar in all bedrooms Licensed Lift Night porter Full central heating Air conditioning in bedrooms Open parking available Covered parking available (charged) Supervised Child discount available 16yrs Open terrace Languages spoken: English,German,Spanish
CARDS: ●● ▭▭ ▭▭ ◑ Travellers cheques

NOIRMOUTIER-EN-L'ILLE Vendée

★ ★ ★ Genéral d'Elbée
pl d'Armes *85330*
☎ 251391029 FAX 251390823
(On the small harbour)
This large rectangular residence dates back to the 18th century and provides a traditional setting for a relaxing holiday. Situated at Noirmoutier, a place frequented by Auguste Renoir who painted its landscape and scenery, the hotel offers attractively furnished bedrooms and cosy public areas. It no longer provides restaurant facilities but recommends those in Punta Lara l'Atlantide for a fine selection of sea food.
Near sea Forest area In town centre
Closed Oct-Mar
26 en suite (bth/shr) (7 fmly) (4 with balcony) No smoking in 7 bedrooms Direct dial from all bedrooms Licensed Full central heating Child discount available 10yrs Outdoor swimming pool Bicycle rental Open terrace Languages spoken: English,Spanish,German
CARDS: ●● ▭▭ ▭▭ ◑

★ ★ ★ Prateaux
Bois de la Chaize, 8 allee du Tambourin *85330*
☎ 251391252 FAX 251394628
(close to the Plage des Dames)
Spacious comfortable bedrooms, all with balcony or terrace overlooking the garden. Two hundred metres from the beach, an atmosphere of calm is influenced by the floral suroundings.

Near sea Near beach Forest area
Closed mid Nov-mid Feb
22 rms (21 bth/shr) (3 fmly) No smoking in 7 bedrooms TV in all bedrooms STV Direct dial from all bedrooms Full central heating Open parking available Child discount available Open terrace Last d 20.30hrs Languages spoken: English
ROOMS: (incl. dinner) s 440-870FF; d 420-650FF
MEALS: Continental breakfast 65FF Lunch 143-298FF Dinner 143-290FF
CARDS: ●● ▭▭ ▭▭ ◑ Travellers cheques

NUAILLÉ Maine-et-Loire

★ ★ Relais des Biches Baumotel
pl de l'Église *49340*
☎ 241623899 FAX 241629624
Surrounded by lush green forests and situated in the heart of a charming village, the hotel welcomes its visitors into a warm atmosphere created by the friendly owners Françoise and Philippe Baume. Comfortable bedrooms with modern amenities, and a cosy restaurant where guests can enjoy a meal with pleasant music in the background, provide the elements for an enjoyable break.
Forest area
13 en suite (bth/shr) (2 fmly) TV in all bedrooms Radio in rooms Direct dial from all bedrooms Mini-bar in all bedrooms Licensed Night porter Full central heating Open parking available Covered parking available (charged) Supervised Child discount available Outdoor swimming pool Boule Bicycle rental Open terrace Last d 22.00hrs
CARDS: ●● ▭▭ ▭▭ ◑ Travellers cheques

OUDON Loire-Atlantique

★ ★ Du Port
10 rue du Port *44521*
☎ 240836858 FAX 240866979
This pleasant village inn is situated near the Loire and features traditionally furnished guest accommodation and a 15th-century dining room which provides an attractive setting for a fine meal.
Near river Forest area In town centre Near motorway
6 en suite (bth/shr) (3 fmly) TV in all bedrooms STV Radio in rooms Mini-bar in all bedrooms Licensed Night porter Full central heating Air conditioning in bedrooms Open parking available Supervised Child discount available 7yrs Outdoor swimming pool Fishing Riding Gym Pool table Mini-golf Bicycle rental Open terrace Covered terrace V meals Last d 22.30hrs Languages spoken: English
MEALS: Full breakfast 55FF Continental breakfast 35FF Lunch 52-62FF&alc Dinner 52-62FF&alc✱
CARDS: ●● ▭▭ ▭▭ ◑ Travellers cheques

PIRIAC-SUR-MER Loire-Atlantique

★ ★ De La Poste
25 rue de la Plage *44420*
☎ 240235090 FAX 240236896
This cheerful family hotel is situated 200 metres from the beach in the small fishing village of Piriac-sur-Mer with half-timbered houses, fishing harbour and marina. It has well equipped bedrooms, a restaurant where seafood features strongly on the menu and attentive owners who provide their visitors with a warm welcome.
Near sea In town centre
Closed 12 Nov-Mar
15 rms (5 bth 5 shr) (1 with balcony) Licensed

contd.

Open terrace Last d 21.45hrs Languages spoken: English
ROOMS: (room only) s 230-320FF; d 230-320FF
MEALS: Continental breakfast 37FF Lunch 80-220FF&alc
Dinner 80-220FF&alc
CARDS: ●● ▦ ▆ Travellers cheques

POIRE-SUR-VIE Vendée

★ ★ Du Centre
pl du Marché *85170*
☎ 251318120 FAX 251318821
Situated in the heart of the Vendée between the sea and
farmlands, the Hotel du Centre is situated in Le-Poiré-sur-Vie.
The establishment has been in the hands of the same family for
three generations and has modern guest accommodation with
good facilities, a bar, a garden with terrace, and a restaurant
which serves a tasty regional cuisine.
In town centre
27 rms (24 bth/shr) TV in all bedrooms Direct dial from all
bedrooms Mini-bar in all bedrooms Licensed Full central
heating Outdoor swimming pool Open terrace Last d
21.00hrs Languages spoken: English
CARDS: ●● ▦ ▆ Travellers cheques

PONT-ST-MARTIN Loire-Atlantique

★ ★ ★ ★ Château du Plessis-Atlantique
44860
☎ 240268172 FAX 240327667
The residence is a classified historic monument which dates
back to the 14th century. Situated in peaceful surroundings,
the building offers fine views over the park and rose gardens.
The guest accommodation is individually decorated with
period furniture and equipped with luxurious en suite
bathrooms, whilst the cuisine consists of a choice of fine
classic dishes.
Near river Near lake
4 rms (3 bth/shr) Mini-bar in all bedrooms Licensed Lift
Night porter Full central heating Open parking available
Covered parking available Supervised Child discount
available 12yrs Boule Bicycle rental Open terrace Covered
terrace Games for children V meals Languages spoken:
English
MEALS: Dinner 250-300FF✱
CARDS: ●● ▦ ▆ ◑

PORNICHET Loire-Atlantique

★ ★ Le Regent
150 bd des Océanides *44380*
☎ 240610568 FAX 240612553
This family hotel offers fine views of the sea and is set in the
bay of Pornichet-La Baule. Recently renovated, it offers the
charm of an old villa and all the comfort of a modern hotel. The
restaurant enjoys a good reputation for its excellent seafood or
a fish dish 'à la maison', whilst on fine days meals are served
on the terrace which offers fine views of the ocean. The
bedroom accommodation is functional with private facilities
and is well maintained.
Near sea Near beach
15 en suite (bth/shr) (2 fmly) (8 with balcony) TV in all
bedrooms Direct dial from all bedrooms Licensed Full central
heating Open parking available Supervised Child discount
available 5yrs Solarium Open terrace Covered terrace
Languages spoken: German, Spanish
ROOMS: (room only) s 305-330FF; d 375-450FF
CARDS: ●● ▦ ▆ ◑ Travellers cheques

PREFAILLES Loire-Atlantique

★ ★ La Flottille
Pointe St-Gildas *44770*
☎ 240216118 FAX 240645172
The hotel is the ideal venue for a relaxing holiday, and offers
exceptional views over La Pointe-Saint-Gildas and the Loire
estuary. It has a friendly, contemporary interior with balconied
guest rooms which are equipped with modern amenities. The
restaurant has a choice of dishes on the menu as well as fresh
seafood, depending on the latest catch.
Near sea Near beach
26 en suite (bth/shr) (2 fmly) (18 with balcony) TV in all
bedrooms STV Direct dial from all bedrooms Mini-bar in all
bedrooms Licensed Full central heating Open parking
available Indoor swimming pool (heated) Fishing Sauna
Solarium Pool table Boule Jacuzzi/spa Bicycle rental Open
terrace V meals Last d 22.00hrs Languages spoken: English &
German
MEALS: Lunch 95-270FF&alc Dinner 150-220FFalc✱
CARDS: ●● ▦ ▆ ◑ Travellers cheques

LES ROSIERS-SUR-LOIRE Maine-et-Loire

★ ★ ★ Jeanne de Laval et Ducs d'Anjou
54 rue Nationale *49350*
☎ 241518017 FAX 241380418
(From Angers take D952)
Near river In town centre Near motorway
10 rms 7 rooms in annexe (3 fmly) TV in all bedrooms Direct
dial from all bedrooms Mini-bar in all bedrooms Licensed
Full central heating Open parking available Supervised Child
discount available 10yrs Open terrace V meals Last d
21.30hrs Languages spoken: English
ROOMS: (room only) s 350-380FF; d 380-400FF
MEALS: Full breakfast 55FF Continental breakfast 55FF Lunch
180-400FF&alc Dinner 180-400FF&alc
CARDS: ●● ▦ ▆ Travellers cheques

SABLES-D'OLONNE, LES Vendée

★ ★ Admiral's Hotel
pl Jean David Nau Port Olonna *85100*
☎ 251214141 FAX 251327123
Near sea Forest area
Closed 25 Dec-2 Jan
32 en suite (bth/shr) (7 fmly) (32 with balcony) TV in all
bedrooms Direct dial from all bedrooms Mini-bar in all
bedrooms Lift Full central heating Open parking available
Child discount available 10yrs Open terrace Covered terrace
CARDS: ●● ▦ ▆ ◑ Travellers cheques

★ ★ Les Hirondelles
44 rue des Corderies *85100*
☎ 251951050 FAX 251323101
Holidays are fun, and when complemented by an hotel like
'Les Hirondelles' they become perfect. Situated in the centre of
town, just 50 metres from the beach, this bright, modern
establishment provides a convivial setting with a friendly
atmosphere. Attractive guest rooms are divided over two
buildings and offer modern appointments, whilst the
restaurant serves well-prepared cuisine based on local fresh
fish produce and seafood.
Near sea In town centre
Closed Sep-30 Mar
65 en suite (shr) 38 rooms in annexe (2 fmly) (21 with balcony)
TV in all bedrooms Direct dial from all bedrooms Licensed

Lift Full central heating Open parking available (charged) Covered parking available (charged) Child discount available 6yrs Bicycle rental Open terrace Last d 21.00hrs Languages spoken: English
MEALS: Continental breakfast 35FF Lunch 140FF&alc Dinner 140FF&alc✱
CARDS: 💳 🔳 💳 Travellers cheques

★ ★ Le Calme des Pins
43 av Aristide-Briand 85100
☎ 251210318 FAX 251215985
The hotel is situated 150 metres from the beach and comprises two renovated fin-de-siecle houses. A warm welcome awaits visitors upon arrival in this informal establishment, where the bedrooms are decorated in soft pastel shades and offer comfortable accommodation. The dining room serves a combination of fresh sea-fish specialities and fine home-grown produce.
Near lake Near sea Near beach Forest area In town centre
Closed Etr-Sep
46 en suite (bth/shr) (7 fmly) (15 with balcony) TV in all bedrooms STV Direct dial from all bedrooms Licensed Lift Full central heating Open parking available (charged) Bicycle rental Open terrace Wkly live entertainment Languages spoken: English,German
CARDS: 💳 💳 Travellers cheques

ST-GILLES-CROIX-DE-VIE Vendée

★ ★ Le Lion d'Or
84 rue de Calvaire 85800
☎ 251555039 FAX 251552284
(Access from La Roche-sur-Yon via D948 and D6)
The hotel is close to the town centre and shops and located 500 metres from the fishing port and yachting harbour. It features a bright, modern interior where individually appointed bedrooms offer a good level of comfort. The menu features local produce, fresh fish and shell fish served by a friendly attentive staff, whilst the congenial bar is open for an after-dinner drink. With a multitude of things to do and discover it is a good venue for a relaxing family holiday.
Near river Near sea In town centre
52 rms (50 bth/shr) (20 fmly) (25 with balcony) TV in 53 bedrooms STV Direct dial from all bedrooms Licensed Full central heating Open parking available Covered parking available (charged) Child discount available 12yrs Indoor swimming pool (heated) Pool table Bicycle rental Open terrace Covered terrace Games for children Last d 21.15hrs Languages spoken: English
ROOMS: (room only) s 155-347FF; d 155-370FF
MEALS: Full breakfast 35FF Continental breakfast 35FF Lunch 73-162FF&alc Dinner 73-162FF&alc
CARDS: 💳 🔳 💳 Travellers cheques

ST-JEAN-DE-MONTS Vendée

★ ★ La Chaumière
103 av d'Orouët 85160
☎ 251586744
(0km from town centre via D38 towards Sables d'Olonne)
This country inn with its thatched roof enjoys a sunny position close to the woods and the sea. Guests receive a friendly reception by the Boucher family who offer comfortable bedrooms with modern amenities and a restaurant which features a fine menu incorporating varied seafood and regional specialities.
Near sea Forest area

Closed Oct-Mar
37 en suite (bth/shr) (8 fmly) (20 with balcony) TV in all bedrooms Radio in rooms Direct dial from all bedrooms Licensed Night porter Full central heating Open parking available Covered parking available (charged) Supervised Child discount available 10yrs Outdoor swimming pool (heated) Tennis Sauna Boule Bicycle rental Open terrace Last d 21.00hrs Languages spoken: English
ROOMS: (room only) d 270-450FF
MEALS: Full breakfast 47FF Continental breakfast 37FF Lunch 80-210FF&alc Dinner 99-210FF&alc
CARDS: 💳 🔳 💳 Travellers cheques

★ ★ La Chaumière
Lieu dit Orouet 85160
☎ 251586744 FAX 251589812
The Boucher family will give you a discreet and friendly welcome at their inn, renowned for its surroundings, close to the woods and sea. The comfortable bedrooms are sound proofed and most have balconies. Chef de Cuisine, Nicholas Boucher, prepares a varied menu of traditional regional dishes using local produce and seafood.
Near sea Near beach Forest area
Closed Oct-Mar
37 en suite (bth/shr) (8 fmly) (20 with balcony) TV in 12 bedrooms Direct dial from all bedrooms Mini-bar in 10 bedrooms Licensed Night porter Full central heating Open parking available Covered parking available (charged) Child discount available Indoor swimming pool (heated) Tennis Sauna Boule Bicycle rental Open terrace V meals Last d 21.00hrs Languages spoken: English

ROOMS: s fr 230FF; d 270-450FF
MEALS: Full breakfast 47FF Continental breakfast 37FF Lunch fr 80FF&alc Dinner 99-210FF&alc
CARDS: 💳 🔳 💳 🅾 Travellers cheques

ST-LAURENT-SUR-SÈVRE Vendée

★ ★ ★ Baumotel et la Chaumière
La Trique-bd du Poitou 85290
☎ 251678081 FAX 251678287
Nestling in beautiful surroundings of a two hectare park with swimming pool you are assured of a warm welcome at La Chaumière. Guests will appreciate the tranquil setting, comfortable bedrooms, panoramic terrace which overlooks the Sèvre Nantaise river, and the gourmet restaurant.
Near river Near lake Forest area Near motorway
20 en suite (bth/shr) (2 fmly) (18 with balcony) TV in all bedrooms Direct dial from all bedrooms Mini-bar in all bedrooms Licensed Full central heating
Open parking available Child discount available 12yrs

contd.

143

Outdoor swimming pool Covered terrace Last d 22.00hrs
Languages spoken: English
ROOMS: (room only) s 290-320FF; d 390-490FF
MEALS: Full breakfast 50FF Continental breakfast 50FF Lunch
95-190FF&alc Dinner 95-190FF&alc
CARDS: ●● ■■ ■■ ●) Travellers cheques

ST-MARTIN-DE-LA-PLACE Maine-et-Loire

★ ★ Auberge du Cheval Blanc
2 rue des Mariniers *49160*
☎ 241384296 FAX 241384262
This former coaching inn was built with volcanic stone, which
gives it a distinct character. It features a cosy lounge and a
country-style restaurant where oak beams and a large fireplace
create an informal setting, and which serves a selection of classic
and fresh-fish specialities. It has a terrace which looks out over
the peaceful garden, and bedrooms with modern facilities.
Near river Near motorway
Closed 5 Jan-5 Feb
12 en suite (bth/shr) (6 fmly) TV in all bedrooms Direct dial
from all bedrooms Licensed Full central heating Open
parking available Covered parking available Supervised
Child discount available 10yrs Boule Open terrace Last d
21.30hrs Languages spoken: English
MEALS: Continental breakfast 30FF Lunch 90-200FF Dinner
90-200FF✱
CARDS: ●● ■■ Travellers cheques

ST-MATHURIN Vendée

Château de la Millière
85150
☎ 251227329 FAX 251227329
Near lake Near sea Forest area
Closed Oct-Apr
5 en suite (bth/shr) (1 fmly) Full central heating Open parking
available
CARDS: ■■

ST-NAZAIRE Loire-Atlantique

★ ★ ★ Hotel Aquilon Arcantis
Rond-Point Océanis, 2 rue Michel Ange *44600*
☎ 240535020 FAX 240531560
Five minutes from La Beaule and a short distance away from the
beach, this modern hotel features well equipped bedrooms
providing the comfort that can be expected from a three star
hotel. It has pleasant grounds with sun-chairs and an assortment
of leisure opportunities. The hotel has a good restaurant also a
grill which provides a selection of quick, tasty meals.
Near lake Near sea Near beach Forest area Near motorway
72 en suite (bth/shr) (4 fmly) (7 with balcony) TV in all
bedrooms STV Direct dial from all bedrooms Licensed Lift
Night porter Full central heating Open parking available
Covered parking available (charged) Supervised Child
discount available 12yrs Outdoor swimming pool Pool table
Boule Bicycle rental Open terrace Covered terrace Last d
23.30hrs Languages spoken: English,German,Spanish
ROOMS: (room only) s 320-450FF; d 340-490FF
Reductions over 1 night Special breaks
MEALS: Full breakfast 45FF Lunch 95-245FF&alc Dinner 95-
245FF&alc
CARDS: ●● ■■ ■■ ●) JCB Travellers cheques

ST-PATERNE Sarthe

Château de St-Paterne
72610
☎ 233275471 FAX 233291671
Forest area Near motorway
7 en suite (bth/shr) (3 with balcony) TV in all bedrooms
Licensed Full central heating Supervised Child discount
available 10yrs Last d 21.30hrs Languages spoken:
English,Spanish
CARDS: ●● ■■ ■■ Travellers cheques

ST-PIERRE-DES-NIDS Mayenne

★ ★ ★ Du Dauphin
53370
☎ 243035212 FAX 243035549
Surrounded by the gentle, peaceful countryside of the region,
the hotel offers three ingredients for an enjoyable stay:
comfort, relaxation and culinary delights. The peaceful guest
rooms have modern facilities, whilst the restaurant offers a
choice of fresh fish and seafood specialities which are skilfully
prepared by the chef.
Forest area In town centre
9 rms (1 fmly) TV in all bedrooms Radio in rooms Direct dial
from all bedrooms Licensed Full central heating Open
parking available Supervised Open terrace V meals Last d
21.00hrs Languages spoken: English,German
MEALS: Continental breakfast 35FF Lunch 92-265FF&alc
Dinner 92-265FF&alc✱
CARDS: ●● ■■ Travellers cheques

ST-SATURNIN Sarthe

★ ★ Climat de France
rte d'Alençon *72650*
☎ 243253121 Cen Res 164460123 FAX 243253379
(from A11 take exit 'sortie Nord' then in direction of Alencon
for hotel on left)
Recently built, the hotel features fully-equipped bedrooms
with private facilities and a restaurant with a choice of
appetising meals which are served in restful surroundings.
Forest area Near motorway
50 en suite (bth) (2 fmly) TV in all bedrooms Radio in rooms
Direct dial from all bedrooms Licensed Full central heating
Open parking available Pool table Open terrace Covered
terrace Languages spoken: English & Spanish
CARDS: ●● ■■

ST-SAUVEUR-DE-LANDEMONT Maine-et-Loire

★ ★ ★ ★ Château de la Colaissière
Claude Cohen *49270*
☎ 240987504 FAX 240987415
Near river Near lake Forest area Near motorway
Closed early Jan-early Feb
16 en suite (bth/shr) (6 fmly) (2 with balcony) No smoking in
1 bedroom TV in all bedrooms STV Radio in rooms Mini-bar
in all bedrooms Licensed Night porter Full central heating
Open parking available Child discount available 14yrs
Outdoor swimming pool (heated) Fishing Boule Open
terrace V meals Languages spoken:
English,German,Italian,Spanish
CARDS: ●● ■■ Travellers cheques

SAULGES Mayenne

★ ★ ★ L'Ermitage
53340
☎ 243905228 FAX 243905661
Near river Forest area
36 en suite (bth/shr) (4 fmly) TV in all bedrooms STV Direct
dial from all bedrooms Licensed Full central heating Open
parking available (charged) Covered parking available
(charged) Supervised Child discount available 12yrs
Outdoor swimming pool (heated) Sauna Solarium Gym
Pool table Boule Mini-golf Jacuzzi/spa Bicycle rental Open
terrace Covered terrace Last d 21.00hrs Languages spoken:
English
MEALS: Full breakfast 52FF Lunch 100-300FF&alc Dinner 100-
300FF&alc✱
CARDS: 💳 💳 💳 Travellers cheques

SAUMUR Maine-et-Loire

★ ★ ★ Anne d'Anjou
32-33 quai Mayaud *49400*
☎ 241673030 FAX 241675100
(autoroute 85)
Near river In town centre
50 rms (5 fmly) (1 with balcony) TV in all bedrooms Direct
dial from all bedrooms Licensed Lift Night porter Full
central heating Open parking available (charged)
Supervised Child discount available 10yrs Languages
spoken: English
ROOMS: (room only) s 330-530FF; d 430-560FF
MEALS: Full breakfast 50FF Lunch 170-370FF
CARDS: 💳 💳 💳 💳 Travellers cheques

★ ★ Central
23 rue Daillé *49400*
☎ 241510578 FAX 241678235
In town centre Near motorway
27 en suite (bth/shr) (2 fmly) (5 with balcony) TV in all
bedrooms Direct dial from all bedrooms Licensed Full
central heating Open parking available (charged) Covered
parking available (charged) Bicycle rental Languages spoken:
English
CARDS: 💳 💳 💳 Travellers cheques

★ ★ Clos des Benedictins
4 rue des Lilas *49400*
☎ 241672848 FAX 241671371
(at Saumur take direction for St Hilaire/St Florent, then follow
arrows to Ecole Nationale d'Equitaion and/or Aerodrome)
Located on a hill overlooking the Loire and Saumur. Several
bedrooms have private balconies or terraces and some have
fine views of the Loire Valley. Originality and regional
specialities are hallmarks of the cuisine.
Near river Forest area
Closed 17 Nov-Feb RS Half board obligatory 15 May-15 Sep
23 en suite (bth/shr) (4 fmly) (6 with balcony) TV in all
bedrooms STV Direct dial from all bedrooms Licensed Full
central heating Open parking available Supervised Child
discount available 12yrs Outdoor swimming pool Open
terrace V meals Last d 21.15hrs Languages spoken: English
ROOMS: (room only) s 300-450FF; d 400-550FF ✱
Reductions over 1 night Special breaks
MEALS: Full breakfast 58FF Lunch 98-320FF&alc Dinner 159-
320FF&alc
CARDS: 💳 💳 💳 Travellers cheques

★ ★ ★ Loire Hotel
rue du Vieux Port *49400*

☎ 241672242 FAX 241678880
Near river In town centre Near motorway
44 en suite (bth) (2 fmly) (4 with balcony) TV in all bedrooms
Direct dial from all bedrooms Mini-bar in all bedrooms
Licensed Lift Night porter Full central heating Open parking
available Covered parking available (charged) Supervised
Child discount available 12yrs Open terrace Last d 21.30hrs
Languages spoken: English,German

ROOMS: (room only) s 360-510FF; d 450-590FF
Reductions over 1 night
MEALS: Full breakfast 48FF Continental breakfast 48FF Lunch
85-198FF&alc Dinner 85-198FF&alc
CARDS: 💳 💳 💳 💳 Travellers cheques

SOLESMES Sarthe

★ ★ ★ Grand Hotel (Minotel)
16 pl Dom-Guéranger *72300*
☎ 243954510 FAX 243952226

The hotels in the Minotel group offer a comfortable interior with
attractive, fully equipped bedrooms and pleasant public areas
where guests can relax or read. The restaurants serve an
excellent cuisine, incorporating dishes with a regional touch and
where local produce has been used to a large extent. Guests
enjoy a special blend of hospitality, provided by attentive staff
who offer personal attention and service at all times.
Near river Forest area
34 en suite (bth) 2 rooms in annexe (6 fmly) (26 with balcony)
TV in all bedrooms STV Direct dial from all bedrooms Mini-
bar in all bedrooms Licensed Lift Full central heating Open
parking available Child discount available 12yrs Sauna
Solarium Jacuzzi/spa Bicycle rental Open terrace Last d
21.30hrs Languages spoken: English

contd.

ROOMS: (room only) s 300-380FF; d 430-480FF
Reductions over 1 night
MEALS: Full breakfast 50FF Lunch 130-200FF&alc Dinner 150-200FF&alc
CARDS: ●● ▤ ▆ ● Travellers cheques

ST-MARS-DES-PRÉS Vendée

Manoir de Ponsay
Chantonnay *85110*
☎ 251469671 FAX 251468007
(From A83 take Chantonnay exit.Take D9600 towards Pontanges. From Puy Belliard follow signs for hotel)
This manor house has been in the hands of the same family since 1644 and is listed as a historic monument. Visitors are welcomed as if they were old friends by the present owners who look after their clientele with attentive service and useful advice about trips in the surrounding region. The guest rooms are comfortable, equipped with modern amenities and provide a good level of comfort.
Near river Near lake Forest area Near motorway
8 en suite (bth/shr) (1 fmly) TV in all bedrooms Licensed Full central heating Open parking available Covered parking available Fishing Open terrace Languages spoken: English
ROOMS: (room only) s 360-570FF; d 360-600FF
MEALS: Full breakfast 45FF Dinner 175FF
CARDS: ▆ ● Travellers cheques

THORIGNÉ-SUR-DUE Sarthe

★ ★ Saint Jacques
pl du Monument *72160*
☎ 243899550 FAX 243765842
(S of Connerré on D302)
A tastefully modernised hotel in a quiet location with comfortable accommodation and a welcoming restaurant.
Near river Forest area
15 en suite (bth/shr) (2 fmly) TV in all bedrooms Direct dial from all bedrooms Licensed Full central heating Open parking available Covered parking available Supervised Child discount available 7yrs Sauna Boule Bicycle rental Open terrace Last d 21.00hrs Languages spoken: English
ROOMS: (room only) s fr 300FF; d 320-460FF **Reductions over 1 night Special breaks**
MEALS: Continental breakfast 48FF Lunch 98-325FF&alc Dinner 98-325FF&alc
CARDS: ●● ▤ ▆ ● Travellers cheques

TRANCHE-SUR-MER, LA Vendée

★ ★ De l'Océan
49 rue Anatole France *85360*
☎ 251303009 FAX 251277010
This handsome seaside hotel has been in the hands of the Guicheteau family since 1925. With the fine golden beach in front and the Atlantic on the horizon it provides a pleasant venue for a stay on the Vendée coast. There is a self-service restaurant on the beach as well as an elegant dining-room on the first floor which serves a choice of dishes, including delicious fresh fish specialities. After a day in the intoxicating sea air, guests can relax in the pleasant bedrooms which offer a good level of comfort.
Near sea Near beach Forest area In town centre
Closed mid Oct-mid Mar
47 rms (5 bth 40 shr) (4 fmly) (3 with balcony) TV in all bedrooms Licensed Full central heating Open parking available Child discount available Last d 22.00hrs
Languages spoken: English & German
MEALS: Continental breakfast 49FF Lunch 90-110FF&alc Dinner 90-110FF&alc✱
CARDS: ●● ▆

VELLUIRE Vendée

★ ★ Auberge de la Riviere
85770
☎ 251523215 FAX 251523742
Set against the backdrop of the Poitiers moors and the canals of 'Venise Verte', this charming establishment has fine views over the surrounding countryside. Handsome polished furniture, copper ornaments and pretty flower arrangements, adorn the rustic interior and pretty bedrooms provide a good level of comfort. The restaurant serves a high quality cuisine with numerous regional dishes, including seafood and fresh water fish specialities.
Near river
Closed Jan-Feb
11 en suite (bth) 9 rooms in annexe (1 fmly) TV in 6 bedrooms Direct dial from all bedrooms Licensed Full central heating Open parking available Supervised Child discount available Open terrace Last d 21.15hrs
ROOMS: (room only) s 380-450FF; d 380-450FF
MEALS: Continental breakfast 60FF Lunch 190-230FF&alc Dinner 190-230FF&alc
CARDS: ●● ▆ Travellers cheques

VOUVANT Vendée

★ ★ Auberge de Maitre Pannetier
pl du Corps-de-Garde *85120*
☎ 251008012 FAX 251878937
Set at the edge of the large Mervent-Vouvant forest, this ancient building welcomes its visitors in friendly family surroundings. The charming guest rooms provide a good level of comfort and meals are served in a beautiful vaulted room, or in the 'cave' cut into the rock face.
Near river Forest area In town centre
7 en suite (bth/shr) TV available Licensed Full central heating Open terrace V meals Languages spoken: English
CARDS: ●● Travellers cheques

Medieval Life in Western Loire

A Summer Day Out in a Recreated Medieval Village

South of the Loire river, amidst unspoilt countryside, lies the theme park at Puy de Fou. From June to September, for a fascinating and unusual family day out, this reconstructed and animated medieval village should give plenty of enjoyment. Set amidst 30 hectares of meadows and woods you can discover a delightful water theatre, hear traditional musicians play, and watch a show of stunt riding and horsemanship staged close to a Renaissance château. See a collection of ancient animal breeds and an awesome display of falconry. In the centre of the park, flanked by towers, a feudal enclosure recreates a bustling Medieval market place. A different world and constantly changing scene lies just across the drawbridge, where you can experience the smell of freshly baked bread and hear the gossip as it echoes round the narrow alleys. A herbalist, glassblower, stone carver and manuscript illuminator display their wares and entertain. Minstrels draw you deeper into this clever illusion until you are part of the dream. An evening at the Cinescenie will draw the day to an unforgettable finale with an impressive display of fireworks, lasers, music and fountains.

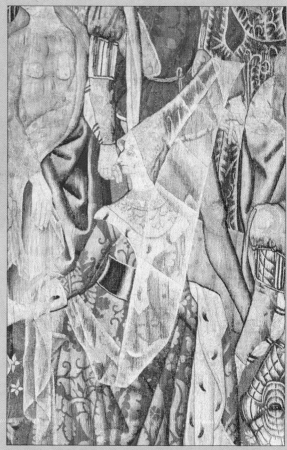

The splendour of medieval life: A detail from the 15th-century tapestry 'Les Bals des Sauvages'

Val de Loire

Described as the "historic cradle of the kingdom of France", the gentle climate of the Loire Valley nurtures some truly beautiful sights. Chief among them are the seemingly limitless number of majestic castles, cathedrals and châteaux: awesome "cathedral of cathedrals" at Chartres, pinnacle of medieval Christian art and architecture; the gothic splendour of St-Etienne Cathedral at Bourges. Vast, sun-drenched vineyards yield characterful wines from Sancerre, Menetou-Salon and Touraine, while famous Orléans, capital city of the old kingdom during the 10th and 11th centuries, basks under the spiritual protection of Joan of Arc.

ESSENTIAL FACTS

DÉPARTEMENTS:	Eure-et-Loire, Loiret, Loir-et-Cher, Indre, Indre-et-Loire, Cher
PRINCIPAL TOWNS	Chartres, Orléans, Blois, Tours, Bourges, Châteauroux
PLACES TO VISIT:	The milky-white Renaissance châteaux of the Loire - there are over 150 in the area so it pays to be selective. The more notable ones include Amboise, Beauregard, Blois, Chambord, Cheverny, Chenonceau and Villesavin. Visit also Sologne - a region of wild forest and heath broken by streams and innumerable lakes.
REGIONAL TOURIST OFFICE	Conseil Regional, 9 r St-Pierre-Lentin, 45041 Orléans. Tel: 38 54 95 42
LOCAL GASTRONOMIC DELIGHTS	Fresh fish: brochet (pike), carpe (carp) and saumon (salmon), cooked with sorrel or butter, vinegar and shallot sauce; asparagus; mushrooms; rillettes, cold potted pork; pork with prunes (a specialty of Tours); tarte Tatin, a caramelized upside-down apple pie.
DRINKS	There are many distinctive wines of the Loire region: dry whites and reds from Touraine, the richer reds from Bourgueil and the flinty-tasting white from Sancerre.
LOCAL CRAFTS WHAT TO BUY	Goat's cheese from Berry; spicy partridge and duck pâté from Chartres; and "cotignac", a delicately coloured quince jelly from Orléans.

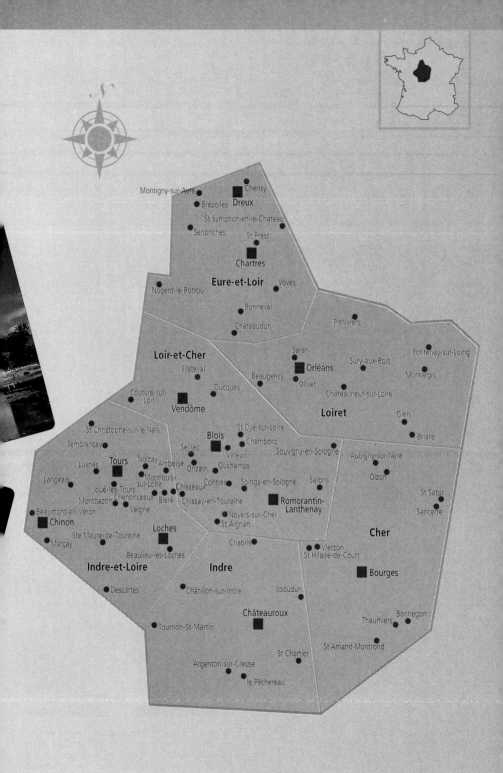

Montigny-sur-Avre • ■ Chérisy
• Brézolles **Dreux**
St Symphorien-le-Château •
Senonches • St Prest •
■
Chartres

Eure-et-Loir
Voves •
Nogent-le-Rotrou •
Bonneval •
Châteaudun •
Pithiviers •

Loir-et-Cher
Saran •
Fréteval • Beaugency • ■ **Orléans** Sury-aux-Bois •
Ouzouer • Olivet • Montargis •
Couture-sur-Loir • Châteauneuf-sur-Loire •
■ **Vendôme**
Loiret
Gien •
St Christophe-sur-le-Nais • St Dyé-sur-Loire • Briare •
Blois
Semblançay • Seillac • ■ • Chambord
Noizay **Tours** Vineuil • Souvigny-en-Sologne •
Luynes • Amboise • Onzain • Ouchamps • Aubigny-sur-Nère •
Langeais • ■ Montlouis-sur-Loire Oizon •
Joué-les-Tours • Chisseaux • Contres • Soings-en-Sologne • Salbris •
Montbazon • Chenonceaux • Bléré St Satur •
Beaumont-en-Véron • Veigne • Chissay-en-Touraine • ■ **Romorantin-Lanthenay** Sancerre •
■ **Chinon** **Loches** Noyers-sur-Cher •
Ste Maure-de-Touraine • ■ St Aignan •
Marçay • Chabris • **Cher**
Beaulieu-les-Loches • Vierzon • ■ **Bourges**
Indre-et-Loire **Indre** St Hilaire-de-Court •
Descartes • Châtillon-sur-Indre • Issoudun •
Bannegon •
■ **Châteauroux** Thaumiers •
Tournon-St-Martin • St Amand-Montrond •
St Chartier •
Argenton-sur-Creuse •
le Pêchereau •

149

EVENTS & FESTIVALS

Mar Beauregard Plant Festival; Donjon des Aigles Birds of Prey at Montrichard; St-Cosme Spring Music Festival

Apr La Bourdaisiere Plant & Garden Festival; Bourges Spring Music Festival

May Orléans Joan of Arc Festival; La Ferté-St-Aubin Plant & Garden Festival; Perche Music Festival; Tours Vocal Music Festival

May-Sep Chambord"The Horse King" equestrian art performances

Jun Chaumont-Sur-Loire International Garden Show; Sully-Sur-Loire Festival; Orléans Jazz Festival; Chambord Game Fair; Chartres Summer Festival; Nohant Romantic Festival

Jul Loches Musical Theatre Festival; Tours Music Festival; Chartres International Organ Festival; La Chatre Chopin Festival;

Aug Chinon Rabelais Market; Berry Jazz Festival; Bué-en-Sancerre Sorcerers' Festival; Chinon Old-fashioned Market;

Sep Tours Jazz Festival; Orléans Horse Festival; Chartres Lyrical Festival; Valençay Music Festival SON ET LUMIÈRES (*Light & Sound Shows*)

May-Sep Azay-le-Rideau - imaginary voyage to the Renaissance by night; Blois Castle "Tale of Blois"

Jun-Aug Villeprevost - a stroll through the park to poetry & music; Semblancay - the history and legend of the Château de la Source; Amboise: Royal Château - a nocturnal renaissance extravaganza featuring 450 characters in period costume each Wed & Sat;

Jun-Jul Beaugency - town centre

Jul Ste-Maure de Touraine in the Château, Cléry St-André outside the Basilica ;

Jul-Aug Chenonceau Château - "In the days of the Ladies of Chenonceau"; Loches "The Knight & The Wolf" - combines history with the fantastic; Valencay Château every Fri & Sat; Argenton-sur-Creuse - based on a play

Sologne

Escape the urban pressure to the rural simplicity of Sologne, an area of the Loire Valley with some 3,000 lakes, deep forests and wild fern moors. The waterways of the Cosson, Beuvron and Sauldre provide excellent angling country; consequently, the local restaurants feature the best in fresh carp, pike, eel, trout and zander dishes. Sologne is also long-established hunting territory, where partridge, duck, hare, wild boar and venison further enhance the region's gourmet cuisine. With all this fresh air and fine food, it's not surprising that Sologne has become popular for hiking holidays.

AMBOISE Indre-et-Loire

★ ★ ★ Bellevue
12 quai Charles Guinot
☎ 247570226 FAX 247305123
With the Loire valley within driving distance, the hotel is situated in the centre of the town and offers well-furnished bedrooms with modern amenities. There is a friendly foyer, an inviting lounge with open fireplace for relaxation, and an attractive restaurant serving a wide range of enjoyable meals.
Near river Forest area In town centre Near motorway
32 en suite (bth/shr) (4 fmly) (4 with balcony) TV in all bedrooms STV Direct dial from all bedrooms Licensed Lift Full central heating Pool table Open terrace Languages spoken: English
CARDS: 💳 💳 Travellers cheques

★ ★ La Brèche ⤝⤝
26 rue Jules Ferry *37400*
☎ 247570079 FAX 247576549
(on right side of river, take street from train station)
Surrounded by all the famous châteaux from the Loire region, the establishment is situated near the town centre where it features attractive bedrooms offering a good level of comfort. It has an informal restaurant which serves a high standard of cooking, whilst in summer, dishes are served in the delightful flower-filled garden.
Near river Forest area Near motorway
RS high season (half board only)
12 rms (11 bth/shr) (5 fmly) (1 with balcony) TV in 10 bedrooms Direct dial from all bedrooms Licensed Full central heating Open parking available Covered parking available Child discount available 10yrs Boule Bicycle rental

Open terrace V meals Last d 21.30hrs Languages spoken: English
ROOMS: s 195-345FF; d 230-380FF
MEALS: Continental breakfast 35FF Lunch 75-170FF&alc Dinner 75-170FF&alc
CARDS: 💳 💳 Travellers cheques

★ ★ ★ Le Choiseul (Relais et Chateaux)
36 quai Charles Guinot *37400*
☎ 247304545 FAX 247304610
(from Amboise, take A10 to Chateau Renault, take D31 and cross bridge, turn right onto D751)

This charming establishment dates back to the 18th-century and is situated near the Loire with a mature park and gardens within its vicinity. Its comfortable bedrooms are attractively furnished - some are in the attic and have sloping ceilings. This family-run hotel offers a friendly professional service.

The restaurant serves a choice of delicious regional dishes. Sporting facilities include table tennis, tennis and mini-golf opposite the hotel.
Near river Forest area
32 en suite (bth/shr) (4 fmly) (7 with balcony) TV in all bedrooms Direct dial from all bedrooms Mini-bar in all bedrooms Licensed Night porter Full central heating Open parking available Covered parking available Supervised Child discount available 12yrs Outdoor swimming pool (heated) Boule Bicycle rental Open terrace Covered terrace Ping pong V meals Last d 21.30hrs Languages spoken: English German & Spanish
ROOMS: (room only) s 600-1350FF; d 600-1350FF
MEALS: Full breakfast 130FF Continental breakfast 85FF Lunch 190-500FF&alc Dinner 280-500FF&alc
CARDS: 😇 💳 💳 🌑 Travellers cheques

★ ★ Le Fleuray
37530
☎ 247560925 FAX 247569397
(From A10 exit 18 take D31 to Autreche, D55 to Dame Marie, then D74 towards Cangey to hotel 2km on left)

This charming French country manor house occupies a peaceful location in unspoilt countryside with the Loire, famous châteaux, vineyards, and the historic towns of Amboise, Tours and Blois nearby. Dating back to 1870, it offers attractively furnished bedrooms, friendly and attentive service from English owners and a restaurant renowned for its excellent cuisine. In summer there is a pretty garden and terrace, whilst in winter guests can relax in front of a welcoming log fire.
Near river Forest area Near motorway
Closed School autumn/winter hols & last wk Feb
11 en suite (bth/shr) 2 rooms in annexe (10 fmly) (2 with balcony) Direct dial from all bedrooms Licensed Full central heating Open parking available Covered parking available Supervised Child discount available 11yrs Boule Open terrace Covered terrace V meals Last d 20.00hrs Languages spoken: English, German & Spanish
ROOMS: s 315-385FF; d 315-475FF **Reductions over 1 night**
MEALS: Full breakfast 58FF Continental breakfast 58FF Dinner 125-235FF&alc
CARDS: 😇 💳 Travellers cheques

★ ★ ★ Novotel Amboise
17 rue des Sabionnières 37400
☎ 247574207 FAX 247304076
Novotel offer their clients good quality accommodation in modern, well-equipped bedrooms and have refined restaurants serving good quality cuisine They have excellent

business meeting and conference facilities and some have food and beverages available 24 hours a day. All their hotels have at least one bedroom for disabled guests.
Forest area
121 en suite (bth) No smoking in 12 bedrooms TV in all bedrooms STV Direct dial from all bedrooms Mini-bar in all bedrooms Licensed Lift Full central heating Open parking available Supervised Child discount available 16yrs Outdoor swimming pool (heated) Tennis Pool table Mini-golf Open terrace Languages spoken: English,German,Italian,Spanish
CARDS: 😇 💳 💳 🌑 Travellers cheques

ARGENTON-SUR-CREUSE Indre

★ ★ Hotel de La Gare et du Terminus
7 rue de la Gare 36200
☎ 254011081 FAX 254240254
A small, charming hotel offering a good standard of accommodation and a restaurant serving a choice of enjoyable, well-flavoured meals. An ideal venue for an overnight stop or to explore the surrounding region.
Near river Forest area In town centre
Closed 4-21 Jan
14 rms (8 shr) (2 fmly) TV in all bedrooms Licensed Full central heating Open parking available Covered parking available Child discount available 10yrs Open terrace Last d 21.00hrs Languages spoken: English
MEALS: Full breakfast 32FF Continental breakfast 32FF Lunch 80-160FF&alc Dinner 80-160FF&alc✱
CARDS: 😇 💳 Travellers cheques

AUBIGNY-SUR-NÈRE Cher

★ ★ La Fontaine ✕✕✕
2 av Général Leclerc 18700
☎ 248580259 FAX 248583680
(from Gien take Bourges/Clermont-Ferrand(greenway) then Lamotte-Bevron by A71 then take Auxerre Way)
This pleasant hotel is situated in a village with 6000 inhabitants, which has got the right measure of peace and animation at the same time. The hotel has comfortable bedrooms equipped with modern facilities which provide an adequate level of comfort, as well as an informal restaurant.
Forest area In town centre Near motorway
Closed 21-31 Dec
16 en suite (bth/shr) (3 fmly) (1 with balcony) TV in all bedrooms STV Mini-bar in all bedrooms Licensed Full central heating Open parking available Child discount available 12yrs Bicycle rental Open terrace V meals Last d 20.30hrs Languages spoken: English & Spanish
ROOMS: (room only) s 260-280FF; d 260-330FF
MEALS: Continental breakfast 35FF Lunch 80FF&alc Dinner 80FF&alc
CARDS: 😇 💳 💳 🌑 Travellers cheques

BANNEGON Cher

★ ★ Auberge du Moulin de Chameron
18210
☎ 248618380 FAX 248618492
The inn was created in 1972 from an 18th-century water mill. It offers good quality cuisine in peaceful, rural surroundings where the well-being of the guests is of prime consideration. The bedrooms are attractively furnished and offer good amenities.
Near river Forest area
Closed mid Nov-early Mar

contd.

13 en suite (bth/shr) TV in all bedrooms Full central heating
Open parking available Outdoor swimming pool (heated)
Open terrace V meals Last d 21.00hrs Languages spoken:
English,German & Spanish
MEALS: Continental breakfast 52FF Lunch 130-195FF Dinner
130-195FF✱
CARDS: ✹ ▬▬ ▆▆

BEAUGENCY Loiret

★ ★ ★ L'Abbaye
2 quai de l'Abbaye *45190*
☎ 238446735 FAX 238448792
Situated on the banks of the River Loire, this former abbey
exudes a historic atmosphere. Many of its original features
have been preserved and through carefully chosen
furnishings, visitors are transported back to a time of tradition
and warm hospitality. The spacious foyer and lounge,
restaurant and bedrooms are decorated in a style befitting the
abbey's origins. The restaurant has a comprehensive menu
where traditional cuisine is complemented by an array of
imaginative dishes.
Near river Forest area Near motorway
18 en suite (bth/shr) (4 fmly) TV in all bedrooms Licensed
Night porter Full central heating Open parking available
Open terrace Close by Last d 22.00hrs Languages spoken:
English
MEALS: Continental breakfast 45FF Lunch fr 190FF&alc
Dinner fr 190FF✱
CARDS: ✹ ▬▬ ▆▆ ☻ Travellers cheques

★ ★ ★ ★ La Tonnellerie
12 rue des Eaux Bleues *45190*
☎ 238446815 FAX 238441001
(3km from Beaugency towards Blois)
Standing at the gateway to Sologne and a region where
châteaux are in abundance, the hotel is evocative of past times
and exudes the discreet charm of an old manor house with the
comfort of modern days. All the bedrooms are individually
decorated with tasteful and high quality furnishings and there
is a shaded garden where breakfast and dinner are served on
fine days. Numerous leisure pursuits to be found nearby. The
restaurant serves the finest of local cuisine and a selection of
Loire Valley wines.
Near river Forest area Near motorway
Closed 2 Jan-28 Feb
20 en suite (bth/shr) (2 fmly) TV in all bedrooms Direct dial
from all bedrooms Licensed Lift Full central heating Open
parking available Child discount available 12yrs Outdoor
swimming pool (heated) Boule Bicycle rental Open terrace V
meals Last d 22.00hrs Languages spoken: English & Spanish
ROOMS: (room only) s 350-660FF; d 450-1240FF
Reductions over 1 night
MEALS: Continental breakfast 65FF Lunch 95-260FF&alc
Dinner 135-260FF&alc
CARDS: ✹ ▬▬ ▆▆ Travellers cheques

BEAULIEU-LÈS-LOCHES Indre-et-Loire

★ ★ Hotel de Beaulieu
37600
☎ 247916080 FAX 247916080
This ancient building dates back to the 16th century and is part
of the Benedictine abbey of Beaulieu, where a tomb contains
the remains of Foulques Nerra, grandfather of England's
Henry II. Situated in the medieval town of Loches, this partly
renovated residence features an old flagstone spiral staircase,

exposed beams, and an attractive interior flower-garden. All
the en-suite guest-rooms have modern facilities.
Near river Near lake Forest area In town centre Near
motorway
Closed early Oct-end March
9 en suite (shr) (2 fmly) Direct dial from all bedrooms
Licensed Boule Bicycle rental Open terrace Last d 23.00hrs
Languages spoken: English
MEALS: Continental breakfast 25FF Lunch 75-100FF&alc
Dinner 75-100FF&alc✱
CARDS: Travellers cheques

BEAUMONT-EN-VÉRON Indre-et-Loire

★ ★ Manoir de la Giraudière
37420
☎ 247584036 FAX 247584606
(From Chinon take road towards Bourgueil for 5km, then turn
left towards Savigny-en-Véron. Hotel 1km on right)

This handsome manor dates back to the 17th century and used
to be a private residence. It is now a welcoming country hotel
surrounded by vineyards, copses and grasslands. It features a
16th-century dovecote, as well as attractively furnished
bedrooms and a terrace, where on fine days guests can enjoy a
drink or a meal.
Near river Forest area
25 en suite (bth/shr) (10 fmly) (2 with balcony) TV in all
bedrooms Direct dial from all bedrooms Licensed Night
porter Full central heating Open parking available
Supervised Child discount available 5yrs Boule Bicycle rental
Open terrace Badminton,Croquet Last d 22.00hrs Languages
spoken: English
ROOMS: (room only) d 200-590FF **Reductions over 1 night**
MEALS: Full breakfast 38FF Lunch 75-160FF&alc Dinner 75-
160FF&alc
CARDS: ✹ ▬▬ ▆▆ Travellers cheques

BLÉRÉ Indre-et-Loire

★ ★ Cheval Blanc
5 pl Ch Bidault *37150*
☎ 247303014 FAX 247235280
Situated amongst the châteaux of the Loire valley, this hotel is the
ideal base for visits to the famous vineyards. The proprietors,
Micheline and Michel Blériot have transformed this 17th-century
house into a welcoming establishment. The comfortable guest
rooms are equipped with private amenities as well as a TV, mini-
bar and direct-dial telephone. The cuisine offers a high standard
of cooking using home-grown, seasonal produce.
Near river Forest area In town centre Near motorway
Closed early Jan-early Feb

12 en suite (bth/shr) TV in all bedrooms STV Direct dial from all bedrooms Mini-bar in all bedrooms Licensed Full central heating Open parking available Covered parking available Supervised Child discount available 8yrs Outdoor swimming pool (heated) Open terrace V meals Last d 21.15hrs
Languages spoken: English
MEALS: Continental breakfast 38FF Lunch 99-270FF Dinner 99-270FF✱
CARDS: ✿ ▩ ▩ ⑨ Travellers cheques

BLOIS Loir-et-Cher

★ ★ ★ Holiday Inn Garden Court (Holiday Inns)
26 av Maudoury *41000*
☎ 254554488 FAX 254745797
(Opposite Palais de Congris convention centre)
This hotel offers guests a special combination of traditional hospitality combined with excellent facilities, and complemented by dedicated staff rendering meticulous service. The interiors have been designed with immaculate attention to detail and ensure that guests have a most satisfying and pleasant stay. Elegant bedrooms are decorated with a touch of class and equipped with outstanding amenities offering the highest level of comfort.
In town centre Near motorway
78 en suite (bth/shr) No smoking in 40 bedrooms TV in all bedrooms Radio in rooms Direct dial from all bedrooms Mini-bar in 40 bedrooms Licensed Lift Night porter Full central heating Open parking available Child discount available 12yrs Bicycle rental Open terrace Last d 22.00hrs
Languages spoken: English & German
ROOMS: (room only) s 430FF; d 470FF
CARDS: ✿ ▩ ▩ ⑨ Travellers cheques

BONNEVAL Eure-et-Loir

★ ★ ★ Hostellerie du Bois Guibert
Hammeau de Guibert *28800*
☎ 237472233 FAX 237475069
Near motorway
14 en suite (bth/shr) (2 fmly) TV in all bedrooms Licensed Full central heating Open parking available Solarium Boule Bicycle rental Open terrace V meals Last d 21.30hrs
Languages spoken: English,German & Spanish
MEALS: Full breakfast 50FF Continental breakfast 50FF Lunch 139-310FF&alc Dinner 139-310FF&alc✱
CARDS: ✿ ▩ ▩ ⑨

BOURGES Cher

★ ★ Climat de France
Z.A.C du Val d'Auron, Av de Robinson *18000*
☎ 248503278 Cen Res 64460123 FAX 248504598
(off N151)
Near river Near lake Near motorway
42 en suite (bth) TV in all bedrooms Direct dial from all bedrooms Licensed Full central heating Open parking available
CARDS: ✿ ▩

BRÉZOLLES Eure-et-Loir

★ ★ Le Relais ✗ ✗ ✗
28270
☎ 237482084 FAX 237482846
In a peaceful, rural setting between the Normandy beaches and the Loire Valley, this hotel offers guests a high standard of comfort and cuisine.

Near river Forest area
Closed Aug
25 en suite (bth/shr) (4 fmly) TV in all bedrooms Direct dial from all bedrooms Licensed Full central heating Open parking available Supervised Child discount available 11yrs Boule Bicycle rental Open terrace V meals Last d 21.30hrs
Languages spoken: English
ROOMS: (room only) s 170-230FF; d 200-250FF
✱ Reductions over 1 night
MEALS: Full breakfast 50FF Lunch 76-200FF Dinner 76-200FF✱
CARDS: ✿ ▩ ▩ ⑨ Travellers cheques

BRIARE Loiret

★ ★ Hotel Le Cerf
22-24 bd Buyser *45250*
☎ 238370080 FAX 238312517
The hotel Le Cerf is located in the town of Briare which has many canals and is situated on the banks of the River Loire. Most of the bedrooms in this attractive establishment have private facilities and provide good comfort. The restaurant has a range of dishes on the menu, which will please most palates and are of good flavour.
Near river In town centre
Closed 21 Dec-4 Jan
21 en suite (bth/shr) 8 rooms in annexe (4 fmly) (2 with balcony) TV in all bedrooms Licensed Full central heating Open parking available Covered parking available (charged) Supervised Child discount available Boule Bicycle rental Open terrace
CARDS: ▩

CHABRIS Indre

★ ★ De la Plage
42 rue du Pont *36210*
☎ 254400224 FAX 254400859
This small country hotel is located near a river and features pleasant bedrooms offering good comfort. The flower-filled interior garden provides the charming setting for lunch and dinner, which include a range of regional dishes and fish specialities. The hotel is very popular with an English clientele who faithfully return every summer.
Near river Forest area In town centre Near motorway
Closed end Jun & early Sept & January
10 en suite (shr) TV in all bedrooms Direct dial from all bedrooms Licensed Full central heating Open parking available Covered parking available Child discount available 2yrs Tennis Boule Bicycle rental Open terrace V meals Last d 21.00hrs Languages spoken: English
MEALS: Full breakfast 31FF Continental breakfast 31FF Lunch 98-220FF&alc Dinner 98-220FF&alc✱
CARDS: ✿ ▩

CHARTRES Eure-et-Loir

★ ★ Climat de France
rue des Pierres Missigualt, Barjouville *28630*
☎ 237353555 Cen Rcs 64460123 FAX 237347212
(3km from town centre, off ring road)
The comfortable bedrooms in this hotel are appointed with modern facilities and offer a good level of comfort. The restaurant serves a decent standard of cooking with an excellent choice from the generous buffet or 'à la carte' menu. Guests are well looked after by friendly staff who provide a helpful and attentive service at all times. *contd.*

Near lake Forest area Near motorway
52 en suite (bth/shr) (9 fmly) No smoking in 24 bedrooms TV
in all bedrooms Radio in rooms Direct dial from all bedrooms
Licensed Night porter Open parking available Open terrace
Covered terrace V meals Languages spoken: English &
German
CARDS: ●● ▆▆

★ ★ ★ Grand Monarque (Best Western)
22 pl des Épars *28005*
☎ 237210072 FAX 237363418
Town centre
This old coaching inn has been improved, enlarged and
updated over the centuries and is now an establishment which
enjoys a good reputation in the region. The elegant guest
rooms offer comfort without sacrificing the building's old
world charm, while the intimate restaurant serves a splendid
cuisine and has acquired a faithful clientele over the years.
In town centre
54 en suite (bth/shr) (8 fmly) TV in all bedrooms STV Radio in
rooms Direct dial from all bedrooms Mini-bar in all bedrooms
Licensed Lift Night porter Full central heating Open parking
available (charged) Covered parking available (charged) Child
discount available 12yrs Open terrace Last d 22.00hrs
Languages spoken: German, Spanish
CARDS: ●● ▆▆ ▆▆ ◑ Travellers cheques

★ ★ De la Poste
3 rue Général Koenig *28000*
☎ 237210427 FAX 237364217
(Follow signs for town centre. Hotel Place des Epars)
This pleasant establishment is situated in the city centre, not
far from all the shops, restaurants and cafés. It features a
genuine interior which comprises sound-proofed bedrooms
with a good level of comfort, and a fine cuisine, augmented by
excellent wines from the renowned house-cellar.
In town centre Near motorway
57 rms (55 bth/shr) (3 fmly) No smoking in 5 bedrooms TV in
all bedrooms STV Direct dial from all bedrooms Licensed
Lift Night porter Full central heating Open parking available
(charged) Covered parking available (charged) Supervised
Child discount available 7yrs Last d 21.30hrs Languages
spoken: English,German
ROOMS: (room only) s 275-310FF; d 300-330FF
MEALS: Full breakfast 41FF Lunch 81-170FF Dinner 81-170FF
CARDS: ●● ▆▆ ▆▆ ◑ Travellers cheques

CHÂTEAUNEUF-SUR-LOIRE Loiret

★ ★ La Capitainerie
Grande Rue *45110*
☎ 238584216 FAX 238584681
Standing next to a magnificent château, this hotel provides the
ideal venue for an overnight stop whilst touring the Loire
valley. It offers attractive guest accommodation with a good
level of comfort, and a traditional cuisine which includes many
superb dishes from the region. In summer meals are served
outside on the terrace.
Near river Forest area In town centre Near motorway
Closed Feb
12 en suite (bth/shr) (3 fmly) (3 with balcony) TV in all
bedrooms Radio in rooms Direct dial from all bedrooms
Licensed Full central heating Open parking available
Supervised Fishing Squash Riding Sauna Solarium Boule
Bicycle rental Open terrace V meals Last d 21.30hrs
Languages spoken: German, Spanish

ROOMS: (room only) d 280-387FF **Reductions over 1 night**
MEALS: Full breakfast 36FF Continental breakfast 36FF Lunch
120-273FF&alc Dinner 120-273FF&alc
CARDS: ●● ▆▆ Travellers cheques

★ ★ Nouvel Hotel du Loiret
4 pl Aristife Briand *45110*
☎ 238584228 FAX 235584399
The hotel is set in the Loire valley on the edge of the beautiful
Sologne region, 100 kilometres from Paris. It offers bedrooms
with modern facilities providing a good level of comfort and a
homely restaurant which serves a classic cuisine where a
choice of tasty, regional dishes feature strongly on the menu.
Near river Near beach Forest area In town centre
Closed 20 Dec-20 Jan
16 en suite (bth/shr) (3 fmly) TV in all bedrooms Licensed
Night porter Full central heating Open parking available
(charged) Covered parking available (charged) Supervised
Open terrace Languages spoken: English
MEALS: Full breakfast 32FF Lunch 80-195FF&alc✷
CARDS: ●● ▆▆ ▆▆

CHÂTEAUROUX Indre

★ ★ Auberge de l'Arc en Ciel
La Forge de l'Isle *36000*
☎ 254340983 FAX 254344674
(On D943 towards Montluçon)
Set on the banks of the River Indre and close to the forest of
Chênes de Châteauroux, the Auberge Arc en Ciel offers its
clientele old-fashioned service in an informal atmosphere. The
bedrooms are comfortable and have good amenities, and
guests can relax in the inviting lounge with its rustic furniture,
or on the terrace. The restaurant, which is situated opposite the
hotel offers enjoyable meals prepared with only fresh produce.
Near river Forest area Near motorway
Closed Last week Dec & first week Jan RS Sun & Mon
25 rms (8 bth 9 shr) (9 fmly) TV in all bedrooms Direct dial
from all bedrooms Licensed Full central heating Open
parking available Child discount available Boule Open
terrace Languages spoken: English
ROOMS: (room only) s 150-210FF; d 175-230FF
MEALS: Continental breakfast 25FF Lunch 60-130FF&alc
Dinner 60-130FF&alc✷
CARDS: ●● ▆▆

Taking your mobile phone to France?
See page 11

CHÂTILLON-SUR-INDRE Indre

★★ Auberge de la Tour
2 rte du Blanc *36700*
☎ 254387217 FAX 254387485
(Approach via N143 & D975)
A warm and friendly welcome awaits visitors upon arrival in this attractive inn, where exposed beams and rustic decorations create a cosy atmosphere. The country-style restaurant serves a choice of regional and traditional dishes, and as soon as the weather permits it, guests can relax on the large terrace. The peaceful bedrooms are equipped with modern facilities and provide a restful night's sleep, whilst the surrounding region is a paradise for nature lovers, and offers excellent walking trails and fishing grounds.
Near river Near lake Forest area In town centre Near motorway
11 rms (1 bth 6 shr) (2 fmly) TV in 6 bedrooms Direct dial from all bedrooms Licensed Full central heating Open parking available Covered parking available (charged) Child discount available Open terrace Covered terrace V meals Last d 22.00hrs
ROOMS: (room only) d 140-260FF
MEALS: Full breakfast 26FF Lunch 55-220FF&alc Dinner 55-220FF&alc
CARDS: ●● ▀▀ Travellers cheques

CHENONCEAUX Indre-et-Loire

★★ Hostellerie de la Renaudière
24 rue du Docteur Bretonneau *37150*
☎ 247239004 FAX 247239051
Located just outside the village, and a few steps away from the castle, this ancient residence welcomes its visitors in peaceful surroundings. Set amidst an attractive park and blessed with the mild climate of the Loire valley, it transports people back in history. The restaurant serves dishes which are based on authentic recipes, complemented by innovative dishes. The bedrooms have modern appointments, whilst the immediate vicinity offers a range of leisure pursuits.
Near river Forest area
15 en suite (bth/shr) 5 rooms in annexe (1 fmly) TV in all bedrooms Direct dial from all bedrooms Mini-bar in all bedrooms Licensed Full central heating Open parking available Supervised Child discount available 8yrs Sauna Solarium Jacuzzi/spa Bicycle rental Open terrace Covered terrace V meals Last d 21.30hrs Languages spoken: English
ROOMS: (room only) s 225FF; d 270-400FF **Reductions over 1 night**
MEALS: Full breakfast 70FF Continental breakfast 25FF Lunch 99-189FF&alc Dinner 99-189FF&alc
CARDS: ●● ▀▀ ▀▀ Travellers cheques

★★ Hostel du Roy
9 rue Bretonneaux *37150*
☎ 247239017 FAX 247238981
(A10 exit Blois direction Montrichard and Chenonceaux or exit Amboise direction Blere and Chenonceaux)
A family atmosphere pervades this charming hotel which is set amongst the Loire Chateaux, in a rustic setting. M Goupil, the chef offers several regional and house specialities accompanied by Loire wines.,
Near river Forest area
37 en suite (bth/shr) 11 rooms in annexe (2 fmly) TV in all bedrooms Direct dial from all bedrooms Licensed Full central heating Open parking available Supervised Boule Covered terrace V meals Last d 21.30hrs

Languages spoken: English, German & Spanish
ROOMS: (room only) s 130-220FF; d 150-256FF
Reductions over 1 night
MEALS: Continental breakfast 30FF Lunch 65-170FF&alc Dinner 65-170FF&alc
CARDS: ●● ▀▀ ▀▀ Travellers cheques

CHERISY Eure-et-Loir

★★★ Domaine de la Reposee
1 rue du Prieuré *28500*
☎ 237438604 FAX 237438351
(from Paris on N12 to Dreux take exit Cherisy. At roundabout, towards Cherisy centre, continue downhill until church then right to Fermaincourt)
A comfortable, peaceful hotel in an attractive garden, where all rooms have character and open onto the garden. This lovely hotel has a 5 acre park by the Eure River and the nearby forest of Anet to add to the peace and calmness of the surroundings.
Near river Forest area Near motorway
7 en suite (bth/shr) TV in all bedrooms STV Direct dial from all bedrooms Licensed Night porter Full central heating Open parking available Indoor swimming pool (heated) Tennis Fishing Riding Sauna Solarium Jacuzzi/spa Open terrace Languages spoken: English
ROOMS: (room only) d 400FF ✱
CARDS: ●● ▀▀ ▀▀

CHINON Indre-et-Loire

★★★★ Château de Danzay
Danzay *37500*
☎ 247584686 FAX 247588435
Château de Danzay was built in 1461 on the remains of a Gallo-Roman villa by the equerry of Louis XI. Nowadays it is a charming Château-hotel surrounded by vineyards, and features elegant guest accommodation decorated with precious rugs, canopy beds and period furniture. The candlelit restaurant serves an outstanding cuisine, accompanied by the great wines of the Loire valley.
Near river Forest area
Closed Nov-Apr
10 en suite (bth/shr) TV in all bedrooms Licensed Full central heating Open parking available Supervised Child discount available Outdoor swimming pool Open terrace Last d 21.30hrs Languages spoken: English, Italian
CARDS: ●● ▀▀ ▀▀ ● Eurocard Travellers cheques

★★ Didérot
4 rue Buffon/7 rue Didérot *37500*
☎ 247931887 FAX 247933710
(45km south west of Tours, take D751 to place Jeanne d'Arc, then rue Buffon & the rue Didérot)
contd.

The Hotel Didérot is housed in a handsome building dating back to the 18th century. Peacefully situated close to the old town and the Place Jeanne D'Arc, the interior features half-timbered walls, a beautiful staircase and a restaurant with a 15th century fireplace where delicious home-made jams are served with breakfast. The bedrooms are individually furnished and equipped with modern facilities.
In town centre
27 en suite (bth/shr) 4 rooms in annexe (4 fmly) No smoking in 4 bedrooms TV in 10 bedrooms Direct dial from all bedrooms Licensed Night porter Full central heating Open parking available Supervised Child discount available Bicycle rental Open terrace Languages spoken: English & Greek

ROOMS: (room only) s 250-320FF; d 300-400FF
CARDS: ●● ▦ ▆▆ ●) Travellers cheques

CHISSAY-EN-TOURAINE Loir-et-Cher

★ ★ ★ Château de la Menaudière
BP 15 41401
☎ 254712345 FAX 254713458
Situated in the heart of the 'Vallée des Rois', surrounded by parklands, this elegant establishment welcomes its guests to a warm, friendly atmosphere. The peaceful bedrooms are beautifully appointed and provide the maximum comfort. The dining room offers an innovative selection of well-prepared dishes, making good use of very high quality produce. Visitors can relax in the congenial bar or for the more energetic there is the tennis-court.
Forest area
Mar-4 Jan
26 en suite (bth/shr) (1 fmly) TV in all bedrooms STV Radio in rooms Direct dial from all bedrooms Mini-bar in all bedrooms Licensed Full central heating Open parking available Supervised Child discount available Outdoor swimming pool (heated) Tennis Boule Bicycle rental Open terrace V meals Last d 22.00hrs Languages spoken: English,German,Spanish
ROOMS: (room only) s 400FF; d 400-800FF
MEALS: Full breakfast 60FF Lunch 90-150FF&alc Dinner 190-290FF&alc✱
CARDS: ●● ▦ ▆▆ ●) Travellers cheques

CHISSEAUX Indre-et-Loire

★ ★ Clair Cottage
27 rue de l'Europe 37150
☎ 247239069 FAX 247238707
(1km from Chenonceaux in direction of Montrichard)
The Hotel Clair Cottage enjoys a peaceful location just one kilometre from the Château de Chenonceaux. The attractive

guest accommodation is housed in an 19th-century outbuilding constructed in the distinct style of the Touraine region, and offers comfortable rooms with good amenities. The restaurant serves a high standard of cooking including regional specialities, personally prepared by the chef-proprietor Mr Bourbonnais.
Near river Near beach Forest area Near motorway
Closed Dec-Feb
20 en suite (bth/shr) 10 rooms in annexe (7 fmly) (3 with balcony) TV in 10 bedrooms Direct dial from all bedrooms Licensed Full central heating Open parking available Child discount available 10yrs Open terrace V meals Last d 21.00hrs Languages spoken: English
ROOMS: (room only) s 230-310FF; d 230-310FF
MEALS: Continental breakfast 35FF Lunch 80-160FF Dinner 80-160FF
CARDS: ●● ▆▆ Travellers cheques

COMBREUX Loiret

★ ★ L'Auberge de Combreux
34 rte du Gatinais 45530
☎ 238468989 FAX 238593619
(from Paris A10 exit Orleans Nord-Montargis N60 then exit Chateauneuf and proceed left to Combreux)
Situated in the tranquillity of a village from the past, the inn offers comfortable rooms of character. Breakfast will be served in your room or may be taken on the terrace. During the day guests may relax by the pool, practise on the golf driving range or use the bicycles available. In the evening you will enjoy the menu offered in the restaurant.
Near river Near lake Forest area Near motorway
Closed 16 Dec-19 Jan
19 en suite (bth/shr) (2 fmly) (3 with balcony) TV in all bedrooms STV Direct dial from all bedrooms Licensed Full central heating Open parking available Child discount available 12yrs Outdoor swimming pool (heated) Tennis Bicycle rental Covered terrace Last d 21.30hrs Languages spoken: English & German
ROOMS: (room only) s 325-495FF; d 325-495FF
MEALS: Continental breakfast 38FF Lunch 90-210FF Dinner 90-210FF&alc✱
CARDS: ●● ▦ ▆▆ Travellers cheques

CONTRES Loir-et-Cher

★ ★ ★ France
33 rue Pierre Henri Mauger 41700
☎ 254795014 FAX 254790295
In the renowned Châteaux of the Loire region, the Hôtel de France and its restaurant 'Les Rois de France' welcome their guests in attractive, peaceful surroundings. The hotel has comfortable bedrooms equipped with modern amenities, and offers three dining-rooms which open on to the terrace with its flowers and fountain. Guests can savour a varied choice of classic and modern cuisine in the regal ambience of the restaurant.
Forest area In town centre
37 en suite (bth/shr) (18 with balcony) TV in all bedrooms STV Radio in rooms Licensed Full central heating Open parking available Covered parking available (charged) Child discount available 12yrs Outdoor swimming pool (heated) Tennis Sauna Jacuzzi/spa Bicycle rental Open terrace V meals Last d 21.15hrs Languages spoken: English,German
CARDS: ●● ▦ ▆▆ Travellers cheques

COUTURE-SUR-LOIR Loir-et-Cher

★★ Le Grand St-Vincent
6 rue Pasteur *41800*
☎ 254724202 FAX 254724155
The village Couture-sur-Loir is the birthplace of the famous poet Pierre de Ronsard and the charming location of this establishment. It has a few guest rooms which are furnished in simple, understated fashion, but are very comfortable, while the restaurant serves dishes to suit all tastes.
Near river Near lake Forest area In town centre
7 en suite (shr) (1 fmly) TV in all bedrooms Licensed Full central heating Open parking available Supervised Child discount available 8yrs Boule Bicycle rental Open terrace Last d 21.00hrs
Rooms: (room only) s 210-240FF; d 240-300FF
✱ **Reductions over 1 night Special breaks**
Meals: Full breakfast 35FF Continental breakfast 25FF Lunch 60-120FF&alc Dinner 60-120FF&alc✱
Cards: ⊛ 〓

DÉSCARTES Indre-et-Loire

★★ Moderne
15 rue Déscartes *37160*
☎ 247597211 FAX 247924490
(Approach from St-Maure via N10)
The hotel is situated in the pretty village of Déscartes, birthplace of the famous philosopher of the same name. Well positioned for visits to the Loire châteaux and Futuroscope, it features well-maintained bedrooms with individual furnishings, whilst the restaurant serves a generous cuisine based on traditional recipes and which can be adapted to individual needs. Guests may want to visit the Déscartes museum and home in the village, stroll around the gardens or visit the nearby chateaux.
Near river Forest area In town centre Near motorway
Closed 21 Dec-4 Jan
11 en suite (bth) (3 fmly) TV in all bedrooms Direct dial from all bedrooms Licensed Full central heating Open parking available Child discount available 12yrs Open terrace V meals Last d 21.30hrs Languages spoken: English,German,Dutch
Rooms: (room only) s 220-285FF; d 258-305FF
✱ **Reductions over 1 night**
Meals: Continental breakfast 38FF Lunch 68-200FFalc Dinner 80-200FFalc
Cards: ⊛ 〓 Carte Bleue Travellers cheques

DREUX Eure-et-Loir

★★ Vidéotel Dreux
8 pl Misirard *28100*
☎ 237456410 FAX 237461911
The hotels in the Vidéotel group all have bedrooms with pleasant furnishings and are equipped with the comfort of their clientele in mind. The restaurants serve a good quality gourmet cuisine with a range of prix-fixe menus, regional specialities and 'eat your fill buffet'. The management couples and their dedicated teams offer a 'round the clock' efficient service, where the well-being and satisfaction of guests is the prime consideration.
In town centre
41 en suite (shr) (9 fmly) No smoking in 8 bedrooms TV in all bedrooms Direct dial from all bedrooms Licensed Lift Night porter Full central heating Open parking available (charged) Child discount available 12yrs V meals Last d 22.00hrs Languages spoken: English
Rooms: (room only) s 250FF; d 250FF
Cards: ⊛ 〓 〓 ⓞ

FONTENAY-SUR-LOING Loiret

★★★ Domaine et Golf de Vaugouard
chemin des Bois *45210*
☎ 238957185 FAX 238957978
(A6 to Lyon exit Dordives, then follow signs to Vangouard from Fontenay-sur-Loing)

An hour's drive from Paris, this stylish renovated farmhouse hotel offers calm, comfort and relaxation.
Near river Near lake Forest area Near motorway
31 en suite (bth/shr) 9 rooms in annexe (9 fmly) (9 with balcony) TV in 40 bedrooms STV Direct dial from 40 bedrooms Mini-bar in all bedrooms Licensed Night porter Full central heating Open parking available Covered parking available Child discount available 12yrs Outdoor swimming pool (heated) Golf Riding Sauna Gym Boule Open terrace Last d 21.30hrs Languages spoken: English
Rooms: (room only) s 450-650FF, d 550-795FF
Reductions over 1 night Special breaks
Meals: Full breakfast 50FF Lunch 90-180FF Dinner 140-180FF✱
Cards: 〓 〓 ⓞ

FRÉTEVAL Loir-et-Cher

★★★ Hostellerie de Rocheux
41160
☎ 254232680 FAX 254230414
This small château is set in extensive grounds. The guest rooms are spacious with large windows overlooking the park and are equipped with up-to-date modern facilities. Meals are served in the intimate restaurant and comprise various imaginative and classic dishes.
Near river Forest area Near motorway
15 en suite (bth) (1 fmly) TV available Mini-bar in all bedrooms Licensed Full central heating Open parking available Child discount available 14yrs Pool table Bicycle rental Open terrace Table Tennis Last d 21.30hrs Languages spoken: English,Italian
Meals: Full breakfast 50FF Lunch 120-235FF&alc Dinner 250-400FFalc✱
Cards: ⊛ 〓 〓 ⓞ

GIEN Loiret

★★★ Rivage
1 quai de Nice *45500*
☎ 238377900 FAX 238381021
(Approach via D940 beside the river)
Near the banks of the Loire, the hotel offers its visitors individually styled bedrooms and suites, tastefully *contd.*

furnished with matching colours and fabrics. There is a spacious
lounge and piano-bar for relaxation, whilst the restaurant serves
an outstanding selection of skilfully executed dishes.
Near river In town centre
19 en suite (bth/shr) TV in all bedrooms STV Direct dial from
all bedrooms Licensed Full central heating Air conditioning
in bedrooms Open parking available Supervised V meals
Last d 21.30hrs Languages spoken: English,German
ROOMS: (room only) s 298FF; d 370-550FF
MEALS: Continental breakfast 48FF Lunch 145-390FF Dinner
145-390FF
CARDS: ●● ▦ ▆ ● Travellers cheques

ISSOUDUN Indre

★ ★ ★ La Cognette
bd Stalingrad 36100
☎ 254212183 FAX 254031303
This is a delightful 19th-century building where the interior
does not seem to have changed over the years. It offers
charming public areas adorned with many antiques, spacious
bedrooms with modern facilities, and a superb restaurant
serving an outstanding selection of dishes, complemented by
great vintage wines.
Forest area In town centre Near motorway
14 en suite (bth/shr) 1 rooms in annexe TV in all bedrooms
STV Radio in rooms Direct dial from all bedrooms Mini-bar
in all bedrooms Licensed Night porter Full central heating
Covered parking available (charged) Child discount available
Open terrace V meals Last d 22.00hrs Languages spoken:
English,German
ROOMS: (room only) d 350-500FF ✱
MEALS: Full breakfast 70FF Continental breakfast 70FF Lunch
200-400FF&alc Dinner 200-400FF&alc✱
CARDS: ●● ▦ ▆ ● Travellers cheques

JOUÉ-LES-TOURS Indre-et-Loire

★ ★ Ariane
8 av du Lac 37300
☎ 247676760 FAX 247673336
The Hotel Ariane is a purpose-built establishment which offers
modern accommodation with good amenities. It stands on the
shores of a lake and features cheerfully decorated bedrooms
and attractive public areas, and because of its location
provides a good base for touring the surrounding area. In
addition there is a good choice of leisure opportunities and
two restaurants nearby.
Near lake Forest area Near motorway
Closed Xmas-early Jan
31 en suite (bth/shr) (5 fmly) TV in all bedrooms STV Direct
dial from all bedrooms Mini-bar in all bedrooms Licensed
Night porter Full central heating Open parking available
Covered parking available (charged) Outdoor swimming pool
(heated) Bicycle rental Open terrace Languages spoken:
English,Spanish
ROOMS: (room only) s 259-289FF; d 259-289FF
CARDS: ●● ▆ Travellers cheques

★ ★ ★ Château de Beaulieu
67 rue de Beaulieu 37300
☎ 247532026 FAX 247538420
Set in delightful gardens, this 17th-century manor house offers
its visitors an enjoyable stay in elegant, sophisticated
surroundings. Smart bedrooms are furnished in character with
the building and offer a high degree of comfort. The
outstanding cuisine is renowned throughout the region for its

skilfully executed dishes containing only the finest ingredients.
19 en suite (bth/shr) 10 rooms in annexe TV in all bedrooms
Direct dial from all bedrooms Mini-bar in all bedrooms
Licensed Full central heating Air conditioning in bedrooms
Open parking available Child discount available Boule Open
terrace Last d 21.30hrs Languages spoken:
English,German,Spanish
ROOMS: (room only) d 390-760FF **Special breaks**
MEALS: Full breakfast 55FF Continental breakfast 55FF Lunch
205-480FF&alc Dinner 205-480FF&alc
CARDS: ●● ▦ ▆ Travellers cheques

LANGEAIS Indre-et-Loire

★ ★ ★ Hosten
2 rue Gambetta 37130
☎ 247968212 FAX 247965672
(in city centre)
Martine and Yannick Errard manage this fashionable inn situated
a few yards from the Langeais medieval castle. The location
makes it an ideal base for visiting the Loire valley castles. The
accommodation comprises ten comfortably furnished rooms, a
bar and the restaurant where Yannick prepares seasonal country
products and local vintages to the greatest effect.
Near river Forest area In town centre Near motorway
Closed 15 Jan-15 Feb
10 en suite (bth/shr) TV in all bedrooms Direct dial from all
bedrooms Licensed Full central heating Open parking
available (charged) Covered parking available (charged)
Bicycle rental Open terrace Last d 21.30hrs Languages
spoken: English
ROOMS: (room only) d 280-550FF
MEALS: Continental breakfast 55FF Lunch 145-195FF&alc
Dinner 145-195FF&alc
CARDS: ●● ▦ ▆ Travellers cheques

LOCHES Indre-et-Loire

★ ★ De France
6 rue Picois 37600
☎ 247590032 FAX 247592866
(In the town centre, beside the Medieval City)
This ancient coaching inn is situated at the foot of the medieval
cité, and offers peacefully situated bedrooms which are
individually appointed and equipped with modern amenities.
There is a flower-filled interior courtyard where, weather
permitting, breakfast and meals are served. The cuisine offers
a high standard of creative and traditional cooking which has a
good reputation locally.
Near river Forest area In town centre
Closed 12 Jan-12 Feb
19 rms (18 bth/shr) (2 fmly) (4 with balcony) TV in all
bedrooms STV Direct dial from all bedrooms Licensed Full
central heating Open parking available (charged) Covered
parking available (charged) Supervised Bicycle rental Open
terrace V meals Last d 21.15hrs Languages spoken: English
ROOMS: (room only) s 225-250FF; d 225-350FF
✱ **Reductions over 1 night**
MEALS: Full breakfast 35FF Continental breakfast 35FF Lunch
85-250FF&alc Dinner 85-250FF&alc
CARDS: ●● ▆ ● Travellers cheques

★ ★ ★ George Sand
39 rue Quintéfol 37600
☎ 247593974 FAX 247915575
Situated in attractive surroundings, the hotel and its friendly
owners, Madame and Monsieur Fortin offer their clientele a

warm welcome. Whether it is for holiday or business, the hotel provides the ideal setting for a successful stay. The pleasant bedrooms are tastefully furnished and the informal restaurant, where exposed beams and rustic furniture create a cosy atmosphere, serves a high standard of cooking.
Near river Near lake Forest area In town centre Near motorway
20 en suite (bth/shr) (3 fmly) TV in all bedrooms Direct dial from all bedrooms Licensed Full central heating Child discount available 12yrs Open terrace V meals Last d 21.00hrs Languages spoken: English
MEALS: Full breakfast 38FF Lunch 90-290FF Dinner 90-290FF✻
CARDS: ●● ▆▆ Travellers cheques

LUYNES Indre-et-Loire

★ ★ ★ ★ Domaine de Beauvois
Le Pont Clouet, rte de Cléré-les-Pins *37230*
☎ 247555011 FAX 247555962
(From A10 exit at Tours Nord take N10 towards Tours and then take N152 to Luynes)
This gracious manor house enjoys a beautiful setting amidst 350 acres of extensive woodlands. The intimate atmosphere of its rustic lounge, sumptuous dining rooms and understated elegance of the guest accommodation create a delightful setting for a relaxing stay. The cuisine is of the highest standard, complemented with outstanding vintage wines from the Loire region.
Near river Near lake Forest area Near motorway
Closed 15 Jan-15 Mar
40 en suite (bth) 2 rooms in annexe (24 fmly) TV in all bedrooms STV Direct dial from all bedrooms Mini-bar in all bedrooms Licensed Lift Night porter Full central heating Open parking available Child discount available 12yrs Outdoor swimming pool (heated) Tennis Fishing Boule Bicycle rental Open terrace boating, hot air ballooning, archery Last d 21.00hrs Languages spoken: English,German,Spanish
MEALS: Full breakfast 130FF Continental breakfast 80FF Lunch fr 350FF&alc Dinner fr 365FF&alc✻
CARDS: ●● ▆▆ ▆▆ ❿ JCB Travellers cheques

MARÇAY Indre-et-Loire

★ ★ ★ ★ Château de Marcay
37500
☎ 247930347 FAX 247934533
This luxurious hotel is housed in a 15th-century fortress surrounded by its own vineyards. The elegant interior combines modern day comfort with exquisite period furnishings and fabrics. The bedrooms are decorated with great taste and have superb en suite facilities, while the restaurant offers an innovative menu served by courteous, attentive staff. After dinner guests can retire to one of the elegant lounges or take a stroll in the splendid wooded park.
Near lake Forest area
38 rms Some rooms in annexe (4 fmly) (6 with balcony) TV in all bedrooms STV Direct dial from all bedrooms Licensed Lift Night porter Full central heating Open parking available Supervised Child discount available Outdoor swimming pool (heated) Tennis Boule Bicycle rental V meals Last d 21.30hrs Languages spoken: English,German,Spanish
MEALS: Full breakfast 130FF Continental breakfast 90FF Lunch 150-425FF&alc Dinner 150-425FF&alc✻
CARDS: ●● ▆▆ ▆▆ ❿ Travellers cheques

MONTARGIS Loiret

★ ★ Climat de France
1250 av d'Antides-Amilly *45200*
☎ 238982021 Cen Res 164460123 FAX 238891916
(off N7, signed Montargis Sud Centre Commercial)
Set in peaceful surroundings at just a few minutes from the town centre, the hotel offers modern bedrooms with good, private facilities, whilst the restaurant serves a traditional cuisine, with generous buffets in the true tradition of the Climat Hotels.
41 en suite (bth) (4 fmly) TV in all bedrooms Direct dial from all bedrooms Licensed Full central heating Open parking available Open terrace Covered terrace Languages spoken: English & French
CARDS: ●● ▆▆

MONTBAZON Indre-et-Loire

★ ★ ★ ★ Château d'Artigny
rte de Monts *37250*
☎ 247262424 FAX 247659279
(highway A10 Paris - Bordeaux, exit 23 towards Montbazon.

When there follow signs Azay-le-Rideau.)
The château is perfectly in keeping with the royal estates surrounding it and reflects in its classical splendour the great past of the Touraine region. The public areas and day rooms feature ornate ceilings and assorted antiques, while the guest accommodation is decorated with high quality furnishings and is completely in style with the building. There is spacious bar-lounge for reading and relaxing, an elegant restaurant and a 65-acre park with unsurpassed leisure facilities.
Near river Forest area
RS 1-9 Jan and 30 Nov-31 Dec.
44 en suite (bth/shr) 11 rooms in annexe (4 fmly) TV in all bedrooms STV Radio in rooms Direct dial from all bedrooms Mini-bar in all bedrooms Licensed Lift Night porter Full central heating Open parking available Child discount available 10yrs Outdoor swimming pool (heated) Golf Tennis Fishing Sauna Gym Boule Jacuzzi/spa Bicycle rental Open terrace Covered terrace Musical evenings,signposted walks V meals Last d 21.30hrs Languages spoken: English,German,Spanish
ROOMS: (room only) s 680-1670FF; d 680-1670FF
MEALS: Full breakfast 140FF Continental breakfast 90FF Lunch 290-450FF&alc Dinner 290-450FF&alc
CARDS: ●● ▆▆ ▆▆ ❿ Travellers cheques

★ ★ ★ Domaine de la Tortinière

Les Gués de Veigné, rte de Ballan-Miré *37250*

☎ 247260019 FAX 247659670

(A10 exit 23 follow Montbazon on N10, 2km N 1st set of traffic lights on left after railway track just outside Montabazon) Halfway between Paris and the Atlantic Coast in the very heart of the Loire Valley and overlooking the Indre Valley. The Domaine de la Tortinière is a charming 19th century manor-house, a place to enjoy the peacefulness of the château country.

Near river Forest area Near motorway

Closed mid Dec-Feb RS Half board compulsory Jul-Sep 21 en suite (bth/shr) 10 rooms in annexe (9 fmly) (6 with balcony) TV in all bedrooms STV Direct dial from all bedrooms Mini-bar in 5 bedrooms Licensed Full central heating Open parking available Outdoor swimming pool (heated) Tennis Fishing Solarium Boule Bicycle rental Open terrace V meals Last d 21.15hrs Languages spoken: English Dutch German Italian & Spanish

ROOMS: (room only) s 480FF; d 590FF **Special breaks**

MEALS: Full breakfast 75FF Lunch fr 220FF&alc Dinner 285-360FF&alc

CARDS: ● ▇ Travellers cheques

Moulins des Planches

28270

☎ 37482597 FAX 37483563

The Moulin des Planches is set in unspoilt countryside. It is situated on the banks of the river Arve, and offers charming accommodation with views over the river or the garden. It has a cosy lounge with open fireplace, and a country style restaurant where exposed beams and terracotta tiled floors create an informal atmosphere. The cuisine includes a choice of well-presented dishes which are based on regional recipes.

Near river Forest area Near motorway

19 en suite (bth/shr) (2 fmly) (1 with balcony) TV in all bedrooms STV Direct dial from all bedrooms Full central heating Open parking available Languages spoken: English

CARDS: ● ▇

★ ★ ★ ★ Château de Noizay

rte de Chancay *37120*

☎ 247521101 FAX 247520464

(8km from Amboise on D78)

This 16th-century building is situated in extensive parklands with mature trees. The individually styled bedrooms are tastefully decorated and offer a high level of comfort, whilst the lounges, dining-rooms and library are all furnished with period pieces and exquisite fabrics.

Near river Forest area Near motorway

Closed mid Jan-mid Mar

14 en suite (bth/shr) (3 fmly) TV in all bedrooms STV Direct dial from all bedrooms Mini-bar in all bedrooms Licensed Full central heating Open parking available Covered parking available Child discount available 12yrs Outdoor swimming pool Tennis Fishing Pool table Boule Bicycle rental Open terrace Covered terrace Last d 21.45hrs Languages spoken: English,German,Spanish

ROOMS: (room only) d 650-1300FF **Reductions over 1 night**

MEALS: Full breakfast 125FF Continental breakfast 85FF Lunch 155-360FF&alc Dinner 240-360FF&alc

CARDS: ● ▇▇ ▇ Travellers cheques

★ ★ ★ Clos du Cher

rte de St-Aignan *41440*

☎ 254750003 FAX 254750379

This former private residence stands in the heart of a shaded park and combines elegance and intimacy in its peaceful interior. The tastefully-furnished bedrooms have private en suite facilities and offer a good standard of comfort. The restaurant offers regional cuisine based on classic recipes incorporating good quality seasonal produce.

Near river Forest area Near motorway

Closed Jan-5 Feb & 12-19 Nov

10 en suite (bth/shr) (3 fmly) TV in all bedrooms STV Direct dial from all bedrooms Mini-bar in all bedrooms Licensed Full central heating Open parking available Child discount available 10yrs Fishing Bicycle rental Open terrace V meals Last d 22.00hrs Languages spoken: English,German,Italian,Spanish

MEALS: Full breakfast 60FF Lunch 135-350FF&alc Dinner 135-350FF&alc*

CARDS: ● ▇▇ ▇ ● Travellers cheques

★ ★ ★ ★ Château de la Verrerie

18700

☎ 248815160 FAX 248582125

(From Aubigny-sur-Nere take D89 to Château)

This majestic 16th-century castle was built by the Stuarts of Scotland and is located close to the Loire Valley and Sancerre vineyards. The guest accommodation is furnished in a style befitting the origin of the building and is situated in the château and its annexe. The restaurant is located in the park and serves a classic cuisine with a wide variety of dishes to suit all palates. With unsurpassed facilities and services on offer, the hotel provides a suitable venue for corporate functions as well as a leisure break.

Near river Near lake Forest area

Closed 16 Dec-14 Jan

12 en suite (bth/shr) 6 rooms in annexe (4 fmly) (1 with balcony) No smoking in 2 bedrooms Direct dial from all bedrooms Licensed Open parking available Covered parking available Supervised Child discount available 12yrs Tennis Fishing Riding Pool table Boule Bicycle rental Open terrace Last d 22.00hrs Languages spoken: English,German, Spanish, Italian,Portuguese

ROOMS: (room only) s 880-1300FF; d 880-1300FF

Reductions over 1 night Special breaks: (walking/biking/riding breaks/golf)

MEALS: Full breakfast 80FF Continental breakfast 60FF Lunch 120-380FF&alc Dinner 135-380FF&alc

CARDS: ● ▇▇ ▇ Travellers cheques

★ ★ ★ Rivage

635 rue de la Reine Blanche *45160*

☎ 238660293 FAX 238563111

Standing under shaded trees on the banks of the River Loiret, this charming establishment offers peaceful accommodation in delightful surroundings. The guest rooms are tastefully furnished with well co-ordinated fabrics and furniture, there is a riverside terrace and a restaurant which serves a combination of fish specialities and game, accompanied by fresh vegetables and excellent wines.

Near river Forest area

17 en suite (bth/shr) (5 fmly) (12 with balcony) TV in all bedrooms Licensed Full central heating Open parking available Supervised Child discount available Tennis Open terrace Pedalos Languages spoken: English
MEALS: Lunch 155-290FFalc✱
CARDS: ♥ 💳 ⅏ ♪)

ONZAIN Loir-et-Cher

★ ★ ★ Château des Tertres
11 rte de Monteaux *41150*
☎ 254208388 FAX 254208921
(A10 from Paris exit Blois then 16kms on N152 direction of Tours)
Located in the middle of the Loire Valley, this 19th century château offers refined décor and antique furniture in a warm atmosphere.
Forest area
Closed 12 Dec-1 Apr
14 en suite (bth/shr) 5 rooms in annexe Direct dial from all bedrooms Licensed Full central heating Open parking available Child discount available 10yrs Bicycle rental Open terrace Languages spoken: English & German
ROOMS: (room only) d 400-520FF
CARDS: ♥ 💳 🔁 Travellers cheques

ORLÉANS Loiret

★ ★ L'Éscale du Port Arthur   ✗ ✗ ✗ ✗
205 rue de l'Église *45160*
☎ 238763036 FAX 238763767
Tucked away between lush vegetation on the banks on the River Loiret, the hotel is surrounded by unspoilt countryside. Completely renovated throughout it now offers tastefully furnished bedrooms with private en suite facilities, three dining-rooms and a shaded terrace with views of the river. A choice of enjoyable meals is served on the terrace in summer or in front of the open fireplace in winter.
Near river Forest area
Closed Closed 4-24 Feb
20 en suite (bth/shr) (3 fmly) No smoking in 2 bedrooms TV in all bedrooms STV Direct dial from all bedrooms Licensed Full central heating Open parking available Child discount available 2yrs Fishing Riding Solarium Boule Bicycle rental Open terrace Covered terrace V meals Last d 22.0hrs Languages spoken: English, Spanish
ROOMS: (room only) s 252-283FF; d 283-325FF
Reductions over 1 night Special breaks: Gastronomic/Cultural/Sports breaks
MEALS: Continental breakfast 37FF Lunch 108-180FF&alc Dinner 108-180FF&alc
CARDS: ♥ 💳 🔁 ♪) JCB Travellers cheques

★ ★ ★ Terminus
40 rue de la République *45000*
☎ 238532464 FAX 238532418
The town of Orléans is steeped in history and associated with the heroine Jeanne d'Arc. With its elegant architecture and the River Loire which flows through the city, it provides the ideal setting for touring the Sologne region with the numerous beautiful castles. The hotel is situated in the town centre, just a stone's throw away from assorted entertainment, shops and restaurants. A discreet, quiet atmosphere prevails throughout and features bedrooms with all modern facilities providing adequate comfort.
Forest area In town centre Near motorway

47 en suite (bth/shr) (3 fmly) (20 with balcony) TV in all bedrooms STV Licensed Lift Night porter Full central heating Languages spoken: English
CARDS: ♥ 💳 🔁 ♪) Travellers cheques

OUCHAMPS Loir-et-Cher

★ ★ ★ Relais des Landes (Best Western)
Les Montils *41120*
☎ 254444040 FAX 254440389
(take A10 exit Blois-Sud south of the Loire, then in direction of Montrichard & onto D751, then onto D764)
This 17th-century mansion stands in its own extensive grounds surrounded by the peaceful countryside of the Sologne region. The bedrooms are individually styled and appointed with en suite facilities. The restaurant offers a wide choice of dishes, alternating between honest simple cooking and a regional cuisine prepared with the finest local produce. Surrounded by the famous chateaux of the Loire, it provides a good base from which to explore the region.
Forest area
Closed end Nov-Feb
28 en suite (bth) TV in all bedrooms Radio in rooms Direct dial from 10 bedrooms Mini-bar in 10 bedrooms Licensed Full central heating Open parking available Child discount available 12yrs Bicycle rental Open terrace V meals Last d 21.30hrs Languages spoken: English & German
ROOMS: (room only) s 495-765FF; d 495-765FF
MEALS: Full breakfast 60FF Lunch 180-235FF&alc Dinner 180-235FF&alc
CARDS: ♥ 💳 🔁 ♪) Travellers cheques

OUCQUES Loir-et-Cher

★ ★ Commerce
9 rue de Beaugency *41290*
☎ 251232011 FAX 254230288
The hotel is situated just a few miles outside Paris and offers a contemporary, cheerful interior where personally-styled bedrooms are equipped with modern facilities offering a good standard of comfort. The cuisine is of a high standard and consists of well-prepared dishes to suit most palates.
In town centre
Closed end Dec-end Jan
12 en suite (bth/shr) (2 fmly) TV in all bedrooms Radio in rooms Direct dial from all bedrooms Mini-bar in 3 bedrooms Licensed Full central heating Covered parking available Child discount available Last d 21.00hrs Languages spoken: English
ROOMS: (room only) s 220-270FF; d 250-290FF
Reductions over 1 night
MEALS: Full breakfast 40FF Lunch 95-265FF&alc Dinner 95-265FF&alc✱
CARDS: ♥ 💳 🔁

PÈCHEREAU, LE Indre

★ ★ ★ Château Hotel du Vivier
rue de Gargilesse *36200*
☎ 254242299 FAX 254011287
(from town centre take D48 towards Gargilesse for 4km. Hotel on right)
This small neo-classical manor house situated in a park with 200 mature cedars. The cosy dining rooms are furnished with period pieces which create a romantic atmosphere. The menu offers a choice of fish specialities and regional dishes;

contd.

weather permitting, meals are also served in the park. The bedrooms offer comfortable accommodation and are well equipped.
Near river Near lake Near beach Forest area Near motorway 6 en suite (bth/shr) (2 fmly) TV in all bedrooms Direct dial from all bedrooms Licensed Night porter Full central heating Open parking available Supervised Child discount available 7yrs Boule Bicycle rental Open terrace V meals Last d 23.00hrs Languages spoken: English, Spanish
ROOMS: (room only) d 350-580FF **Reductions over 1 night**
MEALS: Full breakfast 65FF Lunch 145-395FF&alc Dinner 195-395FF&alc✱
CARDS: ✷ ▦ ▨ ⏺ Travellers cheques

ROMORANTIN-LANTHENAY Loir-et-Cher

★ ★ ★ ★ Grand Hotel du Lion d'Or
69 rue Georges Clemenceau *41200*
☎ 254941515 FAX 254882487
(From Paris A10, A71 to the north of Orleans, towards Bourges, exit Slabris and D724)
In town centre
Closed 17 Feb-20 Mar
16 en suite (bth/shr) (4 with balcony) TV in all bedrooms STV Radio in rooms Direct dial from all bedrooms Mini-bar in all bedrooms Licensed Lift Full central heating Open parking available (charged) Supervised Open terrace Covered terrace Wkly live entertainment V meals Last d 21.30hrs Languages spoken: English
ROOMS: (room only) s fr 600FF; d 900-2100FF
MEALS: Full breakfast 110FF Lunch 420-620FF&alc Dinner 420-620FF&alc
CARDS: ✷ ▦ ▨ ⏺ Travellers cheques

ST-AIGNAN Loir-et-Cher

★ ★ Grand Hotel Saint-Aignan

7-9 quai J-J-Délorme *41110*
☎ 254751804 FAX 254751259
(A10 exit Blois in direction of Vierzon-Chateauroux & continue towards St Aignan, at St Aignan after Le Pont Hotel in a 100mtrs on left)
Located on the banks of the River Cher, the hotel is surrounded by all the famous châteaux of the Loire region, and features pleasant, cosy bedrooms and a traditional and inventive cuisine in a warm and friendly ambience. There are plenty of places to see and out-door activities to experience within a radius of ten kilometres.
Near river Forest area Near motorway
Closed end Nov & end Feb-1st wk Mar
21 rms (5 bth 11 shr) (7 fmly) TV in 9 bedrooms Licensed Full central heating Open parking available Covered parking available (charged) Child discount available 12yrs Open terrace V meals Last d 22.00hrs Languages spoken: English & German
ROOMS: (room only) s 120-310FF; d 120-345FF
MEALS: Continental breakfast 32FF Lunch 87-198FF Dinner 87-198FF
CARDS: ✷ ▦ ▨ ⏺ Travellers cheques

ST-AMAND-MONTROND Cher

Château de la Commanderie
av Farges-Allichamps *18200*
☎ 248610419 FAX 248610184
(A71 exit 8 onto D925 after 5km take D92 until Farges-Allichamps)

One part of this splendid château dates back to the 11th century, when it was the private dwelling of a Commander in the Order of the Knights Templars. The cosy interior is adorned with period furniture and old paintings, and features guest rooms with modern facilities. Guests can enjoy excellent views over meadows and woods, whilst the house is surrounded by a pleasant park with a flower-filled garden.
Near river Forest area
8 en suite (bth/shr) (1 fmly) (2 with balcony) No smoking in 3 bedrooms Licensed Night porter Full central heating Open parking available Covered parking available Supervised Child discount available Riding Boule Bicycle rental Open terrace Languages spoken: English

ROOMS: s fr 500FF; d 850-1200FF **Reductions over 1 night**
MEALS: Dinner fr 350FFalc✱
CARDS: ✷ ▦ ▨ Travellers cheques

ST-CHARTIER Indre

★ ★ ★ Château de la Vallée Bleue
rte de Verneuil *36400*
☎ 254310191 FAX 254310448
Near river Near motorway
Closed Feb
13 en suite (bth/shr) Some rooms in annexe (2 fmly) (1 with balcony) TV in all bedrooms Radio in rooms Direct dial from all bedrooms Mini-bar in all bedrooms Licensed Full central heating Open parking available Child discount available 12yrs Outdoor swimming pool Golf Gym Boule Bicycle rental Open terrace V meals Last d 21.30hrs Languages spoken: English,German,Spanish
CARDS: ✷ ▨

ST-CHRISTOPHE-SUR-LE-NAIS Indre-et-Loire

★ Les Glycines
5 pl Johan d'Alluyé *37370*
☎ 247293750 FAX 247293754
Located on the edge of the popular Touraine region with its fine natural scenery, this small, comfortable establishment has bedrooms which vary in style, and offer a good level of comfort. The cuisine incorporates a selection of well-prepared traditional dishes, served in the informal surroundings of the restaurant.
Near river Forest area In town centre Near motorway
7 rms (6 bth/shr) TV in all bedrooms Direct dial from all bedrooms Mini-bar in all bedrooms Licensed Full central heating Child discount available 12yrs Last d 21.30hrs Languages spoken: English
CARDS: ✷ ▨ Travellers cheques

ST-DYÉ-SUR-LOIRE Loir-et-Cher

★ ★ Manoir de Bel Air
1 rte d'Orleans *41500*
☎ 254816010 FAX 254816534
A comfortable hotel in the heart of the famous castles of the Loire. Enjoy a stay in a peaceful and pretty setting and appreciate the fine specialities and wines.
Near river Forest area Near motorway
Closed 20 Jan-20 Feb
40 en suite (bth) TV in all bedrooms Direct dial from all bedrooms Licensed Full central heating Open parking available Child discount available Bicycle rental Open terrace Last d 21.30hrs Languages spoken: English
ROOMS: (room only) s 240-320FF; d 280-380FF ✱
MEALS: Continental breakfast 36FF Lunch 118-228FF Dinner 118-228FF✱
CARDS: ● ▬ Travellers cheques

ST-HILAIRE-DE-COURT Cher

★ ★ Château de la Beuvrière
45580
☎ 248751463 FAX 248754762
Built as a Protestant stronghold in the 11th century, the château was largely destroyed during the religious wars, and in later centuries renovated by Jacques de la Fond, adviser to Louis IV. Set in extensive grounds, it features stylish guest accommodation equipped with modern appointments and a gourmet restaurant with traditional cuisine based on local recipes. There are elegant lounges for relaxation and a choice of leisure opportunities available.
Near river Forest area Near motorway
Closed 15 Dec-15 Mar
15 rms (10 bth) (1 fmly) (3 with balcony) Direct dial from all bedrooms Licensed Full central heating Open parking available Covered parking available Child discount available Outdoor swimming pool (heated) Tennis Fishing Boule Open terrace Last d 21.00hrs Languages spoken: English
CARDS: ● ▬ ▬ ● Travellers cheques

ST-PREST Eure-et-Loir

★ ★ ★ Manoir des Pres du Roy
allée des Prés du Roy *28300*
☎ 237222727 FAX 237222492
(On D6 N of Chartres)
Near river Forest area Near motorway
18 en suite (bth/shr) (1 fmly) (1 with balcony) TV in all bedrooms STV Direct dial from all bedrooms Mini-bar in all bedrooms Licensed Lift Night porter Full central heating Open parking available Supervised Child discount available 12yrs Tennis Fishing Pool table Bicycle rental Open terrace V meals Last d 21.30hrs Languages spoken: English,German,Spanish
ROOMS: (room only) s 350-380FF; d 350-580FF
Reductions over 1 night Special breaks
MEALS: Full breakfast 48FF Lunch fr 100FF&alc Dinner fr 140FF&alc
CARDS: ● ▬ ▬ ● Travellers cheques

ST-SATUR Cher

★ ★ Le Laurier
29 rue de Commerce *18300*
☎ 248541720 FAX 248540454
(From A6 exit Dordives, then N7 towards Cosne-sur-Loire and Sancerre)

Surrounded by the famous vineyards of Sancerre, this former coaching inn is situated on the banks of the River Loire. A pretty interior enhanced with brass and ancient wood-panelling creates an informal atmosphere, where the bedrooms provide comfortable accommodation, whilst the restaurant serves a choice of enjoyable meals.
Near river Near sea Forest area In town centre Near motorway
Closed 15-30 Nov & 1 Mar-15 Mar
8 rms (5 bth) (1 fmly) TV in all bedrooms Direct dial from all bedrooms Licensed Full central heating Open parking available Supervised Open terrace V meals Last d 22.00hrs Languages spoken: English
ROOMS: (room only) s fr 110FF; d fr 230FF
MEALS: Full breakfast 40FF Lunch 80-250FF Dinner 80-250FF
CARDS: ● ▬ Travellers cheques

ST-SYMPHORIEN-LE-CHÂTEAU Eure-et-Loir

★ ★ ★ ★ Château Hotel d'Ésclimont (Relais et Chateaux)
28700
☎ 237311515 FAX 237315791
Near river Forest area Near motorway
53 en suite (bth/shr) TV in all bedrooms Mini-bar in all bedrooms Licensed Lift Night porter Full central heating Open parking available Supervised Outdoor swimming pool (heated) Golf Tennis Fishing Boule Open terrace V meals Last d 21.30hrs Languages spoken: English
MEALS: Full breakfast 130FF Continental breakfast 85FF Lunch 260-495FF&alc Dinner 320-495FF&alc✱
CARDS: ● ▬ ▬ ● JCB Travellers cheques

STE-MAURE-DE-TOURAINE Indre-et-Loire

★ ★ ★ Hauts de Ste-Maure
2-4 av du Général-de-Gaulle *37800*
☎ 247655065 FAX 247656024
This 16th-century former coaching inn is a building of considerable character; the interior has fine old beams, original stone walls, period furniture, and yet is decorated in 20th-century shades and fabrics. The outbuildings house an astonishing collection of vintage cars and the grounds are full of flowers and shaded spots for lazing around in. The bedrooms provide comfortable accommodation and the restaurant serves a combination of traditional and innovative dishes prepared with home-grown produce.
Near river Near lake Forest area In town centre Near motorway
19 en suite (bth/shr) (3 fmly) No smoking in 2 bedrooms TV in all bedrooms STV Direct dial from all bedrooms Mini-bar in all bedrooms Licensed Lift Night porter Full central heating Air conditioning in bedrooms Open parking available Covered parking available (charged) Supervised Child discount available 10yrs Fishing Bicycle rental Open terrace V meals Last d 21.30hrs Languages spoken: English,Italian
ROOMS: (room only) s 280-380FF; d 300-420FF
Reductions over 1 night Special breaks
MEALS: Full breakfast 65FF Continental breakfast 50FF Lunch 108-240FF&alc Dinner 108-240FF&alc
CARDS: ● ▬ ▬ ● Travellers cheques

★ ★ Le Cheval Blanc
N10 *37800*
☎ 247654027 FAX 247655890
This former coaching inn is situated on the main road from Paris to Bordeaux and features peaceful bedrooms with views of the village and its 16th-century church with a crypt *contd.*

that dates back as far as the 11th century. The guest rooms have modern facilities and the cuisine consists of regional dishes prepared with fresh local produce. The reception is friendly and staff are attentive throughout.
Near river Near lake Forest area In town centre Near motorway
12 rms (3 fmly) TV in all bedrooms Direct dial from all bedrooms Licensed Night porter Full central heating Open parking available Covered parking available Supervised Child discount available 12yrs V meals Last d 21.30hrs Languages spoken: English
CARDS: ● ▨ Travellers cheques

SALBRIS Loir-et-Cher

★ ★ ★ Domaine de Valaudran
av de Romorantin *41300*
☎ 254972000 FAX 254971222
Forest area Near motorway
Closed 6 Jan-2 Mar
31 en suite (bth/shr) No smoking in 2 bedrooms TV in all bedrooms STV Mini-bar in all bedrooms Licensed Night porter Full central heating Open parking available Child discount available 5yrs Outdoor swimming pool (heated) Golf 18 Fishing Riding Solarium Pool table Boule Bicycle rental Open terrace Last d 22.15hrs Languages spoken: English
CARDS: ● ▨▨ Travellers cheques

★ ★ ★ Le Parc
8 av d'Orleans *41300*
☎ 254971853 FAX 254972434
(A71 exit Salbris)
In lush greenery close to the Loire Valley, Le Parc is a house of character and comfort. Owners Sabine and Jean-Pierre Blanquer take pleasure in letting guests share their tasteful home, in the heart of the Sologne region.
Near lake Forest area Near motorway
Closed 15 days in winter RS Restaurant closed Sun eve & Mon Dec-Mar
27 rms (23 bth/shr) (5 with balcony) TV in 24 bedrooms STV Direct dial from 24 bedrooms Licensed Night porter Full central heating Open parking available Covered parking available Supervised Child discount available 12yrs Open terrace Last d 21.00hrs Languages spoken: English
ROOMS: (room only) s 200-400FF; d 220-450FF
Reductions over 1 night
MEALS: Continental breakfast 45FF Lunch 100-170FF&alc Dinner 100-170FF&alc
CARDS: ● ▨ Travellers cheques

SARAN Loiret

★ ★ Climat de France
Par d'Activités d'Ormé-Saran *45770*
☎ 238738080 Cen Res 164460123 FAX 238737878
(off A10 at junction for Orleans Nord then follow signs for Saran Centre)
The peacefully situated bedrooms in this hotel are fitted with modern facilities and provide comfortable accommodation. The restaurant serves a choice of dishes which will suit most palates as well as a delightful selection of desserts.
Near lake Forest area Near motorway
44 en suite (bth/shr) (16 fmly) TV in all bedrooms Radio in rooms Direct dial from all bedrooms Licensed Open parking available Open terrace Covered terrace Languages spoken: English, German, Italian & Spanish
CARDS: ● ▨

SEILLAC Loir-et-Cher

★ ★ Domaine de Seillac
41150
☎ 254207211 FAX 254208288
(from Paris A10, exit Blois towards Angers, take D766, cross the wood and arrive at Molineuf, turn left towards Seillac.)

The hotel is surrounded by an extensive park with a lake and is set in the heart of a village with the famous Loire châteaux nearby. It has been a hotel since 1969 and features bedrooms situated in the main building, whilst the maisonettes with small private terraces can be found in the park. The dining-rooms serve a regional cuisine prepared with fresh local produce and weather permitting, guests can also enjoy breakfast and dinner on the terrace.
Forest area
87 en suite (bth/shr) (70 fmly) (70 with balcony) TV in all bedrooms Direct dial from all bedrooms Licensed Full central heating Open parking available Child discount available 11yrs Outdoor swimming pool (heated) Tennis Fishing Boule Open terrace Covered terrace Table tennis Last d 21.30hrs Languages spoken: English, German
ROOMS: s 290-590FF; d 310-690FF
MEALS: Lunch 120-180FF&alc Dinner 180FF&alc
CARDS: ● ▨▨ ❿ Travellers cheques

SEMBLANÇAY Indre-et-Loire

★ ★ Hostellerie de la Mère Hamard
pl de l'Église *37360*
☎ 247566204 FAX 247565361

Situated in a peaceful village ten minutes from Tours, this delightful residence welcomes its clientele in charming surroundings. The attractive bedrooms offer a good level of comfort, whilst the dining-room, with pretty flower displays,

serves a gourmet cuisine consisting of delicious home-made produce, which is complemented by a good selection of Loire wines.
Forest area
Closed Feb school holidays
9 en suite (bth/shr) (2 fmly) TV in all bedrooms Direct dial from all bedrooms Licensed Full central heating Open parking available Supervised Child discount available Tennis Riding Open terrace V meals Last d 21.00hrs Languages spoken: English,German
ROOMS: (room only) s 160-240FF; d 230-265FF
✱ **Reductions over 1 night**
MEALS: Lunch 99-265FF&alc Dinner 99-265FF&alc
CARDS: ✹ ⚏ Travellers cheques

SENONCHES Eure-et-Loir

★ ★ **De la Forêt**
pl du Champ de Foire *28250*
☎ 237377850 FAX 237377498

The hotel is set in the heart of the Perch region with its unrivalled natural splendour of green fields, large woods and hills. It features a homely interior where comfortable bedrooms have modern amenities, and the country-style restaurant serves a tasty cuisine complemented by a good wine list.
Near lake Forest area
13 en suite (bth/shr) (1 fmly) TV in all bedrooms STV Licensed Full central heating Open parking available Covered parking available Child discount available 12yrs Open terrace V meals
ROOMS: (room only) s 200-350FF; d 200-350FF
Reductions over 1 night
MEALS: Full breakfast 35FF Continental breakfast 35FF Lunch 75-250FF&alc Dinner fr 175FF&alc
CARDS: ✹ ⚏ ⚏ Travellers cheques

SOINGS-EN-SOLOGNE Loir-et-Cher

★ **Les 4 Vents**
rte de Contres *41230*
☎ 254987131 FAX 254987561
Along the route of the Loire châteaux, the hotel has a warm atmosphere throughout and offers its visitors guest rooms which are mostly equipped with modern facilities. The menu features a selection of traditional and char-grilled house specialities to suit most taste, whilst the surrounding area has a multitude of cultural and leisure opportunities to be discovered and experienced.
Near lake Forest area
4 rooms in annexe (3 fmly) TV available Licensed Full central heating Air conditioning in bedrooms Open parking available

Covered parking available Supervised Child discount available Fishing Boule Bicycle rental Open terrace Covered terrace Last d 21.00hrs Languages spoken: English
MEALS: Full breakfast 28FF Continental breakfast 28FF Lunch 58-130FF&alc Dinner 58-130FF&alc✱
CARDS: ✹ ⚏ Travellers cheques

SOUVIGNY-EN-SOLOGNE Loir-et-Cher

★ ★ **Auberge Croix Blanche**
pl de l'Église *41600*
☎ 254884008 FAX 254889106
Near lake Forest area In town centre
Closed Jan-Feb
8 en suite (bth/shr) 8 rooms in annexe Radio in rooms Full central heating Open parking available Supervised Child discount available
MEALS: Lunch 128-255FF&alc Dinner 128-255FF&alc✱
CARDS: ✹ ⚏

SURY-AUX-BOIS Loiret

★ ★ **Domaine de Chicamour**
Chicamour *45530*
☎ 238558542 FAX 238558043
Comfort, relaxation, leisure activities and cuisine inspired by the sea are the features of this charming Breton hotel. In an exceptional location, with panoramic views of the port and islands.
Forest area Near motorway
Closed 16 Nov-14 Mar
12 en suite (bth/shr) Direct dial from all bedrooms Licensed Full central heating Open parking available Covered parking available Child discount available 10yrs Tennis Riding Boule Bicycle rental Open terrace Covered terrace Languages spoken: English, Dutch & German
ROOMS: s 395FF; d 400FF
MEALS: Continental breakfast 50FF✱
CARDS: ✹ ⚏ ⚏ ⓪

THAUMIERS Cher

Château de Thaumiers
18210
☎ 248618162 FAX 248618182
The handsome Château de Thaumiers features bedrooms and suites with private facilities, and because of its extensive corporate services it is a popular venue with business travellers and holiday makers alike. The dining-rooms are exclusively reserved for residents and cater for most tastes. The château offers a choice of varied entertainment and there is no shortage of leisure opportunities and cultural places of interest to visit in the region.
Near river Near lake Forest area
11 en suite (bth) (2 fmly) Direct dial from all bedrooms Licensed Full central heating Open parking available Supervised Outdoor swimming pool (heated) Tennis Fishing Boule Open terrace Languages spoken: English
ROOMS: d 800FF **Reductions over 1 night**
CARDS: ✹ ⚏ Travellers cheques

Taking your mobile phone to France?
See page 11

TOURNON-ST-MARTIN Indre

★ ★ Auberge du Capucin Gourmand

8 rue Bel Air *36220*
☎ 254376685 FAX 254378754
Set in the heart of the Berry countryside, this auberge prides
itself on the excellence of its restaurant's cuisine. Comfortable
bedrooms and a flower-filled garden ensure your stay will be a
pleasant one, but to make it a truly memorable visit you should
try some of the regional specialities on offer in the auberge's
dining room. This is a good base from which to explore the area.
Near river Forest area Near motorway
Closed 2wks Oct–2wks Feb
7 rms (6 bth/shr) (1 fmly) TV in all bedrooms Direct dial from
all bedrooms Licensed Full central heating Open parking
available Supervised Child discount available 10yrs Fishing
Boule Open terrace V meals Last d 21.00hrs Languages
spoken: English
ROOMS: (room only) s 175-270FF; d 225-270FF
✱ **Reductions over 1 night**
MEALS: Continental breakfast 37FF Lunch 80-195FF&alc
Dinner 80-195FF&alc
CARDS: ➋ ▦ ▆ ➒ Eurocard Travellers cheques

TOURS Indre-et-Loire

★ ★ ★ Hotel Alliance Trois Rivières

292 av de Grammount *37200*
☎ 247280080 FAX 247277761
Located just a few minutes away from the town centre the
hotel is surrounded by formal French gardens and offers
bedrooms and suites with every modern day amenity. Situated
in the heart of 'the châteaux de la Loire' it is a good starting
point to discover the glorious past of the region and taste some
of the best wines available. There is a restaurant and congenial
bar as well as a choice of leisure and fitness facilities.
Near river Near lake Near motorway
125 en suite (bth/shr) (6 fmly) (10 with balcony) No smoking
in 6 bedrooms TV in all bedrooms Mini-bar in all bedrooms
Licensed Lift Night porter Full central heating Open parking
available Child discount available 10yrs Outdoor swimming
pool Tennis Pool table Open terrace Last d 22.00hrs
Languages spoken: English,German,Spanish
CARDS: ➋ ▦ ▆ ➒ Travellers cheques

★ ★ ★ Holiday Inn Tours City Centre

15 rue Edward Vaillant *37000*
☎ 247311212 FAX 247385335
The hotel is located in the centre of town, a stone's throw from
the train station and Palais des Congrés. Its bedrooms -
including two suites with mezzanine - are equipped with
modern facilities and provide a high level of comfort. The
restaurant serves a regional cuisine accompanied by renowned
vintage wines, whilst the congenial bar is the ideal spot to
relax with a drink.
In town centre Near motorway
105 en suite (bth/shr) (2 fmly) (2 with balcony) No smoking in
11 bedrooms TV in all bedrooms STV Radio in rooms Direct
dial from all bedrooms Mini-bar in all bedrooms Licensed
Lift Night porter Full central heating Air conditioning in
bedrooms Open parking available (charged) Covered parking
available (charged) Child discount available 19yrs Sauna
Fitness Salon V meals Last d 22.00hrs Languages spoken:
English,German,Spanish
CARDS: ➋ ▦ ▆ ➒ Travellers cheques

★ ★ ★ ★ Jean Bardet

57 rue Croison *37000*
☎ 247414111 FAX 247516872
Situated on the right bank of the River Loire, this magnificent
19th-century building provides the delightful setting for the
hotel. Under the meticulous management of the accomplished
owners Sophie and Jean Bardet, visitors are offered elegant
accommodation with luxurious bathrooms providing excellent
comfort. From the foyer to the dining-room, sophisticated
furnishings of high quality are applied throughout and create a
charming atmosphere. The exquisite cuisine is carefully
executed by Jean Bardet who has acquired many accolades
and is rated one of best cuisiniers in France.
Near river Forest area In town centre
21 en suite (bth/shr) (5 fmly) (4 with balcony) TV in all
bedrooms Radio in rooms Direct dial from all bedrooms
Mini-bar in all bedrooms Licensed Night porter Full central
heating Air conditioning in bedrooms Open parking available
Supervised Child discount available 12yrs Outdoor swimming
pool (heated) Open terrace V meals Last d 22.00hrs
Languages spoken: English,German
CARDS: ➋ ▦ ▆ ➒ Travellers cheques

★ ★ Moderne

1-3 rue Victor Laloux *37000*
☎ 247053281 FAX 247057150
Concealed behind the 19th-century façade of the Hotel
Moderne, lies an interior with a rustic restaurant where period
windows, exposed beams, wood-panelling and a handsome
staircase create a cosy atmosphere. Situated in the heart of
town near the main transport services and business centre, it
features bedrooms with modern amenities which provide a
good level of comfort.
In town centre Near motorway
23 rms (5 fmly) TV in all bedrooms STV Direct dial from all
bedrooms Mini-bar in all bedrooms Licensed Full central
heating Last d 21.30hrs Languages spoken: English
MEALS: Continental breakfast 35FF Dinner 93FF✱
CARDS: ➋ ▦ ▆ Travellers cheques

★ ★ ★ Royal

65 av de Grammont *37000*
☎ 247647178 FAX 247058462
The façade of the Hotel Royal provides a contemporary feature
in one of the prettiest shaded avenues in town. When guests
cross the threshold, they step into an elegant interior which is
reminiscent of a traditional hotel. The comfortable bedrooms
have Louis-style furnishings and are equipped with modern
amenities. Breakfast is served in the winter-garden, whilst the
gracious lounge is the setting for business gatherings and
social events.
In town centre
50 en suite (bth) (4 with balcony) TV in all bedrooms STV
Direct dial from all bedrooms Mini-bar in all bedrooms
Licensed Lift Night porter Full central heating Open parking
available (charged) Covered parking available (charged) Child
discount available 12yrs Languages spoken: German
CARDS: ➋ ▦ ▆ ➒ Travellers cheques

Taking your mobile phone to France?
See page 11

VEIGNE Indre-et-Loire

★ ★ Le Moulin Fleuri
rte du Ripault *37250*
☎ 247260112 FAX 247340471
This 16th-century mill is surrounded by 225 acres of lush parklands, with private fishing, and provides an outstanding setting for an enjoyable stay. Formerly the private residence of the Ducs de Montbazon, it features elegant guest rooms, furnished with period pieces, which provide peaceful accommodation. There is a large lounge with open fire place for relaxing or reading and a restaurant which serves skilfully executed dishes accompanied by a choice of great vintage wines.
Near river Forest area
12 rms (8 shr) (5 fmly) TV in all bedrooms Radio in rooms Direct dial from all bedrooms Mini-bar in 10 bedrooms Licensed Full central heating Open parking available Supervised Fishing Open terrace V meals Last d 21.15hrs Languages spoken: English,Spanish,Italian
ROOMS: (room only) s fr 195FF; d fr 290FF
MEALS: Full breakfast 68FF Continental breakfast 45FF Lunch 170-305FF&alc Dinner 170-305FF&alc
CARDS: 😊 💳 💳 Travellers cheques

VENDÔME Loir-et-Cher

★ ★ ★ Hotel Vendôme
15 Faubourg Chartrain *41100*
☎ 254770288 FAX 254739071

The Hotel Vendôme is an elegant, comfortable hotel situated in the town centre and is run by a team of young, dedicated staff who provide attentive service throughout. The bedrooms are equipped with modern amenities and offer a high degree of comfort, whilst the 15th-century restaurant has served good food and cheer to the pilgrims on their way to Santiago de Compostella for hundreds of years. Nowadays it offers a traditional cuisine which is based on regional recipes with a good measure of seasonal ingredients.
Near river Forest area In town centre Near motorway
35 en suite (bth/shr) (1 fmly) (3 with balcony) TV in all bedrooms STV Radio in rooms Direct dial from all bedrooms Licensed Lift Full central heating Covered parking available (charged) Open terrace Last d 21.30hrs Languages spoken: English
ROOMS: (room only) s 220-335FF; d 280-395FF
Reductions over 1 night
MEALS: Full breakfast 48FF Lunch 95-195FF&alc Dinner 95-195FF&alc
CARDS: 😊 💳 Travellers cheques

VINEUIL Loir-et-Cher

★ ★ *Climat de France*
48 rue des 4 Vents *41350*
☎ 254427022 Cen Res 164460123 FAX 254124381
(off A10 at junction for Vineuil Centre)
Situated in a residential area at three kilometres from the centre of town, the hotel enjoys a peaceful setting. It features comfortable bedrooms with every modern day convenience, as well as a restaurant which serves a comprehensive buffet and a choice of traditional dishes with a regional touch.
Near motorway
58 en suite (bth) (9 fmly) TV in all bedrooms Radio in rooms Direct dial from all bedrooms Licensed Open parking available Boule Open terrace V meals Languages spoken: English, German, Portuguese & Spanish
CARDS: 😊 💳

VOVES Eure-et-Loir

★ ★ ★ Quai Fleuri
15 rue Texier Gallas *28150*
☎ 237991515 FAX 237991120
(On D17)
Situated in lush, green surroundings between Chartres and Orléans, the hotel is set in a large wooded park and provides the suitable setting to relax and unwind. After a drink in the cosy bar, guests can savour a choice of specialities in the restaurant or in 'Le Guillaume ' a private dining-room. The bedrooms have up-to-date modern facilities and there is no shortage of sporting activities at the hotel, whilst the surrounding region offers many places of interest.
Forest area Near motorway
Closed 21 Dec-4 Jan
17 en suite (bth/shr) (2 fmly) No smoking in 2 bedrooms TV in all bedrooms STV Direct dial from all bedrooms Licensed Night porter Full central heating Open parking available Supervised Gym Pool table Boule Bicycle rental Open terrace play room Last d 21.00hrs Languages spoken: English
ROOMS: (room only) s 295-440FF; d 345-440FF
✳ Reductions over 1 night
MEALS: Continental breakfast 45FF Lunch 155-255FF&alc Dinner 155-255FF&alc✳
CARDS: 😊 💳 💳 Travellers cheques

Paris & Ile de France

There's a part of Paris to suit your every mood. History and culture from a host of wonderful galleries and museums, like the famous Louvre which houses important antiquities and many of the world's masterpieces from painting and sculpture. Visit Notre Dame Cathedral, that jewel of medieval architecture, or the Eiffel Tower and the Arc de Triomphe. Shop till you drop for fashionable haute couture, or hunt for bargains and curios among the flea markets. A bite to eat and drink at a street café or a chic bar; a night of revelry at the Pigalle or Moulin Rouge.

(top): The world-famous Notre Dame Cathedral, completed in 1330, and capable of holding nearly 10,000 people.

(bottom): Commissioned by Napoleon, the Arc de Triomphe is a tribute to the Unknown Soldier, and is the central hub of twelve avenues.

ESSENTIAL FACTS

DÉPARTEMENTS:	Paris, Essonne, Hauts de Seine, Seine-et-Marne, Seine-St-Denis, Val-d'Oise, Val-de-Marne, Yvelines
PRINCIPAL TOWNS	Paris, Mantes-la-Jolie, Pontoise, Creil, St Denis, Meaux, Melun, St-Germain
PLACES TO VISIT:	The sights, shops, museums, and boulevards of Paris, Auvers-sur-Oise, the village which inspired the Impressionists, Barbizon, which inspired Rousseau and Millet, the châteaux of Champs, Chantilly and Rambouillet, the Basilica of St-Denis, EuroDisney, and the palaces at Versailles, Vaux-le-Vicomte and Fontainebleau
REGIONAL TOURIST OFFICE	26 av de l'Opéra, 75001 Paris. Tel: 42 60 28 62
LOCAL GASTRONOMIC DELIGHTS	Paris is the place to come for chic food, gourmet food; in fact, every type of food. A la parisienne describes savoury dishes that are typical of Parisian cuisine: soup à la parisienne is made with leeks, potatoes, milk and chervil, while fish à la parisienne is served with heavy mayonnaise, artichoke hearts, hard-boiled eggs and aspic cubes. Other Parisian dishes include sole Dugléré, Anna potatoes, soufflé Rothschild, and Paris-Brest, a ring-shaped éclair filled with praline-flavoured cream.
LOCAL CRAFTS/WHAT TO BUY	Glassware at Soisy-sur-Ecole; the Arts Viaduct which showcases numerous creative and artistic trades, including artistic work in gold, wood, silver, brass, stone, porcelain, and wrought iron, as well as lace and tapestry.

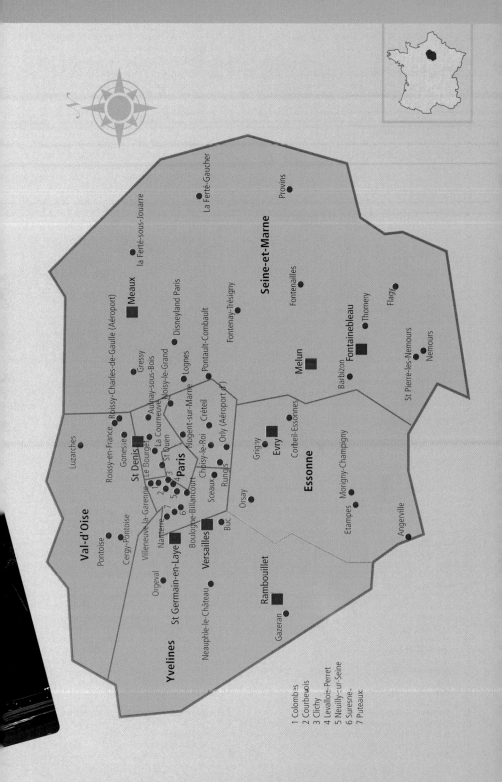

169

EVENTS & FESTIVALS

Jan Val-de-Marne Festival Sons d'Hiver de Fontainebleau (contemporary music and jazz)

Feb Paris Festival de Création Musical (*contemporary music*); Hauts-de-Seine Vocal Music Festival; Bois de Vicennes Bric-à-brac Fair

Mar Maisons-Lafitte Classical Music; Essonne Jazz Festival; Chatou Bric-a-Brac Fair; Coulommiers Wine & Cheese Fair

Mar-May Foire du Trône - fairground in Bois de Vincennes

Apr Hauts-de-Seine French Songs Festival; Seine et-Marne Dance Festival; Paris Parc de la Villette Classical Music Fair; Porte de Versailles Paris Fair

May Seine-et-Marne Music Festival de Meaux ; Essonne Festival d'Etampes (music & dance); Paris Jazz in Montmartre; Châteaufort Historical After-Dark Production; Ris-Orangis Traditional Music Festival; Champeaux Sacred Arts Festival; Conflans-Ste-Honorine Café Théâtre Festival

Jun Samois sur Seine Django Reinhardt Jazz Festival; Ville d'Avray Classical Music Festival; Seine St-Denis Music Festival d'Aubervilliers; aris St-Germain Festival & Fair; Parc de la Villette Jazz Festival; Paris Waiters' Race -

8.3km in uniform with tray on palm of hand; St-Denis Classical Music Festival; Provins Medieval Festival

Jun-Aug Provins Jousting Tournament each Saturday 4pm; St-Germain-en-Laye Fête des Loges (fairground)

Jun-Sep Meaux "On the Road to Europe" historical production after dark staged on one Friday and one Saturday each month;

Jul Hauts-de-Seine Classical Music Festival de l'Orangerie de Sceaux; Paris Tuilleries Gardens Festival

Aug Paris Rimes et Accords (*ancient and classical music*); Paris Sacred Music Festival en l'Ile; Provins Harvest Festival

Sep Paris Musique en Sorbonne ; Paris Autumn Music & Dance Festival; Pontoise Autumn Baroque Music Festival; Bagneux Grape Harvest Festival & Carnival; Arpajon Bean Festival; Blandy-les-Tours Château Traditional Fair

Oct Val-de-Marne French Song Festival; Yvelines Classical Music Festival de l'Abbaye des Vaux de Cernay; Montmartre Grape Harvest Festival; Boissy-St-Léger

Nov Paris Sacred Music Festival de la Ville de Paris; Val-de-Marne Dance Festival

---

ANGERVILLE Essonne

★ ★ ★ Hotel de France
2 pl du Marché, BP14 *91670*
☎ 169951130 FAX 164953959
(from N20 exit Angerville, from A10 exit Allainville or Allaines)
The Hotel de France was originally a coaching inn dating back to 1715 when royalty used to patronise it on their travels. Completely renovated between 1980 and 1982, it has retained its authentic character through the use of beams, terracotta floors and original stones for the walls, chimneys, and tranquil courtyard garden. The home-cooked dishes by the owner are second to none and add to making your stay an enjoyable experience. The geographical location is ideal for making day-trips to Paris, Versailles, Chartres and Orléans.
In town centre Near motorway
17 en suite (bth/shr) (4 fmly) TV in all bedrooms Direct dial from all bedrooms Licensed Lift Full central heating Child discount available Pool table Last d 21.30hrs
MEALS: Full breakfast 40FF Continental breakfast 40FF Lunch 140FF&alc Dinner 140FF&alc✱
CARDS: ●● ▬▬ ▬▬ ❿ Travellers cheques

AULNAY-SOUS-BOIS Seine-St-Denis

★ ★ Les Relais Bleus d'Aulnay
rue Léonard de Vinci *93600*
☎ 248669946 Cen Res 164460616 FAX 2486699216
Les Relais Bleus offer comfortable accommodation and good value at the two star level. They cater for both family and business clientele, with relaxed dining and public areas.
Near motorway
117 en suite (bth/shr) (2 fmly) Licensed Night porter

Full central heating Open parking available Supervised Pool table Open terrace Languages spoken: English,Italian,Spanish

---

BARBIZON Seine-et-Marne

★ ★ ★ Hotellerie du Bas-Breau (Relais et Chateaux)
22 rue Grande *77630*
☎ 160664005 FAX 160692289
Standing at the edge of the forest of Fontainebleau, this 19th-century former hunting lodge has welcomed an impressive array of visitors into its elegant, sophisticated interior. The bedrooms, which vary in style and size, are furnished with flair and offer the highest level of comfort. Guests can relax in the intimate surroundings of the lounge with its open fireplace, or enjoy a meal outside on the shaded terrace.
Forest area
19 en suite (bth/shr) TV in all bedrooms STV Direct dial from all bedrooms Mini-bar in all bedrooms Licensed Night porter Full central heating Air conditioning in bedrooms Open parking available Covered parking available Supervised Outdoor swimming pool (heated) Tennis Bicycle rental Open terrace Last d 21.30hrs Languages spoken: English & Italian
MEALS: Full breakfast 90FF Continental breakfast 150FF Lunch fr 350FF&alc Dinner fr 395FF&alc✱
CARDS: ●● ▬▬ ▬▬ Travellers cheques

BOULOGNE-BILLANCOURT Hauts-de-Seine

★ ★ Hotel Family's
210 bis bd Jean Jaurès *92100*
☎ 146214525 FAX 146216110
Because of their ideal location, the hotels in the Jardin de Paris

group, provide a good base to explore the capital with its many cultural and historic sights. Comfortable bedrooms are equipped with every modern facility and provide a high degree of comfort. There are no restaurant facilities, but a large choice of eating establishments can be found nearby. Forest area In town centre
49 rms TV in all bedrooms STV Direct dial from all bedrooms Lift Night porter Full central heating Child discount available 12yrs Languages spoken: English
CARDS: ●● ▓▓ ▀▀ ● Travellers cheques

BOURGET, LE Seine-St-Denis

★ ★ ★ Bleu Marine
Aéroport Bourget, ZAA Bat 412 *93550*
☎ 149341038 FAX 149341035
(exit A1 at Le Bourget Airport & Zone d'Aviation d'Affaires, hotel off N17)
Near motorway
86 en suite (bth/shr) (4 fmly) No smoking in 43 bedrooms TV in all bedrooms STV Radio in rooms Direct dial from all bedrooms Mini-bar in all bedrooms Room-safe Licensed Lift Night porter Air conditioning in bedrooms Open parking available Supervised Child discount available 12yrs Sauna Gym Open terrace V meals Languages spoken: English German Italian Spanish
CARDS: ●● ▓▓ ▀▀ ● Travellers cheques

BUC Yvelines

★ ★ Climat de France
rue Louis Pasteur *78530*
☎ 139564811 FAX 139568154
(from A86 take D938)
Far from the large hotels in this area of Paris, the hotel features bedrooms equipped with every modern convenience. The restaurant serves a generous and varied cuisine in a friendly atmosphere, and guests can help themselves to as many starters and sweets as they wish from the tempting buffet. Visitors can start off the day with a comprehensive breakfast including pastries, a choice of cheeses and fresh fruit juice.
Forest area Near motorway
44 en suite (bth) TV in all bedrooms Direct dial from all bedrooms Licensed Full central heating Open parking available Open terrace Covered terrace Languages spoken: English
CARDS: ●● ▀▀

CERGY-PONTOISE Val-D'Oise

★ ★ Vidéotel
3 av des Trois Fontaines *95300*
☎ 130309393 FAX 130388520
The hotels in the Videotel group all have bedrooms with pleasant furnishings and are equipped with the comfort of their clientele in mind. The restaurants serve a good quality gourmet cuisine with a range of prix-fixe menus, regional specialities and 'eat your full buffet'. The management couples and their dedicated teams offer a 'round the clock' efficient service, where the well-being and satisfaction of guests is the prime consideration.
Forest area In town centre
133 en suite (shr) (16 fmly) No smoking in 12 bedrooms TV in all bedrooms Direct dial from all bedrooms Mini-bar in all bedrooms Licensed Lift Night porter Full central heating Open parking available Supervised Child discount available

12yrs Pool table Open terrace V meals Last d 22.00hrs Languages spoken: English
ROOMS: (room only) s 285FF; d 285FF
MEALS: Full breakfast 34FF Lunch 52-88FF&alc Dinner 52-88FF&alc
CARDS: ●● ▓▓ ▀▀ ● JCB

CHOISY-LE-ROI Val-de-Marne

★ ★ Climat de France
rue du Docteur Roux *94600*
☎ 146824343 FAX 145732191
The hotel is situated in Choisy Le Roi and features pleasantly decorated, comfortable bedrooms with good modern facilities. The restaurant serves a variety of menus, including a 'no-limits' hors d'oeuvre buffet, as well as the children's 'Soupière Junior'.
Near river Near lake In town centre Near motorway
58 en suite (bth) TV available Direct-dial available Licensed Lift Night porter Full central heating Open parking available Supervised Open terrace Languages spoken: English, German & Spanish
CARDS: ●● ▀▀

CLICHY Hauts-de-Seine

★ ★ ★ Hotel de l'Europe
52 blvd du Général Leclerc *92110*
☎ 147371310 FAX 140871106
Situated in the centre of the city, in a part which oozes that typical Parisian atmosphere, the hotel is close to the metro and a large park. The guest accommodation is functional with modern amenities and a choice of restaurants can be found nearby.
In town centre
71 en suite (bth/shr) 28 rooms in annexe (5 fmly) No smoking in 5 bedrooms TV in all bedrooms STV Direct dial from all bedrooms Licensed Lift Night porter Full central heating Open parking available Covered parking available (charged) Child discount available 12yrs Bicycle rental Languages spoken: English & German
ROOMS: (room only) s 380-450FF; d 380-450FF
CARDS: ●● ▓▓ ▀▀ ● Travellers cheques

★ ★ Hotel Savoy
20 rue Villeneuve
☎ 147371701 FAX 142705517
A charming small hotel, located in a quiet area near La Défense.
45 en suite (bth/shr) TV in all bedrooms STV Direct dial from all bedrooms Lift Open parking available
ROOMS: s 405FF; d 405FF ✱
MEALS: Continental breakfast 40FF✱
CARDS: ●● ▓▓ ●

COLOMBES Hauts-de-Seine

★ ★ Climat de France
1 rue Albert Camus *92700*
☎ 147803230 FAX 147816054
(just off A86 at junct with N309)
Near motorway
58 en suite (bth) (8 fmly) TV available Radio in rooms Direct dial from all bedrooms Licensed Lift Full central heating Open parking available Languages spoken: English
CARDS: ●● ▀▀

CORBEIL-ESSONNES Essonne

★ ★ Aux Armes de France
1 bd Jean Jaurès *91100*

☎ 164962404 FAX 160880400
This 150-year old hotel combines modern day comfort with thoughtful touches from times gone by. Fresh bouquets of flowers and antique silverware on the tables, large walnut armchairs with rich upholstery, and authentic paintings on the wall create an elegant setting for the restaurant. The outstanding cuisine combines classic dishes with innovative creations by the chef, complemented by some fine examples from the wine list.
Near river In town centre
11 en suite (shr) (7 fmly) TV in all bedrooms Licensed Full central heating Open parking available Supervised Child discount available Last d 22.00hrs Languages spoken: English French & Italian
MEALS: Continental breakfast 32FF Lunch 120-235FF&alc Dinner 120-235FF&alc✱
CARDS: ●● ▤ ▆ ①

COURBEVOIE Hauts-de-Seine

★ ★ ★ Novotel Paris la Défense
2 bd de Neuilly-Défense *92400*
☎ 147781668 FAX 147788471
Novotel offer their clients good quality accommodation in modern, well-equipped bedrooms and have refined restaurants serving good quality cuisine They have excellent business meeting and conference facilities and some have food and beverages available 24 hours a day. All their hotels have at least one bedroom for disabled guests.
Near river Forest area Near motorway
280 en suite (bth/shr) (44 fmly) No smoking in 66 bedrooms TV in all bedrooms STV Radio in rooms Direct dial from all bedrooms Mini-bar in all bedrooms Licensed Lift Night porter Full central heating Air conditioning in bedrooms Open parking available (charged) Covered parking available (charged) Supervised Child discount available 16yrs Last d 24.00hrs Languages spoken: English,German,Italian,Spanish
CARDS: ●● ▤ ▆ ① Travellers cheques

★ ★ Hotel la Régence
69 av Gambetta *92400*
☎ 147880698 FAX 147894827
22 en suite (bth/shr) TV in all bedrooms STV Direct dial from all bedrooms Lift Open parking available
ROOMS: s 395FF; d 440FF ✱
MEALS: Continental breakfast 32FF✱
CARDS: ▆

COURNEUVE, LA Seine-St-Denis

★ ★ ★ Climat de France
104 av Jean-Mermoz *93120*
☎ 148383333 FAX 148385884
(off A1, next to the Regional Park of La Courneuve)
Situated near Paris, the owner Mr Eric Georges and his dedicated team welcome visitors in this comfortable, modern establishment. The bedrooms are well equipped and the restaurant offers a traditional cuisine with a choice of special house-starters and a dessert buffet.
Forest area Near motorway
72 en suite (bth/shr) (10 fmly) No smoking in 4 bedrooms TV in all bedrooms STV Radio in rooms Direct dial from all bedrooms Licensed Lift Night porter Full central heating

Open parking available Supervised Child discount available 12yrs Bicycle rental Open terrace Last d 22.00hrs Languages spoken: English, German & Spanish
ROOMS: (room only) s 290-360FF; d 290-360FF **Special breaks**
MEALS: Continental breakfast 45FF Lunch 64-119FF&alc Dinner 79-119FF&alc
CARDS: ●● ▤ ▆

CRÉTEIL Val-de-Marne

★ ★ Climat de France
rue de Archives *94000*
☎ Cen Res 16460123 FAX 169282402
The hotel is situated in the centre of town and features pleasantly decorated, comfortable bedrooms with good modern facilities. The restaurant serves a variety of menus, including a 'no-limits' hors d'oeuvre buffet, as well as the children's 'Soupière Junior'.
Near lake Forest area In town centre Near motorway
51 en suite (bth/shr) No smoking in 10 bedrooms TV available Radio in rooms Direct-dial available Licensed Lift Full central heating Open parking available V meals Languages spoken: English
CARDS: ●● ▆

ÉTAMPES Essonne

★ ★ Climat de France
av de Coquérive, rte de Corbeil *91150*
☎ 160800472 Cen Res 164460123 FAX 160800477
The hotel features pleasantly decorated, comfortable bedrooms with good modern facilities. The restaurant serves a variety of menus, as well as the children's 'Soupière Junior'.
Near lake In town centre Near motorway
44 en suite (bth) TV in all bedrooms Radio in rooms Direct dial from all bedrooms Licensed Full central heating Open parking available Open terrace Languages spoken: English, German & Spanish
CARDS: ●● ▆

ÉVRY Essonne

★ ★ ★ Hotel Mercure Evry Centre
52 bd de Coquibus *91000*
☎ 169473000 FAX 169473010
The hotel Adagio is located in the heart of the town and offers its visitors functional bedrooms with good modern amenities, traditional French cuisine, and a cosy piano bar for relaxation. An informal atmosphere prevails throughout the hotel where friendly staff provide an attentive service.
Forest area In town centre Near motorway
114 en suite (bth/shr) (27 fmly) No smoking in 14 bedrooms TV in all bedrooms STV Radio in rooms Direct dial from all bedrooms Mini-bar in all bedrooms Licensed Lift Night porter Full central heating Open parking available (charged) Covered parking available (charged) Child discount available 14yrs Pool table Open terrace Last d 22.30hrs Languages spoken: English
ROOMS: (room only) s 520FF; d 550FF
MEALS: Continental breakfast 60FF Lunch 95-125FF&alc Dinner 95-125FF&alc✱
CARDS: ●● ▤ ▆ ① Travellers cheques

FERTÉ-GAUCHER, LA Seine-et-Marne

★ ★ Du Bois Frais
32 av des Allies 77320
☎ 164202724 FAX 164203839
(From Paris (A4) take exit for Crécy-La-Chapelle, then take N34
for Coulommiers then on to La Ferté-Gaucher)
The hotel is housed in an 18th-century building and is
surrounded by a large private garden. Staff are friendly and
helpful and create an amiable atmosphere ensuring that guests
are well looked after during their stay. The bedrooms offer a
good level of comfort, whilst the restaurant serves an array of
light, classic dishes.
Near motorway
Closed 24 Dec-15 Jan
7 en suite (bth/shr) (1 fmly) TV in all bedrooms Licensed Full
central heating Open parking available Supervised Child
discount available 10yrs Bicycle rental Open terrace Covered
terrace V meals Last d 21.30hrs Languages spoken: English
ROOMS: (room only) s fr 200FF; d 200-300FF
MEALS: Full breakfast 58FF Continental breakfast 40FF Lunch
100-150FF Dinner 100-160FF
CARDS: ● ■ Travellers cheques

FERTÉ-SOUS-JOUARRE, LA Seine-et-Marne

★ ★ ★ Château des Bondons
47-49 rue des Bondons 77260
☎ 160220098 FAX 160229701
(leave A4 exit 18)
Set in extensive parklands, the château dates back to the 18th
century. With peacocks and ducks freely wandering about, it
has very much preserved its romantic rural atmosphere. The
individually styled bedrooms are equipped with modern
amenities and many little extras. The elegant day rooms
feature wood-panelled walls and carefully co-ordinated items
of furniture.
Near river Forest area
11 en suite (bth/shr) (6 fmly) (4 with balcony) TV in all
bedrooms STV Radio in rooms Direct dial from all bedrooms
Mini-bar in all bedrooms Licensed Night porter Full central
heating Open parking available Supervised Fishing Boule
Mini-golf Bicycle rental Open terrace Languages spoken:
English,German
ROOMS: (room only) s 450-550FF; d 450-550FF
MEALS: Full breakfast 60FF
CARDS: ● ■ ■ ●

FLAGY Seine-et-Marne

★ ★ ★ Au Moulin
2 rue du Moulin 77940
☎ 160966789 FAX 160966951
(from Fontainbleu, take N6 towards Sens and in 18km turn
right towards Nemours then immediately left to Flagy)
Enchanting 13th century water-mill, attractively converted, in
very peaceful surroundings.
Near river Forest area
Closed 21 Dec-22 Jan & 14-24 Sep
10 en suite (bth/shr) (3 fmly) Direct dial from all bedrooms
Licensed Full central heating Open parking available Child
discount available 10yrs Open terrace Last d 21.30hrs
Languages spoken: English, German & Spanish
ROOMS: (room only) s 260-310FF; d 330-500FF
MEALS: Full breakfast 52FF Lunch 160-250FF&alc Dinner 160-
250FF&alc
CARDS: ● ■ ■ ● Travellers cheques

FONTAINEBLEAU Seine-et-Marne

★ ★ ★ Aigle Noir
27 pl Napoléon Bonaparte 77300
☎ 160746000 FAX 160746001
The hotel caters for commercial guests and holiday makers
alike, and behind its imposing façade, it features a traditional
decor combined with contemporary facilities. The guest-
rooms are individually styled and offer modern comfort,
whilst the restaurant serves a light, imaginative cuisine and
has earned a well deserved reputation over the years. In
addition there is a piano-bar and staff provide a friendly,
efficient service.
Forest area In town centre Near motorway
Closed mid-late Aug & late Dec-early Jan
57 en suite (bth/shr) (9 fmly) (4 with balcony) No smoking in
24 bedrooms TV in all bedrooms STV Direct dial from all
bedrooms Licensed Lift Night porter Full central heating Air
conditioning in bedrooms Covered parking available
(charged) Supervised Child discount available 12yrs Indoor
swimming pool (heated) Sauna Solarium Gym Bicycle rental
Open terrace V meals Last d 22.15hrs Languages spoken:
English,Italian,Spanish
MEALS: Full breakfast 95FF Continental breakfast 95FF Lunch
180-450FF&alc Dinner 180-450FF&alc✱
CARDS: ● ■ ■ ● JCB Travellers cheques

★ ★ ★ Hotel de L'Aigle Noir
27 pl Napoléon Bonarparte 77300
☎ 160746000 FAX 160746001
(from Paris A6 in direction Lyon, exit Fontainebleau)
Opposite the castle and gardens of Fontainbleau, the hotel has
been part of the history of France for five centuries. The
individually styled rooms and apartments offer every comfort.
There is a gastronomical restaurant where you can enjoy the
light and imaginative cuisine, a Second Empire styled piano
bar, a spacious and elegant indoor swimming pool, a gym and
sauna.
Forest area In town centre Near motorway
56 en suite (bth/shr) (9 fmly) (4 with balcony) No smoking in
22 bedrooms TV in all bedrooms STV Direct dial from all
bedrooms Mini-bar in all bedrooms Licensed Lift Night
porter Full central heating Air conditioning in bedrooms
Open parking available (charged) Covered parking available
(charged) Child discount available 12yrs Indoor swimming
pool (heated) Sauna Solarium Gym Bicycle rental Open
terrace V meals Last d 22.15hrs Languages spoken: English,
German & Spanish
ROOMS: (room only) s 740-990FF; d 790-2100FF
MEALS: Full breakfast 90FF Continental breakfast 90FF Lunch
180-450FF&alc Dinner 180-450FF&alc
CARDS: ● ■ ■ ● Travellers cheques

FONTAINE-LA-RIVIÈRE Essonne

★ ★ ★ Auberge de Courpain
Courpain
☎ 164956704 FAX 160809902
(follow N20 to Étampes then onto D191 to Pithiviers 8km
further is the auberge)
Near river Forest area Near motorway
Closed 15-28 Feb
17 en suite (bth/shr) (4 fmly) No smoking in 4 bedrooms TV in
8 bedrooms Direct dial from all bedrooms Licensed Night
porter Air conditioning in bedrooms Open parking available
Covered parking available Supervised Child discount
available Fishing Riding Solarium Open terrace V meals

Last d 21.15hrs Languages spoken: English Dutch German & Spanish

ROOMS: (room only) s 350-650FF; d 400-700FF
Reductions over 1 night Special breaks
MEALS: Full breakfast 55FF Continental breakfast 40FF Lunch fr 130FF&alc Dinner fr 180FF&alc
CARDS: ●● ▆▆ ▆ Travellers cheques

FONTENAILLES Seine-et-Marne

★ ★ ★ ★ **Golf de Fontenailles**
Domaine de Bois Boudran 77370
☎ 164605100 FAX 160675212
This is a magnificent building set in extensive grounds where guests can relax in the intimate surroundings of the elegant day rooms or enjoy the comfort of the spacious, well-furnished bedrooms with views over the private golf course. The restaurant serves an array of superb classic French cuisine and seasonal dishes complemented by a good wine list.
Near river Forest area
Closed Dec-Feb
51 en suite (bth) TV in all bedrooms STV Radio in rooms Direct dial from all bedrooms Mini-bar in all bedrooms Licensed Lift Full central heating Open parking available Child discount available Golf Tennis Sauna Bicycle rental Open terrace V meals Last d 21.15hrs Languages spoken: English,Japanese
CARDS: ●● ▆▆ ▆ ⑨ JCB

FONTENAY-TRÉSIGNY Seine-et-Marne

★ ★ ★ ★ **Le Manoir** (Relais et Châteaux)
rte Départementale 402 77610
☎ 164259117 FAX 164259549
This Anglo-Norman manor house is set in a large park with a private lake. All the bedrooms are individually decorated with delicate fabrics and furnished in a style befitting this splendid residence. The excellent cuisine comprises skilfully prepared dishes which are served in the restaurant with its open fireplace. After dinner guests can retire to one of the elegant wood-panelled lounges.
Forest area Near motorway
20 en suite (bth/shr) (7 fmly) (10 with balcony) TV in all bedrooms STV Direct-dial available Mini-bar in all bedrooms Licensed Full central heating Open parking available Covered parking available Child discount available Outdoor swimming pool (heated) Tennis Fishing Pool table Boule Open terrace Covered terrace Table Tennis,Practice Golf,Library Wkly live entertainment V meals Last d 21.00hrs Languages spoken: English,German
CARDS: ●● ▆▆ ▆ ⑨

GAZERAN Yvelines

★ ★ **Auberge Villa Marinette**
20 av Général-de-Gaulle 78125
☎ 134831901 FAX 134831901
The ivy-clad 'Villa Marinette' is an attractive country inn with a rustic decor, where most of the rooms have modern facilities and provide an adequate level of comfort. The restaurant serves good home-cooking by the 'patron' which in summer may be enjoyed on the terrace in the arboured flower-garden.
Near river Forest area Near motorway
Closed Tue evening & Wed. Also seasonal
6 rms (3 shr) Licensed Full central heating Open terrace Last d 21.00hrs Languages spoken: English
ROOMS: (room only) d 140-200FF ✱
MEALS: Full breakfast 35FF Continental breakfast 35FF Dinner 65-190FF✱
CARDS: ●● ▆ Travellers cheques

GONESSE Val-D'Oise

★ ★ **Les Relais Bleus**
7 rte de l'Europe 95500
☎ 139873666 FAX 139873470
Les Relais Bleus offer comfortable accommodation and good value at the two star level. They cater for both family and business clientele, with relaxed dining and public areas.
Near motorway
72 en suite (bth/shr) (25 fmly) TV in all bedrooms STV Direct dial from all bedrooms Mini-bar in all bedrooms Licensed Night porter Open parking available Supervised Child discount available 12yrs Open terrace V meals Last d 22.00hrs Languages spoken: English, German & Spanish
ROOMS: (room only) s 280-305FF; d 280-305FF
Reductions over 1 night Special breaks
MEALS: Full breakfast 36FF Lunch 80-145FF&alc Dinner fr 145FF&alc
CARDS: ●● ▆ Travellers cheques

GRESSY Seine-et-Marne

★ ★ ★ ★ **Manoir de Gressy**
2 rue St-Denis 77410
☎ 160266800 FAX 160264546
(Approach via N2 and D212)

This manor house has been built on the site of an 17th-century farmhouse and has been faithful to the architectural style of days gone by. Attractive wood-panelling, limestone floors, and magnificent pieces of antique furniture contribute to the authentic atmosphere. All individually styled bedrooms have views of the courtyard garden - those on the ground floor have

a private terrace. The menu features classic French cuisine complemented by a choice of select wines.
Near river Forest area In town centre Near motorway
Closed 20 Dec-4 Jan & 4 Jun-14 Jul
88 en suite (bth/shr) (5 fmly) (33 with balcony) No smoking in 15 bedrooms TV in all bedrooms STV Radio in rooms Direct dial from all bedrooms Licensed Lift Night porter Full central heating Open parking available Supervised Child discount available 12yrs Outdoor swimming pool (heated) Tennis Pool table Boule Bicycle rental Open terrace Covered terrace V meals Last d 22.00hrs Languages spoken: English,German,Italian & Spanish
ROOMS: (room only) d 950FF ✱
MEALS: Full breakfast 85FF Lunch 185FF&alc Dinner 185FF&alc
CARDS: ● ▬ ▬ ◑ Travellers cheques

GRIGNY Essonne

★ ★ ★ Château du Clotay
8 rue du Port *91350*
☎ 169258998 FAX 169258022
Surrounded by large trees, the hotel occupies a secluded location on the shores of a lake. It features smartly decorated bedrooms equipped with modern facilities. The menu features an array of well-presented dishes, whilst in summer, breakfast and dinner can be served on the terrace.
Near lake Forest area Near motorway
25 en suite (bth/shr) 15 rooms in annexe (5 fmly) TV in all bedrooms STV Direct dial from all bedrooms Mini-bar in all bedrooms Licensed Full central heating Open parking available Supervised Child discount available 12yrs Outdoor swimming pool Boule Open terrace Covered terrace Languages spoken: English
CARDS: ● ▬ ▬ ◑ Travellers cheques

LEVALLOIS-PERRET Hauts-de-Seine

★ ★ Hotel Espace Champerret
26 rue Louise Michel *92300*
☎ 147572071 FAX 147573139
36 en suite (bth/shr) TV in all bedrooms Direct dial from all bedrooms Lift
ROOMS: s 375FF; d 410FF ✱
CARDS: ● ▬ ◑

LOGNES Seine-et-Marne

★ ★ ★ Hotel Frantour
55 blvd du Mandinet *77185*
☎ 164800250 FAX 164800270
(from Paris take A4 in direction of Metz/Nancy exit at Val Maulriée centre)
A comfortable quiet hotel, located between Paris and Disneyland Paris, combining old world charm and modern convevience.
Near lake Forest area
85 en suite (bth/shr) (5 fmly) (26 with balcony) TV in all bedrooms STV Direct dial from all bedrooms Room-safe Licensed Lift Night porter Full central heating Open parking available Covered parking available Sauna Open terrace Table tennis Last d 22.00hrs Languages spoken: English, German & Spanish
ROOMS: (room only) s 448-488FF; d 493-536FF
MEALS: Continental breakfast 50FF Lunch 69-90FF&alc Dinner 120-200FFalc✱
CARDS: ● ▬ ▬ ◑ Travellers cheques

LUZARCHES Val-D'Oise

★ ★ ★ Hotel Blue Green Mont Griffon

BP 7 *95270*
☎ 134092000 FAX 134680024
(from A1 exit Survilliers follow Chantilly sign, then direction Fosses-Bellefontaine D922. Luzarches (direction Seugy)- Le Mont Griffon (D909) exit hotel after Golf de Montgriffon)
The vast Mont Griffon estate covers more than 600 acres of protected countryside. All the hotel rooms overlook the golf course and forest. An ideal place to relax and enjoy the leisure facilities. Two restaurants provide the choice between an elaborate gourmet menu or lighter meals.
Forest area Near motorway
54 en suite (bth/shr) (24 fmly) No smoking in 6 bedrooms TV in all bedrooms STV Direct dial from all bedrooms Licensed Lift Night porter Open parking available Supervised Child discount available 12yrs Outdoor swimming pool (heated) Golf 18 Sauna Covered terrace Archery Table tennis Last d 21.30hrs Languages spoken: English, Dutch, German & Italian

ROOMS: (room only) s 420-560FF; d 420-560FF **Special breaks: Golf & Cultural breaks**
MEALS: Full breakfast 45FF Continental breakfast 45FF Lunch 65-115FF&alc Dinner 65-115FF&alc✱
CARDS: ● ▬ ▬ ◑

MORIGNY-CHAMPIGNY Essonne

★ ★ ★ Hostellerie de Villemartin
5 allée des Marronniers *91150*
☎ 164946354 FAX 164942468
(From Paris take N20 exit at Etrechy take D148 then D17 towards Morigny. Hotel is on right)
Only 45 kilometres south of Paris, this charming manor house is located in the heart of a magnificent park with mature trees, a lake and a river. Comfortable, country-style decorated bedrooms offer all modern amenities, and the restaurant has the reputation of being one of the best in the region. The surrounding countryside offers many opportunities for walking and cycling.
Near river Near lake Forest area Near motorway
14 en suite (bth/shr) Some rooms in annexe (4 fmly) (2 with balcony) TV in all bedrooms Direct dial from all bedrooms Licensed Night porter Full central heating Open parking available Child discount available Fishing Boule Bicycle rental Open terrace Covered terrace Last d 21.30hrs Languages spoken: English,Spanish
ROOMS: (room only) s 310-450FF; d 350-490FF
Reductions over 1 night
MEALS: Continental breakfast 47FF Lunch 135-285FF&alc Dinner 135-285FF&alc
CARDS: ● ▬ ▬ ◑ Travellers cheques

NANTERRE Hauts-de-Seine

★ ★ ★ Hotel et Résidence Mercure Paris la Defense
17/20 espl Charles de Gaulle, rue des Trois Fontanot *92000*
☎ 146636800 FAX 147254624
(from Paris, ring west, exit La Defense/Porte Maillot, exit 7 (Valmy-Kupka) at 2nd traffic lights)
The hotel is situated in the heart of the lively business centre of 'La Défense' and close to the 'Nanterre Préfecture' RER station, enabling one to reach the centre of Paris in 10 minutes whilst Eurodisney is 40 minutes away. The bedrooms are functional and equipped with modern amenities. There is a restaurant where in the morning a buffet-style breakfast is served.
In town centre Near motorway
160 en suite (bth/shr) (25 fmly) No smoking in 16 bedrooms TV in all bedrooms STV Radio in rooms Direct dial from all bedrooms Mini-bar in all bedrooms Licensed Lift Night porter Full central heating Air conditioning in bedrooms Open parking available (charged) Covered parking available (charged) Supervised Child discount available 16yrs Pool table Last d 22.30hrs Languages spoken: English,German, Arabic
ROOMS: (room only) s 690-1150FF; d 840-1185FF
MEALS: Full breakfast 70FF Lunch 130-210FFalc Dinner 130-210FFalc
CARDS: ●● ▬ ▬ ﾟ Travellers cheques

NEAUPHLE-LE-CHÂTEAU Yvelines

★ ★ ★ Domaine du Verbois
38 av de la République *78640*
☎ 134891178 FAX 134895733
This splendid 19th-century residence stands in extensive parkland and offers fine views across the valley. It features elegant bedrooms furnished with immaculate attention to detail and sophisticated public lounges decorated with high quality furniture and exquisite fabrics. The restaurant serves a rich, traditional cuisine based on classic recipes, where equal emphasis is placed on presentation and flavour.
Forest area
Closed 10-22 Aug
20 en suite (bth/shr) 2 rooms in annexe (6 fmly) TV in all bedrooms STV Radio in rooms Direct dial from all bedrooms Mini-bar in 12 bedrooms Licensed Night porter Full central heating Open parking available Supervised Child discount available 12yrs Tennis Solarium Boule Bicycle rental Open terrace Covered terrace Table tennis V meals Last d 21.30hrs Languages spoken: English,German
ROOMS: (room only) s 490FF; d 490-860FF **Reductions over 1 night Special breaks**
MEALS: Full breakfast 68FF Continental breakfast 68FF Lunch 155FF&alc Dinner 155FF&alc
CARDS: ●● ▬ ▬ ﾟ Travellers cheques

NEUILLY-SUR-SEINE Hauts-de-Seine

★ ★ Hotel Charlemagne
1 rue Charcot *92200*
☎ 146242763 FAX 146371156
In the heart of Neuilly-sur-Seine, close to the metro station and Bois de Boulogne. Hotel Charlemagne is a comfortable hotel with easy access to La Défense area and the Champs Elysées.
40 en suite (bth/shr) TV in all bedrooms Lift
ROOMS: s 395FF; d 450FF ✱
CARDS: ●● ▬

★ ★ ★ Hotel Neuilly Park
23 rue Madeleine Michelis *92200*
☎ 146401115 FAX 146401478
Just beyond the Arc de Triomphe, near the Palais de Congrès and La Défense, but removed from the noise and congestion. Hotel Neuilly Park provides a cosy, warm and peaceful atmosphere.
30 en suite (bth/shr) TV in all bedrooms STV Direct dial from all bedrooms Lift Open parking available
ROOMS: s 650FF; d 770FF ✱
MEALS: Continental breakfast 50FF✱

NOGENT-SUR-MARNE Val-de-Marne

★ ★ Climat de France
1 rue de Nazaré *94130*
☎ 143243737 Cen Res 164460123 FAX 143248404
((off A4, signed Nogent s/Marne)
Standing on the banks of the River Marne, just outside Paris and 20 minutes from Eurodisney, the hotel is a good venue for families and those who want to make day-trips to the capital. The bright bedrooms have good modern facilities and the restaurant serves an honest cuisine incorporating fresh fish specialities and a choice from the comprehensive buffet.
Near river Forest area Near motorway
74 en suite (shr) TV available Direct-dial available Licensed Lift Night porter Full central heating Open parking available Covered parking available Languages spoken: English & German
CARDS: ●● ▬

NOISY-LE-GRAND Seine-St-Denis

★ ★ Climat de France
4 rue du Ballon *93160*
☎ 143052299 Cen Res 164460123 FAX 143041081
(off A4 at Champs s/Marne exit)
Situated in pleasant, leafy surroundings amidst bird song and flowers, the hotel offers a cosy interior where pleasant guest rooms are equipped with private facilities and provide a good quality level of comfort. The restaurant welcomes guests for breakfast, lunches and dinners, and serves besides a generous buffet for appetisers and desserts, classic French cuisine in a warm atmosphere. Young, cheerful staff provide a 'round the clock' attentive service and put a lot of effort into caring for their guests.
Forest area Near motorway
50 en suite (bth/shr) Some rooms in annexe (4 fmly) TV in all bedrooms Radio in rooms Direct dial from all bedrooms Licensed Full central heating Open parking available Boule Open terrace Covered terrace V meals Languages spoken: English, German & Portuguese
CARDS: ●● ▬

ORGEVAL Yvelines

★ ★ ★ Novotel Orgeval
RN 13 *78630*
☎ 139223511 FAX 139754893
Novotel offer their clients good quality accommodation in modern, well-equipped bedrooms and have refined restaurants serving good quality cuisine They have excellent business meeting and conference facilities and some have food and beverages available 24 hours a day. All their hotels have at least one bedroom for disabled guests.
Forest area Near motorway
119 en suite (bth/shr) (15 fmly) No smoking in 27 bedrooms

TV in all bedrooms STV Radio in rooms Direct dial from all bedrooms Mini-bar in all bedrooms Licensed Lift Night porter Full central heating Air conditioning in bedrooms Open parking available Outdoor swimming pool Tennis Boule Open terrace Last d 24.00hrs Languages spoken: English,German,Spanish
CARDS: ✿ 📧 💳 ◑

ORLY (AÉROPORT D') Ile-de-France

★ ★ ★ Novotel Orly Rungis
Zone du Delta, rue du Pont des Halles *94150*
☎ 145124412 FAX 145124413
Novotel offer their clients good quality accommodation in modern, well-equipped bedrooms and have refined restaurants serving good quality cuisine They have excellent business meeting and conference facilities and some have food and beverages available 24 hours a day. All their hotels have at least one bedroom for disabled guests.
Near motorway
181 en suite (bth/shr) (53 fmly) No smoking in 70 bedrooms TV in all bedrooms STV Radio in rooms Direct dial from all bedrooms Mini-bar in all bedrooms Licensed Lift Night porter Full central heating Air conditioning in bedrooms Open parking available (charged) Supervised Child discount available 16yrs Outdoor swimming pool Open terrace Last d 24.00hrs Languages spoken: English
CARDS: ✿ 📧 💳 ◑ Travellers cheques

ORSAY Essonne

★ ★ ★ Novotel Saclay
rue Charles Thomassin *91410*
☎ 169356600 FAX 169410177
Situated close to Paris, the hotel is popular with both business and leisure travellers. It is surrounded by extensive parklands on the edge of the Chevreuse valley and offers comfortable guest accommodation with modern day facilities, a round the clock restaurant and a range of in-house leisure opportunities.
Forest area Near motorway
136 en suite (bth) (136 fmly) No smoking in 50 bedrooms TV in all bedrooms STV Radio in rooms Direct dial from all bedrooms Mini-bar in all bedrooms Licensed Lift Night porter Full central heating Air conditioning in bedrooms Open parking available Supervised Child discount available 12yrs Outdoor swimming pool Tennis Gym Boule Mini-golf Bicycle rental Open terrace Wkly live entertainment Last d 24.00hrs Languages spoken: English
ROOMS: (room only) s fr 550FF; d fr 580FF **Special breaks: Jul-Aug discount weekend breaks**
MEALS: Full breakfast 55FF Lunch fr 120FF&alc Dinner fr 120FF&alc✱
CARDS: ✿ 📧 💳 ◑ Travellers cheques

PARIS

1ST ARRONDISSEMENT

★ ★ Hotel Agora
7 rue de la Cocconerie *75001*
☎ 142334602 FAX 142338099
In town centre
29 en suite (bth/shr) (4 fmly) (11 with balcony) TV in all bedrooms STV Direct dial from all bedrooms Lift Night porter Full central heating Languages spoken: English,Italian,Arabic
CARDS: ✿ 📧 💳 Travellers cheques

★ ★ ★ Hotel du Continent
30 rue du Mont Thabor *75001*
☎ 142607532 FAX 142615222
After an extensive renovation, the hotel finally opened its doors in 1995 and now offers guest rooms which vary in style and size together with an above average level of comfort. Staff provide a friendly and cheerful service and ensure that guests are well looked after.
In town centre
28 en suite (bth/shr) 3 rooms in annexe TV in all bedrooms STV Direct dial from all bedrooms Mini-bar in all bedrooms Licensed Lift Night porter Full central heating Air conditioning in bedrooms Child discount available 12yrs Languages spoken: English,Spanish
CARDS: ✿ 📧 💳 ◑ JCB Travellers cheques

★ ★ ★ ★ Inter-Continental
3 rue Castiglioné *75001*
☎ 144771111 FAX 144771460
This magnificent hotel with its marble columns, crystal chandeliers and painted ceilings is reminiscent of Versailles. Overlooking the beautiful Tuileries Gardens, it features sumptuous lounges which have housed many official celebrations and prestigious fashion shows. The guests' apartments are appointed with immaculate attention to detail and provide sophisticated accommodation. The charming courtyard offers the perfect setting for the elaborate buffets and candlelit dinners that have made the restaurant an absolute favourite amongst chic Parisiennes.
Near river In town centre
450 en suite (bth/shr) (10 fmly) No smoking in 103 bedrooms TV in all bedrooms STV Radio in rooms Direct dial from all bedrooms Mini-bar in all bedrooms Licensed Lift Night porter Full central heating Child discount available 12yrs Open terrace V meals Languages spoken: English,Spanish,Italian,German,Japanese
CARDS: ✿ 📧 💳 ◑ Travellers cheques

★ ★ Hotel Louvre-Forum
25 rue du Bouloi *75001*
☎ 142365419 FAX 142336631
This small cheerful hotel is situated in the centre of Paris with all the main points of interest which the city has to offer not far away. The bedrooms are bright and airy and offer a good standard of comfort. To get the day off to a good start, breakfast is served in the ancient vaulted cellar of the hotel.
Near river In town centre
27 en suite (bth/shr) TV in all bedrooms STV Direct dial from all bedrooms Mini-bar in all bedrooms Licensed Lift Night porter Full central heating Languages spoken: Spanish,German,Italian
CARDS: ✿ 📧 💳 ◑ Travellers cheques

★ ★ ★ Hotel Louvre St-Houoie
141 rue St-Honoré *75001*
☎ 142962323 FAX 142962161
This establishment opened its doors in 1991, and behind its elegant and discreet façade, it features contemporary-style guest-rooms with modern amenities. Breakfast is served in the lounge with its glass pyramid ceiling or in the privacy of your room. The central location makes it a suitable base for sightseeing
In town centre
40 en suite (bth/shr) (5 fmly) (1 with balcony) TV in all bedrooms STV Radio in rooms Direct dial from all bedrooms Mini-bar in 41 bedrooms Licensed Lift Night porter Full central heating Air conditioning in bedrooms

contd.

Child discount available 12yrs Languages spoken:
English,Italian,German
CARDS: ●● ▦ ▉ ◑ JCB Travellers cheques

★ ★ ★ ★ Madelèine Palace
8 rue Cambon *75001*
☎ 142603782 FAX 142603821
(from Porte Maillot onto Avenue de la Grande Armée Place
Etoile, Champs Elysées, Place Concorde & Rue Royal, then turn
1st left into Rue St Honore & at Laura Ashley shop to the right)
Situated in one of the most desirable locations in Paris, the
hotel is popular with both commercial and leisure travellers. 82
rooms and suites provide a high standard of comfort, whilst
the fully equipped and air-conditioned conference room can
accommodate 18-20 delegates. You can enjoy afternoon tea, a
light meal or drink in the English-style bar, whilst dedicated
staff offer a friendly, personal service throughout your stay.
Near river In town centre
82 rms (76 bth/shr) TV in all bedrooms STV Radio in rooms
Direct dial from all bedrooms Mini-bar in 78 bedrooms
Room-safe Licensed Lift Night porter Full central heating y
Languages spoken: English,Spanish,Italian
ROOMS: (room only) s 990-1150FF; d 990-1390FF **Special
breaks**
MEALS: Full breakfast 95FF Continental breakfast 65FF
CARDS: ●● ▦ ▉ ◑ JCB Travellers cheques

★ ★ ★ Hotel Mansart
5 rue des Capucines *75001*
☎ 142615028 FAX 149279744
Ideally located, only a few steps from the art and business
centres of Paris. Each room is unique retaining the character of
an old Parisian residence.
In town centre
57 en suite (bth/shr) (3 with balcony) TV in all bedrooms STV
Direct dial from all bedrooms Mini-bar in all bedrooms
Room-safe Licensed Lift Night porter Full central heating
Languages spoken: English, German & Spanish
ROOMS: (room only) s fr 870FF; d fr 870FF
CARDS: ●● ▦ ▉ ◑ Travellers cheques

★ ★ ★ ★ Meurice (Leading Hotels)
228 rue de Rivoli *75001*
☎ 144581010 FAX 148581015
Situated in the heart of Paris, overlooking the Jardins des
Tuileries, the hotel Meurice occupies a unique position in the
Rue Rivoli. For nearly 200 years it has remained faithful to its
founder's credo; 'no detail too small, no effort too great', and
has been the setting for many of France's political and cultural
occasions. With its exceptional interior and service, the hotel
has been the favourite of many generations of discerning
travellers. Luxurious, individually styled bedrooms are
decorated with assorted antiques and provide sumptuous
accommodation. The restaurant with its turn-of-the-century
decor serves an outstanding cuisine in exquisite surroundings.
Near river In town centre
180 en suite (bth/shr) (3 with balcony) TV in all bedrooms
STV Radio in rooms Direct dial from all bedrooms Mini-bar
in all bedrooms Licensed Lift Night porter Full central
heating Air conditioning in bedrooms Child discount
available 14yrs V meals Last d 22.30hrs Languages spoken:
English,German,Italian,Spanish,Portuguese
CARDS: ●● ▦ ▉ ◑ JCB Travellers cheques

★ ★ ★ ★ Hotel Normandy
70 rue Échelle *75001*
☎ 142603021 FAX 142604581

The Hotel Normandy is a charming establishment set in the
heart of Paris and combines elegance and refinement with
modern comforts. Guests are met upon arrival by friendly and
attentive staff who provide a high level of personal service. The
guest accommodation features discreetly decorated, stylishly
furnished bedrooms and offers the highest level of comfort.
The elegant restaurant serves a superb cuisine in an informal
atmosphere.
Near river In town centre
115 en suite (bth/shr) (4 fmly) (18 with balcony) No smoking
in 22 bedrooms TV in all bedrooms STV Radio in rooms
Direct dial from all bedrooms Licensed Lift Night porter Full
central heating Child discount available 12yrs V meals Last d
22.15hrs Languages spoken:
English,Spanish,Italian,German,Russian
CARDS: ●● ▦ ▉ ◑ Travellers cheques

★ ★ Hotel Prince Albert
5 rue St-Hyacinthe *75001*
☎ 142615836 FAX 142600406
Set in the heart of Paris and ideally located for visits to all the
main attractions, the hotel offers comfortable guest rooms with
modern amenities.
30 rms (22 bth/shr) (3 fmly) (3 with balcony) TV in all
bedrooms STV Radio in rooms Direct dial from all bedrooms
Mini-bar in all bedrooms Licensed Lift Night porter Full
central heating Child discount available 12yrs Languages
spoken: English,Italian,Spanish,Portuguese
CARDS: ●● ▦ ▉ Eurocard Travellers cheques

★ ★ ★ Relais du Louvre
19 rue des Pretres St Germain, l'Auxerrois 19 *75001*
☎ 140419642 FAX 140419644
(in centre of Paris opposite the Louvre Museum)
It is unusual in a busy city to find peace and quiet, but the
Relais du Louvre creates just that within its 18th-century walls.
Restful colour schemes and charming period furniture,
discreetly combined with all modern refinements and services,
provide elegant comfort. Situated between the Louvre and
Notre-Dame.
In town centre
21 en suite (bth/shr) (5 fmly) (1 with balcony) TV in all
bedrooms STV Direct dial from all bedrooms Mini-bar in all
bedrooms Room-safe Licensed Lift Night porter Full central
heating Open parking available (charged) Covered parking
available (charged) Supervised Child discount available 12yrs
Languages spoken: English, German & Italian
ROOMS: (room only) s 600-750FF; d 820-950FF
CARDS: ●● ▦ ▉ ◑

★ ★ ★ Tuileries
10 rue St-Hyacinthe *75001*
☎ 142610417 FAX 149279156
Situated in a quiet street between the Jardins des Tuileries and
the Louvre, this 18th-century house features an interior
adorned with antique rugs, paintings and assorted objects
d'art. The bedrooms are furnished with good taste and offer a
high level of comfort.
In town centre
26 en suite (bth/shr) (12 fmly) (4 with balcony) TV in all
bedrooms STV Radio in rooms Licensed Lift Night porter
Full central heating Air conditioning in bedrooms Languages
spoken: English,German,Spanish,Italian
CARDS: ●● ▦ ▉ ◑ JCB Travellers cheques

★ ★ ★ Hotel Baudelaire Opéra
61 rue Sainte Anne *75002*
☎ 142975062 FAX 142868585
Named after the poet Charles Pierre Baudelaire, the building spans an ancient passageway and is itself around three hundred years old. Within walking distance of most main attractions and shops. The owners, an English/French couple, offer a warm welcome and are very happy to correspond or converse in English or French.

Near river In town centre Near motorway
29 en suite (bth/shr) (5 fmly) (7 with balcony) TV in all bedrooms STV Direct dial from all bedrooms Mini-bar in all bedrooms Licensed Lift Night porter Full central heating Languages spoken: English, German & Spanish
ROOMS: (room only) s 480-520FF; d 610-670FF ✱
MEALS: Continental breakfast 39FF✱
CARDS: ●● 💳 ▆▆ ● Travellers cheques

★ ★ ★ Hotel François
3 bd Montmartre *75002*
☎ 142335153 FAX 140262990
Surrounded by the Opera house, Louvre and shops, the hotel offers its clientele an enjoyable stay where staff are attentive and helpful. The bedrooms are attractively furnished with modern en suite facilities and offer comfortable accommodation in the heart of this lively city.
In town centre
71 en suite (bth/shr) (9 fmly) TV in all bedrooms STV Radio in rooms Direct dial from all bedrooms Mini-bar in all bedrooms Licensed Lift Night porter Full central heating No children Child discount available 12yrs Languages spoken: English,German,Spanish
CARDS: ●● 💳 ▆▆ ● Travellers cheques

★ ★ ★ Gaillon Opéra Best Western (Best Western)
9 rue Gaillon *75002*
☎ 147424774 FAX 147420123
Just a stone's throw away from the Place de l'Opéra, this charming hotel features a cosy interior where assorted antiques and exposed beams create an informal atmosphere. The spacious bedrooms are equipped with modern facilities and provide attractive accommodation. There is a flower-filled courtyard garden for relaxation and staff are more than willing to be of service.
In town centre Near motorway
26 en suite (bth/shr) (9 fmly) (4 with balcony) No smoking in 9 bedrooms TV in all bedrooms STV Radio in rooms Direct dial from all bedrooms Mini-bar in all bedrooms Room-safe Licensed Lift Night porter Full central heating Air

conditioning in bedrooms Child discount available 12yrs Languages spoken: English, Spanish,Portuguese,Italian,German
ROOMS: (room only) s 600-850FF; d 650-950FF ✱ **Special breaks**
CARDS: ●● ▆▆ ▆▆ ● JCB Travellers cheques

★ ★ ★ Grand Hotel de Besançon
56 rue Montorgueil *75002*
☎ 142364108 FAX 145080879
The hotel is located in a pedestrianised street not far from all the favourite tourist attractions. The recently renovated guest-rooms are tastefully furnished and decorated with matching fabrics, and offer a good standard of comfort.
In town centre
20 en suite (bth/shr) No smoking in 5 bedrooms TV in all bedrooms STV Radio in rooms Direct dial from all bedrooms Lift Night porter Full central heating Languages spoken: English
ROOMS: (room only) s 550-620FF; d 650-720FF
CARDS: ●● ▆▆ ▆▆ ●

★ ★ ★ Hotel L'Horset Opéra
18 rue d'Antin *75002*
☎ 144718700 FAX 142665554
(200m from the Opera Garnier & close to Place Vendome, the Louvre, Palais Royal & Tuileries Gardens)
Situated in the heart of the capital, the hotel L'Horset Opéra provides a comfortable and pleasant setting for your stay. Close to the famous department stores, Place Vendôme, the Louvre, the Palais Royal and the Tuilleries gardens it offers its visitors a stay where charm and efficient service go hand in hand. Whether visiting Paris on business or simply for pleasure it has all the advantages of a high-class location. Guest rooms are elegantly furnished to a high degree and equipped with every possible modern amenity. There is a congenial bar and a restaurant.
In town centre
54 en suite (bth/shr) (10 with balcony) TV in all bedrooms STV Radio in rooms Direct dial from all bedrooms Mini-bar in all bedrooms Licensed Lift Night porter Full central heating Air conditioning in bedrooms Child discount available 3yrs Last d 22.30hrs Languages spoken: English,German,Spanish
ROOMS: (room only) s 990-1220FF; d 1100-1350FF
MEALS: Lunch 88FF Dinner 60-150FFalc
CARDS: ●● ▆▆ ▆▆ ● Travellers cheques

★ ★ ★ Jardin de Paris Cusset Opera
95 rue de Richelieu *75002*
☎ 142974890 FAX 142614820
(take direction of Opera, the street of Richelieu is at 500mtrs at the end of the boulevard de Italian starting from the Opera)
The hotel can be found at just five minutes from the Opéra and the big department stores, and is close the to Louvre and the Stock Exchange. Guests will enjoy a comfortable stay in one of the 108 renovated rooms which are equipped with modern facilities. A buffet-style breakfast is served in two 18th-century dining rooms which have fully retained their authentic style.
In town centre
108 en suite (bth/shr) (18 fmly) (3 with balcony) TV in all bedrooms Direct dial from all bedrooms Licensed Lift Night porter Full central heating Child discount available 12yrs Languages spoken: English German & Italian
ROOMS: (room only) s 720-915FF; d 830-1060FF
CARDS: ●● ▆▆ ▆▆ ● JCB Travellers cheques

3RD ARRONDISSEMENT

★ ★ ★ ★ Pavillon de la Reine
28 pl des Vosges *75003*
☎ 142779640 FAX 142776306
Set in the heart of the prestigious Marais district, the hotel features elegant guest accommodation offering a high degree of comfort. The elegant rooms are furnished to suit the character of the house and have views of the flower-filled courtyards. The comfortable public rooms are adorned with period furniture and assorted objets d'art.
Near river In town centre
55 en suite (bth/shr) (6 fmly) (4 with balcony) TV in all bedrooms STV Radio in rooms Direct dial from all bedrooms Mini-bar in all bedrooms Licensed Lift Night porter Full central heating Air conditioning in bedrooms Covered parking available Supervised Languages spoken: Spanish,Italian,German
CARDS: ●● ■■ ■■ ●● Travellers cheques

4TH ARRONDISSEMENT

★ ★ ★ Beaubourg
11 rue Simon le Franc *75004*
☎ 142743424 FAX 142786811
After extensive renovation, the hotel opened its doors in 1986 and features individually styled bedrooms providing very comfortable accommodation. In addition it has a charming private garden, and being located near Notre-Dame and the Pompidou Centre, it is a good base from which to explore all the sights the capital has to offer.
In town centre
28 en suite (bth/shr) 10 rooms in annexe (1 fmly) (1 with balcony) No smoking in 5 bedrooms TV in all bedrooms STV Radio in rooms Direct dial from all bedrooms Mini-bar in all bedrooms Lift Full central heating Languages spoken: English,Arabic,Spanish
CARDS: ●● ■■ ■■ ●● Travellers cheques

★ ★ ★ Hotel de la Bretonnerie
22 rue Ste-Croix-Bretonnerie *75004*
☎ 148877763 FAX 142772678
The house dates back to the 17th century and used to be a private residence. With its ancient stone walls, exposed beams and vaulted cellar it has the charming atmosphere of days gone by. Furnished throughout with great attention to detail it features elegant bedrooms offering a high level of comfort, and inviting public rooms for relaxation.
In town centre
Closed Aug
30 en suite (bth) (5 fmly) TV in all bedrooms STV Direct dial from all bedrooms Mini-bar in all bedrooms Room-safe Lift Night porter Full central heating Languages spoken: English,German
ROOMS: (room only) s 640-790FF; d 640-790FF
CARDS: ●● ■■ Travellers cheques

★ ★ ★ Caron de Beaumarchais
12 rue Vieille du Temple *75004*
☎ 142723412 FAX 142723463
This charming hotel offers bedrooms decorated in 18th-century style furnishings with modern day amenities. Exposed beams, delicate fabrics, and an ancient fireplace create the authentic atmosphere of bygone times and provide the setting for an enjoyable stay.
In town centre
19 en suite (bth/shr) (6 with balcony) TV in all bedrooms STV

Mini-bar in all bedrooms Child discount available 7yrs Languages spoken: English
CARDS: ●● ■■ ■■ ●● Travellers cheques

★ ★ Castex Hotel
5 rue Castex *75004*
☎ 142723152 FAX 142725791
In town centre
27 en suite (bth/shr) 3 rooms in annexe (1 fmly) No smoking on premises Night porter Full central heating Languages spoken: English,Spanish
CARDS: ●● ■■ Travellers cheques

★ ★ ★ Deux-Iles
59 rue St-Louis-en-l'Ile *75004*
☎ 143261335 FAX 143296025
The attractive hotel Des Deux-Iles is housed in a building which dates back to the 18th century and is decorated in cheerful, country-style furnishings. The attractive lounge provides comfortable surroundings for reading or relaxing, whilst the vaulted cellar with its ancient fireplace is the setting for breakfast. Bedrooms are attractive and equipped with modern facilities.
In town centre
17 en suite (bth/shr) TV in all bedrooms Radio in rooms Direct dial from all bedrooms Room-safe Lift Night porter Full central heating Air conditioning in bedrooms Languages spoken: English
ROOMS: (room only) s 710-730FF; d 840FF ✱
CARDS: ●● ■■ ■■ Travellers cheques

★ ★ ★ ★ Jeu de Paumé
54 rue St-Louis-en-l'Ile *75004*
☎ 143261418 FAX 140460276
Standing on the isle of Saint-Louis in the heart of historic Paris, an exclusive hotel has been designed from old royal 'real-tennis' courts. Surrounded by the River Seine and secluded by enchanting gardens it offers excellent accommodation in exquisite surroundings. From the foyer to the bedrooms the hotel has been furnished with great attention to detail in a style befitting its origins.
In town centre
32 en suite (bth/shr) (3 with balcony) TV in all bedrooms STV Radio in rooms Direct dial from all bedrooms Mini-bar in all bedrooms Licensed Lift Night porter Full central heating Sauna Languages spoken: English,German,Italian,Spanish
ROOMS: (room only) s 895-1385FF; d 1195-1385FF
CARDS: ●● ■■ ■■ ●● Travellers cheques

★ ★ ★ Lutèce
65 rue St-Louis-en-l'Ile *75000*
☎ 143262352 FAX 143296025
This cheerful hotel offers comfortable accommodation and is furnished throughout with well matched, country-style furnishings. Its well-equipped bedrooms offer a good standard of comfort, and guests can relax in an informal lounge and breakfast room.
In town centre
23 en suite (bth/shr) TV in all bedrooms STV Radio in rooms Licensed Lift Night porter Full central heating Air conditioning in bedrooms Languages spoken: English,Spanish
CARDS: ●● ■■ ■■ Travellers cheques

★ ★ Place Des Vosges
12 rue Biragué *75004*
☎ 142726046 FAX 142720264

180

Located in a quiet street at just a few steps from one of the most beautiful squares in Paris, this 17th-century establishment is in complete harmony with the surrounding area. It features a cosy, traditional interior, where contemporary bedrooms are well equipped with modern facilities and offer an adequate level of comfort.
In town centre
16 en suite (bth/shr) (6 fmly) TV in all bedrooms STV Lift Night porter Full central heating Child discount available 2yrs Languages spoken: English
ROOMS: (room only) s 330-490FF; d 475-520FF
MEALS: Continental breakfast 30FF✱
CARDS: ● ▆▆ ▆▆ ● Travellers cheques

★ ★ ★ Hotel St-Louis
75 rue St-Louis-en-l'Ile *75004*
☎ 146340480 FAX 146340213
This small, attractive hotel is housed in a 17th-century building and offers modern-day comfort with the charming atmosphere of yesteryear. The guest-rooms have up-to-date facilities and are elegantly appointed. Breakfast is served in the ancient vaulted cellar of the house.
Near river In town centre Near motorway
Licensed Night porter Full central heating Child discount available Languages spoken: English,German,Spanish
CARDS: ● ▆▆ Travellers cheques

★ ★ St-Louis-Marais
1 rue Charles-V *75004*
☎ 148878704 FAX 148873326
This small, charming hotel dates back to the 17th century and has an interior reflecting the atmosphere of those past times. Beamed ceilings, original stone walls, and period furniture feature prominently in this hotel which used to be an outbuilding of a former convent. Bedrooms have good en suite facilities and are attractively furnished.
Near river In town centre Near motorway
Night porter Full central heating Child discount available Languages spoken: English,German,Spanish
CARDS: ▆▆ Travellers cheques

★ ★ ★ St-Merry
78 rue Verrerie *75004*
☎ 142781415 FAX 140290682
This building dates back to the 17th century and used to be the presbytery of the Saint-Merry Church. With its splendid Gothic interior incorporating stone, iron and wood, it provides the exceptional setting for an enjoyable stay. Stylish bedrooms with modern facilities are complemented by public rooms with ornate woodcarvings and assorted antiques.
Near river In town centre
12 rms (10 bth/shr) (3 fmly) Night porter Full central heating Open parking available (charged) Languages spoken: English,German
CARDS: Travellers cheques

★ ★ Hotel Sansonnet
48 rue de la Verrerie *75004*
☎ 147879614 FAX 148873046
A warm welcome by the long-standing proprietors awaits visitors in this 17th-century building, which features sound-proofed bedrooms, most with en suite facilities, and a cosy interior with an ancient wrought-iron staircase leading to the guest accommodation. Centrally located in the heart of Paris, it provides a good base from which to explore the capital.
Near river In town centre
25 rms (21 bth/shr) (3 with balcony) TV in all bedrooms STV

Direct dial from all bedrooms Night porter Full central heating Languages spoken: English
CARDS: ● ▆▆ Travellers cheques

★ ★ ★ ★ Sofitel Paris St-Jacques
17 bd St-Jacques *75014*
☎ 140787980 FAX 145884393
The Sofitel chain comprises of a group of very fine modern, comfortable hotels at the four star level. Bedrooms have been carefully designed to cater to guests' relaxation and well being and the restaurant facilities offer fine cuisine in pleasant surroundings. They cater for business clientele with excellent conference and meeting facilities.
Forest area In town centre Near motorway
797 en suite (bth/shr) No smoking in 116 bedrooms TV in all bedrooms STV Radio in rooms Direct dial from all bedrooms Mini-bar in all bedrooms Licensed Lift Night porter Full central heating Air conditioning in bedrooms Open parking available (charged) Covered parking available (charged) Supervised Child discount available 12yrs Sauna Last d 23.00hrs Languages spoken:
English,Arabic,Danish,German,Italian,Spanish
CARDS: ● ▆▆ ▆▆ ● Travellers cheques

★ ★ ★ Hotel Stella
14 rue Neuve St-Pierre *75004*
☎ 144592850 FAX 144592879
Because of their ideal location, the hotels in the Jardin de Paris group, provide a good base to explore the capital with its many cultural and historic sights. Comfortable bedrooms are equipped with modern facilities and provide a high degree of comfort. There are no restaurant facilities, but a large choice of eating establishments can be found nearby.
In town centre
20 rms TV in all bedrooms Direct dial from all bedrooms Mini-bar in all bedrooms Lift Night porter Full central heating Air conditioning in bedrooms Child discount available 12yrs Languages spoken: English
CARDS: ● ▆▆ ▆▆ ● JCB Travellers cheques

5TH ARRONDISSEMENT

★ ★ ★ Angleterre
44 rue Jacob *76005*
☎ 142603472 FAX 142601693
The elegant hotel Angleterre is set in the very heart of Paris, providing luxury accommodation in sophisticated surroundings; panelled ceilings, waxed beams and period furniture enhance the atmosphere of bygone times. The individually styled guest rooms are spacious and furnished to provide a high level of comfort. In addition there is a delightful, secluded patio with a fountain.
In town centre
27 en suite (bth/shr) TV in all bedrooms STV Direct dial from all bedrooms Room-safe Licensed Lift Night porter Full central heating Languages spoken: English,Spanish
ROOMS: (room only) s 580-850FF; d 680-1500FF
CARDS: ● ▆▆ ▆▆ ● Travellers cheques

★ ★ ★ Hotel Le Colbert
7 rue de l'Hotel Colbert *75005*
☎ 140467950 FAX 143258019
With its iron gates, flower-lined drive, and turn-of-the-century façade, the hotel has the appearance of a smart, private residence. The Hotel Colbert offers an old-world interior with splendid period furniture, complemented by tastefully furnished bedrooms with all modern facilities.

contd.

There are two comfortable lounges, both with fine views.
Near river In town centre
36 en suite (bth/shr) (2 fmly) (1 with balcony) TV in all
bedrooms Radio in rooms Direct dial from all bedrooms
Mini-bar in all bedrooms Room-safe Licensed Lift Night
porter Full central heating Child discount available 12yrs
Languages spoken: English
Rooms: (room only) s fr 890FF; d fr 1030FF
Cards: ✹ ▦ ⚊ ⚈ Travellers cheques

★ ★ Hotel de L'Espérance
15 rue Pascal 75005
☎ 147071099 FAX 143375619
This small, charming hotel is situated near one of the most
picturesque parts of the Quartier Latin. It features cosy
bedrooms, which are tastefully furnished in co-ordinated
shades and fabrics. Fitted with canopy beds and en suite
marbled bathrooms, they offer a high standard of comfort. In
addition there is small, delightful garden in which to enjoy
your breakfast or aperitif.
In town centre Near motorway
38 en suite (bth/shr) TV in all bedrooms STV Direct dial from
all bedrooms Licensed Lift Night porter Full central heating
Child discount available Languages spoken: English,Spanish
Cards: ✹ ▦ ⚊ ⚈ Travellers cheques

★ ★ ★ Grands Hommes
17 pl du Panthéon 75005
☎ 146341960 FAX 143266732
The 18th-century Hotel des Grands Hommes used to be a
popular meeting place for painters and writers during the
1920's. It features individually styled bedrooms, decorated in
pastel shades and wall-coverings, and is furnished with good
quality English-style furniture. Staff are friendly and provide
an attentive and helpful service.
Near river Forest area In town centre
32 en suite (bth/shr) (6 with balcony) TV in all bedrooms STV
Radio in rooms Direct dial from all bedrooms Mini-bar in all
bedrooms Licensed Lift Night porter Full central heating Air
conditioning in bedrooms Languages spoken:
English,German,Polish,Spanish
Rooms: (room only) s 620-700FF; d 720-780FF
Cards: ✹ ▦ ⚊ ⚈ Travellers cheques

★ ★ ★ Hotel de Notre-Dame
19 rue Maître-Albert 75005
☎ 143267900 FAX 146335011
Rustic beams and old furniture confer a certain charm on this
hotel. Completely renovated, it retains some of the atmosphere
of by-gone days while offering modern comfort.
In town centre
34 en suite (bth) TV in all bedrooms STV Direct dial from all
bedrooms Mini-bar in all bedrooms Room-safe Licensed Lift
Night porter Full central heating Languages spoken: English
& German
Rooms: (room only) s 590-750FF; d 590-750FF ✱
Cards: ✹ ▦ ⚊ Travellers cheques

★ ★ ★ Hotel Royal Saint Michel
3 bd St-Michel 75005
☎ 144070606 FAX 144073625
(close to Notre-Dame)
Near river In town centre
39 en suite (bth) (18 with balcony) TV in all bedrooms STV
Direct dial from all bedrooms Mini-bar in all bedrooms
Room-safe Licensed Lift Night porter Full central heating
Air conditioning in bedrooms Child discount available 12yrs

Languages spoken: English Arabic Italian & Russian
Rooms: s 790-990FF; d 930-1160FF **Reductions over 1
night**
Cards: ✹ ▦ ⚊ ⚈ Travellers cheques

★ ★ ★ St-Germain des Prés
36 rue Bonéparte 75005
☎ 143260019 FAX 140468363
The hotel is one of the most popular establishments in the
Quartier Latin and with its exceptional decor, blends very well
with the picturesque character of this district. Charming 18th-
century decorations and furnishings create a special atmosphere
and complement the comfortable, well equipped guest rooms.
In town centre
30 en suite (bth/shr) TV in all bedrooms STV Radio in rooms
Direct dial from all bedrooms Mini-bar in all bedrooms
Licensed Lift Night porter Full central heating Languages
spoken: English,German,Italian,Spanish
Cards: ✹ ▦ ⚊

★ ★ Hotel des Trois Colléges
16 rue Cujas 75005
☎ 143546730 FAX 146340299
Situated near the eminent Sorbonne university this small,
discreet hotel features a predominantly white interior where
bedrooms offer a good level of comfort; some have sloping
ceilings and fine views of the Sorbonne and the Panthéon.
There is a spacious lounge where a delicious breakfast is
served in the morning, and which later in the day provides the
setting for afternoon tea.
In town centre
44 en suite (bth/shr) (3 fmly) TV in all bedrooms STV Direct
dial from all bedrooms Licensed Lift Night porter Full
central heating V meals Languages spoken: Italian,Spanish
Cards: ✹ ▦ ⚊ ⚈ JCB Travellers cheques

6TH ARRONDISSEMENT

★ ★ ★ Aramis St-Germain
124 rue de Rennes 75006
☎ 145480375 FAX 145449929
This charming hotel is situated in the heart of Paris between
Montparnasse and St-Germain-des-Prés and offers modern
comfort in tasteful surroundings. The bedrooms are
comfortable and well-furnished; there is a bar and staff are
always on hand to provide an attentive service.
Near river In town centre Near motorway
42 en suite (bth/shr) (4 with balcony) TV in all bedrooms STV
Radio in rooms Direct dial from all bedrooms Mini-bar in all
bedrooms Licensed Lift Night porter Full central heating
Child discount available 12yrs Jacuzzi/spa Languages spoken:
English
Rooms: (room only) s 600-750FF; d 650-850FF ✱
Cards: ✹ ▦ ⚊ ⚈ J.C.B Travellers cheques

★ ★ ★ Atelier Montparnasse
49l rue Vavin 75006
☎ 146363000 FAX 140510421
This charming, authentic hotel is located on Paris's left bank
with an array of excellent restaurants in the vicinity. The
bedrooms are attractively furnished and have bathrooms with
mosaïc walls, representing famous masterpieces.
In town centre Near motorway
17 en suite (bth/shr) (2 with balcony) TV in all bedrooms
Radio in rooms Direct dial from all bedrooms Mini-bar in all
bedrooms Lift Night porter Full central heating No children
Cards: ✹ ▦ ⚊ ⚈ Travellers cheques

★ ★ **Chaplain**
11 bis rue Jules Chaplain *75006*
☎ 143264764 FAX 140517975
This attractive hotel is located in a quiet residential street away from the bustle of the lively Montparnasse district. The entirely renovated bedrooms are well equipped and offer a good level of comfort, whilst the public rooms are tastefully furnished and provide a comfortable setting for reading or relaxation.
In town centre
25 en suite (bth/shr) (6 fmly) (21 with balcony) TV in all bedrooms STV Direct dial from all bedrooms Lift Night porter Full central heating Supervised Child discount available 12yrs Languages spoken: English,Spanish
CARDS: ● ● ▦ ▬ ▬ ·❱ Travellers cheques

★ ★ ★ **Le Clos Médicis**
56 rue Monsieur-Le-Prince *75006*
☎ 143291080 FAX 143542990
Located in the heart of Saint-Germain-des-Prés and Quartier Latin, this 18th-century building has undergone extensive renovations in recent years and now features a charming Provençale-style interior incorporating quiet, well-equipped bedrooms, a lounge-bar decorated with assorted antiques and open fireplace, and a delightful garden.
In town centre
38 en suite (bth/shr) (4 fmly) (2 with balcony) No smoking in 4 bedrooms TV in all bedrooms STV Direct dial from all bedrooms Mini-bar in all bedrooms Licensed Lift Night porter Full central heating Air conditioning in bedrooms Child discount available 12yrs Open terrace Languages spoken: English,Italian,Spanish
ROOMS: (room only) d 790-1200FF
CARDS: ● ● ▦ ▬ ▬ ·❱ Travellers cheques

★ ★ ★ ★ **L'Hotel**
13 rue des Beaux-Arts *75006*
☎ 144419900 FAX 143256481
Near river In town centre
27 en suite (bth/shr) (2 with balcony) TV in all bedrooms STV Radio in rooms Direct dial from all bedrooms Mini-bar in all bedrooms Licensed Lift Night porter Full central heating Air conditioning in bedrooms Child discount available Languages spoken: English
CARDS: ● ● ▦ ▬ ▬ ·❱ Travellers cheques

★ ★ ★ **Left Bank St-Germain Hotel** (Best Western)
9 rue de l'Ancienne-Comédie *75006*
☎ 143540170 FAX 143261714
Right in the heart of St-Germain-des-Prés, a romantic retreat for visitors to the "old Paris" of poets, students, artists and antiques. A charming hotel with antique furniture, Aubusson tapestries, stone walls, open oak beams and interior gardens.
In town centre
31 en suite (bth/shr) TV in all bedrooms STV Direct dial from all bedrooms Mini-bar in all bedrooms Room-safe (charged) Licensed Lift Night porter Full central heating Air conditioning in bedrooms
ROOMS: (room only) s 750-895FF; d 850-990FF

★ ★ ★ ★ **Hotel Littré**
9 rue Littré *75006*
☎ 145443867 FAX 145448813
The hotel is situated on the left bank between Montparnasse and Saint-Germain-des-Prés and offers traditional hospitality in classic surroundings. The bedrooms feature stylish furnishings and offer a high level of comfort. The public areas and bar have a cosy yet sophisticated atmosphere in which

visitors can unwind after a busy day sightseeing.
In town centre
97 en suite (bth/shr) TV in all bedrooms STV Radio in rooms Direct dial from all bedrooms Mini-bar in all bedrooms Licensed Lift Night porter Full central heating Covered parking available (charged) Languages spoken: English,German,Italian,Portuguese
CARDS: ● ● ▦ ▬ ▬ ·❱ Travellers cheques

★ ★ ★ **Lutétia**
45 bd Raspail *76006*
☎ 149544646 FAX 149544600
The building has one of the most striking façades in Paris which conceals an extraordinary interior of Art-Déco furnishings and decorations. A popular rendezvous amongst those connected to the arts and politics, it is renowned for its traditional hospitality and impeccable service. The bedrooms - some with views of the Eiffel Tower - are furnished with meticulous attention to detail and offer modern amenities; whilst the 'Paris' restaurant has earned many accolades for its outstanding cuisine. In addition the hotel has a popular brasserie with piano bar.
Near river In town centre Near motorway
250 en suite (bth/shr) (50 with balcony) TV in all bedrooms STV Radio in rooms Direct dial from all bedrooms Mini-bar in all bedrooms Licensed Lift Night porter Full central heating Air conditioning in bedrooms Child discount available 12yrs Open terrace V meals Last d 24.00hrs Languages spoken: English,German,Spanish
CARDS: ● ● ▦ ▬ ▬ ·❱ Travellers cheques

★ ★ ★ **Hotel des Marronniers**
21 rue Jacob *75006*
☎ 143253060 FAX 140468356
This comfortable hotel enjoys a peaceful location in the very heart of the 'Quartier Latin', with numerous restaurants and cafes nearby. It has an elegant interior with pleasant bedrooms which are equipped with private facilities and offer a good level of comfort.
In town centre
37 en suite (bth/shr) TV in all bedrooms STV Licensed Lift Night porter Full central heating Air conditioning in bedrooms Languages spoken: English
CARDS: ● ● ▬ Travellers cheques

★ ★ ★ **Hotel Le Montana**
28 rue St-Benoît *75006*
☎ 144397100 FAX 144397129
Because of their ideal location, the hotels in the Jardin de Paris group provide a good base to explore the capital with its many cultural and historic sights. Comfortable bedrooms are equipped with modern facilities and provide a high degree of comfort. There are no restaurant facilities, but a large choice of eating establishments can be found nearby.
In town centre
17 rms (1 fmly) TV in all bedrooms STV Direct dial from all bedrooms Lift Night porter Full central heating Child discount available 12yrs Languages spoken: English
CARDS: ● ● ▦ ▬ ▬ ·❱ JCB Travellers cheques

★ ★ ★ **Hotel Prince de Conti**
8 rue Guénégaud *75006*
☎ 144073040 FAX 144073634
The Hotel Prince de Conti is housed in a renovated 18th-century building set in the historic quarter of Saint-Germain-des-Prés. Most of the guest rooms overlook the interior courtyard and offer peaceful accommodation with modern facilities.
contd.

In town centre
26 en suite (bth/shr) 12 rooms in annexe TV in all bedrooms
STV Direct dial from all bedrooms Mini-bar in all bedrooms
Lift Night porter Air conditioning in bedrooms Child
discount available Open terrace Covered terrace Languages
spoken: English,Italian
CARDS: ♠ ▅▅ ⅏ ⅏ Travellers cheques

★ ★ Hotel Recamier
3 bis pl St-Sulpice *75006*
☎ 143260489 FAX 146332773
The hotel is ideally located in the heart of Saint-Germain-des-
Prés with numerous boutiques and restaurants within walking
distance. There are traditionally furnished, functional
bedrooms equipped with modern amenities offering a good
standard of comfort.
In town centre
30 rms Some rooms in annexe (2 fmly) (10 with balcony) No
smoking on premises Licensed Lift Night porter Full central
heating No children 5yrs Languages spoken:
English,German,Spanish
CARDS: ♠ ▅▅ Travellers cheques

★ ★ ★ ★ Relais St-Germain
9 Carrefour de l'Odéon *75006*
☎ 143291205 FAX 146334530
This 17th-century house has retained much of the original
charm and character of its period. Exposed beams, antique
furniture, and oil paintings complement its charming
atmosphere. The bedrooms are furnished with flair and feature
high quality fabrics combined with luxurious modern amenities.
In town centre
22 en suite (bth/shr) (2 fmly) (2 with balcony) No smoking in 2
bedrooms TV in all bedrooms STV Radio in rooms Direct
dial from all bedrooms Mini-bar in all bedrooms Room-safe
Licensed Lift Night porter Full central heating Air
conditioning in bedrooms V meals Last d 23.00hrs Languages
spoken: English,German,Italian,Portuguese,Spanish
ROOMS: s 1290FF; d 1550-1750FF ✷
MEALS: Full breakfast 75FF Lunch 120-200FFalc Dinner 120-
200FFalc
CARDS: ♠ ▅▅ ⅏ ⅏ Travellers cheques

★ ★ ★ Royal St-Germain
159 rue de Rennes *76006*
☎ 144392626 FAX 145490923
Located near Quartier Latin, this newly renovated hotel offers a
comprehensive range of facilities and services and is therefore
an ideal venue for business travellers as well as leisure guests.
The tastefully appointed bedrooms are fitted with every modern
convenience and offer a good standard of comfort. There is a
restful day room to relax and unwind in after a busy day.
Near river Forest area In town centre
43 en suite (bth/shr) (6 fmly) (4 with balcony) TV in all
bedrooms STV Radio in rooms Direct dial from all bedrooms
Mini-bar in all bedrooms Licensed Lift Night porter Full
central heating Child discount available 12yrs Languages
spoken: English,German,Italian
CARDS: ♠ ▅▅ ⅏ ⅏

★ ★ ★ St-Beuve
9 rue St-Beuvé *75006*
☎ 145482007 FAX 145486752
This small, charming hotel with its elegant interior, has the
intimate atmosphere of a private house. A warm welcome by
exceptionally friendly staff awaits guests upon arrival, and they
ensure that visitors are well looked after during their stay. The

elegant bedrooms are tastefully furnished and offer a high
standard of comfort. Located just a few steps away from the
beautiful Jardin du Luxembourg and the prestigious fashion
boutiques.
In town centre
23 en suite (bth/shr) (5 fmly) (6 with balcony) TV in all
bedrooms STV Direct dial from all bedrooms Mini-bar in all
bedrooms Licensed Lift Night porter Full central heating
Child discount available Languages spoken:
English,German,Spanish
CARDS: ♠ ▅▅ ▅▅ Travellers cheques

★ ★ Hotel de St-Germain
50 rue du Four *75006*
☎ 145489164 FAX 145484622
This small, charming hotel offers a warm and friendly
atmosphere, where newly decorated bedrooms with Laura-
Ashley style furnishings provide attractive guest
accommodation. Helpful staff render an attentive service and
are happy to advice you throughout your stay.
In town centre
30 en suite (bth/shr) (22 with balcony) TV in all bedrooms
STV Direct dial from all bedrooms Room-safe Licensed Lift
Night porter Full central heating Languages spoken:
English,German,Italian,Spanish
ROOMS: (room only) s 415-695FF; d 520-695FF
MEALS: Full breakfast 45FF Continental breakfast 60FF
CARDS: ♠ ▅▅ ▅▅ ⅏ Travellers cheques

★ ★ ★ St-Gregoire
43 rue de l'Abbé Gregoire *75006*
☎ 145482323 FAX 145483395
This establishment dates back to the 18th-century and features
attractively furnished bedrooms with good amenities.
Throughout the hotel, assorted bric-à-brac enhance the
intimate interior. The cosy lounge with attractive open
fireplace lends an informal atmosphere to the place, and
guests can start off the day in the vaulted breakfast room.
In town centre
20 en suite (bth/shr) (2 with balcony) TV in all bedrooms STV
Direct dial from all bedrooms Licensed Lift Night porter Full
central heating Languages spoken:
English,German,Italian,Spanish
ROOMS: (room only) s 690-990FF; d 890-990FF
CARDS: ♠ ▅▅ ▅▅ ⅏ JCB Travellers cheques

★ ★ ★ Hotel des Sts-Pères
65 rue des Sts-Pères *75006*
☎ 145445000 FAX 145449083
This 17th-century private residence is located in one of the
liveliest parts of Paris, St-Germain-des-Prés, where the avant-
garde and historic are combined, and offer a colourful setting
which is popular with many visitors. The hotel has elegant
bedrooms which overlook a pretty interior garden, where
during the summer breakfast is served. There is a cosy lounge
with comfortable armchairs for relaxation, and a congenial bar
for a drink and a chat.
In town centre
39 en suite (bth/shr) TV in all bedrooms STV Direct dial from
all bedrooms Mini-bar in all bedrooms Licensed Lift Night
porter Full central heating Languages spoken:
English,German,Spanish
CARDS: ♠ ▅▅ ▅▅ Travellers cheques

★ ★ ★ ★ Victoria Palace
6 rue Blaise Désgoffé *75006*
☎ 145443816 FAX 145492375

Situated on the left bank, this imposing residence offers entirely renovated bedrooms with traditional French-style furnishings and luxurious en-suite facilities. There is a comfortable lounge-bar where guests can enjoy an aperitif before seeking out one of the many restaurants in the district.
In town centre Near motorway
80 en suite (bth/shr) (2 fmly) (15 with balcony) TV in all bedrooms STV Radio in rooms Direct dial from all bedrooms Mini-bar in all bedrooms Licensed Lift Night porter Full central heating Air conditioning in bedrooms Covered parking available (charged) Child discount available 12yrs Languages spoken: German,Spanish
CARDS: 💳 🏧 🔤 💲 Travellers cheques

7TH ARRONDISSEMENT

★ ★ ★ Hotel de l'Académie
32 rue des St-Pères *75007*
☎ 145498000 FAX 145498010
18th century charming hotel with authentic stone work and mellowed wooden beam décor. A fine base for browsing in the bookshops and antique shops of the Beaux Arts quarter.
In town centre
33 en suite (bth/shr) (8 fmly) (1 with balcony) No smoking in 7 bedrooms TV in all bedrooms STV Direct dial from all bedrooms Mini-bar in all bedrooms Room-safe Lift Night porter Full central heating Air conditioning in bedrooms Open parking available (charged) Covered parking available (charged) Child discount available 12yrs Languages spoken: English & Spanish
ROOMS: (room only) s 590-790FF; d 690-890FF
MEALS: Full breakfast 60FF
CARDS: 💳 🏧 🔤 💲 Travellers cheques

★ ★ ★ Bourdonnais
111 av de la Bourdonnais *75007*
☎ 147054542 FAX 145557554
A charming, quiet hotel situated just a stone's throw away from the Eiffel Tower, it features well equipped, spacious bedrooms, and a delightful winter-garden where breakfast is served. In addition guests will receive helpful service from willing staff.
Near river In town centre
60 en suite (bth/shr) (20 fmly) (10 with balcony) TV in all bedrooms STV Radio in rooms Direct dial from all bedrooms Mini-bar in 6 bedrooms Room-safe Licensed Lift Night porter Full central heating Child discount available Open terrace Languages spoken: English,German,Spanish
ROOMS: (room only) s 540-650FF; d 650-740FF
CARDS: 💳 🏧 🔤 💲 JCB Travellers cheques

★ ★ ★ Hotel Cayre
4 bd Raspail *75007*
☎ 145443888 FAX 145449873
Situated in the heart of Paris, and conveniently located for the fashionable boutiques, antique shops and restaurants as well as the many cultural and historic sights the capital has to offer, the Scandic hotels have an elegant interior where high quality furnishings and fabrics create a luxurious atmosphere. The guest accommodation has excellent en suite facilities with personal touches, and provides the highest level of comfort.
Near river In town centre
118 en suite (bth/shr) TV in all bedrooms Direct dial from all bedrooms Mini-bar in all bedrooms Licensed Lift Night porter Child discount available 12yrs Languages spoken: English,Italian,Spanish
CARDS: 💳 🏧 🔤 💲 Travellers cheques

★ ★ ★ Eiffel Park Hotel
17b rue Améilie *75007*
☎ 147052868
The contemporary Eiffel Park hotel offers its clientele French hospitality the Parisian way. Young, efficient staff provide a warm welcome and ensures that your stay will be a memorable one. There are comfortable bedrooms with up-to-date facilities, a private bar and a attractive terrace where - weather permitting - breakfast is served.
In town centre
36 en suite (bth/shr) (4 with balcony) TV in all bedrooms STV Radio in rooms Direct dial from all bedrooms Mini-bar in all bedrooms Room-safe (charged) Licensed Lift Night porter Full central heating Child discount available 12yrs Open terrace Languages spoken: English,Spanish,German
ROOMS: (room only) s 550-700FF; d 600-780FF
Reductions over 1 night
CARDS: 💳 🏧 🔤 💲 Travellers cheques

★ ★ ★ Elysées Maubourg (Best Western)
35 bd de Latour-Maubourg *75007*
☎ 145561078 FAX 147056508
This charming establishment offers a warm reception to its visitors, and features pleasant public areas, a bar and an interior garden. Close to all the main tourist attractions, it provides fully renovated bedrooms with modern facilities offering a good standard of comfort.
In town centre
30 en suite (bth/shr) (1 with balcony) TV in all bedrooms Direct dial from all bedrooms Mini-bar in all bedrooms Licensed Lift Night porter Full central heating Child discount available 12yrs Sauna Open terrace Languages spoken: English
CARDS: 💳 🏧 🔤 💲 Travellers cheques

★ ★ ★ Hotel Lénox
9 rue de l'Université *75007*
☎ 142961095 FAX 142615283
Situated on the right-bank of the river, the hotel is tucked away in the heart of Saint-Germain-des-Prés. The elegantly furnished bedrooms - each with their own personal style - offer a high standard of comfort and are complemented by old fashioned French hospitality and courteous, attentive service from the staff.
Near river In town centre Near motorway
34 en suite (bth/shr) (4 fmly) (5 with balcony) TV in all bedrooms STV Radio in rooms Direct dial from all bedrooms Licensed Lift Night porter Full central heating No children Languages spoken: English,German,Italian,Spanish,Japanese
CARDS: 💳 🏧 🔤 💲 Travellers cheques

★ ★ ★ ★ Hotel Montalembert
3 rue de Montalembert *75007*
☎ 145496868 FAX 145496949
(located on the left bank, just off the blvd St Germain, on the rue du Bac, not far from the Musee D'Orsay)
Very "left bank" in decoration, with a mixture of classic and contemporary design. Montalembert is the epitome of Parisian charm and style.
In town centre
56 en suite (bth/shr) (17 fmly) TV in all bedrooms STV Direct dial from all bedrooms Mini-bar in all bedrooms Room-safe Licensed Lift Night porter Full central heating Air conditioning in bedrooms Covered terrace Fitness centre Library V meals Last d 22.30hrs Languages spoken: English & Dutch
ROOMS: (room only) d 1695-2200FF
contd.

MEALS: Continental breakfast 60FF Lunch 175-200FFalc
Dinner 250-350FFalc
CARDS: 😊 💳 💳 ⑩ Travellers cheques

★ ★ Hotel du Nevers
83 rue Bac *75007*
☎ 145446130 FAX 142222947
The house dates back to the 18th-century when it was a
convent. It offers fully refurbished bedrooms with modern
amenities and is situated close to all the major tourist sights in
the city.
Near river In town centre Near motorway
11 en suite (bth/shr) (2 with balcony) TV in all bedrooms
Direct dial from all bedrooms Mini-bar in all bedrooms
Licensed Night porter Full central heating Languages
spoken: English

★ ★ ★ Hotel Saxe Résidence
9 Villa de Saxe *75007*
☎ 144497840 FAX 147838547
This establishment is peacefully situated in the heart of the city
and close to all the main sights of interest. The guestrooms are
good-sized and are equipped with modern facilities; there is a
residents' bar where guest can enjoy a pre-dinner drink.
In town centre
49 en suite (bth/shr) (7 fmly) (10 with balcony) TV in all
bedrooms STV Radio in rooms Direct dial from all bedrooms
Mini-bar in all bedrooms Room-safe Licensed Lift Night
porter Full central heating Open parking available Child
discount available 12yrs Languages spoken: English,German
ROOMS: s 650-930FF; d 680-930FF
CARDS: 😊 💳 💳 ⑩ JCB Travellers cheques

★ ★ ★ Hotel St-Romain
5 & 7 rue St-Roch *75007*
☎ 142603170 FAX 142601069
A relaxing stay awaits guests in the newly refurbished hotel
Saint-Romain, where elegance and comfort go hand in hand.
The comfortable bedrooms have luxury marble bathrooms.
Breakfast is served in the privacy of your room or in the
vaulted cellar. The hotel is ideally situated for visits to the
Louvre and other points of interest.
In town centre
34 en suite (bth/shr) (10 fmly) TV in 68 bedrooms STV Direct
dial from all bedrooms Licensed Lift Night porter Full
central heating Child discount available 12yrs Languages
spoken: English,Italian
CARDS: 😊 💳 💳 ⑩ JCB Travellers cheques

★ ★ Solférino
91 rue de Lille *75017*
☎ 147058554 FAX 145555116
The hotel is set in the very heart of Paris yet provides peaceful
accommodation. Decorated throughout with assorted oriental
rugs, pastel shades and attractive furniture, it offers a cosy
setting for an enjoyable stay. In the morning breakfast is
served in the conservatory.
Near river In town centre
Closed 21Dec-3Jan
33 rms (22 bth 5 shr) (1 fmly) (4 with balcony) Lift Night
porter Full central heating Languages spoken: English
CARDS: 😊 💳 Travellers cheques

★ ★ ★ Hotel Thoumieux
79 rue St-Dominique *75007*
☎ 147054975 FAX 147053696
Situated in the ministerial district, between the Eiffel Tower

and Les Invalides, the Hotel Thoumieux offers its clientele an
enjoyable stay in elegant surroundings. The bedrooms are
attractive and equipped with extensive amenities, and the
brasserie-style restaurant serves a wide selection of freshly
prepared food to suit most tastes.
Near river In town centre
Closed 1st May
10 en suite (bth/shr) (3 fmly) TV in all bedrooms Radio in
rooms Direct dial from all bedrooms Night porter Full central
heating V meals Last d 24.00hrs Languages spoken:
English,German,Spanish
CARDS: 😊 💳 💳 Eurocard

★ ★ ★ ★ Tourville
16 av de Tourville *75007*
☎ 147056262 FAX 147054390
The hotel is decorated throughout with soft pastel shades,
period furniture and old paintings which create a warm,
informal atmosphere. The luxurious guest accommodation -
some with private terrace - is spacious and furnished with flair.
In town centre
30 en suite (bth/shr) (3 fmly) (3 with balcony) TV in all
bedrooms STV Direct dial from all bedrooms Licensed Lift
Night porter Full central heating Air conditioning in
bedrooms Child discount available 12yrs Languages spoken:
English,German,Spanish
ROOMS: (room only) s 690-790FF; d 790-1090FF
CARDS: 😊 💳 💳 ⑩ Travellers cheques

★ ★ Hotel de Turenne
20 av de Tourville *75007*
☎ 147059992 FAX 145560604
Situated in one of the most beautiful parts of Paris, the hotel
provides the ideal base from which to explore the city. It has
recently undergone complete renovatation and now offers
comfortable accommodation with luxurious ensuite facilities
and a cosy lounge where guests can enjoy an aperitif before
seeking out one of the many restaurants in the area.
In town centre
34 en suite (bth/shr) (3 fmly) TV in all bedrooms STV Direct
dial from all bedrooms Licensed Lift Night porter Full
central heating Languages spoken: English, German, Spanish,
Dutch
CARDS: 😊 💳 💳 ⑩ Travellers cheques

★ ★ ★ Université
22 r de l'Universite *75007*
☎ 142610939 FAX 142604084
Stay in the heart of Paris, but still be in a quiet area. Comfort is
that expected of a hotel in this category, with the added charm
of an atmosphere of a private residence.
Near river In town centre
27 rms (19 bth 6 shr) No smoking on premises TV in all
bedrooms STV Direct dial from all bedrooms Mini-bar in 15
bedrooms Room-safe Licensed Lift Night porter Full central
heating Air conditioning in bedrooms Languages spoken:
English
ROOMS: (room only) s 500-700FF; d 800-1200FF ✱
CARDS: 😊 💳 💳 Travellers cheques

8TH ARRONDISSEMENT

★ ★ Hotel Amsterdam
53 rue d'Amsterdam *75008*
☎ 148747974 FAX 148783726
Because of their ideal location, the hotels in the Jardin de Paris
group, provide a good base to explore the capital with its many

cultural and historic sights. Comfortable bedrooms are equipped with every modern facilities and provide a high degree of comfort. There are no restaurant facilities, but a large choice of eating establishments can be found nearby.
In town centre
58 rms (2 fmly) TV in all bedrooms STV Radio in rooms Direct dial from all bedrooms Lift Night porter Full central heating Child discount available 12yrs Open terrace Languages spoken: English
CARDS: ●● ▦ ▆▆ ●） Travellers cheques

★ ★ ★ ★ Beau Manoir Best Western (Best Western)
6 rue de l'Arcade *75008*
☎ 142660307 FAX 142680300
Tucked away in leafy surroundings near the Place de la Madeleine and just a few minutes away from all the prestigious shops in the district, the hotel extends a warm welcome to its visitors. The elegant furnishings reflect the atmosphere of this smart area and offer comfortable accommodation. The well equipped bedrooms are spacious and smartly decorated and breakfast is served in the vaulted dining room.
In town centre Near motorway
32 en suite (bth/shr) 32 rooms in annexe TV in all bedrooms STV Radio in rooms Direct dial from all bedrooms Mini-bar in all bedrooms Licensed Lift Night porter Full central heating Air conditioning in bedrooms Open parking available Child discount available 12yrs Languages spoken: English,German,Spanish
ROOMS: s 995-1100FF; d 1155-1300FF ✱
CARDS: ●● ▦ ▆▆ ●） Travellers cheques

★ ★ ★ Hotel de Berne
37 rue de Berne *75008*
☎ 143870892 FAX 143870893
The Hotel Berne is situated in a peaceful area not far from the major shops and sights. It offers its clientele well-furnished bedrooms with modern facilities, and an attractive foyer and lounge. Service is friendly and an overall informal atmosphere prevails.
In town centre
38 en suite (bth) (6 fmly) No smoking in 15 bedrooms TV in all bedrooms STV Radio in rooms Direct dial from all bedrooms Licensed Lift Night porter Full central heating Air conditioning in bedrooms Languages spoken: English,Arabic,German,Italian
CARDS: ●● ▦ ▆▆ ●） Travellers cheques

★ ★ ★ ★ Bristol
112 rue du faubourg St-Honoré *75008*
☎ 153434300 FAX 153434301
This elegant establishment has been entirely renovated and is situated in the prestigious Faubourg district. High quality fabrics and assorted antiques create a warm yet sophisticated atmosphere where guests can unwind and recharge their batteries. The luxurious bedrooms are furnished with impeccable taste and provide a high degree of comfort, whilst the outstanding cuisine has been awarded many accolades.
In town centre
195 en suite (bth/shr) TV in all bedrooms STV Radio in rooms Direct dial from all bedrooms Mini-bar in all bedrooms Room-safe Licensed Lift Night porter Full central heating Air conditioning in bedrooms Open parking available Covered parking available Supervised Child discount available 12yrs Indoor swimming pool (heated) Sauna Solarium Gym Last d 22.30hrs Languages spoken: English,German,Italian,Spanish
ROOMS: (room only) s 2500-2950FF; d 3200-3950FF
CARDS: ●● ▦ ▆▆ ●） Travellers cheques

★ ★ ★ ★ Hotel Châteaubriand
6 rue Châteaubriand *75008*
☎ 140760050 FAX 140760922
Situated in the heart of Paris, and conveniently located for the fashionable boutiques, antique shops and restaurants as well as the many cultural and historic sights the capital has to offer, the Scandic hotels have an elegant interior where high quality furnishings and fabrics create a luxurious atmosphere. The guest accommodation has excellent en suite facilities with personal touches, and provides the highest level of comfort.
In town centre
28 en suite (bth/shr) No smoking in 5 bedrooms TV in all bedrooms Direct dial from all bedrooms Mini-bar in all bedrooms Licensed Lift Night porter Air conditioning in bedrooms Child discount available 12yrs Languages spoken: English,Italian,Spanish
CARDS: ●● ▦ ▆▆ ●） Travellers cheques

★ ★ ★ Hotel Cordelia
11 rue de Greffulhe *75008*
☎ 142654240 FAX 142651181
Situated in the heart of Paris, the hotel extends a warm welcome to its visitors and because of its ideal location, is popular with commercial travellers and tourists alike. After a day of sightseeing guests can unwind in the smartly decorated bedrooms or relax in the cosy lounge with open fire place.
In town centre
30 en suite (bth/shr) TV available STV Radio in rooms Direct dial from all bedrooms Mini-bar in all bedrooms Licensed Lift Night porter Full central heating Air conditioning in bedrooms Languages spoken: English
CARDS: ●● ▦ ▆▆ ●） Travellers cheques

★ ★ ★ Hotel Étoile
3 rue de Ponthieu *75008*
☎ 142257301 FAX 142560139
(between Arc de Triomphe & Concorde near the roundabout with the Champs Elysées)
The Art-Déco interior of this building has enchanted many travellers over the years. The individually appointed bedrooms offer modern facilities and provide comfortable accommodation. The hotel is ideally situated for visits to the nearby historic monuments.
In town centre
25 en suite (bth/shr) (4 fmly) (4 with balcony) TV in all bedrooms STV Direct dial from all bedrooms Mini-bar in all bedrooms Room-safe Licensed Lift Night porter Full central heating Air conditioning in bedrooms Languages spoken: English,Italian,Spanish
ROOMS: (room only) s 590-790FF; d 690-890FF
Reductions over 1 night
CARDS: ●● ▦ ▆▆ ●） Travellers cheques

★ ★ ★ Hotel la Fléche d'Or
29 rue d'Amsterdam *75008*
☎ 148740686 FAX 148740604
(in centre of Paris take direction of the Opera House then towards St Lazare Stn and rue d'Amsterdam)
This hotel has been completely renovated and is close to the Gare St-Lazare, the luxury departments stores and the Opera.
In town centre
61 en suite (bth/shr) (2 fmly) (2 with balcony) No smoking in 15 bedrooms TV in all bedrooms STV Direct dial from all bedrooms Mini-bar in all bedrooms Room-safe (charged) Licensed Lift Night porter Full central heating Air conditioning in bedrooms

contd.

Child discount available 12yrs Languages spoken: English,
German, Italian & Spanish
ROOMS: (room only) s 550-750FF; d 750-850FF
CARDS: � ◑

★ ★ ★ Hotel L'Horset St Augustin
20 rue Roquépine *75008*
☎ 142681164 FAX 142681163
(200m from St Augustin Church & close to the Elysée Palace)
Situated in one of the most beautiful parts of central Paris and
close to the Place de la Madeleine and the Elysée Palace - the
official residence of the French president - the charming
L'Horset Saint Augustin provides its clientele with a pleasant
stay in charming surroundings. The area has a long established
connection with business and the fashion trade, and a visit to
the department stores and the chic boutiques in the celebrated
Rue du Faubourg Saint Honoré is not to be missed. Elegantly
furnished bedrooms provide a high level of comfort and the
quality service rendered by attentive staff is first class.
In town centre
34 en suite (bth/shr) TV in all bedrooms STV Direct dial from
all bedrooms Mini-bar in all bedrooms Licensed Lift Night
porter Full central heating Child discount available 12yrs
Languages spoken: English,Spanish
ROOMS: (room only) s 695-795FF; d 795-895FF
CARDS: ●● ▬ ▭ ◑ Travellers cheques

★ ★ ★ ★ Hotel L'Horset Washington
43 rue Washington *75008*
☎ 149539442 FAX 149539443
The hotel L'Horset Washington is situated just a stone's throw
away from the Champs Elysées and the Arc de Triomphe and
not far away from Paris's most famous sights. Against the
backdrop of one of Paris's prettiest districts, it offers its visitors
a comfortable stay in elegantly furnished surroundings. The
well designed bedrooms are complemented by the
hardworking and attentive staff.
In town centre
17 en suite (bth/shr) TV in all bedrooms Radio in rooms
Direct dial from all bedrooms Mini-bar in all bedrooms
Room-safe (charged) Licensed Lift Night porter Full central
heating Child discount available 12yrs Languages spoken:
English,German
ROOMS: (room only) s 895-1050FF; d 995-1150FF
CARDS: ●● ▬ ▭ ◑ JCB Travellers cheques

★ ★ ★ Hotel Lido (Best Western)
4 passage de la Madeleine *75008*
☎ 142662737 FAX 142666123
The building occupies a peaceful location away from the bustle
of the Place de la Madelaine. The interior, with its old beams
and original stones, is decorated with stylish furniture and
tapestries. The bedrooms are adorned with period pieces and
have luxurious en-suite facilities. In addition the hotel has a
delightful flower garden.
In town centre Near motorway
32 en suite (bth/shr) (11 fmly) TV in all bedrooms STV Radio
in rooms Direct dial from all bedrooms Mini-bar in all
bedrooms Room-safe (charged) Licensed Lift Night porter
Full central heating Air conditioning in bedrooms Child
discount available 12yrs Languages spoken:
English,German,Spanish
ROOMS: s 830-980FF; d 930-1100FF ✳
CARDS: ●● ▬ ▭ ◑ JCB Travellers cheques

★ ★ ★ Mayflower
3 rue Châteaubriand *75008*

☎ 145625746 FAX 142563238
Situated in a quiet street off the Champs-Elysées, the hotel
features an elegant interior incorporating smartly furnished
bedrooms with modern amenities, and an informal lounge
with fireplace. Staff are dedicated and eager to ensure that
guests are well looked after.
In town centre
24 en suite (bth/shr) (4 with balcony) TV in all bedrooms STV
Direct dial from all bedrooms Mini-bar in all bedrooms
Licensed Lift Night porter Full central heating Child
discount available 12yrs Languages spoken:
English,Dutch,German,Italian
CARDS: ●● ▬ ▭ Travellers cheques

★ ★ ★ New Hotel Roblin
6 rue Chauveau-Lagarde *75008*
☎ 144712080 FAX 142651949
The New Hotel group consists of establishments where guests
are offered a combination of 20th-century comfort combined
with traditional hospitality and peaceful interiors for a restful
stay. Bedrooms vary in style and size, are equipped with
modern facilities and offer a high level of comfort.
In town centre
77 en suite (bth/shr) (8 fmly) (2 with balcony) TV in all
bedrooms STV Radio in rooms Direct dial from all bedrooms
Mini-bar in all bedrooms Licensed Lift Night porter Full
central heating Air conditioning in bedrooms Child discount
available 12yrs V meals Last d 22.00hrs Languages spoken:
English,Arabic,Italian,Spanish
CARDS: ●● ▬ ▭ ◑ JCB

★ ★ ★ L'Orangerie
9 rue de Constantinople *75008*
☎ 142220751 FAX 145221649
The Hotel Orangerie offers all the ingredients of a memorable
stay: courteous service and a peaceful interior, complemented
by smartly furnished bedrooms which are equipped with
modern facilities. In addition there is a cosy lounge with
private bar for reading or relaxation.
Forest area In town centre Near motorway
29 en suite (bth/shr) (3 fmly) (10 with balcony) TV in all
bedrooms STV Direct dial from all bedrooms Mini-bar in all
bedrooms Licensed Lift Full central heating Supervised
Child discount available 12yrs Languages spoken:
English,Arabic,German,Italian,Spanish
CARDS: ●● ▬ ▭ ◑ Travellers cheques

★ ★ ★ ★ Plaza-Athénée
av Montaigne *75008*
☎ 153676665 FAX 153676666
Situated on the Avenue Montaigne, the hotel represents
exactly what one associates with Paris; elegance and a
luxurious atmosphere. The lounges and public areas are
adorned with assorted antiques, the guest rooms offer the
highest levels of comfort and are furnished with meticulous
attention to detail, whilst the restaurant is reputed to be one of
the best in the capital. The charming courtyard garden with its
flowers and fountains provides a romantic setting for the
summer restaurant.
Near river In town centre
206 rms No smoking in 42 bedrooms TV in all bedrooms STV
Radio in rooms Direct dial from all bedrooms Mini-bar in all
bedrooms Licensed Lift Night porter Full central heating Air
conditioning in bedrooms Child discount available 12yrs Gym
V meals Last d 21.00hrs Languages spoken:
English,German,Spanish
CARDS: ●● ▬ ▭ ◑ Travellers cheques

★ ★ ★ ★ Residentiale Chambiges

8 rue Chambiges *75008*
☎ 144318383 FAX 140709551
In town centre
33 en suite (bth/shr) TV in all bedrooms STV Direct dial from all bedrooms Mini-bar in all bedrooms Room-safe Licensed Lift Night porter Full central heating Air conditioning in bedrooms Child discount available Open terrace Languages spoken: English
ROOMS: (room only) s 980FF; d 1180FF
CARDS: ⊕ ▆▆ ▆ ⏺ Travellers cheques

★ ★ ★ Hotel Rochambeau

4 rue La Boëtie *75008*
☎ 142652754 FAX 142660381
Situated in the heart of Paris, and conveniently located for the fashionable boutiques, antique shops and restaurants as well as the many cultural and historic sights the capital has to offer, the Scandic hotels have an elegant interior where high quality furnishings and fabrics create a luxurious atmosphere. The guest accommodation has excellent en suite facilities with personal touches, and provides the highest level of comfort.
In town centre
50 en suite (bth/shr) TV in all bedrooms Direct dial from 53 bedrooms Mini-bar in 53 bedrooms Licensed Lift Child discount available 12yrs Languages spoken: English,Italian, Spanish
CARDS: ⊕ ▆▆ ▆ ⏺ Travellers cheques

★ ★ ★ ★ Royal

33 av Friedland *75008*
☎ 143590814 FAX 145636992
Located just a few steps away from the Arc de Triomphe and the Champs Elysées, the hotel exudes elegance and charm. It provides an oasis of peace amidst the lively bustle of the capital and offers traditional hospitality and very comfortable accommodation. The sound-proofed rooms are equipped with modern day amenities and provide a high standard of comfort
In town centre
58 en suite (bth/shr) (12 fmly) (12 with balcony) No smoking in 10 bedrooms TV in all bedrooms STV Radio in rooms Direct dial from all bedrooms Mini-bar in all bedrooms Licensed Lift Night porter Full central heating Air conditioning in bedrooms Open parking available (charged) Covered parking available (charged) Supervised Child discount available 12yrs Languages spoken: English,German,Spanish
CARDS: ⊕ ▆▆ ▆ ⏺ JCB Travellers cheques

★ ★ ★ Hotel Royal Alma

35 rue Jean Goujon *75008*
☎ 153936300 FAX 145636864
The Royal Alma is located in a quiet street in the lively business district near the banks of the River Seine between the Champs Elysées and the Eiffel Tower, with all the major couture houses in the vicinity. There are 64 rooms including suites and apartments which are tastefully decorated and equipped with all the amenities one could expect in a prestigious and renowned establishment such as this. It also has a congenial bar, a restaurant and conference room whilst parking facilities are available.
Near river In town centre
64 en suite (bth/shr) (16 fmly) TV in all bedrooms STV Radio in rooms Direct dial from all bedrooms Mini-bar in all bedrooms Licensed Lift Night porter Full central heating Child discount available 12yrs Last d 23.30hrs Languages spoken: English,Italian,Spanish
ROOMS: (room only) s 1380-2500FF; d 1380-2500FF

Reductions over 1 night

MEALS: Full breakfast 95FF Continental breakfast 95FF Lunch 30-67FF Dinner 30-67FF✱
CARDS: ⊕ ▆▆ ▆ ⏺ Travellers cheques

★ ★ ★ ★ Hotel San Regis

12 rue Jean Goujon *75008*
☎ 144951616
The hotel opened its doors in 1923 and has undergone extensive renovation over the years. It is decorated throughout with beautiful period furniture and the bedrooms are furnished with exquisite taste, providing luxurious en-suite facilities and the highest levels of comfort. With its intimate bar and elegant restaurant, cosy lounges and winter garden, it provides a truly unique setting for a comfortable stay.
In town centre
44 en suite (bth/shr) (6 fmly) (3 with balcony) TV in all bedrooms STV Radio in rooms Direct dial from all bedrooms Mini-bar in all bedrooms Licensed Lift Night porter Full central heating Air conditioning in bedrooms Child discount available Last d 22.00hrs Languages spoken: English,German,Italian,Spanish
CARDS: ⊕ ▆▆ ▆ ⏺ Travellers cheques

★ ★ ★ ★ Sofitel Paris Arc De Triomphe

14 rue Beaujon *75008*
☎ 153895050 FAX 153895051
A haven of calm and quiet close to the Champs-Elysées, built at the turn of the century and completely renovated in 1987. Bedrooms are personalised and some floors are exclusively for non-smokers.
In town centre
135 en suite (bth) (21 fmly) (10 with balcony) No smoking in 80 bedrooms TV in all bedrooms STV Direct dial from all bedrooms Mini-bar in all bedrooms Licensed Lift Night porter Full central heating Air conditioning in bedrooms Bicycle rental Last d 22.30hrs Languages spoken: English, German, Italian, Portuguese & Russian
ROOMS: (room only) s 1950-2400FF; d 2200-2650FF
Reductions over 1 night
MEALS: Full breakfast 120FF Continental breakfast 120FF Lunch 250-390FF&alc Dinner 250-390FF&alc
CARDS: ⊕ ▆▆ ▆ ⏺

★ ★ ★ ★ Sofitel Paris Champs-Elysées

8 rue Jean Goujon *75008*
☎ 140746464 FAX 140746499
With all the modern comfort expected of a hotel in this category, where an entire floor is reserved for the comfort of non-smoking guests. This hotel boasts Napoleon III-style architecture and is located in the heart of Paris.
In town centre
40 en suite (bth) (2 with balcony) No smoking in 14 bedrooms TV in all bedrooms Direct dial from all bedrooms Mini-bar in all bedrooms Licensed Lift Night porter Full central heating Air conditioning in bedrooms Open parking available (charged) Covered parking available (charged) Child discount available 12yrs Open terrace V meals Last d 22.00hrs Languages spoken: English, Brazilian, German & Spanish
ROOMS: (room only) s 1500-1950FF; d 1600-1950FF
MEALS: Full breakfast 150FF Continental breakfast 100FF Lunch 165FF&alc Dinner 165FF&alc
CARDS: ⊕ ▆▆ ▆ ⏺

★ ★ ★ ★ **De la Tremoille**
14 r La Tremoille *75008*
☎ 147233420 FAX 140700108
Built in 1883, the hotel has been completely renovated, but still contains the relaxed style of a fine private house. It offers superb elegance on a small scale and has a special appeal for those seeking peace and privacy in the heart of Paris. The lobby and lounge are furnished in Louis XV style and the wood panelled bar leads to a charming dining room where excellent cuisine is served.
In town centre
107 en suite (bth/shr) (36 with balcony) TV in all bedrooms STV Radio in rooms Direct dial from all bedrooms Mini-bar in all bedrooms Room-safe Licensed Lift Night porter Full central heating Air conditioning in bedrooms Child discount available 12yrs Last d 22.30hrs Languages spoken: English,Italian,Spanish
ROOMS: (room only) s 1360FF; d 2260-2950FF
MEALS: Full breakfast 130FF Continental breakfast 110FF Lunch 220FF&alc Dinner 220FF&alc
CARDS: ● ■ ■ ● JCB Travellers cheques

★ ★ ★ ★ **Vernet**
25 rue Vernet *75008*
☎ 144319800 FAX 144318569
The hotel dates back to the turn of the century and has been entirely renovated in recent years. The building has retained all its original character and offers elegant surroundings with modern comfort. Rooms are furnished to a high standard and equipped with en-suite marbled bathrooms. The restaurant with its Belle-Epoque decor serves an imaginative cuisine in splendid surroundings.
Near river Forest area In town centre Near motorway
57 en suite (bth/shr) (12 with balcony) TV in all bedrooms STV Radio in rooms Direct dial from all bedrooms Mini-bar in all bedrooms Room-safe Licensed Lift Night porter Full central heating Air conditioning in bedrooms Open parking available (charged) Covered parking available (charged) Supervised Child discount available 12yrs Indoor swimming pool (heated) Squash Sauna Jacuzzi/spa Last d 22.30hrs Languages spoken: English,German,Italian,Spanish
ROOMS: (room only) s 1700-1900FF; d 2100-2500FF
Reductions over 1 night Special breaks
MEALS: Full breakfast 160FF Continental breakfast 130FF Lunch fr 310FF&alc Dinner fr 390FF&alc✱
CARDS: ● ■ ■ ● Travellers cheques

★ ★ ★ ★ **Hotel Waldorf-Madelèine**
12 bd Malesherbes *75008*
☎ 142657206 FAX 140071045
Situated in the heart of Paris, and conveniently located for the fashionable boutiques, antique shops and restaurants as well as the many cultural and historic sights the capital has to offer, the Scandic hotels have an elegant interior where high quality furnishings and fabrics create a luxurious atmosphere. The guest accommodation has excellent en suite facilities with personal touches, and provides the highest level of comfort.
In town centre
45 en suite (bth/shr) TV in all bedrooms Direct dial from all bedrooms Mini-bar in all bedrooms Licensed Lift Night porter Air conditioning in bedrooms Child discount available 12yrs Languages spoken: English,Italian,Spanish
CARDS: ● ■ ■ ● Travellers cheques

★ ★ ★ ★ **Hotel le Warwick**
5 rue de Berri *75008*
☎ 145631411 FAX 143590098
This modern hotel is just a few steps away from the Champs-Elysées and the lively bustle of the city. It offers traditional hospitality and charm in contemporary surroundings. The spacious bedrooms provide elegant accommodation and a high standard of comfort, there is a piano-bar and the restaurant is widely known for its imaginative cuisine.
In town centre
147 en suite (bth/shr) (28 with balcony) No smoking in 26 bedrooms TV in all bedrooms STV Radio in rooms Direct dial from all bedrooms Mini-bar in all bedrooms Room-safe Licensed Lift Night porter Full central heating Air conditioning in bedrooms Open parking available (charged) Covered parking available (charged) Supervised Child discount available 12yrs Wkly live entertainment V meals Languages spoken: English,German,Spanish
ROOMS: (room only) s 1700-2100FF; d 2000-2600FF
CARDS: ● ■ ■ ● Travellers cheques

9TH ARRONDISSEMENT

★ ★ ★ **Anjou-Lafayette** (Best Western)
4 rue Riboutte, Angle 82 rue Lafayette *75009*
☎ 142468344 FAX 148000897
In convenient proximity to all the major department stores and sights, the hotel is located in a quiet street. It provides peaceful accommodation and offers well equipped sound-proofed bedrooms. There is a cosy bar-lounge for relaxation.
In town centre
39 en suite (bth/shr) (5 fmly) TV in all bedrooms STV Radio in rooms Direct dial from all bedrooms Mini-bar in all bedrooms Licensed Lift Night porter Full central heating Child discount available 12yrs Languages spoken: English,Spanish,Italian,Portuguese
CARDS: ● ■ ■ ● Travellers cheques

★ ★ ★ **Hotel Blanche Fontaine**
34 rue Fontaine *75009*
☎ 145267232 FAX 142810552
The hotel enjoys a private setting at the foot of Montmartre and features a peaceful atmosphere throughout. The bedrooms are spacious and offer comfortable accommodation, and guests are assured of an attentive and personal service.
In town centre
49 en suite (bth/shr) (10 fmly) (12 with balcony) No smoking in 4 bedrooms TV in all bedrooms STV Radio in rooms Direct dial from all bedrooms Licensed Lift Night porter Full central heating Covered parking available (charged) Supervised Child discount available Open terrace Languages spoken: English,German,Spanish,Italian
CARDS: ● ■ ■ ● Travellers cheques

★ ★ ★ **Brébant**
32 bd Poissonnière *75009*
☎ 147702555 FAX 142466570
The hotel can be found just a few minutes away from the Grands Boulevards and offers the attractive combination of elegant interiors blended with modern day convenience. It has individually styled bedrooms offering a high degree of comfort, and a restaurant where inventive cuisine and select wines feature strongly on the menu.
In town centre
122 en suite (bth/shr) (22 fmly) TV in all bedrooms STV Radio in rooms Direct dial from all bedrooms Mini-bar in all bedrooms Licensed Lift Night porter Full central heating

Child discount available 12yrs Last d 22.30hrs Languages spoken: English,Spanish,Italian,Portuguese
MEALS: Full breakfast 48FF Lunch 98-198FF Dinner 98-198FF✱
CARDS: ✪ ▬ ☱ ⑩ Travellers cheques

★★★ Hotel du Havre
18 rue d'Amsterdam *75009*
☎ 142857274 FAX 148742239
Located in the business and touristic district in the centre of Paris close to the Opéra, the Madeleine and the Champs-Elysées.
In town centre Near motorway
81 en suite (bth/shr) (15 fmly) (5 with balcony) No smoking in 10 bedrooms TV in all bedrooms STV Direct dial from all bedrooms Room-safe Licensed Lift Night porter Full central heating Air conditioning in bedrooms Child discount available 12yrs Languages spoken: English, German & Spanish
ROOMS: (room only) s 400-600FF; d 450-700FF
Reductions over 1 night
MEALS: Full breakfast 49FF Continental breakfast 39FF
CARDS: ✪ ▬ ☱ ⑩ Travellers cheques

★★★ Hotel Marena
27 rue de la Tour d'Auvergne *75009*
☎ 148780133 FAX 140230711
Located between the Opéra and Montmartre and just a few steps away from all the shops, the hotel features peaceful guest accommodation with modern facilities. Attentive staff provide a friendly and efficient service in this informal establishment.
In town centre
36 en suite (bth/shr) TV in all bedrooms STV Direct dial from all bedrooms Lift Night porter Full central heating
Languages spoken: English,Italian,Spanish,German

★★★ Hotel de Morny
4 rue de Liège *75009*
☎ 142854792 FAX 140164484
Situated close to the Saint-Lazare railway station, the Opéra, the big department stores, as well as all the theatres, the hotel is the ideal venue for both tourists and business travellers, who wish to take full advantage of the attractions and business facilities which the capital has to offer.
Forest area In town centre
41 en suite (bth/shr) (5 fmly) (2 with balcony) TV in all bedrooms Direct dial from all bedrooms Mini-bar in all bedrooms Licensed Lift Full central heating Child discount available 12yrs Languages spoken: English,Spanish
ROOMS: s fr 545FF; d fr 710FF ✱
CARDS: ✪ ▬ ☱ ⑩ Travellers cheques

★★ Hotel Parrotel Paris Montholon
11 bis rue Pierre Sémard *75009*
☎ 148782894 FAX 142801115
This popular hotel is ideally located in the heart of Paris and features functional bedrooms with modern amenities. There are pleasant public areas and a cafeteria serves hot and cold drinks. Staff are cheerful and competent.
In town centre
46 en suite (bth/shr) TV in all bedrooms STV Radio in rooms Direct dial from all bedrooms Lift Night porter Full central heating Child discount available 10yrs Languages spoken: English,German

★★ Hotel Riboutte Lafayette
5 rue Riboutté *75009*
☎ 147706236 FAX 148009150
This small peaceful establishment is situated in the centre of

the capital and offers an enjoyable stay in informal surroundings. It features individually styled bedrooms with good modern amenities. The tastefully-decorated public areas are adorned with various objects d'art.
In town centre
24 en suite (bth/shr) TV in all bedrooms STV Direct dial from all bedrooms Lift Full central heating Child discount available 8yrs Languages spoken: English,Italian,Arabic
CARDS: ✪ ▬ ☱ Travellers cheques

★★ Hotel Adix
30 rue Lucien Sampaix *75010*
☎ 142081974 FAX 142082728
Because of their ideal location, the hotels in the Jardin de Paris group, provide a good base to explore the capital with its many cultural and historic sights. Comfortable bedrooms are equipped with modern facilities and provide a high degree of comfort. There are no restaurant facilities, but a large choice of eating establishments can be found nearby.
In town centre
39 rms (4 fmly) TV in all bedrooms Direct dial from all bedrooms Lift Night porter Full central heating Child discount available 12yrs Open terrace Languages spoken: English,German,Italian
CARDS: ✪ ▬ ☱ ⑩ Travellers cheques

★★ Climat de France
31 bd de Strasbourg *75010*
☎ 147702500 Cen Res 164460123 FAX 147703217
(City Centre near Place de la Republique)
Surrounded by the bustling daily life of the capital, the hotel has comfortable bedrooms which provide a restful night's sleep after a day of sightseeing, and which are fitted with good modern amenities. Dedicated staff provide a 'round the clock' service and are always on hand with advice if needed.
In town centre Near motorway
57 en suite (bth/shr) (4 fmly) No smoking in 15 bedrooms TV in all bedrooms Direct dial from all bedrooms Lift Night porter Full central heating Open terrace Languages spoken: English, Italian & Spanish
CARDS: ✪ ☱

★★ Français
13 rue du 8 Mai 1945 *75010*
☎ 140359414 FAX 140355540
The establishment is situated in a lively area not far from all the shops. Over the years it has acquired a faithful following amongst an international clientele and features well equipped bedrooms with extensive facilities offering an above average level of comfort. Arrangements have been made for free parking for guests, 100 metres from the hotel.
In town centre
71 en suite (bth/shr) (4 fmly) (20 with balcony) TV in all bedrooms STV Radio in rooms Direct dial from all bedrooms Mini-bar in all bedrooms Room-safe Licensed Lift Night porter Full central heating Child discount available 16yrs Languages spoken: English,German,Italian,Spanish
ROOMS: (room only) s 300-460FF, d 420-460FF
CARDS: ✪ ▬ ☱ ⑩ Travellers cheques

★★ Hotel Frantour Château-Landon
1/3 rue Château-Landon *75010*
☎ 144653333 FAX 144653320
Located near all the major transport services, the hotel is popular with both commercial and leisure travellers.

contd.

It features comfortable accommodation, various lounges and a congenial bar where guests can enjoy a drink or a quick meal.
In town centre
160 en suite (bth/shr) No smoking in 29 bedrooms TV in all bedrooms STV Radio in rooms Direct dial from all bedrooms Room-safe Licensed Lift Night porter Full central heating Air conditioning in bedrooms Child discount available 11yrs V meals Last d 23.00hrs Languages spoken: English,Spanish,German
ROOMS: s 520FF; d 600FF
MEALS: Full breakfast 40FF Lunch 70-150FFalc Dinner 50-130FFalc✱
CARDS: ●● ▩ ▩ ◑ Travellers cheques

★ ★ ★ ★ Pavillon
38 rue de l'Echiquier *75010*
☎ 142469275 FAX 142470397
(100m from "Grand Boulevards" district)
Located in a quiet street just a few yards away from the bustle of the main shopping streets, the hotel L'Horset Pavillon offers its clientele the charm and genuine atmosphere of a 'Belle Epoque' interior - stained-glass, frescos and wood panelling contribute to an original and enchanting decor. The guest rooms have been entirely refurbished in a style which is completely in keeping with the spirit and style of the area. This district, known as 'Les Grands Boulevards', has numerous theatres, restaurants, cinemas and bistros as well as The Louvre and the Folies Bergères within walking distance.
In town centre
92 en suite (bth/shr) (12 fmly) No smoking in 14 bedrooms TV in all bedrooms STV Radio in rooms Direct dial from all bedrooms Mini-bar in all bedrooms Licensed Lift Night porter Full central heating Air conditioning in bedrooms Child discount available 12yrs V meals Languages spoken: English,German,Italian,Spanish
ROOMS: (room only) s 690-890FF; d 990-1090FF ✱
MEALS: Full breakfast 80FF Continental breakfast 80FF Lunch 90-180FF&alc
CARDS: ●● ▩ ▩ ◑ Travellers cheques

★ ★ ★ Hotel de Rocroy
13 rue Rocroy *75010*
☎ 12811568 FAX 18783081
Not far from all the places of interest in Montmartre, the hotel extends a warm welcome to its visitors and features guest rooms equipped with all modern facilities. It has a cosy bar and is close to some charming little bistros in the area.
In town centre Near motorway
55 en suite (bth/shr) No smoking in 15 bedrooms TV in all bedrooms STV Radio in rooms Direct dial from all bedrooms Licensed Lift Night porter Full central heating Child discount available 12yrs Languages spoken: English,Portuguese
CARDS: ●● ▩ ▩ ◑ Travellers cheques

11TH ARRONDISSEMENT

★ ★ ★ All Suite Hotel
74 rue Amelot *75011*
☎ 140212000 FAX 147008240
In town centre
289 en suite (bth) (8 fmly) No smoking in 18 bedrooms TV in all bedrooms STV Direct dial from all bedrooms Mini-bar in 44 bedrooms Room-safe (charged) Licensed Lift Night porter Full central heating Air conditioning in bedrooms Open parking available (charged) Covered parking available (charged) Supervised Child discount available 12yrs Open

terrace V meals Languages spoken: English, German & Italian
MEALS: Full breakfast 110FF Continental breakfast 60FF Lunch 140-350FF&alc Dinner 140-350FF&alc✱
CARDS: ●● ▩ ▩ ◑

★ ★ ★ ★ Holiday Inn Paris République
10 pl de la République *75011*
☎ 143554434 FAX 147003234
In town centre
318 en suite (bth/shr) (80 fmly) No smoking in 58 bedrooms TV in all bedrooms STV Radio in rooms Direct dial from all bedrooms Mini-bar in all bedrooms Licensed Lift Night porter Full central heating Air conditioning in bedrooms Child discount available 5yrs Open terrace Last d 22.30hrs Languages spoken: English,Dutch
CARDS: ●● ▩ ▩ ◑ Travellers cheques

★ ★ ★ Home Plaza St Antoine
289 bis rue de Faubourg, St Antoine *75011*
☎ 140094000 FAX 140091155

In town centre
89 en suite (bth) (15 fmly) No smoking in 6 bedrooms TV in all bedrooms STV Direct dial from all bedrooms Mini-bar in all bedrooms Room-safe (charged) Licensed Lift Night porter Full central heating Open parking available (charged) Covered parking available (charged) Child discount available Open terrace Languages spoken: English, German, Italian & Spanish
MEALS: Continental breakfast 65FF✱
CARDS: ●● ▩ ▩ ◑

Taking your mobile phone to France?
See page 11

★ ★ Hotel de Mericourt
50 rue de la Folie-Méricourt *75011*
☎ 143387363 FAX 143386613

(exit Périphérique at Porte de Vincennes)
The hotel is located in a quiet street between the the Place de la
République and Opéra Bastille, with all the main tourist
attractions nearby. Completely renovated throughout, it
features sound-proofed bedrooms with private facilities.
Breakfast is served in the delightful winter garden.
In town centre
28 en suite (bth) No smoking in 7 bedrooms TV in all
bedrooms Radio in rooms Direct dial from all bedrooms Lift
Night porter Full central heating No children Special
arrangements for AA Guide users Languages spoken: English
ROOMS: s 360-570FF; d 480-700FF **Special breaks**
CARDS: ● ■ ■ Travellers cheques

★ ★ ★ New Hotel Candide
3 rue Petion *75011*
☎ 143790233 FAX 143790688
This charming hotel is situated not far from the smart Marais
district and offers its visitors the well-balanced combination of
old fashioned hospitality and modern comfort. The guest
accommodation is equipped with modern amenities and to
ensure that you fully enjoy your stay.
In town centre
48 en suite (bth/shr) TV in all bedrooms STV Radio in rooms
Direct dial from all bedrooms Mini-bar in all bedrooms Lift
Night porter Full central heating Child discount available
12yrs Languages spoken: English, Arabic, German, Italian,
Spanish
CARDS: ● ■ ■ ●

12TH ARRONDISSEMENT

★ ★ ★ Hotel Claret
44 bd de Bercy *75012*
☎ 146284131 FAX 149280929
A former coaching inn, the hotel has retained all its original
charm. The comfortable bedrooms have modern amenities and
offer a good level of comfort, whilst the rustic restaurant
serves enjoyable meals in informal surroundings.
In town centre
52 en suite (bth/shr) (1 fmly) No smoking in 10 bedrooms TV
in all bedrooms Licensed Lift Night porter Full central
heating Open parking available (charged) Covered parking
available (charged) Child discount available 12yrs Open
terrace Last d 23.00hrs Languages spoken:
English,German,Spanish

★ ★ Climat de France
9 rue de Reuilly *75012*
☎ 143700404 FAX 143709653
(nr Place de la Nation)
The bedrooms in this establishment are attractively
furnished with well co-ordinated fabrics and shades and
provide comfortable guest accommodation. Friendly staff
provide an attentive service and put a lot of effort into caring
for their guests.
In town centre
43 en suite (bth/shr) (11 with balcony) TV in all bedrooms
Direct dial from all bedrooms Lift Night porter Full central
heating Open parking available (charged) Covered parking
available (charged) Languages spoken: English
CARDS: ● ■

★ ★ Hotel Frantour Paris-Lyon
2 pl Louis-Armand *75012*
☎ 143448484 FAX 143474194
Standing beside the big clock tower of the Gare de Lyon, this
modern and completely renovated hotel offers a comfortable
setting for visits to the major historic sights. All the
bedrooms are equipped with modern facilities and offer a
good level of comfort.
Near river Forest area In town centre Near motorway
315 en suite (bth) (2 with balcony) TV in all bedrooms STV
Radio in rooms Licensed Lift Night porter Languages
spoken: German,Italian,Spanish
CARDS: ● ■ ■ ● Travellers cheques

★ ★ ★ Hotel Lyon Bastille
3 rue Parrot *75012*
☎ 143434152 FAX 143438116
(travel east on Peripherique, leave at Porte de Vincennes &
follow av de la Porte de Vincennes & cont to Place de la
Nation. At rdbt turn onto Blvd Diderot, continue, then turn
right at Av Daumesnil & rue Parrot just a bit further on left)
For more than a century this hotel has proudly maintained the
true traditions of the hotel trade with its warm reception and
personal service. The hotel is constantly upgrading its facilities
to provide the maximum of comfort to its clientele. It features
elegant bedrooms with up-to-date amenities and pleasant
public areas.
In town centre
48 en suite (bth/shr) (5 fmly) (7 with balcony) TV in all
bedrooms Radio in rooms Room-safe (charged) Licensed
Lift Night porter Full central heating Child discount
available 12yrs Languages spoken: English, German, Italian,
Spanish
ROOMS: (room only) s 496-541FF; d 582-652FF
Reductions over 1 night
CARDS: ● ■ ■ ● JCB Travellers cheques

★ ★ ★ Pavillon Bastille
65 rue de Lyon *75012*
☎ 143436565 FAX 143439652
(street is opposite the Opera National de Paris)
This establishment is situated near the Gare de Lyon, and
offers its visitors the informal atmosphere of a private house.
The ancient paved courtyard with 17th century fountain is
complemented by a tastefully decorated interior which is
innovative in design. It features spacious bedrooms with
excellent modern facilities, whilst cheerful and efficient service
is provided by the competent staff.
Near river In town centre Near motorway
25 en suite (bth/shr) (7 fmly) No smoking in 3 bedrooms

contd.

TV in all bedrooms STV Direct dial from all bedrooms Mini-bar in all bedrooms Licensed Lift Night porter Full central heating Air conditioning in bedrooms Open terrace Languages spoken: English
ROOMS: (room only) s 650-955FF; d 650-955FF
CARDS: ●● ▦ ▬ ⑨ Travellers cheques

★ ★ ★ Relais Mercure Nation
61 rue de la Voûte *75012*
☎ 143454138 FAX 143430411
Because of their ideal location, the hotels in the Jardin de Paris group provide a good base to explore the capital with its many cultural and historic sights. Comfortable bedrooms are equipped with modern facilities and provide a high degree of comfort. There are no restaurant facilities, but a large choice of eating establishments can be found nearby.
In town centre
47 rms (8 fmly) TV in all bedrooms Direct dial from all bedrooms Child discount available 12yrs Languages spoken: English
CARDS: ●● ▦ ▬ ⑨ JCB Travellers cheques

13TH ARRONDISSEMENT

★ ★ ★ Holiday Inn Garden Court
21 rue de Toubiac *75013*
☎ 145846161 FAX 145844338
Near river Forest area In town centre Near motorway
71 en suite (bth/shr) TV in all bedrooms STV Direct dial from all bedrooms Mini-bar in all bedrooms Licensed Lift Night porter Full central heating Air conditioning in bedrooms Open parking available (charged) Covered parking available (charged) Child discount available 12yrs Languages spoken: English, German & Spanish
ROOMS: (room only) s 690-890FF; d 690-890FF
MEALS: Full breakfast 65FF
CARDS: ●● ▦ ▬ ⑨ Travellers cheques

14TH ARRONDISSEMENT

★ ★ Ariane Montparnasse
35 rue de la Sablière *75014*
☎ 145456713 FAX 145453949
(between Montparnasse and Porte of Orleans - A6. Close to the metro Pernety - Alesia.)
Located close to the main transport facilities, this hotel offers entirely renovated, modern bedrooms. There is a breakfast room and pleasant lounge and guests are ensured a comfortable stay.
In town centre
30 en suite (bth/shr) (4 fmly) TV in all bedrooms Direct dial from all bedrooms Mini-bar in all bedrooms Lift Night porter Full central heating Child discount available 14yrs Languages spoken: English, Italian, Spanish, German
ROOMS: (room only) s 375-395FF; d 395-425FF
Reductions over 1 night
CARDS: ●● ▦ ▬ ⑨ Travellers cheques

★ ★ Climat de France
55 rue de Plaisance *75014*
☎ 145428143 Cen Res 164460123 FAX 145429787
(near Montparnasse(TGV Station) and 'Parc des Expositions' of Porte de Versailles)
Situated near Montparnasse and the 'Parc des Expositions' the hotel offers easy access to all the business centres and cultural sites in Paris. The comfortable, sound-proofed bedrooms are attractively furnished and vary in style and size. There are no

restaurant facilities in the hotel, but numerous eating establishments can be found in the vicinity.
In town centre
40 en suite (bth/shr) TV in all bedrooms Direct dial from all bedrooms Licensed Lift Night porter Full central heating Languages spoken: English & Spanish
CARDS: ●● ▬

★ ★ ★ Forum Val de Loire
20 bis rue de la Gaîté *75014*
☎ 140643737 FAX 140643749
A charming hotel in the Montparnasse area, all bedrooms are tastefully decorated.
In town centre
14 en suite (bth/shr) (4 fmly) TV in all bedrooms STV Direct dial from all bedrooms Mini-bar in all bedrooms Licensed Lift Night porter Full central heating Air conditioning in bedrooms Open parking available (charged) Child discount available 12yrs Last d 22.30hrs Languages spoken: English, German & Spanish
ROOMS: (room only) s 870-1020FF; d 900-1020FF
Reductions over 1 night Special breaks
MEALS: Full breakfast 65FF Continental breakfast 65FF Lunch 102-165FFalc Dinner 130-165FFalc✱
CARDS: ●● ▦ ▬ ⑨ Travellers cheques

★ ★ Hotel Istria
29 r Campagne-Première *75014*
☎ 143209182 FAX 143224845
Situated near the Jardin du Luxembourg, the Hotel Istria used to be a popular watering hole for painters from the Surrealist movement of the 1920s; the foyer and dining room still bear the hallmarks of that era. Recently renovated, it now offers accommodation with modern-day facilities complemented by a friendly staff providing attentive service.
In town centre
26 en suite (bth/shr) TV in all bedrooms Direct dial from all bedrooms Room-safe Lift Night porter Full central heating Languages spoken: English,Spanish
ROOMS: s 400-510FF; d 610-680FF **Reductions over 1 night Special breaks**
CARDS: ●● ▦ ▬ ⑨ Travellers cheques

★ ★ Hotel la Mascotte
22 rue Hippolyte-Maindron *75014*
☎ 140445151 FAX 140445898
Because of their ideal location, the hotels in the Jardin de Paris group, provide a good base to explore the capital with its many cultural and historic sights. Comfortable bedrooms are equipped with modern facilities and provide a high degree of comfort. There are no restaurant facilities, but a large choice of eating establishments can be found nearby.
In town centre
52 rms (3 fmly) TV in all bedrooms STV Direct dial from all bedrooms Lift Night porter Full central heating Open parking available (charged) Covered parking available (charged) Supervised Child discount available 12yrs Languages spoken: English
CARDS: ●● ▦ ▬ ⑨ JCB Travellers cheques

★ ★ ★ ★ Meridien Montparnasse Paris
19 rue Ct-Réné Mouchotte *75014*
☎ 144364436 FAX 144364900
(from Périphériques exit at Porte d'Orleans, follow direction of Montparnasse towards Gae Montparnasse railway station, hotel behind railway station)
Just a stone's throw away from Saint-Germain-des-Prés and

the Jardin du Luxembourg, this state-of-the-art hotel offers a wide range of unrivalled facilities for both business and leisure travellers. The tastefully decorated guest accommodation provides a relaxing stay in comfortable surroundings. The restaurants serve a wide choice of dishes, which vary from traditional cuisine to brasserie-style cooking.
Near motorway
953 en suite (bth/shr) TV in all bedrooms STV Radio in rooms
Direct dial from all bedrooms Mini-bar in all bedrooms
Licensed Lift Night porter Full central heating Air conditioning in bedrooms Open parking available (charged)
Covered parking available (charged) Supervised Child discount available 12yrs V meals Languages spoken: English,German,Spanish,Italian
ROOMS: (room only) s 1300-2075FF; d 1300-2075FF
Reductions over 1 night Special breaks
MEALS: Full breakfast 115FF Continental breakfast 85FF
Lunch fr 195FF Dinner fr 195FF✱
CARDS: 💳 💳 💳 💳 JCB

★ ★ Hotel Moulin Vert
74 rue du Moulin Vert *75014*
☎ 145436538 FAX 145430886
Situated in a quiet area, the hotel welcomes its visitors in a warm and friendly atmosphere and offers attractively furnished bedrooms with modern facilities. Close to the major transport facilities, it provides a good base to explore the city.
In town centre
28 rms TV in all bedrooms Direct dial from all bedrooms Mini-bar in all bedrooms Lift Night porter Full central heating Child discount available 15yrs Languages spoken: English,Italian
CARDS: 💳 💳 💳 💳 Travellers cheques

★ ★ Hotel Primavera
147 ter rue d'Alésia *75014*
☎ 145420637 FAX 145424456
Because of their ideal location, the hotels in the Jardin de Paris group, provide a good base to explore the capital with its many cultural and historic sights. Comfortable bedrooms are equipped with modern facilities and provide a high degree of comfort. There are no restaurant facilities, but a large choice of eating establishments can be found nearby.
In town centre
70 rms (7 fmly) TV in all bedrooms Radio in rooms Direct dial from all bedrooms Mini-bar in all bedrooms Lift Night porter Full central heating Open parking available (charged)
Covered parking available (charged) Supervised Child discount available 12yrs Languages spoken: English
CARDS: 💳 💳 💳 💳 Travellers cheques

15TH ARRONDISSEMENT

★ ★ ★ Ares (Relais du Silence)
7 rue du Général-de-Larminat *75015*
☎ 147347404 FAX 147344856
This charming hotel is set in the very heart of Paris and offers its clientele a warm reception upon arrival. With historic buildings, numerous restaurants and cafés nearby, it is the ideal venue to explore the capital. In addition, it offers stylish bedrooms with spacious en suite facilities.
In town centre
42 en suite (bth/shr) (12 fmly) TV in all bedrooms STV Direct dial from all bedrooms Mini-bar in all bedrooms Room-safe Lift Night porter Full central heating

Child discount available 12yrs Languages spoken: English,German,Italian,Spanish
ROOMS: (room only) s 525-645FF; d 690-790FF
CARDS: 💳 💳 💳 💳 Travellers cheques

★ ★ ★ Hotel du Bailli de Suffren
149 av de Suffren *75015*
☎ 147345861 FAX 145677582
Individually furnished rooms attractively decorated are available at this charming hotel. Between Montparnasse and Invalides, close to the embassies and ministries along the elegant Avenue de Suffren.
In town centre
25 en suite (bth/shr) TV in all bedrooms STV Direct dial from all bedrooms Mini-bar in all bedrooms Room-safe Lift Night porter Full central heating Child discount available 12yrs Languages spoken: English, German, Portuguese & Spanish
ROOMS: (room only) s 595-670FF; d 725-800FF
MEALS: Continental breakfast 55FF
CARDS: 💳 💳 💳 💳 Travellers cheques

★ ★ Hotel Délos
7 rue du Général-Beuret *75015*
☎ 148282932 FAX 148288846
Located in a residential area close to Montmartre, this peaceful hotel welcomes its visitors into a friendly, informal atmosphere. It offers bright bedrooms providing comfortable accommodation and good amenities.
In town centre
43 rms (33 shr) (4 with balcony) TV in all bedrooms Lift Night porter Full central heating Child discount available 14yrs Languages spoken: English,Spanish
CARDS: 💳 💳 💳 💳 Travellers cheques

★ ★ Hotel Grenelle
140-142 bd de Corenelle *75015*
☎ 145752654 FAX 145777394
In town centre
56 en suite (bth/shr) TV in all bedrooms STV Mini-bar in all bedrooms Licensed Lift Night porter Child discount available 12yrs Languages spoken: English,Italian
CARDS: 💳 💳 💳 💳 Travellers cheques

★ ★ Hotel Lécourbe (Consort)
20 rue Lécourbe *75015*
☎ 147344906 FAX 147346465
In the late 19th century the Laborde-Lécourbe family acquired the house that was to become the Hotel Lécourbe. The family collected many objects d'art, curiosities and books which now adorn the interior of the hotel and create the informal atmosphere of a private house. The guest accommodation is decorated with good taste and has every modern convenience.
contd.

In town centre
47 en suite (bth/shr) (4 fmly) TV in all bedrooms STV Radio in rooms Direct dial from all bedrooms Mini-bar in all bedrooms Lift Night porter Full central heating Supervised

Child discount available 12yrs Languages spoken: English German & Italian
ROOMS: (room only) s 460FF; d 510FF
CARDS: 😊 ▬ ☲ ◑ Travellers cheques

★ ★ ★ **Montcalm** (Best Western)
50 av Félix Faure *75015*
☎ 145549727 FAX 145541505
Located in a residential area of the 15th arrondisement, this peaceful villa-style hotel is surrounded by a delightful flower-filled garden. It features attractively furnished guest-rooms equipped with modern amenities offering a good standard of comfort, complemented by friendly staff who provide courteous service.
Near river In town centre Near motorway
41 en suite (bth/shr) (1 fmly) TV in all bedrooms STV Radio in rooms Direct dial from all bedrooms Mini-bar in all bedrooms Room-safe Licensed Lift Night porter Full central heating Child discount available 12yrs Open terrace Languages spoken: English Arabic Chinese & German
ROOMS: (room only) s 420-610FF; d 490-710FF
Reductions over 1 night
MEALS: Full breakfast 52FF✹
CARDS: 😊 ▬ ☲ ◑ Travellers cheques

★ ★ **Hotel Tour Eiffel**
11 rue Juge *75015*
☎ 145782929 FAX 145786000
As its name indicates this hotel is very close to the Eiffel Tower in the heart of the tourist quarter. Bedrooms have every modern convenience, the hotel was recently completely renovated and redecorated.
In town centre
40 en suite (bth/shr) (5 fmly) (5 with balcony) No smoking in 18 bedrooms TV in all bedrooms STV Direct dial from all bedrooms Lift Night porter Full central heating Covered parking available (charged) Child discount available 12yrs Open terrace Languages spoken: English, German, Italian & Spanish
ROOMS: (room only) s 390-670FF; d 390-670FF
MEALS: Full breakfast 43FF✹
CARDS: 😊 ▬ ☲ ◑ Travellers cheques

Taking your mobile phone to France?
See page 11

★ ★ ★ **Belmont**
30 rue Bassano *75016*
☎ 147237241 FAX 147230970
This turn-of-the century building is situated in one of the most prestigious districts in Paris, and offers all the modern day comfort which one has come to expect from a three star hotel. The bedrooms are tastefully furnished and equipped with up-to-date facilities. Cheerful staff provide an attentive service and ensure that guests are well looked after.
In town centre
79 en suite (bth/shr) (5 fmly) (12 with balcony) TV in all bedrooms STV Radio in rooms Direct dial from all bedrooms Mini-bar in all bedrooms Licensed Lift Night porter Full central heating Child discount available 12yrs Languages spoken: English, Spanish, Portuguese, Italian, Arabic
CARDS: 😊 ▬ ☲ ◑ Travellers cheques

★ ★ ★ ★ **Elysées Régencia** (Best Western)
41 av Marceau *75116*
☎ 147204265 FAX 149520342
In town centre
41 en suite (bth/shr) (4 fmly) No smoking in 12 bedrooms TV in all bedrooms STV Radio in rooms Direct dial from all bedrooms Mini-bar in all bedrooms Room-safe Licensed Lift Night porter Full central heating Air conditioning in bedrooms Open parking available (charged) Covered parking available (charged) Supervised Child discount available 12yrs Languages spoken: English,Spanish
ROOMS: (room only) s 960-1560FF; d 1070-1870FF
Reductions over 1 night Special breaks
CARDS: 😊 ▬ ☲ ◑ Travellers cheques

★ ★ ★ **Hotel Étoile Maillot**
10 rue du Bois de Boulogne *75116*
☎ 145004260 FAX 145005589
A few steps away from the Arc de Triomphe and the Palais des Congrès, a short walk from the Champs Elysées and close to La Défense. Hotel Étoile Maillot offers the charm of a small traditional hotel combining antique furniture with all the modern facilities required today.
28 en suite (bth/shr) (1 fmly) (10 with balcony) TV in all bedrooms STV Direct dial from all bedrooms Mini-bar in all bedrooms Licensed Lift Night porter Full central heating Child discount available 12yrs Languages spoken: English & Spanish
ROOMS: s 615-745FF; d 690-820FF **Special breaks**
CARDS: 😊 ▬ ☲ ◑ Travellers cheques

★ ★ ★ **Holiday Inn Garden Court**
21 rue Gudin *75016*
☎ 146519922 FAX 146510724
(close to Porte St Cloud & Parc des Princes)
Located in a very lively neighbourhood at the corner of the Avenue de Versailles and the Square Porte de St Cloud. A charming quaint, completely renovated 1930's style hotel. The interior architecture has been kept in the 1930's style, but with all the modern comforts.
In town centre
47 en suite (bth/shr) (7 fmly) (10 with balcony) No smoking in 14 bedrooms TV in all bedrooms STV Direct dial from all bedrooms Mini-bar in all bedrooms Room-safe Licensed Lift Night porter Full central heating Air conditioning in bedrooms Child discount available 12yrs Languages spoken: English, German, Russian & Spanish

ROOMS: (room only) s 710-780FF; d 780-980FF
Reductions over 1 night
CARDS: ●● ▆▆ ☲ ●〕Travellers cheques

★ ★ ★ Hotel Résidence Imperiale (Best Western)
155 av Malakoff *75116*
☎ 145002345 FAX 145018882
The hotel dates back to the beginning of this century and was extensively renovated in 1990. It is ideally located, not far from the commercial centre, haute-couture boutiques and tourist attractions. The bedrooms are equipped with modern amenities and those on the fifth floor feature sloping ceilings with authentic exposed beams.
In town centre
37 en suite (bth/shr) (5 fmly) No smoking in 2 bedrooms TV in all bedrooms STV Radio in rooms Direct dial from all bedrooms Mini-bar in all bedrooms Licensed Lift Night porter Full central heating Air conditioning in bedrooms Child discount available 12yrs Languages spoken: English, German, Spanish, Italian
CARDS: ●● ▆▆ ☲ ●〕Travellers cheques

★ ★ Hotel Keppler
12 rue Keppler *75016*
☎ 147206505 FAX 147230229
(near pl de l'Étoile Arc de Triumph)
This small, charming hotel in the heart of Paris, surrounded by the main sights and historic monuments, offers the combination of an informal interior - decorated with period furniture, and assorted antiques - with modern facilities. A cosy atmosphere prevails throughout, and ensures that guests will enjoy their stay in this 'home from home',
In town centre
49 en suite (bth/shr) TV in all bedrooms STV Direct dial from all bedrooms Licensed Lift Night porter Full central heating Child discount available 10yrs Languages spoken: English & Spanish
ROOMS: (room only) s 460-470FF; d 460-470FF
MEALS: Continental breakfast 30FF
CARDS: ●● ▆▆ ☲ Travellers cheques

★ ★ ★ Kléber
7 rue de Belloy *75016*
☎ 147238022 FAX 149520720
The hotel stands in close proximity to the Champs-Elysées and the many museums and fashion boutiques. The interior has recently been completely renovated and now offers very comfortable rooms in a Napoleonic style.
In town centre
22 en suite (bth/shr) (4 fmly) (5 with balcony) No smoking in 6 bedrooms TV in all bedrooms STV Radio in rooms Direct dial from all bedrooms Licensed Lift Night porter Full central heating Open parking available (charged) Supervised Languages spoken: English,Spanish,Arabic,Japanese,Hebrew
ROOMS: (room only) s 690-790FF; d 690-890FF
Reductions over 1 night Special breaks
CARDS: ●● ▆▆ ☲ ●〕JCB Travellers cheques

★ ★ Au Palais de Chaillot
35 av Raymond Poincaré *75116*
☎ 153700909 FAX 153700908
(leave the Périphérique at Porte Maillot in direction of Trocadero Avenues Malakoff then Av Raymond Poincaré)
The establishment is located in one of the residential streets near the Eiffel Tower and was completely renovated in 1996. It offers peaceful accommodation away from the lively bustle of the capital, and comfortable bedrooms with good amenities.

Staff are friendly and helpful and provide an efficient service.
Near river Near lake Forest area In town centre Near motorway
28 en suite (bth/shr) (5 fmly) TV in all bedrooms STV Direct dial from all bedrooms Lift Night porter Full central heating Child discount available 12yrs Open terrace Languages spoken: English,German, Italian,Spanish
ROOMS: (room only) s 450FF; d 520-590FF **Reductions over 1 night**
CARDS: ●● ▆▆ ☲ ●〕Travellers cheques

★ ★ ★ ★ Le Parc Westin Démeure Hotel
55-57 av Raymond Poincaré *75116*
☎ 144056666 FAX 144056600
(follow direction for Périphérique Ouest at Porte Maillot exit take avenue Raymond Poincaré, after Place V-Hugo continue straight ahead until reaching Le Parc on right)
Situated in the heart of the smart 16th arrondissement, the Hotel Le Parc's five buildings are grouped around a delightful private garden. The hotel has been completely renovated under the guidance of the distinguished British interior designer Nina Campbell and now smoothly combines the ultimate comfort and elegance of an English manor house with traditional French hospitality. From the foyer to the elegant bedrooms, fabrics and furnishings blend harmoniously together. Located in a magnificent Parisian town house, the adjacent 'Le Parc' restaurant has the reputation of being one of the best in the world and serves an array of imaginative and inventive dishes.
Forest area In town centre Near motorway
116 en suite (bth/shr) (3 fmly) No smoking in 32 bedrooms TV in all bedrooms STV Radio in rooms Direct dial from all bedrooms Mini-bar in all bedrooms Room-safe Licensed Lift Night porter Full central heating Air conditioning in bedrooms Child discount available 10yrs Gym Pool table Jacuzzi/spa Open terrace Last d 22.30hrs Languages spoken: English,Spanish,Italian,Portuguese,German

ROOMS: (room only) s 1990FF; d 2300-3500FF ✱
Reductions over 1 night Special breaks
MEALS: Full breakfast 135FF Lunch 300-450FFalc Dinner 300-450FFalc✱
CARDS: ●● ▆▆ ☲ ●〕JCB Travellers cheques

▲ ▲ ▲ ▲ Hotel Raphaël
17 av Kléber *75116*
☎ 144280028 FAX 145012150
Stepping over the threshold of the Hotel Raphaël, visitors are transported back into an era of charm and sumptuous elegance. The fabulously decorated public rooms and suites are a testimony to the comfort and tranquillity of bygone times. Splendid wood-panelling and oil-paintings

contd.

197

adorn the hotel throughout and are complemented by spacious guest accommodation with extensive facilities. The cosy English bar is ideal for enjoying a cocktail, whilst the restaurant offers the perfect setting for a memorable meal.
In town centre
90 en suite (bth/shr) (38 fmly) (2 with balcony) No smoking in 16 bedrooms TV in all bedrooms STV Radio in rooms Direct dial from all bedrooms Mini-bar in all bedrooms Room-safe Licensed Lift Night porter Full central heating Air conditioning in bedrooms Open terrace V meals Last d 22.00hrs Languages spoken: English,Spanish,German,Italian
ROOMS: (room only) s 1950-2350FF; d 2350-4200FF
MEALS: Full breakfast 175FF Continental breakfast 135FF Lunch 298FF&alc Dinner 295FF&alc
CARDS: 🐳 💳 🏧 ⑨ JCB Travellers cheques

★ ★ ★ Régina de Pasy
6 av de la Tour *75116*
☎ 145244364 FAX 140507062
The Hotel Regina de Pasy dates back to the 1930's which is apparent in its attractive interior with elegant furnishings and fabrics. It features a spacious foyer, a stylish bar and guest rooms which are decorated in a discreet fashion and equipped with every modern day convenience. Breakfast is served in the rooms or guests can enjoy a comprehensive breakfast-buffet in the downstairs lounge.
Near river In town centre
64 en suite (bth/shr) (4 fmly) (23 with balcony) TV in all bedrooms STV Direct dial from all bedrooms Mini-bar in all bedrooms Licensed Lift Night porter Full central heating Languages spoken: English,German
CARDS: 🐳 💳 🏧 ⑨ Travellers cheques

★ ★ ★ Hotel du Rond Point de Longchamp
86 rue de Longchamp *75116*
☎ 145051363 FAX 147551280
Situated in the 'Golden Triangle' of the Champs Elysées, Trocadéro and the Avenue Victor Hugo, the hotel features an interior where comfort and refined elegance create the setting for an enjoyable stay. A good proportion of the rooms have direct views of the Eiffel Tower, and all are equipped with private facilities. There is an intimate bar for relaxation, whilst Paris offers countless attractions to see and experience.
In town centre
57 en suite (bth/shr) (1 fmly) (6 with balcony) No smoking in 10 bedrooms TV in all bedrooms STV Radio in rooms Direct dial from all bedrooms Mini-bar in all bedrooms Room-safe Licensed Lift Night porter Full central heating Air conditioning in bedrooms Pool table Languages spoken: English & Spanish
ROOMS: (room only) s 606-2006FF; d 812-2012FF
CARDS: 🐳 💳 🏧 ⑨ Travellers cheques

★ ★ ★ ★ Hotel St-James Paris
43 av Bugeaud *75116*
☎ 144058181 FAX 144058182
This magnificent residence is the only chateau-hotel in the whole of Paris. Originally a private house where some of France's most eminent scholars lived and worked, it now features luxurious guest accommodation offering the highest degree of comfort. From its imposing foyer to elegant public rooms it offers a combination of traditional and contemporary styles. It also has a cosy library-bar, an elegant restaurant and a winter-garden.
Near river In town centre Near motorway
48 en suite (bth/shr) 2 rooms in annexe (6 fmly) TV in all bedrooms STV Direct dial from all bedrooms Mini-bar in all

bedrooms Licensed Lift Night porter Full central heating Air conditioning in bedrooms Open parking available Supervised Child discount available 12yrs Sauna Solarium Gym Jacuzzi/spa Open terrace V meals Last d 22.00hrs Languages spoken: English, German, Italian & Spanish
ROOMS: (room only) s fr 1650FF; d 1900-3800FF
MEALS: Full breakfast 135FF Continental breakfast 110FF Lunch 300FF&alc Dinner 300FF&alc✱
CARDS: 🐳 💳 🏧 ⑨ Travellers cheques

★ ★ ★ Hotel de Sevigné
6 rue de Belloy *75116*
☎ 147208890 FAX 140709873
This traditional establishment is situated in a prestigious, residential part of Paris, and just a stone's throw from the Champs-Elysées, it offers attractively furnished guest rooms which provide peaceful accommodation. There is a comfortable lounge for relaxation and guests are well looked after by competent staff who offer an attentive, friendly service throughout their stay.
In town centre Near motorway
30 en suite (bth/shr) (8 fmly) (10 with balcony) TV in all bedrooms STV Radio in rooms Direct dial from all bedrooms Mini-bar in all bedrooms Licensed Lift Night porter Full central heating Open parking available (charged) Covered parking available (charged) V meals Languages spoken: English
CARDS: 🐳 💳 🏧 ⑨ Travellers cheques

★ ★ ★ Hotel Résidence Trocadero (Best Western)
3 av Raymond Poincaré *75116*
☎ 147273330 FAX 147278085
Situated in the prestigious 16th arrondisement the hotel features bedrooms which have been designed to ensure maximum comfort for guests. It caters for business and holiday makers alike and friendly staff ensure that guests are well looked after. Breakfast is served in the cheerful lounge overlooking a flower-decked terrace.
Near river In town centre Near motorway
27 en suite (bth/shr) TV in all bedrooms STV Direct dial from all bedrooms Mini-bar in all bedrooms Room-safe Licensed Lift Night porter Full central heating Child discount available 12yrs Open terrace Languages spoken: English,Spanish,Italian,Arabic
ROOMS: (room only) s 490-670FF; d 560-780FF
Reductions over 1 night
CARDS: 🐳 💳 🏧 ⑨ JCB Travellers cheques

★ ★ ★ Arc de Triomphe Étoile
3 rue de l'Étoile *75017*
☎ 143803694 FAX 144404919
This charming hotel offers its visitors a personal welcome in a family atmosphere where comfortable furnishings create the cosy setting for a relaxing stay in the heart of Paris. It features pleasant bedrooms with good quality amenities, a lounge-library for relaxation and a breakfast room. Entirely renovated, the hotel is now fully adapted to the needs of business travellers.
Forest area In town centre
25 en suite (bth/shr) (10 fmly) TV in all bedrooms STV Radio in rooms Direct dial from all bedrooms Licensed Lift Night porter Full central heating Child discount available 12yrs Languages spoken: English,Italian,Spanish
CARDS: 🐳 💳 🏧 ⑨ Travellers cheques

★ ★ ★ Astor

36 rue P-Démours *75017*
☎ 147646767 FAX 140539134
Situated in one of the smartest districts of Paris, the Hotel Astor offers a combination of elegant comfort and modern convenience. Staff are friendly and provide an attentive round the clock service. The bedrooms are individually appointed, furnished with good taste, and offer high quality accommodation.
In town centre
45 en suite (bth/shr) (6 fmly) (6 with balcony) TV in all bedrooms STV Radio in rooms Direct dial from all bedrooms Mini-bar in all bedrooms Lift Full central heating Child discount available 10yrs Indoor swimming pool (heated) Sauna Jacuzzi/spa Languages spoken: English,Spanish
CARDS: ✿ ▆▆ ▆▆ ➒ Travellers cheques

★ ★ ★ Centre Ville Étoile

6 rue des Acacias *75017*
☎ 143805618 FAX 147549343
(take Périphérique exit Porte Maillot/La Défense in direction of Porte Maillot, at lights keep on left until roundabout of Palais de Congres, take Avenue de la Grande Armée in direction of Arc de Triomphe, Rue des Arcacias is on left)
This Art-Déco style furnished hotel is situated between the Place d'Étoile and Porte Maillot. It features tastefully decorated bedrooms with spacious en suite facilities, and guests are well looked after by an attentive and efficient staff.
Forest area
20 en suite (bth/shr) (2 fmly) No smoking in 5 bedrooms TV in all bedrooms STV Direct dial from all bedrooms Mini-bar in all bedrooms Room-safe Licensed Lift Night porter Full central heating Air conditioning in bedrooms Languages spoken: English,German,Italian,Spanish
ROOMS: (room only) s 590-790FF; d 690-890FF ✱
Reductions over 1 night Special breaks
CARDS: ✿ ▆▆ ▆▆ ➒ JCB Travellers cheques

★ ★ ★ Hotel Champerret-Elysées

129 av de Villiers *75017*
☎ 147644400 FAX 147631058
Located in the residential 17th arrondisement, and just minutes away from the Arc de Triomphe, Opéra and Eiffel Tower, the hotel features well fitted bedrooms - some equipped with the latest communication technology to accommodate business travellers - which provide a high degree of comfort. To start off the day guests are served a comprehensive breakfast-buffet and can relax in the cosy bar-lounge after a day of sight-seeing in the capital.
In town centre
45 en suite (bth/shr) (2 fmly) No smoking in 20 bedrooms TV in all bedrooms STV Direct dial from all bedrooms Mini-bar in all bedrooms Licensed Lift Night porter Full central heating Child discount available 12yrs V meals Languages spoken: English,German,Italian
ROOMS: (room only) s 450-675FF; d 450-685FF
Reductions over 1 night
CARDS: ✿ ▆▆ ▆▆ ➒ Travellers cheques

★ ★ ★ ★ Hotel Concorde la Fayette

3 pl du Général-Koeing *75017*
☎ 140685068 FAX 140685043
Strategically located for business and only five minutes from the L'Arc de Triomphe and La Défense, the hotel is directly connected to the Palais de Congrès de Paris, Europe's largest conference centre, which incorporates varied entertainment, services and shops. It features extensive guest accommodation with excellent facilities, where all the rooms have fine views over the capital. There is a choice of three restaurants where the cuisine alternates between gastronomic dishes and buffet-style and quick-meal eating options. With unsurpassed leisure facilities and services available it is one of the most well appointed contemporary hotels in Paris.
Forest area In town centre Near motorway
No smoking in 96 bedrooms TV in 970 bedrooms STV Radio in rooms Direct dial from 970 bedrooms Mini-bar in 970 bedrooms Licensed Lift Night porter Full central heating Air conditioning in bedrooms Open parking available (charged) Covered parking available (charged) V meals Languages spoken: English,German,Italian,Japanese,Spanish
MEALS: Full breakfast 112FF Continental breakfast 98FF Lunch 56-194FFalc✱
CARDS: ✿ ▆▆ ▆▆ ➒ Travellers cheques

★ ★ ★ Étoile Park Hotel

10 av Mac Mahon *75017*
☎ 142676963 FAX 143801899
A short distance from the Arc de Triomphe, the Étoile Park Hotel is ideally situated for business and sightseeing in Paris.
28 en suite (bth/shr) TV in all bedrooms STV Direct dial from all bedrooms Lift Open parking available
ROOMS: s 600FF; d 650FF ✱

★ ★ ★ Étoile Péreire (Relais du Silence)

146 bd Péreire *75017*
☎ 142676000 FAX 142670290
This small, charming hotel offers bedrooms with modern amenities, most overlooking the peaceful courtyard. It is situated just 10 minutes away from the Place d'Étoile and close to all the main transport facilities. It serves a large breakfast with over 40 different jams to be sampled.
In town centre
26 en suite (bth/shr) (4 fmly) TV in all bedrooms Direct dial from all bedrooms Mini-bar in all bedrooms Licensed Lift Night porter Full central heating Child discount available 6yrs Languages spoken: English,Italian,Spanish
CARDS: ✿ ▆▆ ▆▆ ➒ JCB Travellers cheques

★ ★ ★ Étoile St-Ferdinand (Best Western)

36 rue St-Ferdinand *75017*
☎ 145726666 FAX 145741292
A warm welcome awaits guests in this charming establishment where attentive staff render a friendly service. It has carefully renovated bedrooms offering a good standard of comfort, a pleasant lounge with cosy seating arrangements, and a cheerful dining room where an excellent breakfast is served in the morning.
Near river Forest area In town centre Near motorway
42 en suite (bth/shr) (5 fmly) TV in all bedrooms STV Direct dial from all bedrooms Mini-bar in all bedrooms Licensed Lift Night porter Full central heating Child discount available 12yrs Languages spoken: English,German,Spanish
CARDS: ✿ ▆▆ ▆▆ ➒ Travellers cheques

★ ★ ★ Hotel Fertel Étoile

4 rue des Acacias *75017*
☎ 147667775 FAX 147664790
(from the Périphérique take direction of Porte Maillot, then Avenue de la Grande Armée; drive around the Arc de Triomphe & onto Avenue Carnot, continue to end of street & Rue des Acacias on left)
Between the Arc de Triomphe and Porte Maillot, guests are welcomed to an elegant and refined setting.

contd.

In town centre
51 en suite (bth/shr) TV in all bedrooms STV Direct dial from all bedrooms Licensed Lift Child discount available 12yrs Languages spoken: English, Arabic & Spanish
ROOMS: (room only) s 590-710FF; d 650-770FF
CARDS: ●● ▬▬ ◑

★ ★ ★ Hotel Fertel Maillot
269 blvd Péreire *75017*
☎ 144099292 FAX 144099494
In front of the Palais des Congrès and a short distance from the Arc de Triomphe.
Forest area In town centre
35 en suite (bth/shr) (1 fmly) TV in all bedrooms STV Direct dial from all bedrooms Mini-bar in all bedrooms Lift Night porter Air conditioning in bedrooms Child discount available 12yrs
ROOMS: (room only) s 580FF; d 640FF ✱
MEALS: Continental breakfast 55FF✱
CARDS: ●● ▬▬ ◑

★ ★ Hotel Flaubert
19 rue Rennequin *75017*
☎ 146224435 FAX 143803234
Located near Place des Ternes, just 5 minutes on foot from the Arc de Triumph, this small charming house is built around a pretty garden with birds and an abundance of flowers. The rooms are well appointed and comfortable, and some open on to the garden. There is a friendly, family atmosphere.
37 en suite (bth/shr) TV in all bedrooms Direct dial from all bedrooms Mini-bar in all bedrooms Licensed Lift Night porter Full central heating Open parking available (charged) Covered parking available (charged) Supervised Languages spoken: English, Russian & Spanish
ROOMS: (room only) s 400-480FF; d 480-550FF
CARDS: ●● ▬▬ ▬▬ ◑ Travellers cheques

Frantour Paris Berthier
163 bis av de Clichy *75017*
☎ 140252000 FAX 140252600
In town centre Near motorway
700 rms TV in all bedrooms Direct dial from all bedrooms Licensed Lift Night porter Full central heating Open parking available (charged) Covered parking available (charged) Indoor swimming pool (heated) Sauna Solarium Gym Jacuzzi/spa V meals
ROOMS: s 575FF; d 630FF

★ ★ ★ ★ Le Meriden
81 bd Gouvion St-Cyr *75848*
☎ 140683434 FAX 140683131
'Le Meridien Etoile' is situated in heart of Paris's bustling business centre between 'La Défense' and the Champs Elysées and has an unrivalled range of business facilities on offer. There is Le Club President on two floors, three restaurants including Le Clos Longchamp which is reputed to be one of the Capital's finest and where a superb cuisine incorporating dishes from many corners of the world are served against an elegant decor. The Lionel Hampton jazz club is known as the jazz temple of Paris and provides the ideal setting in which to unwind with many well-known bands and artists performing on a regular basis.
Near lake Forest area In town centre Near motorway
1025 en suite (bth/shr) No smoking in 156 bedrooms TV in all bedrooms STV Radio in rooms Direct dial from all bedrooms Mini-bar in all bedrooms Licensed Lift Night porter

Air conditioning in bedrooms Open parking available (charged) Covered parking available (charged) Child discount available 12yrs V meals
ROOMS: (room only) s 1400-2600FF; d 1400-2600FF
Reductions over 1 night
MEALS: Full breakfast 115FF Continental breakfast 85FF Lunch fr 158FF Dinner fr 158FF✱
CARDS: ●● ▬▬ ▬▬ ◑

★ ★ ★ Eber Monceau (Relais du Silence)
18 rue Léon Jost *75017*
☎ 146226070 FAX 147630101
A small, charming hotel peacefully situated in a quiet street just a few steps away from Parc Monceau and the lively Champs-Elysées. This turn-of-the-century house features cheerfully decorated bedrooms which vary in size, a cosy salon-bar, and a delightful courtyard. The untiring host, Jean-Marc Eber, provides an attentive and friendly service, the satisfaction of the guests being his prime consideration.
In town centre Near motorway
18 en suite (bth/shr) (3 fmly) (1 with balcony) TV in all bedrooms STV Radio in rooms Direct dial from all bedrooms Mini-bar in all bedrooms Licensed Lift Night porter Full central heating Covered parking available (charged) Supervised Child discount available Open terrace Languages spoken: English,Spanish
CARDS: ●● ▬▬ ▬▬ ◑ Travellers cheques

★ ★ ★ Neuville
3 rue Verniquet *75017*
☎ 143802630 FAX 143803855
This former private house dates from the 19th century and is located in a quiet street in a smart residential area. A personal welcome awaits guests on arrival and it features well-appointed bedrooms with all modern conveniences. In addition there is a cosy bar and an attractive garden.
Forest area In town centre Near motorway
28 en suite (bth/shr) (4 fmly) TV in all bedrooms STV Radio in rooms Direct dial from all bedrooms Licensed Lift Night porter Full central heating Open parking available (charged) Covered parking available (charged) Child discount available 12yrs Languages spoken: English,German,Spanish
ROOMS: (room only) s 590-750FF; d 590-750FF
CARDS: ●● ▬▬ ▬▬ ◑ Travellers cheques

★ ★ L'Ouest Hotel
165 rue de Rome *75017*
☎ 142275029 FAX 142272740
The hotel is located just a few steps away from the main sights and historic monuments. The interior is decorated with cheerful, bright colours throughout, whilst the functional bedrooms are equipped with modern facilities and offer a straightforward level of comfort.
48 en suite (bth/shr) TV in all bedrooms Radio in rooms Direct dial from all bedrooms Licensed Lift Night porter Full central heating Supervised Child discount available Languages spoken: English,Arabic,Italian
CARDS: ●● ▬▬ ▬▬ ◑ Travellers cheques

★ ★ ★ Primotel Empire (Best Western)
3 rue Montenotte *75017*
☎ 143801455 FAX 147660433
The hotels in the Primotel group all have modern bedrooms equipped with every modern day convenience and provide a high degree of comfort. Their restaurants serve a high standard of cooking where a choice of traditional and regional dishes feature strongly on the menu; whilst competent staff

offer attentive service and traditional hospitality in a cordial atmosphere.
In town centre
49 en suite (bth/shr) (6 fmly) (9 with balcony) TV in all bedrooms STV Direct dial from all bedrooms Mini-bar in all bedrooms Licensed Lift Full central heating Child discount available 12yrs Languages spoken: English,Italian,Spanish
CARDS: ●● ▦ ▆▆ ❿ Travellers cheques

★ ★ ★ Hotel Regents Garden (Best Western)
6 rue Pierre Demours *75017*
☎ 145740730 FAX 140550142
This charming hotel was built by Napoleon III for his personal physician, and offers an oasis of peace for those who stay here. With its antique furniture, cosy interior, and warm hospitality it represents a typically traditional French hotel. The bedrooms are smartly appointed and overlook the delightful courtyard garden, where on fine days breakfast is served.
In town centre
39 en suite (bth/shr) TV in all bedrooms Radio in rooms Direct dial from all bedrooms Mini-bar in all bedrooms Licensed Lift Night porter Full central heating Open parking available (charged) Child discount available 12yrs Languages spoken: English,German,Italian
CARDS: ●● ▦ ▆▆ ❿ JCB Travellers cheques

★ ★ Hotel St Cyr et des Ternes
101 av des Ternes *75017*
☎ 145748742 FAX 145725755
(in front of the Palais des Congres)
Hotel St Cyr & des Ternes, situated between l'Etoile and La Défense, offers elegant harmony in a contemporary setting.
In town centre Near motorway
34 en suite (bth/shr) (3 fmly) No smoking in 4 bedrooms TV in all bedrooms STV Direct dial from all bedrooms Mini-bar in 18 bedrooms Licensed Lift Night porter Full central heating Child discount available 10yrs Languages spoken: English & Spanish
ROOMS: (room only) s 320-500FF; d 400-530FF
MEALS: Continental breakfast 35FF✱
CARDS: ●● ▦ ▆▆

★ ★ ★ Hotel Stella
20 av Carnot *75017*
☎ 143808450 FAX 147660194
36 en suite (bth/shr) TV in all bedrooms STV Direct dial from all bedrooms Lift
ROOMS: s 546FF; d 572FF ✱
MEALS: Continental breakfast 60FF✱

★ ★ ★ Hotel Ternes Arc de Triomphe
97 av des Ternes *75017*
☎ 153819494 FAX 153819495
An attractive blend of refined decoration and warm colours, designed to offer complete comfort and a friendly atmosphere. Very close to the Champs Elysées and the Arc de Triomphe, the hotel is well situated at the heart of the business district of Paris and just a few minutes from the main historical sights.
In town centre Near motorway
39 en suite (bth/shr) (1 fmly) (3 with balcony) No smoking in 27 bedrooms TV in all bedrooms STV Direct dial from all bedrooms Mini-bar in all bedrooms Licensed Lift Night porter Full central heating Air conditioning in bedrooms Languages spoken: German & Italian
ROOMS: (room only) s 590-830FF; d 590-830FF
CARDS: ●● ▦ ▆▆ ❿ Travellers cheques

18TH ARRONDISSEMENT

★ ★ Climat de France
51 rue Letort *75018*
☎ 142576440 Cen Res 164460123 FAX 142576425
(from Peripherique take Porte de Clignancourt exit)
Guests receive a friendly welcome in this establishment, where staff are attentive and provide competent service throughout. The en suite bedrooms have up-to-date modern amenities and provide a good level of comfort.
In town centre Near motorway
50 en suite (bth/shr) (1 fmly) TV in 51 bedrooms Radio in rooms Direct dial from 51 bedrooms Lift Night porter Full central heating Open terrace Languages spoken: English, German & Spanish
CARDS: ●● ▆▆

★ ★ Eden Hotel
90 rue Ordener *75018*
☎ 142646163 FAX 142641143
Close to the famous flea market and the landmark of Sacré Coeur. The owners offer a warm welcome to their attractive comfortable hotel in a picturesque neighbourhood at the foot of Montmartre.
In town centre
35 en suite (bth/shr) TV in all bedrooms STV Direct dial from all bedrooms Lift Night porter Full central heating Open parking available (charged) Covered parking available (charged) Child discount available Languages spoken: English & German
ROOMS: (room only) s 345-380FF; d 380-420FF
CARDS: ●● ▦ ▆▆ ❿ Travellers cheques

★ ★ Hotel Ordener
131 rue Ordener *75018*
☎ 142529900 FAX 142642816
Because of their ideal location, the hotels in the Jardin de Paris group provide a good base to explore the capital with its many cultural and historic sights. Comfortable bedrooms are equipped with modern facilities and provide a high degree of comfort. There are no restaurant facilities, but a large choice of eating establishments can be found nearby.
In town centre
38 rms TV in all bedrooms Direct dial from all bedrooms Lift Night porter Full central heating Child discount available 12yrs Languages spoken: English
CARDS: ●● ▦ ▆▆ ❿ JCB Travellers cheques

★ ★ Prima Lépic
29 rue Lépic *75018*
☎ 146064464 FAX 146066611
With its trompe-l'oeil decor resembling a flower garden, the hotel has been compared to a spring bouquet in the centre of Montmartre. This charming place has tastefully furnished bedrooms with modern amenities, and cosy public rooms. Situated in the most picturesque part of the city, it offers comfortable accommodation in charming surroundings.
In town centre
38 en suite (bth/shr) (3 fmly) (3 with balcony) TV in all bedrooms Lift Night porter Full central heating Child discount available Languages spoken: English
CARDS: ●● ▆▆ Travellers cheques

★ ★ ★ ★ Terrass Hotel
12 rue Joseph-de-Maistre *75018*
☎ 146067285 FAX 142522911
The Hotel Terrass encapsulates the unique atmosphere of Montmartre. From the foyer to the Provençale-style restaurant, imaginative furnishings and fabrics continue to surprise. The well-appointed bedrooms offer elegant accommodation and a high standard of comfort. The menu features a wide array of inventive dishes, whilst in summer meals are served on the terrace with fine views across the capital.
In town centre
101 en suite (bth/shr) (13 fmly) (12 with balcony) No smoking in 17 bedrooms TV in all bedrooms STV Mini-bar in all bedrooms Licensed Lift Night porter Full central heating Covered parking available (charged) Child discount available 12yrs Open terrace Last d 22.00hrs Languages spoken: English,German
CARDS: ●● ▆▆ ▆▆ ●) Travellers cheques

★ ★ Utrillo
7 rue Aristide Bruant *75018*
☎ 142581344 FAX 142239388
Located in a quiet street in Montmartre, and not far away from the Place du Tetre, the hotel offers contemporary accommodation and comfort. It features a completely renovated interior decorated with reproductions from the famous painter Utrillo. The bedrooms have modern amenities and are very comfortable.
In town centre
30 en suite (bth/shr) (1 fmly) TV in all bedrooms Direct dial from all bedrooms Mini-bar in all bedrooms Lift Night porter Full central heating Child discount available 12yrs Sauna Languages spoken: English,German
CARDS: ●● ▆▆ ▆▆ ●) Travellers cheques

19TH ARRONDISSEMENT

★ ★ ★ ★ Holiday Inn Paris-La-Villette
216 av Jean Jaurès *75019*
☎ 144841818 FAX 144841820
This purpose-built hotel is set in a vast expanding area in the northern part of the city. The spacious bedrooms are well equipped with the up-to-date facilities expected from a four star hotel. There is a congenial bar and the brasserie-style restaurant serves traditional French cuisine, whilst the lounge on the 20th floor offers splendid panoramic views across Paris.
Near river Forest area In town centre Near motorway
182 en suite (bth/shr) (56 fmly) No smoking in 28 bedrooms TV in all bedrooms STV Radio in rooms Direct dial from all bedrooms Mini-bar in all bedrooms Licensed Lift Night porter Full central heating Air conditioning in bedrooms Open parking available (charged) Covered parking available (charged) Child discount available 19yrs Sauna Jacuzzi/spa Open terrace V meals Languages spoken: English,Dutch,German,Spanish
CARDS: ●● ▆▆ ▆▆ ●) Travellers cheques

20TH ARRONDISSEMENT

★ Tamaris
14 rue des Maraichers *75020*
☎ 143728548 FAX 143568175
Situated in a quiet street near the Port de Vincennes, the hotel has pleasant bedrooms with good amenities. It has a TV lounge and breakfast room, and because of its location, it provides a suitable base to explore all the major sights and tourist attractions in the area.

Forest area In town centre Near motorway
42 rms TV available Direct-dial available Lift Night porter Full central heating Languages spoken: English

PONTAULT-COMBAULT Seine-et-Marne

★ ★ ★ Les Relais Bleus
Parc d'Activites des Arpents *77340*
☎ 360294242 Cen Res 164460616
Les Relais Bleus offer comfortable accommodation and good value at the two star level. They cater for both family and business clientele, with relaxed dining and public areas.
Forest area Near motorway
60 en suite (bth/shr) TV in all bedrooms STV Direct dial from all bedrooms Licensed Lift Night porter Full central heating Open parking available Supervised Pool table Languages spoken: English,German,Italian

PROVINS Seine-et-Marne

★ ★ ★ Hostellerie Aux Vieux Remparts
3 rue Couverté-Ville Haute *77160*
☎ 164089400 FAX 360677722
This charming hotel is situated in the medieval heart of the city and offers a flower-decked, shady terrace, comfortable guest accommodation and a splendid restaurant. Situated 85 kilometres from Paris, between Brie and Champagne, it is ideally situated for visits to all the main sights in the town and places of interest in the surrounding region.
Forest area Near motorway
25 en suite (bth/shr) (2 fmly) TV in all bedrooms Radio in rooms Licensed Lift Full central heating Open parking available Supervised Child discount available 12yrs Open terrace Last d 21.30hrs Languages spoken: English, German
MEALS: Full breakfast 50FF Lunch 150-350FF&alc Dinner 150-350FF&alc✱
CARDS: ●● ▆▆ ▆▆ ●) Travellers cheques

PUTEAUX Hauts-de-Seine

★ ★ ★ Hotel le Dauphin
45 rue Jean-Jaurés *92800*
☎ 147737363 FAX 146980882
In the heart of Paris, just a few minutes away from l'Etoile and a short walk from Bois de Boulogne.
30 en suite (bth/shr) TV in all bedrooms Direct dial from all bedrooms Lift Open parking available
ROOMS: s 540FF; d 540FF ✱
CARDS: ▆▆ ●)

★ ★ Hotel de Dion Bouton
19 quai de Dion Bouton
☎ 142043554 FAX 145063951
In a prime location on the banks of the River Seine, facing the Bois de Boulogne. The hotel offers peaceful and pleasant surroundings.
33 en suite (bth/shr) TV in all bedrooms Direct dial from all bedrooms Lift Open parking available
ROOMS: s 460FF; d 460FF ✱
CARDS: ●● ▆▆ ●)

★ ★ ★ Hotel Princesse Isabelle
72 rue Jean Jaurès *92800*
☎ 147788006 FAX 147752520
In the centre of Paris-la-Défense, close to the Champs Elysées. This elegant and comfortably furnished hotel has rooms

overlooking a flowered patio with all modern facilities.
36 en suite (bth/shr) TV in all bedrooms STV Direct dial from
all bedrooms Lift Open parking available
ROOMS: s 685FF; d 685FF ✱
MEALS: Continental breakfast 50FF✱

★ ★ ★ Syjac Hotel
20 quai de Dion-Bouton 92800
☎ 142040304 FAX 145067869
(close to Porte Maillot (air terminal), take direction of La
Défense & drive along the River Seine, hotel near Pont de
Puteaux)
The hotel is at the heart of Puteaux, a district that is being
completely renovated. Reflecting modern elegence and
comfort the rooms are equipped with all the refinements
necessary to make your stay comfortable.
In town centre
33 en suite (bth/shr) (2 fmly) TV in all bedrooms STV Direct
dial from all bedrooms Mini-bar in all bedrooms Lift Full
central heating Child discount available 12yrs Sauna Solarium
Open terrace Languages spoken: English German & Spanish
ROOMS: (room only) s 570-670FF; d 670-750FF
✱ Special breaks: (weekends)
CARDS: 💳 ▣ ▣ ◉

★ ★ ★ Hotel Victoria
85 blvd Richard Wallace 92800
☎ 145065551 FAX 140990597
(Arriving in Paris take the Périphérique Ouest then exit La
Défense, follow signs for Puteaux Centre)
In front of Puteaux station, this provincial hotel in the heart of
Paris offers comfort and tranquillity. Rooms are tastefully
decorated and have every modern convenience.
Near river In town centre
32 en suite (shr) (12 fmly) No smoking in 12 bedrooms TV in
all bedrooms STV Direct dial from all bedrooms Mini-bar in
all bedrooms Room-safe Licensed Lift Night porter Full
central heating Child discount available 12yrs Sauna Solarium
Gym Languages spoken: English, German & Spanish
ROOMS: (room only) s 395-450FF; d 450-540FF
✱ Special breaks
CARDS: 💳 ▣ ▣ ◉ Travellers cheques

RAMBOUILLET Yvelines

★ ★ Climat de France
Lieu dit "La Louvière" 78120
☎ 134856262 Cen Res 164460123 FAX 130592357
(off N306)
The guest rooms in this hotel have pleasant modern
furnishings and provide a good level of comfort. As well as
fully equipped conference rooms, the hotel has a choice of
leisure facilities including a heated swimming pool, tennis
court and mountain bikes to explore the surrounding region.
The restaurant has a comprehensive menu with a choice of
traditional dishes with a regional touch.
Forest area Near motorway
67 en suite (bth/shr) 23 rooms in annexe TV available Direct-
dial available Licensed Night porter Full central heating
Open parking available Supervised Outdoor swimming pool
(heated) Tennis V meals
CARDS: 💳 ▣

ROISSY-CHARLES-DE-GAULLE (AÉROPORT) Val-D'Oise

★ ★ ★ ★ Copthorne Paris Charles de Gaulle
allee du Verger, Zone Hotelière 95700
☎ 134293333 FAX 134290305
(from Paris: A1 or A3 towards Lille, exit Charles de Gaulle-
Roissy en France. Follow Roissy en France-zone Hoteliere.
from Lille: A1 towards Paris, exit Roissy Charles de Gaulle.
zone hoteliere.)
Forest area In town centre Near motorway
237 en suite (bth/shr) (237 fmly) No smoking in 60 bedrooms
TV in all bedrooms STV Radio in rooms Direct dial from all
bedrooms Mini-bar in all bedrooms Licensed Lift Night
porter Full central heating Air conditioning in bedrooms
Open parking available (charged) Covered parking available
(charged) Supervised Child discount available 12yrs Indoor
swimming pool (heated) Sauna Solarium Gym Jacuzzi/spa
Open terrace Covered terrace V meals Languages spoken:
English Italian German Dutch Spanish Portugese
ROOMS: (room only) s 1050-2500FF; d 1050-2500FF
**Special breaks: (weekend package, 650f upon
availability)**
MEALS: Full breakfast 85FF Continental breakfast 60FF Lunch
99-250FF&alc Dinner 99-250FF&alc
CARDS: 💳 ▣ ▣ ◉ JCB Travellers cheques

★ ★ ★ ★ Hotel Holiday Inn Paris Charles de Gaulle
1 allee du Verger BP30 95700
☎ 134293000 FAX 134299052
Forest area Near motorway
243 en suite (bth) (53 fmly) No smoking in 58 bedrooms TV in
all bedrooms STV Radio in rooms Direct dial from all
bedrooms Licensed Lift Full central heating Air conditioning
in bedrooms Open parking available (charged) Supervised
Child discount available 12yrs Indoor swimming pool (heated)
Sauna Gym V meals Last d 22.30hrs Languages spoken:
English, German, Spanish, Dutch
CARDS: 💳 ▣ ▣ ◉ Travellers cheques

★ ★ ★ Novotel Paris Roissy Aéroport de Gaulle
Roissypole Gare 95700
☎ 148620053 FAX 148620011
Novotel offer their clients good quality accommodation in
modern, well equipped bedrooms and have refined
restaurants serving good quality cuisine They have excellent
business meeting and conference facilities and some have food
and beverages available 24 hours a day. All their hotels have at
least one bedroom for disabled guests.
Near motorway
201 en suite (bth) (201 fmly) No smoking in 70 bedrooms TV
in all bedrooms STV Radio in rooms Direct dial from all
bedrooms Mini-bar in all bedrooms Licensed Lift Night
porter Full central heating Air conditioning in bedrooms
Open parking available (charged) Child discount available
12YRS Pool table Languages spoken:
English,German,Spanish
CARDS: 💳 ▣ ▣ ◉ Travellers cheques

★ ★ ★ ★ Sofitel Paris C.D.G. Airport
BP 20248 Zone Centrale 95710
☎ 149192929 FAX 149192900
Personalised, courteous service is offered at this large airport
hotel. The rooms are of contemporary style, luxurious and with
every modern comfort including soundproofing. The L'Escale
restaurant offers dishes for all occasions 24 hours a day. A first
class service is offered for business affairs covering all
requirements including an interpretation service. *contd.*

203

Forest area
352 en suite (bth) (15 fmly) TV in all bedrooms STV Licensed
Lift Night porter Full central heating Air conditioning in
bedrooms Open parking available (charged) Indoor
swimming pool (heated) Tennis Sauna Open terrace V meals
Languages spoken: English German & Spanish
ROOMS: (room only) s 1280-1480FF; d 1280-1480FF ✷
MEALS: Full breakfast 110FF Continental breakfast 80FF
Lunch 99-145FF&alc Dinner 99-145FF&alc✷
CARDS: ● ▬ ▬ ● Travellers cheques

RUNGIS Val-de-Marne

★ ★ Vidéotel
4 rue Mondétour 94656
☎ 145605252 FAX 149780625
The hotels in the Videotel group all have bedrooms with pleasant
furnishings and are equipped with the comfort of their clientele
in mind. The restaurants serve a good quality gourmet cuisine
with a range of fixed price menus, regional specialities and 'eat
your fill buffet'. The management couples and their dedicated
teams offer a 'round the clock' efficient service, where the well-
being and satisfaction of guests is the prime consideration.
Near motorway
82 en suite (bth/shr) (9 fmly) No smoking in 10 bedrooms TV
in all bedrooms Direct dial from all bedrooms Licensed Lift
Night porter Full central heating Air conditioning in
bedrooms Open parking available Supervised Child discount
available 12yrs Open terrace V meals Last d 22.00hrs
Languages spoken: English
ROOMS: (room only) s 345-345FF; d 345-345FF
MEALS: Full breakfast 39FF Lunch 52-88FF&alc Dinner 52-
88FF&alc
CARDS: ● ▬ ▬ ●

ST-GERMAIN-EN-LAYE Yvelines

★ ★ ★ ★ Cazaudéhore et la Forestière
1 av du Prés Kennedy 78100
☎ 139733660 FAX 139737388
Forest area
30 en suite (bth/shr) (6 with balcony) TV in all bedrooms Radio
in rooms Mini-bar in all bedrooms Licensed Lift Night porter
Full central heating Open parking available Child discount
available 8yrs Last d 22.00hrs Languages spoken: English
MEALS: Continental breakfast 75FF Lunch 190-360FF&alc
Dinner 190-360FF&alc✷
CARDS: ● ▬ ▬ JCB Travellers cheques

ST-OUEN Seine-St-Denis

★ ★ ★ Holiday Inn Garden Court
9 rue la Fontaine 93400
☎ 140125197 FAX 140126100
The hotel is situated in the northern part of the capital and can
be easily reached by means of the Peripherique or the Metro.
Close to all the commercial and cultural centres, it features
peaceful guest accommodation complemented by a friendly
and dedicated service. The restaurant serves a comprehensive
choice of good value-for-money dishes.
In town centre Near motorway
120 en suite (bth) No smoking in 40 bedrooms TV in all
bedrooms STV Radio in rooms Direct dial from all bedrooms
Licensed Lift Night porter Full central heating Air
conditioning in bedrooms Open parking available Covered
parking available (charged) Supervised Child discount
available 18yrs Open terrace Languages spoken:

English,German,Spanish,Italian
ROOMS: (room only) s 480FF; d 480FF
Special breaks
MEALS: Full breakfast 55FF Continental breakfast 55FF Lunch
fr 89FF
CARDS: ● ▬ ▬ ● Travellers cheques

ST-PIERRE-LES-NEMOURS Seine-et-Marne

★ ★ Les Roches
av d'Ormesson 77140
☎ 164280143 FAX 164280427
This recently renovated hotel dates back to the turn of the
century and is located at the most southern point of the large
forest of Fontainebleau. Decorated throughout in soft yellow
and green shades, it has peacefully situated bedrooms with
private amenities, and a restaurant which serves a light, refined
cuisine with equal emphasis on presentation and flavour.
Near river Forest area
10 en suite (bth/shr) 5 rooms in annexe (4 fmly) TV in all
bedrooms Licensed Full central heating Open parking
available Covered parking available Child discount available
Solarium Open terrace V meals Last d 21.45hrs Languages
spoken: Spanish
MEALS: Full breakfast 45FF Continental breakfast 30FF Lunch
90-280FF&alc Dinner 145-280FF✷
CARDS: ● ▬ ▬ ● Travellers cheques

SCEAUX Hauts-de-Seine

★ ★ Colbert
20 av Camberwell 92330
☎ 146600221 FAX 147029578
The hotel Colbert has the feel of a private house with the added
convenience of attentive service and modern comfort. Water-
colours, signed engravings, and soft-shaded fabrics create a
cosy atmosphere, where the friendly owner gives her visitors a
personal welcome. The restaurant-brasserie serves a choice of
tasty dishes in an informal and cheerful interior, whilst the
pleasant guest accommodation is well equipped, and provides
a good level of comfort. Situated only 15 minutes from the
centre of Paris, it is a good base for exploring the capital.
Forest area In town centre Near motorway
49 en suite (bth/shr) TV in all bedrooms STV Direct dial from
all bedrooms Mini-bar in all bedrooms Room-safe (charged)
Licensed Lift Night porter Full central heating Open parking
available Child discount available 10yrs Last d 22.00hrs
Languages spoken: English,Italian,Spanish
ROOMS: (room only) s 340FF; d 398FF
MEALS: Full breakfast 38FF Lunch 72-200FFalc Dinner 72-
200FFalc✷
CARDS: ● ▬ ▬ ● Travellers cheques

SURESNES Hauts-de-Seine

★ ★ ★ Hotel Atrium
68-72 blvd Henri Sellier 92150
☎ 142046076 FAX 146977161
(Close to the Bois de Boulogne cross the Pont de Suresnes in
the direction of St Cloud)
Close to La Défense, this charming hotel has unique
architecture and a friendly atmosphere. For relaxation there
are lounges, winter gardens and a fitness club with sauna.
42 en suite (bth/shr) TV in all bedrooms STV Direct dial from
all bedrooms Mini-bar in all bedrooms Room-safe Licensed
Lift Gym
CARDS: ● ▬ ●

★ ★ ★ **Royal Parc de Seine**
6 rue Chevreul *92150*
☎ 146254000 FAX 146254190
Near river Near lake Forest area In town centre Near motorway
97 en suite (bth/shr) (97 fmly) (97 with balcony) TV in all bedrooms STV Licensed Lift Night porter Full central heating Open parking available (charged) Covered parking available (charged) Supervised Child discount available 12yrs Indoor swimming pool Pool table Jacuzzi/spa Open terrace V meals Languages spoken: English,German,Italian,Spanish
ROOMS: (room only) d fr 580FF ✱
MEALS: Full breakfast 50FF Lunch fr 99FF&alc Dinner 99-156FF&alc✱
CARDS: ● ■ Ⅲ☰ ⑩ JCB,Eurocard Travellers cheques

THOMERY Seine-et-Marne

★ ★ ★ **Vieux Logis**
5 rue Sadi Carnot *77810*
☎ 160964477
(6km south east of Fontainebleau, take N6 after Obelisque)
The hotel is situated in the town of Thomery on the banks of the river Seine. It was built in the late 18th century, and features a cheerful interior, where each bedroom is named after a flower and is equipped with modern facilities. There is an inviting bar and a restaurant with a comprehensive menu featuring a varied choice of dishes, which are complemented by an interesting wine list.
Near river Forest area In town centre

28 rms (14 bth/shr) TV in 14 bedrooms Direct dial from 14 bedrooms Licensed Night porter Open parking available Child discount available Outdoor swimming pool (heated) Tennis Bicycle rental Open terrace Last d 21.30hrs Languages spoken: English
ROOMS: (room only) s 400FF; d 400FF
Special breaks
MEALS: Full breakfast 50FF Continental breakfast 50FF Lunch 210-350FF&alc Dinner 155-240FF&alc
CARDS: ● ■ ☰ Travellers cheques

VERSAILLES Yvelines

★ ★ **Relais Mercure**
19 rue Philippe de Dangeau, angle rue Montbauron *78800*
☎ 139504410 FAX 139506511
Situated in the very heart of Versailles near the main stations with connections to Paris, the hotel is set in a quiet, privileged location. Smartly decorated bedrooms have modern facilities and offer a high degree of comfort. Breakfast is served in the attractive lounge and foyer. With Paris and Eurodisney nearby

the hotel is a good base for visits to the capital and its numerous places of interest.
In town centre Near motorway
60 en suite (bth/shr) (11 fmly) TV in all bedrooms STV Direct dial from all bedrooms Lift Night porter Full central heating Open parking available (charged) Covered parking available (charged) Supervised Child discount available 16yrs Languages spoken: English,German,Spanish
ROOMS: (room only) s 365-410FF; d 395-410FF
✱ **Special breaks: Jul/Aug 3 night breaks**
CARDS: ● ■ ☰ ⑩ Travellers cheques

★ ★ ★ **Sofitel Château de Versailles**
2 bis av de Paris *78000*
☎ 139533031 FAX 139538730
The Sofitel chain comprises of a group of very fine modern, comfortable hotels at the four star level. Bedrooms have been carefully designed to cater to guests relaxation and well being and the restaurants facilities offer fine cuisine in pleasant surroundings. they cater for business clientele with excellent conference and meeting facilities.
152 en suite (bth/shr) (31 with balcony) No smoking in 85 bedrooms TV in all bedrooms STV Mini-bar in all bedrooms V meals

★ ★ ★ **Trianon Palace** (Leading Hotels)
1 bd de la Reine *78000*
☎ 130843800 FAX 139490077
This splendid hotel stands on the edge of the former Royal Estate of King Louis XIV at Versailles. Recently renovated and refurbished, it offers excellent facilities and services in a traditional decor. The luxurious bedrooms provide the highest degree of comfort and have excellent en suite appointments, whilst one of the most talented chefs in France, Gérard Vié, presides over the kitchen and is responsible for the delicately flavoured and beautifully presented dishes.
Forest area In town centre Near motorway
94 en suite (bth/shr) Some rooms in annexe TV in all bedrooms STV Radio in rooms Direct dial from all bedrooms Mini-bar in all bedrooms Licensed Lift Night porter Full central heating Air conditioning in bedrooms Open parking available Covered parking available Supervised Child discount available 12yrs Indoor swimming pool (heated) Tennis Sauna Solarium Gym Jacuzzi/spa Bicycle rental Open terrace Covered terrace Wkly live entertainment Last d 22.00hrs Languages spoken: English,German,Spanish, Italian
CARDS: ● ■ ☰ ⑩ JCB Travellers cheques

VILLENEUVE-LA-GARENNE Hauts-de-Seine

★ ★ **Climat de France**
80 bd Charles-de-Gaulle *92390*
☎ 147995600 Cen Res 164460123 FAX 147998866
(Off A1 at St-Ouen, Pte de Clichy exit)
This pleasant hotel is situated in Villeneuve-la-Garenne and features comfortable bedrooms with every modern convenience, as well as a restaurant which serves a comprehensive buffet and a choice of traditional dishes with a regional touch. Staff offer a competent service and provide 'round the clock' personal attention.
Near lake Forest area Near motorway
60 en suite (bth) (2 fmly) TV in all bedrooms Radio in rooms Direct dial from all bedrooms Licensed Full central heating Open parking available Supervised Open terrace Languages spoken: English
CARDS: ● ☰

Burgundy

Lying between the wide open harvest plains of northern France and the industrialised Rhone Valley, Burgundy is a land on undulating hills, woods and unspoilt waterways flowing through a ragged mosaic of fields bordered by centuries-old hedges. Burgundy is a beautiful and fertile land whose wealth is nurtured by wine-growers, farmers and foresters, all applying skills passed down and refined over generations. Burgundians have transformed hospitality into an art form: simple, dignified and sincere. People here understand that the better things in life must be taken with time, naturally.

ESSENTIAL FACTS

DÉPARTEMENTS:	Côte-d'Or, Nièvre, Saône-et-Loire, Yonne
PRINCIPAL TOWNS	Auxerre, Nevers, Dijon, Le Creusot, Monceau-les-Mines, Macon, Chalon-sur-Saône, Beaune
PLACES TO VISIT:	St Madeleine Basilica in Vezelay; Fontenay Abbey; Semur-en-Auxois; Morvan Nature Park; Cluny; Dijon; Beaune - the centre of the wine industry and where there is a famous harvest festival and wine auction in November
REGIONAL TOURIST OFFICE	34 rue de Forges, 21022 Dijon Tel 80 44 11 44
LOCAL GASTRONOMIC DELIGHTS	Burgundy has been described as a gastronomic paradise. Among traditional favourites are boeuf bourguignon (beef casseroled in wine), jambon persillé (ham with parsley) and escargots (snails) in their shells. Dijon mustard is rightly famous and ripe cheeses such as Epoisses, Citeaux and Florentin are delicious
DRINKS	Burgundy produces some of the world's greatest wine, especially in the area around Beaune. Whites include Chablis, Mersault and Montrachet, whilst reds range from Chambertin to everyday Beaujolais. Dijon blackcurrant liqueur (cassis)
LOCAL CRAFTS WHAT TO BUY	Porcelain from Nevers; pottery form Puisaye; paintings on silk from Cluny; art books printed by Benedictine monks at La Pierre-qui-Vivre near St Leger Vauban; aniseed sweets and mustard from Dijon

(Top): A moving memorial to the fallen of World War I at Nevers. The town is also the home of St Bernadette, who lies in a glass tomb at the Couvent St-Gildard.

(Bottom): The dramatic Roche de Solutré dominates the area, and is a popular spot for rock climbers and walkers.

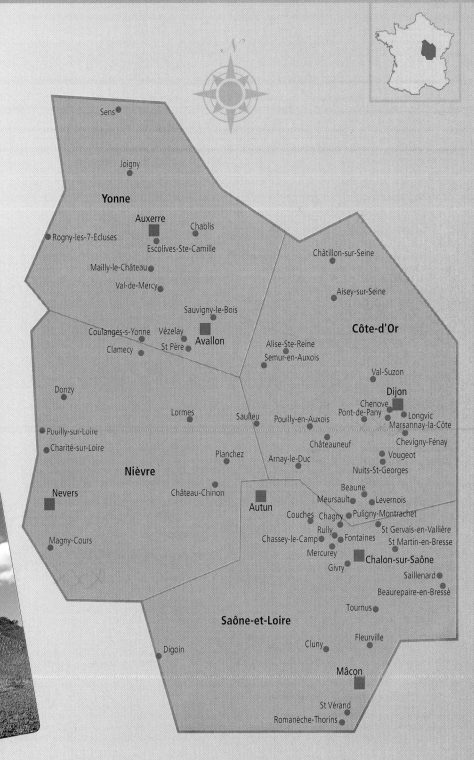

Sens

Joigny

Yonne

Auxerre

Chablis

Rogny-les-7-Ecluses

Escolives-Ste-Camille

Mailly-le-Château

Val-de-Mercy

Châtillon-sur-Seine

Aisey-sur-Seine

Sauvigny-le-Bois

Côte-d'Or

Coulanges-s-Yonne   Vézelay

Clamecy   St Père   **Avallon**

Alise-Ste-Reine

Semur-en-Auxois

Val-Suzon

Donzy

Lormes   Saulieu   Pouilly-en-Auxois   **Dijon**

Chenove   Longvic

Pont-de-Pany   Marsannay-la-Côte

Pouilly-sur-Loire

Châteauneuf   Chevigny-Fénay

Charité-sur-Loire

Planchez   Vougeot

Nièvre   Arnay-le-Duc   Nuits-St-Georges

Château-Chinon   Beaune

Nevers   Meursault   Levernois

Autun   Puligny-Montrachet

Couches   Chagny

Magny-Cours   Rully   St Gervais-en-Vallière

Chassey-le-Camp   Fontaines   St Martin-en-Bresse

Mercurey   **Chalon-sur-Saône**

Givry   Saillenard

Beaurepaire-en-Bressè

Tournus

Saône-et-Loire

Digoin   Fleurville

Cluny

Mâcon

St Vérand

Romanèche-Thorins

EVENTS & FESTIVALS

Jan Rully, Feast of St Vincent, Wine Grower Festival (procession, enthroning)

Mar Chalon-sur-Saône Carnival; Nuits-St-Georges Wine Sales of the Hospices;

May Dijon Antiques Fair; Chalons-sur-Saône 'Montgolfiades' hot air ballooning event; Race of the Maidens & the Footloose Race of the Platter, Semur-en-Auxois; Magny Cours Historic Racing Vehicles;

Jun Donzy Classical Music Festival; St-Jean-de Losne Grand Pardon of the Bargemen (religious procession, blessing of river boats); Le Creusot National Blues Festival; Dijon Music Festival; Beaune Baroque Music Festival (each weekend until end July);

Jul Châtillon-sur-Seine Festival of north Burgundy (classical music & jazz); St Fargeau Castle Historical Show; Rogny-les-Sept Ecluses Fireworks on the Locks; Chalon-sur Saône European Street Theatre meeting; Pouilly-sur-Loire Fête des terroirs; Clamecy Water Jousting; Vézelay Madeleine's Pilgrimage;

Aug Coulanges-sur-Yonne Nautical Jousting; Saulieu Charolais Festival; Autun Augustodunum (Fris & Sats) gallo-roman show in Roman theatre;

Sep Dijon International Folkloriades & Grape Harvest Festival (folklore, dance & music); Alise-Ste-Reine The Mystery of St Reine (reconstruction in period costume of the martyrdom of Ste Reine); Chenove Pressée Festival (tasting & music around medieval wine presses)

Oct Saulieu - Grand Morvan Gourmand Days; Dijon Gastronomic Fair;

Nov International Jazz Festival, Nevers Wine Festival, Chablis Three Glorious Days Wine Festival at Vougeot, Meursault & Beaune; Nevers Jazz Festival; Chablis Wine Festival

Dec Dijon Gingerbread Fair; Dijon Contemporary Music Festival 'Why Note'

The first Burgundians.

In 422 AD, the Romans allowed a wandering tribe from an island off the Swedish coast (today the Danish island of Bornholm) to settle near Geneva. From there they expanded their kingdom across the Burgundy plateau and south to Provence and Marseille. These 'Burgundarholmers' quickly adopted Roman manners and the Christian faith and gave their name to Burgundy.

AISEY-SUR-SEINE Côte-D'Or

★★ Du Roy
21400
☎ 80932163 FAX 80932574
In the heart of the Châtillon region, this hotel welcomes its visitors with old fashioned hospitality complemented by a superb cuisine. The bedrooms are comfortable with good facilities and the cooking is particularly notable for its use of first-class regional produce and ingredients - depending on the season. There is a charming garden and a host of assorted leisure pursuits are to be found nearby.
Near river Forest area Near motorway
Closed Jan
9 rms (5 bth/shr) Direct dial from all bedrooms Licensed Full central heating Open parking available Child discount available 2yrs Open terrace V meals Last d 21.00hrs
ROOMS: (room only) s 1600FF; d 160-260FF ✱
MEALS: Full breakfast 30FF Lunch 70-175FF&alc Dinner 70-175FF&alc✱
CARDS: ●● ▦ ▨ Travellers cheques

ARNAY-LE-DUC Côte-D'Or

★★ Terminus
2 rue de l'Arquébuse 21230
☎ 380900033 FAX 380900130
(approach via Pouilly-en-Auxois towards Autun and Arnay-le-Duc)
Completely renovated in 1994, the hotel now offers comfortable bedrooms with modern amenities. The restaurant serves a wide range of regional specialities skilfully prepared

by the proprietor-chef, and has a selection of good vintage wines on its list. An attractive hotel with an informal, family atmosphere.
In town centre Near motorway
Closed early Jan-early Feb
9 en suite (bth/shr) TV in all bedrooms Direct dial from all bedrooms Licensed Full central heating Open parking available Covered parking available Open terrace V meals Last d 21.00hrs
ROOMS: (room only) s 180-220FF; d 180-300FF
MEALS: Full breakfast 30FF Lunch 90-210FF&alc Dinner 90-210FF&alc
CARDS: ●● ▦ ▨ ⑨ Travellers cheques

AUTUN Saône-et-Loire

★★★ St-Louis
6 rue de l'Arbalete 71400
☎ 385520101 FAX 385863254
A former 17th-century coaching inn in which Napoleon reputedly stayed on three occasions. It occupies an ideal location at the foot of the old city with its Cathedral, museums and shops. Guests can savour well-prepared, traditional and regional cuisine in the friendly, relaxed atmosphere of the restaurant; and explore the surroundings with the Nature Reserve of Morvan and Mount Beuvray nearby.
Near river Near lake Forest area In town centre Near motorway
43 rms (13 bth 25 shr) (4 fmly) (4 with balcony) No smoking in 10 bedrooms TV in all bedrooms Radio in rooms Direct dial from all bedrooms Licensed Night porter Full central heating Open parking available (charged) Covered parking available

(charged) Supervised Child discount available Bicycle rental
Open terrace V meals Last d 22.00hrs Languages spoken:
English & German
ROOMS: (room only) s 250FF; d 350-450FF
MEALS: Full breakfast 90FF Continental breakfast 35FF Lunch
115FF&alc Dinner 185FF&alc
CARDS: ●● ■■ ⅅⅅ

★ ★ De la Tête Noire
1-3 rue de l'Arquébuse *71400*
☎ 385863390 FAX 385863390
Situated in the centre of town and within a stone's throw of the
historic sights, the hotel offers guest rooms with everyday
modern facilities and a restaurant which serves a choice of
both traditional and regional dishes.
In town centre
17 Jan-13 Dec
27 en suite (bth/shr) (6 fmly) No smoking in 18 bedrooms TV
in all bedrooms Direct dial from all bedrooms Licensed Lift
Full central heating Covered parking available (charged)
Supervised Child discount available 12yrs Bicycle rental V
meals Last d 21.45hrs Languages spoken: English
ROOMS: (incl. full-board) s 250-270FF; d 270-310FF
MEALS: Full breakfast 35FF Lunch 59-150FF&alc Dinner 59-
150FF&alc
CARDS: ●● ⅅⅅ Travellers cheques

★ ★ ★ Hotel des Ursulines
14 rue de Rivault *71400*
☎ 385526800 FAX 385862307
Originally a convent dating back to the 17th century, it has now
been extensively renovated. Set in the old quarter of the town,
it offers exceptional views towards the mountains of Morvan,
and is close to the nature reserve and various historic sites.
The bedrooms are very well equipped, offering quality
accommodation, whilst the restaurant has a choice of
specialities on the menu. There is a French-style garden
overlooking the Roman ruins, and attractive function rooms
are available for conferences and social events.
Near lake Forest area Near motorway
38 en suite (bth/shr) (6 fmly) TV in all bedrooms Direct dial
from all bedrooms Mini-bar in all bedrooms Licensed Lift
Night porter Full central heating Open parking available V
meals Last d 21.30hrs Languages spoken:
English,German,Italian & Spanish

★ ★ ★ Le Parc des Marechaux
6 av Foch *89000*
☎ 386514377 FAX 386513172
This sophisticated residence is evocative of a bygone era.
Despite being only a few minutes away from the town centre,
it provides a peaceful oasis amongst mature trees. It has very
well furnished bedrooms with up-to-date facilities.
Near river Near lake Near sea Forest area Near
motorway
25 en suite (bth/shr) (6 fmly) (2 with balcony) TV in all
bedrooms Direct dial from all bedrooms Mini-bar in all
bedrooms Licensed Lift Night porter Full central heating
Open parking available Covered parking available Child
discount available Golf Riding Bicycle rental Open terrace
Languages spoken: English German
CARDS: ●● ■■ Travellers cheques

★ ★ Les Capucins
6 av Paul Doumer *89200*
☎ 386340652 FAX 386345847
(From motorway take exit 6 towards Paris for 5km)
The hotel Les Capucins was entirely renovated in 1997 - the
façade, reception area and restaurant have been completely
refurbished. The restaurant offers a choice of excellent dishes,
prepared with local produce. The garden is full of flowers with
a terrace where meals are served. The guest rooms are
comfortable and mostly equipped with en suite facilities.
Closed Dec-Jan
8 rms (7 bth/shr) (1 fmly) TV in all bedrooms Direct dial from
all bedrooms Licensed Full central heating Open parking
available Child discount available 12yrs Open terrace
ROOMS: d 290-370FF
MEALS: Full breakfast 35FF Lunch 100-195FF&alc
CARDS: ●● ■■ ⅅⅅ Travellers cheques

★ ★ ★ ★ Château de Vault-de-Lugny
11 rue du Château *89200*
☎ 386340786 FAX 386341636
(From Avallon take D957 towards Vézelay,in Pontaubert
take D142)
Built in the 16th century, and situated in extensive wooded
parklands, surrounded by a moat, the chateau was entirely
renovated in 1986, and now offers a luxurious interior where
bedrooms and public areas are furnished in a style befitting
the origin of the building. The guest accommodation has
personally styled bedrooms, with four-poster or canopy beds,
and is equipped with superb modern facilities. In addition
there is a private tennis court and 800 metres of river frontage
for trout fishing at the guest's disposal.
Near river Forest area
Closed mid Nov-mid Mar
12 en suite (bth/shr) (2 fmly) TV in all bedrooms Direct dial
from all bedrooms Room-safe Licensed Full central heating
Open parking available Covered parking available Supervised
Tennis Fishing Boule Bicycle rental Open terrace Hot air
ballooning Wkly live entertainment V meals Last d 23.00hrs
Languages spoken: English,German
ROOMS: s 750-1200FF; d 750-2400FF **Reductions over
1 night Special breaks: 5-10 nights less 8%,over 10
nights less 12%**
MEALS: Full breakfast 90FF Continental breakfast 50FF Lunch
210-280FFalc Dinner 280-430FFalc
CARDS: ●● ■■ ⅅⅅ Travellers cheques

★ ★ ★ Du Moulin des Ruats
Vallée du Cousin *89200*
☎ 386349700 FAX 386316547
This former flour mill was converted into a hotel in 1921 and
enjoys an idyllic setting tucked away in the delightful
surroundings of a valley. All the bedrooms - some with
terraces overlooking the river or garden - are individually
furnished and are very comfortable. Guests can savour the
delicacies on offer in the restaurant with a view of the slowly
turning mill wheel. In summer meals are also served on the
banks of the river.
Near river Forest area Near motorway
Closed mid Nov-early Feb
25 en suite (bth/shr) (3 fmly) (8 with balcony) TV in all
bedrooms STV Direct dial from all bedrooms Licensed Full
central heating Open parking available Open terrace Last d
21.00hrs Languages spoken: English,German & Italian

contd.

ROOMS: (room only) d 370-800FF ✳
MEALS: Full breakfast 50FF Continental breakfast 50FF Lunch fr 155FF Dinner 155-235FF&alc
CARDS: 💳 🏧 💳 ⭕ Travellers cheques

BEAUNE Côte-D'Or

★ ★ ★ Château du Challanges
rue des Templiers-Challanges 21200
☎ 380263262 FAX 380263252
Erected in 1902 on foundations going back to the time of the crusades, this handsome mansion house welcomes visitors in stylish surroundings where good cuisine and exceptional regional wines complement each other. It offers elegant suites and bedrooms decorated in individual styles with luxurious bathrooms. After a long journey, guests can enjoy a glass of Kir or a good Burgundy wine in the sophisticated lounge. A comprehensive buffet-style breakfast is served in the morning.
Near river Forest area Near motorway
Closed end Nov-end Mar
14 en suite (bth/shr) 1 rooms in annexe (5 fmly) (1 with balcony) TV in all bedrooms Direct dial from all bedrooms Licensed Night porter Full central heating Air conditioning in bedrooms Open parking available Covered parking available Supervised Child discount available Golf Tennis Fishing Boule Bicycle rental Open terrace Languages spoken: English,German,Italian & Spanish
CARDS: 💳 🏧 💳 ⭕ Travellers cheques

★ ★ ★ Henry II (Best Western)
12/14 faubourg St-Nicholas 21200
☎ 380228384 FAX 380241513
The hotel stands on the edge of the historic town of Beaune and combines the charm of the past with the modern comfort of the present. With part of the building classified as an historic monument, it offers individually appointed bedrooms furnished in the character of the building. In addition there is a breakfast lounge and a bar.
In town centre Near motorway
50 en suite (bth/shr) (4 fmly) (2 with balcony) TV in all bedrooms STV Direct dial from all bedrooms Mini-bar in all bedrooms Licensed Lift Night porter Full central heating Open parking available (charged) Covered parking available (charged) Supervised Open terrace Languages spoken: English,German
CARDS: 💳 🏧 💳 ⭕ Travellers cheques

★ ★ ★ Novotel
av Charles-de-Gaulle 21200
☎ 380245900 FAX 380245929
(From A6 take Beaune exit. Hotel on right before the Palais des Congrès)
Novotel offer their clients good quality accommodation in modern, well equipped bedrooms and have refined restaurants serving good quality cuisine They have excellent business meeting and conference facilities and some have food and beverages available 24 hours a day. All their hotels have at least one bedroom for disabled guests.
Near motorway
127 en suite (bth/shr) (60 fmly) No smoking in 18 bedrooms TV in all bedrooms STV Radio in rooms Direct dial from all bedrooms Mini-bar in all bedrooms Licensed Lift Night porter Full central heating Air conditioning in bedrooms Open parking available Child discount available 16yrs Outdoor swimming pool Open terrace Covered terrace Last d 24.00hrs Languages spoken: English,German,Spanish
ROOMS: (room only) s 435-450FF; d 485-555FF

MEALS: Full breakfast 55FF Lunch 85-135FF&alc Dinner 85-135FF&alc
CARDS: 💳 🏧 💳 ⭕ Travellers cheques

★ ★ ★ Hotel de la Poste
5 bld Clemenceau 21200
☎ 380220811 FAX 380241971
This handsome building of significant character is situated near the ramparts of the old town of Beaune and features elegantly furnished bedrooms offering a high standard of comfort. The Belle Epoque bar provides a cosy setting for a game of bridge or billiards, and the restaurant serves a fine cuisine along with an extensive choice of wines from the house cellar.
In town centre Near motorway
Closed 24-29 Dec
30 en suite (bth/shr) 4 rooms in annexe (9 fmly) (2 with balcony) TV in all bedrooms STV Mini-bar in all bedrooms Licensed Lift Night porter Full central heating Air conditioning in bedrooms Open parking available (charged) Covered parking available (charged) Supervised Child discount available 13yrs Pool table Open terrace V meals Last d 21.30hrs Languages spoken: English,German,Italian,Spanish
MEALS: Lunch 145-360FF Dinner 145-360FF✳
CARDS: 💳 🏧 💳 ⭕ JCB Travellers cheques

★ ★ Relais Motel 21
rte de Verdun-Rocade Est. 21230
☎ 380241530 FAX 380241610
This is an attractive establishment situated near a motorway exit which makes it a suitable venue for an overnight stop. It offers functional bedrooms with modern facilities and a pleasant restaurant - opening onto the garden and swimming pool - where a wide range of carefully presented dishes, prepared with fresh local produce, feature on the menu. Visitors can relax in the swimming pool with solarium, or play a game of pétanque, whilst assorted games are available for children.
Near river Near lake Forest area Near motorway
42 en suite (bth/shr) (2 fmly) TV in all bedrooms Direct dial from all bedrooms Licensed Full central heating Open parking available Supervised Outdoor swimming pool Solarium Boule Bicycle rental Open terrace V meals Last d 22.00hrs Languages spoken: English
CARDS: 💳 🏧 💳 ⭕ Travellers cheques

★ ★ La Villa Fleurie
19 pl Colbert 21200
☎ 380226600 FAX 380224546
An informal hotel in the centre of Beaune, offering 10 cosy bedrooms and a breakfast room.
In town centre Near motorway
10 en suite (bth/shr) (3 fmly) No smoking on premises TV available Direct-dial available Full central heating Open parking available Supervised Child discount available 14yrs Languages spoken: English & German
ROOMS: (room only) s 270-290FF; d 290-350FF
MEALS: Full breakfast 35FF✳
CARDS: 💳 💳

BEAUREPAIRE-EN-BRESSE Saône-et-Loire

★ ★ Auberge de la Croix Blanche
71580
☎ 385741322 FAX 385741325
Set in unspoilt countryside, this auberge is a converted staging

post. Comfortable bedrooms and a restaurant serving regional specialities including fish from the local lakes help make your stay an extremely pleasant one. Some of the rooms have balconies. Terrace and garden for guests' use.
Near river Near lake Near sea Forest area Near motorway
15 en suite (bth/shr) (1 fmly) (13 with balcony) TV in all bedrooms Licensed Full central heating Open parking available Supervised Child discount available 3yrs Bicycle rental Open terrace V meals Last d 21.30hrs Languages spoken: English,German
CARDS: ● ☰ Travellers cheques

CHABLIS Yonne

★ ★ ★ Hostellerie des Clos
rue Jules Rathier *89800*
☎ 386421063 FAX 386421711
The house was once part of the Chablis Hospices and dates back to the 12th century. The elegant lounges are tastefully decorated with fine fabrics and furnishings, the individually furnished bedrooms, and the outstanding restaurant all create the luxurious setting for a memorable experience. After a day visiting the vineyards, or indulging in energetic sporting activities, guests can pamper themselves with some of the delicious dishes served in the restaurant, accompanied by the finest white wines of Burgundy.
In town centre
Closed 23 Dec-10 Jan
26 en suite (bth/shr) (1 fmly) TV in all bedrooms STV Radio in rooms Mini-bar in all bedrooms Licensed Lift Full central heating Open parking available Covered parking available (charged) Child discount available 12yrs Open terrace V meals Last d 21.30hrs Languages spoken: English,German
MEALS: Full breakfast 50FF Lunch 175-420FF&alc Dinner 175-420FF&alc✱
CARDS: ● ☰ ☲ ⓓ Travellers cheques

★ ★ De l'Étoile
4 rue des Moulins *89800*
☎ 386421050 FAX 386428121
(From A6 exit 'Auxerre Sud' take N65 to Chablis)
This small establishment combines the charming atmosphere of an old private residence with every modern comfort. Bedrooms are comfortable and the restaurant serves a traditional cuisine - which is popular with a large local clientele - and being located in the heart of the Chablis region, is augmented by some excellent examples from the wine list.
Near river Near lake Forest area In town centre Near motorway
Closed 15 Dec-10 Jan RS Nov-Etr
12 rms (7 bth/shr) (4 fmly) Direct dial from all bedrooms Licensed Full central heating Open parking available Covered parking available Supervised Bicycle rental V meals Last d 21.30hrs Languages spoken: English,German,Spanish
ROOMS: (room only) s 180-270FF; d 180-300FF ✱
CARDS: ● ☰ ⓓ Travellers cheques

CHAGNY Saône-et-Loire

★ ★ Auberge La Musardière
30 rte de Chalon *71150*
☎ 385870497 FAX 385872051
(Off N6 near Tuilerie Lambert)
Near river Forest area Near motorway
15 rms (8 bth 5 shr) (1 fmly) (1 with balcony) TV in all bedrooms Direct dial from all bedrooms Licensed Full central heating Open parking available Child discount available 2yrs

Open terrace Covered terrace Last d 21.00hrs
ROOMS: (room only) d 190-225FF ✱
MEALS: Continental breakfast 30FF Lunch 61-195FF Dinner 61-195FF
CARDS: ● ☰ ☲ Travellers cheques

★ ★ ★ ★ Lameloise
36 pl d'Armes *71150*
☎ 305070005 FAX 385870357
(Approach via N74 from Beaune or N6 from S)
This exceptionally charming establishment offers all the ingredients for an enjoyable stay. The smart bedrooms are very comfortable, the tastefully furnished public areas exude an atmosphere of elegant sophistication, whilst the restaurant serves an impressive choice of dishes comprising superb classic cuisine and delicately flavoured specialities of the region.
In town centre Near motorway
Closed mid Dec-late Jan
17 en suite (bth/shr) (3 with balcony) TV in all bedrooms Direct dial from all bedrooms Mini-bar in 7 bedrooms Licensed Lift Night porter Full central heating Air conditioning in bedrooms Covered parking available Last d 21.30hrs Languages spoken: English,German
ROOMS: (room only) d 700-1500FF ✱
MEALS: Full breakfast 95FF Lunch 390-600FF&alc Dinner 390-600FF&alc✱
CARDS: ● ☰ ☲ Travellers cheques

CHALON-SUR-SAÔNE Saône-et-Loire

★ ★ Hotel Clarine (Minotel)
35 pl de Beaune *71100*
☎ 385487043 FAX 385457118

This charming Burgundian house has 50 peacefully situated bedrooms which have pretty furnishings and are all equipped with mini-bar, satellite TV, automatic alarm and direct-dial telephone. Private, covered parking is available in front of the hotel.
Near river Near lake In town centre Near motorway
50 en suite (bth/shr) 23 rooms in annexe (4 fmly) No smoking in 4 bedrooms TV in all bedrooms Radio in rooms Direct dial from all bedrooms Mini-bar in all bedrooms Licensed Full central heating Supervised Sauna Solarium Gym Languages spoken: English,German
ROOMS: (room only) s 260-285FF; d 260-285FF
Reductions over 1 night
CARDS: ● ☰ ☲ ⓓ Travellers cheques

★ ★ ★ Hotel St-Régis (Best Western)
22 bd de la République *71100*
☎ 385480728 FAX 385489088
(From A6 exit 'Chalon Nord' follow signs 'Centre Ville'. Hotel in the same street as the Tourist Office)
The hotel Saint-Régis is an attractive establishment situated in the centre of town. It features tastefully decorated bedrooms with modern amenities. In addition there is a pleasant bar with cosy seating, whilst the cuisine reflects a high standard of home-cooking.
Forest area In town centre Near motorway
40 en suite (bth/shr) (4 fmly) (15 with balcony) TV in all bedrooms Radio in rooms Direct dial from all bedrooms Mini-bar in all bedrooms Licensed Lift Night porter Full central heating Air conditioning in bedrooms Open parking available (charged) Child discount available 12yrs Last d 22.00hrs Languages spoken: English
ROOMS: (room only) s 340-430FF; d 370-520FF ✱

contd.

MEALS: Full breakfast 53FF Lunch 92-330FF Dinner 92-330FF✱

CARDS: ✹ ▦ ▆ ⑩ JCB Travellers cheques

CHARITÉ-SUR-LOIRE Nièvre

★ ★ ★ Le Grand Monarque
33 quai Clemenceau 58400
☎ 386702173 FAX 386696232

Standing on the banks of the river Loire the hotel offers fine views over the river and the 16th-century bridge. The building dates back to the 17th century and features an elegant interior where the bedrooms are individually styled and decorated with flair by the proprietor. There is a delightful garden and the restaurant is popular with a discerning clientele who return time and time again to savour the delicacies on offer.
Near river Forest area In town centre Near motorway
Closed 21 Feb-19 Mar/12-19 Nov
15 en suite (bth/shr) (4 fmly) TV in all bedrooms STV Radio in rooms Licensed Lift Full central heating Open parking available Covered parking available (charged) Child discount available 8yrs Last d 20.45hrs Languages spoken: English, German, Spanish

CARDS: ✹ ▦ ▆ ⑩ Travellers cheques

CHASSEY-LE-CAMP Saône-et-Loire

★ ★ ★ Auberge du Camp Romain
71150
☎ 385870991 FAX 385871151

Tucked away between vineyards and woods in the heart of the Burgundy countryside, the Auberge du Camp Romain provides the perfect hideaway for a peaceful stay. The balconied bedrooms have fine views over the surrounding countryside, whilst the restaurant serves an array of traditional dishes with an imaginative touch, complemented by a good wine list. It has many leisure opportunities on offer and is an ideal venue for energetic guests and nature lovers.
Forest area
Closed Jan
41 en suite (bth/shr) 17 rooms in annexe (7 fmly) (17 with balcony) TV in all bedrooms Licensed Lift Full central heating Open parking available Covered parking available Child discount available 10yrs Indoor swimming pool (heated) Outdoor swimming pool (heated) Tennis Sauna Solarium Pool table Boule Mini-golf Jacuzzi/spa Bicycle rental Open terrace V meals Last d 21.00hrs Languages spoken: English
MEALS: Continental breakfast 37FF Lunch 115-241FF Dinner 115-241FF✱

CARDS: ✹ ▆ Travellers cheques

CHÂTEAU-CHINON Nièvre

★ ★ Au Vieux Morvan
8 pl Gudin 58120
☎ 386850501 386851011 FAX 386850278

The hotel is set in the cheerful centre of Château-Chinon amidst the superb natural scenery of the Burgundy region. With its congenial bar and terrace, it is a popular meeting place for locals, and the traditional cuisine, complemented by selected wines, has a loyal following. The elegant guest rooms are decorated in a discreet fashion and provide comfortable accommodation. The friendly owners Mr and Mrs Duriatti offer traditional hospitality and useful advice about places to visit or areas to explore.
Near river Near lake Forest area In town centre

24 en suite (bth/shr) (8 fmly) TV in all bedrooms Direct dial from all bedrooms Licensed Night porter Full central heating Open parking available Supervised Child discount available 12yrs V meals

CARDS: ✹ ▆ Travellers cheques

CHÂTEAUNEUF Côte-D'Or

★ ★ Hostellerie du Château
rue du Centre 21320
☎ 380492200 FAX 380492127
(Approach via A6 exit 'Bully-en-Auxois)

Situated in the shade of a feudal castle dating back to the 12th century, the Hostellerie du Château offers attractively furnished bedrooms equipped with modern facilities, and a restaurant serving a high standard of cuisine augmented by the finest French wines. Guests can explore the surrounding area where Lake Panthier offers sailing and fishing, or take a walk on the towpath along the picturesque Burgundy Canal.
Near lake Forest area Near motorway
Closed Dec & Jan
17 en suite (bth/shr) 8 rooms in annexe (9 fmly) Direct dial from all bedrooms Licensed Full central heating Child discount available 10yrs Open terrace Last d 21.00hrs Languages spoken: English, German
ROOMS: (room only) d 270FF
MEALS: Full breakfast 50FF Continental breakfast 50FF Lunch 140-220FF&alc Dinner 140-220FF&alc✱

CARDS: ✹ ▦ ▆ ⑩

CHEVIGNY-FÉNAY Côte-D'Or

★ ★ Relais de la Sans Fond
rte de Seurre 21600
☎ 380366135 FAX 380369489

This former coaching inn is situated close to Dijon in rural countryside and is surrounded by the great vineyards of Burgundy. It was completely renovated in 1983 and has undergone further refurbishment in recent years. The cosy bedrooms are fitted with modern amenities, and the restaurant serves tasty, well-prepared meals, complemented by the outstanding wines of the region.
Near lake Forest area Near motorway
17 en suite (bth) (3 fmly) (1 with balcony) No smoking in 1 bedroom TV in all bedrooms Direct dial from all bedrooms Mini-bar in all bedrooms Licensed Full central heating Open parking available Supervised Child discount available 12yrs Boule Bicycle rental Open terrace V meals Last d 21.30hrs Languages spoken: English, German
MEALS: Continental breakfast 32FF Lunch 75-260FF&alc Dinner 75-260FF&alc✱

CARDS: ✹ ▦ ▆ Travellers cheques

CLUNY Saône-et-Loire

★ ★ ★ Bourgogne
pl de l'Abbaye 71250
☎ 385590058 FAX 385590373

This establishment was constructed in 1817 on the site where the Benedictine Abbey of Cluny originally stood. Although simple in outlook, inside it features old stone walls and period furnishings, spacious bedrooms and attractive apartments with assorted 19th century antiques and objets d'art. For relaxation there is a bar and an interior garden. The restaurant serves superb, imaginative dishes complemented by an excellent choice of wines. Many open-air leisure facilities are in the vicinity, and the town of Cluny, with its abbey and Roman

churches, is well worth a visit.
Forest area
15 en suite (bth/shr) (4 fmly) No smoking in 2 bedrooms TV in
35 bedrooms Licensed Full central heating Open parking
available (charged) Covered parking available (charged)
Supervised Child discount available 8yrs Bicycle rental Open
terrace V meals Last d 21.00hrs Languages spoken:
English,German
MEALS: Full breakfast 55FF Continental breakfast 55FF Lunch
fr 160FF&alc Dinner fr 220FF&alc✱
CARDS: ●● ■■ ■■ ⍉ Travellers cheques

COUCHES Saône-et-Loire

★ ★ Des Trois Maures
71490
☎ 385496393 FAX 385495029
This former coaching inn is situated in the village of Couches,
surrounded by the great Burgundy vineyards. Entirely
renovated, it features bedrooms - some have balconies - with
private facilities, one restaurant with a covered terrace, whilst
the other can be found in the spacious grounds. The cuisine
consists of a good standard of traditional home-cooking
prepared with good ingredients.
Forest area
Closed 15 Feb-15 Mar
16 en suite (bth/shr) (2 fmly) TV in all bedrooms Direct dial
from all bedrooms Full central heating Open parking
available Child discount available 15yrs Open terrace
Covered terrace Last d 21.00hrs Languages spoken: Italian
MEALS: Full breakfast 35FF Lunch 78-190FF&alc Dinner 78-
190FF&alc✱
CARDS: ●● ■■ ■■ Travellers cheques

DIGOIN Saône-et-Loire

★ ★ Des Diligences et du Commerce
14 rue Nationale *71160*
☎ 385530631 FAX 385889243
(From Mâcon take N79 through Charolles to Digoin)
This former coaching inn dates back to the 18th century and
has been a popular stopping place for tired travellers
throughout the centuries. Constantly updated to improve the
facilities, it now offers personally styled guest rooms with
every modern convenience and a rustic restaurant where the
menu features a fine traditional cuisine - as well as the chef's
own inventive creations - accompanied by a superb wine list.
Near river In town centre
6 en suite (bth/shr) (3 fmly) (3 with balcony) TV in 15
bedrooms Direct dial from 15 bedrooms Mini-bar in 1
bedroom Licensed Full central heating Open parking
available Covered parking available Supervised Open terrace
Covered terrace V meals Last d 21.30hrs Languages spoken:
English,Spanish
ROOMS: (room only) s 250-300FF; d 250-450FF ✱
MEALS: Full breakfast 35FF Lunch 140-210FF&alc Dinner 140-
210FF&alc
CARDS: ●● ■■ ■■ ⍉

DIJON Côte-D'Or

★ ★ Castel Burgond
3 rte de Troyes, RN 71 *21121*
☎ 380565972 FAX 380576948
(From town centre take N71 towards Troyes. Hotel near last set
of traffic lights on right)
The contemporary Castel Burgond is located just three

kilometres from the historic centre of Dijon. It features a choice
of public rooms and attractive bedrooms with modern
amenities. Guests can enjoy a range of regional dishes
enhanced by some personal inventive creations from the
chef.
Near lake Forest area Near motorway
38 en suite (bth) (13 fmly) (2 with balcony) TV in all bedrooms
Radio in rooms Direct dial from all bedrooms Licensed Lift
Night porter Full central heating Open parking available
Child discount available Pool table Boule V meals Last d
22.00hrs Languages spoken: English,German,Spanish
ROOMS: (room only) s 260-270FF; d 280-290FF
MEALS: Lunch 99-170FF&alc Dinner 99-170FF&alc✱
CARDS: ●● ■■ ■■ ⍉ Travellers cheques

★ ★ Climat de France
15-17 av du Maréchal-Foch *21000*
☎ 380434001 FAX 380431002
(in centre of town, near railway station)
The building dates back to 1891 and was completely renovated
in 1989. Situated in the centre of Dijon opposite the railway
and bus stations, it features pleasantly decorated, comfortable
bedrooms with good modern facilities. The restaurant serves a
variety of menus, including a 'no-limits' hors d'oeuvre buffet,
as well as the children's 'Soupière Junior'.
Near lake In town centre Near motorway
81 en suite (bth/shr) (2 fmly) TV in all bedrooms STV Radio in
rooms Direct dial from all bedrooms Licensed Lift Night
porter Full central heating Air conditioning in bedrooms
Child discount available 12yrs V meals Last d 22.30hrs
Languages spoken: English, German & Italian
ROOMS: s 315-330FF; d 355-365FF
MEALS: Continental breakfast 35FF Lunch 59-126FFalc Dinner
59-126FFalc

★ ★ ★ Hotel des Ducs
5 rue Lamonnoye *21000*
☎ 380673131 FAX 380671951
With completely refurbished and sound-proofed rooms the
hotel now offers comfortable guest accommodation with good
amenities. It features a terrace where breakfast is served in
summer, and there is a billiard room for guests' use. Situated
in the heart of the old town, it provides a suitable base to seek
out the sights.
In town centre
30 en suite (bth/shr) 1 rooms in annexe (13 fmly) (8 with
balcony) TV available STV Radio in rooms Licensed Lift
Night porter Full central heating Open parking available
(charged) Covered parking available (charged) Child discount
available 12yrs Pool table Open terrace Languages spoken:
English
CARDS: ●● ■■ Travellers cheques

DONZY Nièvre

★ ★ Grand Monarque
10 rue de l'Étape *58220*
☎ 386393544 FAX 386393709
(SE of Cosne-sur-Loire on D33)
Standing in the shadow of the old church in the charming
village of Donzy, the hotel is housed in three old stone
buildings and surrounded by 15th-century half-timbered
houses. It features a cosy lounge with magnificent fireplace for
relaxation or reading. The restaurant serves a high quality
regional cuisine prepared with the finest local produce. A 16th-
century spiral staircase leads to the individually styled
bedrooms each in a different colour, with personal

contd.

touches and floral arrangements.
Near river Near lake Forest area In town centre Near motorway
Closed Jan-Feb
(4 fmly) TV in 11 bedrooms Direct dial from 11 bedrooms Licensed Full central heating Open parking available Child discount available Pool table Bicycle rental Open terrace Last d 21.00hrs Languages spoken: English
ROOMS: (room only) d 255-345FF ✳
MEALS: Full breakfast 37FF Continental breakfast 37FF Lunch 83-220FF Dinner 83-220FF✳
CARDS: ● ▓ Travellers cheques

ESCOLIVES-STE-CAMILLE Yonne

★★ Le Mas des Lilas

La Cour Barrée 89290
☎ 386536055 FAX 386533081
(exit 20 from A6 in direction of Auxerre on N65. At roundabout take direction of Avallon/Dijon by N6 after approx 10km from roundablout cross village La Cour Barree. Hotel on right just after bridge)
A charming hotel where a warm welcome and calm

atmosphere awaits guests. All rooms are on the ground floor, with views and direct access to a park.
Near river Near motorway
Closed 15 days autumn & 15 days winter
17 en suite (bth/shr) (2 fmly) No smoking in 2 bedrooms TV in 6 bedrooms Direct dial from all bedrooms Licensed Full central heating Air conditioning in bedrooms Open parking available Child discount available 5yrs Boule Bicycle rental Open terrace Languages spoken: English & Spanish
ROOMS: (room only) s 190-250FF; d 190-250FF
CARDS: ● ▓

FLEURVILLE Saône-et-Loire

★★★ Château de Fleurville
71260
☎ 385331217 FAX 385339534
Near river Near motorway
Closed Nov-Feb
15 en suite (bth) (2 fmly) TV in all bedrooms Licensed Full central heating Open parking available Outdoor swimming pool (heated) Tennis Boule Open terrace Last d 21.30hrs Languages spoken: English,German
MEALS: Continental breakfast 45FF Lunch 100-200FF&alc Dinner 155-250FF&alc✳
CARDS: ● ▓ ◗ Travellers cheques

FONTAINES Saône-et-Loire

★★ Auberge des Fontaines
71150
☎ 35914800
(north of Chalon-sur-Saone close to the N6)

Near river Forest area Near motorway
Closed 21 Dec-9 Jan
9 rms (7 bth/shr) Direct dial from 7 bedrooms Licensed Full central heating Open parking available Supervised Open terrace V meals
ROOMS: (room only) d 180-250FF
MEALS: Continental breakfast 32FF Lunch 70-198FF
CARDS: ● ▓

GIVRY Saône-et-Loire

★ Hostellerie de la Halle
2 pl de la Halle 71640
☎ 385443245 FAX 385444945
This ancient residence used to be the retreat of the monks of the Cluny abbey and dates back to the 16th century. It has a splendid spiral staircase, and the dovecote has also been preserved. Bedrooms have private facilities and provide a straightforward level of comfort. The restaurant serves a choice of good-value dishes which suit most tastes.
In town centre
Closed 2-15 Jan
9 rms (1 fmly) Licensed Full central heating Last d 21.30hrs
CARDS: ● ▓ Travellers cheques

JOIGNY Yonne

★★★ Hotel Rive Gauche

Chemin du Port au Bois, BP 194 89304
☎ 386914666 FAX 386914693
Le Rive Gauche is situated in the town of Joigny, known for its arts and history, on the banks of the river Yonne. The hotel offers its clientele a charming interior with comfortable bedrooms, equipped with well appointed, pretty bathrooms. With its terraces, flower-filled garden and cosy cocktail bar it meets the needs of both tourists and business travellers.
Near river In town centre Near motorway
42 en suite (bth) (5 fmly) (20 with balcony) TV in all bedrooms Direct dial from all bedrooms Mini-bar in all bedrooms Licensed Lift Full central heating Open parking available Child discount available 12yrs Tennis Bicycle rental Open terrace Last d 22.00hrs Languages spoken: English
ROOMS: (room only) s 250-360FF; d 330-660FF
MEALS: Full breakfast 50FF Lunch 98-200FF&alc Dinner 148-200FF&alc
CARDS: ● ▓ ▓

LEVERNOIS Côte-D'Or

★ ★ ★ ★ Hostellerie de Levernois
Chateloy *21200*
☎ 380247358 FAX 380227800
(From A6 exit at Beaune take D970 towards Verdun-sur-le-Doubs)
Built in the tranquil surroundings of a park, this contemporary building offers modern day comfort, where bright, spacious bedrooms and comfortable public areas enjoy a peaceful atmosphere. The bedrooms are well equipped and decorated with good quality fabrics. The friendly restaurant serves a good choice of dishes and offers fine views of the park.
Near river Near motorway
Closed 15 days in Feb, 24-28 Dec
16 en suite (bth/shr) 12 rooms in annexe (6 fmly) TV in all bedrooms STV Mini-bar in all bedrooms Room-safe Licensed Full central heating Open parking available Supervised Tennis Bicycle rental Open terrace Last d 22.00hrs Languages spoken: English, German
MEALS: Full breakfast 95FF Continental breakfast 150FF Lunch 220-550FF&alc Dinner 390-550FF&alc✱
CARDS: ● ▦ ▨ ◑ Travellers cheques

LONGVIC Côte-D'Or

★ ★ Climat de France
7 rue de Beauregard *21600*
☎ Cen Res 164460123
(in direction of Airport off Lyon Par Autoroute)
This charming establishment is peacefully situated, and features pleasant guest accommodation with good modern amenities. There is a flower-decked terrace where on fine days chargrilled dishes are served. The restaurant offers a generous buffet with an extensive choice of specialities as well as an array of traditional dishes.
Near motorway
55 en suite (shr) (3 fmly) TV available Direct-dial available Licensed Full central heating Open parking available Open terrace Covered terrace Languages spoken: English
CARDS: ● ▨

LORMES Nièvre

★ ★ Perreau
8 rte d'Avallon *58140*
☎ 386225321 FAX 386228215
The town of Lormes is situated in the Morvan Regional Park, which has an abundance of hills and mountains, woods and forests to explore, and which also houses the Vézelay Basilica, a famous masterpiece of Romanesque art. Situated in the centre of town, the hotel has renovated guest rooms with modern facilities as well as offering generous and appetising dishes in true Burgundian fashion.
Near lake Forest area In town centre
17 en suite (bth/shr) 9 rooms in annexe (2 fmly) TV in all bedrooms Direct dial from all bedrooms Licensed Full central heating Open parking available Supervised Child discount available Last d 21.00hrs Languages spoken: English
MEALS: Full breakfast 50FF Continental breakfast 30FF Lunch fr 85FF&alc Dinner fr 85FF&alc✱
CARDS: ● ▨

MÂCON Saône-et-Loire

★ ★ ★ Hotel Bellevue
416 quai Lamartine *71000*
☎ 385210404 FAX 385210402
Standing on the banks of the River Saône this establishment maintains a high standard of hospitality and culinary skill. It has spacious bedrooms which offer a high level of comfort and feature many little extras such as bathrobes and toiletries. The menu offers a selection of well-prepared dishes incorporating regional specialities.
Near river In town centre Near motorway
25 rms (24 bth/shr) (6 fmly) (1 with balcony) TV in all bedrooms STV Direct dial from all bedrooms Licensed Lift Night porter Full central heating Open parking available (charged) Covered parking available (charged) Supervised Child discount available 12yrs Last d 22.00hrs Languages spoken: English, German, Italian, Spanish
ROOMS: (room only) s 380-600FF; d 415-700FF
MEALS: Continental breakfast 55FF Lunch 138-290FF&alc Dinner 138-290FF&alc
CARDS: ● ▦ ▨ ◑ JCB Travellers cheques

★ ★ ★ Novotel Mâcon Nord
Sennecé-lès-Mâcon, Péage Mâcon Nord *71000*
☎ 385360080 FAX 385360245
Novotel offer their clients good quality accommodation in modern, well equipped bedrooms and have refined restaurants serving good quality cuisine They have excellent business meeting and conference facilities and some have food and beverages available 24 hours a day. All their hotels have at least one bedroom for disabled guests.
Near motorway
115 en suite (bth) (50 fmly) No smoking in 12 bedrooms TV in all bedrooms STV Radio in rooms Direct dial from all bedrooms Mini-bar in all bedrooms Licensed Night porter Full central heating Air conditioning in bedrooms Open parking available Child discount available 16yrs Outdoor swimming pool Pool table Boule Open terrace volley ball, games for children V meals Last d 24.00hrs Languages spoken: English
CARDS: ● ▦ ▨ ◑ Travellers cheques

★ ★ Terminus
91 rue Victor Hugo *71000*
☎ 385391711 FAX 385380275
(A6 exit29, in town centre)
The Hotel Terminus is constantly upgraded and refurbished to improve the quality of comfort, and has recently received an award for exceptional hospitality in the Burgundy region. It features well-equipped bedrooms, a comfortable lounge, piano-bar and a delightful flower-filled garden. There are three restaurants which cater for most tastes, and weather permitting, serve meals along side the swimming pool.
Near river In town centre Near motorway
48 en suite (bth/shr) (16 fmly) TV in all bedrooms STV Radio in rooms Direct dial from all bedrooms Licensed Lift Night porter Full central heating Covered parking available (charged) Supervised Child discount available Outdoor swimming pool Open terrace V meals Last d 21.30hrs Languages spoken: English, German, Spanish
ROOMS: (room only) s 280FF; d 335-395FF **Reductions over 1 night**
MEALS: Full breakfast 42FF Lunch 94-175FF&alc Dinner 94-175FF&alc
CARDS: ● ▦ ▨ ◑ Travellers cheques

MAGNY-COURS Nièvre

★ ★ ★ Holiday Inn
Ferme du Domaine de Bardonnay *58470*
☎ 386212223 FAX 386212203
The hotel offers a combination of traditional and modern comforts and has peacefully situated bedrooms with good amenities and an attractive restaurant serving gourmet food. With its excellent conference and leisure facilities it also provides a suitable venue for the business traveller.
Near motorway
70 en suite (bth) (33 fmly) (2 with balcony) No smoking in 22 bedrooms TV in all bedrooms STV Radio in rooms Direct dial from all bedrooms Mini-safe Licensed Lift Night porter Full central heating Air conditioning in bedrooms Open parking available Supervised Outdoor swimming pool (heated) Tennis Sauna Gym Pool table Open terrace Table tennis Last d 22.30hrs Languages spoken: English
CARDS: ●● ▆▆ ▇▇ ⑨ Travellers cheques

★ ★ ★ ★ La Renaissance
Ancienne N7 *58470*
☎ 386581040 FAX 386212260
Situated in the town of Magny-Cours the hotel is popular with locals, racing-drivers, and holiday makers alike. The restaurant is decorated in attractive pastel shades and offers a comprehensive choice of regional delicacies complemented by the excellent wines from the Loire region. In addition the bedrooms have good modern amenities and offer high standards of comfort.
Closed 3 weeks Feb/Mar, 2 weeks Aug
9 en suite (bth/shr) (1 fmly) TV in all bedrooms STV Mini-bar in all bedrooms Licensed Full central heating Air conditioning in bedrooms Open parking available Supervised Child discount available 10yrs Open terrace V meals Last d 21.00hrs Languages spoken: English,Italian
CARDS: ●● ▆▆ ▇▇

MAILLY-LE-CHÂTEAU Yonne

★ ★ Castel
pl de l'Église *89660*
☎ 386814306 FAX 386814926
(Between Auxerre & Avallon, leave the autoroute & loin N6, then take D100, onto D950 through Mailly-la-Ville & Mailly-le-Château near the church)
Le Castel is situated near the old church in the elevated part of a peaceful little village which lies between Auxerre and Avallon. The hotel enjoys a quiet position far from the bustle of the heavy traffic and a small distance away from the River Yonne and the Canal du Nivernais. Fishing, swimming, forest walks and watersports are just a stone's throw away.
Near river Forest area In town centre
Closed 16 Nov-14 Mar
12 rms (8 bth 3 shr) (2 fmly) Direct dial from all bedrooms Licensed Full central heating Open parking available Bicycle rental Open terrace V meals Last d 20.30hrs Languages spoken: English,Spanish
ROOMS: (room only) s 150FF; d 300-400FF
MEALS: Full breakfast 37FF Lunch 75-280FF&alc Dinner 75-280FF&alc
CARDS: ●● ▇▇ Travellers cheques

MARSANNAY-LA-CÔTE Côte-D'Or

★ ★ L'Hotellerie de la Côte
rte de Beaune *21160*
☎ 380511000 FAX 380588297
Surrounded by the great vineyards of Burgundy, the hotel offers its visitors comfortable bedrooms, pleasant public areas, and an elegant restaurant where a plentiful, regional cuisine is served. With its excellent facilities and good geographical location it provides a good venue for both business and leisure travellers.
Forest area Near motorway
41 en suite (shr) (6 fmly) No smoking in 14 bedrooms TV in all bedrooms STV Mini-bar in all bedrooms Licensed Full central heating Air conditioning in bedrooms Open parking available Supervised Child discount available 12yrs Pool table Boule Bicycle rental Open terrace V meals Last d 21.00hrs Languages spoken: English,German,Italian,Spanish
MEALS: Full breakfast 35FF Continental breakfast 35FF Lunch 90-170FF&alc Dinner 90-170FF&alc✱
CARDS: ●● ▆▆ ▇▇ ⑨ Travellers cheques

MERCUREY Saône-et-Loire

★ ★ ★ Val d'Or
Grande Rue *71640*
☎ 385451370 FAX 385451845
This former coaching inn is located in the heart of the Burgundy region and offers its visitors a peaceful stay in comfortable surroundings. The architecture and interior are typical of the region and the restaurant offers a first-class cuisine, complemented by some fine examples from the wine list. The bedrooms are traditionally furnished, equipped with modern facilities and offer a good level of comfort.
In town centre
Closed mid Dec-mid Jan
12 en suite (bth/shr) (2 with balcony) TV in all bedrooms Licensed Full central heating Open parking available Covered parking available Supervised Child discount available 12yrs V meals Last d 21.00hrs Languages spoken: English
ROOMS: (room only) d 350-430FF **Reductions over 1 night**
MEALS: Full breakfast 55FF Lunch 120-345FF Dinner 165-345FF✱
CARDS: ●● ▇▇ Travellers cheques

NEVERS Nièvre

★ ★ ★ Hotel de Diane (Best Western)
38 rue du Midi *58000*
☎ 386572810 FAX 386594508
The hotel is situated in the heart of the historic town of Nevers, not far from all the sights and main transport services. The bedrooms offer attractive accommodation and provide good levels of comfort. The restaurant serves an honest country-style cuisine in its vaulted restaurant which dates back to the 14th century.
Near river Near lake Near sea Near beach Forest area In town centre Near motorway
Closed 21 Dec-10 Jan
30 en suite (bth/shr) (2 fmly) No smoking in 4 bedrooms TV in all bedrooms STV Radio in rooms Direct dial from all bedrooms Mini-bar in all bedrooms Licensed Lift Night porter Full central heating Open parking available (charged) Covered parking available (charged) Supervised Child

discount available 12yrs Open terrace V meals Last d
23.00hrs Languages spoken: English, German
ROOMS: (room only) s 440-525FF; d 490-590FF ✱
MEALS: Full breakfast 70FF Continental breakfast 40FF Lunch
79-152FF Dinner 79-152FF
CARDS: ● ● ■■ ■■ ●) Travellers cheques

NUITS-ST-GEORGES Côte-D'Or

★ ★ **Hotel & Restaurant Iris**
1 av Chamboland *21700*
☎ 380611717 FAX 380612633
At the heart of the most prestigious vineyards. The Iris Hotel
provides quiet, comfortable bedrooms and a restaurant with a
wide choice of food.

Near river Near lake Forest area Near motorway
Closed 26 Dec-8 Jan
50 en suite (bth/shr) TV in all bedrooms STV Direct dial from
all bedrooms Licensed Night porter Full central heating
Open parking available Supervised Child discount available
Indoor swimming pool (heated) Outdoor swimming pool
(heated) Tennis Fishing Bicycle rental V meals Last d
21.00hrs Languages spoken: English & German
ROOMS: s fr 295FF; d fr 360FF
MEALS: Full breakfast 35FF Continental breakfast 20FF Lunch
87-130FF&alc Dinner 87-130FF&alc

★ ★ **Le St-Georges**
Carrefour de l'Europe *21700*
☎ 380611500 FAX 380612380
(Near Nuits-St-Georges exit of A31)

This modern establishment provides an attractive base from
which to tour the Burgundy region with its many culinary
delights and excellent wines. Cheerful bedrooms are equipped
with modern facilities and the restaurant offers a refined

Burgundy cuisine as well as specialities such as foie gras,
salmon and freshly smoked magrets de canard.
Forest area Near motorway
47 en suite (bth/shr) 17 rooms in annexe (6 fmly) No smoking
in 9 bedrooms TV in all bedrooms STV Direct dial from all
bedrooms Licensed Night porter Full central heating Open
parking available Covered parking available (charged)
Supervised Child discount available 12yrs Outdoor swimming
pool (heated) Tennis Pool table Boule Open terrace Covered
terrace Last d 21.30hrs Languages spoken:
English,German,Italian,Spanish
ROOMS: (room only) s 290-325FF; d 305-345FF
MEALS: Full breakfast 48FF Lunch 118-246FF&alc Dinner 118-
246FF&alc
CARDS: ● ● ■■ ■■ ●) Travellers cheques

PLANCHEZ Nièvre

★ ★ **Le Relais des Lacs**
58230
☎ 386784168 FAX 386784411
Situated between the lakes of Pannecière and Settons, the
hotel is a popular meeting place for fisherman and hunters
alike so it is no surprise that fresh fish and game feature
strongly on the menu. Guest accommodation features good
modern facilities and offers a good level of comfort.
Near river Forest area In town centre
Closed mid Nov-mid Dec & early Jan-early Mar
36 en suite (bth/shr) (4 fmly) No smoking in 6 bedrooms TV in
all bedrooms Mini-bar in all bedrooms Licensed Full central
heating Open parking available (charged) Child discount
available 12yrs Fishing Pool table Boule Bicycle rental Open
terrace Last d 22.30hrs Languages spoken: English,Spanish
MEALS: Full breakfast 32FF Continental breakfast 32FF Lunch
97-230FF&alc Dinner fr 101FF&alc✱
CARDS: ● ● ■■ ■■ ●) Travellers cheques

PONT-DE-PANY Côte-D'Or

★ ★ ★ ★ **Château la Chassagne**
21410
☎ 380404750 FAX 380236628
Located near the L'Ouche valley just 15 minutes from Dijon,
the hotel is surrounded by a magnificent 40 hectare park.
Elegant days rooms and smartly decorated bedrooms offer the
highest degree of comfort. The cuisine incorporates superb
classic dishes, which on fine days are served on the terrace.
There is an unrivalled choice of leisure facilities and assorted
entertainment available to guests which makes it an unique
setting where to pass an enjoyable stay.
Near river Forest area Near motorway
Closed 16 Nov-14 Mar
12 en suite (bth/shr) (1 fmly) (1 with balcony) TV in all
bedrooms STV Mini-bar in all bedrooms Licensed Lift Full
central heating Open parking available Supervised Outdoor
swimming pool (heated) Golf Tennis Sauna Solarium Gym
Boule Bicycle rental Open terrace Covered terrace
Languages spoken: English,Dutch,German
CARDS: ● ● ■■ ■■ ●) Travellers cheques

POUILLY-EN-AUXOIS Côte-D'Or

★ ★ ★ ★ **Château de Chailly**
Chailly-sur-Armançon *21320*
☎ 380903030 FAX 380903000
This beautiful residence is classified as a historic monument
and luxurious hotel. The elegant bedrooms and suites
contd.

are decorated to a high standard with splendid furnishings and fabrics, and guests have a choice of two restaurants; one serving a gastronomic cuisine, the other has a range of simpler dishes. With its excellent conference and golf facilities it provides a splendid venue for corporate entertainment as well as a leisure break.
Near river Near lake Forest area Near motorway
Closed 19 Dec-11 Jan
45 en suite (bth/shr) TV in all bedrooms STV Radio in rooms Direct dial from all bedrooms Licensed Lift Night porter Full central heating Open parking available Covered parking available Supervised Child discount available 12yrs Outdoor swimming pool (heated) Golf 18 Tennis Pool table Boule Bicycle rental Open terrace Covered terrace Hot air ballooning,wine tasting, karting Last d 21.30hrs Languages spoken: English,German
CARDS: 💳 🏧 💳 🌐 Travellers cheques

PULIGNY-MONTRACHET Côte-D'Or

★ ★ ★ Le Montracher
pl des Marronniers *21190*
☎ 380213006 FAX 380213906
This large pleasant house stands behind the chestnut trees in the village square. A pleasant country atmosphere prevails throughout and extends to the restaurant where a selection of traditional dishes with a personal accent are served. The cosy guest accommodation is attractively furnished, fully equipped, and offers a high level of comfort.
Forest area Near motorway
Closed Dec-9 Jan
32 en suite (bth/shr) 10 rooms in annexe (1 with balcony) TV in all bedrooms STV Direct dial from all bedrooms Night porter Open terrace Wine tasting,vineyard visits Last d 21.30hrs Languages spoken: English,German, Spanish
MEALS: Continental breakfast 55FF Lunch 195-425FF&alc Dinner 195-425FF&alc✱
CARDS: 💳 🏧 💳 🌐 Travellers cheques

ROGNY-LES-SEPT-ECLUSES Yonne

★ ★ Auberge des 7 Ecluses
1 rue Gaspard de Coligny *89220*
☎ 386745290 FAX 386745677
The inn is located beside the Briare canal with its impressive 'staircase' of sluices built in 1605 along the river Loing. It features comfortable bedrooms, a cosy bar and lounge, as well as a restaurant where traditional dishes are combined with fresh sea and shellfish specialities.
Near river Near lake Forest area Near motorway
Closed 1Jan-1Mar
7 en suite (bth/shr) (2 fmly) Licensed Full central heating Open parking available Supervised Child discount available 12yrs Bicycle rental Open terrace Last d 22.00hrs Languages spoken: English,German,Spanish
MEALS: Continental breakfast 35FF Lunch 98-195FF&alc Dinner fr 250FFalc✱
CARDS: 💳 🏧 💳 🌐 Travellers cheques

ROMANÈCHE-THORINS Saône-et-Loire

★ ★ ★ Les Maritonnes
rte de Fleurie *71570*
☎ 385355170 FAX 385355814
(on N6)
An ideal location for exploring the villages and vineyards of the Beaujolais region. A warm welcome is combined with

gourmet food and wooded surroundings which include a swimming pool.
Closed 16 Dec-25 Jan RS closed Sun evening & Mon
20 en suite (bth/shr) TV in all bedrooms Direct dial from all bedrooms Mini-bar in all bedrooms Licensed Full central heating Open parking available Supervised Outdoor swimming pool (heated) Boule Open terrace Last d 21.30hrs Languages spoken: English, German
ROOMS: (room only) s 370-410FF; d 400-550FF
MEALS: Continental breakfast 65FF Lunch 150-420FFalc Dinner 195-420FFalc✱
CARDS: 💳 🏧 💳 🌐 Travellers cheques

SAILLENARD Saône-et-Loire

★ ★ Moulin de Sauvagette
rte de Bletterans *71580*
☎ 385741758
Near river Forest area Near motorway
Closed 15 Jan-13 Mar
9 rms TV in all bedrooms Licensed Full central heating Open parking available Child discount available 7yrs Fishing Boule Bicycle rental Open terrace V meals Languages spoken: English,German

ST-GERVAIS-EN-VALLIÈRE Saône-et-Loire

★ ★ ★ Moulin D'Hauterive
Hameau de Chaublanc *71350*
☎ 385915556 FAX 385918965
Near river Forest area Near motorway
Closed Mon & Tue noon
22 en suite (bth/shr) 3 rooms in annexe (6 fmly) No smoking on premises TV in all bedrooms Mini-bar in all bedrooms Licensed Full central heating Open parking available Supervised Child discount available 12yrs Outdoor swimming pool (heated) Tennis Fishing Sauna Solarium Gym Pool table Boule Jacuzzi/spa Bicycle rental Open terrace Covered terrace Last d 21.00hrs Languages spoken: English
ROOMS: (room only) s fr 530FF; d 600-850FF **Reductions over 1 night**
MEALS: Full breakfast 70FF Lunch 105-165FF Dinner 240-270FF
CARDS: 💳 🏧 💳 🌐

ST-MARTIN-EN-BRESSE Saône-et-Loire

★ ★ Au Puits Enchante
71620
☎ 385477196 FAX 385477458
This friendly family establishment is located in a peaceful little village in Bresse, surrounded by unspoilt countryside and pure, fresh air. The charming guest rooms are individually styled and provide comfortable accommodation. The chef-proprietor, Jacky Chateau works miracles in the kitchen and is responsible for the delicious fresh-water fish specialities and regional good valued dishes based on traditional Burgundy recipes
Forest area
Closed 31 Dec-1 Feb
14 en suite (bth/shr) (1 fmly) No smoking in 8 bedrooms TV in all bedrooms Direct dial from all bedrooms Licensed Full central heating Open parking available Covered parking available Supervised Child discount available 2yrs Fishing Riding Boule Bicycle rental Open terrace V meals Last d 21.00hrs Languages spoken: English,German
ROOMS: (room only) s fr 200FF; d 230-290FF **Special breaks**

MEALS: Full breakfast 38FF Lunch 98-225FFalc Dinner 98-225FFalc
CARDS: ●● ⅠⅠ Travellers cheques

ST-PÈRE Yonne

★ ★ ★ ★ Espérance
89450
☎ 386333910 FAX 386332615
Near river Forest area
35 rms Some rooms in annexe (1 fmly) (1 with balcony) TV in all bedrooms STV Radio in rooms Direct dial from all bedrooms Mini-bar in all bedrooms Licensed Night porter Full central heating Open parking available Outdoor swimming pool (heated) Bicycle rental V meals Last d 22.00hrs Languages spoken: English,German
CARDS: ●● ▭▭ ⅠⅠ ◑ Travellers cheques

ST-VÉRAND Saône-et-Loire

★ Auberge du St-Vérand
71570
☎ 385371650 FAX 385374927
Near river Near motorway
11 rms (3 fmly) (3 with balcony) TV in all bedrooms Licensed Full central heating Open parking available Supervised Boule Open terrace Last d 21.30hrs Languages spoken: English
MEALS: Continental breakfast 35FF Lunch 95-205FF Dinner 95-205FF✱
CARDS: ●● ⅠⅠ

SAUVIGNY-LE-BOIS Yonne

★ ★ ★ Le Relais Fleuri
N6 *89200*
☎ 386340285 FAX 386340998
Near motorway
48 en suite (bth/shr) TV in all bedrooms Radio in rooms Direct dial from all bedrooms Mini-bar in all bedrooms Licensed Night porter Full central heating Open parking available Outdoor swimming pool (heated) Tennis Solarium Boule Table tennis Last d 21.45hrs Languages spoken: English,German

ROOMS: (room only) s 350-400FF; d 350-450FF **Special breaks**
MEALS: Full breakfast 48FF Lunch 95-300FF&alc Dinner 95-300FF&alc
CARDS: ●● ▭▭ ⅠⅠ ◑ Travellers cheques

SEMUR-EN-AUXOIS Côte-D'Or

★ ★ Hotel du Lac
pont et Massène *21140*
☎ 380971111 FAX 380972925
(from A6 exit Bien-les-Semur, turn left, then take first right towards Lac de Pont. After 3km go towards the Hotel de lac.)
Situated in the Burgundy countryside with rolling hills and a rich historic heritage, this beautiful residence is tucked away in a forest on the edge of a lake. A warm and informal atmosphere prevails throughout the establishment, which features attractive guest accommodation with good amenities and a country restaurant which serves an extensive selection of tasty specialities from the region. There is a shaded terrace and garden, whilst also the surrounding area offers a choice of leisure facilities to experience and places to see.
Near river Near lake Near sea Near beach Forest area Near motorway
13 Jan-20 Dec
20 rms (9 bth 10 shr) (5 fmly) (4 with balcony) No smoking in 1 bedroom TV in 15 bedrooms Direct dial from all bedrooms Mini-bar in 5 bedrooms Licensed Full central heating Open parking available Covered parking available (charged) Child discount available 12yrs Open terrace Covered terrace Last d 21.15hrs Languages spoken: English,German
ROOMS: (room only) s 230-250FF; d 260-330FF
Reductions over 1 night
MEALS: Full breakfast 37FF Lunch 90-195FF Dinner 90-195FF
CARDS: ●● ▭▭ ◑ Travellers cheques

SENS Yonne

★ ★ ★ Paris Et De La Poste (Best Western)
97 rue de la République *89103*
☎ 386651743 FAX 386641575
(From Paris (A6) exit Sens Courtenay)
The hotel is set in the town centre, just 50 metres from the cathedral, and offers traditional hospitality in a cordial atmosphere. This delightful building dates back to 1789, and has bedrooms and apartments with modern facilities, a patio, and a flower-decked terrace. The restaurant offers a fine gourmet cuisine which consists of skilfully executed dishes, served by courteous staff.
Near river Forest area In town centre Near motorway
25 en suite (bth/shr) (7 fmly) (1 with balcony) TV in all bedrooms STV Radio in rooms Direct dial from all bedrooms Licensed Lift Full central heating Open parking available (charged) Supervised Child discount available 12yrs Open terrace V meals Last d 22.00hrs Languages spoken: English,Spanish
MEALS: Full breakfast 50FF Continental breakfast 50FF Lunch 99-320FF&alc Dinner 99-320FF&alc✱
CARDS: ●● ▭▭ ⅠⅠ ◑ Travellers cheques

TOURNUS Saône-et-Loire

★ ★ Aux Terrasses
18 av du 23 Janvier *71700*
☎ 385510174 FAX 385510999
The town of Tournus, with its medieval centre, criss-crossed with narrow streets and authentic houses, is one of the most popular tourist sights in southern Burgundy. Henriette and Michel Carrette welcome their visitors in true 'Burgundian' style, and offer comfortable accommodation and a high quality cuisine. There are three dining-rooms, which serve regional specialities skilfully prepared by the proprietor and complemented by the excellent wines of the region.
Near river In town centre Near motorway *contd.*

18 en suite (bth/shr) (3 fmly) TV in all bedrooms Licensed
Full central heating Air conditioning in bedrooms Open
parking available Covered parking available (charged) Child
discount available 12yrs Open terrace V meals Languages
spoken: English
CARDS: ●● ■■ Travellers cheques

★ ★ ★ Le Domaine de Tremont
rte de Plottes *71700*
☎ 385510010 FAX 385321228
Set in the open countryside, and surrounded by wooded hills,
this charming family establishment offers a delightful interior,
adorned with period furniture. Elegant bedrooms offer a
combination of modern comfort and traditional furnishings
and have spacious, well equipped bathrooms. The informal
restaurant serves an honest, traditional cuisine, whilst the
comfortable reading room with harpsichord provides
relaxation.
Forest area
6 en suite (bth/shr) (1 fmly) TV in all bedrooms STV Licensed
Full central heating Open parking available (charged) Child
discount available Boule Open terrace Last d 22.00hrs
Languages spoken: English
CARDS: ●● ■■ Travellers cheques

★ ★ ★ Le Sauvage (Best Western)
pl du Champ-de-Mars *71700*
☎ 385511445 FAX 385321027

The hotel Sauvage is an establishment with the charm of by-
gone times and modern comfort, and features personalised
bedrooms with modern facilities. Some have views of the 13th-
century Saint Philibert church, which is a fine example of
Romanesque art. The restaurant serves a choice of delicacies
such as escargot en coquille and poulet de Bresse,
complemented by some fine examples of Burgundy wines.
Near river In town centre Near motorway
30 en suite (bth/shr) (5 fmly) TV in all bedrooms STV Radio in
rooms Licensed Lift Night porter Full central heating
Covered parking available (charged) Child discount available
12yrs Open terrace Last d 21.00hrs Languages spoken:
English,German
MEALS: Full breakfast 40FF Continental breakfast 40FF Lunch
85-198FF&alc Dinner 85-198FF&alc✱
CARDS: ●● ■■ ■■ ● Travellers cheques

★ ★ ★ La Montagne de Brancion
71700
☎ 385511240 FAX 385511864
(exit A6 at Tournus)
A hilltop position allows beautiful views of the vineyards of the
Maconnais Hills. La Montagne de Brancion is a charmimg,
quiet, family run hotel, with pretty and comfortable bedrooms,
beautiful gardens and fine cooking.
Near sea Forest area
Closed Dec-14 Mar
20 en suite (bth/shr) (1 fmly) (4 with balcony) TV in all
bedrooms Direct dial from all bedrooms Mini-bar in all
bedrooms Room-safe Licensed Full central heating Open
parking available Outdoor swimming pool (heated) Bicycle
rental Open terrace V meals Last d 21.00hrs Languages
spoken: English & German
ROOMS: (room only) s 460-650FF; d 650-760FF
Reductions over 1 night
MEALS: Full breakfast 75FF Continental breakfast 40FF Lunch
160-330FF&alc Dinner 250-330FF&alc
CARDS: ●● ■■ ● Travellers cheques

★ ★ ★ ★ Le Rempart
2-4 av Gambetta *71700*
☎ 385511056 FAX 385517722
(From A6/N6 follow signs for 'Centre Ville' into Tournus)
The building dates back to the 15th century and was built right
on the ramparts of the town. Concealed behind its façade, the
hotel features a renovated interior, where elegantly furnished
guest accommodation, a congenial bar and gourmet cuisine
provide the enjoyable setting for a memorable stay. Upon
arrival guests are met by the friendly Marion family who offer
personal attention and friendly service at all times. Mr Daniel
Rogie presides over the kitchen and is responsible for the well
executed cuisine, which consist of regional dishes prepared
with fresh seasonal produce. Meals are served on a pleasant
covered terrace at the rear of the hotel.
In town centre Near motorway
37 en suite (bth) (5 fmly) TV in all bedrooms STV Radio in
rooms Direct dial from all bedrooms Mini-bar in all bedrooms
Licensed Lift Night porter Full central heating Air
conditioning in bedrooms Open parking available (charged)
Covered parking available (charged) Child discount available
12yrs Open terrace V meals Last d 21.30hrs Languages
spoken: English
ROOMS: (room only) s 398-680FF; d 475-800FF
Reductions over 1 night
MEALS: Full breakfast 50FF Lunch 168-420FF&alc Dinner 168-
420FF&alc
CARDS: ●● ■■ ■■ ● Travellers cheques

VAL-DE-MERCY Yonne

Auberge du Château
3 rue du Pont *89580*
☎ 386416000 FAX 386417328
(from Auxerre take N6 towards Avallon, at Vincelles take D38
to Val-de-Mercy)
Set in the heart of the village, this peaceful inn has comfortable
bedrooms, elegantly furnished in turn-of-the-century style and a
sought-after restaurant, where the chef, who formerly worked
under the guidance of the famous Michel Roux of the Waterside
Inn, invites his guests to sample original French haute cuisine,
enhanced with flavours from different corners of the world.
Forest area Near motorway
Closed 15 Jan-Feb
5 rms (4 bth) TV in all bedrooms Licensed Full central heating
Open parking available Supervised Boule Open terrace
V meals Last d 21.00hrs Languages spoken: English
ROOMS: (room only) s 350-500FF; d 420-500FF
Special breaks
MEALS: Full breakfast 50FF Continental breakfast 70FF Lunch
220-255FF&alc Dinner 220-255FF&alc
CARDS: ●● ■■ ● Travellers cheques

VAL-SUZON Côte-D'Or

★ ★ ★ Hostellerie du Val Suzon
rue du Fourneau *21121*
☎ 380356015 FAX 380356136
This ancient mill is tucked away in a valley in green
surroundings and has maintained its original character. The
two 'livres d'or' contain the names of politicians, royalty and
those connected with the arts who have stayed here. There are
bright, peaceful bedrooms with good modern amenities, and a
restaurant which serves dishes based on traditional recipes,
and complemented by innovative ingredients.
Near river Forest area Near motorway
Closed 16 Nov-14 Dec

15 en suite (bth/shr) 9 rooms in annexe (3 fmly) TV in all
bedrooms STV Direct dial from all bedrooms Mini-bar in all
bedrooms Room-safe Licensed Full central heating Open
parking available Covered parking available Supervised
Child discount available 12yrs Boule Open terrace Last d
21.45hrs Languages spoken: English,Spanish,Portuguese
ROOMS: (room only) s 320-450FF; d 420-520FF
MEALS: Full breakfast 60FF Continental breakfast 40FF Lunch
130-170FF&alc Dinner 200-270FF&alc
CARDS: ● ▦ ▆ ◑ Travellers cheques

VÉZELAY Yonne

★ ★ ★ Residence Hotel Le Pontot
pl du Pontot *89450*
☎ 386332440 FAX 386333005
(at Vezelay, turn right up only street leading into walled city.
Follow one-way signs to parking lot on left. Hotel on other side
of parking lot)
The hotel is housed in a fortified medieval building and
features a charming interior where modern comfort is
combined with elegantly decorated public areas. Just a few
steps away from the Madeleine basilica, it has a walled flower-
garden, where on fine days breakfast and drinks are served,
and bedrooms which are equipped with modern amenities.
From the hotel, guests have fine views of the Morvan hills,
whilst the surrounding area offers a number of adventurous
leisure opportunities.
Near river Near lake Forest area In town centre Near
motorway
Closed 2 Nov-15 Apr
10 en suite (bth/shr) Radio in rooms Direct dial from all
bedrooms Licensed Full central heating Open parking
available Covered parking available (charged) Supervised No
children 10yrs Bicycle rental Open terrace Hot air ballooning
Languages spoken: English
ROOMS: (room only) s 350-700FF; d 600-1050FF
CARDS: ● ▆ ◑ JCB Travellers cheques

VOUGEOT Côte-D'Or

★ ★ ★ ★ Château de Gilly
Gilly les Citeaux *21640*
☎ 380628998 FAX 380628234
(From A31 exit Nuits-St-Georges continue towards Dijon to
Vougeot, then towards Gilly-les-Citeaux)
Situated between Dijon and Beaune, in the heart of the famous
Burgundy vineyards, the Château de Gilly, is a palatial
residence built for the priors of the Cistercian abbey.
Surrounded by a moat, it features bedrooms which are
decorated in style with the architecture and combine modern
comfort with the charm of by gone times. The former cellar
with magnificent vaulted ceiling, is now the setting for an
inspired cuisine accompanied by the best Burgundian wines.
Near river Forest area Near motorway
Closed 26 Jan-7 Mar
48 en suite (bth/shr) 4 rooms in annexe (9 fmly) (2 with
balcony) No smoking in 10 bedrooms TV in all bedrooms STV
Radio in rooms Direct dial from all bedrooms Mini-bar in all
bedrooms Licensed Lift Night porter Full central heating
Open parking available Supervised Tennis Fishing Boule
Bicycle rental Open terrace Croquet Last d 21.30hrs
Languages spoken: English,German
ROOMS: (room only) s 700-1480FF; d 560-2600FF **Special
breaks**
MEALS: Full breakfast 85FF Continental breakfast 130FF
Lunch 195-410FF&alc Dinner 195-410FF&alc
CARDS: ● ▦ ▆ ◑ JCB Travellers cheques

Taking your mobile phone to France?
See page 11

Franche-Comté

Franche-Comté is a region that invites you to experience the great outdoors, where you will find deep forests and a thousand lakes and rivers. Besançon, the fortified capital of the region, nestles inside a loop in the River Doubs and is a city of art and history, hosting prestigious international music festivals in the summer. This region is truly central to Europe, with a 143 mile/230km stretch of its eastern side bordering Switzerland and within reasonably easy reach of both Germany and Italy.

(Top): Salins-les-Bains is home to this stone wine-picker, although the town is chiefly known historically as a major salt producer.

(Bottom): The pretty village of Nans-sous-Ste-Anne, surrounded by greenery.

ESSENTIAL FACTS

DÉPARTEMENTS:	Doubs, Jura, Haute-Saône, Territoire-de-Belfort
PRINCIPAL TOWNS	Besançon, Montbeliard, Luxeuil-les-Bains, Dole,
PLACES TO VISIT:	The route-de-vin from Beaford to Arbois; the Herrisson Falls at the Sout de Doubs; Haut-Jura Nature Park; Cleron Castle; Ornans.
REGIONAL TOURIST OFFICE	9 rue de Pontarlier, 25044 Besançon Tel 81 83 50 47
LOCAL GASTRONOMIC DELIGHTS	Cheeses such as Comté, Morbier, Cancoillote, Bleu de Gex, Mont d'Or or Vacherin du Haut-Doubs; saucisse de Morteaux (smoked sausage); pognes; wild mushrooms; coq au vin jaune; tarts filled with fruit in summer and pumpkin in winter; regional fondu made with blue cheese
DRINKS	The AOC wine from Franche-Comté is Arbois. Three main districts, Arbois, Château-Chalon and L'Etoile, produce red, white or rosé. Château-Chalon also produces vin jaune (yellow wine) and vin de paille (straw wine). Vin jaune is aged in casks for at least six years, whilst vin de paille is made from grapes brought to maturity on beds of straw for three months. Vin fou (crazy or mad wine) is a locally produced sparkling wine. Macvin, a liqueur wine fortified with eau-de-vie, is served with melon, or as an apertif or with dessert.
LOCAL CRAFTS WHAT TO BUY	Watches and clocks from Besançon, lace from Montbéliard and Luxeuil-les-Bains, pottery and earthenware from Mathay and Salins-les-Bain, horn from Jeurre and Lizon, wood crafts and turned products from St Claude, Largillay and Mambelin.

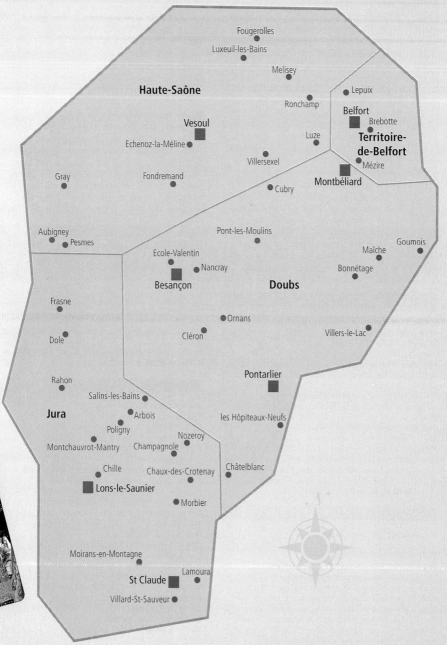

Fougerolles

Luxeuil-les-Bains

Melisey

Haute-Saône

Lepuix

Ronchamp

Belfort

Brebotte

Vesoul

Luze

Territoire-de-Belfort

Echenoz-la-Méline

Mézire

Villersexel

Gray

Fondremand

Montbéliard

Cubry

Aubigney

Pont-les-Moulins

Goumois

Pesmes

Maîche

Ecole-Valentin

Nancray

Bonnétage

Besançon

Doubs

Frasne

Ornans

Dole

Cléron

Villers-le-Lac

Rahon

Pontarlier

Salins-les-Bains

Jura

Arbois

les Hôpiteaux-Neufs

Poligny

Nozeroy

Montchauvrot-Mantry

Champagnole

Chille

Chaux-des-Crotenay

Châtelblanc

Lons-le-Saunier

Morbier

Moirans-en-Montagne

Lamoura

St Claude

Villard-St-Sauveur

EVENTS AND FESTIVALS

Jan Aldenans Flea Market

Feb Morbier Cheese Festival

Mar Besançon Traditional Carnival; St-Valbert Brioche Festival; Pontarlier French Tarot Championship; Audincourt Carnival

Apr Mézire Snail Festival; Nancray Easter Flower Festival; Nancray Vegetable Fair; St-Claude Soufflaculs Festival; Melisey Carnival of the Haute Vallée de l'Ognon

May Sancey-le-Long Trout Festival; Belfort Flower Festival; Villersexel 'Le Triangle Vert' (*sport event*); Dole Festival of Tales & Legends; St Claude, Haut Jura Classical Music Festival; Besançon Comté Fair; Levier Fir Tree Festival

Jun Jazz Festival - St-Claude, Dole, Vesoul, Ornans, Pontarlier, Baume-les-Dames, Arc-et-Senans; Nancray Haymaking; Lavigny Circus Festival; Belfort Cabaret & Theatre at the Castle

Jul Son et Lumière shows at St-Loup sur Semouse, Jougne, Fondremand, Rahon; Moirans-en-Montagne Children's Festival; Brebotte Historical Pageant; Fondremand Arts & Crafts Festival; Arbois Wine Fair; Nozeroy Medieval Fair

Aug Rahon Son et Lumière; Lamoura Local Craft Fair; Frasne Blueberry Festival; Pontarlier, Nights of Joux Festival; Morteau Sausage Festival

Sept Arbios Grape Harvest Ritual; Luxeuil les Bains Art Festival; Besançon Classical Music Festival; Luxeuil les-Bains Son et Lumière; Les Hôpitaux Neufs Descent of the herds from the Alps; Echenoz-la-Méline Honey Festival; MontbéliardVintage Car Rally; Ronchamp Veteran Cars & Motorbikes; Fougerolles Festival of Cherry Eau-de-Vie Tasters

Oct Luze Apple Fair; Montbéliard Model Building Sale; Audincourt Comic Book Festival

Nov Belfort Film Festival

Dec Audincourt Mechanical Figures Fair; Montbéliard Christmas Lights Festival

Route des Vins

If your interests lie in wine-tasting and you wish to increase your knowledge of the origins and making of French wines there are many wine routes suggested and organised by the French Tourist Board for you to explore. The Route des Vins du Jura, for example, provides an itinerary from Arbois (home town and work-place of Louis Pasteur), down to Bealfort with hotels located directly on the route for your gastronomic stopovers. You will be welcomed in these wine villages where gourmets will be able to admire the specialities of Franche-Comte, made of course with Jura wine.

ARBOIS Jura

★ ★ Des Cepages
rte de Villette *39600*
☎ 384662525 FAX 384374962
(A36 exit Dole)
Situated in the wine capital of the Jura, this contemporary establishment features spacious public areas and well equipped bedrooms offering modern comforts. It has an interior garden with a large veranda, where a buffet-style breakfast and dinner offer a choice of varied, high-quality dishes.
Near motorway
33 en suite (shr) TV in all bedrooms Direct dial from all bedrooms Mini-bar in all bedrooms Licensed Lift Open parking available Child discount available 10yrs Open terrace Last d 21.30hrs Languages spoken: English,German
MEALS: Full breakfast 47FF Dinner 48-108FFalc✱
CARDS: ✆ 💳 💳 ⑨ Travellers cheques

AUBIGNEY Haute-Saône

★ ★ Auberge du Vieux Moulin
70140
☎ 384316161 FAX 384316238
(A36 exit Dole(North),20kms follow signs for Gray)
This old water-mill dates back to 1794 and is now a comfortable family inn with an exclusive restaurant. The Mirbey family have worked in the hospitality trade for five generations and offer their guests friendly, attentive service in this charming establishment. The bedrooms provide a high standard of accommodation and are well equipped, and the restaurant features an outstanding choice of dishes

complemented by vintage wines.
Near river Forest area
7 en suite (bth/shr) (4 fmly) TV in all bedrooms Licensed Full central heating Open parking available Fishing Open terrace
MEALS: Continental breakfast 48FF Lunch 100-300FFalc✱
CARDS: ✆ 💳 💳 ⑨ Travellers cheques

BESANÇON Doubs

★ ★ ★ Castan Relais
6 Square Castan *25000*
☎ 381650200 FAX 381830102
(In the town centre. Follow signs for 'Citadelle' and Conseil Régional')
This charming residence offers its clientele the modern comfort of renovated bedrooms in the charming ambience of an 18th-century mansion. Guests receive a degree of personal service which is difficult to match, elegantly furnished bedrooms with thoughtful little extras, and a superb breakfast consisting of house delicacies and regional specialities.
Near river In town centre
Closed 26 Dec-2 Jan & 3 wks Aug
8 en suite (bth/shr) No smoking in 3 bedrooms TV in all bedrooms STV Radio in rooms Licensed Night porter Full central heating Air conditioning in bedrooms Open parking available Supervised Child discount available 13yrs Open terrace Languages spoken: English
ROOMS: (room only) s fr 550FF; d 550-980FF ✱
Reductions over 1 night
CARDS: ✆ 💳 💳 ⑨ Travellers cheques

BONNÉTAGE Doubs

★ ★ Étang du Moulin
25210
☎ 381689278 FAX 381689442
Near river Forest area
Closed 4 Jan-3 Feb
18 en suite (bth/shr) Some rooms in annexe (3 with balcony)
TV in all bedrooms Licensed Full central heating Open parking
available Supervised Child discount available 10yrs Fishing V
meals Last d 21.00hrs Languages spoken: English,German
MEALS: Continental breakfast 45FF Lunch 110-350FF&alc
Dinner 110-350FF✱
CARDS: ●● ☲ Travellers cheques

CHAMPAGNOLE Jura

★ ★ Bois Dormant
rte de Pontarlier *39300*
☎ 384526666 FAX 384526667
(S of town centre towards Lons-le-Saunier)
The hotel opened its doors in 1994 and occupies a very
peaceful location in the middle of a wood. It offers all the
ingredients for a relaxing stay: attractive surroundings,
spacious bedrooms and a restaurant serving an excellent
cuisine. The panelled bedrooms are exceptionally comfortable
and fitted out with attractive pine furniture creating a warm
atmosphere. The restaurant serves a wide array of regional
dishes accompanied by the fine wines of the Jura.
Near river Forest area In town centre Near motorway
36 en suite (bth/shr) (4 fmly) (6 with balcony) TV in all
bedrooms STV Direct dial from all bedrooms Mini-bar in all
bedrooms Licensed Full central heating Open parking
available Child discount available 12yrs Tennis Pool table
Boule Open terrace Covered terrace V meals Last d 22.00hrs
Languages spoken: English,German
ROOMS: (room only) s 290-320FF; d 300-340FF
MEALS: Full breakfast 50FF Continental breakfast 50FF Lunch
88-240FF&alc Dinner 88-240FF&alc
CARDS: ●● ☲ Travellers cheques

★ ★ Grand Hotel Ripotot
av du Maréchal Foch *39300*

☎ 384521545 FAX 384520911
The hotel is situated in Champagnole at an altitude of 1800 feet
at the foot of the Mont-Rivel. The building dates back to 1875,
and has maintained for all those years friendly hospitality and
an excellent service. It features spacious bedrooms - mostly
overlooking the garden - with a personal touch and modern
facilities. There is a delightful restaurant which serves a fine
regional cuisine, accompanied by a selection of good Jura and
Burgundy wines.
Near river Near lake Forest area In town centre Near
motorway
Closed mid Nov-1 Apr
55 rms (45 bth/shr) (8 fmly) (6 with balcony) TV in all
bedrooms STV Direct dial from all bedrooms Licensed Lift
Night porter Full central heating Open parking available
(charged) Covered parking available (charged) Supervised
Child discount available 10yrs Tennis Boule Bicycle rental
Open terrace Last d 21.30hrs Languages spoken:
English,Dutch,Flemish,German,Spanish
ROOMS: (room only) s 140-230FF; d 190-320FF ✱
Reductions over 1 night
MEALS: Continental breakfast 38FF Lunch 90-240FF&alc
Dinner 90-240FF&alc✱
CARDS: ●● ☲ Travellers cheques

Du Parc
★ ★ ★ **Du Parc**
13 rue Paul Crétin *39300*

☎ 384521320 FAX 384522762
(On SW outskirts towards Lons)
In a quiet location close to the River Ain and within 5 minutes
walk of the town centre, the hotel provides a good base for
touring the surrounding region or as an overnight stop en route
to further destinations. It has traditionally furnished bedrooms
with modern appointments, a cosy lounge and a country style
restaurant which serves a choice of regional dishes.
Near river Forest area In town centre Near motorway
40 en suite (bth/shr) (5 fmly) (4 with balcony) No smoking in 2
bedrooms TV in 20 bedrooms STV Radio in rooms Direct
dial from 20 bedrooms Mini-bar in 20 bedrooms Licensed
Full central heating Open parking available Covered parking
available (charged) Supervised Child discount available 10yrs
Fishing Riding Open terrace V meals Last d 22.00hrs
Languages spoken: English,German,Italian
ROOMS: (room only) s 200-250FF; d 260-320FF
Reductions over 1 night Special breaks
MEALS: Full breakfast 35FF Continental breakfast 35FF
Dinner 75-180FF✱
CARDS: ●● ■■ ☲ ➋ Travellers cheques

CHÂTELBLANC Doubs

★ ★ Le Castel Blanc
25240
☎ 381692456 FAX 381691121
The hotel Le Castel Blanc features a country-style interior with
pretty bedrooms, decorated with rustic furniture, which offer a
straight-forward level of comfort. A copious breakfast is
served in the morning, before guests embark on one of the
many leisure opportunities which this beautiful region has to
offer both in summer and winter. In the evening a range of
regional dishes, prepared with fine local ingredients, are
served in the restaurant.
Near lake Near sea Near beach Forest area
11 rms (2 bth 5 shr) (3 fmly) Licensed Full central heating
Open parking available Supervised Child discount available
12yrs Outdoor swimming pool Fishing Sauna Solarium Gym
Boule Bicycle rental Open terrace Last d 20.45hrs Languages
spoken: English,German & Italian
MEALS: Continental breakfast 38FF Lunch fr 85FF&alc Dinner
fr 85FF&alc✱
CARDS: ●● ☲ Travellers cheques

CHAUX-DES-CROTENAY Jura

★ ★ ★ Des Lacs
Pont de la Chaux (N 5) *39150*
☎ 384515042 FAX 384515423
(From A36 exit 'Dole' take N5 via Poligny, Champagnole to
Chaux-des-Crotenay)
Set in the heart of a forest in the Jura region, the hotel has
been in the Monnier family for almost a century. Located in a
region with plenty of lakes and waterfalls, it is the ideal venue
for both a summer and winter holiday. On warm days
swimming, pony rides and fishing are just some of the leisure
opportunities on offer, whilst the winter season offers excellent
skiing grounds. The peaceful bedrooms are furnished in an
understated fashion and have modern facilities, and there is a
rustic restaurant with open fire place which serves tasty
regional dishes.
Near river Near lake Forest area Near motorway
Closed 20 Nov-Jan
30 en suite (bth/shr) (6 fmly) (12 with balcony) TV in all
contd.

bedrooms Direct dial from all bedrooms Licensed Lift Full
central heating Open parking available Covered parking
available Child discount available 13yrs Outdoor swimming
pool (heated) Fishing Sauna Solarium Open terrace Last d
22.00hrs Languages spoken: English
ROOMS: (room only) s 200FF; d 265FF
MEALS: Continental breakfast 32FF Lunch 80-150FF&alc
Dinner 80-150FF&alc
CARDS: ● ▆ Travellers cheques

CHILLE Jura

★ ★ Parenthése
Grande Rue *39570*
☎ 384475544 FAX 384249213
The individually styled bedrooms in this hotel offer cosy
accommodation and are equipped with every modern
convenience. The establishment provides the modern setting
for an enjoyable break, a business meeting or seminar. Public
areas have a relaxed atmosphere and include a restaurant
which serves an array of well prepared dishes accompanied by
select wines.
Near river Forest area Near motorway
31 en suite (bth/shr) (9 fmly) (6 with balcony) TV in all
bedrooms Radio in rooms Direct dial from all bedrooms
Mini-bar in all bedrooms Lift Full central heating Open
parking available Child discount available Outdoor swimming
pool (heated) Solarium Jacuzzi/spa Open terrace V meals
Last d 21.30hrs Languages spoken: German
CARDS: ● ▆ ▆ ● Travellers cheques

CUBRY Doubs

Château de Bournel
25680
☎ 381860010 FAX 381860106
(autoroute Mulhouse/Besancon exit Baume les Dames on right
direction Lure after 14kms turn right)
In the eighty hectares of English style park surrounding the
Château the French architect Robert Berthet has designed an
18 hole golf course using the natural contours and descending
water courses. The accommodation offered is spacious,
comfortable and of the highest standard. In the superb arched
halls of the Château you will discover the traditional and
creative cuisine, using best market and vegetable garden
produce. The extensive cellars include exceptional wines of the
Jura region to compliment your meals.
Forest area
Closed Dec-Feb
13 en suite (bth/shr) (2 fmly) TV in all bedrooms Direct dial
from all bedrooms Mini-bar in all bedrooms Licensed Full
central heating Open parking available Child discount
available 8yrs Golf 18 Bicycle rental Open terrace V meals
Last d 21.30hrs Languages spoken: English & German
ROOMS: (room only) s 640-800FF; d 760-950FF **Special
breaks: Golf breaks**
MEALS: Full breakfast 50FF Lunch 140-190FF&alc Dinner 140-
190FF&alc✱

DOLE Jura

★ ★ ★ La Chaumière
346 av Maréchal Juin *39100*
☎ 384707240 FAX 384792560
Set in country surroundings, and yet just two kilometres from
the town centre, the hotel features bright, attractive bedrooms
with views over the garden offering a high level of comfort.

The restaurant has received many recommendations for its
excellent dishes where fresh local produce is combined with
exotic herbs and spices, offering a delicately balanced cuisine.
Near river Forest area
Closed mid Jun-late Jun
18 en suite (bth/shr) (6 fmly) TV in all bedrooms Radio in
rooms Mini-bar in all bedrooms Licensed Full central heating
Open parking available Covered parking available (charged)
Supervised Outdoor swimming pool (heated) Open terrace
Covered terrace V meals Last d 21.45hrs Languages spoken:
English,German
MEALS: Full breakfast 60FF Continental breakfast 40FF Lunch
95-295FF Dinner 95-295FF✱
CARDS: ● ▆ Travellers cheques

★ ★ Pourchéresse
8 av Duhamel (ex av de Châlon) *39100*
☎ 384820105 FAX 384728150
(On the main road to Lyon & Châlon)
Located in the centre of town and just a few steps away from
the museums and historic sights, the hotel provides a good
base for the many excursions on offer into the surrounding
area. A warm welcome awaits guests upon arrival and they are
invited to sample some of the many cocktails prepared by the
host, of which he alone knows the formula. In addition, the
traditionally furnished bedrooms offer modern amenities and
the restaurant offers a choice of regional dishes.
In town centre
18 en suite (bth/shr) (6 fmly) (6 with balcony) TV in all
bedrooms Direct dial from all bedrooms Licensed Full central
heating Open parking available Open terrace Last d 22.00hrs
Languages spoken: English,German,Italian,Spanish
ROOMS: (room only) s 210FF; d 230FF **Reductions over 1
night**
MEALS: Full breakfast 30FF Lunch 69-175FF Dinner 89-175FF
CARDS: ● ▆ Travellers cheques

ÉCOLE-VALENTIN Doubs

★ ★ Climat de France
rue des Maisonnettes *25480*
☎ 381880411 Cen Res 64460123 FAX 381803133
(off N83 by Esso garage)
A friendly welcome awaits guests by the managers Mr and
Mrs Badie and their dedicated team. The hotel features
pleasantly decorated, comfortable bedrooms with good
modern facilities. The restaurant serves a choice of menus,
including a 'no-limits' hors d'oeuvre buffet, as well as the
children's 'Soupière Junior'. On each floor a 'Tisanière' has
been installed to provide guests with a hot drink at any time
free of charge.
Forest area Near motorway
43 en suite (bth) (11 fmly) No smoking in 9 bedrooms TV in all
bedrooms Radio in rooms Direct dial from all bedrooms
Licensed Full central heating Open parking available Open
terrace Languages spoken: English & German
CARDS: ● ▆ Travellers cheques

GOUMOIS Doubs

★ ★ ★ Taillard
25470
☎ 381442075 FAX 381442615
(Access on A36 via Maïche)
The hotel offers its visitors a peaceful stay in country
surroundings, with warm hospitality and attentive service in
abundant supply. The guest rooms are equipped with modern

amenities and provide maximum comfort. The restaurant has a well-deserved reputation for its light cuisine comprising fresh fish and smoked meats.

Near river Forest area
Closed mid Nov-end Feb
24 rms (17 bth/shr) 7 rooms in annexe (6 fmly) (14 with balcony) TV in all bedrooms Direct dial from all bedrooms Mini-bar in 6 bedrooms Licensed Full central heating Open parking available Covered parking available (charged) Supervised Child discount available 14yrs Outdoor swimming pool (heated) Sauna Pool table Jacuzzi/spa Bicycle rental Open terrace V meals Last d 21.00hrs Languages spoken: English,Italian
ROOMS: (room only) s 275-350FF; d 350-490FF ✱
Reductions over 1 night
MEALS: Full breakfast 55FF Lunch 135-370FF&alc Dinner 135-370FF&alc✱
CARDS: 💳 ▦ 🎫 💳 Travellers cheques

LEPUIX Territoire-de-Belfort

★ ★ **Grand Hotel du Sommet**
90200
☎ 384293060 FAX 384239560
Standing on the peak of the Ballon d'Alsace, the hotel offers splendid views over the surrounding area. In summer the region provides ideal walking country and in winter it is a popular ski-resort. Rooms are well equipped and offer functional accommodation, whilst the restaurant serves dishes to suit all tastes.

Near river Near lake Forest area
19 en suite (shr) (4 fmly) TV in all bedrooms Licensed Full central heating Open parking available Covered parking available Child discount available 14yrs Bicycle rental Open terrace Last d 21.30hrs Languages spoken: English, German
MEALS: Full breakfast 30FF Continental breakfast 30FF Lunch 80-120FF&alc Dinner 80-120FF&alc✱
CARDS: 💳 ▦ 🎫 💳 Travellers cheques

LUXEUIL-LES-BAINS Haute-Saône

★ ★ ★ **Beau Site**
18 rue Georges Moulinard *70300*
☎ 384401467 FAX 384845025
This large residence features architecture typical of the Vosges region and is set in a beautiful well-tended garden. On arrival guests can expect a friendly and informal welcome by courteous staff who provide an attentive service throughout their stay. There are attractively decorated bedrooms with modern facilities offering a high level of comfort and a splendid restaurant serving a good quality cuisine.

Near river Near lake Forest area Near motorway
33 en suite (bth/shr) (6 fmly) (5 with balcony) No smoking in 3 bedrooms TV in all bedrooms Direct dial from all bedrooms Full central heating Open parking available Child discount available 12yrs Outdoor swimming pool (heated) Last d 21.30hrs Languages spoken: English,German, Spanish
CARDS: 💳 🎫 Travellers cheques

MAÎCHE Doubs

★ ★ **Panorama**
36 rue St-Michel *25120*
☎ 381640478 FAX 381640895
Situated on a hillside the hotel has Switzerland on one side and overlooks the little village of Maîche on the other. Pleasant guest rooms and furnished chalets equipped with modern

amenities provide comfortable guest accommodation. There is an attractive terrace skirting the forest as well as a panoramic terrace where a range of appetising dishes is prepared by the chef Christian Puc who uses fresh produce of a high quality.
Forest area
Closed 7-19 Jan
32 en suite (bth/shr) (8 with balcony) TV in 16 bedrooms Direct dial from all bedrooms Mini-bar in 3 bedrooms Licensed Full central heating Open parking available Supervised Child discount available 10yrs Tennis Bicycle rental Open terrace V meals Last d 21.30hrs Languages spoken: English,German
ROOMS: (room only) s fr 220FF; d 260-340FF
MEALS: Full breakfast 39FF Continental breakfast 39FF Lunch 100-245FF&alc Dinner 100-245FF&alc
CARDS: 💳 🎫 Travellers cheques

MONTCHAUVROT-MANTRY Jura

★ ★ **La Fontaine**
Montchauvrot *39230*
☎ 384855002 FAX 384855618
The hotel 'la Fontaine' situated in the Jura region, where mountains, streams and golden vineyards create the natural setting for a enjoyable stay. Rooms have pretty furnishings and offer private facilities, whilst the restaurant serves generous dishes based on regional recipes, and where the chef Mr Belpois incorporates a choice of his own carefully prepared fish specialities.

Near river Near lake Forest area Near motorway
Closed 17 Dec-17 Jan
20 en suite (bth/shr) (3 fmly) (4 with balcony) TV in all bedrooms Licensed Full central heating Open parking available Covered parking available (charged) Child discount available 7yrs Open terrace V meals Last d 21.30hrs Languages spoken: English,German
MEALS: Full breakfast 58FF Continental breakfast 38FF Lunch 90-260FF&alc Dinner 90-260FF&alc✱
CARDS: 💳 🎫

PESMES Haute-Saône

★ ★ **De France**
70410
☎ 384312005
The Hotel de France is a typical Franche-Comté style house which stands on the banks of the River Ognon, and has been in the hands of the Vieille family for several generations. It offers peaceful accommodation with modern amenities and a cosy lounge where guests can relax in front of the open fire. The restaurant serves a classic cuisine and specialities from the region.

Near river Near sea Forest area
10 rooms in annexe (2 fmly) TV available Direct-dial available Licensed Full central heating Open parking available Supervised Child discount available 8yrs Bicycle rental Open terrace V meals Last d 21.30hrs
MEALS: Full breakfast 35FF Continental breakfast 40FF Lunch 80-160FF&alc Dinner 80-160FF&alc✱
CARDS: 💳 ▦ 🎫 Travellers cheques

Taking your mobile phone to France?
See page 11

POLIGNY Jura

★ ★ ★ Domaine Vallée Heureuse
rte de Genève 39800
☎ 384371213 FAX 384370875
Set in a landscape of mauve-coloured hills, this 18th-century mill is an oasis of peace. A romantic garden, a stream full of trout, and three panoramic terraces surrounded by extensive parklands provide the delightful setting for a very enjoyable break. Bedrooms offer up-to-date facilities, and the restaurant serves a creative cuisine, using fresh produce from the region.
Near river Near sea Forest area Near motorway
9 en suite (bth/shr) 1 rooms in annexe (1 fmly) (1 with balcony) No smoking in 1 bedroom TV in all bedrooms Direct dial from all bedrooms Mini-bar in all bedrooms Licensed Full central heating Open parking available Covered parking available (charged) Supervised Child discount available 8yrs Outdoor swimming pool (heated) Fishing Riding Sauna Boule Bicycle rental Open terrace Covered terrace Last d 21.30hrs Languages spoken: English German & Spanish
ROOMS: (room only) s 350-500FF; d 400-550FF
Reductions over 1 night
MEALS: Continental breakfast 55FF Lunch 95-220FF&alc Dinner 135-220FF&alc
CARDS: ● ■ ▆ ▩ ● Travellers cheques

★ ★ ★ ★ Hostellerie des Monts de Vaux
Monts de Vaux 39800
☎ 384371250 FAX 384370907
(off N5 3km E of Poligny)
This 18th-century house was transformed into a coaching inn by Bonaparte, and stands tucked away in a forest on the edge of the Jura plateau. With its wood panelling, rustic period furniture and fabrics, it has retained the charm of times gone by. The guest rooms are cosy and cheerful whilst the dining rooms serves a wide selection of fish and meat specialities accompanied by excellent wines.
Forest area Near motorway
Closed 31 Oct-29 Dec
10 en suite (bth/shr) TV in all bedrooms Direct dial from all bedrooms Mini-bar in 5 bedrooms Licensed Full central heating Open parking available Covered parking available Supervised Tennis Open terrace V meals Last d 21.30hrs Languages spoken: English,German,Italian
ROOMS: (room only) s 500-750FF; d 650-900FF ✱
Reductions over 1 night Special breaks
MEALS: Full breakfast 70FF Lunch fr 80FF&alc Dinner 80-400FF&alc✱
CARDS: ● ■ ▆ ▩ ● Travellers cheques

PONT-LES-MOULINS Doubs

★ ★ Auberge des Moulins
25110
☎ 381840999 FAX 381840444
This hotel has been entirely renovated and offers its visitors a cheerful interior, where the proprietors and their dedicated staff put a lot of effort into caring for their guests. The restaurant provides a high standard of home-cooking and the bedrooms have good amenities and provide straightforward comfort.
Near river Forest area
Closed 17 Dec-22 Jan
11 en suite (bth/shr) No smoking in 1 bedroom TV in all bedrooms Licensed Full central heating Open parking

available Supervised Child discount available 12yrs Open terrace V meals Last d 21.30hrs Languages spoken: English,German,Italian
CARDS: ■ ▆ Travellers cheques

SALINS LES BAINS Jura

★ ★ Grand Hotel des Bains
pl des Allies 39110
☎ 384379050 FAX 384379680
Near river Forest area In town centre Near motorway
Closed 5 Jan-1 Feb
30 en suite (bth/shr) (3 fmly) TV in all bedrooms Direct dial from all bedrooms Mini-bar in all bedrooms Lift Open parking available Covered parking available (charged) Supervised Indoor swimming pool (heated) Sauna Solarium Gym Jacuzzi/spa Bicycle rental Open terrace Languages spoken: English,German
CARDS: ● ▆ Travellers cheques

VILLARD-ST-SAUVEUR Jura

★ ★ Hostellerie 'Au Retour de la Chasse'
39200
☎ 384451132 FAX 384451396
This friendly establishment occupies a dominant position overlooking the Tacon valley. Visitors can expect a warm welcome by proprietor Anny Vuillermoz who looks after their well-being throughout the stay, whilst her husband presides over the kitchen, ensuring guests don't go hungry! The gourmet cuisine consists of fresh local ingredients and is augmented by a selection of fine Jura wines. The comfortable bedrooms have character and provide a good level of accommodation, whilst the surrounding area has a lot of energetic outdoor pursuits to offer.
Forest area
14 en suite (bth/shr) (2 fmly) (2 with balcony) TV in all bedrooms Direct dial from all bedrooms Licensed Full central heating Open parking available Child discount available Tennis Fishing Gym Boule Open terrace Last d 21.30hrs Languages spoken: English
MEALS: Continental breakfast 30FF Lunch 130-350FF&alc Dinner 200-350FFalc✱
CARDS: ● ■ ▆ ▩ ● Travellers cheques

VILLERS-LE-LAC Doubs

★ ★ ★ De France
8 pl M-Cupillard 25130
☎ 381680006 FAX 381680922
This family hotel is located in Villers-Le-lac and has a restaurant with a good reputation which serves a choice of gastronomic dishes, based on a creative and regional cuisine. The bedrooms have modern appointments and offer a high standard of comfort. In addition guests may want to try an excursion to the Haut-Doubs by boat.
Near river Forest area In town centre
Closed 20 Dec-1 Feb
14 en suite (bth/shr) TV in all bedrooms Mini-bar in all bedrooms Licensed Full central heating Last d 21.00hrs Languages spoken: German, English
ROOMS: (room only) s 300-320FF; d 320-340FF
MEALS: Full breakfast 50FF Lunch 160FF&alc Dinner 160FF&alc
CARDS: ● ■ ▆ ▩ ● Travellers cheques

VILLERSEXEL Haute-Saône

★ ★ Du Commerce
1 rue du 13 Septembre *70110*
☎ 384202050 FAX 384205957
The hotel is situated in a small, peaceful village surrounded by
unspoilt countryside and provides the setting for a relaxing
stay far away from the pressures of modern-day life. It features
bedrooms with modern facilities, a comfortable lounge and a
country-style restaurant which offers a selection of regional
dishes of high quality. In addition, various cultural sights and
leisure opportunities are just around the corner.
In town centre
Closed 31 Dec-14 Jan
17 en suite (bth/shr) (3 fmly) TV in all bedrooms STV Direct
dial from all bedrooms Licensed Full central heating Open
parking available Supervised Child discount available 7yrs
Bicycle rental Open terrace Canoeing V meals Languages
spoken: English,German
MEALS: Full breakfast 35FF Continental breakfast 35FF Lunch
60-230FF&alc✷
CARDS: ✷ ☱ Travellers cheques

★ ★ De La Terrasse
70110
☎ 384205211 FAX 384205690
(On D9)
Located near the river, the hotel has all the charm of an old
country inn offering guests a warm welcome and traditional
cuisine.
Near river Forest area
Closed 14 Dec-1 Jan
15 en suite (bth/shr) (5 with balcony) TV in all bedrooms STV
Direct dial from all bedrooms Licensed Full central heating
Open parking available Supervised Child discount available
8yrs Bicycle rental Open terrace Last d 21.15hrs Languages
spoken: English,Spanish
ROOMS: (room only) s 200FF; d 220-300FF
MEALS: Full breakfast 45FF Continental breakfast 30FF Lunch
65-295FF&alc Dinner 65-295FF&alc
CARDS: ✷ ☱ Travellers cheques

Poitou-Charentes

The sunniest region in the west of France with a mild climate even in the winter. Visit the old harbour at La Rochelle with its bustling quayside markets and fashionable bars, or stretch out and soak up the sun on the glorious beaches at the port des Minimes, Aytré and Angoulins. History-lovers should make for Chauvigny and its atmospheric remains of five castles. Royan caters for the sports-minded, offering tennis, squash, and an 18-hole golf course. Further north the villages around the Seudre rear the finest oysters, while in oak casks along the Charente Valley, the famous Cognac brandy matures.

ESSENTIAL FACTS

DÉPARTEMENTS:	Charente, Charente-Maritime, Deux Sèvres, Vienne
PRINCIPAL TOWNS	Angoulême, La Rochelle, Niort, Poitiers, Royan
PLACES TO VISIT:	Parc du Futuroscope; the old harbour at La Rochelle; Cognac and its distilleries, the ruins of five medieval castles at Chauvigny; 'Sleeping Beauty's Castle' at La Roche-Courbon
REGIONAL TOURIST OFFICE	Comité Régional du Tourisme, BP 56, F-86002 Poitiers. Tel: 49 50 10 50
LOCAL GASTRONOMIC DELIGHTS	Fruits de mer including mussels and oysters; entrecôte à la bordelaise; chaudrée, fish soup flavoured with white wine; eels and snails cooked in red wine; saddle of young goat with green garlic; mojettes, haricot beans cooked in butter
DRINKS	Médoc, Sauternes, Graves, St-Emilion, Pomerol and Entre-deux-Mers are the main wine-producing areas, but the Charente Valley is famous for its brandy, produced at the distillery towns of Cognac and Jarnac
LOCAL CRAFTS WHAT TO BUY	Glassware from Tusson, ceramics from Saintes and Thouars, pottery from Cognac

(Top): These colourful puppets are the cast at the Theatre de Marionettes in the main square at Aubeterre-sur-Dronne.

(Bottom): Two 14th-century towers guard the harbour at La Rochelle, which has been called the French Geneva.

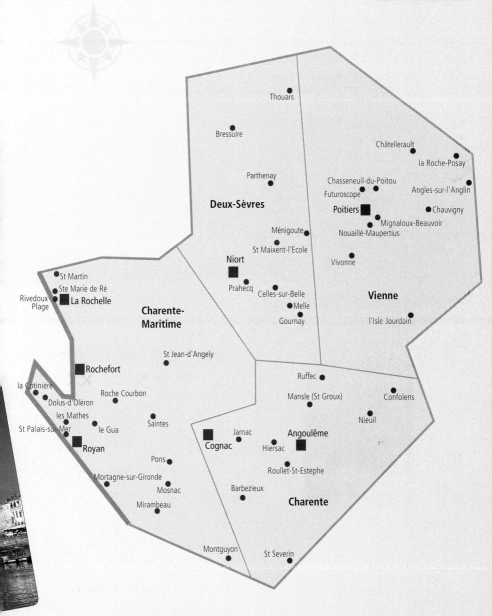

Thouars

Bressuire

Châtellerault

la Roche-Posay

Parthenay

Chasseneuil-du-Poitou

Angles-sur-l'Anglin

Deux-Sèvres

Futuroscope

Poitiers

Chauvigny

Ménigoute

Mignaloux-Beauvoir

Nouaillé-Maupertius

St Maixent-l'Ecole

Niort

Vivonne

Prahecq

Vienne

St Martin

Ste Marie de Ré

Celles-sur-Belle

Rivedoux-Plage

La Rochelle

Melle

Charente-Maritime

Gournay

l'Isle Jourdain

St Jean-d'Angely

Rochefort

Ruffec

la Cotinière

Mansle (St Groux)

Confolens

Roche Courbon

Dolus-d'Oléron

Nieuil

les Mathes

St Palais-sur-Mer

le Gua

Saintes

Cognac

Jarnac

Angoulême

Royan

Hiersac

Pons

Roullet-St-Estephe

Mortagne-sur-Gironde

Mosnac

Barbezieux

Charente

Mirambeau

Montguyon

St Severin

EVENTS & FESTIVALS

Jan Angoulême Comic Strip Festival

Apr Poitiers Spring Music Festival; Cognac International Police Film Festival; Royan Romanesque Festival

May Melle: St-Savinien Music Festival; Angoulême Multiracial Music Festival; La Rochelle International Sailing Week; Parthenay Meat Festival, Châtellerault Jazz Festival; Bressaire Circus Festival; Vivonne Song & Music Festival

Jun Nouaillé-Maupertius Medieval Spectacle; Creations en Val de Charente (*classical music festival*) at Cognac & Jarnac; Roquefort Celebrations

Jul La Rochelle International Film Festival; FLIP Games Festival at Parthenay; Saintes Folk Music & Dance Festival ; Parthenay Jazz Festival; La Rochelle French Language Music Festival; Montguyon World Folk Festival; Chauvigny Summer Festival in the medieval town; Ste-Maxime l'Ecole International Children's Folklore Encounters; Roquefort theatre, street entertainment & music; Thouars Arts Festival; Matha Folklore & Song Festival; Niort Street Art Festival; Son et Lumière at La Rochefoucauld Château & St

Brice Abbey; Château d'Oleron Story-telling Festival

Aug Chauvigny Summer Festival in the medieval town; Confolens International Festival of Folk Music & Dance; Parthenay-en-Gatine Traditional Music Festival; Vitrac St Vincent Music Festival; St-Palais sur Mer World Folklore Festival

Sep Cognac Festival of Street Arts; La Rochelle Boat Show; Angoulême Vintage Car Motor Racing; Fontaine-le-Comte Autumn Music Festival

Oct Ménigoute Ornithological Film Festival

Dec Poitiers Short Film Festival

Cognac

They say serendipity played a part in the creation of the smooth liqueur pineau. An absent-minded vintner accidentally mixed unfermented grape juice with cognac, and wine drinkers have been grateful ever since. But it's brandy that the Charente Valley is famous for, produced in the 20-mile "Golden Circle" region which includes the distillery towns of Cognac and Jarnac. One of the secrets of its luxurious savour is the chalky soil which nurtures a better quality grape juice. You can discover more about the production process by visiting the Cognac Museum or the distilleries which are open throughout the year.

ANGLES-SUR-L'ANGLIN Vienne

★ ★ ★ **Le Relais du Lyon d'Or**
4 rue d'Enfer *86260*
☎ 549483253 FAX 549840228

The hotel is situated in one of the most charming villages of France and dates back to the 14th century. It has been renovated in a style befitting its origins and the bedrooms are furnished to suit the character of the house. The cuisine uses local produce and serves delicacies from the barbecue on the terrace on a daily basis.
Near river Forest area In town centre
Closed 2 wks Nov & Jan-Feb
12 en suite (bth/shr) (5 fmly) TV in all bedrooms Direct dial from all bedrooms Licensed Full central heating Open parking available Supervised Bicycle rental Open terrace V meals Last d 21.00hrs Languages spoken: English

ROOMS: (room only) d 450-370FF **Special breaks**
MEALS: Continental breakfast 40FF Lunch 98-189FF&alc Dinner 98-189FF&alc✱
CARDS: ●●

CELLES-SUR-BELLE Deux-Sèvres

★ ★ **Hostellerie de l'Abbaye**
1 pl des Epoux Laurent *79370*
☎ 549329332 FAX 549797265
The homely Hostellerie de L'Abbaye features a country-style interior with a pleasant guest accommodation equipped with modern amenities. It has a lounge, cocktail bar and an informal restaurant offering a good standard of home-cooking.
Near river Near lake Forest area In town centre Near motorway
17 en suite (bth/shr) TV in all bedrooms STV Direct dial from all bedrooms Licensed Night porter Full central heating Open parking available Supervised Child discount available 10yrs Bicycle rental Open terrace V meals Last d 21.30hrs Languages spoken: English
MEALS: Full breakfast 30FF Continental breakfast 30FF Lunch fr 55FF&alc Dinner fr 70FF&alc✱
CARDS: ●● ● Travellers cheques

CHASSENEUIL-DU-POITOU Vienne

★ ★ ★ **Château du Clos de la Ribaudière**
rue du Champ-de-Foire *86360*
☎ 549528666 FAX 549528632
This gracious building dates back to the 19th century, and was once the private residence of Madame Barbot de la Motte, one of the first women to make a hot-air balloon ascent.

The elegant bedrooms are equipped with modern amenities and offer a high standard of comfort. The restaurant serves skilfully executed dishes from a wide repertoire of regional specialities.
Near river Forest area Near motorway
43 en suite (bth) (4 fmly) (2 with balcony) TV in all bedrooms STV Radio in rooms Direct dial from all bedrooms Licensed Lift Full central heating Open parking available Supervised Child discount available Outdoor swimming pool (heated) Fishing Open terrace V meals Last d 22.00hrs Languages spoken: English

ROOMS: (room only) s 320-620FF; d 380-820FF ✱
MEALS: Full breakfast 50FF Continental breakfast 50FF Lunch 120-285FF&alc Dinner 120-285FF&alc
CARDS: 💳 💳 💳 🐬 Travellers cheques

CHÂTELLERAULT Vienne

★ ★ Le Croissant
15 av Kennedy 86100
☎ 549210177 FAX 549215792
This family hotel is located in the heart of Châtellerault which is the most important trade-centre of the Poitou region. Situated opposite public gardens, it features a restaurant where traditional dishes are enhanced with a modern touch. There are sound-proofed bedrooms with modern facilities, and a comfortable lounge for relaxation.
Near river Forest area
19 rms (6 bth 8 shr) (4 fmly) TV in all bedrooms STV Direct dial from all bedrooms Mini-bar in all bedrooms Licensed Full central heating Open parking available Child discount available 13yrs Open terrace Last d 21.30hrs
CARDS: 💳 💳 💳 Travellers cheques

★ ★ ★ Grand Hotel Moderne
74 bd Blossac 86100
☎ 549213011 FAX 549932519
The handsome Grand Hôtel Moderne can be found in the heart of the town near the banks of the river Vienne. The accommodation is stylishly furnished and comfortable, whilst the restaurant is well known for Christian Proust's cuisine. For the more active there is an 18-hole golf course and fabulous walks in the Vienne valley.
Near river Near lake Forest area In town centre Near motorway
26 en suite (bth/shr) (3 fmly) (6 with balcony) TV in all bedrooms Radio in rooms Mini-bar in all bedrooms Licensed Lift Night porter Full central heating Open parking available (charged) Covered parking available (charged) Open terrace Last d 21.30hrs Languages spoken: English,German
MEALS: Full breakfast 50FF Lunch fr 130FF Dinner fr 180FF✱
CARDS: 💳 💳 💳 🐬 Travellers cheques

COGNAC Charente

★ ★ ★ Hotellerie Les Pigeons Blancs
110 rue Jules Brisson 16100
☎ 545821636 FAX 545822929
The friendly Tachet family offer their visitors traditional hospitality and are always on hand to give advice about exploring this beautiful region. Guests can enjoy a comfortable stay complemented by good quality cuisine, including regional dishes. On fine days meals are served on the terrace whilst the peaceful gardens are just a stone's throw from the old town, the harbour and the famous cognac-cellars.
Near river Forest area In town centre
7 en suite (bth/shr) TV in all bedrooms Licensed Full central heating Open parking available Supervised Child discount available 12yrs Open terrace Covered terrace Last d 21.00hrs Languages spoken: English,German
ROOMS: (room only) s 300-450FF; d 350-600FF
Reductions over 1 night
MEALS: Full breakfast 50FF Lunch 138-250FF&alc Dinner 138-250FF&alc
CARDS: 💳 💳 💳 🐬 Travellers cheques

★ ★ ★ Hotel le Valois
35 rue du 14 Juillet 16100
☎ 545827600 FAX 545827600
Ideally situated in the centre of town, opposite the Palais des Congrès and close to all the famous cognac houses such as Camus, Hennesy, Martell and Remy-Martin, the hotel offers bedrooms with private facilities which provide a high degree of comfort. There is a bright, modern lounge and a bar where a wide choice of splendid cognacs are waiting to be sampled.
Near river Forest area In town centre Near motorway
Closed 23 Dec-2 Jan
45 en suite (bth/shr) (1 fmly) No smoking in 3 bedrooms TV in all bedrooms STV Radio in rooms Direct dial from all bedrooms Mini-bar in all bedrooms Licensed Lift Night porter Air conditioning in bedrooms Open parking available Covered parking available Supervised Sauna Solarium Gym Languages spoken: English
CARDS: 💳 💳 💳 🐬 Travellers cheques

COTINIÈRE, LA Charente-Maritime

★ ★ ★ L'Écallier
65 rue de Port 17310
☎ 546471031 FAX 546471023
The hotel is situated in the picturesque fishing port of La Côtinière on the Atlantic coast, and offers an enjoyable stay with excellent food in a splendid, authentic setting. Guests can savour some of the outstanding dishes whilst enjoying the panoramic view from the restaurant.
Near sea
Closed 15 Nov-1 Feb
8 en suite (bth/shr) (2 fmly) TV in all bedrooms Direct dial from all bedrooms Mini-bar in all bedrooms Licensed Full central heating Air conditioning in bedrooms Open parking available (charged) Supervised Child discount available 14yrs Open terrace Last d 21.30hrs
MEALS: Full breakfast 43FF Continental breakfast 43FF Lunch 150-350FFalc Dinner 150-350FFalc✱
CARDS: 💳 💳 💳 🐬 Travellers cheques

★ ★ ★ Motel Ile de Lumière
av des Pins 17310
☎ 546471080 FAX 546473087

contd.

Surrounded by sand dunes, the hotel looks out over the sea and is situated on the 'Ile Lumineuse', which is connected by a bridge to the mainland. This contemporary establishment offers guest accommodation with private facilities and is a suitable venue for a beach holiday.
Near sea
Closed Nov-Mar
45 en suite (bth/shr) (13 fmly) (32 with balcony) TV in all bedrooms STV Direct dial from all bedrooms Mini-bar in all bedrooms Full central heating Open parking available Covered parking available Child discount available Outdoor swimming pool (heated) Tennis Sauna Bicycle rental Table Tennis,Exercise Studio Languages spoken: English,German,Spanish
CARDS: ●● ▇▇ Eurocard Travellers cheques

DOLUS-D'OLÉRON Charente-Maritime

★ ★ ★ ★ Grand Large
Baie de la Rémigeasse *17550*
☎ 546753789 FAX 546754915
The hotel occupies a seaside location and offers uninterrupted views of the Atlantic ocean. Because of the mild climate, it provides a peaceful oasis for a healthy, relaxing holiday. The restaurant enjoys panoramic views and serves a wide range of sea and shellfish delicacies, and the spacious bedrooms - decorated with restful colours and fabrics - offer a high degree of comfort.
Near sea Forest area
Closed Oct-Apr
(5 with balcony) TV in 26 en suite (bth/shr) all bedrooms STV Radio in rooms Direct-dial available Licensed Full central heating Open parking available Child discount available Indoor swimming pool (heated) Solarium Open terrace Short Tennis Last d 21.15hrs Languages spoken: English,German
ROOMS: (incl. dinner) s 1120-1690FF; d 1560-2630FF
MEALS: Lunch 180-390FF&alc Dinner 280-390FF&alc
CARDS: ●● ▇▇ ▇▇ Eurocard Travellers cheques

GOURNAY Deux-Sèvres

★ ★ Château des Touches
79110
☎ 549299692 FAX 549299747
(NW between D948 and N740)
Guests will enjoy a personal welcome and restful surroundings in this 19th-century château. Bedrooms are equipped with modern facilities, the food is excellent, and a wide choice of leisure opportunities are available.
Forest area Near motorway
13 en suite (bth/shr) (2 fmly) (1 with balcony) Direct dial from all bedrooms Licensed Night porter Full central heating Open parking available Supervised Child discount available 12yrs Pool table Boule Bicycle rental Open terrace V meals Last d 21.00hrs Languages spoken: English
ROOMS: (room only) d 350-500FF **Reductions over 1 night**
MEALS: Full breakfast 45FF Lunch 100-220FFalc Dinner 100-220FFalc
CARDS: ●● ▇▇ ▇▇ Travellers cheques

GUA, LE Charente-Maritime

★ ★ ★ Moulin de Châlons
2 rue du Bassin *17680*
☎ 546228272 FAX 546223107
(Signposted from the centre of the village)

This ancient tidal mill dates back to the 18th century and has been transformed into a traditional hotel where exposed brickwork, waxed beams and period furniture feature strongly. It is situated on the banks of a fishing river. The cuisine consists of regional dishes with a modern touch, where a large choice of assorted fresh sea produce is used. It has comfortable guest rooms with modern amenities, and situated approximately ten kilometres from the sea and not far away from the Gallo-Roman ruins, it is a good base for sight-seeing or a day at the beach.
Near river Forest area Near motorway
Closed 21 Sep-10 May
14 en suite (bth/shr) TV in 6 bedrooms Direct dial from all bedrooms Licensed Full central heating Open parking available Child discount available 8yrs Fishing Open terrace Last d 21.30hrs Languages spoken: English, Spanish
ROOMS: (room only) s 350-465FF; d 350-520FF
MEALS: Full breakfast 62FF Lunch 145-380FF&alc Dinner 160-380FF&alc
CARDS: ●● ▇▇ ▇▇ ◑

HIERSAC Charente

★ ★ ★ Hostellerie du Maine Brun
RN 141 *16290*
☎ 545908300 FAX 545969114
(From Angouleme take N141 towards Cognac)
This former mill is an oasis of peace and provides a relaxed stay amidst the vineyards of the Cognac region. All the luxurious bedrooms, which have private balconies, are decorated with period furniture and offer views over the garden and river. The restaurant serves a wide selection of dishes complemented by some great wines from the house cellar.
Near river Forest area Near motorway
Closed 16 Oct-14 Apr
20 en suite (bth/shr) (20 with balcony) TV in all bedrooms Direct dial from all bedrooms Mini-bar in all bedrooms Licensed Full central heating Open parking available Outdoor swimming pool Open terrace Last d 21.30hrs Languages spoken: English, German
ROOMS: (room only) s 400-450FF; d 570-750FF **✱ Special breaks**
MEALS: Full breakfast 65FF Lunch 98-195FF&alc Dinner 98-195FF&alc✱
CARDS: ●● ▇▇ ▇▇ ◑ Travellers cheques

ISLE-JOURDAIN, L' Vienne

★ ★ ★ Hotel Val de Vienne
Port de Salles *86150*
☎ 549482727 FAX 549484747
(Off D8 towards the River Vienne)
The hotel is situated in a beautiful valley on the banks of the river Vienne. Each bedroom has a private terrace overlooking the river and is equipped with private facilities. Guests can enjoy a pleasant day by the heated swimming pool or take advantage of the various sporting and tourist activities close by, followed by a relaxing dinner in the gourmet restaurant, whilst watching the river flow by.
Near river
Closed 12 Jan-2 Feb RS Sun evening & Mon
20 rms (1 fmly) (20 with balcony) TV in all bedrooms STV Radio in rooms Direct dial from all bedrooms Mini-bar in all bedrooms Licensed Full central heating Open parking available Covered parking available (charged) Child discount available 12yrs Outdoor swimming pool (heated) Fishing

Boule Bicycle rental Open terrace V meals Last d 21.30hrs
Languages spoken: English,German

ROOMS: (room only) d 420-520FF **Reductions over 1 night**
MEALS: Full breakfast 45FF Lunch 95-210FF&alc Dinner 95-210FF&alc✱
CARDS: ✆ ▨ Travellers cheques

MANSLE (ST-GROUX) Charente

★ ★ Les Trois Saules
16230

☎ 545203140 FAX 545227381
This hotel offers a country-style interior where comfortable bedrooms are equipped with good amenities. A picturesque stream flows through the bottom of the pretty garden which provides an attractive setting for a stroll, while the restaurant serves well presented, flavoursome food.
Near river
10 en suite (bth/shr) TV in all bedrooms Direct dial from all bedrooms Licensed Full central heating Open parking available Child discount available Fishing Boule Open terrace Last d 21.00hrs Languages spoken: German,Italian,Spanish
ROOMS: (room only) s 185-195FF; d 200-235FF
Reductions over 1 night
MEALS: Full breakfast 28FF Continental breakfast 28FF Lunch 63-165FF&alc Dinner 63-165FF&alc
CARDS: ✆ ▨ Travellers cheques

MATHES, LES Charente-Maritime

★ ★ Palmyrotel
2 allée des Passereaux, La Palmyre *17570*
☎ 546236565 FAX 546224413
(From A10 (Paris to Bordeaux) exit at Saintes, take N150 to Royan, then D25 To La Palmyre)
Situated in the shade of large pine trees and close to all the large beaches, the hotel offers bedrooms with modern amenities and a good restaurant which serves a wide choice of dishes from the region. From the terrace and the bedrooms guests have fine views of the surrounding gardens.
Near sea Near beach Forest area
Closed 16 Nov-14 Mar RS Half board obligatory Jul-Aug
46 en suite (bth/shr) (14 fmly) (18 with balcony) TV in all bedrooms Direct dial from all bedrooms Licensed Lift Night porter Full central heating Open parking available Child discount available 12yrs Open terrace Covered terrace Wkly live entertainment Languages spoken: English,German
ROOMS: (room only) s 200-355FF; d 250-385FF ✱
MEALS: Full breakfast 35FF Continental breakfast 35FF Lunch 99-195FF Dinner 99-195FF✱
CARDS: ✆ ▨ ⏺ Travellers cheques

MIGNALOUX-BEAUVOIR Vienne

★ ★ ★ Manoir de Beauvoir
635 rte de Beauvoir *86800*
☎ 549554747 FAX 549553195
The Manoir de Beauvoir dates back to the 19th century, and having recently been completely renovated, offers all the facilities expected from a three star hotel. Accommodation consists of apartments equipped with a kitchenette and modern amenities. The wood-panelled restaurant serves a range of regional dishes where the ingredients vary with the seasons, while in summer breakfast is served on the terrace with views of the pond and the golf course.
Near motorway
Closed 16 Dec-2 Jan
46 en suite (bth/shr) 22 rooms in annexe (40 fmly) (10 with balcony) TV available STV Licensed Lift Night porter Full central heating Open parking available Supervised Child discount available 12yrs Golf 18 Open terrace V meals Last d 22.00hrs Languages spoken: English,Italian,Spanish
MEALS: Full breakfast 47FF Lunch fr 100FF&alc Dinner fr 100FF&alc✱
CARDS: ✆ ▨ Travellers cheques

MIRAMBEAU Charente-Maritime

★ ★ ★ Château-Hotel de Mirambeau
rte de Montendre *17150*
☎ 546707177 FAX 546707110
Standing in its own extensive grounds of over 20 acres, this magnificent building dates back to the 12th century. With unsurpassed leisure opportunities on offer it provides an excellent venue for an action-packed stay or cultural holiday. Behind its exterior of towers and gargoyles it conceals a sophisticated interior with elegant furnishings and ornate ceilings. The guest accommodation is furnished to a high standard and equipped with luxurious en suite facilities. The restaurant is noted for its superb cuisine.
Forest area Near motorway
TV available STV Direct-dial available Licensed Lift Night porter Full central heating Open parking available Supervised Indoor swimming pool (heated) Outdoor swimming pool (heated) Golf Tennis Sauna Gym Pool table Jacuzzi/spa Open terrace Languages spoken: English,German,Spanish
CARDS: ✆ ▨ ▨ Access,Eurocard Travellers cheques

MORTAGNE-SUR-GIRONDE Charente-Maritime

★ ★ Auberge de la Garenne
3 Impasse de l'Ancienne Gare *17120*
☎ 546906369 FAX 546905093
With views over the delightful red-tiled roofs and the ancient bell tower of the church, the hotel features guest accommodation which is housed in attractively decorated bungalows and situated in the shaded park. The restaurant offers a choice of well prepared specialities from the Carente region, which on fine days are served on the terrace.
Near river Near sea Near beach Forest area Near motorway
11 rms (8 shr) (6 fmly) (6 with balcony) TV in all bedrooms Direct dial from all bedrooms Licensed Full central heating Open parking available Child discount available 12yrs Outdoor swimming pool Boule Bicycle rental Covered terrace Archery,badminton,table tennis,darts
MEALS: Continental breakfast 32FF Lunch 70-200FF&alc Dinner 70-200FF&alc✱
CARDS: ✆ ▨ Travellers cheques

MOSNAC Charente-Maritime

★ ★ ★ ★ Moulin de la Marcouze
17240
☎ 546704616 FAX 546704814

After having spent eight years in the kitchen of the prestigious 'Tour d'Argent' in Paris, Dominique Bouchet became the proprietor of this establishment, and turned it into the enchanting venue it is today. The spacious guest accommodation offers individually styled bedrooms with balcony or loggia overlooking the garden or river, whilst the restaurant serves delightful, freshly prepared dishes of the highest quality.

Near river Forest area Near motorway
Closed Feb
10 en suite (bth/shr) (5 with balcony) TV in all bedrooms STV Direct dial from all bedrooms Mini-bar in all bedrooms Licensed Full central heating Air conditioning in bedrooms Open parking available Supervised Outdoor swimming pool Fishing Bicycle rental Last d 21.30hrs Languages spoken: English
MEALS: Full breakfast 75FF Continental breakfast 75FF Lunch fr 170FF Dinner fr 250FF★
CARDS: ⬤ 🔳 ⑨

NIEUIL Charente

★ ★ ★ ★ Château de Nieuil
16270
☎ 545713638 FAX 545714645

Surrounded by a moat this elegant chateau was formerly one of François I's hunting lodges. Peacefully situated in 80 acres of wooded parkland, it features individually styled guest rooms and apartments with views of the French-style garden or the immaculate lawns. It has an art gallery housed in the former stables which exhibits paintings and assorted antiques, and the splendid lounges and restaurant are adorned with period furniture and decorated with rich fabrics and furnishings. The high quality cuisine alternates between regional dishes and innovative recipes and uses fresh produce from the Chateau's vegetable garden.

Near river Near lake Forest area
Closed early Nov-Apr
14 en suite (bth/shr) (5 fmly) TV in all bedrooms STV Direct dial from all bedrooms Mini-bar in all bedrooms Licensed Night porter Full central heating Open parking available Covered parking available (charged) Outdoor swimming pool Tennis Fishing Boule Mini-golf Bicycle rental Open terrace Art gallery,antiques V meals Last d 21.00hrs Languages spoken: English,German
CARDS: ⬤ 🔳 🔳 ⑨ Travellers cheques

NIORT Deux-Sèvres

★ ★ ★ Grand Hotel
32-34 av de Paris *79000*
☎ 549242221 FAX 549244241

Near river Forest area In town centre Near motorway
38 en suite (bth/shr) (10 fmly) No smoking in 8 bedrooms TV in all bedrooms Direct dial from all bedrooms Licensed Lift Night porter Full central heating Open parking available Covered parking available (charged) Supervised Open terrace Languages spoken: English
CARDS: ⬤ 🔳 🔳 ⑨ Travellers cheques

★ ★ Le Paris

12 av de Paris *79000*
☎ 549249378 FAX 549282757
(From A10 exit 32 follow signs for town centre)

This peaceful, comfortable hotel can be found in the centre of Niort opposite the restaurants and close to the museums. It features completely renovated and fully equipped rooms, and there is a cosy bar where guests can have a relaxing drink. Numerous leisure activities as well as historic sites to visit may be found in the surrounding region.

Near river In town centre Near motorway
Closed 23 Dec-2 Jan
44 en suite (bth/shr) TV in all bedrooms Direct dial from all bedrooms Licensed Full central heating Open parking available (charged) Covered parking available (charged) Bicycle rental Open terrace Covered terrace Languages spoken: English,German,Spanish
ROOMS: (room only) s fr 250FF; d fr 280FF **Reductions over 1 night**
CARDS: ⬤ 🔳

PARTHENAY Deux-Sèvres

★ ★ Renotel
bd de l'Europe *79200*
☎ 549940644 FAX 549640194

The hotel is surrounded by attractive countryside and yet not far away from the centre of the town. The pleasant bedrooms have modern amenities and are designed to meet individual needs. The restaurant 'Rosalia' is decorated in a fin-de-siecle style and serves a range of enjoyable meals including the house special, 'viande Parthenaise'.

Near motorway
Closed Nov-Etr
42 rms (14 bth 25 shr) TV in all bedrooms STV Direct dial from all bedrooms Licensed Lift Night porter Full central heating Open parking available Supervised Child discount available 12yrs Open terrace Last d 21.00hrs Languages spoken: English
CARDS: ⬤ 🔳 🔳 Travellers cheques

★ ★ St-Jacques
13 av du 114ème Régiment, d'Infanterie *79200*
☎ 549643333 FAX 549940069

Ideally situated in a charming medieval town, the hotel has functional bedrooms with modern amenities. There are no eating facilities available at the hotel, but guests may want to seek out one of the many restaurants close by. An ideal location for visiting the surrounding area, including Futuroscope.

In town centre Near motorway
46 en suite (bth/shr) (10 fmly) TV in all bedrooms STV Mini-bar in 22 bedrooms Licensed Lift Night porter Full central heating Open parking available Child discount available Languages spoken: English
CARDS: ⬤ 🔳 🔳 Travellers cheques

POITIERS Vienne

★ ★ Grand Hotel de l'Europe
39 rue Carnot *86000*
☎ 549881200 FAX 549889730

The hotel is situated in the heart of Poitiers near all the historic monuments, and has easy access to transport services. There is a peaceful interior garden, pleasant public areas, and functional bedrooms which have modern facilities and offer a good level of comfort.

In town centre

88 en suite (bth/shr) Some rooms in annexe (7 fmly) (3 with balcony) TV in all bedrooms Direct dial from all bedrooms Mini-bar in all bedrooms Licensed Lift Night porter Full central heating Open parking available (charged) Covered parking available (charged) Supervised Child discount available 12yrs Open terrace Covered terrace Languages spoken: English,German
CARDS: ●● ▥ ▤ ⋑ Travellers cheques

★ ★ ★ Le Grand Hotel
28 rue Carnot *86000*
☎ 549609060 FAX 549628189
In town centre
47 en suite (bth/shr) (6 fmly) TV in all bedrooms STV Radio in rooms Mini-bar in all bedrooms Licensed Lift Night porter Full central heating Open parking available (charged) Covered parking available (charged) Supervised Bicycle rental Open terrace Languages spoken: English,Spanish
CARDS: ●● ▥ ▤ Travellers cheques

PONS Charente-Maritime

★ ★ ★ Auberge Pontoise
23 av Gambetta *17800*
☎ 546940099 FAX 546913340
(leave A10 at exit 36, hotel in 4km)
The hotel is situated in the medieval town of Pons, once a famous stopping place for pilgrims on their way to Compostella. It has pleasant bedrooms with good modern facilities and an attractive restaurant which serves an array of home-made specialities accompanied by excellent Bordeaux wines. Visitors are well looked after by friendly and cheerful staff who provide an untiring, attentive service.
Near river In town centre Near motorway
Closed 15 Dec-early Feb
22 en suite (bth/shr) (6 fmly) TV in all bedrooms Direct dial from all bedrooms Licensed Night porter Full central heating Open parking available (charged) Covered parking available (charged) Child discount available 10yrs Open terrace V meals Last d 21.30hrs Languages spoken: English
ROOMS: (room only) s 270-380FF; d 270-480FF
Reductions over 1 night
MEALS: Full breakfast 60FF Lunch 160-200FF&alc Dinner 160-200FF&alc
CARDS: ●● ▤ Travellers cheques

PRAHECQ Deux-Sèvres

★ ★ Hotel des Ruralies
autoroute A10, aire des Ruralies *79230*
☎ 549756766 FAX 549758029
A motorway stop-over on the A10. Bedrooms are practical, with some suitable for disabled persons. The restaurant offers regional cuisine and there is a self service cafeteria.
Near motorway
51 rms (50 bth/shr) TV in all bedrooms STV Direct dial from all bedrooms Licensed Lift Night porter Full central heating Air conditioning in bedrooms Open parking available Supervised Child discount available 12yrs Last d 23.00hrs Languages spoken: English & Spanish
ROOMS: (room only) s fr 290FF; d fr 350FF
MEALS: Full breakfast 35FF Continental breakfast 25FF Lunch 80-120FF&alc Dinner 80-120FF&alc
CARDS: ●● ▥ ▤ ⋑ Travellers cheques

RIVEDOUX-PLAGE Charente-Maritime

★ ★ ★ Rivotel
154 av des Dunes *17940*
☎ 546098951 FAX 546098904
Built in 1991, this modern hotel is situated near one of the beautiful beaches of the Ile de Ré, and features bedrooms with excellent private facilities and with views of the sea or the terraced gardens. The restaurant 'Le Lamparo' serves a combination of fresh fish specialities and innovative dishes, skilfully executed by the young, talented chef in charge of the kitchen.
Near sea In town centre
Closed early Oct-end Mar
35 en suite (bth) 26 rooms in annexe (9 with balcony) TV in all bedrooms Licensed Full central heating Open parking available Child discount available 10yrs Outdoor swimming pool (heated) Solarium Jacuzzi/spa Bicycle rental Open terrace Last d 21.45hrs Languages spoken: English,Spanish
CARDS: ●● ▥ ▤

ROCHEFORT Charente-Maritime

★ ★ ★ Hotel La Corderie Royale
rue Audebert *17300*
☎ 546993535 FAX 546997872
Near river
Closed 2-18Feb
53 en suite (bth/shr) (4 fmly) TV in all bedrooms Direct dial from all bedrooms Mini-bar in all bedrooms Licensed Lift Night porter Full central heating Open parking available Supervised Child discount available 12yrs Outdoor swimming pool Sauna Bicycle rental Open terrace Covered terrace Last d 22.00hrs Languages spoken: English
MEALS: Full breakfast 50FF Continental breakfast 50FF Lunch 100-195FF&alc Dinner 140-195FF&alc✱
CARDS: ●● ▥ ▤ ⋑

ROCHELLE, LA Charente-Maritime

★ ★ François-1er
15 rue Bazoges *17000*
☎ 546412846 FAX 546413501
Forest area
38 rms (28 bth/shr) (7 fmly) TV in all bedrooms Direct dial from all bedrooms Night porter Full central heating Open parking available (charged) Supervised Languages spoken: English
CARDS: ●● ▤ Travellers cheques

★ ★ Hotel Frantour
13 rue Sardinerie *17000*
☎ 546417155 FAX 546411076
(exit La Rochelle from A10)
A few steps from the harbour and its famous towers and close to the antique market, the hotel offers the charm and comfort of an old renovated house in the heart of this historic city.
Near sea Near beach In town centre
79 en suite (bth/shr) (2 fmly) TV in all bedrooms STV Direct dial from all bedrooms Licensed Lift Night porter Full central heating Languages spoken: English, German & Italian
ROOMS: s 285-350FF; d 320-425FF
CARDS: ●● ▥ ▤ ⋑ Travellers cheques

★ ★ Frantour St-Nicholas
13 rue Sardinerie *17000*
☎ 546417155 FAX 546417046
(from A10 exit 23 for La Rochelle) *contd.*

The town of La Rochelle became a major port as early as the 12th century, and has colourful streets, lined with ancient houses. Situated a stones throw away from the harbour and its famous towers, the hotel combines the charming atmosphere of an old house with every modern comfort. It features a renovated interior, where comfortable bedrooms, a congenial bar and an exotic winter garden create the setting for a relaxing stay.
Near sea Near beach In town centre
79 en suite (bth/shr) (2 fmly) TV in all bedrooms STV Direct dial from all bedrooms Licensed Lift Night porter Full central heating Open parking available (charged) Covered parking available (charged) Supervised Languages spoken: English, German, Italian & Spanish
CARDS: 💳 📧 💳 💳 Travellers cheques

★ ★ ★ St-Jean d'Acre
4 pl de la Chaine *17000*

☎ 546417333 FAX 546411001
Near sea Near beach In town centre
69 en suite (bth/shr) (6 fmly) (4 with balcony) TV in all bedrooms STV Direct dial from all bedrooms Mini-bar in all bedrooms Licensed Lift Night porter Full central heating Last d 23.00hrs Languages spoken: English German Spanish
ROOMS: (room only) s 360-460FF; d 460-660FF
Reductions over 1 night
MEALS: Continental breakfast 52FF Lunch 85-150FF Dinner 85-150FF
CARDS: 💳 📧 💳 💳 Travellers cheques

★ ★ Trianon et Plage
6 rue de la Monnaie *17000*
☎ 546412135 FAX 546419578
This 19th-century house, once a private residence, has been owned by the same family since 1920, and now offers comfortable accommodation in charming surroundings. Public areas with period furniture and assorted antiques create an elegant atmosphere. The restaurant offers a combination of classic and imaginative cuisine, which uses home-grown produce and as much as possible.
Near sea Near beach In town centre
Closed Jan
25 en suite (bth/shr) (4 fmly) TV in all bedrooms STV Direct dial from all bedrooms Licensed Full central heating Open parking available (charged) Supervised Child discount available 12yrs Mini-golf Bicycle rental V meals Last d 21.00hrs Languages spoken: English,Spanish
ROOMS: (room only) d 360-455FF **Special breaks**
MEALS: Continental breakfast 43FF Lunch 95-188FF&alc Dinner 95-188FF&alc
CARDS: 💳 📧 💳 💳 Travellers cheques

ROCHE-POSAY, LA Vienne

★ ★ ★ Hotel Saint-Roch
4 cours Pasteur *86270*

☎ 549194900 FAX 549194940
(from A10 exit at Chateellerault-Nord/La Roche-Posay)
La Roche Posay is a pretty village renowned for its spa. The hotel is directly linked with spa buildings, guests can enjoy a relaxing stay and also discover the romanesque heritage of the area.
Forest area In town centre
36 en suite (bth/shr) (5 with balcony) TV in all bedrooms Direct dial from all bedrooms Room-safe Licensed Lift Night porter Full central heating Air conditioning in bedrooms Open parking available Child discount available 5yrs Golf Jacuzzi/spa Bicycle rental Open terrace Last d 21.30hrs Languages spoken: English & Spanish

ROOMS: (room only) s 238-300FF; d 325-455FF
Reductions over 1 night Special breaks
MEALS: Continental breakfast 30FF Lunch 69-148FF&alc Dinner 69-148FF&alc
CARDS: 💳 💳 Travellers cheques

ROULLET-ST-ESTEPHE Charente

★ ★ ★ La Vieille Étable
Les Plantes *16440*
☎ 545663175 FAX 545664745
(From Angouleme take N10 towards Bordeaux)
This family farm has been adapted to take guests for over twenty years. A pleasant rural situation but in close proximity to Angouleme. Attractive parkland and good foods.
Near lake
29 en suite (bth/shr) (2 fmly) No smoking in 1 bedroom TV in all bedrooms STV Direct dial from all bedrooms Mini-bar in all bedrooms Licensed Full central heating Open parking available Outdoor swimming pool Tennis Fishing Sauna Bicycle rental Open terrace Covered terrace V meals Last d 21.30hrs Languages spoken: English
ROOMS: (room only) s 295FF; d 295-375FF
MEALS: Full breakfast 36FF Lunch 85-265FF&alc Dinner 85-265FF&alc
CARDS: 💳 💳 Travellers cheques

ROYAN Charente-Maritime

★ ★ ★ Hotel Miramar
173 Conche de Pontaillac *17200*
☎ 546390364 FAX 546392375
The hotel Miramar is situated in a residential area near a fine sandy beach in the elegant seaside resort of Royan. The attractive bedrooms have views of the sea and are stylishly appointed with luxurious private facilities. The surrounding region has a rich historic past and is a paradise for nature lovers, while the restaurant's dishes and wines have earned a well deserved reputation for quality and flavour.
Near sea Near beach
Closed Dec-Mar
25 en suite (bth/shr) 20 rooms in annexe (4 fmly) TV in all bedrooms Direct dial from all bedrooms Night porter Full central heating Open parking available Supervised Child discount available Bicycle rental Open terrace Languages spoken: English
MEALS: Full breakfast 45FF Continental breakfast 45FF✱
CARDS: 💳 📧 💳 💳 Travellers cheques

★ ★ ★ Novotel
bd Carnot *17200*
☎ 546394639 FAX 546394646
Novotel offer their clients good quality accommodation in modern, well equipped bedrooms and have refined restaurants serving good quality cuisine They have excellent business meeting and conference facilities and some have food and beverages available 24 hours a day. All their hotels have at least one bedroom for disabled guests.
Near sea Forest area
83 en suite (bth/shr) (83 fmly) (83 with balcony) No smoking in 10 bedrooms TV in all bedrooms STV Licensed Lift Night porter Full central heating Air conditioning in bedrooms Open parking available Covered parking available (charged) Child discount available 16yrs Indoor swimming pool (heated) Outdoor swimming pool Sauna Solarium Gym Jacuzzi/spa Bicycle rental Open terrace Last d 24.00hrs Languages spoken: English,German
CARDS: 💳 📧 💳 💳

★ ★ ★ Résidence de Rohan
Parc des Fées 17640
☎ 546390075 FAX 546382999

This charming old residence is surrounded by large pine trees and has well-kept lawns leading down to the fine sandy beach. A cosy lounge with comfortable armchairs and open fireplace provides the setting to meet fellow guests, while the peaceful bedrooms - with balcony or private terrace - provide comfortable accommodation. The hotel has no eating facilities but there are more than 20 restaurants nearby.
Near sea Near beach Forest area
Closed 11 Nov-25 Mar
41 en suite (bth/shr) 19 rooms in annexe (5 fmly) (24 with balcony) TV in all bedrooms STV Direct dial from all bedrooms Licensed Full central heating Open parking available Supervised Outdoor swimming pool (heated) Tennis Solarium Boule Open terrace Languages spoken: English, German
ROOMS: (room only) d 400-650FF
CARDS: ●● ■■ ■■ Travellers cheques

SAINTES Charente-Maritime

★ ★ Climat de France
rte de Royan 17100
☎ 546972040 Cen Res 164460123 FAX 546922254
(off A10 at exit 25)
This attractive motel is tucked away amidst lush vegetation on the way to the ocean in the ancient region of Saintonge. It features bedrooms with private facilities and a restaurant which serves, in true tradition of the Climat hotels, an 'eat as much as you can' buffet. The surrounding region with numerous châteaux and historic monuments, is blessed with an exceptional climate which makes it an ideal place for an enjoyable break.
Forest area Near motorway
36 en suite (bth/shr) (1 fmly) TV in all bedrooms Radio in rooms Direct dial from all bedrooms Licensed Night porter Full central heating Open parking available Indoor swimming pool (heated) Outdoor swimming pool (heated) Boule Open terrace Covered terrace V meals Languages spoken: English & Spanish
CARDS: ●● ■■

★ ★ ★ Le Relais du Bois St-Georges
rue de Royan, Cours Genet 17100
☎ 546935099 FAX 546933493
(motorway exit 35 Saintes, head for town centre, at 1st rdbt take 1st right for Saintes Bentre, at next rdbt, 1st right for Relais du Bois, at 3rd rdbt, take 1st right for Relais du Bois.)
Near river Near lake Forest area Near motorway

(18 with balcony) No smoking in 15 bedrooms TV in 30 bedrooms STV Radio in rooms Direct dial from 30 bedrooms Mini-bar in 4 bedrooms Licensed Night porter Full central heating Open parking available Covered parking available (charged) Supervised Indoor swimming pool (heated) Tennis Riding Solarium Boule Jacuzzi/spa Bicycle rental Open terrace Covered terrace Table tennis Croquet V meals Last d 21.45hrs Languages spoken: English, German, Russian, Spanish

ROOMS: (room only) s 390-790FF; d 640-1250FF
Reductions over 1 night
MEALS: Full breakfast 88FF Lunch fr 200FFalc Dinner 195-540FF&alc
CARDS: ●● ■■ ■■ ⑨ Access Travellers cheques

★ ★ Terminus
Esplanade de la Gare, 2 rue Jean Moulin 17100
☎ 546743503 FAX 546972447
(From A10 exit 35 head towards town centre, then the railway station)
An tastefully refurbished 19th century building 600mtrs from the town centre facing a small, shaded square.
Near river Forest area In town centre Near motorway
Closed 23 Dec-4 Jan
28 en suite (bth/shr) (9 fmly) (5 with balcony) TV in all bedrooms Direct dial from all bedrooms Licensed Full central heating Languages spoken: English
ROOMS: (room only) s 200-290FF; d 200-390FF ✱
CARDS: ●● ■■ ■■ ⑨ Travellers cheques

ST-MAIXENT-L'ÉCOLE Deux-Sèvres

★ ★ ★ Logis St-Martin
chemin de Pissot 79400
☎ 549055868 FAX 549761993
(A10 exit 31/32)
This fine 17th-century residence is located in wooded parkland in a region which offers something of interest to everyone. The guest accommodation is cosy with all modern amenities while the elegant restaurant offers a high standard of cooking.
Near river Forest area Near motorway
Closed Jan
11 en suite (bth/shr) (1 fmly) TV in all bedrooms Direct dial from all bedrooms Licensed Full central heating Open parking available Supervised Open terrace V meals Last d 21.30hrs Languages spoken: English, German
ROOMS: (room only) s 390-490FF; d 390-530FF
MEALS: Continental breakfast 62FF Lunch 160-380FF&alc Dinner 160-380FF&alc
CARDS: ●● ■■ ■■ ⑨ Travellers cheques

ST-PALAIS-SUR-MER Charente-Maritime

★★ Hotel de la Plage
1 pl de l'Océan *17420*
☎ 546231032 FAX 546234128
Situated close to the beach and near the forest, as well as having an unrivalled choice of leisure opportunities nearby, the hotel is the ideal venue for a family holiday. It has comfortable guest rooms with modern facilities, and an elegant restaurant with a traditional cuisine - which can be adapted to suit individual needs - and includes seafood specialities.
Near lake Near sea Forest area
Closed mid Nov-mid Feb
20 en suite (bth/shr) (6 fmly) (12 with balcony) TV in 29 bedrooms Radio in rooms Direct dial from 29 bedrooms Licensed Full central heating Child discount available Outdoor swimming pool (heated) Sauna Solarium Gym Open terrace Languages spoken: English
CARDS: ●● 💳 Travellers cheques

★★★ Primavera (Relais du Silence)
12 rue du Brick *17420*
☎ 546232035 FAX 546232878
Near sea Forest area
45 en suite (bth/shr) 2 rooms in annexe (9 fmly) (35 with balcony) TV available Licensed Lift Full central heating Open parking available Child discount available 10yrs Indoor swimming pool (heated) Bicycle rental Last d 21.00hrs
Languages spoken: English,Italian,Spanish
CARDS: ●● ■■ 💳 ●

ST-SEVERIN Charente

★★ De La Paix
16390
☎ 545985225 FAX 545989208
(In the centre of the village)
Located in a small village near the Périgord region, this charming establishment is popular with business travellers and holiday makers alike. Run by the same family for three generations it offers attractive guest accommodation, and a restaurant with views over the gardens, which serves a regional cuisine. The surrounding countryside offers plenty of opportunity for walking, and there is no shortage of sporting activities nearby.

Near river In town centre
Closed 21 Dec-3 Jan
15 en suite (bth/shr) (3 fmly) (1 with balcony) TV in all bedrooms STV Direct dial from all bedrooms Licensed Full central heating Open parking available Covered parking available Child discount available 14yrs Outdoor swimming pool Pool table Bicycle rental Open terrace V meals Last d 23.00hrs Languages spoken: English
ROOMS: (room only) s fr 200FF; d fr 240FF
MEALS: Continental breakfast 30FF Lunch 65-150FF&alc Dinner 65-150FF✱
CARDS: ●● ■■ 💳 Travellers cheques

VIVONNE Vienne

★★ Hotel Le St-Georges
12 Grand'Rue *86370*
☎ 549890189 FAX 549890022
(Approach via N10 & D 742)
Situated in the quiet village of Vivonne in the Poitevin region, the hotel stands on the main street leading into the centre. More than 200 years old, it has been entirely renovated and retained all of its original character. It features a cosy interior where comfortable guest rooms have modern appointments, and a homely lounge with open fire for relaxing or reading. Although the hotel has no restaurant facilities, a meal can be provided on request, whilst there are numerous eating establishments nearby.
Near river In town centre Near motorway
26 en suite (bth/shr) 3 rooms in annexe (5 fmly) TV in all bedrooms STV Radio in rooms Direct dial from all bedrooms Licensed Full central heating Open parking available Supervised Child discount available Open terrace V meals Languages spoken: English
ROOMS: (room only) s 210-220FF; d 220-260FF
CARDS: ●● 💳

Taking your mobile phone to France?
See page 11

Poitou-Charentes

Islands in the Sun

The peaceful seafront at Ile d'Oléron.

Just off the coast lie the delightful islands of Ré, Aix and Oléron. Access to Ré is by car or bicycle via a toll bridge. Once on the island make for the port of La Flotte and its medieval marketplace. Other places of interest are the ruined 12th-century abbey of Les Châteliers and the fort of La Prée. Marked routes for bicycles make this a pleasant way to travel. Oléron's bridge is toll-free and there are regular coaches from Rochefort, Surgères and Saintes. Here, you might like to investigate the Romanesque church at St-Georges, the oyster museum at Le Château, or the marshland bird reserve at Dolus. Its many sandy beaches are recommended, too. Aix is the smallest of the islands, not large enough to require a bridge. The short journey is made by ferry, but you can't take your car. Hired bicycle or horse and carriage are the means of transport. Popular attractions are the mother of pearl workshops and the Napoléon Bonaparte museum. He spent his last hours on French soil here before exile. As you'd expect, fresh seafood is the speciality in all the islands' restaurants.

Futuroscope

Futuroscope Park is just five miles north of Poitiers, capital of the region. An amusement park crossed with a virtual reality cinema, where the screen is seven-storeys high and the seats are mounted on hydraulics to get you moving to the rhythms of the on-screen action. Experience the lightness of flying with a Monarch butterfly as it migrates across America to its mating ground, or the breakneck speed of a Formula 1 racing car as you tear through the streets of a rural village scattering on-lookers. The Devil's Mine is one big dipper ride you won't forget in a hurry! An exhilarating day out for all the family.

Limousin

Many visitors pass through Limousin on their way to the mountains or the coast, yet those who do not stop to explore are missing a region rich in history, architecture, beautiful countryside, and a proud creative and artistic heritage. From the Monédières Mountains and the sound of accordions, to the Plateau de Millevaches and the sound of Limousin cattle; from the peaceful quiet of villages like Mortemart among the Mont de Blond hills, to the bustling markets of the region's capital Limoges, home of some of the world's finest porcelain, Limousin has something to offer to anyone who wishes to glimpse a region rich in both history and culture close to the very heart of France.

(Top): Plates for sale in Limoges, a town which produces some of the world's finest porcelain.

(Bottom): One of the many tapestries produced over the centuries on the looms at Aubusson.

ESSENTIAL FACTS

DÉPARTEMENTS:	Corrèze, Creuse, Haute-Vienne.
PRINCIPAL TOWNS	Limoges, Gueret, Tulle, Aubusson, Ussel, Brive-la-Gaillarde, Rochechouart.
PLACES TO VISIT:	Limoges for porcelain; Aubusson for tapestries; Vassivière for its lake, and Contemporary Art Centre; Brive-la-Gaillarde for its distillery.
REGIONAL TOURIST OFFICE	27, bd de la Corderie, 87031 Limoges. Tel: 55 45 18 80. Fax: 55 45 18 18.
LOCAL GASTRONOMIC DELIGHTS	Côte de boeuf Limousin á la moelle at au vin de Cahors, which uses the deep purple Cahors wine. "Le produits du terroir" such as mushrooms, truffles, cepes, apples, walnuts, chestnuts, and bush fruit such as strawberries, blackberries and raspberries. Red cabbage with chestnuts, creamy potato pie, clafoutis (a form of cherry pie), and a variety of soups.
DRINKS	Fine brandies made of fruits such as cherries, plums and prunes have been produced here for over a century. The area also produces good beers due to the purity of the local water.
LOCAL CRAFTS WHAT TO BUY	Tapestry weaving, porcelain, enamel work. Gentiane (a herbal aperitif), liqueurs, sweetmeats, black pudding with chestnuts, dried mushrooms, madeleines, lace, haute couture fashion, porcelain, pâtè de foie gras.

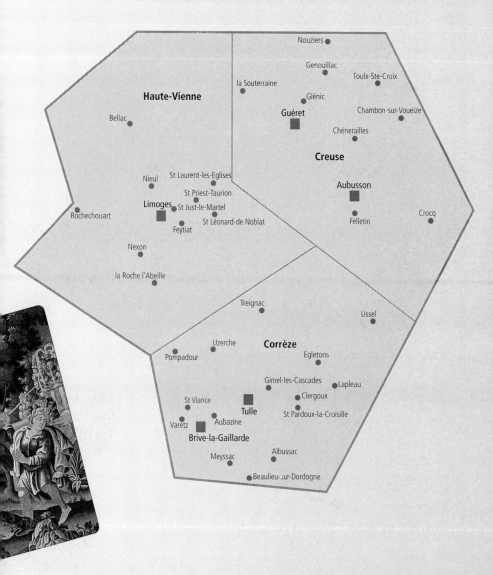

EVENTS & FESTIVALS:

May Chénerailles Horse Market; Beaulieu-sur Dordogne Stawberry Fair; Aubazine Holy Music & Heritage (concerts, readings, light shows);

Jun Glénic Craft Fair; Tours de Merle Light & Sound Show (Son et Lumière); Bellac Festival;

Jul Chénerailles Nocturnal Fantasy Son et Lumière; La Souterraine Arts Festival; Felletin She-lamb Fair; Egletons Medieval Pageant;

Jul/ Aug Le Dorat Light & Sound Show; Rilhac Images, Torches & Lights; Clergoux Music Festival at Château de Sédières; St-Léonard de Noblat Classical Music Summer Festival; Aubusson Classical Music Festival; Nexon Art running to Circus; St-Robert Summer Classical Music Festival; Chambon sur Voueize Son et Lumière at Robeyrie Lake; Tulle International Lace Festival (inc folk entertainment)

Jul/ Sep Annual Limoges Porcelain Exhibition

Aug Toulx-Ste-Croix Theatre Festival; Pays de Trois Lacs Three Lakes Music Festival; Plateau de Millevaches Summer Music Festival; TreignacTraditional Music Festival; Lapleau Festival de la Luzège (theatre); Felletin International Folklore Festival; Brive-la-Gaillarde Orchestrades Universelles (40 youth orchestras); Crocq Horse Festival; Collonges la-Rouge Traditional Market; Nouziers Cider Festival; Pompadour National Stud Presentation of Arab Horses;

Sep Tulle "Les Nuits de Nacre" Accordian Festival;

Sep/Oct Limoges International French-language Festival (Theatre, workshops, exhibitions, music); St-Just-le-Martel International Cartoon Show

Oct Gueret Piano Festival; Limoges Butchers Guild Festival; Limoges Traditional & Gastronomic Festivals

Nov Limoges Jazz Festival

Dec Brive-la-Gaillarde Foie Gras Fair

ALBUSSAC Corrèze

★★ Roche de Vic
Les Quatre Routes *19380*
☎ 555281587 FAX 555280109
The hotel opened its doors and 1951 and has been successfully managed by the same family for three generations. The rustic interior - including the comfortable bedrooms - is constantly upgraded to improve comfort, and the restaurant serves an outstanding cuisine with excellent regional dishes.
Near river Near lake Forest area Near motorway
Closed Jan-1 Mar
13 rms TV in all bedrooms Licensed Full central heating Open parking available Covered parking available Child discount available 12yrs Outdoor swimming pool (heated) Boule Open terrace Covered terrace Last d 21.30hrs Languages spoken: English
MEALS: Full breakfast 35FF Lunch 68-170FF&alc Dinner 68-170FF&alc✱
CARDS: ●● ▆▆

BRIVE-LA-GAILLARDE Corrèze

★★ La Cremaillère ⤬
53 av de Paris *19100*
☎ 555743247 FAX 555179183
This small hotel is situated in the town of Brive and features comfortable, pleasant bedrooms. A range of enjoyable meals to suit most tastes is served in the restaurant.
In town centre
9 en suite (bth/shr) TV in all bedrooms Licensed Full central heating Last d 21.30hrs Languages spoken: English & Spanish
ROOMS: (room only) d 200-260FF ✱

MEALS: Full breakfast 30FF Continental breakfast 30FF Lunch 100-200FF&alc Dinner 100-200FF&alc
CARDS: ●● ▆▆ Travellers cheques

FEYTIAT Haute-Vienne

★★ Climat de France
ZI Le Ponteix-Secteur Laugerie *87220*
☎ 555061460 Cen Res 64460123 FAX 555063893
(Near A20, junction 36)
This pleasant establishment has a warm and friendly interior where attractive bedrooms are equipped with up-to-date modern amenities and an informal restaurant serves a selection of traditional dishes to suit individual tastes, complemented by a good wine list.
Near river Forest area Near motorway
50 en suite (bth) (1 fmly) No smoking in 10 bedrooms TV in all bedrooms STV Radio in rooms Direct dial from all bedrooms Licensed Full central heating Open parking available Supervised Open terrace Languages spoken: English
CARDS: ●● ▆▆

GENOUILLAC Creuse

★★ Le Relais d'Oc
N 940 *23350*
☎ 555807245
Set in a small village in the heart of France this ancient house is about 300 hundred years old. Entirely refurbished and renovated 20 years ago by Madame Hardy and her children, it has retained its old character, and is adorned with period furniture, tools from by-gone times and exposed beams throughout. The service is friendly, whilst the traditional

cuisine has a modern touch and is carefully prepared by the lady of the house and her daughter. Most of the bedrooms have modern facilities and provide a straightforward level of comfort. There is a cosy lounge with open fire and a small delightful garden for relaxation.
Near river Forest area In town centre
Closed 15 Nov-Palm Sunday
7 rms (5 shr) No smoking in 4 bedrooms Licensed Full central heating Open parking available Child discount available 8yrs Last d 20.00hrs Languages spoken: German
MEALS: Full breakfast 34FF Lunch 115-250FF&alc Dinner 115-250FF&alc✱
CARDS: Travellers cheques

GIMEL LES CASCADES Corrèze

★ ★ L'Hostellerie de la Vallée
19800

☎ 555214060 FAX 555213874
(W of Egletons, N89 exit 'The Cascades")
The village of Gimel-les-Cascades is located at an altitude of 446 metres and is counted amongst the most picturesque sites in the Limousin region. The handsome buildings in the village are evidence of a rich architectural heritage, and are complemented by this charming hotel which is situated near the waterfalls. With a fine view over the valley, it offers comfortable bedrooms and a restaurant which caters for most tastes.
Near river Near lake Forest area
Closed Oct-Mar
9 en suite (bth/shr) (1 fmly) TV in all bedrooms Direct dial from all bedrooms Licensed Night porter Full central heating Air conditioning in bedrooms Child discount available 12yrs Boule Open terrace V meals Last d 22.00hrs Languages spoken: English
ROOMS: (room only) d 220-240FF
MEALS: Continental breakfast 25FF Lunch 85-150FF&alc Dinner 115-150FF&alc✱
CARDS: ●● 💳

MEYSSAC Corrèze

★ ★ Relais du Quercy
19500
☎ 555254031 FAX 555253622
Located in the village of Meyssac the hotel has an attractive park and bedrooms are mostly equipped with modern facilities. The cuisine is based on regional recipes with an imaginative accent and is well-known throughout the region. As well as a cocktail bar for a chat and a drink, the hotel organises concert evenings twice a week during the summer season.
Forest area In town centre
12 rms (9 bth/shr) 1 rooms in annexe (2 fmly) TV in all bedrooms Licensed Full central heating Open parking available Covered parking available Child discount available 12yrs Outdoor swimming pool Open terrace Last d 23.00hrs Languages spoken: English,Spanish
MEALS: Full breakfast 35FF Lunch fr 70FF Dinner fr 70FF✱
CARDS: ●● 💳💳 ➤ Travellers cheques

NIEUL Haute Vienne

★ ★ ★ ★ La Chapelle St-Martin
87510
☎ 555758017 FAX 555758950
This splendid country residence is located amidst 30 hectares of private parklands in the hilly countryside towards Limoges. It features comfortable, elegant lounges adorned with rugs

and assorted antiques which create an informal atmosphere. The restaurant is decorated with flair and serves an inventive cuisine only consisting of the finest fresh produce. The guest accommodation is attractive with well co-ordinated fabrics and furniture and provides the highest level of comfort.
Near lake Forest area
12 en suite (bth/shr) (3 with balcony) TV in all bedrooms STV Direct dial from all bedrooms Licensed Night porter Full central heating Open parking available Covered parking available Supervised Child discount available Outdoor swimming pool (heated) Tennis Fishing Sauna Pool table Bicycle rental Open terrace Covered terrace V meals Last d 22.00hrs Languages spoken: English,Spanish
MEALS: Full breakfast 78FF Lunch 250-350FF&alc Dinner 280-380FF&alc✱
CARDS: ●● 💳💳 Travellers cheques

POMPADOUR Corrèze

★ ★ Auberge de la Mandrie
rte de Périgueux *19230*

☎ 555733714 FAX 555736713
The inn is peacefully located in leafy surroundings and features chalet-style guest accommodation situated in large grounds with views over the open countryside. The restaurant has large windows which create a spacious, bright setting, where a choice of regional dishes are served. There are numerous leisure opportunities to be found near the hotel, and the

medieval market town of Ségur le Château is well worth a visit.
22 en suite (bth/shr) TV in all bedrooms Direct dial from all bedrooms Licensed Open parking available Child discount available 10yrs Outdoor swimming pool (heated) Boule Bicycle rental Open terrace Covered terrace Last d 21.15hrs Languages spoken: English
ROOMS: (room only) s 240FF; d 240FF
MEALS: Continental breakfast 36FF Lunch 66-175FF&alc Dinner 66-175FF&alc
CARDS: ●● 💳💳 ➤ Travellers cheques

ROCHE-L'ABEILLE, LA Haute-Vienne

★ ★ ★ Moulin de la Gorce
87800
☎ 555007066 FAX 555007657
Near river Near lake Forest area
Closed Oct-1 Apr
10 en suite (bth/shr) (3 fmly) TV in all bedrooms Licensed Full central heating Open parking available Supervised Child discount available Fishing Boule Open terrace V meals Languages spoken: English
CARDS: ●● 💳💳 ➤ Travellers cheques

ST-LAURENT-LES-ÉGLISES Haute-Vienne

★ ★ **Rallye**
Pont de Dognon *87340*
☎ 555565611 FAX 555565067
This popular hotel is situated next to the Pont du Dognon, near the lake, and has been a family hotel since 1934. It has pretty bedrooms with balconies which offer views of the magnificent forest and a restaurant where freshwater fish delicacies feature strongly on the menu. A number of leisure facilities available for young children as well as for adults makes it a good venue for a family holiday.
Near river Near lake Forest area
Closed end Oct-Etr
18 en suite (bth/shr) (5 fmly) (12 with balcony) TV in 13 bedrooms Direct dial from all bedrooms Licensed Full central heating Open parking available Supervised Child discount available 10yrs Fishing Boule Bicycle rental Open terrace V meals Last d 21.00hrs Languages spoken: English
MEALS: Full breakfast 45FF Continental breakfast 38FF Lunch 80-180FF Dinner 80-180FF✱
CARDS: ✺ ▆ Travellers cheques

ST-PARDOUX-LA-CROISILLE Corrèze

★ ★ ★ **Beau Site**
19320
☎ 552277944 FAX 555276952
The hotel Beau Site is situated in an elevated position at 500 metres in the heart of the 'Green Country'. In this charming family residence visitors are welcomed by the Bidault family; Madame, her son Dominique and his wife Catherine make sure that guests are wanting for nothing. Jean-Claude, 'le père' presides over the kitchen and is responsible for a menu which comprises neo-classical as well as regional dishes. His fish dishes, pâtisserie, desserts and breakfast viennoiserie are highly rated by his clientele who will travel some distance to sample his creations. There is a large choice of leisure facilities available; tennis, fishing, miniature golf and horse-riding are just a few to mention. First-class picnic lunches can be provided on demand.
Near river Near lake Forest area
Closed Oct-Apr
28 en suite (bth/shr) (6 fmly) (2 with balcony) Direct dial from all bedrooms Licensed Full central heating Open parking available Supervised Child discount available 14yrs Outdoor swimming pool (heated) Tennis Fishing Boule Mini-golf Bicycle rental Open terrace Last d 21.00hrs Languages spoken: English
ROOMS: (room only) s 250FF; d 290-330FF
MEALS: Continental breakfast 37FF Lunch 85-240FF&alc Dinner 99-240FF&alc
CARDS: ✺ ▆ Travellers cheques

ST-PRIEST-TAURION Haute-Vienne

★ ★ **Relais du Taurion**
2 chemin des Contamines *87480*
☎ 555397014 FAX 555396763
(12km NE of Limoges)
This friendly inn dates back to the beginning of the century and is located in a park near La Vienne et Taurion. The dining-room has exposed beams which create a cosy atmosphere, and serves an honest cuisine consisting of meat and fish specialities. The bedrooms have modern facilities and provide an adequate level of comfort, whilst the surrounding region offers a large choice of sporting opportunities.

Near river Forest area In town centre
Closed mid Dec-mid Jan
8 en suite (bth/shr) (1 fmly) No smoking on premises TV in all bedrooms Direct dial from all bedrooms Licensed Full central heating Open parking available Supervised Child discount available 12yrs Indoor swimming pool Bicycle rental V meals Last d 21.00hrs Languages spoken: English
ROOMS: (room only) s 240-260FF; d 240-300FF ✱
MEALS: Full breakfast 35FF Continental breakfast 35FF Lunch 110-250FF&alc Dinner 110-250FF&alc
CARDS: ✺ ▆

ST-VIANCE Corrèze

★ ★ **Auberge des pres de la Vezere**
19240
☎ 555850050 FAX 555842536
This delightful country inn is situated just outside the village of St Viance on the threshold of the Périgord region. It has spacious bedrooms with good private facilities, and a comfortable lounge where guests can enjoy a pre or after-dinner drink. The rustic dining-room offers a high-quality regional cuisine, which on fine days is also served on the shaded terrace.
Near river Forest area
Closed mid Oct-end Apr
11 en suite (bth) (2 fmly) TV in all bedrooms Licensed Full central heating Open parking available Child discount available 12yrs Bicycle rental Open terrace Last d 21.30hrs Languages spoken: English
MEALS: Full breakfast 35FF Continental breakfast 35FF Lunch fr 70FF&alc Dinner fr 70FF&alc✱
CARDS: ✺ ▆ ▆ Travellers cheques

SOUTERRAINE, LA Creuse

★ ★ **De La Porte St-Jean**
2 rue des Bains *23300*
☎ 555639000 FAX 555637727
(From N145 follow signs for town centre)
Situated in a pedestrianised area in the historic heart of the town of La Souterraine, the hotel offers very comfortable bedrooms with good modern facilities and has a congenial brasserie-style restaurant which serves dishes to suit most palates. Close to the public gardens and ramparts, it is a suitable venue to explore the town at your own pace.
In town centre Near motorway
32 rms (7 bth 21 shr) 16 rooms in annexe (2 fmly) (2 with balcony) TV in all bedrooms STV Direct dial from all bedrooms Licensed Full central heating Covered parking available (charged) Supervised Child discount available 12yrs Jacuzzi/spa Open terrace V meals Last d 21.00hrs Languages spoken: English,German
ROOMS: (room only) s 169-269FF; d 169-320FF ✱
MEALS: Full breakfast 49FF Continental breakfast 35FF Lunch 83-210FF&alc Dinner 83-210FF&alc✱
CARDS: ✺ ▆ ▆ ➍ Travellers cheques

UZERCHE Corrèze

★ ★ **Teyssier**
rue du Pont Turgot *19140*
☎ 555731005 FAX 555984331
(A20 exit44/45)
Standing on the banks of the river Vézère, the hotel Teyssier has been in the same family for three generations, and provided good food and comfortable accommodation in a

warm and friendly atmosphere. Guests are met upon arrival by the owners Annie and Jean-Michel Teyssier, who both share a passion for refined cuisine; the lady will explain and describe your dishes, whilst her husband creates them with great talent, using market-produce and rare ingredients to a large extent. Most of the bedrooms offer the normal range of amenities, whilst others provide more basic comfort.

Near river Forest area In town centre Near motorway
Closed early Nov-mid Apr
15 rms (5 bth 9 shr) (3 fmly) TV in all bedrooms Direct dial from all bedrooms Licensed Full central heating Open parking available Covered parking available (charged) Open terrace Last d 21.00hrs Languages spoken: English & Spanish
ROOMS: (room only) s 160FF; d 280FF **Reductions over 1 night**
MEALS: Continental breakfast 39FF Lunch 250-320FF&alc Dinner 120-250FF&alc
CARDS: ⬤ 🖩 🖩 ⬤ Travellers cheques

Taking your mobile phone to France?
See page 11

VARETZ Corrèze

★ ★ ★ ★ **Castel Novel**
19240
☎ 555850001 FAX 555850903
This beautiful country château, stands on a wooded hillside and is surrounded by extensive private grounds. The famous writer Colette became the mistress of this residence through her marriage to Henry de Jouvenel and it was here that her daughter Bel Gazou was brought up. It has elegant bedrooms, which provide restful accommodation and the restaurant serves exquisite cuisine where only the finest local ingredients are used. There is a terrace covered with fragrant wisteria, whilst the inviting grounds offer plenty of opportunity to relax.
Near river Forest area
Closed 15 Oct-7 May
37 en suite (bth/shr) 10 rooms in annexe (7 with balcony) TV in all bedrooms STV Mini-bar in all bedrooms Licensed Lift Night porter Full central heating Open parking available Covered parking available Child discount available 12yrs Outdoor swimming pool (heated) Golf 3 Tennis Bicycle rental Open terrace Last d 21.30hrs Languages spoken: English,German,Spanish
CARDS: ⬤ 🖩 🖩 ⬤ Travellers cheques

Auvergne

Auvergne's volcanic terrain offers some of the most wild and breath-taking scenery in France, which is best experienced in its two regional parks. Here, signposted walks designed for the whole family present excellent vantage points from which to view the winding rivers, cascading waterfalls and mountainous slopes. The spectacular gorges of the Haut-Allier are rich in wildlife, including peregrine falcons, red kites, owls and otters. There are water sports, hill walking and hang-gliding activities to challenge the robust and energetic, while the region's castles, Romanesque churches, village inns and spa towns, will inform and refresh those who prefer a gentler pace.

(top): The entombment of Christ is depicted in this late 15th-century tableau at a church in Salers.

(Bottom): The 11th-century chapel of St-Michel d'Aiguilhe tops an enormous dome of volcanic basalt at Le-Puy-en-Velay.

ESSENTIAL FACTS

DÉPARTEMENTS:	Allier, Cantal, Haute-Loire, Puy-de-Dôme
PRINCIPAL TOWNS	Moulins, Clermont-Ferrand, Aurillac, Vichy, Le Puy-en-Velay, Thiers, Montluçon, Issoire, Riom
PLACES TO VISIT:	Parc Régional des Volcans d'Auvergne with its array of old volcanic cones; Le Puy-en-Velay for its outstanding religious art and architecture; Tronçais Forest rich in wildlife, especially deer; the valley of the Dordogne
REGIONAL TOURIST OFFICE	43 av Julien, BP 395, 63011 Clermont-Ferand Tel: 04 73 29 49 49
LOCAL GASTRONOMIC DELIGHTS	Bleu d'Auvergne cheese and others — Auvergne has been called the cheeseboard of France; potée auvergnate, a stew of salt pork and vegetables, coq au vin; cassoulet; vichyssoise, cold leek and potato soup; cousinat, a stew of chestnuts, cream and fruit
DRINKS	Mineral water from the Vichy springs
LOCAL CRAFTS WHAT TO BUY	Honey, jams, cheese, liqueurs, Côtes d'Auvergne wines and many other regional specialities are available at the Village Auvergnat Centre

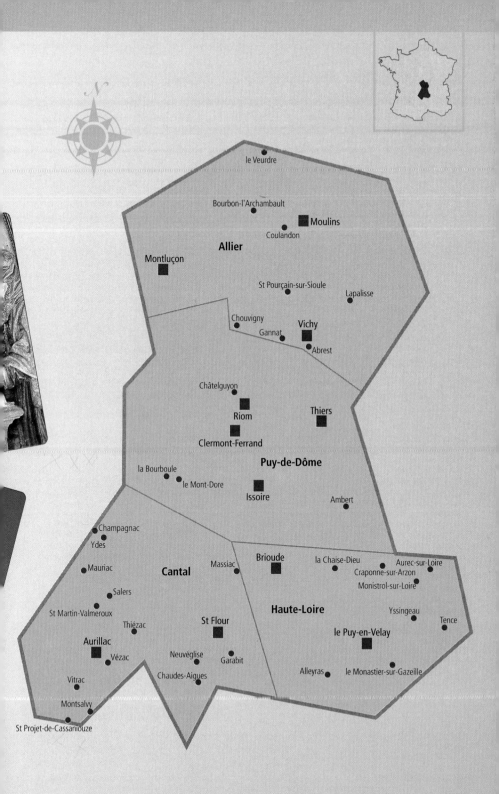

le Veurdre

Bourbon-l'Archambault

Moulins

Coulandon

Allier

Montluçon

St Pourçain-sur-Sioule

Lapalisse

Chouvigny

Vichy

Gannat

Abrest

Châtelguyon

Thiers

Riom

Clermont-Ferrand

Puy-de-Dôme

la Bourboule

le Mont-Dore

Issoire

Ambert

Champagnac

Ydes

Mauriac

Cantal

Massiac

Brioude

la Chaise-Dieu

Aurec-sur-Loire

Craponne-sur-Arzon

Monistrol-sur-Loire

Salers

St Martin-Valmeroux

Haute-Loire

Yssingeau

Thiézac

St Flour

Tence

Aurillac

le Puy-en-Velay

Vézac

Neuvéglise

Garabit

Vitrac

Chaudes-Aigues

Alleyras

le Monastier-sur-Gazeille

Montsalvy

St Projet-de-Cassaniouze

249

EVENTS & FESTIVALS

Jan Clermont-Ferrand International Short Film Festival; St-Bonnet-Le-Froid Monte Carlo Rally

Feb Superbesse motor racing on ice; Le Mont Dore Winter Jazz Festival; Aurillac, Palha Carnival;

Mar Massif Central Chamineige; Montluçon Carnival; Le Puy-En-Velay Street Music Carnival;

Apr Clermont-Ferrand International Video Meeting; Vichy Opera; Yzeure Dare to Dance Festival;

May Yzeure Children's Song Festival; Allanche Pasture Festival; Monistrol-Sur-Loire Springtime Reading;

Jun Riom International Piano Festival; St-Flour Medieval Festival; Chambon-Sur-Lac Hot Air Balloon Rally; Viellevie Cherry Festival; St-Flour Medieval Festival

Jul Ambert World Folk Festival; Yssingeaux Laughter Festival; Riom-ès-Montagnes International Festival of Civilian & Military Music, & Gentian Festival; Lapalisse Laser Nights; Salers Renaissance Festival; Souvigny Medieval Fair and Troubadours' Festival; Charbonnier-le-Mines, Val d'Allier Folk Festival; Le Puy-en-Velay Folk Festival; Issoire

Folklore Festival; Aurillac Horse Festival "Les Crins d'Or"; Hérisson Theatre Festival; Marcoles - strolling players perform in the streets;

Jul/ Aug Hérisson, Bourbonnais Music Festival (medieval & chamber music);

Aug Le Monastier-Sur-Gazeille Brass Music Festival; Champs-Sur-Tarentaine Rock Music Festival; Cunlat Harley Davidson Bike Rally; Le Monastier-sur-Gazeille Brass Music Festival, Murat Dance & Music Festival; Vic-sur-Cère, Carladez Festival (music & folklore); Saint-Germain l'Herm Arts Festival, Pierrefort Festival of Traditions; La Chaise-Dieu Classical Music Festival; Le Puy-en-Velay Marian Feast Day; Braize Donkey Fair; Chalvignac Cheese Fair; St-Pourçain-sur-Sioule Wine Festival

Sep Le Puy-En-Velay Renaissance Festival; Département Du Puy-De-Dôme Concerts & Theatre Festival; St-Martin Valmeroux Cheese Festival; St-Front Festival of The Wind

Oct Chaudes-Aigues Mountain & Adventure Festival; Mourjou Chestnut Fair; Clermont Ferrand Jazz Festival

Nov Le Puy-En-Velay Hot Air Balloon Rally; Monistrol-Sur-Loire Food and Wine Festival; Aurillac Story-telling Festival;

Dec Jaligny Turkey Fair

ABREST Allier

La Colombière
rte de Thiers 03200
☎ 470986915 FAX 470315089
This small, characterful establishment offers panoramic views over the Vallée de l'Allier and features a number of rooms which are equipped with modern amenities. The chef is continuously searching for high quality ingredients to enhance his already excellent classic cuisine.
Near river Near motorway
4 en suite (bth/shr) TV in all bedrooms Licensed Full central heating Open parking available Last d 21.00hrs Languages spoken: English
CARDS: ●● ▆▆ ▆▆ ●)

AIGUEPERSE Puy-de-Dôme

★ ★ ★ Château de la Roche-Aigueperse
La Roche-Chaptuzat 63260
☎ 473636581 FAX 473637679
(A10 S of Paris onto A71 towards Clermont Ferrand. From A71 exit Gannat towards Riom, Clermont Ferrand via N9. On N9 in Aigueperse (10km S of Gannat) turn right to Chaptuzat D7 - map & directions on website http://www.castle-in-france.com)
This feudal castle is the private property of the Marquess de Torcy-Rosey. Three historic bedrooms are available as guest rooms. All with original furniture and canopy-beds of the 17th century. The castle is also open as a museum.
Near motorway
3 en suite (bth/shr) Full central heating Open parking available Covered parking available Supervised Child discount available
ROOMS: d 750-950FF **Reductions over 1 night**

ALLEYRAS Haute-Loire

★ ★ Du Haut Allier
43580
☎ 471575763 FAX 471575799
(From Lyon direction on N88 take D33 towards Cayres and Alleyras)
Situated at the heart of the Massif Central, the hotel Le Haut Allier provides stunning views over the surrounding countryside. It features an attractive interior throughout; bedrooms equipped with modern facilities, and a pleasant restaurant where the menu offers a good choice of well prepared dishes.
Near river Near lake Forest area
Closed mid Nov-early Mar
14 en suite (bth/shr) (7 with balcony) TV in all bedrooms Direct dial from all bedrooms Licensed Lift Full central heating Child discount available 7yrs Boule Bicycle rental Open terrace Covered terrace V meals Last d 21.00hrs Languages spoken: English,Spanish
ROOMS: (room only) d 250-350FF **✱ Reductions over 1 night**
MEALS: Full breakfast 35FF Continental breakfast 35FF Lunch fr 120FF&alc Dinner fr 120FF&alc✱
CARDS: ●● ▆ Travellers cheques

AUREC-SUR-LOIRE Haute-Loire

★ ★ Les Cèdres Bleus
23 rue la Rivière 43110
☎ 477354848 FAX 477353704
(NE towards Bas-en-Basset)
The building stands in a park with cedars, and features attractive bedrooms - all on the ground floor with a view of the

park - equipped with modern amenities. It has a comfortable
day room, a flower-decked terrace for relaxation, and a
restaurant with a comprehensive menu of well-prepared
dishes.
Near river Near motorway
15 en suite (bth/shr) TV in all bedrooms Direct dial from all
bedrooms Licensed Full central heating Open parking
available Supervised Child discount available 10yrs Open
terrace V meals Last d 21.30hrs Languages spoken: English
ROOMS: (room only) s fr 240FF; d fr 290FF
MEALS: Full breakfast 35FF Lunch 120-288FF Dinner 120-
288FF✱
CARDS: 😇 💳 💳 Travellers cheques

AURILLAC Cantal

★ ★ ★ Grand Hotel de Bordeaux (Best Western)
2 av de la République *15000*
☎ 471480184
(A71 exit Massiac Nord)
Situated near the historic centre of the town, the hotel
provides a comfortable setting for an enjoyable stay. It offers a
spacious lounge for reading and relaxing, and a congenial bar
for an aperitif. The bright bedrooms are well equipped with
modern facilities to offer maximum comfort.
In town centre
35 en suite (bth/shr) (8 fmly) No smoking in 12 bedrooms TV
in all bedrooms STV Direct dial from all bedrooms Mini-bar
in all bedrooms Licensed Lift Night porter Full central
heating Open parking available (charged) Covered parking
available (charged) Child discount available 12yrs Bicycle
rental Languages spoken: English & Spanish
ROOMS: (room only) s 350-420FF; d 395-520FF
**Reductions over 1 night Special breaks: special
weekends for walking, riding or clcle tours**
CARDS: 😇 💳 💳 🌑 Travellers cheques

★ ★ ★ Grand Hotel St-Pierre
16 crs Monthyon, Promenade du Gravier *15000*
☎ 471480024 FAX 471648183
The Saint Pierre can be found in the centre of the town of
Aurillac which boasts the title of 'the most sporting town in
France'. Numerous leisure activities are available within the
vicinity, such as a swimming pool, tennis, and golf; or
alternatively one can simply discover the rich cultural and
natural heritage of the area. The hotel has recently been
renovated and has an Art-Déco restaurant with magnificent
wood-panelling where traditional French dishes are served. In
addition, the banqueting facilities can accommodate
conferences, marriage parties and other gatherings.
In town centre
29 en suite (bth/shr) (4 fmly) No smoking in 2 bedrooms TV in
all bedrooms Mini-bar in all bedrooms Lift Full central
heating Open parking available (charged) Covered parking
available (charged) Supervised Child discount available 10yrs
Languages spoken: English & Spanish
CARDS: 😇 💳 💳 🌑 Travellers cheques

BOURBON-L'ARCHAMBAULT Allier

★ ★ Grand Hotel Montespan-Talleyrand
1-3 pl des Thermes *03160*
☎ 470670024 FAX 470671200
(Near the Parc Thermes)
This elegant establishment offers old world charm and
combines traditional hospitality with contemporary
entertainment. The hotel consists of four buildings which date

back to the 16th century, and features ornate French-style
ceilings, period furniture and comfortable bedrooms, some
with private balconies. The restaurant serves outstanding food.
Near lake Forest area Near motorway
Closed 26 Oct-3 Apr
59 rms (10 with balcony) TV in all bedrooms Direct dial from
all bedrooms Licensed Lift Full central heating Covered
parking available Child discount available 10yrs Outdoor
swimming pool (heated) Solarium Jacuzzi/spa Bicycle rental
Open terrace V meals Last d 20.30hrs Languages spoken:
English, German
MEALS: Full breakfast 40FF Lunch 100-160FF&alc Dinner 100-
160FF&alc✱
CARDS: 😇 💳 💳

★ ★ Hotel du Parc et de L'Etablissement
03160
☎ 470670255 FAX 470671395
(next to health spa & leisure centre, hotel is well signposted)
A warm welcome awaits guests at this family owned hotel.
Dating back to 1825 the interior is traditional with modern
comforts.
Forest area In town centre Near motorway
Closed mid Oct-early Apr
52 rms (44 bth/shr) 14 rooms in annexe (6 fmly) (24 with
balcony) Direct-dial available Licensed Lift Full central
heating 22828 open parking spaces Child discount available
10yrs Boule Jacuzzi/spa Bicycle rental Open terrace Last d
20.30hrs

ROOMS: (room only) s 174-185FF; d 220-270FF
Reductions over 1 night Special breaks
MEALS: Continental breakfast 38FF Lunch 70-155FF&alc
Dinner 85-155FF&alc
CARDS: 😇 💳 💳 🌑

BOURBOULE, LA Puy-de-Dôme

★ ★ Aviation Hotel
rue de Metz *63150*
☎ 473813232 FAX 473810285
This friendly establishment is set in the Dordogne valley and
offers cheerful accommodation with good amenities, as well as
a multitude of leisure opportunities which makes it an
excellent venue for a family holiday. In addition it has a cosy
bar and a restaurant which serves a choice of popular dishes to
suit all tastes.
Near river Near lake Forest area In town centre Near
motorway
Closed Oct-19 Dec
50 rms 8 rooms in annexe (28 fmly) (4 with balcony) TV in all
bedrooms Direct dial from all bedrooms Licensed Lift Full

contd.

central heating Covered parking available (charged)
Supervised Child discount available 8yrs Indoor swimming
pool (heated) Pool table Open terrace Last d 20.45hrs

CHAISE-DIEU, LA Haute-Loire

★ ★ Echo et Abbaye
pl de l'Echo *43160*
☎ 471000045 FAX 471000022
This auberge is part of the enclave formed by the splendid La
Chaise Dieu Abbey. The hotel, which is a very old building is
beautifully maintained by Mr Degreze, who extends a warm
welcome to guests. The small bedrooms are charming and
comfortable , some have views of the cloisters. There is a
restaurant dining room decorated in Haute Epoque style,
where the regional Auvergnate cuisine recieves many
compliments.
Near lake Forest area In town centre
Closed 12 Nov-Etr
19 rms (6 bth 5 shr) TV in all bedrooms Direct dial from 11
bedrooms Licensed Full central heating Open parking
available Child discount available 10yrs Fishing Riding Boule
Open terrace V meals Last d 21.15hrs Languages spoken:
English & Spanish
ROOMS: (room only) s fr 250FF; d 295-360FF
MEALS: Continental breakfast 49FF Dinner 95-240FF
CARDS: ●● ■■ ■■ Travellers cheques

CHAMPAGNAC Cantal

★ ★ ★ Château de Lavendes
rte de Neuvic *15350*
☎ 471696279 FAX 471696533
(Access via D15 from Bort-les-Orgues)
Built on the site of an ancient manor house, this 18th-century
residence occupies a secluded location surrounded by three
hectares of private grounds. Converted into a hotel-restaurant
in 1986, it now features an inviting foyer with an imposing
fireplace where visitors can enjoy afternoon tea. There are two
dining rooms, individually furnished with period pieces, which
serve a delicious range of house specialities.
Near river Near lake Forest area
RS 15 Sep-15 May
8 en suite (bth/shr) (1 fmly) TV in all bedrooms Direct dial
from all bedrooms Licensed Full central heating Open
parking available Outdoor swimming pool (heated) Open
terrace Last d 21.00hrs Languages spoken: English
ROOMS: (room only) d 460-700FF **Reductions over 1
night**
MEALS: Full breakfast 85FF Continental breakfast 65FF Lunch
135-195FF&alc Dinner 135-195FF&alc
CARDS: ●● ■■ ■■ Travellers cheques

CHÂTELGUYON Puy-de-Dôme

★ ★ Régence
31 av des États-Unis *63140*
☎ 473860260 FAX 473861249

✗ ✗ ✗ ✗

(From A70/A71 take exit 'Riom Nord' for Châtelguyon, then
follow Thermal drive for 200mtrs)
This turn-of-the-century building is situated in Châtel-Guyon, a
well-known spa town in the Auvergne region. Fully renovated,
it features spacious day rooms adorned with period furniture
and assorted antiques, which create the atmosphere of bygone
times. All the bedrooms are equipped with modern amenities
and offer comfortable accommodation. Guests can enjoy the
sunshine in the garden or on the terrace, before sampling the

fine cuisine, carefully prepared by the chef-proprietor.
Forest area In town centre Near motorway
Closed 20 Oct-15 Apr

27 rms (12 bth 12 shr) (3 fmly) (10 with balcony) Direct dial
from all bedrooms Licensed Lift Full central heating Covered
parking available (charged) Supervised Child discount
available 8yrs Open terrace Covered terrace Last d 21.hrs
Languages spoken: English, Spanish
ROOMS: (room only) d 180-215FF
MEALS: Continental breakfast 45FF Lunch 80-130FF Dinner
75-80FF✱
CARDS: ●● ■■ Travellers cheques

CHAUDES-AIGUES Cantal

★ ★ Beauséjour
9 av Président Pompidou *15110*
☎ 471235237 FAX 471235689
(Access from St-Flour via D921)
The hotel offers a comfortable interior with attractive, fully
equipped bedrooms and pleasant public areas where guests
can relax or read. The restaurant serves an excellent cuisine,
incorporating dishes with a regional touch and where local
produce has been used to a large extent. Guests enjoy a special
blend of hospitality, provided by attentive staff which offer
personal attention and service at all times.
Near river Near lake Forest area
Closed Dec-Mar
40 rms (39 bth/shr) (5 fmly) (3 with balcony) TV in all
bedrooms Direct dial from all bedrooms Licensed Lift Full
central heating Open parking available Covered parking
available (charged) Child discount available Outdoor
swimming pool (heated) Open terrace V meals Languages
spoken: English,Spanish

★ ★ Des Thermes
15110
☎ 471235118 FAX 471235846
The hotel is located at the southern end of the village and
offers guest rooms with modern facilities and a choice of
leisure facilities. There are no restaurant facilities, but guests
may want to seek out the various eating establishments in the
area.
In town centre
Closed Oct-Apr
46 rms (46 with balcony) TV in all bedrooms Direct dial from
all bedrooms Lift Night porter Full central heating Open
parking available Supervised Solarium Jacuzzi/spa
Languages spoken: English
CARDS: ●● ■■

CHOUVIGNY Allier

★ ★ Des Gorges de Chouvigny
03450

☎ 470904211
This family establishment is situated in a beautiful, green valley on the banks of a river. The country-style interior consists of cosy bedrooms and an informal restaurant where Mr Eric Fleury the chef-proprietor, is in charge of the kitchen, whilst the lady of the house provides attentive service in the restaurant. Guests may want to visit the magnificent castle which towers above the hotel, or explore the delightful countryside around.
Near river Forest area Near motorway
Closed Nov-Mar
8 en suite (shr) (2 fmly) Direct dial from all bedrooms Full central heating Open parking available Child discount available 12yrs Open terrace Covered terrace Canoeing,fishing & horseriding nearby Last d 21.00hrs Languages spoken: English
CARDS: 💳 ⚏

CLERMONT-FERRAND Puy-de-Dôme

★ ★ ★ Hotel Frantour Arverne
16 pl Delille *63000*
☎ 473919206 FAX 473916025
The Hotel Frantour Arverne is situated close to the railway station and just a stone's throw from the imposing cathedral with its unrivalled views over the surrounding countryside and the Dômes. If offers pleasant, sound-proofed bedrooms with every modern facility. There are two restaurants, of which one has splendid views of the Puys mountain range, whilst the other - furnished in English style - is suitable for entertaining large parties of up to 300 people. In addition, the four function rooms make it an ideal venue for both the business and leisure traveller.
In town centre Near motorway
57 en suite (bth/shr) (8 fmly) (21 with balcony) TV in all bedrooms STV Radio in rooms Direct dial from all bedrooms Licensed Lift Night porter Full central heating Air conditioning in bedrooms Open parking available (charged) Covered parking available (charged) Supervised Pool table Open terrace Covered terrace V meals Last d 22.30hrs Languages spoken: English,German
CARDS: 💳 ⚏ 🟰 🌐 Travellers cheques

★ ★ ★ Novotel
32-34 rue G-Besse-ZI, Le Brezet Est *63100*
☎ 473411414 FAX 473411400
Novotel offer their clients good quality accommodation in modern, well equipped bedrooms and have refined restaurants serving good quality cuisine They have excellent business meeting and conference facilities and some have food and beverages available 24 hours a day. All their hotels have at least one bedroom for disabled guests.
Near lake Near motorway
96 en suite (bth/shr) (56 fmly) No smoking in 16 bedrooms TV in all bedrooms STV Radio in rooms Direct dial from all bedrooms Mini-bar in all bedrooms Licensed Lift Night porter Full central heating Air conditioning in bedrooms Open parking available Child discount available 16yrs Outdoor swimming pool (heated) Open terrace Covered terrace Last d 24.00hrs Languages spoken: English,German,Italian,Spanish

ROOMS: (room only) s 465-475FF; d 505-530FF ✱
MEALS: Full breakfast 56FF Continental breakfast 56FF Lunch 98-135FF&alc Dinner 98-135FF&alc✱
CARDS: 💳 ⚏ 🟰 🌐 Travellers cheques

COULANDON Allier

★ ★ ★ Le Chalet
03000

☎ 470445008 FAX 470440709
(on D945)
The Hotel Le Chalet is an old country residence dating back to the 19th century. It is situated in three hectares of mature wooded parkland with a private lake. The foyer, lounge, dining-room and bedrooms are spread over three buildings and furnished in a style befitting the character of the house. Meals are served in the elegant restaurant or on the patio with its splendid views of the countryside, whilst the menu is augmented by a wine-list which features the famous Saint-Pourçain and Sancerre wines.
Near river Near lake Forest area
Closed mid Dec-end Jan
28 en suite (bth/shr) Some rooms in annexe (8 fmly) (3 with balcony) TV in all bedrooms STV Licensed Full central heating Open parking available Supervised Child discount available 10yrs Outdoor swimming pool (heated) Fishing Boule Open terrace Last d 21.30hrs Languages spoken: English,German
ROOMS: (room only) s 310-350FF; d 370-480FF ✱
Reductions over 1 night
MEALS: Continental breakfast 48FF Lunch 120-250FF&alc Dinner 120-250FF&alc
CARDS: 💳 ⚏ 🟰 🌐 Travellers cheques

CRAPONNE-SUR-ARZON Haute-Loire

★ ★ ★ Mistou
Pontempeyrat *43500*
☎ 477506246 FAX 477506670
The Hotel Mistou is an ancient mill, tucked away in a delightful valley with splendid parklands and a picturesque river for trout-fishing nearby. Completely renovated in 1930s style, it offers the ideal starting-point from which to discover the Haute-Loire. It has spacious, well equipped bedrooms, a tastefully furnished restaurant serving delightful, freshly prepared food using the finest produce.
Near river Forest area
Closed early Nov-Etr
13 en suite (bth/shr) 10 rooms in annexe (2 fmly) (11 with balcony) Mini-bar in all bedrooms Licensed Open parking available Child discount available 10yrs Open terrace Covered terrace Last d 21.00hrs Languages spoken: English
CARDS: 💳 ⚏ 🟰 Travellers cheques

GARABIT Cantal

★ ★ Garabit-Hotel
15320

☎ 471234275 FAX 471234960
(From A75 exit 30/31 through Le Viaduct de Garabit to hotel)
The hotel stands at the foot of the imposing Garabit viaduct, which bears all the hallmarks of its creator, Gustave Eiffel. It is a pleasant hotel with good accommodation with modern amenities. There is an attractive TV lounge and the dining rooms and terraces are situated on the banks of the lake.
Near river Near lake Forest area Near motorway
RS Nov Mar

contd.

47 en suite (bth/shr) (8 fmly) (16 with balcony) TV in all
bedrooms Direct dial from all bedrooms Mini-bar in all
bedrooms Licensed Lift Open parking available Covered
parking available Child discount available 12yrs Indoor
swimming pool (heated) Fishing Boule Open terrace
Covered terrace V meals Last d 21.30hrs Languages spoken:
English,Dutch,German,Spanish
ROOMS: (room only) d 185-340FF
MEALS: Full breakfast 35FF Lunch 72-175FF&alc Dinner 72-
175FF&alc
CARDS: 💳 💳

MASSIAC Cantal

★ ★ Grand Hotel de la Poste
26 av Général-de-Gaulle *15500*
☎ 471230201 FAX 471230923
Located in a small, pretty town in the Auvergne region, the
hotel is the right venue for a pleasant stay. Whether you want
to get fit or just have a relaxing holiday, it offers something for
everybody. It features excellent leisure facilities and restful
accommodation, while the restaurant offers a wide choice of
eating options.
Near motorway
32 en suite (bth/shr) (2 fmly) TV in all bedrooms Licensed Lift
Full central heating Open parking available Supervised Child
discount available 10yrs Indoor swimming pool (heated)
Outdoor swimming pool (heated) Squash Pool table Mini-golf
Jacuzzi/spa Open terrace Covered terrace V meals Last d
21.00hrs Languages spoken: English
CARDS: 💳 💳 💳 💳 Travellers cheques

MONT-DORE, LE Puy-de-Dôme

★ ★ ★ Panorama
av de la Libération *63240*
☎ 473651112 FAX 473652080
Located in the Auvergne region with its lakes and volcanoes,
the hotel is only 300 metres from the centre of town and the
thermal baths. It has comfortable bedrooms with good
amenities and a restaurant which serves a traditional cuisine
based on fresh regional produce. With its wide in-house range
of leisure opportunities, it is the ideal venue for a summer or
winter holiday.
Near river Near lake Forest area
Closed 14 Oct-24 Dec & 21 Mar-14 May
39 en suite (bth/shr) (2 fmly) TV in all bedrooms Direct dial
from all bedrooms Licensed Lift Full central heating
Open parking available Child discount available 12yrs
Indoor swimming pool (heated) Sauna Pool table Open
terrace Covered terrace Languages spoken: English,
German
CARDS: 💳 💳 Travellers cheques

MONTSALVY Cantal

★ ★ Inter Hotel du Nord
pl du Barry *15120*
☎ 471492003 FAX 471492900
The hotel is located in Montsalvy, a lush green holiday resort
situated at an altitude of 800 metres. It features peacefully
situated rooms with good private facilities, a friendly lounge-
bar and an informal restaurant which serves a splendid cuisine
accompanied by a comprehensive wine list. The surrounding
area has many places of interest to visit well as various leisure
opportunities on offer.
Forest area

Closed Jan-Mar
20 en suite (bth/shr) TV in all bedrooms STV Direct dial from
all bedrooms Mini-bar in all bedrooms Licensed Full central
heating Open parking available Child discount available 12yrs
V meals Last d 21.30hrs Languages spoken: English
MEALS: Full breakfast 40FF Continental breakfast 40FF Lunch
85-250FF&alc Dinner 85-250FF&alc✱
CARDS: 💳 💳 💳 💳 JCB Travellers cheques

MOULINS Allier

★ ★ Le Parc
31 av Général Leclerc *03000*
☎ 470441225 FAX 470467935
(signposted from railway station)
Situated near a peaceful park, the hotel provides a pleasant
venue for a comfortable stay. The bedrooms are attractively
furnished and equipped with modern amenities, while the
restaurant offers a classic cuisine, complemented by a
choice of regional dishes prepared with the finest
ingredients.
In town centre
Closed 10-25 Jul & 2-10 Oct RS Restaurant closed Sat
28 en suite (bth/shr) Some rooms in annexe (8 fmly) (5 with
balcony) TV in all bedrooms Direct dial from all bedrooms
Licensed Night porter Full central heating Open parking
available Supervised Open terrace Last d 21.15hrs
Languages spoken: English, German
ROOMS: (room only) s 200-330FF; d 200-330FF
MEALS: Full breakfast 37FF Lunch 98-210FF&alc Dinner 98-
210FF&alc
CARDS: 💳 💳 Travellers cheques

★ ★ ★ Hotel de Paris-Jacquemart
21 rue de Paris *03000*
☎ 470440058 FAX 470340539
This former coaching inn is situated in the historic heart of the
town. The bedrooms and apartments feature good quality
furniture and up-to-date amenities. The cosy lounge and
elegant restaurant provide the setting for relaxation and
excellent food.
In town centre Near motorway
Closed 1-14 Feb
27 en suite (bth/shr) (4 fmly) TV in all bedrooms STV Direct
dial from all bedrooms Licensed Lift Night porter Full
central heating Open parking available (charged) Supervised
Child discount available 6yrs Outdoor swimming pool (heated)
Open terrace Last d 21.30hrs Languages spoken: English
MEALS: Full breakfast 75FF Continental breakfast 55FF Lunch
120-350FF&alc Dinner 120-350FF&alc✱
CARDS: 💳 💳 💳 💳 JCB

NEUVÉGLISE Cantal

★ ★ Auberge du Pont de Lanau
Lanau *15260*
☎ 471235776 FAX 471235384
This former coaching inn is situated between Saint-Flour and
Chaudes Aigues and provides a good base from which to
explore the Cantal region. An attractive Auverge-style house, it
offers rustic rooms offering good facilities and views of the
surrounding countryside. The splendid cuisine incorporates
regional ingredients with imaginative creations from the chef.
Near river Near lake Forest area Near motorway
Closed Jan & Feb
8 en suite (bth/shr) Some rooms in annexe TV in all bedrooms
Licensed Full central heating Open parking available

Covered parking available (charged) Supervised Last d
21.30hrs Languages spoken: English
MEALS: Full breakfast 35FF Lunch 95-275FF Dinner 95-
275FF✱
CARDS: ✹ ▦

PUY-EN-VELAY, LE Haute-Loire

★ ★ Bristol
7 av Foch *43000*
☎ 471091338 FAX 471095170
Set in the centre of town and with a delightful shaded interior
garden for relaxation, the hotel offers peaceful bedrooms with
modern appointments. It was entirely renovated in 1996 and
features an attractive interior with good quality furniture and
co-ordinated shades and fabrics. There is an elegant dining
room with a 1930s-style decor which offers a high standard of
cooking, whilst in summer a choice of char-grilled dishes are
served on the terrace in the garden.
In town centre
40 en suite (bth/shr) 20 rooms in annexe (2 fmly) TV in all
bedrooms Direct dial from all bedrooms Licensed Lift Night
porter Full central heating Open parking available (charged)
Covered parking available (charged) Supervised Child
discount available 12yrs Open terrace Last d 21.30hrs
Languages spoken: English & German
MEALS: Full breakfast 35FF Lunch 89-145FF Dinner 89-
145FF✱
CARDS: ✹ ▦ ▧ ◑ Travellers cheques

RIOM Puy-de-Dôme

★ ★ Anemotel
Les Portes de Riom *63200*
☎ 473337100 FAX 473640060
This friendly hotel features pleasant bedrooms which are
furnished in an understated fashion and provide a good level
of comfort. The gourmet restaurant caters for all tastes and
opens up to the garden with terrace, while a congenial bar
provides the cosy setting for a chat or a drink.
Near river Near lake Forest area Near motorway
43 en suite (bth/shr) (7 fmly) TV in all bedrooms STV Direct-
dial available Licensed Lift Night porter Full central heating
Air conditioning in bedrooms Open parking available
Supervised Child discount available Boule Open terrace V
meals Last d 22.00hrs Languages spoken: English
MEALS: Full breakfast 36FF Continental breakfast 36FF Lunch
80-160FF&alc Dinner 80-160FF&alc✱
CARDS: ✹ ▧ Travellers cheques

ST-FLOUR Cantal

★ ★ L'Ander
6 bis av du Ct Délorme *15100*
☎ 471602163 FAX 471604640
(Access via A75 exit 28 towards Rodez)
This family run hotel was built in 1988 and has airy bedrooms
with modern appointments, offering an adequate level of
comfort. The restaurant serves regional dishes with a local
accent, which are well prepared by the young chef who is in
charge of the kitchen.
Near river Forest area In town centre Near motorway
50 en suite (bth/shr) (5 fmly) (10 with balcony) TV in all
bedrooms STV Direct dial from all bedrooms Licensed Lift
Night porter Full central heating Air conditioning in
bedrooms Open parking available Covered parking available
Supervised Child discount available 12yrs Indoor swimming

pool Riding Boule Bicycle rental Open terrace V meals Last
d 21.00hrs Languages spoken: English,Spanish
ROOMS: (room only) d 150-220FF **Reductions over 1 night**
MEALS: Full breakfast 30FF Continental breakfast 27FF Lunch
48-55FF&alc Dinner 48-55FF&alc
CARDS: ✹ ▧ Travellers cheques

★ ★ Des Messageries
23 av Charles-de-Gaulle *15100*
☎ 471601136 FAX 471604679
The hotel is set in a quiet part of the town near the station, and
features guest rooms which have modern appointments and
provide a good standard of accommodation. There is a
comfortable TV lounge, and a restaurant which serves good
quality dishes with a large choice of regional specialities.
Near river In town centre Near motorway
Closed Oct-Mar
18 en suite (bth/shr) (3 fmly) (6 with balcony) TV in all
bedrooms STV Direct dial from all bedrooms Mini-bar in all
bedrooms Licensed Full central heating Open parking
available Covered parking available (charged) Child discount
available 12yrs Outdoor swimming pool (heated) Sauna Pool
table Boule Open terrace Last d 21.30hrs Languages spoken:
English
MEALS: Full breakfast 5000FF Continental breakfast 50FF
Lunch 80-99FF&alc Dinner 80-99FF&alc
CARDS: ✹ ▧ Travellers cheques

★ ★ St-Jacques
8 pl de la Liberté *15100*
☎ 471600920 FAX 471603381
Situated at the foot of the medieval cité of St- Flour this
establishment is full of character and furnished with many
period pieces to enhance the charming atmosphere of by-gone
days. The cuisine incorporates a choice of delicious produce
from the Auvergne and the meals - priced to suit anybody's
budget - are served by the fireside in winter or weather
permitting, on the terrace in summer. Outdoor leisure
opportunities are numerous and include; swimming, canoeing,
fishing, tennis and hunting.
Near river Near lake Forest area In town centre Near
motorway
28 en suite (bth/shr) (5 fmly) TV in all bedrooms STV Direct
dial from 280 bedrooms Licensed Lift Full central heating
Open parking available Covered parking available (charged)
Outdoor swimming pool (heated) Bicycle rental Open terrace
V meals Last d 21.00hrs Languages spoken: English
ROOMS: (room only) s 260-310FF; d 260-400FF
Reductions over 1 night
MEALS: Continental breakfast 42FF Lunch 90-235FF Dinner
90-235FF
CARDS: ✹ ▧

ST-MARTIN-VALMEROUX Cantal

★ ★ ★ Hostellerie de la Maronne
Le Theil *15140*
☎ 471692033 FAX 471682822
This Auvergne residence dates back to the 19th century and
offers splendid views over the Cantal mountains and the
beautiful Maronne valley. Situated within the volcano reserve,
six km from Salers, it offers the ideal venue for lovers of
architecture and culture. The guest rooms are decorated in an
attractive fashion and provide peaceful accommodation, whilst
the panoramic restaurant serves a choice of house specialities
skilfully prepared by the proprietor Mme Decock.
Near river Forest area

contd.

Closed 6 Nov-20 Mar
21 en suite (bth) (7 fmly) (9 with balcony) TV in all bedrooms
STV Direct dial from all bedrooms Mini-bar in all bedrooms
Licensed Lift Full central heating Open parking available
Supervised Child discount available 12yrs Outdoor swimming
pool (heated) Tennis Riding Boule Bicycle rental Open
terrace V meals Last d 21.30hrs Languages spoken: English
ROOMS: (room only) s 460-500FF; d 460-700FF
MEALS: Full breakfast 60FF Continental breakfast 60FF
Dinner 150-250FF
CARDS: 😎 ■ ■ ❸ Travellers cheques

ST-POURÇAIN-SUR-SIOUL Allier

★ ★ Le Chêne Vert
35 bd Ledru-Rollin 03500
☎ 470454065 FAX 470456850
(From A71 take exit Montmarault)
The hotel occupies a peaceful village setting in north-central
France and welcomes its visitors in a cosy, intimate interior.
The bedrooms - most with modern amenities - offer adequate
comfort, whilst the homely restaurant serves traditional dishes,
skilfully prepared by Mr Siret and served by courteous,
attentive staff.
Near river In town centre Near motorway
Closed Jan
31 rms (20 bth 8 shr) 14 rooms in annexe (1 fmly) TV in all
bedrooms Direct dial from all bedrooms Mini-bar in 28
bedrooms Licensed Full central heating Open parking
available (charged) Supervised Open terrace Last d 21.00hrs
Languages spoken: English,Spanish
MEALS: Full breakfast 40FF Lunch 90-220FF Dinner 90-220FF
CARDS: 😎 ■ ■ ❸ Travellers cheques

ST-PROJET-DE-CASSANIOUZE Cantal

★ Du Pont
15340
☎ 471494921 FAX 471499610
Set in a quiet village in the Auvergne region, the hotel features
pretty bedrooms which all have fine views over the
surrounding countryside. Situated at 50 metres from the river
Lot, it has a terrace and wooded grounds - where children can
play freely - with a choice of leisure pursuits. The restaurant
offers a choice of regional specialities as well as many
traditional dishes, and because of its central location, the hotel
provides a good base for exploring the sights.
Near river Forest area
Closed Dec-7 Mar
12 rms (7 shr) Direct dial from all bedrooms Licensed Full
central heating Open parking available Supervised Child
discount available 12yrs Boule Bicycle rental Open terrace V

meals Last d 21.30hrs Languages spoken: English,Spanish
ROOMS: (room only) d 180-210FF
MEALS: Full breakfast 38FF Continental breakfast 38FF Lunch
68-126FF&alc Dinner 68-126FF&alc
CARDS: 😎 ■ Travellers cheques

SALERS Cantal

★ ★ Bailliage
15140
☎ 471407195 FAX 471407490
Near river Forest area
Closed 15 Nov-1 Feb
30 rms (4 fmly) (4 with balcony) TV in all bedrooms Licensed
Full central heating Open parking available Covered parking
available (charged) Child discount available 10yrs Outdoor
swimming pool (heated) Boule Open terrace Last d 21.00hrs
Languages spoken: English
ROOMS: (room only) d 230-360FF **Reductions over 1
night**
MEALS: Continental breakfast 37FF Lunch 68-165FF Dinner
68-165FF
CARDS: 😎 ■ ■ ❸ Travellers cheques

★ ★ Le Gerfaut
rte du Puy-Mary 15140
☎ 471407575 FAX 471407345
Near river
Closed 31 Oct-Mar
25 en suite (bth/shr) 3 rooms in annexe (3 fmly) (10 with
balcony) TV in all bedrooms Direct dial from all bedrooms
Licensed Lift Full central heating Open parking available
Child discount available 10yrs Outdoor swimming pool
(heated) Boule Bicycle rental Open terrace Table tennis
Childs play area Last d 21.00hrs Languages spoken:
English,Spanish
ROOMS: (room only) s 250-270FF; d 270-430FF
CARDS: 😎 ■ ■ ❸ Travellers cheques

★ ★ Remparts et Château de la Bastide
Esplanade de Barrouzé 15140
☎ 471407033 FAX 471407532
Near river Forest area In town centre
31 rms (12 bth 17 shr) (8 fmly) (11 with balcony) TV in all
bedrooms Direct dial from all bedrooms Licensed Full
central heating Open parking available Child discount
available 12yrs Open terrace Last d 20.45hrs Languages
spoken: English
MEALS: Continental breakfast 36FF Lunch 68-135FF Dinner
68-135FF★
CARDS: 😎 ■ Travellers cheques

TENCE Haute-Loire

★ ★ ★ Hostellerie Placide
rte d'Annonay 43190
☎ 471598276 FAX 471654446
(Access via A7 or A47)
Tucked away amidst lush vegetation in a peaceful village, the
hotel invites its clientele to enjoy some of the simple pleasures
in life; a restful night's sleep in an attractive bedroom
decorated in pastel shades, followed by a delicious breakfast in
the garden and complemented by a gourmet dinner in the
dining-room with splendid flower displays. Warm hospitality
and excellent food have been a family tradition since the turn-
of-the-century and still feature strongly on the present owners
list of priorities.

Near river Near lake Forest area Near motorway
Closed mid Nov-mid Mar
17 en suite (bth/shr) (6 fmly) (1 with balcony) TV in all
bedrooms Direct dial from all bedrooms Licensed Night
porter Full central heating Open parking available Child
discount available 12yrs Boule Open terrace Last d 21.30hrs
Languages spoken: English, Spanish
Rooms: (room only) s 320FF; d 390-430FF
Meals: Full breakfast 55FF Lunch 85-280FF&alc Dinner 130-
280FF&alc✱
Cards: ●● ▦ ▆ Travellers cheques

THIÉZAC Cantal

★ ★ L'Élanceze et Belle Vallée
15800
☎ 471470022 FAX 471470208
(Off N122)
Set in the heart of the village of Thiezac, this modern hotel
provides the pleasant setting for an enjoyable break in the
Auvergne region. The bedrooms are equipped with modern
facilities, there is reading room, and a garden for relaxation.
The restaurant serves a good standard of cooking
incorporating tasty dishes from the region.
Near river Forest area Near motorway
Closed Nov-20 Dec
41 en suite (bth/shr) 10 rooms in annexe (23 with balcony) TV
in all bedrooms Direct dial from all bedrooms Licensed Lift
Full central heating Open parking available Covered parking
available Child discount available 10yrs Open terrace V meals
Last d 21.00hrs
Rooms: (room only) d 225-260FF **Reductions over 1
night**
Meals: Full breakfast 40FF Continental breakfast 30FF Lunch
89-180FF&alc Dinner 89-180FF&alc
Cards: ●● ▆ Travellers cheques

VEURDRE, LE Allier

★ ★ Pont Neuf
rte de Lurcy Levis *83320*
☎ 470664012 FAX 470664415

The hotel offers a comfortable interior with attractive, fully
equipped bedrooms and pleasant public areas where guests
can relax or read. The restaurant serves an excellent cuisine,
incorporating dishes with a regional touch and where local
produce has been used to a large extend. Guests enjoy a
special blend of hospitality, provided by attentive staff which
offer personal attention and service at all times.
Near river Near sea Forest area Near motorway
Closed 25-31 Oct & 15 Dec-15 Jan

36 en suite (bth/shr) 11 rooms in annexe (4 fmly) No smoking
in 4 bedrooms TV in all bedrooms STV Direct dial from all
bedrooms Licensed Full central heating Open parking
available Covered parking available (charged) Supervised
Child discount available 12yrs Indoor swimming pool
Tennis Fishing Sauna Gym Boule Bicycle rental Open
terrace V meals Last d 21.30hrs Languages spoken:
English, Spanish
Rooms: (room only) s 235-320FF; d 255-350FF
Reductions over 1 night
Meals: Full breakfast 40FF Lunch 85-225FF&alc Dinner 85-
225FF&alc
Cards: ●● ▦ ▆ ☻ Travellers cheques

VÉZAC Cantal

Château de Salles Hostellerie
Château de Salles *15130*
☎ 471624141 FAX 471624414
Near river Forest area
18 en suite (bth/shr) 6 rooms in annexe (6 fmly) TV in all
bedrooms STV Licensed Lift Night porter Open parking
available Child discount available Outdoor swimming pool
Tennis Sauna Gym Pool table Jacuzzi/spa Open terrace
Languages spoken: English, German
Cards: ●● ▦ ▆

VICHY Allier

★ ★ Hotel Arcade
11-13 Av Pierre Coulon *03200*
☎ 470981848 FAX 470977263
Near river Near lake Near beach In town centre
48 en suite (shr) TV in all bedrooms Direct dial from all
bedrooms Lift Full central heating Open parking available
Child discount available 12yrs Indoor swimming pool Sauna
Solarium Open terrace Covered terrace Languages spoken:
English
Rooms: (room only) s 265-300FF; d 300FF **Reductions
over 1 night Special breaks**
Cards: ●● ▦ ▆ Travellers cheques

VITRAC Cantal

★ ★ La Tomette
Centre du Bourg *15220*
☎ 471647094 FAX 471647711
(Access via A75 exit Massiac, then N122 through Aurillac and
St-Mamet)
Surrounded by hills and 25 kilometres south of Aurillac, the
hotel is situated in the charming village of Vitrac, and provides
the peaceful setting for a relaxing stay. Comfortable bedrooms
offer a good level of comfort, in the morning, breakfast is
served in the garden, whilst at dinner a choice of enjoyable
dishes with an 'Auvergne' touch are served in the restaurant.
The immediate vicinity has a range of leisure facilities on offer,
or guests may want to explore the Cantal mountains nearby.
Forest area
Closed 16 Dec-1 Apr
15 en suite (bth/shr) 15 rooms in annexe (6 fmly) TV in all
bedrooms STV Direct dial from all bedrooms Licensed Full
central heating Open parking available Supervised Child
discount available 12yrs Outdoor swimming pool (heated)
Sauna Pool table Boule Bicycle rental Open terrace Covered
terrace Last d 21.00hrs Languages spoken: English

contd.

ROOMS: (room only) d 260-320FF
MEALS: Full breakfast 40FF Lunch 90-200FF&alc Dinner 90-200FF&alc
CARDS: 🐡 📷 💳 Travellers cheques

YDES Cantal

★ ★ ★ Château de Trancis
Trancis *15210*
☎ 471406040 FAX 471406213
(From Bort-les-Orgues take D922 towards Mauriac for 6km then left onto D15 towards Saignes. Hotel 200mtrs on right)
Near river
Closed Mid Oct-mid Mar

7 en suite (bth/shr) (1 with balcony) TV in all bedrooms STV Direct dial from all bedrooms Mini-bar in all bedrooms Licensed Full central heating Open parking available Supervised Outdoor swimming pool Open terrace V meals Last d 22.00hrs Languages spoken: English
MEALS: Lunch fr 280FF Dinner fr 280FF✱
CARDS: 🐡 📷 💳 Travellers cheques

Taking your mobile phone to France?
See page 11

EXPLORING AUVERGNE

Outdoor Pursuits

Auvergne is a haven for fitness and health. Hikers and walkers are well served with numerous signposted and regularly maintained paths around the lakes, volcanoes and valleys of the region. Mountain biking, cycling and pony-trekking provide other ways to enjoy the fresh air of the countryside, and special routes have been mapped out for the needs of the beginner or the more experienced explorer. Useful topological guides are available. For a 'hands-on' approach, there are over 50 climbing areas to suit all levels of ability. Or why not see the sights from the air with a dizzying choice of hang gliding, paragliding, microlights, parachuting or ballooning. Those

Volcano Country: Le Parc Regional des Volcans D'Auvergne is ideal for walking and exploring.

who were born to be wild can go bungee jumping from the Récoumène Viaduct in Haute-Loire. Down in the Gorges de l'Allier the river flows between imposing rock-faces upon which are Romanesque chapels, fortresses, abbeys, and the villages of St-Illpize, St-Arcons and Chanteuges. The gorges are a suitable venue for exciting water sports, ranging from canoeing and windsurfing, to kayaking and canyon-rafting.

Auvergne Cuisine

Cuisine in Auvergne is simple and generous. Cabbage soup with pork, locally known as "potée", is a favourite hotpot dish. In fact, the abundance of pork provides the foundation for a number of popular meals, including pigs' trotters coated with breadcrumbs or cooked in white wine, sausages cooked in local brandy, and salt pork ("petit salé") served with green lentils from Le Puy; the latter are often served with the fine salmon caught from the River Allier. Auvergne is also proud of its distinctive cheeses, such as Cantal, Saint-Nectaire, Bleu d'Auvergne and Fourme d'Ambert which make a deliciously smooth "aligot" with mashed potato. And what better to accompany the local cheeses, than a light and fruity local wine like Châteaugay or Saint-Pourçain.

Rhône Alpes

Wonderfully situated at the meeting point of northern and southern Europe, and bordering Italy and Switzerland, the Rhône Alpes scenery is a spectacle of vivid contrasts: from snow-covered peaks and vast glaciers, to dense woodland and rich pastures. A paradise for outdoor leisure activities and sporting holidays. With 70 winter ski resorts, the Savoie is the largest ski area in the world, while the Ardèche is a veritable adventure playground of magnificent caves and gorges. And when the playing's done, relax with a glass of local wine. A Beaujolais, or Côte du Rhône, or Savoie - so many to choose from.

(Top): The impressive clock tower of the 17th-century church at Hauteluce dominates the village and surrounding countryside.

(Bottom): Among the outdoor pursuits offered in the region, canoeing is one of the most popular.

ESSENTIAL FACTS

DÉPARTEMENTS:	Ain, Ardèche, Drôme, Isère, Loire, Rhône, Haute-Savoie, Savoie
PRINCIPAL TOWNS	Lyon, St-Etienne Bourg-en-Bresse, Roanne, Villefranche-sur-Saône, Vienne, St-Chamond, Romans-sur-Isère, Valence, Montélimar, Grenoble, Chamonix, Annecy, Chambéry, Aix-les-Bains
PLACES TO VISIT:	The gorges of the Ardèche including the Grottes de St Marcel; the Roman buildings and Renaissance quarter in Lyon; Mont Blanc; the Parc National de la Vanoise; the Alpine region for skiers; the spa resorts of Aix-les-Bains, Evian and Thoron
REGIONAL TOURIST OFFICE	104 bis, route de Paris, 69260 Charbonnières-les-Bains. Tel: 72 59 21 59
LOCAL GASTRONOMIC DELIGHTS	Matelote, a fish stew made with red wine; chard, a green leaf vegetable served with well-seasoned white sauce; roast thrush; braised boar; nougat from Montélimar; various forms of raclette and fondue, including Savoyade made from three local cheeses; walnut from Grenoble; fruit tarts made from wild strawberries and blueberries
DRINKS	The Beaujolais region, where small villages prepare their world-famous wines; the green and yellow Chartreuse liqueur, originally produced by the monks at La Grand Chartreuse.
LOCAL CRAFTS WHAT TO BUY	Chocolate production at Pérouges; silks, clothes and textiles from St-Jorioz

EVENTS & FESTIVALS

Jan Avoriaz Film Festival

Feb Chamonix 24-hour Ice Race; Lyon Art Fair

Mar St-Gervais-les-Bains Comedy & Theatre Festival; Grenoble Jazz Festival; Isère Festival of the Story; Chamrousse International Husky Sleigh Race; Meribel Red Ski Show (*son et lumière acrobatic skiing*); Flaine Snow Jazz Festival

Apr Bourg-d'Oisans International Mineral & Crystal Market ; Valloire International Chess Festival; Lyons International Fair

May Chamonix Festival of Science, Earth & Mankind; Condrieu Wine Festival; St-Etienne Music Festival

Jun International Chime & Bell Festivals at Annecy, Lyon, Miribel, St Genis Laval, St Nicholas, Aussois, Farnay, Taninges; Historical Reconstruction of the First Airship Flight at Annonay; Gex Bird Festival (*fairground, music, comic parade*); Annonay Street Art Festival

Jun/Jul Grenoble Theatre Festival; Jazz in Vienne; Son et Lumière at Val Grangent & St-Just-St Rambert

Jul St-Gervais Alpine Festival; Montélimar Miniature Art Festival; Albertville Military Music Festival; Buis-les-Baronnies Lime Blossom Fair; Olive Festivals at Nyons & Les Vans; Saoû Picodon Cheese Festival; Les Aillons Bread Oven Festival; Tournon-sur-Rhône Musical Nights; Grignan Nocturnal Festival at the Château; Folklore Festivals at Bourg-St Maurice, Chambery & Voiron; Mègève Jazz Contest; La Plagne Kite Festival; St-Antoine l'Abbaye Medieval Nights

Aug Tarentaise Baroque Music & Art Festival; Crest Acoustic Art Festival; Aix-les-Bains Steam Festival; Les Saises Lumberjack Competition; Coligny Traditional Fair; Ruoms Ardèche Vintners' Festival; Aix-les-Bains Flower Festival; La Rosière Shepherds' Festival at Col de Petit St Bernard; Châtel Alpine Festival

Sep Romans Brioche Festival; Charlieu Weaver Festival; Tain l'Hermitage Vintage Wine Festival;

Oct Montbrison Cheese Fair; Montbrison Folklore & Gastronomic Event; Lyons Pottery Festival "Foire aux Tupiniers"

Nov Grenoble Contemporary Music Festival; Villefranche-sur-Saône Official Launching of Beaujolais Nouveau Wine; Bourg-en-Bresse Flower Festival

Dec Autrans Snow, Ice & Adventure Film Festival; Lans-en-Vercors Festival of Children's Films; Val Thorens Motor Race on snow & ice

---

AIGUEBELETTE-LE-LAC Savoie

★ ★ De La Comné
73610
☎ 479360502 FAX 479441193
Quality is the hallmark of this hotel, situated in the magnificent Savoy countryside, with fabulous views over the lake and mountains. It has been in the hands of the same family for five generations, and is widely known for its warm hospitality and outstanding cuisine. Airy bedrooms with modern facilities offer a high standard of comfort, and a selection of regional dishes and fresh fish specialities from the lake are served in the restaurant or on the shaded terrace of the flower-filled garden.
Near lake Near sea Forest area Near motorway
9 rms (2 bth 3 shr) (4 with balcony) TV in all bedrooms STV Direct dial from all bedrooms Licensed Full central heating Open parking available Child discount available 8yrs Open terrace V meals Last d 21.30hrs Languages spoken: English
CARDS: ● ■ Travellers cheques

AIX-LES-BAINS Savoie

★ ★ ★ Agora
rue de Chambéry *73100*
☎ 479342020 FAX 479342030
(in the town centre in the direction of Aix-Les-Bains)
This brand-new hotel is designed to meet a guest's every need. It occupies an excellent location in the heart of Aix within walking distance of the sights. Sound-proofed bedrooms offer every modern amenity, the fully equipped conference rooms can accommodate up to 80 people and the heated indoor swimming pool with jacuzzi, sauna, Turkish bath and massage-shower are directly accessible by lift. In the restaurant, a large range of traditional dishes are served in a friendly atmosphere.
Near lake Near beach Forest area In town centre Near motorway
64 en suite (bth/shr) (8 fmly) TV in all bedrooms STV Direct dial from all bedrooms Licensed Lift Night porter Full central heating Covered parking available (charged) Supervised Child discount available 12yrs Indoor swimming pool (heated) Sauna Solarium Body Building V meals Last d 21.30hrs Languages spoken: English, German & Spanish
MEALS: Full breakfast 95FF Continental breakfast 95FF Lunch 80-148FF&alc Dinner 80-148FF&alc✱
CARDS: ●● ■■ ■■ ●) Travellers cheques

★ ★ Dauphinois et Nyvolet
14 av de Trésserve *73100*
☎ 479612256 FAX 479340462
This charming hotel occupies a peaceful location in a residential area. It features individually appointed bedrooms, offering a good standard of comfort with views over the well-tended flower garden. The restaurant serves a good choice of regional dishes. Weather permitting, guests can enjoy their meal on the shaded terrace.
Near lake Forest area In town centre Near motorway
Closed mid Dec-mid Feb
83 rms (48 bth/shr) 75 rooms in annexe (14 with balcony) Licensed Lift Night porter Full central heating Open parking available Supervised Child discount available 10yrs Open terrace Last d 21.30hrs Languages spoken: German
MEALS: Full breakfast 39FF Lunch 105-175FF&alc Dinner 105-175FF&alc✱
CARDS: ●● ■■ ■■ ●) Travellers cheques

★ ★ ★ **Le Manoir** (Relais du Silence)
37 rue Georges Ier, BP512 *73100*
☎ 479614400 FAX 479356767
Le Manoir was converted into a hotel from what were
originally the out-buildings of the old luxury hotel Splendide-
Royale. This friendly country establishment now offers
individually appointed bedrooms with views of the garden or
the open countryside. Banqueting facilities are available for
seminars or large dinner parties of up to 250 people. There is a
lovely mature garden in which to relax. The more energetic
visitors can make use of an indoor swimming pool with
Jacuzzi, sauna and Turkish bath.
Near lake Near beach Forest area Near motorway
73 en suite (bth/shr) 10 rooms in annexe (5 fmly) (30 with
balcony) TV in all bedrooms STV Licensed Lift Night porter
Full central heating Open parking available Covered parking
available (charged) Supervised Child discount available 12yrs
Indoor swimming pool (heated) Sauna Pool table Jacuzzi/spa
Covered terrace Body Building V meals Last d 21.30hrs
Languages spoken: English,German,Italian & Spanish
MEALS: Full breakfast 55FF Continental breakfast 55FF Lunch
135-245FF&alc Dinner 135-245FF&alc✱
CARDS: ● ■ ▆ ⬤ Travellers cheques

★ ★ ★ **La Pastorale**
221 av Grand Port *73100*
☎ 479634060 FAX 479634426
Near lake Near beach Forest area Near motorway
Closed early Feb-mid March
30 en suite (bth/shr) (6 fmly) TV in all bedrooms STV
Licensed Lift Full central heating Open parking available
Child discount available 10yrs Last d 21.30hrs Languages
spoken: English, German & Italian
CARDS: ● ■ ▆ ⬤ Travellers cheques

★ ★ **Thermal**
2 rue Davat *73100*
☎ 479352000 FAX 479881648
The Hotel Thermal offers its visitors an enjoyable stay in
pleasant surroundings. Spacious bedrooms provide a high
standard of comfort and there is an attractive public lounge for
relaxation. The restaurant, which serves a range of classic
dishes, also prepares meals to meet individual needs.
Near lake Forest area In town centre Near motorway
80 en suite (bth/shr) (50 fmly) (45 with balcony) TV in all
bedrooms Direct dial from all bedrooms Licensed Lift Night
porter Full central heating Open parking available Covered
parking available (charged) Supervised Child discount
available Open terrace Last d 21.00hrs Languages spoken:
English,German
MEALS: Full breakfast 25FF Lunch 85FF&alc Dinner
85FF&alc✱
CARDS: ● ■ ▆ ⬤ Travellers cheques

ALBY-SUR-CHÉRAN Haute-Savoie

★ ★ **Alb'Hotel**
Sur N201 *74540*
☎ 450682493 FAX 450681301
Conveniently located close to Italy and Geneva, as well as all
the major ski-resorts, the hotel features attractive bedrooms
equipped with modern comforts. It has a shaded park and
good leisure facilities. The restaurant, which is situated nearby,
serves an array of commendable dishes.
Near river Near lake Forest area Near motorway
37 en suite (bth/shr) (1 fmly) STV Direct dial from all
bedrooms Mini-bar in all bedrooms Licensed Night porter

Full central heating Open parking available Child discount
available 12yrs Outdoor swimming pool Boule Open terrace
Covered terrace Last d 22.00hrs Languages spoken:
English,Arabic,German,Spanish
CARDS: ● ■ ▆ ⬤ Travellers cheques

ALLEVARD-LES-BAINS Isère

★ ★ **Pervenches** (Relais du Silence)
rte de Grenoble *38580*
☎ 476575073 FAX 476450952
(equi-distant between Grenoble and Chambery)
The hotel and outbuildings are surrounded by a large shaded
park with swimming pool, tennis, bowls and table tennis.
Peacefully situated, it offers bedrooms with private facilities,
TV and telephone, and glorious views of the open countryside.
There is a pleasant public lounge with open fireplace to play a
game of bridge or just to relax in. The restaurant serves a
range of traditional dishes.
Forest area Near motorway
Closed 16 Oct-Jan
25 en suite (bth/shr) 16 rooms in annexe (6 fmly) (1 with
balcony) TV in all bedrooms Direct dial from all bedrooms
Licensed Full central heating Open parking available Child
discount available 10yrs Outdoor swimming pool (heated)
Tennis Pool table Boule V meals Last d 21.00hrs
CARDS: ● ■ ▆ ⬤ Travellers cheques

★ ★ **Speranza**
rte du Moutaret *38580*
☎ 476975056
Amidst the delightful scenery of a flower-filled park, the hotel
offers its visitors an enjoyable stay in the peaceful atmosphere
of the surrounding mountains. It features attractive
accommodation equipped with modern facilities, and the
restaurant serves enjoyable meals, incorporating largely local
produce.
Near lake Forest area
Closed Oct-mid May
18 rms (11 bth 6 shr) (6 fmly) (5 with balcony) Direct dial from
all bedrooms Licensed Full central heating Open parking
available Supervised Child discount available 12yrs Boule
Open terrace Last d 22.00hrs
ROOMS: (room only) d 190-270FF ✱ **Reductions over 1
night**
MEALS: Full breakfast 35FF Lunch 105-140FF Dinner 95-
105FF
CARDS: Travellers cheques

AMBILLY Haute-Savoie

★ ★ ★ **New Hotel Genève**
38 rte de Genève *74100*
☎ 450387066 FAX 450387223
Situated near the unique tourist attractions of the Haute Savoie
and the French-Genevan trade centre, the New Hôtel Genève
offers the perfect combination of a traditional French Hotel
complemented by friendly courteous service to both
commercial and leisure guests. Because of its ideal
geographical location, visitors can enjoy lovely Alpine walks
and sailing on Lake Geneva. With the border only 800m from
the hotel, excursions can be made into Italy, Austria or
Switzerland. Function rooms can accommodate up to 130
people and the restaurant Casa Savoia serves predominantly
Italian cuisine.
Near river Near lake Forest area In town centre

contd.

263

Near motorway
93 en suite (bth) (3 fmly) TV in all bedrooms STV Mini-bar in
all bedrooms Licensed Lift Night porter Full central heating
Air conditioning in bedrooms Open parking available
Covered parking available (charged) Supervised Child
discount available 12yrs Discount at Sports Complex
Languages spoken: English German & Spanish
CARDS: ●● ▦ ▆▆ ◑ Travellers cheques

ANDRÉZIEUX-BOUTHÉON Loire

★ ★ ★ Les Iris
42160
☎ 477360909 FAX 477360900
Tucked away amongst the ancient cedars of its park, the hotel
provides a haven of tranquillity. Built in early 1900, this
handsome building offers tastefully furnished guest
accommodation with everyday modern facilities. The elegant
restaurant serves a classic cuisine, whilst on fine days guests
can enjoy breakfast on the terrace or beside the pool.
Near river Forest area In town centre Near motorway
Closed 1-5 Jan & 9-17 Aug
10 en suite (bth) No smoking in 2 bedrooms TV in all
bedrooms STV Direct dial from all bedrooms Mini-bar in all
bedrooms Licensed Open parking available Outdoor
swimming pool Solarium Boule Bicycle rental Open terrace
Table Tennis Children's playground Last d 21.30hrs
Languages spoken: English,German,Spanish
ROOMS: (room only) s fr 420FF; d fr 420FF
MEALS: Full breakfast 48FF Continental breakfast 48FF Lunch
110-265FF&alc Dinner 110-265FF&alc
CARDS: ●● ▆▆ JCB Travellers cheques

ANNECY Haute-Savoie

★ ★ ★ Atria Novotel Annecy Centre
1 av Berthollet *74000*
☎ 450335454 FAX 450455068
Novotel offer their clients good quality accommodation in
modern, well equipped bedrooms and have refined
restaurants serving good quality cuisine They have excellent
business meeting and conference facilities and some have food
and beverages available 24 hours a day. All their hotels have at
least one bedroom for disabled guests.
Near lake Near beach In town centre Near motorway
95 en suite (bth/shr) (35 fmly) No smoking in 29 bedrooms TV
in all bedrooms STV Radio in rooms Direct dial from all
bedrooms Mini-bar in all bedrooms Licensed Lift Night
porter Full central heating Air conditioning in bedrooms
Open parking available (charged) Covered parking available
(charged) Supervised Child discount available 16yrs Open
terrace V meals Last d 24.00hrs Languages spoken:
English,German,Italian,Portuguese,Spanish
ROOMS: (room only) s 440-495FF; d 495-560FF
Reductions over 1 night
MEALS: Lunch 69-130FF Dinner 89-130FF
CARDS: ●● ▦ ▆▆ ◑ Travellers cheques

★ ★ ★ Hotel Carlton (Best Western)
5 rue des Gilieres *74000*
☎ 450454775 FAX 450518454
This attractive hotel is situated in the old quarter of the town
with the lake and mountains not far away. Stylish,
contemporary furnishings feature throughout and help to
create an informal atmosphere. The guest rooms are well
equipped and offer comfortable accommodation, whilst the
cuisine combines classic dishes with innovative creations.

Near river Near lake Forest area In town centre Near
motorway
55 en suite (bth/shr) (4 fmly) (23 with balcony) TV in all
bedrooms Licensed Lift Night porter Full central heating
Covered parking available (charged) Supervised Open terrace
Covered terrace Last d 22.00hrs Languages spoken:
English,German,Italian,Spanish
CARDS: ●● ▦ ▆▆ ◑ Travellers cheques

★ ★ ★ Au Faisan Doré
34 av d'Albigny *74000*
☎ 450230246 FAX 450231110
Situated a stone's throw from the beauty spots and all the
major attractions, the hotel is suitable for either a short break
or a holiday. It features a spacious day-room, well-furnished
bedrooms offering above average levels of comfort, and a
traditional cuisine featuring regional dishes and fish
specialities from the nearby lake.
Near lake Near sea Forest area In town centre
Closed early Dec-late Jan
40 en suite (bth/shr) (2 fmly) (2 with balcony) TV in all
bedrooms Licensed Lift Full central heating Open parking
available (charged) Supervised Open terrace Last d 20.45hrs Languages
spoken: English,German
MEALS: Continental breakfast 45FF Lunch 150-250FF&alc
Dinner 100-200FF&alc✱
CARDS: ●● ▆▆ Travellers cheques

ANNECY-LE-VIEUX Haute-Savoie

★ ★ ★ ★ Abbaye
15 chemin de l'Abbaye *74940*
☎ 450236108 FAX 450277765
This beautiful residence dates back to the 16th century. With its
wooden gallery surrounding the courtyard and its original
stone staircase it provides a haven of charm and tranquillity.
The beautifully furnished bedrooms and individually
appointed apartments offer a high standard of comfort, whilst
the restaurant, with its arched ceiling, exudes an atmosphere
of elegant sophistication and serves imaginative, skilfully
prepared dishes, which in summertime can also be enjoyed on
the shaded terrace.
Near lake In town centre
18 en suite (bth/shr) (3 fmly) (1 with balcony) No smoking in 4
bedrooms TV in all bedrooms STV Radio in rooms Mini-bar
in all bedrooms Licensed Full central heating Open parking
available Child discount available V meals Last d 23.00hrs
Languages spoken: English & Spanish
ROOMS: (room only) s 400-1200FF; d 400-1200FF
Reductions over 1 night Special breaks
MEALS: Full breakfast 65FF Dinner fr 125FF&alc
CARDS: ●● ▦ ▆▆ ◑ Travellers cheques

ANNEMASSE Haute-Savoie

★ ★ Maison Blanche
41 rte de St-Julien *74100*
☎ 450920101 FAX 450376050
(A40 exit14 from Paris signed Annemasse, turn right after
50mtrs and left through a small bridge. From Annemasse
1.5km towards St Julien)
This establishment has recently undergone extensive
refurbishment and has also been extended with a large
veranda along the width of the façade, which is complemented
by a terrace with mature horse-chestnut trees, and a pretty
arboured garden. Situated near all the main access roads and
at 80 kilometres from the Mont Blanc Tunnel, it is a good base

for touring the region, or explore the border areas of France, Switzerland and Italy all in one day. The guest rooms are equipped with modern facilities and provide a good level of comfort, whilst the restaurant serves a cuisine which suits most palates.
Near river Forest area Near motorway
12 en suite (bth/shr) TV in all bedrooms Direct dial from all bedrooms Full central heating Child discount available Open terrace Last d 21.30hrs Languages spoken: English,Italian
ROOMS: (room only) s 200-220FF; d 220-280FF ✱
MEALS: Continental breakfast 35FF Lunch 65-170FF Dinner 65-170FF✱
CARDS: ✱ ▤ ▤ ➌ Travellers cheques

ANSE Rhône

★ ★ St-Romain
rte de Graves 69480
☎ 474602446 FAX 474671285
This old farm house has been completely renovated and stands off the beaten track in leafy surroundings. Pleasant bedrooms with attractive furnishings offer a good level of accommodation. The rustic restaurant offers an adequate choice of well-prepared regional dishes.
Near river Forest area Near motorway
Closed Dec
24 en suite (bth/shr) (2 fmly) TV in all bedrooms Radio in rooms Licensed Full central heating Open parking available Supervised Child discount available Tennis Boule Mini-golf Bicycle rental Open terrace V meals Last d 21.30hrs Languages spoken: English,German
MEALS: Full breakfast 35FF Lunch 98-300FF&alc Dinner 98-300FF&alc✱

ATTIGNAT Ain

★ ★ Dominique Marcepoil
481 Grande Rue 01340
☎ 474309224 FAX 474259348
This old ancestral farmhouse has been renovated with good taste and flair. It offers a spacious foyer and an attractive restaurant with a view of the well-stocked wine cellar. The menu features an extensive choice of classic and imaginative, modern dishes from the chef. Drinks and snacks are also served outside in the shaded garden.
Near river Near lake Near beach Forest area Near motorway
10 en suite (bth/shr) (3 fmly) TV in all bedrooms Direct dial from all bedrooms Licensed Air conditioning in bedrooms Open parking available Supervised No children Child discount available 12yrs Open terrace Covered terrace V meals Languages spoken: English
CARDS: ✱ ▤ ▤

AUBENAS Ardèche

★ ★ La Pinède
rte du Camping des Pins 07200
☎ 475352588 FAX 479930642
The hotel is situated amidst natural parklands with meadows and pine trees at one kilometre from Aubenas. It provides the ideal venue for a family holiday; peace and quiet for parents, whilst children can play freely. There are comfortable bedrooms, which are mostly with modern facilities and panoramic restaurant with fine views of the surrounding area. On fine days lunch is served on the shaded terrace, whilst the immediate vicinity has a choice of sporting options on offer.
Forest area

30 rms 10 rooms in annexe (6 fmly) TV in all bedrooms Licensed Full central heating Open parking available Covered parking available Child discount available 12yrs Outdoor swimming pool Boule Open terrace V meals Last d 21.00hrs
MEALS: Full breakfast 37FF Continental breakfast 37FF Lunch 98-180FF&alc Dinner 98-180FF&alc✱

AUSSOIS Savoie

★ ★ Le Choucas
15 Le Plan Champ 73500
☎ 479203277 FAX 479203987
(From Chambery take A43 (direction Albertville) then take N6 to Modane. D215 to Aussois)
The hotel occupies a sunny location with stunning views towards the peaks of the surrounding mountain range. It offers several sun-terraces, comfortable bedrooms with good amenities, and a host of assorted leisure facilities. The restaurant specialises in dishes from the Savoy region as well as more traditional cuisine.
Forest area
Closed May & Oct-Nov
28 en suite (bth) (4 fmly) TV in all bedrooms STV Licensed Full central heating Open parking available Child discount available 6yrs Solarium Gym Pool table Open terrace V meals Last d 21.00hrs Languages spoken: English, Italian
ROOMS: (room only) s 195-215FF; d 295-325FF
Reductions over 1 night
MEALS: Full breakfast 50FF Continental breakfast 36FF Lunch 85-120FF&alc Dinner 85-120FF&alc
CARDS: ✱ ▤ ➌ Travellers cheques

AUTRANS Isère

★ ★ De La Buffe
38880
☎ 476947070 FAX 476957248
Situated in the very heart of the village, the hotel 'La Buffe' is widely known for its warm hospitality and excellent cuisine. Surrounded by beautiful countryside, it offers well equipped guest accommodation with modern facilities, whilst the restaurant serves a wide choice of menu and à la carte dishes.
Near river Near beach Forest area
23 en suite (bth) (2 fmly) (16 with balcony) TV in all bedrooms STV Direct dial from all bedrooms Mini-bar in all bedrooms Licensed Full central heating Open parking available Child discount available 12yrs Sauna Solarium Pool table Jacuzzi/spa Bicycle rental Open terrace Covered terrace V meals Last d 21.00hrs Languages spoken: English
MEALS: Full breakfast 52FF Continental breakfast 52FF Lunch 77-150FF Dinner 100-150FF✱
CARDS: ✱ ▤ ▤ Travellers cheques

★ ★ ★ De La Poste   ✕ ✕ ✕
"Le Village" 38880
☎ 476953103 FAX 476953017
This hotel of character enjoys a splendid setting in the heart of the park of Vercours. It features individually designed bedrooms which vary in style and size, a congenial bar, and a restaurant which has earned many accolades for its outstanding cuisine. An excellent place for an active holiday or relaxation amidst the peaceful countryside.
Forest area Near motorway
Closed Nov
29 en suite (bth/shr) (1 with balcony) TV in all bedrooms STV

contd.

Direct dial from all bedrooms Licensed Lift Full central heating Child discount available 8yrs Indoor swimming pool (heated) Sauna Solarium Gym Pool table Jacuzzi/spa Open terrace Table tennis V meals Last d 21.00hrs Languages spoken: English, Italian, Spanish
ROOMS: (room only) s 250-300FF; d 270-320FF
MEALS: Full breakfast 45FF Lunch 80-230FF&alc Dinner 80-230FF&alc✱
CARDS: ●● ェ Travellers cheques

AVIERNOZ Haute-Savoie

★ ★ **Auberge Cameila**
74570
☎ 450224424 FAX 450224325
(from N203 towards Chamonix take D175 towards Villaz, then left onto D5 to Aviernoz. Hotel on left)
A warm welcome awaits visitors to this attractive establishment which is situated in peaceful, rural surroundings, and where the untiring hosts will do everything to make your stay an enjoyable one. It offers attractive, airy bedrooms with modern facilities, a terrace, and delightful gardens. The menu features good quality home-cooking served by a helpful and friendly staff.
Near river Near lake Near beach Forest area Near motorway
12 en suite (bth/shr) (3 fmly) (3 with balcony) TV in all bedrooms Direct dial from all bedrooms Licensed Full central heating Open parking available Supervised Child discount available 12yrs Open terrace V meals Last d 20.30hrs Languages spoken: English
ROOMS: (room only) s 235-305FF; d 370-510FF ✱
Reductions over 1 night Special breaks
MEALS: Full breakfast 42FF Continental breakfast 32FF Lunch 90-130FF&alc Dinner 90-130FF&alc✱
CARDS: ●● ェ Travellers cheques

BAGNOLS Rhône

★ ★ ★ **Château de Bagnols**
Le Bourg *69620*
☎ 474714000 FAX 474714049
This 13th century building has been lovingly renovated and is furnished to suit the character of the house. Assorted antiques and silk draperies enhance the elegant interior, and the comfortable bedrooms are tastefully decorated. There is a delightful garden and terrace where guests can relax under lime trees, whilst the restaurant offers an innovative selection of dishes combining superb classic cuisine with the finest regional delicacies.
Forest area
20 en suite (bth) TV in all bedrooms STV Licensed Lift Night porter Full central heating Open parking available Covered parking available Child discount available 10yrs Bicycle rental Open terrace Last d 21.00hrs Languages spoken: English,German,Italian,Spanish
CARDS: ●● ▦ ェ ●》 Travellers cheques

BEAUMONT Ardèche

★ ★ **Le Sentier des Arches**
Le Gua, rte de Valgorge *07110*
☎ 475394409 FAX 475395589
(From A7 take exit Loriol/Montelimar, then go to Aubenas. In Aubenas take the road to Alès, then in Joyeuse take the road to Valgorge. In Le Gua follow signs)
In the calm of a chestnut-grove along the River La Beaume, with many activities close-by.

Near river Forest area
Closed Nov-Mar
12 en suite (bth) (3 fmly) (12 with balcony) Open parking available Child discount available 10yrs Bicycle rental Last d 20.30hrs Languages spoken: English
ROOMS: s 250FF; d 320FF ✱ **Reductions over 1 night**
MEALS: Dinner 80FF

BEAUREPAIRE Isère

★ ★ **Fiard-Zorelle**
av des Terreaux *38270*
☎ 474846202 FAX 474847113
The Hotel Fiard is a comfortable setting for an overnight stop or a pleasant holiday. Individually styled bedrooms, decorated in co-ordinated fabrics offer modern amenities and good comfort. The menu includes many dishes to suit most tastes, complemented by a selection of fresh fish specialities. The cosy bar provides a relaxed atmosphere for a drink or a chat.
Near river Forest area In town centre Near motorway
Closed 15 Jan-15 Feb
15 en suite (bth/shr) (2 fmly) TV in all bedrooms Direct dial from all bedrooms Licensed Full central heating Covered parking available (charged) Child discount available 10yrs V meals Last d 21.00hrs Languages spoken: English,German,Spanish
ROOMS: (room only) s 250-300FF; d 300-400FF ✱
Reductions over 1 night
MEALS: Full breakfast 60FF Continental breakfast 40FF Lunch 140-350FF&alc Dinner 140-350FF&alc
CARDS: ●● ▦ ェ ●》 Travellers cheques

BELLEGARDE-SUR-VALSERINE Ain

★ ★ ★ **Belle Époque**
10 pl Gambetta *01200*
☎ 450481446 FAX 450560171
(Approach via A40 exit 10 or 11)
The turn-of-the century hotel La Belle Époque offers its visitors a warm welcome in elegantly refurbished surroundings. The proprietors look after their clientele - Pierrette Sévin offers a friendly smile upon guests' arrival and her husband introduces them to the finest examples of regional cooking. The bedrooms are individually styled, decorated with great taste and offer a high level of comfort.
Near river Forest area In town centre Near motorway
Closed 6-21 Jul & 9 Nov-1 Dec
20 en suite (bth/shr) TV in all bedrooms Direct dial from all bedrooms Licensed Full central heating Air conditioning in bedrooms Open parking available Covered parking available (charged) Supervised V meals Last d 21.00hrs Languages spoken: English,German
ROOMS: (room only) s 250-350FF; d 300-400FF
MEALS: Full breakfast 45FF Continental breakfast 45FF Lunch 125-270FF&alc Dinner 155-270FF&alc
CARDS: ●● ェ Travellers cheques

BONNE Haute-Savoie

★ ★ **Baud**
74380
☎ 450392015 FAX 450362896
The history of this establishment goes back to 1860 an over the years the art of hospitality has been polished to perfection. It features a delightful garden going down to banks of the river and bedrooms decorated with flair. The outstanding cuisine

includes many house delicacies such as terrines, patisseries and home-made confitures.
Near river Near lake Forest area Near motorway
8 rms (7 bth/shr) (1 fmly) (1 with balcony) TV in all bedrooms Licensed Full central heating Open parking available Covered parking available (charged) Supervised Child discount available 10yrs Fishing Boule Open terrace V meals Last d 21.00hrs Languages spoken: English,German,Italian
CARDS: ● ■ ⊞ Travellers cheques

BONSON Loire

★ Des Voyageurs
4 av de St-Rambert *42160*
☎ 477551615 FAX 477367633
Hotel in a small village situated 12 km from St Etienne. Functional bedrooms and gourmet restaurant serving traditional French dishes. Good location for an overnight stop.
In town centre
Closed Aug
7 rms (1 bth 3 shr) TV in all bedrooms Licensed Full central heating Open terrace Covered terrace Last d 21.00hrs
Languages spoken: English & German
ROOMS: (room only) s fr 215FF; d fr 235FF ✱
MEALS: Full breakfast 28FF Lunch 60-135FF&alc Dinner 72-135FF&alc
CARDS: ● ■ ⊞ ⓪ Travellers cheques

BOURG-EN-BRESSE Ain

★ ★ ★ Le Mail
46 av du Mail *01000*
☎ 474210026 FAX 474212955
(Leave town centre via the tunnel under the railway line towards Villefranche. Hotel on right)
This informal family-run hotel stands at the edge of the town Bourg-en-Bresse. The bedrooms are well furnished with modern amenities and the menu features a selection of regional dishes and fish specialities skilfully prepared by the owner Roger Charolles.
Closed 15 Jul, 4 Aug & 24 Dec-7 Jan
9 en suite (bth/shr) (1 fmly) (1 with balcony) TV in all bedrooms Direct dial from all bedrooms Licensed Full central heating Air conditioning in bedrooms Open parking available Bicycle rental Open terrace V meals Last d 21.30hrs
Languages spoken: English
ROOMS: (room only) d 200-280FF ✱
MEALS: Full breakfast 35FF Lunch 120-320FF&alc Dinner 120-320FF&alc
CARDS: ● ■ ⊞ ⓪ Travellers cheques

BOURGOIN-JALLIEU Isère

★ ★ Les Relais Bleus
Hôtel-de-Launay, Porte Medicis- R.N.6 *38300*
☎ 474283800 Cen Res 64460616 FAX 474283200
Les Relais Bleus offer comfortable accommodation and good value at the two star level. They cater for both family and business clientele, with relaxed dining and public areas.
Forest area In town centre Near motorway
61 en suite (bth/shr) (9 fmly) (8 with balcony) TV in all bedrooms Direct dial from all bedrooms Licensed Lift Night porter Full central heating Air conditioning in bedrooms Open parking available Covered parking available Supervised Pool table Bicycle rental V meals Languages spoken: English,German

BOURG-ST-ANDÉOL Ardèche

★ ★ Le Prieuré
Quai Fabry *63760*

☎ 475546299 FAX 475546373
This handsome manor house was built by the canons of St Ruf and stands on the banks of the river Loire. It features an attractive interior furnished in a style befitting the origin of the building. Guests will especially appreciate the architecture, the French ceilings and the furniture chosen with great attention to detail. The bedrooms are comfortable; the attractive dining room offers traditional cuisine served by courteous staff.
Near river Forest area In town centre Near motorway
16 en suite (bth/shr) (7 fmly) (3 with balcony) TV in all bedrooms Licensed Full central heating Child discount available 4yrs Boule Open terrace Covered terrace Last d 21.30hrs Languages spoken: English,Italian
CARDS: ● ■ ⊞

BOUVANTE Drôme

★ Auberge du Pionnier
26190
☎ 475485712 FAX 475485826
(Access via D131 or D331)
The auberge is situated in the Parc du Vercors and enjoys a secluded position surrounded by large grasslands and forests. It provides a good holiday base in both summer and winter and has numerous leisure opportunities on offer. An informal atmosphere prevails throughout and with its bar, terrace and peaceful garden, it provides the ideal setting for those visitors who want to get away from it all. The bedrooms offer straightforward facilities and the restaurant serves good quality home-cooking.
Near lake Forest area
9 rms (6 shr) (4 fmly) Direct dial from all bedrooms Licensed Full central heating Open parking available Covered parking available Child discount available 10yrs Boule Open terrace Last d 20.00hrs Languages spoken: English,Italian
ROOMS: (room only) d 155-230FF
MEALS: Continental breakfast 35FF Lunch 52-160FF Dinner 52-160FF
CARDS: Travellers cheques

BRIDES-LES-BAINS Savoie

★ ★ ★ Grand Hotel Des Thermes
73570
☎ 479552977 FAX 479552829
This large hotel is situated in the heart of the town of Brides-les-Bains, and was recently renovated to provide up-to-date modern comfort, whilst preserving a traditional atmosphere. Dynamic staff offer a 'round the clock' competent service which is difficult to match and are always on hand with a smile and useful advice if necessary. The rooms offer a high standard of comfort, whilst the restaurant caters for most tastes. Many leisure facilities are on offer in the vicinity as well as varied entertainment organised by the hotel.
Near river Forest area In town centre
102 en suite (bth/shr) (6 fmly) (78 with balcony) TV in all bedrooms STV Radio in rooms Licensed Lift Night porter Full central heating Open parking available Covered parking available (charged) Supervised Child discount available 12yrs Outdoor swimming pool Tennis Sauna Gym Pool table Boule Jacuzzi/spa Bicycle rental Open terrace Covered terrace Wkly live entertainment Casino V meals Languages spoken: English
CARDS: ● ■ ⊞ Travellers cheques

CARROZ-D'ARÂCHES, LES Haute-Savoie

★ ★ Les Belles Pistes
56 rte du Pernand *74300*
☎ 450900017 FAX 450903070
(from A40 exit at junction Cluses Central and take N205. Take turn for Les Carroz/Flaine(10km)
The hotel Les Belles Pistes is situated just a few minutes walk from Les Carroz, a traditional village in the heart of the Grand Massif. Owned and managed by a friendly British family, the hotel has undergone extensive refurbishment in recent times. It now offers pleasant bedrooms equipped with modern amenities, a cosy lounge-bar, TV room, small shop and a sun terrace, ideal for watching the nursery slope or enjoying afternoon tea.
Near lake Forest area In town centre Near motorway
Closed Apr-Jun & Sep-Dec
18 en suite (bth/shr) (7 fmly) (2 with balcony) No smoking in all bedrooms Radio in rooms Direct dial from all bedrooms Licensed Full central heating Open parking available Supervised Child discount available 11yrs Open terrace Last d 21.00hrs Languages spoken: English
MEALS: Full breakfast 50FF Continental breakfast 35FF Lunch 55-65FF&alc Dinner fr 95FF&alc✱
CARDS: ✺ ☲ Access Travellers cheques

CELLIERS Savoie

★ ★ Le Grand Pic
73260
☎ 479240372 FAX 479243878
This hotel stands in the heart of a small mountain village, offering pleasant guest rooms with cosy wood-panelling, a vaulted restaurant, and a south facing terrace surrounded by plants and flowers. The restaurant serves a high standard of home-cooking in good Savoyard tradition with many house specialities. The surrounding area provides good skiing ground in winter, whilst in summer it offers many places to discover and explore.
Forest area
Closed 26 Sep-25 Dec & 16 Apr-24 May
15 rms (4 shr) 6 rooms in annexe (5 fmly) (13 with balcony) Licensed Full central heating Open parking available Supervised Child discount available 7yrs Open terrace Library V meals Last d 21.00hrs Languages spoken: English,German
CARDS: ✺ ☲ Travellers cheques

CHAMBÉRY Savoie

★ ★ Aux Pervences
600 Chemin des Charmettes *73000*
☎ 479333426 FAX 479600252
(take the direction of Chambery centre, then Carre Curial and the Jean Jacques Rousseau's Museum to Charmettes)
Set in an area of natural beauty, with shaded terraces, the hotel offers traditional home made cooking and a warm welcome to guests.
Near lake Forest area
11 rms (2 bth) (1 fmly) TV in 8 bedrooms Direct dial from all bedrooms Licensed Full central heating Open parking available Covered parking available Boule Open terrace Last d 22.00hrs Languages spoken: English, German, Italian & Spanish
ROOMS: (room only) s 140-190FF; d 140-190FF
MEALS: Full breakfast 27FF Continental breakfast 27FF Lunch 95-160FF Dinner 95-160FF
CARDS: ✺ ■ ☲ Travellers cheques

★ ★ ★ ★ Château de Candie
rue du Bois de Candie *73000*
☎ 479966300 FAX 479966310
Set in the tranquil surroundings of landscaped parklands with ornamental ponds, fountains and lakes, the Château de Candie offers a warm welcome to its clientele. Each of the guest-rooms have individually styled interiors and feature canopy beds, wood-panelling, columns, and frescoes, while the restaurant serves regional Savoie dishes and wines.
Forest area Near motorway
19 en suite (bth/shr) 3 rooms in annexe (5 fmly) (4 with balcony) TV in all bedrooms Direct dial from all bedrooms Licensed Lift Full central heating Open parking available Supervised Child discount available 12yrs Open terrace V meals Last d 21.30hrs Languages spoken: English,German,Italian,Spanish
ROOMS: (room only) d 500-950FF
MEALS: Full breakfast 80FF Continental breakfast 80FF Lunch 145-300FF&alc Dinner 145-300FF&alc
CARDS: ✺ ■ ☲ Travellers cheques

★ ★ ★ France
22 fbg Réclus *73000*
☎ 479335118 FAX 479850630
Situated in the very heart of Chambéry at 200 metres from the station, the hotel features a interior which combines charming furnishings, a convivial atmosphere and functional facilities. It has bedrooms with balconies which are equipped with private facilities, a congenial bar and comfortable lounges. Guests can start off the day with a generous buffet-breakfast, before visiting some of the many tourist attraction in the area.
In town centre Near motorway
48 en suite (bth/shr) (42 with balcony) No smoking in 16 bedrooms TV in all bedrooms STV Radio in rooms Direct dial from all bedrooms Licensed Lift Night porter Full central heating Air conditioning in bedrooms Open parking available (charged) Covered parking available (charged) Supervised Languages spoken: English,German
CARDS: ✺ ■ ☲ ☻ Travellers cheques

★ ★ ★ Hotel des Princes
4 rue de Boigne *73000*
☎ 479334536 FAX 479703147
The Hotel des Princes is a building with plenty of character and can be found right in the historic heart of Chambery, close to the Cathedral and 'La Fontaine des Elephants'. The guest rooms are equipped with modern amenities and the friendly hosts Jasmine and Yannick Pérrenes are on hand to assist their guests in discovering the charming sights of the Old Town.
Near lake In town centre Near motorway
45 en suite (bth/shr) (6 with balcony) TV in all bedrooms STV Direct dial from all bedrooms Lift Night porter Full central heating Languages spoken: English
ROOMS: (room only) s fr 300FF; d fr 350FF **Reductions over 1 night**
MEALS: Full breakfast 35FF Continental breakfast 55FF
CARDS: ■ ☲ ☻

★ ★ Savoyard
35 pl Monge *73000*
☎ 479333655 FAX 479852570
Located in the historic centre of the capital of the Savoy, the hotel is just a stone's throw away from the pedestrianised area. It features comfortable bedrooms with modern facilities, and pleasant dining rooms which serve a wide choice of regional dishes.

Near river Near sea Forest area In town centre Near motorway
10 en suite (shr) (3 fmly) (3 with balcony) TV in all bedrooms STV Licensed Full central heating Air conditioning in bedrooms Open parking available Supervised Child discount available 12yrs Open terrace V meals Last d 22.30hrs
Languages spoken: English,Italian,Spanish
MEALS: Full breakfast 32FF Continental breakfast 32FF Lunch 75-180FF Dinner 75-180FF&alc✱
CARDS: 😄 ▆ 🎴

CHAMONIX-MONT-BLANC Haute-Savoie

★ ★ De l'Arve
rue Valot quai de l'Alpina *74400*
☎ 450530231 FAX 450535692
Standing on the banks of the River Arve the hotel enjoys a peaceful location. The foyer, lounge and dining room have been recently completely renovated and provide a pleasant setting for an relaxing stay. The bedrooms have private facilities and balconies; there is a resident's bar and a first-class restaurant with stunning views of the Mont-Blanc.
Near river Forest area In town centre
Closed Nov-19 Dec
39 rms (26 bth 9 shr) (4 fmly) (29 with balcony) TV in all bedrooms Direct dial from all bedrooms Licensed Lift Night porter Full central heating Open parking available Child discount available 10yrs Pool table Open terrace Last d 20.30hrs Languages spoken: English,German
ROOMS: (room only) s 213-229FF; d 272-460FF
MEALS: Full breakfast 38FF Continental breakfast 38FF Lunch 75-110FFalc Dinner 75-110FFalc
CARDS: 😄 ▆ 🎴 ➍ Travellers cheques

★ ★ Hotel Frantour
39 rue des Allobroges *74400*
☎ 450530756 FAX 450535479
Set in a stunning location right at the heart of the famous ski resort of Chamonix, this recently renovated chalet-style residence offers its guests a combination of warm hospitality and modern facilities, with breathtaking views of the Alps. A wide range of leisure facilities such as sauna, solarium, Jacuzzi, cinema and private night-club are available. The guest-rooms with private verandas are well equipped, and the restaurant 'La Cordée' provides an excellent selection of dishes.
Near river Near lake Forest area In town centre Near motorway
Closed mid Oct-mid Dec
133 en suite (bth) 45 rooms in annexe (66 fmly) (133 with balcony) TV in all bedrooms STV Direct dial from all bedrooms Licensed Lift Night porter Full central heating Open parking available (charged) Covered parking available (charged) Supervised Child discount available 11yrs Sauna Solarium Pool table Jacuzzi/spa Open terrace Covered terrace Last d 21.30hrs Languages spoken: English,Dutch,German,Italian,Spanish,
CARDS: ▆ 🎴 ➍ Travellers cheques

★ ★ Au Relais des Gaillands
964 rte des Gaillands *74400*
☎ 450531358 FAX 450558506
The Relais des Gaillands is an informal chalet-style hotel which offers its visitors comfortable bedrooms and a cuisine which combines classic dishes with specialities from the Savoy region.
Near lake Forest area
Closed 16 Oct-20 Dec

21 en suite (shr) (6 fmly) (8 with balcony) TV in all bedrooms STV Direct dial from all bedrooms Licensed Full central heating Open parking available Child discount available 10yrs Pool table Open terrace Last d 22.00hrs Languages spoken: English,Italian
ROOMS: s 300FF; d 380FF ✱
MEALS: Continental breakfast 35FF Lunch fr 100FFalc Dinner fr 100FFalc
CARDS: 😄 🎴 Travellers cheques

CHAMPAGNY-EN-VANOISE Savoie

★ ★ L'Ancolie
Les Hauts du Crey *73350*
☎ 479550500 FAX 479550442
The hotel is situated in the charming village of Champagny and is surrounded by the magnificent scenery of the Savoy region. Indoors, the untiring proprietors Anne and Philippe will do their utmost to make your stay an enjoyable one. The comfortable bedrooms have en suite facilities, there is a cosy-bar with open fire place, and the restaurant serves a range of tasty dishes from the region.
Forest area
Closed May & Oct-Nov
31 en suite (bth/shr) (7 fmly) (24 with balcony) TV in all bedrooms STV Direct dial from all bedrooms Licensed Lift Full central heating Open parking available Covered parking available (charged) Child discount available Outdoor swimming pool (heated) Sauna Solarium Pool table Jacuzzi/spa Open terrace Covered terrace V meals Last d 21.30hrs Languages spoken: English,German
MEALS: Full breakfast 50FF Continental breakfast 50FF Lunch 95-95FF&alc Dinner 115-115FF&alc✱

CHAMPIER Isère

★ ★ Auberge de la Source
36260
☎ 474544044 FAX 474545036
(15km from Bourgoin-Jallieu on N85)
This country inn has offered warm hospitality and good food for 25 years. Transformed from a derelict farm into a cosy hotel by the present owners, it features comfortable bedrooms which mostly have good amenities, and a spacious restaurant. Situated 55 km from Lyon and at the same distance from Grenoble it is a good base for touring the surrounding region.
Forest area
10 rms (2 bth 7 shr) (3 fmly) TV in all bedrooms Radio in rooms Direct dial from all bedrooms Licensed Full central heating Open parking available Child discount available 12yrs Outdoor swimming pool Open terrace Covered terrace V meals Last d 21.00hrs Languages spoken: English
ROOMS: (room only) s fr 170FF; d 200-260FF
MEALS: Full breakfast 28FF Lunch 80-230FF&alc Dinner 80-230FF&alc
CARDS: 😄 🎴

CHAPAREILLAN Isère

★ De l'Avenue
38530
☎ 476452335 FAX 476455650
Situated in green surroundings at the foot of Mont Granier, and at the cross-roads of the main ski resorts and the Savoy vineyards the hotel offers a restaurant with fine cuisine consisting of regional specialities. The comfortable bedrooms have private facilities, whilst leisure facilities include numerous

contd.

walking tracks, fishing, swimming and tennis nearby.
Near river Forest area Near motorway
25 rms 4 rooms in annexe (5 fmly) Direct dial from all
bedrooms Licensed Full central heating Open parking
available Covered parking available Child discount available
7yrs Boule Open terrace Languages spoken: English
CARDS: ●●

CHARAVINES Isère

★ ★ Hostellerie du Lac Bleu
Lac de Paladru *38850*

☎ 476066048 FAX 476066681
(Access from A43/A48)
The hotel is situated in leafy surroundings on the shores of Lac
de Paladru. Shaded, flower-decked terraces, a restaurant and
veranda with views of the lake and guest rooms with every
modern convenience create the pleasant setting for an
enjoyable stay. The restaurant serves an array of specialities
including fresh fish from the lake, whilst a beach bar, serves
ice cream and snacks near the shoreline. The hotel has a range
of leisure facilities on offer, whilst varied entertainment can be
found nearby.
Near lake Forest area Near motorway
Closed 15 Oct-15 Mar
12 en suite (bth/shr) (1 fmly) TV in 5 bedrooms Direct dial
from all bedrooms Licensed Full central heating Open
parking available Child discount available 10yrs Fishing
Solarium Boule Open terrace Covered terrace Last d
21.00hrs Languages spoken: English,German
ROOMS: (room only) s 200FF; d 270FF
MEALS: Continental breakfast 38FF Lunch 70-180FF&alc
Dinner 70-180FF&alc✱
CARDS: ●● ⬛ Travellers cheques

★ ★ De la Poste
965 rue Principale *38850*
☎ 476066041 FAX 476556242
Just a two minute walk from Lac de Paladru, this former
coaching inn is peacefully situated in leafy surroundings. It has
a conservatory with pretty flowers and old stables which now
serve as the banqueting rooms. The bedrooms are individually
appointed and decorated with attractive fabrics and
furnishings. The restaurant serves a traditional cuisine,
augmented by fresh fish specialities from the lake.
Near lake Near beach Forest area In town centre Near
motorway
Closed 3-10 Nov & 15-28 Feb
15 en suite (bth/shr) 5 rooms in annexe (2 fmly) TV in all
bedrooms STV Direct dial from all bedrooms Licensed Full
central heating Child discount available 5yrs Pool table Boule
Open terrace Last d 21.30hrs Languages spoken: English,
Spanish
MEALS: Full breakfast 38FF Continental breakfast 38FF Lunch
98-260FF&alc Dinner 98-260FF&alc✱
CARDS: ●● ■■ ⬛ Travellers cheques

CHARLIEU Loire

★ ★ Relais de l'Abbaye
42190
☎ 477600088 FAX 477601460
Located in the charming medieval town of Charlieu, the hotel
is set amidst leafy surroundings on the banks of the river
Sornin. The guest rooms have private facilities and provide a
good level of comfort, whilst the restaurant serves a carefully
prepared cuisine, which in summer can be enjoyed on the

terrace. Numerous historic places of interest are well worth a
visit, such as the Benedictine Abbey, the silk and hospital
museum, as well as the Romanesque churches and castles.
Near river
27 en suite (bth/shr) (8 fmly) TV in all bedrooms Direct dial
from all bedrooms Licensed Full central heating Open
parking available Boule Bicycle rental Open terrace V meals
Last d 21.15hrs Languages spoken: English,German
CARDS: ●● ■■ ⬛ Travellers cheques

CHÂTILLON-SUR-CHALARONNE Ain

★ ★ De la Tour
01400
☎ 474550512 FAX 474550919
This village is adorned with flowers throughout and has quite
rightly won the highest distinction for floral displays by the
French Tourist Board. Standing in the centre is the charming
hotel de la Tour which was transformed into an hotel during
the time of the 'Belle Époque'. It has renowned traditional
cuisine based on regional recipes, and pretty guest rooms with
modern amenities, whilst some have authentic beamed
bathrooms. In addition there is comfortable lounge and a
congenial bar to relax with a drink.
Near river
13 rms (6 fmly) TV in all bedrooms Licensed Full central
heating Open parking available (charged) Covered parking
available (charged) Child discount available Open terrace V
meals Last d 21.30hrs Languages spoken: English
CARDS: ●● ⬛ Travellers cheques

CHÂTILLON-SUR-CLUSES Haute-Savoie

★ ★ Le Bois du Seigneur
Col de Châtillon *74300*
☎ 450342740 FAX 450348020
Located close to all the popular ski resorts and with a
multitude of leisure facilities on offer, the hotel provides a good
venue for both winter and summer holidays. Comfortable
bedrooms with modern amenities offer peaceful
accommodation, there is a garden with terrace, and the
country-style restaurant with its rustic open fireplace provides
the informal setting for an enjoyable meal.
Near river Near lake Forest area
10 en suite (bth/shr) (2 fmly) No smoking in 5 bedrooms TV in
all bedrooms Direct dial from all bedrooms Licensed Full
central heating Open parking available Supervised Child
discount available 12yrs Open terrace V meals Last d
22.00hrs Languages spoken: English, German
MEALS: Full breakfast 34FF Continental breakfast 34FF Lunch
79-280FF&alc Dinner 79-280FF&alc✱
CARDS: ●● ■■ ⬛ 🔵 Travellers cheques

CHAZELLES-SUR-LYON Loire

★ ★ Château Blanchard
36 rte de St-Galmier *42140*
☎ 477542888 FAX 477543603
(Approach via A72 or A6 and D11)
A tastefully restored former hat maker's house, situated in a
shaded park. The bedrooms are furnished in 1930s style and
the restaurant serves carefully prepared regional dishes.
Near river Near lake Forest area In town centre Near
motorway
12 en suite (bth/shr) (2 fmly) No smoking in 1 bedroom TV in
all bedrooms Direct dial from all bedrooms Licensed Full
central heating Open parking available Supervised Child

discount available Boule Mini-golf Bicycle rental Open
terrace Children's play area V meals Last d 21.15hrs
Languages spoken: English
ROOMS: (room only) d 280-380FF
MEALS: Full breakfast 35FF Continental breakfast 35FF Lunch
88-245FF&alc Dinner 88-245FF&alc
CARDS: ●● ▆▆ ▆▆ ⍉ Travellers cheques

CLELLES Isère

★ ★ **Ferrat**
38930
☎ 476344270 FAX 476344747
Situated below Mont-Aiguille at an altitude of 800 metres, the
hotel provides a comfortable setting for a restful break.
Attractive guest rooms with modern amenities, pleasant
grounds, swimming pool with snack bar, and various leisure
opportunities in the surrounding region make it a good venue
for a family holiday.
Forest area Near motorway
Closed Dec-14 Feb
23 en suite (bth/shr) 7 rooms in annexe (2 fmly) (7 with
balcony) TV in all bedrooms Licensed Full central heating
Open parking available Covered parking available (charged)
Supervised Child discount available Outdoor swimming pool
Boule Bicycle rental Open terrace Table tennis, volley ball
Last d 21.00hrs Languages spoken: English, Italian
MEALS: Full breakfast 30FF Continental breakfast 40FF Lunch
90-180FF&alc Dinner 90-180FF&alc*
CARDS: ●● ▆▆ ⍉ Travellers cheques

CLUSAZ, LA Haute-Savoie

★ ★ **Le Bellachat**
74220
☎ 450326666 FAX 450326584
This chalet-style hotel provides the ideal setting for both
summer and winter holidays. With breathtaking views of the
Aravis mountains it features comfortable bedrooms with
modern day amenities. After a day in the fresh mountain air
guests can savour some of the splendid dishes on offer in the
restaurant or relax in the cosy bar.
Near lake Forest area
Closed 21 Apr-May & 21 Oct-14 Dec
30 en suite (bth/shr) (8 fmly) (13 with balcony) TV in all
bedrooms STV Licensed Full central heating Air
conditioning in bedrooms Open parking available Supervised
Child discount available 7yrs Open terrace Table
tennis,playroom Last d 21.00hrs Languages spoken: English
MEALS: Continental breakfast 40FF Lunch 75-200FFalc Dinner
75-200FFalc*
CARDS: ●● ▆▆ ▆▆

COISE Savoie

★ ★ ★ ★ **Château de la Tour du Puits**
Le Puits *73800*
☎ 479288800 FAX 479888801
On the ancient historic route from Lyon to Turin, the Château
de la Tour de Puits occupies a splendid location amid seven
hectares of woodland and lush green scenery. It offers
luxurious bedrooms which vary in style and size and are
equipped with all modern amenities. There is a shaded terrace
with panoramic views. Sporting facilities include a fitness
room, outdoor heated swimming pool and putting green. The
restaurant serves an outstanding choice of delightful
specialities from the region.

Forest area Near motorway
Closed Jan RS Sun evening & Mon
7 en suite (bth/shr) No smoking in 4 bedrooms TV in all
bedrooms STV Radio in rooms Direct dial from all bedrooms
Licensed Full central heating Open parking available
Supervised Child discount available 12yrs Outdoor swimming
pool (heated) Solarium Gym Bicycle rental Open terrace
Covered terrace Wkly live entertainment Last d 21.30hrs
Languages spoken: English

ROOMS: (room only) d 750-950FF **Reductions over 1 night**
MEALS: Full breakfast 80FF Lunch 120-450FF&alc Dinner 195-
450FF&alc
CARDS: ●● ▆▆ ▆▆ ⍉ Travellers cheques

COL DU MONT-SION Haute-Savoie

★ ★ **La Clef des Champs et Hotel Rey**
St-Blaise *74350*
☎ 450441329 FAX 450440548
The restaurant La Clef des Champs and the Hotel Rey combine
the best of both worlds; excellent food and comfortable
accommodation. Set in the splendid scenery of the Mont Sion
Pass at an altitude of 2600 feet, they offer elegant guest rooms
with every modern convenience and a choice of dishes to suit
all tastes. On fine days guests can enjoy delicious finger-
buffets in the garden or meals served on the terrace.
Near lake Forest area Near motorway
Closed 6-26 Jan & 25 Oct-15 Nov
30 en suite (bth/shr) (3 fmly) TV in all bedrooms STV Direct
dial from all bedrooms Mini-bar in 20 bedrooms Room-safe
Licensed Lift Full central heating Open parking available
Child discount available Outdoor swimming pool Tennis
Boule Open terrace Last d 21.00hrs Languages spoken:
English,German
CARDS: ●● ▆▆ Travellers cheques

CONFRANÇON Ain

★ ★ ★ **Auberge La Sarrasine**
RN79 Entre Macon et Bourg-, en-B *01310*
☎ 474302565 FAX 474252423
This charming, ancient Bresse farmhouse has been converted
to offer its guests an enjoyable stay in delightful flower-filled
surroundings. The bedrooms are furnished to provide the
maximum comfort and the restaurant offers an innovative
selection of freshly prepared dishes. The hotel is ideally
situated for excursions to various tourist attractions in the area.
Near river Near lake Near motorway
11 en suite (bth) (2 fmly) TV in all bedrooms STV Radio in
rooms Mini-bar in all bedrooms Licensed Night porter Full
central heating Open parking available Supervised Child

contd.

271

discount available Outdoor swimming pool (heated) Open terrace Covered terrace V meals Last d 21.30hrs Languages spoken: English
MEALS: Full breakfast 55FF Continental breakfast 30FF Lunch 98-320FF&alc Dinner 98-320FF&alc✱
CARDS: 🏧 💳 🎫 ① Travellers cheques

CORPS Isère

★ ★ De la Poste
rte Napoléon *38970*
☎ 476300003 FAX 476300273
The hotel is situated near the old Route Napoléon. It offers its visitors attractive guest rooms with excellent en suite facilities and a restaurant - furnished with period pieces and original paintings - where the cuisine consists of classic dishes and specialities from the Dauphin region.
Near lake Forest area In town centre Near motorway
Closed Dec-mid Jan
29 en suite (bth/shr) 9 rooms in annexe (4 fmly) (2 with balcony) TV in all bedrooms Direct dial from all bedrooms Licensed Full central heating Air conditioning in bedrooms Open parking available Covered parking available Supervised Child discount available 10yrs Tennis Fishing Sauna Boule Bicycle rental Open terrace Covered terrace Wkly live entertainment V meals Last d 22.00hrs Languages spoken: English
ROOMS: (room only) s 200-300FF; d 235-450FF ✱
Reductions over 1 night Special breaks
MEALS: Full breakfast 40FF Continental breakfast 40FF Lunch 100-220FF&alc Dinner 100-220FF&alc✱
CARDS: 🏧 💳 🎫 Travellers cheques

COTEAU, LE Loire

★ ★ ★ Artaud
133 av de la Libération *42120*
☎ 477684644 FAX 477722350
Located in the heart of the Loire region, much importance is attached to culinary skill and use is made of high quality, fresh ingredients. The bedrooms are decorated in modern style, some split-level.
In town centre Near motorway
Closed 26 Jul-16 Aug
25 en suite (bth/shr) (3 fmly) (2 with balcony) TV in all bedrooms STV Direct dial from all bedrooms Licensed Full central heating Covered parking available (charged) Supervised Child discount available 8yrs V meals Last d 21.30hrs Languages spoken: English
ROOMS: (room only) s 250-380FF; d 250-390FF ✱
Reductions over 1 night
MEALS: Full breakfast 38FF Continental breakfast 38FF Lunch 98-350FF&alc Dinner 98-350FF&alc✱
CARDS: 🏧 💳 🎫 Travellers cheques

COURCHEVEL Savoie

★ Les Allobroges
St-Bon le Haut *73120*
☎ 479081015
This charming hotel is housed in a building full of character and typical of the Savoy region. The bedrooms, were entirely refurbished two years ago and are equipped with modern facilities. The surrounding countryside is filled with flowers during the summer, whilst the winter season changes it into a white fairy tale landscape. The vaulted restaurant with open fire place and exposed brickwork dates back to the 17th

century, and serves candlelit meals with soft background music.
Near lake Forest area
9 rms (6 fmly) (8 with balcony) TV in all bedrooms Licensed Full central heating Open parking available Covered parking available Child discount available Boule Open terrace V meals Last d 22.30hrs Languages spoken: English
MEALS: Full breakfast 40FF Continental breakfast 30FF Lunch 80-230FF&alc Dinner 80-230FF&alc✱
CARDS: 🏧 💳 ① Travellers cheques

★ ★ ★ Hotel Bellecote
73120
☎ 479081019 FAX 479081716
Just 100 metres from the ski-station and right on the edge of the Bellecôte slopes, this chalet-style hotel offers a breathtaking view over the surrounding snow-capped mountains. Furnished throughout with a combination of stylish period furniture from the Savoy and Afghanistan, it offers very comfortable bedrooms with modern facilities, a cosy bar for evening relaxation, a gym and a fantastic indoor swimming pool. The menu features a wide range of superb dishes which are skilfully presented and beautifully flavoured.
Forest area
Closed mid Dec-mid Apr
56 en suite (bth/shr) TV in all bedrooms STV Radio in rooms Mini-bar in all bedrooms Licensed Lift Night porter Full central heating Open parking available Covered parking available (charged) Child discount available Indoor pool (heated) Golf Sauna Solarium Gym Pool table Jacuzzi/spa Open terrace Covered terrace Gym Last d 22.30hrs Languages spoken: English,German,Italian,Spanish
MEALS: Continental breakfast 100FF Lunch fr 250FF Dinner fr 360FF✱
CARDS: 🏧 💳 🎫 ①

★ ★ ★ Hotel Carlina
73120
☎ 479080030 FAX 479080403
This grand mahogany chalet offers its guests all the comforts of a large winter palace. There are several lounges with cosy seating arrangements to relax in, a bar with live piano music, and luxurious bedrooms - thoughtfully designed, and furnished to a high standard. The restaurant serves a combination of traditional and innovative cuisine in sumptuous surroundings; or guests can enjoy their meals on the terrace while basking in the sunshine.
Forest area In town centre
63 en suite (bth/shr) TV in all bedrooms STV Radio in rooms Licensed Lift Night porter Full central heating Open parking available Covered parking available (charged) Indoor swimming pool (heated) Sauna Solarium Gym Jacuzzi/spa Open terrace Covered terrace Last d 22.30hrs Languages spoken: English,German,Italian,Spanish
MEALS: Continental breakfast 100FF Lunch fr 250FF Dinner fr 360FF✱
CARDS: 🏧 💳 🎫 ①

★ ★ ★ Hotel Les Ducs de Savoie
73120
☎ 479080300 FAX 479081630
Forest area
Closed mid Dec-mid Apr
70 en suite (bth/shr) TV in all bedrooms STV Radio in rooms Licensed Lift Night porter Full central heating Open parking available Covered parking available (charged) Indoor swimming pool (heated) Sauna Solarium Gym Pool table

Jacuzzi/spa Open terrace Covered terrace Last d 22.30hrs
Languages spoken: English,German,Italian,Spanish
MEALS: Continental breakfast 80FF Lunch fr 195FF Dinner fr 270FF✱
CARDS: 💳 ▬ ▬ ⓪

★ ★ ★ ★ Nèiges
73121
☎ 479080377 FAX 479081870
The Hotel des Neiges occupies an exceptional location alongside the ski-slope. It has a south-facing terrace which can be reached without having to take off one's skis. The elegant bedrooms provide a tranquil haven. Guests can dine in the elegant surroundings of the restaurant with its exquisite décor, open fireplace and delightful orchid garden, whilst listening to entertaining live background piano music.
Forest area
Closed mid Dec-mid Apr
42 en suite (bth/shr) (5 fmly) (30 with balcony) TV in all bedrooms STV Radio in rooms Licensed Lift Night porter Full central heating Open parking available Covered parking available (charged) Child discount available Sauna Pool table Jacuzzi/spa Open terrace Last d 21.30hrs Languages spoken: English,Italian,Spanish
MEALS: Full breakfast 85FF Lunch 300FF Dinner 355FF✱
CARDS: 💳 ▬ ▬ ⓪ Travellers cheques

★ ★ ★ Peupliers
Le Praz - St-Bon *73120*
☎ 479084147 FAX 479084505
For 30 years the hotel Les Peupliers has gained a well-earned reputation for offering traditional hospitality to its clientele. By making good use of wood and stone materials, it has created an atmosphere in which guests can relax and enjoy breathtaking views of the surrounding mountains. The elegant bedrooms offer modern amenities and have stunning vistas. The 'Carnozet' restaurant serves a comprehensive choice of traditional Savoie specialities based on authentic recipes. Furthermore there is a lounge with open fireplace and a sauna and fitness room.
Near lake Forest area
30 en suite (bth/shr) (3 fmly) (20 with balcony) TV in all bedrooms STV Radio in rooms Direct dial from all bedrooms Licensed Lift Full central heating Open parking available Child discount available 13yrs Fishing Sauna Gym Pool table Boule Bicycle rental Open terrace Last d 21.00hrs Languages spoken: English,Spanish
ROOMS: (room only) d 350-750FF
MEALS: Continental breakfast 50FF Lunch 100-190FF&alc Dinner 135-210FF&alc✱
CARDS: 💳 ▬ ▬ ⓪ Travellers cheques

★ ★ ★ ★ Pralong 2000
rte de l'Altiport *73120*
☎ 479082482 FAX 479083641
Situated at 1850 metres on the peak of Courchevel, this grand hotel offers its visitors a warm and friendly welcome with courteous service by competent staff in an informal atmosphere. The bedrooms are tastefully furnished to provide maximum comfort. The inviting restaurant features classic French cuisine on the menu, offering a well-balanced combination of flavours and fresh ingredients. Extensive sporting facilities include a fully equipped fitness centre, large indoor pool, massage rooms and a solarium.
Forest area
Closed mid Dec-early Apr
65 en suite (bth/shr) (37 with balcony) TV in all bedrooms

STV Radio in rooms Direct-dial available Licensed Lift Night porter Full central heating Air conditioning in bedrooms Open parking available Covered parking available (charged) Indoor swimming pool (heated) Sauna Solarium Pool table Covered terrace Last d 21.30hrs Languages spoken: English,German
CARDS: 💳 ▬ ▬ ⓪ Travellers cheques

★ ★ ★ La Sivolière
73120
☎ 479080833 FAX 479081573
(from Paris A6 - Bourg en Bresse, A7 - Lyon, A47 Albertville-Moutiers-Courchevel)
Set in a forest on the edge of the ski-slopes, the hotel enjoys a sheltered position away from the bustle. Inside, the cosy, tastefully furnished interior of this mountain chalet provides a relaxing atmosphere where guests can sample good quality Savoyard dishes in the dining room, and afterwards enjoy a 'digestif' in front of a roaring log fire, before retiring to one of the comfortable wood-panelled bedrooms.
Forest area
Closed 29 Nov-3 May
33 en suite (bth/shr) (6 fmly) (18 with balcony) TV in 30 bedrooms STV Direct dial from all bedrooms Room-safe Licensed Night porter Full central heating Open parking available (charged) Covered parking available (charged) Child discount available Sauna Solarium Pool table Open terrace Covered terrace Languages spoken: English & Spanish
ROOMS: (room only) d 870-2250FF
MEALS: Full breakfast 78FF Lunch fr 150FF Dinner fr 280FF
CARDS: 💳 ▬ ▬

COURS-LA-VILLE Rhône

★ ★ Le Pavillon
Col du Pavillon *69470*
☎ 474898355 FAX 474647026
The completely renovated hotel Le Pavillon has a bright green façade which blends in with the surrounding countryside. The unusual architecture conceals a modern interior with two bars and lounges as well as a top class restaurant which serves traditional, generously-portioned cuisine.
Near lake Near beach Forest area Near motorway
21 en suite (bth/shr) (2 fmly) (2 with balcony) TV in all bedrooms Direct dial from all bedrooms Licensed Night porter Full central heating Open parking available Child discount available Boule Open terrace V meals Last d 21.00hrs Languages spoken: English,German, Italian
ROOMS: (room only) s fr 270FF; d fr 330FF **Reductions over 1 night**
MEALS: Continental breakfast 39FF Lunch 84-280FF Dinner 99-280FF
CARDS: ▬ Travellers cheques

CREST Drôme

★ ★ Grand Hotel
60 rue de l'Hôtel-de-Ville *26400*
☎ 475250817 FAX 475254642

This charming hotel is situated right in the centre of a small medieval village of only 8000 inhabitants. It offers comfortable bedrooms with modern facilities including direct-dial telephone and TV. There is a cosy lounge and meeting room for social functions. The restaurant serves a good choice of specialities from the region.
Near river In town centre Near motorway
Closed end Dec-end Jan *contd.*

20 rms (3 bth 6 shr) (2 fmly) TV in 15 bedrooms Direct dial from all bedrooms Licensed Full central heating Covered parking available (charged) Last d 21.00hrs Languages spoken: English
ROOMS: (room only) s fr 140FF ✱
MEALS: Full breakfast 33FF Lunch 90-200FF&alc Dinner 90-200FF&alc
CARDS: 💳 ▆ Travellers cheques

CREST-VOLAND Savoie

★ ★ Hotel du Mont Charvin
73590
☎ 479316121 FAX 479318210
This pleasant chalet-style hotel is located in the Savoy region, in a resort which is popular in winter as well as in summer. A friendly family atmosphere prevails throughout, and is complemented by sunny guest rooms with private facilities, as well as a restaurant which serves a selection of dishes from the set and à la carte menus. Guest can relax in the cosy bar and TV lounge, or go hiking along some of the many marked footpaths which start from the resort.
Near river Forest area In town centre
23 rms (6 fmly) (6 with balcony) Direct dial from all bedrooms Licensed Night porter Full central heating Open parking available Covered parking available (charged) Supervised Child discount available 7yrs Boule Open terrace V meals Last d 20.30hrs Languages spoken: English
MEALS: Full breakfast 30FF Continental breakfast 30FF Lunch 88-120FF&alc Dinner 88-120FF&alc✱
CARDS: 💳 ▆

DARDILLY Rhône

★ ★ Ibis Hotel
Porte de Lyon - A6 *69570*
☎ 478660220 FAX 478474793
(A6 exit Limonest/Dardilly from the N after Villefranche/Toll, from S take Feyzin Lyon Centre in direction of Paris)
Modern hotel in regional style with quiet comfortable bedrooms. Forest area Near motorway

64 en suite (bth/shr) (12 fmly) No smoking in 11 bedrooms TV in all bedrooms STV Direct dial from all bedrooms Licensed Night porter Full central heating Open parking available Child discount available 12yrs Outdoor swimming pool Boule Covered terrace French billards Table tennis Last d 22.30hrs Languages spoken: English, German, Italian & Spanish
ROOMS: (room only) s 325-335FF; d 355-365FF
MEALS: Full breakfast 38FF Lunch fr 95FF&alc Dinner fr 95FF&alc
CARDS: 💳 ▆▆ ▆ 🔵 Travellers cheques

★ ★ ★ Novotel Lyon Nord
Porte de Lyon-Autoroute A6 *69570*
☎ 472172929 FAX 478350845
Near motorway
107 rms TV in all bedrooms Direct dial from all bedrooms Mini-bar in all bedrooms Lift Air conditioning in bedrooms Open parking available Outdoor swimming pool Pool table Boule Open terrace Languages spoken: English,German,Spanish

DÉSAIGNES Ardèche

★ ★ Des Voyageurs 🖊 🖊
07570
☎ 475066148 FAX 475066443
The hotel is situated in the medieval village of Désaignes at an altitude of 500 metres. It offers a quiet, family setting for those visitors who want to get away from it all, and a good standard of home-cooking including traditional and regional dishes. All the bedrooms have modern amenities, whilst the gardens, private tennis courts and swimming pool provide excellent relaxation.
Near river Forest area
Closed end Sep-Etr
40 rms (18 bth/shr) TV in all bedrooms Licensed Full central heating Open parking available Covered parking available Child discount available Outdoor swimming pool Tennis Boule Open terrace Covered terrace V meals Last d 21.00hrs
CARDS: 💳 ▆ Travellers cheques

DEUX-ALPES, LES Isère

★ ★ ★ ★ La Berangère
11 rte de Champamé *38860*
☎ 476792411 FAX 476795508
The hotel enjoys a sunny position with fine views of the Oisans mountain range. It is constantly upgrading it facilities to offer its clientele a comfortable stay with good modern amenities. There is a drawing room with open fire place and a cosy bar for an aperitif or after-dinner liqueur. The menu offers an extensive choice of specialities from the region and imaginative creations from the chef.
Near lake Forest area
Closed 2 May-19 Jun & 2 Sep-Nov
59 en suite (bth/shr) (6 fmly) (59 with balcony) TV in all bedrooms STV Radio in rooms Direct dial from all bedrooms Licensed Lift Night porter Full central heating Open parking available Child discount available 9yrs Indoor swimming pool (heated) Outdoor swimming pool (heated) Sauna Solarium Pool table Boule Jacuzzi/spa Bicycle rental Open terrace V meals Last d 21.30hrs Languages spoken: English, Italian, Spanish, German
MEALS: Full breakfast 65FF Continental breakfast 65FF Lunch 140-220FF&alc Dinner 220FF&alc✱
CARDS: 💳 ▆▆ ▆

★ ★ ★ La Mariande
38860
☎ 476805060 FAX 476790499

The hotel is peacefully located in the heart of the Oiseans mountain range and offers exceptional views over the surroundings. With its comfortable bedrooms, lounge-bar with open fireplace and the generous, enjoyable meals served in the restaurant it is the ideal place for both summer and winter breaks.
26 en suite (bth/shr) (4 fmly) (14 with balcony) TV in all bedrooms Licensed Full central heating Open parking

available Child discount available Outdoor swimming pool (heated) Tennis Sauna Solarium Pool table Jacuzzi/spa Open terrace Last d 21.00hrs Languages spoken: English, German
MEALS: Full breakfast 50FF Lunch 120-170FF Dinner 120-170FF✱
CARDS: ●● ▆▆ Travellers cheques

DIE Drôme

★★ Des Alpes
87 rue C Buffardel *26150*
☎ 472221583 FAX 475220939
In the heart of the Clairette region, this former coaching inn dates back to the 14th century, and has entirely renovated rooms with adequate modern facilities. The area is blessed with a mild climate, whilst the hotel offers a fine mountain view and is ideally placed for visits to the Vercors, Les Grands Goulets and the Chloranche caves.
Near river Forest area In town centre Near motorway
24 en suite (bth/shr) (5 fmly) TV in all bedrooms STV Direct dial from all bedrooms Full central heating Covered parking available (charged) Languages spoken: English,German
CARDS: ●● ▆▆ ▆▆ Travellers cheques

★★ St-Domingue
44 rue C Buffardel *26150*
☎ 475220308 FAX 475222448
Forest area In town centre
26 en suite (bth/shr) Direct dial from all bedrooms Licensed Full central heating Covered parking available (charged) Child discount available Outdoor swimming pool V meals Last d 22.00hrs Languages spoken: English,Spanish
MEALS: Full breakfast 30FF Continental breakfast 30FF Lunch 70-135FF&alc Dinner 70-135FF&alc✱
CARDS: ●● ▆▆ ▆▆ Travellers cheques

DIVONNE LES BAINS Ain

★★ Bellevue Marquis
av du Mont-Mussy *01220*
☎ 450200216 FAX 450202655
Situated in green surroundings with a garden and a terrace at the foot of the Jura, the hotel offers cosy guest accommodation and a cuisine which alternates between healthy dishes and a choice of gourmet meals. Set in the village of Divonne-les-Bains with thermal baths and excellent leisure facilities, it is a good venue for relaxing holiday.
Near lake Forest area
Closed Nov-early Mar
15 en suite (bth/shr) (6 with balcony) TV in all bedrooms Licensed Full central heating Open parking available Child discount available Open terrace V meals Last d 21.30hrs
CARDS: ●● ▆▆ ▆▆ ●

★★★★ Château de Divonne
115 rue des Bains *01220*
☎ 450200032 FAX 450200373
(Approach via Gex on N5)
This beautiful white 19th-century residence is situated in a park and offers panoramic views over the surrounding countryside. The spacious bedrooms with en suite facilities are furnished in a style befitting the house, and feature personal touches including fresh flower arrangements. The elegant lounges and dining room are complemented by the superb cuisine which is widely acknowledged for its comprehensive choice of dishes and fabulous desserts.
Near lake Forest area Near motorway

27 en suite (bth/shr) TV in all bedrooms STV Direct dial from all bedrooms Mini-bar in all bedrooms Licensed Lift Night porter Full central heating Open parking available Covered parking available (charged) Outdoor swimming pool (heated) Tennis Boule Bicycle rental Open terrace Last d 22.00hrs Languages spoken: English, German
ROOMS: (room only) s 500-1200FF; d 970-1480FF
MEALS: Full breakfast 95FF Lunch 240-290FF&alc Dinner 280-490FF&alc
CARDS: ●● ▆▆ ▆▆ ● JCB Travellers cheques

DOUSSARD Haute-Savoie

★★ Arcalod Grand Parc
74210
☎ 450443022 FAX 450448503
(From Duingt take N508 to Doussard)
Located on the south side of Lake Annecy, standing at an altitude of 450 metres, the hotel enjoys an exceptionally peaceful and sunny location. Set in a rural position and with a wide choice of leisure facilities on hand it provides a pleasant setting for either an active and relaxing holiday. The attractive bedrooms offer modern amenities and the restaurant serves regional specialities as well as the chef's personal imaginative creations.

Near river Near lake Forest area
Closed Nov-Mar
33 en suite (bth/shr) (10 fmly) (18 with balcony) No smoking in 10 bedrooms TV in all bedrooms STV Direct dial from all bedrooms Licensed Lift Full central heating Air conditioning in bedrooms Open parking available Covered parking available Supervised Child discount available 12yrs Outdoor swimming pool (heated) Gym Pool table Boule Mini-golf Bicycle rental Open terrace Covered terrace V meals Last d 20.30hrs Languages spoken: English,Italian
ROOMS: s 220-300FF; d 250-350FF ✱ **Reductions over 1 night**
MEALS: Continental breakfast 45FF Lunch 110-155FF&alc Dinner 110-155FF&alc
CARDS: ●● ▆▆ ▆▆ ● Travellers cheques

★★★ Marceau-Hotel
115 ch de la Chapellière *74210*
☎ 450443011 FAX 450443944
(N508 in direction of Albertville)
The establishment was originally an ancient house which has been converted to a comfortable, charming hotel. Situated in the heart of the countryside, it offers lovely views of the surroundings, and it has a good reputation for its comfortable accommodation and high quality cuisine.
Near lake Forest area

contd.

16 en suite (bth/shr) (6 fmly) (6 with balcony) TV in all bedrooms Radio in rooms Direct dial from all bedrooms Licensed Full central heating Open parking available Covered parking available (charged) Tennis Boule Open terrace Table tennis Childrens play area Languages spoken: English
ROOMS: (room only) s 400FF; d 480-680FF
CARDS: ●● ▆▆ ▆▆ ⓞ Travellers cheques

ÉCHENEVEX Ain

★ ★ ★ Auberge des Chasseurs
Naz-Dessus *01170*
☎ 450405407 FAX 450419061
(Leave Fernay Voltaire in the direction of Gex, 2km before Gex turn left)
Standing at the foot of the Jura mountains, facing the Alps and close to Switzerland, the Auberge des Chasseurs has all the attractive features of a country house. The decor in the guest rooms combine elegance and comfort. Whilst the restaurant offers cuisine rich in the flavours of French gastronomy.
Near river In town centre
Closed mid Nov-early Mar
15 en suite (bth/shr) (1 fmly) (4 with balcony) TV in all bedrooms STV Direct dial from all bedrooms Licensed Night porter Full central heating Open parking available Outdoor swimming pool (heated) Tennis Open terrace V meals· Last d 21.30hrs Languages spoken: English, Italian & Spanish
ROOMS: (room only) s 430-530FF; d 480-650FF
MEALS: Continental breakfast 55FF Lunch 75-280FF&alc Dinner 165-280FF&alc
CARDS: ●● ▆▆ ▆▆ Travellers cheques

ÉCHETS, LES Ain

★ ★ Marguin
916 rte de Strasbourg *01700*
☎ 478918004 FAX 478910683
At 15 kilometres from Lyon, located in the beautiful Dombes region, the Marguin family has offered its visitors warm hospitality and attentive service since 1906. This small hotel serves a traditional cuisine which is skilfully prepared by the talented Jacques Marguin and his equally accomplished son Christophe. The guest accommodation consists of very comfortable bedrooms mostly appointed with modern facilities.
Near lake Near motorway
8 rms (7 bth/shr) (2 fmly) (4 with balcony) TV in 19 bedrooms Licensed Full central heating Open parking available Boule Open terrace V meals Last d 21.00hrs Languages spoken: English, German
CARDS: ●● ▆▆ ▆▆

ÉVIAN-LES-BAINS Haute-Savoie

★ ★ Panorama
Grande Rive *74500*
☎ 450751450 FAX 450755912
The hotel is situated in Evian, a town with a faithful following of regular visitors: those who come to take the waters and those who like to spend an evening in the casino. The Panorama hotel offers splendid views over the blue waters of Lake Geneva and features balconied bedrooms with modern facilities offering good comfort, private grounds with a sunny terrace, and an excellent cuisine incorporating fresh fish delicacies from the lake.
Near lake Near motorway

Closed early Oct-end Apr
29 en suite (bth/shr) (5 fmly) (26 with balcony) TV in all bedrooms Licensed Full central heating Child discount available Open terrace V meals Last d 21.30hrs Languages spoken: English
MEALS: Full breakfast 50FF Continental breakfast 35FF Lunch 72-175FF&alc Dinner 72-175FF✱
CARDS: ●● ▆▆ ▆▆ Travellers cheques

★ ★ ★ ★ Verniaz
rte d'Abondance *74500*
☎ 450750490 FAX 450707892
The hotel is housed in various ancient houses and chalets which are situated in a magnificent flower-filled park. It offers unrivalled views of the surrounding countryside and features charming bedrooms, a congenial bar, and a cosy restaurant with large open fireplace.
Near lake Forest area Near motorway
Closed mid Nov-mid Feb
34 en suite (bth) (28 with balcony) TV in all bedrooms Direct dial from all bedrooms Licensed Lift Night porter Full central heating Open parking available Outdoor swimming pool (heated) Golf Tennis Riding Solarium Pool table Open terrace Last d 21.00hrs Languages spoken: English, German
ROOMS: (room only) s 600-700FF; d 800-1300FF ✱
MEALS: Full breakfast 75FF Lunch 200-350FF Dinner 200-350FF
CARDS: ●● ▆▆ ▆▆ ⓞ Travellers cheques

EYBENS Isère

★ ★ ★ Château de la Commanderie
17 av d'Echirolles *38320*
☎ 476253458 FAX 476240731
This is an enchanting residence set in fabulous, peaceful grounds just within minutes of the town of Grenoble. Its interior is adorned with antiques, tapestries, ancestral portraits and 18th-century wood-panelling. The superb dining room serves an excellent cuisine in elegant surroundings, and the bedrooms are tastefully decorated with high quality fabrics and furnishings, and offer a high level of comfort.

Forest area Near motorway
25 en suite (bth/shr) (6 fmly) (3 with balcony) TV in all bedrooms STV Radio in rooms Direct dial from all bedrooms Mini-bar in all bedrooms Licensed Night porter Full central heating Open parking available Outdoor swimming pool Pool table Boule Open terrace Covered terrace Last d 21.15hrs Languages spoken: English, Spanish
ROOMS: (room only) s 430-665FF; d 470-705FF
MEALS: Lunch 165-265FF&alc Dinner 197-265FF&alc
CARDS: ●● ▆▆ ▆▆ ⓞ Travellers cheques

FARGES Ain

★ ★ Château de Farges
01550
☎ 450567171 FAX 450567127
This hotel provides a peaceful setting for a relaxing holiday and is decorated throughout in rustic style. It offers spacious guest-rooms, most of which are equipped with modern amenities, and a sunny terrace looking out over a large park. The restaurant serves a selection of fine dishes including regional specialities.
Near river Forest area Near motorway
34 rms (10 bth 16 shr) TV in all bedrooms Licensed Full central heating Open parking available Covered parking available Child discount available 12yrs Open terrace V meals Last d 21.15hrs Languages spoken: English,German
CARDS: 💳 ▆▆ ▆▆

FAVERGES Haute-Savoie

★ ★ Genève
34 rue de la République *74210*   ✗ ✗✓
☎ 450324690 FAX 450444809
This coaching inn dates back to the 18th century and was entirely renovated in 1991. The bedrooms are spacious with good quality beds and offer all modern conveniences. It features a peaceful lounge, cosy bar and attractive garden. Enjoyable meals are served in the informal restaurant where staff provide a friendly and attentive service.
Forest area In town centre
30 en suite (bth/shr) (4 fmly) (7 with balcony) TV in all bedrooms STV Direct dial from all bedrooms Licensed Lift Full central heating Open parking available Supervised Child discount available 12yrs Open terrace Last d 21.00hrs Languages spoken: English,Portuguese
MEALS: Full breakfast 35FF Lunch 59-110FF&alc Dinner 59-110FF&alc✱
CARDS: 💳 ▆▆ ▆▆ 🌐 Travellers cheques

FERNEY-VOLTAIRE Ain

★ ★ Hotel de France
1 rue de Genève *01210*
☎ 450406387 FAX 450404727
This is a small hotel offering traditionally furnished bedrooms with modern amenities. The cuisine features classic dishes complemented by a selection of fine wines from the house cellar. In addition, the hotel features a winter garden and has a shaded terrace.
Near lake Forest area In town centre Near motorway
14 en suite (shr) Some rooms in annexe TV in all bedrooms STV Radio in rooms Mini-bar in all bedrooms Licensed Full central heating Open parking available Child discount available 11yrs Fishing Squash Riding Pool table Boule Bicycle rental Open terrace Covered terrace V meals Last d 22.00hrs Languages spoken: English
MEALS: Full breakfast 40FF Lunch fr 115FF&alc Dinner fr 165FF&alc✱

★ ★ ★ Novotel Genève Aéroport
rte de Meyrin *01210*
☎ 450408523 FAX 450407633
Near lake Forest area Near motorway
80 en suite (bth/shr) (40 fmly) No smoking in 2 bedrooms TV in all bedrooms STV Radio in rooms Direct dial from all bedrooms Mini-bar in all bedrooms Licensed Night porter Full central heating Air conditioning in bedrooms Open parking available Outdoor swimming pool Tennis Open terrace Covered terrace Last d 24.00hrs Languages spoken: English,German,Portuguese,Spanish
CARDS: 💳 ▆▆ ▆▆ 🌐 Travellers cheques

FONTANIL-CORNILLON Isère

★ ★ Les Relais Bleus
8 av de Louisiane *38120*
☎ 476752738 Cen Res 164460616 FAX 476756779
Les Relais Bleus offer comfortable accommodation and good value at the two star level. They cater for both family and business clientele, with relaxed dining and public areas.
Forest area Near motorway
50 en suite (bth) TV in all bedrooms STV Direct dial from all bedrooms Licensed Full central heating Open parking available Outdoor swimming pool Pool table Open terrace V meals Languages spoken: English,Spanish

GRAND-BORNAND, LE Haute-Savoie

★ ★ Le Cortina
74450
☎ 450270022 FAX 450270631
(From Annecy take D909 to St Jean-de-Sixthen take D4 to Le Chinaillon)
Summer or winter the mountains always provide a splendid setting for a relaxing holiday. The guest accommodation is comfortable and the cuisine served in the panoramic dining room includes a choice of regional specialities. In addition, the hotel and surrounding countryside offer many leisure opportunities.
Near river Near lake Forest area
Closed 16 Apr-19 Jun & 15 Sep-19 Dec
30 en suite (bth/shr) (24 with balcony) TV in all bedrooms Direct dial from all bedrooms Licensed Lift Full central heating Child discount available Outdoor swimming pool (heated) Pool table Open terrace Table tennis(summer only) Last d 21.00hrs Languages spoken: English, Italian
CARDS: 💳 ▆▆ Eurocard Travellers cheques

GRENOBLE Isère

★ ★ ★ Angleterrie
pl Victor-Hugo *38000*
☎ 476873721 FAX 476509410
Set in the heart of the town and surrounded by attractive gardens, the hotel features bedrooms with modern facilities, attractively decorated public areas and fine views towards the Vercors mountain range.
In town centre
66 en suite (bth) (2 fmly) (30 with balcony) No smoking in 5 bedrooms TV in all bedrooms STV Direct dial from all bedrooms Mini-bar in all bedrooms Licensed Lift Night porter Full central heating Air conditioning in bedrooms Languages spoken: English,German,Italian,Spanish
CARDS: 💳 ▆▆ ▆▆ 🌐 Travellers cheques

★ ★ ★ Grand Hotel
5 rue de la République *38000*
☎ 476444936 FAX 476631406
This 19th-century building is situated in the old part of the town and features a cosy interior. A warm atmosphere prevails throughout. The bedrooms provide comfortable accommodation with good quality beds and are equipped with modern amenities.
In town centre

contd.

51 en suite (bth/shr) (6 fmly) (18 with balcony) No smoking in 5 bedrooms TV in all bedrooms STV Direct dial from all bedrooms Mini-bar in all bedrooms Licensed Lift Night porter Full central heating Air conditioning in bedrooms Child discount available 12yrs Golf Languages spoken: English,Italian
CARDS: ➌➌ ▨▨ ▨▨ ◑ Travellers cheques

GRESSE-EN-VERCORS Isère

★ ★ ★ Le Chalet
38650
☎ 476343208 FAX 476343106
Located in the regional nature reserve of the Vercors at the foot of the French Dolomites the hotel is the ideal venue for a summer as well as a winter holiday. A family establishment for 50 years, bedrooms are comfortable, with modern facilities, whilst the cosy restaurant with open fire place serves dishes skilfully prepared by Paul and Christophe Prayer.
Near river Near lake Forest area
Closed Apr-7 May & 20 Oct-20 Dec
25 en suite (bth/shr) 14 rooms in annexe (6 fmly) (14 with balcony) TV in all bedrooms Mini-bar in all bedrooms Licensed Full central heating Open parking available Covered parking available (charged) Supervised Child discount available 10yrs Outdoor swimming pool (heated) Tennis Boule Open terrace Last d 21.00hrs Languages spoken: English
MEALS: Continental breakfast 44FF Lunch 94-290FF&alc Dinner 94-290FF&alc✱
CARDS: ➌➌ ▨▨ Travellers cheques

GRIGNAN Drôme

★ ★ ★ ★ Manoir de la Roseraie
rte de Valréas *26230*
☎ 475465815 FAX 475469155
(Approach via A7 & N7)
The residence is set in extensive grounds amidst rose gardens and immaculate lawns. It features elegant bedrooms with individual furnishings, and in the restaurant guests can enjoy a delicious cuisine prepared with home-grown produce and complemented by fine wines personally selected by the sommelier.
Near river Forest area
Closed 5 Jan-16 Feb

15 en suite (bth/shr) 2 rooms in annexe No smoking in 1 bedroom TV in all bedrooms STV Radio in rooms Direct dial from all bedrooms Licensed Full central heating Open parking available Supervised Child discount available 4yrs Outdoor swimming pool (heated) Tennis Boule Bicycle rental

Open terrace V meals Last d 21.15hrs Languages spoken: English,German,Dutch
ROOMS: (room only) s 690-1100FF; d 690-1680FF
MEALS: Full breakfast 90FF Lunch 195-250FF&alc Dinner 195-250FF&alc
CARDS: ➌➌ ▨▨ ▨▨ ◑ Travellers cheques

HOUCHES, LES Haute-Savoie

★ ★ ★ Le Mont Alba
475 av des Alpages *74310*
☎ 450545035 FAX 450555087
Situated in the village of Les Houches at the foot of the Mont Blanc mountain range, Le Mont Alba combines an olde-worlde atmosphere with modern services and facilities. The chalet-style hotel features spacious bedrooms with private en suite amenities, a cosy bar and a restaurant which serves a range of freshly prepared dishes.
Near lake Forest area Near motorway
Closed Nov-15 Dec
43 en suite (bth/shr) (1 fmly) (39 with balcony) TV in all bedrooms STV Radio in rooms Direct dial from all bedrooms Mini-bar in all bedrooms Licensed Lift Full central heating Open parking available Covered parking available (charged) Child discount available 12yrs Indoor swimming pool (heated) Sauna Open terrace Last d 21.30hrs Languages spoken: English
CARDS: ➌➌ ▨▨ ▨▨ Travellers cheques

JULIÉNAS Rhône

★ ★ Chez la Rose
69840
☎ 474044120 FAX 474044929
This charming building is situated amidst hills and vineyards. It features individually styled bedrooms with tasteful furnishings offering a high degree of comfort. The cuisine incorporates meticulously prepared dishes accompanied by great vintage wines.
Forest area Near motorway
Closed 17 Nov-17 Dec & 23 Feb-3 Mar
10 en suite (bth/shr) 5 rooms in annexe (4 fmly) (1 with balcony) TV in all bedrooms STV Direct dial from all bedrooms Licensed Full central heating Open parking available Child discount available 12yrs Open terrace V meals Last d 21.30hrs Languages spoken: English
ROOMS: (room only) s 200-450FF; d 200-550FF
MEALS: Full breakfast 80FF Continental breakfast 40FF Lunch 98-275FF&alc Dinner 98-275FF&alc
CARDS: ➌➌ ▨▨ ▨▨ ◑ Travellers cheques

LANARCE Ardèche

★ ★ Le Provence
07660
☎ 466694606 FAX 466694156
Set in a tiny village of only 250 inhabitants at an altitude of 1250 metres and surrounded by woods and plains, the hotel has pleasant bedrooms with modern facilities which provide a good level of comfort. It has a cosy lounge and a panoramic restaurant which serves carefully prepared dishes with an imaginative touch.
Near river Forest area Near motorway
Closed 15 Nov-15 Mar
15 en suite (bth/shr) (3 fmly) TV in all bedrooms Direct dial from all bedrooms Licensed Full central heating Open parking available Covered parking available Child discount available 14yrs Fishing Boule

Open terrace Last d 21.00hrs Languages spoken: English
MEALS: Full breakfast 25FF Lunch 75-170FF Dinner 75-
170FF✱
CARDS: ●● ☎ Travellers cheques

LANSLEBOURG Savoie

★ ★ ★ Alpazur
73480
☎ 479059369 FAX 479058655
The hotel is situated at the foot of the slopes and features
balconied bedrooms with views of the mountain. There is a
comfortable lounge and a cosy bar for some après-ski
entertainment in winter and relaxation in summer. But best of all
is the restaurant with open fireplace, where the chef-proprietor
offers a traditional cuisine served in generous portions.
Near river Forest area Near motorway
Closed 20 Apr-30 May and 21 Sep-19 Dec
24 en suite (bth/shr) (2 fmly) (14 with balcony) No smoking in
10 bedrooms TV in all bedrooms Direct dial from all
bedrooms Licensed Full central heating Open parking
available Covered parking available Child discount available
12yrs Bicycle rental Open terrace V meals Last d 21.00hrs
Languages spoken: English,Italian
ROOMS: (room only) d 290-360FF **Special breaks: skiing
and walking breaks**
MEALS: Full breakfast 60FF Continental breakfast 40FF Lunch
100-260FF&alc Dinner 100-260FF&alc✱
CARDS: ●● ☎ ☎ ◑ Travellers cheques

LYON Rhône

★ ★ ★ Hotel Bristol Promotour
28 Cours Verdun *69002*
☎ 478375655 FAX 478370258
Standing in the bustling centre of Lyon and close to the main
travel services and exit roads, the hotel provides the ideal venue
for a business trip as well as a leisure holiday. Sound-proofed
bedrooms with modern amenities, a pleasant bar and spacious
public areas offer a comfortable setting for a relaxing stay.
In town centre Near motorway
113 en suite (bth/shr) No smoking in 24 bedrooms TV in all
bedrooms STV Radio in rooms Direct dial from all bedrooms
Licensed Lift Night porter Full central heating Air
conditioning in bedrooms Child discount available 12yrs Pool
table Languages spoken: English, German, Spanish
CARDS: ●● ☎ ☎ ◑ Travellers cheques

★ ★ ★ Hotel Carlton (Best Western)
4 rue Jussieu *69002*
☎ 478425651 FAX 478421071
The hotel is located in the bustling centre of Lyon, with many
shops and restaurants nearby, and combines good old-
fashioned hospitality with modern comfort. Whether it is a
business trip or leisure break, it provides comfortable
accommodation and excellent service in informal
surroundings. To start off the day, guests can enjoy a high
quality buffet-breakfast in the dining room.
In town centre Near motorway
83 en suite (bth/shr) (83 fmly) (62 with balcony) TV in all
bedrooms STV Radio in rooms Direct dial from all bedrooms
Mini-bar in all bedrooms Licensed Lift Night porter Full
central heating Air conditioning in bedrooms Child discount
available 12yrs Languages spoken: English, Spanish, German
ROOMS: (room only) s 400-730FF; d 490-780FF
MEALS: Full breakfast 58FF✱
CARDS: ●● ☎ ☎ ◑ JCB Travellers cheques

★ ★ ★ Grand Hotel des Beaux-Arts (Best Western)
73-75 rue du Prés E Herriot *69002*
☎ 478380950 FAX 478421919
Constructed in typical Lyonnais style, the hotel features
comfortable bedrooms with modern facilities. Elegantly
furnished in Art-Déco style, it provides the ideal venue for a
business, gastronomic or cultural visit to this city.
In town centre
75 en suite (bth/shr) (20 with balcony) No smoking in 11
bedrooms TV in all bedrooms STV Radio in rooms Direct
dial from all bedrooms Mini-bar in all bedrooms Room-safe
(charged) Licensed Lift Night porter Full central heating Air
conditioning in bedrooms Child discount available 12yrs
Languages spoken: English, German, Italian, Spanish
ROOMS: (room only) s 495-750FF; d 550-750FF ✱
CARDS: ●● ☎ ☎ ◑ JCB Travellers cheques

★ ★ ★ Hotel Royal (Best Western)
20 pl Bellecour *69002*
☎ 478375731 FAX 478370136
The Hotel Royal is located on the Place Bellecour and enjoys a
popular reputation in Lyon. With its individually styled
bedrooms, courteous staff and elegant decor, it provides a
comfortable environment for a memorable stay. Surrounded
by commercial centres, shops and restaurants and with its
numerous facilities and services, it is the ideal venue for both
business and leisure guests.
Near river In town centre Near motorway
80 en suite (bth/shr) (7 fmly) (44 with balcony) No smoking in
13 bedrooms TV in all bedrooms STV Radio in rooms Direct
dial from all bedrooms Mini-bar in all bedrooms Room-safe
Licensed Lift Night porter Full central heating Air
conditioning in bedrooms Open parking available (charged)
Covered parking available (charged) Supervised Child
discount available 12yrs V meals Last d 22.00hrs Languages
spoken: English, German, Spanish, Italian,Arabic
ROOMS: (room only) s 590-1300FF
**Reductions over 1 night Special breaks: Weekend
breaks**
MEALS: Full breakfast 72FF Lunch 65-142FF&alc Dinner 128-
142FF&alc
CARDS: ●● ☎ ☎ ◑

★ ★ ★ Sofitel Lyon
20 quai Gailleton *69002*
☎ 472412020 FAX 472400550
The Sofitel chain comprises of a group of very fine modern,
comfortable hotels at the four star level. Bedrooms have been
carefully designed to cater to guests' relaxation and well being
and the restaurant facilities offer fine cuisine in pleasant
surroundings. They cater for business clientele with excellent
conference and meeting facilities.
Near river In town centre Near motorway
167 en suite (bth/shr) TV in all bedrooms STV Radio in rooms
Mini-bar in all bedrooms Licensed Lift Night porter Full
central heating Air conditioning in bedrooms Open parking
available (charged) Supervised Child discount available Last
d 22.30hrs Languages spoken: German,Italian
CARDS: ●● ☎ ☎ ◑

★ ★ ★ La Tour Rose (Small Luxury Hotels)
22 rue du Boeuf *69005*
☎ 478372590 FAX 478422602
The hotel La Tour Rose is housed in three buildings which go
back as far as the 15th century. Its sumptuous interior is
adorned with rich silks in numerous shades and textures
complemented by elegant furniture. The guest accommodation
contd.

is exquisitely furnished and offers a high level of comfort whilst the lounges, terraces and gardens provide a relaxing ambience for an enjoyable stay. The restaurant combines culinary as well as architectural innovations in the former chapel with its glass roof, and serves an extensive array of imaginative dishes.

In town centre Near motorway

12 en suite (bth/shr) 5 rooms in annexe (5 fmly) (2 with balcony) TV in all bedrooms Direct dial from all bedrooms Mini-bar in all bedrooms Licensed Lift Full central heating Air conditioning in bedrooms Open parking available (charged) Covered parking available (charged) Supervised Child discount available 15yrs Open terrace Covered terrace Wkly live entertainment V meals Last d 22.30hrs Languages spoken: English,Spanish,Italian

ROOMS: (room only) s 950-1200FF; d 1200-2800FF ✱
MEALS: Full breakfast 95FF Continental breakfast 120FF Lunch fr 400FFalc Dinner fr 500FFalc
CARDS: ●● ■■ ✖ ⬤ JCB Travellers cheques

MALATAVERNE Drôme

★ ★ ★ Domaine du Colombier
rte de Donzère *26780*
☎ 475908686 FAX 475907940
(exit A7 at Montelimar Sud in the direction Malataverne, pass through village and take direction of Donzere for 4km)
The house is an old "Bastide" from the 13th century. Each room has attractive individual décor, with floral design a feature of the furnishings. Gastronomic and regional dishes are served in the vaulted restaurant.

Forest area

25 en suite (bth/shr) (8 fmly) (6 with balcony) TV in all bedrooms Direct dial from all bedrooms Licensed Full central heating Open parking available Outdoor swimming pool Bicycle rental Covered terrace 4ha park V meals Last d 21.30hrs Languages spoken: English, German & Italian

ROOMS: (room only) s 280-860FF; d 315-1200FF
MEALS: Lunch 150-360FF&alc Dinner 195-360FF&alc
CARDS: ■■

MÉAUDRE Isère

★ ★ Auberge du Furon
38112
☎ 476952471 FAX 476952471
The Auberge du Furon is situated on the edge of a wood. With many leisure opportunities on offer it is the ideal venue for both a summer and winter holiday. The pleasant guest rooms provide fine views over the countryside and the restaurant - a popular meeting place for the locals - serves a range of well-presented dishes based on traditional recipes and local produce.

Forest area

Closed mid Nov-mid Dec

9 en suite (bth) (1 fmly) (3 with balcony) TV in all bedrooms STV Direct dial from all bedrooms Licensed Full central heating Open parking available Child discount available 12yrs Boule Open terrace Covered terrace Last d 21.00hrs Languages spoken: English
CARDS: ●● ■■ Travellers cheques

MEGÈVE Haute-Savoie

★ ★ ★ Les Fermes de Marie
chemin de Riante Colline *74120*
☎ 450930310 FAX 450930984

Visitors find it hard to believe that they have arrived at an hotel when they step over the threshold of 'Les Fermes de Marie'. The interior has been designed to resemble a typical Savoyard house and by using original materials, an enchanting rustic environment has been created. From the lounge with open fireplace and antique furniture, to the restaurant where large meals are served, a warm atmosphere prevails.

Closed mid Sep-mid Dec

68 en suite (bth) (60 with balcony) TV in all bedrooms STV Direct dial from all bedrooms Mini-bar in all bedrooms Licensed Lift Night porter Full central heating Open parking available (charged) Covered parking available (charged) Supervised Child discount available Indoor swimming pool Outdoor swimming pool Sauna Solarium Pool table Jacuzzi/spa Bicycle rental Open terrace Covered terrace Wkly live entertainment Casino Last d 22.00hrs Languages spoken: English,Italian
CARDS: ●● ■■ ✖

MERCUROL Drôme

★ ★ De La Tour
Le Village, 11 rue de la République *26600*
☎ 475074007 FAX 475074620
(exit A7 at Tain L'Hermitage-Romans and follow signs Mercurol-Romans, then take 1st left to village of Mercurol)
Calm and good hospitality are the focus of this lovely hotel, in a village just three kilometres from the A1 motorway.

Forest area Near motorway

20 rms (5 bth 12 shr) (8 fmly) TV in 13 bedrooms Direct dial from all bedrooms Licensed Night porter Full central heating Covered parking available (charged) Child discount available 12yrs Boule V meals Last d 22.00hrs Languages spoken: English

ROOMS: (room only) d 165-270FF **Reductions over 1 night**
MEALS: Full breakfast 30FF Continental breakfast 30FF Lunch 75-125FF&alc Dinner 75-125FF&alc
CARDS: ●● ✖

MÉRIBEL-LES-ALLUES Savoie

★ ★ Orée du Bois
rte du Belvédère *73550*
☎ 479005030 FAX 479085752
Situated in the heart of 'Les Trois Vallées', this hotel provides a comfortable setting for an enjoyable break. Balconied bedrooms are equipped with modern amenities and have panoramic views over the surrounding mountains. After a day in the fresh mountain air, guests can enjoy the tasty cuisine served in the informal atmosphere of the restaurant.

Forest area

Closed Etr,Jul,Aug & Xmas

35 rms (26 bth 6 shr) (2 fmly) (35 with balcony) TV in all bedrooms STV Radio in rooms Direct dial from all bedrooms Licensed Lift Full central heating Open parking available Covered parking available (charged) Child discount available Outdoor swimming pool Golf Solarium Bicycle rental Open terrace Last d 21.00hrs Languages spoken: English
CARDS: ●● ■■ ✖ Travellers cheques

MEYLAN Isère

★ ★ ★ Hotel Alpha
34 av de Verdun *38240*
☎ 476906309 FAX 476902827
Because of its easy access, the hotel is ideally situated for the town centre and tourist sights as well as exploring the

surrounding region. With ski-slopes less than 30 minutes away it is a good venue for a winter stay and features two styles of guest accommodation to meet individual requirements, and a restaurant which serves meals alternating between traditional dishes and a popular 'Bistro'-style cuisine.
Near river Forest area In town centre Near motorway
85 en suite (bth/shr) TV in all bedrooms STV Radio in rooms Direct dial from all bedrooms Mini-bar in all bedrooms Licensed Lift Night porter Full central heating Open parking available Covered parking available (charged) Child discount available 12yrs Outdoor swimming pool Pool table Open terrace Covered terrace Last d 23.00hrs Languages spoken: English,Spanish,German,Italian
CARDS: ●● ■■ ⅢⅡ ⅅ Travellers cheques

MEYZIEU Rhône

★ ★ ★ Mont Joyeux
av Victor Hugo-Le Carreau 69330
☎ 478042132 FAX 472028572
(off A46)
Located just a few minutes outside Lyon, the hotel offers its clientele a complete change of scenery and a peaceful stay. Situated opposite a large lake it offers attractive bedrooms with balconies, a restaurant with fine views over the water and a terrace for relaxation. The cuisine consists of a wide range of dishes including light pastries, fresh fish and regional specialities skilfully executed by the chef-proprietor Jean-Bernard Mollard.
Near lake Forest area Near motorway
20 en suite (bth) (2 fmly) (8 with balcony) TV in all bedrooms STV Radio in rooms Direct dial from all bedrooms Mini-bar in all bedrooms Licensed Full central heating Open parking available Child discount available Outdoor swimming pool Fishing Boule Open terrace V meals Last d 21.30hrs Languages spoken: English,German,Spanish
ROOMS: (room only) s 415-455FF; d 445-475FF
MEALS: Full breakfast 55FF Lunch fr 130FF&alc Dinner fr 130FF&alc
CARDS: ●● ■■ ⅢⅡ ⅅ Travellers cheques

MIRMANDE Drôme

★ ★ Capitelle
rue du Rémpart 26270
☎ 475630272 FAX 475630250
Located in an medieval village, this former private Renaissance residence used to be the house of the painter André Lhóte. All the bedrooms are individually appointed and have modern facilities; there is a restaurant, where the beams and open fireplace create a warm and informal atmosphere, and a pleasant terrace.
Forest area Near motorway
Closed Tuesday and Wednesday noon
11 en suite (bth/shr) (2 fmly) (3 with balcony) Full central heating covered parking spaces (charged) Supervised Child discount available 10yrs Open terrace Last d 21.30hrs Languages spoken: English
CARDS: ●● ■■ ⅢⅡ ⅅ Travellers cheques

MONTAILLEUR Savoie

★ ★ Tour de Pacoret
73460
☎ 479379159 FAX 479379384
The hotel is an ancient watch-tower which dates back to the 14th century and is an oasis of peace amidst beautiful green

scenery. It combines all the virtues associated with the countryside; restful accommodation, a warm and friendly atmosphere and a high standard of cooking. The pretty bedrooms have panoramic views over the surrounding area, while the restaurant serves an excellent cuisine based on regional produce, accompanied by a choice of select wines.
Near river Near lake Forest area
Closed end of Oct-Etr
9 en suite (bth/shr) TV in all bedrooms Direct dial from all bedrooms Licensed Full central heating Open parking available Covered parking available (charged) Boule Open terrace Last d 21.30hrs Languages spoken: English
CARDS: ●● ■■ Travellers cheques

MONTBOUCHER-SUR-JABRON Drôme

★ ★ ★ Castel
Le Castel 26740
☎ 475460816 FAX 475014409
During the 13th century the château was the private residence of the Adhémars, vassals under the Dukes of Poitiers. Its towers were brokn in half during the Revolution and have been transformed into terraces. The interior is splendidly decorated with oriental carpets, beautiful engravings, velvet and lace, as well as assorted antiques. The bedrooms are furnished with flair and a good eye for detail and provide a high standard of comfort, whilst the vaulted restaurant serves an outstanding cuisine augmented by some good Côte du Rhone wines.
Near river Forest area Near motorway
12 en suite (bth/shr) (1 fmly) (2 with balcony) TV in all bedrooms STV Mini-bar in all bedrooms Licensed Full central heating Open parking available Supervised Child discount available 12yrs Outdoor swimming pool Tennis Boule Open terrace V meals Last d 21.00hrs Languages spoken: English & Hungarian
MEALS: Full breakfast 48FF Lunch 149-350FF&alc Dinner 149-350FF&alc✱
CARDS: ●● ■■ ⅢⅡ Travellers cheques

MONTÉLIMAR Drôme

★ ★ Le Printemps
8 ch de la Manche 26200
☎ 475013263 FAX 475460314
The hotel is peacefully situated in Provence, and has functional bedrooms with good amenities and a pleasant restaurant which serves a choice of enjoyable meals to suit most tastes. Guests can also relax or have a meal on the attractive terrace under the plane trees.
Closed 1-15 Dec
25 rms (2 fmly) (2 with balcony) TV in all bedrooms STV Direct dial from all bedrooms Mini-bar in all bedrooms Licensed Full central heating Open parking available Supervised No children 14yrs Outdoor swimming pool Open terrace Last d 21.00hrs
CARDS: ●● ■■ ⅢⅡ

MONTHIEUX Ain

★ ★ ★ ★ Gouverneur
Lieu-dit Le Breuil 01390
☎ 472264200 FAX 472264220
(On D82)
Once home to the Governer of the Dombes, this 14th century castle is now the biggest golf resort in the Rhône-Alpes region

contd.

and offers extensive facilities and services to its visitors. The bedrooms are situated in the ancient outbuildings and contemporary extension, and feature very comfortable bedrooms with excellent en suite facilities. The restaurant serves a classic cuisine prepared with fresh ingredients from the region.

Near river Near lake Forest area
Closed 15-30 Dec
53 en suite (bth/shr) (8 fmly) TV in all bedrooms STV Radio in rooms Direct dial from all bedrooms Mini-bar in all bedrooms Licensed Lift Night porter Full central heating Air conditioning in bedrooms Open parking available Supervised Child discount available 12yrs Outdoor swimming pool (heated) Golf 45 Tennis Fishing Pool table Boule Bicycle rental Open terrace V meals Last d 21.30hrs Languages spoken: English,German
ROOMS: (room only) s 460-500FF; d 540-590FF
CARDS: ● ▆▆ ▆ ● Travellers cheques

MORZINE Haute-Savoie

★ ★ Des Bruyères
Im des Champs de la Plagne *74110*
☎ 450791576 FAX 450747009
This lovely chalet-hotel is situated in the heart of the village and provides the atmosphere of a private home with the added convenience of attentive service and excellent comfort. It is ideally situated for an action-packed holiday and has unsurpassed sporting opportunities for young guests as well as adults in the immediate vicinity. It features cosy bedrooms with balconies and fine mountain views, a congenial bar for a drink and a chat, and a restaurant which serves traditional cuisine with a special 'Savoy' touch.
Near river Near lake Forest area In town centre Near motorway
Closed 21 Apr-19 Jun & 11 Sep-19 Dec
24 en suite (bth/shr) 4 rooms in annexe (12 fmly) (24 with balcony) TV in all bedrooms Direct dial from all bedrooms Full central heating Open parking available Child discount available 12yrs Outdoor swimming pool (heated) Sauna Pool table Bicycle rental Open terrace Last d 20.30hrs Languages spoken: English
MEALS: Continental breakfast 40FF Lunch 110-120FF Dinner 110-120FF✱
CARDS: ● ▆ Travellers cheques

NOAILLY Loire

★ ★ ★ Château de la Motte
rte D4- La Motte *42640*
☎ 477666460 FAX 477666438
Near river Forest area Near motorway
Closed 2 Jan-Mar
12 en suite (bth/shr) (1 with balcony) TV in all bedrooms Direct dial from all bedrooms Licensed Night porter Full central heating Open parking available Child discount available Outdoor swimming pool Fishing Riding Boule Open terrace Covered terrace ping pong,cruise on canal V meals Last d 21.30hrs Languages spoken: English,German,Italian,Russian,Spanish
MEALS: Full breakfast 50FF Continental breakfast 50FF Lunch 95-290FF Dinner 135-290FF✱
CARDS: ● ▆ Travellers cheques

NOTRE-DAME-DE-BELLECOMBE Savoie

★ ★ Bellevue
73590
☎ 479316056 FAX 479316984
Standing opposite Mount Chavin and the Aravis mountain range, this small friendly hotel is situated in the heart of the village. An informal atmosphere prevails in this establishment, where the rooms have private facilities and the restaurant serves a high standard of cooking. For the more energetic, sporting opportunities include cross-country skiing, para-gliding, and mountain biking, as well as more relaxed pastimes.
Forest area In town centre Near motorway
Closed 20 Apr-20 Jun & 10 Sep-20 Dec
18 rms (15 bth/shr) (9 with balcony) TV in all bedrooms Direct dial from all bedrooms Licensed Full central heating Open parking available Child discount available 10yrs Solarium Boule Open terrace Last d 21.00hrs Languages spoken: English
MEALS: Continental breakfast 36FF Lunch 100-150FF&alc Dinner 100-150FF&alc✱
CARDS: ● ▆

NYONS Drôme

★ ★ ★ Auberge du Vieux Village d'Aubres
Aubres *26110*
☎ 475261289 FAX 475263810
(3km NE of Nyons on D94)
This traditional inn has been built on the site of a medieval castle and thanks to the mild local climate guests can enjoy breakfast on the terrace all year round. It features very comfortable bedrooms - most with terrace - which are equipped with modern amenities, while the restaurant offers a cuisine which includes classic dishes.
Near river Forest area

23 en suite (bth/shr) (6 fmly) (20 with balcony) TV in all bedrooms STV Radio in rooms Direct dial from all bedrooms Mini-bar in all bedrooms Room-safe Licensed Full central heating Open parking available Child discount available Outdoor swimming pool (heated) Sauna Solarium Gym Boule Jacuzzi/spa Bicycle rental Open terrace Covered terrace ping pong,library V meals Last d 20.30hrs Languages spoken: English,German
ROOMS: (room only) s 300-780FF; d 450-780FF
Reductions over 1 night
MEALS: Full breakfast 52FF Lunch 80-178FF&alc Dinner 80-178FF&alc✱
CARDS: ● ▆▆ ▆ ● Travellers cheques

PEISEY-NANCROIX Savoie

★ ★ La Vanoise
Plan Peisey *73210*
☎ 479079219 FAX 479079748
Closed early Sep-late Dec
34 en suite (bth/shr) (5 fmly) (20 with balcony) TV in all
bedrooms Licensed Full central heating Open parking
available Child discount available Outdoor swimming pool
(heated) Pool table Boule Bicycle rental Open terrace V
meals Last d 20.30hrs
CARDS: ●● ▆▆ Travellers cheques

POËT-LAVAL, LE Drôme

★ ★ ★ Hospitaliers
Vieux Village *26160*
☎ 475462232 FAX 475464999
Standing at the foot of a castle in a medieval village, the hotel
consists of four buildings. Most of the comfortable bedrooms
offer a magnificent view over the valley and the foothills of the
Alps. The attractive restaurant serves a range of appetising
meals where special attention has been paid to ingredients and
presentation.
Near river Forest area In town centre Near motorway
Closed 16 Nov-14 Mar
23 rms (4 fmly) (1 with balcony) TV in all bedrooms Licensed
Full central heating Open parking available Outdoor
swimming pool Open terrace Last d 21.15hrs Languages
spoken: English
CARDS: ●● ▆▆ ▆▆ 〇 Travellers cheques

PONT-D'AIN Ain

★ ★ Des Allies
01100
☎ 474390009 FAX 474391366
Situated in a location where good food and numerous beauty
sights are in abundance, the hotel offers modern amenities for
a business trip or leisure stay. Bedrooms provide a good level
of comfort, while the surrounding region is ideal for hunting,
fishing and walking.
Near river Near lake Forest area In town centre Near motorway
Closed 31 Oct-Jan
18 rms (14 bth/shr) (4 fmly) TV in all bedrooms Radio in
rooms Direct dial from all bedrooms Licensed Full central
heating Covered parking available (charged) Supervised
Languages spoken: English
ROOMS: (room only) s 175-295FF; d 175-350FF ✱
CARDS: ●● ▆▆ 〇 Travellers cheques

PONT-DE-CHERUY Isère

★ Bergeron
3 rue Giffard *38230*
☎ 478321008 FAX 478321170
This traditional hotel with its informal atmosphere is situated
next to the church in Pont de Cheruy. After extensive
refurbishment it now offers pleasant bedrooms with modern
facilities which provide a good level of comfort and a
restaurant which caters for all tastes.
Near river Near lake Near sea Forest area In town centre
Near motorway
16 rms 8 rooms in annexe (2 fmly) (1 with balcony) Full
central heating Open parking available Covered parking
available (charged) Open terrace
CARDS: ●● ▆▆

PONT-DE-VAUX Ain

★ ★ Le Raisin
2 pl Michel Poosat *01190*
☎ 385303097 FAX 385306789
(leave A6 at Tournus onto N6 in direction of Macon)
Le Raisin is situated in the very heart of France between
Tournus and Mâcon. It has a pleasant interior with functional
bedrooms offering an adequate level of comfort, whilst the
restaurant serves good quality cooking which suits all palates
and pockets.
Near river Forest area
18 en suite (bth/shr) (3 fmly) TV in all bedrooms Direct dial
from all bedrooms Licensed Full central heating Open
parking available Supervised Boule Open terrace V meals
Last d 21.00hrs Languages spoken: English & Spanish
ROOMS: (room only) s 270-320FF; d 270-320FF
MEALS: Continental breakfast 42FF Lunch 115-350FF&alc
Dinner 115-350FF&alc
CARDS: ●● ▆▆ ▆▆ 〇 Travellers cheques

PRAZ-DE-CHAMONIX, LES Haute-Savoie

★ ★ Eden
35 rte des Gaudenays *74400*
☎ 450531843 FAX 450535150
This very comfortable hotel offers pleasant guest rooms
decorated with light-wood furniture, which have fine views of
the Mont Blanc mountain range. For just a weekend or longer
stay, it features an attractive interior where guests can relax
and savour the excellent cuisine prepared by owners Mr and
Mrs Lesage.
Forest area Near motorway
20 rms (3 with balcony) TV in all bedrooms STV Direct dial
from all bedrooms Mini-bar in all bedrooms Licensed Open
parking available Supervised Child discount available 10yrs
Languages spoken: English,Italian
CARDS: ●● ▆▆ ▆▆ 〇 Travellers cheques

QUINCIÉ-EN-BEAUJOLAIS Rhône

★ ★ Le Mont Brouilly
69430
☎ 474043373 FAX 474690072
(leave A6 at Bellville/Saône in direction of Beaujolais approx
8km)
Standing at the foot of Mont Brouilly, the hotel features all the
facilities necessary for a successful holiday. Comfortable guest
accommodation equipped with modern amenities, dining
rooms, terrace and extensive private grounds with various
leisure opportunities. The warm welcome by the proprietor,
combined with the excellent cuisine of Yves Bouchacourt,
makes this an excellent venue in the Beaujolais region.
Near river Forest area Near motorway
Closed Feb
29 en suite (bth/shr) (1 fmly) TV in all bedrooms Direct dial
from all bedrooms Licensed Full central heating Open
parking available Covered parking available (charged)
Supervised Child discount available 10yrs Outdoor swimming
pool Open terrace Last d 21.00hrs Languages spoken:
English
ROOMS: (room only) s 220-310FF **Reductions over 1
night**
MEALS: Continental breakfast 35FF Lunch 90-230FF Dinner
90-230FF
CARDS: ●● ▆▆ ▆▆ Travellers cheques

REPLONGES Ain

★ ★ ★ Hostellerie Sarrasine
79 Mâcon-Est *01750*
☎ 385310241 FAX 385311174
Near river Near lake Near sea Near motorway
7 en suite (bth) (2 fmly) TV in all bedrooms STV Radio in
rooms Direct dial from all bedrooms Mini-bar in all bedrooms
Licensed Night porter Full central heating Open parking
available Covered parking available Supervised Child
discount available Bicycle rental Open terrace Covered
terrace Wkly live entertainment Casino V meals Last d
21.30hrs Languages spoken: English,German,Italian
MEALS: Full breakfast 65FF Continental breakfast 30FF Lunch
98-320FF&alc Dinner 98-320FF&alc✱
CARDS: 💳 🏧 ⚑ 🌐 JCB Travellers cheques

REVENTIN-VAUGRIS Isère

★ ★ Le Reventel
38121
☎ 4474788350 FAX 4474852788
(Access via N7 towards Valence)
Near motorway
Closed Xmas & late Aug-early Sep
16 rms (2 bth 11 shr) (2 fmly) TV in all bedrooms Direct dial
from all bedrooms Licensed Full central heating Open
parking available Covered parking available Open terrace V
meals Last d 21.15hrs Languages spoken: English
ROOMS: (room only) s 220-280FF; d 220-320FF ✱
MEALS: Full breakfast 30FF Continental breakfast 30FF Lunch
60-175FF&alc Dinner 60-175FF&alc
CARDS: 💳 🏧 ⚑ 🌐 Travellers cheques

ROANNE Loire

★ ★ ★ Grand Hotel
18 cours de la République *42300*
☎ 477714882 FAX 477704240
(situated close by the railway station)
In town centre
Closed 1-18 Aug & Xmas
33 en suite (bth/shr) TV in all bedrooms STV Direct dial from
all bedrooms Mini-bar in all bedrooms Licensed Lift Night
porter Full central heating Open parking available (charged)
Supervised Child discount available 12yrs Languages spoken:
English
CARDS: 💳 🏧 ⚑ 🌐 Travellers cheques

★ ★ ★ ★ Troisgros
pl de la Gare *42300*
☎ 477716697 FAX 477703977
In town centre
Closed 2 wks Feb & 2 wks Aug
18 en suite (bth/shr) (2 fmly) (1 with balcony) TV in all
bedrooms Direct dial from all bedrooms Mini-bar in all
bedrooms Licensed Lift Night porter Full central heating Air
conditioning in bedrooms Open parking available Covered
parking available Supervised Child discount available Open
terrace Last d 21.30hrs Languages spoken: English, German
& Spanish
ROOMS: (room only) s 700-1900FF; d 700-1900FF
MEALS: Full breakfast 110FF Lunch 620-750FF&alc Dinner
620-750FF&alc
CARDS: 💳 🏧 ⚑ 🌐 JCB Travellers cheques

ROCHE-SUR-FORON, LA Haute-Savoie

★ ★ Foron
50 Imp de l'Étang *74800*
☎ 450258276 FAX 450258154
Forest area Near motorway
Closed 20 Dec-5 Jan
26 en suite (bth/shr) (1 with balcony) TV in all bedrooms
Direct dial from all bedrooms Full central heating Open
parking available Covered parking available (charged) Child
discount available 12yrs Languages spoken: English,Italian
CARDS: 💳 🏧 ⚑ 🌐 Travellers cheques

ST-AGNAN-EN-VERCORS Drôme

★ ★ Veymont
26420
☎ 475482019 FAX 475481034
Forest area
Closed Nov-Dec

17 en suite (bth/shr) (2 fmly) Direct dial from all bedrooms
Licensed Full central heating Open parking available Child
discount available 15yrs Sauna Jacuzzi/spa Open terrace V
meals Last d 20.30hrs Languages spoken: English
ROOMS: (room only) d 220-235FF **Reductions over 1 night**
MEALS: Continental breakfast 35FF Lunch 85-115FF&alc
Dinner 85-115FF&alc
CARDS: 💳 ⚑ Travellers cheques

ST-CIRGUES-EN-MONTAGNE Ardèche

★ ★ ★ Domaine du Lac Ferrand
07510
☎ 475389557 FAX 475389558
Near lake Forest area
Closed 16 Nov-30 Dec
18 en suite (bth/shr) TV in all bedrooms STV Direct dial from
all bedrooms Licensed Full central heating Open parking
available Supervised Child discount available 10yrs Fishing
Sauna Gym Boule Jacuzzi/spa Open terrace Languages
spoken: English,Portuguese,Spanish
CARDS: 💳 🏧 ⚑ 🌐

ST-DONAT-SUR-L'HERBASSE Drôme

★ ★ ★ Chartron
1 av Gambetta *26260*
☎ 475451182 FAX 475450136
(take Tain-l'Hermitage exit from A7 in the direction of Romans,
continue towards Chanos Curson then turn right & follow road
to St Donat-sur-l'Herbasse)

This former coaching inn is situated in the heart of the 'Drôme des Collines' and was completely renovated in 1990. With exposed brickwork on the outside, it features a contemporary interior and the well equipped bedrooms have modern facilities. The restaurant offers various truffle specialities, complemented by fine wines from the region.
Near river Near lake In town centre
7 en suite (bth/shr) TV in all bedrooms Mini-bar in all bedrooms Licensed Full central heating Open parking available Covered parking available (charged) Child discount available Open terrace Languages spoken: English
CARDS: ●● ■■ ⅈ ⓓ Travellers cheques

ST-GENIS-POUILLY Ain

★ ★ Climat de France
85 rte de la Faucille *06130*
☎ 450420520 Cen Res 164460123 FAX 450420814
(on D984 off N1)
This pleasant hotel features an attractive, modern interior where a cosy atmosphere creates the setting for a relaxing stay. Bedrooms are fitted with modern appointments, whilst the restaurant offers a choice from the plentiful buffet as well as traditional dishes.
Near river Forest area Near motorway
42 en suite (bth/shr) TV in all bedrooms STV Radio in rooms Direct dial from all bedrooms Full central heating Open parking available Open terrace Covered terrace Last d 22.00hrs Languages spoken: English & German
ROOMS: (room only) s fr 270FF; d fr 270FF ✷
MEALS: Continental breakfast 30FF Lunch 59-130FFalc Dinner 59-130FFalc✷
CARDS: ●● ■■ ⅈ ⓓ Travellers cheques

ST-JEAN-D'ARDIÈRES Rhône

★ ★ ★ Château de Pizay
rte de Villie Morgon *69220*
☎ 474665141 FAX 474696563
(From A6 exit 'Belleville' take N6 towards Mâcon to hotel on left)
Situated just 30 minutes from Lyon and Mâcon in the heart of Beaujolais country, this magnificent 14th century castle is surmounted by an imposing tower. There are a number of luxurious guest rooms with private terraces on the ground floor while others have views over the swimming pool. The restaurant serves a cuisine where delicate flavours blend with high quality ingredients and is augmented by the excellent vintage wines from the castle's private cellar.
Forest area Near motorway
Closed 24 Dec-2 Jan
62 en suite (bth/shr) (8 fmly) TV in all bedrooms STV Radio in rooms Direct dial from all bedrooms Mini-bar in all bedrooms Licensed Night porter Full central heating Air conditioning in bedrooms Open parking available Supervised Child discount available 12yrs Outdoor swimming pool Tennis Pool table Boule Bicycle rental Open terrace Last d 21.30hrs Languages spoken: English,German,Italian
ROOMS: (room only) s 535-700FF; d 655-1040FF
MEALS: Full breakfast 65FF Continental breakfast 65FF Lunch 200-395FF&alc Dinner 200-395FF&alc
CARDS: ●● ■■ ⅈ ⓓ Travellers cheques

ST-MARTIN-DE-BELLEVILLE Savoie

★ ★ ★ Novotel
pl de la Lombarde-Val Thorens *73440*
☎ 479000404 FAX 479000593
Novotel offer their clients good quality accommodation in modern, well equipped bedrooms and have refined restaurants serving good quality cuisine They have excellent business meeting and conference facilities and some have food and beverages available 24 hours a day. All their hotels have at least one bedroom for disabled guests.
In town centre
Closed Dec-Apr
104 rms (104 fmly) No smoking in 52 bedrooms TV in all bedrooms STV Radio in rooms Direct dial from all bedrooms Licensed Lift Night porter Full central heating Open parking available (charged) Covered parking available (charged) Supervised Child discount available 16yrs Solarium Pool table Open terrace yoga,snow scoot V meals Last d 22.00hrs Languages spoken: English,German,Japanese
MEALS: Full breakfast 50FF Lunch fr 145FF&alc Dinner fr 145FF&alc✷
CARDS: ●● ■■ ⅈ ⓓ

ST-PAUL-EN-CHABLAIS Haute-Savoie

★ ★ Bois Joli
74500
☎ 450736011 FAX 450736528
(From Thonon or Evian head towards St Paul and Bernex)
A pleasant hotel in a mountain valley offering guests spectacular views, a restful stay and fine food.
Near lake Near sea Forest area
Closed late Feb-late Mar & mid Oct-mid Dec
24 rms (20 bth/shr) 4 rooms in annexe (2 fmly) (24 with balcony) TV in all bedrooms Open parking available Child discount available Outdoor swimming pool (heated) Tennis Sauna Solarium Pool table Boule Bicycle rental Open terrace Last d 20.30hrs Languages spoken: English
ROOMS: (room only) s 280-360FF; d 320-360FF ✷
MEALS: Continental breakfast 40FF Lunch 98-230FF Dinner 98-230FF✷
CARDS: ●● ■■ ⅈ ⓓ

ST-PIERRE-DE-CHARTREUSE Isère

★ ★ L'Atre Fleuri
38380
☎ 4768868021 FAX 476886497
The hotel is close to the village of St Pierre-de-Chartreuse and has stunning views over the surrounding mountain peaks. The bedrooms are pleasantly appointed and there is a terrace overlooking a small mountain stream. The restaurant serves fine cuisine, including regional specialities.
Near river Forest area
Closed mid Oct-end Dec
7 en suite (bth/shr) Licensed Full central heating Open parking available Supervised Child discount available Open terrace Last d 21.00hrs Languages spoken: English, Spanish
MEALS: Full breakfast 50FF Continental breakfast 30FF Lunch 96-215FF&alc Dinner 96-215FF&alc✷
CARDS: ●● ⅈ Travellers cheques

ST-SORLIN-D'ARVES Savoie

★ ★ Beausoleil
73530
☎ 479577142 FAX 479597525
Excellent skiing country in winter, and splendid green scenery in summer, ideal for a holiday in either season. This cheerful chalet-style hotel offers individually appointed, cosy bedrooms which have excellent views over the surrounding countryside. The restaurant serves a choice of regional dishes with a hint of Savoy, prepared with fresh seasonal produce.
Near river Near lake Forest area
Closed May-late Jun & mid Sep-mid Dec
23 rms (21 bth/shr) (6 fmly) (15 with balcony) TV in all bedrooms STV Direct dial from all bedrooms Licensed Full central heating Open parking available Supervised Child discount available 10yrs Boule Bicycle rental Open terrace Last d 21.00hrs Languages spoken: English,Italian
ROOMS: (room only) s 195-220FF; d 230-270FF ✱
MEALS: Full breakfast 38FF Continental breakfast 38FF Lunch 98-160FF&alc Dinner 98-160FF&alc✱
CARDS: ⬤ ▤

STE-EULALIE Ardèche

★ ★ Hotel de la Poste
07510
☎ 475388109
The Hotel de la Poste is located in St Eulalie, a small mountain village, surrounded by grasslands, forests, and numerous little streams which provide the splendid scenery for a relaxing stay. The bedrooms are equipped with modern facilities and there is a shaded garden and a lounge with a good choice of reading material, as well as a restaurant.
Near river Near sea Forest area
Closed 1 Oct-30 Dec
10 rms (6 shr) (2 fmly) (1 with balcony) Direct dial from all bedrooms Licensed Full central heating Open parking available Supervised Child discount available 9yrs Boule Open terrace Last d 20.30hrs Languages spoken: English
MEALS: Continental breakfast 30FF Lunch 75-130FF Dinner 75-130FF✱

SAMOËNS Haute-Savoie

★ ★ ★ Les Sept Monts
pl des 7 Monts *74340*
☎ 450344058 FAX 450341389
Near river Near lake Forest area In town centre Near motorway
Closed 15 Sep-20 Dec & 15 Apr-1 Jun
31 en suite (bth/shr) 6 rooms in annexe (22 with balcony) TV in 18 bedrooms STV Licensed Lift Full central heating Open parking available Covered parking available (charged) Supervised Child discount available Indoor swimming pool (heated) Outdoor swimming pool (heated) Riding Sauna Solarium Gym Pool table Boule Mini-golf Bicycle rental Open terrace Covered terrace V meals Last d 21.00hrs Languages spoken: English,Italian
MEALS: Full breakfast 40FF Continental breakfast 35FF Lunch fr 100FF&alc Dinner fr 100FF&alc✱
CARDS: ⬤ ▤ ▤ Travellers cheques

SATILLIEU Ardèche

★ ★ ★ Gentilhommière (Best Western)
07290
☎ 475692323 FAX 475349192
Near river Forest area
49 en suite (bth/shr) 15 rooms in annexe TV in all bedrooms STV Direct dial from all bedrooms Licensed Lift Full central heating Open parking available Supervised Child discount available Indoor swimming pool (heated) Outdoor swimming pool (heated) Tennis Riding Sauna Solarium Gym Pool table Boule Mini-golf Jacuzzi/spa Bicycle rental Open terrace Covered terrace V meals Last d 20.30hrs Languages spoken: English
ROOMS: (room only) s 250-320FF; d 320-450FF
Reductions over 1 night
MEALS: Full breakfast 45FF Continental breakfast 45FF Lunch 90-240FF&alc Dinner 90-240FF&alc
CARDS: ⬤ ▤ Travellers cheques

SÉRÉZIN-DU-RHÔNE Rhône

★ ★ La Bourbonnaise
69360
☎ 478028058 FAX 478021739
Located 5 kilometres south of Lyon, and close to the main access routes, La Bourbonnaise has peacefully situated bedrooms and a choice of two restaurants with views over the garden. Because of its ideal location its is a good venue for an overnight stop en route to more southern holiday destinations.
Near river Near motorway
39 rms (34 bth/shr) 13 rooms in annexe (1 fmly) No smoking in 2 bedrooms TV in all bedrooms Radio in rooms Licensed Full central heating Open parking available Supervised Child discount available 12yrs Solarium Boule Bicycle rental Open terrace Covered terrace V meals Last d 21.45hrs Languages spoken: English,German
CARDS: ⬤ ▦ ▤ ⬤ CB Travellers cheques

SEVRIER Haute-Savoie

★ ★ La Fauconnière
Lieu-dit Letraz-Chuguet *74320*
☎ 450524118 FAX 450526333
The hotel is situated on the shores of the lake just two kilometres from Annecy, and welcomes its visitors in pleasant surroundings. It features comfortable bedrooms with modern appointments, whilst the restaurant serves a high standard of cooking by Jean-Claude Raffatin, who has presided over the kitchen for the last 20 years.
Near lake Near sea Near beach Forest area Near motorway
29 rms (4 bth 21 shr) (4 fmly) (8 with balcony) TV in all bedrooms Direct dial from all bedrooms Licensed Full central heating Open parking available Covered parking available Child discount available 10yrs Boule Open terrace V meals Last d 21.00hrs Languages spoken: English
MEALS: Full breakfast 39FF Lunch 110-200FF&alc Dinner 110-200FF&alc✱
CARDS: ⬤ ▤ ▤ ⬤ Travellers cheques

★ ★ Inter Hotel Beaurégard
rte d'Albertville *74320*
☎ 450524059 FAX 450524471
(from Annecy in direction of Albertvilleon N508)
The hotel Beauregard was renovated and extended in 1992 and stands just two kilometres from Annecy and the old town, on the banks of what is reputedly the cleanest lake in Europe. The

guest rooms - most with panoramic views - have functional, modern facilities, whilst the gardens with terraces and play area for children provide carefree relaxation. The restaurant serves a traditional cuisine where only the finest local produce is used.
Near lake Near sea Near beach Forest area Near motorway
Closed 15Dec-15Jan
46 rms (29 bth 16 shr) (12 fmly) (20 with balcony) TV in all bedrooms STV Direct dial from all bedrooms Licensed Lift Full central heating Open parking available Covered parking available (charged) Child discount available Boule Bicycle rental Open terrace Table tennis,water ski-ing Last d 21.25hrs Languages spoken: English
ROOMS: (room only) s 250-380FF; d 250-380FF ✱
MEALS: Full breakfast 37FF Lunch 97-195FF&alc Dinner 97-195FF&alc✱
CARDS: 💳 💳 💳 Travellers cheques

★ ★ Les Tonnelles
rte d'Albertville *74320*
☎ 450524158 FAX 450526005
Surrounded by a mountainous landscape with pastures and chestnut trees, and close to beautiful Lake Annecy, the 'Auberge Les Tonnelles' provides the relaxing setting for a carefree stay. In summer guests can enjoy lunch on the terrace at the foot of the mountain, and in winter there is the attractive dining room. Bedrooms are fitted with modern amenities and offer a good level of comfort, whilst the restaurant serves an array of regional specialities including fresh fish from the lake.
Near lake Forest area Near motorway
26 rms (9 bth 1 shr) 7 rooms in annexe (5 fmly) (2 with balcony) TV in all bedrooms STV Direct dial from all bedrooms Licensed Full central heating Open parking available Child discount available 10yrs Open terrace Last d 21.45hrs Languages spoken: English
CARDS: 💳 💳 💳 Travellers cheques

★ ★ Rhône
10 quai Charles de Gaulle *01420*
☎ 450592030
This family hotel, where the accent is on informality, has a traditional decor where comfortable bedrooms are fitted with modern amenities and provide an adequate level of comfort. The restaurant has a good reputation in the area and offers a classic cuisine. Weather permitting meals are served on the terrace with fine views over the river.
Near river Forest area In town centre Near motorway
10 rms (5 bth/shr) (1 fmly) TV in all bedrooms STV Licensed Full central heating Outdoor swimming pool (heated) Fishing Boule Open terrace Languages spoken: English,Spanish
MEALS: Full breakfast 30FF Lunch 95-150FF✱
CARDS: 💳 💳 Eurocard Travellers cheques

★ ★ Climat de France
15 rue Docteur Schweitzer *38180*
☎ 476217612 Čen Řes 164460123 FAX 476217880
(off A480 junction 5B)
Situated two kilometres from the centre of town the hotel stands at the foot of the Mouchererotte. Twelve kilometres from the nearest ski station, it features comfortable guest accommodation, a spacious sun terrace and a choice of leisure facilities. The restaurant serves a popular buffet as well as a choice of traditional dishes.

Near river Forest area Near motorway
45 en suite (bth/shr) TV in all bedrooms Radio in rooms Direct dial from all bedrooms Licensed Night porter Full central heating Open parking available Supervised Tennis Sauna Pool table Mini-golf Open terrace Covered terrace Languages spoken: English & German
CARDS: 💳 💳

★ ★ Ferme St-Michel
26130
☎ 475981066 FAX 475981909
The 'Ferme St-Michel' dates back to the 16th-century and is located in the heart of the 'Drôme Provençal' surrounded by vineyards and lavender fields. All the bedrooms have private facilities and are attractively furnished, whilst the vaulted restaurant serves a high standard of honest, home-cooking including a choice of truffle specialities. There is no shortage of sights in the area; the castle of the famous Marquis de Sévigné, and Château Suze de la Rousse with its world famous wine-university, are well worth a visit.
Forest area
14 rms (13 bth) (1 fmly) TV in all bedrooms Direct dial from all bedrooms Full central heating Open parking available Child discount available Outdoor swimming pool Boule Open terrace Last d 21.15hrs
CARDS: 💳 💳 Travellers cheques

★ ★ Hotel du Parc
73500
☎ 479205173 FAX 479205173
Near river Forest area
Closed Sep-22 Dec & 31 Mar-29 Jun
30 rms (24 fmly) (10 with balcony) Direct dial from 10 bedrooms Licensed Full central heating Open parking available Supervised Child discount available 12yrs Solarium Pool table Boule Open terrace V meals Languages spoken: English,Italian
CARDS: 💳 💳 Travellers cheques

★ ★ Relais du Château
26790
☎ 475048707 FAX 475982600
This handsome residence is situated in a park of 12000 square metres, opposite the Château de Suze-la-Rousse. It has bright, spacious bedrooms with views of the château or the park, and a restaurant which serves a distinct Provençale cuisine as well as an array of seasonal dishes. Breakfast and dinner can also be enjoyed on the shaded terrace with the lingering scent of the surrounding lavender.
Near river Forest area
Closed early Jan-end Feb & early Nov-mid Nov
39 en suite (bth/shr) (4 fmly) (8 with balcony) TV available Licensed Lift Full central heating Open parking available Supervised Outdoor swimming pool Tennis Boule Bicycle rental Open terrace V meals Last d 22.00hrs Languages spoken: English,German,Italian
CARDS: 💳 💳 💳 💳 Travellers cheques

TALLOIRES Haute-Savoie

★ ★ ★ ★ Auberge du Père Bise
rte du Port *74290*
☎ 450607201 FAX 450607305
This delightful country inn has been in the capable hands of
the Bise family for four generations and offers a warm and
friendly atmosphere with comfortable accommodation and
excellent food. Splendidly located on the shores of Lac Annecy
it features elegantly decorated bedrooms with good quality
furnishings and fabrics, as well as luxurious en suite facilities.
The rich cuisine incorporates regional specialities and fresh
fish delicacies.
Near lake Near sea Near beach Forest area
Closed 2 Nov-8 Feb
34 en suite (bth/shr) 24 rooms in annexe (6 fmly) (20 with
balcony) TV in all bedrooms STV Direct dial from all
bedrooms Mini-bar in all bedrooms Licensed Lift Full central
heating Open parking available Supervised Child discount
available Boule Open terrace V meals Last d 21.00hrs
Languages spoken: English,German,Italian,Japanese
CARDS: 💳 💳 💳 💳 Travellers cheques

★ ★ ★ ★ Le Cottage
Au Bord du Lac *74290*
☎ 556607110 FAX 550607751
Le Cottage offers stunning views over the lake, and
surrounded by flower-filled gardens it provides a delightful
setting for a memorable holiday. Attractive bedrooms with
modern facilities are complemented by a renowned, authentic
cuisine.
Near lake Near sea Near beach Forest area
Closed approx Oct-Apr
35 en suite (bth/shr) Some rooms in annexe (20 with balcony)
TV in all bedrooms STV Direct dial from all bedrooms
Licensed Lift Night porter Full central heating Open parking
available Covered parking available (charged) Supervised
Child discount available 12yrs Outdoor swimming pool
(heated) Boule Bicycle rental Open terrace V meals Last d
21.30hrs Languages spoken: English,German,Italian
ROOMS: (room only) d 450-1100FF ✱ **Reductions over 1
night Special breaks**
MEALS: Full breakfast 70FF Lunch 140-270FF&alc Dinner 140-
270FF&alc
CARDS: 💳 💳 💳 💳 Travellers cheques

★ ★ ★ ★ Prés du Lac
Marie-Paule Conan *74290*
☎ 450607611 FAX 450607342
(From Annecy follow road to 'Centre Congrès, Veyrier,
Menthon and Talloires)
The hotel occupies a privileged position with a private beach,
on the banks of the lake. The bedrooms with private terraces
and balconies, are divided over three houses, and overlook the
lake. Breakfast is served at any time in the morning in the
apartments or the garden and light refreshments are available
from room service during the day. Guests can relax on the
private beach whilst taking in the splendid natural
surroundings and, in addition, there is a reading and day
room, as well as a large choice of leisure facilities and
restaurants nearby.
Near lake Forest area In town centre Near motorway
Closed Nov-1 Mar
16 en suite (bth/shr) 7 rooms in annexe (3 fmly) (15 with
balcony) TV in all bedrooms STV Radio in rooms Direct dial
from all bedrooms Mini-bar in all bedrooms Room-safe
Licensed Night porter Full central heating Air conditioning in

bedrooms Open parking available Covered parking available
(charged) Supervised Child discount available Tennis
Solarium Mini-golf Open terrace Languages spoken:
English,German,Italian
ROOMS: (room only) d 860-1200FF
CARDS: 💳 💳 💳 💳 Travellers cheques

★ ★ ★ Villa des Fleurs
rte du Port *74290*
☎ 450607114 FAX 450607406
This turn-of-the century mansion is situated in wooded
grounds near the Talloires Bay and is surrounded by
mountains. It was discovered on a fine autumn morning, by
the present owners Charles and Marie-France Jaegler, who
transformed it into an inn of outstanding character. The
bedrooms are on two floors and are equipped with modern
facilities, whilst the restaurant has earned many
recommendations in French and international food guides.
The menu features a selection of regional dishes prepared with
a combination of traditional and imaginative ingredients.
Near lake Near sea Forest area
Closed 15 Nov-15 Dec
8 en suite (bth/shr) (1 fmly) TV in all bedrooms Direct dial
from all bedrooms Mini-bar in all bedrooms Licensed Full
central heating Open parking available Supervised Child
discount available 10yrs Golf Bicycle rental Last d 21.30hrs
Languages spoken: English,German
ROOMS: (room only) d 450-480FF ✱
MEALS: Continental breakfast 60FF Lunch fr 150FF&alc
Dinner fr 150FF&alc✱
CARDS: 💳 💳 💳 Travellers cheques

TAPONAS Rhône

★ ★ Auberge des Sablons
69220
☎ 474663480 FAX 474663522
Surrounded by lush foliage and flowers, this recently
constructed hotel is situated at 300 metres from the River
Saône. The peaceful bedrooms have fine views of the
countryside and are equipped with modern facilities. Two
country-style dining-rooms and a shaded terrace provide the
homely setting for a traditional cuisine and regional specialities.
Near river Near beach Forest area Near motorway
15 en suite (bth/shr) TV in all bedrooms Direct dial from all
bedrooms Licensed Night porter Full central heating Open
parking available Supervised Child discount available Fishing
Open terrace V meals Last d 21.30hrs Languages spoken:
English
MEALS: Full breakfast 34FF Lunch 85-220FFalc Dinner fr
150FFalc✱
CARDS: 💳 💳 Travellers cheques

TASSIN-LA-DEMI-LUNE Rhône

★ ★ ★ Novotel Lyon Tassin Vaise
av Victor Hugo *69160*
☎ 478646869 FAX 478646111
Novotel offer their clients good quality accommodation in modern, well equipped bedrooms and have refined restaurants serving good quality cuisine They have excellent business meeting and conference facilities and some have food and beverages available 24 hours a day. All their hotels have at least one bedroom for disabled guests.
Near motorway
104 en suite (bth) (39 fmly) No smoking in 26 bedrooms TV in all bedrooms STV Radio in rooms Direct dial from all bedrooms Mini-bar in all bedrooms Licensed Lift Night porter Full central heating Air conditioning in bedrooms Open parking available Covered parking available (charged) Child discount available 16yrs Outdoor swimming pool Open terrace Last d 24.00hrs Languages spoken:
English,German,Italian,Spanish
CARDS: ● ■ ▆ ● Travellers cheques

THUEYTS Ardèche

★ ★ Des Marronniers
07330
☎ 475364016 FAX 475364802
The hotel is located in an authentic village in the Ardèche region, surrounded by the volcanic landscape of the Cévennes mountain range. The cosy interior features a comfortable lounge, bedrooms with modern facilities, and a restaurant with a charming, shaded terrace. The surrounding area has numerous sporting activities to offer as well as cultural points of interest.
Near river Forest area In town centre Near motorway
Closed 21 Dec-6 Mar
19 rms TV in all bedrooms Direct dial from all bedrooms Licensed Full central heating Open parking available Child discount available 10yrs Outdoor swimming pool Boule Open terrace Last d 21.00hrs Languages spoken: English,German
CARDS: ▆

TOURNON Ardèche

★ ★ ★ Hotel du Château
Quai Marc-Seguin *07300*
☎ 475086022 FAX 475070295
Close to the banks of the Rhône, comfortable rooms and tempting menus await guests at Hotel du Château.
Near river In town centre Near motorway
14 en suite (bth/shr) TV in all bedrooms STV Direct dial from all bedrooms Mini-bar in all bedrooms Licensed Full central heating Covered parking available (charged) Supervised Open terrace Covered terrace V meals Last d 21.00hrs Languages spoken: English
ROOMS: (room only) s fr 290FF; d 330-370FF
MEALS: Continental breakfast 40FF Lunch 100-295FF&alc Dinner 100-295FF&alc
CARDS: ● ■ ▆ ● Travellers cheques

VALMOREL Savoie

★ ★ ★ Planchamp
Hameau Planchamp *73260*
☎ 479098391 FAX 479098393
The hotel is located in Valmorel which is an equally popular resort in summer as in winter. It features fully equipped apartments which provide spacious accommodation with excellent views, and are complemented by a full range of services to ensure a relaxing stay. The informal restaurant serves an array of specialities from a wide repertoire of dishes.
Near river Forest area Near motorway
Closed 15 Apr-1 Jul, 30 Aug-15 Dec
37 en suite (bth/shr) 12 rooms in annexe (8 fmly) (8 with balcony) TV in all bedrooms STV Direct dial from all bedrooms Mini-bar in 25 bedrooms Licensed Full central heating Air conditioning in bedrooms Child discount available Tennis Fishing Riding Solarium Pool table Boule Bicycle rental Open terrace V meals Last d 22.00hrs Languages spoken: English,German,Spanish
ROOMS: s 410-500FF; d 540-660FF ✱
MEALS: Lunch fr 170FF&alc Dinner 170-180FFalc✱
CARDS: ● ▆ Travellers cheques

VAL-THORENS Savoie

★ ★ ★ Fitz Roy Hotel
73440
☎ 479000478 FAX 479000611
Located in Val Thorens, in the heart of des Trois Vallées, this large chalet-style hotel features a stunning interior where wood-panelling, paintings, and intimate public areas create the cosy, relaxing setting for a enjoyable holiday. Visitors are welcomed by a roaring log fire in the main foyer, furnished with comfortable armchairs, whilst the bedrooms are decorated in pastel shades and equipped with excellent modern amenities. A sumptuous dinner is served in the candlelit restaurant after a day skiing and enjoying fresh mountain air, and a large choice of fitness and leisure facilities as well as beauty treatments are available in the hotel.
Closed Dec-5 May
36 en suite (bth) (3 fmly) (36 with balcony) TV in all bedrooms STV Radio in rooms Direct dial from all bedrooms Mini-bar in all bedrooms Licensed Lift Night porter Full central heating Child discount available Indoor swimming pool (heated) Sauna Solarium Gym Jacuzzi/spa Open terrace Beauty salon Last d 22.00hrs Languages spoken: English,German,Spanish
CARDS: ● ■ ▆ ●

VARCES-ALLIÈRES-ET-RISSET Isère

★ ★ ★ Relais l'Escale
pl de la République, RN 75 *38760*
☎ 476728019 FAX 476729258
The hotel is situated at 15 minutes from Grenoble, and consists of a number of attractive chalets scattered around the delightful garden. Fitted with modern amenities, they provide comfortable accommodation and a restful night's sleep. The restaurant serves gourmet cuisine in the informal dining room, or, weather permitting, under the mature plane trees in the garden.
Forest area In town centre Near motorway
Closed Early Nov, Sun evening & Mon RS Half board obligatory at high season
7 en suite (bth) (7 with balcony) TV in all bedrooms Radio in rooms Direct dial from all bedrooms Mini-bar in all bedrooms Licensed Air conditioning in bedrooms Open parking available Supervised Outdoor swimming pool Solarium Open terrace Last d 21.00hrs Languages spoken: English,German,Italian
ROOMS: (room only) s fr 490FF; d 490-590FF
MEALS: Full breakfast 50FF Lunch 145-298FF&alc Dinner 145-290FF&alc
CARDS: ● ■ ▆ Travellers cheques

VEYRIER-DU-LAC Haute-Savoie

★ ★ ★ ★ Auberge de l'Eridan
13 Vieille rte de Pensières *74290*
☎ 450602400 FAX 450602363
Surrounded by a park, the hotel is set on shores of Lac d'Annecy against the backdrop of the mountains. The proprietor, Marc Veyrat, loves the colour blue, which is apparent in the elegant interior of this establishment. The modern, spacious bedrooms have private terraces and provide the highest level of comfort. The lovely dining room has a panoramic view of the lake and mountains and offers the ideal setting to enjoy an outstanding meal in delightful surroundings.
Near lake
11 en suite (bth/shr) TV in all bedrooms STV Radio in rooms Mini-bar in all bedrooms Licensed Lift Night porter Full central heating Air conditioning in bedrooms Open parking available Covered parking available Supervised Open terrace Last d 22.00hrs Languages spoken: English,German,Italian,Spanish
CARDS: ●● ■■ ▆▆ ◑ Travellers cheques

★ ★ ★ ★ Demeure de Chavoire
71 rte d'Annecy - Chavoire *74290*
☎ 450600438 FAX 450600536
When guests cross the threshold of 'La Demeure de Chavoire' they receive a warm and friendly welcome in an interior which has been decorated with their well-being in mind. Magnificent parquet flooring in the lounge and splendid flower displays, wood-panelling and meticulous attention to detail create a country-house atmosphere. The bedrooms are individually styled, furnished with period pieces, and feature many little extras, whilst modern amenities blend harmoniously with the elegant fabrics and furnishings.
Near lake Near sea Near beach Forest area Near motorway
13 en suite (bth/shr) (3 fmly) (2 with balcony) TV in all bedrooms Radio in rooms Direct dial from all bedrooms Mini-bar in all bedrooms Licensed Night porter Full central heating Open parking available Supervised Open terrace Languages spoken: English
CARDS: ●● ■■ ▆▆ ◑

VIENNE Isère

★ ★ ★ Château des 7 Fontaines
Les 7 Fontaines *38200*
☎ 474852570 FAX 474317447
The château is set on the Vienne Hills in the Rhône Valley, and surrounded by a lush green park, it provides a peaceful setting for a relaxing stay. It features spacious bedrooms, decorated in a discreet fashion and equipped with modern appointments, complemented by indoor and outdoor leisure facilities.
Near motorway
Closed Oct-May
16 en suite (bth/shr) (2 fmly) TV in all bedrooms Direct dial from all bedrooms Licensed Night porter Full central heating Open parking available Child discount available Tennis Solarium Boule Open terrace Languages spoken: English,German,Spanish
CARDS: ●● ■■ ▆▆ ◑

VILLIÉ-MORGON Rhône

★ ★ Villon
Le Bourg *69910*
☎ 474691616 FAX 474691681
In the very heart of the Beaujolais vineyards and surrounded by an extensive park with splendid mature trees, the hotel offers pleasant guest rooms equipped with modern facilities and a restaurant with fine views of the park which serves a high quality gourmet cuisine, accompanied by the excellent wines of the region.
Forest area In town centre
45 en suite (bth/shr) (2 fmly) (15 with balcony) TV in all bedrooms Direct dial from all bedrooms Licensed Night porter Full central heating Open parking available Child discount available 11yrs Outdoor swimming pool Tennis Boule Open terrace Last d 21.00hrs Languages spoken: English,German
MEALS: Full breakfast 38FF Lunch 110-235FF&alc Dinner 110-235FF&alc✱
CARDS: ●● ▆▆ Travellers cheques

VIOLAY Loire

★ ★ Perrier
pl de l'Église *42780*
☎ 474639101 FAX 474639177
Entirely renovated in 1991, the hotel is situated in a small village at an altitude of 830 metres. It features a peaceful interior, where most of the bedrooms have modern amenities and provide straight-forward comfort. The restaurant offers high quality, enjoyable dishes of good flavour.
Near lake Forest area In town centre Near motorway
10 rms (8 bth) TV in all bedrooms Licensed Full central heating Covered parking available Child discount available 12yrs Open terrace Last d 14.00hrs
MEALS: Full breakfast 35FF Continental breakfast 35FF Lunch 60-168FF&alc Dinner 80-168FF✱
CARDS: ▆▆

VONNAS Ain

★ ★ ★ ★ Georges Blanc
pl du Marché *01540*
☎ 474509090 FAX 474500880
Situated in Vonnas, this charming traditional establishment offers 20th-century comfort combined with lavish hospitality of by-gone times. Its delightful interior with exposed beams, period furniture and authentic tapestries features comfortable bedrooms with private facilities, whilst the beautiful restaurant serves outstanding cuisine, complemented by fine examples from the wine list .
Near river
Closed 2 Jan-10 Feb
48 en suite (bth/shr) (15 fmly) (12 with balcony) TV in all bedrooms STV Mini-bar in all bedrooms Lift Night porter Full central heating Air conditioning in bedrooms Open parking available Supervised Outdoor swimming pool (heated) Golf Tennis Fishing Mini-golf Bicycle rental Open terrace Last d 21.30hrs Languages spoken: English,German,Spanish
MEALS: Full breakfast 105FF Lunch 460-730FF&alc Dinner 460-730FF&alc✱
CARDS: ●● ■■ ▆▆ ◑ Travellers cheques

Taking your mobile phone to France?
See page 11

RHÔNE ALPES

The Castles of the Rhône

The Rhône Alpes region has over 400 castles. One of the oldest is Château des Allinges. Positioned on the hill of Allinges, this site of pilgrimage for St-François-de-Sales has an 11th-century chapel with frescos which are the oldest surviving pictorial art in Savoie. Château de Sur-le-Comtal, a fortified castle built by the Forez Counts, also originally dates from the 11th century, containing several splendidly decorated rooms. Built at high altitude by the Dauphins of Vienne, the 13th-century Château des Allymes at Ambérieu-en-Bugey is a memorable example of medieval military architecture, and has now been adapted to hold archaeological and historical exhibitions. Tour de Crest, in the Drôme province, is another example of fine medieval architecture, yet its principal claim to fame is for having the highest dungeon in France.

Lyon

Capital of Rhône Alpes, Lyon is France's second largest city. A major centre of historical and cultural significance, it is divided into nine districts. The Old Lyon quarters of Saint Jean, Saint-Georges and Saint Paul comprise an exceptional collection of 15th and 17th-century Renaissance buildings, huddled together in the narrow streets, once the heart of the old city's thriving political and intellectual life. In contrast, the Presqu'Ile is a pedestrian-only haven for shoppers, including many establishments which will be

The Basilique Notre-Dame in the Fourvière district of Lyon.

of interest to collectors of antiques. Museums and galleries include the Musée des Beaux Arts which is the largest in France after the Louvre, and the Institut Lumière, devoted to the innovative work of early film pioneer Louis Lumière. Also, as the "world capital of gastronomy", Lyon boasts the largest number of star French chefs.

Aquitaine

Aquitaine is situated in the basin of the Garonne extending inland to the Dordogne, between the Atlantic and the Pyrénées. It is a region of huge variety, from mountains and valleys to vast surf-washed beaches and shady forests, as well as countless leisure and sporting opportunities. There are many reminders of the Renaissance and Middle Ages, particularly in the hills of Perigord, Agen and the Basque country which are dotted with castles, monuments and dwellings from prehistory. Towns such as Pau and Bordeaux are rich in medieval and classical heritage and contain many museums documenting the area's history. Festivals are excellent occasions to experience firsthand local traditions and sample the many gastronomic delights.

Two contrasting scenes of Aquitaine's rich heritage. (Top): The Lascaux II caves, which contain exact replicas of the prehistoric cave paintings which were discovered at the nearby village of Lascaux.

(Bottom): Two colourful characters at a fair in Bayonne, which has a strong Basque heritage.

ESSENTIAL FACTS

DÉPARTEMENTS:	Dordogne, Gironde, Landes, Lot-et-Garonne, Pyrénées-Atlantiques
PRINCIPAL TOWNS	Agen, Bayonne, Bergerac, Biarritz, Bordeaux, Dax, Mont-de-Marsan, Pau, Périgueux, Sarlat
PLACES TO VISIT:	Caves at Betharram-Ste Pé, Combarelles, Font-de-Gaume, Sare, Isturiz & Oxocelhaya; prehistoric sites in the Vézère valley; the cliffs at Vautours; narrow-gauge railways at Artouste Fabreges & La Rhune; St-Jean-Pied-de-Port, a 13th century town with Bishops' Prison; St-Jean-de-Luz including waxwork museum & Florenia floral valley; Kakouetta Gorge nr Ste-Engrâce.
REGIONAL TOURIST OFFICE	23 Parvis des Chartrons, 33074 Bordeaux. Tel 05 56017000 Fax 05 56017007. E.mail: Tourisme@cr-aquitaine.fr
LOCAL GASTRONOMIC DELIGHTS	goose or duck confit, foie gras, woodpigeon, wild boar, hare, trout, salmon, garbure - a rich, local stew, charcuterie, Bayonne ham, sauce béarnaise, poule au pot - a chicken casserole, Béarn Pastis - a cake not a drink, cheeses, Pyrénéen chocolates - with an ice-cool filling, lamprey, truffles.
DRINKS	Bordeaux wines from Bergerac, Medoc, Sauternes, St-Emilion, Graves; brandy from Armagnac; rosé from Béarn

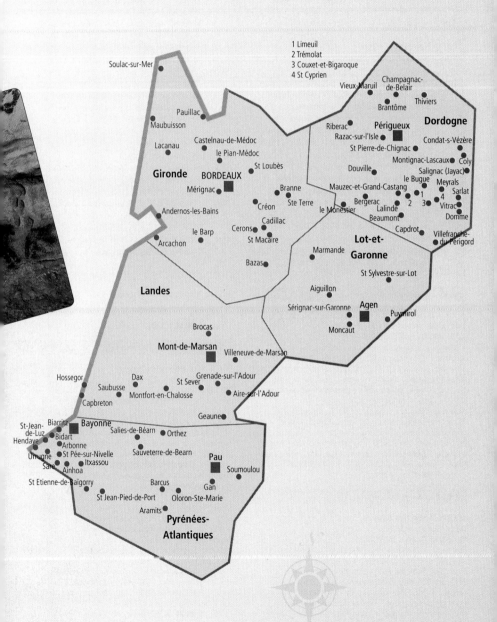

EVENTS & FESTIVALS

Feb Bordeaux Antiques Fair; St Macaire Carnival; Bazas Traditional Promenade des Boeufs Gras

Mar Biarritz Carnival; Béarnais Carnival at Pau; Bayonne Ham Fair; Lacanau Windsurf Festival; St Emilion Concert & Wine Tasting

Apr Biarritz Musical Fair (classical); Bordeaux International Festival of Young Soloists; Ste Terre Fish Festival;

May Soulac-sur-Mer Theatre Festival; Thivier foie gras market

June Pau Festival; St-Sever International Folklore Festival; Aire sur l'Adour Feria; Bordeaux Wine Fair; St-Sever Feria; Mourenx Celebrations; St Emilion Vine Flowering Festivals; Montflaquin wine & cheese market;

July Terrasson Puppet Festival; Mont-de-Marsan Flamenco Festival; Oloron-Ste-Marie Jazz Festival; Biarritz International Folk Festival; Festival around Bergerac; Bayonne Jazz Festival; Capbreton Storytelling Festival; Perigord Noir Festival (Dordogne music); Montignac World Folklore Festival; Andernos les-Bains Jazz Festival; Sarlat Theatre Festival; St-Jean de Luz Tunafish Festival; Biarritz Surf Festival; Bayonne Medieval Fair; Orthez Fair & Cavalcade; Mont de Marsan Feria; Pau

Festival; St-Etienne de Baigorry Basque Game Festival; Son et Lumière at Bazas & Castillon la Bataille; Eymet Medieval Festival; La Junte de Roncal (*traditional Pyrenean celebrations*)

Aug Bayonne Festival; Biarritz Andalusian Feria; Oloron-Ste-Marie Pyrenean Folk Festival; Périgueux Mime Festival; Uzeste Art & Music festival; Marmande Song & Music Festival; Gujan-Mestras Oyster Fair; St Palais Basque Tug-of-War Festival; Arcachon Ocean Festival; Montflaquin Medieval Festival

Sep Dax Holy Art Festival; St-Sever Crossover Music Festival; Biarritz classical & modern dance festival; Oloron-Ste-Marie "La Garburade"; Eugénie-les-Bains Imperial Festival; Marathon of Médoc & Graves Châteaux; Salies de Béarn Salt Festival; Aramits Shepherds' Festival; Siros Song Festival (local dialect)

Oct St-Jean de Luz Country Choir Festival; Espelette Capsicum Pepper Festiva; Geaune Vintage Festival; Marcillac Vintage Festival

Nov Sarlat Film Festival; Hossegar European Kite Festival; Maubuisson Armistice Sailing Grand Prix

Dec Bazas Traditional Christmas Celebration; Monségur foie gras market

---

AGEN Lot-et-Garonne

★ ★ ★ ★ **Hotel Chateau des Jacobins**
1 ter, pl des Jacobins, 2 r Jacob *47000*
☎ 553470331 FAX 553470280
The hotel is centrally situated opposite the 12th-century Jacobine church in peaceful surroundings. The comfortable bedrooms have modern amenities and are decorated with rich silks and velvets in keeping with the style of the original building. Close to several golf-courses and organised visits of the area can be arranged on request.
Near river Near lake In town centre Near motorway
15 en suite (bth/shr) (1 fmly) (1 with balcony) TV in all bedrooms Direct-dial available Mini-bar in all bedrooms Full central heating Air conditioning in bedrooms Open parking available Supervised Languages spoken: English & Spanish
Rooms: (room only) s 400-450FF; d 550-600FF ✱
Cards: ✺ ▦ ▅ Travellers cheques

AIGUILLON Lot-et-Garonne

★ ★ **Le Jardin des Gygnes**
rte de Villeneuve *47190*
☎ 553796002 FAX 553881022
(from A62 exit6, take direction Aiguillon and avoid 'centre-ville'. Hotel on road to Villeneuve on leaving town)
Near river Near lake Forest area Near motorway
24 en suite (bth/shr) (5 fmly) (9 with balcony) TV in all bedrooms Direct dial from all bedrooms Full central heating Open parking available Child discount available 12yrs Outdoor swimming pool Fishing Solarium Boule Bicycle rental Open terrace Covered terrace Last d 21.30hrs Languages spoken: English,Spanish

Rooms: (room only) s 170-245FF; d 195-280FF
Meals: Full breakfast 32FF Lunch 60-165FF&alc Dinner 60-165FF&alc✱
Cards: ✺ ▦ ▅ Travellers cheques

AINHOA Pyrénées-Atlantiques

★ ★ ★ **Argi Eder** (Best Western)
rte de la Chapelle *64250*
☎ 559937200 FAX 559937213
Amidst the stunning natural scenery of the Basque countryside, situated at the foot of the Pyrenees and just 200m outside the attractive village of Aïnhoa, the Hotel Argi-Eder offers its visitors comfortable bedrooms with en suite bathrooms - some of them with therapeutic baths and minibar. A cocktail can be enjoyed before sampling some of the exclusive dishes for which the proprietor-chef is famous in the region. In addition, there are banqueting facilities, a swimming pool and two tennis courts.
Forest area
Closed mid Nov-end Mar RS 15 Jun-14 Sep (half-board only)
36 en suite (bth/shr) (4 fmly) (30 with balcony) TV in all bedrooms Direct dial from all bedrooms Mini-bar in all bedrooms Licensed Full central heating Open parking available Supervised Child discount available 12yrs Outdoor swimming pool Boule Bicycle rental Open terrace V meals Last d 21.00hrs Languages spoken: English & Spanish
Rooms: (room only) s 550-600FF; d 600-650FF
Meals: Full breakfast 52FF Continental breakfast 54FF Lunch 135-235FF&alc Dinner 135-235FF&alc
Cards: ✺ ▦ ▅ ➋ JCB Travellers cheques

★ ★ ★ **Ithurria**
pl du Fronton *64250*
☎ 559299211 FAX 559298128
The Hotel Ithurria is set in Aïnhoa, without a doubt one of the most picturesque villages in the Basque Country. Situated on the walled market square, this former 17th-century coaching inn is classified as an historic monument and serves a choice of delicious dishes prepared with fresh local produce in a friendly, relaxed atmosphere. The bedrooms are attractively furnished in local style and provide fine views over the rolling countryside.
Near river Near lake Near sea Near beach In town centre
Closed early Nov-end March
27 en suite (bth/shr) (3 fmly) (13 with balcony) TV in all bedrooms Direct dial from all bedrooms Licensed Full central heating Open parking available Outdoor swimming pool
Squash Sauna Gym Boule Open terrace Last d 21.15hrs
CARDS: ● ▬ ▬ ● Travellers cheques

★ ★ **Oppoca**
r Principale *64250*
☎ 559299072 FAX 559298103
This 17th century inn is situated near the 'place du fronton' in the village of Aïnhoa in the Basque country. It features comfortable bedrooms with views of the Pyrenees, which are fitted with modern facilities, and the restaurant serves a choice of regional dishes, complemented by fine wines.
Near river Near lake Forest area Near motorway
12 en suite (bth/shr) (5 with balcony) Licensed Full central heating Open parking available Child discount available 10yrs
Open terrace Last d 21.00hrs Languages spoken: English
ROOMS: (room only) d 220-320FF ✱
MEALS: Full breakfast 35FF Lunch 95-175FF&alc Dinner 95-175FF&alc✱
CARDS: ● ▬ Travellers cheques

★ ★ ★ **Hotel Laminak**
rte de St-Pée *64210*
☎ 559419540 FAX 559418765
(From A63 exit 4, follow signs Biarritz Centre and then Arbonne)
Situated between the sea and mountains, this old farmhouse offers a delightful setting for your holiday. Charming guest-rooms provide maximum comfort, the lounges afford a panoramic view over the rolling countryside, and a generous breakfast comprising home-made jams and pastries is served on the colonial-style veranda or terrace.
Near river Near lake Near beach Forest area Near motorway
Closed mid Nov-mid Mar
10 en suite (bth/shr) TV in all bedrooms Direct dial from all bedrooms Mini-bar in all bedrooms Room-safe Licensed Full central heating Open parking available Supervised Open terrace Covered terrace Languages spoken: English, Spanish
CARDS: ● ▬ ▬ Travellers cheques

★ ★ **Hotel de Gascogne**
79 cours Héricart-de-Thury *33120*
☎ 556834252 FAX 556831555
Near sea Forest area In town centre Near motorway
33 rms (32 bth/shr) 5 rooms in annexe (4 fmly) (10 with balcony) TV available Licensed Lift Full central heating
Open parking available Last d 23.00hrs Languages spoken: English & Spanish
CARDS: ● ▬ ▬ ● Travellers cheques

★ ★ **Le Nautic**
20 bd de la Plage *33120*
☎ 556830148 FAX 556830467

The hotel is ideally situated just a few steps away from the yachting harbour and the beaches. A whole range of sporting facilities such as tennis courts, 3 18-hole golf courses, sailing and horse-riding can be found in the vicinity. The friendly staff will also be happy to assist you in booking offshore fishing or a cruise. The bedrooms offer a good level of comfort and have modern facilities, and there is one apartment with kitchenette and large patio and a superb view of the harbour.
Near sea Near beach Forest area In town centre
44 en suite (bth/shr) (1 fmly) (39 with balcony) TV in all bedrooms Direct dial from all bedrooms Licensed Lift Night porter Full central heating Open parking available
Supervised Child discount available 10yrs Close by
Languages spoken: English & Spanish
ROOMS: (room only) d 295-450FF
CARDS: ● ▬ ▬ ● Travellers cheques

★ ★ ★ **Villa Térésa-Hôtel Semiramis**
4 allée de Rebsomen *33120*
☎ 556832587 FAX 557522241
The hotel is classified as an historic monument and has the discreet charm and refined architecture of a typical Arcachonnaise villa. Guests can enjoy meals prepared with fresh market produce, under the watchful eyes of the cherubs painted on the ceiling of the elegant restaurant, or relax by the swimming pool near the Petit Pavillon in the garden.
Near sea Near beach Forest area
20 en suite (bth/shr) 8 rooms in annexe (3 fmly) (12 with balcony) TV in all bedrooms Direct dial from all bedrooms
Full central heating Open parking available No children 2yrs
Outdoor swimming pool Open terrace Last d 21.0hrs
Languages spoken: English & Spanish
ROOMS: (room only) s 450-720FF; d 450-720FF
Reductions over 1 night Special breaks
MEALS: Full breakfast 63FF Continental breakfast 63FF
Dinner fr 180FF✱
CARDS: ▬ ▬ Travellers cheques

★ ★ **Hotel Chilo**
64130
☎ 559289079 FAX 559289310
(From Pau take D24 towards Mauleon)
The hotel Chilo has been in the hands of the same family for three generations, and is situated in the heart of a village surrounded by the breathtaking scenery of the Pyrenees. It features a cosy interior and individually styled attractive *contd.*

bedrooms, providing a soothing atmosphere for a relaxing stay. Delicious dishes are served in the restaurant.
Forest area
Closed 15 Jan-10 Feb & 1 wk end Mar
10 en suite (bth/shr) 2 rooms in annexe (1 fmly) TV in all bedrooms Direct dial from all bedrooms Licensed Full central heating Open parking available Child discount available Outdoor swimming pool Boule Open terrace V meals Last d 21.30hrs Languages spoken: English, Spanish, Portuguese
CARDS: ●● ■■ ■■ ❿ Travellers cheques

BARP, LE Gironde

★ ★ Le Resinier
N10 *33114*
☎ 556886007 FAX 556886737
Located on the edges of the Landes de Gascogne regional park. It features pleasant bedrooms with modern amenities and serves a high standard of home-cooking incorporating fresh local produce.
Near river Near lake Near sea Near beach Forest area Near motorway
TV in 9 bedrooms Mini-bar in 9 bedrooms Full central heating Open parking available Child discount available Open terrace Last d 22.00hrs Languages spoken: English, Spanish

BAYONNE Pyrénées-Atlantiques

★ ★ ★ Hotel Loustau
1 pl de la République *64100*
☎ 559550808 FAX 559556936
Located in the centre of Bayonne, on the banks of the river Adour, the hotel offers its visitors a warm welcome. The guest accommodation is attractively furnished, well equipped, and offers comfortable surroundings for a relaxing stay. The menu features a range of commendable dishes prepared with the best local produce, served in the rustic decor of the restaurant where willing staff provide attentive service.
Near river Near sea Near beach Forest area In town centre Near motorway
44 en suite (bth/shr) (8 fmly) (2 with balcony) No smoking in 5 bedrooms TV in all bedrooms Radio in rooms Licensed Lift Night porter Full central heating Supervised Child discount available Sauna Gym Bicycle rental Open terrace Last d 22.00hrs Languages spoken: English, Spanish
CARDS: ●● ■■ ■■ ❿ Travellers cheques

BAZAS Gironde

Château d'Arbieu
33430
☎ 556251118 FAX 556259052
Forest area
6 rms (5 bth/shr) Direct dial from all bedrooms Full central heating Open parking available Child discount available 10yrs Outdoor swimming pool Pool table Boule Bicycle rental Languages spoken: English
MEALS: Dinner fr 160FF✱
CARDS: ●● ■■ ■■ Travellers cheques

BEAUMONT Dordogne

Château de Régagnac
Montferrand-Cadouin *24440*
☎ 553632702
Set in the heart of the south-west of France this delightful 18th-century residence stands in 10 acres of peaceful parkland.

It has remained faithful to the rules of traditional hospitality and offers comfortable accommodation and excellent food.
Near river Near lake Forest area
5 en suite (bth/shr) Open parking available Supervised No children 13yrs Tennis Fishing Open terrace Languages spoken: English, Spanish
MEALS: Dinner 400FF✱
CARDS: Travellers cheques

BERGERAC Dordogne

★ ★ ★ Bordeaux
38 pl Gambetta *24100*
☎ 553571283 FAX 553577214
(From Bordeaux direction cross the bridge and follow signs for 'Centre Ville' to the cathedral)
Situated in the centre of town, close to the historic quarter, the hotel is an oasis of calm and tranquility. Pretty gardens and an outdoor pool all add to this impression. Although the hotel has been going since 1855, inside it has been thoroughly modernised with the result that bedrooms are comfortable, with all modern amenities. Bar and restaurant on site.
Near river In town centre
40 en suite (bth/shr) (1 fmly) No smoking in 5 bedrooms TV in all bedrooms STV Direct dial from all bedrooms Licensed Lift Night porter Full central heating Open parking available (charged) Covered parking available (charged) Child discount available 12yrs Outdoor swimming pool Pool table Open terrace Last d 22.00hrs Languages spoken: English,German,Spanish
ROOMS: s 306-376FF; d 422-512FF
MEALS: Full breakfast 46FF Lunch 100-240FF Dinner 100-240FF
CARDS: ●● ■■ ■■ ❿ JCB Travellers cheques

★ ★ Climat de France
24100
☎ 553572223 Cen Res 164460123
Situated in the 'Périgord Pourpre' and surrounded by the famous vineyards of Bergerac, the hotel offers a good base for visits to the places of historic interest in the region. It features bedrooms equipped with every modern convenience. The restaurant serves a generous and varied cuisine in a friendly atmosphere, and guests can help themselves to as many starters and sweets as they wish from the tempting buffet.
Near river Near motorway
46 en suite (bth/shr) Licensed Night porter Full central heating Air conditioning in bedrooms Open parking available Covered parking available Supervised Outdoor swimming pool Mini-golf Open terrace V meals Languages spoken: English
CARDS: ●● ■■

★ ★ Commerce
36 pl Gambetta *24100*
☎ 553273050 FAX 553582382
(In town centre near the cathedral)
Situated in the heart of Bergerac, close to the town's old quarters, this hotel offers bright airy bedrooms with modern amenities, whilst its restaurant 'Le Bistro Gambetta' serves a good choice of freshly prepared food in a relaxed atmosphere.
In town centre
35 en suite (bth/shr) (1 fmly) (6 with balcony) TV in all bedrooms STV Licensed Lift Night porter Full central heating Open parking available (charged) V meals Last d 21.45hrs Languages spoken: English

ROOMS: (room only) d 195-380FF **✷ Reductions over 1 night**
MEALS: Full breakfast 40FF Lunch 95-160FF&alc Dinner 95-160FF&alc✷
CARDS: ✇ ▆▆ ▆▆ ⑩ Travellers cheques

BIARRITZ Pyrénées-Atlantiques

★ ★ ★ Café de Paris
5 pl Bellevue *64200*
☎ 559241953 FAX 559241820
(From motorway take exit Biarritz La Négresse and continue into town centre. Hotel 50 metres from the Grande Plage)
The hotel Café de Paris is situated in a small square opposite the beach in the very heart of Biarritz. With the famous Grande Plage and the Rocher de la Vierge nearby it offers spacious bedrooms with fine views of the sea. Decorated in soothing pastel shades, they provide a good level of comfort. In addition there is a bistro for a quick meal and an a la carte restaurant.
Near sea Near beach In town centre Near motorway
19 en suite (bth) (1 fmly) (5 with balcony) TV in all bedrooms STV Mini-bar in all bedrooms Licensed Lift Night porter Full central heating Open terrace Last d 22.00hrs Languages spoken: English,Spanish
ROOMS: (room only) s 600-1100FF; d 700-1200FF
MEALS: Full breakfast 85FF Continental breakfast 85FF Dinner 170-450FFalc✷
CARDS: ✇ ▆▆ ▆▆ ⑩ Travellers cheques

★ ★ ★ Château du Clair de Lune
48 av Alan Séeger, rte d'Arbonne *64200*
☎ 559415320 FAX 559415329

This enchanting residence and its colonial-style hunting lodge are set in a park surrounded by ancient trees. The interior combines elegance with intimacy and is adorned with many exquisite antiques and objects d'art. The charming bedrooms with views of the rose-garden are furnished with immaculate taste and offer a high degree of comfort. There is a library, a large lounge with a grand piano, and a flower-decked terrace overlooking the magnificent garden set against the backdrop of the Pyrenees.
Near sea Forest area Near motorway
15 en suite (bth/shr) 8 rooms in annexe (4 fmly) (8 with balcony) TV in all bedrooms STV Mini-bar in all bedrooms Licensed Full central heating Open parking available Boule Open terrace Languages spoken: English
ROOMS: (room only) d 450-750FF
CARDS: ✇ ▆▆ ▆▆ ⑩ Travellers cheques

★ ★ Climat de France
RN 10 Aéroport de Parme *64200*
☎ 559234041 Cen Res 164460123 FAX 559412611
(off N10 near Airport)
Near lake Near sea In town centre Near motorway
74 en suite (bth/shr) Some rooms in annexe TV in 60 bedrooms Radio in rooms Direct-dial available Room-safe Licensed Night porter Full central heating Open parking available Open terrace Covered terrace V meals Languages spoken: English & Spanish
CARDS: ✇✇ ▆▆

★ ★ ★ ★ Miramar
13 rue Louison Bobet *64200*
☎ 559413000 FAX 559247720
(Halfway between the town centre and the lighthouse)
This contemporary hotel offers visitors a different kind of experience, where modern comfort and relaxation, but most of

all the physical well-being of guests, are placed high on the list of priorities. With its avant-garde architecture it cuts a distinctive silhouette against the Atlantic coastline. The public areas feature a combination of modern comforts with stylish elegance. The luxuriuosly appointed bedrooms have balconies providing stunning views over the ocean, and the restaurant offers a choice of skilfully prepared classic cuisine or low-calorie dishes.
Near sea Near beach In town centre
126 en suite (bth/shr) (126 with balcony) TV in all bedrooms Radio in rooms Direct dial from all bedrooms Mini-bar in all bedrooms Room-safe Lift Night porter Full central heating Air conditioning in bedrooms Covered parking available (charged) Supervised Child discount available 12yrs Indoor swimming pool (heated) Outdoor swimming pool (heated) Sauna Solarium Gym Pool table Jacuzzi/spa Open terrace Covered terrace Last d 22.00hrs Languages spoken: English & Spanish
ROOMS: (room only) s 1375-2425FF; d 1585-2700FF
Special breaks
MEALS: Full breakfast 100FF Continental breakfast 100FF Lunch 290FF&alc Dinner 290FF&alc
CARDS: ✇ ▆▆ ▆▆ ⑩ Travellers cheques

★ ★ Hotel Palacito
1 rue Gambetta *64200*
☎ 559240489 FAX 559243343
Near sea Near beach In town centre Near motorway
30 en suite (bth/shr) TV in all bedrooms Lift Full central heating Child discount available 15yrs Languages spoken: English & Spanish
ROOMS: (room only) s 190-225FF; d 220-365FF
CARDS: ✇ ▆▆ ▆▆ ⑩ Travellers cheques

BIDART Pyrénées-Atlantiques

★ ★ ★ Bidartéa (Best Western)
rte d'Espagne - RN 10 *64210*
☎ 559549468 FAX 559548382
A large chalet-style building decorated in typically Basque fashion, set in parkland. Bedrooms are cheerful and comfortable, and there's a restaurant and bar to help you unwind. On sunny days you can enjoy your pre-dinner drink on the terrace. This hotel is ideal as a holiday centre; it is situated very close to the beach as well as to many places of interest - Biarritz, St-Jean-de-Luz and Bayonne are all nearby.
Near river Near sea Forest area In town centre Near motorway
Closed Apr-15 Oct
26 en suite (bth/shr) 6 rooms in annexe (7 fmly) (18 with balcony) TV in all bedrooms Licensed Lift Full central heating Open parking available Covered parking available (charged) Supervised No children Child discount available 12yrs Outdoor swimming pool Boule Mini-golf Open terrace Languages spoken: English,Basque,Spanish
CARDS: ✇ ▆▆ ▆▆ ⑩

BORDEAUX Gironde

▲ ▲ ▲ Burdigala
115 rue Georges Bonnac *33000*
☎ 556901616 FAX 556931506
In town centre
83 en suite (bth/shr) (7 fmly) TV in all bedrooms STV Mini-bar in all bedrooms Licensed Lift Night porter Full central heating Air conditioning in bedrooms Open parking available (charged) Covered parking available (charged)

contd.

Supervised Child discount available 12yrs Jacuzzi/spa V
meals Last d 22.00hrs Languages spoken:
English,Dutch,German,Japanese,Spanish
MEALS: Full breakfast 80FF Continental breakfast 80FF Lunch
180-280FF&alc Dinner 180-280FF&alc✱
CARDS: ☎ ▬ ▭ ◑ JCB Travellers cheques

★ ★ Etche-Ona
11 rue Mautrec *33000*
☎ 556443649 FAX 556445958
Near river In town centre
Closed late Dec-early Jan
33 rms (14 bth 12 shr) (4 fmly) TV in all bedrooms Direct dial
from all bedrooms Child discount available 12yrs Languages
spoken: English & Spanish
CARDS: ☎ ▬ ▭ ◑ Travellers cheques

★ ★ ★ Grand Hotel Francais (Best Western)
12 rue du Temple *33000*
☎ 556481035 FAX 556817618
This hotel is one of the great buildings in Bordeaux, reflecting
the prestigious 17th-century architecture of this city. Situated
near the cultural and business centres, it is the ideal setting for
commercial and leisure travellers alike. Elegantly furnished
throughout, it provides sophisticated surroundings for a
enjoyable stay, while the attractive bedrooms offer modern
amenities and provide a high level of comfort.
In town centre
35 en suite (bth/shr) (7 with balcony) TV in all bedrooms STV
Mini-bar in all bedrooms Lift Night porter Full central
heating Air conditioning in bedrooms Languages spoken:
English,German,Spanish
CARDS: ☎ ▬ ▭ ◑ Travellers cheques

★ ★ ★ Holiday Inn Garden Court
28-30 rue de Tauqia *33000*
☎ 556922121 FAX 556910806
Near river In town centre Near motorway
89 en suite (bth) No smoking in 45 bedrooms TV in all
bedrooms STV Radio in rooms Direct dial from all bedrooms
Mini-bar in all bedrooms Licensed Lift Night porter Full
central heating Air conditioning in bedrooms Open parking
available (charged) Supervised Child discount available 12yrs
Gym Pool table Open terrace V meals Last d 22.00hrs
Languages spoken: English,German & Spanish
CARDS: ☎ ▬ ▭ ◑ Travellers cheques

★ ★ ★ Normandie
7 crs du 30 Juillet *33000*
☎ 556521680 FAX 556516891
Situated in the heart of Bordeaux, on the banks of the
Garonne, this hotel is ideally situated near the shops,
restaurants, museums and cinemas. Whether for business or
leisure, you are bound to enjoy your stay here. Bedrooms offer
all modern comforts and a warm welcome awaits you at the
private bar and public lounges.
In town centre
100 en suite (bth/shr) (12 with balcony) TV in all bedrooms
STV Radio in rooms Licensed Lift Night porter Full central
heating Child discount available 3yrs Languages spoken:
English,Spanish
CARDS: ☎ ▬ ▭ ◑ Travellers cheques

★ ★ ★ Novotel Bordeaux Centre Meriadeck
45 crs Mal-Juin *33000*
☎ 556514646 FAX 556982556
Novotel offer their clients good quality accommodation in

modern, well equipped bedrooms and have refined
restaurants serving good quality cuisine They have excellent
business meeting and conference facilities and some have food
and beverages available 24 hours a day. All their hotels have at
least one bedroom for disabled guests.
In town centre
138 en suite (bth/shr) No smoking in 36 bedrooms TV in all
bedrooms STV Radio in rooms Direct dial from all bedrooms
Mini-bar in all bedrooms Licensed Lift Night porter Full
central heating Air conditioning in bedrooms Child discount
available 16yrs Open terrace Last d 24.00hrs Languages
spoken: English,Spanish
MEALS: Full breakfast 51FF Lunch 150-220FFalc Dinner 150-
220FFalc✱
CARDS: ☎ ▬ ▭ ◑ Travellers cheques

★ ★ ★ Hotel de Sézé
23 allées de Tourny *33000*
☎ 556526554 FAX 556443183
Set in the historic heart of Bordeaux, between de Place de
Tourny and the Esplanade des Quinconces visitors are assured
of a warm welcome in this 18th-century building, once a
private residence. The cosy interior combined with the elegant
furnishings create an atmosphere of well-being enhanced by
the attentive service of friendly staff. The bedrooms are
tastefully furnished and offer a high level of comfort and the
surrounding area offers a a wide range of restaurants, shops
and assorted entertainment.
In town centre Near motorway
24 en suite (bth/shr) (4 fmly) (5 with balcony) TV in all
bedrooms Direct dial from all bedrooms Mini-bar in all
bedrooms Lift Night porter Full central heating Covered
parking available (charged) Supervised Child discount
available 16yrs Languages spoken: English,Spanish
CARDS: ☎ ▬ ▭ ◑

★ ★ ★ ★ Sofitel Aquitania
bd J G Doumergue *33000*
☎ 556508380 FAX 556397375
The Sofitel chain comprises of a group of very fine modern,
comfortable hotels at the four star level. Bedrooms have been
carefully designed to cater to guests relaxation and well being
and the restaurants facilities offer fine cuisine in pleasant
surroundings. Business clientele will find excellent conference
and meeting facilities.
Near lake Near motorway
Closed 15 Dec-12 Jan
190 en suite (bth/shr) No smoking in 56 bedrooms TV in all
bedrooms STV Radio in rooms Direct dial from all bedrooms
Mini-bar in all bedrooms Licensed Lift Night porter Full
central heating Air conditioning in bedrooms Open parking
available Child discount available 12yrs Outdoor swimming
pool Pool table Open terrace Last d 22.30hrs Languages
spoken: German,Italian,Portuguese
CARDS: ☎ ▬ ▭ ◑ Travellers cheques

BRANNE Gironde

★ ★ De France
7-9 pl du Marché *33420*
☎ 557845006 FAX 557799951
Located in the area of Entre-Deux-Mers, this hotel is very close
to the vineyards of Saint-Emilion. The same family have been
running it for five generations and have perfected the art of
hospitality. As well as cosy surroundings and comfortable
bedrooms, the restaurant serves traditional dishes using only
the freshest local produce.

Near river In town centre Near motorway
13 rms (3 bth 1 shr) TV in all bedrooms Licensed Full central
heating Covered parking available (charged) Child discount
available 2yrs V meals Last d 21.00hrs Languages spoken:
English,Spanish
CARDS: 💳 ▦

BRANTÔME Dordogne

★ ★ ★ Chabrol
57 rue Gambetta *24310*
☎ 553057015 FAX 553057185
(Approach via D939 Angoulême-Périgueux)
Near river Forest area In town centre
Closed Feb & mid Nov-mid Dec
20 en suite (bth/shr) 8 rooms in annexe (3 fmly) (6 with
balcony) TV in all bedrooms Direct dial from all bedrooms
Licensed Full central heating Child discount available Open
terrace Covered terrace Last d 21.30hrs Languages spoken:
English
ROOMS: (room only) s 260-400FF; d 280-400FF ✱
MEALS: Full breakfast 45FF Continental breakfast 45FF Lunch
160-420FF&alc Dinner 160-420FF&alc
CARDS: 💳 ▦ ▦ ⑤ Travellers cheques

★ ★ ★ Domaine de la Roseraie
rte d'Angoulême *24310*
☎ 553058474 FAX 553057794
(Approach via D939 Angoulême-Périgueux)

This completely renovated 17th-century 'Charterhouse' is
situated in 4 hectares of grounds at the gateway of Brantôme,
which is known as the 'Green Venice of Périgord', and
regarded as a harbour of peace and tranquillity by historians,
painters, writers and nature lovers. The proprietors Evelyne
and Denis Roux offer their visitors a pleasant, relaxing stay,
with the traditional, high quality cuisine of the area. The
spacious guest rooms are immaculate and furnished with
antique family heirlooms. They are equipped with modern
amenities and have private en suite facilities.
Near river Forest area
Closed 15 Nov-15 Mar
8 en suite (bth/shr) (2 fmly) (8 with balcony) No smoking in 4
bedrooms TV in all bedrooms STV Radio in rooms Direct
dial from all bedrooms Licensed Full central heating Open
parking available Outdoor swimming pool (heated) Tennis
Solarium Boule Open terrace V meals Last d 21.30hrs
Languages spoken: English & German
ROOMS: (room only) s fr 400FF; d 400-680FF
MEALS: Full breakfast 50FF Lunch 145-225FF&alc Dinner 115-
225FF&alc
CARDS: 💳 ▦ ▦ ⑤ Travellers cheques

BROCAS Landes

★ De la Gare
rte de Bélis *40420*
☎ 558514067
This newly renovated establishment is situated near the peaceful
Etang de Brocas. The bedrooms have private facilities and the
restaurant serves innovative cuisine incorporating varied dishes
prepared with fresh local produce, and game specialities such
as wood pigeon with cêpe mushrooms, when in season.
Near lake Forest area
7 en suite (shr) (2 with balcony) Direct dial from all bedrooms
Licensed Full central heating Open parking available Child
discount available Boule Open terrace Last d 22.00hrs
Languages spoken: English,German
MEALS: Continental breakfast 30FF Lunch 95-160FF&alc
Dinner 95-160FF&alc✱
CARDS: 💳 ▦

BUGUE, LE Dordogne

★ ★ L'Auberge du Noyer
Le Reclaud-de-Bouny-Bas *24260*
☎ 553071173 FAX 553545744
(5kms W of Le Bugue on the D703, direction Ste Alvère)
A converted 18th century Perigordian farmhouse in peaceful
countryside. Tastefully renovated, the good sized bedrooms,
have beams and exposed stone walls, or are furnished in
romantic country style with well equipped bathrooms. The
simple carte menu features local produce bought at market
each morning and served in an attractive rustic dining-room.
Near river Forest area
Closed 2 Nov-Palm Sun
10 en suite (bth) Direct dial from all bedrooms Licensed Full
central heating Open parking available Covered parking
available Child discount available 16yrs Outdoor swimming
pool Boule Bicycle rental Open terrace Last d 20.30hrs
Languages spoken: English, Arabic, German, Italian & Spanish
ROOMS: (room only) s fr 280FF; d 380-480FF
MEALS: Continental breakfast 48FF Dinner 160FF
CARDS: 💳 ▦ Travellers cheques

★ ★ ★ Royal Vézère (Best Western)
24260
☎ 553072001 FAX 553035180
(From Bergerac take then D29 to Sauve Boeuf. Take D703 to Le
Bugue)
The hotel is situated in the heart of the picturesque village of
Le Bugue, and occupies a splendid location on the banks of the
river Vézère. It features attractive bedrooms decorated in co-
ordinating colours and fabrics which offer a good standard of
comfort. An array of outstanding regional dishes are served in
the restaurant, whilst there is also a cosy bar and the brasserie-
style Le Jardin for a quick meal.
Near river Forest area In town centre
Closed Oct-May
52 en suite (bth/shr) (4 fmly) (48 with balcony) TV in 39
bedrooms Direct dial from all bedrooms Mini-bar in 15
bedrooms Licensed Lift Night porter Full central heating
Open parking available Covered parking available (charged)
Child discount available 12yrs Outdoor swimming pool Open
terrace Last d 21.00hrs Languages spoken: English
ROOMS: (room only) s 300-505FF; d 315-545FF
Reductions over 1 night
MEALS: Full breakfast 45FF Continental breakfast 45FF Lunch
92-245FF&alc Dinner 92-245FF&alc
CARDS: 💳 ▦ ▦ ⑤ Travellers cheques

CADILLAC Gironde

★ ★ ★ Château de la Tour
10 av de la Libération *33410*
☎ 556769200 FAX 556621159
Ideally situated, only 20 minutes from the centre of Bordeaux and 40 minutes from the nearest airport, the Château de la Tour combines traditional hospitality with modern comforts. The sound-proofed bedrooms are tastefully furnished with attractive fabrics and equipped with modern amenities. The panoramic restaurant offers a stunning vista of the Château des Ducs d'Epernon and serves an array of delicious regional dishes, traditional recipes, as well as the chef's own creations. In addition, the hotel boasts four highly advanced conference rooms for seminars and functions.
Near river Forest area In town centre
31 en suite (bth) (1 fmly) TV in all bedrooms STV Direct dial from all bedrooms Mini-bar in all bedrooms Licensed Lift Full central heating Open parking available Covered parking available (charged) Child discount available 12yrs Outdoor swimming pool Sauna Gym Pool table Boule Jacuzzi/spa Open terrace Languages spoken: English,Spanish
CARDS: ■ Travellers cheques

CAPBRETON Landes

★ ★ ★ L'Océan
85 av Georges Pompidou *40130*
☎ 558721022 FAX 558720843
(NW of town centre towards the marina and the lighthouse)
The hotel is a 1950s building, and stands on the water's edge, close to the marina and a fine sandy beach. It features a cheerful, bright interior with modern furnishings. The attractive bedrooms are individually appointed and equipped with modern amenities, whilst an attractive restaurant with terrace offers fine views across the water.
Near river Near sea Forest area
Closed mid Oct-Etr
27 rms (24 bth/shr) (17 with balcony) TV in 25 bedrooms Direct dial from all bedrooms Licensed Lift Night porter Full central heating Open parking available Child discount available Languages spoken: English,German
ROOMS: (room only) s 260-350FF; d 410-440FF
CARDS: ● ■ ● Travellers cheques

CAPDROT Dordogne

★ ★ Hostellerie le St-Hubert
04540
☎ 553234491 FAX 553366690
Situated in the small hamlet of Capdrot and three kilometres from one of the most beautiful fortified towns in Europe Monpazier, this peaceful venue offers the ideal setting where guests can relax and enjoy the splendid scenery of the Périgord countryside. The bedrooms have private facilities and the restaurant serves an imaginative cuisine with a regional touch, incorporating fresh local produce.
Forest area In town centre
11 en suite (bth) (1 fmly) Direct dial from all bedrooms Licensed Full central heating Open parking available Child discount available Outdoor swimming pool Tennis Fishing Riding Pool table Boule Bicycle rental Open terrace Languages spoken: English
CARDS: ● ■ ■ ● Travellers cheques

CASTELNAU-DE-MÉDOC Gironde

Chateau de Foulon
33480
☎ 556582018 FAX 556582343
Near river Near lake Near sea Forest area
5 en suite (bth) (1 fmly) Bicycle rental
CARDS: Travellers cheques

CÉRONS Gironde

★ ★ Grillobois
N113 *33720*
☎ 556271150 FAX 556270404
Surrounded by the vineyards of Graves and Sauternes, this small hotel features comfortable bedrooms with private facilities, whilst the restaurant serves a choice of delicious grilled dishes, cooked over 'vignotte' embers made from vine trunks. The hotel organises special dinner-dances with live music on a regular basis. Guests can relax on the terrace alongside the swimming pool, or visit the nearby châteaux, vineyards and varied tourist sights.
Near river Forest area Near motorway
Closed 2-28 Jan
10 en suite (shr) (5 fmly) TV in all bedrooms Direct dial from all bedrooms Licensed Full central heating Open parking available Child discount available 12yrs Outdoor swimming pool Tennis Sauna Solarium Boule Bicycle rental Open terrace Covered terrace V meals Last d 22.30hrs Languages spoken: English,Spanish
CARDS: ●● ■ Travellers cheques

CHAMPAGNAC-DE-BELAIR Dordogne

★ ★ ★ ★ Moulin du Roc
24530
☎ 553028600 FAX 553542131
(6km from Brantôme)

Nestling on the banks of the river Dronne, the hotel Le Moulin du Roc welcomes visitors to its lavish interior. The exquisitely appointed bedrooms offer a high degree of comfort and throughout the delightful public areas, period furniture and delicate fabrics make this a truly exceptional residence. The menu offers a selection of tantalising dishes, whilst meals are served on the terrace with a lovely view of the river. Leisure facilities include a sauna, solarium and fitness room, swimming pool and tennis court.
Near river
Closed Jan & Feb
14 en suite (bth) (3 fmly) (2 with balcony) TV in all bedrooms STV Radio in rooms Direct dial from all bedrooms

Mini-bar in all bedrooms Licensed Full central heating Open parking available Covered parking available Indoor swimming pool (heated) Outdoor swimming pool (heated) Tennis Fishing Boule Bicycle rental Open terrace Covered terrace V meals Last d 21.30hrs Languages spoken: English,Spanish
ROOMS: (room only) d 410-720FF ✱
MEALS: Full breakfast 65FF Lunch 160-290FF&alc Dinner 220-290FF&alc✱
CARDS: ✸ 🖪 ⚏ ➒ Travellers cheques

COLY Dordogne

★ ★ ★ Manoir d'Hautégente
24120
☎ 553516803 FAX 553503852
(From Perigueux take N89 towards Brive. Take D704 towards Montignac, then D62 to Coly)

Because of its location, the Manoir de Hautegente provides an ideal base for touring the region. The interior is tastefully decorated with fine fabrics and antique furniture which create the cosy, informal atmosphere of a private residence. The cuisine includes a range of regional specialities, prepared with ingredients from the private vegetable garden. After dinner guests can enjoy a 'digestif' in one of the drawing rooms with open fireplace, or retire to the elegant guest rooms which have views of the park.
Near river Forest area
1 Apr-3 Nov
14 en suite (bth) (2 fmly) (1 with balcony) TV in all bedrooms Direct dial from all bedrooms Mini-bar in all bedrooms Licensed Full central heating Open parking available Child discount available 12yrs Outdoor swimming pool (heated) Fishing Bicycle rental Open terrace V meals Last d 21.00hrs Languages spoken: English
ROOMS: (room only) s 470-520FF; d 970FF ✱
MEALS: Full breakfast 65FF Lunch fr 150FF&alc Dinner fr 220FF&alc
CARDS: ✸ 🖪 ⚏ Travellers cheques

CONDAT-SUR-VÉZÈRE Dordogne

★ ★ ★ Château de la Fléunie
24570
☎ 553513274 FAX 553505898
Near river Forest area Near motorway
Closed Oct-Apr
33 en suite (bth) 8 rooms in annexe (12 fmly) (7 with balcony) TV in all bedrooms Direct-dial available Mini-bar in 17 bedrooms Licensed Full central heating Open parking available Supervised Child discount available 10yrs Outdoor

swimming pool Tennis Pool table Boule Bicycle rental Open terrace Last d 21.30hrs Languages spoken: English, German, Spanish
CARDS: ✸ 🖪 ⚏ Travellers cheques

COUX-ET-BIGAROQUE Dordogne

Petit Chaperon Rouge
La Faval *24220*
☎ 553293779 FAX 553294663
Overlooking the Dordogne valley, this property, called 'The Little Red Riding Hood', is a haven of peace and tranquillity. On-site restaurant specialises in regional and gastronomic dishes. Bathing, fishing and canoeing available. English spoken.
Near river Near beach Forest area
11 rms (6 bth/shr) (3 fmly) Direct dial from 6 bedrooms Licensed Full central heating Open parking available Child discount available 6yrs Open terrace Last d 22hrs Languages spoken: English & German
ROOMS: (room only) d 140-195FF
MEALS: Continental breakfast 35FF Lunch 60-178FF&alc Dinner 60-178FF&alc
CARDS: ✸ 🖪 ⚏ Travellers cheques

CRÉON Gironde

★ ★ ★ Hostellerie Château Camiac
rte de Branne D121 *33670*
☎ 556232085 FAX 556233884
A stunning building which occupies a dominant position overlooking the rolling countryside. It offers an elegant interior where modern amenities have been carefully blended with old-world charm and hospitality. The tastefully furnished bedrooms offer a high standard of comfort, and the restaurant serves traditional French cuisine complemented by the great Bordeaux wines from its own prestigious wine-cellar.
Near lake Forest area
21 en suite (bth) 12 rooms in annexe (3 fmly) No smoking in 15 bedrooms TV in all bedrooms Radio in rooms Licensed Lift Full central heating Open parking available Child discount available Outdoor swimming pool Tennis Fishing Riding Pool table Boule Bicycle rental Open terrace Covered terrace Archery V meals Last d 21.45hrs Languages spoken: English,German,Spanish
MEALS: Full breakfast 75FF Continental breakfast 15FF Lunch fr 130FF&alc Dinner fr 160FF&alc✱
CARDS: ✸ 🖪 ⚏ ➒ Travellers cheques

DAX Landes

★ ★ Jean le Bon
12-14 rue Jean le Bon *40100*
☎ 558742914 FAX 558900304
To take advantage of all the benefits the town of Dax has to offer - it is the largest spa town in France - what better place to stay than in a hotel located in the centre of town. It offers peaceful accommodation with modern facilities and a restaurant which serves delicious regional cuisine. Being a native of the area, the chef knows all the best places to buy the high quality produce for his outstanding dishes.
Near river Forest area
27 rms (1 fmly) (6 with balcony) TV in all bedrooms STV Direct dial from all bedrooms Licensed Night porter Full central heating Open parking available Covered parking available (charged) Supervised Child discount available 16yrs Outdoor swimming pool (heated) Solarium Boule *contd.*

Bicycle rental Open terrace Last d 22.00hrs Languages spoken: English,Italian,Spanish
MEALS: Full breakfast 30FF Continental breakfast 30FF Lunch 75-150FF&alc Dinner fr 75FF&alc✱
CARDS: ✷✷ ▉▉ ▭▭

DOMME Dordogne

★ ★ ★ **Esplanade**
24250
☎ 553283141 FAX 553284992
Situated within the fortifications of the village of Domme, the hotel commands a stunning view over the valley. The rustic restaurant, where cheerful table linen offers a dramatic contrast with the furnishings, has been awarded many accolades for its outstanding cuisine. A number of the bedrooms are housed in the old stone houses of the village and are furnished with many period pieces.
Near river In town centre
Closed ear Nov-mid Feb
25 en suite (bth/shr) 10 rooms in annexe (5 fmly) (1 with balcony) TV in all bedrooms Licensed Full central heating Child discount available 12yrs Open terrace Last d 21.15hrs Languages spoken: English,German,Spanish
CARDS: ✷✷ ▉▉ ▭▭ Travellers cheques

DOUVILLE Dordogne

★ ★ **Le Tropicana**
Maison Jeannette *24140*
☎ 553829831 FAX 553804550
The hotel is situated at equal distance from Bergerac and Périgueux and is close to the prestigious sites which have made the Périgord region famous. A welcome and convivial atmosphere meets visitors upon arrival, complemented by comfortable rooms and a restaurant which serves gastronomic cuisine which will delight the most discerning gourmet. There is a congenial bar with a sunny terrace, as well as a choice of leisure facilities for all ages.
Near river Forest area Near motorway
23 en suite (bth/shr) (17 with balcony) TV in all bedrooms Direct dial from all bedrooms Licensed Full central heating Open parking available Supervised Child discount available 10yrs Outdoor swimming pool Fishing Open terrace Last d 21.00hrs
CARDS: ✷✷ ▭▭

GAN Pyrénées-Atlantiques

★ ★ **Le Clos Gourmand**
40 av Henri IV *64290*
☎ 559215043 FAX 559215663
(On left at the entrance to the town via N134)
The house is situated on the banks of a river and provides an ideal venue for an overnight stop. Surrounded by the vast vineyards of the region it combines comfortable guest accommodation with a choice of fine, good-value dishes.
Near river Forest area Near motorway
8 en suite (bth/shr) (2 fmly) TV in all bedrooms Direct dial from all bedrooms Licensed Full central heating Open parking available Supervised Child discount available 10yrs Fishing Boule Bicycle rental Open terrace Table Tennis,Volley Ball Last d 21.00hrs Languages spoken: English,Spanish
ROOMS: (room only) d 220-250FF ✱
MEALS: Full breakfast 55FF Continental breakfast 35FF Lunch 88FF Dinner 100FF✱
CARDS: ✷✷ ▭▭ ✺ Travellers cheques

GRENADE-SUR-L'ADOUR Landes

★ ★ ★ **Pain Adour et Fantaisie**
14-16 pl des Tilleuls *40270*
☎ 558451880 FAX 558451657
(From Bordeaux A62 exit Mont-de-Marsan and continue on N124)
Situated in the heart of the south-west, this attractive building dates back to the 17th century and offers spacious, brightly decorated bedrooms providing good modern comfort. The menu features an imaginative cuisine prepared with superb ingredients from the region. When the weather is fine, guests can also enjoy meals on the terrace with views over the river Adour.
Near river Near lake Forest area Near motorway
11 en suite (bth/shr) (8 with balcony) TV in all bedrooms Direct dial from all bedrooms Mini-bar in all bedrooms Room-safe Licensed Night porter Full central heating Air conditioning in bedrooms Open parking available Covered parking available (charged) Child discount available 11yrs Bicycle rental Open terrace Covered terrace Last d 22.00hrs Languages spoken: English,Spanish
ROOMS: (room only) d 380-700FF
MEALS: Full breakfast 75FF Lunch 150-360FF&alc Dinner 150-360FF&alc
CARDS: ✷✷ ▉▉ ▭▭ ✺ Travellers cheques

HENDAYE Pyrénées-Atlantiques

★ ★ **Chez Antoinette**
pl Pellot *64700*
☎ 59200847 FAX 59481164
(exit autoroute a St Jean-de-Luz Sud, Plage Hendaye in direction 'Centre Ville'. After third roundabout, second road on left)
This small, traditional hotel is situated near one of the most beautiful beaches in the south-west of France. Most rooms are equipped with modern facilities and offer an adequate level of comfort. A warm, convivial atmosphere prevails throughout and is complemented by a good measure of personal service at all times.
Near sea Near beach Forest area In town centre Near motorway
Closed Oct-Mar
16 en suite (shr) 7 rooms in annexe (2 fmly) (1 with balcony) TV in all bedrooms Direct dial from all bedrooms Licensed Full central heating Open parking available Open terrace Languages spoken: English,Spanish,German,Basque
ROOMS: (room only) d 220-250FF ✱
CARDS: ✷✷ ▭▭ Eurocard Travellers cheques

HOSSEGOR Landes

★ ★ **Les Helianthes**
av de la Côte-d'Argent *40150*
☎ 558435219 FAX 558439519
The establishment is set in tranquil surroundings between the lake and the sea. An informal, friendly atmosphere prevails throughout and visitors are offered a relaxing stay in comfortable accommodation with an extensive array of leisure pursuits available.
Near lake Near sea Near beach Forest area Near motorway
Closed mid Oct-end Mar
18 rms (14 bth/shr) (12 fmly) TV in all bedrooms Radio in rooms Direct dial from all bedrooms Licensed Full central heating Open parking available Child discount available

Indoor swimming pool Outdoor swimming pool Bicycle rental Open terrace Covered terrace Languages spoken: English,German, Spanish
CARDS: ●● ☴ Travellers cheques

★ ★ Lacotel
av du Touring Club de France *40150*
☎ 558439350 FAX 558434949
Located between the lake and pine forests the hotel enjoys an exceptional position with beaches just a stones throw away. Modern bedrooms with balconies offer a good level of comfort, whilst the restaurant serves regional cuisine as well as seafood specialities. Because of its superb location and splendid surroundings it is an excellent venue for families who want a relaxing stay and a carefree place for children to play.
Near lake Near sea Near beach Forest area
Closed 16 Dec-14 Jan RS Half board obligatory high season
42 en suite (bth) (4 fmly) (42 with balcony) TV in all bedrooms Direct dial from all bedrooms Licensed Full central heating Open parking available Child discount available 15yrs Outdoor swimming pool Open terrace Covered terrace Last d 21.30hrs Languages spoken: English,German
ROOMS: (room only) d 295-330FF
MEALS: Full breakfast 38FF Continental breakfast 38FF Lunch 90-120FF&alc Dinner 90-120FF&alc✱
CARDS: ●● ☴ ⚬ Travellers cheques

ITXASSOU Pyrénées-Atlantiques

★ ★ Du Fronton
La Place *64250*
☎ 559297510 FAX 559292350
(From Bayonne take D932 to Cambo, then D918 turn right to Itxassou.)

Set at the foot of a mountain in the heart of the Basque village of d'Itxassou, the hotel offers its visitors a relaxing stay in warm and friendly surroundings. Apart from comfortable accommodation, it serves a range of enjoyable dishes prepared with high quality ingredients from the region. On fine days, guests can dine on the terrace with splendid views of the rolling countryside.
Forest area
Closed Jan-15 Feb
14 en suite (bth/shr) (4 fmly) TV in all bedrooms Direct dial from all bedrooms Licensed Full central heating Open parking available Child discount available 12yrs Outdoor swimming pool Open terrace V meals Last d 21.00hrs Languages spoken: English, Spanish
MEALS: Full breakfast 35FF Lunch 85-170FF&alc Dinner 85-170FF&alc
CARDS: ●● ☷ ☴ ⚬

LACANAU Gironde

★ ★ ★ Vitanova
Domaine de l'Ardilouse *33680*
☎ 556038000 FAX 556263555
This Scandinavian-style hotel is an ideal venue for those who like an active holiday. It offers excellent up-to-date facilities, bedrooms with a cosy seating area and balcony, bar and an intimate lounge with open fire place. The restaurant serves a range of regional cuisine and Scandinavian specialities.
Near lake Near sea Forest area
65 en suite (bth/shr) (35 fmly) (30 with balcony) TV in all bedrooms STV Radio in rooms Direct dial from all bedrooms Licensed Night porter Open parking available Covered parking available Child discount available 5yrs Indoor swimming pool (heated) Outdoor swimming pool Sauna Solarium Gym Boule Jacuzzi/spa Bicycle rental Open terrace Covered terrace V meals
CARDS: ●● ☷ ☴ ⚬ Travellers cheques

LALINDE Dordogne

★ ★ ★ Château
1 rue de la Tour *24150*
☎ 553610182 FAX 553247460
This is a small château which dates back to the 18th century and has excellent views of the River Dordogne. Though situated in the centre of town, it offers a restful stay in pleasant surroundings. The bedrooms have modern-day amenities and are of a good size. It is ideally situated for visits to the surrounding vineyards.
Near river Forest area In town centre Near motorway
Closed early Jan-early Feb
7 en suite (bth/shr) (2 with balcony) TV in all bedrooms Radio in rooms Full central heating Outdoor swimming pool Fishing Open terrace Covered terrace Last d 20.45hrs Languages spoken: English
CARDS: ●● ☷ ☴ ⚬

LIMEUIL Dordogne

★ ★ Beau Regard et Les Terrasses
rte de Trémolat *24510*
☎ 553633085 FAX 553245355
(Approach via D31)Le Bugue-Trémolat)
Set in the open countryside and surrounded by the towns of Bergerac, Périgueux, and Sarlat, the hotel provides a good base for three holiday musts: touring, food and sporting facilities. It offers bedrooms with modern facilities and an attractive restaurant with an extensive choice of well-prepared dishes.
Near river Near beach Forest area
Closed Oct-Apr
8 en suite (bth/shr) Direct dial from all bedrooms Licensed Open parking available Supervised Child discount available 12yrs Boule Open terrace Covered terrace V meals Last d 21.30hrs Languages spoken: English, Spanish
ROOMS: (room only) d 220-280FF **Reductions over 1 night**
MEALS: Full breakfast 40FF Continental breakfast 40FF Lunch 90-280FF&alc Dinner 90-280FF&alc
CARDS: ●● ☴ Travellers cheques

MAUZAC-ET-GRAND-CASTANG Dordogne

★ ★ ★ Métairie
24150
☎ 553225047 FAX 553225293
(from Toulouse: take autoroute exit Mamande towards *contd.*

Bergerac - Calinde, look for signs. from Paris: take exit Libourne, towards Bergerac - Calinde.)
The hotel Metairie provides the perfect setting for a relaxing break in country surroundings. Set in the very heart of the Périgord region, it offers stylish bedrooms, an informal atmosphere and a restaurant which serves a choice of traditional dishes with a contemporary twist. On fine days meals are also served by the side of the swimming pool or on the flower-decked terrace.
Near river Forest area
Closed Nov-end Mar
10 en suite (bth) (2 fmly) (6 with balcony) TV in all bedrooms STV Direct dial from all bedrooms Mini-bar in all bedrooms Licensed Full central heating Open parking available Supervised Child discount available Outdoor swimming pool Boule Bicycle rental V meals Last d 21.30hrs Languages spoken: English,German,Spanish
ROOMS: (room only) s 450-550FF; d 450-1050FF
Reductions over 1 night Special breaks
MEALS: Full breakfast 60FF Lunch 120-260FF&alc Dinner 155-235FF&alc∗
CARDS: 😊 💳 🔟 Travellers cheques

MÉRIGNAC Gironde

★ ★ ★ Novotel Bordeaux Aéroport
av Kennedy *33700*
☎ 556341025 FAX 556559964
Novotel offer their clients good quality accommodation in modern, well equipped bedrooms and have refined restaurants serving good quality cuisine They have excellent business meeting and conference facilities and some have food and beverages available 24 hours a day. All their hotels have at least one bedroom for disabled guests.
In town centre Near motorway
137 en suite (bth/shr) (47 fmly) No smoking in 22 bedrooms TV in all bedrooms STV Direct dial from all bedrooms Mini-bar in all bedrooms Lift Night porter Air conditioning in bedrooms Open parking available Child discount available Outdoor swimming pool Open terrace Languages spoken: English,German,Spanish
CARDS: 😊 💳 🔟 Travellers cheques

MEYRALS Dordogne

★ ★ ★ Hotel de la Ferme Lamy
24220
☎ 553296246 FAX 553596141

(from Sarlat towards Perigueux/Les Eyzies on D6, then D47 after 2km. Drive 9km on D47. At cross called Benives, turn left on the road C3 towards Meyrals and drive for 1.5km.)

The hotel is located between the medieval capital of Sarlat and Les Eyzies with its prehistoric heritage. Individually styled bedrooms feature high quality beds and tasteful furnishings. A delicious breakfast consisting of freshly baked brioche and home-made jam is served in the lounge or outside on the shaded terrace under the lime trees.
Near river Forest area
12 en suite (bth/shr) (7 fmly) (10 with balcony) TV in all bedrooms Direct dial from all bedrooms Mini-bar in 10 bedrooms Licensed Full central heating Open parking available Supervised Outdoor swimming pool Jacuzzi/spa Open terrace Languages spoken: English,German,Italian
ROOMS: (room only) d 310-800FF ∗ **Special breaks: (4 nights for 3 paid, ex high season)**
CARDS: 😊 💳 🔟 Travellers cheques

MONESTIER, LE Dordogne

★ ★ ★ ★ Château des Vigiers
24240
☎ 553615000 FAX 553615020
(From Bergerac take D936 then D18)
This handsome residence dates back to 1597 and was locally known as 'Le Petit Versailles'. Entirely renovated throughout, it offers individually styled bedrooms decorated in a style befitting the origin of the house. The elegant dining room serves a range of excellent dishes complemented by select vintage wines.
Near lake Forest area
47 en suite (bth/shr) TV in all bedrooms STV Direct dial from all bedrooms Mini-bar in all bedrooms Room-safe Licensed Lift Night porter Full central heating Open parking available Covered parking available (charged) Child discount available 18yrs Outdoor swimming pool (heated) Golf 18 Tennis Fishing Sauna Gym Pool table Boule Bicycle rental Open terrace Covered terrace V meals Last d 21.30hrs Languages spoken: English, German,Swedish, Dutch
ROOMS: (room only) d 790-1280FF **Reductions over 1 night**
MEALS: Full breakfast 85FF Continental breakfast 85FF Lunch fr 100FF&alc Dinner 100-385FF&alc
CARDS: 😊 💳 🔟 Travellers cheques

MONTFORT-EN-CHALOSSE Landes

★ ★ Tauzins
rte d'Hagetmau *40380*
☎ 558956022 FAX 558984579
Situated between the Landes and the Pyrenees, the town of Dax is the most important thermal spa in the whole of France. The hotel is a large white building which welcomes its visitors in the true tradition of the south-west. The guest accommodation is comfortable with good amenities, whilst the dining room serves a selection of regional specialities including choice fish delicacies from the Atlantic ocean. The surrounding area has a range of leisure facilities as well as cultural places which are worth visiting.
Near lake Forest area
Closed Jan & 1-15 Oct
16 en suite (bth/shr) (5 fmly) (10 with balcony) TV in all bedrooms STV Licensed Night porter Full central heating Open parking available Covered parking available (charged) Supervised Child discount available 10yrs Outdoor swimming pool (heated) Golf Pool table Boule Mini-golf Bicycle rental Open terrace Close to a lake and riding stables V meals Last d 22.00hrs Languages spoken: English,Spanish
CARDS: 😊 💳 🔟 Travellers cheques

MONTIGNAC Dordogne

★ ★ ★ ★ Château de Puy Robert
24290
☎ 553519213 FAX 553518011
Near river Forest area
Closed 16 Oct-Apr
38 en suite (bth/shr) 23 rooms in annexe (4 fmly) (14 with balcony) TV in all bedrooms STV Direct-dial available Mini-bar in all bedrooms Licensed Lift Night porter Full central heating Open parking available Supervised Child discount available 12yrs Outdoor swimming pool Bicycle rental Open terrace V meals Last d 21.30hrs Languages spoken: English,German
ROOMS: (room only) s 660-1050FF; d 660-1750FF ✱
MEALS: Full breakfast 85FF Lunch 195-410FF&alc Dinner 195-410FF&alc
CARDS: 💳 🏧 ⚉ 🔾 Travellers cheques

MONTIGNAC-LASCAUX Dordogne

★ ★ ★ Hostellerie le Relais du Soleil d'Or
16 rue du 4 Septembre *24290*
☎ 553518022 FAX 553502754
(from Motorway, A20 exit at Brive, Then go towards Montignac - Lascaux N89. Located in town centre)
This former coaching inn is situated in a park with mature trees and offers its visitors old fashioned hospitality combined with modern comfort. The guest accommodation consists of well maintained bedrooms with modern facilities. The restaurant serves a modern cuisine based on the traditional, well-known recipes from the Périgord region.
Near river In town centre
Closed 19 Jan-13 Feb
32 en suite (bth) (13 fmly) TV in all bedrooms Direct dial from all bedrooms Mini-bar in all bedrooms Licensed Full central heating Open parking available Outdoor swimming pool Boule Open terrace Last d 21.30hrs Languages spoken: English,Spanish
ROOMS: (room only) s 320-350FF; d 350-430FF
MEALS: Full breakfast 55FF Lunch 130-250FF&alc Dinner 130-250FF&alc
CARDS: 💳 🏧 ⚉ 🔾 Travellers cheques

★ ★ ★ La Roseraie
pl d'Armes *24290*
☎ 553505392 FAX 553510223
(Approach via N20 towards Brive, then N89 to Montignac)
In the heart of the medieval village of Montignac stands this 19th-century mansion with views over the river Vézère. The bedrooms have modern amenities and offer a good level of comfort, while the restaurant offers a high standard of home-cooking. Guests may want to take a stroll and relax in the park with its mature trees and fragrant rose garden.
Near river Forest area In town centre
Closed 4 Nov-2 Apr
14 en suite (bth/shr) (4 fmly) TV in all bedrooms Direct dial from all bedrooms Night porter Full central heating Open parking available Child discount available 12yrs Outdoor swimming pool Solarium Open terrace Last d 21.30hrs Languages spoken: English
ROOMS: (incl. dinner) d 350-430FF
MEALS: Full breakfast 60FF Lunch 100-190FF&alc Dinner 130-190FF&alc
CARDS: 💳 ⚉

OLORON-STE-MARIE Pyrénées-Atlantiques

★ ★ ★ Alysson Hotel
bd des Pyrénées *64400*
☎ 559397070 FAX 559392447
34 en suite (bth/shr) No smoking in 5 bedrooms TV in all bedrooms STV Direct dial from all bedrooms Licensed Lift Full central heating Open parking available Child discount available 12yrs Outdoor swimming pool Bicycle rental Open terrace Last d 21.30hrs Languages spoken: English, Spanish
CARDS: 💳 🏧 ⚉ Travellers cheques

ORTHEZ Pyrénées-Atlantiques

★ ★ Au Temps de la Reine Jeanne
44 rue Bourg Vieux *64300*
☎ 559670076 FAX 559690963
(From A64 Orthez Centre Ville)
Near river Near lake In town centre Near motorway
20 en suite (bth/shr) (2 fmly) (4 with balcony) TV in all bedrooms Direct dial from all bedrooms Licensed Full central heating Child discount available 14yrs Pool table Mini-golf Bicycle rental Open terrace Last d 22.oohrs Languages spoken: English, Spanish
MEALS: Continental breakfast 30FF Lunch 85-180FF&alc Dinner 85-180FF&alc✱
CARDS: 💳 🏧 ⚉ Travellers cheques

PAU Pyrénées-Atlantiques

★ ★ ★ Gramont
3 pl Gramont *64000*
☎ 559278404 FAX 559276223
Town centre
This former coaching inn has for centuries been a favourite overnight stop for tired travellers. It features a pleasant foyer, where friendly staff offer a warm welcome to visitors, as well as attractive guest accommodation decorated with good quality furniture and fabrics which create a homely atmosphere. There is a comfortable lounge and a congenial bar for a pre-dinner drink or a chat.
In town centre Near motorway
36 en suite (bth/shr) (5 fmly) No smoking in 1 bedroom TV in all bedrooms STV Licensed Lift Night porter Full central heating Open parking available Covered parking available Supervised Pool table Open terrace Covered terrace Languages spoken: English
CARDS: 💳 🏧 ⚉ 🔾 Travellers cheques

PAUILLAC Gironde

★ ★ ★ ★ Château Cordeillan-Bages
rte des Chareaux *33250*
☎ 556592424 FAX 556590189
(A10 exit 7, in direction of Le Verdonn then D2)
This pleasant establishment is set in the centre of town and has sound-proofed bedrooms which are fitted with modern appointments and provide a good level of comfort. The restaurant serves a quality cuisine which consists of a range of dishes based on regional recipes. The surrounding region offers plenty of opportunities for hiking and cycling, whilst golf, tennis and swimming can be found nearby.
Near river Forest area
Closed 8 Dec-1 Feb RS Restaurant closed Sat/Mon lunchtime
25 en suite (bth/shr) (1 fmly) (1 with balcony) TV in all bedrooms STV Radio in rooms Direct dial from all bedrooms Mini-bar in all bedrooms Room-safe Licensed Lift   *contd.*

Night porter Full central heating Open parking available
Supervised Child discount available 12yrs Boule Bicycle
rental Open terrace Last d 21.30hrs Languages spoken:
English,German
ROOMS: (room only) d 720-900FF
MEALS: Full breakfast 75FF Continental breakfast 95FF Lunch
185-235FF&alc Dinner fr 300FF&alc
CARDS: ♠♠ ▦ ▆▆ ⑨ Travellers cheques

PIAN-MÉDOC, LE Gironde

★ ★ ★ Le Pont Bernet
rte du Verdon 33290
☎ 556702019 FAX 556702290
The hotel is surrounded by a park and situated close to the
Médoc vineyards. Guests can expect a warm welcome upon
arrival by friendly staff who will ensure that they are well
looked after, whilst Christian Sauvage is in charge of the
kitchen and responsible for the high standard of cooking. All
the guest rooms have modern en suite facilities and are
decorated in a pleasant fashion.
Near river Forest area Near motorway
18 en suite (bth/shr) TV in all bedrooms STV Direct dial from
all bedrooms Mini-bar in all bedrooms Full central heating
Open parking available Supervised Child discount available
8yrs Outdoor swimming pool (heated) Golf Tennis Fishing
Last d 21.30hrs Languages spoken: English,Spanish
CARDS: ♠♠ ▦ ▆▆ ⑨

PORT-DE-LANNE Landes

★ ★ ★ La Vieille Auberge
pl de l'Eglise 40300
☎ 558891629 FAX 558891289
(off N117 28km E of Bayonne)
Standing in the shadow of a 13th-century church this Virginia
creeper-clad hotel, with beautiful garden, offers warm
hospitality to its guests. In the dining room the aroma of
ancestral recipes blended with the very best local ingredients
fills the air. All the natural flavours are combined in the cuisine
of Mireille, a commander of the Cordons Bleus of France.
Near river Forest area
Closed mid Sep-mid May
10 en suite (bth/shr) TV in all bedrooms Direct dial from all
bedrooms Licensed Full central heating Open parking
available Child discount available 10yrs Outdoor swimming
pool Fishing Boule Open terrace V meals Last d 21.30hrs
Languages spoken: English, German & Spanish
ROOMS: (room only) s 200-250FF; d 320-400FF ✱
Reductions over 1 night
MEALS: Continental breakfast 45FF Lunch 120-250FF Dinner
120-250FF✱

PUYMIROL Lot-et-Garonne

★ ★ ★ ★ Les Loges de l'Aubergade (Relais et Chateaux)
52 rue Royale 47270
☎ 553953146 FAX 553953380
This ancient residence dates back to the 12th century when it
was the private dwelling of the Counts of Toulouse. Situated in
an elevated position in the small fortified village of Puymirol it
offers splendid views over the surrounding countryside. The
bedrooms have modern facilities and provide good comfort,
while the restaurant has a choice of menus to suit all tastes.
Near lake Forest area Near motorway
Closed Feb
10 en suite (bth/shr) (10 fmly) (2 with balcony) TV in all

bedrooms STV Direct dial from all bedrooms Mini-bar in all
bedrooms Room-safe Licensed Full central heating Air
conditioning in bedrooms Open parking available Covered
parking available (charged) Supervised Child discount
available Indoor swimming pool Outdoor swimming pool
Solarium Boule Jacuzzi/spa Open terrace V meals Last d
21.30hrs Languages spoken: English, Spanish,Italian
CARDS: ♠♠ ▦ ▆▆ ⑨ Travellers cheques

RAZAC-SUR-L'ISLE Dordogne

★ ★ ★ Château de Lalande
24430
☎ 553545230 FAX 553074667
(On N89 W of Périgueux)
Set in the heart of Périgord, this splendid building provides a
handsome setting for an enjoyable stay. The elegant lounges,
attractive restaurant and comfortable bedrooms are furnished
in keeping with the architecture of the building, while the
surrounding area is steeped in history and offers a great many
places to visit.
Near river Forest area Near motorway
Closed 16 Nov-14 Mar
22 en suite (bth/shr) (5 fmly) TV in all bedrooms Direct dial
from all bedrooms Full central heating Open parking
available Child discount available 10yrs Indoor swimming
pool Outdoor swimming pool Boule Open terrace Last d
21.30hrs Languages spoken: English
ROOMS: (room only) d 270-460FF
MEALS: Continental breakfast 40FF Lunch 98-300FF&alc
Dinner 98-300FF&alc✱
CARDS: ♠♠ ▦ ▆▆ ⑨ Travellers cheques

RIBÉRAC Dordogne

★ ★ France
3 rue Marc-Dufraisse 24600
☎ 553900061 FAX 553910605
Near river Near lake Forest area In town centre Near motorway
20 rms (8 bth 9 shr) 4 rooms in annexe (4 fmly) TV in all
bedrooms STV Direct dial from all bedrooms Licensed Full
central heating Child discount available 10yrs Open terrace V
meals Last d 21.30hrs Languages spoken: English,Dutch
MEALS: Full breakfast 30FF Continental breakfast 30FF Lunch
70-250FF&alc Dinner 70-250FF&alc✱
CARDS: ♠♠ ▆▆ Travellers cheques

ST-CYPRIEN Dordogne

★ ★ ★ Abbaye
rue de l'Abbaye 24220
☎ 553292048 FAX 553291585
Near river
Closed 15 Oct-15 Apr
24 en suite (bth/shr) 10 rooms in annexe (4 fmly) (3 with
balcony) Radio in rooms Direct dial from all bedrooms
Licensed Full central heating Open parking available Child
discount available 10yrs Outdoor swimming pool Open terrace
V meals Last d 21.00hrs Languages spoken: English,German
ROOMS: s 410-460FF; d 500-780FF ✱
CARDS: ♠♠ ▦ ▆▆ Travellers cheques

★ ★ De La Terrasse
pl Jean Ladignac 24220
☎ 553292169 FAX 553296088
(from Sarlat take direction of Bergerac, hotel is in village, in
direction of Les Eyzies)

The Périgord region features old houses built into the hillsides, and wooded scenic spots. The hotel de 'La Terrasse' is an accurate presentation of the warm hospitality and excellent food which has made this region so popular. The pleasantly furnished guest rooms offer a good level of comfort and provide relaxing accommodation. The cuisine offers a high standard of home-cooking, where regional dishes take pride of place, and which are also served on the terrace in summer.
Near river Forest area In town centre
Closed 15 Dec-15 Feb
19 rms (4 bth 12 shr) TV in 11 bedrooms Direct dial from all bedrooms Licensed Full central heating Child discount available 12yrs Boule Bicycle rental Open terrace V meals Last d 22.00hrs Languages spoken: English,German,Spanish
ROOMS: (room only) s 210-350FF; d 210-350FF
Reductions over 1 night
MEALS: Continental breakfast 35FF Lunch 80-180FF&alc Dinner 80-180FF&alc
CARDS: 💳 ▩ ▆ Travellers cheques

ST-ÉTIENNE-DE-BAIGORRY Pyrénées-Atlantiques

★ ★ ★ Arce
64430
☎ 559374014 FAX 559374027
(From the church head towards 'Col d'Ispéguy' and turn left after the bridge)
Near river Forest area
Closed mid Nov-mid Mar
23 en suite (bth/shr) 3 rooms in annexe (3 fmly) (14 with balcony) TV in all bedrooms Direct dial from all bedrooms Licensed Full central heating Open parking available Supervised Outdoor swimming pool (heated) Tennis Pool table Open terrace Last d 20.45hrs Languages spoken: English,Spanish
ROOMS: (room only) s 315-370FF; d 335-1080FF ✱
MEALS: Full breakfast 50FF Lunch 110-215FF&alc Dinner 110-215FF&alc✱
CARDS: 💳 ▆

ST-JEAN-DE-LUZ Pyrénées-Atlantiques

★ ★ ★ ★ Parc Victoria
5 rue Cépe *64500*
☎ 559267878 FAX 559267808
This 19th-century residence is situated in Saint-Jean-de-Luz, a colourful fishing port on the Atlantic ocean. Surrounded by a flower garden and park with mature trees, bedrooms are decorated in 1930s decor and equipped with marble bathrooms. There is a delightful terrace where guests can enjoy a generous breakfast or a drink, and the restaurant serves a choice of enjoyable meals.
Near sea In town centre
Closed 15 Nov-15 Mar
12 en suite (bth/shr) 2 rooms in annexe (2 fmly) (2 with balcony) TV in all bedrooms STV Radio in rooms Mini-bar in all bedrooms Licensed Lift Night porter Full central heating Open parking available Supervised Child discount available 6yrs Outdoor swimming pool (heated) Boule Open terrace Covered terrace Languages spoken: English
CARDS: 💳 ▩ ▆ ▪ Travellers cheques

ST-JEAN-PIED-DE-PORT Pyrénées-Atlantiques

★ ★ Central
1 pl Ch-de-Gaulle *64220*
☎ 559370022 FAX 559372779
Saint-Jean-Pied-De-Port is the last stopping place on the road

to Santiago de Compostella and combines the beauty of the Pyrenees with the charm of the Basque region. The Central Hotel enjoys a riverside position and features rustic bedrooms with modern facilities as well as a restaurant offering a regional cuisine rich in flavour and prepared with fresh local produce.
Near river Near lake Forest area In town centre
Closed 15 Dec-15 Feb
13 en suite (bth/shr) Some rooms in annexe (8 fmly) (9 with balcony) No smoking in 2 bedrooms TV in all bedrooms STV Licensed Full central heating Child discount available 10yrs Open terrace V meals Languages spoken: English,German,Spanish
CARDS: 💳 ▩ ▆ ▪ Travellers cheques

★ ★ ★ Les Pyrénées
19 pl Ch-de-Gaulle *64220*
☎ 559370101 FAX 559371897
This friendly hotel is located in the pretty village of Saint-Jean-Pied-De-Port and features a cheerful interior with a restaurant where the dishes reflect the colours and flavours of the regional cuisine prepared by the chef-proprietor Firmin Arrambide. The guest accommodation comprises attractive rooms with up-to-date facilities which provide a good level of comfort.
In town centre
Closed 5-28 Jan
(6 fmly) (5 with balcony) TV available Direct-dial available Lift Full central heating Air conditioning in bedrooms Covered parking available (charged) Outdoor swimming pool (heated) Open terrace Last d 21.00hrs
MEALS: Full breakfast 85FF Lunch 230-500FF Dinner 230-500FF✱

ST-LOUBES Gironde

★ ★ Au Vieux Logis
33450
☎ 556789299 FAX 556789118
Both the hotel and its restaurant are housed in a 19th-century building which has retained the atmosphere of a private house with the added convenience of the comfort and attentive service of an hotel. Bedrooms are well equipped with modern facilities. There is a small restaurant and located within a short driving distance from Bordeaux and St Emilion, it is a good base for visits to the surrounding vineyards.
In town centre Near motorway
6 en suite (bth/shr) TV in all bedrooms Direct dial from all bedrooms Mini-bar in all bedrooms Licensed Full central heating Last d 22.00hrs Languages spoken: English
ROOMS: (room only) s fr 250FF; d fr 290FF ✱
MEALS: Continental breakfast 40FF Lunch 80-260FF Dinner 130-260FF✱
CARDS: 💳 ▩ ▆ ▪ Travellers cheques

ST-PÉE-SUR-NIVELLE Pyrénées-Atlantiques

★ ★ Bonnet (Minotel)
Quartier Ibarron *64310*
☎ 559541026 FAX 559545315
Near river Near lake
RS 3 Jan-10 Feb
75 en suite (bth/shr) 2 rooms in annexe (4 fmly) (30 with balcony) TV in all bedrooms Licensed Lift Full central heating Open parking available Child discount available Outdoor swimming pool (heated) Tennis Boule Open terrace Last d 21.00hrs Languages spoken: English,Spanish

contd.

MEALS: Full breakfast 42FF Continental breakfast 42FF Lunch 59-93FF&alc Dinner 59-93FF&alc✱
CARDS: ●● ■ ■ ■ ⊕ Travellers cheques

ST-PIERRE-DE-CHIGNAC Dordogne

★ ★ Le Saint Pierre
pl de la Halle *24330*
☎ 553075504 FAX 553082647
Close to the Vézère valley the hotel is a good base for exploring the world-famous prehistoric sites and the medieval city of Sarlat. Visitors receive a warm welcome in this establishment, where comfort and traditional, local cuisine go hand in hand. The bedrooms - two with terraces - have modern appointments, there is a shaded terrace, a garden where children can play freely, whilst the surrounding area offers a choice of outdoor activities.
Near river Forest area Near motorway
Closed Feb-Mar
13 en suite (bth/shr) Some rooms in annexe (4 fmly) (2 with balcony) TV in all bedrooms STV Licensed Full central heating Open parking available Covered parking available (charged) Indoor swimming pool (heated) Outdoor swimming pool (heated) Open terrace Last d 21.00hrs Languages spoken: English
CARDS: ●● ■ Travellers cheques

ST-SYLVESTRE-SUR-LOT Lot-et-Garonne

★ ★ ★ ★ Château Lalande
47140
☎ 553361515 FAX 553361516
This handsome residence provides the luxurious setting for a memorable holiday or corporate stay. It features an elegant interior with a fine range of facilities and services on offer, including elegant bedrooms, decorated with period furniture and providing the highest level of comfort. The two restaurants serve cuisine which alternates between light dishes and classic specialities. The surrounding region has a lot to offer for those who prefer more energetic pastimes.
Near river Near lake Forest area In town centre
22 en suite (bth/shr) TV in all bedrooms STV Direct dial from all bedrooms Mini-bar in all bedrooms Licensed Lift Full central heating Open parking available Covered parking available Child discount available 13yrs Outdoor swimming pool (heated) Tennis Sauna Solarium Gym Pool table Boule Jacuzzi/spa Open terrace V meals Last d 22.00hrs Languages spoken: English
CARDS: ●● ■ ■ ■ ⊕

SALIGNAC (JAYAC) Dordogne

★ ★ Coulier
24590
☎ 553288646 FAX 553282633
Closed 15 Dec-15 Jan
15 rms (13 shr) (3 fmly) TV in all bedrooms Mini-bar in all bedrooms Full central heating Open parking available Child discount available 12yrs Outdoor swimming pool Open terrace
CARDS: ●● ■ Travellers cheques

SARE Pyrénées-Atlantiques

★ ★ ★ Arraya
64310
☎ 559542046 FAX 559542704
(From A63 exit at St Jean de Luz Nord, take D918 towards d'Ascain-Sare)

The Hotel Arraya offers its clientele the charm of a private country house with the added convenience of discreet but efficient service. The interior is decorated in the style of the finest 17th-century Basque residences, and features a foyer, cosy accommodation and a bar. The dining room serves a splendid cuisine which is renowned in the area and includes a choice of regional specialities.
Near river Forest area In town centre
Closed mid Nov-mid Apr
21 en suite (bth/shr) (4 fmly) (7 with balcony) TV in all bedrooms Direct dial from all bedrooms Licensed Night porter Full central heating Air conditioning in bedrooms Open parking available Supervised Child discount available Open terrace Last d 22.00hrs Languages spoken: English, Spanish
CARDS: ●● ■ ■

SAUBUSSE Landes

★ ★ Complexe Aubusse Thermal
40180
☎ 558574000 FAX 558573737
(autoroute A64 exit 8, direction for Dax, complex signposted)
The complex, which can offer health treatments, incorporates a hotel-restaurant set in a forest landscape. There are various activities including a gym and swimming pool and the beaches of the Atlantic coast are nearby.
Near river Forest area Near motorway
Closed Dec-Feb
48 en suite (bth/shr) 10 rooms in annexe (2 fmly) (6 with balcony) TV in all bedrooms Direct dial from all bedrooms Room-safe Licensed Night porter Full central heating Open parking available Child discount available 12yrs Indoor swimming pool (heated) Outdoor swimming pool Sauna Solarium Gym Pool table Boule Jacuzzi/spa Bicycle rental Open terrace Last d 20.00hrs Languages spoken: English,Spanish
ROOMS: (room only) s 250-300FF; d 250-300FF
Reductions over 1 night Special breaks
MEALS: Full breakfast 37FF Continental breakfast 37FF Lunch 79-215FF Dinner 79-215FF
CARDS: ●● ■ Travellers cheques

SAUVETERRE-DE-BEARN Pyrénées-Atlantiques

★ ★ Hotel de Vieux Pont
64390
☎ 559389511 FAX 559389910
Near river Near sea Near motorway
Closed Nov-Mar
7 en suite (bth/shr) (2 fmly) (5 with balcony) TV in all bedrooms STV Direct dial from all bedrooms Licensed Full central heating Open terrace Last d 21.15hrs Languages spoken: English,German
CARDS: ●● ■ Travellers cheques

SÉRIGNAC-SUR-GARONNE Lot-et-Garonne

★ ★ ★ Le Prince Noir
rte de Mont-de-Marsan *47310*
☎ 553687430 FAX 553687193
The 17th-century hotel Le Prince Noir is situated in the heart of Lot-et-Garonne, near the Landes region. The restaurant, where exposed brickwork and a beamed ceiling create an informal, cosy atmosphere, serves a range of enjoyable dishes. All the bedrooms are personally styled and feature varied furnishings and fabrics. In addition, there is a peaceful interior courtyard,

and a shaded park with good leisure facilities.'
Near river Forest area Near motorway
22 en suite (bth/shr) (2 fmly) TV in all bedrooms Direct dial
from all bedrooms Licensed Full central heating Open
parking available Supervised Outdoor swimming pool Tennis
Boule Bicycle rental Open terrace Last d 20.45hrs Languages
spoken: English,Spanish
CARDS: ●● ■■ ■■ Travellers cheques

SOUMOULOU Pyrénées-Atlantiques

★★ Bearn
14 rue de Las Bordes 64420
☎ 559046009 FAX 559046333
A warm welcome by the friendly owners, the Chabat family,
awaits visitors upon arrival in this charming establishment.
Surrounded by parkland, and with views of the Pyrenees, it
provides the charming setting for a holiday in this region full
of places to visit and discover. The spacious, gourmet
restaurant offers a regional cuisine, accompanied by a choice
of fine wines. There are pleasant sound-proofed bedrooms, a
cosy TV lounge and bar, as well as a terrace for relaxation.
Near river Forest area Near motorway
14 en suite (bth/shr) (3 fmly) TV in all bedrooms Direct dial
from all bedrooms Licensed Night porter Full central heating
Open parking available Covered parking available (charged)
Child discount available Boule Open terrace Languages
spoken: English,Spanish
MEALS: Full breakfast 40FF Lunch 67-195FF&alc✱
CARDS: ●● ■■ ■■ ●) Travellers cheques

THIVIERS Dordogne

★★★ Château de Mavaleix
24800
☎ 553528201 FAX 553620380
This handsome building was erected in the 13th century to
stand guard over the valley and ensure the safety of travellers.
A refuge for nobles on the way to Santiago de Compostella, it
provided a haven of rest and good cheer for the pilgrims. The
château has retained its simplistic, geometrical lines from the
early Middle Ages. Restored in later centuries, it is now a listed
property. Surrounded by parkland it exudes an atmosphere of
peace and serenity which is reflected in its interior. The
bedrooms are decorated in a discreet fashion and provide a
high level of comfort, whilst the restaurant serves dishes to
suit most palates.
Near river Near lake Forest area
Closed 8 Jan-6 Feb
15 en suite (bth/shr) 10 rooms in annexe (1 with balcony) TV
in all bedrooms Licensed Full central heating Open parking
available Child discount available Outdoor swimming pool
Fishing Boule Bicycle rental Open terrace V meals Last d
21.00hrs Languages spoken: English,Spanish
ROOMS: (room only) s 380-390FF; d 410-450FF ✱
MEALS: Full breakfast 60FF Lunch 130-180FF&alc Dinner 130-
180FF
CARDS: ●● ■■ Travellers cheques

TRÉMOLAT Dordogne

★★★ Le Vieux Logis et ses Logis des Champs
24510
☎ 553228006 FAX 553228489
In the heart of the Périgord region, the hotel 'Le Vieux Logis'
features the comfort and the warm restful interior of a
luxurious private residence. All the bedrooms and apartments

are tastefully decorated and equipped with modern facilities.
The restaurant serves an honest, creative cuisine which
incorporates fresh local produce to a large extent.
Near river Near lake Forest area
24 en suite (bth/shr) (6 fmly) TV in all bedrooms Direct dial
from all bedrooms Mini-bar in all bedrooms Licensed Full
central heating Open parking available Covered parking
available Child discount available 10yrs Outdoor swimming
pool Pool table Boule Open terrace Cycle hire nearby V
meals Languages spoken: German,Spanish
ROOMS: (room only) d 780-1360FF
MEALS: Full breakfast 95FF Continental breakfast 85FF Lunch
190-390FF&alc
CARDS: ●● ■■ ■■ ●) Travellers cheques

URRUGNE Pyrénées-Atlantiques

Château d'Urtubie
64122
☎ 559543115 FAX 559546251
Near sea Near beach Forest area Near motorway
Closed 15 Feb-23 Dec
6 rms (4 bth 1 shr) Licensed Full central heating Open
parking available Covered parking available Child discount
available Tennis Fishing Bicycle rental Open terrace
Languages spoken: English,Spanish
CARDS: ■■ ■■

USTARITZ Pyrénées-Atlantiques

★★★ Hotel la Patoula
rue Principale 64480
☎ 559930056 FAX 559931654
This charming hotel is situated in a pretty Basque village by
the River Nive. Quiet bedrooms have stylish décor and the
restaurant produces local cuisine with fresh ingredients.
Near river Near sea Near beach Forest area Near motorway
Closed 6 Dec-14 Feb
9 en suite (bth/shr) TV in 8 bedrooms Direct dial from all
bedrooms Mini-bar in 2 bedrooms Full central heating Open
parking available Fishing Open terrace V meals Last d 22.00hrs
ROOMS: (room only) d 350-470FF
MEALS: Continental breakfast 60FF Lunch 100-200FF&alc
Dinner 100-200FF&alc
CARDS: ●● ■■ Travellers cheques

VIEUX-MARUIL Dordogne

★★★ Château de Vieux Mareuil
24340
☎ 553607715 FAX 553564933
Situated on a small hill, this magnificent 15th-century
residence offers fine views over the surrounding woods and
meadows of the Périgord Vert. It features tastefully decorated
guest rooms which provide the highest level of comfort, a
comfortable lounge for relaxation, and a small, intimate
dining-room which serves widely acknowledged cuisine,
consisting of outstanding, well-presented dishes, which in
summer also can be enjoyed on the panoramic terrace.
Near river Near lake Forest area Near motorway
Closed 2 Jan-1 Mar
14 en suite (bth/shr) (4 fmly) (5 with balcony) No smoking in 7
bedrooms TV in all bedrooms STV Direct dial from all
bedrooms Mini-bar in all bedrooms Licensed Night porter
Full central heating Open parking available
Covered parking available Supervised Child discount
available 10yrs Outdoor swimming pool (heated)

contd.

Fishing Riding Solarium Boule Jacuzzi/spa Bicycle rental
Open terrace V meals Last d 22.00hrs Languages spoken:
English,German, Italian, Spanish
MEALS: Continental breakfast 60FF Lunch 130-290FF&alc
Dinner 130-290FF&alc✱
CARDS: ✹ ▰ ▱ ⍟ Travellers cheques

VILLEFRANCHE-DU-PÉRIGORD Dordogne

★ ★ La Clé des Champs
Mazeyrolles 24550
☎ 553299594 FAX 553284296
This old inn is located in the heart of the rolling countryside
of the Périgord Noir and reflects in its charming interior
local history and traditions. This region has reputedly the
best cuisine in France and the restaurant does this
reputation justice. In addition comfortable bedrooms offer
restful accommodation and are equipped with every modern
facility.
Forest area
Closed Nov-end Apr
13 en suite (bth/shr) (13 with balcony) TV in all bedrooms
STV Direct dial from all bedrooms Mini-bar in all bedrooms
Licensed Full central heating Open parking available
Covered parking available Child discount available 12yrs
Outdoor swimming pool (heated) Tennis Pool table Boule
Bicycle rental Open terrace Last d 21.00hrs Languages
spoken: English
MEALS: Full breakfast 40FF Continental breakfast 25FF Lunch
98FF&alc Dinner 98FF&alc✱
CARDS: ✹ ▰ ▱ ⍟ Travellers cheques

VILLENEUVE-DE-MARSAN Landes

★ ★ ★ Francis Darroze
Grande-Rue 40190
☎ 558452007 FAX 558458267
The hotel Francis Darozze is an example of a success story
which started a century ago. In the following years the art of
hospitality and high quality cooking have been passed on from
father to sons and daughters in this charming establishment,
which features individually appointed guest rooms with
excellent facilities. The restaurant serves an outstanding
cuisine based on authentic recipes with an imaginative touch,
as well as exquisite desserts, complemented by the finest
vintage wines.
Forest area In town centre
15 en suite (bth) (6 fmly) (12 with balcony) No smoking in 1
bedroom TV in all bedrooms Radio in rooms Licensed Full
central heating Open parking available Covered parking
available Supervised Child discount available 12yrs Outdoor
swimming pool Tennis Boule Open terrace Covered terrace

V meals Last d 22.00hrs Languages spoken:
English,German,Spanish
CARDS: ✹ ▰ ▱ ⍟ Travellers cheques

VITRAC Dordogne

★ ★ De Plaisance
Le Port 24200
☎ 553283304 FAX 553281924
Surrounded by numerous places of interest, the hotel is built
against a hillside in the little village of Vitrac. Each generation
of the family have continued to offer the real Périgord tradition
of a lovingly prepared classic cuisine and cosy
accommodation. The surrounding countryside offers many
fascinating prehistoric sites to discover as well as splendid
scenery to explore.
Near river
Closed 16 Nov-6 eb
42 en suite (bth/shr) Some rooms in annexe TV in all
bedrooms Licensed Lift Full central heating Open parking
available Child discount available 12yrs Outdoor swimming
pool Tennis Boule Mini-golf Open terrace Last d 20.45hrs
Languages spoken: English
CARDS: ✹ ▰ ▱ ⍟

★ ★ ★ Domaine de Rochebois
rte de Montfort 24200
☎ 553315252 FAX 553293688
The 'Domaine de Rochebois' was fully renovated and
refurbished with a distinct Italian touch and is now a splendid
hotel where the interior consists of a congenial bar, billiards
room, an elegant restaurant, and guest rooms with excellent
modern facilities, providing the highest level of comfort.
Surrounded by beautiful gardens it offers outstanding leisure
facilities including a fabulous nine hole golf course, which was
opened in 1989, and harmoniously blends with the
surrounding landscape.
Near river Forest area
Closed end Oct-mid Apr
40 en suite (bth/shr) (35 with balcony) TV in all bedrooms
STV Direct dial from all bedrooms Mini-bar in all bedrooms
Licensed Lift Night porter Full central heating Open parking
available Supervised Child discount available 12yrs Outdoor
swimming pool Golf 9 Tennis Solarium Gym Pool table
Boule Bicycle rental Open terrace V meals Last d 21.30hrs
Languages spoken: English,German
CARDS: ✹ ▰ ▱ ⍟ Travellers cheques

Taking your mobile phone to France?
See page 11

Aquitaine

The French Beret

The traditional French beret originated from Béarn and was part of the traditional costume of the Ossau Valley as early as the middle ages. Traditionally, the beret was worn from breakfast until bedtime and was even occasionally used as a purse. It was the mark of a man and a means of identifying him as a Béarnais. The door of the 13th-century church at Bellocq has a beret on it. Today the beret is worn by thousands,

Does the beret aid contemplation? Perhaps this citizen can provide the answer.

many having no idea of its origin, save that it came from France. Two local companies export the beret worldwide and it remains a local symbol as well as being a practical or fashionable hat for both men and women.

Périgord: a treasure trove of prehistoric sites

Périgord is home to a treasure trove of caves and sites and almost half the cave paintings found in France. Both the topography and climate of the Vézère valley in particular suited prehistoric man providing food and natural shelters in abundance. So it was here that much enterprise and development took place. The largest wall-painting representing aurochs known in Europe can be found at the caves of Lascaux as well as beautiful paintings of bulls and horses. The cave at Villars is home to a blue horse, whilst mammoths can be found on the ceiling of Rouffignac cave. The cave-dwelling fortress at the Roque St Christophe near Le Moustier is also worth a visit, as are wonderful caves full of stalagmites and stalactites at Les Eyzies and the chasm of Proumeyssac at Audrix.

Midi-Pyrénées

Midi-Pyrénées is a region of rich culture and natural beauty just waiting to be discovered. This is the place to enjoy some of the many colourful and traditional festivals which sometimes involve whole départements or just a village or town. Appreciate too the wonderful choice of music festivals staged throughout the year that offer something for every taste from local folk singing through to sacred music or jazz. Standing on the banks of the Garonne River, Toulouse is a lively city where the arts and modern technology live comfortably side by side amongst the characteristic squares and streets.

(Top): The beautiful village of Calvignac stands atop a vertical rock face above the river. The Tour de Gourdon has secret dungeons and a fine Renaissance gallery.

(Bottom): French bread - famous the world over for its freshness and flavour.

ESSENTIAL FACTS

DÉPARTEMENTS:	Ariège, Aveyron, Haute-Garonne, Gers, Lot, Tarn, Tarn-et-Garonne, Hautes-Pyrénées
PRINCIPAL TOWNS	Albi, Castres, Foix, Lourdes, Montauban, Tarbes, Toulouse, Millau
PLACES TO VISIT:	Archeological sites at La Graufenesque & Montmaurin; Beaulieu-en-Rouergue Abbey; Castles at Assier, Castelnau-Bretenoux & Gramont; Carmelite Chapel at Toulouse; boyhood home of Marshal Foch at Tarbes; Bagnères-de-Bigorre, a spa town since Roman times; the National Stud at Tarbes with their beautiful Anglo-Arabs; the pilgrimage town of Lourdes.
REGIONAL TOURIST OFFICE	54 boulevard de l'Embouchure, BP2166, 31022 Toulouse Tel 0561 13 55 55 Fax 05 61 47 1716
LOCAL GASTRONOMIC DELIGHTS	Cassoulet, a casserole of white haricot beans with a selection of fresh pork, smoked pork or garlic sausages, bacon, preserved goose or duck; foie gras, goose liver pâté; magret de canard; cabecou, small cheeses; croustades, small pies containing meat, game or poultry, often deep-fried.
DRINKS	Armagnac

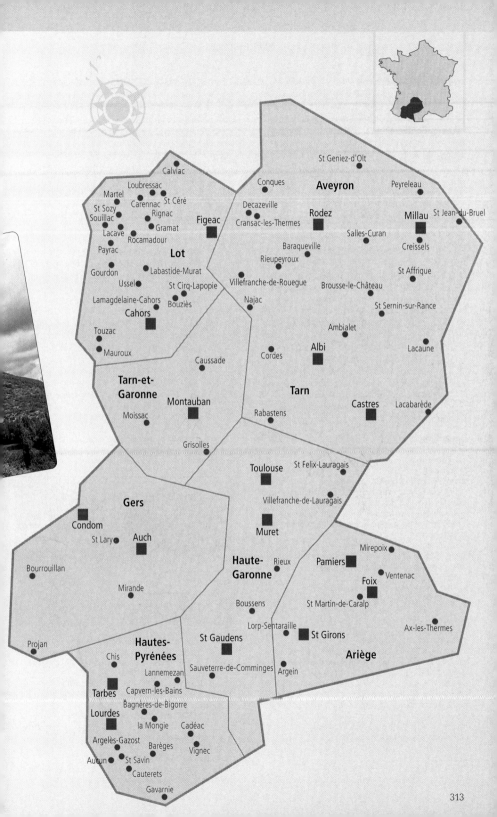

St Geniez-d'Olt

Calviac

Conques **Aveyron** Peyreleau

Loubressac
Martel St Céré Decazeville Rodez Millau St Jean-du-Bruel
St Sozy Carennac Rignac Cransac-les-Thermes
Souillac Figeac Salles-Curan Creissels
Lacave Gramat
Rocamadour **Lot** Baraqueville
Payrac Rieupeyroux St Affrique

Gourdon Labastide-Murat Villefranche-de-Rouegue Brousse-le-Château
Ussel St Cirq-Lapopie Najac St Sernin-sur-Rance
Lamagdelaine-Cahors Bouziès
Cahors Ambialet Lacaune

Touzac Caussade Cordes **Albi**
Mauroux

Tarn-et- **Tarn**
Garonne Castres Lacabarède
Montauban Rabastens
Moissac

Grisolles

Toulouse St Felix-Lauragais

Villefranche-de-Lauragais
Gers
Condom **Muret**
St Lary **Auch** Mirepoix
Pamiers
Bourrouillan **Haute-** Rieux Ventenac
Garonne **Foix**
Mirande St Martin-de-Caralp
Boussens
Lorp-Sentaraille Ax-les-Thermes
Projan **Hautes-** St Gaudens **St Girons**
Chis **Pyrénées** **Ariège**
Lannemezan Sauveterre-de-Comminges Argein
Tarbes Capvern-les-Bains
Lourdes Bagnères-de-Bigorre
la Mongie Cadéac
Argelès-Gazost Barèges Vignec
Aucun St Savin
Cauterets
Gavarnie

313

EVENTS & FESTIVALS

Mar Lourdes International Festival of Sacred Music; Toulouse International Fair; St-Félix de Lauragais Cocagne Traditional Fair;

Apr Albi Jazz Festival; Tarbes French Song Festival; Auterive Medieval Festival

May Toulouse International Children's Theatre Festival; Montauban French Song Festival; Festival at Condom; Haute-Garonne Départment Poilus Rally for pre-1914 cars; Bourg St Bernard 'Pré de la Fadaise' Traditional Celebration

June Auch Classical Music Festival; Cahors Spring Festival; Villefranche-de-Rouergue European Festival Gramont Music Festival in the Castle; Vic Fezensac Whit Sunday Feria; Comminges Thermal Spa Rally for cycle-cars between 1914-1935; Toulouse Grand Férétra Festival

Jul Foix Medieval Pageant; Moissac Musical Evenings in the Abbey; Puylaurens Summer Festival; Saujac Light & Sound Show; St-Girons Folklore & Dance Festival; Germ-Louron Jazz Festival; St-Félix Lauragais Classical & Traditional Music Festival; Toulouse Summer Festival; Mirande Country Music Festival; Gourdon Summer Festival (classical & jazz); Jazz Festivals at Luz-St-Sauveur, Souillac & Montauban; Sylvanès

Sacred Music Festival; Castres Goya Festival Galvarnie Theatre Festival; Tarbres Equestria; Montréal-du-Gers Festival; St-Lizier Classical Music Festival; Cordes Festival of the Great Falconer; Lisle sur Tarn Wine Festival; Mirepoix Medieval Festival

Aug Moissac Musical Evenings in the Abbey; St Félix Lauragais Classical & Traditional Music Festival; Toulouse Summer Festival; Sylvanès Sacred Music Festival (*music, dance, theatre*); Gourdon Summer Festival (classical & jazz); Mirepoix International Puppet Festival; Capvern les Bains Latin American Festival; Assier Festival (theatre, music, attractions); Aveyron Département Folklore Festival; Vaour Comedy Festival; Fleurance Festival of the Heavens; Marciac Jazz Festival; Hauts-Pyrénées Département 'On the paths to Santiago de Compostela'; St-Paul Cap de Joux Historical Festival; Wine Festivals at Gaillac & Madiran; Trie sur- Baïse Pourcailhade (pig) Festival; Sauveterre-du-Rouergue Festival of Light; Peyrusse-le-Roc Medieval Festival;

Sep Toulouse Jacobin Piano Festival; Cordes Gastronomic Festival; Moissac Chasselas Grape Festival;

Oct Auch Festival of Contemporary Music & Dance; Toulouse Jazz Festival

---

ALBI Tarn

★ ★ Lapérouse   ✗✗✗✗
21 pl Laperouse *81000*
☎ 563546922 FAX 563380369
Set in the very heart of the town, and a stone's throw from all the sights, the establishment provides comfortable bedrooms, each with their own personal touch. There is a delightful terrace, with pot-plants situated around the swimming pool. In town centre
24 rms (9 bth 13 shr) (1 with balcony) TV in all bedrooms STV Direct dial from all bedrooms Licensed Full central heating Outdoor swimming pool Languages spoken: English,Portuguese
ROOMS: (room only) s 150-200FF; d 200-320FF
CARDS: ●● ☲ Travellers cheques

★ ★ ★ ★ La Réserve (Relais et Chateaux)
rte de Cordes *81000*
☎ 563608080 FAX 563476360
On the way to Cordes, just outside Albi and situated on the bank of the river Tarn, the hotel La Réserve provides an oasis of tranquillity and enjoyment. Privately owned by a family who over five generations have perfected the art of hospitality, it offers bedrooms with private facilities, TV, direct-dial telephone and also has an outdoor swimming pool, and clay tennis-courts. Albi, with its magnificent cathedral dating back to the 13th century and its famous Toulouse-Lautrec museum, offers many places of historic interest.
Near river
Closed early Nov-late Apr
24 en suite (bth/shr) 4 rooms in annexe (4 fmly) (12 with balcony) No smoking in 10 bedrooms TV in all bedrooms STV

Direct dial from all bedrooms Mini-bar in all bedrooms Room-safe Licensed Night porter Full central heating Air conditioning in bedrooms Open parking available Supervised

Child discount available 12yrs Outdoor swimming pool (heated) Tennis Fishing Solarium Pool table Boule Bicycle rental Covered terrace V meals Last d 21.00hrs Languages spoken: English, German & Spain
ROOMS: (room only) s 490-750FF; d 750-1300FF
MEALS: Full breakfast 70FF Lunch 120-300FF&alc Dinner 160-360FF&alc
CARDS: ●● ■■ ☲ ◑ Travellers cheques

★ ★ ★ ★ St-Antoine
17 rue St-Antoine *81000*
☎ 563540404 FAX 563471047
The Hostellerie Saint-Antoine is one of the most peaceful and comfortable of its kind in the region, and amongst the oldest in

314

the whole of France. Founded in 1734 and renovated in both 1964 and 1989, it has been in the capable hands of the same family for five generations. The bedrooms are equipped with private facilities, TV and direct-dial telephone. The restaurant is renowned for its extensive range of regional specialities. Guests can use the swimming pool and tennis courts of the hotel La Réserve which is owned by the same family.
In town centre
44 en suite (bth/shr) (4 fmly) No smoking in 10 bedrooms TV in all bedrooms STV Mini-bar in all bedrooms Licensed Lift Night porter Full central heating Air conditioning in bedrooms Open parking available (charged) Supervised Child discount available 12yrs Bicycle rental Open terrace V meals Last d 21.00hrs Languages spoken: English, German & Spanish
MEALS: Full breakfast 60FF Lunch 80-140FF&alc Dinner 140-280FF&alc✱
CARDS: 💳 🏧 🔁 💳 Travellers cheques

AMBIALET Tarn

★ ★ Du Pont
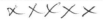
81430
☎ 563553207 FAX 563533721
The hotel Du Pont stands on the banks of the river Tarn and has been passed on from father to son for nearly two centuries. The individually appointed bedrooms are spacious and offer maximum comfort. There is a sunny terrace with fine views over the swimming pool and surrounding countryside. The imaginative cuisine places the emphasis on presentation and utilises high quality ingredients from the region.
Near river Forest area
Closed mid Nov-mid Dec
20 en suite (bth/shr) 6 rooms in annexe (6 fmly) (6 with balcony) TV in all bedrooms STV Direct dial from all bedrooms Licensed Full central heating Open parking available Child discount available Outdoor swimming pool (heated) Tennis Bicycle rental Open terrace V meals Last d 21.30hrs Languages spoken: English
ROOMS: (room only) d 300-315FF
MEALS: Full breakfast 40FF Lunch 100-200FF&alc Dinner 100-200FF&alc
CARDS: 💳 🏧 🔁 💳 Travellers cheques

ARGEIN Ariège

★ ★ La Terrasse
09140
☎ 561967011
The small Hotel 'La Terrasse' is the ideal venue for a restful holiday accompanied by excellent food. The restaurant serves a choice of carefully prepared dishes comprising fresh-water fish and regional specialities. The country-style furnishings in the guest rooms and public area create a warm and friendly atmosphere.
Near river Near beach In town centre
Closed mid Nov-end Jan
10 rms (5 bth 3 shr) (1 fmly) (1 with balcony) Licensed Night porter Child discount available 12yrs Open terrace Last d 21.00hrs
MEALS: Continental breakfast 30FF Lunch 90-160FFalc Dinner 70-170FF&alc✱

Taking your mobile phone to France?
See page 11

ARGELÈS-GAZOST Hautes-Pyrénées

★ ★ Beau Site
10 rue Capitaine Digoy 65400
☎ 562970863 FAX 562970601
(in the town centre near the Office de Tourisme)
Situated in a picturesque street in the old part of the town, the hotel features a comfortably furnished, cosy lounge and bedrooms equipped with all the modern amenities. There is a delightful garden, and the terrace offers panoramic views over the beautiful surrounding countryside. The restaurant provides a selection of well-presented dishes made with fresh local produce.
Near river Near lake Forest area In town centre Near motorway
Closed 5 Nov-5 Dec
16 en suite (bth/shr) 5 rooms in annexe (6 with balcony) No smoking on premises TV in all bedrooms STV Direct dial from all bedrooms Licensed Child discount available 10yrs Open terrace V meals Last d 20.00hrs Languages spoken: English, Italian
ROOMS: (room only) d 240-250FF **Reductions over 1 night**
MEALS: Continental breakfast 30FF Lunch 80-85FF Dinner 80-85FF✱
CARDS: 💳 🔁 Travellers cheques

★ ★ Bon Répos
av du Stade 65400
☎ 562970149 FAX 562970397
This friendly establishment has a convivial atmosphere throughout and is a popular meeting place for locals and tourists alike. The pretty guest-rooms have fine views of the surrounding mountains and are equipped with modern day facilities. The restaurant serves a range of well-presented dishes, prepared with fresh local produce.
Near river Forest area
Closed Oct-mid May
18 en suite (bth/shr) (10 fmly) (7 with balcony) TV in all bedrooms Licensed Full central heating Open parking available Covered parking available (charged) Outdoor swimming pool Boule Open terrace Languages spoken: English, Spanish
CARDS: 💳 🔁 Travellers cheques

★ ★ Hostellerie Le Relais
25 rue Maréchal Foch 65400
☎ 562970127 FAX 562979000
In town centre
Situated amongst the magnificent scenery of the Pyrenees, the hotel has an informal atmosphere throughout. The public room is bright and cheerful, and the bedrooms have more than adequate facilities. Guests can relax on the shaded, flower-decked terrace, whilst the restaurant serves enjoyable meals in a friendly atmosphere.
In town centre Near motorway
Closed Nov-Jan
23 en suite (bth/shr) TV in all bedrooms STV Direct dial from all bedrooms Licensed Full central heating Open parking available Supervised Child discount available Open terrace Last d 21.00hrs Languages spoken: English, Spanish
MEALS: Continental breakfast 30FF Lunch 70-220FF&alc Dinner 70-220FF✱
CARDS: 💳 🔁 Travellers cheques

AUCH Gers

★ ★ ★ ★ Hotel de France (Relais et Chateaux)
2 pl de la Libération *32003*
☎ 562617171 FAX 562617181
Situated in the heart of the ancient town of Auch between the cathedral and the Town Hall, this imposing building used to be a coaching inn. The establishment has retained all of its superb original décor. Bedrooms are spacious and offer modern facilities to provide maximum comfort. An elegant restaurant ensures guests dine in an atmosphere of sophistication.
Near river Near lake In town centre Near motorway
29 en suite (bth/shr) (3 fmly) TV in all bedrooms STV Radio in rooms Mini-bar in all bedrooms Licensed Lift Night porter Full central heating Open parking available (charged) Covered parking available (charged) Supervised Child discount available 12yrs Open terrace Boutique Wkly live entertainment Languages spoken: English,German & Spanish
MEALS: Full breakfast 80FF Lunch 185-505FF&alc✱
CARDS: ●● ■■ ⬛ ⬤ Travellers cheques

AUCUN Hautes-Pyrénées

★ ★ Le Pocors
rte de l'Aubisque *65400*
☎ 562974090 FAX 562974156
Located in rural surroundings with magnificent views of the countryside, the hotel offers a relaxing stay for weary guests. The bedrooms are airy and well equipped with up-to-date facilities. There is an attractive restaurant with a good range of tasty dishes.
Near river Near lake Forest area
48 en suite (bth) (8 fmly) TV in all bedrooms Direct dial from all bedrooms Licensed Lift Full central heating Open parking available Child discount available 10yrs Indoor swimming pool (heated) Tennis Sauna Pool table Boule Open terrace Covered terrace V meals Last d 21.30hrs Languages spoken: English
ROOMS: (room only) d 260-290FF
MEALS: Full breakfast 40FF Continental breakfast 40FF Lunch 60-180FF Dinner 60-180FF
CARDS: ●● ■■ ⬛ Travellers cheques

AX-LES-THERMES Ariège

★ ★ Lauzéraie
prom du Couloubret *09110*
☎ 561642070 FAX 561643850
The Hotel L'Auzeraie lies in the heart of the wild, unspoilt Pyrenees in the peaceful spa resort of Ax-Les-Thermes and on the main routes for holiday destinations and Andorra. Just opposite the casino and close to the shops, it welcomes visitors in a friendly, relaxed atmosphere and offers sound-proofed bedrooms with modern facilities. Its is complemented by the restaurant which invites guests to sample some of the many renowned specialities of the region.
Near river Forest area In town centre Near motorway
Closed mid Nov-mid Dec
33 en suite (bth/shr) (1 fmly) (15 with balcony) TV in all bedrooms STV Direct dial from all bedrooms Licensed Lift Full central heating Open parking available Child discount available 11yrs Open terrace V meals Last d 21.00hrs Languages spoken: English,Spanish
MEALS: Full breakfast 34FF Continental breakfast 35FF Lunch 80-220FF&alc Dinner 80-220FF&alc✱
CARDS: ●● ■■ ⬛ Travellers cheques

BARAQUEVILLE Aveyron

De l'Agriculture
449 av du Centre *12160*
☎ 565690979
(From Rodez take N88 to Baraqueville)
This small informal hotel is situated in tranquil, leafy surroundings. The untiring hosts provide a round the clock attentive service, and offer their visitors pleasant bedrooms - most with modern facilities - and a friendly restaurant which serves a good range of dishes.
Near lake Forest area In town centre Near motorway
10 rms (3 bth) 20 rooms in annexe Licensed Full central heating Open parking available Covered parking available (charged) Open terrace Last d 21.30hrs
CARDS: ●● ⬛⬛ ⬤

BARÈGES Hautes-Pyrénées

★ ★ Richelieu
rue Ramond *65120*
☎ 562926811 FAX 562926600
The hotel can be found in the village of Barèges which occupies a stunning location amidst splendid mountainous scenery. It features comfortable bedrooms with good amenities and a range of leisure pursuits to suit everyone's needs. There is a comfortable lounge-bar, games room and an attractive restaurant which serves regional cuisine.
Near river Forest area In town centre Near motorway
Closed 11 Apr-May & Oct-19 Dec
35 en suite (bth/shr) (4 fmly) (14 with balcony) TV available Licensed Lift Full central heating Child discount available 10yrs Pool table Open terrace Last d 21.00hrs Languages spoken: English, Spanish
MEALS: Full breakfast 50FF Continental breakfast 50FF Lunch 90FF&alc Dinner 90FF&alc✱
CARDS: ●● ■■ ⬛ ⬤ Travellers cheques

BOURROUILLAN Gers

★ ★ Moulin du Comté
32370

☎ 562090672 FAX 562091049
(NW off N124)
Tucked away in the Gers countryside, this former 18th-century mill is situated in a park filled with flowers and trees. Guests can relax in the rustic interior which offers attractive bedrooms with modern facilities and a charming restaurant which serves local and regional specialities.
Near river Near lake Forest area
10 en suite (bth/shr) (6 fmly) (6 with balcony) TV in all bedrooms Direct dial from all bedrooms Licensed Full central heating Open parking available Supervised Child discount available 12yrs Outdoor swimming pool Fishing Boule Open terrace Covered terrace V meals Last d 22.00hrs Languages spoken: English,Spanish
ROOMS: (room only) s 250-350FF; d 250-450FF ✱
Reductions over 1 night
MEALS: Full breakfast 30FF Continental breakfast 30FF Lunch 65-280FF&alc Dinner 65-280FF&alc
CARDS: ●● ⬛⬛ ⬤

BOUSSENS Haute-Garonne

Du Lac
7 promenade du Lac *31360*
☎ 561900185 FAX 561971557
A pretty hotel on the shores of the lake, surrounded by a
flower-filled terrace. Peace and calm are assured if you stay
here. Bedrooms are comfortable and a restaurant serves
regional food using seasonal fresh produce.
Near river Near lake Forest area Near motorway
Closed 1-15 Feb
12 rms (2 fmly) (6 with balcony) TV in all bedrooms Mini-bar
in all bedrooms Licensed Night porter Full central heating
Open parking available Supervised No children Child
discount available 10yrs Boule Open terrace Last d 21.30hrs
Languages spoken: Portuguese,Spanish
CARDS: ➋ ■ ☰

BOUZIÈS Lot

★ ★ Les Falaises
46330
☎ 565312683 FAX 565302387
Situated amidst green surroundings in a tiny village of only 68
inhabitants on the banks of the river Lot, the hotel is the ideal
venue for an active holiday. Organised excursions and a
multitude of leisure facilities are available to the guests. The
bedrooms are comfortable and equipped with modern
amenities, complemented by a cosy bar, crêperie and a
restaurant.
Near river Forest area
Closed Dec-2 Feb
39 en suite (bth/shr) (11 fmly) (1 with balcony) TV in all
bedrooms Direct dial from all bedrooms Licensed Full central
heating Open parking available Child discount available
Outdoor swimming pool (heated) Tennis Fishing Pool table
Boule Bicycle rental Open terrace Table tennis,canoeing V
meals Last d 21.00hrs Languages spoken:
English,German,Spanish
MEALS: Full breakfast 40FF Lunch 79-230FF&alc Dinner 79-
230FF&alc✱
CARDS: ➋ ■ ☰ Travellers cheques

BROUSSE-LE-CHÂTEAU Aveyron

★ ★ Le Relays du Chasteau
12480
☎ 565994015 FAX 565994015
Situated in a medieval village, this establishment offers its
visitors tranquil surroundings and good food. The pleasant
bedrooms are newly decorated with matching shades and
fabrics and are equipped with modern amenities. Guests can
relax in the cosy surroundings of the bar, lounge or terrace,
and enjoy a good cuisine which incorporates richly flavoured
dishes from the south-west region.
Near river Forest area
12 en suite (bth/shr) (1 fmly) Licensed Full central heating
Open parking available Child discount available Boule Open
terrace Last d 21.00hrs Languages spoken: English,Spanish
CARDS: ➋ ☰ Travellers cheques

CADÉAC Hautes-Pyrénées

★ ★ Val d'Auré
rte de St-Lary *65240*
☎ 562986063 FAX 562986899
The informal hotel Val d'Aure is located in 7 acres of

magnificent, wooded parklands with views of the Pyrenean
mountain range. A warm and friendly atmosphere prevails
throughout, and with its well equipped, spacious bedrooms,
bar with billiard table and attractive garden, it provides the
ideal setting for a family holiday. The tastefully decorated
dining room offers panoramic views over the valley and serves
a range of enjoyable meals.
Near river Near lake Forest area
Closed Oct-19 Dec
23 en suite (bth/shr) 4 rooms in annexe (7 fmly) (9 with
balcony) TV in all bedrooms Radio in rooms Direct-dial
available Licensed Night porter Air conditioning in
bedrooms Open parking available Covered parking available
Supervised Child discount available Outdoor swimming pool
Golf Tennis Fishing Pool table Boule Bicycle rental Open
terrace Covered terrace Languages spoken: English,Spanish
MEALS: Full breakfast 42FF Lunch 65-120FF Dinner 65-
120FF✱
CARDS: ➋ ☰ Travellers cheques

CAHORS Lot

★ ★ Climat de France
Rond Point de Régourd *46000*
☎ 565300000 Cen Res 164460123 FAX 565225619
(at junction with D911 and D662)
This contemporary hotel is popular with holiday makers and
business travellers alike and features attractively furnished
bedrooms with modern amenities as well as fully equipped
conference facilities. The restaurant serves a traditional cuisine
of good quality and flavour as well as a generous buffet with
an extensive choice of specialities, complemented by a popular
menu for the younger guests.
In town centre Near motorway
68 en suite (bth/shr) 27 rooms in annexe (12 fmly) No
smoking in 2 bedrooms TV in all bedrooms STV Radio in
rooms Direct dial from all bedrooms Licensed Night porter
Full central heating Open parking available Pool table Boule
Open terrace Languages spoken: English
CARDS: ➋ ☰

CALVIAC Lot

★ ★ Le Ranfort
Lieu-dit Pont de Rhodes *46190*
☎ 565330106 FAX 565330132
Situated in wide open countryside, on the edge of the Lot and
Cantal region, this rustic hotel has a traditional interior with
well equipped bedrooms. It offers an informal restaurant
where a choice of traditional dishes features on the menu, and
which are also served on the panoramic terrace alongside the
swimming pool.
Near river Forest area
Closed 25 Sep-15 Oct
27 rms (4 fmly) No smoking in 11 bedrooms TV in all
bedrooms Direct dial from all bedrooms Licensed Full central
heating Open parking available Child discount available 10yrs
Outdoor swimming pool (heated) Boule Open terrace V
meals Last d 21.00hrs
MEALS: Full breakfast 30FF Lunch 60-190FFalc Dinner 60-
190FFalc✱
CARDS: ➋ ☰ Travellers cheques

CAPVERN-LES-BAINS Hautes-Pyrénées

★ ★ Bellevue
rte de Mauvezin 65130
☎ 562390029
The hotel stands 800 metres from the thermal baths and offers stunning views over the Pyrenean mountain range with the magnificent Pic du Midi de Bigorre in the distance, and the medieval Mauvezin castle nearby. It has pleasant guest rooms, which are mostly equipped with private facilities and a panoramic restaurant which serves honest regional cuisine. With a choice of comfortable lounges for relaxation and varied games it is an attractive venue for a restful holiday amidst outstanding countryside.
Near river Forest area
Closed early Oct-early May
33 rms (22 shr) 15 rooms in annexe (3 fmly) Full central heating Open parking available Covered parking available Solarium Boule Open terrace Covered terrace Last d 20.30hrs Languages spoken: English & Spanish
CARDS: ● ● Travellers cheques

CARENNAC Lot

★ ★ Hostellerie Fenelon

46110
☎ 565109646 FAX 565109486
This charming hotel is situated in the heart of the picturesque village of Carennac. The guest rooms are comfortable and well equipped;, and some have splendid views of the river Dordogne and l'Ile Calypso. The restaurant is noted for its excellent cuisine and offers carefully prepared dishes, produced with the finest, fresh local produce. Leisure activities on offer nearby are: boating on the river Dordogne, fishing, walking and tennis.
Near river Forest area
Closed 7 Jan-9 Mar RS Fri-Sat
15 en suite (bth/shr) (2 fmly) TV in all bedrooms STV Direct dial from all bedrooms Licensed Full central heating Open parking available Child discount available 12yrs Outdoor swimming pool (heated) Riding V meals Last d 21.00hrs
Languages spoken: English
ROOMS: (room only) s 240-280FF; d 270-340FF
Reductions over 1 night
MEALS: Full breakfast 45FF Lunch 95-270FF Dinner 95-270FF
CARDS: ● ● Travellers cheques

CAUSSADE Tarn-et-Garonne

★ ★ Dupont
25 rue des Récollets 82300
☎ 563650500 FAX 563651262
This ancient coaching inn is located between Cahors and Montauban. The restaurant offers a gastronomic menu where a choice of local ingredients take pride of place. The cosy interior consists of bedrooms with private facilities, which provide an adequate level of comfort, whilst the historic sights of Cordes and St-Cirq-Lapopie are noteworthy places to visit.
Forest area In town centre Near motorway
Closed Nov-Mar
30 en suite (bth/shr) 8 rooms in annexe (8 with balcony) TV in all bedrooms Direct dial from all bedrooms Licensed Full central heating Open parking available Covered parking available Supervised Child discount available 10yrs V meals
Languages spoken: English,Spanish
MEALS: Full breakfast 40FF Continental breakfast 30FF✱
CARDS: ● ● Travellers cheques

★ ★ Larroque
av de la Gare 82300
☎ 563651177 FAX 563651204
(Opposite the railway station)
This establishment has been owned by same family since 1886 and has provided genuine hospitality and good food for six generations. It features a charming interior, enhanced by a permanent exhibition of contemporary art, where well equipped bedrooms provide a good level of comfort. Creative cuisine based on regional recipes is served in the restaurant with its fine open fireplace, in winter, and on the terrace by the side of the swimming pool in summer.
Near river Near lake Forest area In town centre Near motorway
Closed 21 Dec-15 Jan
18 en suite (bth) 8 rooms in annexe (4 fmly) (1 with balcony) TV in all bedrooms Direct dial from all bedrooms Mini-bar in 2 bedrooms Licensed Night porter Full central heating Open parking available Supervised Child discount available 12yrs Outdoor swimming pool Bicycle rental Open terrace ping pong V meals Languages spoken: English,Spanish
ROOMS: s 180-220FF; d 215-265FF ✱ **Reductions over 1 night**
MEALS: Full breakfast 50FF Lunch 65-195FF&alc✱
CARDS: ● ● ● ● Travellers cheques

CAUTERETS Hautes-Pyrénées

★ ★ ★ Hotel Asterides
9 blvd Latapie Flurin 65110
☎ 562925043 FAX 562926489
(head towards Lourdes then to Pierrefitte-Nestalas at traffic lights turn right to Cauterets, 8km)
A quiet comfortable hotel offering friendly attentive service.
Near lake Forest area In town centre
Closed Nov-4 Dec
12 en suite (bth) (3 fmly) (7 with balcony) TV in all bedrooms Direct dial from all bedrooms Licensed Lift Full central heating Child discount available Open terrace Last d 20.30hrs
Languages spoken: English
ROOMS: s 240-350FF; d 320-500FF
MEALS: Full breakfast 40FF Continental breakfast 40FF Lunch fr 110FF Dinner fr 110FF✱

★ ★ ★ Club Aladin
av du Gen Leclerc 65110
☎ 562926000 FAX 562926330
This high quality hotel has much to offer and is especially suited to those who prefer an active holiday. Staff provide an efficient and friendly service, and the bedrooms are comfortable with up-to-date facilities. It features an indoor swimming pool, sauna, Turkish bath and fitness centre. The restaurant has a comprehensive menu of well prepared dishes, and in the evening guests can relax in the lounge or piano-bar.
Near river Forest area In town centre
Closed May & Oct-mid Dec
(15 fmly) (90 with balcony) TV in 126 bedrooms STV Direct dial from 126 bedrooms Licensed Lift Night porter Full central heating Open parking available (charged) Child discount available 12yrs Indoor swimming pool Squash Sauna Solarium Gym Last d 20.30hrs Languages spoken: English,Italian,Spanish
CARDS: ● ● ● Travellers cheques

★ ★ Etche Ona
20 rue de Richelieu *65110*
☎ 562925143 FAX 562925499
(S of Lourdes via N21 and D920)
'Etche Ona' means 'home sweet home' in the Basque
language, and that is exactly what this attractive establishment
offers: 'a home from home'. Set in the heart of the resort, it
offers a very comfortable stay in informal surroundings,
pleasant bedrooms with modern amenities and a restaurant
which serves an array of delicacies from the region
Near river Forest area
Closed May & Oct-Nov
30 rms (28 bth/shr) (7 fmly) (4 with balcony) TV in all
bedrooms Direct dial from all bedrooms Licensed Lift Full
central heating Child discount available 6yrs Sauna Solarium
Open terrace Last d 20.45hrs Languages spoken:
English,Spanish
ROOMS: (room only) d 250-320FF
MEALS: Full breakfast 35FF Continental breakfast 35FF Lunch
110-195FF&alc Dinner 110-195FF
CARDS: 🐱 💳 💳 Travellers cheques

★ Le Pas de l'Ours
21 rue de la Raillère *65110*
☎ 562925807 FAX 562920649
(S of Lourdes via N21 and D920)
This small, pretty hotel is managed by François and Blandine
Barret, who besides being hotel-owners are accomplished
mountain guides and are always willing to give useful advice
about the surrounding Pyrenees. It has comfortable bedrooms
with modern facilities, a TV lounge and a restaurant which
serves a refined cuisine which can be adapted to individual
needs.
Near river Near lake Forest area In town centre
Closed 15 Apr-1 May & 30 Sep-1 Dec
13 en suite (bth/shr) (6 fmly) (5 with balcony) No smoking on
premises Direct dial from all bedrooms Licensed Full central
heating Child discount available 12yrs Sauna Open terrace
Last d 22.00hrs Languages spoken: English
ROOMS: (room only) d 220-240FF
MEALS: Full breakfast 40FF Lunch 70-80FF&alc Dinner 70-
80FF&alc
CARDS: 🐱 💳

CHIS Hautes-Pyrénées

★ ★ De la Tour
65800
☎ 562362114 FAX 562366810
The beautiful countryside is reflected in this charming hotel,
which offers a good measure of warm hospitality, an attractive
decor and modern comfort. Guests can enjoy a healthy
breakfast at the foot of the tower, whilst the lounges and the
bar provide relaxation. The menu features rich, local dishes
where numerous fish specialities take pride of place. Just a few
minutes from the town of Tarbes, and half an hour's drive from
Lourdes, it is a good base to explore the splendid surrounding
area.
Near river Near lake Forest area Near motorway
10 en suite (bth/shr) (1 fmly) (1 with balcony) TV in all
bedrooms Direct dial from all bedrooms Licensed Full central
heating Open parking available Supervised Outdoor
swimming pool Boule Bicycle rental Open terrace Last d
20.00hrs Languages spoken: English,Spanish
CARDS: 🐱 💳 💳 Travellers cheques

CONDOM Gers

★ ★ ★ Hotel des Trois Lys
38 rue Gambetta *32100*
☎ 562283333 FAX 562284185
The hotel Trois Lys with it 18th century façade combines old-
fashioned hospitality and courteous service with all the
modern comforts of this day and age. It has a splendid outdoor
swimming pool and offers its clientele well equipped
bedrooms and conference facilities, making it equally suitable
for both commercial and leisure traveller. `
In town centre
Closed Feb
10 rms (9 bth/shr) (3 fmly) TV in all bedrooms Direct dial from
all bedrooms Licensed Full central heating Open parking
available Supervised Outdoor swimming pool Open terrace
Last d 21.30hrs
ROOMS: (room only) s 260FF; d 380-560FF
MEALS: Full breakfast 42FF Continental breakfast 42FF Lunch
80-140FFalc Dinner 80-140FFalc
CARDS: 🐱 💳 💳 💿 Travellers cheques

★ ★ Logis des Cordeliers
rue de la Paix *32100*
☎ 562280368 FAX 562682903
This charming inn is peacefully situated in leafy surroundings
not far from the bustling centre of Condom, the capital of
Armagnac. All bedrooms have modern facilities and a shaded
terrace which looks out over a superb private swimming pool.
The restaurant is housed in a 14th century chapel. The menu is
based on fine quality ingredients and offers a good choice of
dishes.
Near river Near lake Forest area In town centre Near
motorway
(11 with balcony) TV in 21 bedrooms Direct dial from 21
bedrooms Licensed Full central heating Open parking
available Covered parking available (charged) Outdoor
swimming pool Bicycle rental Open terrace Languages
spoken: English,Spanish
CARDS: 🐱 💳 Travellers cheques

CONQUES Aveyron

★ ★ Auberge St-Jacques
12320
☎ 565728636 FAX 565728247
The hotel St-Jacques is situated in one of the side streets which
filter off the main road going through the town of Conques
and the Place de la Basilique. It has a panoramic terrace on the
first floor which has views over the basilica, and comfortable
bedrooms with ancient exposed beams which create an
authentic atmosphere.
Forest area
13 en suite (bth/shr) No smoking in 1 bedroom Licensed Full
central heating Air conditioning in bedrooms Open parking
available Open terrace V meals Last d 21.30hrs Languages
spoken: English
MEALS: Full breakfast 35FF Continental breakfast 29FF Lunch
fr 100FF Dinner 185 140FF&alc ♥
CARDS: 🐱 💳 💳 💿

★ ★ ★ ★ Ste-Foy
12320
☎ 565698403 FAX 565728104
The hotel Sainte-Foy occupies a splendid location opposite the
Romanesque abbey in Conques, which is one of the main
resting places on the pilgrim-route to Santiago de   *contd.*

Compostella. This 17th century inn offers its visitors a combination of relaxation and culture with an efficient, courteous staff on hand to ensure that your stay will be a memorable experience. It has private lounges, a number of delightful shaded terraces, conference rooms equipped with up-to-date communication facilities, and a restaurant serving a cuisine cooked to the highest standards.
Near river Near lake Forest area In town centre
Closed Dec-Etr
17 en suite (bth/shr) (6 fmly) TV available Licensed Lift Full central heating Air conditioning in bedrooms Open parking available (charged) Covered parking available (charged) Child discount available Open terrace Covered terrace Last d 21.30hrs Languages spoken: English,Italian,Spanish
CARDS: 💳 🏧 💳 Travellers cheques

CORDES Tarn

★ ★ ★ Hostellerie du Vieux Cordes
rue St-Michel *81170*
☎ 563560012 FAX 563560247
This ancient dwelling stands in the medieval heart of the 13th century village of Cordes, and guests can expect a warm welcome in a relaxed and friendly atmosphere. It offers tastefully furnished, functional bedrooms; and the restaurant has an ambitious menu with regional specialities - which make much use of duck and salmon - featuring prominently.
Forest area In town centre
Closed Jan
21 en suite (bth/shr) 8 rooms in annexe (5 fmly) TV available Licensed Night porter Full central heating Open terrace V meals Last d 21.30hrs Languages spoken: English,Spanish
CARDS: 💳 🏧 💳 💳

CRANSAC-LES-THERMES Aveyron

★ ★ Du Parc
rue Général Louis Artous *12110*
☎ 565630178 FAX 565632036
The hotel is surrounded by a large park with beautiful trees and features pleasant bedrooms which are equipped with modern amenities offering a good level of comfort. Guests can enjoy a traditional meal in the informal restaurant or relax on the terrace with views of the park.
Near lake Forest area In town centre
Closed Nov-Mar
25 rms 15 rooms in annexe (4 fmly) TV in all bedrooms Direct dial from all bedrooms Licensed Full central heating Open parking available Covered parking available Supervised Child discount available 10yrs Outdoor swimming pool Fishing Riding Solarium Boule Mini-golf Bicycle rental Open terrace Covered terrace Last d 21.00hrs
MEALS: Full breakfast 55FF Continental breakfast 35FF Lunch 75-175FF Dinner 75-175FF✱
CARDS: 💳 🏧 💳 Travellers cheques

CREISSELS Aveyron

★ ★ Château de Creissels
rte de St-Affrique *12100*
☎ 565601659 FAX 565612463

This ancient building dates back to the 12th century. In 1960, extensive renovation turned it into a country inn offering modern comfort without sacrificing its old-world charm. The elegant furnishings are evocative of the past, the bedrooms are individually appointed and offer a high standard of comfort, whilst the first-class cooking places equal emphasis on

presentation and flavour. From the terrace, guests can enjoy exceptional views over the River Tarn. Leisure facilities within the vicinity include climbing, rafting, canoeing and horse-riding.
Near river Forest area
Closed Jan
31 en suite (bth/shr) (4 fmly) (5 with balcony) TV available STV Direct-dial available Licensed Full central heating Open parking available Child discount available 10yrs Fishing Pool table Boule Open terrace Covered terrace V meals Last d 21.30hrs Languages spoken: English,Spanish
MEALS: Full breakfast 45FF Lunch 70-130FFalc Dinner fr 118FFalc✱
CARDS: 💳 🏧 💳 💳 Travellers cheques

DECAZEVILLE Aveyron

★ ★ Du Pont
Port d'Agrès *12300*
☎ 565640265 FAX 565640909
(8km N of Decazville off D963 Decazville to Maurs road)
Situated in the heart of the Lot valley, between Figeac and Conques, the traditional family hotel du Pont features bedrooms with well equipped private facilities, a congenial bar, comfortable day room and a restaurant which serves good quality cuisine with a choice of house specialities. With numerous sights of cultural and historic importance nearby, it provides a good starting point for excursions in the region.
Near river Forest area Near motorway
Closed Nov-mid Mar
23 en suite (bth/shr) 8 rooms in annexe (3 fmly) (2 with balcony) TV in 3 bedrooms STV Licensed Full central heating Open parking available Covered parking available Child discount available 10yrs Outdoor swimming pool Tennis Fishing Boule Bicycle rental Open terrace Table tennis V meals Last d 21.00hrs Languages spoken: English
MEALS: Full breakfast 30FF Continental breakfast 35FF Lunch 80-160FF Dinner 80-160FF✱
CARDS: 💳 💳 Travellers cheques

FIGEAC Lot

Château du Viguier du Roy
rue Droite (Emile Zola) *46100*
☎ 565500505 FAX 565500606
Situated in the heart of the medieval city, the hotel is housed in several buildings which feature a harmonious combination of varied architectural styles. Exquisitely decorated throughout, it offers elegant bedrooms with modern amenities. In addition, the interior terraced gardens create a delightful setting for an enjoyable stay.
Near river Forest area In town centre
Closed mid Nov-mid Dec & Jan-mid Mar
20 en suite (bth/shr) (2 fmly) (4 with balcony) No smoking in 12 bedrooms TV in all bedrooms Licensed Lift Full central heating Air conditioning in bedrooms Open parking available (charged) Covered parking available (charged) Supervised Outdoor swimming pool (heated) Solarium Jacuzzi/spa Open terrace Languages spoken: English,German,Spanish

GAVARNIE Hautes-Pyrénées

★ ★ ★ Hotel Club Vignemale
BP *2 65120*
☎ 562924000 FAX 562924008
Enjoy fresh mountain products in a relaxed peaceful atmosphere. Vignemale was built at the beginning of the

century and all the rooms are individually decorated. In the heart of the Pyrénées National Park, there are fine views of the Cinque de Gavarnie glacier.
Near river Forest area
RS 15 Apr-May & mid Sep-mid Oct
25 en suite (bth/shr) (2 fmly) (7 with balcony) No smoking in 13 bedrooms TV in all bedrooms STV Direct dial from all bedrooms Licensed Lift Full central heating Open parking available Supervised Child discount available 5yrs Fishing Riding Solarium Bicycle rental Open terrace Languages spoken: English & Spanish
ROOMS: (room only) s 560FF; d 560-620FF
MEALS: Full breakfast 58FF
CARDS: 😊 💳 ▦

★★ Le Marbore
65120
☎ 562924040 FAX 562924030
The hotel dates back to the beginning of the century and features 1930s decor. It is situated at the very heart of a park and offers its visitors a warm welcome in friendly surroundings. The bedrooms are well equipped and provide a good level of comfort. In addition, there is a cosy bar and a restaurant.
Near river Forest area
25 en suite (shr) (6 with balcony) TV in all bedrooms STV Licensed Full central heating Open parking available Child discount available 10yrs Sauna Gym Pool table Open terrace Covered terrace Wkly live entertainment V meals Last d 21.30hrs Languages spoken: English,German,Italian,Spanish
MEALS: Continental breakfast 32FF Lunch 95-190FF&alc Dinner 95-190FF&alc✱
CARDS: 😊 💳 ▦ 🌐 Travellers cheques

GOURDON Lot

★★★ Hostellerie de la Bouriane
pl du Foirail 46300

☎ 565411637 FAX 565410492
(From Cathedral take first on right and continue for 100yds)
This 19th century country inn has taken its name from the region and is situated just a stone's throw from the centre of the village. It features attractive, well furnished rooms with modern amenities, a cosy lounge, and a restaurant with an impressive fireplace, which serves tasty regional dishes.
Near lake Near sea Forest area
Closed mid Jan-early Mar
20 en suite (bth/shr) (5 fmly) TV in all bedrooms STV Radio in rooms Direct dial from all bedrooms Licensed Lift Full central heating Open parking available Supervised Open terrace V meals Last d 21.00hrs Languages spoken: English
ROOMS: (room only) d 280-350FF ✱
MEALS: Full breakfast 40FF Lunch 85-250FF&alc Dinner 85-250FF&alc✱
CARDS: 😊 💳 ▦ 🌐 Travellers cheques

★★★ Hostellerie Domaine du Berthiol
46300
☎ 565413333 FAX 565411452
(SE of Gourdon on D704)
This characterful residence is situated amidst green scenery and features peaceful bedrooms equipped with modern day conveniences. The restaurant serves a wide choice of regional dishes which are complemented by the excellent wines of the Cahors.
Forest area
Closed Nov-Mar

29 en suite (bth/shr) (4 fmly) (2 with balcony) TV in all bedrooms Direct dial from all bedrooms Licensed Lift Night porter Full central heating Open parking available Child discount available 8yrs Outdoor swimming pool Tennis Solarium Boule Open terrace Last d 21.30hrs Languages spoken: English,German
MEALS: Full breakfast 55FF Lunch 100-270FF Dinner 170-270FF✱
CARDS: 😊 💳 ▦ 🌐 Travellers cheques

GRAMAT Lot

★★ Du Centre
pl de la République 46500
☎ 565387337 FAX 565387366
A warm welcome by the friendly proprietors awaits guest upon arrival in this informal establishment. Whether you travel alone or with the family, an attentive service and cheerful smile is always present. The restaurant serves a choice of commendable dishes and the bedrooms are very comfortable.
In town centre Near motorway
14 en suite (bth/shr) (4 fmly) TV in all bedrooms STV Direct dial from all bedrooms Licensed Full central heating Open parking available Covered parking available (charged) Child discount available 10yrs Open terrace Last d 21.00hrs Languages spoken: English
ROOMS: (room only) s 230-300FF; d 280-350FF
MEALS: Full breakfast 40FF Lunch 80-200FF&alc Dinner 80-200FF&alc
CARDS: 😊 💳 ▦ 🌐 Travellers cheques

★★★ Le Lion d'Or

8 pl de la République 46500
☎ 565387318 FAX 565388450
(Approach via N140 from Figeac or Bretenoux)
This ancient building with its rustic stone façade offers renovated rooms with modern amenities. It has a 15th century fire place which has retained all of its original features and creates a cosy atmosphere. The elegant dining room serves an excellent choice of dishes based on local produce, which are complemented by fine vintage wines from the Cahors region.
Near river Forest area In town centre Near motorway
Closed mid Dec-mid Jan
15 en suite (bth/shr) TV in all bedrooms STV Radio in rooms Direct dial from all bedrooms Licensed Lift Full central heating Air conditioning in bedrooms Open parking available Covered parking available (charged) Child discount available 10yrs Tennis Riding Sauna Gym Boule Bicycle rental Open terrace Covered terrace Last d 21.15hrs Languages spoken: English
ROOMS: (room only) d 270-390FF ✱
MEALS: Full breakfast 50FF Continental breakfast 50FF Lunch 100-300FF&alc Dinner 100-300FF&alc✱
CARDS: 😊 💳 ▦ 🌐 Travellers cheques

★★ Relais des Gourmands
2 av de la Gare 46500
☎ 565388392 FAX 565387099
A comfortable hotel in a quiet location in the heart of the Quercy region. There is a peaceful garden complete with recreational facilities and the restaurant serves an appetising selection of local cuisine.
16 en suite (bth) (4 fmly) No smoking in 1 bedroom TV in all bedrooms STV Direct dial from all bedrooms Licensed Full central heating Child discount available 12yrs Outdoor swimming pool Open terrace V meals Last d 21.00hrs Languages spoken: English,German

contd.

ROOMS: (room only) s 285-360FF; d 285-450FF
MEALS: Full breakfast 45FF Lunch 85-225FF&alc Dinner 85-225FF&alc
CARDS: ●● ☲ Travellers cheques

GRISOLLES Tarn-et-Garonne

★ ★ Relais des Garrigues
rte de Fronton 82170
☎ 563673759/563673159 FAX 563641376
(W, off N20 towards Fronton)
Situated en route to the Pyrenees and Spain, the hotel stands just a few steps away from the Canal du Midi. Located on the garden side, the functional bedrooms have private facilities, whilst the restaurant serves regional cooking of good flavour.
Near river Forest area Near motorway
Closed 23 Dec-15 Jan
15 en suite (bth/shr) (1 fmly) (5 with balcony) TV in all bedrooms Direct dial from all bedrooms Licensed Full central heating Open parking available Covered parking available (charged) Supervised Child discount available Boule Open terrace Covered terrace V meals Last d 22.00hrs Languages spoken: English,Spanish
ROOMS: (room only) s 190-200FF; d 200-210FF ✱
Reductions over 1 night
MEALS: Continental breakfast 30FF Lunch 45-72FF&alc
Dinner 45-72FF&alc
CARDS: ●● ☲ Travellers cheques

LABASTIDE-MURAT Lot

★ ★ Climat de France
pl de la Mairie 46240
☎ 565211880 Cen Res 164460123 FAX 565211097
(off A20 onto D667, hotel in village centre)
This handsome building dates back to 1226 and combines a warm and friendly interior with generous hospitality of by-gone times. Under the meticulous management of Hélène and Jan Recour, guests are offered attractive bedrooms which are equipped with up-to-date modern amenities and an informal restaurant which serves a selection of traditional dishes, complemented by regional specialities.
Forest area In town centre
Closed 16 Dec-14 Jan
20 en suite (bth/shr) TV in all bedrooms Radio in rooms Direct dial from all bedrooms Licensed Full central heating Child discount available 13yrs Open terrace V meals Last d 22.00hrs Languages spoken: English & Spanish
ROOMS: (room only) s 305-340FF; d 305-340FF **Special breaks**
MEALS: Continental breakfast 38FF Lunch 65-130FF&alc
Dinner 89-130FF&alc
CARDS: ●● ▭▭ ☲ ·▫ Travellers cheques

LACABARÈDE Tarn

★ ★ ★ Demeure de Flore   ¼ ✗ ✗
106 Grande Rue 81240
☎ 563983232 FAX 563984756
(On N112 opposite the FINA service station)
The house is set in landscaped gardens with mature trees, and offers its clientele an oasis of peace combined with modern day comfort. Its delightful interior is adorned with assorted antiques, whilst the bedrooms are furnished with flair and well co-ordinated colours and fabrics. Meals are served in the intimate restaurant or in summer, guests can enjoy lunch by

the side of the swimming pool or on the terrace overlooking the garden.
Near river Near lake Forest area Near motorway
11 en suite (bth/shr) 3 rooms in annexe (3 fmly) (7 with balcony) TV in all bedrooms Direct dial from all bedrooms Licensed Full central heating Open parking available (charged) Outdoor swimming pool Open terrace Covered terrace V meals Last d 20.30hrs Languages spoken: English
ROOMS: (room only) s 370-420FF; d 430-480FF
MEALS: Full breakfast 56FF Continental breakfast 56FF Lunch 95-125FF&alc Dinner 95-125FF&alc
CARDS: ●● ☲ Travellers cheques

LACAUNE Tarn

★ ★ ★ Central Hotel Fusies
2 rue de la République 81230
☎ 563370203 FAX 563371098
This traditional hotel has been in the Fusies family for 300 years. The art of lavish hospitality and culinary skills have been passed on from generation to generation and the hotel offers the unique combination of old world charm and modern day comfort. The guest-rooms are equipped with up-to-date facilities, the restaurant serves a good choice of dishes, whilst the surrounding countryside provides the perfect setting for an enjoyable stay.
Near river Near lake Forest area In town centre
120 rms (104 bth/shr) (10 fmly) (10 with balcony) TV in all bedrooms Direct dial from all bedrooms Licensed Lift Night porter Full central heating Open parking available Covered parking available Supervised Child discount available 11yrs Outdoor swimming pool (heated) Tennis Boule Bicycle rental Open terrace Covered terrace V meals Last d 21.00hrs Languages spoken: English, Spanish
MEALS: Lunch 80-300FF&alc Dinner 80-300FF&alc✱
CARDS: ●● ▭▭ ☲ ·▫ Travellers cheques

LACAVE Lot

★ ★ ★ ★ Château de la Tréyne (Relais et Châteaux)
46200
☎ 565276060 FAX 565276070
This magnificent castle is set in a dominant position overlooking the River Dordogne. It offers delightful, shaded French gardens and is decorated throughout with immaculate attention to detail. Dinner is served in the candlelit drawing room with its Louis XIII furniture, whilst the bedrooms combine the charm of bygone times with modern comfort.
Near river Forest area Near motorway
Closed mid Nov-Etr
14 en suite (bth) (4 fmly) TV in all bedrooms STV Direct dial from all bedrooms Licensed Lift Open parking available Supervised Child discount available 10yrs Outdoor swimming pool (heated) Tennis Fishing Riding Pool table Open terrace Last d 21.30hrs Languages spoken: English,Italian
ROOMS: (room only) s 700-980FF; d 700-1600FF
MEALS: Full breakfast 80FF Lunch 220-360FF&alc Dinner 320-360FF&alc
CARDS: ●● ▭▭ ☲ ·▫ Travellers cheques

LAMAGDELAINE-CAHORS Lot

Claude Marco
Lamagdelaine 46090
☎ 565353064 FAX 565303140
(From N20 take D653 take left turn for Lamagdelaine)
The house is set in a secluded location and features a small

number of charming bedrooms situated around the swimming pool. The superb vaulted cellar is the setting for the elegant restaurant whose outstanding cuisine has been awarded many accolades over the years.
Near river Forest area Near motorway
Closed 5 Jan-5 Mar
4 en suite (bth/shr) TV in all bedrooms STV Radio in rooms Direct dial from all bedrooms Mini-bar in all bedrooms Room-safe Licensed Full central heating Open parking available Supervised Child discount available 10yrs Outdoor swimming pool Open terrace V meals Last d 21.30hrs Languages spoken: English, Spanish
MEALS: Full breakfast 50FF Lunch 130-295FF&alc Dinner 130-295FF&alc✱
CARDS: ✹ ▆▆ ☰

LANNEMEZAN Hautes-Pyrénées

★ ★ **Pyrénées** (Minotel)
33 rue Didérot-pl des Pyrénées 65300
☎ 562980153 FAX 562981185
In town centre Near motorway
30 en suite (bth/shr) (1 fmly) (6 with balcony) TV in all bedrooms Direct dial from all bedrooms Licensed Lift Full central heating Open parking available Covered parking available Child discount available Open terrace V meals Last d 21.00hrs Languages spoken: English,Spanish
CARDS: ✹ ▆▆ ☰ ◑ Travellers cheques

LORP-SENTARAILLE Ariège

★ ★ **Horizon 117**
rte de Toulouse 09190
☎ 561662680 FAX 561662608
This rustic establishment is situated near the 2000-year old village of Saint-Lizier. It has a delightful garden and a range of leisure facilities. The bedrooms are well equipped with modern amenities and there is a cosy restaurant where guests can savour a choice of regional specialities.
20 en suite (bth/shr) (2 fmly) (20 with balcony) TV in all bedrooms Direct dial from all bedrooms Licensed Full central heating Open parking available Child discount available Outdoor swimming pool Tennis Sauna Solarium Boule Open terrace Covered terrace Last d 21.15hrs Languages spoken: English
ROOMS: (room only) d 260-310FF **Reductions over 1 night**
CARDS: ✹ ▆▆ ☰ ◑ Travellers cheques

LOUBRESSAC Lot

★ ★ ★ **Relais de Castelnau**   ✗ ✗ ✗✗
rte de Padirac, Rocamadour 46130
☎ 565108090 FAX 565382202
(Access on D20 via Bretenoux)
The village of Loubressac is reputed to be one of the most beautiful in France, and the hotel occupies a stunning location, offering unrivalled views over the Dordogne valley and the Château de Castelnau. Attractively furnished bedrooms with modern facilities offer pleasant accommodation, and there is also a restaurant and a pretty garden.
Near river Forest area Near motorway
Closed 12 Nov-19 Mar
40 en suite (bth) (4 fmly) (9 with balcony) TV in all bedrooms Direct dial from all bedrooms Mini-bar in all bedrooms Licensed Full central heating Open parking available Child discount available 12yrs Outdoor swimming pool Tennis

Boule Open terrace Last d 21.00hrs Languages spoken: English, Spanish
ROOMS: (room only) d 299-550FF
MEALS: Full breakfast 45FF Lunch 89-170FF Dinner 105-170FF
CARDS: ✹ ▆▆ ☰

LOURDES Hautes-Pyrénées

★ ★ ★ **America Hotel**
6 rue de la Rine Astrid 65100
☎ 562422525 FAX 562947169
Situated in the pilgrims' town of Lourdes the hotel is a fine example of the latest in hotel design and offers contemporary accommodation with everyday modern amenities which are complemented by a spacious foyer and bar where marble and exotic woods create a warm atmosphere.
127 en suite (bth/shr) (12 fmly) TV in all bedrooms STV Radio in rooms Direct dial from all bedrooms Licensed Lift Night porter Full central heating Air conditioning in bedrooms Open parking available Supervised Child discount available Languages spoken: English,Italian,German
CARDS: ☰ Travellers cheques

MARTEL Lot

★ ★ **Les Falaises**
a Gluges 46600
☎ 565373359 FAX 565373419
The hotel is situated in Gluges, a medieval village on the banks of the Dordogne. The bedrooms are peaceful and equipped with all modern amenities, there is a cosy lounge with TV and a shaded terrace where on fine days meals are served. The traditional cuisine is based on fresh, regional produce.
Near river Near sea Forest area
Closed 31 Oct-Feb
16 en suite (bth/shr) Some rooms in annexe (4 fmly) (2 with balcony) Direct dial from all bedrooms Licensed Full central heating Open parking available Covered parking available (charged) Supervised Child discount available Boule Open terrace Canoeing V meals Last d 21.30hrs Languages spoken: English,German,Italian,Spanish
MEALS: Continental breakfast 38FF Lunch 85-85FF&alc Dinner 98-198FF&alc✱
CARDS: ✹ ☰ Travellers cheques

MAUROUX Lot

★ ★ **Hostellerie le Vert**
Le Vert 46700
☎ 565365136 FAX 565365684
The charming hotel Le Vert is set amidst the great vineyards of the Cahors region and offers comfortable accommodation with good amenities. The restaurant has acquired a good reputation locally for its inventive cuisine and serves meals on the terrace which looks out over an attractive garden.
Near river Forest area
Closed early Nov-mid Feb
8 en suite (bth/shr) 2 rooms in annexe (1 with balcony) TV in all bedrooms Licensed Full central heating Open parking available Child discount available 10yrs Outdoor swimming pool Bicycle rental Open terrace V meals Languages spoken: English,German
MEALS: Continental breakfast 38FF Lunch 100-155FF&alc✱
CARDS: ✹ ▆▆ ☰ Travellers cheques

MIREPOIX Ariège

★ ★ ★ La Maison des Consuls
09500
☎ 561688181 FAX 561688115
(from Toulouse or Narbonne A61 exit Bram Mirepoix)
Recently renovated old historical house of the 14th century, in the heart of the city. Spacious bedrooms, each one decorated in different historical style.
Near river Near lake Forest area In town centre Near motorway
8 en suite (bth/shr) No smoking in 1 bedroom TV in all bedrooms Direct dial from all bedrooms Mini-bar in all bedrooms Licensed Full central heating Child discount available 8yrs Languages spoken: English & Spanish
ROOMS: (room only) s 420-680FF; d 420-680FF
Reductions over 1 night
MEALS: Full breakfast 40FF Continental breakfast 60FF
CARDS: 🍱 💳 Travellers cheques

NAJAC Aveyron

★ ★ Hotel Oustal Del Barry
pl du Bourg *12270*
☎ 565297432 FAX 565297532
(20km from Villefranche de Rouesgue. Najac is signposted from Villefranche.)
The establishment is set in Najac, reputedly one of the most beautiful villages in France. It offers bedrooms and a restaurant which serves a selection of superb dishes from an inspired regional menu. In addition there is a delightful garden with fine views over the surrounding region.
Near river Forest area In town centre Near motorway
Closed Nov-1 Apr
21 rms (7 bth 10 shr) (1 fmly) (2 with balcony) TV in all bedrooms Direct dial from all bedrooms Licensed Lift Full central heating Open parking available Covered parking available Supervised Child discount available 12yrs Boule Bicycle rental Open terrace Covered terrace Last d 21.30hrs Languages spoken: English
ROOMS: (room only) s fr 260FF; d fr 300FF
MEALS: Full breakfast 48FF Continental breakfast 48FF Lunch 130-260FF&alc Dinner 130-260FF&alc
CARDS: 🍱 💳 Travellers cheques

PAMIERS Ariège

★ ★ De France
5 rue Dr Rambaud, 13 rue Hospice *09100*
☎ 561602088 FAX 561672948
This attractive hotel has been thoroughly renovated and offers individually styled bedrooms equipped with modern facilities and offering a good standard of comfort. The art of hospitality has been passed down for three generations and the hotel is now in the capable hands of Maïté and José Raja, who provide an attentive service for their guests.
Near river Forest area In town centre Near motorway
30 en suite (bth/shr) (4 fmly) (10 with balcony) No smoking in 2 bedrooms TV in all bedrooms Direct dial from all bedrooms Night porter Full central heating Open parking available Covered parking available (charged) Supervised Child discount available 10yrs Solarium Boule Bicycle rental Open terrace V meals Last d 21.30hrs Languages spoken: English,Spanish
MEALS: Continental breakfast 35FF Lunch 90-230FF Dinner 90-230FF✱
CARDS: 🍱 💳 Travellers cheques

★ ★ De La Paix
4 pl Albert Tournier *09100*
☎ 561671271 FAX 561606102
Standing in a quiet, shady square only a stone's throw from the shops, the hotel has been a part of the town's history for over 200 years. Formerly a coaching inn, it has retained all of its original character and features an authentic interior with superb Empire period ceilings. The cosy bedrooms together with the attentive service and the excellent cuisine make it a desirable venue for a enjoyable stay.
Near river Near sea Forest area In town centre Near motorway
16 en suite (bth/shr) (7 fmly) TV in all bedrooms STV Direct dial from all bedrooms Licensed Night porter Full central heating Air conditioning in bedrooms Open parking available Covered parking available Supervised Child discount available 4yrs Boule Bicycle rental Open terrace V meals Last d 22.30hrs Languages spoken: English & Spanish
ROOMS: (room only) s 160-190FF; d 220-250FF ✱
Reductions over 1 night Special breaks
MEALS: Continental breakfast 35FF Lunch 49-150FF&alc Dinner 79-150FF&alc
CARDS: 🍱 💳 Travellers cheques

PAYRAC Lot

★ ★ Petit Relais
Calès *46350*
☎ 565379609 FAX 565379593
(N20 to Payrac and take direction for Rocamadour)
The hotel Le Petit Relais is ideally situated for those who want to explore the numerous places of interest in the surrounding region, and provides a peaceful setting for a pleasant stay. The restaurant serves a range of classic and regional dishes in rustic surroundings, whilst on fine days guests can also enjoy a drink or meal on the shaded terrace. The guest accommodation is attractive with modern amenities and offers a good level of comfort.
Near river Near motorway
Closed 20 Dec-10 Jan
15 en suite (bth/shr) (2 fmly) TV in all bedrooms Direct dial from all bedrooms Licensed Full central heating Open parking available Supervised Child discount available 10yrs Outdoor swimming pool Boule Open terrace Covered terrace Last d 21.30hrs Languages spoken: English & Spanish
ROOMS: (incl. full-board) s 150-190FF; d 240-370FF
Reductions over 1 night
MEALS: Full breakfast 36FF Lunch 75-220FF&alc Dinner 75-220FF&alc
CARDS: 🍱 💳 Travellers cheques

PEYRELEAU Aveyron

★ ★ ★ Grand Hotel de la Muse et du Rozier
12720
☎ 565626001 FAX 565626388
(take D907 along river Tarn, at Rozier roundabout head in direction of Sainte Enimie. Hotel further 500 metres)
On the banks of the Tarn, this striking hotel offers a warm welcome combined with a calm and relaxing situation. The well appointed bedrooms have views of the river and mountains as does a wide terrace where guests can eat in fine weather.
Near river Near beach Forest area
Closed 6 Nov-15 Mar
38 en suite (bth/shr) (3 fmly) (14 with balcony) TV in all bedrooms STV Direct dial from all bedrooms Licensed Lift

Full central heating Open parking available Covered parking
available (charged) Child discount available 8yrs Outdoor
swimming pool (heated) Tennis Fishing Bicycle rental Open
terrace Canoeing V meals Last d 21.30hrs Languages
spoken: English,German,Italian
ROOMS: (room only) s 350-430FF; d 420-565FF
Reductions over 1 night
MEALS: Full breakfast 65FF Continental breakfast 65FF Lunch
95-220FF&alc Dinner 160-220FF&alc
CARDS: ●● ▬▬ ▬▬ ●

PROJAN Gers

Château de Projan
32400
☎ 562094621 FAX 562094408
(located 3km from road between Aire-sur-Adour and Pau. In
Aire-sur-Adour follow direction of Pau, drive through village
of St Agnet then turn left to Riscle and follow signs to Projan)
The Château de Projan is situated in the heart of the
countryside. This big house is surrounded by mature oak trees
and has an amazing interior where 18th-century furniture and
contemporary works of art form the decor, and it offers its
visitors a beautiful venue in which to relax. The guest rooms
each have carefully chosen, individual furnishings and are in
complete harmony with the rest of the house.
Near river Forest area Near motorway
Closed Oct-Mar
9 rms (1 bth 3 shr) (1 fmly) No smoking in 2 bedrooms Direct
dial from all bedrooms Licensed Full central heating Open
parking available Covered parking available Child discount
available 12yrs Tennis Fishing Open terrace Table tennis Last
d 21.00hrs Languages spoken: English, German & Spanish
ROOMS: (room only) s 290-500FF; d 290-500FF **Special
breaks**
MEALS: Full breakfast 40FF Continental breakfast 25FF
Dinner fr 100FF

RABASTENS Tarn

★ ★ **Du Pré Vert**
54 promenade des Lices *81800*
☎ 563337051 FAX 563338258
(On outskirts towards Toulouse)
Near river In town centre
Closed Jan
27 rms (4 bth 8 shr) (2 fmly) TV in 9 bedrooms Direct dial
from 14 bedrooms Licensed Full central heating Open
parking available Child discount available 10yrs Mini-golf
Open terrace V meals Languages spoken: English,Italian
ROOMS: (room only) s 180-220FF; d 260-300FF ✱
MEALS: Full breakfast 34FF Lunch 88-180FF&alc✱
CARDS: ●● ▬▬ ▬▬ ● Travellers cheques

RIEUPEYROUX Aveyron

★ ★ **Du Commerce**
12240
☎ 565655306 FAX 565655658
Near lake Forest area
Closed end Dec-mid Jan
(3 fmly) (3 with balcony) TV available Licensed Lift Full
central heating Open parking available Covered parking
available Child discount available 6yrs Outdoor swimming
pool Boule Open terrace V meals Last d 21.00hrs Languages
spoken: English
CARDS: ●● ▬▬ ▬▬ Travellers cheques

RIGNAC Lot

★ ★ ★ **Chateau de Roumegouse**
☎ 565336381 FAX 565337118
Located on top of a hill overlooking the Causse of
Rocamadour, the building is surrounded by 12 acres of private
grounds. The interior is adorned with period furniture,
paintings and flower arrangements which create a warm and
friendly atmosphere. The smartly furnished bedrooms provide
elegant accommodation and the restaurant with its
magnificent open fireplace serves a sophisticated cuisine
which will satisfy any discerning gourmet.
Forest area
10 Apr-18 Oct
15 en suite (bth/shr) (2 fmly) (1 with balcony) TV in all

bedrooms Mini-bar in all bedrooms Licensed Full central
heating Open parking available Child discount available 12yrs
Outdoor swimming pool Bicycle rental Open terrace V meals
Last d 22.00hrs Languages spoken: English,Spanish
ROOMS: (room only) s 500-1000FF; d 680-1300FF
MEALS: Full breakfast 80FF Continental breakfast 65FF Lunch
105-330FF&alc Dinner 185-350FF&alc
CARDS: ●● ▬▬ ▬▬ ● Travellers cheques

ROCAMADOUR Lot

★ ★ ★ **Beau Site** (Best Western) ✗ ✗ ✗ ✗
Cité Medievale *46500*
☎ 565336308 FAX 565336523
Forest area In town centre
43 en suite (bth/shr) (5 fmly) TV in all bedrooms STV Direct
dial from all bedrooms Licensed Lift Full central heating
Open parking available Covered parking available (charged)
Child discount available 12yrs Bicycle rental Open terrace
Last d 21.00hrs
ROOMS: (room only) s 290-410FF; d 360-480FF
MEALS: Full breakfast 49FF Continental breakfast 49FF Lunch
98-210FF&alc Dinner 98-210FF&alc
CARDS: ●● ▬▬ ▬▬ ● JCB Travellers cheques

★ ★ ★ **Hotel Domaine de la Rhue**
La Rhue *46500*
☎ 565337150 FAX 565337248
(from Rocamadour take D673 in direction of Brive, then N140
for 1km & take small road on left)
The accommodation at the hotel is in former 19th century
stables, which now provide spacious, comfortable rooms of
character. This is an excellent location for walking, bicycling,
riding, canoeing or ballooning adventures, or more restfully
relaxing by the swimming pool. Although there is not a

contd.

restaurant at the hotel there are many in the surrounding area.
Closed mid Oct-Etr
12 en suite (bth/shr) 2 rooms in annexe (2 fmly) TV in 2
bedrooms Direct dial from all bedrooms Mini-bar in 2
bedrooms Full central heating Open parking available
Supervised Child discount available 3yrs Outdoor swimming
pool Bicycle rental Open terrace Languages spoken: English
& German
ROOMS: s 370-570FF
CARDS: ●● ▆▆ Travellers cheques

★ ★ Terminus Hotel et Des Pelerins
pl de la Carretta *46500* ✗ ✗ ✗✗
☎ 565335214 FAX 565337210
(from Brive N140 to Rocamadour the city at the first gate, cross
the street, the hotel is situated between 2nd and 3rd gates)

Near river
Closed Nov - Etr
12 en suite (bth/shr) (1 fmly) (3 with balcony) TV in all
bedrooms Direct dial from all bedrooms Licensed Full central
heating Open parking available Child discount available 10yrs
Open terrace V meals Last d 21.30hrs Languages spoken:
English
ROOMS: (room only) s 210-270FF; d 250-330FF
CARDS: ●● ▆▆ ▆▆ ●) Travellers cheques

★ ★ Troubadour
Le Belvéyré *46500*
☎ 565337027 FAX 565337199
Near river Forest area
Closed 15 Nov-15 Feb
10 en suite (bth/shr) (2 fmly) (10 with balcony) TV in all
bedrooms STV Direct dial from all bedrooms Licensed Air
conditioning in bedrooms Open parking available Covered
parking available Supervised Child discount available 10yrs
Outdoor swimming pool Boule Bicycle rental Open terrace
Last d 21.00hrs Languages spoken: English
CARDS: ●● ▆▆ Travellers cheques

★ ★ Vielles Tours
Lafage *46500*
☎ 565336801 FAX 565336859
Near river Forest area
Closed 12 Nov-29 Mar
18 en suite (bth/shr) (7 fmly) TV in all bedrooms Full central
heating Open parking available Child discount available 12yrs
Outdoor swimming pool Bicycle rental Open terrace Last d
21.00hrs
CARDS: ●● ▆▆ ▆▆ Travellers cheques

RODEZ Aveyron

★ ★ ★ Tour Maje
bd Gally *12000*
☎ 565683468 FAX 565682756
In town centre
41 en suite (bth/shr) (3 fmly) TV in 44 bedrooms STV Direct
dial from 44 bedrooms Mini-bar in 44 bedrooms Licensed Lift
Night porter Full central heating Covered parking available
(charged) Pool table Open terrace Languages spoken:
English
ROOMS: (room only) s 295-350FF; d 330-380FF
Reductions over 1 night
CARDS: ●● ▆▆ ▆▆ ●) Travellers cheques

ST-AFFRIQUE Aveyron

★ ★ Moderne
54 av A Pezet *12400*
☎ 565492044 FAX 565493655
En route to the Pyrenees and the seaside, the town of Saint-
Affrique is a good starting point to discover the Aveyron
region. The hotel provides the permanent setting for an art
exhibition, with numerous paintings adorning the walls, and
features refurbished guest rooms, decorated in pretty shades
and fabrics. Guests can savour the local cuisine , given an
added personal touch by the chef-proprietors, and enjoy an
after-dinner drink in the cosy bar.
Near river Forest area
Closed 20 Dec-20 Jan
35 en suite (bth/shr) 7 rooms in annexe (4 fmly) (8 with
balcony) No smoking in 1 bedroom TV in all bedrooms Direct
dial from all bedrooms Licensed Full central heating Covered
parking available (charged) Supervised Child discount
available 7yrs Pool table Open terrace library V meals Last d
21.30hrs Languages spoken: English,Spanish
MEALS: Full breakfast 38FF Lunch 90-270FF&alc Dinner 90-
270FF&alc✱
CARDS: ●● ▆▆ Travellers cheques

ST-CÉRÉ Lot

★ ★ ★ De France
181 av François de Maynard *46400* ✗ ✗ ✗
☎ 565380216 FAX 565380298
A few steps away from the medieval centre of Saint-Ceré, the
hotel invites its visitors to a carefree stay in friendly
surroundings. Spacious guest rooms with a balcony overlook
the garden, there is an intimate lounge with comfortable
seating, and the restaurant serves a gourmet cuisine which
captured the rich flavours and colours of the Quercy region.
Forest area In town centre
Closed Nov-15 Mar
23 en suite (bth/shr) (2 fmly) (12 with balcony) TV in all
bedrooms STV Direct dial from all bedrooms Licensed Full
central heating Open parking available Covered parking
available (charged) Supervised Child discount available 10yrs
Outdoor swimming pool (heated) Open terrace Last d
21.15hrs
MEALS: Full breakfast 45FF Continental breakfast 45FF Lunch
75-130FF&alc Dinner 75-130FF&alc✱
CARDS: ●● ▆▆ Travellers cheques

★ ★ ★ Ric
rte de Leyne *46400*
☎ 565380408 FAX 565380014
Forest area

Closed Dec-Mar
5 en suite (bth/shr) TV in all bedrooms Licensed Full central
heating Open parking available Child discount available
Outdoor swimming pool Boule Bicycle rental Open terrace
Last d 21.30hrs Languages spoken: English
MEALS: Full breakfast 45FF Lunch 110-250FF&alc Dinner 110-
250FF&alc✱
CARDS: ✸ ▆

★★ **Le Victor Hugo**
7 av des Marquis *46400*
☎ 565381615 FAX 565383991
This pretty house has a façade adorned with flowers and
enjoys a privileged position on the banks of a river. The guest
rooms are decorated with taste and provide a good level of
comfort, whilst the restaurant serves a first-class cuisine
consisting of skilfully executed dishes which are
complemented by fine wines from an excellent cellar.
Near river Near lake Forest area In town centre
9 en suite (bth/shr) (3 fmly) TV in all bedrooms Direct dial
from all bedrooms Licensed Night porter Full central heating
Open parking available Open terrace V meals Languages
spoken: English
ROOMS: (room only) s fr 240FF; d fr 240FF
MEALS: Continental breakfast 35FF Lunch 90-210FF✱
CARDS: ✸ ▆ ➍ Travellers cheques

ST-CIRQ-LAPOPIE Lot

★★★ **Pelissaria**
Le Bourg *46330*
☎ 565312514 FAX 565302552
Near river
Closed 16 Nov-Mar
10 en suite (bth) 3 rooms in annexe (3 fmly) (4 with balcony)
TV in all bedrooms Full central heating Outdoor swimming
pool (heated) Open terrace Languages spoken:
English,German
MEALS: Full breakfast 50FF Continental breakfast 50FF
Dinner fr 200FF✱
CARDS: ✸ ▆ Travellers cheques

ST-GAUDENS Haute-Garonne

★★★ **Hostellerie des Decres**
Villeneuve-de-Rivière *31800*
☎ 561893600 FAX 561883104
Forest area Near motorway
24 en suite (bth/shr) (5 fmly) (5 with balcony) TV in all
bedrooms STV Radio in rooms Licensed Night porter Full
central heating Open parking available Supervised Child
discount available 12yrs Outdoor swimming pool Tennis Gym
Boule Open terrace Covered terrace V meals Last d 21.30hrs
Languages spoken: English,Spanish
MEALS: Full breakfast 65FF Lunch 110-260FF Dinner 155-
260FF✱
CARDS: ✸ ▆ Travellers cheques

★★ **Pedussaut**
9 av de Boulogne *31800*
☎ 561891570 FAX 561891126
This large, 1930s-style house is situated in the centre of town,
and features an interior courtyard and garden as well as an
abundance of delightful features which create a cosy
atmosphere. The friendly owners Brigitte and Antoine Gay and
their dedicated staff offer a degree of personal service which is
difficult to match. The cuisine is based on traditional recipes

from the region, consisting of fresh market produce, whilst the
bright, airy bedrooms have attractive furnishings and provide
good comfort. The region with its fascinating historic and
cultural past, offers a great many places to discover and
explore.
In town centre Near motorway
25 rms (5 bth 15 shr) (5 fmly) (1 with balcony) TV in all
bedrooms STV Direct dial from all bedrooms Licensed Full
central heating Open parking available Covered parking
available Child discount available 12yrs Open terrace Last d
21.30hrs Languages spoken: English,Spanish
ROOMS: (room only) s 150-200FF; d 150-240FF ✱
MEALS: Continental breakfast 30FF Lunch 70-180FF&alc
Dinner 70-180FF&alc
CARDS: ✸ ▆ Travellers cheques

★★ **Tuilère**
Sur RN 117 *31800*
☎ 561890851 FAX 561892164
Pleasant bedrooms with modern facilities provide a good level
of comfort in this hotel, which because its convenient location
is a good venue for an overnight stop. The restaurant has a
choice of eating options alternating between fast meals and a
traditional menu.
Near river Forest area Near motorway
20 en suite (shr) (13 fmly) TV in all bedrooms Direct dial from
all bedrooms Mini-bar in all bedrooms Licensed Night porter
Full central heating Open parking available Child discount
available 8yrs Outdoor swimming pool Open terrace
Languages spoken: Italian,Spanish
MEALS: Full breakfast 50FF Continental breakfast 30FF✱
CARDS: ✸ ▆ Travellers cheques

ST-GENIEZ-D'OLT Aveyron

★★ **Du Lion d'Or**
12130
☎ 565474332 FAX 565474980
Situated in a former Augustinian monastery and surrounded
by the cloister's ancient turreted residences and the 'cours-
haut' promenade with mature limes, the hotel provides the
charming setting for a restful stay. The saying goes 'the proof
of the pudding is in the eating', which is certainly true of the
high quality cuisine, skilfully prepared by Mr Rascalou which
incorporates a choice of innovative dishes and house
specialities. After a copious dinner, guests can relax to the cosy
day room with 16th-century fire place or retire to the pleasant
bedrooms.
Near river Forest area In town centre
Closed Jan-1 Mar
12 en suite (bth/shr) (1 with balcony) TV in all bedrooms
Licensed Night porter Full central heating Open parking
available Child discount available 10yrs Boule Bicycle rental
Open terrace Last d 22.00hrs Languages spoken: English
CARDS: ✸ ▆ ➍ Travellers cheques

ST-GIRONS Ariège

★★★ **Château de Seignan**
rte de Foix *09200*
☎ 561960880 FAX 561960820
(On D117)
This charming residence is set in the middle of a park with
mature horse-chestnut trees, flowers and a river. Set amidst
unspoilt countryside it features elegant bedrooms furnished to
a high standard, and equipped with modern amenities. The
restaurant with splendid open fire place serves an array of
contd.

traditional dishes of very good quality.
Near river Forest area
Closed 31 Oct-1 Apr
9 en suite (bth/shr) (3 fmly) TV in all bedrooms Direct dial
from all bedrooms Mini-bar in all bedrooms Licensed Full
central heating Open parking available Child discount
available 12yrs Outdoor swimming pool Tennis Open terrace
V meals Last d 22.00hrs Languages spoken: English,Spanish
ROOMS: (room only) s 380-450FF; d 450-980FF
MEALS: Full breakfast 47FF Continental breakfast 47FF Lunch
150-250FF&alc Dinner 150-250FF&alc
CARDS: ●● ■■ ■■ ●)

★ ★ ★ Eychenne

8 av Paul Laffont 09200
☎ 561040450 FAX 561960720
(A64 exit Saint Girons)
This friendly hotel has been in the hands of the same family for
six generations and features pleasant bedrooms equipped with
modern en suite facilities and a restaurant which serves a
classic cuisine complemented by the fine wines chosen by
Michel Bordeau. In addition, there is a swimming pool
surrounded by a lovely flower garden.
Near river
42 en suite (bth/shr) (7 fmly) (2 with balcony) TV in all
bedrooms STV Direct dial from all bedrooms Mini-bar in all
bedrooms Licensed Night porter Full central heating Open
parking available Covered parking available Supervised
Child discount available 12yrs Outdoor swimming pool
(heated) Open terrace V meals Last d 21.30hrs Languages
spoken: English
ROOMS: (room only) s fr 290FF; d 390-565FF **Reductions
over 1 night**
MEALS: Full breakfast 48FF Continental breakfast 48FF Lunch
135-320FF&alc Dinner 135-320FF&alc
CARDS: ●● ■■ ■■ ●) Travellers cheques

ST-JEAN-DU-BRUEL Aveyron

★ ★ Midi-Papillon
pl Albin Lémasson 12230
☎ 565622604 FAX 565621297
This hotel is set in a picturesque valley amidst hills and
chestnut trees. It has been managed by the Papillon family for
four generations and now features comfortable bedrooms with
modern facilities and a restaurant which offers a traditional
cuisine combined with more innovative dishes prepared with
the finest local produce.
Near river
Closed 11 Nov-Palm Sunday
19 rms (5 fmly) (5 with balcony) Direct dial from all bedrooms
Licensed Full central heating Open parking available
Covered parking available (charged) Child discount available
7yrs Outdoor swimming pool (heated) Jacuzzi/spa Open
terrace Last d 21.30hrs Languages spoken: English,
Spanish
MEALS: Continental breakfast 24FF Lunch 74-139FF&alc
Dinner 74-139FF&alc*
CARDS: ●● ■■ Travellers cheques

ST-MARTIN-DE-CARALP Ariège

★ ★ Le Grandgousier
09000
☎ 561029002
This sympathetically decorated hotel offers its visitors a warm
and friendly welcome. It has pleasant bedrooms equipped with

modern facilities and a restaurant which specialises in regional
dishes and fresh fish specialities.
Near river Forest area Near motorway
8 en suite (bth/shr) Licensed Full central heating Open
parking available Child discount available Open terrace Last
d 21.30hrs Languages spoken: English,Spanish
CARDS: ●● ■■ Travellers cheques

ST-SAVIN Hautes-Pyrénées

★ ★ ★ Le Viscos
65400
☎ 562970228 FAX 562970594
The hotel Le Viscos is situated in Saint-Savin, close to the spa
resorts and winter sports. The surrounding area has numerous
places of interest to visit or explore including the famous Col
d'Aubisque and the pilgrim town of Lourdes. After a day of
sightseeing, the comfortable bedrooms provide the necessary
relaxation, whilst the restaurant with its distinct cuisine of the
region serves a choice of excellent dishes, skilfully executed by
the chef-proprietor Jean-Pierre Saint-Martin.
In town centre
16 en suite (bth/shr) TV in all bedrooms Licensed Open
parking available Child discount available 3yrs Open terrace
V meals Last d 21.30hrs Languages spoken: English,Spanish
MEALS: Full breakfast 36FF Lunch fr 108FF&alc Dinner fr
108FF&alc*
CARDS: ●● ■■ ■■ Travellers cheques

ST-SERNIN-SUR-RANCE Aveyron

★ ★ Carayon
pl du Fort 12380
☎ 565981919 FAX 565996926
Between Albi and the Gorges du Tarn, in South Aveyron, half
the guest rooms at this hotel have their own balcony
overlooking a peaceful private park. Here guests can enjoy
various activities including mini-golf, swimming pools, water
slide and tennis. Discover the produce of the Rouergue in the
gourmet restaurant, where the chef and his team prepare
traditional, yet imaginative cooking.
Near river Forest area In town centre
60 en suite (bth/shr) 6 rooms in annexe TV in all bedrooms
STV Direct dial from all bedrooms Mini-bar in all bedrooms
Licensed Lift Full central heating Open parking available
Covered parking available (charged) Child discount available
Outdoor swimming pool Tennis Fishing Sauna Solarium
Gym Boule Mini-golf Jacuzzi/spa Bicycle rental Covered
terrace V meals Languages spoken: English & Spanish
ROOMS: (room only) s 199-389FF; d 199-389FF
Reductions over 1 night Special breaks
MEALS: Full breakfast 40FF Lunch 76-300FFalc Dinner 120-
300FFalc
CARDS: ●● ■■ ■■ ●) Travellers cheques

ST-SOZY Lot

★ ★ Grangjier
46200
☎ 565322014 FAX 565322797
Near river Forest area
Closed Feb
13 rms (1 bth 9 shr) 7 rooms in annexe (2 fmly) TV in all
bedrooms Licensed Full central heating Open parking
available Child discount available 12yrs Boule Open terrace
V meals Last d 20.45hrs Languages spoken: English
CARDS: ●● ■■ Travellers cheques

SALLES-CURAN Aveyron

★ ★ Hostellerie du Levézou
12410
☎ 565463416 FAX 565460119
Near lake Forest area
Closed Nov-Etr
20 rms 4 rooms in annexe TV in all bedrooms Licensed Full central heating Open parking available Child discount available 12yrs Bicycle rental Open terrace V meals Last d 22.00hrs Languages spoken: English
CARDS: ■ ➠ CB

SAUVETERRE-DE-COMMINGES Haute-Garonne

★ ★ ★ Hostellerie des 7 Molles (Relais et Chateaux)
31510
☎ 561883087 FAX 561883642
With a backdrop of mountains, the Hostellerie is set at the foot of the Pyrenees in an quiet scenic setting. Gilles Ferran prepares local dishes with flair and originality and the grounds include tennis courts and a swimming pool. Three golf courses are within easy reach.
Near river Forest area
Closed Jan-mid Mar
19 en suite (bth/shr) (2 fmly) (19 with balcony) TV in all bedrooms STV Direct dial from all bedrooms Mini-bar in all bedrooms Licensed Lift Full central heating Open parking available Child discount available Outdoor swimming pool (heated) Tennis Pool table Boule Open terrace Covered terrace V meals Last d 21.30hrs Languages spoken: English,Spanish
ROOMS: (room only) s 420-560FF; d fr 650FF
MEALS: Full breakfast 75FF Continental breakfast 75FF Lunch 190-295FFalc Dinner 190-295FFalc
CARDS: ●● ▦ ▥ ➠ Travellers cheques

SOUILLAC Lot

★ ★ ★ Hotel Renaissance (Minotel)
2 rue Jean-Jaurès *46200*
☎ 565327804 FAX 565370759
The hotels in the Minotel group offer a comfortable interior with attractive, fully equipped bedrooms and pleasant public areas where guests can relax or read. The restaurants serve an excellent cuisine, incorporating dishes with a regional touch and where local produce has been used to a large extent. Guests enjoy a special blend of hospitality, provided by attentive staff which offer personal attention and service at all times.
Near river In town centre Near motorway
Closed Jan-Feb
27 en suite (bth/shr) 6 rooms in annexe (4 fmly) TV in all bedrooms Direct dial from all bedrooms Licensed Lift Full central heating Open parking available Covered parking available Child discount available Indoor swimming pool (heated) Outdoor swimming pool (heated) Open terrace V meals Last d 21.00hrs Languages spoken: English
CARDS: ●● ▥

★ ★ Inter Hotel Le Quercy
rue de la Recégé *46200*
☎ 565378356 FAX 566370722
All the hotels in the Inter Hotel group offer guest accommodation which is designed with the individual needs of its clientele in mind. Whether situated in the capital or in a seaside resort, they offer old-fashioned hospitality and up-to-

date modern amenities. Staff are friendly and helpful throughout, and provide a degree of personal service which is difficult to match and make a stay, whether for business or pleasure an enjoyable experience to look back upon.
Near river Near motorway
Closed early Dec-mid Mar
25 en suite (bth/shr) (3 fmly) (20 with balcony) TV in all bedrooms STV Direct dial from all bedrooms Licensed Night porter Full central heating Covered parking available (charged) Outdoor swimming pool (heated) Bicycle rental Open terrace Languages spoken: English
ROOMS: (room only) s 200-290FF; d 290FF
CARDS: ●● ▥ ➠ Travellers cheques

★ ★ ★ La Vielle Auberge

46200
☎ 565327943 FAX 565326519
Situated in a quiet part of the little town of Souillac and offering a peaceful setting for a relaxing holiday. The gastronomic restaurant offers numerous regional specialities, complemented by an extensive wine list, whilst the pretty bedrooms are equipped with modern facilities and offer a good level of comfort. The hotel has a good range of leisure facilities, and there is no shortage of out-door activities in the surrounding area.
Near river In town centre
19 en suite (bth/shr) (8 fmly) TV in all bedrooms STV Direct dial from all bedrooms Mini-bar in all bedrooms Licensed Full central heating Open parking available Covered parking available (charged) Child discount available Indoor swimming pool (heated) Outdoor swimming pool (heated) Sauna Solarium Gym Jacuzzi/spa Bicycle rental V meals Last d 21.30hrs Languages spoken: English, German
ROOMS: (room only) s 240-280FF; d 280-360FF
MEALS: Full breakfast 40FF Lunch 100-320FF&alc Dinner 100-320FF&alc
CARDS: ●● ▦ ▥ ➠ Travellers cheques

TOULOUSE Haute-Garonne

★ ★ ★ Hotel des Beaux-Arts
1 pl du Pont Neuf *31000*
☎ 561234050 FAX 561220227
(follow signs centre ville hotel is situated on the banks of river Garonne next to the Pont Neuf bridge)
Behind 18th century façades, on the banks of the River Garonne. Each room is an elegant blend of charm and modern international requirements.
Near river In town centre
19 en suite (bth/shr) No smoking in 6 bedrooms TV in all bedrooms STV Direct dial from all bedrooms Mini-bar in all bedrooms Room-safe Licensed Lift Night porter Full central heating Air conditioning in bedrooms Open parking available (charged) Child discount available Languages spoken: English, German & Spanish
ROOMS: (room only) s 450-950FF; d 550-950FF
CARDS: ●● ▦ ▥ ➠ Travellers cheques

★ ★ ★ Hotel Frantour
78 rue Bayard *31000*
☎ 561625090 FAX 561992102
(A61 Carcassonne to Nice exit Centre Ville or Gare Matabiau)
On the banks of the Canal du Midi, facing the railway station, the Hotel Frantour is a modern, comfortable hotel in a yesteryear atmosphere.
In town centre
Closed Xmas & New Year
contd.

71 en suite (bth/shr) (5 fmly) (32 with balcony) TV in all bedrooms Direct dial from all bedrooms Mini-bar in 38 bedrooms Licensed Lift Night porter Full central heating Air conditioning in bedrooms Open parking available (charged) Covered parking available (charged) Languages spoken: English, German & Spanish
ROOMS: (room only) s 250-325FF; d 250-380FF
MEALS: Full breakfast 45FF Lunch 55-68FF Dinner 55-68FF✱
CARDS: 〓 〓 〓 ⑨ Travellers cheques

★ ★ ★ Grand Hotel Capoul (Best Western)
13 pl Wilson *31000*
☎ 561107070 FAX 561219670
Just a few steps away from the Capitol, opposite the gardens and fountain of the Place Wilson, the hotel Capoul is a charming establishment which has preserved its own distinct style, through a personalised, high quality decor. The spacious bedrooms are furnished in a contemporary style and have every modern day convenience, whilst guests can choose from a number of restaurants with a 'sans frontières' cuisine.
Near river Near lake Near sea Forest area Near motorway 140 rms Some rooms in annexe No smoking on premises Radio in rooms Night porter Open parking available Covered parking available No children Indoor swimming pool (heated) Outdoor swimming pool (heated) Golf Tennis Fishing Squash Riding Sauna Solarium Gym Pool table Boule Mini-golf Jacuzzi/spa Bicycle rental Last d 23.30hrs Languages spoken: English,Italian,German,Spanish

★ ★ ★ ★ Grand Hotel de l'Opera
1 pl du Capitole *31000*
☎ 561218266 FAX 561234104
(from motorway 61 or 62 follow exit 15 then follow signs to Capitole)
In the very heart of the historic centre of Toulouse. The hotel welcomes guests to an elegant setting of a 17th-century monastery. While respecting its traditions and architecture, the owner has renovated it wiht great care. Spacious rooms, luxury suites and conference rooms with quality is the result.
In town centre
46 en suite (bth/shr) (1 fmly) (2 with balcony) No smoking in 5 bedrooms TV in all bedrooms Direct dial from all bedrooms Mini-bar in all bedrooms Licensed Lift Night porter Full central heating Air conditioning in bedrooms Indoor swimming pool (heated) Sauna Solarium Gym Jacuzzi/spa Open terrace Covered terrace V meals Last d 0.30hrs Languages spoken: English & Spanish
ROOMS: (room only) s 490-690FF; d 890-950FF
Reductions over 1 night
MEALS: Full breakfast 82FF Continental breakfast 82FF Lunch fr 129FF&alc Dinner 200-300FFalc
CARDS: 〓 〓 〓 ⑨ Travellers cheques

★ ★ ★ ★ Holiday Inn-Crowne Plaza
7 pl du Capitole *31000*
☎ 561611919 FAX 561237996
Fifteen minutes drive from the international airport, in the centre of the "Ville Rose", on one of the most attractive squares in Europe. The Holiday Inn Crowne Plaza is among the most exclusive hotels in Toulouse.
In town centre Near motorway
162 en suite (bth) No smoking in 21 bedrooms TV in all bedrooms STV Direct dial from all bedrooms Mini-bar in all bedrooms Licensed Lift Night porter Full central heating Air conditioning in bedrooms Child discount available 12yrs Sauna Solarium Jacuzzi/spa Open terrace V meals

Languages spoken: English, Dutch, German, Italian & Spanish
ROOMS: (room only) s 850-1100FF; d 850-1100FF
CARDS: 〓 〓 〓 ⑨

★ ★ ★ Jean Mermoz
50 rue Matabiau *31100*
☎ 561630404 FAX 561631564
In the heart of the town, with its courtyard gardens and an Art-Deco interior, the hotel offers exceptionally peaceful accommodation in Toulouse, known as 'the pink city'. The quiet bedrooms have modern facilities and provide a high level of comfort, whilst guests can start off the day with a generous buffet breakfast in the winter garden with terrace.
In town centre
52 en suite (bth) (6 fmly) (1 with balcony) TV in all bedrooms STV Direct-dial available Mini-bar in all bedrooms Licensed Lift Night porter Full central heating Air conditioning in bedrooms Covered parking available (charged) Child discount available 12yrs Open terrace Languages spoken: English,Italian,Spanish
CARDS: 〓 〓 〓 ⑨ Travellers cheques

★ ★ ★ Novotel Toulouse Aeroport
23 Impasse de Maubec *31000*
☎ 561150000 FAX 561158844
(From city centre take exit 1 towards Auch)
Novotel offer their clients good quality accommodation in modern, well equipped bedrooms and have refined restaurants serving good quality cuisine They have excellent business meeting and conference facilities and some have food and beverages available 24 hours a day. All their hotels have at least one bedroom for disabled guests.
In town centre Near motorway
123 en suite (bth) (40 fmly) No smoking on premises TV in all bedrooms STV Radio in rooms Direct dial from all bedrooms Mini-bar in all bedrooms Room-safe Licensed Lift Night porter Full central heating Air conditioning in bedrooms Open parking available Supervised Outdoor swimming pool Tennis Boule Open terrace Last d 24.00hrs Languages spoken: English,German,Spanish
ROOMS: (room only) s 460-580FF; d 480-600FF
MEALS: Full breakfast 55FF Continental breakfast 55FF Lunch fr 140FFalc Dinner fr 140FFalc✱
CARDS: 〓 〓 〓 ⑨ Travellers cheques

★ ★ ★ ★ Sofitel Toulouse Centre
84 allée Jean-Jaurès *31000*
☎ 561102310 FAX 561102320
The Sofitel chain comprises of a group of very fine modern, comfortable hotels at the four star level. Bedrooms have been carefully designed to cater to guests relaxation and well being and the restaurants facilities offer fine cuisine in pleasant surroundings. They cater for business clientele with excellent conference and meeting facilities.
In town centre Near motorway
119 en suite (bth/shr) (2 fmly) No smoking in 51 bedrooms TV in all bedrooms STV Radio in rooms Direct dial from all bedrooms Mini-bar in all bedrooms Licensed Lift Night porter Full central heating Air conditioning in bedrooms Open parking available (charged) Covered parking available (charged) Child discount available V meals Last d 23.00hrs Languages spoken: English,Spanish
CARDS: 〓 〓 〓 ⑨ Travellers cheques

★ ★ Videotel

77 bd de Liembouchure *31200*
☎ 5561573477 FAX 5561235474
The hotels in the Videotel group all have bedrooms with pleasant furnishings and are equipped with the comfort of their clientele in mind. The restaurants serve a good quality gourmet cuisine with a range of prix-fixe menus, regional specialities and 'eat your fill buffet'. The management couples and their dedicated teams offer a 'round the clock' efficient service, where the well-being and satisfaction of guests is the prime consideration.
Near river In town centre Near motorway
90 en suite (bth/shr) (2 fmly) No smoking in 10 bedrooms TV in all bedrooms Direct dial from all bedrooms Mini-bar in all bedrooms Licensed Lift Night porter Full central heating Air conditioning in bedrooms Open parking available Covered parking available (charged) Supervised Child discount available 12yrs Pool table Open terrace V meals Last d 22.00hrs Languages spoken: English
ROOMS: (room only) s 280-280FF; d 280-280FF
MEALS: Full breakfast 34FF Lunch 52-88FF&alc Dinner 52-88FF&alc
CARDS: ● ▦ ▩ ◉

TOUZAC Lot

★ ★ ★ Source Bleue

Moulin de Léygues *46700*
☎ 565365201 FAX 565246569
(On D911, 6km W of Puy-l'Évêque on the left bank of the River Lot)

This charming hotel is situated on the banks of a river and has a park with giant bamboo trees. The residence has been in same family for 12 generations and offers guest accommodation with good modern facilities as well as a restaurant which serves dishes to suit most palates.
Near river Near lake Forest area
Closed Jan-Feb
15 en suite (bth/shr) (2 fmly) No smoking in 2 bedrooms TV in all bedrooms Direct dial from all bedrooms Licensed Night porter Full central heating Open parking available Supervised Child discount available 10yrs Outdoor swimming pool Fishing Sauna Solarium Gym Boule Jacuzzi/spa Bicycle rental Open terrace V meals Last d 21.00hrs Languages spoken: English,Spanish
ROOMS: (room only) s 300-320FF; d 395-495FF ✱
MEALS: Continental breakfast 35FF Lunch fr 150FFalc Dinner 100-240FF✱
CARDS: ● ▦ ▩ Travellers cheques

USSEL Lot

★ Relais du Pouzat

RN20 Le Pouzat *46240*
☎ 565368654 FAX 565368472
Situated in the Lot region with its glorious, natural splendour, sweeping valleys, caves and prestigious monuments, the hotel is a good starting point to discover and explore these places, without having to venture too far away. The comfortable bedrooms have modern amenities and there is a shaded flower-decked terrace A choice of tasty dishes - lovingly prepared by the lady of the house - are served in the dining-room, where original stone walls and exposed beams create a homely atmosphere.
Near lake Forest area Near motorway
14 en suite (bth/shr) (2 fmly) (4 with balcony) TV in all bedrooms Direct dial from all bedrooms Mini-bar in 10 bedrooms Licensed Full central heating Open parking available Child discount available 10yrs Open terrace Last d 22.00hrs
ROOMS: (room only) s 145-200FF; d 185-260FF
Reductions over 1 night Special breaks
MEALS: Continental breakfast 32FF Lunch 100-160FFalc Dinner 100-160FFalc
CARDS: ● ▩ ◉ Travellers cheques

VENTENAC Ariège

★ ★ ★ Domaine de Guinot

09120
☎ 561607001 FAX 561670081
The hotel enjoys a secluded location amidst extensive woodlands at the foot of the Pyrenees. The pretty guest rooms have country-style furnishings where the combination of wood and original stone create an authentic and homely atmosphere. The restaurant serves a choice of tasty dishes which are prepared with fresh market produce. The hotel is a good base to visit the nearby Carthares châteaux, and whilst walking in the woods guests can come across deer and wild boar.
Near lake Near beach Forest area
Closed 30 Sep-1 Apr
8 rms (7 shr) (1 fmly) (1 with balcony) Full central heating Open parking available Supervised Child discount available 8yrs Outdoor swimming pool Tennis Boule Bicycle rental Open terrace Last d 21.00hrs Languages spoken: English,Spanish,Italian
CARDS: ● ▩

VIGNEC Hautes-Pyrénées

★ ★ De La Neste

Vignec *65170*
☎ 562394279 FAX 562395877
Located opposite the beautiful thermal baths of Saint-Lary, the hotel is situated on the banks of the trout fishing grounds of the Neste d'Aure. It features well equipped bedrooms with panoramic views and a restaurant which serves regional dishes as well as special creations by the chef-proprietor. Friendly staff are always on hand to provide useful advice about the magnificent surroundings or the historic heritage of the valley.
Near river Near lake Forest area
Closed 1-31 May & Oct-14 Dec
22 en suite (bth/shr) (4 fmly) (6 with balcony) No smoking in 15 bedrooms TV in all bedrooms STV Radio in rooms Direct dial from all bedrooms Mini-bar in all bedrooms Licensed Night porter Full central heating Air conditioning in *contd.*

bedrooms Open parking available Supervised Child discount available 10yrs Outdoor swimming pool (heated) Fishing Solarium Jacuzzi/spa Open terrace Covered terrace V meals Last d 21.00hrs Languages spoken: English,Spanish
MEALS: Full breakfast 40FF Continental breakfast 35FF Lunch 70-160FF&alc Dinner 100FF&alc✱
CARDS: ● ■ Travellers cheques

★ ★ ★ Le Relais de Farrou
rte de Figeac *12200*
☎ 565451811 FAX 565453259
This pleasant establishment offers its visitors a fully up-to-date setting which combines ancient wood-paneling and original stone walls with 20th century facilities. It has well equipped bedrooms, a comfortable lounge with open fire place and a charming restaurant. In addition, it offers unsurpassed fitness and leisure facilities, for both young and older guests.
Near river Forest area Near motorway

26 en suite (bth/shr) (4 fmly) (15 with balcony) No smoking in 8 bedrooms TV in all bedrooms STV Radio in rooms Direct dial from all bedrooms Licensed Night porter Full central heating Open parking available Covered parking available (charged) Supervised Child discount available 12yrs Outdoor swimming pool Tennis Sauna Solarium Boule Mini-golf Jacuzzi/spa Bicycle rental Open terrace Last d 21.30hrs
MEALS: Continental breakfast 44FF Lunch 122-216FF&alc Dinner 122-216FF&alc✱
CARDS: ● ■ Travellers cheques

Taking your mobile phone to France?
See page 11

PILGRIMAGE AT LOURDES

The Miraculous Shrine at Lourdes

More than four million people a year visit Lourdes, most of them bound for the grotto where, in 1858 Bernadette Soubirous (later to become Ste Bernadette) first saw visions of the Virgin Mary. Napoleon III ordered the grotto opened to the public, and when the sick were dipped into the water of a spring there they were

Ste Bernadette's grotto.

Lourdes' Basilique du Rosaire

said to be cured. The hope of a miraculous cure for illness has made Lourdes into the site of the largest pilgrimage in the world. A new, underground basilica with a capacity of some 20,000 had be constructed in the late 1950s after crowds became too large to fit into the Basilique du Rosaire. It was consecrated on the centenary of Bernadette's visions. Not long after she saw her famous visions Bernadette became a nun at Nevers, and later nursed the wounded of the Franco-Prussian War.

Languedoc-Roussillon

A bird's eye view of Languedoc-Roussillon would show a plain enclosed by a semicircle of mountains and a coastline that is half sand and half rock. The relatively simple geography hides diverse landscapes and as a result a rich variety of vistor locations. The gentle volcanic plains of Languedoc are thick with orchards whose gold-vermillion fruits fill the landscape. Further south, Roussillon is home to the breathtaking east range of the Pyrénées. The juxtaposition of French, Catalan and Spanish cultures creates a fascinating variety of traditions.

ESSENTIAL FACTS

DÉPARTEMENTS:	Aude, Gard, Hérault, Lozère, Pyrénées-Roussillon
PRINCIPAL TOWNS	Perpignan, Beziers, Banyuls, Nimes, Carcassonne, Narbonne, Mende, Montpellier
PLACES TO VISIT:	Dolomite blocks at Aveyron, north of Montpellier; Bronze-age finds at Mende; underground river, grotto and swallow-hole just outside Meyrueis; the Fou canyon at Arles-sur-Tech.
REGIONAL TOURIST OFFICE	20 rue de la Republique, 34000 Montpellier. Tel: 67 58 05 10 Quai de Laittre-de-Tassigny, BO 540, 66005 Perpignan. Tel: 68 34 29 94
LOCAL GASTRONOMIC DELIGHTS	Snails served with a sauce aux noix: a Narbonne speciality made from crushed walnuts, ham, shallots and parsley; ollada: a Catalan soup made from pork, beans & vegetables; lou-kenkas: a spicy sausage; le suguet: a fish soup; chipirones guipuzcoanes: tiny squid stewed with onions, garlic and paprika; gâteau Basque: cake made with lemon & cherries.
DRINKS	Vin Collioure: a strong aromatic wine aged in oak barrels; Blanquette de Limoux: a sparkling white wine; the amber Rancio wines.
LOCAL CRAFTS WHAT TO BUY	Carved wood and cork ornaments, decorative ironwork, ceramics, espadrilles

(Top): Legend has it that the mountain village of Castelbouc is haunted by a decadent noble in the shape of a giant billy goat!

(Bottom): Cattle-farming is popular throughout the Pyrénées regions.

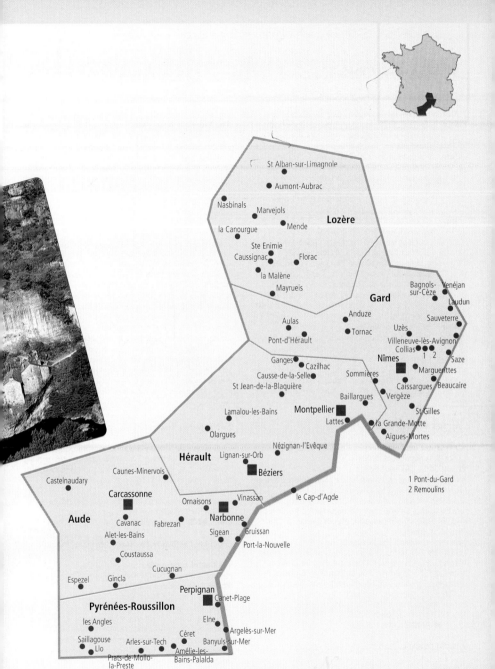

St Alban-sur-Limagnole

Aumont-Aubrac

Nasbinals
Marvejols
Lozère
la Canourgue
Mende

Ste Enimie
Caussignac
Florac
la Malène
Mayrueis

Bagnols-
sur-Cèze
Venéjan

Laudun
Gard
Anduze
Sauveterre
Aulas
Tornac
Uzès
Pont-d'Hérault
Villeneuve-lès-Avignon
Collias
1 2
Nîmes
Saze
Ganges
Cazilhac
Marguerittes
Causse-de-la-Selle
Sommières
St Jean-de-la-Blaquière
Caissargues
Beaucaire
Baillargues
Vergèze
Lamalou-les-Bains
Montpellier
St Gilles
Lattes
Olargues
la Grande-Motte
Aigues-Mortes
Nézignan-l'Evêque
Hérault
Lignan-sur-Orb
Caunes-Minervois
Castelnaudary
1 Pont-du-Gard
2 Remoulins
Carcassonne
Ornaisons
Vinassan
le Cap-d'Agde
Aude
Cavanac
Fabrezan
Narbonne
Alet-les-Bains
Sigean
Gruissan
Coustaussa
Port-la-Nouvelle
Cucugnan
Espezel
Gincla
Perpignan
Canet-Plage
Pyrénées-Roussillon
Elne
les Angles
Céret
Argelès-sur-Mer
Saillagouse
Arles-sur-Tech
Banyuls-sur-Mer
Llo
Amélie-les-
Prats-de-Mollo-
Bains-Palalda
la-Preste

EVENTS AND FESTIVALS:

Jan -

Mar Limoux Traditional Carnival (every weekend)

Feb Arles-sur-Tech Bear Festival;

Mar Cap d'Agde Cerfvolantissimo;

Apr Gruissan Easter Monday Pilgrimage to Seamens' Cemetery; La Canourgue Bachelors' Festival; Nîmes Jazz Festival;

Jun Nîmes Whit Monday Feria; Uzès Garlic Fair; Amélie-les-Bains Mule Driver Festival; Venejan Musical evenings; Uzès Contemporary Dance Festival; Laudun Music at Lascours Castle; St Guilhem le Desert Music Season in Gellone Abbey (till mid-Aug); Montpellier Dance Festival;

July Bagnoles-sur-Ceze Blues Festival; Céret Feria; St Ambroix Volo Biou (flying beef) Legend Festival (traditional parade, theatre show); Beaucaire Summer Festival (inc Ste Madeleine's Fair, medieval procession); Cap d'Agde Sea Festival; Carcassonne Festival; Le Grau-du-Roi/Port-Camargue Jazz Festival; Ouveillan Fontcalvy Festival (music, street theatre); Béziers Classical Music Festival; Jazz in Junas; Lamalou-les-Bains Operetta Festival (to mid Aug); Béziers Orb Valley Music Festival (to mid Aug);

Aug Béziers Feria; Aigues-Mortes St Louis Festival (historical parade, street entertainment etc); Béziers Orb Valley Music Festival; Lamalou-les-Bains Operetta Festival; Villeveyrac Musical weeks at Valmagne Abbey; Amélie-les-Bains Folklore Festival

Sep Cap d'Agde Catamaran Sailing Trophy; Arles-sur Tech Medieval Festival; Mialet Protestant gathering

at Mas Soubeyran (1st Sun); Nîmes Grape Harvest Feria;

Nov Garons Salon des Santons (Christmas ornament fair)

The Wines of Roussillon

Vines were first planted in the region in the seventh and eighth centuries BC, thanks to the temporary colonisation of Greek sailors bringing cargoes of iron from Corinth. Vine growing here is essentially a family affair and almost every wine-producing village has its own co-operative. The saying is that the vine is the longest thread in the social fabric of the region.

The different soils and terrain of Roussillon's vineyards produce wine from Vins de Pays to Appellation Contrôlée. The latter reach their peak after two years and many are aged in wood to give greater character. Appellation Contrôlée wines include Collioure, Côtes du Roussillon, Côtes du Roussillon-Villages and Vins Doux Naturels.

There are many variations of Vin Doux Naturels. Both Banyuls and Rivesaltes are particularly good with melon and are often drunk as an aperitif or as a dessert wine, while Muscats de Rivesaltes has a particularly flowery bouquet. Rancio wines are amber in colour with a characteristic green tinge and it is said that they never leave the taster indifferent. You will either love them or hate them.

Coullioure produces warm, aromatic wines which go well with meat and game. Côtes du Roussillon can be either red, white or rosé, whilst Côtes du Roussillon-Villages are exclusively red. All are most enjoyable.

Whatever your preference in wine, you will find it here.

AIGUES-MORTES Gard

★ ★ ★ **Hotel les Templiers**
23 rue de la République *30220*
☎ 466536656 FAX 466536961
(leave A9 at Gallargues (between Nîmes and Montpellier) and follow signs)
Situated in the centre of Aigues-Mortes this 17th century residence offers eleven Provençale guest rooms. It is an ideal place for exploring the Camargue with its special light and festive atmosphere.
Near sea Near beach In town centre
Closed Nov-Feb
10 rms (6 bth 3 shr) (3 fmly) (1 with balcony) TV in all bedrooms STV Direct dial from all bedrooms Licensed Full central heating Air conditioning in bedrooms Open parking available Languages spoken: English
ROOMS: (room only) s 500-780FF; d 500-780FF
MEALS: Continental breakfast 25FF
CARDS: ● ▬ ▬ Travellers cheques

ALET-LES-BAINS Aude

L'Évêché
11580
☎ 468699025 FAX 468699194
This old bishop's residence is surrounded by an extensive park and situated in a medieval village on the banks of the River Aude. It has spacious bedrooms which are mostly equipped with modern facilities, banqueting halls for business meetings and social events, as well as a restaurant which serves a choice of classic dishes and popular meals to suit most tastes. At 30 kilometres form Carcassone it is well placed for visits to the Cathares castles.

Near river Near lake Forest area In town centre Near motorway
Closed Nov-Mar
30 rms (6 fmly) Licensed Full central heating Open parking available Child discount available 7yrs Bicycle rental Open terrace V meals Last d 21.00hrs Languages spoken: English,Spanish
MEALS: Continental breakfast 32FF Lunch 65-210FF&alc Dinner 65-210FF&alc✱
CARDS: ● ▬ Travellers cheques

AMÉLIE-LES-BAINS-PALALDA Pyrénées-Orientales

★ ★ **Castel Emeraude**
rte de la Corniche *66112*
☎ 468390283 FAX 468390283
Near river Near sea Forest area
Closed early December-end January
59 en suite (bth/shr) (6 fmly) (34 with balcony) TV in all bedrooms Direct dial from all bedrooms Mini-bar in all bedrooms Licensed Lift Full central heating Open parking available Supervised Child discount available Solarium Boule Jacuzzi/spa Bicycle rental Covered terrace V meals Last d 21.00hrs Languages spoken: English German Portuguese & Spanish

ANDUZE Gard

★ ★ **Porte des Cévennes**
2300 rte de St-Jean-du-Gard *30140*
☎ 466619944 FAX 466617365
The newly opened hotel La Porte des Cévennes, features peacefully situated bedrooms with modern amenities and

private loggias. A high standard of home cooking, complemented by good local wines, is served in the country-style dining-room with terrace overlooking the valley.
Near river Near sea Forest area Near motorway
Closed Nov-Mar
37 en suite (bth/shr) (2 fmly) (34 with balcony) TV in 34 bedrooms STV Direct dial from all bedrooms Night porter Open parking available Supervised Child discount available 10yrs Indoor swimming pool (heated) Solarium Open terrace Children's playground Last d 21.00hrs Languages spoken: English
ROOMS: (room only) s 260-330FF; d 260-330FF
MEALS: Full breakfast 45FF Continental breakfast 45FF Dinner 90-150FF✱
CARDS: 💳 📳 ⚏ ⬢ Travellers cheques

ANGLES, LES Pyrénées-Orientales

★★ Llaret Hotel
12 av de Balcere *66210*
☎ 468309090 FAX 468309166
The hotel is situated at an elevated position and offers unrivalled views of the lake and the magnificent Pyrenees. The airy bedrooms are cheerfully decorated and offer good modern amenities. There is an English-style pub, and the restaurant combines high quality cuisine with a panoramic vista over the surrounding countryside.
Near river Near lake Near beach
Closed mid May-mid Jun & Oct-mid Dec
26 en suite (bth/shr) (8 fmly) (20 with balcony) No smoking on premises TV in all bedrooms Radio in rooms Mini-bar in all bedrooms Licensed Full central heating Open parking available Supervised Child discount available 12yrs Solarium Boule Bicycle rental Open terrace Last d 21.30hrs Languages spoken: English,Spanish
MEALS: Full breakfast 35FF Lunch 95-140FF&alc Dinner 95-140FF&alc✱
CARDS: 💳 ⚏

ARGELÈS-SUR-MER Pyrénées-Orientales

★★★ Cottage (Relais du Silence)
21 rue Arthur Rimbaud *66700*
☎ 468810733 FAX 468815969
(From A9 exit 'Le Boulou' circle town following 'Centre Plage' signs)
Just 30 minutes from the Spanish Border, the Hotel Le Cottage is ideally located to discover the vineyards and the historic and cultural heritage of Roussilon. Only 1500 metres from the sea, it offers visitors a peaceful and relaxing stay surrounded by lush orange trees and bougainvillaea. It has attractive, comfortable bedrooms with modern facilities. Leisure facilities include a play area for children, table tennis, golf practice and tennis courts nearby. The cuisine consists of delicately flavoured Mediterranean dishes made from fresh local produce.
Near sea
Closed 16 Oct-8 Apr
32 en suite (bth/shr) (8 fmly) (21 with balcony) TV in all bedrooms STV Direct dial from all bedrooms Mini bar in 10 bedrooms Room-safe Licensed Full central heating Open parking available Covered parking available (charged) Supervised Child discount available 11yrs Outdoor swimming pool Solarium Pool table Boule Mini-golf Open terrace Covered terrace Last d 21.30hrs Languages spoken: English,German,Spanish
ROOMS: (room only) s 290-580FF; d 300-720FF

MEALS: Full breakfast 54FF Continental breakfast 44FF Lunch 85-265FF&alc Dinner 150-265FF&alc
CARDS: 💳 📳 ⚏ Eurocard Travellers cheques

AULAS Gard

★★ Le Mas Quayrol
☎ 467811238 FAX 467812384
(From Nîmes-Montpellier motorway take Ganges exit to Le Vigan, then through Le Mont Aigoual to Aulas)
Le Mas Quayrol is situated right in the middle of the countryside not far from Mont Aigoual and some of the famous sites of the Midi-Languedoc, it is surrounded by chestnuts and green oak trees. From the restaurant as well as the bedrooms guests can enjoy panoramic views over the low foothills of the Cévennes. Bedrooms are well equipped. The hotel offers its visitors a comfortable stay with lounges, bars and terraces for relaxation and an excellent cuisine.
Near river Forest area
Closed Dec-Mar
16 en suite (bth/shr) (4 fmly) TV in all bedrooms STV Licensed Full central heating Open parking available Supervised Child discount available 5yrs Outdoor swimming pool Tennis Open terrace Last d 21.20hrs Languages spoken: English, Spanish
ROOMS: (room only) s 350FF; d 375FF **Reductions over 1 night Special breaks**
MEALS: Full breakfast 37FF Lunch 95-235FF&alc Dinner 95-235FF&alc
CARDS: 💳 ⚏

AUMONT-AUBRAC Lozère

★★★ Grand Hotel Prouhéze
2 rte du Languedoc *48130*
☎ 466428007 FAX 466428778
(From A75, exit 35)
This handsome residence offers its visitors a memorable stay in delightful surroundings. The interior is decorated throughout with flair and great attention to detail. The restaurant offers a creative selection of inspired dishes, and combines the finest fresh produce with delicately flavoured herbs from the region. Bedrooms are smartly furnished and well equipped with modern amenities. Staff are dedicated, and offer a friendly service.
Forest area Near motorway
Closed 31 Oct-Mar
27 en suite (bth/shr) (4 fmly) TV in all bedrooms Radio in rooms Licensed Full central heating Open parking available Child discount available 10yrs Open terrace Last d 21.00hrs Languages spoken: English
MEALS: Full breakfast 80FF Lunch 135-500FF Dinner 195-500FF✱
CARDS: 💳 📳 ⚏

BAGNOLS-SUR-CÈZE Gard

★★★★ Château de Montcaud
Hameau de Combe-Sabran *30200*
☎ 466898000 FAX 466896001
(On entering Bagnols, turn towards Alès on D6, then right at first crossing after 4km)
Whether your stay is a holiday or just a short break, this manor house is the ideal venue to explore the lovely countryside of Provençe or visit the famous Côte du Rhone vineyards. It stands in the leafy surroundings of a large park. The individually styled bedrooms are generous in size and *contd.*

incorporate elegant furnishings and the highest level of comfort. The menu features a wide selection of well-presented dishes consisting of good quality ingredients, with equal emphasis being placed on presentation and flavour. In addition there is a heated swimming pool, sauna, Turkish bath, fitness centre and tennis court.
Near river Forest area Near motorway
Closed 2 Jan-4 Apr
32 en suite (bth/shr) (2 fmly) (2 with balcony) TV in all bedrooms STV Radio in rooms Direct dial from all bedrooms Mini-bar in all bedrooms Licensed Lift Full central heating Air conditioning in bedrooms Open parking available Covered parking available (charged) Supervised Child discount available 12yrs Outdoor swimming pool (heated) Tennis Sauna Gym Boule Jacuzzi/spa Bicycle rental Open terrace V meals Last d 21.45hrs Languages spoken: English,German,Spanish,Italian
ROOMS: (room only) s 990-1250FF; d 1050-1550FF
Reductions over 1 night
MEALS: Full breakfast 100FF Lunch 150-330FF&alc Dinner 250-420FF&alc
CARDS: 💳 ▓▓ 💳 💳 JCB

BAILLARGUES Hérault

★ ★ ★ **Golf Hotel de Montpellier Massané**
Domaine de Massane *34670*
☎ 467878787 FAX 467878790
(from Montpellier A9 exit number 28 in the direction of Nîmes or N113 in the direction of Nîmes)
This modern hotel is part of the golf course complex Montpellier Massane, and therefore ideal for golfers. The modern Club House, with its splendid open fire place, cosy bar and seating arrangements provides relaxation in a friendly atmosphere. The restaurant 'La Lucques', serves a well balanced cuisine, prepared with the finest fresh produce from the region. The bedrooms - with views over the gardens and golf course - are well equipped with modern facilities.
Near sea Near beach
32 en suite (bth/shr) (16 fmly) No smoking in 2 bedrooms TV in all bedrooms STV Radio in rooms Direct dial from all bedrooms Mini-bar in all bedrooms Room-safe Licensed Night porter Full central heating Air conditioning in bedrooms Open parking available Supervised Outdoor swimming pool Golf 18 Tennis Sauna Solarium Pool table Boule Bicycle rental Open terrace Covered terrace Jaccuzzi Languages spoken: English,German & Spanish
ROOMS: (room only) s 410-460FF; d 470-520FF **Special breaks: Golfing Breaks**
MEALS: Full breakfast 63FF Continental breakfast 46FF
CARDS: 💳 ▓▓ 💳 💳

BANYULS-SUR-MER Pyrénées-Orientales

★ ★ **Les Elmes**
Plage des Elmes *66650*
☎ 468880312 FAX 468885303
(On N114 between Collioure and Cerbère)
Standing on the edge of a blue cove and just metres away from a fine sandy beach, this cheerful, modern hotel offers charming guest rooms with modern facilities. The restaurant with shaded terrace affords wonderful views of the surrounding countryside and serves a delicately flavoured, light cuisine, accompanied by excellent local wines.
Near sea Near beach Near motorway
Closed 6-20 Jan & 4-19 Dec
31 en suite (bth/shr) (14 fmly) (7 with balcony) TV in all

bedrooms STV Direct dial from all bedrooms Licensed Night porter Full central heating Air conditioning in bedrooms Open parking available Covered parking available (charged) Supervised Child discount available 12yrs Boule Bicycle rental Open terrace Boating Languages spoken: English, German
ROOMS: (room only) d 190-500FF ✷ **Special breaks**
MEALS: Full breakfast 40FF Continental breakfast 40FF Lunch 100-260FF&alc
CARDS: 💳 ▓▓ 💳 💳 Travellers cheques

BEAUCAIRE Gard

★ ★ ★ **Robinson**
rte de Remoulin *30300*
☎ 466592132 FAX 466590003
(Approach via A9 and D986)

This large house is surrounded by lush scenery and features an attractive interior carefully decorated with well matching fabrics and furnishings. The foyer-lounge with open fire opens into the gardens, where in the summer meals are served on the terrace. The bedrooms offer good amenities and the restaurant serves a range of dishes to suit all tastes. Run by the same family for four generations it provides a pleasant setting for a relaxing holiday in Provence.
Near river Forest area
30 en suite (bth/shr) (12 fmly) TV in all bedrooms Direct dial from all bedrooms Licensed Full central heating Open parking available Covered parking available (charged) Child discount available Outdoor swimming pool (heated) Tennis Solarium Boule Open terrace Covered terrace V meals Last d 21.30hrs Languages spoken: English, German & Italian
ROOMS: (room only) s 270-300FF; d 295-350FF
MEALS: Full breakfast 45FF Lunch 100-200FF&alc Dinner 100-200FF
CARDS: 💳 💳 Travellers cheques

CAISSARGUES Gard

★ ★ ★ **Les Aubuns** (Best Western)
30132
☎ 466701044 FAX 466701497
(On D442, 2km from the airport)
This typical Provençale hotel is set in the open countryside just outside Nîmes. Surrounded by lush oleander bushes it offers comfortable, well equipped bedrooms providing relaxing accommodation. With its multitude of leisure facilities and beautiful surroundings, it is the ideal venue for both energetic guests and nature lovers.
Forest area Near motorway
26 en suite (bth/shr) (4 fmly) (26 with balcony) TV in all bedrooms STV Radio in rooms Direct dial from all bedrooms Licensed Night porter Full central heating Open parking available Child discount available 10yrs Outdoor swimming pool Golf 18 Tennis Riding Solarium Boule Open terrace Last d 21.30hrs Languages spoken: English,Spanish
ROOMS: (room only) s 420FF; d 485FF
MEALS: Full breakfast 46FF Continental breakfast 46FF Lunch 125-155FF Dinner 125-155FF
CARDS: 💳 ▓▓ 💳 💳 Travellers cheques

CANET-PLAGE Pyrénées-Orientales

★ ★ ★ **Galion**
20 bis av du Grand Large *66140*
☎ 468802823 FAX 468732441
The hotel is set in Canet-Plage 12 kilometres from Perpignan

and close to the Spanish border. With sunshine all year round, fine sandy beaches and unsurpassed leisure facilities nearby, it provides the ideal setting for an enjoyable holiday. The bedrooms are pleasantly furnished and have modern facilities, whilst the restaurant serves high quality cuisine where a choice of seafood and fish specialities feature high on the menu.
Near lake Near sea In town centre
Closed Sep-Apr
28 en suite (bth/shr) (10 fmly) (28 with balcony) TV in all bedrooms Direct dial from all bedrooms Licensed Lift Night porter Full central heating Open parking available Child discount available 10yrs Outdoor swimming pool Bicycle rental Open terrace pedalos Last d 21.00hrs Languages spoken: English,Spanish
MEALS: Full breakfast 40FF Continental breakfast 40FF Lunch fr 80FF&alc Dinner fr 80FF&alc✱
CARDS: 💳 📠 Travellers cheques

★ ★ St-Georges
45 prom Côte Vermeille *66140*
☎ 468803377 FAX 468806504
The hotel enjoys a seafront location in the heart of Canet Plage. It features a modern, informal interior with pleasant bedrooms, comfortable public areas and a pretty garden. The restaurant serves a good choice of regional dishes and traditional French cuisine.
Near sea In town centre
Closed Oct-Apr
41 en suite (bth/shr) (10 fmly) (27 with balcony) TV in all bedrooms STV Licensed Lift Night porter Full central heating Open parking available Child discount available 12yrs Outdoor swimming pool Last d 2.45hrs Languages spoken: English,German,Spanish,Swedish
MEALS: Full breakfast 30FF Lunch 60-95FF Dinner 60-95FF✱
CARDS: 💳 📠 Travellers cheques

LE CAP-D'AGDE Hérault

★ ★ ★ Hotel du Golf
Ile des Loisirs *34300*
☎ 467268703 FAX 467262689
This attractive establishment is tucked away amidst 5000 square metres of delightful gardens. It offers a wide array of attractive features - there are sunny terraces, an open-air swimming pool and a solarium, with golf, tennis and water-sports nearby. Meals can be enjoyed in the gourmet restaurant or on the shaded terrace beside the swimming pool.
Near sea
Closed early Nov-late Mar
50 en suite (bth/shr) 20 rooms in annexe (4 fmly) (20 with balcony) TV in all bedrooms Mini-bar in all bedrooms Licensed Night porter Full central heating Air conditioning in bedrooms Open parking available Covered parking available (charged) Supervised Child discount available Outdoor swimming pool (heated) Solarium Pool table Boule Bicycle rental Open terrace Covered terrace Last d 23.00hrs Languages spoken: English,German,Spanish
CARDS: 💳 📠 Travellers cheques

CARCASSONNE Aude

★ ★ ★ Bristol
7 av Foch M Sartore *11000*
☎ 468250724 FAX 468257189
The hotel is set in the centre of the historic town of Carcassonne and offers comfortable accommodation and an

excellent cuisine. The spacious foyer, attractive dining rooms and popular wine bar, complement the tastefully furnished bedrooms which are equipped with modern facilities.
Near river In town centre
Closed Jan & Feb
59 rms (56 bth/shr) (4 fmly) TV in all bedrooms STV Direct dial from all bedrooms Licensed Lift Night porter Full central heating Covered parking available (charged) Last d 21.30hrs Languages spoken: English,Italian & German
CARDS: 💳 📠 Travellers cheques

★ ★ ★ Domaine d'Auriac
rte de St-Hilaire *11000*
☎ 468257222 FAX 468473554
The establishment is set in the leafy surroundings of a 300 year old park, just a stone's throw from Carcassonne, between Montagne Noire and Pays Cathare. Le Domaine d'Auriac offers its guests a restful atmosphere, comfortable amenities and culinary delights. The swimming pool, tennis, walks, billiard room and a nine-hole golf course will add to an enjoyable stay at the foot of the medieval Cité de Carcassonne.
Near river Near lake Forest area Near motorway
25 en suite (bth/shr) 2 rooms in annexe (12 fmly) (6 with balcony) TV in all bedrooms Mini-bar in all bedrooms Licensed Lift Night porter Full central heating Air conditioning in bedrooms Open parking available Covered parking available Supervised Child discount available 12yrs Outdoor swimming pool Golf Tennis Fishing Pool table Boule Open terrace Covered terrace Languages spoken: English,German & Spanish
CARDS: 💳 📠 Travellers cheques

★ ★ ★ Hotel Le Donjon (Best Western)
2 rue Comte Roger *11000*
☎ 468710880 FAX 468250660
The traditional hotel Le Donjon is situated in the medieval heart of the city and dates back to the 16th century. With its half-timbered façade, mullion windows, exposed beams and ornate French-style ceilings it reflects the atmosphere of times past. Most of the bedrooms are decorated in Louis XIII style and offer good comfort.
In town centre Near motorway
38 en suite (bth/shr) (2 fmly) TV in all bedrooms STV Radio in rooms Licensed Lift Night porter Full central heating Air conditioning in bedrooms Open parking available (charged) Supervised Child discount available 12yrs Open terrace V meals Last d 23.00hrs Languages spoken: English,Italian & Spanish
MEALS: Continental breakfast 25FF Lunch 73-128FF Dinner 73-128FF✱
CARDS: 💳 📠 Travellers cheques

★ ★ ★ Trois Couronnes
2 r des Trois Couronnes *11000*
☎ 468253610 FAX 468259292
Situated opposite the medieval city, the hotel has a splendid view of the imposing fortress. From the panoramic restaurant on the fourth floor, guests can enjoy the splendour of the castle whilst savouring some of the many specialities on the menu. The hotel also boasts a fitness room, indoor swimming pool, and billiards - tennis and golf can be found in the near vicinity.
Near river In town centre
68 en suite (bth) (5 fmly) (44 with balcony) No smoking in 20 bedrooms TV in all bedrooms STV Mini-bar in all bedrooms Licensed Lift Night porter Full central heating Air conditioning in bedrooms Open parking available (charged) Covered parking available (charged) Supervised Child

contd.

discount available Indoor swimming pool (heated) Tennis
Sauna Solarium Gym Jacuzzi/spa Bicycle rental V meals
Last d 22.30hrs Languages spoken: English,German,Spanish
MEALS: Full breakfast 60FF Continental breakfast 60FF Lunch
fr 100FF&alc Dinner 150-275FF&alc✱
CARDS: ●● ▉▉ ▇▇ ●) Travellers cheques

CASTELNAUDARY Aude

★ ★ Grand Hotel Fourcade
14 rue des Carnes *11400*
☎ 468230208 FAX 468941067
In the heart of the region, well known for its famous cassoulet,
this small, charming hotel is situated in a picturesque street.
Most of the bedrooms have modern facilities and guests can
sample the tasty house speciality 'cassoulet Fourcade' in the
cosy atmosphere of the restaurant.
Near river Near lake In town centre Near motorway
12 rms (8 bth/shr) (4 fmly) (3 with balcony) TV in 29 bedrooms
Mini-bar in 29 bedrooms Licensed Full central heating Open
parking available Covered parking available (charged)
Supervised Child discount available Last d 21.30hrs
Languages spoken: English,Italian
CARDS: ●● ▉▉ ▇▇ ●) Travellers cheques

CAUNES-MINERVOIS Aude

★ ★ Hotel d'Alibert
pl de la Marie *11160*
☎ 468780054
Situated in a splendid Renaissance residence the Hotel Alibert
has become a 'must' for a holiday in the Minervois region.
With its ribbed vaults, spiral staircase and century-old
sculptures it has retained a heritage of family hospitality. The
guest rooms are mostly equipped with modern facilities and
offer a good level of comfort, whilst the restaurant serves
regional cuisine in a traditional interior.
Forest area In town centre
Closed Xmas-end Feb
7 rms (2 bth 3 shr) (3 fmly) Licensed Full central heating
Open parking available Covered parking available Bicycle
rental Open terrace V meals Languages spoken: English
CARDS: ●● ▇▇

CAUSSE-DE-LA-SELLE Hérault

★ ★ Hostellerie le Vieux Chêne
34380
☎ 467731100 FAX 467731054
En route to the pilgrim resort of Santiago de Compostella and
situated between the mountains and the sea, this charming
establishment features a delightful restaurant serving the very
best specialities from the region. Exquisite dishes incorporate;
truffles, foie gras and crayfish and are accompanied by superb
vintage wines. The tastefully decorated bedrooms offer a high
quality of comfort and are equipped with modern facilities.
Near river Forest area In town centre
3 en suite (bth/shr) 2 rooms in annexe (1 fmly) (1 with
balcony) TV in all bedrooms STV Radio in rooms Direct dial
from all bedrooms Mini-bar in all bedrooms Licensed Full
central heating Open parking available Supervised Solarium
Boule Open terrace Covered terrace V meals Last d 21.30hrs
ROOMS: (room only) d fr 310FF
MEALS: Continental breakfast 45FF Lunch 110-150FF&alc
Dinner 110-150FF&alc
CARDS: ●● ▉▉ ▇▇ Travellers cheques

CAUSSIGNAC Lozère

★ ★ Les Aires de la Carline
rte de l'Aven Armand *48210*
☎ 466485479 FAX 466485759

Near river Forest area
Closed Oct-Mar
12 en suite (bth/shr) (2 fmly) TV in all bedrooms Direct dial
from all bedrooms Full central heating Air conditioning in
bedrooms Open parking available Child discount available
10yrs Boule Open terrace Last d 22.00hrs Languages spoken:
English
ROOMS: (room only) d 260-280FF **Reductions over 1
night**
MEALS: Continental breakfast 35FF Dinner 90-130FF
CARDS: ●● ▉▉ ▇▇ ●)

CAVANAC Aude

★ ★ ★ Château de Cavanac
11570
☎ 468796104 FAX 468797967
(5km from Carcassonne via D104 to St-Hilaire)
The 17th century Château de Cavanac offers its clientele
charming bedrooms - with four-poster or canopy beds and
excellent en suite facilities - accompanied by a traditional cuisine
prepared over a wood fire and served in the former stables
which now provide the informal setting for the restaurant.
Forest area
Closed mid Jan-mid Feb
15 en suite (bth/shr) (3 fmly) No smoking in 1 bedroom TV in
all bedrooms Direct dial from all bedrooms Room-safe
Licensed Lift Open parking available Outdoor swimming
pool Tennis Sauna Pool table Open terrace Covered terrace
V meals Last d 22.00hrs Languages spoken: English
ROOMS: (room only) d 350-670FF
MEALS: Full breakfast 45FF Continental breakfast 45FF
Dinner fr 195FF&alc✱
CARDS: ●● ▇▇

CAZILHAC Hérault

★ ★ ★ Auberge les Norias
254 av des Deux Ponts *34190*
☎ 467735590 FAX 467736208
This large former mill stands in leafy surroundings near the
River Herault. Bedrooms have private facilities and overlook a
tranquil park. The cuisine offers a choice of regional and
inventive dishes served in the rustic setting of the dining
room, whilst in summer guests can relax on the flower-filled
terrace.

Near river
11 en suite (bth) 1 rooms in annexe (1 with balcony) TV in all
bedrooms Licensed Full central heating Open parking
available Covered parking available (charged) Child discount
available 10yrs Open terrace Covered terrace Wkly live
entertainment Last d 21.30hrs Languages spoken:
English,German
MEALS: Full breakfast 35FF Continental breakfast 40FF Lunch
fr 100FF&alc Dinner fr 100FF&alc✱
CARDS: 🍴 💳 💳 Travellers cheques

CÉRET Pyrénées-Orientales

★ ★ ★ Mas Trilles
Pont de Reynes *66400*
☎ 468873837 FAX 468874262
This ancient Catalan farmhouse dates back to the 17th century
and is tucked away on a hillside overlooking the river.
Completely renovated throughout, its has retained all of its
original character. Modern amenities have been carefully
blended with old-world charm and hospitality. Charming,
individually appointed bedrooms - many with private patios or
gardens - terraces, and a heated swimming pool in lush
surroundings, will contribute to an enjoyable stay.
Near river Forest area Near motorway
Closed mid Oct-mid April
10 en suite (bth) (7 fmly) (8 with balcony) TV in all bedrooms
Direct dial from all bedrooms Licensed Full central heating
Open parking available Supervised Child discount available
Outdoor swimming pool (heated) Fishing Boule Bicycle
rental Open terrace Last d 20.30hrs Languages spoken:
English,Italian
CARDS: 🍴 💳 💳

★ ★ ★ ★ Terrasse au Soleil
rte de Fontfrède *66400*
☎ 468870194 FAX 468873924
(From A9, take D115 to Céret. Hotel signposted from town
centre)
This old Catalan farmhouse occupies a dominant position on a
hillside overlooking Céret. The house is decorated throughout
in rich ochres, Mediterranean blues and mosaics. The restful,
airy guest-rooms, equipped with modern amenities,
magnificent terrace and cool shaded garden combine to make
your stay a memorable one. A swimming pool, flood-lit tennis
court and a driving range are available.
Forest area
Closed 15 Oct-14 Mar
27 en suite (bth/shr) 14 rooms in annexe (8 fmly) (20 with
balcony) No smoking in 1 bedroom TV in all bedrooms Direct
dial from all bedrooms Mini-bar in all bedrooms Room-safe
Licensed Night porter Full central heating Air conditioning in
bedrooms Open parking available Child discount available
Outdoor swimming pool (heated) Golf Tennis Boule Open
terrace Covered terrace Last d 21.30hrs Languages spoken:
English,Spanish
ROOMS: (room only) d 695-1200FF ✱
MEALS: Lunch 160-240FF Dinner fr 240FF✱
CARDS: 🍴 💳 💳 ⓓ JCB

COLLIAS Gard

★ ★ ★ Hostellerie du Castellas
Grand'rue *30210*
☎ 466228888 FAX 466228428
(A9 exit Remoulins. Take D981 direction Uzes, then left turn for
Collias)

This enchanting establishment with its pale stone walls and
green shutters offers its visitors lavish hospitality and
dedicated, personal service. The interior exudes an
atmosphere of elegant sophistication through the use of
exquisite fabrics and art nouveau/art déco furniture in the
bedrooms and public areas. The vaulted restaurant serves
delicately flavoured specialities combining fresh ingredients
with herbs and spices from the region. There is a fully
equipped function room to cater for business travellers;
sporting facilities include canoeing, hiking and climbing;
whilst Le Pont du Gard, Nimes, Uzes and Avignon represent
places of cultural and historic interest to visit.
Near river
Closed Jan-early Mar
17 en suite (bth/shr) (3 fmly) (5 with balcony) TV in all
bedrooms Direct dial from all bedrooms Mini-bar in all
bedrooms Licensed Full central heating Air conditioning in
bedrooms Open parking available Supervised Child discount
available 5yrs Outdoor swimming pool Open terrace V meals
Last d 21.30hrs Languages spoken: English,German
ROOMS: (room only) d 480-1000FF ✱
MEALS: Full breakfast 70FF Lunch 90-350FF Dinner 170-
360FF✱
CARDS: 🍴 💳 💳 ⓓ

COUSTAUSSA Aude

★ ★ Peyré Picade
87500

☎ 468741111 FAX 468740037
A far cry from the standard package available in most hotels,
this establishment offers a personalised interior as well as a
service which is difficult to match, and provides a haven of
peace far away from stress and pollution. The guest rooms are
well furnished with good modern amenities and the cuisine
consists of an array of delicious meals prepared with fine local
produce. Leisure facilities include a riding centre with 20
horses, which offers unforgettable rides through the
countryside, rowing, rafting and cycle rides in the woods.
Forest area
10 en suite (bth/shr) (1 fmly) (3 with balcony) Open parking
available Covered parking available Supervised Child
discount available 12yrs Outdoor swimming pool Riding
Solarium Pool table Boule Open terrace V meals Last d
21.00hrs Languages spoken: English,Spanish
MEALS: Full breakfast 25FF Continental breakfast 25FF Lunch
95-150FF&alc Dinner 95-150FF&alc✱
CARDS: 🍴 💳 💳 ⓓ

CUCUGNAN Aude

★ ★ Auberge du Vigneron
2 rue A Mir *11350*
☎ 468450000 FAX 468450308
This 100-year old country inn is peacefully situated in Cathar
countryside. The restaurant is reminiscent of a wine cellar; its
superb oak wine barrels providing a rustic setting for an
enjoyable meal. The country-style bedrooms with exposed
brickwork offer comfortable accommodation. The surrounding
vineyards produce the famous Corbières wines and are well
worth a visit.
Near river Near lake Forest area
Closed 16Dec-15Feb
6 en suite (shr) TV in all bedrooms Direct dial from all
bedrooms Licensed Full central heating Open parking
available Covered parking available (charged) Boule Open
terrace V meals Last d 21.30hrs   *contd.*

ROOMS: (room only) s 210-240FF; d 220-260FF **
MEALS: Full breakfast 35FF Continental breakfast 35FF Lunch 80-185FF&alc Dinner 80-185FF&alc
CARDS: ●● ▆ Travellers cheques

ELNE Pyrénées-Orientales

★ ★ Week-End
29 av Paul Reig *66200*
☎ 468220668 FAX 468221716

This family hotel is situated in the charming Pyrenean village of Elne, four kilometres from the sea and close to the mountains. Housed in ancient barn with hundred-year old oak beams, it has been renovated in authentic Catalan style, and features comfortable bedrooms and a restaurant which serves regional cuisine prepared with the best seasonal produce available.

Near river Near lake Near sea Near beach Forest area Near motorway
Closed 7 Nov-14 Feb
8 en suite (shr) (2 fmly) (4 with balcony) TV in all bedrooms Direct dial from all bedrooms Full central heating Air conditioning in bedrooms Covered parking available (charged) Supervised Child discount available 12yrs Bicycle rental Last d 22.00hrs Languages spoken: English,Dutch,German,Italian,Spanish
ROOMS: (room only) d 215-240FF **Reductions over 1 night Special breaks**
MEALS: Lunch 78FF Dinner 95-150FF
CARDS: ●● ▆▆ ▆ ⑩ Travellers cheques

ESPEZEL Aude

★ Grau
11340
☎ 468203014
This small, family hotel has been recently renovated and upgraded to two star standard. It is situated in a Pyrenean village at an altitude of 900 metres and is surrounded by forests. The restaurant offers excellent home-cooking by the proprietor and the bedrooms, equipped with modern amenities, guarantee a good night's sleep.
Near river Near lake Forest area In town centre
8 en suite (bth/shr) (2 fmly) No smoking in 2 bedrooms Licensed Full central heating Open parking available Child discount available 12yrs Fishing Boule V meals Last d 20.55hrs Languages spoken: English,Spanish
CARDS: ●● ▆ Travellers cheques

Taking your mobile phone to France?
See page 11

FABREZAN Aude

★ ★ Le Clos des Souquets
av de Lagrasse *11200*
☎ 468435261 FAX 468435676
Originally an ancient wine-cellar, this small hotel has been completely renovated and offers individually appointed bedrooms, each with their own personal style. The restaurant serves exotic fish specialities from Africa, which are brought in twice a week. In addition, it features a shaded terrace and an interior garden.
Near river Forest area
Closed early Nov-April
5 en suite (bth) TV in all bedrooms Licensed Full central heating Open parking available Supervised Outdoor swimming pool Pool table Boule Bicycle rental Open terrace Covered terrace V meals Last d 21.45hrs Languages spoken: English,Spanish
CARDS: ●● ▆ ⑩

FLORAC Lozère

★ ★ ★ Grand Hotel du Parc
47 av Jean Honestier *48400*
☎ 466450305 FAX 466451181

The Grand Hotel du Parc is very close to the city centre, but provides quiet surroundings. Bedrooms are comfortable and the restaurant serves gastronmic and regional specialities. The Gleize family have owned the hotel since 1922.
Near river Forest area In town centre
Closed Dec-14 Mar
60 rms (36 bth 18 shr) 26 rooms in annexe (10 fmly) (4 with balcony) TV in 54 bedrooms Direct dial from all bedrooms Licensed Lift Full central heating Open parking available Covered parking available Outdoor swimming pool (heated) Boule Covered terrace Last d 20.45hrs Languages spoken: English, German & Spanish
ROOMS: (room only) s 230-260FF; d 230-300FF
MEALS: Full breakfast 37FF Lunch 92-185FF&alc Dinner 92-185FF&alc
CARDS: ●● ▆▆ ▆ ⑩ Travellers cheques

★ ★ Le Rochefort
RN 106 *48400*
☎ 466450257
(2km N)
Located in this unspoilt corner of France, in the heart of the Cévennes National Park, between Chardons and Chataignes, the hotel 'Le Rochefort' offers its clientele spacious, comfortable rooms with balconies. The restaurant 'Le Dolmen' with a panoramic view over the surrounding countryside,

serves a choice of innovative and tasty dishes.
Near river Forest area Near motorway
Closed Nov-Etr
24 en suite (bth/shr) (6 fmly) (8 with balcony) TV in all
bedrooms Direct dial from all bedrooms Licensed Full central
heating Open parking available Child discount available 14yrs
Boule Open terrace V meals Last d 21.30hrs Languages
spoken: English
ROOMS: (room only) s 270-350FF; d 290-350FF
MEALS: Continental breakfast 35FF Lunch 60-185FF&alc
Dinner 80-185FF&alc
CARDS: ✿ 💳 Travellers cheques

GANGES Hérault

★ ★ ★ ★ **Château de Madières Hostellerie**
Madières *34190*
☎ 467738403 FAX 467735571
A delightful building situated in an exceptional setting. It
features a spacious lounge with an imposing fireplace and
assorted antiques. The magnificent vaulted restaurant serves a
large selection of outstanding regional specialities. The
individually styled bedrooms offer a high degree of comfort
and complement the warm atmosphere which prevails
throughout.
Near river Forest area Near motorway
Closed Nov-Mar
12 en suite (bth/shr) (4 fmly) TV in all bedrooms STV Direct
dial from all bedrooms Mini-bar in all bedrooms Licensed
Full central heating Open parking available Child discount
available 10yrs Outdoor swimming pool (heated) Fishing
Gym Boule Bicycle rental Open terrace Covered terrace V
meals Last d 21.30hrs Languages spoken:
English,German,Spanish
MEALS: Continental breakfast 80FF Lunch 145-380FF&alc
Dinner 195-380FF&alc✱
CARDS: ✿ 💳 💳 🌑 Travellers cheques

GINCLA Aude

★ ★ **Hostellerie du Grand Duc**   ✗ ✗✗
2 rte de Boucheville *11140*
☎ 468205502 FAX 468206122
(Head towards Foix on N117 at Lapradelle Puylaurens turn left
onto D22 & continue for 7km)
Your hosts will give you a warm welcome to their hotel at the
edge of the Boucheville Forest. Bedrooms are charming and
full of character, and open onto attractive gardens. Discover
local cuisine and rich flavours in the restaurant.
Near river Forest area
Closed mid Nov-mid Mar
10 en suite (bth/shr) TV in all bedrooms Direct dial from all
bedrooms Licensed Full central heating Open parking
available Child discount available 10yrs Open terrace V meals
Last d 21.00hrs Languages spoken: English & German
ROOMS: (room only) s 250-270FF; d 280-330FF
Reductions over 1 night
MEALS: Full breakfast 40FF Dinner 120-250FFalc✱
CARDS: ✿ 💳 Travellers cheques

GRANDE-MOTTE, LA Hérault

★ ★ ★ **Hotel Frantour**
1641 av du Golf *34280*
☎ 467298888 FAX 467291701
(From Nimes leave A9 at exit Gallargues and follow 'Golf'
signs)

This peaceful establishment offers luxurious bedrooms with
private terraces and an extensive range of modern facilities.
The menu features a choice of superb dishes which can be
served on the sunny terrace.
Near lake Near sea Near motorway
Closed Nov-Mar
81 en suite (bth) (42 fmly) (81 with balcony) No smoking in 5
bedrooms TV in all bedrooms STV Radio in rooms Direct
dial from all bedrooms Mini-bar in all bedrooms Room-safe
Licensed Lift Night porter Full central heating Air
conditioning in bedrooms Open parking available Supervised
Child discount available 12yrs Outdoor swimming pool Golf
Sauna Solarium Pool table Boule Bicycle rental Open terrace
Covered terrace V meals Languages spoken: English,German
ROOMS: (room only) s 471-712FF; d 602-774FF
MEALS: Full breakfast 50FF Lunch fr 100FF
CARDS: ✿ 💳 💳 🌑 Travellers cheques

LAMALOU-LES-BAINS Hérault

★ ★ ★ **Hotel de la Paix**   ✗ ✗✗ ✗ ✗
rue Alphonse Daudet *34240*
☎ 467956311 FAX 467956778
(From A9 exit Béziers Est, take D909 towards Bédarieux)
Situated close to the Regional Park Haute-Languedoc, in the
charming spa town of Lamalou-les-Bains, this turn-of-the-
century hotel is surrounded by lush vegetation, and features
comfortable bedrooms with private appointments and a
restaurant which serves an authentic cuisine consisting of
varied dishes depending upon the season. When the weather
is fine, meals are served on the terrace which is surrounded by
ancient plane trees.
Near river Forest area In town centre
31 en suite (bth/shr) (4 fmly) TV in all bedrooms Direct dial
from all bedrooms Licensed Lift Full central heating Open
parking available Covered parking available (charged) Child
discount available 12yrs Open terrace Covered terrace V
meals Last d 21.30hrs Languages spoken: English,German
ROOMS: (room only) s 180-220FF; d 190-280FF
Reductions over 1 night
MEALS: Continental breakfast 35FF Lunch 80-250FF&alc
Dinner 80-250FF&alc✱
CARDS: ✿ 💳 💳 🌑 Travellers cheques

LATTES Hérault

★ ★ **Mas de Couran**
rte de Fréjorgues *34970*
☎ 467655757 FAX 467653756
(Off D172)
Far away from the hectic bustle of the city of Montpellier, this
19th-century manor house offers a peaceful stay in the
delightful surroundings of a park with pine trees. It features
individually appointed bedrooms with modern amenities and a
restaurant serving traditional cuisine and excellent regional
specialities.
Near sea
18 en suite (bth/shr) (2 fmly) (1 with balcony) TV in all
bedrooms Direct dial from all bedrooms Mini-bar in all
bedrooms Licensed Night porter Open parking available
Supervised Child discount available 12yrs Outdoor swimming
pool Bicycle rental Open terrace Covered terrace V meals
Last d 21.30hrs Languages spoken: English,Spanish
ROOMS: (room only) s 360-395FF; d 375-475FF
MEALS: Full breakfast 45FF Continental breakfast 45FF Lunch
100-235FF&alc Dinner 100-235FF&alc
CARDS: ✿ 💳 💳 🌑 Travellers cheques

LIGNAN-SUR-ORB Hérault

★ ★ ★ Château de Lignan
34490
☎ 467379147 FAX 467379925
(From A9 exit at Beziers Est, follow signs for Beziers centre
then take D19)
The château stands in its own private grounds just 20
kilometres from the sea and the Cévennes, a region well
known for its historic interests and gastronomic delights. The
tastefully furnished bedrooms are fitted with luxury en suite
bathrooms and offer a high level of comfort. The menu
features an extensive choice of seafood specialities and
regional dishes. With its cosy lounge, piano-bar and numerous
facilities it provides the perfect setting for a relaxing stay.
Near river Forest area In town centre Near motorway
49 en suite (bth/shr) (1 fmly) TV in all bedrooms STV Direct
dial from all bedrooms Mini-bar in all bedrooms Licensed
Lift Night porter Full central heating Air conditioning in
bedrooms Open parking available Supervised Outdoor
swimming pool Sauna Solarium Boule Bicycle rental Open
terrace Last d 22.00hrs Languages spoken: English, German,
Spanish
ROOMS: (room only) s 305-340FF; d 305-340FF **Special
breaks**
MEALS: Continental breakfast 38FF Lunch 65-130FF&alc
Dinner 89-130FF&alc
CARDS: ●● ▀▀ ▀▀ ▶ Travellers cheques

LLO Pyrénées-Orientales

★ ★ ★ L'Atalaya
66800
☎ 468047004 FAX 468040129
(From N116 at Saillagouse take D33 to Llo)
Situated in a peaceful village on the border between Andorra
and Spain, this delightful residence features a charming
interior, decorated with good taste and flair. Pretty guest-
rooms offer a high level of comfort, and an attractive
restaurant serves an outstanding cuisine including, fresh
regional ingredients and excellent desserts.
Forest area
Closed 11 Jan-Mar & 16 Oct 19 Dec RS Mon & Tue lunchtine
13 en suite (bth/shr) 3 rooms in annexe (2 fmly) (4 with
balcony) TV in all bedrooms STV Direct dial from all
bedrooms Mini-bar in all bedrooms Room-safe (charged)
Licensed Night porter Full central heating Open parking
available Covered parking available Child discount available
5yrs Outdoor swimming pool Open terrace Last d 21.30hrs
Languages spoken: English, Spanish
ROOMS: (room only) s 495FF; d 650FF
MEALS: Full breakfast 60FF Lunch 160-200FF&alc Dinner 160-
200FF&alc
CARDS: ●● ▀▀ ▀▀ Eurocard Travellers cheques

MALÈNE, LA Lozère

★ ★ ★ Manoir de Montesquiou
48210
☎ 466485112 FAX 466485047
This handsome manor house stands in the heart of the Tarn
Gorge and used to be the private dwelling of the eminent
Montesquiou family. The bedrooms are individually furnished
and offer modern facilities, whilst the restaurant serves a
classic cuisine based on the best available regional produce.
Near river
Closed 31 Oct-Mar

12 rms TV in all bedrooms Direct dial from all bedrooms Full
central heating Open parking available Solarium Open
terrace Last d 21.00hrs Languages spoken: English
CARDS: ●● ▀▀ ▶ Travellers cheques

MARGUERITTES Gard

★ ★ Climat de France
La Panché Sud-RN 86 *30320*
☎ 466263050 Cen Res 164460123 FAX 466264466
The hotel occupies a convenient location near the main access
route and features fully equipped bedrooms which offer a
good level of comfort. The restaurant serves a range of popular
dishes which suit most pockets and palates.
Near sea Forest area Near motorway
46 en suite (shr) (1 fmly) TV available Radio in rooms Direct-
dial available Licensed Lift Night porter Open parking
available Supervised Outdoor swimming pool Solarium
Open terrace
CARDS: ●● ▀▀

MARVEJOLS Lozère

★ ★ De la Gare et des Rochers
pl de la Gare *48100*
☎ 466321058 FAX 466323063
Situated on a rocky outcrop, the hotel offers splendid views
over the valley. The bedrooms are comfortable and have good
facilities, whilst the restaurant serves honest, simple food.
Near river Forest area Near motorway
Closed 15 Jan-10 Mar
30 rms (18 bth 10 shr) (4 fmly) (12 with balcony) TV in all
bedrooms Direct dial from all bedrooms Licensed Lift Full
central heating Open parking available Covered parking
available Open terrace V meals Last d 21.00hrs Languages
spoken: Spanish
MEALS: Continental breakfast 36FF Lunch 75-145FF&alc
Dinner 75-145FF&alc
CARDS: ●● ▀▀ Travellers cheques

MENDE Lozère

La Boulene
Aspres *48000*
☎ 466492337 FAX 466493443
This ancient 18th century farm has been built of granite on
three different levels. Now completely restored in the
traditional country style, it is surrounded by a forest and
grazing grounds with adjoining stables, and is the ideal venue
for those who are looking for a holiday with outdoor pursuits.
Walking, fishing and horse-riding feature highly in this area.
The accommodation is comfortable with private facilities and
offers stunning views over the Lot valley, Mont Lozère, and the
Cévennes.
Near river Near lake Forest area Near motorway
Closed 6 Nov-Mar
9 en suite (bth/shr) 2 rooms in annexe Direct dial from all
bedrooms Licensed Full central heating Open parking
available Child discount available Indoor swimming pool
Outdoor swimming pool Riding Boule Bicycle rental Open
terrace V meals Languages spoken: English
ROOMS: (room only) s 210FF; d 210FF **Reductions over 1
night Special breaks**
MEALS: Full breakfast 35FF Continental breakfast 35FF Lunch
100FF
CARDS: ●● ▀▀ ▀▀ ▶ Travellers cheques

MEYRUEIS Lozère

★ ★ ★ Château d'Ayres
48150
☎ 466456010 FAX 466456226
This attractive 12th century inn is located in the Cévennes National Park and provides a delightful setting for a visit to the Tarn Gorges or other points of interest in the area. Elegantly furnished bedrooms provide restful accommodation and a high level of comfort, while the cuisine consists of a range of innovative dishes skilfully prepared by the proprietor and her son.
Near river Forest area
Closed mid Nov-late Mar RS Half board obligatory 10 Jul-26 Aug
27 en suite (bth/shr) (7 fmly) (3 with balcony) TV in all bedrooms STV Direct dial from all bedrooms Mini-bar in 24 bedrooms Licensed Full central heating Open parking available Supervised Child discount available 7yrs Outdoor swimming pool (heated) Tennis Riding Boule Open terrace V meals Last d 22.00hrs Languages spoken: English
ROOMS: (room only) s 410-520FF; d 510-845FF
MEALS: Full breakfast 65FF Continental breakfast 65FF Lunch 110-255FF&alc Dinner 152-255FF&alc
CARDS: 💳 📰 💳 💳 Travellers cheques

★ ★ Le Renaissance
rue de la Ville *48150*
☎ 466456019 FAX 466456594
La Renaissance is an old 16th century manor house, located between a medieval alleyway and a wonderful shaded garden, and guarantees complete tranquillity for its guests. Bedrooms at this authentic Renaissance residence are individually furnished. For those visitors who like outdoor pursuits there is tennis, a swimming-pool, horse-riding, mountain-biking, and plenty of walks to be found in the vicinity.
In town centre
Closed mid Nov-late Mar
18 en suite (bth/shr) (2 fmly) TV in 12 bedrooms Direct dial from all bedrooms Licensed Child discount available 7yrs Open terrace Last d 22.00hrs Languages spoken: English
ROOMS: (room only) s 200-230FF; d 200-300FF
MEALS: Continental breakfast 40FF Lunch 100-320FF&alc Dinner 100-320FF&alc
CARDS: 💳 📰 💳 Travellers cheques

MONTPELLIER Hérault

★ ★ ★ Hotel Le Guilhem
18 rue Jean-Jacques Rousseau *34000*
☎ 467529000 FAX 467606767
(From A9 exit 'Montpellier Est' follow signs for 'Centre Historique')
This charming hotel is set in the historic heart of Montpellier, with gardens, museums and handsome old buildings nearby. Each guest room has its own personal style and character, offering up-to-date facilities and panoramic views over the city. A delicious breakfast is served on the terrace, from where you can see St Peters cathedral.
In town centre Near motorway
33 en suite (bth/shr) 9 rooms in annexe TV in all bedrooms STV Direct dial from all bedrooms Mini-bar in all bedrooms Licensed Lift Night porter Full central heating Air conditioning in bedrooms Open terrace Languages spoken: English,German
ROOMS: (room only) d 330-650FF
CARDS: 💳 📰 💳 💳 Travellers cheques

★ ★ ★ Holiday Inn Métropole
3 rue Clos Réné *34000*
☎ 467581122 FAX 467921302
(From A9 exit 'Montpellier Sud' follow signs for city centre/railway station)
The hotel was built in 1898 in the heart of Montpellier. It has all the charm of a stylish private residence with the comfort associated with a four star hotel. The guest accommodation has excellent amenities and all rooms are furnished with attention to detail. The restaurant opens up to the interior garden with lush vegetation, which provides an oasis of peace amidst the bustle of the town.
In town centre
81 en suite (bth/shr) (4 fmly) No smoking in 20 bedrooms TV in all bedrooms STV Direct dial from all bedrooms Mini-bar in all bedrooms Room-safe Licensed Lift Night porter Full central heating Air conditioning in bedrooms Open parking available (charged) Covered parking available (charged) Supervised Child discount available 14yrs Pool table Last d 22.00hrs Languages spoken: English,Arabic,German,Spanish
ROOMS: (room only) d 680FF
MEALS: Full breakfast 70FF Continental breakfast 70FF Lunch 70-130FFalc Dinner 70-130FFalc✱
CARDS: 💳 📰 💳 💳 JCB Travellers cheques

★ ★ ★ New Hôtel du Midi
22 bd Victor Hugo *34000*
☎ 467926961 FAX 467927363
The New Hôtel group consists of establishments where guests are offered a combination of 20th-century comfort combined with traditional hospitality and peaceful interiors for a restful stay. Bedrooms vary in style and size, are equipped with modern facilities and offer a high level of comfort.
In town centre
47 en suite (bth/shr) (6 fmly) (10 with balcony) TV in all bedrooms STV Direct dial from all bedrooms Mini-bar in all bedrooms Licensed Lift Night porter Full central heating Air conditioning in bedrooms Languages spoken: English,German,Italian,Spanish
ROOMS: (room only) s 380-500FF; d 400-540FF ✱
Reductions over 1 night

★ ★ ★ Novotel
125 bis av de Palavas *34000*
☎ 467640404 FAX 467654088
(From A9 take exit 'Montpellier Sud' to the city centre, then follow signs for 'Palavas' and 'Prés d'Arenes')
Novotel offer their clients good quality accommodation in modern, well equipped bedrooms and have refined restaurants serving good quality cuisine They have excellent business meeting and conference facilities and some have food and beverages available 24 hours a day. All their hotels have at least one bedroom for disabled guests.
Near sea Near motorway
162 en suite (bth) (40 fmly) No smoking in 16 bedrooms TV in all bedrooms STV Radio in rooms Direct dial from all bedrooms Mini-bar in 113 bedrooms Licensed Lift Night porter Full central heating Air conditioning in bedrooms Open parking available Supervised Child discount available 16yrs Outdoor swimming pool Pool table Open terrace Last d 24.00hrs Languages spoken: English,German,Italian
ROOMS: (room only) s fr 460FF; d fr 495FF **Reductions over 1 night**
MEALS: Full breakfast 55FF Continental breakfast 55FF Lunch fr 98FF&alc Dinner fr 98FF&alc
CARDS: 💳 📰 💳 💳 Travellers cheques

NARBONNE Aude

★ ★ Climat de France
chemin des Hoteliers, Z.I. Plaisance *11100*
☎ 468410490 Cen Res 164460123 FAX 468413413
(from A9 take N113 Narbonne exit then at 2nd rbt take 3rd exit and next right)
This recently constructed hotel offers rooms with modern amenities which provide comfortable accommodation. Because of its location it is a good venue for an overnight stop, and with its flexible conference facilities it is a popular venue with business travellers and holiday makers alike. The restaurant serves a traditional cuisine of good quality and an excellent choice of desserts.
Near motorway
40 en suite (bth) TV in all bedrooms Radio in rooms Direct dial from all bedrooms Licensed Open parking available (charged) Covered parking available (charged) Supervised Languages spoken: English, German & Spanish
CARDS: ☎ ☲

★ ★ ★ Novotel
Quartier Plaisance, rte de Perpignan *11100*
☎ 468427200 FAX 468427210
Novotel offer their clients good quality accommodation in modern, well equipped bedrooms and have refined restaurants serving good quality cuisine They have excellent business meeting and conference facilities and some have food and beverages available 24 hours a day. All their hotels have at least one bedroom for disabled guests.
Near motorway
96 en suite (bth/shr) (40 fmly) No smoking in 20 bedrooms TV in all bedrooms STV Radio in rooms Direct dial from all bedrooms Mini-bar in all bedrooms Licensed Lift Night porter Full central heating Air conditioning in bedrooms Open parking available Child discount available 16yrs Outdoor swimming pool Pool table Open terrace Covered terrace V meals Languages spoken: English,German,Italian,Spanish
ROOMS: (room only) s 420-440FF; d 470-490FF
Reductions over 1 night
MEALS: Full breakfast 55FF Continental breakfast 55FF Lunch 120-180FFalc✱
CARDS: ☎ ☲ ☲ ➋ Travellers cheques

NASBINALS Lozère

★ ★ La Maison de Rosalie
Montgros *48260*
☎ 466325514 FAX 466325646
An old restored farmhouse in local style, with comfortable bedrooms tastefully decorated
Near river Near lake Forest area
Closed 4 Nov-24 Apr
9 rms (4 bth 3 shr) Some rooms in annexe (8 fmly) Direct dial from all bedrooms Licensed Full central heating Open parking available Child discount available 10yrs Sauna Gym Boule Open terrace V meals Last d 21.00hrs Languages spoken: English, German & Spanish
ROOMS: (room only) d 255FF ✱
MEALS: Continental breakfast 33FF Lunch 89-195FF&alc Dinner 108-195FF&alc✱
CARDS: Travellers cheques

NÉZIGNAN-L'ÉVÊQUE Hérault

★ ★ ★ Hostellerie de St-Alban
31 rte d'Agde *34120*
☎ 467811138 FAX 467989163
This charming establishment is housed in a mansion which dates back to the 19th century. Located in the Languedoc-Roussillon region it is ideally located for visits to the seaside or exursions inland. The guest accommodation offers a high degree of comfort and have modern facilities, there are two restaurants and up-to-date leisure facilities.
Near river Near lake Near sea Near beach Near motorway
14 en suite (bth) (4 fmly) (9 with balcony) TV in all bedrooms STV Licensed Full central heating Open parking available Child discount available 7yrs Outdoor swimming pool Tennis Solarium Jacuzzi/spa Open terrace V meals Last d 21.00hrs Languages spoken: English
CARDS: ☎ ☲ Travellers cheques

NÎMES Gard

★ ★ ★ ★ Hôtel Imperator Concorde
quai de la Fontaine *30900*
☎ 466219030 FAX 466677025
Twelve miles from the famous Pont de Gard aqueduct, this haven of tranquility is located in the heart of Nîmes. The hotel is one hundred and fifty yards from Fotaine Garden, the Roman Temple, the Amphitheatre and the Contemporary Art Centre.
In town centre Near motorway
63 en suite (bth/shr) (6 fmly) (5 with balcony) No smoking in 3 bedrooms TV in all bedrooms Direct dial from all bedrooms Mini-bar in all bedrooms Licensed Lift Night porter Full central heating Air conditioning in bedrooms Open parking available (charged) Covered parking available (charged) Supervised Child discount available 12yrs Covered terrace V meals Last d 22.00hrs Languages spoken: English, German, Italian & Spanish
ROOMS: (room only) s 530-850FF; d 680-1000FF
Reductions over 1 night
MEALS: Full breakfast 80FF Continental breakfast 65FF Lunch 140-330FF Dinner 140-330FF
CARDS: ☎ ☲ ☲ ➋ Travellers cheques

★ ★ ★ New Hôtel la Baume
21 rue Nationale *30000*
☎ 466732842 FAX 466732845
(Follow signs 'Centre Ville')
The New Hôtel group consists of establishments where guests are offered a combination of 20th century comfort combined with traditional hospitality and peaceful interiors for a restful stay. Bedrooms vary in style and size, are equipped with modern facilities and offer a high level of comfort.
In town centre Near motorway
33 en suite (bth/shr) (2 fmly) (2 with balcony) TV in all bedrooms STV Radio in rooms Direct dial from all bedrooms Mini-bar in all bedrooms Licensed Lift Night porter Full central heating Air conditioning in bedrooms Child discount available 12yrs Open terrace Last d 22.00hrs Languages spoken: English,German,Spanish
ROOMS: (room only) s 320-550FF; d 320-600FF
MEALS: Full breakfast 52FF Continental breakfast 40FF Lunch 50-85FF&alc Dinner 80-105FF&alc
CARDS: ☎ ☲ ☲ ➋ JCB Travellers cheques

★ ★ ★ Hotel L'Orangerie
755 rue Tour de l'Évêque *30000*
☎ 466845057 FAX 466294455
This modern hotel is situated in a historic area, right in the heart of the tourist region and only 40 kilometres from the Mediterranean. Surrounded by a park with mature plane trees it is both beatiful and welcoming. The spacious bedrooms with private terrace have modern facilities and offer good comfort, while the elegant dining rooms serve a traditional cuisine with a regional accent.
Forest area In town centre Near motorway
31 en suite (bth/shr) (5 fmly) (16 with balcony) TV in all bedrooms STV Direct dial from all bedrooms Mini-bar in all bedrooms Licensed Night porter Full central heating Air conditioning in bedrooms Open parking available Supervised Child discount available 10yrs Outdoor swimming pool Boule Jacuzzi/spa Open terrace ping pong Last d 22.00hrs
Languages spoken: English
CARDS: ●● ▬▬ ▭▭ ⦿ Travellers cheques

OLARGUES Hérault

★ ★ ★ Domaine de Rieumége
rte de St-Pons *34390*
☎ 467977399 FAX 467977852
(From A9 exit at Beziers Est,follow directions for Bedarieuse/Herepian/Olargues)
This 17th century establishment is surrounded by private grounds of 35 acres and provides a charming and comfortable setting for those visitors who love unspoilt countryside. Standing at the foot of the Cévennes, it features a warm, informal interior incorporating pleasant bedrooms with modern facilities, a cosy lounge with open fireplace and a restaurant where exposed brickwork and beams create a cosy atmosphere.
Near river Forest area
Closed early Nov-Etr
14 en suite (bth/shr) 6 rooms in annexe (4 fmly) TV in 10 bedrooms Direct dial from all bedrooms Room-safe Licensed Full central heating Open parking available Supervised Child discount available 16yrs Outdoor swimming pool Tennis Fishing Bicycle rental Open terrace V meals Last d 21.30hrs Languages spoken: English
ROOMS: (room only) s 355-395FF; d 395-490FF
Reductions over 1 night Special breaks
MEALS: Full breakfast 65FF Lunch 100-160FF&alc Dinner 135-240FF&alc
CARDS: ●● ▬▬ ▭▭ Carte Bleue Travellers cheques

ORNAISONS Aude

★ ★ ★ Relais du Val d'Orbieu
11200
☎ 468271027 FAX 468275244
(From A9 exit Narbone Sud, take N113 towards Lezignan-Corbieres, then D24)
Situated in the heart of the rolling countryside of the Corbières region, the inn occupies a peaceful location. It features tastefully decorated guest rooms with en suite facilities offering a good levels of comfort. There is a summer restaurant, shaded by a pergola, and another indoors. Both serve a high standard of cooking. Open all year round, this charming residence provides the ideal place for an overnight stop or a longer break.
Near river Forest area
Closed Dec-Jan
20 en suite (bth/shr) (5 fmly) (8 with balcony) TV in all

bedrooms STV Direct dial from all bedrooms Mini-bar in all bedrooms Licensed Full central heating Open parking available Supervised Outdoor swimming pool Tennis Boule Bicycle rental Open terrace Covered terrace Practice golf V meals Last d 21.00hrs Languages spoken: English & Spanish

ROOMS: (room only) s 390-450FF; d 490-750FF
MEALS: Full breakfast 70FF Continental breakfast 70FF Lunch 125-295FF&alc Dinner 125-295FF&alc
CARDS: ●● ▬▬ ▭▭ ⦿ Travellers cheques

PERPIGNAN Pyrénées-Orientales

★ ★ De La Poste et de la Perdrix
6 rue Fabriques Nabot *66000*
☎ 468344253 FAX 468345820
The hotel reflects the spirit of this Catalan city and is situated right in the heart of the old town. Its authentic cuisine is based on classic recipes and includes only the finest local produce. The bedrooms are furnished with modern facilities and offer a good standard of comfort, whilst the town itself and the surrounding area offer a choice of leisure pursuits.
Near sea In town centre Near motorway
38 rms (10 bth 20 shr) (35 with balcony) TV in 29 bedrooms Direct dial from all bedrooms Lift Night porter Full central heating Child discount available 10yrs V meals Last d 21.15hrs Languages spoken: English,German,Spanish
ROOMS: (room only) s 140-240FF; d 170-270FF
MEALS: Continental breakfast 30FF Lunch 90-110FF&alc Dinner 90-110FF&alc
CARDS: ●● ▬▬ ▭▭ ⦿ Travellers cheques

PONT-D'HÉRAULT Gard

★ ★ Château de Rey
Le Rey *30570*
☎ 467824006 FAX 467824779
Near river Forest area
Closed Jan
13 en suite (bth/shr) (2 fmly) TV in all bedrooms STV Direct dial from all bedrooms Full central heating Open parking available Covered parking available Supervised Child discount available Fishing Open terrace V meals Last d 22.00hrs Languages spoken: English
CARDS: ●● ▭▭

PONT-DU-GARD Gard

★ ★ ★ Vieux Moulin
Pont-du-Gard *30210*
☎ 466371435 FAX 466372648
The hotel 'Le Vieux Moulin' is a genuine flour mill which
contd.

overlooks the river opposite the famous 2000 year-old 'Pont du Gard'. From the shaded terraces and dining-room, guests can enjoy fine views of this imposing aqueduct, whilst savouring a delicious cuisine, complemented by good local wines. The sunny bedrooms have individual Provençal-style furnishings and provide a good level of comfort.
Near river Near sea Near beach Forest area Near motorway Closed 16Oct-15Mar
17 rms (7 bth 3 shr) (5 fmly) (5 with balcony) Direct dial from all bedrooms Licensed Full central heating Open parking available Child discount available 10yrs Boule Open terrace V meals Last d 22.00hrs Languages spoken: English,German
CARDS: ● ▩ Travellers cheques

PORT-LA-NOUVELLE Aude

★ ★ ★ Méditerranée
Front de Mer 11210
☎ 468480308 FAX 468485381
(from Narbonne travel S on A9 and exit Sigean and take Port la Nouvelle N9)

The hotel offers fine views over the beach and the sea and contains pleasant bedrooms with balconies. The menu offers a choice of tasty dishes and fresh fish specialities take pride of place. A good venue for a seaside holiday.
Near sea Near beach Near motorway
31 en suite (bth/shr) (10 fmly) (17 with balcony) No smoking in 1 bedroom TV in all bedrooms Direct dial from all bedrooms Mini-bar in 6 bedrooms Licensed Lift Night porter Full central heating Air conditioning in bedrooms Covered parking available (charged) Supervised Child discount available 14yrs Open terrace V meals Last d 21.30hrs Languages spoken: English, German & Spanish
ROOMS: (room only) s 200-395FF; d 260-395FF **Special breaks: Fishing breaks**
MEALS: Full breakfast 55FF Continental breakfast 35FF Lunch 65-190FF&alc Dinner 65-190FF&alc
CARDS: ● ▤▤ ▩ ◑ Travellers cheques

PRATS-DE-MOLLO-LA-PRESTE Pyrénées-Orientales

★ ★ Bellevue
Le Foiral 66230
☎ 468397248 FAX 468397804
The Bellevue is built in the style of a typical Catalan house. Set in the heart of the Catalonian region it offers views of the medieval town and the Presta spa nearby. The guest rooms are pleasantly furnished and offer a good level of comfort, while the restaurant with terrace serves regional dishes based on local and home-grown produce.
Forest area In town centre

Closed 3 Nov-Mar(except school hols)
18 rms (11 bth 5 shr) (3 fmly) (5 with balcony) TV available Direct dial from all bedrooms Licensed Full central heating Open parking available Supervised Child discount available 12yrs Boule Open terrace Last d 20.45hrs Languages spoken: English,Spanish,Catalan
MEALS: Full breakfast 40FF Continental breakfast 33FF Lunch 90-180FF&alc Dinner 90-180FF&alc✱
CARDS: ●● ▩ Travellers cheques

REMOULINS Gard

★ ★ ★ Le Vieux Castillon
Castillon-du-Gard 30210
☎ 466376161 FAX 466372817
(From A9 take N86 towards Montelimar, then D19A towards Alès)
With its medieval architecture, patios and sandstone-tiered terraces, this hotel is renowned throughout the region as a centre for musical events. The guest rooms are exquisitely furnished, and the vaulted ceilings and exposed beams enhance the traditional atmosphere. Guests can pamper their palates with the outstanding delicately flavoured regional cuisine, augmented by a wine-list featuring the fine wines of the Côtes du Rhône.
Closed Jan-early Mar
35 en suite (bth/shr) 12 rooms in annexe TV in all bedrooms STV Direct dial from all bedrooms Mini-bar in all bedrooms Room-safe Licensed Lift Night porter Full central heating Air conditioning in bedrooms Outdoor swimming pool Sauna Pool table Open terrace Last d 21.00hrs Languages spoken: English,German
ROOMS: (room only) d 850-1750FF **Special breaks**
MEALS: Full breakfast 90FF Lunch 270-550FF&alc Dinner 270-550FF&alc
CARDS: ●● ▤▤ ▩ ◑ Travellers cheques

SAILLAGOUSE Pyrénées-Orientales

★ ★ Planes "La Vieille Maison Cerdane"
pl de Cerdagne, BP34 66800
☎ 468047208 FAX 468047593
Forest area Near motorway
Closed 16 Oct-19 Dec
20 rms 20 rooms in annexe (16 with balcony) TV in all bedrooms Direct dial from all bedrooms Licensed Lift Full central heating Open parking available Child discount available Outdoor swimming pool (heated) Solarium Pool table Last d 21.00hrs Languages spoken: English,Spanish
MEALS: Continental breakfast 35FF Lunch 140-250FF&alc Dinner 140-250FF&alc✱
CARDS: ●● ▤▤ ▩ Travellers cheques

ST-ALBAN-SUR-LIMAGNOLE Lozère

★ ★ ★ Relais St-Roch
Chateau de la Chastre 48120
☎ 466315548 FAX 466315326
(A75 exit 34 in direction of St Alban)
This beautiful, pink-granite residence stands in the heart of the town of Saint-Alban in the Margeride region and is the ideal place for those who are looking for a peaceful stay, fresh air, attentive service and good cuisine. The guest rooms are very comfortable and the restaurant 'La Petite Maison' with its charming interior, offers an extensive choice of specialities, more than 150 different brands of whiskies and a very large wine selection. Outdoor activities include first-class fishing

waters, paths for hiking and nature parks housing wolves and European bison.
Near river Near beach Forest area
Closed Nov-Mar
9 en suite (bth/shr) (2 fmly) (1 with balcony) TV in all bedrooms STV Radio in rooms Direct dial from all bedrooms Mini-bar in all bedrooms Licensed Night porter Full central heating Open parking available Child discount available 12yrs Outdoor swimming pool (heated) Fishing Boule Bicycle rental Open terrace V meals Last d 21.30hrs Languages spoken: English German & Spanish

ROOMS: (room only) s 540-720FF; d 540-720FF
Reductions over 1 night
MEALS: Full breakfast 58FF Continental breakfast 58FF Lunch 88-268FF&alc Dinner 128-268FF&alc
CARDS: ●● ▦ ▦ ● Travellers cheques

ST-GILLES Gard

★★ **Le Cours**   ✗ ✗ ✗ ✗ ✗
10 av François Griffcuille *30800*
☎ 466873193 FAX 466873183
Situated close to the centre of Saint-Gilles-du-Gard, on the edge of the Camargue, the hotel offers its visitors the opportunity to experience the charming ambience of a southern French village. The bedrooms offer good comfort and have modern facilities, and guests can enjoy regional specialities - cooked to perfection by Mr Peyrol - in the attractive dining room or on the terrace under the plane trees.
In town centre
15 Dec-1 Mar
33 en suite (bth/shr) (5 fmly) TV in all bedrooms STV Radio in rooms Direct dial from all bedrooms Licensed Lift Full central heating Open parking available Child discount available 2yrs Open terrace V meals Last d 22.00hrs Languages spoken: English,Italian
ROOMS: (room only) d 200-250FF ✱ **Reductions over 1 night**
MEALS: Full breakfast 33FF Continental breakfast 33FF Lunch 50-150FF&alc Dinner 50-150FF&alc
CARDS: ●● ▦ ▦ ● Travellers cheques

ST-JEAN-DE-LA-BLAQUIÈRE Hérault

★★★ **Le Sanglier**
Domaine de Cambourras *34700*
☎ 467447051 FAX 467447233
(From A75 exit 54/56 to St-Jean-de-Blaquière)
The hotel is surrounded by splendid countryside of unrivalled beauty and was completely renovated in recent years. It has charming bedrooms and one apartment, all with modern

facilities, whilst the restaurant serves an array of commendable dishes including char-grilled specialities, complemented by the finest of Languedoc wines.
Forest area
Closed 25 Oct-23 Mar
10 en suite (bth) (3 fmly) (8 with balcony) TV in all bedrooms Direct dial from all bedrooms Licensed Full central heating Open parking available Covered parking available Supervised Child discount available Outdoor swimming pool Tennis Solarium Boule Open terrace V meals Last d 21.00hrs Languages spoken: English,Spanish
ROOMS: (room only) d 400FF ✱ **Reductions over 1 night**
MEALS: Full breakfast 48FF Continental breakfast 48FF Lunch 100-220FF&alc Dinner 100-220FF&alc✱
CARDS: ●● ▦ Travellers cheques

STE-ENIMIE Lozère

★★★★ **Hotel Château de la Caze**
La Malène *48210*
☎ 466485101 FAX 466485575
(5km from La Malène towards Ste-Enimie)
This 15th-century château was built under the reign of Charles VIII and has retained all of its original character. It has an extensive park with a natural spring which cascades into the castle moat, and formal French gardens which were created to celebrate the 500th anniversary of the building. The peaceful bedrooms are discreetly decorated with excellent furnishings and provide a high level of comfort. The cuisine is imaginative, incorporates fresh produce from the region, and is served in the elegant restaurant with imposing fire place. Every year a series of musical events is organised at the castle which have become popular over the years, and are concluded with a candlelit dinner.
Near river Forest area Near motorway
Closed 15 Nov-1 Apr
19 en suite (bth) 6 rooms in annexe (7 fmly) (5 with balcony) TV in all bedrooms STV Direct dial from all bedrooms Mini-bar in 6 bedrooms Licensed Open parking available Covered parking available Supervised Child discount available 12yrs Outdoor swimming pool (heated) Fishing Open terrace Table tennis Canoeing Last d 21.30hrs Languages spoken: English,Dutch
ROOMS: (room only) s 500-600FF; d 500-750FF
MEALS: Full breakfast 65FF Continental breakfast 65FF Lunch 130-320FF&alc Dinner 175-320FF&alc
CARDS: ●● ▦ ▦ Travellers cheques

SAUVETERRE Gard

★★★ **Hostellerie de Varenne**
pl St-Jean *30150*
☎ 466825945 FAX 466828483
Near river Forest area Near motorway
14 en suite (bth/shr) (3 fmly) (2 with balcony) TV in all bedrooms Radio in rooms Mini-bar in all bedrooms Licensed Full central heating Open parking available Boule Open terrace V meals
CARDS: ▦ ●

SAZE Gard

★★ **Auberge la Gelinotte**   ∝ ✗ ✗ ✗
N100 *30650*
☎ 490317213 FAX 490269583
(from Avignon towards Nimes for 12km. From A9 Remoulins towards Avignon for 7km.)   *contd.*

Forest area Near motorway
Closed 15 Nov-1 Mar
10 en suite (bth/shr) 5 rooms in annexe (4 fmly) Direct dial
from all bedrooms Licensed Full central heating Open
parking available Child discount available 12yrs Outdoor
swimming pool Boule Open terrace Covered terrace
Volleyball Table tennis V meals Last d 21.00hrs Languages
spoken: English
ROOMS: (room only) d 275-290FF
MEALS: Continental breakfast 35FF Lunch fr 120FF&alc
Dinner fr 120FF&alc
CARDS: ● ▆ Travellers cheques

SIGEAN Aude

★ ★ ★ ★ Château de Villefalse
Le Lac *11130*
☎ 468485429 FAX 468483437
Surrounded by extensive vineyards, as well as woods and
rivers, and a few steps away from the flamingo colonies, the
château offers the charm and lavish hospitality of the past
times combined with modern comfort. The restaurant serves a
gourmet cuisine where the menu features a choice of dishes
depending on the season as well as fresh fish produce from
the lake. With easy access and unrivalled fitness and sporting
facilities on offer, it provides a good venue for an action packed
holiday.
Near river Near lake Near sea Near beach Forest area Near
motorway
25 en suite (bth) Some rooms in annexe TV in all bedrooms
Licensed Lift Full central heating Air conditioning in
bedrooms Open parking available Child discount available
Indoor swimming pool (heated) Outdoor swimming pool
Tennis Fishing Sauna Solarium Gym Pool table Jacuzzi/spa
Open terrace Covered terrace V meals Languages spoken:
English,Spanish
CARDS: ● ▆ ▆ ● Travellers cheques

SOMMIÈRES Gard

★ ★ ★ Auberge du Pont Romain ✗ ✗ ⋏ ✗
2 rue Emile Jamais *30250*
☎ 466800058 FAX 466803152
(Access via A9 exit Lunel)
This 17th century inn is located in the medieval town of
Sommières, which provides an ideal starting points for visits to
the Camargue and the seaside. It has a delightful interior with
peaceful bedrooms overlooking a park, three dining-rooms
which serve an inventive cuisine including home-made duck
foie gras and fresh fish specialities. In addition there is a
shaded park, flower-decked terrace, and a patio with a
fountain as well a range of out-door leisure facilities nearby.
Near river Forest area Near motorway
Closed 15 Jan-15 Mar & Nov
19 rms (14 bth 4 shr) 3 rooms in annexe (2 fmly) (1 with
balcony) Direct dial from all bedrooms Licensed Lift Full
central heating Open parking available Child discount
available Outdoor swimming pool (heated) Bicycle rental
Open terrace Covered terrace V meals Last d 21.30hrs
Languages spoken: English,Spanish
ROOMS: (room only) s 240-360FF; d 285-450FF ✱
MEALS: Full breakfast 50FF Lunch 170-250FF Dinner 170-
250FF✱
CARDS: ● ▆ ▆ ● Travellers cheques

TORNAC Gard

★ ★ ★ Démeures du Ranquet
rte de St-Hippolyte du Fort *30140*
☎ 466775163 FAX 466775562
(Access via D982)
In the ancient language of the Languedoc the word 'ranquet'
means 'rocky hill', and it is on the slopes of the hill where this
former ancient farmhouse is situated. It has spacious guest
accommodation, equipped with modern facilities and private
terraces, and offers a high standard of cooking by owner Anne
Majourel. Ideally situated for exploring this region with its
fascinating past and magnificent landscapes.
Forest area
Closed Nov-Mar
10 en suite (bth/shr) (10 with balcony) No smoking in 2
bedrooms TV in all bedrooms Radio in rooms Direct dial
from all bedrooms Mini-bar in all bedrooms Room-safe
Licensed Air conditioning in bedrooms Open parking
available Supervised Child discount available 10yrs Outdoor
swimming pool Boule Bicycle rental Open terrace V meals
Last d 21.30hrs Languages spoken: English,Spanish
ROOMS: (room only) s 660-720FF; d 800-900FF
MEALS: Full breakfast 80FF Lunch 180-380FF&alc Dinner 180-
380FF&alc
CARDS: ● ▆ Travellers cheques

UZÈS Gard

★ ★ Hotel D'Entraigues
8 rue de la Colodé *30700*
☎ 466223268 FAX 466225701
Situated opposite buildings of architectural significance, the
hotel features a combination of period and contemporary
furnishings. It has bedrooms, studios and apartments with
modern facilities - some also with balconies and terraces - and
restaurants - of which one operates on the terrace and garden
in the summertime.
Near river Forest area In town centre Near motorway
35 en suite (bth) (9 fmly) TV in all bedrooms Direct dial from
all bedrooms Licensed Lift Full central heating Air
conditioning in bedrooms Open parking available Covered
parking available (charged) Supervised Child discount
available 12yrs Outdoor swimming pool Solarium Open
terrace V meals Last d 22.00hrs Languages spoken:
English,German
MEALS: Full breakfast 50FF Continental breakfast 50FF Lunch
110-270FF&alc Dinner 110-270FF&alc✱
CARDS: ● ▆ ▆ ●

★ ★ ★ Hotel Marie D'Agoult
Château d'Arpaillargues *30700*
☎ 466221448 FAX 466225610
Far from the madding crowd of holiday makers rushing to
the southern beaches, the hotel provides a peaceful stopping
place 3 miles from the town of Uzès. Once the private
residence of Marie d'Agoult - a talented writer who eloped
with the composer Franz Liszt - it conceals behind its
massive walls the charming atmosphere of a Provençale
mansion. The guest accommodation, decorated with flair and
a good eye for detail, is equipped with excellent en suite
facilities. The dining-rooms with exposed brickwork and
vaulted ceilings serve outstanding cuisine which is difficult
to match.

Closed beg Nov-beg Apr
28 en suite (bth) (4 fmly) (8 with balcony) TV in all bedrooms
Direct dial from all bedrooms Mini-bar in 26 bedrooms
Room-safe Full central heating Air conditioning in
bedrooms Open parking available Outdoor swimming pool
Tennis Open terrace Last d 21.30hrs Languages spoken:
English & German

ROOMS: s 450-600FF; d 450-800FF
MEALS: Full breakfast 65FF Lunch 145-230FF&alc Dinner
230FF&alc✱
CARDS: 😄 ▦ ▦ 🌑 Travellers cheques

VERGÈZE Gard

★ ★ **La Passiflore**
1 rue Neuve *30310*
☎ 466350000 FAX 466350921
(exit A9 at Gallargues, then take RN113 towards Nimes. At first
traffic lights in Codognan turn left and follow signs to Vergeze
centre ville.)
Situated in the peaceful surroundings of a pretty village, this
18th-century farmhouse has undergone extensive renovation
whilst retaining all of its original character. Each of the
peaceful guest rooms have private facilities and overlook the
courtyard or the garden. The menu offers a wide choice of
dishes prepared by 'La Patronne', and is served in the
candlelit courtyard in summer or in the informal dining-room
in winter. Because of its convenient location the hotel
'Passiflore' is the ideal venue for an overnight stop or
extended stay to explore the surrounding Provence,
Camargue and Cévennes.
Forest area In town centre Near motorway
11 rms (2 bth 8 shr) (1 fmly) (1 with balcony) Licensed Full
central heating Air conditioning in bedrooms Open parking
available Supervised Child discount available 7yrs Open
terrace Last d 21.30hrs Languages spoken: English
ROOMS: (room only) d 225-325FF
MEALS: Continental breakfast 38FF Dinner 135FF&alc✱
CARDS: 😄 ▦ ▦ Travellers cheques

VILLENEUVE-LÈS-AVIGNON Gard

★ ★ **Hotel de L'Atelier**
5 rue de la Foire *30400*
☎ 490250184 FAX 490258006
This charming hotel is housed in an ancient building which
dates back to the 16th century, and has individually styled
bedrooms decorated with period furniture and equipped with
modern day amenities. Close to cultural and historic places of
interest as well as the fabulous surrounding regions of
Provence, Lubéron and Camargue, it provides a good starting
point for day trips, and has a large choice of sporting facilities
in the vicinity.
Near lake
Closed beg Nov-beg Dec
19 en suite (bth/shr) (3 fmly) TV in all bedrooms Direct dial
from all bedrooms Licensed Night porter Full central heating
Solarium Open terrace
CARDS: 😄 ▦ ▦ 🌑 Travellers cheques

★ ★ **Résidence les Cédres**
39 av Pasteur Bellevue *30400*
☎ 490254392 FAX 490251466
Not far from the town of Avignon this late 18th century house
is surrounded by a shaded park full of flowers and ancient
cedar trees. All the bedrooms - some housed in bungalows in
the garden - are attractively furnished and equipped with
modern facilities. The informal restaurant serves traditional
and regional dishes, whilst there is also a choice of leisure
facilities on the premises.
Closed 16 Nov-15 Mar
21 en suite (bth/shr) (5 fmly) TV in all bedrooms Direct dial
from all bedrooms Mini-bar in all bedrooms Licensed Full
central heating Open parking available Supervised Child
discount available 2yrs Outdoor swimming pool Boule Open
terrace Last d 21.30hrs Languages spoken: English,German
MEALS: Full breakfast 40FF Lunch 108-158FF Dinner 108-
158FF✱
CARDS: 😄 ▦ Travellers cheques

VINASSAN Aude

★ ★ **Aude Hotel**
Aire Narbonne Vimmattan Nord *11110*
☎ 468452500 FAX 468452520
Located in a peaceful poplar grove near the rest area of the
Narbonne-Vinassan motorway (A9), the hotel is not far away
from the beaches. The sound-proofed bedrooms have modern
amenities and provide a peaceful night's sleep. From an early
hour a delicious breakfast is served in a spacious day room,
whilst dinner consists of regional specialities accompanied by
a selection of the finest vintages.
Near motorway
59 en suite (bth/shr) (9 fmly) TV in 30 bedrooms STV Direct
dial from 30 bedrooms Licensed Lift Night porter Full central
heating Air conditioning in bedrooms Open parking available
Covered parking available (charged) Supervised Open terrace
Last d 21.30hrs Languages spoken: English,German,Spanish
ROOMS: (room only) s 290FF; d 330FF
MEALS: Full breakfast 35FF Continental breakfast 35FF
Dinner 75-150FF&alc
CARDS: 😄 ▦ ▦ 🌑 Travellers cheques

Provence

Imagine peaceful Romanesque villages nestling in mountain folds, Gothic palaces perched on hilltops giving way to enchanting olive groves and vineyards, the heady aroma of lavender fields bathed in clear sunshine and you are halfway to discovering one of the most diverse and dramatic regions of France. If action is on the agenda, the snow-clad Alpes are made for sport of all kinds and if a spot of people-watching is needed, head for the glamorous resorts in the south with their sublime coastlines of sandy beaches, caves and rocky inlets waiting to be explored.

(Top): The mountain town of Séguret has a 12th-century church, a 15th-century fountain, and a ruined castle.

(Bottom) One of Provence's best known products is sweet-smelling lavender, which is used as a basic ingredient in most of France's world-famous perfumes.

ESSENTIAL FACTS

DÉPARTEMENTS:	Alpes-de-Haute-Provence, Bouches-du-Rhône, Hautes-Alpes, Var, Vaucluse
PRINCIPAL TOWNS	Arles, Avignon, Carpentras, Gap, Sisteron, Digne les Bains, Aix-en-Provence, Marseille, Toulon
PLACES TO VISIT:	The Carmague with its white horses; the Roman remains at Arles; the Popes' Palace at Avignon; Cezanne's studio at Aix-en-Provence; Les Ecrins, the National Nature Park in Hautes-Alpes.
REGIONAL TOURIST OFFICE	13 rue Roux de Brignoles, 13006 Marseille Tel: 91 13 84 13; 5 rue Capitaine de Bresson, 05000 Gap Tel: 92 53 62
LOCAL GASTRONOMIC DELIGHTS	Bouillabaisse, fish stew; calissons, small diamond shaped almond-paste biscuits; rascasse, spiny fish; salade Niçoise, tuna fish salad; daube, a casserole; poutargue, a roe paste; pissaladière, an onion tart; tapenade, an olive paste; local cheeses such as Brousse du Rove, Arles & Le Ventoux Tome, Champsaur & Le Queyras Tome.
DRINKS	Red wines such as Châteauneuf-du-Pape and Gigondas. The herbal aperitif from Forcalquier 'pastis', an aniseed-flavoured aperitif usually diluted with water; local spirits such as Vieux Marc de Provence, Elixir du Révérend Père Gaucher, Eau de vie de Poire, and Genepy des Alpes.
LOCAL CRAFTS WHAT TO BUY	Provencal fabrics, honey perfumed with lavender and rosemary, pottery and earthenware, olive oil, lavender products, ornamental 'santons', crystallised fruits.

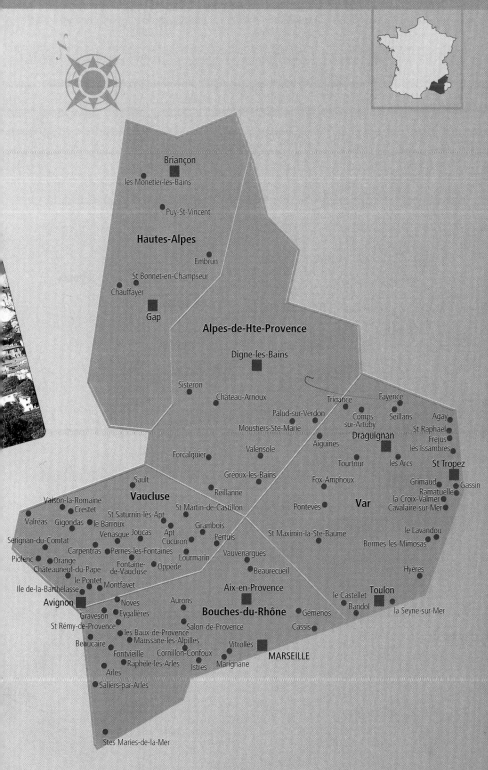

Briançon
les Monetier-les-Bains
Puy-St-Vincent

Hautes-Alpes

Embrun
St Bonnet-en-Champseur
Chauffayer
Gap

Alpes-de-Hte-Provence

Digne-les-Bains

Sisteron
Château-Arnoux
Trigance
Fayence
Palud-sur-Verdon
Comps-sur-Artuby
Seillans
Agay
Moustiers-Ste-Marie
St Raphaël
Aiguines
Draguignan
Fréjus
les Issambres
Forcalquier
Valensole
Tourtour
les Arcs
St Tropez
Gréoux-les-Bains
Fox-Amphoux
Grimaud
Gassin
Sault
Reillanne
Ramatuelle
Vaucluse
la Croix-Valmer
Vaison-la-Romaine
St Martin-de-Castillon
Pontevès
Cavalaire-sur-Mer
Crestet
Var
Valréas
St Saturnin-les-Apt
Gigondas
le Barroux
Grambois
le Lavandou
Venasque
Joucas
Apt
Pertuis
Serignan-du-Comtat
Cucuron
St Maximin-la-Ste-Baume
Bormes-les-Mimosas
Carpentras
Pernes-les-Fontaines
Lourmarin
Piolenc
Orange
Fontaine-
Oppède
Vauvenargues
Hyères
Châteauneuf-du-Pape
de-Vaucluse
le Pontet
Beaurecueil
Ile-de-la-Barthelasse
Montfavet
Aix-en-Provence
le Castellet
Toulon
Avignon
Noves
Aurons
Bandol
Graveson
Eygalières
Bouches-du-Rhône
Gémenos
la Seyne-sur-Mer
St Rémy-de-Provence
Salon-de-Provence
Cassis
les Baux-de-Provence
Beaucaire
Maussane-les-Alpilles
Vitrolles
Fontvieille
Cornillon-Confoux
MARSEILLE
Raphele-les-Arles
Istres
Marignane
Arles
Saliers-par-Arles

Stes Maries-de-la-Mer

EVENTS & FESTIVALS

Jan	Coudoux Wine Festival
Mar	Les Orres Comic Book Festival; Digne-les Bains Film Festival; Aix Wine Fair
Apr	Brignoles Agricultural Wine-Growing Fair & Exihibition
May	Les Mées Olive Tree Festival; Flower Shows at Tarascon & Sanary-sur-Mer; Stes-Maries-de-la-Mer Gypsy Pilgrimage with Procession of Ste-Sarah to the Sea
Jun	Cassis Fishermans Festival; Marseille Garlic Festival; Stes-Maries-de-la-Mer 'Jornadido Biou' (the day of the bull); Manosque Medieval Fair; Valréas Petit St Jean Night (since 1504); Le Val Holy Art Festival; Gréoux-les-Bains Craft Fairs; Trets Wine Festival; Wine Fairs at Gemenos & La Destrousse
Jul	Ferrassieres Lavender Festival; Jazz Festivals at Toulon, Chateau-Arnoux, St Raphael, Salon-de-Provence, Forcalquier, Ramatuelle; Martigues Venetian celebrations; Visan Wine & Harvest Festival; Stes-Maries-de-la-Mer Festival of the Virgin Mary; Châteauvallon Contemporary Dance Festival; Folklore Festival at Cavaillon, Marseille (Château Gombert); Arles International Photo Workshop & Exhibitions; Festivals at Avignon, Vaison-la-Romaine, Colmars-les-

	Alpes, Marseille, Carpentras; St-Etienne-les-Orgues Herb & Craft Fair
Aug	Frejus Grape Festival; Chateauneuf-du-Pain Medieval Festival of La Veraison; Monfort Wine Festival; Châteauneuf-du-Pape Medieval Celebration of Fruit Harvest; Draguignan 'Draguifollies' (jazz, rock, blues, street artists); Pont de Cervières 'Bacchu-ber' ancient sword dance parade; Castellane Craft Fair; Salon de Provence Chamber Music Festival (Chateau de l'Emperi); Brignoles Jazz Festival; Sault Notre Dame Fair & Lavender Festival; Forcalquier Provence Products Fair;
Sep	Peyruis Apple & Fruit Festival; Le Val Sausage Fair; Marseille International Fair; Allemagne-en-Provence Old Crafts Festival; Riez Honey & Lavender Fair; Plan-de-la-Tour Fortified Wine (Vin Cuit) Festival
Oct	Apt Wine Harvest Festival; Draguignan Jazz Festival; Stes-Maries-de-la-Mer Gypsy Festival & Pilgrimage
Nov	Marseille 'Santons' Fair; Aups Truffle Market; Avignon Naming of Côtes du Rhône Wine; Marseilles Christmas Ornaments Fair; Wine Fairs at Istres & Martiques
Dec	Istres Sheperds Festivals; Bandol Wine Festival, Seguret Yule Evening

---

AGAY Var

★ ★ Le Lido
bd de la Plage 83530
☎ 494820159 FAX 494820975
Located on the waterfront in the harbour of Agay, against the backdrop of the red rocks of the Esterel mountains, the hotel has bedrooms with every modern convenience - some also have a terrace overlooking the sea. There is a private sandy beach, a terrace and a restaurant which serves an array of seafood specialities and a delicious 'bouillabaisse'.
Near river Near lake Near sea Forest area Near motorway
25 en suite (shr) (1 fmly) (8 with balcony) TV in all bedrooms STV Direct dial from all bedrooms Licensed Full central heating Open parking available Supervised Boule V meals Languages spoken: English,Italian

---

AIGUINES Var

★ ★ Du Grande Canyon du Verdon (Minotel)
Falaise des Cavaliers 83630
☎ 494769131 FAX 494769229
This attractive mountain inn is perched like an eagle's nest 800 feet above the Verdon river on the 'Corniche Sublime'. The restaurant dates back to 1928 and was extended with an hotel in 1983. It features comfortable bedrooms with modern amenities, whilst the pizza-grill restaurant serves a range of dishes which suit most palates. The magnificent surrounding countryside offers a choice of high energy, as well as relaxing out-door activities.
Near river Forest area
Closed mid Oct-end Mar
16 en suite (bth/shr) (6 fmly) (10 with balcony)

TV in all bedrooms Licensed Full central heating Open parking available Child discount available 12yrs Solarium Pool table Boule Open terrace Last d 21.00hrs Languages spoken: English,Italian
CARDS: 💳 ▨▨ 🌑 Travellers cheques

AIX-EN-PROVENCE Bouches-du-Rhône

Château de la Pioliné
13546
☎ 442200781 FAX 442599612
This magnificent residence is situated in splendid parkland. It exudes an atmosphere of elegance and sophistication and is furnished throughout with meticulous attention to detail. It provides a haven of charm and tranquillity for those who are on holiday or attending a conference, and yet is just 20 minutes away from the Marseille-Provence airport. The menu offers an extensive range of imaginatively cooked dishes made from fresh local produce. A unique place where the owners offer warm hospitality and attentive service to satisfy the every need of their guests.
Near river Forest area Near motorway
TV in 21 bedrooms Mini-bar in 21 bedrooms Lift Night porter Full central heating Open parking available Outdoor swimming pool

★ ★ ★ ★ ★ Hotel Mascotte
av de la Cible 13100
☎ 442375858 FAX 442375859
Just a stone's throw from the town centre stands the easily assessable Hotel Mascotte. It affords views across the Aix countryside and offers comfortably equipped sound-proofed bedrooms all with direct-dial telephone and satellite TV.

After an aperitif in the relaxed atmosphere of the bar, guests can sample an array of traditional French and regional dishes on the terrace beside the pool.
Forest area In town centre Near motorway
93 en suite (bth/shr) No smoking in 20 bedrooms TV in all bedrooms STV Direct dial from all bedrooms Mini-bar in all bedrooms Licensed Lift Night porter Full central heating Air conditioning in bedrooms Open parking available Child discount available 12yrs Outdoor swimming pool (heated) Solarium Pool table Mini-golf Open terrace V meals Last d 22.30hrs Languages spoken: English & Spanish
CARDS: 💳 💳 💳 💳 Travellers cheques

★ ★ ★ Mas de la Bertrande
Beaurecueil *13100*
☎ 442667575 FAX 442668201
(leave the road from Nice at Canet and take the N7 and turn right for Beaurecueil)
An authentic Provençal farm at the foot of the Sainte Victoire mountain. A carefully prepared fixed price menu and also à la carte is offered. The comfortable rooms are located on the ground floor and have private terraces, there is a salt water pool where guests can relax and enjoy the tranquil atmosphere.
Forest area
Closed 16 Feb-9 May
10 en suite (bth/shr) (5 fmly) TV in all bedrooms STV Direct dial from all bedrooms Mini-bar in all bedrooms Licensed Full central heating Open parking available Child discount available 12yrs Outdoor swimming pool Boule Bicycle rental Open terrace Covered terrace Last d 21.30hrs Languages spoken: English
ROOMS: (room only) s 380-550FF; d 380-550FF
MEALS: Full breakfast 45FF Continental breakfast 45FF Lunch 90-150FF&alc Dinner 130-150FF&alc
CARDS: 💳 💳 💳 Travellers cheques

★ ★ ★ ★ Mas d'Entremont
RN7 *13090*
☎ 442174242 FAX 442211583
(follow Avignon-Sisteron-Celony)
Set in extensive parkland 3 km from the centre of Aix-en-Provence, the Hotel Le Mas d'Entremont offers bedrooms which all overlook the beautiful garden with its earthenware pots abundant with flowers. Weather permitting, meals are served on the terrace and guests can enjoy the view of old stone fountains and the pond with waterlillies. Combined with the warm hospitality of the hosts and the authentic local cuisine, guests will find this a place to remember.
Forest area Near motorway
Closed 2 Nov-15 Mar
17 en suite (bth) 12 rooms in annexe (2 fmly) (17 with balcony) TV in all bedrooms STV Direct dial from all bedrooms Mini-bar in all bedrooms Room-safe Licensed Lift Full central heating Air conditioning in bedrooms Open parking available Supervised Child discount available 15yrs Outdoor swimming pool Tennis Solarium Boule Bicycle rental Open terrace Covered terrace Last d 21.30hrs Languages spoken: English & Italian
ROOMS: (room only) s 580-650FF; d 650-850FF
MEALS: Full breakfast 76FF Lunch 200-240FF&alc Dinner 200-240FF&alc
CARDS: 💳 💳 Travellers cheques

★ ★ ★ Mas des Ecureuils
chemin de Castel Blanc, petite rte des Milles *13090*
☎ 442244048 FAX 442392457
The Hotel Le Mas des Ecureuils is situated in a typically

Provençale pine forest. It has well equipped bedrooms, some with airconditioning, terraces and small libraries. Guests can enjoy their breakfast in the lounge, on their private terrace, or alongside the swimming pool. Leisure facilities include a Turkish bath, pétanque, table tennis or jogging in the 8 hectare pine forest. The restaurant La Carraire serves an excellent traditional cuisine.
Forest area
23 en suite (bth/shr) (6 fmly) (15 with balcony) TV in all bedrooms Direct dial from all bedrooms Mini-bar in all bedrooms Room-safe Licensed Night porter Full central heating Open parking available Supervised Child discount available Outdoor swimming pool (heated) Sauna Boule Bicycle rental Open terrace V meals Last d 22.00hrs Languages spoken: English German & Spanish
ROOMS: (room only) s 380-660FF; d 480-760FF ✱
MEALS: Continental breakfast 50FF Lunch 128-250FF&alc Dinner 128-250FF&alc✱
CARDS: 💳 💳 💳 💳 Travellers cheques

★ ★ Hotel des 4 Dauphins
54 rue Roux-Alphéran *13100*
☎ 442381639 FAX 442386019
A small charming hotel set right in the heart of historic Aix en Provence. The hotel has been recently renovated and equipped with every modern comfort, and decorated throughout in the traditional Provençal style. Cafés, restaurants, museums and boutiques are all within walking distance of the hotel..
In town centre
12 en suite (bth/shr) TV in all bedrooms Direct dial from all bedrooms Mini-bar in 4 bedrooms Night porter Full central heating Languages spoken: English
ROOMS: (room only) s 293-333FF; d 376-396FF
CARDS: 💳 💳 Travellers cheques

★ ★ ★ ★ Villa Gallici (Relais et Chateaux)
av de la Violette *13100*
☎ 442232923 FAX 442963045
Peaceful as the countryside and yet in the middle of the town, the Hotel Villa Gallici is more like a private elegant residence than a hotel. Furnished throughout with sumptuous materials, it has luxurious and sophisticated bedrooms (all individually furnished) and a courteous staff providing attentive service. A delicious breakfast is served in the shade of plane trees A Florentine garden with ancient cypress trees also contains a swimming pool. Villa Gallici will transport visitors back to the days of elegance and lavish hospitality.
In town centre
19 en suite (bth/shr) (11 with balcony) TV in all bedrooms STV Radio in rooms Direct dial from all bedrooms Mini-bar in all bedrooms Licensed Night porter Full central heating Air conditioning in bedrooms Open parking available Supervised Outdoor swimming pool Tennis Solarium Boule Jacuzzi/spa Open terrace Last d 21.30hrs Languages spoken: English, German, Italian
MEALS: Full breakfast 100FF Continental breakfast 70FF Dinner fr 350FFalc✱
CARDS: 💳 💳 💳 💳 Travellers cheques

APT Vaucluse

★ ★ ★ Auberge du Luberon
8 pl du Faubourg du Ballet *84400*
☎ 490741250 FAX 490047949
This typical Provençale residence offers comfortable accommodation and good food. It provides warm hospitality to the tired traveller and features good quality guest

contd.

accommodation comprising individually appointed bedrooms. The lounge with open fire place has an informal atmosphere, whilst the restaurant serves a selection of dishes utilising the delicate flavours of the region.
Near river Forest area In town centre Near motorway
15 en suite (bth/shr) 7 rooms in annexe (5 with balcony) TV in all bedrooms STV Direct dial from all bedrooms Mini-bar in 8 bedrooms Licensed Night porter Full central heating Covered parking available (charged) Supervised Child discount available 12yrs Open terrace V meals Last d 21.30hrs Languages spoken: English,Spanish
ROOMS: (room only) s 290-340FF; d 290-550FF
MEALS: Full breakfast 52FF Continental breakfast 52FF Lunch 155-395FF&alc Dinner 155-395FF
CARDS: ●● ■■ ▄▄ ●) Eurocard Travellers cheques

★ ★ ★ Auberge du Presbytère
pl de la Fontaine *84400*
☎ 490741150 FAX 490046851
(highway to Avignon, N100 to Apt, 3.5km on the Lueron above Apt)
A family hotel renowned for its hospitality with a truly international clientele. Guests from many different countries including Australia, New Zealand, Japan and America stay at this charming auberge.
Forest area In town centre Near motorway
10 en suite (bth/shr) (2 fmly) (2 with balcony) TV in all bedrooms Licensed Full central heating Child discount available 12yrs Open terrace Last d 21.00hrs Languages spoken: English, Italian & Spanish
ROOMS: (room only) d 240-450FF **Reductions over 1 night**
MEALS: Continental breakfast 50FF Lunch 165FF&alc Dinner 165FF&alc
CARDS: ●● ■■ ▄▄ Travellers cheques

ARLES Bouches-du-Rhône

★ ★ ★ Arlatan
26 rue du Sauvage *13200*
☎ 490935666 FAX 490496845
The hotel is steeped in history with an architectural heritage dating back to the fourth century, and once served as the private residence of the Comtes d'Arlatan de Beaumont. Guests receive a warm welcome in this truly handsome property, with its period furniture, gothic crosses from the 16th century and 17th century ceilings. The hotel offers elegant bedrooms with modern facilities in historical surroundings.
Near river Near sea In town centre Near motorway
41 en suite (bth/shr) (6 fmly) TV in all bedrooms Direct dial from all bedrooms Mini-bar in all bedrooms Lift Night porter Full central heating Air conditioning in bedrooms Open parking available (charged) Covered parking available (charged) Supervised Languages spoken: English
CARDS: ●● ■■ ▄▄ ●) Travellers cheques

★ ★ ★ Atrium
1 rue Emile Fassin *13200*
☎ 490499292 FAX 490933859
(opposite the Office du Tourisme)
Situated in the heart of Arles and within the vicinity of the unspoilt Camarque countryside, the Hotel Atrium offers its visitors a range of facilities to meet everyone's needs: comfortable sound-proofed bedrooms, an informal restaurant serving traditional regional dishes; large, well equipped function rooms and a swimming pool. The competent staff provides a friendly, efficient service.
In town centre

91 en suite (bth) (6 fmly) (10 with balcony) TV in all bedrooms STV Direct dial from all bedrooms Mini-bar in all bedrooms Licensed Lift Night porter Full central heating Air conditioning in bedrooms Open parking available (charged) Covered parking available (charged) Supervised Child discount available 12yrs Outdoor swimming pool Solarium Open terrace Last d 21.30hrs Languages spoken: English,Italian & Spanish
ROOMS: (room only) s 470-550FF; d 520-630FF ✱
MEALS: Full breakfast 55FF Continental breakfast 55FF Lunch 65-120FF&alc Dinner 65-120FF&alc
CARDS: ●● ■■ ▄▄ ●) Travellers cheques

★ ★ Hotel Calendal
22 pl du Dr Pomme *13200*
☎ 490961189 FAX 490960584
(from town centre follow signs for 'Amphitheatre')
Located in the heart of the town, between the arena and the ancient theatre, the hotel is the ideal location for an excursion to the Roman ruins as well as a visit to the many shops. The pretty bedrooms are furnished with flair in Provençale style and either overlook the arena or the delightful garden with its mature trees and palms.
In town centre
27 en suite (bth/shr) (10 fmly) (3 with balcony) TV in all bedrooms STV Direct dial from all bedrooms Licensed Night porter Full central heating Child discount available 10yrs Open terrace Last d 21.00hrs Languages spoken: English, Italian
ROOMS: (room only) s 250-350FF; d 250-420FF
MEALS: Full breakfast 36FF Lunch 50-100FFalc Dinner 50-100FFalc
CARDS: ●● ■■ ▄▄ ●) JCB Travellers cheques

★ ★ ★ ★ Grand Hotel du Nord Pinus
14 pl du Forum *13200*
☎ 490934444 FAX 490933400
(from Arles center take direction Place de la Republique then Place du Forum)
Many international artists have stayed in this charming hotel situated in a pleasant area amid plane trees.
Near river Near sea Near beach Forest area In town centre Near motorway
23 en suite (bth/shr) TV in all bedrooms STV Mini-bar in all bedrooms Licensed Lift Night porter Full central heating Air conditioning in bedrooms Open parking available (charged) Covered parking available (charged) Last d 21.15hrs Languages spoken: English, Dutch & German
ROOMS: (room only) s fr 770FF; d 840-990FF
MEALS: Full breakfast 75FF Lunch fr 120FF&alc Dinner fr 160FF&alc✱
CARDS: ●● ■■ ▄▄ Travellers cheques

★ ★ ★ ★ Jules César (Relais et Chateaux)
9 bd des Lices *13631*
☎ 490934320 FAX 490933347
(on autoroute A54 exit 5)
Originally a convent dating back to the 17th century, this splendid residence offers its visitors that magical combination of elegance, modern comfort and excellent food. Because of its unique location, guests can make day trips to Saint-Trophime, the Arènes or explore the countryside which inspired Van Gogh. Bedrooms with modern facilities are furnished to a high standard; there is large lounge, 2 courtyard gardens and an outdoor heated swimming pool. The restaurant serves a wide choice of traditional, imaginatively cooked dishes and specialities from the region.

In town centre Near motorway
Closed 12 Nov-23 Dec
56 en suite (bth/shr) TV in all bedrooms STV Radio in rooms
Direct dial from all bedrooms Mini-bar in all bedrooms
Licensed Night porter Full central heating Air conditioning in
bedrooms Open parking available (charged) Covered parking
available (charged) Supervised Child discount available 10yrs
Outdoor swimming pool (heated) Solarium Open terrace
Covered terrace Last d 21.30hrs Languages spoken: English,
German, Italian & Spanish

ROOMS: (room only) s 650-1000FF; d 750-1250FF
MEALS: Full breakfast 85FF Continental breakfast 85FF Lunch
150-420FF&alc Dinner 200-420FF&alc✱
CARDS: ●● ■■ ▀▀ ◑ JCB Travellers cheques

★ ★ ★ ★ Le Mas de Peint
Le Sambuc *13200*
☎ 490972062 FAX 490972220
(from A55 or N113 at Arles follow the road to Stes Maries
D570, then D36 direction Salin de Giraud after 20kms, cross the
village of le Sambug and in 2kms turn left)
In the heart of the dramatic Camargue region just outside
Arles, Le Mas de Peint is set on a 500 hectare estate dating
back to the 17th century. The ground floor provides spacious
rooms for meeting and relaxing and there is an authentic
kitchen serving home cooked delicacies. There are eight
spacious bedrooms and two suites featuring wood beamed
ceilings and antique furniture. Jacques Bon is always on hand
to describe his land, rice fields, horses and pure blood
camargue bulls.
Near beach
Closed 6 Jan-20 Mar
10 en suite (bth/shr) (1 fmly) (2 with balcony) TV in all
bedrooms STV Direct dial from all bedrooms Mini-bar in all
bedrooms Room-safe (charged) Licensed Full central heating
Air conditioning in bedrooms Open parking available
Covered parking available Child discount available Outdoor
swimming pool Riding Bicycle rental Open terrace Last d
21.30hrs Languages spoken: English & German
ROOMS: (room only) d 1050-1500FF **Reductions over 1
night Special breaks**
MEALS: Full breakfast 85FF Lunch fr 185FF Dinner fr 230FF
CARDS: ●● ■■ ▀▀ ◑ Travellers cheques

★ ★ ★ Mireille
2 pl St-Pierre *13200*
☎ 490937074 FAX 490938728
(cross River Rhône via rue Gambetta (heading north). Hotel on
right)
Away from the throng of ancient Arles and situated on the
right bank of the River Rhône, the Hotel Mireille is an

absolute oasis of peace. It offers extensively renovated rooms -
each furnished in a different style - with direct access to the
mature garden and attractive swimming pool. The restaurant
serves a buffet-style breakfast, and at dinner time visitors can
sample the creative well-presented dishes typical of the
Provençe and Camarque. Ideally situated for exploring the
countryside.
Closed Nov-Mar
34 en suite (bth/shr) 4 rooms in annexe (1 fmly) TV in all
bedrooms STV Radio in rooms Mini-bar in all bedrooms
Licensed Night porter Full central heating Air conditioning in
bedrooms Open parking available Covered parking available
(charged) Outdoor swimming pool Boule Mini-golf Bicycle
rental Open terrace Ping-pong V meals Languages spoken:
English, Italian
ROOMS: (room only) d 320-620FF
CARDS: ●● ■■ ▀▀ ◑ Travellers cheques

★ ★ ★ New Hotel Arles Camargue
45 av Sadi-Carnot *13200*
☎ 490994040 FAX 490933250
In town centre Near motorway
67 en suite (bth/shr) (7 fmly) (1 with balcony) TV in all
bedrooms STV Radio in rooms Direct dial from all bedrooms
Mini-bar in all bedrooms Licensed Lift Night porter Full
central heating Air conditioning in bedrooms Open parking
available Covered parking available (charged) Supervised
Child discount available 16yrs Indoor swimming pool (heated)
Outdoor swimming pool (heated) Pool table Open terrace
Covered terrace V meals Last d 22.30hrs Languages spoken:
English,German,Italian & Spanish
CARDS: ●● ■■ ▀▀ ◑ JCB Travellers cheques

★ ★ ★ Primotel Camargue
Face au Palais des Congrés *13200*
☎ 490939880 FAX 490499276
The hotels in the Primotel group all have modern bedrooms
equipped with every modern day convenience and provide a
high degree of comfort. Their restaurants serve a high
standard of cooking where a choice of traditional and regional
dishes feature strongly on the menu; whilst competent staff
offer attentive service and traditional hospitality in a cordial
atmosphere.
Near river In town centre Near motorway
144 en suite (bth/shr) TV in all bedrooms Direct dial from all
bedrooms Licensed Lift Night porter Full central heating Air
conditioning in bedrooms Open parking available Child
discount available 12yrs Outdoor swimming pool Tennis Pool
table Open terrace Last d 22.00hrs Languages spoken:
English,German,Italian & Spanish
CARDS: ●● ■■ ▀▀ ◑ Travellers cheques

AURONS Bouches-du-Rhône

★ ★ Domaine de la Reynaude
Les Sonnaillets *13121*
☎ 490593024 FAX 490593635
(from Marseille take A7 and follow signs Montpellier take the
exit Salon-centre, follow the sign Pelossanne and then Aurons,
hotel is approx 1kms after Auron)
Relax in the magnificent setting of the heart of Provence. The
charming 18th century coaching inn provides well appointed
rooms, all with bay windows opening onto surrounding
countryside. Many leisure activities are offered within the
grounds.
Forest area

contd.

32 en suite (bth/shr) 2 rooms in annexe (6 with balcony) TV in all bedrooms Direct dial from all bedrooms Licensed Full central heating Open parking available Supervised Child discount available Outdoor swimming pool (heated) Tennis Boule Covered terrace Last d 21.30hrs Languages spoken: English & Spanish
ROOMS: (room only) s 280FF; d 320-600FF
MEALS: Continental breakfast 40FF Lunch 110-200FF Dinner 110-200FF*
CARDS:

AVIGNON Vaucluse

★ ★ ★ **Hotel Bristol** (Best Western)
44 cours Jean Jaurès *84009*
☎ 490822121 FAX 490862272
(In town centre near the railway station)
The Hotel Bristol is a traditional establishment, renovated throughout to provide a high standard of accommodation. Staff are friendly and courteous. It features spacious public areas, a cosy bar and comfortable modern bedrooms.
In town centre Near motorway
67 en suite (bth/shr) (3 fmly) (6 with balcony) No smoking in 5 bedrooms TV in all bedrooms STV Direct dial from all bedrooms Mini-bar in all bedrooms Room-safe Licensed Lift Night porter Full central heating Air conditioning in bedrooms Covered parking available (charged) Supervised Sauna Bicycle rental Languages spoken: English,German,Spanish,Italian
ROOMS: s 469FF; d 518-618FF
CARDS: Travellers cheques

★ ★ ★ ★ **Mirande**
4 pl de l'Mirande *84000*
☎ 490859393 FAX 490862685
(from Marseille or Lyon on A8/A7 take the Avignon Nord exit and drive towards city centre until you reach the gate 'porte de la Ligne', hotel is signposted)

La Mirande, originally a Cardinal's Palace dating from the times of the Popes in Avignon, is now transformed into a luxury hotel. Located in a tranquil cobbled square at the foot of the Popes' Palace, protected from the bustle of the town, the hotel offers the comfortable elegance of 18th century interiors, a secluded garden and terraces.
Near river In town centre Near motorway
20 en suite (bth/shr) (2 fmly) (3 with balcony) TV in all bedrooms Direct dial from all bedrooms Mini-bar in all bedrooms Room-safe Licensed Lift Night porter Full central heating Air conditioning in bedrooms Open parking available (charged) Covered parking available (charged) Child discount available Open terrace Last d 21.45hrs Languages spoken: English, German, Italian Spanish & Swedish
ROOMS: (room only) s 1850-2400FF; d 1850-2400FF
MEALS: Full breakfast 170FF Lunch 135-380FF&alc Dinner 210-380FF&alc
CARDS: Travellers cheques

★ ★ ★ **Primotel Horloge**
1 rue Felicien David *84000*
☎ 490868861 FAX 490821732
(approach from A9 exit Remoulins or A7 exit Avignon Nord)
The hotels in the Primotel group all have modern bedrooms equipped with every modern convenience and provide a high degree of comfort. Their restaurants serve a high standard of cooking where a choice of traditional and regional dishes feature strongly on the menu; whilst competent staff offer attentive service and traditional hospitality in a cordial atmosphere.
In town centre
70 en suite (bth/shr) 13 rooms in annexe (1 fmly) (5 with balcony) TV in all bedrooms STV Radio in rooms Direct dial from all bedrooms Mini-bar in all bedrooms Licensed Lift Night porter Full central heating Air conditioning in bedrooms Child discount available 12yrs Languages spoken: English,German,Italian,Spanish
ROOMS: (room only) s 350-555FF; d 390-605FF
CARDS: JCB Travellers cheques

BANDOL Var

★ ★ ★ **Le Provençal**
rue des Escoles *83150*
☎ 494295211 FAX 494296757
This comfortable hotel is peacefully situated near the Plage de Renecros and offers splendid views over the sea and mountains. The attractively decorated bedrooms have good facilities and the restaurant with its flower-decked terrace serves a choice of tasty dishes in a friendly atmosphere. In addition there is a congenial bar and TV lounge for relaxation.
Near sea Near beach
22 rms (20 bth/shr) Licensed Full central heating Open parking available Covered parking available Child discount available 5yrs Open terrace V meals Last d 22.00hrs Languages spoken: English,Spanish
CARDS: Travellers cheques

BARROUX, LE Vaucluse

★ ★ **Hostellerie François Joseph**
chemin des Rabassières *84330*
☎ 490625278 FAX 490623354
(Leave A7 onto D950 until Carpentras through Carpentras take D938 until village of Barroux)
The Hostellerie François Joseph is situated at the foot of Mont-Ventoux in parklands filled with the flowers, trees and heady fragrances which are so typical of Provençe. It consists of three country houses, painted in pink and ochre, featuring spacious guest-rooms with private balconies overlooking the delightful grounds, a shaded terrace and an attractive swimming pool.
Forest area
Closed Dec-Feb
18 en suite (bth/shr) (4 fmly) (4 with balcony) TV available Direct dial from all bedrooms Night porter Full central heating Open parking available Supervised Solarium Bicycle rental Open terrace Wkly live entertainment Languages spoken: English & French
CARDS: Travellers cheques

★ ★ Géraniums
pl de la Croix *84330*
☎ 490624108 FAX 490625648
In the heart of a picturesque village guarded by a 12th-century medieval castle, Agnes and Jacques Roux extend a warm welcome to their visitors. Surrounded by olive trees, vineyards and orchards, the hotel 'Les Géraniums' offers comfortable bedrooms with good facilities and a high standard of cooking which uses regional ingredients.
Near lake Forest area
Closed early Jan-end Feb
22 en suite (bth/shr) 9 rooms in annexe (2 fmly) (4 with balcony) Licensed Full central heating Open parking available Supervised Child discount available 12yrs Solarium Boule Open terrace V meals Last d 21.00hrs Languages spoken: English,Spanish
CARDS: ●● ■■ ■■ ●) Travellers cheques

BAUX-DE-PROVENCE, LES Bouches-du-Rhône

★ ★ ★ La Benvengudo
Vallon de l'Arcoulé *13520*
☎ 490543254 FAX 490544258
Against the backdrop of the Alpilles, the creeper-covered farmhouse 'Auberge La Benvengudo' is set in peaceful, rural surroundings. Run by the enthusiastic Beaupied family, it offers its clientele an enjoyable stay amidst the lovely scenery of the Provençale countryside. Guests can savour a host of regional delicacies, skilfully prepared by Daniel Beaupied who presides over the kitchen. A selection of leisure pursuits are on offer such as a swimming pool, tennis courts and boules.
Forest area
Closed end Oct-early Feb
20 en suite (bth/shr) (4 fmly) (3 with balcony) TV in all bedrooms Licensed Night porter Full central heating Air conditioning in bedrooms Open parking available Covered parking available Supervised Outdoor swimming pool Tennis Boule Open terrace V meals Last d 21.45hrs Languages spoken: English, German,Italian & Spanish
MEALS: Continental breakfast 60FF Dinner fr 240FF&alc✱
CARDS: ●● ■■ ■■ Travellers cheques

★ ★ ★ La Cabro d'Or (Relais et Chateaux)
13520
☎ 490543321 FAX 490544598
Visitors return again and again to 'La Cabro d'Or. This enchanting establishment possesses many attributes to make your stay a memorable experience. A unique setting surrounded by a delightful garden, olive trees and orchards, while charming bedrooms and elegantly furnished public areas cannot fail to please.
Forest area Near motorway
31 en suite (bth/shr) TV in all bedrooms STV Radio in rooms Mini-bar in all bedrooms Full central heating Air conditioning in bedrooms Open parking available Covered parking available Outdoor swimming pool Tennis Riding Open terrace V meals Languages spoken: English & German
CARDS: ●● ■■ ■■ ●) Travellers cheques

★ ★ ★ ★ Oustau de Daumanière
Vallon de la Fontaine *13520*
☎ 490543307 FAX 490544046
The house is situated at the gateways of the Val d'Enfer where according to legend Dante found the inspiration for the 'Divine Comedy'. Surrounded by olive trees, vines and blue skies it features elegantly furnished rooms which combine tradition with modern comfort and provide a luxurious setting for a

memorable stay. The restaurant serves skilfully executed dishes incorporating the finest produce from l'Ousteau's garden, which are accompanied by an extensive selection of wines from the house cellar.
Forest area
Closed 15 Jan-1 Mar
20 en suite (bth/shr) 1 rooms in annexe (8 fmly) (3 with balcony) TV in all bedrooms STV Radio in rooms Direct dial from all bedrooms Room-safe Full central heating Air conditioning in bedrooms Open parking available Outdoor swimming pool Riding Open terrace Covered terrace V meals Last d 21.30hrs Languages spoken: English
CARDS: ●● ■■ ■■ ●) Travellers cheques

BEAURECUEIL Bouches-du-Rhône

★ ★ ★ Relais Sainte Victoire
13100
☎ 442669498 FAX 442669649
(10km from Aix en Provence)
Just a few minutes from Aix-en-Provence, at the foot of the St Victoire mountains, surrounded by landscapes made familiar by the paintings of Cézanne, sits Le Relais Sainte Victoire. Rooms which overlook gardens with swimming pool and mini tennis are equipped with every comfort including air-conditioning and jacuzzi. In the restaurant the Jugy-Bergès family offer an imaginative and refined menu of authentic Provence dishes.
Forest area Near motorway
Closed 1st wk Nov & Jan also 2 wks Feb
10 en suite (bth) (1 fmly) (2 with balcony) TV in all bedrooms Direct dial from all bedrooms Mini-bar in all bedrooms Licensed Full central heating Air conditioning in bedrooms Open parking available Child discount available 12yrs Outdoor swimming pool Riding Solarium Boule Jacuzzi/spa Mini tennis Last d 21.30hrs Languages spoken: English
ROOMS: (room only) s 400-600FF; d 400-600FF
MEALS: Full breakfast 70FF Dinner 145-400FF
CARDS: ■■ ■■ ●)

BORMES-LES-MIMOSAS Var

★ ★ ★ Hostellerie de la Reine Jeanne
Foret du Dom *83230*
☎ 494150083 FAX 494647789
(mid way between Toulon and St Tropez on N98)

Halfway between St Tropez and Toulon and only a few minutes from the beaches in the calm shade of the Dom forest. Reine Jeanne is pleased to welcome guests to the eight individually styled guestrooms offering a subtle harmony of up-to-date comfort and the soft charm of timeless Provence.

contd.

8 en suite (bth/shr) (3 fmly) (8 with balcony) TV in all bedrooms STV Direct dial from all bedrooms Mini-bar in all bedrooms Room-safe (charged) Licensed Full central heating Open parking available Child discount available 12yrs Outdoor swimming pool Solarium Boule Bicycle rental Covered terrace V meals Last d 22.00hrs Languages spoken: English, German & Italian
ROOMS: (room only) s 500-700FF; d 650-750FF
Reductions over 1 night Special breaks
MEALS: Full breakfast 70FF Continental breakfast 50FF Lunch 150-280FF&alc Dinner 150-280FF&alc✱
CARDS: ●● ▆ Travellers cheques

CARPENTRAS Vaucluse

★ ★ ★ **Les 3 Colomes**
148 av des Garrigues *84200*
☎ 490660701 FAX 490661154
The attractive hotel Les 3 Colomes enjoys a secluded setting in a shaded park. Sheltered from the ever blowing Mistral, it offers peaceful accommodation with a wide range of modern facilities. Skilfully prepared dishes, including delicately flavoured regional specialities, are served on the pool-side terrace or dining room.
Forest area
Closed Jan-Feb
30 en suite (bth/shr) (6 fmly) (9 with balcony) No smoking in 6 bedrooms TV in all bedrooms STV Direct dial from all bedrooms Licensed Full central heating Open parking available Supervised Child discount available 12yrs Outdoor swimming pool Tennis Gym Pool table Boule Bicycle rental Open terrace V meals Last d 21.30hrs Languages spoken: English,Italian
MEALS: Full breakfast 50FF Lunch 120-230FF&alc Dinner 120-230FF✱
CARDS: ●● ▆ ▆ Travellers cheques

★ ★ ★ **Hostellerie du Blason de Provence**
rte de Capentras a Montreux *84200*
☎ 490663134 FAX 490668305
The charming family-run hotel is set in an attractive garden and provides the peaceful setting for a relaxing holiday. Courteous, attentive service, an excellent cuisine and comfortable guest rooms add to an enjoyable stay. Surrounded by unspoilt countryside and numerous picturesque, hill-top villages it provides a suitable setting for both summer and winter holidays.
Near river Forest area Near motorway
Closed mid Dec-mid Jan
20 en suite (bth/shr) (4 fmly) (2 with balcony) TV in all bedrooms Mini-bar in all bedrooms Licensed Full central heating Open parking available Supervised Child discount available 12yrs Outdoor swimming pool Tennis Boule Open terrace Last d 21.30hrs Languages spoken: English,Dutch,German,Spanish
MEALS: Full breakfast 50FF Lunch fr 95FF&alc Dinner 135-265FFalc✱
CARDS: ●● ▆ ▆ ⑨ Travellers cheques

★ ★ ★ **Safari**
1 av J H Fabre *84200*
☎ 490633535 FAX 490604999
(From town centre take Avignon road and hotel is on the right just before the large rdbt)
A charming residence set in attractive, leafy surroundings; it offers smart bedrooms with every conceivable amenity and a welcoming restaurant serving outstanding Provençale cuisine with perfectly balanced flavours and the fresh ingredients of

the region. It has a swimming pool, excellent conference facilities, and is an ideal base for visits to Avignon.
Closed Jan-Feb
42 en suite (bth/shr) 14 rooms in annexe (3 fmly) (21 with balcony) TV in all bedrooms STV Radio in rooms Direct dial from all bedrooms Licensed Lift Night porter Full central heating Open parking available Supervised Child discount available 10yrs Outdoor swimming pool Boule Open terrace

Last d 22.00hrs Languages spoken: English,German
MEALS: Full breakfast 55FF Continental breakfast 55FF Lunch fr 135FF&alc Dinner fr 168FF&alc
CARDS: ●● ▆ ▆ ⑨ Travellers cheques

CASTELLET, LE Var

★ ★ ★ **Castel Lumière**
1 rue Portail *83330*
☎ 494326220 FAX 494327033
Near motorway
Closed Jan
6 rms TV in all bedrooms Licensed Full central heating Air conditioning in bedrooms Child discount available 6yrs Boule Open terrace Last d 22.00hrs Languages spoken: English,Italian,Spanish
MEALS: Full breakfast 55FF Continental breakfast 55FF Lunch 120-250FF&alc Dinner 120-250FF&alc✱

CAVALAIRE-SUR-MER Var

★ ★ **Raymond**
av des Allies *83240*
☎ 494640732 FAX 494640273
(Approach from A8 via Le Muy & Ste-Maxime)
This informal establishment offers all the facilities which make it a good venue for an enjoyable holiday. It has a bar, comfortable day room, sunny terrace and a flower filled garden, well equipped bedrooms and a restaurant, whilst the surrounding area provides a extensive choice of leisure pursuits.
Near sea Forest area
Closed mid Oct-mid Feb
36 en suite (bth/shr) (5 fmly) (24 with balcony) No smoking in 4 bedrooms TV in all bedrooms STV Direct dial from all bedrooms Licensed Full central heating Open parking available Covered parking available Supervised Child discount available 12yrs Outdoor swimming pool Pool table Boule Bicycle rental Open terrace Last d 21.30hrs Languages spoken: English, German, Italian
ROOMS: (room only) d 260-420FF **Reductions over 1 night**
MEALS: Continental breakfast 37FF Lunch 80-230FF&alc Dinner 100-230FF&alc
CARDS: ●● ▆ ▆ Travellers cheques

CEILLAC Hautes-Alpes

★ ★ La Cascade
05600
☎ 492450592 FAX 492452209
Peacefully situated in a majestic setting at an altitude of 1700m, the hotel provides a good base for both summer and winter breaks. Most of the rooms are equipped with modern facilities, there is a cosy reading room with open fire place, a panoramic terrace and a restaurant which caters for all tastes.
Near river Forest area
Closed 11 Apr-end May & 11 Sep-19 Dec
23 rms (15 bth 6 shr) (5 fmly) (11 with balcony) TV in all bedrooms Direct dial from all bedrooms Licensed Full central heating Open parking available Child discount available 12yrs Last d 21.00hrs Languages spoken: English
MEALS: Full breakfast 42FF Dinner 70-105FF✱

CHÂTEAU-ARNOUX Alpes-de-Haute-Provence

★ ★ ★ ★ Bonne Étape
chemin du Lac *04160*
☎ 492640009 FAX 492643736
(In front of the castle)
This 18th-century coaching inn occupies an enviable position in the lush hills of the Provençal countryside with its extraordinary light that has inspired so many painters through the centuries. Surrounded by ancient olive trees, meadows and the delicate fragrances of the region, it welcomes visitors into its charming interior and offers warm hospitality and comfortable guest rooms, but above all, an outstanding cuisine. Leisure facilities include a splendid outdoor heated swimming pool with an 18-hole golf-course and horse-riding centre nearby.
Near river Near lake Forest area Near motorway
Closed early Jan-mid Feb RS Nov-Mar
18 en suite (bth/shr) (2 fmly) (2 with balcony) TV in all bedrooms STV Radio in rooms Direct dial from all bedrooms Mini-bar in all bedrooms Licensed Full central heating Air conditioning in bedrooms Open parking available Covered parking available Supervised Outdoor swimming pool (heated) Open terrace Covered terrace V meals Last d 21.30hrs Languages spoken: English,German,Italian,Spanish
ROOMS: (room only) d 600-1500FF
MEALS: Full breakfast 85FF Continental breakfast 30FF Lunch 225-595FF&alc Dinner 225-595FF&alc✱
CARDS: 💳 📧 📧 ⓓ Travellers cheques

CHÂTEAUNEUF-DU-PAPE Vaucluse

★ ★ ★ Sommellerie
rte de Roquemaure *84230*
☎ 490835000 FAX 490835185
(exit A7 Orange to Châteauneuf-du-Pape, in the village follow directions to Roquemaure for 2km you will find La Sommellerie on the D17)
Set amid famous vineyards, La Sommellerie, once an ancient sheep-fold of the 17th century, is now a charming and comfortable country house where Annie Paumel will recieve you like friends. Pierre Paumel, Master Chef of France creates provençal specialities served with the matching wines. In summer meals can be enjoyed in the arbour or at the pool side, where barbecue specialities are available from the charcoal grill. In winter a warm fire awaits you in the dining room.
Near river Forest area
Closed 15-18 Feb
14 en suite (bth/shr) (2 fmly) TV in all bedrooms Direct dial

from all bedrooms Licensed Full central heating Open parking available Supervised Outdoor swimming pool Solarium Boule Open terrace Last d 21.30hrs Languages spoken: English & German

ROOMS: (room only) s 400-475FF; d 400-475FF
MEALS: Continental breakfast 55FF Lunch 150-360FF Dinner 150-360FF
CARDS: 💳 📧 📧 Travellers cheques

CHAUFFAYER Hautes-Alpes

★ ★ Le Bercail
05800
☎ 492552221 FAX 492553155
Situated at 75 kilometres south of Grenoble, the hotel stands a small distance away from the road at the entrance of the village. Set amidst shady linden trees, it is tucked away in lush vegetation on the edge of two large Alpine valleys. The bedrooms are appointed with modern facilities and the menu features a range of enjoyable meals, which in summer are served on the shaded terrace.
Near river Forest area Near motorway
11 en suite (bth) (2 fmly) TV in all bedrooms Radio in rooms Direct dial from all bedrooms Licensed Night porter Full central heating Open parking available Supervised Child discount available Boule Bicycle rental Open terrace Covered terrace V meals Last d 22.00hrs Languages spoken: English,German
ROOMS: (room only) s 170FF; d 200-250FF ✱ **Reductions over 1 night**
MEALS: Full breakfast 35FF Continental breakfast 35FF Lunch 70-140FF Dinner 70-140FF
CARDS: 💳 📧 📧 ⓓ Travellers cheques

COMPS-SUR-ARTUBY Var

★ ★ Grand Hotel Bain
83840
☎ 494769006 FAX 494769224
(at S exit for Gorges du Verdon)
This hotel has been in the hands of the same family for centuries. The pleasant bedrooms are furnished in an understated fashion and provide a good level of comfort. The restaurant offers a high standard of cooking, where good use has been made of fresh local produce.
Near river Forest area Near motorway
18 en suite (bth/shr) (5 fmly) TV in all bedrooms Direct dial from all bedrooms Licensed Full central heating Covered parking available (charged) Supervised Tennis Pool table Boule Open terrace V meals Last d 21.00hrs Languages spoken: English

contd.

ROOMS: (room only) d 250-345FF
MEALS: Full breakfast 38FF Continental breakfast 38FF Lunch
78-195FF&alc Dinner 78-195FF&alc
CARDS: 💳 💳 💳 ⚡

CORNILLON-CONFOUX Bouches-du-Rhône

★ ★ ★ Le Devem de Mirapier
rte de Grans-D19 *13250*
☎ 490559922 FAX 490558614
Constructed in a typical Provençal style and situated 4 km from
Salon, the hotel enjoys a peaceful position amidst pine trees
and offers guests tranquillity and plenty of sunshine. A
welcoming ambience and good quality cooking mean that
many visitors return as old friends.
Forest area
15 en suite (bth/shr) TV in all bedrooms STV Direct dial from
all bedrooms Licensed Full central heating Air conditioning
in bedrooms Open parking available Child discount available
8yrs Outdoor swimming pool Tennis Solarium Pool table
Boule Open terrace Covered terrace V meals Languages
spoken: English & Italian
ROOMS: (room only) s 400-600FF; d 520-700FF
CARDS: 💳 💳 💳

CRESTET Vaucluse

★ ★ Mas de Magali
quartier Chante Coucou *84110*
☎ 490363991 FAX 490287340
(leave A7 at exit Bollèe, follow direction Vaison-la-Romaine,
continue direction of Malaucene-Cardentras, then follow hotel
signs)
In a park of oak trees and traditional provencal countryside,

the interior of the hotel is romantically decorated to create a
cosy atmosphere. Rooms are spacious, some have terraces
with beautiful views. In the restaurant guests can enjoy the
flavours of the region.
Near river Near lake Near sea Forest area Near motorway
Closed 19 Oct-14 Mar
9 en suite (bth/shr) (2 fmly) (4 with balcony) No smoking in 2
bedrooms TV in all bedrooms STV Direct dial from all
bedrooms Licensed Full central heating Open parking
available Child discount available 10yrs Outdoor swimming
pool Sauna Boule Bicycle rental Open terrace V meals Last d
20.30hrs Languages spoken: English, Dutch, German & Spanish
ROOMS: (room only) s 295-335FF; d 295-335FF
MEALS: Full breakfast 45FF Continental breakfast 45FF
Dinner 125-145FF✱
CARDS: 💳 💳 💳 Travellers cheques

CROIX-VALMER, LA Var

★ ★ ★ Les Moulins de Paillas (Best Western)
plage de Gigaro *83420*
☎ 494797111 FAX 494543705
The hotel comprises two charming houses built in Provençale
style with stunning views over the Mediterranean. The
individually appointed bedrooms are well equipped; some
have balconies whilst others have a view of the garden. The
hotel offers various eating options and is surrounded by
enormous shaded grounds.
Near sea Forest area
Closed Oct-mid May
30 en suite (bth) 38 rooms in annexe (15 with balcony) TV in
all bedrooms Radio in rooms Direct dial from all bedrooms
Mini-bar in all bedrooms Licensed Full central heating Air
conditioning in bedrooms Open parking available Child
discount available 7yrs Outdoor swimming pool Solarium
Open terrace Last d 22.30hrs Languages spoken:
English,German,Italian
CARDS: 💳 💳 💳 Travellers cheques

CUCURON Vaucluse

L'Arbre de Mai
rue de l'Église *84160*
☎ 490772510 FAX 490772510
(from Cavaillon (A7) take turning for Pertuis, after Cadenet
turn left signed Cucuron)
The building dates back to the 18th century and is situated in
the heart of a picturesque village. Inside, it has a superb
Renaissance staircase which leads to the pleasant country-style
bedrooms. There is a small restaurant in the hotel which
serves good home-made food.
Near river Near lake Forest area In town centre Near motorway
Closed Nov-Feb
6 en suite (shr) (3 fmly) (1 with balcony) Licensed Full central
heating Child discount available 5yrs Open terrace Last d
21.30hrs Languages spoken: English, Spanish, Italian
ROOMS: d 340-360FF
MEALS: Continental breakfast 30FF Lunch 90-140FF&alc
Dinner fr 140FF&alc
CARDS: 💳 💳 Travellers cheques

EMBRUN Hautes-Alpes

★ ★ De la Mairie
pl Barthélon *05200*
☎ 492432065 FAX 492434702
This attractive hotel is situated in the centre of the old town. It
features bright, cheerfully decorated bedrooms with good
amenities. In addition, there is a bar and an informal restaurant
serving a good selection of enjoyable meals.
Near lake In town centre
Closed Dec-May
24 en suite (bth/shr) (5 fmly) TV in all bedrooms Direct dial
from all bedrooms Licensed Lift Full central heating Child
discount available Open terrace Casino Last d 21.30hrs
Languages spoken: English,German
CARDS: 💳 💳 💳 ⚡ Travellers cheques

EYGALIÈRES Bouches-du-Rhône

★ ★ Auberge Crin Blanc
rte d'Orgon *13810*
☎ 490959317 FAX 490906062
Set at the foot of the Alpilles in the heart of the

enchanting Provence region, this country inn is surrounded by an extensive park with pine trees. All the bedrooms are situated on ground-floor level and feature facilities associated with a two star hotel. The restaurant which overlooks the swimming pool, serves regional dishes with a distinct Provençale flavour. There is a delightful garden to relax in, complete with water-lily pond, and a tennis court for the more energetic.

Forest area

Closed 16 Nov-14 Mar

10 en suite (bth/shr) (10 fmly) Direct dial from all bedrooms Licensed Open parking available Supervised Child discount available 11yrs Outdoor swimming pool Tennis Boule Last d 21.30hrs Languages spoken: English
MEALS: Full breakfast 45FF Continental breakfast 25FF Lunch 150-250FF&alc Dinner 150-250FF&alc✱

FAYENCE Var

★ ★ ★ Moulin de la Camandoule
chemin Notre Dame des Cyprès *83400*
☎ 494760084 FAX 494761040

This authentic mill is situated in the village of Fayence, which reputedly has more hours of sun in a year than anywhere else in France, and the purest air too. Located in the hinterland of the Côte d'Azur, it features an exceptional interior where the old millstones and presses have been preserved and can be found in the lounge and restaurant. The rooms vary in style and size, but are all equipped with modern appointments, whilst the cuisine consists of classic dishes based on regional recipes and ingredients which are augmented by a selection of fine wines.

Near river Near lake Forest area

12 en suite (bth/shr) (1 fmly) TV in all bedrooms Licensed Full central heating Open parking available Outdoor swimming pool Solarium Boule Open terrace Covered terrace V meals Last d 21.30hrs Languages spoken: English,Italian,German
CARDS: 💳 💳 Travellers cheques

FONTAINE-DE-VAUCLUSE Vaucluse

★ ★ Hotel du Parc
Les Bourgades *84800*
☎ 490203157 FAX 490202703
(Off N100 Apt/Avignon)

Standing on the banks of the River Sorgue and surrounded by a shaded park, the Hotel du Parc has well equipped guest rooms, and a restaurant which serves a range of gastronomic dishes, complemented by an exceptional wine-list featuring over 250 vintages from the house-cellar.

Near river

Closed 2 Jan-15 Feb

12 en suite (bth/shr) (2 fmly) (6 with balcony) Direct dial from all bedrooms Licensed Full central heating Open parking available Child discount available 8yrs Fishing Open terrace V meals Last d 21.30hrs Languages spoken: Italian,Spanish
ROOMS: (room only) d 280FF
MEALS: Full breakfast 40FF Continental breakfast 40FF Lunch 99-149FF&alc Dinner 99-149FF&alc
CARDS: 💳 💳 💳 💳 Travellers cheques

FONTVIEILLE Bouches-du-Rhône

★ ★ ★ ★ La Régalido (Relais et Châteaux)
rue Frederic Mistral *13990*
☎ 490546022 FAX 490546429

(Approach via D17 from Arles)

This is a charming creeper-clad residence displaying all the attributes which makes Provençe so popular. Decorated in the distinct style of the region and featuring individually styled bedrooms with modern amenities, a spacious foyer, and varied small cosy lounges. In addition, there is a shaded terrace beside the flower-filled garden where in summer, breakfast and other meals are served.

Forest area

Closed 2-31 Jan

15 en suite (bth/shr) (3 fmly) (3 with balcony) TV in all bedrooms STV Direct dial from all bedrooms Mini-bar in all bedrooms Licensed Night porter Full central heating Air conditioning in bedrooms Open parking available Supervised Open terrace V meals Last d 21.15hrs Languages spoken: German,Spanish

ROOMS: (room only) s 470-690FF; d 690-1570FF **Special breaks**
MEALS: Full breakfast 80FF Continental breakfast 40FF Lunch 165-400FF&alc Dinner 270-400FF&alc
CARDS: 💳 💳 💳 💳 Travellers cheques

★ ★ La Ripaille
rte des Baux *13990*
☎ 490547315 FAX 490546069
Near river Near lake Near sea Forest area In town centre Near motorway

Closed mid Oct-mid Mar

20 en suite (bth/shr) (2 fmly) (9 with balcony) TV in all bedrooms Direct-dial available Licensed Full central heating Open parking available Supervised Child discount available 9yrs Outdoor swimming pool (heated) Riding Solarium Boule Open terrace Last d 21.00hrs Languages spoken: English,Spanish
MEALS: Full breakfast 50FF Lunch 90-135FF&alc Dinner 135FF&alc✱
CARDS: 💳 💳 Travellers cheques

★ ★ Hostellerie de la Tour
3 rue des Plumelets *13990*
☎ 490547221
(Just before entering Fontvieille from the direction of Arles turn left towards Tarascon. Hotel 800mtrs)

Located in leafy surroundings, just a few minutes on foot from a charming village, visitors receive a warm, personal welcome in this characterful establishment. It features bedrooms with private terraces, which are equipped with modern amenities and provide a good level of comfort.

Forest area Near motorway

Closed 31 Oct-1 Mar

10 en suite (shr) (1 fmly) Direct dial from all bedrooms Licensed Night porter Full central heating Open parking available Child discount available 2yrs Outdoor swimming pool Open terrace V meals Languages spoken: English,German
ROOMS: (room only) s fr 220FF; d 275-355FF
MEALS: Continental breakfast 45FF Lunch fr 85FF&alc Dinner fr 95FF&alc
CARDS: 💳 💳 Travellers cheques

FORCALQUIER Alpes-de-Haute-Provence

★ ★ ★ Hostellerie des 2 Lions
11 pl du Bourguet *04300*
☎ 492752530 FAX 492750641

This ancient coaching inn dates back to the 17th century and stands at the foot of the medieval city. The establishment is an

ideal setting for an overnight stop and offers elegant
bedrooms and old-fashioned French hospitality. The cuisine
has earned a good reputation in the region and incorporates
classic and innovative dishes.
In town centre Near motorway
Closed Jan-Mar
16 en suite (bth/shr) (2 fmly) No smoking on premises TV in all
bedrooms STV Mini-bar in all bedrooms Licensed Full central
heating Open parking available (charged) Child discount
available 10yrs Last d 21.15hrs Languages spoken: Italian
MEALS: Full breakfast 50FF Lunch 150-300FF&alc Dinner 150-
300FF&alc✱
CARDS: ●● ■■ ▥ Travellers cheques

FOX-AMPHOUX Var

★ ★ ★ Auberge du Vieux Fox
pl de l'Église 83670
☎ 494807169 FAX 494807838
Near lake Forest area
8 en suite (bth/shr) (1 fmly) TV in all bedrooms Licensed Full
central heating Child discount available Pool table Open
terrace V meals Last d 21.30hrs Languages spoken:
English,German
CARDS: ●● ■■ ▥ ❿ Travellers cheques

GAP Hautes-Alpes

★ ★ Fons-Regina
13 av de Fontreyne 05000
☎ 492539899 FAX 492515451
(Off the main road to Marseille)
Surrounded by three acres of parkland, the hotel has a
pleasant restaurant, attractively furnished bedrooms, and a
delightful garden with tables and chairs alongside the
swimming pool. There is a cosy bar for a chat and a drink, or
guests may want to seek out the 18-hole golf course nearby.
Forest area
25 en suite (bth/shr) TV in all bedrooms STV Direct dial from
all bedrooms Full central heating Open parking available
Child discount available 10yrs Outdoor swimming pool
(heated) Open terrace V meals
ROOMS: (room only) s 160-190FF; d 228-248FF ✱
CARDS: ●● ■■ ▥ ❿ Travellers cheques

★ ★ Pavillon
Chabanas rte de Veynes 05000
☎ 492520273 FAX 492533472
Standing amidst green scenery and located not far from the
forest, the hotel offers bedrooms with up-to-date facilities. The
pleasant dining rooms serve a combination of classic dishes
and specialities from the Alsace. The park features a shaded
terrace and provides varied leisure facilities.
Forest area
Closed Xmas-early Jan
82 en suite (bth/shr) 50 rooms in annexe (30 fmly) (50 with
balcony) TV in all bedrooms STV Licensed Full central
heating Open parking available Covered parking available
Child discount available Indoor swimming pool (heated)
Tennis Boule Mini-golf Bicycle rental Open terrace Covered
terrace Languages spoken: English,German,
CARDS: ●● ■■ ▥ ❿ Travellers cheques

GASSIN Var

★ ★ ★ ★ Domaine de l'Astragale
chemin de la Gassiné 83580
☎ 494894898 FAX 494971601
This charming building stands a few steps away from the
famous harbour of St Tropez and its popular beaches. It
offers the warm hospitality of yesteryear combined with
modern comfort. Elegant bedrooms are complemented by
tastefully furnished public areas, whilst the restaurant is
particularly noted for its skilfully prepared dishes,
combining local produce with the delicately flavoured herbs
of the region.
Near sea Near motorway
Closed mid Oct-mid May
34 en suite (bth/shr) (16 fmly) (18 with balcony) TV in all
bedrooms STV Radio in rooms Direct dial from all bedrooms
Mini-bar in all bedrooms Licensed Night porter Full central
heating Air conditioning in bedrooms Open parking available
Covered parking available Child discount available 7yrs
Outdoor swimming pool (heated) Tennis Solarium Boule
Jacuzzi/spa Open terrace Table Tennis Last d 22.00hrs
Languages spoken: English,German,Italian
CARDS: ●● ■■ ▥ ❿ Travellers cheques

★ ★ ★ ★ Le Mas de Chastelas
quartier Bertaud 83580
☎ 494567171 FAX 494567156
(leave A8 exit Le Muy in direction of Ste-Maxime, follow signs
to St Tropez, pass Port Grimaud, on arrival at lights crossing at
La Foux continue on D98, main St Tropez road, turn right at
big sign "Domaine Bertaud Relieu")
A very calm and relaxing place close to St Tropez and with
unique surroundings. The main building is 18th century, in
provençal style and in the middle of a spacious park.
Near sea Near beach Forest area Near motorway
30 rms (28 bth/shr) 6 rooms in annexe (4 fmly) (6 with
balcony) TV in all bedrooms STV Direct dial from all
bedrooms Mini-bar in 18 bedrooms Room-safe Licensed Lift
Night porter Air conditioning in bedrooms Open parking
available Supervised Child discount available Outdoor
swimming pool Open terrace Last d 21.30hrs Languages
spoken: English German Italian & Spanish
ROOMS: (room only) s 1200-2000FF; d 1200-2000FF
MEALS: Full breakfast 70FF Lunch 210-265FF&alc Dinner 210-
265FF&alc
CARDS: ●● ■■ ▥ ❿

★ ★ Relais Bon Accueil
Presqu'île de Giens 83580
☎ 494582048 FAX 494589046
A warm welcome awaits visitors at the hotel, which offers a
peaceful, informal atmosphere as well as a range of culinary
delights. Set in the heart of the Giens peninsula with its mild
climate, it is surrounded by flowers and lush vegetation. There
is an attractive restaurant with rustic furnishings providing the
setting for an enjoyable meal, while bedroom accommodation
is cosy with good facilities.
Near sea Near beach
10 rms 1 rooms in annexe TV in all bedrooms Licensed Full
central heating Open parking available Child discount
available Languages spoken: English,German,Italian
CARDS: ●● ■■ ▥ Travellers cheques

Taking your mobile phone to France?
See page 11

GÉMENOS Bouches-du-Rhône

★ ★ ★ ★ Relais de la Magdeleine
rte d'Aix-en-Provence *13420*
☎ 442322016 FAX 442320226
(Access via A50 exit Toulon)
Set in a park, this residence offers its visitors a friendly reception in informal surroundings. The pleasant bedrooms have good amenities and in summer meals are served on the terrace in the shade of the plane trees.
Near river Forest area Near motorway
Closed Dec-15 Mar
24 en suite (bth/shr) (3 fmly) TV in all bedrooms STV Direct dial from all bedrooms Licensed Lift Full central heating Open parking available Supervised Child discount available 7yrs Outdoor swimming pool Boule Open terrace Covered terrace V meals Last d 21.30hrs Languages spoken: English, German
ROOMS: (room only) s 440-580FF; d 590-790FF ✳
Reductions over 1 night
MEALS: Full breakfast 75FF Lunch 160-250FF&alc Dinner 250FF&alc✳
CARDS: ●● 💳 Travellers cheques

GIGONDAS Vaucluse

★ ★ Florets
rte des Dentelles *84190*
☎ 490658501 FAX 490658380
Located at the foot of the Dentelles de Montmirail, and surrounded by the famous Gigondas vineyards, this friendly hotel has been in the same family for 36 years. The restaurant offers a high standard of cooking, which combines traditional dishes with regional ingredients, and on fine days is served on the shaded terrace. The hotel is a good starting point for many country walks, whilst also wine-tasting and visits to the wine cellars on the family estate can be arranged. There are cheerful bedrooms with a good level of comfort and which provide a restful night's sleep.
Forest area
Closed end Dec-Mar
13 en suite (bth/shr) 4 rooms in annexe (4 with balcony) TV in all bedrooms Direct dial from all bedrooms Full central heating Open parking available Supervised Child discount available Boule Open terrace Covered terrace V meals
Languages spoken: English & Spanish
CARDS: ●● 💳 💳 ● Travellers cheques

GORDES Vaucluse

★ ★ ★ ★ Les Bories
rte de l'Abbaye de Senanque *84220*
☎ 490720051 FAX 490720122
(Motorway to Avignon-Sud in direction of Apt. Before Gordes centre turn left rte de l'Abbaye de Sénanque)
Les Bories is in the heart of the Luberon on a hill overlooking the village of Gordes. Delightful guest rooms and extensive grounds with scented footpaths, where the terraces are shaded by holm oaks and olive trees. Fine local cuisine modern and traditional is prepared by the chef.
Forest area In town centre Near motorway
Closed mid Nov-mid Feb
18 en suite (bth/shr) 8 rooms in annexe (1 fmly) (10 with balcony) TV in all bedrooms STV Direct dial from all bedrooms Mini-bar in all bedrooms Licensed Lift Full central heating Air conditioning in bedrooms Open parking available Indoor swimming pool (heated) Outdoor swimming pool

Tennis Solarium Boule Open terrace Last d 21.00hrs
Languages spoken: English & German
ROOMS: s 840-1790FF; d 930-1980FF
MEALS: Full breakfast 95FF Lunch 190-300FF&alc Dinner 230-300FF&alc
CARDS: ●● 💳 💳 ● Travellers cheques

GRAMBOIS Vaucluse

★ ★ ★ Le Clos des Sources
Quartier Le Brusquet *84240*
☎ 490779355 FAX 490779296
The establishment is set in an elevated position with lovely views over the Provençale countryside. It features a spacious foyer, a cosy bar, and comfortable bedrooms with private terrace. The panoramic restaurant serves a range of regional specialities in elegant surroundings; in addition guests can relax on the patio with its charming fountain.
Near river Forest area Near motorway
Closed mid Nov-end Feb
(3 fmly) (12 with balcony) No smoking in 4 bedrooms TV in 12 bedrooms Licensed Night porter Full central heating Open parking available Supervised Child discount available Outdoor swimming pool Golf Solarium Boule Open terrace Last d 22.00hrs Languages spoken: English,Italian
CARDS: ●● 💳 Travellers cheques

★ ★ ★ Clos des Sources
quartier le Breusquet *84240*
☎ 490779738 FAX 490779296
(Leave A7 at Cavaillon/Aix-en-Provence take direction of Pertuis on D973 continue to La Tour d'Aigues and onto Grambois)
In the southern Luberon amid seasonal aromas and beautiful walks, this hotel is a charming place offering refinement and comfort.
Forest area
Closed Jan
12 en suite (bth/shr) (3 fmly) (12 with balcony) No smoking in 2 bedrooms TV in all bedrooms STV Direct dial from all bedrooms Licensed Night porter Full central heating Open parking available Supervised Child discount available 10yrs Outdoor swimming pool Solarium Boule Open terrace Wkly live entertainment Last d 21.15hrs Languages spoken: English & Italian
ROOMS: (room only) s 620FF; d 700FF **Reductions over 1 night**
MEALS: Continental breakfast 60FF Lunch 150-230FF&alc Dinner 180-320FF&alc
CARDS: ●● 💳 💳 Travellers cheques

GRAVESON Bouches-du-Rhône

★ ★ Mas des Amandiers
rte d'Avignon *13690*
☎ 490958176 FAX 490958518
A warm reception awaits visitors to this charming establishment, where courteous staff provide an attentive service. Peacefully situated bedrooms are well equipped and have good facilities, it also has a restaurant and a delightful garden. The hotel is a good base from which to explore the beautiful surrounding countryside.
Near motorway
Closed mid Oct-mid Mar
25 en suite (bth) (3 fmly) (1 with balcony) TV in all bedrooms Direct dial from all bedrooms Licensed Full central heating Open parking available Supervised Outdoor swimming pool

(heated) Tennis Fishing Boule Bicycle rental Open terrace
Languages spoken: English,Spanish
ROOMS: (room only) s 280-290FF; d 290-320FF
CARDS: 😊 📰 🔁 🌓 Travellers cheques

GRÉOUX-LES-BAINS Alpes-de-Haute-Provence

★ ★ ★ Hotel Villa Borghése
av des Thermes *04800*
☎ 492780091 FAX 492780755
(Access via A51 exit 'Manosque')

This enchanting villa lies tucked away in leafy surroundings
near the lavender fields and lakes of the Verdon region, and
provides an ideal base for excursions into the countryside. The
restaurant offers a wide choice of dishes prepared with the
delicate herbs of the region. The guest-rooms are equipped
with modern facilities and provide comfortable
accommodation.
Near river Near lake Forest area In town centre Near
motorway
Closed end Nov-end Mar
67 en suite (bth/shr) (4 fmly) (36 with balcony) TV in all
bedrooms STV Radio in rooms Direct dial from all bedrooms
Mini-bar in all bedrooms Licensed Lift Night porter Full
central heating Air conditioning in bedrooms Open parking
available Covered parking available (charged) Child discount
available 12yrs Outdoor swimming pool (heated) Tennis
Sauna Solarium Boule Jacuzzi/spa Open terrace Covered
terrace Last d 21.30hrs Languages spoken:
English,German,Italian
ROOMS: (room only) s 380-510FF; d 510-680FF
MEALS: Full breakfast 60FF Continental breakfast 60FF Lunch
160-250FF Dinner 160-250FF
CARDS: 😊 📰 🔁 🌓 Travellers cheques

GRIMAUD Var

★ ★ ★ Hotel de La Boulangerie
rte de Collobrières *83310*
☎ 494432316 FAX 494433827
A pleasant hotel in a Mediterranean park overlooking the
Maures mountain range. The freshest ingredients of the day's
market are used on the menu.
Forest area
Closed 11 Oct-Mar
10 en suite (bth/shr) (1 fmly) (1 with balcony) TV in 4
bedrooms STV Direct dial from all bedrooms Mini-bar in 1
bedroom Licensed Full central heating Open parking
available Outdoor swimming pool Tennis Open terrace
ROOMS: d 680-760FF

HYÈRES Var

★ ★ Inter Hotel Centrotel
45 av Edith Cavell *83400*
☎ 494383810 FAX 494383773
All the hotels in the Inter Hotel group offer guest
accommodation which is designed with the individual needs of
its clientele in mind. Whether situated in the capital or in a
seaside resort, they offer old-fashioned hospitality and up-to-
date modern amenities. Staff are friendly and helpful
throughout, and provide a degree of personal service which is
difficult to match and make a stay, whether for business or
pleasure an enjoyable experience to look back upon.
Near sea In town centre Near motorway
24 en suite (bth/shr) (5 fmly) (2 with balcony) TV in all
bedrooms Direct dial from 23 bedrooms Mini-bar in 4
bedrooms Full central heating Air conditioning in bedrooms
Covered parking available (charged) Supervised Child
discount available 12yrs Languages spoken: English,German
ROOMS: (room only) s 250-330FF; d 280-420FF
Reductions over 1 night Special breaks
CARDS: 😊 📰 🔁 🌓 Travellers cheques

★ ★ ★ Le Manoir
Ile de Port-Cros *83400*
☎ 494059052 FAX 494059089
This charming residence dates back to 1830. After several
renovations it has retained all its original character and
combines modern comfort with old world charm. The
bedrooms are spacious with every conceivable amenity, and
guests can enjoy meals outside on the terrace which offers
stunning views over the sea.
Near sea Near beach Forest area
Closed 1 Oct-Apr
22 en suite (bth/shr) 2 rooms in annexe (5 fmly) (8 with
balcony) Mini-bar in all bedrooms Room-safe Licensed Full
central heating Child discount available 10yrs Solarium Boule
Open terrace Covered terrace Last d 21.00hrs Languages
spoken: English, Italian
CARDS: 😊 🔁 Travellers cheques

★ ★ Du Parc
7 bd Pasteur *83400*
☎ 494650665 FAX 494659328
Located on the edge of the medieval quarter of the town, this
friendly family hotel welcomes its clientele in informal
surroundings. Under the 'hands on' management of the
Moreau family visitors are offered comfortable accommodation
and a high standard of cooking which includes regional dishes
prepared with local produce. The mild and sunny climate of the
area makes it a pleasant place for walking, cycling or
discovering the natural splendour of the Var region.
In town centre Near motorway
42 en suite (bth/shr) (13 fmly) TV in all bedrooms Direct dial
from all bedrooms Licensed Full central heating Open
parking available Child discount available Last d 20.30hrs
Languages spoken: English,Italian,German,Russian,Spanish
MEALS: Full breakfast 45FF Lunch 49-120FF Dinner fr 89FF✱
CARDS: 😊 🔁 Travellers cheques

ILE-DE-LA-BARTHÉLASSE Vaucluse

★ ★ La Ferme
chemin des Bois, Ile de la Barthelasse *84000*
☎ 490825753 FAX 490271547
(From A7 exit at Avignon Nord, towards Avignon, take N100
over bridge turn right onto D228, hotel is 5kms)

The house stands peacefully amidst leafy surroundings just minutes away from the bustle of the town. It offers a delightful garden and in the summer meals are served on the terrace. The bedrooms are comfortable and equipped with modern facilities, there is a congenial bar, and a high standard of home-cooking is achieved by the proprietor.
Near river Forest area
Closed Nov-Mar
20 en suite (bth/shr) No smoking in 3 bedrooms TV in all bedrooms Direct dial from all bedrooms Licensed Full central heating Open parking available Outdoor swimming pool Open terrace Last d 21.30hrs Languages spoken: Italian
ROOMS: (room only) s 330-360FF; d 360-450FF
MEALS: Continental breakfast 50FF Lunch 110-210FF Dinner 110-210FF
CARDS: ●● ▦ ▆ JCB Travellers cheques

ISSAMBRES, LES Var

★ ★ La Quiétude
N98 *83380*
☎ 494969434 FAX 494496782
Near sea Near beach Near motorway
Closed 15 Oct-20 Feb
19 en suite (bth/shr) (6 fmly) (17 with balcony) TV in all bedrooms Direct dial from all bedrooms Room-safe Licensed Full central heating Open parking available Supervised Child discount available 12yrs Outdoor swimming pool Open terrace Covered terrace Last d 21.30hrs Languages spoken: English Spanish
MEALS: Continental breakfast 36FF Lunch 90-170FF&alc Dinner 90-170FF&alc✱
CARDS: ●● ▆ Travellers cheques

JOUCAS Vaucluse

★ ★ Hostellerie des Comandeurs
Le Village *84220*
☎ 490057801 FAX 490057447
The hotel enjoys a peaceful setting in a small village, surrounded by lavender and rosemary fields. It features comfortable bedrooms - most with fine views over the surrounding countryside - and a restaurant which serves a range of Provençale dishes.
Forest area
Closed 1 wk Nov & Jan
13 en suite (shr) TV in all bedrooms Radio in rooms Direct dial from all bedrooms Licensed Full central heating Open parking available Supervised Child discount available 10yrs Outdoor swimming pool Boule Open terrace V meals Last d 21.00hrs Languages spoken: English, German
CARDS: ●● ▆ Travellers cheques

LAVANDOU, LE Var

★ ★ Auberge de la Falaise
34 bd de la Balèine, St-Clair *83980*
☎ 494710135 FAX 494717948
This small, charming inn offers splendid views over the deep-blue sea and the Rochers de la Baleine. There is a delightful garden and beyond that a fine sandy beach, which makes it the ideal venue for a seaside holiday. The pleasant bedrooms offer a good level of comfort, furthermore there is a sunny terrace and a restaurant which serves dishes to suit all tastes.
Near sea Near beach
Closed 26 Oct-24 Mar
30 rms (29 bth/shr) 1 rooms in annexe (7 with balcony) TV in

all bedrooms Licensed Night porter Full central heating Open parking available Supervised Open terrace Languages spoken: English, German, Italian
CARDS: ●● ▆ Travellers cheques

★ ★ ★ Belle Vue
St-Clair *83980*
☎ 494710106 FAX 494716472
Located on the beautiful Côte-D'Azur, the hotel Belle-Vue affords stunning views over the bay and beaches. Amidst green scenery it offers all the ingredients for a relaxing holiday; tranquillity, plenty of sunshine, and deep blue skies. The well equipped bedrooms are complemented by the restaurant which serves a choice of delightful regional specialities.
Near sea Near beach
Closed Nov-Mar
19 en suite (bth/shr) (7 with balcony) TV in all bedrooms STV Radio in rooms Direct dial from all bedrooms Mini-bar in all bedrooms Full central heating Open parking available Covered parking available (charged) Languages spoken: English, German
CARDS: ●● ▦ ▆ ⑩ Travellers cheques

★ ★ ★ Hotel Les Roches
1 av des 3 Dauphins-Aiguebelle *83980*
☎ 494710507 FAX 494710840
(from Toulon A57 towards Hyeres-Le Lavandou. D559 until Aiguebelle)
Nestling in a rocky cliff facing the Iles D'Or, terraces cascade down to a private beach. The comfortable rooms are furnished with antiques and original paintings by Provencal artists adorn the walls. The restaurant features fresh local seafood and a selection of cheese from the surrounding hills, an interesting wine list is offered to complete your meal.
Near sea Near beach Forest area Near motorway
Closed Nov-Mar
38 en suite (bth/shr) (12 fmly) (38 with balcony) No smoking in 2 bedrooms TV in all bedrooms STV Direct dial from all bedrooms Mini-bar in all bedrooms Room-safe Licensed Night porter Full central heating Air conditioning in bedrooms Open parking available Outdoor swimming pool Solarium Open terrace Last d 22.00hrs Languages spoken: English, German, Italian & Spanish
ROOMS: d 1900-2500FF
MEALS: Lunch 250-350FFalc Dinner 320-520FF&alc✱
CARDS: ●● ▦ ▆ ⑩ Travellers cheques

LOURMARIN Vaucluse

★ ★ ★ Guilles
rte de Vaugines *84160*
☎ 490683055 FAX 490683741
(From A7 exit at Senas follow signs for Mallemort(D23), then take D973 to Lauris,then D27 to Lourmarin)
Forest area
Closed 6 Nov-end Feb
28 en suite (bth) (1 fmly) (8 with balcony) TV in all bedrooms Mini-bar in all bedrooms Licensed Night porter Full central heating Open parking available Supervised Child discount available 12yrs Outdoor swimming pool Tennis Boule Open terrace Covered terrace Last d 21.15hrs Languages spoken: English,Italian
MEALS: Continental breakfast 65FF Lunch fr 145FF&alc Dinner 185-320FF&alc✱

MARIGNANE Bouches-du-Rhône

★ ★ ★ Sofitel Marseille Aéroport
Aéroport de Marseille Provence *13700*
☎ 442784278 FAX 442784270
The Sofitel chain comprises of a group of very fine modern, comfortable hotels at the four star level. Bedrooms have been carefully designed to cater to guests relaxation and well being and the restaurants facilities offer fine cuisine in pleasant surroundings. They cater for business clientele with excellent conference and meeting facilities.
Near sea Near motorway
179 en suite (bth) No smoking in 22 bedrooms TV in all bedrooms STV Radio in rooms Mini-bar in all bedrooms Licensed Lift Night porter Full central heating Air conditioning in bedrooms Open parking available Supervised Child discount available Outdoor swimming pool Tennis Sauna Solarium Gym Boule Jacuzzi/spa Open terrace Covered terrace ping pong Last d 24.00hrs Languages spoken: English,Arabic,German,Italian,Spanish
MEALS: Full breakfast 70FF Lunch 135-195FF Dinner 135-195FF✱
CARDS: 🌑 💳 🌑 Travellers cheques

MARSEILLE Bouches-du-Rhône

★ ★ Climat de France
6 rue Beauvau *13001*
☎ 491330233 Cen Res 164460123 FAX 491332134
(adjacent to the port area)
Right on the border of the 'Vieux Port' and the historic centre, the hotel Climat de France features attractively furnished bedrooms which offer comfortable accommodation. There is a cosy bar to relax or have a chat, whilst the restaurant serves a high standard of cooking consisting of regional dishes of good flavour.
Near sea In town centre
49 en suite (bth) No smoking in 25 bedrooms TV in all bedrooms Direct-dial available Licensed Lift Night porter Air conditioning in bedrooms Bicycle rental Languages spoken: English & Spanish
CARDS: 🌑 💳

★ ★ Climat de France
13 rue Lafon *13006*
☎ 491333434 FAX 491541059
(from highway take direction of "Prefecture" until boulevard "d'Athene" continue to green bridge then 1st street on the right (rue Dreudré), then 1st on left (rue Longate), then 1st street on right)
Situated in the heart of Marseille near the Préfecture, and only five minutes from the Old Port, the hotel offers comfortable bedrooms with private facilities. Guests can enjoy a meal on the sunny patio or sample a variety of tasty dishes. as well as a generous buffet and delicious desserts.
Near sea In town centre
83 en suite (bth) (17 fmly) No smoking in 4 bedrooms TV in all bedrooms Direct dial from all bedrooms Licensed Lift Night porter Full central heating Open parking available Covered parking available Supervised Child discount available 12yrs Open terrace Covered terrace Last d 22.00hrs Languages spoken: English & German
ROOMS: (room only) s 305FF; d 305FF **Reductions over 1 night**
MEALS: Continental breakfast 35FF Lunch 88-118FF Dinner 88-118FF
CARDS: 🌑 💳 🌑 Travellers cheques

★ ★ ★ Holiday Inn Marseille
103 av du Prado *13008*
☎ 491831010 FAX 491798412
The hotel is located on the well-known Avenue du Prado close to some of the main tourist attractions. With its easy access, it offers well furnished bedrooms equipped with modern amenities. In the restaurant 'Le Mytilus' guests can enjoy traditional Provençal fare.
Near sea Near beach In town centre Near motorway
119 en suite (bth/shr) (4 fmly) (8 with balcony) No smoking in 22 bedrooms TV in all bedrooms STV Radio in rooms Direct dial from all bedrooms Mini-bar in all bedrooms Room-safe Licensed Lift Night porter Full central heating Air conditioning in bedrooms Open parking available (charged) Covered parking available (charged) Supervised Child discount available 12yrs Open terrace V meals Languages spoken: English,Spanish
ROOMS: (room only) s 510-950FF; d 510-950FF
MEALS: Full breakfast 55FF Continental breakfast 55FF✱
CARDS: 🌑 💳 🌑 Travellers cheques

★ ★ ★ New Hotel Bompard
2 rue des Flots Bleus *13007*
☎ 491521093 FAX 491310214
Set in the leafy surroundings of a park, this large beautiful building provides an oasis of peace. Situated near the bustling town centre and not far from the sea, it features a large salon-bar, comfortable bedrooms decorated in pastel shades, and a shaded terrace with views of the park. The hotel does not have restaurant facilities, but there is choice of eating options nearby.
Near sea Forest area Near motorway
46 en suite (bth/shr) (4 fmly) (9 with balcony) TV in all bedrooms STV Radio in rooms Direct dial from all bedrooms Mini-bar in all bedrooms Licensed Lift Night porter Full central heating Air conditioning in bedrooms Open parking available Supervised Indoor swimming pool Outdoor swimming pool Solarium Boule Open terrace Covered terrace Languages spoken: English,German
CARDS: 🌑 💳 🌑 Travellers cheques

★ ★ ★ Novotel Marseille Est-La Valentine
St-Menet *13011*
☎ 491439060 FAX 491270674
Novotel offer their clients good quality accommodation in modern, well equipped bedrooms and have refined restaurants serving good quality cuisine They have excellent business meeting and conference facilities and some have food and beverages available 24 hours a day. All their hotels have at least one bedroom for disabled guests.
131 en suite (bth/shr) (25 fmly) No smoking on premises TV in all bedrooms STV Radio in rooms Direct dial from all bedrooms Mini-bar in all bedrooms Licensed Lift Night porter Full central heating Air conditioning in bedrooms Open parking available Supervised Child discount available 16yrs Outdoor swimming pool Tennis Solarium Boule Open terrace Covered terrace Last d 24.00hrs Languages spoken: English,German,Italian
CARDS: 🌑 💳 🌑 Travellers cheques

★ ★ ★ St-Ferréol's Hotel
19 rue Pisançon *13001*
☎ 491331221 FAX 491542997
Set in the most picturesque pedestrian street in Marseille, and 150 metres from the Old Port and the Canebière, this attractive hotel has a cosy, elegant interior. Stylish rooms - with decorations which are inspired by famous painters, such as

Cézanne, Gauguin and van Gogh - offer a high standard of comfort and are equipped with luxurious marble bathrooms. There is a congenial bar which is the ideal spot to relax or get acquainted with fellow guests.
In town centre
Closed 1-21 Aug
20 rms (2 fmly) TV in all bedrooms STV Radio in rooms Direct dial from all bedrooms Lift Night porter Child discount available 4yrs Jacuzzi/spa Languages spoken: English,German,Spanish,Arabic
CARDS: ● ▬ ▬ Travellers cheques

MAUSSANE-LES-ALPILLES Bouches-du-Rhône

★ ★ Hostellerie Les Magnanarelles
104 av Vallée des Baux *13520*
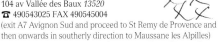
☎ 490543025 FAX 490545004
(exit A7 Avignon Sud and proceed to St Remy de Provence and then onwards in southerly direction to Maussane les Alpilles)
In a pretty village at the heart of Provence. Everything at the hotel is dedicated to the sun, tranquility and the flavours of the Provençal countryside, and the bedrooms also reflect this.
Forest area In town centre Near motorway
Closed 3 Jan-28 Feb
18 en suite (bth/shr) Some rooms in annexe (2 fmly) (1 with balcony) TV in 1 bedroom Direct dial from all bedrooms Licensed Full central heating Open parking available (charged) Supervised Child discount available 7yrs Tennis Covered terrace Last d 21.00hrs Languages spoken: English & Spanish
ROOMS: (room only) s fr 230FF; d 250-280FF
MEALS: Full breakfast 35FF Lunch 150-220FFalc Dinner 150-220FFalc
CARDS: ● ▬

★ ★ ★ Hotel Val Baussenc
132 av de la Vallée-de-Baux *13520*
☎ 490543890 FAX 490543336
This Provençal villa is surrounded by pine trees and orchards. All the individually appointed bedrooms have a private terrace and offer fine views over the delightful countryside.
Forest area
Closed Jan-end Feb
21 en suite (bth/shr) (18 with balcony) TV in all bedrooms Licensed Open parking available Supervised Child discount available 12yrs Outdoor swimming pool Open terrace Covered terrace Last d 21.00hrs Languages spoken: English,German,Spanish
MEALS: Dinner 180-240FF✱
CARDS: ● ▬ ▬ ᴑ Travellers cheques

MONETIER-LES-BAINS, LES Hautes-Alpes

★ ★ ★ Auberge du Choucas
17 rue de la Fruitière *05220*
☎ 492244273 FAX 492245160
Situated in the ancient alpine village of Monetier-Les-Bains, this charming country inn warmly welcomes its visitors. The bedrooms are very comfortable, and guests can relax in the intimacy of the lounge with its open fireplace. The vaulted restaurant serves an excellent cuisine including regional specialities.
Near river Forest area Near motorway
Some rooms in annexe No smoking in 2 bedrooms TV available Radio in rooms Direct-dial available Licensed Full central heating Air conditioning in bedrooms Child discount available Open terrace Languages spoken: English
CARDS: ● ▬ Travellers cheques

MONTFAVET Vaucluse

★ ★ Auberge de Bonpas
rte de Cavaillon *84140*
☎ 490230764 FAX 490230700
Traditional inn with comfortable bedrooms and a restaurant serving gastronomic meals.
Near river Near motorway
11 rms (7 bth 3 shr) (3 fmly) TV in all bedrooms STV Direct dial from all bedrooms Mini-bar in 3 bedrooms Licensed Full central heating Open parking available Supervised Child discount available Outdoor swimming pool Riding Solarium Bicycle rental Open terrace Table tennis Last d 22.00hrs Languages spoken: English & Spanish
ROOMS: (room only) s 190-360FF; d 230-420FF ✱
Reductions over 1 night
MEALS: Full breakfast 48FF Continental breakfast 48FF Lunch 100-268FF&alc Dinner 100-268FF&alc✱
CARDS: ● ▬ ▬ ᴑ Travellers cheques

★ ★ ★ Frènes
av des Vertes Rives, Montfavet *84140*
☎ 490311793 FAX 490239503
This beautiful 19th-century residence is set in the shade of a flower-filled park close to Avignon. The comfortable spacious bedrooms in the main house are full of antique furniture whereas those in the annexes are furnished in a more contemporary style. The restaurant serves a delicious Provençal cuisine accompanied by an excellent wine list featuring great wines such as Châteauneuf-du-Pape and Côte de Provence vintages. The hotel is featured on the cover of this guide.
Forest area
Closed Nov-1 Apr
20 en suite (bth/shr) (4 fmly) (2 with balcony) TV in all bedrooms STV Radio in rooms Mini-bar in all bedrooms Licensed Lift Night porter Full central heating Air conditioning in bedrooms Open parking available Covered parking available Supervised Child discount available 15yrs Outdoor swimming pool Sauna Solarium Pool table Jacuzzi/spa Open terrace Covered terrace V meals Last d 21.30hrs Languages spoken: English,German,Italian,Spanish
MEALS: Full breakfast 90FF Lunch 195-400FF&alc Dinner 195-400FF&alc✱
CARDS: ● ▬ ▬ ᴑ Travellers cheques

MOUSTIERS-STE-MARIE Alpes-de-Haute-Provence

★ ★ ★ Bastide de Moustiers
quartier St-Michel *04360*
☎ 492704747 FAX 492704748
A secluded 17th-century fortified farmhouse, offering secluded peace, tucked away at the start of the Verdon Gorge. La Bastide de Moustiers has been restored in the traditional regional manner.
Near river Near lake Forest area
Closed Jan-mid Mar
12 en suite (bth/shr) 7 rooms in annexe TV in all bedrooms Direct dial from all bedrooms Mini-bar in all bedrooms Room-safe Licensed Night porter Full central heating Air conditioning in bedrooms Open parking available (charged) Outdoor swimming pool (heated) Bicycle rental Open terrace V meals
ROOMS: (room only) s 800-1400FF; d 900-1500FF

NOVES Bouches-du-Rhône

★ ★ ★ ★ **Auberge de Noves**
rte de Châteaurénard *13550*
☎ 490941921 FAX 490944776
The Auberge de Noves is a charming establishment set in the beautiful Provençal countryside. Surrounded by tall trees and fragrant flowers it has been in the capable hands of the Lalleman family for three generations and offers all the ingredients for a memorable stay. A generous breakfast is served under the shady trees, country-style guest rooms offer comfortable accommodation, and a candlelit restaurant serves a host of excellent dishes from the region.
Near river Forest area Near motorway
23 en suite (bth/shr) (3 fmly) (13 with balcony) TV in all bedrooms STV Licensed Lift Night porter Full central heating Air conditioning in bedrooms Open parking available Covered parking available (charged) Supervised Child discount available 8yrs Outdoor swimming pool (heated) Tennis Fishing Boule Bicycle rental Open terrace V meals Last d 22.00hrs Languages spoken: English,German,Italian
CARDS: ●● ▩ ▆ ● Travellers cheques

OPPÈDE Vaucluse

★ ★ ★ **Mas des Capélans**
Le Plan des Capelans N100 *84580*
☎ 490769904 FAX 490769029
(From A7 exit Avignon Sud, follow directions for Apt on N100. After Coustellet follow signs for Oppede)
This 18th-century house has been splendidly converted in modern day accommodation. The spacious, comfortable bedrooms command stunning views over the surrounding countryside. During summer meals are served in the courtyard under the mulberry trees, whilst in winter the restaurant with open fireplace provides a cosy setting.
Near river Forest area
RS 16 Nov-14 Feb
10 en suite (bth/shr) (2 fmly) (1 with balcony) No smoking on premises TV in all bedrooms Radio in rooms Licensed Full central heating Open parking available Supervised Outdoor swimming pool (heated) Solarium Pool table Boule Open terrace Last d 20.30hrs Languages spoken: English,German
ROOMS: (room only) d 600-900FF ✱ **Reductions over 1 night**
MEALS: Full breakfast 55FF Dinner 155FF
CARDS: ●● ▩ ▆ Travellers cheques

ORANGE Vaucluse

★ ★ ★ **Arène**
pl de Langes *84100*
☎ 490341095 FAX 490349162
(from A7 exit Orange in the direction of the town centre)
This attractive hotel stands in a small square under mature plane trees in the historic heart of Orange. It offers individually styled bedrooms equipped with every modern day convenience which provide a high level of comfort. In addition it has an attractive flower-decked terrace and a delightful restaurant which serves a wide range of dishes.
In town centre Near motorway
Closed early-end of Nov
30 en suite (bth/shr) (4 fmly) (12 with balcony) TV in all bedrooms STV Direct dial from all bedrooms Mini-bar in all bedrooms Room-safe Licensed Night porter Full central heating Air conditioning in bedrooms Open parking available

(charged) Covered parking available (charged) Child discount available Open terrace V meals Last d 21.30hrs Languages spoken: English German & Spanish
ROOMS: (room only) s 340-500FF; d 340-500FF
Reductions over 1 night
MEALS: Lunch 100-350FF&alc Dinner 100-350FF&alc
CARDS: ●● ▩ ▆ ● Travellers cheques

PALUD-SUR-VERDON, LA Alpes-de-Haute-Provence

★ ★ **Le Panaoramic**
rte de Moustiers *04120*
☎ 492773507 FAX 492773017
(on the D952 west of La Palud-sur-Verdon)
From everywhere in the hotel guests have splendid views of the Verdon Gorge. With a multitude of leisure opportunities on offer in the surrounding area, it is the ideal venue for a sporting holiday. Comfortable bedrooms with balcony or terrace are equipped with modern amenities and a range of delicious dishes is served in the attractive restaurant.
Near river Near lake Forest area
Closed 12 Nov-Etr
20 en suite (bth/shr) (3 fmly) (8 with balcony) TV in all bedrooms STV Direct dial from all bedrooms Licensed Full central heating Open parking available Supervised Child discount available Outdoor swimming pool (heated) Boule Open terrace Covered terrace V meals Last d 21.00hrs Languages spoken: English
ROOMS: (room only) s 350-410FF; d 370-430FF
MEALS: Full breakfast 40FF Continental breakfast 40FF Dinner fr 110FF&alc
CARDS: ●● ▆ Travellers cheques

PERNES-LES-FONTAINES Vaucluse

★ ★ **L'Hermitage**
rte de Carpentras *84210*
☎ 490665141 FAX 490613641
Centrally located for visits to all the places of interest in the region, this attractive establishment is set in a park with a large salt-water swimming pool. The shaded terrace with wisteria, the magnificent plane trees in the garden and terracotta pots with flowers make the park an idyllic setting.
20 en suite (bth) (5 fmly) (2 with balcony) TV in all bedrooms Direct dial from all bedrooms Licensed Open parking available Supervised Child discount available 6yrs Outdoor swimming pool Boule Open terrace Languages spoken: English
ROOMS: (room only) s 280-370FF; d 300-380FF ✱
CARDS: ●● ▩ ▆ ● Travellers cheques

PERTUIS Vaucluse

★ ★ ★ **Sévan** (Best Western)
rte de Manosque *84120*
☎ 490791930 FAX 490793577
Tucked away amidst the magnolias and olive trees, this modern hotel offers its visitors a warm and friendly welcome. The gourmet restaurant serves a distinct, robust Provençal cuisine. The spacious bedrooms, equipped with modern amenities, are complemented by an unsurpassed range of leisure facilities available to the guests.
Near river Forest area
Closed 3 Jan-14 Jan
36 en suite (bth/shr) (4 fmly) (20 with balcony) TV in all bedrooms STV Direct dial from all bedrooms Mini-bar in all bedrooms Licensed Lift Night porter Open parking available

Supervised Child discount available 12yrs Outdoor swimming pool Tennis Sauna Pool table Boule Mini-golf Bicycle rental Open terrace Table tennis,night club,volley ball Last d 22.00hrs Languages spoken: English,German,Spanish
ROOMS: (room only) s 360-500FF; d 460-600FF
MEALS: Full breakfast 59FF Continental breakfast 46FF Lunch 135-180FF Dinner 135-180FF
CARDS: ✷ ▦ ▨ ◑ Travellers cheques

PIOLENC Vaucluse

★ ★ Auberge de L'Orangerie
4 rue de l'Ormeau *84420*
☎ 490295988 FAX 490296774

(from North follow A7 South from Lyon and exit at South Montelimar, following N7 south. After 40km -in Piolenc, turn left at post officeand hotel is in park.)
Set in the heart of a pretty village in Provence, this 18th century inn is situated in the shade of old trees. It features cosy guest accommodation decorated with period pieces, providing a good level of comfort. The cuisine is based on regional recipes with well balanced flavours and ingredients.
Near river Forest area In town centre Near motorway
6 rms (5 bth/shr) (2 fmly) (1 with balcony) TV in 5 bedrooms Direct dial from 4 bedrooms Licensed Full central heating Open parking available Supervised No children Solarium Open terrace V meals Last d 21.30hrs Languages spoken: English German Spanish
ROOMS: (room only) d 300-480FF
MEALS: Full breakfast 45FF Lunch 90-200FF Dinner 140-200FF
CARDS: ✷ ▨ Eurocard Travellers cheques

PONTET, LE Vaucluse

★ ★ ★ ★ Hostellerie des Agassins
Lieu-dit Le Pigeonnier *84130*
☎ 490324291 FAX 490320829
The hotel des Agassins is located just outside Avignon. It has an enchanting interior with cosy lounges, tiled floors and bedrooms with flower-filled balconies. Together with a lovely collection of paintings adorning the walls and its restaurant, reputedly the best in the region, it offers a charming stetting for a relaxing stay.
Near river Near lake Forest area Near motorway
Closed Jan-1 Feb
30 en suite (bth) (26 with balcony) No smoking in 5 bedrooms TV in all bedrooms STV Radio in rooms Mini-bar in all bedrooms Licensed Lift Night porter Full central heating Air conditioning in bedrooms Open parking available Supervised Child discount available 6yrs Outdoor swimming pool (heated) Tennis Solarium Boule Bicycle rental Open terrace Covered

terrace Last d 22.00hrs Languages spoken: English,German,Italian,Spanish
MEALS: Full breakfast 75FF Continental breakfast 75FF Lunch 100-380FF&alc Dinner 185-380FF&alc ✱
CARDS: ✷ ▦ ▨ ◑ Travellers cheques

PONTEVES Var

★ ★ ★ Le Rouge Gorge
83670
☎ 494770397
Situated in open countryside between the Verdon Gorge and the Côte d'Azur, the hotel offers a relaxing stay with plenty of fresh air in a mild climate. Bedrooms are furnished in a comfortable fashion and offer all modern facilities. The restaurant serves regional dishes and the surrounding countryside offers plenty of walking opportunities.
Near river Forest area
10 en suite (bth/shr) (2 fmly) No smoking on premises TV in all bedrooms Direct dial from all bedrooms Full central heating Open parking available Supervised Child discount available Outdoor swimming pool Boule Bicycle rental Open terrace Covered terrace Last d 21.00hrs Languages spoken: English
CARDS: ✷ ▨ Travellers cheques

PUY-ST-VINCENT Hautes-Alpes

★ ★ La Pendine
05290
☎ 492233262 FAX 492234663
The hotel is situated at the foot of the slopes in the international winter sport resort of Puy-Saint-Vincent. Accommodation is comfortable with modern facilities, there are two restaurants which serve a high standard of cooking, a bar and a garden with terrace where on fine days meals and drinks are served.
Forest area
Closed 11 Apr-19 Jun & 11 Sep-15 Dec
28 rms 6 rooms in annexe (2 fmly) TV in all bedrooms Direct dial from all bedrooms Licensed Full central heating Open parking available Child discount available 8yrs Pool table Boule Open terrace Last d 21.45hrs Languages spoken: Italian
CARDS: ✷ ▨ Travellers cheques

RAMATUELLE Var

★ ★ ★ Hotel les Bouis
rte de Pampelonne *83350*
☎ 494798761 FAX 494798520
(3km NE of Ramatuell, off D93)
A welcoming Provencal house, nestling among a forest of umbrella pines, lawns stretch from the panoramic terraces down to the pool with its loungers, parasols and an open dining area for barbecues. The decor inside the house is warm and light, air conditioned guest rooms offer breathtaking views from private terraces.
Near sea Near beach Near motorway
Closed mid Oct-mid Mar
17 en suite (bth/shr) (17 with balcony) TV in all bedrooms STV Direct dial from all bedrooms Mini-bar in all bedrooms Room-safe Licensed Night porter Full central heating Air conditioning in bedrooms Open parking available Supervised Outdoor swimming pool Solarium Bicycle rental Open terrace Languages spoken: English & German
ROOMS: (room only) d 950-1180FF ✱
MEALS: Lunch 120-140FFalc
CARDS: ✷ ▦ ▨ Travellers cheques

★ ★ ★ Ferme d'Augustin
Plage de Tahiti *83350*
☎ 494559700 FAX 494974030
(Close to the Tahiti Beach)
Near sea Forest area
Closed Oct-Mar
46 en suite (bth/shr) (16 fmly) (6 with balcony) TV available
Radio in rooms Direct dial from all bedrooms Mini-bar in all
bedrooms Room-safe Licensed Lift Night porter Full central
heating Air conditioning in bedrooms Open parking available
Supervised Outdoor swimming pool (heated) Solarium
Jacuzzi/spa Bicycle rental Open terrace Languages spoken:
English,German,Italian,Spanish
ROOMS: (room only) s fr 580FF; d 1800FF ✱
CARDS: ●● ▉▉ ▆▆ Travellers cheques

<hr>

RAPHÈLE-LES-ARLES Bouches-du-Rhône

★ ★ ★ Auberge La Feniere
N453 *13280*
☎ 490984744 FAX 490984839
Near river Near lake Near sea Forest area Near motorway
25 en suite (bth/shr) (2 fmly) (3 with balcony) TV in all
bedrooms Licensed Full central heating Open parking
available Covered parking available (charged) Supervised
Child discount available 6yrs Boule Open terrace Covered
terrace Last d 21.30hrs Languages spoken: English
MEALS: Continental breakfast 60FF Lunch 100-160FF&alc
Dinner 100-160FF&alc✱
CARDS: ●● ▉▉ ▆▆ ⓓ Travellers cheques

<hr>

REILLANNE Alpes-de-Haute-Provence

Auberge De Reillanne
04110
☎ 492764595
Near motorway
RS Wed
7 en suite (bth/shr) (2 fmly) Direct dial from all bedrooms
Mini-bar in all bedrooms Licensed Night porter Full central
heating Open parking available Child discount available 10yrs
Last d 21.00hrs Languages spoken: English,German
ROOMS: (room only) s 280FF; d 380FF
MEALS: Full breakfast 50FF Continental breakfast 50FF
Dinner 135-185FF
CARDS: ●● ▆▆

<hr>

ST-BONNET-EN-CHAMPSEUR Hautes-Alpes

★ ★ La Cremaillère
05500
☎ 492500060 FAX 492500157
The hotel enjoys a tranquil, leafy setting on the edge of the
village of Saint Bonnet with its healthy dry and sunny climate.
It has guest rooms with modern appointments and a shaded
park with a terrace from where guests have magnificent views
towards the Dévoluy mountain range.
Near river Near lake Forest area Near motorway
Closed Oct-Mar
21 en suite (bth/shr) TV in all bedrooms Direct dial from all
bedrooms Licensed Full central heating Open parking
available Covered parking available (charged) Supervised
Child discount available Boule Open terrace Covered terrace
Last d 21.00hrs Languages spoken: English,German
MEALS: Continental breakfast 35FF Lunch 100-180FF Dinner
100-180FF✱
CARDS: ●● ▆▆ Travellers cheques

STES-MARIES-DE-LA-MER Bouches-du-Rhône

★ ★ ★ Hotel Clamador
route d'aigues Mortes *13460*
☎ 490978426 FAX 490979338
The hotel Clamador is a large, white farmhouse peacefully
situated one kilometre from the beach, between the Rhône and
the lakes. The bedrooms with modern facilities offer a good
level of comfort, and are complemented by a congenial bar
and a quiet reading room.
Near river Near sea Near beach
Closed 31 Oct-1 April
20 en suite (bth/shr) (7 with balcony) TV in all bedrooms STV
Direct dial from all bedrooms Licensed Night porter Full
central heating Open parking available Covered parking
available Child discount available 12yrs Outdoor swimming
pool Riding Solarium Boule Mini-golf Bicycle rental Open
terrace Languages spoken: English,Italian
ROOMS: (incl. full-board) s 290-360FF; d 365-420FF
Reductions over 1 night
CARDS: ●● ▉▉ ▆▆ ⓓ Travellers cheques

★ ★ ★ Mas de la Fouques
Stes-Maries *13640*
☎ 490978102 FAX 490478102
The hotel is situated in the heart of the Camargue, with its wild
horses, bulls and numerous birds in abundance. Located in a
peaceful spot away from the road, it features a sunny interior
which harmoniously blends with the delightful surroundings.
The bedrooms are bright and airy with large, good quality
beds offering the highest level of comfort, whilst the restaurant
serves a superb cuisine incorporating regional specialities.
Guests can also enjoy a drink or a meal on the poolside terrace
or relax in the cosy bar.
Near river Near lake Near sea Near beach
Closed 2 Nov-24 Mar
14 en suite (bth/shr) (1 fmly) (14 with balcony) TV in all
bedrooms Direct dial from all bedrooms Mini-bar in all
bedrooms Licensed Full central heating Air conditioning in
bedrooms Open parking available Supervised Child discount
available 7yrs Outdoor swimming pool (heated) Tennis
Fishing Riding Solarium Boule Bicycle rental Open terrace
Covered terrace V meals Last d 21.30hrs Languages spoken:
English,Italian
MEALS: Full breakfast 75FF Lunch 170-225FF&alc Dinner 225-
395FF&alc✱
CARDS: ●● ▉▉ ▆▆ ⓓ Eurocard Travellers cheques

★ ★ ★ Le Mithra
rte d'Aigues Mortes *13460*
☎ 490979940 FAX 490979773
(4kms from village, on D38)
The guest rooms at this hotel are built around a patio with
swimming pool. Mithra is right in the heart of the Camargue,
only four kilometres away from Les Saintes-Maries-de-la-Mer.
Near beach
20 en suite (bth/shr) TV in all bedrooms Direct dial from all
bedrooms Licensed Full central heating Open parking
available Supervised Child discount available 10yrs Outdoor
swimming pool Boule Bicycle rental Covered terrace Last d
22.00hrs
ROOMS: (room only) s 250-400FF; d 250-400FF
MEALS: Full breakfast 35FF Continental breakfast 35FF Lunch
100FF&alc Dinner 100FF&alc
CARDS: ●● ▆▆ ⓓ Travellers cheques

★★ Hostellerie du Pont de Gau

rte d'Arles *13460*
☎ 490978153 FAX 490979854
The Camargue region is a mass of lagoons and reeds, populated by pink flamingos and white horses. The hotel is located right in the heart of the Ornithological Park in a setting that is typical of the region. Visitors are offered warm hospitality and a distinct regional cuisine which incorporates game, meats, fresh water and sea fish.
Near motorway
Closed 5 Jan-20 Feb
9 en suite (bth) TV in all bedrooms STV Direct dial from all bedrooms Licensed Full central heating Open parking available Child discount available 10yrs Last d 21.30hrs
Languages spoken: English
MEALS: Full breakfast 32FF Lunch 98-255FF Dinner 98-255FF✱
CARDS: 💳 💳 💳 Travellers cheques

ST-MARTIN-DE-CASTILLON Vaucluse

★★ Lou Caleu

84750
☎ 490752888 FAX 490752549
The hotel is set in the nature Park of Luberon, in the very heart of Provence. The bedrooms are divided over two detached houses, situated in extensive wooded grounds and heath lands. The restaurant serves from a large choice of set menus which feature traditional dishes and regional specialities. The hotel has its own riding-school and is therefore a good base to explore the countryside on horseback.
Near river Forest area Near motorway
16 en suite (bth/shr) (8 fmly) (11 with balcony) TV in all bedrooms STV Mini-bar in all bedrooms Licensed Full central heating Open parking available Covered parking available Supervised Child discount available 10yrs Outdoor swimming pool Tennis Riding Boule Bicycle rental Open terrace Covered terrace V meals Last d 22.00hrs Languages spoken: English,German
MEALS: Lunch 85-185FF Dinner 85-185FF✱
CARDS: 💳 💳 💳 Travellers cheques

ST-MAXIMIN-LA-SAINTE-BAUME Var

★★★ France

1-3 av Albert *83470*
☎ 494780014 FAX 494598380
(off A8)
This former coaching inn is located in the centre of town and provides a good base for trips to the Verdon Gorge, the Var coast and other places of interest in Provence. It offers pleasant bedrooms with modern amenities offering a high level of comfort and a well-known restaurant with a loyal following of discerning gourmets. The building itself is built on a plateau of overhanging rocks and waterfalls.
In town centre Near motorway
26 en suite (bth/shr) (2 fmly) TV in all bedrooms STV Direct dial from all bedrooms Night porter Full central heating Open parking available (charged) Covered parking available (charged) Supervised Child discount available 6yrs Outdoor swimming pool Open terrace Last d 22.00hrs Languages spoken: English, Italian
ROOMS: (room only) s 270-300FF; d 330-360FF
MEALS: Continental breakfast 45FF Lunch 120-240FF&alc Dinner 120-240FF&alc
CARDS: 💳 💳 💳 Travellers cheques

ST-RAPHAËL Var

★★★ Excelsior

193 bd Felix Martin *83700*
☎ 494950242 FAX 494953382
(Adjacent to the Casino)
The family hotel Excelsior enjoys an excellent position on the sea front promenade in St Raphaël, at 30 metres from the seafront attractions. The restaurant and terrace serve a superb Provençal cuisine, whilst the English-style pub boasts a selection of draught beers and exotic cocktails. The newly refurbished bedrooms are equipped with every modern convenience and offer a high standard of comfort. There is a choice of leisure opportunities and adult pursuits available in the vicinity.
Near sea In town centre
36 rms (34 bth/shr) (3 fmly) (3 with balcony) TV in all bedrooms STV Direct dial from all bedrooms Mini-bar in all bedrooms Licensed Lift Night porter Full central heating Air conditioning in bedrooms Open parking available (charged) Child discount available 8yrs Golf Open terrace V meals Last d 22.30hrs Languages spoken: English,German,Italian
ROOMS: s 230-280FF; d 620-720FF ✱ Reductions over 1 night
MEALS: Full breakfast 55FF Continental breakfast 55FF Lunch 128-190FF&alc Dinner 140-190FF&alc✱
CARDS: 💳 💳 💳 💳 Travellers cheques

★★★ Golf de Valescure

av Paul l'Hermité *83700*
☎ 494528500 FAX 494824188
Forest area
Closed 7-31 Jan & 14 Nov-22 Dec
40 en suite (bth) (40 with balcony) TV in all bedrooms STV Direct dial from all bedrooms Licensed Lift Night porter Full central heating Air conditioning in bedrooms Open parking available Supervised Child discount available 12yrs Outdoor swimming pool Golf Tennis Solarium Pool table Boule Mini-golf Open terrace Covered terrace Last d 22.00hrs Languages spoken: English,Dutch,German,Italian
CARDS: 💳 💳 💳 💳 Travellers cheques

★★★ La Potinière (Relais du Silence)

169 av de Boulouris *83700*
☎ 494952143 FAX 494952910
(N of N98)

Near sea Near beach Forest area
29 en suite (bth/shr) (11 fmly) (26 with balcony) No smoking in 1 bedroom TV in all bedrooms STV Radio in rooms Direct dial from all bedrooms Mini-bar in all bedrooms   *contd.*

Room-safe (charged) Night porter Full central heating Open parking available Covered parking available (charged) Supervised Child discount available 11yrs Indoor swimming pool (heated) Outdoor swimming pool Sauna Solarium Boule Bicycle rental Open terrace Wkly live entertainment Last d 21.00hrs Languages spoken: English Dutch Italian German
ROOMS: (room only) s 290-470FF; d 390-790FF
Reductions over 1 night Special breaks
MEALS: Full breakfast 70FF Continental breakfast 50FF Lunch 140FF Dinner fr 140FF&alc
CARDS: ●● ■■ ▆▆ ◐ Travellers cheques

ST-RÉMY-DE-PROVENCE Bouches-du-Rhône

Château de Roussan
rte de Tarascon
☎ 490921163 FAX 490925059
(the château is 2.5km from the centre of St Remy on the left hand side of the D99 towards Tarascon)
At the beginning of the 18th century, the Marquis of Ganges built this residence on the land of his ancestor Nostradamus. Located in peaceful countryside, in 6 hectares of park, the Château de Roussan ensures its guests a quiet pleasant stay in attractive and romantic surroundings.
Near motorway
21 en suite (bth/shr) Direct dial from all bedrooms Night porter Full central heating Open parking available Child discount available 14yrs Boule Open terrace Last d 21.30hrs Languages spoken: English, German & Spanish
ROOMS: (room only) s 430-750FF; d 430-750FF ✱
MEALS: Continental breakfast 60FF Lunch fr 89FF&alc Dinner 150-275FFalc✱
CARDS: ●● ■■ ▆▆ Travellers cheques

★ ★ ★ ★ **Domaine de Valmouriane**
petite rte des Baux *13210*
☎ 490924462 FAX 490923732
(exit Cavaillon motorway and follow signs to St Remy (D99), near St Remy take direction Beaucaire/Tarascon still on D99, in approx 2kms turn left direction Les Baux D27, hotel in 2kms on the right)
Discover the true Provence in this 18th century house halfway between St Remy-de Provence and Les Baux. Enjoy the peace of a wooded valley in the the heart of the Alpilles, in individual rooms with modern comforts.
Forest area
14 en suite (bth/shr) (2 fmly) (5 with balcony) TV in all bedrooms STV Direct dial from all bedrooms Mini-bar in all bedrooms Room-safe Licensed Lift Night porter Full central heating Air conditioning in bedrooms Open parking available Supervised Child discount available 12yrs Outdoor swimming pool (heated) Tennis Solarium Boule Jacuzzi/spa Covered terrace Last d 21.30hrs Languages spoken: English, German, Portugese & Spanish
ROOMS: (room only) s 890-1310FF; d 890-1310FF
MEALS: Continental breakfast 70FF Lunch 150-340FF&alc Dinner 200-340FF&alc
CARDS: ●● ■■ ▆▆ ◐ Travellers cheques

★ ★ ★ ★ **Hostellerie du Vallon de Valrugues**
Chemin Canto Cigalo *13210*
☎ 490920440 FAX 490924401
(From A7 exit Cavaillon head towards St-Rémy. At entrance to the town turn left and follow signs)
A Roman style villa with elegant bedrooms and a fine restaurant specialising in local cuisine.
Near lake Forest area

53 en suite (bth) (2 fmly) (30 with balcony) TV in all bedrooms STV Direct dial from all bedrooms Mini-bar in all bedrooms Licensed Lift Night porter Full central heating Air conditioning in bedrooms Open parking available Supervised Child discount available 14yrs Outdoor swimming pool Tennis Sauna Gym Pool table Boule Mini-golf Jacuzzi/spa Open terrace Wkly live entertainment Last d 21.30hrs Languages spoken: English, German, Italian, Spanish
ROOMS: s 680-870FF; d 1160-1480FF
MEALS: Full breakfast 95FF Continental breakfast 95FF Lunch 165-195FF&alc Dinner 280-460FF&alc
CARDS: ●● ■■ ▆▆ JCB Travellers cheques ●● ■■ ▆▆

★ ★ ★ **Le Mas des Carassins**
1 chemin Gaulois *13210*
☎ 490921548 FAX 490926347
(located near the Roman ruins, 10mins by foot from the town centre, by the D5)
An old house typical of the south of France, located in the tranquility of the Provençal countryside. Located at the foot of the Alpilles hills, ten minutes by foot from the village centre. A large garden and two lounges are available for guests use.
Near lake Forest area
Closed Nov-Mar
10 en suite (bth/shr) (2 fmly) Direct dial from all bedrooms Licensed Night porter Full central heating Open parking available Supervised Covered terrace Languages spoken: English & Italian
ROOMS: (room only) s 380FF; d 400-570FF
CARDS: ●● ▆▆ Travellers cheques

ST-SATURNIN-LÈS-APT Vaucluse

★ ★ **Des Voyageurs**
84490
☎ 490754208
This hotel is located in a small village, which has a 17th-century castle and fortified walls as well as pre-historic caves. A family-run establishment, it offers its visitors comfortable bedrooms, and a regional cuisine featuring game specialities when in season. The surrounding region offers varied leisure pursuits including walking and fishing.
Near lake Forest area In town centre
14 rms (5 fmly) (3 with balcony) Licensed Full central heating Open terrace V meals Languages spoken: English, German
CARDS: ●● ▆▆

ST-TROPEZ Var

★ ★ ★ ★ **La Mandarine**
rte de Tahiti *83990*
☎ 494790666 FAX 494973367
Near sea Forest area
Closed early May-mid Oct
43 en suite (bth) (12 fmly) (34 with balcony) TV in all bedrooms STV Direct dial from all bedrooms Mini-bar in all bedrooms Licensed Night porter Full central heating Air conditioning in bedrooms Open parking available Covered parking available (charged) Child discount available 7yrs Outdoor swimming pool (heated) Solarium Open terrace Last d 22.30hrs Languages spoken: English, German, Italian, Spanish
CARDS: ●● ■■ ▆▆ Travellers cheques

★ ★ ★ ★ **Ponche**
pl du Révelin, Port des Pêcheurs *83990*
☎ 494970253 FAX 494977861
Near sea Forest area In town centre

Closed Dec-Mar
18 en suite (bth/shr) 2 rooms in annexe (2 fmly) (4 with balcony) TV in all bedrooms STV Mini-bar in all bedrooms Licensed Lift Night porter Full central heating Air conditioning in bedrooms Open parking available (charged) Covered parking available (charged) Child discount available Open terrace V meals Last d 24.00hrs Languages spoken: English,Italian,German
CARDS: ●● ▧▧ ▨▨ Travellers cheques

★ ★ ★ ★ Residence de la Pinede
Plage de la Bouillabaisse *83991*
☎ 494970421 FAX 494977364
Near sea
Closed Nov-Apr
50 rms (4 fmly) (46 with balcony) TV available STV Radio in rooms Mini-bar in all bedrooms Licensed Lift Night porter Full central heating Air conditioning in bedrooms Open parking available Supervised Outdoor swimming pool (heated) Fishing Open terrace V meals Last d 22.30hrs Languages spoken: English,German,Italian,Spanish
CARDS: ●● ▧▧ ▨▨ ●》 Travellers cheques

★ ★ ★ Hotel Sube
quai Suffren *83990*
☎ 494973004 FAX 494548908
(A8 exit Le Muy take direction Sainte Maxime)
The only hotel in the old port of St Tropez, Le Sube will enchant you with intimate atmosphere. Fully renovated in Provençal style offering every comfort.
Near sea Near beach Forest area In town centre
30 en suite (bth/shr) (4 fmly) (9 with balcony) TV in all bedrooms STV Direct dial from all bedrooms Licensed Night porter Full central heating Air conditioning in bedrooms Open terrace Languages spoken: English & Italian
ROOMS: (room only) s fr 590FF; d 890-1500FF ✱
CARDS: ●● ▧▧ ▨▨ ●》 Travellers cheques

★ ★ ★ Les Cabanettes
N572 *13200* ✗✗✗✗✗✗
☎ 466873153 FAX 466873539
Near motorway
Closed 25 Jan-28 Feb
29 en suite (bth) (1 fmly) (29 with balcony) TV in all bedrooms Radio in rooms Direct dial from all bedrooms Mini-bar in all bedrooms Licensed Full central heating Air conditioning in bedrooms Open parking available Covered parking available (charged) Child discount available 12yrs Outdoor swimming pool Open terrace Covered terrace Last d 21.00hrs Languages spoken: German English Italian
ROOMS: (room only) d 435-435FF **Reductions over 1 night**
MEALS: Full breakfast 50FF Continental breakfast 50FF Lunch 130-190FF&alc Dinner 130-190FF&alc
CARDS: ●● ▧▧ ▨▨ ●》 Travellers cheques

★ ★ ★ ★ Abbaye de Sainte-Croix
rte du Val de Cuech *13300*
☎ 490562455 FAX 490563112
A restored 12th century monastery located at the foothills of the Alpilles. The original Roman style with vaulted ceilings and small windows has been retained and the abbey stands above the medieval city in a quiet and remote location with superb views over Provence.

Forest area
Closed early Nov-mid Mar RS half board obligatory at certain times
24 en suite (bth/shr) (1 fmly) (9 with balcony) TV in all bedrooms Direct dial from all bedrooms Mini-bar in all bedrooms Room-safe Licensed Full central heating Air conditioning in bedrooms Open parking available Supervised Child discount available 12yrs Outdoor swimming pool Boule Bicycle rental Open terrace Covered terrace Park Last d 21.30hrs Languages spoken: English,Italian,Spanish
ROOMS: (room only) s 760-1330FF; d 760-1330FF
MEALS: Full breakfast 130FF Continental breakfast 85FF Lunch 270-395FF&alc Dinner 395-440FF&alc
CARDS: ●● ▧▧ ▨▨ ●》 Travellers cheques

★ ★ Domaine de Roquerousse

rte d'Avignon *13300*
☎ 490595011 FAX 490595375
30 en suite (bth/shr) (8 with balcony) TV in all bedrooms Direct dial from all bedrooms Licensed Full central heating Open parking available Supervised Outdoor swimming pool Tennis Gym Pool table Boule Bicycle rental Covered terrace riding stables near by Last d 21.15hrs Languages spoken: English,Spanish
CARDS: ●● ▧▧ ▨▨ ●》 Travellers cheques

★ ★ ★ ★ Le Mas du Soleil
38 Chemin de Ste-Comé *13300*
☎ 490560653 FAX 490562152
Forest area
10 en suite (bth) TV in all bedrooms Direct dial from all bedrooms Mini-bar in all bedrooms Licensed Night porter Full central heating Air conditioning in bedrooms Open parking available Supervised Outdoor swimming pool Jacuzzi/spa Open terrace Covered terrace Last d 21.30hrs Languages spoken: English
CARDS: ●● ▧▧ ▨▨ Travellers cheques

★ ★ ★ Hostellerie du Val de Sault
Ancien chemin d'Aurel *84390*
☎ 490640141 FAX 296641274
Forest area
Closed 6 Nov-28 Mar
11 rms (11 fmly) (11 with balcony) TV in all bedrooms Mini-bar in all bedrooms Full central heating Open parking available Supervised Outdoor swimming pool (heated) Tennis Sauna Solarium Gym Open terrace Last d 21.30hrs Languages spoken: English,Italian
MEALS: Full breakfast 59FF Continental breakfast 59FF Lunch 123-480FF&alc Dinner 149-480FF&alc✱
CARDS: ●● ▧▧ ▨▨

★ ★ ★ Deux Rocs
pl Font d'Amont *83440*
☎ 191760732 FAX 191760060
The hotel is located in the historic village of Seillans, which inspired the famous painter Max Ernst, who spend the last years of his life here. Facing two huge rocks and sheltered by the ramparts of the village, the hotel is an 18th-century manor house where a traditional interior is combined with modern comfort. All the bedrooms are personally styled with different wall-paper and curtains, and offer comfortable
contd.

accommodation. The restaurant serves a classic cuisine, which in summer also can be enjoyed on the terrace under the plane trees, with the cicadas singing in the background.
In town centre
Closed Nov-Mar
14 en suite (bth/shr) Direct dial from all bedrooms Licensed Full central heating Child discount available 12yrs Open terrace V meals Last d 21.00hrs Languages spoken: English,German,Dutch
ROOMS: (room only) s fr 280FF; d 280-550FF
MEALS: Continental breakfast 45FF Lunch 90-220FF&alc Dinner 145-220FF&alc
CARDS: ●● ▆▆ Travellers cheques

SÉRIGNAN-DU-COMTAT Vaucluse

★ ★ ★ Hostellerie du Vieux Chateau
rte de St-Cécile *84830*
☎ 490700558 FAX 490700562
This 18th-century farmhouse is situated in a small village along the wine route and surrounded by lush, green countryside. A warm, cheerful welcome awaits guests upon arrival by the owners Anne-Marie and Jean-Pierre Truchot. Meals are served in the informal dining-room or in summer in the shade of an ancient plane tree. The attractive guest accommodation has private facilities and offers a high standard of comfort.
Near river Forest area In town centre
Closed 20-30 Dec
7 en suite (bth/shr) TV in all bedrooms Licensed Full central heating Open parking available Supervised Child discount available Outdoor swimming pool Solarium Jacuzzi/spa Open terrace V meals Last d 21.30hrs Languages spoken: English
CARDS: ●● ▆▆ ▆▆ Travellers cheques

SEYNE-SUR-MER, LA Var

★ ★ ★ Novotel Toulon la Seyne
La Camp Laurent *83500*
☎ 494630950 FAX 494630376
Novotel offer their clients good quality accommodation in modern, well equipped bedrooms and have refined restaurants serving good quality cuisine They have excellent business meeting and conference facilities and some have food and beverages available 24 hours a day. All their hotels have at least one bedroom for disabled guests.
Near motorway
86 en suite (bth/shr) (20 fmly) No smoking in 17 bedrooms TV in all bedrooms Mini-bar in all bedrooms Licensed Lift Night porter Full central heating Air conditioning in bedrooms Open parking available Supervised Child discount available 16yrs Outdoor swimming pool Pool table Open terrace Last d 24.00hrs Languages spoken: English
CARDS: ●● ▆▆ ▆▆ ▆▆ Travellers cheques

SISTERON Alpes-de-Haute-Provence

★ ★ Touring Napoléon
04200
☎ 492610006 FAX 492610119
The town of Sisteron is known as the pearl of Haute-Provence, set on the side of a cliff and dominated by its famous citadel. The hotel is located 300 metres from the town centre and was recently completely renovated. It has functional guest rooms with modern facilities as well as a homely restaurant.

Near river Forest area In town centre Near motorway
28 en suite (bth/shr) (6 fmly) (14 with balcony) TV in all bedrooms STV Direct dial from all bedrooms Licensed Full central heating Open parking available (charged) Covered parking available (charged) Supervised Child discount available 2yrs Bicycle rental Open terrace Last d 21.30hrs Languages spoken: English,German,Italian
CARDS: ●● ▆▆ ▆▆ ▆ Travellers cheques

TOULON Var

★ ★ ★ Holiday Inn Garden Court
1 av Ragéotdé la Touché *83000*
☎ 494920021 FAX 494620815
Set right in the centre of Toulon, a shaded garden shelters the hotel from the lively bustle of the town. The spacious bedrooms offer quality accommodation and provide a high level of comfort against a very competitive price. The restaurant offers a traditional cuisine consisting of tasty dishes, which are also served on the terrace by the side of the swimming pool.
Near sea In town centre Near motorway
81 en suite (bth/shr) No smoking in 40 bedrooms TV in all bedrooms STV Radio in rooms Direct dial from 18 bedrooms Mini-bar in all bedrooms Licensed Lift Night porter Full central heating Air conditioning in bedrooms Open parking available Covered parking available Child discount available 12yrs Outdoor swimming pool Pool table Open terrace Last d 22.30hrs Languages spoken: English,Italian
CARDS: ●● ▆▆ ▆▆ ▆ Travellers cheques

★ ★ ★ New Hotel Amirauté
4 rue A Guiol *83000*
☎ 296221967 FAX 296093672
Near sea In town centre Near motorway
58 en suite (bth/shr) (6 with balcony) TV in all bedrooms STV Radio in rooms Mini-bar in all bedrooms Licensed Lift Full central heating Air conditioning in bedrooms Child discount available 5yrs Languages spoken: English,Dutch,German,Italian,Spanish
CARDS: ●● ▆▆ ▆▆ ▆ JCB Travellers cheques

★ ★ ★ New Hotel Tour Blanche
83200
☎ 494244157 FAX 494224225
Basking in the warm Provençale sunshine for most of the year, and with views of one of the most beautiful bays in the Mediterranean, the hotel provides the privileged setting for an overnight stop or longer break. Inside, modern comfort and tradition blend perfectly; there are fully equipped bedrooms, offering a high level of comfort, whilst a panoramic restaurant and adjoining bar provide the opportunity to enjoy an excellent meal and have an aperitif and a chat.
Near sea Forest area Near motorway
91 rms (6 fmly) (42 with balcony) TV in all bedrooms STV Radio in rooms Mini-bar in all bedrooms Licensed Lift Night porter Full central heating Air conditioning in bedrooms Open parking available Supervised Child discount available 5yrs Outdoor swimming pool Golf Solarium Pool table Boule Open terrace Last d 23.00hrs Languages spoken: English,Dutch,German,Italian,Spanish
MEALS: Full breakfast 50FF Continental breakfast 50FF Lunch 90-150FF&alc Dinner 90-150FF&alc✱
CARDS: ●● ▆▆ ▆▆ ▆ JCB Travellers cheques

TOURTOUR Var

★ ★ ★ Auberge de Saint-Pierre
83690
☎ 494705717
This 16th-century house enjoys a peaceful, green setting and has pretty guest rooms which are equipped with modern amenities. The cuisine is of outstanding quality, which is no surprise, as the chef-proprietor is a former disciple of the famous Auguste Escoffier. There is a comfortable lounge were the original stone walls and exposed beams create an authentic atmosphere, and a number of leisure facilities available. Guests can venture out on a 45 minutes walk which will take them to an altitude of 850 metres will reward them with a stunning vista over the surrounding region.
Near river Forest area
Closed Oct-Mar
16 en suite (bth/shr) (4 fmly) (9 with balcony) TV in 5 bedrooms Licensed Full central heating Open parking available Outdoor swimming pool (heated) Tennis Fishing Sauna Boule Bicycle rental Open terrace V meals Last d 21.00hrs
CARDS: 🚾 Travellers cheques

★ ★ ★ ★ Bastide de Tourtour
83690
☎ 494705730 FAX 494705490
At an altitude of 650 metres, close to the medieval village of Tourtour, the establishment provides the peaceful setting for a restful holiday. Because of its geographical position it is a good base for touring the surrounding region or visiting St-Tropez and Cannes on the coast. The bedrooms are tastefully furnished and have panoramic views, whilst the cosy restaurant serves a gastronomic cuisine in informal surroundings.
Forest area
Closed mid Nov-mid Dec
25 rms (13 fmly) (12 with balcony) TV in all bedrooms STV Direct dial from all bedrooms Mini-bar in all bedrooms Licensed Lift Full central heating Open parking available Supervised Child discount available 12yrs Outdoor swimming pool (heated) Tennis Pool table Boule Jacuzzi/spa Bicycle rental Open terrace V meals Last d 21.00hrs Languages spoken: English,German

ROOMS: (room only) s 380-530FF; d 520-890FF
Reductions over 1 night
MEALS: Full breakfast 75FF Lunch 160-280FF&alc Dinner 230-280FFalc
CARDS: 🚾🚾🚾 🐠 Travellers cheques

TRIGANCE Var

★ ★ ★ Château de Trigance
83840
☎ 494769118 FAX 494856899
(A8 exit Le Muy/Draguignau onto D955 in direction of Castellane after Jabron 4km on left)
This ancient fortress was built by monks in the ninth century, and became in later years the private residence of the Comtes de Provence. Set in an elevated position, it overlooks the small, Provençale village of Trigance and offers bedrooms decorated with medieval furnishings, including canopy beds and period furniture. The vaulted, candlelit restaurant provides the magnificent setting for an enjoyable meal, whilst the terrace offers panoramic views over the surrounding countryside.
Near river Forest area
Closed Nov-22 Mar
10 en suite (bth) (2 fmly) (1 with balcony) TV in all bedrooms STV Direct dial from all bedrooms Licensed Night porter Full central heating Open parking available Supervised Tennis Solarium Boule Bicycle rental Open terrace Last d 21.30hrs Languages spoken: English & German
ROOMS: (room only) d 600-900FF **Reductions over 1 night**
MEALS: Continental breakfast 68FF Lunch 210-290FF&alc Dinner 210-290FF&alc
CARDS: 🚾🚾🚾 🐠 Travellers cheques

★ ★ Le Viel Amandier
Montée de St-Roch *83840*
☎ 494769292 FAX 494856865
Situated at the foot of the of the magnificent village of Trigance, the hotel provides a peaceful setting for a relaxing stay as well as a good starting point for exploring the Gorges du Verdon on foot. Guests receive a warm welcome, and are well looked after by the friendly owners and their dedicated team. A selection of well prepared dishes are served in the restaurant or on fine days, guests can enjoy their meals on the terrace.
Near river Forest area
Closed 11 Nov-1 Apr
12 en suite (bth/shr) TV in all bedrooms Open parking available Child discount available 14yrs Outdoor swimming pool Solarium Open terrace Covered terrace Last d 21.00hrs Languages spoken: English,Italian
ROOMS: (room only) d 260-320FF ✱
MEALS: Continental breakfast 40FF Lunch fr 100FF&alc Dinner 120-80FF&alc✱
CARDS: 🚾 🚾 Travellers cheques

VAISON-LA-ROMAINE Vaucluse

★ ★ Le Logis du Château
84110
☎ 490360998 490362424 FAX 490361095
The hotel is situated in the popular town of Vaison-La-Romaine at the foot of the Mont Ventoux and opposite the medieval cité and the chateau des Comtes de Toulouse. It has comfortable rooms and a gastronomic cuisine, which combines Provençale specialities with traditional dishes.
Forest area
Closed end Oct-early Apr
45 en suite (bth/shr) (1 fmly) (6 with balcony) TV in all bedrooms STV Direct dial from all bedrooms Licensed Lift Full central heating Open parking available Covered parking
contd.

available Supervised Child discount available 10yrs Outdoor swimming pool Tennis Open terrace Covered terrace Area for children to play games V meals Languages spoken: English
CARDS: ◘◘ ▥

VALENSOLE Alpes-de-Haute-Provence

★ ★ ★ ★ Hostellerie la Fuste
Lieu dit La Fuste *04210*
☎ 392720595 FAX 392729293
Located in the heart of the enchanting Provençal countryside, this large 17th century house is surrounded by olive trees, and mature plane trees, and provides the charming setting for a relaxing stay in unspoilt surroundings. The comfortable bedrooms have homely furnishings and offer restful accommodation, whilst the restaurant serves cuisine which combines traditional recipes with creative dishes from the chef.
Near lake Forest area Near motorway
Closed 10 Jan-1 Mar
14 en suite (bth/shr) (8 with balcony) No smoking in 4 bedrooms TV in all bedrooms Direct dial from all bedrooms Mini-bar in all bedrooms Night porter Full central heating Air conditioning in bedrooms Open parking available Covered parking available Indoor swimming pool (heated) Outdoor swimming pool (heated) Solarium Boule Jacuzzi/spa Open terrace V meals Last d 22.30hrs Languages spoken: English,Italian,Spanish
CARDS: ◘◘ ▥ ▥ ◍ Travellers cheques

★ ★ Pies
04210
☎ 392748313
Located in the vicinity of Moustiers and its celebrated pottery works, the hotel is set amidst the quiet, sunny atmosphere of a Provençale village. Opened in 1968, and nowadays managed by father and son, it has pleasant bedrooms with modern appointments, and a restaurant which serves a high standard of cooking consisting of trout, truffles, morel mushrooms and game when in season. In addition there is a comfortable lounge, bar and a delightful garden with terrace.
Forest area
Closed Dec-Mar
16 rms (3 fmly) (12 with balcony) TV in all bedrooms Direct dial from all bedrooms Mini-bar in all bedrooms Full central heating Open parking available Child discount available 10yrs Boule Bicycle rental Open terrace
CARDS: ◘◘ ▥ Travellers cheques

VALRÉAS Vaucluse

★ ★ Grand Hotel
28 av General de Gaulle *84600*
☎ 490350026 FAX 490356093
Owned by the same family since 1954, the hotel offers modern comforts and good cooking.
Forest area In town centre
RS 21 Dec-28 Jan
15 en suite (bth/shr) No smoking in 2 bedrooms TV in all bedrooms STV Direct dial from all bedrooms Licensed Full central heating Open parking available (charged) Covered parking available (charged) Child discount available 12yrs Outdoor swimming pool Boule Open terrace Covered terrace Last d 21.00hrs Languages spoken: English, German & Italian
ROOMS: (room only) s 260-280FF; d 300-350FF
MEALS: Continental breakfast 40FF Lunch 98-300FF&alc Dinner 98-300FF&alc
CARDS: ◘◘ ▥

VAUVENARGUES Bouches-du-Rhône

★ Au Moulin de Provence
13126
☎ 442660222 FAX 442660121
In lovely countryside at the foot of Mount Sainte Victoire, in front of Picasso's castle. A small, but cosy friendly hotel with a good atmosphere.
Near river Forest area
Closed 2 Nov-Feb RS Jan-Mar
12 rms (9 bth/shr) (5 with balcony) Direct dial from all bedrooms Licensed Full central heating Open parking available Open terrace Covered terrace V meals Last d 21.00hrs Languages spoken: English
ROOMS: (room only) s fr 120FF; d 210-280FF
MEALS: Continental breakfast 35FF Lunch 90-110FF&alc Dinner 90-110FF&alc
CARDS: ◘◘ ▥ Travellers cheques

VENASQUE Vaucluse

Auberge La Fontaine
pl la Fontaine *84210*
☎ 490660296 FAX 490661314
This ancient ivy-clad house is located in Venasque, reputedly one of the most beautiful villages in France. The owners Ingrid and Christian Soehlke have made a dream come true, and created a setting where guests feel at home the minute they step over the threshold and are free to treat the house as their own. It features suites with excellent facilities and a cosy dining room, where seasonal dishes include truffles, wild asparagus, game and Mediterranean fish and seafood.
RS (restaurant closed mid Nov -mid Dec)
5 en suite (bth/shr) (5 fmly) (4 with balcony) TV in all bedrooms Direct dial from all bedrooms Mini-bar in all bedrooms Licensed Air conditioning in bedrooms Open parking available Child discount available Boule Bicycle rental Open terrace Covered terrace Last d 22.00hrs Languages spoken: English,German,Spanish
ROOMS: (room only) d 800FF **Reductions over 1 night Special breaks: 3 day breaks**
MEALS: Lunch 80-150FF&alc Dinner 80-220FF&alc
CARDS: ◘◘ ▥ EC Travellers cheques

VITROLLES Bouches-du-Rhône

★ ★ Hotel Loiisiana
Aéroport de Marseille Provence, Imp Pythagoré - La Couperigné *13127*
☎ 442108500 FAX 442108501
This cheerful hotel-complex has pleasant bedrooms with high quality bedding offering a straight-forward level of comfort. Situated near the airport, it is popular with business travellers and a good venue for an overnight stop. There is a bar and a restaurant which caters for most tastes as well as a number of well appointed meeting rooms.
Near lake Forest area Near motorway
100 en suite (bth/shr) 20 rooms in annexe No smoking in 10 bedrooms TV in all bedrooms STV Direct dial from all bedrooms Licensed Night porter Open parking available Supervised Child discount available Outdoor swimming pool Sauna Boule Open terrace Covered terrace Last d 22.00hrs Languages spoken: English,Spanish,German,Italian
CARDS: ◘◘ ▥ Travellers cheques

★ ★ ★ Primotel Aeroport Marseille Provence
13127
☎ 442797919 FAX 442896918

The hotels in the Primotel group all have modern bedrooms equipped with every modern day convenience and provide a high degree of comfort. Their restaurants serve a high standard of cooking where a choice of traditional and regional dishes feature strongly on the menu; whilst competent staff offer attentive service and traditional hospitality in a cordial atmosphere.

Near motorway

120 en suite (bth/shr) TV in all bedrooms STV Radio in rooms Direct dial from all bedrooms Licensed Lift Night porter Full central heating Air conditioning in bedrooms Open parking available Child discount available 12yrs Outdoor swimming pool Tennis Open terrace V meals Last d 23.00hrs

Languages spoken: English

CARDS: ● ▦ ▥ ● Travellers cheques

Côte D'Azur

Summer and winter here are positively packed with arts festivals, many of which are famous the world over. But if you take the time to experience the gentler pace of life in the villages perched on the hillside and leisurely drive along some of the breath-taking roads through forests, past Roman churches, Gothic palaces and breathe in the scent from fields of lavender or the rosemary and thyme growing wild, you will experience something very different to the pace of life in the smart towns of Cannes and Nice.

(Top): A typical Côte D'Azur countryside landscape

(Bottom): The village of Cotignac was built in the 17th and 18th centuries, although previous inhabitants lived in the caves and tunnels in the 80m-high cliff.

ESSENTIAL FACTS

DÉPARTEMENTS:	Alpes-Maritimes
PRINCIPAL TOWNS	Grasse, Cannes, Antibes, Nice
PLACES TO VISIT:	Cannes for the shopping; Grasse for the perfume museum and tours at the Molinard, Fragonard or Galimard Perfumeries (the latter two are also in Eze Village); Mercantour national nature park; Villa Ephrussi de Rothschild at St-Jean-de-Cap-Ferrat; Picasso Museum
REGIONAL TOURIST OFFICE	Palais des Festival, 06400 Cannes Tel 04 93 39 24 53 Fax 04 93 99 37 06; 55 Promenade des Anglais, BP 602 Nice 06011 Tel 04 93 37 78 78 Fax 04 93 86 01 06
LOCAL GASTRONOMIC DELIGHTS	bouillabaisse, a fish stew; aïoli, garlic-flavoured mayonnaise; calissons, small diamond shaped almond-paste biscuits; rascasse, a spiny fish; salade Niçoise, tuna fish salad; pissaladière, an onion tart from Nice; tapenade, an olive paste; ratatouille; pistou soup, a thick vegetable soup with basil and garlic; squid; bourride, fish soup; anchoïade, an anchovy mixture.
DRINKS	Pastis, an aniseed-flavoured aperitif usually diluted with water to make a long drink; sweet aperitif wines such as Muscat des Beaume de Venise and Rasteau; or try some of the Provençal spirits - Vieux Marc de Provence, Elixir du Révérend Père Gaucher, Eau de vie de Poire, Genepy des Alpes.
LOCAL CRAFTS WHAT TO BUY	soaps and perfume from Grasse, lavender honey, Provençal fabrics, herbs, olive oil, crystallised fruit

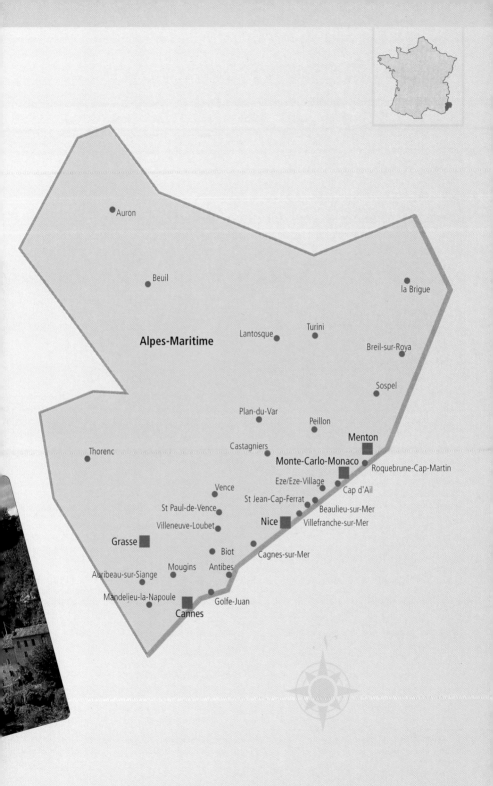

Auron

Beuil

la Brigue

Alpes-Maritime

Lantosque

Turini

Breil-sur-Roya

Sospel

Plan-du-Var

Peillon

Thorenc

Castagniers

Menton

Monte-Carlo-Monaco

Roquebrune-Cap-Martin

Vence

Eze/Eze-Village

Cap d'Ail

St Paul-de-Vence

St Jean-Cap-Ferrat

Beaulieu-sur-Mer

Villeneuve-Loubet

Nice

Villefranche-sur-Mer

Grasse

Biot

Mougins

Antibes

Cagnes-sur-Mer

Auribeau-sur-Siange

Mandelieu-la-Napoule

Golfe-Juan

Cannes

EVENTS & FESTIVALS

Feb Cannes International Games Festival; Antibes/Juan-les-Pins Jazz Festival; Menton Lemon Festival; Nice Carnival; Cagnes-sur Mer International Flower Exhibition; Mandelieu-la-Napoule Mimosa Festival

Mar Antibes Golden Dove Magic Festival; Nice International Fair; Antibes Antiques Show

Apr Antibes Antiques Show

May Antibes Bridge Festival; Cannes International Film Festival; Cannes Contemporary Art Market (*Palais de Festivals*); Cagnes-sur-Mer Comic Book Festival; May Festivals at Nice, Menton, Roquebrune; Grasse International Flower Show; Monaco (Monte Carlo) Formula One Grand Prix;

Jun Cannes International Festival of Actors' Performances (*humour, theatre, music hall*); Antibes International Young Soloist Festival

Jul Nice Jazz Festival; Antibes/Juan-les-Pins Jazz Festival in the pine forest; Nice, Cimiez Monastery Cloister Festival (chamber & choral music); Menton Music Festival (*chamber music, recitals*)

Aug Cagnes-sur-Mer Medieval Festival; Nice, Menton Music Festival (*chamber music, recitals*)

Oct Antibes World Festival of Underwater Photography & Film;

Nov Antibes Maritime & Military Film Festival; Cannes International Dance Festival

Lavender

This delicate amethyst blue plant has been described as the 'soul of Upper Provence, its coat-of-arms'. It is hard to imagine the landscape without the endless expanse of blue which stretches to the horizon and fills the peaceful villages and beauty spots with its fragrance. Lavender origins lie in Persia; it was brought to Provence in ancient times and is an integral part of Provençal culture. The lavender flourishes in the stony ground and the flowers bloom for just a short time during mid-summer.

Harvest time brings with it a time for colourful celebration, of numerous festivals including displays of both modern and traditional methods of lavender distillation. The local tourist boards organise many sight-seeing tours taking in the region's architectural gems during this interesting time.

D'ANGERS (NEAR CANNES) Alpes-Maritimes

★ ★ ★ ★ **Hotel Cristal**
13 Rond Point Duboys d'Angers *06400*
☎ 493394545 FAX 493386466
(From A8, follow signs for town centre, then for 'Croisette' and 'Rond Point duboys d'Angres)
The Hotel Cristal is located just 100 metres from the sea and offers all the services and facilities which can be expected from an establishment of this calibre. It features an elegant interior with smart public areas and attractive guest-rooms equipped with every modern convenience. Courteous staff provide an attentive service and nothing is too much trouble. There is a panoramic restaurant and terrace on the sixth floor where a bar and outstanding leisure facilities complement this prestigious setting.
Near sea Near beach In town centre
Closed 20 Nov-25 Dec
51 en suite (bth) No smoking in 12 bedrooms TV in all bedrooms Direct dial from all bedrooms Mini-bar in all bedrooms Licensed Lift Night porter Full central heating Air conditioning in bedrooms Covered parking available (charged) Child discount available 12yrs Outdoor swimming pool Solarium Open terrace Last d 22.00hrs Languages spoken: English,German,Italian,Spanish
ROOMS: (room only) s 550-870FF; d 575-1010FF
Reductions over 1 night
MEALS: Full breakfast 95FF Continental breakfast 72FF Lunch 140-250FF&alc Dinner 140-250FF&alc✱
CARDS: ●● ▆▆ ▆▆ ◗ JCB Travellers cheques

ANTIBES Alpes-Maritimes

★ ★ **Climat de France**
2317 chemin de St-Claude *06600*
☎ 493748001 Cen Res 164460123 FAX 493952248
(800 m from de Antibes Jaun-les-Pins motorway exiting the new activity area of Nova Antipolis)
Situated just three kilometres from the beaches of Antibes and Juan-les-Pins, the hotel features bedrooms equipped with every modern convenience. The restaurant serves a generous and varied cuisine in a friendly atmosphere, and guests can help themselves to as many starters and sweets as they wish from the tempting buffet.
Near sea Near beach In town centre Near motorway
46 en suite (bth/shr) TV in all bedrooms Direct dial from all bedrooms Licensed Lift Full central heating Air conditioning in bedrooms Open parking available Child discount available 13yrs Outdoor swimming pool Solarium Open terrace Covered terrace Languages spoken: English & Greek
CARDS: ▆▆ ◗ Travellers cheques

★ ★ **Le Ponteil**
11 Impasse Jean Mensier *06600*
☎ 493346792 FAX 493344947
Situated in leafy surroundings in the old quarters of the town, the hotel features a day room to relax in and bedrooms equipped with modern amenities. Good quality home cooking incorporating fine regional ingredients is served on the shaded terrace.
Near sea Near beach In town centre
Closed mid Nov-late Dec & mid Jan-early Feb RS Jun-Sep (half board only)

15 rms (3 bth 7 shr) (1 fmly) (1 with balcony) TV in all bedrooms Direct dial from all bedrooms Room-safe Licensed Full central heating Open parking available Supervised Child discount available 2-7yrs Open terrace Languages spoken: English,German,Italian
ROOMS: (room only) s fr 262FF; d 322-484FF
CARDS: ☎ ▦ ☲ Travellers cheques

AURIBEAU-SUR-SIAGNE Alpes-Maritimes

★ ★ ★ ★ Auberge de la Vignette Haute
370 rte du Village 06810
☎ 493422001 FAX 493423116
The Auberge de la Vignette Haute is situated just 10 minutes from Cannes and Grasse, and one hour from St Tropez and Monaco. It can be found on a rocky peak amidst peaceful and verdant countryside there are lots of golf courses in the area. This enchanting establishment offers its visitors luxurious, individually appointed bedrooms where refined comfort is complemented by numerous pieces of antique furniture, reminiscent of by-gone days. There is a private museum 'Le Curiosa' and the gastronomic restaurant is lit only by oil lamps and has a view on the 'Bergerie' and its animals.
In town centre
12 en suite (bth/shr) (1 fmly) (10 with balcony) TV available STV Mini-bar in all bedrooms Licensed Full central heating Air conditioning in bedrooms Open parking available Covered parking available (charged) Child discount available Outdoor swimming pool Fishing Boule Jacuzzi/spa Bicycle rental Open terrace V meals Last d 22.00hrs Languages spoken: English,Italian
MEALS: Full breakfast 120FF Continental breakfast 80FF Lunch 160-300FF&alc Dinner 380-520FF&alc✱
CARDS: ☎ ▦ ☲ Travellers cheques

BEAULIEU-SUR-MER Alpes-Maritimes

★ ★ ★ ★ Le Metropole (Relais et Chateaux)
15 bd Maréchal Leclerc 06130
☎ 493010008 FAX 493011851
(From A8 exit 50 or 58 follow signs for 'Basse Corniche')

This Italian palatial-style hotel occupies a splendid beach-front position with breathtaking views over the Mediterranean. It features a delightful flower garden with terrace. The smart bedrooms with good quality furniture and matching fabrics offer maximum comfort. The restaurant has earned a good reputation for its outstanding cuisine, where meat specialities and fresh seafood, combined with seasonal ingredients, feature strongly on the menu.
Near sea Near beach In town centre
Closed 20 Oct-20 Dec

43 en suite (bth/shr) (20 with balcony) TV in all bedrooms STV Direct dial from all bedrooms Room-safe Licensed Lift Night porter Full central heating Air conditioning in bedrooms Open parking available Supervised Child discount available 15yrs Outdoor swimming pool (heated) Solarium Open terrace Covered terrace Last d 22.00hrs Languages spoken: English,German & Italian
ROOMS: (room only) s 900-1900FF; d 1200-3000FF
MEALS: Continental breakfast 120FF Lunch 300-500FF&alc Dinner 400-500FF&alc
CARDS: ☎ ▦ ☲ Travellers cheques

BEUIL Alpes-Maritimes

★ ★ L'Escapade
06470
☎ 493023127
A chalet-style small hotel at an altitude of 1400m in a pretty hamlet one hour's drive from Nice. This is the perfect holiday location in both summer and winter, when the hotel is popular with skiers. Bedrooms are small but comfortable, and a restaurant, bar and terrace all help to make your stay a very relaxing one.
Forest area
Closed 15 Nov-19 Dec
11 rms (9 bth/shr) (2 fmly) (6 with balcony) TV in all bedrooms STV Direct dial from all bedrooms Mini-bar in all bedrooms Licensed Full central heating Child discount available 10yrs Boule Bicycle rental Open terrace Last d 21.30hrs Languages spoken: English,Italian
ROOMS: (room only) d 220-310FF
MEALS: Full breakfast 50FF Lunch 105-150FF&alc Dinner 105-150FF&alc
CARDS: Travellers cheques

BIOT Alpes-Maritimes

★ ★ ★ Hotel le Domaine du Jas
625 rte de la Mer 06410
☎ 493655050 FAX 296650201
The hotel reflects the atmosphere and style of the Mediterranean region, and offers exceptionally furnished bedrooms with terrace and full range of modern amenities. Set against the backdrop of the historic and picturesque village of Biot - a favourite residence for many artists - it provides the ideal venue for a sun-filled luxurious holiday.
Near sea Forest area Near motorway
Closed Jan-Feb
17 en suite (bth/shr) (3 fmly) (17 with balcony) TV in all bedrooms Direct dial from all bedrooms Night porter Full central heating Open parking available Covered parking available Supervised Outdoor swimming pool Solarium Open terrace Covered terrace Languages spoken: English,Italian,Spanish
CARDS: ☎ ▦ ☲ Travellers cheques

BREIL-SUR-ROYA Alpes-Maritimes

★ ★ Castel du Roy
rte de Tende 06540
☎ 493044366 FAX 493049183
(Approach via A8 and D2204 through Sospel)
The hotel occupies a fine position, situated in 5 acres of parkland beside the River Roya and close to the picturesque Vallée des Merueilles.
Near river Near lake Forest area
Closed 31 Oct-1 Mar

contd.

19 en suite (bth/shr) (1 fmly) TV in all bedrooms Direct dial from all bedrooms Mini-bar in all bedrooms Licensed Full central heating Open parking available Supervised Child discount available 3yrs Outdoor swimming pool (heated) Fishing Boule Bicycle rental Open terrace Badminton Last d 21.00hrs Languages spoken: English

ROOMS: (room only) s 310FF; d 380-420FF

MEALS: Full breakfast 40FF Continental breakfast 40FF Lunch 110-210FF&alc Dinner 110-210FF&alc

CARDS: 💳 💳 💳 Travellers cheques

★ ★ Le Roya
pl Biancheri *06540*
☎ 493044810 FAX 493049270
This hotel is situated in the centre of town opposite a lake and mountains. The bedrooms are large and comfortable and the restaurant - 40 metres away from the main hotel, in an old windmill - serves a French/Italian cuisine.
Near river Near lake Forest area In town centre
18 en suite (bth/shr) (5 fmly) (3 with balcony) TV in all bedrooms Radio in rooms Licensed Full central heating Open parking available Covered parking available (charged) Supervised Child discount available Open terrace V meals Last d 22.30hrs Languages spoken: Italian

MEALS: Full breakfast 90FF Continental breakfast 30FF Lunch 90FF&alc Dinner 90FF&alc✱

★ ★ Le Mirval
06430
☎ 493046371 FAX 493047981
This turn-of-the century hotel is located in the medieval village of La Brigue, known for its shrine; Notre Dame de la Fontaine. Entirely renovated throughout, it offers a delightful setting for an enjoyable stay. Well equipped bedrooms, a garden with terrace on the banks of the stream, and a panoramic restaurant create an attractive ambience. The cuisine features dishes from a repertoire of Italian and French cooking.
Near river Forest area
Closed 3 Nov-Mar
18 en suite (bth/shr) (6 fmly) (4 with balcony) TV in all bedrooms Direct dial from all bedrooms Licensed Full central heating Open parking available Child discount available 12yrs Solarium Boule Open terrace Last d 20.30hrs Languages spoken: Italian

MEALS: Continental breakfast 35FF Lunch 90-150FF Dinner 90-150FF✱

CARDS: 💳 💳 💳 Travellers cheques

★ ★ ★ Cannes Palace Hotel (Best Western)
14 av de Madrid *06400*
☎ 493434445 FAX 493434130
Situated in a residential area, the hotel offers modern guest accommodation with extensive facilities. It features spacious lounges and a restaurant which serves classic cuisine in elegant surroundings. Located near the beach, it is the ideal venue for a seaside holiday.
Near sea In town centre Near motorway
Closed 11 Nov-23 Dec
101 en suite (bth) (6 fmly) (41 with balcony) No smoking in 5 bedrooms TV in all bedrooms STV Radio in rooms Direct-dial available Mini-bar in all bedrooms Licensed Full central heating Air conditioning in bedrooms Open parking available (charged) Covered parking available (charged)

Supervised Child discount available 12yrs Outdoor swimming pool Sauna Fitness Studio V meals Last d 21.45hrs
Languages spoken: English,Arabic,Dutch,German,Spanish
CARDS: 💳 💳 💳 💳 Travellers cheques

★ ★ ★ ★ Croisette Beach Hotel
13 rue du Canada *06400*
☎ 493949450 FAX 493683538
(A8 exit Cannes centre, take direction city centre/centre croisette, behind the Carlton hotel)
Located 50mtrs from the famous Croisette, the hotel offers fully renovated well equipped bedrooms, a terrace with bar that opens onto the garden and pool. Private garaging is available.
Near beach In town centre
Closed 21 Nov-25 Dec
94 en suite (bth/shr) (10 fmly) (55 with balcony) No smoking in 16 bedrooms TV in all bedrooms STV Direct dial from all bedrooms Mini-bar in all bedrooms Room-safe Licensed Lift Night porter Full central heating Air conditioning in bedrooms Covered parking available (charged) Supervised Child discount available 16yrs Outdoor swimming pool (heated) Sauna Solarium Covered terrace Languages spoken: English, German, Italian & Spanish

ROOMS: (room only) s 565-765FF; d 565-765FF

CARDS: 💳 💳 💳 💳 Travellers cheques

Hotel Embassy
6 rue de Bone *06400*
☎ 493387902 FAX 493990798
(Between the Voie Rapide and rue d'Antibes)
The hotels in the Quality group offer a comfortable interior with attractive, fully equipped bedrooms and pleasant public areas where guests can relax or read. The restaurants serve an excellent cuisine, incorporating dishes with a regional touch and where local produce has been used to a large extend. Guests enjoy a special blend of hospitality, provided by attentive staff which offer personal attention and service at all times.
Near sea Near beach In town centre Near motorway
60 en suite (bth/shr) (3 fmly) TV in all bedrooms STV Radio in rooms Direct dial from all bedrooms Mini-bar in all bedrooms Room-safe Licensed Lift Night porter Full central heating Air conditioning in bedrooms Open parking available (charged) Covered parking available (charged) Supervised Child discount available Solarium Pool table Jacuzzi/spa Open terrace Wkly live entertainment Last d 22.00hrs
Languages spoken: English,Dutch,German,Italian

ROOMS: s 450-620FF; d 580-750FF

CARDS: 💳 💳 💳 💳 Travellers cheques

★ ★ ★ Hotel de l'Olivier
5 rue des Tambourinaires *06400*
☎ 493395328 FAX 493395585
(NE of junction of Voie Rapide with avenue Dr-Picaud)
Situated in the old quarters of Cannes called 'Le Suquet', the Hôtel de l'Olivier extends a warm welcome to its clientele. It features charming bedrooms with modern amenities, a restful terrace surrounded by a delightful garden, a superb lounge and swimming pool. An array of restaurants and cafés are nearby, whilst the beach, casino and old yachting harbour are only 300 metres from the hotel.
Near sea In town centre Near motorway
24 en suite (bth/shr) (6 with balcony) TV in all bedrooms Direct dial from all bedrooms Licensed Night porter Full central heating Air conditioning in bedrooms Open parking available Child discount available 8yrs

Outdoor swimming pool Pool table Languages spoken:
English,German
ROOMS: (room only) s 525-715FF; d 615-815FF ✳
MEALS: Continental breakfast 52FF
CARDS: ✹ ▦ ▨ ⫶ Travellers cheques

★ ★ ★ Hotel de Paris
34 bd d'Alsace *06400*
☎ 493383089 FAX 493390461
Amidst abundant, leafy surroundings and set around a
swimming pool, the Hotel de Paris with its ochre-coloured
façade is in complete harmony with the beautiful scenery of
the Côte d'Azur. Just 300 metres from the beach, it offers
traditional hospitality together with modern comfort. The
bedrooms all have up-to-date facilities; the hotel also has a bar,
Turkish bath, Jacuzzi and a shady park with swimming pool.
Near sea In town centre
Closed 15 Nov-26 Dec
50 en suite (bth/shr) (2 fmly) (15 with balcony) TV in all
bedrooms STV Radio in rooms Direct dial from all bedrooms
Room-safe Licensed Lift Night porter Full central heating
Air conditioning in bedrooms Open parking available
(charged) Covered parking available (charged) Supervised
Child discount available 12yrs Outdoor swimming pool Golf
Solarium Jacuzzi/spa Open terrace Languages spoken:
English,German,Italian
ROOMS: (room only) s 450-650FF; d 520-720FF
CARDS: ✹ ▦ ▨ ⫶ JCB Travellers cheques

★ ★ ★ Primotel Canberra
120 rue d'Antibes *06400*
☎ 493382070 FAX 492980347
Situated in the 'city of the stars' and only 100 m from the
famous sea-front 'La Croisette', the hotel offers spacious,
sound-proofed guest rooms with private facilities, mini-bar,
satellite TV and direct-dial telephone. Within easy reach of the
famous Rue d'Antibes and its luxury boutiques, it offers its
visitors a comfortable stay in elegant surroundings.
Near sea Near beach In town centre Near motorway
44 en suite (bth/shr) (6 fmly) (6 with balcony) TV in all
bedrooms STV Direct dial from all bedrooms Mini-bar in all
bedrooms Room-safe Licensed Lift Night porter Full central
heating Air conditioning in bedrooms Open parking available
(charged) No children Child discount available 12yrs
Languages spoken: English,German,Italian
ROOMS: (room only) s 420-590FF; d 500-680FF
CARDS: ✹ ▦ ▨ ⫶ Travellers cheques

CAP-D'AIL Alpes-Maritimes

★ ★ La Gigogne
rte de la Plage Mala *06320*
☎ 493782960 FAX 493418662
(Approach from town centre via N98)
The hotel La Cigogne enjoys a peaceful location at five minutes
from the beach and the town centre. Surrounded by the splendid
scenery of the Riviera, it features bedrooms with private
facilities, a cosy lounge and attractive bar, whilst the modern
restaurant with terrace which serves a Provençale cuisine.
Near sea Near beach Near motorway
Closed 15 Jan-15 Mar
15 rms (7 bth 7 shr) (3 fmly) TV in 10 bedrooms STV Direct
dial from all bedrooms Licensed Full central heating Open
parking available No children 4yrs Child discount available
10yrs V meals Last d 21.00hrs Languages spoken:
English,German,Italian

ROOMS: s 280-320FF; d 380-420FF
MEALS: Full breakfast 40FF Continental breakfast 40FF Lunch
100-130FF Dinner 100-130FF
CARDS: ✹ ▨

CASTAGNIERS Alpes-Maritimes

★ ★ Servotel
1976 rte de Grenoble *06670*
☎ 493082200 FAX 493290366
(From A8 exit 'Nice St-Isidore' follow N202 towards Digne for
8km)
This contemporary hotel complex includes bedrooms and a
number of fully equipped apartments. It is situated in a large
park and features an attractive interior with spacious public
rooms, a pleasant bar and a multitude of leisure opportunities.
Under the family ownership of Mr and Mrs Servella guests
receive a warm welcome upon arrival and want for nothing
during their stay. The bedrooms are furnished with matching
colours and fabrics, whilst the restaurant is widely known for
its splendid cuisine.
Near river Near motorway
44 rms (38 bth/shr) 31 rooms in annexe (2 fmly) (44 with
balcony) No smoking in 5 bedrooms TV in all bedrooms STV
Direct dial from all bedrooms Licensed Lift Full central
heating Open parking available Covered parking available
Supervised Child discount available Outdoor swimming pool
Tennis Riding Sauna Solarium Gym Boule Jacuzzi/spa
Open terrace Covered terrace Beauty Salon V meals Last d
21.30hrs Languages spoken: English,Italian,German
ROOMS: (room only) d 280-330FF ✳
MEALS: Full breakfast 40FF Lunch 90-190FF&alc Dinner 90-
190FF&alc✳
CARDS: ✹ ▦ ▨ Travellers cheques

EZE Alpes-Maritimes

★ ★ ★ ★ Château Eza
rue de la Pise *06360*
☎ 493411224 FAX 493411664
This attractive building has been the private residence of
European royalty throughout this century. From both the
restaurant and terrace it offers stunning views over the Côte
d'Azur and the Mediterranean. All the guest-rooms are
individually appointed and offer elegant accommodation
combined with modern amenities. The cuisine encompasses an
outstanding repertoire of dishes carefully prepared with
regional ingredients, herbs and spices.
Near sea Near motorway
Closed Nov-end Mar
10 en suite (bth/shr) (2 fmly) (7 with balcony) TV in all
bedrooms Radio in rooms Licensed Night porter Full central
heating Air conditioning in bedrooms Open parking available
Supervised Open terrace Covered terrace V meals Last d
22.30hrs Languages spoken: English,German,Italian
CARDS: ✹ ▦ ▨ ⫶ Travellers cheques

EZE-VILLAGE Alpes-Maritimes

★ ★ L'Hermitage du Col d'Eze
06360
☎ 493410068 FAX 493412405
Forest area
Closed mid Dec-mid Jan
14 en suite (bth/shr) (3 fmly) (2 with balcony) TV in all
bedrooms STV Direct dial from all bedrooms Licensed Full
central heating Open parking available   *contd.*

Outdoor swimming pool Boule Open terrace Last d 21.00hrs
Languages spoken: English,Italian
MEALS: Lunch 90-180FF&alc Dinner 90-180FF&alc✱
CARDS: ✹ ▓ ▆ Travellers cheques

GOLFE-JUAN Alpes-Maritimes

★ ★ ★ Beau Soleil
Impasse Beau Soleil *06220*
☎ 493636363 FAX 493630289
Set in a quiet location between Cannes and Antibes in the
heart of the Côte d'Azur, the hotel is only 500 metres from the
fine sandy beach. It features entirely renovated bedrooms with
modern facilities and a shaded terrace where breakfast and
lunch are served.
Near sea In town centre Near motorway
Closed 15 Oct-24 Mar
30 en suite (bth/shr) (2 fmly) (10 with balcony) TV in all
bedrooms STV Direct dial from all bedrooms Room-safe
Licensed Lift Night porter Full central heating Air
conditioning in bedrooms Open parking available Covered
parking available Child discount available 12yrs Outdoor
swimming pool Tennis Boule Open terrace Covered terrace
Last d 21.00hrs Languages spoken: English
ROOMS: (room only) d 500-570FF
MEALS: Full breakfast 50FF Lunch 89-135FF&alc Dinner 98-
135FF&alc
CARDS: ✹ ▓ ▆ Travellers cheques

★ ★ De Crijansy
av Juliette Adam *06220*
☎ 493638444 FAX 493634204
Quietly located only 300 metres from the fine sandy beaches,
the hotel has a modern restaurant where a range of generous
well-presented meals are served. The guest rooms have private
facilities and provide a good degree of comfort. There is a
delightful garden with terrace, and there is direct access from
the hotel to the beach.
Near sea Near motorway
20 en suite (bth/shr) (13 with balcony) TV available Child
discount available Boule Open terrace Last d 21.00hrs
Languages spoken: English
CARDS: ✹ Travellers cheques

GRASSE Alpes-Maritimes

★ ★ ★ Hotel des Parfums (Best Western)
bd Eugene Charabot *06130*
☎ 493361010 FAX 493363548
The Hotel des Parfums is a building with character which is
located in the heart of the town with views across the
surrounding Grasse region. Guest rooms and apartments with
balconies or terraces have modern appointments, and there
are two restaurants as well as a panoramic terrace. The cosy
piano-bar is a good place for a chat with fellow guests, or for
those who want to work out there are fitness and leisure
facilities.
In town centre
71 en suite (bth/shr) (9 fmly) (60 with balcony) TV in all
bedrooms STV Direct dial from all bedrooms Mini-bar in all
bedrooms Licensed Lift Night porter Full central heating Air
conditioning in bedrooms Open parking available Supervised
Child discount available 12yrs Outdoor swimming pool Sauna
Jacuzzi/spa Open terrace Last d 22.00hrs Languages spoken:
English,German,Italian

LANTOSQUE Alpes-Maritimes

★ ★ ★ Hostellerie de l'Ancienne Gendarmerie
06450
☎ 493030065 FAX 493030631
This hotel, is as the name suggests, an old police station. It is
situated in rural surroundings and offers stunning views over
the beautiful countryside. The luxurious bedrooms, elegant
restaurant and terrace all overlook the river. The cuisine offers
classic and regional dishes with high quality produce from the
Côte d'Azur area.
Near river Forest area
Closed early Nov-mid Dec
8 en suite (bth/shr) (1 with balcony) TV in all bedrooms Direct
dial from all bedrooms Mini-bar in all bedrooms Licensed
Night porter Full central heating Open parking available
Supervised Outdoor swimming pool Fishing Jacuzzi/spa
Open terrace Covered terrace Last d 21.30hrs Languages
spoken: English,German
CARDS: ✹ ▓ ▆ ➒ Travellers cheques

MANDELIEU-LA-NAPOULE Alpes-Maritimes

★ ★ ★ ★ Ermitage du Riou
av Henri Clens *06210*
☎ 493499556 FAX 492976905
Situated opposite the deep blue waters of the Mediterranean
and near Cannes, this charming hotel offers a homely
atmosphere with completely renovated and personally styled
bedrooms, a delightful garden with swimming-pool, and a
popular restaurant which serves delicious seafood specialities.
Near river Near sea Forest area In town centre Near
motorway
41 en suite (bth/shr) 5 rooms in annexe (4 fmly) (29 with
balcony) No smoking in 8 bedrooms TV in all bedrooms STV
Radio in rooms Direct dial from all bedrooms Mini-bar in all
bedrooms Licensed Lift Night porter Full central heating Air
conditioning in bedrooms Open parking available Covered
parking available (charged) Supervised Child discount
available Outdoor swimming pool Solarium Gym Boule
Open terrace Last d 22.00hrs Languages spoken:
English,German,Italian
CARDS: ✹ ▓ ▆ ➒ Travellers cheques

★ ★ ★ ★ Royal Hôtel Casino
605 av du Général de Gaulle *06212*
☎ 492977000 FAX 493495150
(situated just off A8 (Marseille-Nice) exit 40 and follow red and
white sign posts)
With a combination of facilities under one roof including twenty
lounges, two restaurants, three bars, a casino and a night club,
the Royal Hôtel Casino offers real international luxury. The
bedrooms have either views of the sea or the golf course.
Near river Near sea Near beach
213 en suite (bth/shr) (213 fmly) (213 with balcony) No
smoking in 5 bedrooms TV in all bedrooms STV Direct dial
from all bedrooms Mini-bar in all bedrooms Licensed Lift
Night porter Full central heating Air conditioning in
bedrooms Open parking available (charged) Supervised
Child discount available 10yrs Indoor swimming pool
Outdoor swimming pool Tennis Sauna Solarium Open
terrace Casino Last d 22.30hrs Languages spoken: English,
German, Italian & Spanish
ROOMS: (room only) d 690-1620FF
MEALS: Full breakfast 110FF Continental breakfast 95FF
Lunch 205-260FF&alc Dinner 205-260FF&alc✱
CARDS: ✹ ▓ ▆ ➒ JCB

MENTON Alpes-Maritimes

★ ★ ★ Hotel Prince de Galles (Best Western)
4 av Général-de-Gaulle 06500
☎ 493282121 FAX 493359591
The town of Menton is known throughout France as 'the pearl of the Riviera' and lies within a short distance of Monaco. The hotel is situated in the smart residential part of the town and is surrounded by a large garden. It features attractive, refurbished bedrooms with modern amenities. The cosy bar with terrace offer splendid views over the sea, whilst the restaurant 'Le Petit Prince' is situated in the garden and serves a cuisine where Mediterranean dishes take a prominent place on the menu.
Near sea In town centre
68 en suite (bth/shr) (4 fmly) (40 with balcony) TV in all bedrooms STV Direct dial from all bedrooms Licensed Lift Night porter Full central heating Open parking available Supervised Child discount available 12yrs Open terrace Last d 21.00hrs Languages spoken: English,German,Italian,
MEALS: Full breakfast 42FF Continental breakfast 25FF Lunch 90-95FF&alc Dinner 90-95FF&alc✱
CARDS: ✸ ▓▓ ▨▨ ⑨ Travellers cheques

MOUGINS Alpes-Maritimes

★ ★ ★ ★ Mas Candille
Clement-Rebuffel 06520
☎ 493900085 FAX 492928556

Just 10 minutes from Cannes, the 18th century hotel Mas Candille is set in lush surroundings with olive and cypress trees, and offers stunning views over the valley. The lounges with their beams and exposed brickwork reflect the distinct atmosphere of Provence, while the guest rooms feature co-ordinated shades and fabrics and provide comfortable accommodation. The panoramic restaurant serves a superb cuisine which incorporates the delicate flavours and fragrances of the region.
Forest area Near motorway
Closed Nov-Apr
23 en suite (bth/shr) (4 fmly) TV in all bedrooms STV Radio in rooms Direct dial from all bedrooms Mini-bar in all bedrooms Room-safe Licensed Night porter Full central heating Air conditioning in bedrooms Open parking available Supervised Child discount available 12yrs Outdoor swimming pool (heated) Golf 18 Tennis Open terrace Last d 22hrs Languages spoken: English, German, Italian
ROOMS: (room only) s 680-1200FF; d 980-1200FF **Special breaks**
MEALS: Continental breakfast 85FF Lunch fr 165FF&alc Dinner 195-270FF&alc
CARDS: ✸ ▓▓ ▨▨ ⑨ Travellers cheques

★ ★ ★ ★ Moulin de Mougins
Quartier Notre Dame de Vie 06250
☎ 490757824 FAX 493901855
This old mill dates back to the 16th century and is tucked away amidst leafy surroundings. It has a delightful, fragrant garden where thyme, basil and lavender grow in abundance. The restaurant enjoys an outstanding international reputation and the proprietor Roger Vergé, who presides over the kitchen, has written many books on the art of fine cuisine. The guest rooms provide peaceful accommodation and offer a good level of comfort for those visitors who do not want to travel on after a delicious meal.
Near sea Near beach Forest area Near motorway
Closed 11 Feb-11 Mar
7 en suite (bth/shr) (2 fmly) (2 with balcony) TV in all bedrooms STV Licensed Night porter Full central heating Air conditioning in bedrooms Open parking available Supervised Open terrace V meals Last d 22.30hrs Languages spoken: English, German, Italian
MEALS: Lunch fr 315FF Dinner 615-740FF✱
CARDS: ✸ ▓▓ ▨▨ ⑨ Travellers cheques

NICE Alpes-Maritimes

★ ★ ★ ★ Acropolé-Nice-Hôte
25 bd Dubouchage 06000
☎ 493805733 FAX 493626911
This elegant establishment features the distinct architectural style of the Riviera and is located in the heart of Nice, close to the beautiful beaches and splendid gardens. The bedrooms are furnished with taste and offer a high degree of comfort, whilst the staff provide round the clock service. The day begins with an enormous buffet-style breakfast.
Near sea Near beach In town centre
130 en suite (bth/shr) (5 fmly) (12 with balcony) No smoking in 10 bedrooms TV in all bedrooms STV Mini-bar in all bedrooms Licensed Lift Night porter Full central heating Air conditioning in bedrooms Open parking available (charged) Covered parking available (charged) Child discount available 6yrs Bicycle rental Open terrace Languages spoken: English, German, Italian, Spanish
CARDS: ✸ ▓▓ ▨▨ ⑨ Travellers cheques

★ ★ ★ Hotel Albert 1er
4 av des Phocéens 06000
☎ 493857401 FAX 493803609
The hotel occupies an enviable location in the centre of town, opposite the splendid municipal gardens and just a stone's throw from the sea. It has a cosy lounge and fully equipped guest accommodation offering a good level of comfort.
Near sea Near beach In town centre
79 en suite (bth/shr) (10 with balcony) TV in all bedrooms Lift Night porter Full central heating Air conditioning in bedrooms Child discount available 6yrs Bicycle rental Languages spoken: English, German, Italian
CARDS: ✸ ▓▓ ▨▨ ⑨ Travellers cheques

★ ★ ★ Boréal (Minotel)
9 rue Paul Déroulède 06000
☎ 493820606 FAX 493820191
The hotel has recently been renovated and now offers high quality, attractively decorated bedrooms with every modern convenience. The public areas are spacious and decorated in contemporary furnishings and colours, which create a cheerful atmosphere. Located in the town centre, it is close to the beach and the shops.
Near sea Near beach Forest area In town centre   *contd.*

Near motorway
45 en suite (bth/shr) (5 fmly) No smoking in 5 bedrooms TV in all bedrooms STV Radio in rooms Direct dial from all bedrooms Room-safe (charged) Licensed Lift Night porter Full central heating Air conditioning in bedrooms Child discount available 12yrs Open terrace V meals Last d 22.30hrs Languages spoken: English, Spanish
ROOMS: (room only) s 295-395FF; d 395-495FF **Special breaks**
MEALS: Continental breakfast 40FF Lunch 75-100FF&alc Dinner 75-100FF&alc
CARDS: ✿ 💳 ⚎ Travellers cheques

★ ★ ★ Hotel Chatham
9 rue Alphonse Karr *06000*
☎ 493878061 FAX 493823097
The Chatham is located in a popular tourist area in Nice close to the famous public gardens of the Place Massena, the Promenade des Anglais and the beaches. Open all year round, it features sound-proofed bedrooms with modern appointments which provide a high degree of comfort. There are no restaurant facilities in the hotel, but a large choice of eating establishments in the vicinity.
Near sea Near beach In town centre
49 en suite (bth/shr) TV in all bedrooms Direct dial from all bedrooms Lift Night porter Full central heating Air conditioning in bedrooms Child discount available Languages spoken: English, German, Spanish, Italian
CARDS: ✿ 💳 ⚎ ⏏ JCB Travellers cheques

★ ★ Climat de France
6 rue E Philibert *06300*
☎ 493558000 Cen Res 164460123 FAX 493558030
(from A8 take exit 50, signed Nice Centre and follow signs to The Port)
This contemporary hotel has sound-proofed bedrooms with private facilities which offer a good level of comfort. Situated near the old, picturesque centre, and at 200 metres from the port, it features a pleasant, modern interior where the restaurant serves a choice of dishes alternating between regional specialities and classic cuisine.
Near sea Forest area In town centre
110 en suite (shr) (11 fmly) TV in all bedrooms Direct dial from all bedrooms Licensed Lift Night porter Full central heating Air conditioning in bedrooms Open parking available (charged) Covered parking available (charged) Supervised Open terrace Covered terrace V meals Languages spoken: English, German, Italian & Spanish
CARDS: ✿ ⚎

★ ★ ★ ★ Négresco
37 Promenade des Anglais *06000*
☎ 493166400 FAX 493883568
(exit Autoroute A8 Nice West and take direction Town Centre/Promenade des Anglais)
For most people the hotel Négresco represents the era of the Belle Epoque combined with traditional hospitality and meticulous French courtesy. Classified as a historic monument, this great white palace with its sparkling chandeliers and inlaid gold, is universally recognised as one of France's most magnificent hotels. The furnishings throughout are worthy of a museum, original works of art, rare and costly antiques line its corridors and it has a number of exquisitely decorated restaurants serving the finest cuisine, which is as delightful to the eye as to the palate.
Near sea Near beach In town centre Near motorway
143 en suite (bth/shr) (5 with balcony) TV in all bedrooms

STV Direct dial from all bedrooms Mini-bar in all bedrooms Licensed Lift Night porter Full central heating Air conditioning in bedrooms Open parking available (charged) Covered parking available (charged) Supervised Open terrace Private beach Gymnasium opening soon Wkly live entertainment Last d 23.30hrs Languages spoken: English, Italian, Spanish, Russian, Arabic
ROOMS: (room only) s 1300-2450FF; d 1300-2450FF **Special breaks**
MEALS: Full breakfast 190FF Continental breakfast 130FF Lunch 170-590FF&alc Dinner 170-590FF&alc✱
CARDS: ✿ 💳 ⚎ ⏏ Travellers cheques

★ ★ ★ ★ La Pérouse (Best Western)
11 quai Rauba Capeu *06000*
☎ 493623463 FAX 493625941
Just a stone's throw from the old part of Nice and its delightful flower market, the hotel occupies a beautiful location overlooking the Baie des Anges. The peacefully situated spacious bedrooms and the flower-decked terraces with panoramic views over the deep blue sea provide a charming setting for a memorable stay. From May to September guests can dine in the garden under the shady lemon trees.
Near sea Near beach Forest area In town centre Near motorway
64 en suite (bth/shr) (60 with balcony) TV in all bedrooms STV Radio in rooms Direct dial from all bedrooms Mini-bar in all bedrooms Room-safe Licensed Lift Night porter Full central heating Air conditioning in bedrooms Child discount available 16yrs Outdoor swimming pool Sauna Solarium Jacuzzi/spa Open terrace Covered terrace Last d 22.00hrs Languages spoken: English, German,Spanish,Italian
ROOMS: (room only) s 545-1380FF; d 920-1380FF
MEALS: Continental breakfast 99FF Lunch fr 170FF&alc Dinner fr 170FF&alc✱
CARDS: ✿ 💳 ⚎ ⏏ Travellers cheques

★ ★ ★ Petit Palais
10 av E Bickert *06000*
☎ 493621911 FAX 493625360
The hotel is located near Nice's Matisse and Chagall museums. It is one of the best hotels of its kind in town, and features comfortable bedrooms with views over the Baie des Anges and the rooftops of the old quarter.
Near sea Near beach In town centre Near motorway
25 en suite (bth/shr) (1 fmly) (10 with balcony) TV in all bedrooms STV Direct dial from all bedrooms Licensed Lift Full central heating Open parking available (charged) Child discount available 12yrs Solarium Open terrace Languages spoken: English, German, Spanish
MEALS: Full breakfast 50FF Lunch 50-150FFalc Dinner 50-150FFalc✱
CARDS: ✿ 💳 ⚎ ⏏ Travellers cheques

★ ★ ★ Primotel Suisse
15 quai Rauba Capeu *06300*
☎ 493623300 FAX 493853070
The hotels in the Primotel group all have modern bedrooms equipped with every convenience and provide a high degree of comfort. Their restaurants serve a high standard of cooking where a choice of traditional and regional dishes feature strongly on the menu; whilst competent staff offer attentive service and traditional hospitality in a cordial atmosphere.
Near sea In town centre Near motorway
42 en suite (bth/shr) (30 with balcony) TV in all bedrooms Radio in rooms Direct dial from all bedrooms

Mini-bar in all bedrooms Licensed Lift Full central heating
Air conditioning in bedrooms Child discount available 12yrs
Languages spoken: English,German,Italian
CARDS: 💳 🏧 🔜 💳 Travellers cheques

★★ Les Relais Bleus
58 bd Risso *06300*
☎ 493262060 Cen Res 164460616 FAX 493260034
Les Relais Bleus offer comfortable accommodation and good
value at the two star level. They cater for both family and
business clientele, with relaxed dining and public areas.
Near sea In town centre
70 en suite (bth/shr) TV in all bedrooms STV Lift Night
porter Full central heating Air conditioning in bedrooms
Open terrace Languages spoken: English,Italian,Spanish

★★ Hotel St-Gothard
20 rue Paganini *06000*
☎ 493881341 FAX 493822755
Situated in the heart of the town, close to the big department
stores and 800 metres from the Promenade des Anglais and
the beaches, the hotel features bright spacious bedrooms, a
friendly foyer and lounge, complemented by personal
attention and service by friendly staff at all times. There are no
in-house restaurant facilities, but there is a wide choice of
eating establishments nearby.
Near sea Near beach In town centre
64 en suite (bth/shr) (12 fmly) (10 with balcony) TV in all
bedrooms STV Radio in rooms Direct dial from all bedrooms
Lift Night porter Full central heating Child discount available
12yrs Special rates for AA Guide users Last d 21.00hrs
Languages spoken: English Italian & Spanish
ROOMS: (room only) s 190-240FF; d 250-300FF
Reductions over 1 night
CARDS: 💳 🏧 🔜 💳 Travellers cheques

★★★★ Splendide Hotel
50 bd Victor-Hugo *06000*
☎ 493164100 FAX 493164270
(from A8, exit to airport/Promenade des Anglais, follow
seaside road into town (about 5 miles). After Négresco Hotel,
turn left into rue Meyerbeer)
The Hotel Splendide was built in 1883 and combined with its
excellent location in the centre of town, it has offered
outstanding service and warm hospitality for three
generations. The bedrooms are comfortably furnished and
offer the highest level of comfort. The restaurant specialises in
traditional French cuisine, with relaxing outdoor dining in the
summer. Being close to the Promenade des Anglais and all the
main shopping areas, it's an ideal venue for a holiday in Nice.
Near sea Near beach
128 en suite (bth/shr) (10 fmly) (100 with balcony) No smoking
on premises TV in all bedrooms STV Radio in rooms Direct
dial from all bedrooms Mini-bar in all bedrooms Licensed
Lift Night porter Full central heating Air conditioning in
bedrooms Covered parking available (charged) Supervised
Child discount available 12yrs Outdoor swimming pool
Jacuzzi/spa Open terrace V meals Last d 22.00hrs Languages
spoken: English, German, Spanish, Italian
ROOMS: (room only) s 795-950FF; d 795-950FF
Reductions over 1 night
MEALS: Full breakfast 80FF Continental breakfast 38FF Lunch
120-150FF&alc Dinner 150FF&alc
CARDS: 💳 🏧 🔜 💳 Travellers cheques

★★★ Auberge de la Madone
pl du Village *06440*
☎ 493799117 FAX 493799936
(A8 exit Nice-Est towards Sospel, take D21 into Peillon)
Perched on a narrow rocky spur approximately 17km form
Nice when ascending the Paillon Valley, Peillon is one of the
most beautiful and genuine villages of the Maritime Alps. A
genuine warm welcome awaits you at the hotel with its
atmosphere of peace and quiet.
In town centre
Closed 20 Oct-20 Dec & 7-24 Jan
20 en suite (bth/shr) 6 rooms in annexe (2 fmly) Full central
heating Open parking available Child discount available
Riding Solarium Boule Open terrace V meals Languages
spoken: English & Italian
ROOMS: (room only) s 450-600FF; d 480-800FF
MEALS: Continental breakfast 60FF Lunch 140-380FF&alc
Dinner 200-380FF&alc*
CARDS: 💳 🔜

★★ Cassini
231 av de la Porte des Alpes, (RN 202) *06670*
☎ 493089103 FAX 493084548
Near river Forest area Near motorway
12 rms (3 bth 7 shr) (1 with balcony) TV in all bedrooms
Licensed Full central heating Covered parking available
(charged) Child discount available 10yrs Open terrace Last d
22.00hrs Languages spoken: English,German,Italian
MEALS: Continental breakfast 30FF Lunch 85-130FF&alc
Dinner 85-130FF&alc*
CARDS: 💳 🏧 🔜 💳 Travellers cheques

★★★★ Grand Hotel du Cap Ferrat
bd Général-de-Gaulle *06230*
☎ 493765050 FAX 493760452
(In a private park at the southernmost end of the Cap Ferrat
peninsula)
The hotel occupies a splendid position on the tip of the Cap
Ferrat with views over the Mediterranean. Surrounded by pine
woods, it is ideally situated near Nice's international airport and
Monte-Carlo. Its magnificent interior has been decorated with
minute attention to detail and features elegant guest rooms
where carefully chosen period furniture blends in with modern
amenities. The restaurant serves an extensive choice of inventive
local dishes which will not disappoint the most demanding
gourmet. With unsurpassed facilities and services on offer, it is
an excellent venue for a relaxing stay on the Côte d'Azur.
Near sea Near motorway
Closed Jan & Feb
57 en suite (bth/shr) 6 rooms in annexe (11 fmly) (7 with
balcony) TV in all bedrooms STV Radio in rooms Mini-bar in
all bedrooms Room-safe Licensed Lift Night porter Full
central heating Air conditioning in bedrooms Open parking
available Covered parking available (charged) Supervised
Child discount available 12yrs Outdoor swimming pool
(heated) Tennis Solarium Bicycle rental Open terrace Last d
21.45hrs Languages spoken: English,German,Italian,Spanish
ROOMS: d 1900-2500FF
MEALS: Full breakfast 170FF Continental breakfast 120FF
Lunch 300-490FF&alc Dinner 420-490FF&alc*
CARDS: 💳 🏧 🔜 💳

ST-PAUL-DE-VENCE Alpes-Maritimes

★★★ Hameau
528 rte de la Colle *06570*
☎ 549332804 FAX 5493325575
Forest area
Closed end Dec-early Jan
17 rms (5 fmly) (3 with balcony) Licensed Full central heating
Air conditioning in bedrooms Open parking available
Outdoor swimming pool Boule Open terrace Languages
spoken: Italian
CARDS: ♣ ☲ Travellers cheques

★★★★ Mas d'Artigny
rte de la Colle *06570*
☎ 493328454 FAX 493329536
(From A8 or N7 exit Cagnes-sur-Mer towards St-Paul and
Vence. After La Colle-sur-Loup turn left and follow signs)
Surrounded by wooded gardens, the hotel offers comfortable
accommodation and fine regional and traditional cuisine.
Forest area
85 en suite (bth/shr) Some rooms in annexe (40 with balcony)
TV in all bedrooms STV Direct dial from all bedrooms
Licensed Lift Night porter Full central heating Air
conditioning in bedrooms Open parking available Covered
parking available (charged) Supervised Child discount
available 10yrs Outdoor swimming pool (heated) Tennis Pool
table Boule Bicycle rental Open terrace Last d 22.00hrs
Languages spoken: English,Dutch,German,Italian,Spanish
ROOMS: (room only) s 800-1670FF; d 980-1850FF
MEALS: Full breakfast 100FF Continental breakfast 140FF
Lunch 290-400FF&alc Dinner 290-400FF&alc
CARDS: ♣ ☲ ☲ ➲ JCB Travellers cheques

★★★★ Saint-Paul Relais et Chateaux (Relais et
Châteaux)
86 rue Grande *06570*
☎ 493326525 FAX 493325294
18 en suite (bth/shr) (1 with balcony) No smoking in 1
bedroom TV in all bedrooms STV Mini-bar in all bedrooms
Licensed Lift Night porter Full central heating Air
conditioning in bedrooms Open terrace y V meals
Languages spoken: English,Italian,Spanish
CARDS: ♣ ☲ ☲ ➲ Travellers cheques

SOSPEL Alpes-Maritimes

★★ L'Auberge Provencale
rte du Col de Castillon *06380*
☎ 493040031
This country inn is set in an oasis of peace and tranquillity and
occupies an elevated position overlooking one of the most
beautiful medieval villages in the Menton area. It has a
panoramic terrace shaded by oleanders and horse-chestnut
trees, comfortable guest rooms and a high standard of home-
cooking, which consists of regional dishes prepared with fresh
local produce.
Near river Forest area
Closed 11 Nov-11 Dec
9 rms (2 fmly) (6 with balcony) Licensed Full central heating
Open parking available Supervised Child discount available
Boule Open terrace Languages spoken: English,Italian
CARDS: Travellers cheques

THORENC Alpes-Maritimes

★★ Auberge les Merisiers
24 av de Belvédère *06750*
☎ 493600023 FAX 493600217
(Leave motorway at Cannes and follow directiopns to Grasse.
Then follow the N85 to St Vallier. Turn right on leaving St
Vallier and follow the signs to Thorenc- approx 25km)
This old country inn is situated in the village of Thorenc, set in
the hills around Grasse, and because of its close proximity to
the ski resorts of Gréolières-les-Neiges and Audibergue, and
only an hour's drive away from the Côte d'Azur, it is a popular
place for both a winter and summer holiday. After a complete
face-lift in recent years, it now features peaceful bedrooms,
which are equipped with modern facilities, and a restaurant
which serves a high standard of cooking, consisting of
generous, well prepared dishes by the chef-proprietor
Edouard Maurel.
Near lake Forest area Near motorway
12 rms (9 shr) (1 fmly) (4 with balcony) TV in all bedrooms
Direct dial from all bedrooms Licensed Full central heating
Covered parking available Child discount available 10yrs
Open terrace Last d 21.00hrs Languages spoken:
English,Italian
ROOMS: (room only) s 230-250FF; d 230-250FF
MEALS: Continental breakfast 30FF Lunch 99-159FF Dinner
99-159FF
CARDS: ♣ ■ ☲ Travellers cheques

★★ Des Voyageurs
av de Belvédère *06750*
☎ 493600018 FAX 493600351
The third generation of their family to run this establishment,
Claudette and Albert Rouqier offer warm hospitality, good
food and comfortable accommodation to their visitors. The
quiet bedrooms have modern facilities and offer splendid
views of the mountains, whilst the restaurant serves a fine
cuisine incorporating classic and regional dishes.
Near river Near lake Forest area Near motorway
Closed 15 Nov-Jan
12 en suite (bth/shr) (3 fmly) TV in all bedrooms Licensed
Full central heating Open parking available Covered parking
available Supervised Child discount available 12yrs Solarium
Boule Open terrace V meals Last d 20.30hrs Languages
spoken: English,Spanish,Italian
MEALS: Full breakfast 32FF Continental breakfast 32FF Lunch
89-145FF Dinner 89-145FF✹
CARDS: ♣ ☲ Travellers cheques

TURINI Alpes-Maritimes

★★ Trois Vallees
Col de Turini *06440*
☎ 493915721 FAX 493795362
At 30 miles from Nice, the hotel enjoys a pleasant setting, on
the edge of the Mercantour Park amidst dense forests. It is a
good venue for all seasons; in winter cross-country skiing, in
springtime and summer, a refreshing climate and walking
opportunities, whilst the autumn offers an array of natural
produce such as wild mushrooms and strawberries in the
woods. The bedrooms have a terrace, are fitted with modern
amenities and provide relaxing accommodation, whilst the
restaurant with splendid open fire place serves traditional
cuisine of good quality.
Forest area
30 en suite (bth/shr) 11 rooms in annexe (3 fmly) TV in all
bedrooms STV Licensed Full central heating Open parking

available Supervised Child discount available 12yrs Outdoor swimming pool (heated) Sauna Boule Jacuzzi/spa Bicycle rental Open terrace Last d 22.00hrs Languages spoken: English,Dutch,German,Spanish
CARDS: 💳 🏧 💳 💳 Travellers cheques

VENCE Alpes-Maritimes

★ ★ ★ ★ Chateau Saint-Martin
av des Templiers *06140*
☎ 493580202 FAX 493240891
The Château Saint Martin is located between Cannes and Monaco, close to the medieval villages of Vence and Saint-Paul. All the bedrooms, lounges and public areas are decorated with beautiful Persian carpets, tapestries from Flanders and are adorned with period furniture. In addition to the main house, cottages are spread over the wooded estate and offer guest accommodation of the highest standard. As well as other parts of the hotel, the restaurant has recently undergone a face-lift and has been extended with terraces and a shaded patio. The outstanding cuisine consists of a choice of gastronomic dishes which are renowned throughout the area.

Closed Oct-Apr
38 en suite (bth/shr) 11 rooms in annexe (27 with balcony) TV in all bedrooms STV Radio in rooms Direct dial from all bedrooms Mini-bar in 5 bedrooms Licensed Lift Night porter Full central heating Air conditioning in bedrooms Open parking available Covered parking available Supervised Outdoor swimming pool (heated) Tennis Boule Open terrace Last d 22.00hrs Languages spoken: English,Italian,German
ROOMS: (room only) d 3000-4000FF
MEALS: Full breakfast 120FF Lunch 430-490FF&alc Dinner 430-490FF&alc✱
CARDS: 💳 🏧 💳 💳 Travellers cheques

★ ★ La Roseraie
av Henri Giraud *06140*
☎ 493580220 FAX 493589931
This beautiful old Mediterranean-style villa dates back to the turn of the century and is surrounded by the lush vegetation of palm trees, yuccas, magnolias and lovely roses. With spectacular views over the medieval village of Vence and Bayou hill, it provides the charming setting for a peaceful stay. The bedrooms are decorated in the pretty Provençale style and have fine views over the surrounding countryside. A generous breakfast consists of home-baked croissants and traditional preserves and is served on the terrace in the delightful garden.

Forest area
12 en suite (bth/shr) (2 fmly) (5 with balcony) TV in all bedrooms Licensed Open parking available

Outdoor swimming pool Boule Bicycle rental Open terrace Covered terrace Childrens Play area Languages spoken: English,German,Italian
CARDS: 💳 🏧 💳 Travellers cheques

★ ★ Mas de Vence
539 av Emile Hugues *06140*
☎ 493580616 FAX 493240421
Located in the cultural centre of Vence, in the heart of the Côte d'Azur, this contemporary hotel offers modern bedrooms in pleasant, traditionally designed surroundings. In a good location, convenient for the sea, as well as the charming old villages in the hills nearby. The restaurant serves an honest, tasty cuisine where Provençale specialities take pride of place on the menu.
41 en suite (bth/shr) 3 rooms in annexe (5 fmly) (35 with balcony) TV in all bedrooms Direct dial from all bedrooms Licensed Lift Night porter Full central heating Open parking available Covered parking available Supervised Child discount available 10yrs Outdoor swimming pool Solarium Boule Open terrace V meals Last d 21.30hrs Languages spoken: English,German,Spanish,Italian
ROOMS: (room only) s 350-380FF; d 440-475FF
Reductions over 1 night
MEALS: Continental breakfast 40FF Lunch 155FF&alc Dinner 155FF&alc
CARDS: 💳 🏧 💳 💳 Travellers cheques

VILLEFRANCHE-SUR-MER Alpes-Maritimes

★ ★ ★ Hotel Bahia (Best Western)
Basse Corniche, Pont St Jean *06230*
☎ 493013232 FAX 493012977
Overlooking the famous bay of Villefranche-sur-Mer, between Nice and the Principality of Monaco, the hotel Bahia offers modern comfort in a pleasant atmosphere with personal attention and service at all times. Elegantly decorated rooms are fitted with up-to-date facilities, whilst its gastronomic restaurant, terrace, swimming pool and bar, situated on the fifth floor, offer a stunning vista over the Mediterranean sea. The cuisine consists of a choice of exquisite dishes, skilfully prepared by the chef.
Near sea Near motorway
58 en suite (bth/shr) (4 fmly) (58 with balcony) TV in all bedrooms STV Radio in rooms Direct dial from all bedrooms Mini-bar in all bedrooms Licensed Lift Night porter Full central heating Air conditioning in bedrooms Open parking available Covered parking available Supervised *contd.*

Child discount available 12yrs Outdoor swimming pool Solarium Open terrace Covered terrace Languages spoken: English,German,Italian
CARDS: 🌐 💳 💳 ⦿ Travellers cheques

★ ★ ★ La Flore
bd Princesse Grace de Monaco *06230*
☎ 493763030 FAX 493769999
This charming establishment dates back to the turn of the century, and after thorough renovation opened its doors in 1994. Situated in a quiet location at five minutes from the beach, it features individually styled bedrooms which provide a very high level of comfort, and have terraces or balconies overlooking the Bay of Villefranche. The attractive restaurant serves a high quality classic and regional cuisine consisting of the finest local produce.
Near sea Near beach Near motorway
31 en suite (bth/shr) 8 rooms in annexe (6 fmly) (20 with balcony) TV in all bedrooms STV Direct dial from all bedrooms Mini-bar in all bedrooms Room-safe Licensed Lift Night porter Full central heating Air conditioning in bedrooms Open parking available Covered parking available (charged) Supervised Child discount available 2yrs Outdoor swimming pool Solarium Open terrace Last d 22.00hrs Languages spoken: English,Italian
ROOMS: (room only) s 300-500FF; d 300-1060FF
Reductions over 1 night
MEALS: Full breakfast 60FF Lunch 130-230FFalc Dinner 210FF&alc
CARDS: 🌐 💳 💳 ⦿ Travellers cheques

★ ★ ★ Welcome
1 quai Amiral Courbet *06230*
☎ 493767693 FAX 493018881
(A8 exit 50, through Nice along Promenade des Anglais; then to Villefranche-sur-Mer, follow 'centre ville, plage' down to sea.)
Ideally situated on one of the most beautiful stretches of the Côte d'Azur, and just a few minutes away from Nice and Monaco, the hotel offers a tastefully decorated interior with fully equipped bedrooms and a renowned restaurant, where a choice of superb dishes is served by competent, attentive staff.
Near sea Near beach
Closed 20 Nov-20 Dec
32 en suite (bth/shr) (3 fmly) (27 with balcony) TV in all bedrooms STV Direct dial from all bedrooms Mini-bar in all bedrooms Room-safe (charged) Licensed Lift Night porter

Full central heating Air conditioning in bedrooms Covered parking available (charged) Supervised Child discount available 12yrs Open terrace Last d 22.00hrs Languages spoken: English Italian Spanish German

ROOMS: s 400-720FF; d 495-950FF **Reductions over 1 night Special breaks**
MEALS: Lunch 140-255FF Dinner 140-255FF
CARDS: 🌐 💳 💳 ⦿ Travellers cheques

VILLENEUVE-LOUBET Alpes-Maritimes

★ ★ ★ Inter Hotel Hamotel
Les Hameaux du Soleil, rte de la Colle *06270*
☎ 493208660 FAX 493733394
All the hotels in the Inter Hotel group offer guest accommodation which is designed with the individual needs of its clientele in mind. Whether situated in the capital or in a seaside resort, they offer old-fashioned hospitality and up-to-date modern amenities. Staff are friendly and helpful throughout, and provide a degree of personal service which is difficult to match and make a stay, whether for business or pleasure, an enjoyable experience to look back upon.
Near river
30 en suite (bth) (30 with balcony) TV in all bedrooms STV Radio in rooms Mini-bar in all bedrooms Licensed Lift Night porter Full central heating Open parking available Covered parking available Child discount available 12yrs Languages spoken: English,Portuguese
CARDS: 🌐 💳 💳 ⦿ Travellers cheques

INDEX